1,001

Exemplary Practices

In America's Two-Year Colleges

McGraw-Hill's **College Custom Series** consists of products that are produced from camera-ready copy. Peer review, class testing, and accuracy are primarily the responsibility of the author(s).

1,001 EXEMPLARY PRACTICES
IN AMERICA'S TWO-YEAR COLLEGES

1 2 3 4 5 6 7 8 9 0 SEM SEM 9 0 9 8 7 6 5 4

ISBN 0-07-048597-6

Custom Series Editor: Judy T. Ice

Cover Design: Lynn R. Hammond

Cover Art: William Finley

Page Layout & Design: Marc S. A. Glasgow

Printer/Binder: Quebecor Printing Semline, Inc.

 This book is printed on recycled paper containing a minimum of 50% total recycled fiber with 10% postconsumer de-inked fiber.

1,001
Exemplary
Practices
In America's Two-Year Colleges

Editors
John E. Roueche
Dale Parnell
Carl M. Kuttler, Jr.

With
Patty C. Jones

Foreword by
Terrel H. Bell

McGraw–Hill, Inc.
College Custom Series

New York St. Louis San Francisco Auckland Bogotá
Caracas Lisbon London Madrid Mexico Milan Montreal
New Delhi Paris San Juan Singapore Sydney Tokyo Toronto

TABLE OF CONTENTS

TABLE OF CONTENTS

John E. Roueche and Dale Parnell dedicate this book to the innovative and creative faculties in America's community and technical colleges who make a daily difference in the lives of the students they teach.

Carl M. Kuttler, Jr. dedicates this book to his mentor, Dr. Michael M. Bennett, president emeritus of St. Petersburg Junior College; to John E. Roueche, who has inspired innovation; to Dale Parnell, who has encouraged national leadership; and to the District Board of Trustees of St. Petersburg Junior College, who have fostered creativity.

Editors' Note

Without the contributions of hundreds of institutions, this book – the first of this magnitude in at least 25 years – would have been impossible. In May of 1992, and again in November of the same year, leaders of thousands of community, junior and technical colleges were asked to submit descriptions of programs that they believe "merit national attention… for a variety of reasons: impact, uniqueness, visibility, profitability or inherent value." In addition, the institutions were asked to choose their submissions in a deliberative manner and to document any outside recognition that had been received. During the ensuing year, hundreds of institutions prepared and submitted descriptions of exemplary practices. As late as December of 1993, we still were receiving new entries and updates of entries earlier submitted. Because the institutions were given so much freedom, many entries vary in length and content. Entries have been edited for clarity, readability and length while trying to maintain the spirit and accuracy of the original text. No submission was rejected.

The future is here – and everywhere. It's in all 50 states and beyond. It's at Prince William Sound Community College in the cold north of Alaska and Miami-Dade Community College in sunny Florida. The future is technological and multicultural, it's progressive and responsive, cooperative and curricular. To successfully compete in such a world requires practical, quality preparation. Where are millions turning for that preparation? To the hundreds of community, technical and junior colleges that have made two-year institutions the fastest-growing segment of U.S. education.

That these institutions are successful at meeting diverse educational demands is obvious throughout this book, compiled under the qualified direction of John E. Roueche, Dale Parnell and Carl M. Kuttler, Jr. – three men I personally know and respect for their ground-breaking work in this facet of higher education. Dr. Roueche, director of the Community College Leadership Program at the University of Texas at Austin, can be credited with re-energizing hundreds of colleges and their faculty to provide the best teaching-and-learning experience. Dr. Parnell, former president of the American Association of Community and Junior Colleges and the author of *The Neglected Majority*, remains the nation's leading advocate of technical education and the integration of academic and vocational education. And Dr. Kuttler, president of St. Petersburg Junior College of Florida, presides over an institution that has received many prestigious awards, has been honored by the White House and is on the cutting edge of technological advances.

This ambitious and accessible book is perhaps the most exhaustive compilation of exemplary programs of community, technical and vocational colleges, and is sure to become a standard reference for college faculty and administrators nationwide. Never before has information of this scope been available in one source. While these three men deserve the credit for undertaking such a project, the institutions herein represented deserve credit for seeing the advantage of sharing their successes. A strength of community, technical and junior colleges is, after all, a willingness to grow and learn from each other.

Thanks to the contributing institutions, vitality and innovation pervade this book. The programs in these pages are as diverse and driven as the populations they serve. The programs represent manifold topics, from aerospace technology to coal mining technology, from fundraising to parenting, and from total quality management to wildlife management. Peruse this book and it becomes obvious why enrollment at community, technical and junior colleges is increasing so dramatically: These dynamic institutions are meeting needs, fulfilling dreams and attacking the future head on. Drs. Roueche, Parnell, Kuttler and the hundreds of contributing colleges deserve our gratitude and praise for having the foresight to make two-year institutions – and this project – a valuable resource in today's ever-changing, ever-challenging world.

–Terrel H. Bell
United States Secretary of Education (1981-1985)

Can the community college movement still be called a national movement? No other major sector of education can be called a movement, yet community college leaders still refer to themselves as being involved in a movement. A quick review of this book on exemplary practices in community, technical and junior colleges reveals why the term still is appropriate and applicable.

The authors of this book set upon a mission to collect exemplary practices in community, technical and junior colleges. The purpose of this effort was to catalog a nationally representative sample of good ideas and model practices. Thus, college leaders can avoid "reinventing the wheel" and save time and money when considering some innovative proposals. However, we discovered much more than exemplary practices and innovations.

We discovered that the community college movement is very much alive. The exemplary practices outlined in this book reveal a creativity and an energy that is missing in so much of education at other levels. There has been no attempt in this collection of exemplary practices to be inclusive or exclusive. Rather, the purpose has been to be representative. Exemplary practices exist in small as well as large colleges, in rural as well as urban settings, in occupational education as well as the liberal arts, and in teaching as well as administrative practices. No attempt has been made to evaluate practices, that function has been left to the reader.

A major purpose in developing this anthology of exemplary practices is to provide a service to those who work in community colleges and in other sectors of education. In this volume one can find a reference to most of the grassroots innovations developed or being developed in the community, technical and junior colleges of the United States.

This collection of exemplary practices also has been developed to help inspire the creation of new models and new ideas in education reform efforts. Leaders in all levels of education are urged to utilize this book to expand the innovations dialogue where it already is in progress, and to initiate the discussion where it has yet to begin. We are thankful to the hundreds of our colleagues who have furnished us with this treasure trove of material.

Finally, we would like to recognize those who did so much work in the development and production of this book. In addition to Patty Curtin Jones, our thanks go to Daniel G. Caudill, Diane Clark, Kim Corry, Marc S.A. Glasgow, Lynn R. Hammond, Valerie Kurdys, Josephine E. Smith and Kathy Federico.

John E. Roueche
Professor
University of Texas at Austin
Texas

Dale Parnell
Professor
Oregon State University
Oregon

Carl M. Kuttler, Jr.
President
St. Petersburg Junior College
Florida

John E. Roueche has been professor and director of the Community College Leadership Program at the University of Texas at Austin since 1971. The Texas doctoral program in Community College Leadership is the nation's oldest and has produced more presidents, vice presidents and deans of American community colleges than any other university graduate program. He holds the Sid W. Richardson Regents Chair in Community College Leadership, the first endowed faculty position in the community college field. He is a community college graduate (Mitchell Community College) and has a bachelor's degree from Lenoir-Rhyne College and received his Ph.D. in higher education administration from Florida State University. He has served as a high school history and English teacher, community college dean of students and instruction dean, and faculty member at UCLA and Duke University before joining the Texas faculty. He has directed 12 national research and development projects at The University of Texas at Austin and currently co-directs (with Terry O'Banion) the $2.8-million W.K. Kellogg Foundation National Leadership Project (1989-1994). He has spoken to more than 1,200 colleges and universities on teaching and leadership excellence. Dr. Roueche is the author of 29 other books and more than 100 articles and chapters focused on leadership, teaching and learning in American colleges and universities.

Dale Parnell, professor of education at Oregon State University, is a former national president of the American Association of Community and Junior Colleges. His book, *The Neglected Majority*, was chosen as the best national association book in 1985 and his proposal to establish a Tech Prep/Associate Degree Program between high schools and colleges has gone from an original idea to a federally funded program being implemented across the nation. He is a former high school teacher, principal, school superintendent, state superintendent of public instruction, and commissioner of Oregon's community colleges. In addition, he was president of San Joaquin Delta College, the first chancellor of the San Diego Community College System in California and was founding president of Lane Community College in Oregon. He holds a doctoral degree from the University of Oregon and has been named the outstanding alumnus of the year by the University of Oregon, College of Education, and by his undergraduate alma mater, Willamette University in Oregon. He helped draft and secure passage of the 1986 Higher Education Act, and the 1990 Perkins Vocational and Applied Technology Act. He was appointed by the U.S. President to chair the National Advisory Council on Equal Educational Opportunity. Dr. Parnell, a popular lecturer and prolific writer, has authored several books, chapters and articles on significant education issues.

Carl M. Kuttler, Jr. was graduated from St. Petersburg Junior College in Florida and has been its president since 1978. He also holds degrees from Florida State University and Stetson University College of Law. He was the first community college president to be appointed, in 1988, to the National Advisory Council on Education Research and Improvement, the commission formed to advise the U.S. President and Secretary of Education on education policies. In partnership with the American Association of Community and Junior Colleges, he developed a series of U.S. Presidential Leadership Seminars that have been held at the Jimmy Carter Center in Atlanta and at the Gerald R. Ford Library in Grand Rapids. He was named Honorary Rector of Leningrad (now St. Petersburg) State University in Russia in 1990, and Honorary President of Baoji Teachers College in China in 1992. He received the International Leadership Award from the National Institute for Staff and Organizational Development, for his global innovativeness. In 1991, Phi Theta Kappa (two-year academic honor fraternity) named him one of four outstanding college presidents in the United States. The United States Information Agency selected Dr. Kuttler in 1993 to visit Russia and assist that country in developing a community college system.

Patty Curtin Jones, Assistant to the President of St. Petersburg Junior College, is responsible for coordinating special projects for the college. She is a former newspaper reporter who covered a number of beats, including education, government and the criminal justice system, for the *St. Petersburg Times* of Florida. Ms. Jones was familiar with community colleges and their strengths long before reporting on them or working for one; she is the daughter of a former SPJC faculty member as well as a graduate of the institution, where she served as editor of the student newspaper while attending. She completed her higher education at the University of Florida.

PARTNERSHIP WITH NORTHWEST AIRLINES

▩ *Through the partnership, the airline conducts some courses and* ▩
lends jet engine components and special tools and equipment

The mathematics program is strengthened, students are exposed to the real-world work of aviation technology and females and minorities have increased opportunities in aviation education through a partnership between Alabama Aviation and Technical College and Northwest Airlines.

Northwest Airlines conducts some courses and lends jet engine components and special tools and equipment to the college as part of the partnership, which directly led to a three-year grant of $289,525 from the National Science Foundation (NSF) Private Sector Partnership grant program. Northwest Airlines has contributed engineering and technical personnel resources and equipment to AATC the value of which meets or exceeds the NSF grant resulting in a project of approximately $600,000. Examples of partnership activities include:

- Engineers and technicians assisted the college in developing three new mathematics courses and refining existing instructional units to meet the competencies required in the aviation industry workplace.
- Northwest personnel conducted Boeing 727, DC-9 and avionics familiarization courses on the AATC campus.
- Northwest hosted a Tech Prep conference for the college and its Tech Prep partners at the Atlanta facility and continues to host tours for other college constituencies.
- Northwest Airlines regularly lends jet engine components and special tools and equipment to the college for laboratory instruction.
- Northwest personnel conduct training for AATC faculty on special equipment.
- Northwest Airlines hosted field trips and employment interviews with hundreds of AATC students.
- Northwest Airlines provided AATC with valuable recruiting materials for minorities and females.

Because of Northwest Airlines' extraordinary commitment to Alabama Aviation and Technical College, the college nominated the organization for the Exemplary Business or Labor Involvement category of the National Association of State Councils on Vocational Education Awards 1992. Northwest Airlines received the national award in a special ceremony held in Washington, D.C. on June 12, 1992.

Contact:
Sandra H. Flowers, Institutional and Student Development
(205) 774-5113

Alabama Aviation and Technical College
PO Box 1209
Ozark, AL 36361
Total headcount enrollment-Credit: 582
Campuses/sites: 2; Full-time faculty: 25

FEDERAL AVIATION ADMINISTRATION
EDUCATION RESOURCE CENTER

▩ *The Center maintains and provides quantities of the FAA printed materials and* ▩
makes available to the public other audio-visual and computer software resources

In September 1989, Alabama Aviation and Technical College became the first two-year college in the nation designated an official Federal Aviation Administration Education Resource Center. Other resource centers are typically located on university campuses.

The FAA Education Resource Center functions as an information distribution center for free FAA aviation education, curriculum, career guidance materials and other resources. These materials and resources are available for use by the media, the public, and the educational community – kindergarten through college. The Center maintains and provides quantities of the FAA printed materials and makes available to the public other audio-visual and computer software resources. Center personnel also answer general information requests, provide duplication services, conduct workshops, and make aviation-related presentations utilizing the FAA career materials.

In 1991, when AATC hosted its first open house, approximately 40 teachers and counselors received packages of aviation career materials from the Center for use in aviation career units in elementary and secondary education programs.

Continues on Page 10

One of the FAA education publications included in the Center, Women In Aviation And Space, was developed by college personnel. As a result of the success of this publication, AATC received a commendation from the FAA for its efforts to provide career opportunities for women in aviation.

The FAA Education Resource Center has been an excellent tool for publicizing both aviation education and the college. The college is listed in FAA publications, which are distributed nationally and internationally. As a result, hundreds of inquiries about college programs are received annually from across the United States. Also, the staff in the FAA Education Resource Center will continue to conduct additional workshops in the community and throughout the state to increase the awareness of its resources.

Contact:
Megan Johnson, Director, Learning Resources Center
(205) 774-5113

Alabama Aviation and Technical College
PO Box 1209
Ozark, AL 36361
Total headcount enrollment-Credit: 582
Campuses/sites: 2; Full-time faculty: 25

POLYSOMNOGRAPHIC (SLEEP DISORDERS) TECHNOLOGY

The program aims to raise professional standards in the field while alleviating the shortage of qualified personnel

In the spring of 1991, the Alabama Commission on Higher Education granted approval to Calhoun State Community College to offer an associates in applied science degree in Polysomnographic Technology, the study of sleep disorders. Approval of this program made Calhoun the first college in the nation to offer a formal training program for sleep disorder technicians.

The program, which is being offered through a cooperative agreement between Calhoun and Huntsville Hospital in Huntsville, Alabama, is designed to prepare individuals for employment in the field of polysomnographic technology. Other aims of the program are to raise the professional standards of the field of polysomnography; to alleviate the shortage of qualified personnel to fill positions; and to decrease the migration to the field from respiratory care and electroencephalography, areas from which many of the current polysomnographic technologists have come and both of which also are experiencing personnel shortages.

Calhoun is one of the first educational institutions in the country to propose a program in polysomnographic technology. The only programs existing until the implementation of the Calhoun program were two-week programs available only to individuals already working in sleep disorders centers.

Students enrolled in the program receive three-quarters of general education at Calhoun, with the technical component of four quarters of study taught by staff of the Huntsville Hospital Sleep Disorders Center.

Offering this program has been cost-effective for both Calhoun and Huntsville Hospital because the college was already offering a general education curriculum, and the hospital has already been doing training in the technical aspects of the profession. The program has been advantageous to both the college and the hospital in that the college is able to provide trainees for the technical training portion of the program who have a demonstrated level of education.

Contact:
Jorge Kuzmicic, Dean of Instruction
(205) 306-2500

Calhoun State Community College, John C.
PO Box 2216
Decatur, AL 35609-2216
Total headcount enrollment-Credit: 8,200 Non-Credit: 1,000
Campuses/sites: 3; Full-time faculty: 140

ENGLISH AND MATHEMATICS DIVISION LEARNING CENTER

The English and math faculty have come to rely on the lab as a support for their classroom instruction

The English and Mathematics Division Learning Center, unlike such centers elsewhere, is designed for all students – not just developmental students. It was created after the 1990 merger of the Calhoun Community College junior college and technical college divisions. Key to the merger was the establishment of a new academic division – the English and Mathematics Division, housing a Department of English, a Department of Mathematics, and Developmental Studies.

The Division was created based upon the premise that all Calhoun students take basic courses within this division; that almost all developmental courses are either writing, reading, or math; and that students in English and math all need the opportunity to receive individual attention in a lab setting. The Learning Lab is situated directly in the middle of the building, an easily accessible place for students and faculty.

The Learning Center is an individualized lab with several options available for students and faculty. Students may drop in for individual tutoring, computer-assisted tutoring, small group learning, or viewing video lectures.

Several math faculty video-tape their lectures daily, allowing students in need of additional learning time to either view the tapes in the lab or check them out for home viewing. Other courses have video back-ups for students to review difficult concepts. The Learning Center is staffed by a director, two bachelor's degree instructors, and a host of part-time teachers/tutors. It is open during all hours Calhoun College is open for students.

Any student wishing help in English or math is invited to come. Students may be directed (required) to visit the lab, but most faculty find students taking advantage of the lab with only minimal encouragement. The English and math faculty have come to rely on the lab as a support for their classroom instruction. Faculty spend time in the lab with their students, and counselors have volunteered their time in the lab.

Administratively, the new division and the Learning Center have enabled costs to be minimized (one lab instead of three) and have assured that a large group of faculty communicate with each other as a means of aiding students.

Contact:
Jorge Kuzmicic, Dean of Instruction
(205) 306-2500

Calhoun State Community College, John C.
PO Box 2216
Decatur, AL 35609-2216
Total headcount enrollment-Credit: 8,200 Non-Credit: 1,000
Campuses/sites: 3; Full-time faculty: 140

JOBS NATIONAL WORKPLACE LITERACY GRANT

The primary training site for the project is a mobile learning lab at a job-shop metal casting industry

Central Alabama Community College takes its workplace skills straight to the client through a mobile learning lab, on site at the industry.

The lab primarily goes to Robinson Foundry, Inc., of Alexander City, the largest job-shop metal-casting industry using a new technology known as "lost foam." They have reinvested capital into research and development, and have produced a world-class process and technology for the metal-casting industry. For their current work force to maintain job stability and advancement, Robinson Foundry must meet the certification requirements of its major suppliers. Basic workplace skills deficiencies have been documented a major barrier to meeting certification standards.

So in 1991, Robinson Foundry, Inc., entered a partnership with Central Alabama community College and was awarded $242,000 from the U.S. Department of Education to fund a National Workplace Literacy Project. This partnership focuses on the identification, development and implementation of a comprehensive workplace basic-skill training effort through which reading, math, language, problem-solving, critical thinking and communication skills are taught in the context of the specific job training material for all hourly employees. The training is required and the corporation compensates every employee regular hourly wage for participation in the training.

The primary training site for the project is a mobile learning lab which is on site at the industry. The lab is equipped with 10 IBM-compatible computer stations that

Continues on Page 12

are networked. To facilitate curriculum development, Tel-A-Train's Course Creator was installed. At the heart of the project is the development, validation and implementation of a training process that incorporates the research-supported strategies of curriculum design and effective teaching from CACC faculty.

The JOBS project, an acronym for Job Oriented Basic Skills, trained 216 people by the end of the first grant period of 8/30/92. Surveys indicated 70 percent to 85 percent of participants considered the JOBS project to have helped them to improve skills in reading, writing, computation, problem-solving, working as team members and using computers. Although the TABE locator test does not produce verifiable results, the summary data reflect average achievement gains of two to three grade levels.

Industrial outcomes were similarly positive with supervisors reporting a 73 percent improvement in job attitude and 63 percent increase in job knowledge.

A subsequent grant has been funded, bringing the total expenditures to $500,000. This iteration has expanded the project to three other companies under the Robinson corporate umbrella, including a goal of training 300 employees.

The JOBS project has been recognized in *Modern Castings*, a publication of the American Foundrymen's Society, in an article titled "New Training Program Receives Top Grades at Robinson Foundry." Example lessons from the workplace-specific curriculum have been posted on the ERIC database.

Contact:
Robert E. Stone, Director
(205) 234-6346

Central Alabama Community College
PO Box 699
Alexander City, AL 35010
Total headcount enrollment-Credit: 2,563 Non-Credit: 1,017
Campuses/sites: 6; Full-time faculty: 53

PRACTICAL NURSING

Job opportunities are excellent for program graduates,
who excel on the licensure examination

Because the Practical Nursing program at J.F. Drake State Technical College is so popular and enjoys a solid reputation, many students must wait one or more quarters for admission. The program is popular because it's effective.

The Practical Nursing program, begun in 1965, is a comprehensive course of study that combines theory with clinical practice. The curriculum is designed to provide qualified individuals an opportunity to acquire the knowledge, attitudes and skills that will enable them to become safe and competent practitioners of Practical Nursing. To become licensed, graduates of this program must successfully write the National Council Licensure Examination (NCLEX-PN).

The typical student who attends this program full-time and whose academic and clinical progress are satisfactory should complete the course of study in four quarters. Students are admitted to the program during the Spring, Fall and Winter Quarters.

Graduates of the Practical Nursing program are well-prepared to function efficiently as Practical Nurses. Job opportunities are excellent and many of our graduates are hired by affiliating clinical agencies. Graduate performance on the Licensure Examination is very good with 90 percent to 100 percent of our graduates successfully passing the examination the first time. Students successfully completing the fundamentals phase of the First Quarter are eligible to make application for certification as a nursing assistant. This allows students to work during the time they are in the program.

The Practical Nursing program is divided into two levels, first and second quarter courses are Level I and third and fourth quarter courses are Level II. In order to meet Level requirements, the practical nursing faculty structures the program in a manner designed to assist graduates with accomplishing several program objectives.

The Practical Nursing program has an active Advisory Committee composed primarily of members of the Health Community. This committee functions to assist instructors in remaining knowledgeable of new trends, equipment, materials and techniques in nursing procedures. In addition, it aids in recruitment of students, and in the attainment of new equipment for the department.

Contact:
Annice Conaway, Instructor-In-Charge
(205) 539-8161

J.F. Drake State Technical College
3421 Meridian Street North
Huntsville, AL 35811
Total headcount enrollment-Credit: 33,237 Non-Credit: 16,992
Campuses/sites: 1; Full-time faculty: 24

ELECTRONICS TECHNOLOGY

▨ Each quarter, local industry representatives are invited to the college to review ▨
curriculum, textbooks, course outlines, lab exercises and student special projects

A mix of theory, practical experience and strong ties with local industry mean Electronics Technology students at J.F. Drake State Technical College are well-trained for entry-level employment or for applying updates to the world of basic electronics.

The program has two options for students:

1) Associate in Applied Technology Degree (21 months, 7 quarters); and

2) Certificate (12 months, 4 quarters).

The first major strength of the program lies in its structure. The Electronics Program offers a broad field of theory, supported with "hands-on" experiences. Students are taught theory and are given testing, and problem-solving exercises. They are required to select, build and present a technical project to the Electronics instructors, Electrical Engineers, and local industry personnel. The knowledge and skills that the students have mastered in the various electronics and related courses are climaxed in these projects at the end of each quarter.

The second major strength of the program is the unique relationship it has with local electronics industries. Each quarter, local industry representatives are invited to the college to review the curriculum, textbooks, course outlines, laboratory exercises, and graduating senior's special projects. This activity gives students in the program up-to-date knowledge in the electronics field. Industry participants receive firsthand exposure to the program's content and student potential, and the instructors are kept up-to-date on the rapid changes of industry as a result of this activity. It is this unique relationship that has helped to make Drake Tech's Electronics Program a success.

Because much of the success of the Electronics Department depends upon the relationship established with local industries, stronger linkages and partnerships with industry through various programming experiences have been fostered by the college and department for many years. These linkages and partnerships include:

- Employment: More than 95 percent of the Electronics Department graduates are employed as electronic technicians.

- Cooperative Education Training: A very high quality and rapidly growing Cooperative Education Program supports training and academics. Five major industries/companies participate in Drake Tech's Co-op efforts.

- Training for Industries: Training for industries is an ongoing program that allows industries to provide their employees with up-to-date training in the rapidly changing technological world of work. Six major industries participate in our TBI efforts.

- Electronics Repair/Technical Support Partnership: The Electronics Repair/Technical Support

Partnership is an agreement between J.F. Drake State Technical College's Electronics Department and McDonnell Douglas Corporation, located in Huntsville, Alabama. This partnership provides Drake Tech's electronics students with hands-on knowledge in failure isolation, and repair of electrical components and the upgrading of personal computers. This agreement has proven to be a valuable component in our Microcomputer System Repair course.

In the summer of 1991, Drake Tech's Electronics Department and SCITEK, Inc. of Huntsville developed the first Memorandum of Understanding. Under this well-structured partnership, SCITEK and Drake Tech acted cooperatively in pursuit of minority business and educational opportunities afforded by Federal Government agencies and federally operated research institutes. The partnership bore fruit in the summer of 1991 whereby Drake Tech and SCITEK teamed up to deliver seven microportable computers. Drake Tech provided the necessary engineering, service, facilities and manpower to assemble the electronic package and interfaces for the seven micro-portable computers. This convenient PC-based micro-portable computer offers immediate data input/output capabilities within fingertip control at all times.

The system was developed to support SCITEK's Inventory and Property Book Management System Software/Database System.

The success of the MPC project with SCITEK led to another highly successful project. In June of 1992, Drake Tech was awarded a small procurement of $25,000 by the U.S. Army Missile Command Research Development and Engineering Center, Advanced System Concept Office to conduct a feasibility study of a "Virtual Reality Simulator." The VRS project was finalized in the early fall of 1992. We eagerly await the opportunity to put the VRS Feasibility into hardware reality.

The Electronics Department has a broad field of more than 40 years of combined instructional experiences. The faculty's educational background vary from the Associate Degree level to the Educational Specialist level. A vast quantity of military training (missile and electronic), industrial application, and teaching at the senior college level in science, electronics and physics affords the college a strong teaching faculty.

The faculty serves on many of the State of Alabama education committees including the: Curriculum Review and Leadership Committee for Electronics, etc. The AVA Trade and Industrial Section - Post Secondary Division, named Drake's Electronics instructor "Teacher of the

Continues on Page 14

Year" for 1983. The faculty plays a major role in Drake's Local Professional Development activities and Drake's Tech Prep efforts.

The faculty and students of the Electronics Department teach and learn in five spacious, well-equipped laboratories. The estimated value of these laboratories is $2-million. The faculty and Drake's staff write proposals on both the Federal and State levels over $80,000.00 in the last five years.

The Department of Electronics is well-known throughout the city of Huntsville and the state of Alabama for producing highly trained electronics technicians. For the last 15 years, the Electronics Department has produced first place, second place, or third place winners on the State level during the annual Skill Olympics - VICA. During the same period, we have represented the State of Alabama at the National Skills Olympics - VICA level.

Contact:
Bobby Petty, Instructor-In-Charge
(205) 539-8161

J.F. Drake State Technical College
3421 Meridian Street North
Huntsville, AL 35811
Total headcount enrollment-Credit: 33,237 Non-Credit: 16,992
Campuses/sites: 1; Full-time faculty: 24

TRAINING WITH INDUSTRY

Students in the program take one course at a time over a shorter period rather than a few courses at once over a traditional quarter

The Training With Industry Program at Jefferson Davis Community College is a unique service because both the academic calendar and teaching strategies have been modified to meet the needs of employees of a local textile mile. All programs are credentialed and taught on-site by members of the college faculty to employees as a group.

In the traditional fashion, students who attend Jefferson Davis enroll for 10 to 15 credit hours and take two to three courses per week for a 10-week period. But in the Industry Program, students who enroll for 10 credit hours will take the first course twice a week for the first half of the 10-week quarter and the second course twice a week for the remaining five weeks of the quarter. Students in the

program are able to focus on one subject at a time and concentrate on their studies while juggling a full-time job and families.

Special support and recognition of this program has been reflected by the contributions of textbooks to all students by a private donor. A testament to the success of this project is the graduation of 10 employee/students with an Associate of Arts degree in the spring of 1992. A special dinner and awards ceremony was provided by the college for these graduates.

Five additional industry programs have been initiated since 1989 following this format.

Contact:
Sherry Martin, Assistant to the Academic Dean
205-867-4832, ext. 87

Jefferson Davis Community College
220 Alco Drive
Brewton, AL 36426
Total headcount enrollment-Credit: 1,723 Non-Credit: 11
Campuses/sites: 2; Full-time faculty: 50

SUCCESS CENTER

The Center serves as an umbrella organization for a variety of support services, including free GED preparatory classes

The Success Center at Jefferson Davis Community College aims to improve the lot of people in its economically depressed, rural area of Alabama where only 47 percent of adults older than 25 have a high school diploma and where only 6.7 percent of the two-county service area population are college graduates.

Located on the Brewton campus, the Success Center s is designed to: 1) enhance the skills of successful students as well as provide developmental assistance; 2) provide adults an opportunity to earn a GED certificate; and 3) provide basic adult literacy training by a professional staff.

Continues on Page 15

The Success Center is a unique service; seed money for pre-operational support services – such as scholarship and counseling sessions targeting high-risk adults wishing to enter post secondary programs for the first time – was provided by local funds. Also, funds for start-up personnel, equipment and supplies, were provided by the U.S. Department of Education through Title III funds. The program has been so successful that state funds were allocated to replicate the program on the college's Atmore campus.

The Center now serves as the umbrella organization for a variety of support services. Through the donation of a private benefactor, the college has been able to establish a comprehensive GED testing and services program. The college provides free GED preparatory classes and administers the GED exam free of charge on a weekly rotation basis between its two campuses.

Approximately 200 adults have taken the exam this past year through this program. To encourage adults who earn a GED certificate to further their education and show its commitment to the adult population, the college offers scholarships on a competitive basis to individuals who score above average on the exam. GED certificate holders are the largest single category of students enrolled at Jefferson Davis Community College.

Through a Community-Based Organization Grant, the college has entered into a cooperative venture with the Brewton Area Adult Reading Council to provide basic reading and writing instruction to adults with little or no reading ability. Volunteers from the community are trained by the Success Center staff to provide tutoring sessions for those seeking assistance and to establish an individualized plan to help each learner meet his or her goals. Since 1990, 20 tutors have been trained by the staff and have provided more than 1,000 hours of instruction.

In addition to these services, New Horizons and Second Career Opportunity Programs provide tuition scholarships, textbooks and childcare to displaced homemakers, single parents, unemployed adults, and individuals wishing to change careers or to enter employment for the first time. The scholarship program through this service is made available through federal funds and the donation of a local trust. Preparatory classes in study skills, time management and assertiveness are conducted to address the ongoing needs of this group.

Contact:
Sherry Martin, Assistant to the Academic Dean
205-867-4832, ext. 87

Jefferson Davis Community College
220 Alco Drive
Brewton, AL 36426
Total headcount enrollment-Credit: 1,723 Non-Credit: 11
Campuses/sites: 2; Full-time faculty: 50

CULINARY APPRENTICESHIP

Area chefs collaborated with college personnel to design and implement the program

The Culinary Apprenticeship Program at Jefferson State Community College is a joint venture that showcases an education-business partnership at its best. The program was initiated by the college in 1985 at the request of the Birmingham, Alabama Chapter of the American Culinary Federation, Inc. College personnel in the Food Management Technology program and Birmingham chefs have collaborated closely in implementing the program as designed by the American Culinary Federation Educational Institute (ACFEI).

Students in the program complete their academic studies, including 38 hours of general education and 60 hours of foods and nutrition (FNT) courses at Jefferson State. In addition, they acquire a solid foundation of cooking skills, techniques and knowledge through 6,000 hours of on-the-job training in a local qualified food-service establishment, under the supervision of a certified chef. Upon completion of the program, the apprentice is awarded an AAS Degree from Jefferson State and a certificate of completion from the American Culinary Federation Educational Institute. The graduate also will have the required number of certification points to apply to the American Culinary Federation as a Certified Cook, the first level of certification for chefs.

Since its initiation in spring of 1986, enrollment in the program has grown from seven to 24, and its graduates are in high demand in the area. The Birmingham chefs have continued to provide support for the program, not only as instructors and supervisors for apprentices, but also through donations of equipment, supplies and money. The program received its accreditation from the American Culinary Federation Educational Institute Accrediting Commission in 1992.

Contact:
Janie Greene, Coordinator, Food Services Management Program
(205) 853-1200, ext. 1538

Jefferson State Community College
2601 Carson Road,
Birmingham, AL 35215
Total headcount enrollment-Credit: 7,493 Non-Credit: 397
Campuses/sites: 2; Full-time faculty: 151

LEARNING SUCCESS CENTER

In consultation with the Center, some faculty members have implemented study skills lectures and have printed materials for their students

Jefferson State Community College recruits a diverse student population and promotes academic success for all students entering the college through its Learning Success Center (LSC).

The purposes of the LSC are:

1) to assist students in developing and implementing objectives that lead to attainment of educational goals; and

2) to assist faculty and staff with developing and implementing strategies, techniques, and materials for classroom and laboratory settings that foster active learning.

The LSC implemented in 1988, provides individual and group study skills instruction, computer- and video-assisted learning, and tutoring for students. The Learning and Study Skills Inventory is used to assess strengths and weaknesses of individual students. Prescriptions based on these assessments are developed utilizing resources within the open lab setting. Instructional software is available for developmental as well as college-level topics. Software topics include mathematics, English, biology, chemistry,

physics, accounting, history, geography, nursing, word processing, psychology and sociology. Instructional videotapes, ranging from basic mathematics to calculus, are available. Individual and small-group tutoring is provided for courses identified as high-risk for entering students.

The LSC encourages faculty and staff to participate in LSC activities. LSC staff members provide guest lectures regarding effective study and learning strategies in content courses. In consultation with the LSC staff, some faculty members have implemented study skills lectures and print materials for students enrolled in their classes. If a faculty member is unable to address a specific learning or study problem, a referral may be made to the LSC. Joint projects for the LSC and academic divisions have included development of a vocabulary-building course and a mathematics study skills course.

The LSC is open 56 hours per week. From its inception, the LSC has realized tremendous growth, from 519 students in 1989 to 1,867 in 1991. Development of the LSC was made possible through Title III Part A Strengthen Institutions Program funds.

Contact:
Linda J. Hooton, Director, Academic Services
(205) 853-1200, ext. 1536

Jefferson State Community College
2601 Carson Road
Birmingham, AL 35215
Total headcount enrollment-Credit: 7,493 Non-Credit: 397
Campuses/sites: 2; Full-time faculty: 151

CONCEPTS OF SCIENCE COURSE

The interdisciplinary course is designed for students who have only a 10-hour science requirement in their programs

The explosion of new information in all scientific fields and the increasing importance of science in our daily lives have made an understanding of the function and role of science of the utmost importance. Unfortunately, science illiteracy is increasing.

To bridge the information gap for students not majoring in science, Southern Union State Junior College developed an interdisciplinary course called Concepts of Science for students who have only a 10-hour science requirement in their programs.

Concepts of Science is a non-lab course that introduces the basic concepts, stresses the interactions between structure and energy, and stresses the impact of the sciences on

everyday life. The course is designed to enable the student to: 1) demonstrate an understanding of the structure of science; 2) demonstrate an understanding of energy; 3) demonstrate an understanding of the interaction of structure and energy; and 4) demonstrate an understanding of the interaction between the sciences and humanities.

In its first year the course enrolled approximately 100 students in the six sections that have been offered. Efforts have been made to expand understanding and appreciation of the sciences through explorations of historical aspects of science and through external reading by students. Additionally, an understanding and use of the scientific method has been stressed through computer simulations that require students to apply appropriate methods in problem solving.

Because textbooks currently do not exist for this type of course, much effort has been put into the development of an appropriate text.

Concepts of Science at SUSJC will continue to grow in enrollment, and it is expected that up to 500 students eventually will be enrolled annually in the course.

Contact:
Ron Estridge, Instructor
(205) 395-2211

Southern Union State Junior College
Roberts Street
Wadley, AL 36276
Total headcount enrollment-Credit: 3,366 Non-Credit: 1,972
Campuses/sites: 3; Full-time faculty: 52

MACHINE SHOP TECHNOLOGY AND COMPUTER NUMERICAL CONTROL

⁜ The hi-tech computerized machining program has been equipped, ⁜ with input from industry, with state-of-the art equipment

In 1975, Wallace State Community College at Hanceville launched a multi-million-dollar project to develop the most progressive hi-tech computerized machining program within the Southeast. It continues to have tremendous success.

The project was a response to the demand by a hi-tech industrial area surrounding the college. This industry had a high demand for machining employees with numerical control, computer numerical control, computer numerical control, computer assist programming and graphics programming. None of the traditional machine shop training programs had the equipment or instructors to provide this type training.

The college, working closely with industry, equipped and developed a state-of-the-art computerized machining center now recognized as one of the top machining training programs in the nation. The program has been equipped with NC horizontal and vertical mills, CNC lathes, CNC wire E.D.M. with four axis, a four-axis milling machine, Intergraph Interact 220 CAD/CAM Computers, a computerized coordinate measuring machine plus numerous manually operated lathes, mills, grinders, boring mills and shapers.

The program has experienced great success with the percentage of graduate placement in the high 90's. Graduates have experienced phenomenal success in positions including machinist, tool-die makers, computer assist programmers, inspectors and engineering technicians. Students competing in the VICA State Skills Competition placed first for a span of nine consecutive years plus a first-place national winner.

Contact:
Herb Black
(205) 352-6403

Wallace State Community College
801 Main Street Northwest
Hanceville, AL 35077
Total headcount enrollment-Credit: 4,566 Non-Credit: 725
Campuses/sites: 2; Full-time faculty: 115

PHYSICAL THERAPIST ASSISTANT

⁜ The two-year program prepares graduates for employment in hospitals, rehab centers, ⁜ nursing homes, home health care agencies and private practices

In April of 1992, the Physical Therapist Assistant Program at Wallace State Community College in Hanceville received accreditation by the Commission on Accreditation in Physical Therapy Education. The program is a two-year Associate in Applied Science degree. The first year consists of general education courses while the second year consists of classroom and clinical instruction.

The Physical Therapist Assist (PTA) is a skilled technical health worker who, under the supervision of a licensed

Continues on Page 18

physical therapist, assists in the patient's treatment program. A planned patient care program is carried out by the assistant following established procedures. Duties of the Physical Therapist Assistant are varied but include rehabilitation of orthopedic, neurological and pediatric impairments, and sports related problems. Physical Therapist Assistants are employed in general hospitals, rehabilitation centers, nursing homes, home health care agencies, private practices and other specialized health care settings.

The student must complete the first year of program prerequisites before being eligible for the Physical Therapist Assistant Program. Second-year classes begin in the fall and four quarters are necessary to complete the final year of the program. The second year includes technical and clinical experience at a variety of health care settings where the student works under the supervision of a Registered Physical Therapist.

Contact:
Melinda Campbell
(205) 352-6403

Wallace State Community College
801 Main Street Northwest
Hanceville, AL 35077
Total headcount enrollment-Credit: 4,566 Non-Credit: 725
Campuses/sites: 2; Full-time faculty: 115

FISHING VESSEL OIL SPILL RESPONSE TRAINING

*The college developed this multi-year training program
as a direct result of the Exxon Valdez oil spill*

The Fishing Vessel Oil Spill Response Training program, a direct result of the 1989 Exxon Valdez oil spill, trains crews how to respond to oil spills.

This multi-year training program followed the oil industry's establishment of the Ship Escort/Response Vessel System (SERVS) in Valdez. The SERVS mission is to prevent oil spills by escorting tankers throughout Prince William Sound, and to provide initial response personnel and equipment in the event that a spill occurs. Part of the SERVS plan to respond to a major spill in the area is to employ fishing vessels from the ports of Prince William Sound and the Northwestern Gulf of Alaska to assist in a spill cleanup.

In the fall of 1992 SERVS approached Prince William Sound Community College with a request to develop the multi-year training program for fishing vessel crews involved in oil spill operations. A contract to develop and deliver oil spill training was signed by SERVS and PWSCC in November of 1992.

Because fishing vessel crews are not available for training between mid-April and mid-September, the training had to be developed and delivered in a very short time. For their expertise in industrial and safety training, the Mining and Petroleum Training Service (MAPTS) of the University of Alaska was brought into the course development process in the earliest stages. MAPTS has been conducting industrial training in Alaska since 1979. SERVS personnel played a large role in the training development. SERVS equipment operators were the logical choice to teach the classroom and hands-on equipment and machinery portions of the class.

In January and February of 1993 as intensive effort by PWSCC, MAPTS and SERVS resulted in the development of a two-day training course. In March and April the class was presented in four coastal communities, with some communities receiving multiple sessions to meet the local need for trained crews. A total of 263 students were trained by mid-April.

Once all crews in the fishing vessel oil response fleet have been through the basic training class, a yearly refresher/advanced training course will be instituted to upgrade and enhance their skills. New personnel will receive basic training through regularly scheduled classes. Specialty training, such as wildlife rescue techniques, will be developed and delivered as needed. Keeping track of qualified personnel through the college's record-keeping system is an important component of the program.

Prince William Sound Community College's oil spill response training project has demonstrated that partnerships in training development with industry can meet critical needs in a timely and cost-effective manner.

Contact:
Vince Kelly, Director, Vocational Education and Training
(907) 835-2943

Prince William Sound Community College
PO Box 97
Valdez, AK 99686
Total headcount enrollment-Credit: 1,989 Non-Credit: 831
Campuses/sites: 3; Full-time faculty: 10

CENTER FOR TEACHING EFFECTIVENESS

*The Center addresses the challenge to develop a systematic approach
to faculty retention, appraisal and development*

Continuous feedback is the impetus for continuous improvement at Arizona Western College's Center for Teaching Effectiveness. Founded on the belief that the faculty of a college is its most important human resource, the AWC Center for Teaching Effectiveness addresses the challenge to develop a systematic approach to faculty retention, appraisal and continuous development. The Center serves as a catalyst for change as faculty move to new life stages; societal changes result in more complexity; technology advances at alarming rates; and the cultural mix of students becomes increasingly diversified.

The Arizona Western College model ties assessment activities at three levels to development actions on three corresponding levels with continuous feedback. Holistically looking at issues raised through personnel appraisal, program review and organizational climate assessment touches all parts of the organization resulting in substantive organizational transformation. Prior to the creation of the Center for Teaching Effectiveness, Arizona Western College had a faculty appraisal system which had been abandoned for several years.

The strategy used to implement a systematic approach to faculty development included a Title III proposal to establish the Center for Teaching Effectiveness. The leadership structure for the Center supports the need for high visibility, faculty empowerment and integration into academic decision making. Pivotal to its success is the delineation of the CTE director's role. Critical structural elements include faculty status of the directorship, rotating tenureship in the role, direct reporting relationship to the Vice-President for Academic Affairs and membership on the College Academic Council.

Complementing the organizational structure is strong fiscal resource allocation. The operational funds for the Center for Teaching Effectiveness are allocated from three areas: institutional operating funds, Title III funds, and division funds that support faculty travel. The total amount of the operating budget from institution and grant funds was $136,295 for 1992-93. The individual division budgets contain professional development travel funds that totaled $62,136 for 1992-93. Together these monies account for 1.4 percent of the college operating budget.

The implementation strategy that provides the backbone for broad-based support is the committee structure. Committees, primarily composed of faculty (although some include students, classified employees and professional administrators), help guide the assessment, development and implementation of the program. All receive clerical, budget and facilitation support.

The objectives of the Center for Teaching Effectiveness as identified by the Professional Development Committee include: promoting professional and personal development of the faculty; developing a better understanding and support of the college mission and goals; providing needs-based programs and ongoing activities for professional and personal development; acquainting faculty with college resources and services; promoting an environment of trust, professionalism and teamwork; expanding assistance to associate faculty; and increasing student learning outcomes.

Changes in teaching effectiveness are evidenced in many ways. Most importantly, there is a change in the organizational climate throughout the entire campus. The focus is on improving teaching and learning through everything the college does. Specific examples of recent successes at Arizona Western College include:

- a new center where faculty can come for resources and input into instructional issues;
- the integrated use of computers within the curriculum in several divisions;
- the development of an Open Access Computer lab to support faculty computer-based assignments;
- an overall 3 percent improvement rate in the retention since 1989;
- a Faculty Appraisal System that focuses on both formative and summative opportunities for improvement;
- a Faculty Mentor Program to orient new full time and associate faculty to Arizona Western College;
- a Flex Program to provide for the individually selected professional growth opportunities of the faculty;
- a Ranch Experience modeled after the national model for Great Teacher Seminars; and
- presentations on CTE programs have been given at various prestigious conferences and meetings.

The CTE will focus for the next three years on the development of a Program Review model, the implementation of Renaissance Projects (Mini-grants) tied to outcomes of appraisal and program review, and the institutionalization of grant funds that support the Center.

Contact:
Kathy Watson, Director
(602) 344-7756

Arizona Western College
PO Box 929
Yuma, AZ 85366
Total headcount enrollment-Credit: 7,401
Campuses/sites: 5; Full-time faculty: 86

AVIATION

*⊠ The program is strengthened by some 30 jet and piston ⊠
aircraft based at the college's on-campus airport*

Besides the fundamentals only learned through hands-on training, Cochise College incorporates critical thinking, problem-solving and applied math across the aviation curriculum. The aviation program is also strengthened by a multi-million dollar facility, including some 30 jet and piston aircraft based at the college's own on-campus airport.

The need for such a program is obvious. There has been a dramatic increase in the amount of air travel over the last 40 years, creating a need for additional trained pilots, mechanics and communication systems repair persons. Cochise College has provided professional pilot and aviation maintenance technician programs since 1968 and has recently added avionics to its nationally recognized aviation program.

The aviation program offers students a variety of study alternatives for aviation careers, including courses culminating in FAA Certificates for Commercial Pilots, Flight Instructors and Airline Transport Pilots, as well as Airframe, Power Plant and Avionics Technicians. The Aviation Program allows students to choose the area in which they wish to concentrate and offers degrees up to the Associate of Applied Science level.

Courses are designed to ensure that graduates have practical, hands-on training combined with academic and technical knowledge that will enhance their ability to compete in the global aviation arena. The Cochise College aviation division also recognizes the value of applied academics and has incorporated critical thinking, problem solving and applied mathematics across the curriculum.

Fully accredited by the FAA, the college's southern Arizona location contributes to the successful training with its optimal year-round climate.

The Aviation Program has grown to include 12 full-time instructors and is supplemented by several adjunct faculty and placement services. The annual budget for this program approaches $1-million, indicating a strong commitment from the residents of the community in providing students with training that leads to rewarding careers in the aviation industry.

Contact:
Lee Oppeheim, Chairman
(602) 364-0302

Cochise College
Route 1, Box 100
Douglas, AZ 85607
Total headcount enrollment-Credit: 5,000 Non-Credit: 634
Campuses/sites: 3; Full-time faculty: 100

TECH PREP

*⊠ Tech Prep has required unprecedented cooperation between secondary ⊠
and post secondary instructors, resulting in better training for students*

The critical shortage of skilled workers has created a sense of urgency in many business managers throughout the country who recognize global competitiveness depends on a highly trained work force. Cochise College answered this need by establishing and implementing core and technical skills within college curriculum in conjunction with seven local area high schools. Tech Prep has required unprecedented cooperation between secondary and post secondary instructors. Through this effort, students are more technically prepared, can solve problems and work in groups, and will help bring our nation back to its former competitive level.

Tech Prep, combines the last two years of high school with two years of advanced technical training at the college level to enable graduates to enter industry at a higher level of preparedness.

These core skills were developed with the help of business and industry and will prepare all students for: 1) higher degree programs at the community college level; and 2) rewarding employment upon completion of an Associates Degree. Technical skills will complement core skills by providing students with the competitive edge needed in today's work place.

Cooperation between secondary and post secondary instructors has flourished allowing for alignment of curriculum. This reduces duplication of courses and enhances student success at the community college. High school students now can begin programs in their junior year leading to degrees in Avionics, Media-Communications and Hospitality, three areas once only reserved for college students. Alignment of curriculum to incorporate employability and technical skills involved partnerships with local, state and national industries. These

Continues on Page 22

relationships serve to provide an evaluation of the program offerings by ensuring curriculum and outcomes mirror industry needs.

Emphasis on academic and vocational integration and applied course work (applied math, principles of technology and applied communication) has moved instructors from a traditional lecture-based methodology to hands-on learning. In-service days at both the secondary and post secondary levels have provided instructors with information on applied teaching methodologies, student outcomes and performance standards and measures.

Contact:
Ray Nadolny, Program Coordinator
(602) 458-7880, ext. 110 or (602) 458-4994

Cochise College
Route 1, Box 100
Douglas, AZ 85607
Total headcount enrollment-Credit: 5,000 Non-Credit: 634
Campuses/sites: 3; Full-time faculty: 100

MOHAVE COMMUNITY COLLEGE

EMERGENCY DISPATCH TRAINING

Local police leaders and directors of 911 dispatch centers advise the program, and experienced dispatchers help teach

When far too few qualified dispatchers could be found for the county's new 911 system, Mohave Community College helped develop what became the first Emergency Dispatch Training program in Arizona.

Working with five law-enforcement agencies in the county and the Association of Public Communications Officers, Mohave Community College in 1991 developed a certificate of 23 hours and an AAS degree program were developed. One of the courses developed proved to have a much wider appeal than the EDT students. Spanish for Protective Services Personnel has a growing enrollment of police officers not in EDT programs.

Local police leaders and the directors of the 911 dispatch centers serve as an active advisory committee. Experienced dispatch personnel from the different agencies agreed to serve as associate faculty. Dispatch equipment was provided by one of the agencies and in the spring of 1992 classes began at two locations in the county.

The response to the program by the law enforcement agencies, students and the communities served has been significant and positive. Many of those enrolled were referred to the program by local law-enforcement departments. Upon completion of the certificate program students are permitted to sit for the APCO certifying examination. This exam is administered by Mohave Community College.

Contact:
Annabelle Lewis, Dean, Community/Occupational Services
(602) 757-0898

Mohave Community College
1971 Jagerson Avenue
Kingman, AZ 86401
Total headcount enrollment-Credit: 6,219
Campuses/sites: 14; Full-time faculty: 46

MOHAVE COMMUNITY COLLEGE

CASINO GAMING

The program, which has its own training facility, has consistently placed 93 percent of its graduates

It was no gamble for Mohave community College to start a Casino Gaming program, complete with its own training facility. In 1990, the first students completed a certificate program in this unique aspect of hospitality, the most significant industry for the twin cities of Bullhead City, Arizona, and Laughlin, Nevada.

The curriculum and teaching manuals were developed locally with support from the major casinos in Laughlin.

These same casinos have continued to provide experienced associate faculty for the program. Mohave Community College constructed a training facility and began a program that has consistently placed more than 93 percent of its graduates. In the initial year 50 students were enrolled. The enrollment now consistently tops 140.

The program is staffed by a full-time director who has extensive management experience in casino gaming. The faculty is comprised of 10 associates who are practicing and highly skilled employees from the major casinos. The casinos not only hire beginning employees, but also are sending some of their existing personnel back for additional training leading to the Casino Dealer Master certificate.

Mohave Community College's sister college, Colorado Mountain College, requested and was given the curriculum to aid them in the development of their program. The director of the program for MCC has served as a consultant and source of information to several developing programs across the country.

Contact:
Dina Glasser, Director
(602) 758-3926

Mohave Community College
1971 Jagerson Avenue
Kingman, AZ 86401
Total headcount enrollment-Credit: 6,219
Campuses/sites: 14; Full-time faculty: 46

THE EAGLE NETWORK:
EXPANDING THE LEARNING EXPERIENCE

Because the college services such a vast service area, students may attend class electronically and at community learning centers

Serving a district with only seven people per square mile over a vast 21,000-square-mile area would be nearly impossible for Northland Pioneer College without television, a shuttle system and community centers. But with these and other innovations, the college, itself a small, rural, isolated institution, reaches a highly diverse cultural and economic populace.

The college's service area encompasses Navajo and Apache counties, general municipalities, and three reservations for the Apache, Hopi and Navajo tribes. The total service area is 100 miles wide and 250 miles long. The largest city in the district has fewer than 9,000 residents. The district's population density is seven people per square mile.

In addition to four main campuses with headcount enrollments between 500 and 1,300 each, 15 additional college locations provide extended service satellite community learning centers in approximately 15 additional towns. A unique ground-transportation shuttle system of vans and cars daily and weekly delivers students, instructors, supplies and equipment to campuses and outlying community learning centers. To minimize travel time and costs for students, class scheduling was concentrated to primarily one day per week time blocks of three to four hours.

Because even all these adaptations are not enough, in the early 1980's the college moved forward with an approximate $25,000 purchase and installation of a DAROME live audio telephone line conference bridging system. Using desktop microphones, the system was able to link one instructor with students from any of 10 communities to create classes large enough (15-plus people) to make previously lower enrollment courses feasible to offer. Also, travel 20-to-100-plus miles each way was greatly reduced for many students. For others their waiting time of two

semesters to four semesters for a needed class to actually get enough enrollment in their community, no longer was needed. The primordial Eagle Network was born.

The Eagle Network has grown in many technical and philosophical ways to expand the district's learning experiences, services and support operations. Based on this initial success NPC developed a plan to construct a two-way interactive video system. A microwave path study confirmed possible radio site locations and possible repeater sites to penetrate six of the main communities in the district as well as several others. With the help of a Title III federal grant of $1.2-million spread over three years, and $300,000 from the institution over the same period, an extensive microwave backbone system has been developed and used successfully since 1988. Since then the system has been expanded to carry telecommunications signals for the audio classes, audio-video classes, multiple types of meetings such as faculty, classified staff, administrators, advisory councils and others, and telefacsimile transmission. In 1991, the telecommunications department assumed control of the college's entire telephone systems. It now literally is a telephone and data communications company for the district with respect to connecting all campuses and learning centers across the service area. The system has received area and national engineering award recognition.

The annual operating budget for this system is stable at $160,000. Prior to the system's current use, annual outside source equipment costs to the district were $33,000 per year with an estimated cost of $133,000 per year for area telephone companies long distance and service charges. It is a goal of the Eagle Network personnel to effect a further reduction in cost of 20 percent to 25 percent.

Thirty-five to 40 classes are offered per semester over

Continues on Page 24

both the audio and video subsystems of the Eagle Network. The network annually serves 1,500-plus students (380-plus full-time student equivalent). Plans include interconnecting the system with Northern Arizona University's similar, but much smaller, system, in order to make available more upper division and higher degree course work throughout northeastern Arizona. Additional opportunities abound for rural professional organization in-service training as other linkages are refined and partnerships entered into.

Contact:
Brian Siemens, Technical Coordinator, Telecommunications
Gary Passer, Vice President, Instructional Services
(602) 524-1993

Northland Pioneer College
PO Box 610
Holbrook, AZ 86025
Total headcount enrollment-Credit: 2, 200
Campuses/sites: 19; Full-time faculty: 57

MOBILE COSMETOLOGY PROGRAM

The mobile facility has 20 student-training cosmetology stations, plus other stations for such things as dryers

Northland Pioneer College's entire Mobile Cosmetology program is moved annually between two cities 90 miles apart in order to better serve a vast and sparsely populated region.

At one time, a very small private cosmetology school in one of the most centralized communities of the college service area had been struggling to stay open for some time. A needs assessment in the early 1980's showed a need for additional cosmetologists to be trained in the college's service area, but not enough to have a continuing program in any one community. The spirit of "taking the education/training to the people" philosophy was what NPC was founded on. In the early years it consisted of duplicating small facilities or leasing them for multiple simultaneous offerings in multiple small communities. However, a traveling cosmetology program was instead designed to alternate the program's location at opposite ends of the service area in alternate years. This meant moving the entire program annually between Winslow, Arizona, and Show Low, Arizona, a distance of 90 miles.

Using minimal funds, an extra-wide mobile facility was designed with 20 student-training cosmetology stations inside the shell area of a typical larger single-wide mobile home. Ten stations were created along each side. Additional stations for dryers, shampooing, clinic management/instructor work and supply storage were put at one end. Each of the 20 training stations consists of mirror, locking overhead and under counter storage, and a special cosmetologist's client chair. Classroom lecture space is borrowed from nearby buildings as needed at the host site of the program each year, as is the library, student lounge and other common service areas. A permanent "modular building parking pad" with utility connections has been created at each site to round out minimal facility needs.

Curricular/calendar modifications from traditional schools of cosmetology to meet the state's cosmetology board's 1600 hours training minimum include concentrating the program from one of "open-entry/open-exit flexible hours" to a program that meets five days a week for eight hours a day through a 10-1/2 month total-immersion program from August through mid-June.

For practical student training and community service the program provides "open to the public" cosmetology services beginning in November of each year on a "cost recovery-only" basis. This is attractive to regular college students, staff, special clientele such as persons on low incomes, and others. All students are expected to take and pass the state licensing examination at the end of the program. The retention and success rate are consistently higher than those of private schools.

Institutional and community economic feasibility has been gained by a 10-year continuing history of full classes each year. Only a few seriously interested and qualified students are turned away each year, matching fairly closely the interest level to space availability, market demand, and the instructor/coordinator personnel costs. If students do drop out, their training station is filled with licensed cosmetologists seeking instructor license training or manicurist hours, both requiring much less than 1,600 hours of training. The mobile cosmetology program is staffed by one full-time instructor/coordinator.

Students annually compete and do very well in regional and state hair styling and other related competitions. Over the past 10 years the program has consistently performed well as an anchor occupational program of the institution in a unique rural geographical setting that for students, staff, and communities is literally "on-the-move" every year!

Contact:
Flo Finch, Instructor/Coordinator
(602) 537-2976/289-4633

Northland Pioneer College
PO Box 610
Holbrook, AZ 86025
Total headcount enrollment-Credit: 2, 200
Campuses/sites: 19; Full-time faculty: 57

AFRICAN-AMERICAN HISTORY PROJECT

▦ Project participants are developing the first comprehensive ▦
history of a predominantly Black neighborhood in Tucson

The first comprehensive oral history of a predominantly Black neighborhood in Tucson is but one result of the ongoing African-American History Project (AAHIP), which has brought the college and its community closer together.

The project (AAHIP) was begun in the spring of 1987 as a joint project of Pima County Community College District and Arizona Historical Society Southern Division to provide college credit for students interested in training to collect the oral histories of Tucson's older Black residents. As a result of their efforts, students were provided a scholarship by the Arizona Historical Society after successful completion of this project.

The Training of student interns, which was the original intent of the AAHIP has continued as the major focus. However, several related activities have occurred including a teacher in-service for teachers in Tucson School District #1 (the largest district in the city) to assist them in the preparation of materials and class outlines for Black culture month. Further, members of the project have been involved in the sponsorship of the Buffalo Soldier Round Up held in Tucson in August 1991; and a presentation at the Phoenix Art Museum on the Buffalo Soldiers depicted by Frederick Remington in his 1888 prints, sketches and oils.

This year the AAHIP participants are working on a display for the Arizona Historical society that will trace the history of the South Park Neighborhood. The AAHIP in cooperation with Tucson Urban League and the Arizona Humanities Council will develop the first comprehensive history of a predominantly Black neighborhood in Tucson. The oral histories and artifacts will be displayed by the Historical Society in the fall of 1994.

In the five years of its existence, the AAHIP has trained more than 24 interns, recorded 30 oral histories and generated $8,000 in scholarships to attend Pima College and the University of Arizona. AAHIP is an example of how community colleges, working with community groups, can enhance their scholarship base while providing enriching educational experiences for students.

Contact:
Michael S. Engs, Associate Dean
(602) 884-6194

Pima County Community College District
PO Box 3010
Tucson, AZ 85702-3010
Total headcount enrollment-Credit: 40,800 Non-Credit: 13,184
Campuses/sites: 7; Full-time faculty: 303

INSTRUCTIONAL TECHNOLOGY AND DISTANCE EDUCATION

▦ The college offers courses via such venues as television, print, audiographic ▦
teleconference and interactive video teleconference

Besides providing more accessible education, Instructional Technology at Rio Salado Community College fosters integration of technology in design, development, delivery and management of educational programs and services.

But the greatest impact of the distance program has been and continues to be service to those students who have been unserved or underserved by the campus environment. The distance program appeals to students who may be full-time employees, shift workers, incarcerated, homebound, parents or rural residents. This program enables students at a distance to complete all their Associate of Arts Degree or Associate of General Studies Degree requirements. Travel is limited, the time frame is as unrestrictive as possible, and the cost is the same as a classroom student would pay.

Rio Salado Community College has a long history of distance delivery in higher education. Beginning with the establishment of the college in 1978, Instructional Technology has grown from a department offering five to six telecourses in a semester to a program of more than 45 different courses offered through eight different delivery systems: broadcast and cable television, print, audio cassette, audio teleconference, audiographic teleconference, computer conference and interactive video teleconference.

To support the goals of Instructional Technology and to ensure a quality program, several factors are required such as: certified faculty to conduct each course, proctored testing, a faculty evaluation process, an efficient support staff, an efficient messaging system to facilitate communication between faculty and students, and attentiveness and responsiveness to student needs. Instructional Technology

Continues on Page 26

conducts ongoing program review and evaluation – continually updating and revising the instructional approach, delivery method and informative materials associated with each course. Ongoing evaluation has led to an expanded format for offering classes. "IT" now has a tri-semester format available for most courses and is experimenting with multiple start dates to accommodate the courses, such as Reading or Sociology, that have an extremely high demand .

In addition to addressing instructional and operational needs, Instructional Technology also invests staff time and allocates resources to research and development activities. These activities keep Instructional Technology on the forefront of new approaches to distance education. The most recent development project is an animated graphics system that will be compatible with both the audiographics and video teleconference deliveries.

Rio Salado Community College's Department of Instructional Technology has been a leader in distance education and alternative delivery systems for more than a decade. It is considered by many institutions to be one of the most far-ranging and innovative in the country and in the world. Instructional Technology welcomes visitors from the United States and international visitors on a nearly monthly basis to discuss the distance program. The college staff also participates in conferences and programs held by organizations such as the Instructional Telecommunications Consortium, the Association for Educational Communications and Technology, the National University Teleconference Network and the Annenberg/CPB Project.

Contact:
Betsy Frank
(602) 223-4201

Rio Salado Community College
640 North First Avenue
Phoenix, AZ 85003
Total headcount enrollment-Credit: 27,000 Non-Credit: 11,000
Campuses/sites: 250; Full-time faculty: 10

INSTITUTE FOR CULTURE AND LANGUAGE LEARNING

Thirteen foreign languages are offered in a variety of time formats ranging from two weeks to six weeks

The Institute for Culture and Language Learning (ICLL) provides educational experiences that contribute to the promotion of better understanding of diverse cultures through language instruction, cultural activities and related course instruction.

Located centrally in Maricopa County and easily accessible via interstate from all parts of the region, the ICLL offers 13 foreign languages in a variety of time formats and methods.

The best-attended courses are those offered in the activated/accelerated formats and methodologies. These courses range in length from two weeks to six weeks, and utilize activities that support immersion learning such as dance, games, drama, music, costuming, art projects and other experiential activities. Spanish, French, German and Italian are offered in this format. For these courses, classrooms are highly decorated with artifacts, souvenirs, posters and products from the nations in which these languages are spoken. The rooms also are equipped with permanent stereo sound systems and audio visual equipment utilized in the accelerated method to provide learning experiences that appeal to different human senses.

In addition to accelerated courses, other languages are offered in more traditional formats and using more conventional methods: Portuguese, Chinese, Japanese, Korean, Arabic, Greek, Hebrew, Latin and Russian.

French, German and Italian also are offered in traditional as well as activated methods.

The ICLL was initially established primarily to meet the need of school teachers who are required to facilitate the teaching of Spanish in their classrooms. By combining the activated/accelerated methodology with the desirability of having permanent, decorated, fully equipped classrooms dedicated to language instruction, Rio Salado was able to meet the needs of these teachers quickly during the summer months. However, once established, it was discovered that there are many employee groups throughout the county seeking foreign language instruction in more convenient and effective delivery methods, so expansion of the ICLL offerings was indicated. Additional languages, methods, and formats were added, and the success of the entire enterprise has been overwhelming. Approximately 1,500 people each semester avail themselves of the opportunities to vary their learning schedules and intensity at the ICLL.

Staffed with a full-time administrator and a full-time clerical person, the ICLL operates with a streamlined work force and relies heavily on adjunct faculty. Instructors have been carefully selected and trained in the activated methodology and are constantly evaluated and supported by two full-time foreign-language instructors who have undergone extensive training themselves. Materials have been developed for each language taught at the ICLL and placed permanently in appropriately designed classrooms. Some classrooms have large amounts of peripherals, and other hands-on materials are displayed to support a rich, relaxed yet challenging environment for learning.

In addition to language instruction, other activities occur at the ICLL or are planned for the future. Sponsorship of special events such as theater, debate, art, film, music or dance is part of the effort, and cultural understanding and awareness seminars and workshops are included in the plans.

The ICLL and the accelerated teaching methods used there have been featured in several local publications. In addition, representatives involved with the project have presented papers and demonstrations at local, national and international conferences and meetings.

Plans for the future for the ICLL include expansion of language courses and cultural activities, as well as activating/accelerating more of the languages currently taught there. A technology-based international learning center is on the agenda for future development, along with utilization of distance learning opportunities for overseas English as a Second Language instruction. Further and expanded training in the accelerated method is planned, and specially developed instructional packages and/or courses for community college foreign language instructors will be offered nationally. Refinement of current efforts will be undertaken as well, in order to assure learners at the Institute for Culture and Language Learning the finest opportunities to develop increased awareness, tolerance and appreciation of other cultures of the world.

Contact:
Carol Wilson
(602) 231-8659

Rio Salado Community College
640 North First Avenue
Phoenix, AZ 85003
Total headcount enrollment-Credit: 27,000 Non-Credit: 11,000
Campuses/sites: 250; Full-time faculty: 10

SOUTH MOUNTAIN COMMUNITY COLLEGE

ACE (ACHIEVING A COLLEGE EDUCATION)

High school students "at risk" of dropping out enter the program, which encourages higher education, after their sophomore year

High school students once at-risk of dropping out now are graduating and even pursuing higher education, thanks to a partnership of South Mountain Community College and Arizona State University. In 1991, for instance, SMCC's class valedictorian was a student who once had been considered a likely high school dropout.

The ACE (Achieving a College Education) program, students enroll in college classes during the summer following their sophomore year in high school. Private scholarships pay for their education until high school graduation. ACE students attend "summer institutes" and college classes during regular school year at South Mountain Community college (after regular school hours).

The goal of the program is to ensure that students complete high school and, eventually earn a baccalaureate

degree. Ninety-two percent of the ACE groups who started in 1988 and 1989 have graduated from high school, 65 percent are enrolled in higher education, and 2 percent enlisted in military service. Overall rates from Phoenix high schools were 57 percent in 1990 and 51 percent in 1991.

In May of 1991, the ACE program brought 160 new recruits to South Mountain Community College's campus. The program is in its fourth year and currently is tracking 468 students. On average, 200 ACE students are enrolled in college classes each semester either on Saturdays, or during evenings and summer sessions. A total of 6,590 credits were earned by ACE students from June 1988 to August 1991. Most of these credits were taken by high school students.

Contact:
Stella Torres
(602) 243-8000

South Mountain Community College
7050 South 24th Street
Phoenix, AZ 85040
Total headcount enrollment-Credit: 3,053
Campuses/sites: 3; Full-time faculty: 40

LIBRARY OUTREACH

▨ The program strives to make attending college ▨
a natural progression for children

In an attempt to demystify college, South Mountain Community College offers several reading and arts activities for pre-school through elementary school children. This Library Outreach Program began in 1986 with the ultimate goal of making attending college a natural and comfortable progression for young children in the community. Programming includes "story hours" for pre-school children, reading and arts activities for elementary-school-age children, after school and evenings, as well as field trips, summer reading programs, summer day camps, computer workshops and family reading programs.

The program also attracts community members to use the library. For many area residents, the two existing public libraries are difficult to reach. South Mountain Community College seeks to fill that need with extended library services to the community.

An average of 35 school-age children visit the college's library each day. The program has recorded more than 8,000 contacts with children since July of 1990, 2,800 of those since August 1991.

In addition to students and employees, more than 3,000 community members hold college library cards.

Contact:
Isabel Leroy
(602) 243-8000

South Mountain Community College
7050 South 24th Street
Phoenix, AZ 85040
Total headcount enrollment-Credit: 3,053
Campuses/sites: 3; Full-time faculty: 40

STUDENT SUPPORT SERVICES

*▨ Academically underprepared students get some extra help through ▨
this program, including tutoring and transfer assistance*

Assessment, counseling, tutoring and transfer assistance are offered to new students, who too often are academically underprepared when they arrive at Garland County Community College. The Arkansas Freshman Assessment and Placement Program, established by the Arkansas Legislature in 1987, requires all new freshmen at public colleges and universities in the state to be assessed to determine their college course placement in English, mathematics and reading. Those who do not meet placement cut-off scores set by the State Board are assigned to developmental courses in their area(s) of need. From this group approximately 225 students who qualify as first generation or low-income or have a physical disability are selected to participate in the federally funded Student Support Services Program.

The Student Support Services Program is staffed by a director, a counselor/disability specialist, a counselor/transfer specialist, a tutor supervisor/math specialist and a program secretary.

Additional assessment is provided to qualifying students not meeting cut-off scores. Tests include: the Test of Adult Basic Education (TABE) to determine specific functional level in reading, math and English; Learning Styles Inventory to determine students' learning mode preference; Goal Setting and Attainment Analysis to determine students' ability to set and attain realistic goals; and a Study Skills Inventory to determine students' ability to study effectively.

Academic, financial aid and personal counseling are provided to qualifying students on an individual and group basis. Students are assisted in the development of their degree plan and scheduling of classes according to their test scores. Financial aid counseling is provided to low-income students including identification of grant and loan opportunities and assistance in completing application forms. Personal and group counseling are provided according to need.

Tutoring in most academic subject areas is provided by peer and professional tutors. Small group instruction is provided in mathematics by a math specialist. An open-entry, open-exit math lab also is available.

Academic support services provided to students with learning and physical disabilities include: an evaluation of need for support services; consultation with faculty concerning needed classroom and testing accommodations; assistance with ordering recorded textbooks; coordination of note taking, reading and interpreting services with state and community rehabilitative agencies; and assistance with class scheduling and early registration.

Transfer assistance is provided to students wishing to continue their education at a four-year institution. Transfer assistance includes matriculation, housing, financial aid, counseling and, in some situations, networking with appropriate social services agencies.

The Student Support Services Program has been in existence at Garland County Community College for 13 years.

Contact:
Linda Swofford, Director
(501) 767-9371

Garland County Community College
100 College Drive
Hot Springs, AR 71913
Total headcount enrollment-Credit: 2,209   Non-Credit: 1,360
Campuses/sites: 1; Full-time faculty: 52

LEARNING ACCELERATION CENTER

*▨ The Center features computer-assisted instruction for students ▨
who are or will be enrolled in occupational programs*

More than 90 percent of Garland County Community College's entering students must enroll in pre-college level math, reading, writing or study skills – a stunning fact that requires significant action. But because the need so outweighs available teaching resources, GCCC developed the Learning Acceleration Center.

The Center, funded by the Carl D. Perkins Vocational and Applied Technology Education Act of 1990, features a Computer Assisted Instruction (CAI) Lab that supports

academic enhancement for the students who are or will be enrolled in occupational programs. The program provides for an assessment of academic skills, individualized prescriptive instruction, and pre- and post-testing to evaluate growth and achievement.

All students enrolled at Garland County Community College are qualified to receive CAI tutorial services in the Learning Acceleration Center. The LAC Lab operates as a

Continues on Page 30

"open-entry, open-exit" program. Students may begin CAI tutorials at any time during the semester and continue instruction until goals have been accomplished.

The Center's diagnostic and prescription system identifies a student's present level of functioning. It also provides a computerized printout identifying skills to be mastered in order to enhance student's potential for success in her/his academic and occupational program of study.

The Center's basic skills course offers more than 400 modules that teach individual reading, writing and math skills. Each course includes a pre-test, tutorial and post-test. A computer management system is used to organize, analyze, track, monitor and provide reports for students and teachers.

The Center has a director/instructor, secretary, lab assistant, faculty members who volunteer time, and a group of retired professionals from Hot Springs Village who volunteer time. The grant has provided $300,000 for the first two years. The Center is equipped to serve 20 students per hour. The lab is fully accessible for students with visual disabilities with the addition of adaptive equipment that includes a Braille printer, print enlarger, voice synthesizer and the computer magnifying system.

The Director has been invited to present this unique program to the American Vocational Association's National Conference in St. Louis. Articles in the local and school newspapers have featured the Center. The Director presented a workshop on this program to the state and local chapters of the American Association of University Women.

Contact:
Dianne Rogers, Director
(501) 767-9371, ext. 237

Garland County Community College
100 College Drive
Hot Springs, AR 71913
Total headcount enrollment-Credit: 2,209 Non-Credit: 1,360
Campuses/sites: 1; Full-time faculty: 52

BUSINESS AND INDUSTRY RESOURCE CENTER

The Center is a key component of college-sponsored economic development activities

Strategically located in an industrial park, the Business and Industry Resource Center at Mississippi County Community College provides training, retraining and information to area businesses and industries. From its inception, the BIRC developed a strong linkage to existing industries in Mississippi County.

The Center's roots reach back to 1985, when the State of Arkansas initiated the establishment of an Economic Development Office in every state-supported college and university. The Business and Industry Resource Center (BIRC) at Mississippi County Community College was established at this time to provide a mechanism for disseminating the information and requisite resources of state and federal agencies as well as the community college to the area businesses and industries.

The initial activities of the BIRC were conducted by a full-time coordinator and part time secretary. During the past six years, the demands for the services of the BIRC have required the addition of personnel, facilities and equipment. In 1990, the Harold F. Ohlendorf Institute for Economic Development was created as a component of the BIRC function. The Institute was created specifically to direct the economic development initiative to the southern half of Mississippi County Community College's service district. This program has continued to grow at the college's Osceola center by adding an additional computer laboratory as well as a developmental education lab with interactive computer capabilities.

A concerted effort by the BIRC has been to provide the training and retraining necessary for today's work force. In 1990, Mr. Harry L. Crisp, Chairman and CEO of Pepsi Cola Bottling of Marion, Illinois, donated a relatively new, 26,000-square-foot, $1-million facility to Mississippi County Community College for use in its economic development activities. This facility is located in the Blytheville Industrial Park and has been heavily utilized as an industry training location as well as a business incubator.

Additional activities underway include the hiring of an industrial training coordinator to be used in a local industry with specific responsibilities for the completion of a comprehensive training program for the industry's 500 employees. All of this activity exemplifies the crucial role community colleges can play in providing service for the purpose of economic development.

Contact:
Robin Myers, Associate Dean, Continuing and Community Education
(501) 763-6222

Mississippi County Community College
PO Box 1109
Blytheville, AR 72316
Total headcount enrollment-Credit: 3,264 Non-credit: 2,479
Campuses/sites: 3; Full-time faculty: 38

COMMUNITY COLLEGE RESPONSE TO BASE CLOSURE

▨ The loss of a military base crystallized the region's resolve ▨
to overcome the adversity through community development

Under the leadership of Mississippi County Community College, the loss of a military base was transformed into a positive push for community development.

The change was not easy. Mississippi County Community College is a medium-sized rural community college that had approximately 57,000 persons in its service district as of 1990. But Eaker Air Force Base, located in Blytheville, Arkansas, was slated for closure in December 1990. Through 1989 the total base-related personnel equaled 3,775, both military and civilian. A total of 8,532 military or civilian employees and their dependents will be extracted from the county's population as a result of the closure of Eaker Air Force Base.

Mississippi County Community College was actively engaged in defense of the base closure during the Spring of 1991. The president and several administrators from the college were involved in the newly formed Chamber of Commerce Eaker Committee presentation to the Defense Base Closure and Realignment Commission. These presentations focused on the importance of the mission, the efficiency and effectiveness of the Air Force Base, and the linkage and economic dependence that the community maintained with Eaker Air Force Base.

The defense of the base proved to be unsuccessful but the experience crystallized the region's resolve to overcome this adversity and laid the foundation for the creation of the Blytheville-Gosnell Development Authority.

The president of the community college served as Chairman of the Education Subcommittee of the Eaker Redevelopment Committee, which was responsible for recommending all education reuses to the Development Authority. The most viable educational proposals from the community included plans to establish:

- a residential statewide Mathematics and Science High School utilizing dormitories, classrooms and recreation facilities;

- a University Center coordinated by the community college that would host visiting universities in providing bachelor and graduate degree programs to area citizens;
- an educational consortium consisting of the community college, the area technical institute and the six county public school districts to utilize facilities and to capitalize on activities that can be mutually beneficial to all institutions;
- a regional educational cooperative and the requisite resources through audio visual support and other media;
- a county-wide alternative school operated by the educational cooperative;
- an environmental training facility;
- a crash fire training and hazardous waste academy. A corporate training park with requisite recreational facilities and other amenities; and
- a pilot training program.

Many of the employees of Mississippi County Community College have been heavily involved in the development, analysis and implementation of these plans. College employees have worked closely with the Development Authority officials in creating the educational reuse plan for the Air Force Base. This involvement has included direct contact with state and federal agencies, trips to Washington, D.C., lobbying the state legislature for special legislation, and countless meetings and interviews as well as extensive assistance and leadership in the preparation of grant applications and proposals. The community truly has looked to the college for leadership and as a resource for a project of this size and importance to the region. This level of involvement by the college is an indication of the importance of the college's role in the overall development and leadership of the area.

Contact:
Robin Myers, Associate Dean, Continuing and Community Education
(501) 763-6222

Mississippi County Community College
PO Box 1109
Blytheville, AR 72316
Total headcount enrollment-Credit: 3,264 Non-credit: 2,479
Campuses/sites: 3; Full-time faculty: 38

ASPIRE

*⧉ ASPIRE (A Student Paper in an Interdisciplinary Research Environment) ⧉
involves the student and the student's instructor working as a team*

At North Arkansas Community Technical College, a student required to write a research paper in English Composition I, Ethic and Introductory Biology could write one paper encompassing all three areas. Thus, the student learns how disciplines relate and, because one paper addresses multiple subjects, has time to prepare a quality paper.

Developed by four faculty, ASPIRE (A Student Paper in an Interdisciplinary Research Environment) involves the student and his/her instructors working as a team to develop one paper. For instance, that paper for English, Ethics and Biology could cover: "The cost of a product must include environmentally-safe disposal of all wastes." Each instructor grades the paper for his/her discipline; the recorded grade for all the classes is the average of these grades. All papers submitted through ASPIRE are graded by an instructor of composition.

At the beginning of the semester, all interested students and instructors are invited to a meeting. At this meeting, two coordinators hand out an information packet that includes rationale for ASPIRE, guidelines, procedures, submission deadlines, suggested topics, list of workshops, a thesis proposal form, and grading policies. Throughout the semester, the North Arkansas Community Technical College oordinators meet with the students and instructors as needed. (The coordinators are instructors in the program.)

We have a designated "drop box" for student submissions. When a student submits his/her thesis proposal, each instructor evaluates it from the perspective of his/her discipline and either approves or revises it; the student picks it up at the same place. This same procedure applies to submission of a list of sources, working outline, rough draft and final draft. At any point in the process a student or instructor may request a meeting with one or all involved parties. At the end of the process the student is required to submit a corrected "clean" copy of his/her paper to put on file.

Since we began the project, we have seen topics for student papers change from such topics as "Maslow has an interesting theory of self actualization" to "Sister Carrie's character development can be understood through Maslow's theory of self actualization;" and from "Hiroshima is a national disgrace" to "Scientists have a moral responsibility for their inventions." We also have students, now attending four year institutions, returning to tell us how much ASPIRE has helped them with writing papers. The faculty involved agree that ASPIRE has helped us clarify our expectations of research papers, state requirements clearly and identify specific grading techniques. The time demanded of the faculty is a problem; we hope to refine the process to reduce the required time.

Contact:
Marty Terrill, Coordinator
(501) 743-3000

North Arkansas Community Technical College
Pioneer Ridge
Harrison, AR 72601
Total headcount enrollment-Credit: 2,500 Non-Credit: 2,300
Campuses/sites: 3; Full-time faculty: 62

INTERDISCIPLINARY ISSUES AND IDEAS: AN HONORS PROGRAM

*⧉ In all honors classes, instructors develop work around collaborative learning, ⧉
individual inquiry, discussion and projects*

Set in a region somewhat culturally devoid and economically deprived, North Arkansas Community Technical college tries to enhance the lives of its honors students through an interdisciplinary program. In all honors classes, instructors develop work around collaborative learning, individual inquiry, discussions and projects.

Begun in 1988, the program consists of honors sections of general education courses required for most majors and accepted for transfer, plus three interdisciplinary courses developed specifically for the honors program. Lecture is

kept to a minimum.

The three courses developed for the honors program are Critical Thought (required for graduation from the honors program) Philosophy and the Sciences, and History of Great Ideas. Critical Thought begins with an introduction to the terminology of critical thinking and then considers unsolvable problems in the disciplines. The unit in psychology, for example, might explore the nature vs. nurture issue; or the evolution vs. creation debate.

Philosophy and the Sciences begins with an overview of

philosophy, the story of its development. Then visiting professors come in to team teach units on physical, natural, biological and social sciences.

History of Great Ideas is a series of seminars covering 15 ideas that have shaped western culture. Each seminar is led by a person knowledgeable in that field. For example, the seminar "The Rise of the Greek Civilization – Historical Perspective" is taught by a professor of western civilization. "The Development of Individual Rights" is taught by a lawyer. This class is open to visitors from the college and local communities.

The program uses faculty mentors to provide personal contact with each student enrolled in an honors class. The mentors meet with the students, either one-on-one or in groups at least four times during the semester.

The honors program offers extracurricular activities each semester such as a trip to the Shakespearean Festival in Canada, a visit to an art museum, or local activities such as touring Ayley's Underground Lab. On campus, we have pizza parties, cookie days, dip-n-chip days – a variety of celebrations. The students also have a study room equipped with computers, a cooking area (complete with microwave) and storage space for their books and materials.

The program began with 25 students and has grown to 123. Ten faculty members work part-time in honors.

Contact:
Marty Terrill, Coordinator
(501) 743-3000

North Arkansas Community Technical College
Pioneer Ridge
Harrison, AR 72601
Total headcount enrollment-Credit: 2,500 Non-Credit: 2,300
Campuses/sites: 3; Full-time faculty: 62

PHILLIPS COUNTY COMMUNITY COLLEGE

JOHN DEERE AG TECH

The tailor-made program was created to upgrade technical competence and professional level of the incoming dealership technician

Today's high tech equipment in the farming industry is constantly demanding new training for service technicians, and through a joint partnership, Phillips County Community College (PCCC) and John Deere are providing this training through the new John Deere Ag Tech Program.

The days of using basic mechanical skills to work on farm machinery are over, and John Deere dealers say they need trained professionals who can use their minds as well as their hands to work on computerized equipment.

John Deere Ag Tech is a two-year ag-mechanics program designed to upgrade the technical competence and professional level of the incoming dealership technician. Phillips County Community College is currently one of only three colleges in the United States participating in the program and the only junior college taking part. Nineteen students are enrolled in the PCCC program.

The program involves attending classroom lecture and laboratory experiences on John Deere equipment at PCCC and a unique opportunity for the students to get valuable experience working at a John Deere dealership.

The overall aim of the program is to let dealers recruit their own future service personnel locally and, if the deal-ership chooses to, sponsor the students' participation in the program.

The total program is completed in four semesters, or about 24 months, and is designed to make the employee more effective for the dealer. At the same time, the student obtains a two-year associate degree in applied science.

By recruiting locally, dealers think they will have a better chance at keeping the newly trained service technicians at home working in their dealership.

The course covers specialized training in such areas as hydraulics, electrical and electronics systems, tillage, harvesting and planting equipment, and consumer products, as well as basic training in such subjects as math, physics, social science and communications.

Through a team effort by the student, the dealer, John Deere and PCCC, the sponsors believe they are helping the agri-industry to grow in an area of the Delta that is in need of an economic boost. The John Deere Ag Tech Program has been featured in a special segment of the Channel 3 evening news in Memphis, Tennessee.

Contact:
John Baker, Dean of Occupational Education
(501) 338-6474

Phillips County Community College
PO Box 785
Helena, AR 72342
Total headcount enrollment-Credit: 1,563 Non-Credit: 516
Campuses/sites: 1; Full-time faculty: 88

YOUNG PEOPLE'S WORKSHOP IN THE ARTS

※ *Students entering grades 3 through 12 are eligible for the six-week summer program,* ※
which includes dance, drama, music and art

For the past 20 years, Phillips County Community College (PCCC) has introduced area children to a unique blend of music, dance, drama and art during a summer program known as Young People's Workshop in the Arts.

Students eligible to apply for this six-week program are those entering grades 3 through 12. The program has grown so popular among area young people that for the past several years, the number of applicants has far exceeded the 100 slots available.

The students attend classes in dance, drama, music and art from 8 a.m. to 11:30 a.m. Mondays through Thursdays. The classes are taught by professional instructors in the PCCC Fine Arts Department. At the end of the six weeks, the students incorporate what they've learned in each class into a final production that is free and open to the public.

The 1992 performance was a special salute to Walt Disney entitled "When You Wish Upon a Star."

A special guest instructor in the '92 summer workshop was Ron Hutchins of Nashville, Tennessee, who is a professional singer, dancer, and actor. An established dance teacher and choreographer, Hutchins is the recipient of the Tennessee Arts Commission Fellowship for excellence in dance performance. He spent two seasons at Opryland USA where he was assistant choreographer. Hutchins has danced for The Country Music Awards, The Riviera in Las Vegas, and The Palace Theatre in Los Angeles.

An added plus for PCCC employees is that their children are eligible to take the summer workshop at a far-reduced rate. Of the 100 children enrolled in the '92 summer program, 32 were children of PCCC administrators, faculty and staff.

Contact:
Kirk Whiteside, Speech and Theatre Instructor
(501) 338-6474

Phillips County Community College
PO Box 785
Helena, AR 72342
Total headcount enrollment-Credit: 1,563 Non-Credit: 516
Campuses/sites: 1; Full-time faculty: 88

BUSINESS AND INDUSTRIAL INSTITUTE

※ *The Institute provides direct management support and technical help* ※
for several industries trying to compete in the global market

Perhaps then-Governor Bill Clinton said it best in 1990: "There are models that work. In my state, Westark Community College in Fort Smith is an adult education center, a traditional community college, and the biggest and best tech program we've got. It conducts industry training programs for companies all over Arkansas."

Just eight years earlier, in 1982, Westark Community College had recognized the need for retraining the existing work force in Western Arkansas. Westark expanded its mission to respond through a Business and Industrial Institute (BII) to growing requests for direct management support and technical assistance from several industries struggling to adjust to new levels of non-seasonal, global competition, requiring real-time information.

Using the special talents and expertise of existing Westark faculty and having recruited seasoned professional business faculty to help industry implement new technology, it is not unusual to find BII instructors and part-time adjunct staff delivering on-site, customized training classes from 6 a.m. to 2 a.m., Monday through Saturday, in any given week. They are busy providing 150 training courses to all levels of employees in a multitude of modern technologies and computer resources.

Several cases and reports from manufacturing companies have shown annual savings of hundreds of thousands of dollars per plant as a result of implementing systems and problem-solving techniques for which Westark has provided training.

Structurally, the Business and Industrial Institute director reports to the chair of the Business Division at the college. The BII consists of three major, integrated components: Quality Technology, Management Technology, and Computer Resources. Introductory, intermediate and advanced training needs and applications for business and industry may be found to be in common for all manufacturing industries and service organizations within these three Westark BII components.

Quality Technology training instructors deliver an array of beginning to advanced level courses in all aspects of Total Quality Management. Total Quality Management and process measurement courses are tailored to the needs of each industry, as well as each individual company's

WESTARK COMMUNITY COLLEGE

RESOURCE DEVELOPMENT

※ *The Foundation Board now is the premier board in town and does significant friend- and fund-raising*

Contact:
Stephen D. Lease, Director
(501) 788-7762

Westark Community College
PO Box 3649
Fort Smith, AR 72913-3649
Total headcount enrollment-Credit: 5,472. Non-Credit: 1,780
Campuses/sites: 1; Full-time faculty: 11

In just a few years, Westark Community College's Foundation Board has become the premier board in town and does significant friend- and fund-raising. The rise in prestige and impact can be traced to July 1988, when: 1) the Director of Development had begun to understand the concept of philanthropy and to practice the process of fund-raising; 2) competent outside counsel had been obtained to help the college begin a model development program; 3) a favorable feasibility study for a major gifts campaign had been completed; and 4) approximately 200 significant community leaders, former donors, and older alumni had been cultivated (this included the 15-member Foundation Board of Directors).

The 1989-90 year was devoted primarily to carrying out a major gifts campaign designed to raise $1-million for scholarship endowment, $2-million for equipment endowment and $500,000 for outright purchase of equipment.

Continues on Page 36

terminology and operations. In-plant training is frequent, and the non-credit curriculum and work examples are updated regularly with client input, especially employee post-evaluations, of each completed course.

To maximize individual and group productivity, there is a family of human resources behavioral techniques available that go hand-in-hand with quality management. This management technology element of the BII program is focused on improvement in supervisory communication and individual/team performance by hourly employees and management of local business and industry.

The implementation and practice of quality management systems and performance management techniques cannot be successfully accomplished without harnessing and directing the powers of computer literacy and applications to a company's management, support, sales and production operations, from enhanced just-in-time inventory techniques to internal/external customer satisfaction.

A unique personal computer in-plant training project was developed in BII with mobile labs to provide a flexible, high-quality source of training in all areas of business needs for computer competence. The goal of the program is to be flexible enough to accommodate a wide range of students from basic technical or office skills, through all levels of management and executive positions, or from Basic Keyboarding to Advanced Production Simulation and CAD/CAM.

Since 1988, the Business and Industrial Institute has conducted 255,804 training hours involving 21,211 employees. Total training enrollment for the FY 1991-92 year was 7,571. The institute conducted 77,348 total training hours during the past year, a 522 percent increase since FY1988-89.

With no original funding base for the Business and Industrial Institute, the college obtained "seed money" of $122,000 from a four-year Arkansas Department of Higher Education grant in 1988. Leveraging that money with one-time funding from the Arkansas Business Council and local client sources, the college put together enough of a funding base to purchase three mobile lap-top computer labs for use in on-site training and to pay for salaries and release time for a small nucleus of specialized full-time faculty and adjunct faculty to develop customized curriculum and provide training. The evolution of course content is continuous.

Since 1988, in-plant training and customized technical assistance has been provided to 91 different companies and numerous governmental agencies all over Arkansas. Cooperative agreements have been developed with other two-year and four-year higher education institutions, enhanced by ADHE and Arkansas Industrial Development Commission support.

The budget for the FY1992-93 year totals about $800,000 for personnel, equipment and general operations. The program is funded through an ADHE grant of $241,500, with $450,000 in customer fees, and the balance from Westark in the form of facilities overhead and personnel benefits support. BII has held local client charges at $85 per instructional hour for the past three years.

In addition to the director, there are eight full-time instructors in the Business and Industrial Institute, three regular part-time instructors and 12 to 15 adjunct business/technical faculty, who are continuously used to carry out the actual training programs. The office support staff includes one secretary/receptionist, one secretary/office manager and one desktop publisher.

Contact:
Carolyn Branch, Vice President, Institutional Advancement
(501) 788-7021

Westark Community College
PO Box 3649
Fort Smith, AR 72913-3649
Total headcount enrollment–Credit: 5,472. Non-Credit: 1,780
Campuses/sites: 1; Full-time faculty: 11

The campaign lasted nine months with approximately 400 volunteers raising $5.3-million in cash and pledges. This is a record for a public two-year college for this time period. The overall goal is to annually generate an average of $1-million in gifts from the private sector, build the Foundation endowment to $20-million by the year 2000, and develop a model comprehensive development program based on private sector fund raising for a medium-size community college.

Outstanding outcomes to date include:

1) actual dollars processed through the Development Office has exceeded $1-million for the past four years, with $1.9-million in 1991-92 and $1.4-million the previous year;

2) the endowment has increased from zero to more than $5-million;

3) the Foundation has given more than $1-million to the college for scholarships, equipment, and other needs since 1988; It will provide nearly $1-million during this current fiscal year.

4) the first $1-million cash gift was obtained;

5) the well-trained Foundation Board is now the premier board in town and it does significant friend- and fund-raising;

6) a budget of $150,000 provides a staff of 2.5 people and all direct costs for operating a program including annual, major and planned giving, as well as special projects;

7) Westark's image has been elevated significantly and President Joel Stubblefield is on a first-name basis with area power brokers who stand behind the college's mission with their own philanthropy; and

8) the program's status among its peers has been recognized in these ways: AIMS Award "Special Recognition for Total Development Effort" (1991 and 1992); named among the top 10 to 12 colleges with private sector fund-raising since 1989 by the Council for Aid to Education; the president and development officer have made several presentations about the program; the college's image has been elevated significantly and the president is on a first-name basis with area power brokers who stand behind the college's mission with their own philanthropy.

WELDING TECHNOLOGY TRAINING CENTER

※ *Partner manufacturers and suppliers have become a link between the college and local welding companies*

A partnership among national manufacturers, local suppliers and Allan Hancock College has sparked a new direction for the Allan Hancock College Welding Program.

The Welding Technology Training Center has been established with the cooperation of the Lincoln Electric Company, ALTAIR Gases and Equipment, Inc., Liquid Air Corp. and local welding companies. Lincoln Electric Company, a national manufacturer of welding equipment and materials, provides equipment, technology, technical expertise, and research and development opportunities to the Training Center. ALTAIR, Inc. and Liquid Air, Inc., local welding supply and equipment dealers, provide supplies, technical support, training and education assistance. The Center concept represents a real win-win situation for all partners. Manufacturers and suppliers are providing the college with the resources and expertise to train new and experienced welders on state-of-the-art equipment with the latest welding techniques. This includes access to prototype equipment and technological advances as they are being developed. The partners have joined with the college to provide seminars and workshops to welding shop owners/operators, high school and college welding instructors, sales and technical representatives and college students.

Partner manufacturers and suppliers are given the opportunity to field-test equipment, train field representatives and increase their exposure within the local industry. They have become a connecting link between the college and local welding companies. Working through the

Continues on Page 38

Contact:
Liz Regan, Coordinator, Early Childhood Studies
(805) 922-6966

Allan Hancock College
800 South College Drive
Santa Maria, CA 93454
Total head count enrollment-Credit: 8,168; Non-Credit: 8,646
Campuses/sites: 3; Full-time faculty: 112

BILINGUAL/BICULTURAL TEACHER PREPARATION

※ *The program calls for developing Spanish fluency and prepares students for spontaneous conversation*

Reaching a minority population and meeting needs of the local schools for bilingual aides and teachers are the twin goals of the Bilingual/Bicultural Teacher Preparation Program and Spanish Language Institute of Allan Hancock College. Through the program, instructors recruit potential students across a wide range of ages and backgrounds. A special target group is instructional aides, who are already working in classroom settings and are highly motivated to complete a degree or certificate.

The teacher preparation program offers students three options: an associate degree or certificate in Early Childhood Studies with a bilingual/bicultural emphasis, an associate degree or preparation for transfer. The certificate and associate degree options prepare students as instructional aides while the transfer option leads to a career as a bilingual/bicultural teacher. Instructors in the program provide students with an environment within which they can excel, one of active, cooperative learning. The curriculum is based on the implementation of cooperative learning and anti-bias principles.

If the student is non-Spanish speaking, the program calls for developing Spanish fluency through the Spanish Language Institute. The Institute prepares students to use the language in spontaneous conversation in a variety of situations. During the school year, Spanish courses are offered at the local elementary schools or high schools. In the summer, students may travel to Mexico for a five-week intensive language program.

Students entering the program receive specific support services. In addition to attending a semester-long orientation course, they are assigned to an academic counseling assistant, attend workshops on study skills, math anxiety, and time management, and work with representatives of the local state university in preparation for transfer as juniors.

Initially, the program, begun in 1991, was funded through a loan from the California Community Colleges Chancellor's Office.

The program has increased the number of students who are entering the Early Childhood Studies Program or who are preparing for a career in teaching and has served to attract a number of English second language students interested in becoming teachers.

Contact:
Sharon McCuen, Dean, Research and Development
(916) 484-8306

American River College
4700 College Oak Drive
Sacramento, CA 95841
Total head count enrollment-Credit: 23,000
Campuses/sites: 4; Full-time Faculty: 267

AMERICAN RIVER COLLEGE

TEACHING RESOURCES CENTER

⌘ *The Center is equipped with the latest computer hardware and software, as well as written and recorded material for faculty to use*

Despite having few dollars and no new resources or staff to implement it, American River College established the Teaching Resources Center (T.R.C.) that soon became a nationwide model.

Established in 1980, the T.R.C. is located in a large room of the college library, where the professional collection is housed. The room is large enough to accommodate the many workshops, symposiums and speakers that the T.R.C. regularly features. Most often programs feature American River faculty who share ideas and expertise; faculty also are brought in from a half dozen nearby universities for special presentations (usually for a small honorarium) – hence the T.R.C.'s motto: "Teachers Teaching Other Teachers."

The T.R.C. is staffed by a Faculty Director (on partial reassigned time) and T.R.C. Assistant (classified support position), with a large Faculty Advisory Committee. The directorship is rotated, with a new faculty director each year. This brings new ideas, perspectives and energy to the program.

Equipped with the latest computer hardware and software for faculty to learn and experiment, the T.R.C. also has video and audio tapes and written materials on a wide variety of teaching issues.

The T.R.C. offers many services: one-on-one computer assistance, video feedback of lectures, midterm student feedback for specific courses, assistance in constructing tests or writing course objectives and assessment of reading level of materials. Mini grants are awarded for departments to bring speakers on discipline-specific topics. A monthly newsletter is published.

A fall Teaching Week features a full slate of activities relating to teaching. Also, each year the T.R.C. sends one faculty member (selected by lottery) to attend the California Great Teachers Seminar; that faculty member then replicates the experience for 10 ARC faculty (also selected by lottery) on a three-day weekend in the fall. Use of the T.R.C. has remained high over the years. An unduplicated count recently showed that 72 percent of the regular faculty and 22 percent of the part-time faculty use the Center at least once during the year.

Contact:
Ray Hobson, Dean of Academic Affairs
(805) 922-6966

Allan Hancock College
800 South College Drive
Santa Maria, CA 93454
Total head count enrollment-Credit: 8,168; Non-Credit: 8,646
Campuses/sites: 3; Full-time faculty: 112

college, the partners are able to offer technical assistance to local industry in developing customized manufacturing processes and in providing on-site training to their employees.

The Welding Technology Training Center creates long-term financial benefits for the partner manufacturers and suppliers, however their commitment goes far beyond monetary gains, and instead anchors on their desire to help the community. The goals of the Center are to help local welding companies be competitive, and to provide them with a work force trained in developing technologies.

This partnership allows the college to maintain on site some of industry's newest equipment. Partners are provided the opportunity to field-test prototype equipment in college labs, utilizing welding students. Where equipment is not available for housing in college facilities, Lincoln Electric Company makes its training facilities in Southern California available to college instructors and local employers. Field trips are hosted in this facility for college students in order to introduce them to new equipment and processes.

It is critical for Allan Hancock College to offer training on the most modern equipment available. The Welding Technology Training Center provides this capability with the cooperation of all partners. This program has been so successful that the college expects to extend this partnership concept into other industrial technology training programs.

HIGH SCHOOL/COLLEGE ARTICULATION COUNCIL

*▩ The school districts and college not only share resources, ▩
but have joint in-service activities as well*

Because the teaching profession continues to need more multicultural diversification, a local High School/College Articulation Council broadened the traditional 2+2 agreement to include a 2+2+2 program for under-represented students who want to become high school teachers.
Other successes of the Council include:

- college courses offered on high school sites;
- high school students tested for admission to subsequent college courses through 2+2 agreements;
- the Partnership to Assure College Entry (PACE) program conducts tours for middle school students and sponsors a four-week summer academy for 150 students;
- joint in-service activities for college and high school faculty; and
- joint development of tech-prep curriculum in engineering and health careers.

These partnerships date back to 1988, when the superintendents of Grant Union High School District and San Juan Unified School District and the president of American River College began the formation of an Articulation Council. In 1989, Center Unified School District became a member, and in 1990 the president of California State University, Sacramento, appointed a liaison person to the council. Five subcommittees were established to address key issues set forth by the CEOs. Four co-chairs (a second-level administrator from each district/college) then were appointed to coordinate the operation of the council and its subcommittees. Council meetings occur quarterly, and responsibility for the meeting rotates among the four constituent co-chairs who function as equal partners.

The Council has five subcommittees and initiatives: 1) College Composition Project; 2) Curriculum: Faculty-to-Faculty; 3) College Courses on High School Campuses; 4) At-risk Students; and 5) Counselor Liaison. The co-chairs in spring 1991 reviewed the accomplishments of the council and unanimously and strongly affirmed its continuation.

Through these initiatives, college and high school managers and faculty have developed "first name basis" working relationships that are helpful in regards to grants, in sharing facilities and in responding to budget reductions.

All in all, the American River College/Center Unified/Grant Union/San Juan Unified Articulation Council has been the framework with which many activities and programs have been initiated. Within this framework, it is expected that new or expanded activities will be initiated over the years ahead.

Contact:
Stephen M. Epler, Vice President, Instruction
(916) 484-8411

American River College
4700 College Oak Drive
Sacramento, CA 95841
Total head count enrollment-Credit: 23,000
Campuses/sites: 4; Full-time faculty: 267

ENTREPRENEURIAL PARTNERSHIP PROGRAM

*▩ Potential entrepreneurs targeted for this program include ▩
commuters, laid-off aerospace workers and minorities*

The Antelope Valley Entrepreneurial Partnership Program is a first ever valley-wide cooperative effort aimed at assisting people intending to start their own businesses. Specific groups targeted for this program include commuters and laid-off aerospace workers. The consortium also seeks to reach women, minorities, new businesses and other potential entrepreneurs.

The Antelope Valley Entrepreneurial Partnership Program is unlike any other in the nation in that it is composed of four individual programs: Entrepreneurial Outreach Forum, Training Institute, Funding Programs, and Technical Assistance Network. While none of the four programs is necessarily unique, by combining them together the consortium has developed a very comprehensive, step-by-step system designed to map out the path to starting and succeeding in a new business. This unique approach is a joint undertaking by Antelope Valley College, the cities of Palmdale and Lancaster, chambers of commerce in both cities, the local chapter of the Small Business Administration SCORE, and the Antelope Valley Local Development Corporation.

The first step, the Entrepreneurial Outreach Forum, is a half-day seminar that attempts to accomplish three objec-

Continues on Page 40

tives: communicate to the community the value each member of the consortium places on assisting new and growing small businesses; offer initial suggestions from forum speakers; and introduce the other parts of the Entrepreneurial Partnership Program. Participants then were asked to take the second step in the process and take the first part of the training program.

Antelope Valley College spearheads the training portion of the program. The Training Institute consists of two courses. Course I is a 12-hour, two-day workshop that helps participants evaluate whether they have "what it takes" to be an entrepreneur and to analyze his/her business idea, form of business organization and initial financing needs. At various times throughout this intensive workshop, a successful small business owner, a lawyer or accountant, and a local banker will be invited to speak to the class. The course's presenter walks the participants through a carefully compiled manual. This course also discusses the Urban Business Identification System. This study of the local business base helps identify industry types that are under-supplied or over-supplied. Using the study, participants can evaluate their own business concepts in terms of potential level of competition. Everyone must complete Course I to be eligible for Course II.

The second course is a 10 week, 30-hour class designed to produce a comprehensive business plan. Using a standard textbook on entrepreneurship, students are assisted in developing their plans in carefully designed stages. As each part is completed, it is evaluated by the course instructor and by the appropriate specialists in that area. These specialists are local SCORE representatives, marketing professionals, accountants, lawyers and bankers. Each participant who successfully completes a business plan will be able to meet with a lender and have it critiqued in terms of how a lending institution would view it.

Part three of the program is a "smorgasbord" of funding options. Those who successfully complete their business plan can look for money from a greater number of potential sources than is generally available to the average entrepreneur who is not part of this program. In addition to conventional loans and traditional SBA loans, this funding program attempts to offer city-linked deposits, bank CDC micro loans, Antelope Valley Local Development Corporation revolving loans, and a venture capital forum to introduce participants to potential investors with capital to invest.

The last step of the program is the Technical Assistance Network, also known as the Passport Program. Developed in Pennsylvania, one of the purposes of this program is to reduce the start-up costs, thus increasing the chance of success. It includes a network of business service providers offering their services to these new businesses at initially reduced rates. A second function of the Passport Program is to offer as much local assistance as possible. Such assistance would come from SCORE, Antelope Valley Local Development Corporation's incubator and assistance program, and local city ombudsman offices.

After Course II is underway, the consortium begins the cycle over again. The Outreach Forum and Courses I and II will be offered on a continuous basis.

We believe the joint effort and coordinated program will help develop the local small business community and provide many new job opportunities while increasing the success rate of new businesses.

Contact:
Tom Miller, Dean, Business Division
(805) 943-3241, ext. 301

Antelope Valley College
3041 West Avenue K, Lancaster
Lancaster, CA 93536-5426
Total head count enrollment-Credit: 18,463; Non-Credit: 405
Campuses/sites: 1; Full-time faculty: 121

ANTELOPE VALLEY COLLEGE

REGIONAL CAREER PREP COUNCIL

Major accomplishments of the council include a career education plan for all K-14 students and significant private industry involvement

The total articulation among school districts of the Antelope Valley has led to unique work ethic partnerships between schools and businessmen, with business leaders teaching elements of a work ethic program at the high school and adult school – extending down to elementary level. Twenty employers have been brought into classrooms of northern Los Angeles County. A thrust to involve the academics in career preparation is prime to the program.

This is but one result of a grant from the California Community College Chancellor for an articulation plan, which was developed with input from business, industry, the military and seven school districts. Under the 1991 state grant, a sequential career education plan for all K-14 students involving partnerships between business, industry and all public schools in the Antelope Valley was developed.

Features of the program include a Regional Career Prep Council involving a full-time regional coordinator with salary paid jointly by the Antelope Valley Union High School District and private industry. A maximum limit of $5,000 is imposed on private industry contributors to allow a greater number of participants to "buy-in" to the program.

Through the Council, a Medical-Technical Magnet was established at one high school campus. A school-wide Health Care Consortium with articulation as a major part of the program dedicated to developing a bridge between secondary and college level allied health programs is one example of the general mission of the Antelope Valley Regional Career Prep Council.

The military sponsors an annual Salute to Youth day that opens the local Air Force base to junior and senior high school students for exposure to military activities and related opportunities not usually available to the public.

Direct contact with pilots, astronauts, support personnel, FM officials, and college airframe and power plant personnel is provided.

Other items include Junior Achievement, Applied Economics, college information nights, Career School Fair, employer workshops, Principal for a Day, Educational Total Quality Management Training for school administrators. Business, industry, board of trade, chambers of commerce and all area school districts are a part of the Antelope Valley Regional Career Prep Council.

Contact:
California Community Colleges Chancellor's Office
June Battey, Antelope Valley Union HS District Office
(805) 948-7655

Antelope Valley College
3041 West Avenue K, Lancaster
Lancaster, CA 93536-5426
Total head count enrollment-Credit: 18,463; Non-Credit: 405
Campuses/sites: 1; Full-time faculty: 121

THE CHAMBER SCHOLARS PROGRAM

The college and Chamber of Commerce developed the scholarship program for under-represented students, including American Indians and Pacific Islanders

African American, American Indian, Chicano/Latino, disabled, and Pacific Island students who are seeking a university education get an extra boost from a partnership between local businesses and Butte College.

The Butte College Transfer Center, in partnership with the local Chamber of Commerce, has developed a textbook scholarship program for students participating in the Transfer Center's TRUST (Targeting Resources to under-represented Student Transfer) Program. TRUST has been recognized as an exemplary program by the Northern California Regional Transfer Project and has been featured at numerous conferences.

These scholarships are designed to cover a portion of the cost of textbooks for a maximum of four years. They are awarded to students attending Butte College and support continues after transfer to a university. For example, a student who transferred one year after receiving the scholarship uses it for as many as three years after transfer (this could include one year of graduate study).

Fully enrolled students currently spend more than $200 per term for textbooks. By funding a $1,000 scholarship, the donor will contribute $125 each term for eight terms. The grants are awarded in the form of a voucher issued by the scholarship committee to the campus bookstore.

Through work experience and internship programs, participating Chamber of Commerce members have the option of a more extensive involvement with the student to which their individual scholarship is awarded. Butte College's Cooperative Education Program connects the business community to students pursuing degrees in related fields. Experiential education has shown itself to be a valuable tool for the student as well as a benefit to the employer. Participation in this program allows Chamber members to target students in majors most appropriate to their business.

Some positive features of this program include:

•the program addresses an identified and immediate need in our community and throughout the nation; more students from under-represented groups must graduate from universities, complete graduate degrees and enter the professional world; this pool of talent no longer can be ignored; through this program the local Chamber of Commerce is identified as an organization doing its part to make this need a reality;

•the Cooperative Education option is an ideal vehicle for local businesses wishing to access this talented pool of potential employees; through work experience and internship programs both the employer and the student profit; the student gains relevant experience and the employer receives quality support; and

•the eight-term span of support not only helps students transfer but, more importantly, also helps them graduate from universities; the graduation of Chamber Scholars from universities and their entry into postgraduate work and the professional community will build a network of community leaders who will be a potential source of support for future students.

Contact:
Larry Newman, Transfer Center Coordinator
(916) 895-2453

Butte College
3536 Butte Campus Drive
Oroville, CA 95965
Total head count enrollment: 13,000
Campuses/sites: 3; Full-time faculty: 160

THE PUENTE PROJECT

*⌗ The retention project, designed for Mexican-American/Chicano ⌗
students, requires students to meet quarterly with their mentors*

The Puente Project at Chabot College addresses the low transfer and retention rates of Mexican-American/Chicano students. The team approach used by the Puente Project (founded in 1981) includes a Mexican-American counselor, an English teacher and mentors from the Mexican-American/Chicano community.

Students are selected at the beginning of the year based on a personal interview, writing sample and test scores (for guidance purposes only). Students must commit to remaining in the Project the entire year. They must meet on a quarterly basis with their mentors (professionals who are in their same field of interest).

Class content uses teaching materials that are ethnic related to the students in the class. The class is structured in such a way that it greatly encourages students to develop their writing fluency. Students are expected to do a great deal of writing and draft revisions based on an eight-step model.

During the year, the students meet with their mentors; these meetings also become a basis for one of their papers in the class. Mentors act as a role models as well as advocates for their students. Students often comment on how inspired they were after meeting with their mentors. They have this feeling that they too can succeed in the professional world. Statistics over the past 10 years show a greatly improved retention and transfer rate for student participating in the Puente Project.

In 1991 the American Association of Community and Junior Colleges (AACJC) recognized the Puente Project as one of six national exemplary projects in the United States. The Project has been so successful that it has been replicated in 23 other community colleges in California. The state-wide Puente staff and the Chabot College Puente staff have given numerous presentations on the model.

Contact:
Ruth L. Self, Project Director
Ramon Parada, Project Coordinator
(510) 786-6982

Chabot-Las Positas Community College District
25555 Hesperian Boulevard
Harvard, CA 94545
Total head count enrollment-Credit: 21,438; Non-Credit: 3,500
Colleges in district: 2; Full-time faculty: 250

THE DARAJA PROJECT

*⌗ This year-long writing/counseling/mentoring program ⌗
uses the team approach to help black students succeed*

Where the aforementioned Puente Project targets Mexican American/Chicano students, the Daraja Project offers much the same to black students. The Daraja Project (translated to mean "steps to success") also uses the team approach. The team includes a black counselor who advises and coordinates the project, a black counselor who is in charge of the mentor component, an English teacher and black professionals from the community who act as mentors.

The Daraja Project is a year-long writing, counseling and mentoring program aimed at black students with a special emphasis on recruiting black males to participate. Students must commit to the entire year The counselor advises and provides support to the students throughout the year. Students are placed with black professionals in the same career major of interest. Students are required to meet with the mentors each quarter. The students use these meetings to write "mentors" papers.

The project uses an eight-step writing process to develop the students writing fluency. Class content uses teaching materials that are ethnic-related to the students in the class.

Parents and family members are an integral part of the project. An orientation is held for parents and students at the beginning of the year. Students are encouraged to share their classroom assignments and activities with their parents. An end-of-year programs recognizes the students who completed the project.

The Daraja Project has presented the model to numerous California organizations. The Project has been recognized for its outstanding efforts by Bay Area Black organizations.

Contact:
Ruth L. Self, Project Director
Carolyn Greene, Counselor/Project Coordinator
(510) 786-6718

Chabot-Las Positas Community College District
25555 Hesperian Boulevard
Harvard, CA 94545
Total head count enrollment-Credit: 21,438; Non-Credit: 3,500
Colleges in district: 2; Full-time faculty: 250

CENTER FOR INTERNATIONAL TRADE DEVELOPMENT

The Center provides extensive assistance in international marketing, exporting and importing,
financing exports and operating and overseas business

Small- and medium-sized businesses that want to secure a niche in the international marketplace can turn to the Center for International Trade Development (CITD). The Center provides training to all segments of the business community, from manufacturing to service providers to agribusiness.

CITD programs are designed to provide a background and extensive technical assistance in international marketing, exporting and importing, financing exports and operating a business overseas. Specific goals of the CITD include: 1) provide individualized one-on-one international trade counseling and advising; 2) establish an international trade library; 3) provide international trade resource and referral services; 4) provide technical assistance; 5) conduct international trade workshops, seminars and classes; and 6) provide specialized training.

The CITD was established in 1990 in partnership with Mt. San Antonio College and California State Polytechnic University, Pomona. The CITD is located with Mt. San Antonio College's Small Business Development Center in the city of Pomona. The partnership also includes affiliations with Rio Hondo and Fullerton colleges.

The Center's director is the executive vice president of instruction at Citrus College. The day-to-day operations are assigned to a manager, who works at the Pomona site. An advisory board, composed of business leaders and college administrators, meets quarterly to evaluate the center's operation. In addition, an in-house advisory committee also provides guidance to the CITD.

The CITD has extensive support from local Chambers of Commerce, economic development units, private sector specialists, and state and federal agencies. The Center works closely with the California State World Trade Commission, Office of Export Development, and with the U.S. and Foreign Commercial Service and U.S. Department of Commerce. In addition, the CITD meets the requirements for participation in ED Net (California Community Colleges Economic Development Network).

The CITD is funded through the Economic Development Program of the California Community College Chancellor's Office. Local funds and private-sector contributions also support the Center. Citrus College provides in-kind funding for specific components, including technical libraries and resource centers. California State Polytechnic University, Pomona, provides access to an international trade collection, a teleconferencing facility and the Cal Poly International Center. International trade consultants have donated significant resources to the CITD project.

Since 1990, the CITD has expanded its operations from the Pomona location. Several cities have contracted with the CITD for consulting services in their city offices. The CITD has also sponsored seminars on the Citrus College campus in conjunction with private and non-profit international trade organizations, including the Export Managers Association of California.

Contact:
Ralph Jagodka, Director
(909) 629-2223

Citrus College
1000 West Foothill Boulevard
Glendora, CA 91741
Total head count enrollment-Credit: 10, 685; Non-Credit: 4,000
Campuses/sites: 1; Full-time faculty: 136

SUMMER HIGH SCHOOL

The tuition-free program helps students earn more high school
credits and gives the college an opportunity to recruit

Responding to an unmet need in a local school district, Citrus College developed a community college funded, tuition-free summer school program for high school students at Claremont High in 1987.

For several years, local school districts had been unable to provide high school classes for their students because the districts were not generating enough ADA to fund such programs. A private university was providing summer classes for Claremont students at $100 per course. Many parents could not afford to pay this much tuition to send their children to summer school.

High school and Citrus College trustees and administrators discussed the possibility of administering a summer high school program through Citrus College. Citrus personnel explored ways to establish a contractual agree-

Continues on Page 44

ment with the local district and decided that a free high school program could be provided under an adult education agreement.

The college's goals are: 1) to provide high school students with a way to earn additional high school credits or make up deficiencies at no cost to their families; 2) to be cost effective for the college; 3) to create a sense of goodwill with Claremont community residents; 4) to establish a closer identity between Claremont High School students and Citrus College; and 5) to offer an avenue for recruiting students to Citrus.

The program is supported by non-credit and basic skills education funds and is administered by the college's non-credit education department. The college district hires a high school administrator to serve as coordinator of the program at each site. Citrus College employs the instructors, who are certified to teach both non-credit courses at Citrus as well as high school courses. The college pays a rental fee for textbooks, instructional supplies and use of the facility.

The first summer, 900 students attended the program and earned about 1,400 credits that generated 180 ADA. The next year, a second high school in the District requested a Citrus administered program. In addition, an out-of-district high school asked Citrus to sponsor a summer program.

In 1991, 1,520 students generated 176 ADA at Claremont High; 829 students generated 121 ADA at Monrovia High; and 1,681 students generated 199 ADA at Upland High.

Contact:
James Gulli, Dean of Instruction, Continuing Education & Extended Day
(818) 914-8562

Citrus College
1000 West Foothill Boulevard
Glendora, CA 91741
Total head count enrollment-Credit: 10,685; Non-Credit: 4,000
Campuses/sites: 1; Full-time faculty: 136

HOTEL AND RESTAURANT PROGRAM

The program prepares students for all aspects of the hospitality industry

Students and instructors in City College of San Francisco's Hotel and Restaurant Program get a regular taste of the hospitality industry, as they prepare and serve about 6,000 breakfasts, lunches and dinners daily. This service to faculty and staff is but one aspect of the program, which prepares students for a wide range of careers concerned with food, service and/or lodging, including hotels, restaurants, clubs, institutions and corporations.

The hospitality field is divided into two general categories: "back of the house," where one does not usually deal with the public; and "front of the house," where public contact is an important part of the work.

"Front of the house" careers include ownership and/or management of hotels, clubs, restaurants. "Back of the house" careers include food preparation, housekeeping, purchasing, and accounting.

The CCSF H & R program includes a non-credit program at the Downtown campus focusing on food and wine service; a Chinese Cooks training program at the Chinatown/North Beach campus; and a Hotel and Restaurant Operations program at the Phelan campus.

The Hotel and Restaurant credit program limits enrollment to 86 students per semester. The program requires a commitment of a minimum of 30 hours per week of class work for four semesters, or two academic years.

Resources include the Alice Statler Library, which houses one of the most complete collection of books and periodicals about the industry in the West. In addition, students have access to some of the leading hotels and restaurants in the Bay Area as one-semester interns.

Contact:
Linda Hirose, Hotel and Restaurant Department
(415) 239-3152

City College of San Francisco
50 Phelan Avenue, Conlan Hall
San Francisco, CA 94112
Total head count enrollment-Credit: 35,000; Non-Credit: 50,000
Campuses/sites: 8; Full-time faculty: 1,000

AFRICAN AMERICAN ACHIEVEMENT PROGRAM

The program, designed to improve retention, provides individual and group counseling services and specialized instructional material

To increase the retention rate of African American students and reverse the decline of City College's African American student enrollment., City College of San Francisco developed a comprehensive, innovative counseling and instructional model that is successfully serving under-represented and under-served student populations. It can be easily replicated for other student groups and in other colleges.

The African American Achievement Program has been recognized by the California Community Colleges State Chancellor's Office and by professional organizations as an outstanding regional program.

The program has served more than 175 students since spring 1990, and helped 74 students complete English 1A, and has assisted in the transfer of 40 students to baccalaureate institutions.

AAAP provides individuals and group counseling services, which include personal, educational career planning, and transitional support counseling after students have completed the AAAP English 1A course. AAAP prepares and challenges African American students to be successful in English courses and in the uses of the library. Classes include English 5B/S (Basic Composition and Reading), English 12T (Expository Reading and Writing), and English 1A (Reading and Composition). The program features original instructional materials designed especially for African American students.

AAAP coordinates a mentor component so students have the support of professional mentors in the field of their interest who encourage them to succeed with their educational and career plans.

AAAP staff are African American educators and other professionals who believe that it is their responsibility to help African American students succeed in college. The staff consists of a counselor/coordinator, an English Instructor, a librarian, two mentor counselors/coordinators and two student office assistants.

Contact:
Debra Stewart, African American Achievement Program
(415) 239-3137

City College of San Francisco
50 Phelan Avenue, Conlan Hall
San Francisco, CA 94112
Total head count enrollment-Credit: 35,000; Non-Credit: 50,000
Campuses/sites: 8; Full-time faculty: 1,000

TRAUMATIC HEAD-INJURY PROGRAM

The program readies students – who, due to injury were unable to return to school or work – for vocational training and placement

Although traumatic head injuries once kept people out of the work force and from academia, that's no longer so for the more than 250 students a year who find new hope through a special program at Coastline Community College. As part of its special education program, Coastline Community College embarked on a pilot program to provide educational services to adults who had sustained traumatic brain injuries. That pilot project, which began with 15 students, evolved into a comprehensive Traumatic Head-Injury Program – the first such community college program in the nation.

The goal of Coastline's THI Program is to prepare students for vocational training and placement, continuing education, and/or community independence. To accomplish this goal, the THI Program offers a structured, two-year, full-time course of study which includes a unique staff-designed curriculum. Based on a hierarchy of cognitive functioning, the curriculum begins with primary thinking skills related to attention and concentration and advances to higher-level reasoning and problem solving skills. The program also features computer-assisted instruction, neuropsychological assessment and follow-up, individual and group counseling, student/family orientations and support seminars, and a transitional community course to assist students in reentering community and work environments.

The full-time program is complemented by a Mild/Moderate Head-Injury Program (a part-time, limited duration program for adults who have sustained milder types of head injuries) and a "Job Club" that is designed to facilitate job acquisition and retention. Outcome studies conducted at Coastline have shown positive results. Pre- and post- neuroeducational testing shows significant gains and, even more importantly, students and their families report positive changes in independence, reasoning and

Continues on Page 46

social skills. Approximately 80 percent of all graduates do transition into work training, regular college programs, or employment upon leaving the program.

Coastline's THI Program team includes the program administrator, a four-member neuropsychological and neuroeducational team, eight special education instructors, one full-time counselor and two part-time counselors, a career development instructor/coordinator, and part-time job developers and instructional aides/associates. The THI Program also provides approximately 10 internships each semester for undergraduate and graduate students and has attracted interns from as far away as the University of Edinburgh. Case management teams are utilized to coordinate program and service planning for individual students, and services to THI Program students are further enhanced by joint research projects with community professionals and nearby universities.

The THI Program is supported by a combination of funding sources, including California community college attendance-based apportionment and direct excess cost funding for disabled student programs, government grants, private and corporate donations, and local fund-raising efforts. Enrollment fees for the six-unit per semester THI Program are the same as for other California community college courses.

The program has garnered extensive and highly complimentary media attention, including articles in *The Los Angeles Times*, Orange County's *Register*, and the local *Daily Pilot*. Additionally, the THI Program has been featured on the NBC *Today Show*, KABC-TV, and KOCE-TV. The THI Program hosts more than 100 visiting professionals each year and routinely provides information to assist others in starting similar programs, and Coastline's THI Program served as the model for many components of *The ABI Handbook* (a guide to serving students with acquired brain injury), which was developed by a consortium sponsored by the Chancellor's Office for California Community Colleges. The computer-assisted component of the THI Program was also the inspiration for the California Community College/Department of Rehabilitation High Tech Center Grants, which resulted in the funding of more than 58 High Tech Centers to serve students with acquired brain injuries and learning disabilities.

Contact:
Pat Arlington, Associate Dean, Special Programs
(714) 751-9776

Coastline Community College
11460 Warner Avenue, Fountain Valley
CA 92708-2597
Total head count enrollment-Credit: 31,400; Non-Credit: 8,300
Campuses/sites: 4; Full-time faculty: 47

INTERNATIONAL BUSINESS CERTIFICATE CURRICULUM

⌗ *The program helps California businesses stay abreast* ⌗
of the ongoing internationalization of the marketplace

The burgeoning field of International Business has especially impacted Orange County, California, one of the fastest-growing centers of international business in the nation. Coastline Community College and the World Trade Center Association of Orange County have responded to that growth by establishing a World Trade Center Institute (WTCI).

The WTCI was the entity used to obtain a grant from the U.S. Department of Education in the fall of 1986. The initial grant funded a variety of WTCI projects, including the development of an international business curriculum and certificate program to be offered through Coastline; and the development and expansion of current international trade resource materials and information for the use of students and small- and medium-sized businesses.

Coastline, through advisory meetings with the business community, developed an international business curriculum and International Trade Resource Center to serve small-sized and medium-sized business.

Since 1988, more than 1,500 students have enrolled in Coastline's international business curriculum. A large percentage of these students are already employed and are anticipating their first international assignment or the challenge of developing international accounts. Other students are seeking careers in this exciting but technical field. Non-credit seminars, workshops, and conferences, co-sponsored by the World Trade Center Association of Orange County and other international organizations, supplement the curriculum.

In recognition of Coastline's leadership role in the international business instructional arena, Coastline was awarded two further California State funded grants during 1989-90. The purpose of the grants was to prepare international business curriculum guides for faculty in the 107 California community colleges. These curriculum guides were intended to enable faculty at all of the colleges to prepare and teach international business courses.

In December 1990, 40 different international business

curriculum guides were completed and distributed to the 107 California Community Colleges.

In 1991-92, Coastline was awarded another federally funded grant from the U.S. Department of Education's Business and International Education Program. This grant was to expand the distribution of the curriculum guides to more than 600 community colleges throughout the United States. Approximately 12 regional workshops and/or presentations, with an average attendance of 25, were conducted.

During the past six years, Coastline's International Business Certificate Program has offered training to more than 1,500 students under the internationally-experienced tutelage of full-time and adjunct instructors.

Contact:
Charlanne T. Nee, Dean, Business and International Studies
(714) 759-7058

Coastline Community College
11460 Warner Avenue, Fountain Valley
CA 92708-2597
Total head count enrollment-Credit: 31,400; Non-Credit: 8,300
Campuses/sites: 4; Full-time faculty: 47

HELPING STUDENTS WITH PSYCHOLOGICAL DISABILITIES

Because it is often difficult to return to college after mental illness, a special program helps students reenter the education environment

Mental illness most often strikes people during their late teens and early 20's, at which time many are students whose education is interrupted by the onset of their illness. Returning to college after an extended absence caused by mental illness can be difficult, if not impossible, without the availability of educational support services. Functional limitations requiring accommodation, lack of self-confidence and temporary loss of social and academic skills all present formidable barriers to be overcome.

In response to the special needs of students with psychological disabilities, the College of San Mateo established its "Transition to College" program, which combined Disabled Student Programs and Services support services, specialized instruction, peer support, and community participation to assist students with psychological disabilities to succeed in college. Participating students have rated these services very helpful to their reentry. Preliminary research combined with staff observations indicates program success in fulfilling its goals of achieving greater student retention, improving interpersonal, classroom and study skills, and increasing students' self-esteem.

Educational support services provided are identical to those traditionally provided to students with other types of disabilities and are arranged by a project counselor and peer counselors. These services include individual assessment of functional limitations, prescriptive academic programming, special registration, monitoring of student progress, and liaison with college instructors and community providers.

Specialized instruction consists of a reentry course for students with psychological disabilities, entitled "Transition to College." The course focuses on college orientation, career exploration, disability management, and academic and social skills development. Taught in an informal manner, the course encourages student interaction and peer support. Following completion of the course, students are invited to attend a peer-led support group.

The local community participates in the project through a Community/College Coalition that includes local mental health services, agencies and consumer groups, who assist the project staff in providing consultation and in-service training to college personnel, assessment and recruitment of students, monitoring of student progress, formulation of joint educational and rehabilitation plans, grant writing, book scholarships and political advocacy.

The program was initially established in 1991 under a grant from the State Chancellor's Office, testing a state-recommended approach to services for these students, and is a continuing participant in a national study on supported education for students with psychological disabilities directed by Boston University's Center for Psychiatric Rehabilitation.

In addition to providing research data to Boston University, project staff have presented their findings at numerous state and national educational organizations conferences. Among these are the California Association of Post-Secondary Educators for the Disabled, Community College League of California, American College Personnel Association and International Association of Psychosocial Rehabilitation Services. The program's "Transition to College" course has been included as a model in the recently published Resource Guide for Serving Students with Psychological Disabilities, developed by the California State Chancellor's Office. In recognition of its success, this program is one of five recipients of the Pyramid Award

Continues on Page 48

(October 1992) for outstanding achievement in student development, awarded by a consortium of three national Student Services organizations: the American College Personnel Association, the National Association of Student Services Administrators, and the National Council on Student Development.

Present funding for the program is provided by partial reassignment of existing college staff, community grants, and some funding from the Vocational and Applied Technology Education Act (VATEA). The program serves 100 students per year at an approximate total cost of $21,500.

Contact:
Patricia Griffin, Vice President, Student Services, (415) 574-6118,
Arnett Caviel, Dean, Special Programs and Services, (415) 574-6434

College of San Mateo
1700 West Hillsdale Boulevard
San Mateo, CA 94402
Total head count enrollment-Credit: 14,569
Campuses/sites: 1; Full-time faculty: 204

COLLEGE OF THE CANYONS

TEACHING IMPROVEMENT FOR ADJUNCT FACULTY

Adjuncts, who traditionally receive few rewards, are designated "Associates" and get a consequent increase in pay

Because the faculty development needs of adjunct instructors always have been slighted in comparison to their full-time counterparts, College of the Canyons decided to design a program of faculty development specifically for adjunct instructors. The program was designed in 1989 to address four ongoing problems: 1) a weak sense of connection and commitment to the institution for most part-time faculty; 2) very little interaction between part-time faculty and other faculty members; 3) a dearth of opportunities for faculty development for part-time faculty; and 4) an absence of incentives and rewards for pursuing professional improvement.

Called the Associate Program, it leads to the designation of adjunct instructors as "Associates" and a consequent increase in pay. The program has three phases. The first phase is the completion of an Instructional Skills Workshop (ISW). The ISW is a 24-hour course for instructional improvement and is based on a micro-teaching approach: Instructors actually practice teaching while being videotaped and observed by other faculty members. Two facilitators (full-time faculty) and five or six participants (adjunct faculty) compose one workshop. The workshop emphasizes very specific, fundamental teaching skills including the basics of an effective lesson, planning and preparing for a lesson, and the use of teaching aids. Each participant must present a series of three 10-minute presentations that are videotaped and reviewed by the group. Moreover, each participant assumes the role of a student during the other lessons.

The second phase of the program is an eight-hour Advanced Teaching Workshop (ATW). The ATW is designed to provide exposure to teaching topics beyond the basics introduced in the first workshop. The content of the workshop varies and, in part, has been based on the requests of participants for additional coverage of specific teaching topics. As an example, faculty members have presented workshops on questioning techniques, critical thinking in the classroom, and classroom research. This portion of the Associate Program simply is an opportunity to explore current issues of interest in greater depth and with few restrictions in format.

The final phase in the program is a Teaching Analysis. During both workshops teachers are urged to explore and experiment with new skills and techniques. The analysis phase presents an opportunity for feedback about real-world applications of those skills and techniques. Therefore, participants are asked to choose some specific aspect of their teaching and, in cooperation with a full-time faculty member, analyze its use and effectiveness.

Participants are paid a small stipend for each of the workshops they attend and Associate Adjuncts are permanently paid at a rate that is 10 percent higher than other part-time instructors. The Associate Program has cost the College between $5,000 and $6,000 a year, principally to pay full-time faculty to conduct workshops and for small stipends for part-time faculty who participate. Ten to 15 adjunct instructors participate each year.

Contact:
Russell C. Richardson, Instructor, Department of Political Science
(805) 259-7800, ext. 387

College of the Canyons
26455 North Rockwell Canyon Road
Valencia, CA 91355
Total head count enrollment-Credit: 6,200
Campuses/sites: 1; Full-time faculty: 70

INDUSTRIAL MAINTENANCE TECHNICIAN TRAINING

The two-semester course was formed with help from businessmen who demand rigor and significantly high level competencies

When confronted with the imminent closure of a poorly attended machining program, the Vocational Dean sought advice from a Chamber of Commerce committee of businessmen called the Roundtable. The result: a new Industrial Maintenance Technician Training Program replaced the machining class. The Chamber/Business Advisory Committee assisted the college with course content, length of training, instructor selection, equipment for the laboratory, and made a commitment to hire the students who completed the first class.

There are several factors that make this program a model partnership. The program did not exist prior to the recommendation of the advisory committee. Industry had a need for trained maintenance workers and asked the college to help. The Advisory Committee committed many hours of time to assist with the specific training skills and content for the curriculum required for this program. They

further assisted with the design for the new laboratory and donated a significant amount of equipment and materials necessary to start the class.

In order to meet the needs of industry, the course lasts one year (two semesters) and meets Monday through Friday from 8 a.m. to 2 p.m. The Advisory Committee demanded rigor and significantly high level competencies allowing the college to offer 12 AA/AS degree level units for each semester of the class. The course articulates 12 units of credit toward a BA for students transferring to the California State University, Fresno, and majoring in Industry and Technology.

The Advisory Committee, instrumental in forming this course, has been nominated for a Partnership Award for their efforts in meeting the needs of industry and education.

Contact:
David C. Bockman, Dean of Instruction, Applied Sciences
(209) 730-3808

College of the Sequoias
915 South Mooney Boulevard
Visalia, CA 93277
Total head count enrollment-Credit: 9,128; Non-Credit: 250
Campuses/sites: 1; Full-time faculty: 162

College of the Sequoias

SUCCESS PROGRAM

The college recognizes it is important for under-prepared students to develop critical thinking skills and camaraderie with peers

Because students needing help in just one area may still impact the entire campus community, the entire campus community at College of the Sequoias responds. How? Through the Success Program first offered in 1986 to students without all the skills needed for success.

Before the Success Program, the English and mathematics departments had developed and offered developmental studies courses for those students. Instructors often felt frustrated, however, because the problems these students were having were not limited to English and math. Their problems included lack of study skills, lack of knowledge about the college as an institution, lack of life-coping skills, and lack of ability to set goals and meet those goals.

Under the leadership of the Associate Dean of Precollegiate Studies, precollegiate programs are administered by the Precollegiate Studies Board. The Board has been charged with:

- encouraging participation by all campus divisions and service areas on the board;
- taking responsibility for the development of policy

affecting under-prepared students;
- taking responsibility for the oversight of the precollegiate program on campus; and
- working with the Associate Dean, Precollegiate Studies to assess/evaluate policies and programs.

This group is made up of representatives from each of the academic divisions as well as representatives from counseling, EOP&S, classified employees and students. The Precollegiate Studies Board surveys current research in adult learning, applying those findings to benefit students. A prime example of this approach is the Success Program.

Several assumptions represented the theoretical underpinning for the Success Program:

1) although the college curriculum divides the world into disciplines of study, this isn't the way we confront it every day; it is important that students "center" their learning, developing a consciousness and voice of their own which can be used to make

Continues on Page 50

sense of the world;

2) critical thinking is the essence of a precollegiate program; reading/writing/computing are only aspects of critical thinking;

3) thinking/reading/writing/computing cannot be learned in isolation; and

4) an effective precollegiate program is set up as a "community of learners," where students, teachers, advisors and counselors get to know each other, so they are able to provide the support needed by under-prepared and insecure students.

The number of challenges faced by these students demanded a more unified approach than simply offering courses in the math and English departments. The Success Program attempted to meet these needs by:

1) placing the responsibility for precollegiate students on the shoulders of the entire college community rather than simply on the shoulders of the math and English divisions;

2) coordinating efforts to help precollegiate students;

3) providing a full-time class load (14 units), integrating English and math skills with a content course where Skills were applied;

4) assigning faculty advisors to each student to monitor student progress and to service as a resource for students, helping students get through the college bureaucracy and referring students to campus resources;

5) assisting students in developing career goals and college survival skills; and

6) balancing the need for academic rigor with the individual attention many of these students require.

The Success Program includes two levels, each a semester in length. The first level was designed for students who, in general, are working with basic communication skills. The second level was designed for those students with more advanced communication skills.

Contact:
Dale Norton, Associate Dean, Precollegiate Studies
(209) 730-3823

College of the Sequoias
915 South Mooney Boulevard
Visalia, CA 93277
Total head count enrollment-Credit: 9,128; Non-Credit: 250
Campuses/sites: 1; Full-time faculty: 162

COLLEGE OF THE SISKIYOUS

HISTORY OF WRITING FOR PUBLICATION: ENGLISH 21

Several students from this popular course have successfully published their works

In 1988, in response to student petitions containing more than 200 names requesting a class to teach the necessary skills for marketing and publishing written material, instructor, Eve Thompson, created Writing for Publication. The first night's enrollment was 75 students and has remained consistently high.

The goals of the class are simple: to teach the skills necessary for successful marketing for publication. Assignments include: developing and maintaining an idea file, developing idea angle sheet, writing query letters, analyzing markets, conducting interviews, synthesizing research, and photography and professional preparation of the manuscript. Students are expected to prepare and submit at least one manuscript for publication during the semester. Other assignments cover the business aspects of writing: maintaining records for taxes, copyright laws, and desktop publishing.

Several students have successfully published their works since the classes' inception. Some have published in magazines, other have won contests. The cumulative total of earnings is well over $250,000. This mark was passed by the publication of *The Second Fifty Years* in 1992. Co-authored by two former students, this book has been praised by *Publisher's Weekly*. Additionally, two previous students are magazine editors and two are newspapers editors.

The class is a boon to the amateur and professional writer alike as marketing techniques can be used either for a one-time publication of a successfully written essay in response to an academic assignment or to earn an income for a lifetime.

Contact:
Eve Thompson, Instructor
(916) 938-5322

College of the Siskiyous
800 College Avenue
Weed, CA 96094
Total head count enrollment-Credit: 8,815; Non-Credit: 1,449
Campuses/sites: 2; Full-time faculty: 55

ELEMENTARY STATISTICS SUMMER COURSE

▦ The course, which is team-taught, meets for eight weekends ▦
and relies on user-friendly statistical software

Statistics students and instructors can become so involved in the arithmetic and getting the right answer that they sometimes lose sight of the real reasons for studying statistics. Real-world problems become too cumbersome for paper, pencil and a hand-held calculator. So the College of the Siskiyous designed an Elementary Statistics course to be special in several ways:

1) The course relies heavily on a student version of a statistical software program called Execustat. Each student purchases their own software for about $35. We chose Execustat because it is menu driven, uses as a statistical report generator in business, and it has an interpret feature that reinforces the vocabulary of statistics. We hope this user friendly statistical software enhances the students' over-all understanding of statistics as well as motivate students through discovery learning.

2) The course meets for eight Saturdays and Sundays from 8 a.m. to 5 p.m. We want to make the course available to people who cannot enroll in weekday classes because of jobs or other scheduling problems. The long days create a special challenge to maintain course content without overwhelming the students with hours and hours of lecture.

3) The course is team-taught by two mathematics instructors. Team teaching allows students to be exposed to different types of instruction styles, which give the lectures more variety. It also serves as a teacher mentoring program, where a seasoned statistics teacher is teamed with an instructor relatively inexperienced in teaching statistics.

4) Cooperative learning is used extensively to reinforce ideas immediately after the lectures. This gives students an opportunity to get up and move around as well as talk with others in the group. Worksheets are designed for both class work and computer-lab group work to provide a greater variety of activities.

5) Students are asked to do a statistical study that supports a particular opinion which is not necessarily accurate. The report could include deceptive charts, exclusion of information that does not support their point of view, and biased methods of collecting information. The instructors believe students should be made aware of the accidental and deliberate misuses of statistics in order to critically analyze statistical information presented to them at work and from the news media.

Beyond the items listed above, the course is very much like an ordinary statistics course. Problems are assigned and collected from the text, some of which involve larger sets of data. Students are encouraged to use the software to do homework. Three tests and a final exam are given in class over the material in the text. Students are allowed to use the software to solve selected problems on the exams. Students also complete a standard statistical report using honest and ethical methods of summarizing the information collected.

Student response to this course is very favorable. It is extremely important to keep the students and instructors active. A typical morning begins with 45 minutes of lecture, 30 minutes of in-class group work, 10 minute break, 30 minutes of lecture, 30 minutes of a in-class group activity, 10 minute break, 20 minutes of lecture, and approximately one hour of group activity using the computer software. Some students stay in the computer lab and work on the software right through lunch, others play volleyball, jog or join the instructors for lunch. The schedule is repeated in the afternoon, fitting in as much lecture as possible in short segments. It is best to have several activity options prepared just in case interest dims in the late afternoon.

Contact:
Jerry Pompa, Instructor, (916) 938-5259
Barb Odegard, Instructor, (916) 938-5267

College of the Siskiyous
800 College Avenue
Weed, CA 96094
Total head count enrollment-Credit: 8,815; Non-Credit: 1,449
Campuses/sites: 2; Full-time faculty: 55

FIRE TECHNOLOGY

The program's operating fire department prepares students for a career with increasingly demanding criteria for employment

Columbia College is one of the few community colleges in the nation to operate its own fire department staffed by students enrolled in the program. Through mutual aid agreements with other agencies, emergency responses provide practical experience for students as well as a vital community service.

The Fire Technology Program prepares students for careers in all areas of Fire Service. A two-year program combining technical and manipulative training with selected General Education courses is offered to allow the student to earn an Associate degree. A certificate program also is available for those students who wish to pursue only the technical aspects of this challenging field. The Program provides the basic training requirements for California State Firefighter I certification, preparing students for entry-level positions or transfer to four-year colleges and universities.

The Fire Service offers careers in a variety of challenging and rewarding settings. In California, rapid population growth has resulted in the expansion of fire fighting agencies to meet the increased demand. Positions are available in city, county, state and federal fire service units as well as those maintained by the military, private and insurance industries and investigative agencies. The employment picture is similar across the nation and overseas.

Educational requirements for individuals seeking employment in the Fire Service are becoming increasingly demanding. The need for highly skilled technical experts in fire fighting and related fields is so great that many departments require the two-year Associate in Science degree and most agencies require firefighter certification prior to employment. The existence of a functional training facility provides students the opportunity to acquire hands-on experience that has proven to be a significant advantage when competing for employment positions.

Fire Service is a profession. Career firefighters must prepare for advancement. Through promotions, they realize greater career and goal achievement while providing an increased service to the community. Columbia College also is geared for this in-service student. Many current leaders in the field began their careers at Columbia College and continue to support and endorse this outstanding program.

In keeping with the philosophy of the college, the emphasis is on the quality of the program rather than its size. This commitment has not been compromised despite increasing demand for enrollments during recent years.

Contact:
George Melendrez, Program Coordinator and Fire Chief
(209) 532-1191

Columbia College
PO Box 1849
Columbia, CA 95310
Total head count enrollment-Credit: 3,500
Campuses/sites: 1; Full-time faculty: 50

CULINARY ARTS (HOSPITALITY MANAGEMENT)

The program prepares students for careers as chefs, restaurant managers/owners and hoteliers

A historic hotel open to the public is the training site for Columbia College's Hospitality Training Program, which students help operate. The college has been operating the hotel since 1976, when The City Hotel Corporation was formed to reopen and operate the 1870 hotel in Columbia State Park, Columbia, CA.

Tourism is the largest industry in this part of the state, followed by forestry (lumber) and mining. Columbia is located in the heart of the old Mother Lode gold fields and is one of a string of historical Mother Lode gold mining towns preserved, in varying degrees, to enrich our heritage. The City Hotel was the "fanciest" of its day. The restaurant at the City Hotel continues today to be the benchmark by which all restaurants in the Mother Lode are measured.

The Hospitality Management Program prepares its students for careers as chefs, restaurant manager/owners and as hoteliers. Culinary students are trained in the restaurant kitchen and dining room on campus during the first two semesters of their studies. Advanced third and fourth semester students are passed to the City Hotel for the completion of their theory lectures and practical education. The management staff at the hotel who also function as adjunct faculty are the manager, chef, dining room manager and beverage manager. The restaurant has a white tablecloth, fine dining theme featuring multicourse menus and full service including some a la cart service. The menus feature local and air-freighted fresh foods from around the world. It is a "scratch" kitchen, meaning all foods are prepared at the restaurant including breads, stocks, soups, sauces, ice creams, pastries and, of course, appetizers and entrees. The cuisine takes an eclectic contemporary approach to classical food preparation.

Students pass through all stations in the kitchen and take lecture/lab classes in the dining room and the "saloon" in order to complete their practical training at the Hotel. Wines, marketing, employer-employee relations, laws, baking, food presentation, restaurant design and operation, recipe writing/computer-aided costing, safety and sanitation, nutrition, meat cutting, and curing/smoking are taught on campus.

The college has a matriculation program that tests all incoming students on language and math skills. Free tutorial services are available to all students. Educationally disadvantaged students are given special counseling and assistance in learning and testing. A low teacher-student ratio in labs that averages 1:5 assures students of close supervision and training.

On-campus student (dorm) housing is available at Columbia. Full financial aid also is available. In-state tuition is minimal. Student expenses for tools, books and uniforms are partly defrayed by the program's own scholarship fund.

The uniqueness of the City Hotel as our training site sets Columbia College apart from and ahead of other Community Colleges teaching Culinary Arts. The Hotel has been recognized in *Gourmet Magazine*, metropolitan newspapers across the country and its wine list is a consistent award winner (*Wine Spectator*). The training is overseen by a program coordinator and administered by two full-time instructors and the four adjunct faculty mentioned above.

An advisory board of local restaurant, banking and lodging professionals plus the City Hotel board of directors assist in curriculum development. The college is fully accredited by the Western Association of Schools and Colleges.

Graduates are easily placed in local and distant, hotels and restaurants. Preference to graduates is given by the City Hotel. Graduates are found working throughout the Mother Lode and well beyond in responsible, challenging positions as sous-chefs, chefs and owners of their own establishments.

Contact:
Francis Lynch, Program Coordinator
(209) 533-5135

Columbia College
PO Box 1849
Columbia, CA 95310
Total head count enrollment-Credit: 3,500
Campuses/sites: 1; Full-time faculty: 50

COSUMNES RIVER COLLEGE

HEALTH INFORMATION TECHNOLOGY

Community partnerships help sustain this program, which offers all courses in the evening and/or on Saturday

In its quest to offer quality programs without substantially increasing its budget, Cosumnes River College designed a Health Information Technology Program that shares courses, classrooms and labs with other programs. Plus, convenient evening and Saturday classes may be scheduled.

Established in August 1989 with an enrollment of approximately 30 students, the program was initially accredited by the Committee on Allied Health Education and Accreditation in May 1991, in time for the first graduating class. The program is designed to train health information professionals with the knowledge and skills to process, analyze, disseminate and maintain health care information. A career as a health information professional offers a unique opportunity to combine an interest in health information, business and computer information science. The third class graduated in May 1993. So far all graduates who sat for national certification have passed the examination. In the fall of 1992, a record number of students entered the freshmen class, giving strong indication that the program is on a growth curve.

The program shares core courses in allied health and anatomy/physiology, as well as classroom and laboratory facilities, with our nationally accredited Medical Assisting program. The net effect: scarce resources can be better utilized, to the betterment of both programs. Secondly, a close departmental relationship with computer science faculty and the staff of the main College Computer Lab have resulted in improved student access to computer services.

Some courses are offered at the hospital sites; others are available at campus outreach facilities as well. Additionally, accommodations have been made by other college departments to ensure that these students are served. For example, the liaison counselor to the program has visited Saturday classes to provide assistance to new students. The library is closed on Saturdays; however, important print

Continues on Page 54

and media are housed in the classroom facility for easy access by students.

In addition to college innovations, a number of community partnerships sustain this program. Software vendors have donated key pieces of software to the program. Area hospital medical record departments provided a library of diversified medical records for student projects; and the local professional association provided staff time to "sanitize" these records so that they could be used for instruction. Additionally, students participate in a two-semester directed practice in area medical facilities. Moreover, local facilities provide staff time to advise the program director on a regular basis. Also, the Sacramento Valley Health Information Association, which worked with the college to develop the initial program and hire the first program faculty, continues to have a close relationship with the college. This organization allows students to attend professional functions at low or no cost. The professional association has donated supplies, furniture and cash to the program. The organization also participates in career fairs and other activities to promote the program in the community.

The college motto is "commitment, quality and innovation." This program exemplifies each of these important goals from the multiple perspectives of program, college and community involvement.

Contact:
Sharon Stith, Program Director, (916) 688-7244
Janis Caston, Dean, Business, Allied Health & Family Science, (916) 688-7226

Cosumnes River College
8401 Center Parkway
Sacramento, CA 95823
Total head count enrollment-Credit: 9,500
Campuses/sites: 3; Full-time faculty: 80

EMERGENCY MEDICAL TECHNICIAN-PARAMEDIC

Students receive extensive training through affiliations with 12 medical facilities and a network of fire service agencies and ambulance services

As the primary trainer of Emergency Medical Technicians and Paramedics in San Bernardino and Riverside Counties, Crafton Hills College offers its Emergency Medical Technician-Paramedic students a flexible but formidable program. Approved by the Inland Counties Emergency Medical Agency and the Riverside County Emergency Medical Services department, the EMT-Paramedic program also received its initial five-year accreditation by the Committee on Allied Health Education and Accreditation (CAHEA) of the American Medical Association in April 1985 and was awarded a five-year renewal in 1990. It is the only community college paramedic program in California to have CAHEA accreditation.

Crafton Hills College maintains affiliations with 12 medical facilities, as well as a network of fire service agencies and ambulance services. Paramedic students receive extensive training and experience through these affiliations. The course consists of four components: classroom, laboratory, clinic (externship) and field (externship). Students have the option of either a six-month or one-year training program. The thrust of the training is to develop specific skills and to develop general principles of assessment and treatment based on fundamentals of normal anatomy and physiology. Students are encouraged to apply the general knowledge and principles presented in the course to a broad spectrum of specific patient conditions. Because of the field schedules, each student ends the program at a different time. Only upon successful completion of a field preceptorship, as well as the previous didactic and clinical phases, will the student be eligible for the State of California paramedic examination and the Inland Counties Emergency Medical Agency and Riverside County accreditation examinations. The student receives 30 units towards an associate degree and may elect to continue with the general education courses necessary for completion of degree requirements.

The Emergency Medical Services program is staffed by four full-time faculty. They are supported by numerous part-time instructors, facilitators and preceptors. An emergency-room physician serves as the medical director for the program.

Contact:
James Holbrook, Program Director
(909) 794-2161

Crafton Hills College
11711 Sand Canyon Road
Yucaipa, CA 92399
Total head count enrollment-Credit: 5,883
Campuses/sites: 1; Full-time faculty: 66

RADIOLOGIC TECHNOLOGY

*A partnership between the college and a hospital
has greatly enhanced recruitment efforts*

Crafton Hills College and the San Bernardino County Medical Center jointly provide Radiologic Technology training, which has strengthened the program and students' employment outlook. The partnership, begun in 1985, effectively removed weaknesses in the program that had threatened its accreditation, and it added a two-year, high-tech training program to the college's occupational education offerings that would not otherwise have been possible. For the first time, students in the program were able to receive college credit for the course work and to obtain an Associate of Science degree by completing general education requirements. In addition, the Medical Center folded its hospital-based training program into the college's.

The Medical Center's ability to recruit highly qualified students has been greatly enhanced by the partnership. Selection of students is conducted by Medical Center staff through an application and interview process. All books are supplied to the students by the Medical Center, and a stipend that increases the second year is paid to the students. Students must pay the state-mandated community college enrollment fee.

The director of the program is a Medical Center employee, but he receives a monthly stipend from the college to provide administrative coordination between the two institutions. He is also paid as a part-time faculty member to teach an Introduction to Radiologic Technology class each fall semester that is separate from the core professional program. In addition, the college reimburses the Medical Center for the full cost of a Clinical Instructor position, which was added to meet accreditation standards. Other regular staff members of the Medical Center Radiology Department serve as instructors.

Students must complete a 24-month training period, which includes more than 600 hours of classroom instruction and more than 3,500 hours of supervised clinical training. Clinical training and experience is gained from each area of the Radiology Department on a rotational basis. These include all sections of Diagnostic X-ray, Nuclear Medicine, Radiation Therapy, Ultrasound, and Angiography. These areas utilize many types of radiographic equipment and provide varied experience and training in the care of patients of all ages and with various stages of illness. The program is accredited by the Council on Medical Education of the American Medical Association. Students who complete the training are eligible for certification by the American Registry of Radiologic Technologists.

Contact:
Ron Kibby, Assistant Dean, Occupational Education
(909) 794-2161

Crafton Hills College
11711 Sand Canyon Road
Yucaipa, CA 92399
Total head count enrollment-Credit: 5,883
Campuses/sites: 1; Full-time faculty: 66

Cuesta College

STUDENT LIFE ORIENTATION DAYS

*A two-day orientation program for first-year students
precedes each autumn semester*

During the first year of college, students face many daunting tasks, including setting educational goals, socializing with new peer groups, and reevaluating personal values and attitudes. These tasks can be particularly challenging for students uncertain of their new environment and future. A Student Life Orientation (SLO), a two-day program before each fall semester, is Cuesta College's attempt to make the adjustment easier.

The comfort and confidence that occur through becoming acquainted with the people, programs, physical surroundings, policies and expectations are clearly related to student retention and success offered through Student Life Orientation (SLO) Days.

Therefore, the mission of the SLO Days program provides for continuing services and assistance that:
• aids new students in their transition to Cuesta College;
• exposes new students to the broad educational opportunities of Cuesta College;
• integrates new students into the life of Cuesta College; and

Continues on Page 56

- informs new students of the campus resources available to assist them in their educational and personal development.

Broad-base involvement, including faculty and staff, in the planning and implementation of orientation activities is the key to meeting the goals of the SLO Days program. To accomplish these goals, the orientation activities are divided into areas that provide major focus on academic orientation and adjustment, social adjustment, and orientation to the campus and community. Also included is a program for parents to help them gain insight into the kinds of adjustments students face during their college years.

This program is made possible with many financial partnerships between the college and members of the private sector as well as fees generated by participants' registration. SLO Days has been recognized by the National Orientation Directors Association (NODA) as unique to community colleges, and has been presented in educational sessions for the National Association for Campus Activities (NACA).

Contact:
Karen Bergher, Director, Student Development
(805) 546-3289

Cuesta College
PO Box 8106
San Luis Obispo, CA 93403-8106
Total head count enrollment-Credit: 7,769
Campuses/sites: 3; Full-time faculty: 130

PROGRAM ASSISTING STUDENT-ATHLETE SUCCESS (PASS)

The program not only stresses academics,
but also personal development

Student athletes, valued for their roles in the classroom as well as on the playing field, get a broad range of support from Cuesta College. In 1989, the College inaugurated the PASS program in an effort to provide assistance for student-athletes. The six-component program is consistent with the Knight Foundation Report as well as the emphasis on academic rigor of the California Community College Commission on Athletics.

The six components of the PASS program are:
- academic advisement, orientation, preregistration, transferring, etc.;
- academic status unit checks, progress reports, etc.;
- learning assistance learning skills, tutoring, math/science labs, writing clinics, etc.;
- Student-Athlete Success Class (three units of learning, living and survival skills);
- scholarship recognition (top 10 scholar athletes, honor roll, team scholarship awards); and
- personal development (substance abuse prevention, family relationships, eating disorders awareness, etc.).

PASS provides confidential, professional and voluntary assistance to support students with issues that may be adversely affecting their academic, athletic or personal performance. Educational programs are provided to offer preventive information, assist in identifying problems and promote the general well-being of student athletes. Appropriate referrals to campus and community resources will be made.

Contact:
Warren E. Hansen, Director of Athletics
(805) 546-3210

Cuesta College
PO Box 8106
San Luis Obispo, CA 93403-8106
Total head count enrollment-Credit: 7,769
Campuses/sites: 3; Full-time faculty: 130

PRECOLLEGIATE ACADEMY

▣ The program helps under-represented/at-risk students in grades eight through 12 ▣
who might not otherwise pursue higher education

Because the path to college begins long before a student gets that high school diploma, Diablo Valley College in 1991 joined with the University of California, Berkeley, the University of California, Davis, and the Mt. Diablo Unified School District to form the Precollegiate Academy, UC Partnership Program.

This program helps support under-represented/at-risk students grades eight to 12 who do not have adequate information or incentives to develop higher education goals. The program develops instructional strategies and support activities to help students make the decision to attend college and prepare them academically to be persistent and successful in college-level course work.

It requires strong collaboration and includes:
- formal partnership agreements;
- outreach and recruitment of special need students;
- campus tours;
- Saturday academic enrichment classes in English and math;
- student and parent conferences and workshops; and
- student counseling and mentoring.

The program has about 50 students in it each year. It is expanding to include a College Success Program, which will offer more courses and serve more students.

Contact:
Pamela Hawkins, Assistant Dean, Economic Development
(510) 685-1230, ext. 439

Diablo Valley College
321 Golf Club Road
Pleasant Hill, CA 94523
Total head count enrollment-Credit: 23,800
Campuses/sites: 2; Full-time faculty: 300

PHYSIC/MATH INTERDISCIPLINARY COURSE/GRANT

▣ The course assumes team-teaching makes it easier for engineering ▣
and physics students to understand how the subjects relate

Team-teaching physics and calculus, Diablo Valley College has found, not only more easily demonstrates the interrelationship of those subjects but also is more attractive to women and minorities. The Diablo Valley formula for team-teaching was developed by physicist Oshri Karmon and mathematician David Johnson, along with Dean of Instruction Elaine Cohen. The work is funded by a three-year, $236,802 grant from the Department of Education.

Karmon and Johnson say this approach will increase the number of community college students, particularly under-represented students who transfer to four-year institutions and eventually receive degrees in physics and engineering.

This represents a dramatic change from the impact the traditional way of teaching calculus and physics separately had on beginning students: many who might otherwise have gone on to become successful physicists or engineers were eliminated when they encountered their freshman physics and calculus courses.

Contact:
Elaine Cohen, Dean of Instruction
(510) 685-1230, ext. 203

Diablo Valley College
321 Golf Club Road
Pleasant Hill, CA 94523
Total head count enrollment-Credit: 23,800
Campuses/sites: 2; Full-time faculty: 300

CREATIVE WRITING

The program here, along with those at three universities,
serves as a focus for the Bay Area writing community

The writing program at Foothill College impacts more than the students in classrooms, it reaches the Bay Area writing community as well.

The change, however, was slow in coming. From its earliest days in the late 1950's, Foothill College provided an assorted sequence of Creative Writing courses year round, leading to a certificate or a major for the AA degree. Then in 1975, the Foothill College Writing Conference was born.

Since then, the Creative Writing Program also serves as a focus for the active and prolific Bay Area writing community, along with the three major university programs at Stanford, Berkeley and San Francisco State.

The six-day conference, coordinated by regular members of the English faculty, each June attracts fledgling writers from as far away as Colorado and Washington state. The attraction, to be sure, has been economic: for less than $75, participants can attend up to 16 workshops, all of the daily noon and evening readings and even get a one-on-one evaluation of a short manuscript. They have rubbed elbows over the years with Grace Paley, Galway Kinnell, John Ciardi, Donald Hall, Nikki Giovanni, Ishmael Reed, just to mention a few of the "name" writers. What has kept people coming back, however, cannot be explained by the low cost. The professional writers of fiction, poetry and biography come here as a personal commitment – it cannot be the very limited honoraria they receive. They are here to teach, visit one another, and inspire their less experienced fellow writers, not to parade their talents. Over the years the college has invited back a core group of primarily Northern California writers (several of whom teach at the universities mentioned above) that has given the conference its reputation as a

teaching conference rather than entertainment. This core group has evolved slowly as young professional writers (most recently, Rudolfo Anaya and Jane Hirshfield, for example) "try out" and are asked back.

Since our regular staff of Creative Writing instructors are part of this core group, they naturally attract conference participants into their courses during the ensuing summer, fall, winter and spring quarters, generating a fairly stable supply of students. With very few exceptions over the past few years, each quarter we have offered two sections of short fiction, the novel, poetry, autobiography, film-writing, and the literary journal. Except for our Introduction to Creative Writing, where students are exposed to several genres, all courses, which are generally taught in a workshop format, contain writers at several levels of expertise.

Salaries for the instructors and for the coordinators of the Writing Conference comes out of instructional funds, as with any academic program. Honoraria of the visiting faculty, publicity and other expenses associated with the conference are borne by the non-instructional budget of the Language Arts Division. The total cost of the conference, including those in instruction, amounts to about $25,000 and brings in over $60,000 in FTE from the state.

Foothill College, furthermore, works with two local independent bookstores in shared events, such as a recent Native-American literature workshop and book fair featuring the writer and scholar Greg Sarris. A number of years ago, "alumni" of the program founded the Waverly Writers, a small monthly poetry journal. The Creative Writing Program thus has become a vehicle for a community of local writers who can share the interests and concerns in what is generally a lonely practice.

Contact:
Jim Mauch, Division Dean, Language Arts
(415) 949-7250

Foothill College
12345 El Monte Road
Los Altos Hills, CA 94022
Total head count enrollment-Credit: 13,694; Non-Credit: 445
Campuses/sites: 95; Full-time faculty: 260

DIAGNOSTIC / CARDIAC ULTRASOUND TECHNOLOGY

The programs are monitored by an advisory committee comprising members
of the medical, business and education communities

There has been a well-documented shortage of medical Ultrasound Technologists within the health care community. The community college as its mission statement is the natural setting for this type of vocational training. Since

1985, the Diagnostic Ultrasound Technology program has been in existence at Foothill College. In 1990, a program in Cardiac Ultrasound Technology was added.

The programs were a response to the needs of the

medical community. To ensure the course objectives and curriculum accurately reflected the requirements of the profession a Community Advisory Committee was established. The members were from the medical, business and education community. Their collective direction and guidance gave rise to the present program.

The programs were established to become 12 months and full-time for individuals with Allied Health credentials. The programs fulfill the requirement of the American Registry of Diagnostic Medical Sonography, the only nationally recognized organization which administers the appropriate credentials.

The Ultrasound Technology programs are designed to:
 1) ensure graduates have current job skills in order to practice;
 2) ensure the medical community has a labor pool by which to fill vacancies; and
 3) to support the clinical affiliates through updates and continuing education. The programs are continually evaluated by students, faculty, medical and business community. The result is a progressive and well-respected program.

The medical ultrasound technology programs requires a network of medical affiliates to provide the necessary clinical instruction. A cooperative arrangement is essential between education and business to ensure medical personnel with the didactic and practical skills. There is emphasis in independent thinking, decision making and practical performance.

Contact:
Mary Ann Pavic, Division Dean, Biological and Health Sciences
(415) 949-7249

Foothill College
12345 El Monte Road
Los Altos Hills, CA 94022
Total head count enrollment-Credit: 13,694; Non-Credit: 445
Campuses/sites: 95; Full-time faculty: 260

BUILDING CONSTRUCTION

Students receive true hands-on training by constructing a custom
residential home, from the foundation through to the landscaping

Constructing a custom residential home is the practical and marketable experience students receive in the Fresno City College Building Construction Program. Under the supervision of the college's staff, the construction of the home brings together the varied departments of the college's trade programs including electrical, mill cabinet shop, sheet metal shop, and heating and air conditioning. The program builds motivation, increases pride and develops skills, all of which are essential to the assurance of a quality vocational program.

Each year, the Building Industry Association selects a highly respected developer for the cooperative venture. The project is entirely coordinated and completed by the Building Construction Program of Fresno City College's Technical-Industrial Division.

While several of the college's trade programs are involved at various stages of construction, the instructor serves as general contractor. The students fulfill the role of construction crew. Their responsibilities include everything from foundation and framing to roofing, finishing work and landscaping. The project is a one-year program that includes two academic semesters. Students are on the construction site 20 hours a week, August through May.

The Building Construction Program is dedicated to providing a hands-on vocational experience that combines small group instruction and individual tutoring with practical application. Work values are taught, the highest expectations for quality levels are maintained, and adherence to deadlines and fiscal constraints are enforced. As a result, the students become more than students; the program allows them the opportunity to be apprentice tradesmen, actually applying what they are learning. Graduates of the program are able to obtain and maintain steady employment in the construction field as a result of the quality hands-on training experience.

The Building Industry Association of the San Joaquin Valley has endorsed the program from the beginning and continues to do so. Its effectiveness in training young people in the construction industry is best exemplified by the number of graduating students hired by the builder. A 95 percent placement rate has been maintained for the last several years.

Each year, without fail, the college has sold the homes constructed through the program for a profit. The homes each year have become increasingly more complex and are now located in custom residential developments.

Over the last several years, the program has won numer-

Continues on Page 60

ous awards. It received the 1988 Governor's Citation for Excellence in Vocational Education, and the homes are a regular feature in the Building Industry Association's "Parade of Homes – an annual showing of "the best" model homes in the Fresno area. The program received the Building Industry Outstanding Educational Program Award and the National Association of Home Builders has requested one of Fresno City College's contracts with developers to be used as a national model.

Contact:
Arthur D. Ellish, Dean of Instruction
(209) 442-4600

Fresno City College
1101 East University Avenue
Fresno, CA 93741
Total head count enrollment-Credit: 22,937; Non-Credit: 2,837
Campuses/sites: 1; Full-time faculty: 248

LVN TO RN ARTICULATION

Articulation students have one intensive year of classroom instruction and clinical experience before taking the licensing exam

Fresno City College has been in the forefront of a state movement to facilitate the articulation of Licensed Vocational Nurses to become Registered Nurses in no more than 30 semester units of instruction. Fresno City College, among the first in the state to implement this program, serves as a model for other California community college nursing programs.

The first year of the articulation component was funded by the California Area Health Education Consortium (AHEC) as a special project promoting academic upward mobility in health care education. This specific articulation process facilitated Licensed Vocational Nurses moving upward academically to eventual licensing as Registered Nurses. This is done through one intensive year of classroom instruction and clinical experience that qualifies these students to take the registered nurse licensing examination.

The nursing courses taken are the second year courses of the two-year nursing program. Licensed Vocational Nurses entering the Licensed Vocational Nurse to Registered Nurse articulation component of the Fresno City College Registered Nursing Program enter the second year of that program. They are assigned to instructors whose main focus is to assist these students with mastery of clinical skills and with the transition unique to Vocational Nurses articulating to Registered Nurses. Articulation students attend all the second-year nursing lecture courses along with the students in the generic component of the program.

Since the inception of the program, 215 Licensed Vocational Nurses have entered the program and 176 have completed the program successfully and have been licensed as Registered Nurses in California. Initially 10 students entered the program each fall. In 1986 the number was increased to 15, and in the fall 1992 semester, this number was increased to 30. Currently two full-time nurse faculty members are assigned to the Licensed Vocational Nurse to Registered Nurse articulation component of the two-year Associate in Science Degree Nursing Program. Both the instructors bold Master's degrees in Nursing.

Articulation students are local residents with roots in the local community. Their average age is 37. Hospitals employ these Licensed Vocational Nurses and are highly supportive of their endeavors to acquire the education requisite for licensing as Registered Nurses. Since the inception of the Licensed Vocational Nurse to Registered Nurse articulation component of the nursing program, area hospitals have continued to make a concerted effort to collaborate with the college nursing program to offer quality clinical learning experiences for the students.

Contact:
Gordon Ogden, Director of Nursing
(209) 442-4600

Fresno City College
1101 East University Avenue
Fresno, CA 93741
Total head count enrollment-Credit: 22,937; Non-Credit: 2,837
Campuses/sites: 1; Full-time faculty: 248

INTERCULTURAL CENTER

▦ The Center has fostered international and intercultural sensitivity ▦
on the college campus

The entire campus, not just a classroom or club, is considered an intercultural center for Golden West College. This mind set began to tangibly catch on in the fall of 1989, when college president Judith Valles encouraged three staff members to call together a task force to establish a center to promote intercultural interaction and harmony, and provide learning activities and support services.

A task force of interested faculty, administrators and students was called together by the Associate Dean of Language Arts and Social Sciences. The task force formulated the mission statement, goals and name (Intercultural Center) that were subsequently approved by a survey of staff and students. More than just a facility with isolated concerns, the center was designed to be broad-based in mission and function and foster the notion that the entire campus is an intercultural center.

The IC goals are: 1) to encourage a focus on intercultural/international experiences in GWC educational activities; 2) to promote events that explore cultural diversity, recognize interdependence, and foster harmony and mutual understanding; 3) to provide a supportive and enriched atmosphere for all students, and assistance to ethnic minorities so that they can better realize their potential in the larger cultural context; and 4) to act as an intercultural/international information and communication center for the college community. Current activities include an ESL support program wherein some 100 community volunteers assist students, discussion groups, staff development, study abroad, international student recruitment and assistance, celebrations, children's programs, and assistance to relevant campus and community groups.

The Intercultural Center is supervised by an instructional dean and coordinated by a faculty member working with a full-time staff assistant (classified employee) and some hourly employees. The dean and coordinator serve on and are advised by a 20-person advisory committee of faculty, staff, students and administrators. The operational budget of $16,200 is currently supplemented by tuition from newly recruited international students. Once the center becomes self-supporting from increased tuitions, additional tuition income will be dispersed to other college programs.

As a result of the IC, international and intercultural sensitivity and activity are a reality throughout the GWC campus. Within 15 months of the formation of the IC, it had been showcased at five major state and national conferences such as AACJC. In the summer of 1990, GWC was named as a Beacon College because of the IC, and the IC is featured in the Beacon publication Beyond the Classroom: International Education and The community College, Vol. 11, Internationalizing the Campus Environment, 1992, pp. 3-17.

Contact:
Donna E. Willoughby, Dean, Social Sciences, Intercultural Center
(714) 895-8790

Golden West College
15744 Golden West Street
Huntington Beach, CA 92647-0592
Headcount not provided
Campuses/sites: 1; Full-time faculty: 209

TELEMEDIA SERVICES

▦ College-produced programs are shown on campus, in the media center, ▦
via satellite, and on local PBS and cable channels

The Telemedia Services of Golden West College have influenced people far beyond the local TV viewing area. Many college-produced programs have been sold to institutions nation-wide, with royalty monies going to faculty developers and the college.

It all began in 1976, when Golden West College established Telemedia Services to support faculty development of instructional video programs. A number of benefits for students, faculty and the college resulted from teaming faculty with Telemedia's two-person professional staff.

Telemedia Services' main mission is to support instruction with time made available for public relations and campus-wide projects. Programs produced are shown on campus, in the library media center, broadcast via satellite, local PBS and local cable channels.

The success of the department is due to a number of factors such as faculty participation, the process developed for prioritizing projects, staffing Telemedia with professionals whose backgrounds include educational as well as

Continues on Page 62

TV expertise, streamlining production, facility coordination of various district and campus facilities, and distribution of programs.

The faculty interest for developing video programs has created a backlog of requests since the facility opened in 1976. A two-tier scheduling process was developed to meet this demand.

A few major projects are produced each year. Major projects proposed by faculty are reviewed by the Telemedia Review Committee, which has a standard criteria for prioritizing projects. Faculty time and production costs are funded for these projects with royalties being shared by faculty and the college. Faculty also have the right to buy back their projects and own the rights to the project.

The remaining time is left open for less complex faculty projects. Faculty are scheduled on a first-come-first-served basis. This is Telemedia Services "Open Door" to faculty and where many faculty learn of the possibilities of utilizing video for instructional development. This introduction with simpler projects often leads faculty members to proposing a major project.

GWC Telemedia Services was awarded the Visual Communication Department of the year award by Apple Computers and the Visual Communicators Association. Also, Telemedia has received three Emmy Awards, 13 Emmy nominations for Instructional Programs and numerous Educational and Instructional awards.

Contact:
Douglas Larson, Associate Dean, Telemedia Services
(714) 895-8236

Golden West College
15744 Golden West Street
Huntington Beach, CA 92647-0592
Total head count not provided
Campuses/sites: 1; Full-time faculty: 209

GROSSMONT COLLEGE

PROJECT INVEST (SKILLED INSURANCE CLERK TRAINING)

Project Invest is designed to combine skill-building with help making the transition from welfare to school to insurance work

More than 2-million Californians receive $5.7-billion in Aid to Families with Dependent Children (AFDC) payments; welfare payments have increased 32 percent since 1985. California has 26 percent of the total AFDC cost in the nation (with only 12 percent of the total population) and a budget shortfall exceeding $6-billion.

In response to this fiscal crisis, the insurance industry and Grossmont College have formed a partnership to train disadvantaged students for entry-level jobs in the insurance industry. With funding from the Job Training Partnership Act (JTPA), Project Invest students attend school as a 25-member cohort group for 20 units of intensive training in typing, microcomputer applications, English and job search. To prepare students for the rigors of college, they all participate in a four-week pre-training module, taking courses in reading, math review, life skills and keyboarding.

Project Invest is unique because of its "career continuum" approach to employment training; it provides entry-level skills training that articulates to the next level of occupational training and flows into transfer programs at four-year institutions.

Because they are recipients of welfare, unemployment benefits and disability payments, Project Invest students bring a variety of personal, financial and family problems to school with them. To prevent these factors from interfering with their ability to stay in school and subsequently find employment, Project Invest has been designed to combine skill-building with assistance in making the transition from welfare to school to work. Emergency funds are available to help students through crisis; a clothing bank helps students prepare for job interviews. Peer group support is cultivated among students. Functioning collaboratively, engaging in critical thinking and asking for help are important skills students learn to develop.

For many Project Invest students, school has meant failure due to language barriers, learning disability or chaos in the home. To help students overcome these feelings of academic inadequacy, a teaching methodology called PQ3R has been developed. Students are aided in navigating difficult college textbooks by learning to Preview, Question, Read, Record and Review (PQ3R). This technique is incorporated into all of the classroom instruction. These methods are so successful that 40 percent of the high-risk welfare students go on to pursue additional college course work after finishing the Project Invest curriculum.

Enthusiastic industry participation is a key feature. Project Invest is supported by the Independent Insurance Agents Association, which works with Grossmont College to develop curriculum, provide scholarships and structure internships for students. At a recent Insurance Industry Conference, the Independent Agents Association donated a booth to Project Invest that resulted in several permanent placements for students. Project Invest is publicized in local and state-wide insurance publications and has received a national award for the Outstanding Educational Program by the Independent Agents Association.

Prospective employers call Grossmont College directly to employ students.

A Project Invest national teleconference is planned for Spring 1993 to be down-linked to hundreds of community colleges nationwide. Local insurance agencies are encouraged to work with their local community college campuses to develop Project Invest sites for their local communities.

Contact:
Michele Nelson, Vice President, Instruction
(619) 465-1700, ext. 608

Grossmont College
8800 Grossmont College Drive
El Cajon, CA 92020-1799
Total head count enrollment-Credit: 17,484
Campuses/sites: 1; Full-time faculty: 220

GROSSMONT COLLEGE

CENTER FOR THE VOCATIONALLY CHALLENGED

The Center prepares students with disabilities for today's evolving job market by constantly updating curricula and technology

Recognizing the employment barriers that uninformed employers pose to persons with disabilities, coupled with the acknowledgment that companies can only hire job-qualified disabled people, Grossmont College established the Center for the Vocationally Challenged (CVC) in 1986.

The CVC is a joint venture between the College District, about 40 local area businesses who serve as Business Advisory Council (BAC) members, the State Department of Rehabilitation, IBM and the Private Industry Council. The Center offers three computer-training programs for the disabled that are unique to the California Community College system. The programs, Programmer, PC Support Specialist and LAN (Local Area Network) Support Specialist Training for the Physically Challenged, are conducted in two dedicated computer labs and one classroom.

Annually enrolled in these accelerated programs are 100 disabled students. Programs are designed to help persons rapidly enter or reenter the job market. Graduates earn a certificate in seven to 10 months. Students who additionally complete general education requirements earn an AS degree. A whopping 84 percent of CVC graduates enter computer related jobs with starting salaries of $18,000 to $25,000 per year! A tribute to effective program design and dedicated staff, 70 percent of students who enter training, graduate. The Center employs 15 full-time staff, and offers instruction for a wide spectrum of disabled women and men. These include persons who are blind or visually impaired, deaf and hearing impaired, the learning disabled, as well as those with cerebral palsy, orthopedic disabilities, spinal injuries, and recovering drug and alcohol abusers.

The CVC is unique in three distinct ways. First, in collaboration with 42 local businesses and campus personnel, the CVC regularly modifies curricula to stay abreast with emerging computer technologies. Consequently,

programs are established that meet local employer needs and participating disabled students are given a competitive edge when seeking employment. Second, community and business professionals are extensively involved to ensure program and student success through mentors, periodic student evaluations, mock interviews, classroom presentations and career fairs. In addition, registration fees, books, transportation, parking fees, clothing allowances and guidance are provided by State Department of Rehabilitation Counselors. Third, agreements and contracts are in place with several public and private organizations. Consequently, $600,000 worth of equipment and software has been donated and nearly $4-million in contracts generated.

Since the inaugural computer program for the disabled in 1987, literally dozens of articles about the Center for the Vocationally Challenged programs have appeared in local newspapers. In addition, articles have appeared in business and rehabilitation journals and local company newsletters. Last Spring, the Center was selected from 107 campuses by the California Community College Chancellor's Office as one of nine "Exemplary Vocational Education Programs for Special Populations" More recently, the National Committee on Disability selected the CVC program as one of 15 "Centers of Energy" in the nation; a coveted designation for post secondary programs that serve disabled people and have demonstrated influence on other colleges. Finally, the National Council of Instructional Administrators identified the CVC program as one of two Exemplary Degree Programs.

Co-sponsorship, co-direction and joint funding require flexible, adaptable management with the vision to bridge the bureaucracy in creative and innovative ways that respond to local community and special population needs. A coalition of private employers, public organizations and

Continues on Page 64

Grossmont College have helped hundreds of persons with disabilities earn impressive entry-level salaries in jobs with great career potential. By doing so, state and national recognition follow, operational funds expand, additional opportunities grow and students are better served.

Contact:
Scott Barr, Director, Center for the Vocationally Challenged
(619) 465-1700, ext. 608

Grossmont College
8800 Grossmont College Drive
El Cajon, CA 92020-1799
Total head count enrollment-Credit: 17,484
Campuses/sites: 1; Full-time faculty: 220

HOSPITALITY PROGRAM

The main objective of the program is to improve the hospitality/service level on the South Shore of Lake Tahoe

The Hospitality Program at Lake Tahoe Community College fits perfectly with the local economic landscape. Tourism, a huge part of the area economy, thrives in the Sierra Nevada, on Lake Tahoe's southern shore.

The Lake Tahoe Hospitality Program is designed to support and assist local businesses in the areas of front-line employee training, staff development and to create an awareness that each person's performance makes a difference.

The main objective of this program is to improve the hospitality/service level on the South Shore of Lake Tahoe in order to facilitate and enhance the guest's stay. Two methods to achieve this goal are improve the quality of information and its delivery system and improve the quality of behavior toward guests. We believe well-trained employees will be better able to handle demanding situations and are a key to success. The Lake Tahoe Hospitality Program can ensure a better informed employee.

Training is offered as part of the Lake Tahoe Community College Hotel and Restaurant Management Program. Students receive college credit for the classes they attend and a certificate of course completion. The following classes are offered on a rotating basis on site at the college or at a business site by request of a member business:

- Lake Tahoe Tourist Orientation;
- Dealing with the Difficult Customer;
- Time Management on the Job;
- Stress Management on the Job; and
- Serving the International Guest

Since July 1991, the program has trained 1,000 employees and will continue to grow to meet the needs of our community. Special Topic classes have been added as requests and needs assessment require. The Hospitality Program has offered the following classes as Special Topics:

- Quality Control in a Service, Health and Administrative Environment;
- Presentation Skills;
- Americans with Disabilities Act; and
- Managers Guide to Customer Service.

Contact:
Lori Gaskin, Dean
(916) 541-4660, ext. 230

Lake Tahoe Community College
One College Drive
South Lake Tahoe, CA 96150-4524
Total head count enrollment-Credit: 6,000
Campuses/sites: 1; Full-time faculty: 26

BI-CULTURAL CONVERSATION COURSE

The innovative language course pairs English-speaking students with Spanish-speaking students, which also promotes cultural understanding

An innovative bilingual conversation course pairing English-speaking students studying Spanish and Spanish-speaking students studying English was Lake Tahoe Community College's innovative response to the needs of a rapidly growing Hispanic population.

The course is made up of 50 percent ESL Students and 50 percent Spanish-language students. The Bicultural Conversation courses are designed to meet both the ESL student's needs as well as the needs of the Spanish-language student (whose first language is English).

The goal of the course for one half of the students is to provide the ESL students the opportunity to speak, practice and build their English oral skills with native English speakers on a one-on-one basis. The goal for the second half of the students is to build skills in oral Spanish. The students work in pairs, using a wide range of vocabulary from greetings and expressions of courtesy to topical vocabulary which include such topics as shopping, employment and foods. Students are required to speak English or Spanish for the majority of the class and help to correct the Spanish of their English-speaking partners (or correct the English of their Spanish speaking partners).

The course focuses on oral proficiency and offers the students a living language laboratory.

The students from the ESL group must have taken at least one quarter of ESL and the students from the Spanish group must have had at least two quarters of Spanish.

In the past year, the course has proved very popular, and the college is considering adding sections and expanding the experiment. It has proved to be very beneficial for both groups of students. Their pronunciation and vocabulary have increased and the two groups of students have begun to learn more about each other and their cultures.

Contact:
Diane Rosner, Instructor-in-Charge
(916) 541-4660, ext. 255

Lake Tahoe Community College
One College Drive
South Lake Tahoe, CA 96150-4524
Total head count enrollment-Credit: 6,000
Campuses/sites: 1; Full-time faculty: 26

LANEY COLLEGE

PROJECT BRIDGE

Culturally sensitive to its mostly minority learners, this basic skills program emphasizes a student-centered approach

Unlike most basic skills programs that focus on skill instruction, Laney College's Project Bridge was founded on the notion that people learn literacy practices in the service of understanding ideas, and through collaborative work in an academic learning community.

In this interdisciplinary program, ideas and skills are brought together to empower students. Students enter the program with skills that place them two to seven years below college level on placement tests, and often bring with them a history of school failure. The program is designed to help students see themselves as learners and to help them become skilled enough to succeed in the vocational or academic programs of their choice. The program offers reading, writing, math, computer science and social science or ethnic studies.

The content of the curriculum is culturally sensitive to the program's mostly minority learners; the pedagogy emphasizes a student-centered approach, and support is a program watchword: both in the classroom via tutorial assistance and in a special counseling component which trouble-shoots crises such as child-care problems and advises "next steps" so that students leaving Bridge find viable programs for academic work and vocational training.

The course registers 80 students per semester and retains 75 percent of them. As program evaluation showed in 1986, students completing Project Bridge are twice as likely to continue in school as students enrolled in conventional remedial classes on the campus. Of those who continue in school after completing Bridge, more than half register for college-level work and show a grade point average higher than that of remedial students from the campus at large. A new follow-up study is currently being launched to determine if a new emphasis on linkages between Bridge and the next step program have been effective.

Project Bridge has received state funding and, through FIPSE, national funding as well. An ongoing private foundation grant allows the counseling and advisement component and a cultural enrichment component to continue. Bridge has been honored as Peralta Community College District's most innovative program, and several research studies conducted on under-prepared learners have been conducted at this site.

Contact:
Margot Dashiell or Smokey Wilson, Coordinators
(510) 464-3411)

Laney College
900 Fallon Street
Oakland, CA 94607
Total head count enrollment-Credit: 22,602; Non-Credit: 190
Campuses/sites: 1; Full-time faculty: 152

DEAF CAN

▦ In addition to academic work, the program for Deaf students encompasses vocational ▦
and linguistic aspects of personal development

Because minority deaf people face especially tough obstacles to equal education, the Deaf CAN program at Laney College includes self-contained Deaf classes taught by fluent signers, at least some of whom are Deaf and African-American, Hispanic or Asian. The program offers a bilingual/bicultural program of basic skills as a preparation for college and vocational programs.

This model program presents a comprehensive approach to basic skill development for Deaf adults in English, math, computer literacy preparation and problem-solving skills. The program encompasses psychosocial, vocational and linguistic aspects of the participants' development, as well as academic work. In these classes where American Sign Language and English overlap and interweave, a rich language environment promotes the slogan "Deaf CAN!" Students enter the program with skills that place them far below college level on placement tests; many (particularly refugee Deaf persons from politically oppressed home-

lands) have never been to school before at all. The program goal is to help Deaf students succeed to in the vocational or academic programs of their choice.

The course registers a maximum of 15 students per semester and retains 90 percent of them. As program evaluation has shown, significant improvements occur in students' reading and writing abilities; many complete Deaf CAN and move into productive lives: continuing in mainstream courses at the college, transferring to other institutions or acquiring jobs in which they find satisfaction. One student, for example, who could neither read nor write upon entry in Deaf CAN, is now working as a computer operator and earning a good salary.

Deaf CAN has received State funding and national recognition. It has been honored as an innovative program, and identified as a Model by the University of California Center on Deafness and the pedagogy disseminated in a conference in 1992.

Contact:
Smokey Wilson, (510) 464-3411
Rocky Gomez, (510) 464-3400 (TDD)

Laney College
900 Fallon Street
Oakland, CA 94607
Total head count enrollment-Credit: 22,602; Non-Credit: 190
Campuses/sites: 1; Full-time faculty: 152

THE FRESHMAN CONNECTION: A LEARNING COMMUNITY

▦ An interdisciplinary block of courses for entering students includes ▦
coed PE, U.S. History and psychology

An interdisciplinary block of courses for entering students unifies courses from a number of disciplines and unifies support systems. This creates natural links for students to form study groups, while providing staff development opportunities for faculty in working with other faculty outside their own discipline.

As offered in the fall of 1991, the 13.5-unit block of linked classes, called The Freshman Connection, included a co-educational physical education class, a precollege English class in a learning laboratory setting, introduction to health, library skills, United States history and a psychology course called The College Experience. The courses all were regular course offerings, but were identified by a block in the schedule that allowed easy registration for all classes within the block. The instructors all maintained one office hour in common, facilitating planning for the classes.

The faculty met for one day during the summer to:
- develop loosely linked themes and to plan teaching schedules so that major projects and tests would not be scheduled for the same day in several classes;
- collaborate on means of intervening to provide help to individual students;
- develop strategies to encourage collaborative learning, and on sharing learning and teaching strategies to become more effective presenters;
- use topics from the library skills course for student reports as the basis for some library exercises and in other cases, used assignments directly from the courses; and
- grade the students in his or her own class independently from the teachers of the other linked classes.

The students were encouraged to participate in the program by emphasizing the opportunities for making new friends quickly, becoming involved in informal activities at the college, and by offering a full load of classes in prime-time (all classes were held between 8:30 a.m. and 12:30 p.m., with time set aside for participation in the library course, which is self-paced).

The first Freshman Connection was offered for students whose English skills were assessed to be at a precollege level. Other Freshman Connections are being considered for entering students in science/math majors, business or vocational students, and one for potential transfer students without specific majors.

Contact:
Don Milanese, Dean of Instruction
(510) 373-5803

Las Positas College
3033 Collier Canyon Road
Livermore, CA 94550-9797
Total head count enrollment-Credit: 6,335; Non-Credit: 27
Campuses/sites: 3; Full-time faculty: 68

STUDENT SUPPORT PROGRAM

The program, which supports drug- and alcohol-free lifestyle choices, includes weekly support groups and a special course

The rise in the incidence of drug and alcohol abuse among college students motivated Las Posits College to create a Student Support Program.

This program began in 1990 with counseling staff employing a professional expert to train more than 40 volunteer faculty and staff in recognition and referral techniques for alcohol- and drug-dependent students. A large poster placed in each classroom and throughout the campus identified by photograph and by name the trained faculty and staff who were available to help students with substance abuse problems.

A continuing 20-member faculty, staff, and student group led by a counselor met monthly to establish this important program which developed the following activities:

- established a weekly support group for students choosing a drug- and alcohol-free lifestyle;
- organized a contemporary studies psychology course designed to deal with interpersonal problems associated with substance dependency;

- sponsored a Community and College Challenge Day as a training activity for persons dealing with substance abuse, personal and interpersonal problems;
- drafted a drug-free workplace policy for the college;
- developed procedures for dealing with substance abuse emergencies;
- developed an information and referral resource listing for the college community;
- piloted a Peer Support Network (made up of student volunteers) with weekly training sessions led by a counselor and psychology instructor; and
- developed a "Listening Post" program; joined community "we say no" efforts.

In two years the Las Positas College Student Support Program has grown into a successful college and community cooperative effort that continues to develop and serve the needs of the college community who choose to live a substance-free lifestyle.

Contact:
Dee Roshong, Associate Dean, Student Services, (510) 373-5820
Art Tenbrink, Counselor, (510) 373-5817

Las Positas College
3033 Collier Canyon Road
Livermore, CA 94550-9797
Total head count enrollment-Credit: 6,335; Non-Credit: 27
Campuses/sites: 3; Full-time faculty: 68

ASSOCIATE DEGREE NURSING

*Student retention has improved through a
mentoring project with area nurses*

Besides the traditional course work, Long Beach City College's Associate Degree Nursing program pairs students with mentors already working in the field. This, a joint effort of the program and six local health care agencies, began in 1987.

But the Long Beach City College Associate Degree Nursing Program first admitted students in 1959. There have been 2,756 graduates since that time. The program's pass rate for first time takers on a recent state board examination was 91 percent.

The purpose of the associate degree nursing program at Long Beach City College is to meet the Long Beach area need for entry-level registered nurses. Clinical rotation planning for the program is done in collaboration with other associate and baccalaureate degree nursing programs and representatives of local health care facilities. In 1989, the program was one of the first nursing programs in California to start a nurse worker program with local area hospitals. The student nurse worker program is an outgrowth of changes in state board regulations designed to encourage innovative collaborations between nursing schools and health care facilities.

The program has had a nursing career ladder in place for many years. Applicants holding nursing assistant certificates are granted advanced placement into the first module of the program and applicants holding vocational (practical) nurse licenses who successfully complete an advanced placement examination receive credit by exami-

nation for all first year courses. Generic and advanced placement graduates of the program who successfully complete a chemistry course are eligible for advanced placement into the junior year of local bachelor's degrees in nursing programs.

Program faculty (16 full-time and five part-time) write, produce, review and update course syllabi for all major courses in the program. Nursing students also have access to the multi-media Nursing and Health Technologies Learning Center. The Health Care Associates, a volunteer fund raising organization of representatives from local health care agencies, provide funding for extended Learning Center hours, textbooks, tutoring, and emergency funds for students in need.

In 1987, the program initiated a mentoring project in which staff nurses in local agencies volunteered to mentor nursing students. The main purpose of the project was to increase retention of students in the nursing program and was a joint effort of the program and six local health care agencies. The most successful activity of the project is an annual Shadow Your Mentor Day in the spring.

Clinical experience for nursing students increases from nine hours of clinical practice per week in the first semester to 24 hours per week in the fourth and last semester of the program. An effort is made to ensure that each student has clinical experience in as wide a variety of clinical agencies as possible.

Contact:
Marilyn Balint, Department Head, (310) 420-4160
Mary Cavalier, Program Director, (310) 420-4533

Long Beach City College
4901 East Carson Street
Long Beach, CA 90808
Total head count enrollment-Credit: 40,394; Non-Credit: 8,972
Campuses/sites: 2; Full-time faculty: 322

COMMERCIAL MUSIC

*The department's hands-on training environment has helped it flourish,
at a time when other college's music programs wilt*

Long Beach City College's effort to embrace the essentials of technology without abandoning the historic and artistic traditions of music is paying off.

In contrast to a statewide decline in enrollment, the Long Beach City College's Music/Radio/TV Department has shown a steady increase in enrollment since the fall of 1978. Such success has come specifically because of a knowledgeable staff, state-of-the-art facilities, comprehensive course offerings and a dedication to reflect the

changing demands and technologies of the professional world of music.

The primary impact of this program can be seen in the number of LBCC music students who are prepared for and find placement in the music business. After investing an ongoing amount of time and research in music technologies and their impact on the job market, the department has developed a hands-on training environment, a computer-run record-keeping system, and state-of-the-art recording facilities that allow students to prepare product for the market place. Commercial Music students have benefited from the Commercial Music Program because they have been able to access the current technology and learn current music business trends. Staying up-to-date with the world of commercial music is always a great challenge, however, the faculty and staff of the LBCC Music/Radio/TV Department realize this challenge and strive not to abandon the quality of tradition upon which the program was founded.

Each student entering into the Commercial Music Program is a unique individual with goals and needs tied to the real immediate needs of academia. For this reason, the Long Beach City College Music/Radio/Television Department, like all other departments at LBCC, has as one of its primary missions the responsibility of providing a quality educational experience for any and all members of the community. The LBCC Music/Radio/Television Department has intensified this educational experience over the years by providing a highly qualified faculty and staff, by offering a diversified curriculum, and by constantly striving to offer state-of-the-art facilities in which students can pursue their academic, artistic and creative goals.

The most recent offering to the community by LBCC is a state-of-the-art multimedia production facility in which individuals can utilize the latest technology to develop the skills and craftsmanship necessary to pursue their immediate goals in music, radio and television. By embarking on this highly ambitious undertaking, LBCC is striving to embrace the essentials of technology in today's highly technological society while not abandoning the historic and artistic traditions that have charted the course for the present degree of success at LBCC.

The Commercial Music Program's goals are to maintain a program that is valuable to the novice musician, the college musician, and the returning professional, as well as to provide students with real-life musical experience and generate enthusiasm by bringing students into contact with professionals and big-name artists in the field.

The LBCC Music/Radio/TV Department was chosen as a representative for a national educational advertisement campaign for Apple Computers, and has received a major technology music grant from Kawai America.

Contact:
Priscilla Remeta, Department Head
(310) 420-4314

Long Beach City College
4901 East Carson Street
Long Beach, CA 90808
Total head count enrollment-Credit: 40,394; Non-Credit: 8,972
Campuses/sites: 2; Full-time faculty: 322

LOS ANGELES CITY COLLEGE

STUDENT ASSISTANCE CENTER

A multi-lingual student staff provide the large immigrant student population with information in their native languages

Los Angeles City College continues to be an ethnic melting pot, where students of different language and background converge – but, due to their unfamiliarity with English, have varying degrees of success. However, an on-campus multi-lingual student staff is helping improve the odds and increase enrollment.

At the heart of this effort is the LACC Student Assistance Center, which provides students with a variety of important services to help them with the admissions process. Unique within the nine-college district, the Center employs a multi-lingual student staff who help LACC's large immigrant student population by providing them with college information in their native languages.

Indeed, it is the Center's staff who are the first persons to greet LACC's newest students when they come to campus to enroll. Among their duties, the staff helps students fill out the application forms and schedules their English placement tests. The staff is also there to answer any questions students might have regarding the college's programs, offices and services. In short, the Center helps LACC's student integrate into the college environment.

The Center is headed by one project manager and a clerical assistant. Its nine student assistants are fluent in Spanish, Armenian, Korean, Russian, Portuguese and French.

The Center's physical layout has been designed so that students can be processed as quickly as possible. Only a low counter separates the staff from the students, and students don't have to wait in lines to be helped. As soon as a student reaches the counter, a staff person is there to help them.

The Student Assistance Center has had a dramatic impact on the general operations of the Admissions Office. Long lines at the admissions office are a thing of the past, for now students arrive with correctly completed application forms that can be processed quickly. The admissions clerks also no longer need to serve as general information counters.

The Student Assistance Center also serves a number of other functions. It provides class schedules, keeps active housing listings and a job board, as well as information on

Continues on Page 70

child care. Referrals are also made for students requesting psychological, family planning or substance-abuse counseling. In addition, information is provided on legal aid, food stamps, and low-cost medical and dental clinics.

One of the many pluses of the Center is that its staff is composed of student peers who can easily relate to the newcomers, especially students of their own ethnic group. They are aware of which psychological approach to take in handling each student's question or problem. The student assistants often form a close bond with the incoming students, who often return to the same persons for assistance.

The Center was set up initially under a Federal Title III grant and currently is funded through California matriculation funds.

The office is open weekdays from 8 a.m. to 4:30 p.m. The Center also handles telephone requests for information on its two telephone lines.

Contact:
Elaine Geismar, Director, Student Assistance Center
(213) 953-4340

Los Angeles City College
855 North Vermont Avenue
Los Angeles, CA 90029
Total head count enrollment-Credit: 17,300
Campuses/sites: 1; Full-time faculty: 190

ENGLISH/ESL DEPARTMENT

Through unusual efforts, such as a Readathon and
Reading Series, language comes alive

Successful writers who personally share their work and students who participate in a three-day reading marathon are just two things that make the Los Angeles City College English/ESL Department stand alone.

Specifically, the innovative programs that enhance the curriculum and greatly benefit LACC's students include the City Works reading series, the semi-annual Readathon, the English Conversation Center, and the Writing Lab. Here is a brief description of each.

The City Works reading series, begun in 1989, presents five to six readings each year by major writers and poets. The intent of the series is to highlight writers who are relevant to LACC's broad, multi-ethnic mix of students and can speak to that diversity. The series has presented readings by such writers as Sandra Cisneros, June Jordan, Gwendolyn Brooks, Gary Soto and Eduardo Galeano.

English/ESL teachers use the readings as focal points for their classes' curriculum, further enhancing the events. For example, students were assigned to read Cisneros' book, *The House on Mango Street* before Cisneros came to campus. To have met the author after having read her work was truly an inspiration for the students. Similarly, the poems and writings of other authors were distributed for study in English/ESL classes prior to the writers' arrival on campus. The readings are very popular and attended by as many as 700 students. The events are held both during the day and in the evening. Although a number of writers have appeared at LACC for free, most are given an honorarium. The funds used to support the City Works series come from the college's Readathon event which has been held twice, in 1990 and in 1992.

The Readathon is, in part, an expansion of the City Works series, in which as many as 45 writers read from their work or those of others. In addition, more than 2,000 to 3,000 students participate in the three-day event. It customarily begins on Wednesday at 10 a.m. and continues day and night through the following Friday at noon, during a week in May. This year's Readathon raised $15,000 through corporate contributions, grass roots fund-raising and private sponsorship of students reading during the event. The Readathon also is cosponsored by the PEN International Writers Association. An additional purpose of the event is to encourage reading among students by making reading a social event. Reading becomes a focus of campus life and it is highlighted in a very public way.

Each Readathon has a theme and in 1990 it was a celebration of multi-cultural literacy. In 1992 the Readathon highlighted writers of conscience, whose work is banned in their native countries. Students wrote more than 400 letters to the heads of various governments in support of persecuted writers. The Readathon also served as a focal point for a number of other events held on campus. The English ESL Department held a book sale and sold t-shirts and buttons; independent book sellers were also on hand. The Child Development Department promoted children's books and literature and the Foreign Language Department presented readings in more than a dozen foreign languages. The Disabled Student Services office provided information on learning disabilities instruction. The Art Department designed a logo for the event. The Theater Department presented excerpts from its stage production of "The Grapes of Wrath" as part of the opening ceremony. In addition, the nearby Braille Institute demonstrated electronic reading for the blind.

The English Conversation Center, one of the department's newest programs is the English Conversation Center. The Center was set up to provide entry-level ESL students an opportunity to practice their conversational skills in a relaxed, non-academic atmosphere. Students take part in roundtable discussions and are encouraged to express their thoughts by an English-speaking facilitator. Because LACC's ESL classes are filled to capacity, the English Conversation Center provides increased English practice for students.

The Writing Lab is a place students can go for additional help in improving their reading, writing, and note-taking skills. Operated as a "drop in" center, the lab employs a staff of full-time tutors and it features 20 personal computers with a various word-processing programs. The lab takes a holistic approach to the writing process and helps students with pre-writing, brainstorming, drafting, editing and grammar. The lab also has a lending library available to students. Students receive one-half unit of academic credit for 10 hours of work each semester in the lab.

Contact:
Gary Columbo, Chairperson, English - ESL Department
(213) 953-4232

Los Angeles City College
855 North Vermont Avenue
Los Angeles, CA 90029
Total head count enrollment-Credit: 17,300
Campuses/sites: 1; Full-time faculty: 190

BILINGUAL PROFESSIONAL EXPRESSWAY PROJECT

The program for foreign-trained professionals includes accelerated English language instruction, transcript evaluation and special workshops

Los Angeles Mission College has a relatively new student group to serve: a large number of foreign-trained professionals now achieving permanent residency in the U.S. through the Amnesty Program or through the New Immigration Reform Act. The Bilingual Professional Expressway is designed to create an identification, matriculation, transfer and placement process to assist immigrant professional teachers to integrate into the American job market in an effective manner.

The program includes a specialized matriculation process, self-paced accelerated English language instruction, concrete transcript evaluation, general education course completion, university transfer assistance, credential and certification assistance and continuous support services through specially designed workshops and seminars.

In addition to the existing college ESL sequence of courses, a special ESL conversation class was created to improve the participants English communication skills. Another special class was designed to help the students understand the American Educational System and to provide information on job networking strategies.

As a direct result of an intensive recruitment process, 2,845 foreign professionals were identified More than 80 percent of the Professional expressway students come from Latin American countries, with Mexico leading with more than 50 percent. The remaining professionals come from countries such as Thailand, China, Ethiopia, Czechoslovakia, Taiwan, Korea, Japan, Brazil, India, Iran, Pakistan, Philippines, Russia, Spain, Sri Lanka and the United States

A large portion of the participants hold degrees of higher education ranging from Associate of Arts Degrees to Ph.D.'s. The degrees for the most part are in Education, Engineering, Business Administration, Computer Science and Health-related fields.

An ongoing dissemination plan consists of presentations at schools, colleges, universities and associations. A brochure that emphasizes the purpose of the program was developed. A step-by-step manual on "how to" implement the project is being prepared. The manual will be distributed to educational institutions that might be interested in establishing a similar program. With our assistance, five California community colleges have implemented a similar project.

The Bilingual Professional Expressway Project has developed partnerships that involve the community, the local school district and institutions of higher learning.

A $300,000 grant from the U.S. Department of Education's Fund for the Improvement of Post Secondary Education (FIPSE) was awarded to Los Angeles Mission College to assist immigrant bilingual teachers to become educators in this country. The program is run by the program director, a secretary and a program assistant. Also, a part-time counselor guides and counsels students in the program.

Contact:
Renee S. Baez, Director
(818) 364-7735

Los Angeles Mission College
13356 Eldridge Avenue
Sylmar, CA 91342
Total head count enrollment-Credit: 6,432; Non-Credit: 1,200
Campuses/sites: 2; Full-time faculty: 66

HONORS PROGRAM

Active student participation and extensive reading and writing assignments make this transfer program tough to enter

Although Honors classes have been taught at Pierce College for many years, not until relatively recently did they get new vigor and direction. Diverse courses were brought together in the form of a highly integrated and purposeful program.

This exciting change was due to the leadership of individuals from both the faculty and the administration who had concluded that the college should make available a different type of academic environment that would meet the needs and interests of some of its varied student body. In addition to the college's initiatives, there also were external factors; the University of California at Los Angeles (UCLA) was committed to increasing the number of community college students transferring to that institution. The result was the Pierce College Honors Program.

The Honors Program offers students the opportunity to enroll in an enriched curriculum of general education classes. Designed for academically prepared and highly motivated students who are planning to transfer to a demanding four-year university, requirements for entry into the program are rigorous. Approximately three-quarters of those who apply are denied admittance to the program because of insufficient grade point average and/or a lack of writing and reading abilities.

Limited to 25 students per class, the program offers 12 to 14 courses every semester. Active participation by the students is required and extensive reading and writing assignments make the classes challenging but rewarding, both to students and faculty. In the several years of its existence the Honors Program has attracted to it the best from the student body and from Pierce faculty.

The Pierce College Honors Program, in conjunction with several other community colleges in Southern California, is a member of the Transfer Alliance Program with UCLA. As part of the TAP agreement, Pierce Honors Program students are required to take at least eight Honors courses along with their other classes and maintain a minimum of a 3.25 GPA before they can be certified for admission to UCLA, which has thus far accepted all Pierce Honors Program students who have completed the requirements.

The program, however, is more than just the Transfer Alliance Program with UCLA. There are many students in the program who plan to transfer to other major universities and who believe that the challenge and environment of the Honors classes can better prepare them to succeed; there are some studies which indicate that Pierce College Honors students do maintain higher grades upon transferring than their non-Honors peers.

Also, in conjunction with Phi Theta Kappa, the national community college academic fraternity, the Honors Program sponsors debates and discussions of major issues during the academic year. These events often involve students and faculty not directly involved in the Honors Program. In conclusion, since its restructuring several years ago, the entire Pierce College community, from the administration downward, has been greatly supportive of the program, and its success has prompted inquiries from other community colleges interested in establishing or improving their own programs.

Contact:
Eugene Larson, Director
(818) 719-6455

Los Angeles Pierce College
6201 Winnetka Avenue
Woodland Hills, CA 91371
Total head count enrollment-Credit: 18,200
Campuses/sites: 1; Full-time faculty: 252

PROJECT FOR ADULT COLLEGE EDUCATION (PACE)

Not a basic skills program, this project targets non-traditional students seeking associate and bachelor's degrees

Non-traditional students get non-traditional treatment at Los Angeles Pierce college, where "adult education" means far from remedial education.

This curriculum trend began in the mid 1980's, when Los Angeles Pierce College started to formulate a response to the needs of a newly emerging student population, comprised of an increasing number of adults returning to education after spending time in professional and personal pursuits. What became apparent in discussions within the college and between the college and its community was that an alternate mode of educating a working adult population had to be designed and implemented if Pierce was to meet its educational obligations toward the community.

The "adult education" programs throughout the state, and certainly many within the Los Angeles area, primarily emphasize basic skills education. Realizing that this area was being addressed elsewhere, the conclusion was reached that Pierce both needed to and could modify its presentational modes in order to offer a General Education, transfer program appropriate to the working adult while continuing to offer a "regular schedule" of transfer courses for the college's other populations. Given these concerns, along with demographic and psychological factors where the students were concerned, it was quite apparent that a traditional curriculum format would not fit, nor would a transfer program be workable if it would take several years to complete – for example, as long as it typically would take a "regular" student to complete General Education requirements.

The Project for Adult College Education was established at Pierce College in 1986 to meet the needs of a student population composed of adults who, most typically have been out of any formal educational environment for at least five to 10 years; worked, or are currently employed; had to meet family obligations, often since the time they last attended school thus being prevented from continuing their formal education; completed high school, either through graduation or the GED.; expressed the goal of earning an Associate degree from Pierce College and a Bachelor's (and perhaps also an advanced) degree from a four-year university; and English skills assessed above the "regular" student population at Pierce College.

A very basic overview of the Project for Adult College Education shows that it is a:

- curriculum package of General Education, transfer course work;
- curriculum package of course work that can meet requirements at most public and private universities in California;
- program through which a student can matriculate in five semesters, earning 60 units of credit;
- program into which a student may enter at the beginning of any semester, in anticipation of completing the requirements for graduation 2 1/2 years later; and
- program designed and maintained for working adult students, a population comprised largely of under-represented students and minorities.

With an enrollment of approximately 400 students each semester since its inception, PACE has provided educational, professional and personal growth to approximately 5,000 non-traditional, under-represented students. The PACE program may be measured in terms of the quantity of students who have been enrolled and who have graduated, although the academic quality of our program is an even more valid indicator of the results generated. For example, although in any given semester PACE accounts for approximately 5 percent of the Pierce College Enrollment, approximately 40 percent of the Dean List students are from our program. In recognition of the outstanding contributions our program has made to the academic offerings at Los Angeles Pierce College, the California Community College Board of Governors presented PACE with its 1991/92 Exemplary Program Award.

Contact:
Jeff Cooper, Director
(818) 719-6455

Los Angeles Pierce College
6201 Winnetka Avenue
Woodland Hills, CA 91371
Total head count enrollment-Credit: 18,200
Campuses/sites: 1; Full-time faculty: 252

THE FASHION CENTER

The Center has in-house study collections, sponsors seminars and offers tech-prep articulation

The Fashion Center of Los Angeles Trade-Technical College, a leader since 1920 in preparing students to move to the front of companies in the California fashion industry, continues to push the limits of fashion education and innovation.

The Fashion Center has been a state-wide leader in creating a consortium of fashion educators to support community college fashion programs by organizing an annual fashion symposium. This program includes 50+ industry speakers, a fashion show, statewide contest for fashion design and merchandising students, and promotional activities to stimulate attendance in public fashion programs. This symposium model has been exported to the northern part of California and is supported by a grant from the Community College State Chancellor.

Other innovations include: an in-house study collection of historic costumes and textiles numbering more than 8,000; an annual seminar for professionals in industry entitled "Fashion Update;" and a tech-prep articulation model

Continues on Page 74

in Fashion Merchandising that has been funded as a statewide model program.

Designed to provide specialized training in the latest technology, with training leading to careers in fashion design, pattern technology, production supervision, buying, store management, sales, fashion consulting as well as entrepreneurs in retailing and manufacturing, the fashion program has turned out many graduates who own and work at companies that are the leaders of the California fashion industry. Examples include: Carol Little, Owner/Designer St. Tropez; Tadashi Shoji, Owner/Designer, Tadashi; Carl Jones, Owner, Cross Colors; and Robin Picone, Owner/Designer, Body Glove. The fashion community contributes to the programs on a continuous basis. Scholarships are donated by professional groups and companies. Industry members participate as

lecturers, mentors, work-experience employers and advisors. The college has the only computer-assisted grading, marking and pattern development system in a public institution in the western United States (this was partially donated by Gerber Scientific Industries).

Sixteen full-time instructors, and more than 30 part-time professionals staff the department. Instructors include authors who are recognized authorities in the field because of the foundation text books they have written. These include Helen Armstrong, author of *Patternmaking for Fashion Design*, and Sharon Tate, author of *Inside Fashion Design*, *The Complete Book of Fashion Illustration*, *The Fashion Coloring Book*, and *The Fashion Handbook, A Guide to Your Visual Image*. Instructors are widely sought as guest lecturers around the nation on their areas of expertise.

Contact:
Sharon Tate, Dean, Academic Affairs
(213) 744-9004

Los Angeles Trade-Technical College
400 West Washington Boulevard
Los Angeles, CA 90015
Total head count enrollment-Credit: 14,828; Non-Credit: 529
Campuses/sites: 1; Full-time faculty: 187

CONSTRUCTION TECHNOLOGIES

▓ *The program features a variety of disciplines, including cabinet-making,* ▓
carpentry, plumbing and refrigeration mechanics

Some of the most complete and comprehensive Construction Technologies programs in the Western States are at Los Angeles Trade-Technical College, which has a proud heritage of producing well-qualified candidates to meet the needs of industry in the areas of construction and maintenance for residential, commercial and light industrial projects.

The college's reputation for high standards and quality instruction is well-established throughout Southern California. Unique offerings include the disciplines of Air Conditioning and Refrigeration Technology, Cabinet making and Millwork, Carpentry, Electrical Construction and Maintenance Technology, Plumbing and Refrigeration and Air Conditioning Mechanics. Because the institution is a state-funded community college, our programs are very affordable and accessible to state residents.

The faculty consists of 22 full-time employees and 32 part-time employees who also hold jobs in industry. Our faculty members possess many years of experience in industry as well as academic accomplishment. Among our faculty are those who are frequently published in trade journals and periodicals as well as authors of textbooks.

Currently we are exploring tech prep programs with local high schools and regional occupational centers. A department member was one of an 11-member team that recently represented California at the National Center for Research in Vocational Education Conference on Tech Prep. Faculty members also have participated in assisting developing countries to establish vocational programs similar to our own.

Contact:
Bobby R. McNeel, Associate Dean
(213) 744-9467

Los Angeles Trade-Technical College
400 West Washington Boulevard
Los Angeles, CA 90015
Total head count enrollment-Credit: 14,828; Non-Credit: 529
Campuses/sites: 1; Full-time faculty: 187

SOUTHEAST ASIAN PROJECT

The project helps meet the needs of Southeast Asian refugees trying to acculturate into the Western world

Merced College's program to help Laotian refugees acculturate to America doesn't stop with teaching them English. Knowing the process of assimilating is not one-sided, the college also teaches the English-speaking community the Hmong language.

The need for such a program began in 1984, when the Southeast Asian population began rapidly growing in the Central San Joaquin Valley of California. Most of these refugees in and around Merced are from Laos. Among the Laotians, approximately 8,000 are Hmong, 1,500 Mien, 1,500 Lao and 500 others representing groups such as Vietnamese and Chinese. Many Southeast Asian Refugees requiring acculturation into the Western world not only need to acquire survival language skills and techniques, but

also academic and professional skills and social skills. In response to the needs of these refugees, Merced College has developed, or refocused, specific services to assist them in their transition to Western society.

In addition to English as a Second Language classes, developmental studies and tutorial assistance, and the class in the Hmong language, Merced College has an Asian student center, which provides the student with a setting where they can receive support from their peers.

Also, staff of the college work closely with the leaders of the Southeast Asian community to sponsor special programs of interest, and to assist in the coordination of special services to the refugee populations within the district's boundaries.

Contact:
Jonas Vangay, Counselor
(209) 384-6000

Merced College
3600 M Street
Merced, CA 95340
Total head count enrollment-Credit: 11,599; Non-Credit: 9,963
Campuses/sites: 2; Full-time faculty: 147

HONORS PROGRAM

The curriculum includes general education transfer courses and special-topics seminars

In just a few years, enrollment in the Merced College Honors Program grew tenfold, from only 10 students to more than 100. Designed to meet the needs of exceptional students by providing them with an enriched educational environment, the program challenges students to reach their full potential and to better prepare themselves for the academic demands of a four-year college or university.

The curriculum for the program, which began in 1988, consists of two basic components: honors-designated sections of general education transfer courses, and special seminars designed to give students the opportunity to do advanced reading and research on topics of interest to them. The general education classes offer smaller enrollments than non-honors sections, and there is increased emphasis on class discussion, critical thinking, writing and independent research. The special seminars are often interdisciplinary in nature, and the topics covered are usually selected by honors students themselves.

One of the more unique advanced seminars is a one-unit interdisciplinary seminar, "Big Questions in the Arts and Sciences," which is offered each summer during the first two weeks of summer school. Six different instructors

participate in the seminar, with each of them having two and one-half hours to deal with a topic of special interest to them. In the past, topics have been extremely diverse, running from soil science to calligraphy to the philosophy of religion. The course is open to high school juniors and seniors as well as to Merced College students. Thus, it serves as a tool of recruitment, as well as a vehicle to allow more instructors to participate in honors program teaching.

A new two-unit honors seminar allows honors students to vote on the topic to be covered. In the first round of balloting the top three vote-getters were "The 60's Experience," "The Vietnam War," and "The Philosophy of Sex and Love." Topics covered by past advanced seminars include "The Harlem Renaissance," "Methods of Meditation," "The Paradox of Freedom," and "Joseph Campbell and the Power of Myth."

In addition to special curriculum, honors program students are given the opportunity to participate in field trips and enrichment activities. These have included a geography field trip to Yosemite National Park, a humani-

Continues on Page 76

ties field trip to a Renaissance fair, several trips to Town Hall lecture series in Fresno, and a trip to hear speakers and poets at nearby colleges and universities.

Recently, students attended the Western Regional Honors Council convention in Lake Tahoe and National Collegiate Honors Council convention in Los Angeles. A highlight of each trip was a presentation involving two Merced honors students, a former Merced College honors student now attending U.C. Davis and the Honors Program Coordinator. The presentation was entitled "Multicultural Diversity and the Hmong Experience."

One of the rewards of the program for those instructors who have taught in it is learning about the successes of former students. Although the program is still fairly new, we have seen many cases of such success. To list just a few one of our first Honors Program students is now attending Harvard Divinity School, and another is enrolled in law school at the University of San Francisco. A third is pursuing a graduate degree in Buddhist studies through the Graduate Theological Union, while a fourth is pursuing a graduate degree in anthropology at Northern Arizona University.

Contact:
Max O. Hallman, Program Coordinator
(209) 384-6327

Merced College
3600 M Street
Merced, CA 95340
Total head count enrollment-Credit: 11,599; Non-Credit: 9,963
Campuses/sites: 2; Full-time faculty: 147

MIRA COSTA COMMUNITY COLLEGE DISTRICT

MIRA COSTA STUDENT AMBASSADORS

▒ The ambassadors have been the primary tool in the School ▒
Relations/Minority Outreach program's recruitment

Students themselves have shown to be the best college recruiters of under-represented students.

Initiated as a pilot project during the fall 1990 semester, the student ambassadors have become a permanent and integral part of the college's outreach team.

The 15 culturally diverse student ambassadors, under the direction of the Mira Costa College office of School Relations/Minority Outreach, are interviewed, hired and trained during the summer months in preparation for their work, which begins each fall semester. They are supported by an annual budget of $18,000, which covers all student payroll and training costs.

The Office of School Relations/Minority Outreach is responsible for implementing student outreach services that are designed to help the college meet its strategic goals to enhance the ethnic and cultural diversity of the student body and to make Mira Costa the college of choice for students in the local schools.

As part of this plan, the ambassadors have undertaken a comprehensive set of duties which have enabled the college to secure its presence in the high schools, bring the college message to students in middle and elementary schools, and effectively target students from ethnic minority backgrounds.

With cooperation from the district high schools, each ambassador holds weekly on-site peer counseling sessions at an assigned school. These sessions cover the first stages of the admissions process and ensure that interested students receive ongoing pre-enrollment advising. The ambassadors have also been instrumental in the expansion of the early outreach program by delivering regular on- and off-campus college workshops for middle school and elementary school students. These workshops are designed to reach students at an early age in order to encourage them to stay in school and someday pursue a college education. Most importantly, the ambassadors have provided a variety of target outreach services for minority high school students. These include serving as mentors for students in the College Bound program; providing workshops for Advancement Via Individual Determination (AVID), Migrant Education, English as a Second Language, and other support programs for under-represented and educationally disadvantaged students; and holding weekly bilingual peer-counseling appointments at each feeder high school.

The student ambassadors have enjoyed a great deal of success since the advent of the program. Recent high school graduates consider Mira Costa to be a very attractive college option as evidenced by the fact that the average age of the student body has decreased by more than two years, while the number of students enrolled full-time has nearly doubled. Ambassador efforts have also contributed to the increasing diversity of the student body as the percentages of Asian-Pacific, African-American and Latino students have climbed steadily over the past few years. The program has also received recognition both on-

and off-campus. During the spring of 1992, the student ambassadors received Mira Costa's "Excel-erator of the Year" award for being an innovative and effective college program. In addition, the ambassadors were selected to be workshop presenters for the 1992 annual convention of the Community League of California.

Contact:
Paul Schlossman, Coordinator, School Relations & Minority Outreach
(619) 757-2121, ext. 279

Mira Costa Community College District
One Barnard Drive
Oceanside, CA 92056
Total head count enrollment-Credit: 9,400; Non-Credit: 2,168
Campuses/sites: 2; Full-time faculty: 127

MISSION COLLEGE

CULTURAL PLURALISM

*Integrating Cultural Pluralism throughout the curriculum has meant
changing syllabi and celebrating cultural holidays*

An entire year of research and planning was done before Mission College embarked on a multicultural path that included adjusting curricula, developing new courses and establishing a speaker series.

The change came following the fall of 1986, when the Governing Board of the West Valley-Mission Community College district directed West Valley College and Mission College to look into what it called "cultural pluralism" and to make recommendations to the Board. At Mission College, the recommendations of a committee were presented to the Board in June 1987. Besides changes in courses, they included: celebrations of cultural events of various ethnic groups, providing staff development opportunities for professional growth and developing a cultural pluralism requirement within the existing Associate Degree Area Requirements.

The approach recommended by the committee was to integrate Cultural Pluralism throughout the curriculum and across the campus. At least 17 course outlines have been significantly modified to include culturally pluralistic content, and two new courses are being offered that were designed to address multicultural issues. So far more than 20 faculty members have participated in a series of in-service workshops to accomplish their curriculum revisions. Many faculty members added statements of Cultural Pluralism to their course outlines as they made revisions mandated by Title V. Most Flex Day (staff development) programs have included a session on Cultural Pluralism. Guest speakers have been brought to campus each semester. Cultural holidays have been celebrated their significance publicized. New instructional materials (media, books) have been purchased.

What is Cultural Pluralism About? (10/89: Jane Patton, Mission College)

1) Retention: Using a variety of teaching strategies can help all students succeed; It fosters an understanding and appreciation of cultural differences.

2) Critical thinking: Looking at contrasting views from other cultures; comparing and contrasting ideas; less dogmatic thinking.

3) Effective teaching and faculty development opportunities: Focusing on adapting teaching to the students' needs; making the content relevant to diverse students.

4) Program improvement: Adding new courses to the curricula; modifying existing courses.

5) Meeting the needs of diverse students: Immigrant and native-born students with diverse needs are a focal point.

6) Affirmative action: The very existence of the Cultural Pluralism program is an affirmative action; Cultural Pluralism goals include retaining under-represented students in higher education via improved teaching strategies; faculty and staff awareness of diversity is increased through development experiences.

7) It is for vocational students: Many "new majority" students are enrolled in vocational programs and Cultural Pluralism across the curriculum assists them via improved teaching strategies and culturally sensitive curricula.

8) It is for transfer students: Various courses in transfer program include Cultural Pluralism components; improved teaching strategies sensitive to diversity can assist in the transfer function of under-represented students and in the Cultural Pluralism knowledge of all students.

9) It is for the faculty and staff members' continuing enrichment: Developing opportunities are an underlying goal of the program.

Contact:
Marc Accornero, Committee Chair
(408) 988-2200, ext. 3359

Mission College
3000 Mission College Boulevard
Santa Clara, CA 95054-1897
Total head count enrollment-Credit: 9,394
Campuses/sites: 1; Full-time faculty: 124

ENGLISH AS A SECOND LANGUAGE

*▓ Instruction is delivered via small group work, ▓
role-playing, video and computer learning*

An unprecedented increase in the number of immigrants coming to the U.S. in the last 15 years has resulted in the need for unprecedented college-level English-language instruction. At Mission College, this includes instruction delivered through such techniques as pair-group and small-group work, role-playing, video learning and computer learning.

The English as a Second Language program is designed to maximize second language acquisition. There are 22 courses, five adjunct labs and six open-labs courses, plus 13 Workplace ESL courses. The course work is divided into four skills (reading and vocabulary, grammar and writing, listening and speaking, and pronunciation) at five levels of proficiency. The four linguistic skills are integrated within each course, but to ensure each skill is addressed thoroughly, separate courses are devoted to each. Courses have been articulated with other departments that teach communication skills.

During matriculation, students' language skills are carefully assessed for successful assimilation into the program; in addition, each semester students receive academic advice from their ESL instructors. Students are encouraged to take other academic courses concurrently with ESL courses.

Instruction in English as a Second Language is delivered in an interactive, participatory mode. Acquiring a second language is a complex task that demands diligence and determination on the part of the student, and a great deal of encouragement and flexibility from well-trained instructors.

The college provides strong counseling and academic support for the ESL program through special orientations, a well-equipped language laboratory, an English Computer-Writing Lab and a Learning Center, where students can work with a tutor or independently with printed material, audiotapes, videotapes, computer software and a special book collection in the library.

The English as a Second Language Programs has grown at Mission College from two courses in 1979, to eight courses (39 sections) in fall 1986, to 22 courses (75 sections) on campus and 13 courses in Workplace ESL in 1993. This provides a rigorous and comprehensive program for more than 1,200 students each semester. According to spring 1992 figures, more than one third of Mission College's students (36 percent) are non-native speakers of English. The student taking ESL courses are from many cultures, but currently the two largest groups are Asian (74 percent) and Hispanic (23 percent).

The ESL Department has provided leadership for other campus programs and activities. ESL instructors helped develop Mission's Cultural and Global Awareness Program, write a successful grant for ED> Net (now directed by an ESL faculty member) and hold staff development workshops for associate faculty each semester. There are 5.5 full-time faculty and 22 associate faculty. In spring 1993, an ESL faculty member coordinated the new Mission College Bangkok campus program, and since the inception of Mission's Corporate Training Program in 1990, faculty have taught 44 Workplace ESL courses in 15 companies here in Silicon Valley. Mission ESL faculty are also active on boards of professional organizations such as CATESOL (California Teachers of English to Speakers of Other Languages) and in TESOL, the international branch.

Mission's successful ESL curriculum was replicated at our sister institution, West Valley College, around 1990. Mission College's English as a Second Language program recently received an Exemplary Program Award in spring 1993 from the Board of Governors of California Community Colleges.

Contact:
JoAnn Hacker, Department Chair
(408) 748-2792, ext. 3404

Mission College
3000 Mission College Boulevard
Santa Clara, CA 95054-1897
Total head count enrollment-Credit: 9,394
Campuses/sites: 1; Full-time faculty: 124

PRINTING TECHNOLOGY

Students get experience solving complex color printing and proofing problems through internship and work experience programs

In the Silicon Valley, there is a growing need for employees working in the printing industry to have electronic publishing and pre-press skills. Mission College has the only accredited community college printing department in the South Bay that offers the full range of skills needed for employability in the printing industry.

The Printing Technology Department has designed courses to keep up with the continually changing technology in Silicon Valley. Our graduates are taught: the historical development of the industry; the traditional methods of image development and reproduction; electronic publishing using software common to the industry; and digital imaging, pre-press and electronic stripping.

Our classes regularly tour and preview the ever-changing state-of-the-art equipment used in print shops throughout the South Bay. They get first-hand experience in problem-solving complex color printing and proofing problems through our internship and work experience programs. Recently, the department was selected as one of two colleges in the United States to engage in a training partnership with Aldus Corporation to teach digital image assembly using PressWise software.

In the past year, Mission College's Printing Technology Program has seen 22 of its certificated students or graduates get placed in high-level printing jobs in local industry. Employers of our students include some of the largest shops in the Santa Clara valley, including: the Mercury New, the House of Printing, Mueler Printing, Keedie Imaging, Consolidated Publications Inc., Pizzazz Printing, LinoText, Campbell Printing and Adobe Systems.

Contact:
Printing Department
(408) 988-2200

Mission College
3000 Mission College Boulevard
Santa Clara, CA 95054-1897
Total head count enrollment-Credit: 9,394
Campuses/sites: 1; Full-time faculty: 124

TELEPHONE REGISTRATION

Besides shortening the on-campus registration period, the system reduces the need for temporary clerical help

On-campus semester registration at Mt. San Antonio College has been reduced from 15 days to five days, thanks to a newly designed computer system for telephone registration.

Originally implemented in spring 1990 for continuing students, this was a major undertaking because Mt. SAC has a comprehensive system of course prerequisites and student eligibility requirements. Therefore, the target pilot population of continuing students were advised of their need to establish eligibility for courses prior to telephone registration. To further advise students of their eligibility, more than 30,000 eligibility notices were sent to continuing students to clearly inform them of these new requirements, their eligibility codes, and the opportunity to take placement tests for establishing skill levels at a higher level than those established by completion of prerequisite courses. (New eligibility by testing triggered second and third notices of updated eligibility.)

With this advance notice, publicity, and carefully worded class schedule instructions, approximately 65 percent of the continuing students successfully registered by telephone between the established hours of 6 a.m. to 11 p.m.

With the success of the telephone registration system for continuing students, the system was expanded for all students to use in subsequent terms. Students received registration permits in the mail that emphasized telephone registration priority dates, but included on-campus registration dates routinely scheduled two to three weeks later. Students were free to call back and make program changes as often as they wished, but actual registration was not complete until fees were paid. Fees were due and payable at the Bursar's office by mail or in person within a published five-day period. The system allowed students to search for open sections of closed classes and allowed students to verify their schedule and check fees repeatedly. There were very few time periods when all lines were busy.

Continues on Page 80

Although a few problems were experienced regarding payment deadlines and obligations for fee payments, the system has worked exceedingly well. In addition to the shorter registration period, the hourly as-needed for temporary registration clerical costs have been dramatically reduced. In addition to these reductions, the same system is used for students to access their semester grades. More than 90 percent of the students register by telephone and a similarly high percentage of students obtain their grades by this same computer response system.

Contact:
Rob Rennie, Director, Information Services, (909) 594-5611, ext. 4365
Lynn Hanks, Director, Admissions, (909) 594-5611, ext. 4415

Mt. San Antonio College
1100 North Grand Avenue
Walnut, CA 91789
Total head count enrollment-Credit: 39,892; Non-Credit: 37,640
Campuses/sites: 1; Full-time faculty: 325

MT. SAN ANTONIO COLLEGE

ADAPTIVE LEARNING LAB

Students with disabilities have made impressive gains through the lab's open format

Mt. San Antonio College's Adaptive Learning Lab for individuals with disabilities has an open-entry/open-exit format that means, for instance, if a student with disabilities has medical setbacks, he will not have to formally withdraw or risk a poor grade.

This flexibility was built into a project co-developed by the State Department of Rehabilitation and the California Community College Foundation. The need is obvious: The number of disabled students accessing the community college environment has increased fivefold in the past decade as the range of curricula involving computer technology has also significantly expanded. Fortunately, the potential for disabled students to access curricula through computer technology, both conceptually and physically, has likewise expanded.

High-tech centers established throughout the state received similar initial equipment and training, but then were allowed to develop in unique directions that best-suited their individual campuses' needs. Mount San Antonio College's High Tech Center was developed in 1988. Its unique development suggested that the title, Adaptive Learning Lab, would be more appropriate.

The Adaptive Learning Lab has had three primary goals: 1) to facilitate students' learning ability for improved success in post secondary education; 2) to provide access to computers and curricula for students with physical or visual disabilities; and 3) to promote transfer of their abilities and access into all areas of our campus. The lab has been succeeding beyond its initial dreams.

From the beginning, this lab decided against structured course schedules in favor of an open-entry/open exit design with students working individually in their own area of need. As a result, a hearing-impaired student studying grammar may be seated next to a learning disabled student studying math. Nearby, a couple of students with acquired brain injuries may be working together on memory skills. This design has been important for several reasons. Once students have been identified with a disability or discovered that they are having unexpected difficulty with a class, they can begin immediately in a lab in which they can schedule work around their current classes. Students with acquired brain injury can begin in the lab upon (or even before) discharge from the rehabilitation hospital and prepare for the upcoming semester. If there are medical setbacks, the student may stop without having to formally withdraw or risk a poor grade. For working students, an evening section is available. Two full-time instructors run the lab: one is a specialist in learning disabilities and adaptive computer technology; the other is a specialist in acquired brain injury and communication.

Gains for the students have been impressive. A special project, "Classroom Preparation and Study Skills Development for Brain Injured Students," designed and implemented structures specifically for preparing acquired brain injury students to begin or return to mainstream classes. Services for the acquired brain injury students focus on smoothing the transfer from the rehabilitation setting to the educational setting and, when appropriate, coordinating with the Department of Rehabilitation. Hearing-impaired students, for whom research has documented a .2 grade level advance per year in language skills after completion of high school, are advancing two to three grade levels when a semester of lab time is added to their remedial level reading and writing classes. Early data strongly suggests that learning disabled students who have used the lab to supplement their classes advance more quickly through the required curricula to transferable classes.

Visually limited students function independently in word-processing and computer programming when provided with a "user-friendly" screen enlarger that is compatible with most current software. The lab proposed use of this enlarger in the Computer Information Systems lab (used by students in computer classes), and is proposing its use in the Technology Learning Center for faculty and staff use. Overall, there has been increased interaction with instructors on campus, with better coordination of our services and education for instructors about disabilities.

Contact:
Stephen Lange or Christine Tunstall
(909) 594-5611, ext. 4290

Mt. San Antonio College
1100 North Grand Avenue
Walnut, CA 91789
Total head count enrollment-Credit: 39,892; Non-Credit: 37,640
Campuses/sites: 1; Full-time faculty: 325

OHLONE COLLEGE

BUSINESS ROUNDTABLE

The roundtables raise money for the college foundation while providing businesses with practical, hands-on applications of concepts

To survive and succeed, community colleges must have good relationships with the local business community. The Business Roundtables was initiated in 1989 as an annual fund-raising project with the two goals: 1) increasing the competitiveness of local businesses; and 2) raising funds for the college's foundation.

The Ohlone College Business Roundtable is a multi-day conference that focuses on a different theme each year. The conference includes more than 50 speakers addressing topics related to seven tracks. One of the distinguishing features of the Roundtable is its emphasis on practical, hands-on applications. Most speakers are practitioners rather than consultants, and participants take tours of local companies that stress the theme of the conference.

The key to the success of the Business Roundtable is the relationship between the business sponsor and the college. The sponsor companies give the Foundation generous donations, volunteer leadership for the Roundtable committees and provide access to other corporate resources. Additional benefits to the college include curriculum enhancement and improvement in the college's own quality processes.

The first Ohlone College Business Roundtable began with five sponsors and 10 speakers. With a theme of "Managing a Volatile Future," 270 participants were attracted and $27,000 was raised for the non-profit Ohlone College Foundation. The second Roundtable, "Managing the Workforce of the Future," attracted 250 people and raised $43,000. Then the Roundtable's volunteer steering committee decided to place emphasis on the quality theme. As a result, the third Roundtable in 1991, "Countdown to Quality," was very successful. It sold out weeks ahead of time, with 500 participants, and raised $53,000 for the foundation. The 1992 Roundtable, "Leading the Quality Commitment," was the largest and most successful yet, with 16 corporate sponsors. The 1992 event sold out two months in advance and raised $93,000 for the foundation's programs. Ohlone College plans to expand its 1993 Business Roundtable by involving more businesses and other organizations in its planning and by moving the conference to a larger facility.

Forming good partnerships with businesses has proven to be extremely worthwhile. Corporate employees have not only loaned their expertise to help the college's programs but also have made contributions to help the foundation's monetary reserves. The Business Roundtable is by far the college foundation's biggest annual fund-raiser and has resulted in tremendous positive publicity for the college.

The Ohlone College Business Roundtable has been featured in the National Council for Resource Development Association's *Foundation Development Abstracts* and in a nationwide video conference on charitable giving.

Contact:
Peter Hoffman, Executive Director
(510) 659-6020

Ohlone College
43600 Mission Boulevard
Fremont, CA 94539-5884
Total head count enrollment-Credit: 9,935; Non-Credit: 130
Campuses: 1; Full-time faculty: 134

REGISTERED NURSING MENTOR PROJECT

*▨ Students are placed with mentors who share their ethnic ▨
identity, and they visit their mentor's work site monthly*

In 1991, Ohlone College Department of Nursing began the Ethnic Minority Registered Nursing Mentor Project, developed to increase the retention, graduation rates, and NCLEX-RN pass rates for ethnic minority nursing students through the provision of social support. Ethnic nursing students are placed with RN mentors who share the student's same ethnic identity.

Registered nurses, including Ohlone nursing alumni, are recruited from surrounding community hospitals and clinics and undergo specialized training for their role as mentors. The intent is to create a pool of trained mentors. A contract established jointly by both mentor and student protege after their initial interaction sets guidelines and structure for the relationship during the academic year. Mentors and proteges have frequent contact by telephone and the proteges visit the mentor's work site once a month, for observation only, as a condition of mentor participation in the program.

Mentors keep logs of contacts and submit them to the project office monthly. Project staff monitor relationships, provide support to mentors and proteges and plan social/cultural/professional events during the academic year. Mentors also establish networks in order to help one another.

Preliminary descriptive evaluative data indicate that mentors and proteges alike have experienced many benefits from participating in this planned mentoring program. Reported benefits include increased self-confidence, availability of ethnic role models, insights into real-life nursing and into working effectively as part of a team, and increased abilities to solve problems and provide opportunities to establish networks. It seems reasonable to deduce that these reported benefits will impact student success positively.

Project recruitment, development and evaluation are coordinated through the grant office by a nursing faculty member/grant coordinator and a college educational counselor. This project is made possible by a four-year (1990-1994) grant from the Robert Wood Johnson Foundation to address the nursing shortage and the future supply of ethnic minority nurses.

Project participants and nursing faculty enthusiastically support the continuation of the project beyond the funding period and efforts are underway to institutionalize the project once grant funding ceases. To date, two articles have been published in *Nurseweek*, a newspaper that reaches California registered nurses. The articles are entitled "Minority RN's Mentor Ohlone Nursing Students," and "Minority Mentor Program Competes First Year." In addition, inquiries have been received from nursing programs in several states and from health care institutions in California that wish to establish a similar project.

Contact:
Bernadette Van Deusen, Project Coordinator
(510) 659-6155, ext. 6287

Ohlone College
43600 Mission Boulevard
Fremont, CA 94539-5884
Total head count enrollment-Credit: 9,935; Non-Credit: 130
Campuses/sites: 1; Full-time faculty: 134

POLYSOMNOGRAPHIC (SLEEP DISORDERS) TECHNOLOGY

*▨ Program graduates are employed in Sleep Disorder Centers, ▨
which are in medical centers, hospitals or clinic/office settings*

Orange Coast College is one of no less than two institutions nationwide offering a vocational program in Polysomnographic Technology, an Allied Health specialty for the diagnosis and treatment of sleep disorders and daytime alertness.

Ranked among America's largest single-campus community colleges, OCC's Polysomnographic Technology program is the only such program in California.

The range of sleep disorders is varied, but includes common disorders such as narcolepsy, sleep apnea, insomnia and many others. PSG Technologists operate a variety of sophisticated electronic monitoring devices which record brain activity (EEG), muscle and eye movement, respiration, blood oxygen and other physiological events. Technologists are also involved in evaluation of various treatment methods.

PSG technologists are employed in Sleep Disorder Centers, which can be located in medical centers, hospitals, or clinic/office settings. Orange Coast College's PSG program provides lectures, laboratory on campus, clinical experience at accredited sleep centers, and physician lectures. A major emphasis of the program is to prepare technologists for Board Registration by the Association of PSG Technologists.

Graduates from OCC's Neurodiagnostic Technologists or Respiratory Care programs may complete the PSG certificate program with one additional year's study. Many courses from these programs are directly related to polysomnography. Students without those backgrounds can complete this certificate within two years.

The preferred admission procedure to the program is done by completion of OCC's course, Introduction to Health Occupations. In this course, prospective students take general aptitude examinations in which reading comprehension and math skills are considered important for success in the program. Currently, no students are denied admission to the program because of low test scores. However, if test scores are low, the student will be advised on how to improve their basic skills.

Contact:
Pat Stanley, Administrative Dean of Instruction, Career Education (714) 432-5628
Algeania Freeman, Division Dean, Consumer and Health Sciences, (714) 432-5702

Orange Coast College
2701 Fairview Road
PO Box 5005
Costa Mesa, CA 92628-5005
Total head count enrollment-Credit: 26,000
Campuses/sites: 1; Full-time Faculty: 331

ELECTRONIC MEDIA

Students have career opportunities in such areas as graphics or software development, the aerospace industry and the film industry

Orange Coast College's new Electronic Media department is an interdisciplinary program that links such seemingly diverse fine arts disciplines as computer graphics, digital photography, commercial art, music and film/video. Visual literacy is seen as the common thread that ties all its aspects together. Students are encouraged to independently explore various areas of application. The Electronic Media facilities at OCC include an extensive open lab that is set aside for Electronic Media usage only.

The timing is perfect because Electronic Media is a field experiencing accelerating expansion. The computer is used as a powerful communication tool in virtually every field from advertising to engineering; i.e., education, medicine, law, business, cartography, and fine arts.

The curriculum was developed and is reviewed on a regular basis by educators and industry representatives to ensure that course offerings accurately reflect current industry standards. Local industry often offers internships, access to specialized equipment, and training positions.

Orange County is a major industrial center and attracts many hi-tech industries. The proximity of Orange Coast College to the Irvine Industrial Complex increases local job prospects. Los Angeles is one of the world's centers in the field of electronic media.

Many students become entrepreneurs and start their own companies in presentation graphics or software development. Others are hired by aerospace industries, the film industry or other large corporations. Some choose to go on to four-year institutions for further training.

Required courses may include study in two-dimensional color and design, contemporary art history, photo/computer graphics, lettering and typography, basic photography and introduction to humanities.

Contact:
Pat Stanley, Administrative Dean of Instruction, Career Education, (714) 432-5628
Ted Baker, Division Dean, Fine Arts, (714) 432-5629

Orange Coast College
2701 Fairview Road
PO Box 5005
Costa Mesa, CA 92628-5005
Total head count enrollment-Credit: 26,000
Campuses/sites: 1; Full-timeFaculty: 331

STAFF DEVELOPMENT

Each full-time faculty member annually designs a professional development contract, which undergoes peer review

While many colleges in California and elsewhere have adopted flexible calendar programs, Palomar's program is uniquely flexible. Every year each full-time faculty member designs a professional development contract.

Part-time faculty design contracts each semester. The activities are submitted to a peer-review committee for approval. With the flexible calendar, which was adopted in 1986, up to 15 days of the year may be set aside for staff, professional, organizational and instructional development. Palomar College elected to have nine days of professional development opportunities for faculty to expand their professional competence, to improve their workplace effectiveness, and to contribute to the organizational dynamics of the college.

Mini conferences and workshops are developed as common interests and expressed needs are identified. The contracting process and program development are managed by the professional development coordinator, who is a faculty member with 80 percent release time for a two-year term, and a full-time staff assistant.

In practice professional development offers the gift of time to recreate faculty enthusiasm for both subject-matter and learning. This passion has led to substantial innovations in curricula and in teaching strategies. Some faculty have chosen to make a direct connection between professional development and student learning by including students in extracurricular activities such as: student/faculty art and photography exhibitions; field trips facilitated by faculty from the earth science, journalism, disabled student program, and physical education depart-

ments; and cross-age and cross-course tutoring programs. Also, some faculty have created professional development activities that will shape new learning environments. One such faculty-initiated activity is a study circle. The study circle format consists of a group of five to 20 participants who come together a specified number of times to discuss a particular topic of mutual interest. The initial topic selected by faculty participants was "Great Learning." A life science professor agreed to facilitate the discussions, and the professional development office coordinated the activity. Reading material always was disseminated prior to the meetings, and the discussions have been thoughtful and lively. Discussions about collaborative learning, study skills across the curriculum, and Gardner's theories of multiple intelligence have inspired and encouraged faculty to explore and expand their teaching. New study circles are forming to discuss learning communities/coordinated course curriculum and multi-media. This process would have great nationwide appeal for the following reasons:

1) participant-generated topics ensures that it will meet their needs and interest;
2) opportunity for in-depth discussion;
3) topic specificity and time limitations;
4) the Study Circle Resource Center in Connecticut will provide support with ideas for appropriate materials on certain topics;
5) could be used by any employee group with an interest in a specific topic; and
6) low cost.

Contact:
Leigh Squires, Professional Development Assistant
(619) 744-1150, ext. 2250

Palomar College
1140 West Mission Road
San Marcos, CA 92069-1487
Total head count enrollment: 26,000
Campuses/sites: 1; Full-time faculty: 298

COMPUTER LITERACY FOR FACULTY

Any faculty member may produce a peer-reviewed project using computer-assisted instruction

Porterville College encourages technological growth among its faculty through a program allowing each faculty member who volunteers for the program to produce a final project using computer-assisted instruction, used in a classroom and reviewed by peers.

The use of computers for instructional purposes has

been well-documented in educational research. The growing literature on the effectiveness of computer-assisted instruction (CAI) in combination with traditional classroom lecture/discussion has shown that CAI increases student achievement, decreases time needed to master the subject matter and increases positive attitudes to the subject matter.

Developing such an instructional capability is crucial in providing the college with the ability to harness CAI's promise to strengthen educational programs and improve the retention of students in general and academically disadvantaged students in particular. To achieve this goal, however, faculty development in computing had to become a priority of the institution.

An ongoing program to meet the objective of (re)educating the faculty in computer skills/possibilities was instituted in 1992. Under the auspices of the Federal Title III program, a designated percentage of Porterville College faculty fellows voluntarily participate in the program which espouses the following objectives:

- increase the computer literacy of the faculty at the college;
- improve the instructional delivery system;
- provide alternate learning styles to (re)train students;
- increase reputation for currency and academic breadth;
- increase enrollment;
- utilize campus-wide interfacing computers to assist faculty in using/developing computer-assisted instructional packages;
- faculty review/evaluation of existing instructional software;
- train faculty to develop software to integrate into courses; and
- provide advanced training to a cadre of faculty in software development.

Each faculty member produces a final project that utilizes CAI in an actual classroom setting which is viewed and discussed by fellow faculty members.

As each new group of faculty complete the program, Porterville College's ability to enhance the educational experience of its students is geometrically increased.

Contact:
Linda Prentiss, Associate Dean, Development/Title III
(209) 781-3130, ext. 270

Porterville College
100 East College Avenue
Porterville, CA 93257
Total head count enrollment-Credit: 2,940; Non-Credit: 858
Campuses/sites: 1; Full-time faculty: 54

ADAPTIVE PHYSICAL EDUCATION

Each physically challenged student has an individualized program prescribed that helps remediate specific physical limitations

Physically disadvantaged individuals have been, for the most part, left out of the fitness revolution. To ameliorate this oversight, Porterville College developed a course to address the special needs of the physically challenged student. Since 1988, this course has allowed the physically challenged student to take part in a program designed to maximize his/her physical potential. Adaptive Physical Education is designed to allow physically challenged students to participate in an adapted physical education program.

Once a physician has referred someone to the program, an individual interview is required to assess the needs of the patient and the suitability (physically and mentally) of the prospect. Each student has an individualized program prescribed which will help remediate specific physical limitations. Each student is personally challenged to achieve attainable goals developed within the parameters necessitated by his/her own situation. Thus motivated, the individual is able to aspire to fitness levels which were hitherto unavailable to him/her, with the guidance of our specially trained instructors.

After admittance, the personal trainer develops a program centered around the fitness center. (This gives the student a health club environment for workouts.) Specially designed benches and handrails allow the student access to the workout stations, while modifications to the equipment allows the student to utilize the same equipment physically advantaged students employ. This "mainstreaming" has a positive mental effect on the student and enhances self-esteem.

Cardiovascular, cardiopulmonary, multiple sclerosis, muscular dystrophy and cerebral palsy patients/students as well as paraplegics and quadriplegics find benefits in this special course – benefits that last a lifetime.

Contact:
Ron Glahn or Darryl Williams
(209) 781-3130, ext. 274

Porterville College
100 East College Avenue
Porterville, CA 93257
Total head count enrollment-Credit: 2,940; Non-Credit: 858
Campuses/sites: 1; Full-time faculty: 54

OCCUPATIONAL THERAPY ASSISTANT PROGRAM

There are no prerequisites for admission to the program, which is offered only in the evening to accommodate people working full-time day jobs

The Occupational Therapy Assistant Program at Sacramento City College was created to fill a local professional need while remaining sensitive to the time crunch many modern students are under. Thus, the program is offered only in the evenings to accommodate people working full-time day jobs.

During 1987, shortly after the professional community requested such a program, an advisory committee was formed, a needs survey was developed and distributed, a relationship was established with the appropriate accrediting body and the curriculum was drafted. By Christmas the program and curriculum was approved by the campus curriculum committee. After approval by the Board of Trustees of the Los Rios Community College District, the package was submitted for state approval. State approval to begin offering the program was received in July of 1988; less than two years had elapsed since the initial contact from the community. Two months later the first students registered in the first introductory course. The coordinator of the program and the faculty are all occupational therapy professionals who work part-time in the OTA Program. They bring to the Program a commitment to the profession and a knowledge of the current practices in the field. From the student's perspective the program offers an excellent opportunity to make a job change. There are no prerequisites for admission and the program is offered only in the evening to accommodate people who are working in full-time day jobs.

Graduates from the program are prepared to assist registered occupational therapists in the administration of therapy to patients. This requires that the assistants have skills and knowledge to help patients develop physically, psychologically and socially; these are the professionals who work most closely with patients as they learn to adapt and perform at their maximum level in their occupational pursuit under new personal conditions. The first class was graduated in December 1991. All the graduates took and passed the certification examination in January 1992.

The success of this program is built on the obvious, long-accepted components of initial industry involvement, established community need, and continuing direct professional involvement with an institution dedicated to quality occupational programs.

Contact:
Doreen Chan, Dean, Allied Health
(916) 558-2275

Sacramento City College
3835 Freeport Boulevard
Sacramento, CA 95822
Total head count enrollment-Credit: 16,669; Non-Credit: 20
Campuses/sites: 5; Full-time faculty: 250

EARLY START PROGRAM

After a tour of the college, at-risk middle school students are sent a letter about the program and asked to respond

Sacramento City College, an inner-city college located on a main boulevard that acts as a dividing line between several racial and socioeconomic groups, is a natural place for the very diverse South Sacramento population to come together. This provides an exciting atmosphere for the college but it also places a special responsibility on the staff to be responsive to the many needs in the immediate community, at-risk young people being a particularly important and relevant challenge.

In 1985 the college started a program for at-risk students of junior high age called the Early Start Program, ESP. The purpose of the program is to provide "a continuous orientation, prevention, and support program that begins in the eighth grade with visits to Sacramento City College." The program has six goals: 1) to provide information about the college on-site to eliminate barriers concerning students being on a college campus; 2) to reinforce academic instruction; 3) to increase participants self-esteem and motivation; 4) to promote school retention; 5) to increase minority graduation from high school; and 6) to develop specific student's skills and prepare them for a successful college career.

Under the direction of a full-time coordinator, a variety of activities have become part of the program over the years. However, it is built on a few important building blocks. Throughout the academic year young people are brought on-campus from many of the local middle schools for tours and a general orientation to the college; approximately 2,000 12 to 15 year old's see the campus through the tours each year. With the aid of the middle school faculty and administration, a group of at-risk students are identified from those who toured and sent a special letter describing the ESP and asking them to respond if they are interested. Further informational materials are sent to those who respond with an application for the Summer Early Start Program.

This central activity is designed to engage the young people and begin to reshape their attitudes about themselves and the possibilities for their lives. The Summer Early Start Program happens on the college campus and lasts for the month of July, four days a week, seven and a half hours a day. It is filled with new experiences designed to meet the goals noted earlier and is run by the full-time coordinator with summer help from ESP alumni. This is followed up during the year with a twice monthly, Saturday academy, regular tutoring sessions during the week and

other special events to continue to reinforce the ethic of success started in the summer. Students continue in the program through their sophomore year in high school. Another key element is parent involvement. Parents are continually encouraged to be part of the program as parent advisors and program volunteers. The program is packed with recognition, ceremonies and events to spark commitment and a can-do attitude.

The success of the program is primarily anecdotal. There are many stories of how students began to improve academically, changed their circle of friends, graduated from high school and went on to college. Individual successes are the proof of the program. Graduation rates for those who first came to a Summer ESP are now around 90 percent.

During the 1992 summer, 71 young people took part in the Summer Early Start Program. In five years we hope for 100 percent high school graduation from these 71 students; that's what the staff expects from them. High expectation will reap high performance.

Contact:
Earnestine McKnight, ESP/Articulation Specialist
(916) 558-2191

Sacramento City College
3835 Freeport Boulevard
Sacramento, CA 95822
Total head count enrollment-Credit: 16,669; Non-Credit: 20
Campuses/sites: 5; Full-time faculty: 250

SADDLEBACK COLLEGE

RADIO BROADCASTING, KSBR-FM

KSBR-FM, run by faculty and students, features a respected jazz format and an acclaimed news department

KSBR-FM at Saddleback College is no run-of-the-mill college radio station. It has developed a highly successful contemporary jazz format and has been asked to report its weekly play lists to three major trade magazines.

Operated by faculty and students, the Radio Broadcasting program is an independent, community-service radio station consolidated with the existing radio and television department. Saddleback College stresses: 1) excellence in teaching and learning by allowing the 610 students enrolled in radio and television to use broadcasting facilities as part of the instructional program; 2) a professional-sounding, high-quality radio station with an emphasis on public programs and community service; and 3) minimal cost during a time of limited resources.

Saddleback College offers a comprehensive program in all aspects of radio production and station operations. KSBR, a "Class A" FM station, operates as a broadcast laboratory 24 hours a day, 365 days a year while utilizing student and community volunteer operators. Students are required to complete two introductory radio courses before auditioning for a weekly air shift, which may be repeated up to four semesters. In addition to their air shifts, students are required to elect additional roles in

station operations in conjunction with an advanced radio broadcasting course. These activities include engineering, production, programming, promotion, public affairs and research. Students are encouraged to enroll in the Communication Arts Internship Program, which offers valuable professional broadcast experience in the Los Angeles and Orange County areas. KSBR has been very successful in placing graduates in paid professional positions.

KSBR's music format has gained the respect and support of the music industry. The college FM station reports its weekly play lists to trade magazines *Radio and Records*, *The Gavin Report* and *The MAC Report*. These periodicals establish the industry standard for music air play. While contemporary jazz is generally considered to be a "niche" format, the programming elements used by the students during their air shifts are applicable to a wide range of formats used throughout the commercial radio industry. This has enabled Saddleback College students to attain professional positions at stations using diverse formats such as country, album rock, adult contemporary, news/talk, adult alternative and top-40.

Continues on Page 88

In addition to music, KSBR-FM hosts a highly acclaimed news department, broadcasting news each half hour, mornings and evenings, and hourly throughout the day. The station has received numerous awards from the Associated Press for excellence in news coverage. Under the supervision of a professional news director, the news department is staffed by students who are enrolled in radio, television news, and public affairs classes.

The staff responsible for operating the station consists of three full-time college employees, a station manager, a program director, a news director and 55 students and community volunteers. Through a very successful underwriting program and annual fund-raiser, KSBR generates the funding necessary to maintain a "state-of-the-art" broadcast facility featuring the latest in computer and digital technology. At present, the instructional radio program enrolls approximately 610 students in all classes, generating 5,385 weekly student contact hours (WSCH) annually. This results in approximately 174 FTE's each year, generating approximately $495,900 in apportionment.

Contact:
Mark Schiffelbein, General Manager, Radio/Television
(714) 582-4882

Saddleback College
28000 Marguerite Parkway
Mission Viejo, CA 92692
Total head count enrollment-Credit: 18,549; Non-Credit: 4,325
Campuses/sites: 1; Full-time faculty: 237

LEGAL ASSISTING

The curriculum stresses understanding and reasoning rather than rote learning of facts

Although the field of legal assisting is relatively new, Saddleback College didn't take long to create a quality Legal Assisting Program. Since its inception in 1981 under the supervision of the Business Science Division, many articles have been published praising the program, and attorneys and legal administrators have indicated a growing need for legal assistants. Two reports, the *Employment Projections for 1995* and *California Projection of Employment 1987-2000*, show that legal assisting is one of the top 10 areas of higher employment in Orange County and throughout the United States.

In 1987, Saddleback College made several long-term commitments to the Legal Assisting Program. A full-time instructor, who was a former practicing attorney, was employed to direct, expand, and enrich the program. Additionally, the instructor developed and implemented a law library and established American Bar Association (ABA) approval for the program. Final approval, following reviews of the program and site visitations, was received from the ABA in August 1991.

The law library, which has received thousands of dollars for subscriptions and new purchases, is used by both students in the Legal Assisting Program and the public. Saddleback College has received donations for the law library to assist in the expansion and maintenance of the holdings. There are 400 students enrolled in the program. Two full-time and 10 associate faculty (eight with juris doctorates, one paralegal and one law office administrator) teach the 23 courses that make the curriculum for the program.

The primary concern of the Legal Assisting program has been to develop occupational competence in trained legal assistants to assist attorneys in their daily tasks. This contribution assists in providing a more economical and efficient delivery of legal service in the private and public sectors. The current objectives of the program focus are on ensuring that students are introduced to the law and the legal system, the role and ethics of the paralegal, basic writing skills, methods of legal research, advanced on-line legal research, critical thinking through legal reasoning and the analysis of a lawsuit, and basic computer skills in legal applications. The curriculum stresses understanding and reasoning rather than rote learning of facts. The technical courses emphasize how the subject matter is applied in the practice of law and focuses on principles and procedures common to many types of law-related activities.

In addition to the educational requirements, the Legal Assisting Program meets the previously stated objectives by requiring all students with this major to complete successfully the following courses: Introduction to Legal Assisting, Law Office Management and Ethics, Civil Litigation and Procedures (A and B), Business Law, Legal Drafting and Writing, Introduction to Legal Research, Real Property Law and Procedures, Business Law Procedures, Advanced Legal Research, Law Office Computer Applications, and an Internship. In addition, students choose two from the four elective courses offered in various areas of the law, such as, Family Law and

Procedures, Estate Planning, Probate Procedures, and/or Bankruptcy Law and Procedures which give them increased skills and knowledge needed to assist lawyers in these areas. Completion of the program qualifies graduates to serve various legal needs of the community and contribute to the advancement of the legal profession.

Contact:
Marly Bergerud, Dean, Business Science Division
(714) 582-4500

Saddleback College
28000 Marguerite Parkway
Mission Viejo, CA 92692
Total head count enrollment-Credit: 18,549; Non-Credit: 4,325
Campuses/sites: 1; Full-time faculty: 237

SAN BERNARDINO VALLEY COLLEGE

ATHLETIC ACADEMIC SUPPORT

The program promotes success by integrating the student athlete's academic and athletic goals

Nationally, the educational goals of student athletes are often a secondary concern, while their athletic successes are the top priority. This is not the case at San Bernardino Valley College, where the philosophy is to provide accessible educational programs of quality that enable students to develop their potentialities and achieve their educational and career goals. In the college's view, student athletes are student first and athletes second.

The Athletic Academic Support Program is designed to promote success by integrating students' academic and athletic goals and carefully monitoring progress toward those goals.

Student athletes complete the same initial assessment/advisement sequence as other new students. The Athletic Academic Support Program builds on this initial sequence and monitors student progress through:

1) Athletic advising. In addition to academic advisement, students work with the Athletic Academic Advisor, who specializes in NCAA regulations and guides students in obtaining and maintaining NCAA regulation status.

2) Pre-sport verification. A student athlete cannot participate in a sport unless the Athletic Academic Advisor verifies to the college, the Foothill Conference and the California Commission on Athletics that the student has met, and continues to meet, the established academic requirements;

3) Mid-semester reviews. In addition to the preregistration sessions with the counselor, each student athlete is required to meet twice during the semester with the Athletic Academic Advisor to discuss her/his athletic and academic progress.

4) Grade checks. During student athletes' sports season, their professors complete grade checks to verify if the student athletes are having academic or attendance problems. If a faculty member indicates that a student athlete needs help, the Athletic Academic Advisor assigns the student to a tutor and monitors his/her academic progress with that tutor.

5) Required course. Student athletes are required to complete a one-unit Human Development course with the Athletic Academic Advisor, which includes the state and NCAA regulations for athletes, introduction to various basic skills programs, such as Hooked on Phonics, and techniques for grade improvement. During this course, each student athlete completes an Educational Goal Plan, which outlines the student's semester-by-semester course of study and identifies the support services the student may need to successfully achieve his/her academic goal.

In the first three years of implementation, 770 student athletes participated in the Athletic Academic Support Program. And it works! For example, all 31 sophomore football players met the NCAA qualifications by the end of Fall semester, 1992, with an overall GPA of 2.82. The Women's Volleyball team has a combined GPA of 3.1, and has been nominated for California's Scholar Athletic Team of the Year. Our college's Athletic Academic Support Program has recently been designated a model program of athletic academic advising by the California Commission on Athletics.

This program demonstrates that athletics and academics are compatible! In Fall, 1992, the San Bernardino Valley College football team won the Foothill Conference Championship and the Southern California Bowl, and

Continues on Page 90

was rated third in California and fifth nationally for community college teams. Five SBVC players were named to the All-State football team, and two were named to the Junior College All-American team. Also in the fall of 1992, the college's Men's Cross-country Team won the Foothill Conference Championship and finished sixth in the state.

Contact:
Carl Ferrill, Counselor/Athletic Academic Advisor
(909) 888-6511, ext. 1475

San Bernardino Valley College
701 South Mt. Vernon Avenue
San Bernardino, CA 92410
Total head count enrollment-Credit: 25,025
Campuses/sites: 1; Full-time faculty: 170

HONORS PROGRAM

Student may participate by either taking a single honors course or by entering the full program of seminar-format honors courses

Honors programs no longer may be unusual for community colleges, but the San Bernardino Valley Honors Program differs from the prototypical model in three unique ways.

First, the honors courses in our program are advanced courses rather than honors-designated sections of introductory courses. One concern about establishing an honors program has been the worry that such programs will drain the brightest and best students from the rest of the introductory sections. To alleviate this concern, the honors courses at San Bernardino Valley College are three-unit advanced courses that students may take concurrently with the introductory course or after completing the introductory course. We offer honors courses in 12 disciplines: art, chemistry, economics, geography laboratory, mathematics, political science, philosophy, psychology, sociology, and Spanish.

The second unique feature of our college's Honors Program is that students may participate in one of two ways: 1) they may take a single honors course in an area of interest provided that they earn an A or B in the prerequisite introductory level course, or 2) they may qualify for admission into the full Honors Program if they satisfy specific admission criteria. This flexibility allows a wider range of students to experience the enriched, seminar-format of honors courses and to benefit from the designation of honors courses on their transcripts.

The third unique feature of our college's Honors Program is the requirement that students participate in public service/interest activities in addition to maintaining above-average grades. In order to complete the Honors Program students must complete four public service/interest points, which are earned through a range of activities, such as serving on college committees, participating in a college performance or sport, writing articles for the Honors Program newsletter, or volunteering for off-campus activities (such as political campaigns). This public service/interest criteria fosters students' leadership skills and broadens their exposure to events within the college community as well as the larger community.

The Honors Program has offered three to five classes per semester with 15-30 students per class. The first two students graduated from the Honors Program in June 1992, and 10 students were scheduled to graduate in June 1993. The Honors Program has become an integrated part of the college community, producing a newsletter twice a semester and offering a student-designed seminar to the entire college three times per year.

The Honors Program recently received a positive review from the Director of the Transfer Alliance Program at the University of California at Los Angeles, and consequently, our college's honors students who wish to transfer to UCLA are eligible for first-priority consideration for admission.

Contact:
Susan Spagna, Program Coordinator
(909) 888-6511, ext. 1194

San Bernardino Valley College
701 South Mt. Vernon Avenue
San Bernardino, CA 92410
Total head count enrollment-Credit: 25,025
Campuses/sites: 1; Full-time faculty: 170

PROJECT FLAMINGO

A new information system allows for timely access to data about student success measures, class schedules, facilities use and program goals

In 1990, San Diego City College undertook the development of a Management Decision Support System, which calls for the development of a new information system that will support strategic planning and strengthen the college's management capabilities. It addresses and resolves the problems of not having timely access to essential information about student success measures, class schedule conflicts, facilities utilization and program goals.

Each component of the DSS is designed to improve efficiency, strengthen decision making and improve management outcomes and trends. The components to be developed are:

- a Student Outcome and Follow-up System that can provide retention/attrition and graduation data by academic discipline and also incorporate follow-up data on student transfer and employment outcomes;
- a Facilities Management System that can reduce staff time and conflicts involved in class and event scheduling as well as improve facilities planning and utilization;
- a Program Cost/Revenue System that can give decision makers accurate cost and revenue data by program, thus improving the college's ability to target and allocate resources and identify priorities

on a cost-benefit basis; and

- a Program Evaluation and Planning System that can provide critical information regarding program productivity, census data, employment trends, student profiles and demographic data in order to improve planning and evaluation of institutional effectiveness.

Each component is designed to be completed over the period of approximately one year, with a fifth year devoted to the integration of the four components.

In addition to the development of the components, the DSS calls for the incremental networking of 30 individuals via LAN technology, among them, managers, department chairpersons and clerical staff

The development of the DSS requires the annual resources of a 0.5 FTE project director, a full time technical analyst, a part time technical trainer, 0.5 FTE of clerical assistance and the resulting applicable benefits. In addition, the project also requires hardware, software and peripherals to network six microcomputer stations.

The average annual cost is $140,000 and funding for it is being made possible through a Federal Title III Grant.

Contact:
Candace Richard N. Massa, Dean, School of Mathematics and Sciences
(619) 230-2520

San Diego City College
1313 12th Avenue
San Diego, CA 92101
Total head count enrollment-Credit: 14,000
Campuses/sites: 1; Full-time faculty: 175

WORLD CULTURES PROGRAM

The curriculum increasingly emphasizes non-western as well as western cultures, and links some humanities and English courses

San Diego City College's World Cultures Program grew from a dual emphasis on developing a more global curriculum and creating "learning communities."

The curriculum avoids the exclusively western focus of many humanities courses and includes often-neglected regions in the world. The courses increasingly emphasize non-western as well as western cultures. In addition, some sections of humanities are now linked with English courses so student skills are strengthened and learning is enhanced.

The structure of the classroom also goes beyond the traditional classroom setting. The courses are team taught and their curricula are inter-related. Reading and writing

assignments in the English classes, for example, reinforce and expand on topics studied in the humanities classes. Students are encouraged to work together and attend small group study sessions. English skills are emphasized and writing workshops are available. Students from any major are welcome in the program.

Students may choose from more than 10 humanities courses to satisfy general education requirements for the associate degree (6 units) or for transfer to a four-year college, as well as the multicultural requirement for graduation. The interdisciplinary perspective, according to former students, prepares City College graduates for rigor-

Continues on Page 92

ous upper-division work. The faculty agree that essay writing is an essential skill for both liberal and vocational arts students and meet regularly to discuss ways to strengthen students' writing, reading and critical thinking skills.

In the last three years, the Humanities faculty have introduced several innovations in an attempt to make the curriculum more accessible to a diverse student body.

In a district where many "humanities" classes still focus on uniquely western cultures, the City College approach has been both innovative and popular. Students report that they are intrigued by the exposure to new cultures and that they enjoy the sense of community engendered by the team-taught courses and the study sessions. Similarly, the block-scheduled classes and the team-teaching format have elicited rage reviews from the faculty. Faculty learn from each other in the context of the classroom as well as outside that context. They are often surprised to discover differences in approaches to learning, teaching strategies, expectations for students, and requirements for successful writing and problem solving extant in another discipline. They report feeling a sense of renewal and shared commitment to student success after a semester or two of team teaching in World Cultures.

Goals include:

- integrating the teaching of English and humanities by scheduling English composition and Introduction to the Humanities in a three-hour block twice each week, assigning faculty to teach both courses, and by integrating course curricula so that ideas, selected readings and other materials, assignments and key themes are presented over six hours each week;
- demonstrating how "cultural diversity" might become an intrinsic element of every course just as reading, writing and critical thinking are seen as essential elements on the curriculum; this is done by developing model assignments that illustrate how the curriculum may be expanded and providing a model for integrating material from various disciples;
- strengthening students' skills in reading, writing and critical thinking by providing for small group study by hiring experienced tutors in English and the humanities, linking assignments to the requirements of the humanities course so that students see the application of their skills immediately, and by providing a model for helping students to be successful by challenging them and providing the necessary assistance to enable them to meet expectations.

Contact:
Candace Waltz, Professor, Humanities
(619) 230-2512

San Diego City College
1313 12th Avenue
San Diego, CA 92101
Total head count enrollment-Credit: 14,000
Campuses/sites: 1; Full-time faculty: 175

THE SAN DIEGO CAREER CENTER

For laid-off workers, the Center conducts an assessment of skills, education and special interests before helping with a job search

San Diego's changing economy, influenced by national and international trends, is causing a substantial increase in worker displacements and the need to retrain people for new careers.

Recognizing this change, the San Diego Community College District, the San Diego Consortium and Private Industry Council and the California Employment Development Department entered into a collaboration to establish the San Diego Career Center. The first of its kind in California, the Career Center, opened in the fall of 1991, is a one-stop center for career assessment, job training, retraining and placement for San Diego County residents. It also provides services to laid-off workers and employers facing plant closures and layoffs.

For laid-off workers, the Career Center staff conducts a one-on-one assessment of an individual's skills, educational background and special interests. Job search assistance, including interview techniques and resume development is available. Laid-off workers also benefit from immediate job referral for those workers with marketable skills; retraining for new skills; and other support services, including financial counseling, transportation assistance and child care referral.

For the job seeker, the Career Center has access to the Employment Development Department's computerized Job Match system. Existing job openings are matched to an individual's skills, experience and desired work location. Career Center staff also assist in career assessment, resume preparation and interview skills training.

For the career explorer, the Career Center offers a variety of educational classes for those seeking to improve job skills or needing additional training to move into a new career field. The Career Center also features a "state-of-the-art" computer lab. Classes are conducted in computer/office skills, high school diploma/GED preparation, and literacy/reading.

For the employer facing a layoff, the Career Center can tailor services to help employers prepare for a layoff. Services available include planning sessions with management, union officials or employee representatives, as well as meetings with workers to explain services and developing customized programs to assist workers.

For the employer hiring employees, the Career Center serves as a referral source for reliable, skilled workers. The Career Center serves employers by carefully screening applicants to meet employer specifications; reducing employers' total recruitment, hiring and training costs; and providing services at no cost to the employer.

Contact:
Valerie Edinger, Associate Dean, Continuing Education Center
(619) 627-2545

San Diego Community College District
3375 Camino del Rio South
San Diego, CA 92108-3883
Total head count enrollment-Credit: 84,043; Non-Credit: 92,132
Campuses/sites: 13; Full-time faculty: 547

SAN DIEGO COMMUNITY COLLEGE DISTRICT

WORK PLACE LEARNING RESOURCE CENTER

✳ *Participation with the business community fosters a dynamic environment* ✳
to guide educational programs for the community

The Work Place Learning Resource Center (WPLRC) of the San Diego Community College District allows education to work closely with the business community to monitor and respond to workplace changes on a long-term basis. The goal of the Center is to meet the work force training needs of business and industry through contract education. Some of the objectives of the Center include: 1) providing direct services to assist companies, unions and government agencies in defining work force preparation needs; 2) offering instruction tailored to the needs of the work force as determined by an on-site assessment of needs; 3) serving as a demonstration site for model programs, curricula and services related to workplace learning; and 4) providing technical assistance and staff development to SDCCD and other community colleges in this region.

The WPLRC, funded by the California Community Colleges Chancellor's Economic Development Network, represents a significantly different form of partnership between education and business. This new relationship will allow education to work closely with the community of businesses to monitor and respond to the changes in the workplace on an ongoing basis. This new connection with the business community will help SDCCD Continuing Education see and keep track of the accelerating changes in the workplace from more of an "insider's position," because the nature of the contract will be to address the educational needs of the work force. Our participation in contract education and specifically through the WPLRC will provide the means for aligning our curriculum in more

"traditional" programs we offer. Our participation with the business community will provide us with a dynamic environment to guide the development and maintenance of both existing and new educational programs for our community.

The participation of education in the arena of the workplace will help to provide SDCCD instructors with added insight into how they can better serve our students. Instructor participation in workplace instruction will be a dynamic way for the SDCCD to respond to the rapid changes in the workplace. These same instructors will be instrumental in revising district curriculum in order to better align our instruction to changing community needs.

Recently, the Workplace Learning Resource Center has provided a Vocational English as a Second Language (VESL) program to the line workers of an electronics company. The company was implementing a Total Quality Management (TQM) program and wanted the VESL instruction to help include workers in addressing the issues of quality. Workshops have been provided to companies on: "Balancing Work and Home Responsibilities," "Conflict Resolution and Effective Communications," "Money Management," and "Cross-Cultural Awareness Training for Supervisors."

The focus of the WPLRC recently has been toward the small business. How can we establish closer relationships with small business? How do we assess their changes? What new models for delivering educational services are needed for the small business sector?

Contact:
Alma McGee, Continuing Education ABE/ESL Office
(619) 265-3458

San Diego Community College District
3375 Camino del Rio South
San Diego, CA 92108-3883
Total head count enrollment-Credit: 84,043; Non-Credit: 92,132
Campuses/sites: 13; Full-time faculty: 547

AVANZA PROJECT

The project aims to help Latino immigrants break their dependence on social services

Breaking the cycle of poverty for both parents and their children is the focus of the San Diego Community College District Avanza Project. The district's Harbor View Continuing Education Center reflects national and statewide patterns concerning the education of Latino immigrants are reflected locally at the San Diego Community College District's (SDCCD).

Among the post-amnesty participants enrolled in job training and continuing educational programs, women, particularly single parents, show low participation rates and extremely high attrition. The reasons most often mentioned are related to the lack of life management skills. Generally speaking, the lack of these skills tends to lock Latino immigrants into a pattern of poverty. With limited access to job training, transportation, child care facilities, or any educational facility, single female parents and pregnant women face an unending cycle of long-term dependency on social services. The project addresses the need to involve these new Californians (post-amnesty immigrants) in education and prepare them for skilled vocational training or college enrollment.

Within the scope of this project, three general areas of need are being addressed:

1) Improving Communications. A locally designed Spanish language outreach recruitment and community resource linkage effort targeted to the needs of this new Californian has been implemented. A bilingual Resource Directory identifying community- based social services agencies and local training programs has been developed, produced and distributed to program participants. The directory has been made available to more than 400 educational and community services providers.

2) Appropriate Bilingual Materials. A replicable, bilingual job skills training program model, including instructional materials and job readiness instrument materials has been locally developed. These culturally sensitive materials are geared to helping the new Californians improve their life management skills and education. The bilingual materials are designed to meet JTPA (Department of Labor) guidelines for employability training and include information on how to change jobs and how to work effectively with others. Issues of decision-making and problem-solving have been addressed as well.

3) Individualized Instruction. A guided, pre-job or school entry readiness program which helps this population improve their life management and job skills while they explore vocational and educational options has been developed. The program addresses the major barriers to learning by providing child care facilities, transportation, individual counseling, job development, job placement and other special support services.

During the fall of 1992, all 50 participants completed the program and are now enrolled in further job training in credit or non-credit programs. An additional 50 students were expected to complete the program in August 1993. Avanza has had a 100 percent completion rate this year with a population that traditionally has experienced high attrition in educational programs. Avanza Project information has been sent to 107 California community colleges and to local and regional agencies that serve the new Californians.

Contact:
Cruz Rangel and Elizabeth Urtecho, Harbor View
(619) 230-2895

San Diego Community College District
3375 Camino del Rio South
San Diego, CA 92108-3883
Total head count enrollment-Credit: 84,043; Non-Credit: 92,132
Campuses/sites: 13; Full-time faculty: 547

MESA ACADEMY

Dedicated to the academic and personal success of African-American students, the program includes mentoring and transfer planning

San Diego Mesa College is committed to reversing the trend of lower enrollment of African-American students.

The college's Mesa Academy is a seven-component program dedicated to the academic and personal success of African-American students. Through the program students are able to gain a better knowledge of the academic system, personal knowledge, and skills to be more successful in class and in achieving their goals. They also are able to feel better plugged in and more connected to the educational process. The Mesa academy provides:

1) college orientation through high school outreach, registration assistance, placement testing and preliminary educational planning, and identification of campus and community resources;

2) mentorship from African-American faculty, community members, business and industries leaders, and speakers from the campus and community;

3) peer support through training in group study techniques and learning to assist one another;

4) Student Success Seminar, a three-credit course in study skills, time management, test-taking skills, life skills and developing a healthy self-concept through implementing the Nguzo Saba – The Seven Principles (unity, self-determination, collective work and responsibility, cooperative economics, purpose, creativity, and faith in self);

5) cultural awareness through participation in and attendance at Afro-centric cultural and social events, discussion of contemporary African-American issues, and involvement in cross-cultural experiences;

6) career and educational guidance by development of a long-range educational plan, occupational interest inventories, individual counseling and access to faculty and industry representatives; and

7) transfer planning through workshops on admissions, financial aid, and campus resources made by four-year representatives as well as visitation to four-year institutions.

Mesa Academy provides a valuable service to African-American students and to the campus as well. The college is enhanced by involvement in activities that are responsive to student needs. Knowledge is gained about the unique cultural learning style of the African-American student that can be instrumental in exposing the faculty to the need for developing a variety of teaching styles. The program is administered by three African-American Counseling faculty who have been very willing to share the knowledge they have gained for the benefit of campus curriculum transformation. They are developing a Summer Bridge component and a math and English component.

Contact:
Barbara Armstrong, Dennard Clendenin or Judy Sundayo
(619) 627-2535

San Diego Mesa College
7250 Mesa College Drive
San Diego, CA 92111
Total head count enrollment-Credit: 26,983
Campuses/sites: 1; Full-time faculty: 259

MESA HUMANITIES INSTITUTE

Several guest speakers, including Rosa Parks, have interacted with students and faculty to enrich classroom experiences

The administration and faculty at San Diego Mesa College have, in the past, wanted to enrich campus life by bringing guest speakers, holding faculty workshops and adding diversity to the curriculum. But there was little time, support staff or money to do these activities and good ideas were not acted upon or people were overwhelmed with the extra work involved.

That is, until 1990, when the Board of Trustees established the Mesa College Humanities Institute. The objectives of the Institute were: 1) enhancement of experiences/communication in the arts and humanities among faculty, students, professional artists and the community; 2) implementation of an organizational vehicle for support of programs, projects, activities and events; and 3) sponsorship of staff development programs. In 1991, the responsibility for curriculum transformation (diversity in all curriculum) was added to the list of objectives.

In its first two years, the Humanities Institute accomplished much and made an impact on the community and campus. There have been more than 120 guest speakers or performers; these individuals have interacted with students and faculty to enrich classroom experiences. Workshops for faculty from elementary through college have been held on Chinese and African Art and Literature, the Native American Experience, and Islam. The first Spanish language production on the campus was the San Diego premier of "Our Lady of the Tortilla." The Borderlands Issues Conference was a major bi-national conference with more than 30 speakers/planners. Mesa's outreach to high schools included two student congresses and two high school speech tournaments held on campus. One of the most successful events was the 79th birthday celebration for civil rights leader Rosa Parks. Over two days, four events were held: 1) a press conference where Mrs. Parks spoke and took questions from local press and television reporters as well as high school and college student reporters; 2) a fund-raiser birthday party where Mrs. Parks was honored by 1,700 people from the community for her contribution to civil rights; 3) a gathering of 1,800 elementary and junior high school students who wished Mrs. Parks a happy birthday and to learn how one person can make a difference; and 4) a luncheon for 100 civil rights workers, where Mrs. Parks was presented with a $10,000 check for the Rosa and Raymond Parks Institute for Self Development from monies raised at the benefit birthday

Continues on Page 96

party.

Work on curriculum transformation has included an assessment of materials in the Mesa College library and development of resource lists. Model projects were developed in 11 departments, each one based on goals set by the department. A major project is the Coalition Against Institutional Racism, which has sponsored a one-day workshop called "Between Utopia and Armageddon: A Day of Planning for the Future."

The Institute has one faculty coordinator at full reassigned time, two half-time clerks, and four faculty members each semester with 20 percent reassigned time to work on special projects. The coordinator oversees all programs, budget, fund raising and works with the departments to plan curriculum transformation activities. One clerk handles all publicity and media coverage and the other deals with workshops and activities held for elementary through college faculty.

More than $22,000, after expenses, has been raised. This money has been used to support activities, help other programs on campus and make donations to off-campus programs that foster the humanities and improved communication.

In addition to receiving strong board approval and support and very good media coverage, the community and campus have embraced the activities. As a result, Mesa's reputation and visibility have improved. Faculty who have needs or ideas are encouraged to contact institute personnel who plan, make arrangements and cover expenses for project implementation. Ideas become reality, needs are met, the faculty feel supported and all are enriched.

Contact:
Pat Olafson, Coordinator
(619) 627-2783

San Diego Mesa College
7250 Mesa College Drive
San Diego, CA 92111
Total head count enrollment-Credit: 26,983
Campuses/sites: 1; Full-time faculty: 259

THE PLACE

The PLACe is a learning center that empowers students to learn how to learn, not just stop by for specific class assignments

The PLACe, whose acronym stands for Personal Learning Assistance Center, offers a wide variety of free services to any student enrolled at Miramar College: tutoring, diagnosis, tutorials, and small group study and review sessions.

Students may use The PLACe to get help with a class assignment, on the recommendation of a faculty member or because they choose to use it on their own. No funds are necessary. Faculty may either direct a student to The PLACe during the center's open hours or may write a note to the coordinator or the tutor if a particular need has been identified or if the instructor has ideas about what would be most useful for the student.

•Tutorials: all students (even those doing well) may request one-to-one skills and/or content tutoring to support their learning. Skills tutoring includes formal and informal diagnosis of needs in math, reading, writing, or study skills, and a review of the skills required to learn the material effectively and efficiently. Content tutoring focuses on the specific content of a course and will be presented only by tutors who have been certified by Miramar College academic departments as qualified experts in a subject area. Students may schedule an appointment for tutoring or drop in for assistance and be seen by the first available tutor. The PLACe is equipped with computers, on audio cassette system,

video player, and self-paced tutorial books and materials. Learning assistance tools may be used independently or with the guidance of the Place tutors to build skills and course-specific knowledge.

•Diagnosis: All tutors are trained to use inquiry, standardized tests and computerized assessment tools to diagnose common learning problems in reading. writing, math and study skills. Faculty specialists provide more in-depth diagnosis of skill knowledge, levels, strengths and weaknesses.

•Small Group Study and Review Sessions: Students who wish to study together in a course may request a scheduled tutorial where tutors will provide a learning and review session that may include suggestions for studying, guided problem solving practice, test preparation and review of the course material.

During its first eight weeks, The PLACe boasted more than 2,300 peer tutoring hours to 675 students. Its success began with the vision of a learning center that would empower students to learn how to learn rather than provide tutors for specific classroom assignments.

Developmental stages included surveys completed by 63 members of college faculty, staff and administration from 25 disciplines. Faculty predicted the need for services in reading, reasoning and writing for more than 50 percent of their students. A working committee representing a variety of instructional areas developed a $70,000 staffing plan for the first year of set-up and operation, which included: design of The PLACe logo and signage; purchases for software, hardware, books, cassettes, videos and audio-visual equipment; a facility renovation project; and the tutoring hiring and training process.

Current staffing includes: a coordinator for ESL, reading and study skills, and math specialists – a combined 1.6 FTE; one instructional lab technician (38 hours per week), one clerk (15 hours per week), and 37 tutors (averaging 15 hours per week). It is hoped that hours of operation and staffing will increase in coming years.

Contact:
Robert Carlson, Executive Dean of Instruction
(619) 536-7350

San Diego Miramar College
10440 Black Mountain Road
San Diego, CA 92126
Total head count enrollment-Credit: 8,500
Campuses/sites: 1; Full-time faculty: 62

SAN JOAQUIN DELTA COLLEGE

ELECTRON MICROSCOPY (EM)

Much of the instruction is done on an individualized or small-group basis by the instructors, a laboratory aide or peer student groups

San Joaquin Delta College is the only community college in the United States offering electron microscopy training in both biological and crystalline materials as a professional/vocational two-year program.

The program is designed to prepare students for employment as EM technologists. Students become qualified to operate and maintain electron microscopes that are used in research, academic and industrial fields. They learn to prepare physical and biological/medical samples for observation on both the transmission electron microscope (TEM) and the scanning electron microscope (SEM), to take and develop the micrographs, to operate ancillary equipment, and to interpret results from energy dispersive wavelength and spectrometers.

Enrollment in the program, which has been part of the Science and Mathematics Division since 1989, consists of both men and women, and ranges from those who have just graduated from high school to those already possessing advanced or professional degrees. Some have a Baccalaureate Degree and have returned to acquire specific EM skills that will assist them in their research or industrial careers.

The curriculum requires a solid foundation in science, mathematics, computer science, and physics. All certificate courses require a grade of "C" or better and technical report writing is strongly emphasized. Classes have regularly scheduled lecture and lab hours assigned. Much of the instructional work on the TEM and SEM must be done outside of the scheduled class time. Students, therefore, sign up for time on the microscopes, which are in continuous daily operation. Much of the instruction is done on an individualized or small-group basis by the instructors, a laboratory aide, or peer student groups. The students have a high degree of commitment and motiva-tion. Their withdrawal rate has been lower and their success rate has been higher than the college averages.

Students have a well-equipped laboratory with a wide range of scientific, technical equipment and specialized preparation equipment. There are four transmission electron microscopes, specialized cutting devices and two scanning electron microscopes. The two scanning microscopes have attached to them energy dispersive spectrometers and a wave length spectrometer for identification of elements and compounds in the samples. There are three specimen preparation rooms, one ultramicrotome room, a physical testing laboratory and two photographic dark rooms. Specimens for use in the program come from industrial, medical, and biological research sources.

Graduates are employed in major universities (Stanford, UC Davis, UC Berkeley, University of Colorado, Texas, Baylor, Cal Tech, Harvard, etc.), where they participate as laboratory supervisors or research assistants, as well as in some of the world's foremost research laboratories (Lawrence Livermore National Lab, Bell Labs, Sandia National Laboratory, Solar Research Institute, General Electric, Hewlett Packard, JEOL-USA, etc.).

In addition to strong financial support from the College, the EM faculty and its EM Council actively solicit donations from the private sector. More than $300,000 of equipment has been donated by industrial firms. In addition, other manufacturers of EM equipment have sold the college equipment at a substantial discount.

Throughout the program's 22 years, the college, EM faculty and its EM Council have constantly worked together to monitor the program's progress, to recommend new courses and course revisions, to identify equipment

Continues on Page 98

needs, etc. The EM faculty continue to benefit from feedback from graduates regarding their activities, needs, and achievements. Employer surveys have given excellent endorsement of this program and some have made valuable recommendations for additional modifications to meet the changing needs of industry and research groups.

In 1987, the EM Program received the Governor's Citation for Excellence in Vocational Education. The EM Program has gained both a national and international reputation for the quality of instruction and the capabilities of its students. SJDC has been visited by electron microscopists from West Germany, South Africa, Australia and China as well as numerous educators, research experts and industrial representatives from across the United States.

Contact:
Judy Murphy (209) 474-5284/5249
Frank Villalovoz (209) 474-5249

San Joaquin Delta College
5151 Pacific Avenue
Stockton, CA 95207-6370
Total head count enrollment-Credit: 16,521; Non-Credit: 1,965
Campuses/sites: 1; Full-time faculty: 230

SUCCESS WITHIN REACH

⊠ Program goals for retaining minority students include providing mentors, varying instructional methods ⊠
and increasing students' self-esteem, aspirations and retention

Success Within Reach (SWR) is aimed at reducing the high drop-out rates among minorities.

The goals of the program are to: 1) provide mentors as role models for students; 2) use instructional methods that reflect the learning styles of different minority groups; 3) increase students' self-esteem; 4) increase students' career knowledge and aspirations; 5) improve students' skills in written and oral language; and 6) increase retention within the term and persistence from term to term.

Nineteen African-American, 31 Asian, and 37 Hispanic students were enrolled in the SWR program. They were compared to a group of similar students not enrolled in the program. The students in both groups were not eligible for transfer English courses, and were enrolled in English 79, which is one level below transferability. The SWR students were enrolled in a guidance course for the first semester.

Courses were not team-taught, but instructors sat in on each other's classes. The counselor was present in all classes. The guidance counselor always was a member of the same ethnic group as the students.

At the end of the first semester, SWR students had attempted 15.8 units and completed 10.9 units, with a GPA of 2.6. During the same period, the comparison student attempted 13.6 units and completed 9.8 students, with a GPA of 2.2. Seventy-three percent of the SWR students enrolled at the college the following semester, compared to 66 percent of the students not in SWR.

On the question of course success, 67 percent of the SWR students received an A, B or C in English 79, compared to 58 percent of the comparison students. Seventy-six percent of the returning SWR students completed English 1A, and 91 percent of the 46 students who enrolled in Speech 1A were successful. Among the comparison students, 12 of the 17 (70 percent) who attempted English 1A were successful, and two of the four who enrolled in Speech 1A completed it.

While many of the initial results are encouraging, the program is continuing to modify its methods and approaches.

The project initially was funded with a $25,000 grant from the State Chancellor's Office. It is not funded by the college.

Contact:
Elliott R. Chambers, EOPS Director
(209) 474-5682

San Joaquin Delta College
5151 Pacific Avenue
Stockton, CA 95207-6370
Total head count enrollment-Credit: 16,521; Non-Credit: 1,965
Campuses/sites: 1; Full-time faculty: 230

COOPERATIVE AGENCIES RESOURCES FOR EDUCATION

⚙ CARE students are single parents who depend on welfare ⚙
but want to become self-sufficient

Social service agencies across the nation for years have been seeking a viable program to assist welfare-dependent single heads of household break the cycle of poverty. Single parents comprise a significant segment of the community college population in California. At Santa Barbara City College and other California community colleges, the CARE (Cooperative Agencies Resources for Education) Program gives students one main contact person who facilitates all aspects of enrollment, from providing special counseling to coordinating child care.

Individuals served by the Cooperative Agencies Resources for Education (CARE) Program are not only single parents, but also are low-income, educationally disadvantaged, and dependent upon welfare assistance. In 1982, Santa Barbara City College identified a genuine, long-term need to provide support for single parents in our community, and began with a state-funded special project, serving 33 families. Today, of 107 California Community Colleges, 44 provide a CARE program, providing support services designed to ensure academic and personal success.

At SBCC, a part of the state CARE network since 1984-85, the CARE Program provides access for and equity to welfare recipients who with proper support, could break the welfare dependency cycle through education and job training. The CARE Program is a supplemental program of the Extended Opportunity Programs and Services (EOPS), providing additional dollars for student grants and allowances for child care, transportation, textbooks and supplies. This supplement is designed to strengthen the retention and persistence of students who are welfare-dependent single parents with preschool-aged children.

Besides counseling and child care, support services provided to CARE students include: books/supplies and transportation costs; personal development activities and/or curriculum (including self-esteem, parenting, study skills); group support courses and peer networking; and help from peer advisors who are often single parents themselves.

Emphasis is placed on a holistic approach to each student. CARE students have one main contact person who facilitates all aspects of enrollment, including financial aid, registration, scheduling and counseling, as well as coordinating child-care services and addressing the specific individual concerns of this special population. Group orientations provide an arena to meet peers and reduce the anxieties inherent in the reentry experience. Peer advising is a key component, and provides each student with a trained and knowledgeable fellow single-parent student contact to increase retention and encourage the use of campus and community resources.

The impact of CARE on these families is tangible and immediate. The increase in self-esteem and confidence coming from accomplishing course work across the curriculum and an awareness of one's intelligence and abilities not formerly recognized, added to the security of a quality child care environment, provide a means for the entire family unit to develop and blossom. Personal growth is monumental, as this unique group of students realizes they have the power and the means to control their lives. Single-parent students are highly motivated, seeing this opportunity for a post secondary education as their only chance to escape the cycle of welfare dependency. Though the unique demands on their time and skills sometimes interferes with or interrupts successful completion of course work, our overall success rate is exceptional.

In the 1991-92 academic year, 201 single parent students were served by CARE – 23 received AA/AS degrees and/or Certificates of completion, 13 were accepted for transfer, 61 scholarships were awarded, and 13 students earned a place on the President's Honor Roll with a GPA of 3.5 or better. A combination of state funding totaling $112,328 was augmented by exceptional financial support from the community in the form of a $25,000 endowment, a $50,000 child-care grant and personal contributions from community supporters of $8,000.

The Board of Governors of the California Community Colleges named the Santa Barbara City College CARE Program one of the two top Exemplary Programs statewide, with an award of $4,000 from state lottery funds. CARE at SBCC owes its success to the demonstrated coordination of effort between student services and the instructional component, which assures the highest level of communication and cooperation to benefit students.

Contact:
Patricia Canning
(805) 965-0581, ext. 2384

Santa Barbara City College
721 Cliff Drive
Santa Barbara, CA 93109
Total head count enrollment-Credit: 12,264; Non-Credit: 37,631
Campuses/sites: 3; Full-time faculty: 216

TRANSFER ACHIEVEMENT

The program is designed to boost the number of under-represented ethnic minority students who transfer to four-year institutions

The Transfer Achievement Program(TAP), a component of the Transfer Center, addresses the need to increase the number and percentage of under-represented ethnic minority students who transfer from Santa Barbara City College to four-year institutions.

In contrast to "smorgasbord" efforts common to community colleges, this project introduced a comprehensive and systematic approach for increasing minority student transfer rates. Key elements included: aggressive outreach; a program that students join; providing structure and involvement through a developmental "map" of specific transfer-related tasks, the Transfer Task inventory; offering academic support in math and English; providing regular feedback and personal support; and proactive transfer transition intervention.

The project's guiding objectives were to increase to a level at parity with the general student body, the number and percentage of SBCC's minority students:

- who commit to transfer as an educational goal;
- who are involved in a greater number of transfer-related activities as outlined in the Transfer Task Inventory;
- who succeed in and persist in math and English courses; and
- who apply for, are accepted by and enroll at four-year institutions.

The following parts of the project have been institutionalized by Santa Barbara City College since the program's inception in 1988: one half-time Program Coordinator; one half-time Special Program Advisor; one half-time College Work Study Peer Advisor; one hourly Math Group Instructor/Coordinator; three hourly Math Group Student Facilitators; and transportation, mailing and duplicating costs.

The Transfer Achievement Program has received national recognition by the American Association of Junior and Colleges and state-wide recognition by the California Community College Chancellor's Office as an exemplary minority student success program. The program is currently funded by the Funds for the Improvement of Post Secondary Education (FIPSE) through the U.S.. Department of Education. This $270,00 award, which began in the 1991-92 academic year, will continue through 1994, at which time institutionalization will take place.

There are more than 1,000 students who have received transfer-related services from TAP. The number of transfer applicants has increased 100 percent since the program began in 1988. A comparison of TAP members with non-TAP members revealed that TAP members on average complete 39 units, whereas under-represented students completed 22, and that the average GPA among TAP members in Spring 1992 was 2.4, exceeding the 2.0 GPA of under-represented students.

Contact:
Victoria Noseworthy
(805) 965-0581, ext. 2544

Santa Barbara City College
721 Cliff Drive
Santa Barbara, CA 93109
Total head count enrollment-Credit: 12,264; Non-Credit: 37,631
Campuses/sites: 3; Full-time faculty: 216

WORK OF LITERARY MERIT

All sections of freshman composition study a single literary work, sparking lively campus-wide discourse among faculty and students

In 1981, the English Department of Santa Rosa Junior College initiated its Work of Literary Merit (WOLM) Program, which incorporates the teaching of a single literary work – usually a major novel – into all sections of freshman composition.

The purpose of the program is to encourage students to read literature while helping them to improve their critical thinking, writing and research abilities. The WOLM also provides a bridge between the first semester of freshman composition and the second, which focuses on the study of writing and literature.

For each WOLM the department arranges four or five public lectures delivered by members of the department, by faculty in other departments or by professors from local colleges. These noon lectures, well attended by the composition students and others, provide students and faculty with a lively, stimulating forum. Each lecture is videotaped for use in classrooms or for viewing by students in the library. Some sets of WOLM lectures have been compiled into a booklet that serves as a resource and provides models of writing and research.

In addition to the energy generated by the faculty lectures, there is quite a bit of spontaneous discussion on campus, among students as well as faculty. With more than 40 class sections reading the same book, anything can happen. Faculty inevitably share ideas for writing assignments and teaching approaches, and occasionally indulge in written debates via the department newsletter, or oral ones at each other's homes. The library staff pitch in by helping to assemble a body of research materials for each WOLM (a binder listing these and containing photocopied articles is made available). The librarians also offer specialized bibliographic instruction tailored to the WOLM selection.

Indeed, one of the best things about the WOLM is that it serves as a unifying influence on campus. It is not just an "instructional" program it is a cultural celebration of something that has value for everyone. It reminds us that literature can and should be a part of everyone's intellectual life and that it offers avenues into such related disciplines as history, art and religion. (An SRJC philosophy instructor, for example, spoke on Hinduism in connection with Forster's *A Passage to India*)

Each WOLM project is different, the differences depending not only on the book selected but also on the faculty who get involved in the planning. Some WOLM's have produced tee-shirts, and some have resulted in marathon oral readings (Huck Finn had both). When Shakespeare's *The Tempest* was the WOLM, the college's Theater Arts Department obliged by putting on a production of the play – students had the benefit of writing reviews of the local productions as well as comparing it with those available on video. When *Steppenwolf* and *Frankenstein* were WOLM's, there was a series of film showings in the library.

The WOLM program has sparked interest and imitation at community colleges in California, and has been written up in *inside english*, the journal of the English Council of California Two-Year Colleges (ECCTYC; March 1986 and May 1988).

Contact:
Ron Taylor, English Chair
(707) 527-4351

Santa Rosa Junior College
1501 Mendocino Avenue
Santa Rosa, CA 95401
Total head count enrollment-Credit: 25,426; Non-Credit: 7,850
Campuses/sites: 4; Full-time faculty: 280

SANTA ROSA JUNIOR COLLEGE

COLLEGE SUCCESS

The program for at-risk students emphasizes reading and writing as well as personal confidence and study skills

The College Success Program at Santa Rosa Junior College focuses on primary academic skills, is multiculturally integrated, interdisciplinary and challenges students to learn from one another. Its integrated curriculum of English, guidance, behavioral science and mathematics courses, designed to serve the special needs of the "high risk" student.

Developed by members of the Counseling and English Department staffs in 1974, it initially targeted reentry high school drop-outs, veterans and drug-rehabilitation students. Today it retains as its goal the matriculation of students who most likely would drop out of college.

The program spans the academic year, is skill-based and features a drive to accelerate student growth in cultural literacy.

The College Success curriculum includes developmental classes in reading, composition, guidance, psychology and math. Of these, the English and guidance courses form the core and must be taken concurrently. The emphasis is on development of primary academic skills – reading and writing – as well as personal confidence and study skills.

Integration takes the form of a dual focus on themes and on skills:

1) as far as practicable, the courses are organized around common themes that are relevant to the lives and needs of the students: autonomy, family, functionality/dysfunctionality, the individual in a diverse society, communication/alienation;

2) skills instruction is also, where feasible, integrated; guidance for example, includes instruction in library skills, while English includes reading and essay assignments that take advantage of those skills; when the students go on a field trip to visit a University of California campus or to see a musical in San Francisco, their English and their guidance instructors go along.

The College Success student is also provided with academic support. There are scheduled study hours when tutorial assistance is provided, and students meet with their instructors in private conferences. There are guest lecturers who not only provide additional stimulation, but also can serve as role models for students from disadvantaged backgrounds. Every effort is made to bring students into the life of the college, and to encourage them to utilize support services and staff.

Continues on Page 102

A chief distinguishing characteristic of the College Success Program is the coordination among the faculty who teach the courses. Because College Success courses are scheduled as a block, the instructors are able to meet on a regular basis (weekly or biweekly, in recent years) to discuss the students' progress and current needs. Once problems are identified, they are dealt with immediately. This adds to the retention of the students in the program.

College Success instructors also demand a high level of accountability from students, along with respect for the instructor, other students and themselves. They know that unless students complete work, participate in class activity, and feel successful as students, those students will probably not gain the confidence needed to continue succeeding once out of the program.

Students are considered successful if they do one or more of the following:
- maintain a GPA of 2.0 in academic mainstream classes;
- make progress toward or complete an AA degree or certificate program;
- transfer to a four-year institution; and/or
- continue in the College Success Program.

Since 1978 College Success has achieved a 61 percent success rate using these criteria. In more recent years (1989-91), the rate has climbed to 70 percent.

The college was particularly proud that the College Success Program was awarded the Exemplary Program Award in the spring of 1991, followed by a PBS broadcast in the fall of 1991.

Contact:
Evelyn Pollard, Dean, Counseling and Guidance Services
(707) 527-4689

Santa Rosa Junior College
1501 Mendocino Avenue
Santa Rosa, CA 95401
Total head count enrollment-Credit: 25,426; Non-Credit: 7,850
Campuses/sites: 4; Full-time faculty: 280

FIELD EXPERIENCE PROGRAM

*▦ Students are exposed to diverse environmental management techniques ▦
and the many implications of protection/preservation*

Biological, geological and earth sciences are included in the study of natural sciences or the study of nature – but nature exists outside of the classroom.

Lectures are essential to provide the natural science student with the tools with which to construct an understanding. Laboratories are effective but incomplete.

Sierra Community College believes the field experience is essential to complete the learning process by observing, classifying, measuring and analyzing nature using the methodologies acquired in lecture and laboratory. Maintaining this extensive program requires the purchase and maintenance of numerous transport vans, buses and field equipment.

Field experience components augmenting the traditional lecture/laboratory curriculum at Sierra Community College have been a tradition in the biological and physical sciences since the inception of the Rocklin campus. Maintaining this exceptional field program has been and continues to be a college goal as the curriculum strives to send experienced and competent biologists, geologists and students of related disciplines into field-oriented careers or to upper-division work in the sciences. The most active field programs at Sierra Community College are found in the departments of biological, geological and earth sciences.

In addition to brief field experiences within the normal lecture/lab course offerings, the Biological Sciences, Earth Science and Geology departments offer specialized field curricula.

The Biological Sciences department offers a comprehensive curriculum for biology majors and non-major students working toward an Associate Degree or toward upper-division transfer. Additionally, the department offers 25 separate field courses that provide the Sierra student opportunities to examine and study local, regional and distant natural areas in detail. These field courses take students into myriad ecosystems in California and the western states. Study sites include numerous desert ecosystems, diverse locations of the Sierra Nevada, coastal forests and coastal marine environments. Field courses have been designed to provide understanding of virtually all of California's most important bio-regions. Students conduct collegiate biological exercises, sharpening their skills in taxonomy, systematic, sampling, measurement, data collection, ecosystems analysis, biogeography and other related sub-disciplines.

The Earth Science department, in addition to general courses in earth science and oceanography, allows students to choose from four field courses that explore earthquake, volcanic, glacial and tectonic phenomena. Study sites include the city of San Francisco and surrounding bay area, Yosemite National Park, Mt. Lassen National Park and Pt. Reyes National Seashore.

The Geology department offer courses in physical, historical, California and environmental geology. Each course may be augmented with a laboratory component.

Additionally, students may enroll in a field program that includes eight separate regional courses in field geology. Unique and diverse geological sites in California and western North America are examined closely by teams of Sierra students. Identification, mapping, collecting and analysis help prepare students for the rigorous aspects of field geology. Through this field program and via the Sierra Community College Science Club, students participate in collegiate and professionally directed paleontological digs. Numerous sites in the west have been excavated, studied and cataloged. Specimens have been acquired and placed in the Sierra Community College Museum and numerous regional museums neighboring each dig. Sierra Community College digs have ranged from South Dakota to Nevada, Wyoming and California.

Cooperative activities (joint biology-geology) occur as much of the paleontological efforts are naturally cross-disciplinary. Sierra Community College students have worked together in teams on many of these digs to study the paleobiology of the western states.

Interdisciplinary field experiences annually occur between the departments of biology, earth science and geology. In addition to scores of important scientific sites in California ranging from high mountain sites to foothill, valley, desert and coastal sites, Sierra students travel to Alaska, the western provinces of Canada, throughout the Pacific Northwest (Washington, Oregon and Northwestern California), and as far south as Baja California, Mexico.

In addition to real-life studies in identification and classification of biological and physical phenomena, students hone their skills in observation, measurement, data collection and analysis of these field sites. Field skills are developed in numerous scientific sub-disciplines. Spin-off benefits of field courses include development of observational skills, photographic skills, electronic audio/video media experience and reporting/writing skills.

As students frequently take more than one field course in more than one department, important linkages between scientific disciplines occur. Students are provided the opportunity to synthesize broader interpretations of scientific phenomena as they relate them to other fields of biological or physical study.

Students are exposed to processes of local, regional, state and federal management techniques of parks, reserves, forests and other biogeographic regions. Students are also exposed to the realities of social, economic and political implications of protection/preservation efforts in western North America. Students also develop teamwork and leadership skills and are exposed to various potential careers in the biological and physical sciences.

Contact:
Joe Medeiros, Biological Science Department
(916) 624-3333, ext. 2225

Sierra Community College
5000 Rocklin Road
Rocklin, CA 95677
Total head count enrollment-Credit: 13,813; Non-Credit: 54
Campuses/sites: 3; Full-time faculty: 154

SIERRA COMMUNITY COLLEGE

GET AWAY SPECIAL

The college prepared a self-contained payload of three experiments to fly aboard the Space Shuttle

In 1989, Sierra Community College faculty began its involvement with NASA's Get Away Special (GAS) program. The GAS program allows individuals to build and fly a self-contained automated payload aboard the Space Shuttle. Educational institutions can fly a 5.0 cubit foot payload for $10,000.

Sierra Community College's GAS payload was to house three experiments: one on insulin tagging, another on Artemia physiology and the third on ion diffusion. All three experiments required the micro-gravity environment of the Space Shuttle.

The secondary objectives of the three experiments focused on educating students about all aspects of scientific experiments. Sierra Community College students were responsible for seeking funding, designing, manufacturing and constructing the experiments, for testing the experiments and all other phases of the project.

Dr. Ronald Nelson originally carried out experiments on insulin tagging in the mid 1960's. His results showed that the gravity field of Earth would not allow two materials of vastly differing molecular weights to combine. The creation of tagged insulin starts with the injection of chemicals in a mixing chamber. The materials are pumped periodically during a 24-hour period and then transferred to a dialysis chamber for cleaning and storage. The tagged insulin is ready for experiments on Earth to determine the transport mechanism of insulin through cell walls.

The Brine shrimp Artemia experiment was to determine the physiological effects of micro-gravity on cysts (eggs)

Continues on Page 104

hatched in space. After injecting a saline solution into a growth chamber, a video camera was to recorded the hatching and life cycle of the brine shrimp. Upon return from space, local elementary schools were to receive copies of the video tape, brine shrimp eggs, and a growth chamber so they could compare their Earth hatched shrimp with those from space.

The ion diffusion experiment tracks the flow of salt ions through a series of three separating chambers. A computer was to record conductivity and temperature readings for comparison with a control experiment held on Earth.

Approximately 100 students, 12 staff members, and 15 local corporate sponsors worked on the project. Students have had exposure to fund raising, computer hardware design, software development (more than 3,000 lines of

code), structural analysis, manufacturing, safety report generation, photography and video tape recording.

The GAS project forces students to apply the skills they have learned in class to a problem that will be solved, designed and built. The students worked with the knowledge that their experiments was to fly aboard the Space Shuttle. They are exposed to the NASA space vehicle safety process – the most rigorous design standard in the world.

NASA confirms the flight of the Sierra Community College GAS experiments aboard flight STS-57, which was scheduled for lift off on April 15, 1993. Students and staff were to travel to Cape Kennedy three times: to deliver the experiment, for launch, and for return of the experiment from the cargo bay of the Space Shuttle.

Contact:
Michael Dobeck, Computer Science Department
(916) 624-3333

Sierra Community College
5000 Rocklin Road
Rocklin, CA 95677
Total head count enrollment-Credit: 13,813; Non-Credit: 54
Campuses/sites: 3; Full-time faculty: 154

TEAM TEACHING ENGLISH AND CONTENT AREA COURSES

In addition to seeing the relevance of writing skills, students also develop close bonds from working together in the two classes

At Solano Community College (SCC), faculty have, for the past few years, been linking college composition (English I) with introductory classes in other disciplines. Faculty have taught English I with American History, Introduction to Biology, and Child Development. Plans are in the works for links of English I to courses in: Western Civilization, Minority Group Relations, Nutrition, Art History, and American Government.

The idea of linking English composition with so-called "content area" classes (classes that emphasize mastery of factual content such as history, rather than classes that emphasize mastery of a process such as composition) arises from concerns expressed by instructors in several disciplines at Solano Community College. English teachers express frustration that composition students often perceive reading and writing assignments as exercises without relevance to other course work or tasks outside school. Teachers in other fields complain that students who have had freshman English seem unable to write coherently or read textbooks independently.

Solano Community College first tried linking college composition (English I) to content area classes in 1989-90, without team teaching. All students in a particular composition class enrolled in a designated biology or history section (Barth 1985 describes a similar set-up). The college now calls this the "scotch-tape" model and found that the two classes remained essentially separate despite being "scotch-taped" together.

Barth describes a "social" benefit that we also found in linked classes: students developed close bonds from sharing two classes and worked together and supported each other much more than students in other classes.

Another discovery in two pilot-linked classes was that students wrote well and produced substantive content for two readers: a content area expert to whom they wanted to demonstrate in-depth knowledge, and a writing expert inexperienced in the content area, for whom they wanted to write clearly and explain concepts fully. Students could not count on the content instructor "reading between the lines" of unclear writing to figure out what they meant. English teachers benefited from papers with substantial content rather than content gathered halfheartedly for the "exercise" of writing an English paper. In other words, the content area class offered students a context for their reading and writing.

Some drawbacks to "scotch-taping" include:
1) instructors spent large amounts of time typing to update each other on what had been said in the two separate classes;
2) each instructor separately discussed with the students the relevance of the two fields (e.g., English and biology) to each other, but connections were at best delayed in students' eyes; and
3) our content area teachers preferred to lecture, so the burden of discussing the links between

reading/writing and the content area fell heavily on English instructors.

We also observed during our first semester of "scotch-taped" classes that when we did manage to appear in each other's classes, students' writing was invariably more substantive and clear than for assignments given by only one of the teachers.

Solano Community College felt it could capitalize on the advantages of "scotch-taped" classes and solve problems of communication and continuity by teach-teaching. The presence of both instructors in the classroom allows immediate answers to questions relating to either discipline or to the links between the fields. Having both instructors present allows students to see a connection between disciplines rather than being told about it. In addition, team-taught classes magnify the "community" effect that we had already observed in our first linked classes. Students can form relationships with each other and with a pair of teachers; students can see a "team" on their side. Under-prepared students, in particular, can benefit from two concerned teachers whose teamwork often brings problems to light faster than they might surface in an ordinary class and whose two heads are often better than one for brainstorming solutions to problems.

Linked classes are scheduled back-to-back and in the same room. Both instructors are present for both hours, so in reality they have a block of instructional time to use however they wish. (Each instructor receives a full class of reassigned time in his/her teaching schedule to allow for the double teaching time.) Classes are limited to the size of a regular English I class, which is 30 students. All students are required to take both classes and cannot drop one without dropping the other. Both teachers grade all or nearly all papers. Students receive grades and full credit for both classes.

Faculty experience as well as student evaluations and performance in the linked classes we have taught so far suggest the following conclusions:

1) Students who take these classes do express, at the end of the term, an understanding of the relevance of reading and writing to learning in other fields. Student evaluations included comments on the value of using reading strategies such as mapping for classes other than the content class to which English was linked. Students also expressed the idea that using English as a tool for learning the content area material was valuable. A number of students commented that they felt they were weak in one of the two areas (e.g., I'm good at English but not so hot at biology and so the English helped me stay motivated to study biology).

2) The link allowed students to read primary materials in the content area rather than relying solely on a text.

3) The reading of primary materials in some cases helped students relate personally to what they were learning. Primary texts, chosen carefully, can help "dry facts" become "real" for students.

4) Teachers need time to continue to teach classes like these. The idea that reassigned time can be offered for team-teaching or coordination on a temporary basis, "until the project gets off the ground," does not take into account the continuing preparation and the demands of team teaching. Although it's true that faculty teaching together for the second or third time had a better understanding of each other's goals and methods, each still needed to prepare both her own materials and her teaching partner's in order to be able to help students make fresh connections. Just as an English teacher rereads *Jane Eyre* each time s/he teaches it, so s/he can have all its nuances fresh in her mind, so the English teacher must reread his/her teaching partner's biology or history or child development assignments. Also, Solano has found that both teachers need to read all papers, which means the content area teacher has a much heavier paper-grading load than normal.

5) Faculty development and rejuvenation are a wonderful byproduct of the classes. As faculty work together and learn from each other, respect and collegiality follow. One interesting change in teaching style has occurred with the content teachers involved in the project, who have, as a result of the linked classes, tended to decrease time spent lecturing in favor of more group and discussion-oriented activities.

6) Students seem more reluctant to drop linked classes than they are to drop ordinary sections of English I or other classes. This has even been true for students who are clearly doing very poorly in one of the two classes. The reasons may be that dropping one means dropping the other where they might still succeed, and dropping both means losing a large number of units.

7) The counselors are key players in the success of these classes. At SCC, counselors are the primary contacts students have when planning schedules, as the college has no faculty advising program. So SCC feels we need to enlist counselors in directing to the classes students who might be interested and in helping students understand the demands of interdisciplinary study.

Does Solano Community College believe these classes work to help students apply reading and writing skills for learning in other fields, and to help students form a sense

Continues on Page 106

of community (often missing on the commuter campuses of community colleges? Yes. Does Solano Community College think linked classes are the right option for every student? No. Does Solano Community College have definitive proof of our impressions? No. More research remains to be done, and we hope to do some of it at Solano.

Contact:
Nan Wishner, English Department
(707) 864-7000, ext. 206

Solano Community College
4000 Suisun Valley Road
Suisun, CA 94585
Total head count enrollment-Credit: 11,791
Campuses/sites: 3; Full-time faculty: 147

COMPUTER ACCESS CENTERS

*Students with disabilities have access to the centers, which
helps them achieve academic or vocational goals*

Computer access centers for people with disabilities at every state community college in Colorado provide training on specialized, adaptive computer equipment. The overall goals of the centers are to aid students to achieve academic or vocational goals and enhance employability.

Classes frequently consist of students with a variety of disabilities learning how to use specialized computer programs. A blind student may be working on a computer with a screen reading program, while someone with mild to severe orthopedic disabilities may be using a modified keyboard. Often, four or five students receive instructions for the same exercise but each uses tailored adaptive devices to fulfill the requirement of the assignment.

The centers serve students who are totally or partially blind, deaf, orthopedically disabled, learning disabled or have acquired brain injury. Adaptations available include:

advanced speech synthesizers combined with screen-reading programs for the blind; screen magnifiers to enlarge text and graphics through a variety of magnification and color modifications; special word processing and other adaptations to reduce written language difficulties for the deaf; smart word processors and keyboard modifications to aid the orthopedically disabled produce written materials at an increased pace; automatic, phonetically based spell-checkers, screen readers, text enlargers and smart word processors to facilitate the writing process for the learning disabled; and strategies designed to improve learning potential, organizational strategies and academic skills for students with acquired brain injury.

The centers were established under a three-year, $1.1-million grant from the Colorado Rehabilitation Service and with help from the Governor's Job Training Office.

Contact:
Susie Bell, Director
(303) 620-4000

Colorado Community College and Occupational Education System
1391 North Speer, Suite 600
Denver, CO 80204-2554
Total headcount enrollment-Credit: 136,693
Number of colleges: 15; Full-time faculty: 1,119

COLORADO COMMUNITY COLLEGE AND OCCUPATIONAL EDUCATION SYSTEM

COLORADO CORE TRANSFER CURRICULUM

*Faculty from two-year and four-year institutions review
and revise the core transfer curriculum together*

Articulation agreements with other institutions have improved the quality, consistency and continuity of community college courses throughout the Colorado system.

The Colorado Core Transfer Program began with the passage of two Colorado House bills; one required two- and four-year institutions of higher education to develop transfer agreements, the other required Colorado community colleges to develop and implement a core transfer program in cooperation with the state's four-year institutions.

Aided by a one-year Quality Incentive Grant from the Colorado Commission on Higher Education, the Colorado Community College and Occupational Education System (CCCOES) began the Core Transfer Consortium Project. In the spring of 1986, CCCOES hired a project director and assembled a faculty task force. Each of the state's 15 community colleges sent a task force member who represented their college and a specific discipline or area of study within general education. The project's goal was to improve the AA/AS degree.

Over a two-year period, the Task Force met frequently, constructing a 33- to 34-credit core curriculum which was reviewed and revised in coordination with the Educational Services Council of community college vice presidents/deans or instruction and student services. The effort was augmented by annual meetings of two- and four-year faculty, where further review and revision was undertaken. This combined faculty process still continues to discuss transfer and curriculum issues related to the core, commonly described transfer electives, and issues of general interest to each discipline committee.

After the core curriculum was approved both the two- and four-year faculty and administrations, CCCOES signed articulation agreements in June 1987, with all state four-year colleges and universities. These agreements guarantee the requirements at each receiving institution when a community college student completes the core with grades of "C" or better and receives a core completed stamp on his/her transcript. At many colleges and universities, the entire AA/AS degree is accepted for transfer.

Continues on Page 108

The community college Faculty Task Force, now renamed the Faculty Transfer Curriculum Council (FTCC), meets quarterly to consider revisions to the core and to assist CCCOES staff in matters related to AA/AS degree transfers. Additionally, 25 faculty discipline committees which developed the curriculum meet twice a year in an annual community college general education faculty meeting and an annual two-four year faculty meeting.

Contact:
Dale Beckmann, Director
(303) 620-4000

Colorado Community College and Occupational Education System
1391 North Speer, Suite 600
Denver, CO 80204-2554
Total headcount enrollment-Credit: 136,693
Colleges: 15; Full-time faculty: 1,119

DEVELOPMENTAL STUDIES

Both student enthusiasm and the retention rate soared as the result of a well-developed basic skills curriculum

Colorado Mountain College has 18 learning labs, with both day and evening classes providing accessibility, flexibility and a well-developed curriculum for adult basic education and remediation. It all began in 1982 with three learning labs were established in Rifle, Glenwood Springs and Carbondale, using the Learning Unlimited software and materials. Student enthusiasm for the new program and the greatly improved retention rate determined the future strategy for adult basic education at Colorado Mountain College.

Over the next several years Colorado Mountain College established learning labs at the various locations throughout the college district. In addition, the faculty (all part-time, except one) researched and developed an outstanding cross-reference to supplement the Learning Unlimited Program materials.

When the state of Colorado recently mandated the use of the Comprehensive Adult Student Assessment System (CASAS) for placement testing, Colorado Mountain College faculty developed the curriculum for the reading component. The reading component could be used in the same system with the Learning Unlimited program, giving students and instructors the use of both an academic and the skills curriculum. CASAS is now being used throughout the state and now also includes a math curriculum.

Today, Colorado Mountain College has 18 learning labs, five full-time faculty and 19 adjunct faculty serving 1,300 students on an individual basis. Counselors are available at each location; two full-time special populations coordinators provide assistance for learning disabled students.

Contact:
Shirley Bowen, Director
(303) 945-8691

Colorado Mountain College
PO Box 10001
Glenwood Springs, CO 81602
Total headcount enrollment-Credit: 19,441 Non-Credit: 1,482
Campuses/sites: 7; Full-time faculty: 68

ENVIRONMENTAL TECHNOLOGY

Students conduct various field projects, such as high-altitude revegetation experiments with local mine waste

Situated in a historic mining town located in the heart of the Colorado Rocky Mountains, Colorado Mountain College's Timberline Campus enjoys a unique environmental setting and proximity to the EPA's Superfund site at California Gulch. It is an ideal setting for the Environmental Technology (ET) program.

The ET program has been training two-year technicians in land reclamation since 1974, and in water quality and waste management since 1988. The program includes an appropriate mix of general academic courses including math, English composition, speech, technical writing, computer applications, biology, chemistry, earth science and ecology, etc. Program-specific courses depend upon the area of specialization, land or water, and include classes in soils, plant science, land rehabilitation, heavy equipment operations, surveying, hydrology, soil and water chemistry, water and waste water treatment, hazardous and non-hazardous waste management, etc.

The most exciting aspects of the program are its practical, hands-on components in the laboratory and in the field. Students carry on a variety of experiments under the guidance of their instructors. One ongoing project involves high-altitude revegetation experiments with local mine waste. Student experiments revealed that both the mine slag and dolomitic limestone that make up much of the mine waste in the area, can be used to create a satisfactory growing medium in reclaiming pyritic soils and mine tailings. Another field project undertakes continuous and comprehensive studies of local stream environments. Students work in pairs to take measurements, collect samples, perform analyses and record field observations on their stream segment. This project extends throughout the students' entire two-year program. As their course work progresses, the scope of their field assignments is expanded.

Additionally, all ET students must complete a summer practicum in the environmental field between their first and second year of study. Instructors assist students in finding paid internship positions with government agencies or private industry and then monitor their progress throughout the summer. This work/study practicum provides the students with summer income as well as valuable work experiences and references for their resumes. The experiential learning aspects of the ET program produces meaningful environmental data, provide students with essential experiences in field research and documentation, increase their enthusiasm for the field and develop their self-confidence.

Small class sizes also contribute to the success of CMC's ET program and students. With classes averaging around 15 students, instructors always have ample time and energy to focus their attention on students' special questions and needs.

Student success is measured in two ways. The primary measure is from comparisons of program entry and exit scores on three curriculum related exams. The second measure of student success is employer response to our graduates.

We have been graduating ET students since 1976, and many now hold leadership positions in their fields. Some earlier graduates today manage the environmental departments of their companies, others are superintendents of water and waste water treatment plants. Companies that have hired our graduates appreciate the quality of their knowledge and skills and continue to recruit newer graduates.

The ET program won the 1988 Colorado Governor's Mined Land Reclamation Award. The program, located in the town of Leadville, has been featured in regional papers such as the High Country News and in numerous professional journals such as Pollution Engineering. Many of its graduates have gone on to assume leadership positions in the environmental field, and today the college receives more job placement offers than it has graduates.

Contact:
Peter Jeschofnig, Associate Professor
(719) 486-2015

Colorado Mountain College
PO Box 10001
Glenwood Springs, CO 81602
Total headcount enrollment-Credit: 19,441 Non-Credit: 1,482
Campuses/sites: 7; Full-time faculty: 68

COMMUNITY COLLEGE OF AURORA

TEACHING FOR A CHANGE: FACULTY DEVELOPMENT

The college's instructional philosophy is that faculty should use diverse teaching methods suited to various learning styles

Because "telling is not teaching," the Community College of Aurora encourages faculty to use a variety of teaching methods suited to various learning styles.

After, all, what is a community college, if not a community of learners? Faculty as well as students must value learning, strive to enhance their skills and weave a common design of excellence in teaching and learning. The Faculty Development Program at Community College of Aurora (CCA), a comprehensive, non-traditional training model, supports instructional excellence for all faculty in all disciplines; encourages faculty to use experiential, student-centered learning approaches; and helps instructors equip students with the critical thinking skills, teamwork strategies and ethical perspective required for effective life-long learning.

Faculty members often use interactive learning – classroom activities designed to get students, rather than faculty, to "cover the material."

The CCA Faculty Development Program includes a number of components:
•Faculty Mentor Program;
•New Faculty Orientation;
•Effective Community College Teaching;
•Educational Topics and Issues;
•Mini-Grants for Teaching and Learning Excellence;

Continues on Page 110

- Individual Teaching Consultations;
- Independent Study;
- Teaching Resource Center/Idea Bank;
- Videotape Production;
- Conference Attendance;
- Annual International Faculty Development;
- Conference & Mini-Conferences;
- Consultation with other Colleges; and
- Opportunities to Facilitate Seminars Publications.

CCA received an $81,000 Quality Incentive Grant from the Colorado Commission on Higher Education to develop its interdisciplinary critical thinking infusion project. FIPSE (the Fund for Improvement of Post Secondary Education) awarded the College $225,000 for its ethics infusion project.

CCA has designed a consultation process that enables colleges interested in starting or enhancing faculty development programs of their own to come to CCA for study and training. CCA has also sponsored two International Faculty Development Conferences at Vail, Colorado.

CCA's Faculty Development Program was named a Colorado Program of Excellence in 1989 and has received $750,000 to date, as a result. National awards have included:

1) The Institutional Award for a Single Campus from the National Council for Staff, Program, and Organizational Development, an AACJC affiliate council, 1991;

2) Exemplary Faculty Development Program from the National Council of Instructional Administrators, 1992; and

3) The AACJC/Kellogg Beacon Grant from the American Association of Community and Junior Colleges, 1992. As a Beacon College, CCA will help six other community colleges develop ethics-across-the-curriculum projects.

Contact:
Karen Hewett, Director of Faculty/Staff/Organizational Development
(303) 360-4830

Community College of Aurora
16000 East CentreTech Parkway
Aurora, CO 80011-9036
Total headcount enrollment-Credit: 4,700 Non-Credit: 1,500
Campuses/sites: 1; Full-time faculty: 25

COMMUNITY COLLEGE OF AURORA

VICTIM ASSISTANCE CERTIFICATE/TRAINING

The college's answer to the rapidly expanding area of crime victim assistance is to turn out sophisticated, knowledgeable professionals

As the only institution in Colorado and one of the few in the nation providing comprehensive crime victim assistance training, Community College of Aurora's use of practicing professionals brings unprecedented credibility to the classroom.

CCA, recognizing changing community/career needs, in 1986 developed and implemented the certificate program in crime victims assistance. The program represents a unique educational opportunity that prepares current and future professionals to assume successful roles as crime victim advocates or program administrators.

This program initially offered a certificate in "direct services." Due to expert advice from professionals on the Victim Assistance Advisory Board and requests from students, in 1990 an "administrative" component was added providing a dual tract option. Faculty in this program were chosen for their instructional expertise and their continuing commitment to this field. Recognition of the fact that the knowledge and skills offered through this program would generally benefit the criminal justice system, and crime victims in particular, was quick in coming. Due to its recognized value and growth, in the summer term of 1992 the college expanded its options by adding a Victim Assistance Emphasis within the Criminal Justice Associate of Applied Science degree.

Because of its uniqueness, CCA is attracting a great deal of attention from local service agencies and criminal justice professionals as well as recognition from Colorado's statewide victims assistance membership agency, the Colorado Organization for Victims Assistance.

Because of our standing in the criminal justice community, CCA's program has opened lines of communication with national victim service organizations – both private and governmental. This dialogue will prove invaluable in future program and curriculum development as well as enhancing career alternatives for students.

Contact:
Les Moroye, Division Chair, Business & Public Service Programs
(303) 360-4731

Community College of Aurora
16000 East CentreTech Parkway
Aurora, CO 80011-9036
Total headcount enrollment-Credit: 4,700 Non-Credit: 1,500
Campuses/sites: 1; Full-time faculty: 25

HAZARDOUS MATERIALS TECHNOLOGY (HAZMAT)

With this program, the college provides training and retraining for environmental scientists, geologists, engineers and technicians

More than half of those enrolled in the Hazardous Materials Technology program at Front Range Community College already have bachelor's or master's degrees, demonstrating how progressive the program remains. Though only developed in 1988, the HAZMAT program has become a model for at least 20 other American colleges.

In the United States, the hazardous waste cleanup business is a $10-billion-a-year industry, according to Denver's Environmental Protection Agency office. In the western region alone, there are 2,000 different sources of hazardous wastes. Additionally, federal, state and local regulations governing the handling, use, transportation and disposal of hazardous and politically hazardous chemicals or wastes have created a critical need for thousands of educated hazardous materials specialists in Colorado, both at technical and professional levels.

In response to this huge demand, Front Range Community College developed an Associate of Science degree program that teaches students how to store, analyze, collect, dispose, recycle and transport hazardous materials. In four years, more than 3,700 students took courses in this nationally and internationally recognized program.

The Associate of Science degree is designed to allow students to easily transfer their credits toward a baccalaureate degree program in environmental health, environmental science or environmental engineering. Students may also choose to complete the certificate program or attend both credit and non-credit studies to update their skills in subjects like transportation of hazardous materials, asbestos removal, waste minimization, response tactics, air monitoring, environmental laws, and radiation protection. With this program, the college provides training and retraining for environmental scientists, geologists, engineers and technicians.

In 1990, the Colorado Commission on Higher Educational (CCHE) declared that the HAZMAT program was one of five higher education "Programs of Excellence" in the state of Colorado. Along this prestigious award, CCHE authorized additional funding for the program for the next five years. (With this funding, the college hopes to develop a 10,000-square-foot field-training site for ground water monitoring, underground storage tanks, drum sampling and emergency response training. A special classroom devoted to industry training has also been requested.)

Since it was developed, the HAZMAT program has generated more than $1-million in training contracts for business and industry. Recently a training contract was completed for Browning-Ferris Industries at Last Chance, Colorado. The year-long project included curriculum development and training manuals for 70 hazardous materials specialists at the plant. The HAZMAT program extends beyond Colorado's boundaries as well. In partnership with the National Environmentally Health Association, the college recently won a training contract with the state of Nevada's Division of Environmentally Protection. Assistance for this project will be provided by four Nevada community colleges and the University of Nevada at Las Vegas.

Contact:
Richard Barth, Department Chair, EnviroTech
(303) 466-8811

Front Range Community College
645 West 112th Avenue
Westminster, CO 80030
Total headcount enrollment-Credit: 10,500 Non-Credit: 20,000
Campuses/sites: 3; Full-time faculty: 352

FRONT RANGE COMMUNITY COLLEGE

SELF-SUFFICIENCY NURSING

This welfare-to-work program includes a deliberate attempt to move students toward problem-solving their own issues

Offsetting the state's nursing shortage and getting students off welfare are two main goals of the Self-Sufficiency Nursing Program at Front Range Community College.

At its inception in 1988, four major objectives were established for the program: 1) to provide Aid for Families of Dependent Children (AFDC) recipients a viable alternative for financial self-sufficiency through education in a profession; 2) to enhance participants' self-esteem through achieving success in a demanding academic program and making a meaningful contribution to health-care delivery;

Continues on Page 112

3) to assist welfare recipients in becoming positive role models for their children; and 4) to increase the number of registered nurses practicing in the state of Colorado, in an effort to reduce the state's nursing shortage.

This unusual focus was made possible through the partnership efforts of the college, Governor Roy Romer, Colorado Department of Social Services, Colorado Commission on Higher Education, Colorado Community College and Occupational Education System, and various job-training agencies in northern Colorado.

With the commitment from five state agencies to provide financial support to the students, the college's nursing faculty began to develop an accelerated Associate Degree Nursing curriculum. (Many students required preparatory academic courses before they could be admitted into the program.) Curriculum included a deliberate attempt to move students toward problem-solving their own life issues. Before entering the program, students were required to attend a workshop on self-esteem and co-dependency based on the 12-step model on breaking the poverty cycle. Nursing faculty attend these workshops with the students.

Ten students graduated from the nursing program in that first year, with an outstanding 100 percent "first time" pass rate on the RN licensing exam and are currently working as RNs. Since 1988, several more students have completed the program, and have jobs as registered nurses or licensed practical nurses. Today there are 27 self-sufficiency students enrolled in various levels of the college's nursing program, with more than 600 potential students on the waiting list.

Contact:
Alma Mueller, Department Chair
(303) 466-8811

Front Range Community College
645 West 112th Avenue
Westminster, CO 80030
Total headcount enrollment-Credit: 10,500 Non-Credit: 20,000
Campuses/sites: 3; Full-time faculty: 352

FARM AND RANCH BUSINESS MANAGEMENT

The program is uniquely delivered on-site, at the respective students' farms and ranches

The Farm and Ranch Business Management program at Morgan Community College is uniquely delivered on-site to individuals who currently own and/or operate farms and ranches in the college's 11,000-square-mile service area.

In Colorado and other western states that are agri-business intensive, the numbers easily demonstrate the need for such a program that emphasizes how to assure profitability at farms and ranches . While less than 10 percent of Americans are engaged in agricultural careers, those working in or owning/managing farms and ranches meet an expanding national and international demand for goods and services produced and marketed in agriculture.

Students begin this credit program of studies by defining their assets and liabilities in real and measurable terms. Thereafter, students are introduced to construction of cost-center management, and defining of "enterprise centers" which can be managed toward acceptable profitability. Students thus use their own business operation as both a case study profile, and to improve costs/income measures which are desirable. The college supports use of a traveling "computer van" equipped fully with hardware and software which students learn and use in completing the program. Ultimately, students acquire their own computer material toward completion of the program. The computer is the primary instructional and management modality used by students during and after graduation, to learn about and improve the management of their farm and ranch operations.

The Farm and Ranch Business Management Program, begun in 1980, serves 200-plus students per year and uses three full-time and 10 part-time faculty. Students enrolled typically represent husband and wife teams. Seventy-five to 90 students complete the program each year. The program has received wide recognition and has appeared in national journals dedicated to agriculture and was featured on national television by Charles Kuralt. Scores of potential farm and ranch bankruptcies have annually been averted due to intervention by the program.

Contact:
Mike Olearnick, Chair, Division of Extended Studies
(303) 867-3081

Morgan Community College
Fort Morgan, CO 80701
Total headcount enrollment-Credit: 2,000 Non-Credit: 1,000
Campuses/sites: 5; Full-time faculty: 45

PHYSICAL THERAPIST ASSISTANT

▩ Students complete a rounded liberal arts and science curriculum, infused ▩
with classroom skills and enhanced through clinical training

The need for highly skilled allied health professionals, including Physical Therapy Assistants, is growing at exponential rates as America races toward the year 2000. This is even true at Morgan Community College, which has a large service area (11,000 square miles), sparse population (less than 50,000 residents) and a smattering of health care facilities that number fewer than the state's more populated regions. Morgan's PTA program is one of the strongest rural-delivered programs nationwide.

Designed in 1989, the program educates professionals who work under the direct supervision of physical therapists, carrying out treatment plans using a variety of treatment modalities, including but not limited to exercise, heat, sonic and related associated treatment methods. Students complete a rounded liberal arts and sciences curriculum, infused with classroom PTA skills and knowledge development, and enhanced through many hours of supervised clinical-setting training.

The PTA Program serves students from Western states and places students in their clinical assignments in states as far west as California. Graduates of the PTA Program have been placed in states across the nation. The program is accredited by the American Physical Therapy Association. Two full-time faculty and scores of extended clinical outreach faculty provide classroom and skill instruction as students navigate the program. Faculty in the program are leaders in the physical therapy profession at state, regional and national levels.

The PTA Program typically enrolls in a "Pre-PTA" curricular track, up to 50 students each academic year, and enrolls 40 to 50 regular PTA students. Twenty-plus students complete the degree program annually. Qualified student demand for admission to the PTA Program is great.

Contact:
Phyllis Gertge, Chair, Division of Health Sciences & Applied Technologies
(303) 867-3081

Morgan Community College
Fort Morgan, CO 80701
Total headcount enrollment-Credit: 2,000 Non-Credit: 1,000
Campuses/sites: 5; Full-time faculty: 45

CENTER FOR TEACHING EXCELLENCE

▩ The Center includes a library of tapes, books, journals and ▩
articles as well as faculty computers, printers and a VCR

To create and nurture an atmosphere where students and faculty feel challenged to excellence, Red Rocks Community College established its Center for Teaching Excellence in September 1991. It quickly became an integral part of the college's learning community.

Discussions about a Center began earlier – in strategic planning meetings in January 1991 as representatives from all areas of the college met to set priorities for the future. To assist Red Rocks' faculty and staff to meet the challenges of technology in education, to respond to the changing needs of the diverse students who come to community colleges, and to encourage professional development among its faculty, the idea of the Center was born. At this time, the Center was envisioned as a resource for the college.

The idea of a Resource Center became real over the next 10 months. The college was able to build a library of tapes, books, journals and articles and to set aside a physical location for these library materials and for faculty computers, printers and a VCR.

The Center has sponsored many professional development opportunities for faculty and staff, including workshops on critical thinking, learning styles, tech-prep programs, distant learning and environmental scanning. In 10 months, 100 percent of full-time faculty attended at least one workshop offered through the Center for Teaching Excellence. Some of the most popular workshops offered through the Center were the 15, three-hour computer workshops we sponsored in fall semester 1991 and spring semester 1992. Almost 25 percent of Red Rocks' full-time faculty participated in these seminars, many of them using a computer for the first time. The Center invited adjunct faculty to attend and participate in all of these activities; about 50 adjunct faculty have participated in Center-sponsored activities during this time. The college published two editions of *The Red Letter*, a forum for faculty to discuss and debate teaching and education. The Center for Teaching Excellence is a resource for the college and its community.

Continues on Page 114

The greatest success has been the level of faculty involvement in the Center and in Center projects. The Center coordinator is a full-time faculty member who is given release time to direct the Center's activities. Also in place is a seven-member Steering Committee that communicates with the faculty and advises the coordinator. Inviting participation from all faculty – academic, remedial, "soft" vocational and hard shops; adjunct and full-time; those who have a 20-year history with the college and those who have a two-year history with the college – has helped to ensure that the Center's programs meet the needs of the whole college and that all faculty feel invited to participate. And our faculty do participate. Red Rocks Community College faculty designed and facilitated the workshops and seminars offered. Inviting our faculty to be the Center has built interest, trust and commitment.

In addition to building upon our successes, we continue to find ways to nurture excellence among the faculty and the college. Projects for 1992-1993 included a semester project in critical thinking developed and facilitated by Red Rocks' faculty; a Summer Institute for Teachers; integration of a vocational course with an academic course; integration of academic courses; and adaptation of curricula to technology, including computer-assisted instruction, interactive video instruction, and two-way audio, two-way video classes delivered via T-1.

Red Rocks Community College's Center for Teaching Excellence was highlighted in a lead editorial in the Denver Post and was featured in an article in the *AACJC Times*.

Contact:
Marilyn Smith, Coordinator,
(303) 988-6160, ext. 439

Red Rocks Community College
13300 West Sixth Avenue
Lakewood, CO 80401-5398
Total headcount enrollment-Credit: 11,500
Campuses/sites: 2; Full-time faculty: 7

RED ROCKS INSTITUTE

This business and industry institute serves corporations, small businesses, public agencies and non-profit organizations

In the fall of 1989, Red Rocks Community College expanded its services to include a business and industry division, the Red Rocks Institute. Created to specifically meet the work force demands of the 21st Century, the Institute quickly became a leader in all levels of corporate training.

Services of the Institute focus on assisting companies to meet their goals of employee productivity and business profitability. The parameters under which the Institute operates are clearly defined in its mission statement: to provide quality, customer focused, cost effective training and consulting to "Give Business the Power of Human Potential."

The Red Rocks Institute serves corporations, small businesses, public agencies and non-profit organizations in a four-county area. Although the services of the Institute are many, they consist of three primary components: 1) Customized Training and Consulting; 2) Small Business Strategies; and 3) Apprenticeship and Work Based Learning. Specifically, the services include:

- Project Analysis. Client service managers assist employers in identifying resource needs and in developing programs to meet those needs. The managers have planning and analysis expertise to counsel clients throughout the process.
- Management Assistance. Small business consultants assist business owners in planning, marketing, personnel and financial management. Specialized

assistance in areas such as loan packaging, procurement and foreign trade is available.

- Employee Development. Professional trainers and instructional designers customize self-paced modules, seminars and courses to develop the knowledge, skills, technical expertise and managerial qualities that employees need to be part of a productive work force.
- Resource Coordination. Client-service managers coordinate college, public and private-sector resources to best serve the client. The college services include assessment and development, career counseling and aptitude testing, and computer access and training. Job placement, cooperative education and apprenticeship programs are also available.

Although very young at the time, 1990 was a year of significant achievement for the institute. Partnerships were formed with more than 20 businesses, resulting in more than 80 training programs and services provided to more than 2,000 employees. The majority of the businesses are local, but the Institute serves several national organizations such as: American Express, BALL Aerospace, BALL Metal Container, COBE Laboratories, Coors Brewery, Kaiser Permanent, Merrill Lynch, U.S. Department of Interior, U.S. Department of Veterans Affairs and the U.S. Postal Service. Business clients of the Institute recognize it as being a unique resource for providing high-quality training that otherwise may not be attainable.

A large factor in the success of the Institute is its in-house expertise. Subject experts range from small business consulting, to developing on-site literacy/learning centers, to the development of customized training courses such as supervisory and leadership skills, listening and communication effectiveness, total quality management and statistical process control.

Striving to continually "Give Business the Power of Human Potential," the Red Rocks Institute prides itself in the ability to establish long-term partnerships with its clients, thus making it possible to be "partners in work force development."

Contact:
Shelli Bischoff, Executive Director
(303) 987-0313

Red Rocks Community College
13300 West Sixth Avenue
Lakewood, CO 80401-5398
Total headcount enrollment-Credit: 11,500
Campuses/sites: 2; Full-time faculty: 7

DISABILITIES AWARENESS AND OUTREACH

▣ *The college and community work together* ▣
to provide accessibility and support

Asnuntuck Community College sponsors and houses the REACH (Resources, Education, Advocacy, Counseling, Help) program, which heightens student, staff and community awareness regarding the disabled and their needs. This program was originally funded via a VISTA grant. At the present time, the program is staffed entirely by volunteers. Specific achievements of this program include:

1) disabilities awareness workshops for faculty, staff, students and the community;
2) a quarterly publication with specific news devoted to access and awareness issues for the disabled (current mailing list contains 250 addresses);
3) direct input to the architect during college renovations costing more than $6-million (this input involved a collaborative effort on the part of the college, the REACH program and the architect to ensure that the renovated facility was appropriately accessible for the disabled);
4) collaborative efforts with the town of Enfield, Connecticut to properly ramppolling places;
5) collaborative efforts with the town of Enfield to

provide optimum service for the disabled via the Dial-a-Ride Program;
6) the writing and publication of two pamphlets that provided discount information provided by local merchants for the disabled and which provided referral services for disabled persons and their families; and
7) a swimming program for disabled persons at a local school.

Recognition:

- Cited 1982 through 1991 for contributions to improve the lives of disabled persons by the National Organization for Disabilities (NOD). Specifically, acknowledged in 1985 with a monetary award for their efforts;
- Awarded the Joseph E. O'Connor Distinguished Service Award from the North Central Connecticut Chapter of the Governor's Committee on Employment of the Handicapped in 1985; and
- Cited by the Connecticut State General Assembly in 1981, 1985 and 1989 for its work with the disabled.

Contact:
Jo-Ann Bellantuono, Assistant Director, Community Services
(203) 253-3001

Asnuntuck Community College
170 Elm Street
Enfield, CT 06082
Total head count enrollment-Credit: 2,000; Non-Credit: 550
Campuses/sites: 1; Full-time faculty: 26

COMPUTER AND INFORMATION SYSTEMS

▣ *The program is designed to serve both students* ▣
and the business community

Because almost every job today requires some contact with a computer, the Computer and Information Systems curriculum at Asnuntuck Community College tries to provide a broad range of skills including computer programming, systems analysis, word processing, as well as a variety of other "application" skills such as spreadsheets and databases.

The Computer and Information Systems Program at Asnuntuck Community College has, in the last 10 years, seen steady growth. In the last few years the needs of the students have shifted from career programming skills to more general application skills. The introduction of a new Personal Computer Specialist Certificate is one example of how Asnuntuck has attempted to meet this need. The CIS

Program is designed to provide a two-year, college level curriculum to meet the needs of the business community for personnel with training in the concepts, procedures, and applications of computer systems and equipment. An additional objective of the program is to provide students with the fundamentals for potential transfer to a four-year institution. The curriculum provides for instruction in practical application of theory through interaction with a computer system as well as courses in related fields of general education.

The technical courses included in the Computer Science curriculum cover the areas of data processing application, operation of computer terminals by students, and programming in high-level languages – COBOL, C, Pascal and FORTRAN 77. Other courses cover systems development and design, data processing management, teleprocessing design, database design, and software concepts. Students are assigned a variety of projects that cover complete applications from input record and form design through program development practices in both business and scientific applications.

Graduates have received training qualifying them for a range of computer-related positions from programmer trainee through to systems analyst and supervisory management roles.

Asnuntuck Community College has four computer labs, each with 25 workstations. Three of the labs are controlled by two local area networks: a Banyan Vines System and a Digital Equipment Corporation Pathworks System. The college has a wide assortment of software. In teaching, the focus is on application software as well as programming languages.

Computer and Information Systems has grown to include five full-time faculty.

Contact:
Fredric Stefanowicz, Coordinator
(203) 253-3128

Asnuntuck Community College
170 Elm Street
Enfield, CT 06082
Total head count enrollment-Credit: 2,000; Non-Credit: 550
Campuses/sites: 1; Full-time faculty: 26

CAPITAL COMMUNITY-TECHNICAL COLLEGE

MATHEMATICS DEVELOPMENT CENTER

A key element in the Center's operation is the role of the tutor-liaisons, each of whom is assigned to a class

The Mathematics Development Center not only helps students succeed in math, but also it is a catalyst for developing new curricular options.

Supported by Title III funds, the Mathematics Development Center was created as a model for other institutions with similar problems.

The Mathematics Development Center, both a physical facility and an organizational structure, is a multi-functional unit that provides additional resources and coordinates existing ones in support of math students. The Center is staffed by a full-time coordinator/counselor, part-time tutor-liaisons, peer tutors and student workers. Through interaction with a Mathematics Planning and Advisory Group, the Center is a catalyst for developing new curricular options and instructional formats such as a Problem Solving and Learning Strategies Course, Small Group Collaborative Learning Methods, Computer Assisted Instruction, Alternative Testing, Incorporation of Technology into Curriculum and Instruction, a Math Learning Strategies Video Series, etc.

Any student enrolled in a math course may use the services of the Center. A key element in the Math Development Center's operation is the role of the tutor-liaisons, each of whom is assigned to a class. Such an attachment provides a vital communication link among the Center, students, class activities and instructors. This encourages early identification of student problems and enables the Center, in conjunction with the instructor, to make appropriate and rapid responses to them. In developmental math courses, the tutor-liaison attends each class and works with the instructor to enhance the learning process. With respect to credit math courses, the tutor-liaison periodically visits the class and consults with the instructor. In the Center, the tutor-liaison tutors on an individual basis and in small groups, while fostering students' self-esteem and helping them to develop good learning strategies. In addition, the tutor-liaison helps students access other resources in the Center such as computer-assisted instruction. The underlying goal is to help students move toward becoming more independent learners.

Establishing a computer-based student monitoring and tracking system as a basis for evaluation and program revision is another important function of the Center. The monitoring system organizes information about our students in developmental math and the tracking system follows their progress through mathematics at Capital.

Whether evaluated in terms of staff and student attitudes or by cold statistics, the Math Development Center has proven to be an effective agent for advancing student participation and success in mathematics. Formal surveys of student and staff perceptions about the Center's effectiveness have been overwhelmingly positive. Moreover, student success rates in developmental math courses have increased from a pre-grant low of 45 percent, to a current rate in excess of 70 percent. Preliminary statistics also indicate improvement in success rates and enrollment for credit math courses.

Contact:
Rama Chaturved, Division Director, Science & Math
(203) 520-7836

Capital Community-Technical College
61 Woodland Street
Hartford, CT 06105-2354
Total head count enrollment-Credit/Non-Credit: 4,395
Campuses/sites: 7; Full-time faculty: 103

THE BUSINESS AND INDUSTRY SERVICES NETWORK

*The Network addresses workplace issues through programs
dealing with basic math and literacy skills*

The Business and Industry Services Network of the Community-Technical Colleges of Connecticut promotes cooperation between business, education and government. A collaborative effort of the 12 community-technical colleges in the state designed to provide training and education for the state's work force and employers. The Network uses the educational resources and expertise of the public two-year colleges in the Connecticut system to meet the needs of business and industries throughout the state. The Network can deliver single courses and seminars on a wide array of business-related, technical or educational topics, as well as complete certificate or degree programs.

The colleges' facilities, equipment, libraries and faculty provide a valuable resource to support the economic development of the state and its citizens. The colleges and their business partners have been actively involved, since the Network's inception in 1986, in addressing workplace issues through programs dealing with basic math and literacy skills along with courses designed to help Connecticut's businesses and their employees remain current with the rapidly changing technology involved in computer-integrated manufacturing and biomedical engineering.

The Network serves as the connection between business, education and state government and promotes cooperative efforts with other state colleges, universities and agencies. The Network's directors act as brokers for other state services to business. The Network directors' familiarity with state and federal programs and funding can simplify the often complex business of dealing with government and can assist Connecticut businesses and industries to find the resources needed to support their development and growth.

Contact:
Judith K. Resnick, Director
(203) 725-6619

Community Technical Colleges of Connecticut
61 Woodland Street
Hartford, CT 06105
Total head count enrollment-Credit: 45,655
Colleges: 12

FIRE TECHNOLOGY AND ADMINISTRATION

*The combination of general education and specialized courses
makes the student well-prepared for today's complex world*

A combination of liberal arts, science and career education, the Fire Technology and Administration Program, of the Community Technical Colleges of Connecticut is a cooperative effort of the five comprehensive community-technical colleges in the system in Hartford, New Haven, Norwalk, Norwich and Waterbury. It provides advanced training and college-level education to students interested in leadership roles in fire protection, prevention, and administration. The programs also train personnel of insurance companies and of industries involved in fire prevention and protection practices.

The fire technologists trained through the program work in career or volunteer fire departments, in local, state and federal agencies, in industry or insurance companies, in architectural firms, or related areas. They serve their industries and their communities by establishing and promoting educational programs directed at fire prevention, fire safety and fire code enforcement. The fire technologist can enhance community safety and greatly reduce the suffering caused by uncontrolled fire.

The program requires courses in English, literature, communications, psychology, as well as in chemical principles, codes and standards, hydraulics, building construction and investigation techniques. This combination of general education and specialized courses makes the Fire Technology and Administration degree program the perfect combination of liberal arts, science and career education needed to be successful in today's complex and changing economic environment.

A system coordinator oversees program development and delivery at all five of the participating colleges and is responsible for recruitment of students, program promotion, and outreach to business and industry throughout the state.

Contact:
George Munkenbeck, Naugatuck Valley Community-Technical College
(203) 566-8760

Community Technical Colleges of Connecticut
61 Woodland Street
Hartford, CT 06105
Total head count enrollment-Credit: 45,655
Colleges: 12 colleges

INSTRUCTIONAL TELEVISION

Mothers of small children, adults with full-time jobs and people with disabilities take advantage of televised courses

The Instructional Television network of the Community Technical Colleges of Connecticut may minimize student commuting, but it doesn't take away from essential support services such as teacher conferences, library services and counseling.

In the fall of 1992, the Community-Technical Colleges began their 10th year of broadcasting via the Community College Instructional Television Network (CCIT). CCIT was established in 1983 in cooperation with Connecticut Public Television and participating cable systems around the state. The network provides ready access to college credit courses for those adults who have difficulty commuting to a college campus on a regular basis. Mothers with small children, adults with full-time jobs, or disabled persons for whom distance is a barrier to education and self-improvement often find the televised course to be an ideal solution.

With transmitters throughout the state, CCIT broadcasts from 8 a.m. until 11 p.m., seven days a week, and reaches more than 500,000 homes in Connecticut through its 18 participating cable stations. CCIT programming is repeated three times in five-hour blocks daily, so cable coverage is available on all participating cable systems at some time during every day. Students can sign up for credit courses on a flexible schedule, with the added benefit of reviewing material through repeat programming.

Students enroll at one of the participating colleges in the 12-college system, purchase books at the college book store, attend a minimum of three seminars and two exams on campus during each semester, and view the actual programs on television at home.

The director of Televised Services and a technical assistant work with program delivery, from course selection and program promotion to college coordination and technical support.

Contact:
Daniel McAuliffe, Director, Televised Instruction
(203) 725-6618

Community Technical Colleges of Connecticut
61 Woodland Street
Hartford, CT 06105
Total head count enrollment-Credit: 45,655
Colleges: 12

TEACHING PARTNERS

Business, education and human services sectors help students with disabilities gain culinary skills

Eight students with developmental disabilities learn professional culinary skills through a one-year non-credit program combining lecture, laboratory and work experience at Manchester Community-Technical College. Additionally, the program educates hospitality management degree student in supervisory skills necessary in training and supporting special needs employees within industry jobs. All this is possible through a unique partnership between Manchester Community College, Hospitality Management Department and Community Enterprises/Windsor ICE Division.

Upon completion of the two-semester course of study, Supported Education students receive assistance in the transition toward each individual's optimal employment capability. With support, students expand their skills in employment in order for them to be competitive in career oriented, hospitality positions.

The unique partnership between business, higher education, human service agencies and persons with disabilities provides many opportunities students with disabilities gain culinary skill competencies necessary for employment in the hospitality industry, while hospitality management students are learning skills to train the disabled in the work setting. The program offers individuals with disabilities the opportunity to be in a social and educational environment that has traditionally been closed to them, while encouraging the college community to become more inclusive. The nation's hospitality industry has a new source of dedicated and trained culinary professionals as well as a new group of management professionals experienced at working with this new labor force.

The Supported Education Program at Manchester Community College received the Vocational Improvement Practices Award from the State of Connecticut, Department of Education and the National "Yes, I Can" award given to a 1991 Supported Education graduate, for excellence in meeting employment challenges.

Continues on Page 120

The program is made possible by the financial partnership between the College, Community Enterprises, public agencies and the private sector. The program was also the recipient of the underwriting grant, Job Training Partnership Act, City of Hartford, Employment Resources and Development Agency.

Contact:
Sandra Jenkins, Hospitality Management Department Chair
(203) 647-6121

Manchester Community-Technical College
PO Box 1046, 60 Bidwell Street
Manchester, CT 06045-1046
Total head count enrollment-Credit: 6,134; Non-Credit: 1,054
Campuses/sites: 1; Full-time faculty: 95

HUMANITIES WEEKEND

The weekend exposes about 100 students to the interrelationships among various liberal arts disciplines

One intense weekend, Manchester Community-Technical College has found, can do more to drive home the interrelationships among various liberal arts disciplines than any standard interdisciplinary effort. The Humanities Weekend dates back to the spring and summer of 1985, when a committee of Liberal Arts faculty met to design a unique program that would add to an innovative component to traditional classes in the form of a two-day weekend experience that would immerse students in activities in the various areas of the humanities.

A "pilot weekend" was held in the spring 1986 semester and was so successful that the Weekend Experience courses, including the two-day weekend component, have been offered every semester since.

Each semester, two sections of Introduction to Literature and one section of Introduction to Humanities are offered as four-credit courses that include, in addition to the traditional requirements of these courses, attendance at the two-day weekend of activities, as well as pre- and post-weekend assignments that enable students to understand the interrelationship among the various liberal arts disciplines, such as music, poetry, history, philosophy, fine arts, photography, and to help students develop skills in reading, writing, critical thinking, and cross-cultural understanding.

Under the umbrella theme of "Freedom and Constraint," students spend a weekend (Friday from 1 p.m. to 11 p.m. and Saturday from 9 a.m. to 4 p.m.) in a series of activities including presentations, demonstrations, workshops, discussions, and even games that introduce them to the liberal arts, give them a sense of personal enrichment that these disciplines have to offer, and encourage them to include more liberal arts courses in their programs of study. A workbook, developed by the Humanities Division faculty, provides topical readings and written assignments to prepare students for the weekend activities and to help them assess what they have learned after the weekend. A student evaluation form helps keep the program relevant and effective.

Approximately 100 students enroll in the weekend courses each semester. They are required to complete the workbook assignments and attend and participate in all weekend activities in order to earn the four credits for these courses. All expenses are paid for by the sale of the workbook, a required text for students in the WE courses, and by the fees charged of the guests who attend the weekend.

The coordinator of the Humanities Weekend Experience program is assisted by members of the Humanities Division in teaching the three courses, in writing and revising the workbook each semester, and in acting as presenters, mentors and behind-the-scenes helpers during the weekend, which includes providing (for students and their guests) a formal dinner on Friday night, and a Continental breakfast and Pizza Party lunch on Saturday. Division members offer their time and talents each semester, without remuneration, to help make the weekend a success.

Contact:
Elaine Horne, Assistant Professor, English/Weekend Coordinator
(203) 647-6253

Manchester Community-Technical College
PO Box 1046, 60 Bidwell Street
Manchester, CT 06045-1046
Total head count enrollment-Credit: 6,134; Non-Credit: 1,054
Campuses/sites: 1; Full-time faculty: 95

SATURDAY ACADEMY

▓ *The program is an effort to excite* ▓
seventh-graders about education

School on Saturday? One hundred and twenty 7th–grade students and their parents choose to spend 10 weeks attending Saturday classes and workshops each year in Middletown, CT. They are part of a program called The Saturday Academy, sponsored through an educational partnership between Middlesex Community-Technical College, Aetna Life and Casualty, and three public middle schools.

Saturday Academy specifically works with "average" kids – those who are not receiving the benefits of school enrichment or remediation programs – in an effort to excite them about education and keep them in school. Through weekly hands-on classes in four subject areas and educational field experiences, Saturday Academy is designed to foster in students a higher level of confidence in their academic abilities; strengthen communication, math, science, and computer skills; and motivate participants to achieve future educational goals.

For parents, Saturday Academy also offers 10 full weeks of enrichment. Parents participate in a weekly workshop series covering topics ranging from developing self esteem in children to financing higher education. In these sessions, adults from three different local communities have the opportunity to discuss shared social, emotional and educational concerns.

Following their workshop, parents join their children for two academic classes. While parents enjoy the teaching and applied exercises in these classes, they most appreciate the unique opportunity to witness their child's development through first hand observation of academic skills, behavior and learning styles.

In the past eight years, Aetna Life and Casualty has funded four Saturday Academies – in Hartford and Middletown, CT., Atlanta, GA., and Washington, D.C.

Contact:
Edith A. Fuld, Coordinator, Saturday Academy Program
(203) 343-5872

Middlesex Community-Technical College
100 Training Hill Road
Middletown, CT 06457
Total head count enrollment-Credit: 3,289; Non-Credit: 860
Campuses/sites: 8; Full-time faculty: 50

LEARNING DISABILITIES PROGRAM

▓ *The long-range goal is to increase* ▓
employability and life success

Reflecting a trend at other colleges, the number and types of learning disabled students has steadily increased at Naugatuck Valley Community-Technical College from 49 identified LD students in 1988 to 107 identified LD students in 1992. In response to this need, the college sought and was awarded considerable funding to develop a comprehensive LD Program. Through the Carl Perkins Grant, there has been a dramatic increase of professional services provided to learning disabled students.

Facets of the Learning Disabilities Program at Naugatuck Valley Community-Technical College include:
 1) academic advising;
 2) early registration;
 3) vocational transfer counseling;
 4) tutoring;
 5) faculty sensitivity training;
 6) demonstration of alternative teaching models;
 7) student and parent orientations;
 8) student support groups;
 9) personal counseling; and

10) community outreach.

The program is staffed by an instructor/coordinator, a counselor and numerous tutors. The most important goal for the staff is to assure student access to vocational career programs. The long-range goal is to increase employability and life success.

As soon as students enter the program, they are placed in a tracking system that continues through successful completion of their vocational programs. The staff closely monitors program retention rates, course withdrawal rates, course and program completion rates, graduation rates and GPA. Students are also tracked for one year following graduation in an effort to provide follow-up information on the program's effectiveness and success.

During the time students remain in the program, a team approach is employed to insure each student's success. The instructor/coordinator, counselor, tutors other college offices and the student him/herself are committed to working together to achieve identified goals. At weekly

Continues on Page 122

staff meetings individual student problems are brain stormed and changes in instructional delivery are recommended. These recommendations are then shared with faculty. The most exciting development has been the creation of professional teams working together to promote excellence in teaching by improving classroom instruction and providing accommodations for learning disabled students.

Contact:
Carolyn Curtis, Coordinator, (203) 575-8052
Joseph V. Cistulli, Dean of Instruction, (203) 575-8046

Naugatuck Valley Community-Technical College
750 Chase Parkway
Waterbury, CT 06708
Total head count enrollment-Non-Credit: 2,606
Campuses/sites: 1; Full-time faculty: 125

ACADEMIC SKILLS DEVELOPMENT: INTRODUCTION TO THINKING AND LEARNING STRATEGIES

The course teaches linguistic and topical knowledge as well as rules of inference and conventional discourse

A significant improvement in retention rates is proof that teaching students four kinds of knowledge that are needed to glean meaning from written text is working at Naugatuck Valley Community-Technical College.

Such basic teaching is needed because the process of comprehending written text may not be implicit for developmental students. That process requires the reader to use a combination of what is written, what the reader already knows, and a variety of general processes such as inferencing, noting connections and organizing, to construct a reasonable account of what the author presumable intended.

Thus, Naugatuck Valley Community-Technical College's reading/learning strategies assist students in their comprehension of written text and directly instruct them in learning strategies that can increase their success in college-level courses. The course is required of all students who score within a specific range of scores on their placement test. Students may also opt to take the course, regardless of their placement test score.

Introduction to Thinking and Learning Strategies intends to directly and specifically instruct readers (thereby, forcing metacognitive knowledge) in four kinds of knowledge necessary to construct meanings for texts.

1) Linguistic knowledge or knowledge about how sentences are formed and the rules of forward and backward reference assists students to understand relationships within and between sentences. This provides a linking agent to action to object which allows the reader to construct a coherent set of events and relationships.

2) Topical knowledge, which refers to the text's subject matter, is usually automatic for expert readers but not so automatic for developmental readers. Students are given direct instruction in how to activate their prior knowledge as it relates to the text's subject matter.

3) Rules of inference also appears to function automatically for skilled readers but not so for developmental readers. Again, students are taught strategies for drawing inferences as well as recognizing when these strategies are breaking down.

4) Finally, knowledge of conventional discourse structures assist the process of text interpretation.

Academic Skills Development: Introduction to Thinking and Learning Strategies is an outgrowth of the college's traditional reading program. To ensure that the reading strategies taught in the course address students' levels of competencies, outcomes assessment for content mastery is required and a detailed item analysis for the program, as well as for individual sections of the course, are conducted. Students' scores on outcomes assessment is averaged into their final grade, thereby adding ownership on the part of students for their learning. The most crucial aspect of the program is reflected in the curriculum changes which result from item analysis.

Also, to further ensure that course objectives are being met, the course is continually evaluated by students and faculty. Faculty evaluation of content and instructional style takes the form of peer observations and team teaching. Faculty meet formally once every two weeks, informally every day to share ideas and materials and to develop a common mid-term and final exam thereby assuring that course objectives are being addressed by all instructors. All students enrolled in the course are also required to complete an extensive research project requiring complete familiarity with the college library and its data base systems. The sign of a competent student is reflected in his/her ability to access information.

The course is one of the few of its kind to utilize a customized computer program specifically designed to provide practice and reinforcement of specifically taught reading and learning strategies. A 25-station computer lab was developed for this distinctive program. The lab is staffed with an educational assistant and several tutors.

Becoming a Master Student is the textbook used for learning strategies such as test-taking techniques, improving memory and note taking. A book of readings on a wide variety of topics with high student interest is used for the reading strategies portion of the course. All reading materials/lessons are developed in-house by teams of teaching faculty.

In two years, ASD has improved the rate of student mastery of reading strategies from 35 percent to 70 percent. Even more noteworthy, a limit of only eight to 10 weeks per semester are devoted to reading strategies. Retention rates for students enrolled in the course have also significantly improved from an average of 65 percent in 1990 to 80 percent in 1992.

Contact:
Carolyn Curtis, Coordinator, (203) 575-8052
Joseph V. Cistulli, Dean of Instruction, (203) 575-8046

Naugatuck Valley Community-Technical College
750 Chase Parkway
Waterbury, CT 06708
Total head count enrollment-Non-Credit: 2,606
Campuses/sites: 1; Full-time faculty: 125

INTERPRETING FOR THE DEAF AND DEAF STUDIES

The Deaf Studies Certificate may be pursued in conjunction with other degree programs

Deaf and hard-of-hearing people who, through federal legislation have the right to equal access in all aspects of public life can pursue more opportunities – thanks partly to an increasing number of interpreters learning from Northwestern Connecticut Community-Technical College (NCCTC).

NCCTC offers an Associates of Science Degree and a Certificate in Interpreting for the Deaf. The Interpreting for the Deaf Program trains generalist interpreters to work in a variety of settings, i.e., educational, medical, employment and social services settings. The interpreter acts as a communication facilitator as well as a bilingual/bicultural mediator between deaf or hard-of-hearing persons and hearing persons.

The Interpreting for the Deaf Program is augmented by the Certificate of Deaf Studies. This program can be pursued prior to the Interpreting for the Deaf Associate in Science or Certificate Programs or it can be used as an entry into other fields working with deaf or hard-of-hearing persons. The Deaf Studies Certificate trains students in American Sign Language and Deaf Culture. This can be pursued in conjunction with other degree programs such as Human Services, Recreation, Early Childhood Education, etc.

All American Sign Language and Interpreting courses extensively use video resources and nationally recognized curricula. All aspects of the interpreting process are addressed – consecutive and simultaneous interpretation, transliteration, sign-to-voice interpretation and transliteration, oral interpretation, and ethics and professional standards.

Upon completion of the Interpreting for the Deaf Program, students are encouraged to pursue national certification from the Registry of Interpreters for the Deaf.

The program employs two full-time faculty and several adjuncts. Several of the courses are available at off-campus sites. NCCTC has also entered into a transfer articulation agreement with Central Connecticut State University. Interpreting for the Deaf graduates can transfer into CCSU's Communications Department.

Contact:
Tammy S. Cantrell, Assistant Professor
(203) 738-6390

Northwestern Connecticut Community-Technical College
Park Place
Winsted, CT 06098
Total head count enrollment-Credit: 2,053
Campuses/sites: 7; Full-time faculty: 35

MEDICAL ASSISTING

The program includes a specialized course devoted to medical laws and ethics

Medical Assisting is a career program that, at its completion, grants an Associate of Science Degree and high probability of immediate employment. Its practitioners, as with any professional field, also need more than straight medical training. That's why Northwestern Connecticut Community-Technical College's program includes a specialized course devoted to medical laws and ethics.

This program is accredited by the Committee on Allied Health Education and Accreditation (CAHEA). Graduates primarily are employed in physician's offices, ambulatory care centers or hospitals.

Medical assistants are multi-skilled professionals who function as an integral part of a health care delivery system. They can perform a variety of clinical and administrative skills.

Administrative skills include patient reception and registration, preparing and maintaining medical records, basic secretarial skills and transcription, maintaining supplies and office equipment, processing medical insurance forms and maintaining a billing-and-collection system.

Clinical duties can include taking patient histories, assisting the physician with procedures, taking vital signs, performing basic sterile procedures, maintaining sterile equipment and supplies, collecting and processing of spec-imens, performing basic laboratory tests and obtaining electrocardiograms.

The curriculum includes specific courses designed to ensure competency in all skills prior to 160 hours of field work experience. Other related courses include medical terminology, microcomputers of the medical office, human biology and microbiology.

The specialized course devoted to the discussion of medical laws and ethics relating to health professionals is a semester course divided into two components. One section is devoted to specific laws governing the actions of health professionals. The final section is designed to discuss contemporary medical issues. It is constructed to allow students to critically analyze medical issues allowing for a deeper understanding of the dilemmas that face many patients as well as health care professionals. Students have opportunities to discuss options and express views of issues. Listening skills are enhanced by hearing what another is saying without passing judgment.

The Medical Assisting Career Program continues to grow each year. The college has made a commitment to offer courses both on a day and evening basis to allow for part-time as well as full-time students.

Contact:
Barbara Berger, Assistant Professor
(203) 738-6378

Northwestern Connecticut Community-Technical College
Park Place
Winsted, CT 06098
Total head count enrollment-Credit: 2,053
Campuses/sites: 7; Full-time faculty: 35

CENTER FOR TEACHING

Faculty members help each other improve their teaching effectiveness through observation and student interviews

Exploring a variety of innovative techniques and strategies for educating a diverse population is the focus of Norwalk Community-Technical College's Center for Teaching (CFT). Established in 1987, the CFT serves as a testing ground for new ideas and acts as a clearinghouse for information in journals and books on instructional techniques for college learning.

Each year, the CFT sponsors a series of lectures by prominent educators on issues related to teaching and learning, attended by at least 100 members of the college's professional staff. Faculty and staff at the other state community-technical colleges are invited.

The CFT at NCTC also sponsors, in cooperation with the statewide Center for Teaching, Teaching Partners, a program in which faculty members pair off to help each other improve their teaching effectiveness. Each partner observes his counterpart and is in turn observed in a classroom setting. After interviewing each other's students, the partners can compare notes on what students liked about the teacher's presentation, his teaching style and overall effectiveness in holding the student's attention and interest.

CFT also provided support for NCTC's participation in the Sears Project at Columbia University. Under this two-year grant, NCTC was one of six colleges chosen to participate in a partnership consortium with Teachers

College to train a team of faculty from each institution to promote more effective teaching aimed at the diverse population of students found in today's classrooms.

The Integrated Skills Reinforcement Program focuses on development of teaching strategies that incorporate all language skills – reading, writing, speaking and listening – for content mastery. Each instructor prepares a learning guide to assist students with employing these strategies in covering course content. These language-based activities are designed to encourage critical thinking and learning that can move with the student across the curriculum. These strategies improve student learning as well as the ability to communicate and build skills to last a lifetime.

According to the ISR chairperson Arlette Werner, faculty "have already made some changes in course outlines, in their teaching and in the format of their testing. One of the strengths of this program is the immediate application to the classroom. There is no substitute for the group process that we experience with ISR. It is my privilege to be part of the ISR program. It continues to enrich my teaching skills and it feeds my teaching soul.

The concept of the CFT was developed by President William H. Schwab. Funding comes through state grants and the college foundation. Faculty take full responsibility for implementing the programs.

The CFT has been a powerful stimulus for faculty morale and performance, which in turn leads to greater student satisfaction. Between spring 1988 and spring 1993, returning student enrollment grew by more than 20 percent. The professional demands and commitment that the CFT has engendered challenged faculty and motivated changes.

Contact:
William H. Schwab, President
(203) 857-7001

Norwalk Community-Technical College
188 Richards Avenue
Norwalk, CT 06854-1655
Total head count enrollment-Credit: 5,015; Non-Credit: 4,500
Campuses/sites: 1; Full-time faculty: 77

TECHWAY

The program helps recruit students interested in such things as underwater robotics, mechanics and electronics.

Norwalk Community-Technical College's Techway program has forged a partnership between faculty and staff from high school and college to ease the transition for high school students who wish to pursue a degree in technical education. Thanks to a $25,000 Carl D. Perkins Tech-Prep Education grant, the program helps recruit students interested in careers in technology and also prepare them for technological studies.

The Summertech 1992 program, part of the Techway project, consisted of two sessions, each of two weeks duration, attended by 40 high school students. Four NCTC faculty in the Division of Technology were involved in conducting the program. The first summer course introduced students to underwater robotics, mechanics and architecture. The second summer course involved computers and electronics.

During the academic year, the Techway committee meets to review curriculum so that vocational and technical courses in the high schools can be realigned with the NCTC curricula to provide a smooth transition from high school to college.

During the 1992-1993 academic year, high school students were enrolled in the realigned courses. The college staff met with high school faculty to provide feedback on Summertech. Continuing curriculum revision will involve the faculty at the college and the high schools.

Contact:
John Fisher, Dean of Technology
(203) 857-7309

Norwalk Community-Technical College
188 Richards Avenue
Norwalk, CT 06854-1655
Total head count enrollment-Credit: 5,015; Non-Credit: 4,500
Campuses/sites: 1; Full-time faculty: 77

ASSESSMENT OF PRIOR LEARNING (APL)

Students learn how to prepare a portfolio based on their learning

The Mohegan Campus of Three Rivers Community Technical College in Norwich, Connecticut, offers a unique and innovative program for adult learners. The program, Assessment of Prior Learning, is the only one of its kind in the state which offers an actual course in the preparation of a portfolio based on a student's learning. The course consists of teaching a student how to prepare his/her portfolio. The student receives four college credits upon completion of the course. He/she then may submit the portfolio for evaluation to a committee of college evaluators. As a result of the evaluation a student may receive up to 30 credits which may be used toward a Three Rivers degree.

The retention rate for the students who take the portfolio development course and submit a portfolio is impressive and interesting. Ninety-eight percent of all the students who enroll in the course complete it and submit a portfolio for evaluation. Of that 98 percent, 95 percent continue at the college and complete their Associate's degree. Of that 95 percent, 89 percent transfer to a four-year school.

Contact:
Licia E. Tronco, Director of Assessment
(203) 886-1931

Three Rivers Community-Technical College–Mohegan Campus
Mahan Drive
Norwich, CT 06360
Total head count enrollment-Credit: 3,220
Campuses/sites: 5; Full-time faculty: 42

NUCLEAR ENGINEERING TECHNOLOGY

When established, it was the only such program in the Northeast and one of six nationwide

Three Rivers Community/Technical College – Thames Valley Campus encourages minorities and women to break traditional barriers and enter the field of Nuclear Engineering Technology. Developed and sponsored jointly by the Connecticut State Community-Technical College System and Northeast Utilities, the program is a perceived outgrowth of the Three Mile Island and Chernobyl nuclear "incidents," which led to the correct assessment that the federal Nuclear Regulatory Commission (NRC) would require at least a two-year Associate's Degree for all nuclear power plant watch-standing personnel by 1991.

With no such available two-year nuclear program existing in the entire Northeast, the Nuclear Engineering Technology Program at Thames Valley State Technical College became only the sixth such program nationally. With strong guidance from its 16-member Nuclear Advisory Committee (NAC), a TAC/ABET-accreditable curriculum was developed, satisfying three major goals: 1) a strong technical program which would fully satisfy the NRC's academic licensing requirements for commercial nuclear power personnel; 2) a recognized, accredited two-year technology program which would prepare the graduate for an easy transition into a four-year baccalaureate engineering degree; and 3) a quality nuclear education program which would allow the graduate to successfully find employment in any of the numerous nuclear science or engineering-related businesses in the Northeast.

The nuclear program permits only 25 full-time students to enter each year. Of these, up to 15 positions are set aside for full scholarships offered by corporate members of our NAC. These full scholarships provide: 1) all tuition and student fees; 2) all textbook costs; 3) a monthly stipend of $400; and 4) guaranteed summer internship employment for both summers at one of our NAC member's facilities. Most importantly, the student incurs no obligations by accepting a scholarship. Upon graduation he or she is free to pursue any educational or employment goal.

To date, there have been 127 graduates from the program. The majority, some 74 percent, have opted to immediately accept employment in the nuclear field, while the remaining 26 percent have gone on to work toward their baccalaureate degree. Virtually all of these continuing students have opted for the Nuclear Engineering program at the University of Lowell or Mechanical Engineering programs at the University of Connecticut or the University of New Haven. As our NAC membership includes the respective department chairmen from these three ABET-accredited universities, our graduates can complete their baccalaureate work with two additional years and one summer of continued study. Not only have our graduates successfully completed baccalaureate degree programs, but also several have gone on to receive their master's degrees in Nuclear Engineering at the University of Lowell, and one is now enrolled in a nuclear doctoral program at MIT.

As the nuclear industry work force has historically been comprised primarily of white male, ex-military personnel, the college has made a concerted effort to encourage women and minorities in this demanding technical field. The College is proud of its results, as this effort addresses the number one recommendation as put forth in "Building Communities" (an AACJC-sponsored national teleconference held November, 1980). An average 21 percent of the graduates are women or minorities. Similarly, the degree program has been fully expanded into the evenings to permit the full-time worker the opportunity to return to college to obtain their degree – currently some 122 part-time evening students. The program to date enjoys a phenomenal success rate. All of our continuing four-year degree program students have performed well, and the employer demand for our graduates far exceeds our graduation numbers even in these recessionary times. Once employed, our graduates have also documented a positive track record in their chosen employment field.

The program has just undergone its second TAC/ABET accreditation visit in November 1991, and the college remains the only TAC/ABET-accredited two-year nuclear degree program in the country. The nuclear program has been designated as a Center of Excellence within the state of Connecticut. Our nuclear program was selected as the best two-year degree program in the country in 1992 by the National Council of Instructional Administrators in their Exemplary Program competition.

In December 1991, the college accepted delivery of an advanced principles nuclear reactor simulator. This is a one-of-a-kind, state-of-the-art simulator that provides an unparalleled education tool. It becomes the ultimate "what-if" device, that permits the student to study any aspect of a Pressurized Water Reactor (PWR) and understand their operational control on the safe operation of that nuclear plant. Since this is a simulator and not a real reactor, nuclear "accidents" lead to a better knowledge of nuclear engineering technology not environmental catastrophe. A $1.5-million nuclear laboratory was formally dedicated on February 13, 1992. A recent TAC/ABET evaluator was so impressed with the curriculum/laboratory equipment that he said it was the most comprehensive two-year program he had ever seen, and compared it quite favorably with four-year programs.

We feel this nuclear program is the premier nuclear Associate's Degree in the nation, and one of the most noteworthy two-year programs of any type. This is due to the documented success of our graduates and our reciprocal cooperation with the nuclear industry and academia through our scholarship program and the support of our Nuclear Advisory Committee.

Contact:
James Sherrard
(203) 886-0177

Three Rivers Community-Technical College–Thames Valley Campus
574 New London Turnpike
Norwich, CT 06360-6598
Total head count enrollment-Credit: 1,064
Campuses/sites: 5; Full-time faculty: 34

THREE RIVERS COMMUNITY-TECHNICAL COLLEGE–THAMES VALLEY CAMPUS

COMPUTER INTEGRATED MANUFACTURING (CIM)

❈ *The program boosts the regional economy* ❈
and provides state-of-the-art training

Thames Valley, one of only 50 colleges and universities across the country to participate in an IBM/CIM in Higher Education Alliance, agreed to develop and teach computer integrated manufacturing courses, seminars and curricula in return for $500,000 in hardware and software. IBM made this commitment to ensure a well-trained work force and to promote the CIM concept as a means of survival and success to businesses of all sizes.

Although Thames Valley has made a commitment to CIM prior to its membership in the CIM alliance, the honor certainly gave additional impetus to concerted efforts in focusing on expedient CIM course development.

A CIM team was subsequently formed from TVSTC faculty and administration, and IBM branch personnel in Hamden, Connecticut. Approximately 36 seminars were developed as prescribed by IBM needs. Course seminars were initially presented to IBM'ers and their customers, and were later available to area businesses.

CIM courses were then incorporated into the Manufacturing Engineering Technology curriculum. Graduates of this associate's degree, a TAC/ABET accredited program, are trained technicians equipped to design and operate "factories of tomorrow."

In October 1990, our CIM lab was dedicated. Equipped with state-of-the-art equipment in robotics, the plant floor capabilities gave further opportunities for hands on instruction. Because of IBM's initial investment, state bond monies and grants were forthcoming to finance the new lab.

Because of the CIM initiative, Thames Valley has provided special apprentice programs for 150-200 Pratt &

Continues on Page 128

Whitney employees, assisted in implementation of the CIM concept in small businesses in the area, and have earned a reputation as an excellent provider of CIM/Manufacturing instruction.

This program is exemplary because it provides a real boost to business in southeastern Connecticut and western Rhode Island during very difficult economic times. The college is providing trained technicians and business consulting opportunities for those who need it most.

Contact:
Harry Ogden
(203) 886-0177

Three Rivers Community-Technical College–Thames Valley Campus
574 New London Turnpike
Norwich, CT 06360-6598
Total head count enrollment-Credit: 1,064
Campuses/sites: 5; Full-time faculty: 34

NURSING

The college is hospital-based, giving students valuable insight into their future career

The single-purpose mission of the Wilcox College of Nursing focuses on the education of the nurse in an environment approximating the health care system in which the nurse will function upon graduation. This is possible largely because the college in 1991 was licensed as the first hospital-based college of nursing in the State of Connecticut to offer a program in nursing leading to an associate of science degree.

The program in nursing prepares the individual for a career in nursing as a professional practitioner. In addition, the program establishes the foundation for graduates to continue their education in a senior college.

The general education courses supporting the program in nursing are contracted from the local community college. This unique arrangement effectively utilizes community resources by bringing private and public institutions of higher education together in a sharing modality. In addition to the arrangement with the community college, graduates of the College of Nursing can complete their baccalaureate degree in nursing through an articulated arrangement with an area state university.

The student has the opportunity to enroll in either full-time or part-time study, as the college offers the nursing program through a day or evening division. The program of study for full-time study is two years in length and for part-time study is 3-1/2 years in length. This innovative and flexible educational environment recognizes the diverse backgrounds of the student population.

The graduate of the program utilizes the nursing process, critical thinking, decision making, collaboration, advocacy and delegation in the role of provider of care and manager of care. In addition to maintaining a commitment to continuous learning and self-development as a member of the nursing discipline.

The program in nursing has 10 full-time and two part-time nursing faculty members. The traditional academic and student services are maintained to provide the students with the best education.

The Wilcox College of Nursing is accredited by the State of Connecticut Department of Higher Education and has candidacy status from the New England Association of Schools and Colleges. The program in nursing is approved by the Connecticut State Board of Nurse Examiners.

Contact:
Dean for Academic Affairs
(203) 344-6402

Wilcox College of Nursing
28 Crescent Street
Middletown, CT 06457
Total head count enrollment-Credit: 200
Campuses/sites: 1; Full-time faculty: 11

ECONOMIC DEVELOPMENT

*Industrial training reaches current Delaware companies
and those seeking to relocate*

With four campuses strategically located throughout the state, Delaware Tech provides education and training to all sectors of the population. One of its hallmarks is the industrial training that takes place for numerous businesses and industries. It is not unusual for Delaware Tech to serve more than 400 corporations in the course of a year, and train or retrain more than 5,000 employees. The companies served are both large and small – from thousands of employees to just a handful.

Delaware Tech has built a reputation of quality so that when corporations have a need to be addressed, they turn to Delaware Tech. Delaware Tech also has a close relationship with the Delaware Development Office, which is the arm of government responsible to retain businesses in the state as well as to seek the relocation of other industries to Delaware. The office helps to identify needs in business and industry, and then contacts are made with the Delaware Tech campus in close proximity to the plant site, or with another Delaware Tech campus that has particular expertise to satisfy the identified need.

Delaware Tech also has a close relationship with the statewide Private Industry Council (PIC), and is the largest provider of services in partnership with the statewide PIC. Additionally Delaware Tech has a unique agreement with the American Institute of Banking (AIB). The AIB partnership is one in which a combination of AIB courses and Delaware Tech courses are conducted to produce an associate degree program in banking. With regard to industrial affiliations, the college recently completed a massive retraining program at the General Motors assembly plant in northern Delaware, where Delaware Tech was the exclusive provider. More than 4,500 employees were retrained during a five-year period with $6-million in funding. Examples of special activities that take place in support of the corporate community include a certified Asbestos Abatement program and a Burn Lab, which is part of the Fire Science Technology program, allowing for product testing in a controlled environment. Each of the campuses of Delaware Tech has an industrial training division, and each division has been responsive to requests for assistance from business and industry. It is anticipated that these divisions will be asked to do even more in the future, as industries recognize the cost-effectiveness and quality of Delaware Tech's training programs.

Contact:
Thomas S. Kubala, President
(302) 739-4053

Delaware Technical & Community College
P.O. Box 897
Dover, DE 19903
Total head count enrollment-Credit: 17,000; Non-Credit: 19,000
Campuses/sites: 4; Full-time faculty: 236

ALLIED HEALTH PROGRAMS

▩ The 14 programs, from Dental Hygiene to Ultrasound Technology, ▩
produce graduates who are in great demand

Delaware Tech has taken on the responsibility of helping to make the residents of the State of Delaware healthier. The college has always been responsive to the needs of the state and its thousands of citizens, and has kept its programs up to date with contemporary content and equipment. Of particular note has been the development of several health-related technologies to address current and future medical needs. These programs are:

- Dental Assistant°;
- Dental Hygiene;
- Histotechnician;
- Medical Laboratory Technology;
- Medical Office Assistant;
- Medical Transcriptionist°;
- Nuclear Medicine Technology;
- Associate Degree Nursing;
- Occupational Therapy Assistant;
- Practical Nursing;
- Physical Therapist Assistant;
- Radiologic Technology;
- Respiratory Therapy; and
- Ultrasound Technology

All of the programs are AAS degree offerings, except for the two one-year diploma programs indicated with an asterisk (°). Graduates of these programs have been extremely successfully in passing national exams to obtain licensure where that is required in order to carry out job responsibilities. In addition, the graduates are in great demand by employers in Delaware and other states in the East.

Contact:
Thomas S. Kubala, President
(302) 739-4053

Delaware Technical & Community College
P.O. Box 897
Dover, DE 19903
Total head count enrollment-Credit: 17,000; Non-Credit: 19,000
Campuses/sites: 4; Full-time faculty: 236

INSTITUTE FOR SPACE TECHNOLOGY

The college offers educational and training opportunities to employees of NASA and its contractors at the Kennedy Space Center

Brevard Community College has contributed to the success of America's Space Program in many unique ways and BCC's Space Technology Program is the latest such way. In the words of former Kennedy Space Center Director, Forrest S. McCartney, "Brevard Community College has rightfully earned its reputation as one of the nation's very best community colleges. It has certainly served Brevard County, Kennedy Space Center and America's space program with distinction and vigor."

Through the Institute for Space Technology, Brevard Community College offers educational and training opportunities to the employees of NASA and its contractors at the Kennedy Space Center, Cape Canaveral Air Force Station, and the employees of local high-technology business and industry. In cooperation with NASA, the contractors and the private sector industry of Brevard County, the Institute utilizes only the best instructor-experts in their respective fields as adjunct classroom faculty. In addition to the traditional credit programs, students, through the Institute, have available a wide range of BCC support services including enrollment, placement testing, on-site registration, student development and program advisement. Day and evening courses are available not only at Kennedy Space Center, but also at numerous industry sites throughout the county. Three state-of-the-art programs exist within the Institute: Quality Assurance Technology, Logistics Systems Technology and Space Engineering Technology. Additionally, there also is

an Associate of Arts degree in Quality Assurance Technology for those interested in pursuing upper division studies. A few significant accomplishments of the past year include:

- expanding the area of the Institute focus beyond the confines of the Kennedy Space Center to embrace all parts of Brevard County and coordinating two Institute programs, Quality Assurance Technology and Logistics Systems Technology;
- relocating the Institute to our Melbourne Campus to provide broader county coverage and promotional base; providing full-time student services at two locations on the Space Center; one in the NASA headquarters area and the other at the populous Launch Complex 39; and
- delivering non-credit training courses to NASA employees in mathematics, statistical process control, practical TQM measurements, benchmarking and goal-setting in direct support of the space agency's implementation of Total Quality Management and Structured Services.

The Institute has been recognized nationally on CNN and at a U.S. Congressional Hearing on Science and Mathematics Education. As Forrest S. McCartney said, "Today Brevard Community College continues to meet the demands of the space program here in Brevard County through its high professional standards and innovative curriculum."

Contact:
Donald Pulket
(407) 459-3879

Brevard Community College
1519 Clearlake Road
Cocoa, FL 32922
Total head count enrollment-Credit: 15,000; Non-Credit: 50,000
Campuses/sites: 5; Full-time faculty: 232

DIVERSITY PROGRAMS

In three years, the number of black first-time students at the college increased 133 percent and overall black enrollment rose by 41 percent

Brevard Community College's diversity programs range from Women-In-Transition to the Center for Career Development and BCC's Office of Minority Recruitment, Retention and Advisement.

BCC's President, Dr. Maxwell C. King, issued a moral challenge to all employees to join him in this effort to make BCC one of America's most committed colleges to diversity. At the time he stated that all employees should

help him "for one single reason: It is the right thing to do." Dr. King also met with community leaders through out the county and asked their help. The results speak for themselves.

In three years, the number of BCC's black students in their first time in college increased 133 percent, the overall black enrollment increased by 41 percent, and degree

Continues on Page 132

completions of black students increased 25 percent. The percentage of BCC employees who are black increased by 14 percent during the same period.

One of the highest honors received by BCC was that of the National Association for the Advancement of Colored People (NAACP) honoring BCC President Maxwell C. King for "his lifelong profile in courage in standing up for blacks." Said the NAACP officers: "BCC, under the personal initiatives of Dr. King, is one of the most effective colleges in the nation in providing financial aid for minorities."

The National Association of Community College Trustees (ACCT) recognized BCC as "one of the two most outstanding community colleges in the nation in terms of providing equal opportunity." BCC received one of two first annual ACCT Kennedy Equity Awards. According to ACCT Executive Director, Ray Taylor, "Brevard was chosen because it has established an exemplary record of achievement in providing opportunity for all individuals... BCC has one of America's most effective financial aid programs for minorities... your WENDI program is one of the country's very best in providing opportunities for women... and your president, Maxwell King, is among the nation's most respected CEOs for his courage in standing up for minority rights."

Taylor also said, "The efforts of BCC's president and board of trustees are inspiring and well above and beyond the norm in the area of equity."

Contact:
Maxwell C. King, President
(407) 632-1111, ext. 2000

Brevard Community College
1519 Clearlake Road
Cocoa, FL 32922
Total headcount enrollment-Credit: 15,000; Non-Credit: 50,000
Campuses/sites: 5; Full-time faculty: 232

AVIATION TECHNOLOGY

The program includes components in aviation administration, aviation maintenance management and professional pilot training

Broward Community College is the only community college in Florida teaching a tripartite Associate of Science program, preparing students for employment in one of the nation's largest and most exciting industries. Air transportation and its allied activities are growing at a phenomenal rate and economic forecasts indicate this growth will continue in the next decade. Opportunities for management and technically trained personnel are almost limitless, especially in South Florida, where the tourist industry and airlines are inextricably linked.

The components of Brevard's Aviation Technology program include aviation administration, aviation maintenance management and professional pilot training.

The aviation administration program prepares students for employment or advancement in management positions or as air traffic controllers. The aviation management program leads to Federal Aviation Administration airframe and power plant certification and employment within the general aviation sector. The professional pilot program prepares students for FAA certification as private pilot, commercial pilot, instrument rating and flight instructor.

The college has broken ground on its South Campus for a $3.7-million Aviation Institute, which should be complete by August 1994, it will contain a 7,000-foot hangar, flight simulation wing, classroom wing, office wing and meteorology laboratory. The increase in space provided by the new facility should allow the aviation technology program to double its student enrollment from its present 200.

Contact:
Ursula Davidson, Department Head
(305) 963-8910

Broward Community College
225 East Las Olas Boulevard
Fort Lauderdale, FL 33301
Total head count enrollment-Credit: 38,000; Non-Credit: 13,000
Campuses/sites: 6; Full-time faculty: 300

TEACHER EDUCATION ALLIANCE

This joint teacher education program operates with Atlantic University and Broward County Public Schools

Approximately 70 percent of Florida's public school teachers begin their college preparation in a state community college. The Teacher Education Alliance is a joint teacher education program operated by Broward Community College, Florida, Atlantic University and the Broward County Public Schools.

After a year of planning, the program enrolled 14 students at BCC for the 1992-93 school year. The program was slated to enroll about 50 students for the 1993-94 term.

"The main curriculum themes are technology, multicultural education and the ability to use varied teaching strategies," said Dr. Suzanne Kinzer, the Alliance's executive director.

The program also puts considerable emphasis in placing the prospective teachers into classroom and tutorial situations earlier than other traditional teacher education programs.

"Instead of waiting for their junior and senior years, we're putting the students into the classrooms from the beginning," said Dr. Kinzer.

TEA instructors at all levels are hand-picked for their assignments, both for knowledge of the subject matter and their ability to inspire and interact with the prospective teachers.

The TEA program is designed so its graduates will be able to conduct classroom research, use reflective teaching practices, obtain a level of teacher readiness that does not require initial retraining, recognize the need for parental involvement in the classroom situation, and be technologically literate and able to use technology in instructional settings.

Contact:
Suzanne M. Kinzer, Executive Director
(305) 760-7344

Broward Community College
225 East Las Olas Boulevard
Fort Lauderdale, FL 33301
Total headcount enrollment-Credit: 38,000; Non-Credit: 13,000
Campuses/sites: 6; Full-time faculty: 300

ARTIST-IN-RESIDENCE

An essential element of the program is a downtown studio in a centrally located, storefront setting

Central Florida Community College's artist-in-residence program is a prime example of the cultural activity a community college can sponsor to present a powerful resource learning while meeting community needs and serving as an image-builder for the college.

CFCC became involved with the artist-in-residence concept through a grant program partially funded by the Florida Department of State (Division of Cultural Affairs) and the Florida Department of Education (Division of Community Colleges) in August 1991. The intent was for the artist-in-residence to work as a community arts resource and cultural ambassador for the college.

The artist-in-residence is expected to provide one-on-one exposure to art and art form in the community. The community college provides a grassroots approach to an individual community, and the artisan works among the people. Through the diverse community contacts afforded by the college, artists-in-residence can touch the lives of individuals as yet untouched by the arts.

An essential element to the program is a downtown studio in a centrally located, storefront setting. Downtown development organizations are happy to make empty, deteriorating facilities available, usually on a rent-free basis. Improvements and positive activity often create more interest and provide an incentive for additional activity in the downtown area. While revitalizing the downtown area of any city, the location also enables those that would not normally have access to the arts a central location within which to converge to partake of the arts.

Artists-in-residence must come into contact with as many area public school children as possible in their educational settings. As students learned from the artist-in-residence, they developed a desire to go to the artist's downtown studio for further interaction. In many cases, parents accompanied those children which further expanded the impact of the program within the community.

Continues on Page 134

This interaction helps to fulfill (in part) the goal of increasing the cultural awareness not only of the public student, but also that of the parents and surrounding community. Many citizens had their first contact and interaction with the college through the artist-in-residence program. More than 10,000 people in CFCC's service area had some exposure to this cultural awareness venture.

The community college has also gained from this experience. New and innovative relationships were formed with the public schools and other community agencies and organizations. The college was able to act on one of the institution's strategic goals: "To expand the role of the college in the cultural life of the community."

The artist-in-residence functions without controversy, produces good relations with the community, and enhances the college's visibility and image. The program manages to be all this and still provides immeasurable assets, such as impacting young children into possible career avenues, providing the surrounding community with cultural opportunities, and possible economic improvements to this nation's cities and towns.

Contact:
Oel G. Wingo, Assistant to the President, (904) 237-2111
John Briggs, Artist in Residence, (904) 732-6119

Central Florida Community College
PO Box 1388
Ocala, FL 32678
Total headcount enrollment-Credit: 10,000; Non-Credit: 10,000
Campuses/sites: 3; Full-time faculty: 110

RADIATION PROTECTION

Though the oldest AS degree program in the United States, the program remains in the forefront of enrolling equal numbers of men and women

Central Florida Community College's Radiation Protection program, formerly male-dominated, now boasts an equal enrollment of men and women.

Implemented in 1962, the Radiation Technology Program (now the Radiation Protection Program) came into existence in response to the need to monitor the environment as a result of the rapid expansion of nuclear material in new and ever-changing ways.

The program remains the oldest AS degree program in the United States, the only Radiation Program at a community college in the state of Florida, and recognized as one of the three outstanding programs among all colleges in the United States. The Radiation Protection Technology Program provides education to international students from many countries such as Brazil, Finland and England, while continuing to educate the students of the United States. Their governments and other private companies often refer these students. Students seeking a higher degree must obtain an AA degree, and then may receive a bachelors, masters or doctorate in health physics. Students receiving an AS degree have not had any problems obtaining positions. The only remaining challenge the students face is being able to graduate before being recruited. The average salary for a graduate is $30,000. The program also boasts a 90 percent or higher placement rate.

The Radiation Protection Technology Program prepares graduates for employment in various areas concerned with monitoring radiation of the environment. Students learn monitoring techniques to ensure that recommended concentration levels of radiation are not being exceeded. They are also trained to collect, prepare and analyze samples of radioactivity and to collect and analyze data regarding human exposure in radioisotope laboratories, nuclear fuel processing facilities, particle accelerator complexes, and nuclear reactor installations. Graduates may work in nuclear power plants, hospitals, shipbuilding facilities, for the government, or anywhere radioactive substances are extensively used.

The program has an active advisory committee consisting of individuals from the Department of Radiation Protection, nuclear power plants and a number of small businesses. This committee ensures that the program offers a current, constantly upgraded curriculum. The newest addition to the curriculum assists graduates to work in restoration and reclamation of soil in power plants.

Contact:
Rhonda Rawls
(904) 237-2111, ext. 376

Central Florida Community College
PO Box 1388
Ocala, FL 32678
Total headcount enrollment-Credit: 10,000; Non-Credit: 10,000
Campuses/sites: 3; Full-time faculty: 110

SCIENCE DEMONSTRATION PROGRAM

A decline in standardized test scores in science prompted the college to take entertaining demonstrations to area schoolchildren

Chipola Junior College sponsors entertaining demonstrations to stimulate an interest in science among students in area schools, grades 4 through 10.

This strategy resulted from national testing results that has shown a decline in standardized test scores in the area of science. Enrollments show fewer students choosing to study in the area of both pure and applied science.

It is believed that early stimulation of both teachers and students by the use of selected demonstrations in the area of chemistry and physics will lead to an increased awareness of the need for study in both the physical and biological sciences.

A non-exhaustive list of attention-getting and entertaining demonstrations was selected and tested. Area schools were then contacted via letter outlining the type of program available and offering it to them on a cost-free basis. Mutually agreed upon date and time of presentation was made. The date and time of presentation is dependent upon the schedule and availability of the presenter. Materials used were included in the physical science

budget for the initial year (1992-93) of the presentations.

Following the presentations, a letter requesting comments from teachers participating was left with each teacher. Some teachers, in addition to their own personal responses encouraged their students to write expressing their reaction to the presentations. These comments are available for review upon request from the department head of the natural science department.

Initial comments have been very favorable. Requests for a return engagement later in the year with a different presentation have been made. Most of the presentations have been devised to produce smoke, flame or explosions. An effort has been made in the talk given with the presentation to explain in simple terms what is occurring and in most cases, to tie it in with current or recent past events. A list of demonstrations, materials needed, methods of preparation and safety precautions is being prepared to be given to elementary teachers on request. The current presenter is Crayton C. Coleman, half-time instructor in the natural sciencedepartment.

Contact:
Lou Cleveland
(904) 526-2761

Chipola Junior College
3094 Indian Circle
Marianna, FL 32446-2053
Total headcount enrollment-Credit: 4,423; Non-Credit: 4,036
Campuses/sites: 1; Full-time faculty: 71

LITERATURE/LANGUAGE FESTIVAL

The festival is for high school students, who compete in writing, speech, oral interpretation, grammar/mechanics/usage, literature and humanities

The Chipola Junior College Literature/Language Festival improves articulation between area high schools and Chipola Junior College, provides a forum for communication between college faculty and high school teachers and provides high school students with information about special CJC offerings. In addition, the academically talented students and their teachers receive recognition for excellence in the humanities.

The CJC Literature/Language Festival, begun in 1991, is an interscholastic competition consisting of six contests: writing, speech, oral interpretation, grammar / mechanics / usage, literature and humanities. Participants in the festival must be currently enrolled juniors and seniors from one of the high schools in the CJC district. The districts include Calhoun, Holmes, Jackson, Liberty and Washington counties. A single school may have a maximum of 12 contestants participating in the festival. Contests are first

held on the high school campuses to determine which contestants will compete on the college campus. Recognition at CJC is given to first, second and third places and honorable mentions in each contest. Thus widespread learning and inquiry in the humanities is rewarded at the high school and the college.

The festival schedule begins with a general session for all participants where mechanics of the competition is explained. Then students disperse to compete in the individual contests. The writing contest consists of an impromptu expository essay written in one 90-minute period and based on a choice made from three topics provided at the contest. The essay is evaluated on specified criteria by a panel of college faculty. The speech contest consists of an impromptu three-minute speech on a randomly selected subject provided by the judges three

Continues on Page 136

minutes before presentation. Speeches are evaluated on specified criteria by a panel of college faculty. The oral interpretation contest consists of a two- to three-minute oral interpretation of a literary work of the contestant's own choosing. Oral interpretations are evaluated on specified criteria by a panel of college faculty. The grammar/mechanics/usage contest consists of a multiple-choice, 50-item examination. Time allotted for the exam is 60 minutes. The literature contest consists of a multiple-choice, 100-item examination covering American and English literature. Time allotted for the exam is 60 minutes. The humanities contest consists of a multiple-choice, 50-item exam covering art, art history, architecture, music and World literature. This exam is also 60 minutes.

Contact:
Sarah Clemmons
(904) 526-2761, ext. 213

Chipola Junior College
3094 Indian Circle
Marianna, FL 32446-2053
Total headcount enrollment-Credit: 4,423; Non-Credit: 4,036
Campuses/sites: 1; Full-time faculty: 71

SOUTHEAST MUSEUM OF PHOTOGRAPHY

Exhibitions have included work by such masters as Arthur Rothstein, Robert Frank, Gordon Parks and Sally Mann

The Southeast Museum of Photography is a community-oriented educational institution that fulfills the college's mission through the presentation of exhibitions, lectures, workshops and symposia that address all aspects of photography – both as art and as a source of information. Programs provide students and non-students with access to a wide range of images and ideas and the opportunity for self-directed and self-paced learning in a non-competitive environment.

The museum began in 1980 as a modest series of one-person exhibitions designed to complement an ambitious pro gram of lectures and symposia featuring photographers who spoke about their work. In 1984, the first of several gifts of photographs was made to the college by a private collector in recognition of excellence in public programs. In 1992, the college opened the museum's new building featuring more than 7,000 square feet of exhibition space, state-of-the-art storage facilities, a photography research library and conference/classroom facilities. In addition to a year-round schedule of exhibitions and lectures, the museum presents K-12 programming, weekend parent-child activities, short-term community workshops in photographic techniques, and produces catalogues, a newsletter and other publications. The museum offers courses in Museum Studies that combine practical and theoretical approaches to work in a museum or gallery. Internships, through the department of art or the department of photography, are also available.

Exhibitions have included work by such masters as Arthur Rothstein, Robert Frank, Gordon Parks and Sally Mann, as well as shows that have explored new concepts of landscape, the photojournalism of the Gulf War, photographic post-modernism and the historical depiction of Florida's Seminoles. Living artists, women and artists of color are aggressively scheduled for both exhibitions and programs. Regional audiences are drawn from a radius of several hundred miles, and the museum's status as a tourist attraction is increasing national and international visitation to Daytona Beach.

The museum earns income through workshop tuition and through the production of exhibitions that are rented to other institutions. It has been successful, as well, with grant support on the local, state, national and international levels. Community support is equally strong, with a friend's group of several hundred, who donate both money and time to museum operations.

As one of the college's major outreach efforts, the museum educates, informs and entertains its growing constituency, while maintaining its national place as one of the only museums of photography and the only one associated with a community college.

Contact:
Alison Nordstrom, Director
(904) 254-4469

Daytona Beach Community College
PO Box 2811
Daytona Beach, FL 32120-2811
Total headcount enrollment-Credit: 19,414; Non-Credit: 18,608
Campuses/sites: 5; Full-time faculty: 214

PROGRAM FOR APPLIED ACADEMICS AND TECHNICAL STUDIES

A ladder concept was used to allow students to choose between employment and future education at multiple completion points

The Program for Applied Academics and Technical Studies, offered by Daytona Beach Community College and the Volusia County School System, develops an effective and efficient delivery system of career planning and preparation for students, and provides an improved structure for supplying the business sector with a well-prepared work force.

Guiding principles are that students should be prepared academically as well as technically so that continuation of education can be encouraged. A ladder concept was used that allows students to choose between employment and future education at multiple completion points. Also guiding the development was a belief that students interested in technical programs generally learn academic subjects better in an applied manner. That is, when practical concepts are taught in a real world setting, they are more easily understood.

Major goals of the program begun in the 1991-92 academic year are: 1) to establish a four-way partnership between the college, the school system, business and industry, and local government agencies; 2) to offer coordinated career exploration and planning; 3) to offer innovative delivery methods; 4) to build articulated programs; and 5) to provide coordinated curriculum planning.

Major components of the program are: 1) student and parent career education, planning and goal-setting beginning at the middle school level and continuing throughout high school; 2) a joint steering committee (college, schools, business, local government); 3) articulated 2 + 2 programs; 4) innovative delivery mechanisms such as dual enrollment and distance learning through the college's interactive instructional TV system; 5) college/school instructor discipline groups that work together on an ongoing basis; 6) student mentoring; 7) instructor and counselor upgrading through internships with local businesses and government agencies; 8) coordinated counseling programs; and 9) cooperative work study.

During the planning stage, the Program for Applied Academics and Technical studies was presented to education, business and community groups in a series of input sessions and workshops. As a result, a great deal of support from the community has been achieved and the working relationship between the college and the school system has been significantly improved. Most importantly, students will now have a coordinated, sensible program of career preparation available to them – one that prepares them for employment at multiple levels, but that simultaneously encourages them to continue their education as far as possible.

Contact:
Howard Turner, Dean of Technologies
(904) 255-8131, ext. 3702

Daytona Beach Community College
PO Box 2811
Daytona Beach, FL 32120-2811
Total headcount enrollment-Credit: 19,414; Non-Credit: 18,608
Campuses/sites: 5; Full-time faculty: 214

CITRUS TECHNOLOGY

The program was created in direct response to requests from Florida's citrus industry

As the citrus industry has become more dominant in South Florida, so has the need for more people skilled in its operation. So at a direct response to requests from Florida's citrus industry, Edison Community College began an Associate in Science degree program in Citrus Technology in 1991, offering classes in conjunction with the Institute of Food and Agricultural Sciences (IFAS) of the University of Florida. The citrus industry provides direct support to fund the program.

The general education requirements for the AS degree in Citrus Technology consist of 21 hours, as well as 10 hours of electives. Much of the course work can be completed by taking courses offered at the IFAS Center or at outreach sites near where the targeted students are located. The program is designed to meet the growing need for mid-level managers in the citrus industry, and prepares students for employment in grove production,

Continues on Page 138

sales and service to the citrus and nurseries industry.

Edison is working on an articulation agreement with the University of Florida that will allow graduates of the Citrus Technology Program to move directly into the baccalaureate degree program in agriculture at the university.

Contact:
Suzanne Pahl, Citrus Technology Counselor
(813) 732-3711

Edison Community College
PO Box 06210
Fort Myers, FL 33906-6210
Total headcount enrollment-Credit: 13,927; Non-Credit: 12,000
Campuses/sites: 3; Full-time faculty: 150

LEARNING RESOURCES

Merged library collections mean the college and a university campus have more than 85,000 books available to students

Edison Community College formed a very beneficial alliance with the Fort Myers Branch of the University of South Florida in 1982, when the university branch was built on a site adjoining Edison. The library collections of the two institutions were merged, providing a joint collection of more than 85,000 books. The collections were merged and the books of the two colleges were integrated under the Library of Congress Cataloging System.

The advantage to Edison Community College was not limited to a larger book collection. The journal and periodical subscription list was increased significantly and more research materials were made available since the library needed to be equipped to serve the needs of not only lower-division studies but also upper-division and graduate students.

A further advantage came in the installation of Library User Information Services (LUIS), an on-line cataloging system that gave both community college and university students and faculty access to library materials throughout the state university system. The library now has access to 5-million bibliographic titles.

The staff of the Learning Resources are all employed by Edison Community College, but both institutions contributed proportionally to the budget, according to their FTE.

Contact:
Charles Ritchie, Director, Learning Resources
(813) 489-9219

Edison Community College
PO Box 06210
Fort Myers, FL 33906-6210
Total head count enrollment-Credit: 13,927; Non-Credit: 12,000
Campuses/sites: 3; Full-time faculty: 150

CENTER FOR THE ADVANCEMENT OF TEACHING & LEARNING

The Center is bridging the gap between educational theory and day-to-day classroom practices

Corresponding with an increasing interest in determining the impact of instructors' teaching on learning has been a national concern for improved performance by both instructor and student. Often, this has led college instructors to alter the teaching/learning environment of the college classroom. The Center for the Advancement of Teaching and Learning at Florida Community College at Jacksonville helps instructors do this by bridging the gap between educational theory and day-to-day classroom practices. The Center believes teachers should be the primary means to improve and measure teaching and learning.

In general, the Center acts as a catalyst to enhance teaching and learning at FCCJ. The specific objectives of the Center include:

1) supporting the development and use of teaching and learning procedures to promote student success and retention;
2) providing training in classroom research to promote effective, innovative teaching and assess

learning;

3) assisting faculty in using learning outcomes;
4) establishing a forum for communicating research results;
5) studying perennial and emerging issues in higher education; and
6) studying the application of new educational technologies.

To accomplish these goals, the Center has implemented a wide variety of teaching and learning projects. It has encouraged innovation in college teaching and learning by sponsoring workshops on critical thinking, learning styles, collaborative learning and academic technology. The Center has provided mini-grants to support more than 40 faculty research projects. Some of these projects have resulted in: a new curriculum for high-risk English and reading students; videotapes on listening skills for ESL students; a freshman writing sampler; and computer-assisted instruction for biology classes.

Through the Center, FCCJ faculty have written and published cases on college teaching through the AAHE teachers' initiative while others have developed teaching portfolios. The Center has also supported faculty who present at national conferences or who publish in national journals.

Since its inception, the Center has been organized and directed by faculty members. The Steering Committee members, including an adjunct faculty member, come from all five campuses and represent liberal arts and vocational programs. All segments of the college benefit from the Center's activities. The key reason for the Center's success is that it is faculty-driven. Unlike many conventional programs where a gap exists between what administrators or faculty development staff create and what faculty desire, FCCJ faculty are both designers and experimenters. As a result, the Center has been instrumental in shifting college values from administration-controlled to faculty-driven professional development as shown by budgetary and administrative support with the assignment of an Associate Vice President mentor. Moreover, the Center has served as a model for the creation of other faculty centers at FCCJ and as a resource for other community colleges and universities.

Finally, the Center has created a national and even international impact on teaching and learning through the National Conference on College Teaching, Learning, and Technology. This conference draws faculty of all disciplines from both two-year and four-year colleges and universities, hosting more than 300 participants each year. FCCJ faculty can thus meet and exchange ideas with leading national educators across the nation. Juried papers from this conference have been published in two issues of the *Community/Junior College Quarterly of Research and Practice* and the *Interactive Learning International* journal.

Contact:
Arnold Wood, Chairperson, Center Steering Committee
(904) 646-2341

Florida Community College at Jacksonville
501 West State Street
Jacksonville, FL 32202
Total headcount enrollment-Credit/Non-Credit: 87,883
Campuses/sites: 9; Full-time faculty: 415

FLORIDA COMMUNITY COLLEGE AT JACKSONVILLE

URBAN RESOURCE CENTER

⊞ *Program goals include developing work force readiness skills and facilitating* ⊞
innovative uses of technology to support instruction

Jacksonville's work force needs are changing, and the communities that comprise the Jacksonville metropolitan area are looking to Florida Community College at Jacksonville to adapt to those changes and meet the educational needs of the 21st Century work force.

Fifty-two percent of today's jobs require post secondary education. By the year 2000, that figure will rise to 80 percent. The Jacksonville Community Council, Inc., reported recently in its Future Work Force Needs Study that among the greatest work force problems was "extremely high unemployment among youth and minorities worsened by insufficient work training and education opportunities." Among its recommendations: "Florida Community College at Jacksonville should be encouraged to continue and expand its efforts as a major local provider of work force-related education and training." The state of Florida mandated that FCCJ take a proactive role in work force development by participating in the economic development of the community, upgrading the community's work force skills and increasing minority employment opportunities. FCCJ is uniquely qualified to accomplish these tasks because of its experience in educational and vocational training, its proven track record with special needs groups and the development of custom training programs for business and industry.

Between 1987 and 1990, FCCJ's work force-related training increased from 100,000 to 1-million hours annually. During that period, Jacksonville's economic development blossomed, creating some 12,000 jobs per

Continues on Page 140

year. Concern was expressed as to the ability of the community to provide the work force required for continued expansion. In February 1990, the District Board of Trustees approved the concept of the Urban Resource Center, a high-level, educational entity - that will change according to the specific needs of business and industry. The Center will serve as the area's central skills assessment and job training/retraining asset for the area work force, designed to upgrade skills in the local labor market and to attract additional businesses to the area. The Urban Resource Center will serve current and future FCCJ students, the unemployed and under-employed of Northeast Florida, currently employed residents and other special needs groups. It will help position FCCJ as an institution that can and will adapt to the needs of a diverse student body, and it will help position Northeast Florida as an area that can meet current and future needs of individuals and the economic community at large.

The Northeast Florida business/civic community has become a complete partner in the development of the Urban Resource Center. An advisory council representing leaders from business, industry, community organizations and government agencies was formed to provide input on training and employment needs, to create partnerships and to act as a liaison to the community. Extensive personal interviews were conducted with more than 100 Northeast Florida business and civic leaders representing more than 70 organizations to assess their training needs and work force problems and to exchange information about the

Urban Resource Center Advisory Council and the Northeast Florida economic community. These interviews led to the development of the Urban Resource Center's 11 program initiatives.

Program goals are to facilitate the development of work force readiness skills in FCCJ students, facilitate innovative uses of technology to support instruction, facilitate the development of appropriate curriculum to meet the educational needs of FCCJ students and businesses, facilitate the development of workplace literacy skills, and facilitate matching employer job openings with qualified job applicants. To accomplish these goals – and based upon survey and interview results – program facilities include three multipurpose assessment testing rooms, one large work evaluation lab, a career resource room and educational advising facilities, two computer information system labs, one computer aided drafting and design/computer aided manufacturing (CADD/CAM) lab, two electronic classrooms, two microcomputer labs, one business data processing lab, one multi-skills lab, three interdisciplinary computer labs, one "Office of the Future" lab, one interdisciplinary laboratory (distant learning center), three multi-media conference rooms, and one economic development office. All Urban Resource Center facilities are accessible to and adapted for disabled persons. Total building square footage is 62,160 gross square feet, total projected facility cost is $12-million (includes site acquisition, renovation, and furniture and equipment).

Contact:
Stan Block, Executive Director, Community Economic Development Center
(904) 633-8149

Florida Community College at Jacksonville
501 West State Street
Jacksonville, FL 32202
Total headcount enrollment-Credit/Non-Credit: 87,883
Campuses/sites: 9; Full-time faculty: 415

FLORIDA KEYS COMMUNITY COLLEGE

MARINE PROPULSION TECHNOLOGY

Because of its unique location in the Florida Keys, the program draws students from across the nation and around the world

Started in 1968, the Marine Propulsion Technology Program at Florida Keys Community College is unique in the country for offering, under one roof, technician training in four key areas of the now $18-billion-dollar-a-year recreational boating industry. These areas are: Marine Diesel Repair, Gas Engine Outboard and Inboard/Outboard Repair, Fiberglass Repair and Maintenance, and Marina Management. Additionally, in 1991 a 4,000-square-foot welding lab oratory was built for the Marine Propulsion program so students could learn the ancillary skills of pipe welding and fabrication while pursuing the four mainline programs.

The college is ideally situated for this training, as Florida now holds the number one position in the nation for new

boat sales, number of dealers, and number of boat builders. Because of its uniqueness and location, the program draws students from across the country and many foreign students as well. Students from Columbia, Venezuela, Bermuda, Puerto Rico, Bahamas, Singapore, Trinidad and Canada have been trained alongside those from Maine, Ohio, New York and Alaska. The college also offers other marine-related programs and attracts students to Florida Keys Community College. There is a two-year 68/74 semester hour program which leads to an Associate in Science degree in Marine Propulsion Technology. Credits earned in the certificate program are transferable to the Associate in Science program. More than 700 students have completed the program as either degree or certificate graduates.

The Marine Propulsion program occupies an 8,500-square-foot main facility and the above-mentioned welding laboratory. Two full-time instructors, four part-time instructors and one full-time laboratory assistant. The total annual capital outlay to support this program in 1992-93 was $133,000.

The Marine Propulsion department is a member of Nautical Marine Manufacturers Association (NMMA); the American Welding Society (AWS); the Society of Accredited Marine Surveyors (SAMS); and the Nautical Fire Prevention Association (NFPA). Individual faculty have membership in the American Boat and Yacht Council (ABYC). The department is seeking recognition by the Society of Naval Architects and Marine Engineers (SNAME). By special arrangement, the department can send students to a technician training facility in West Palm Beach, Florida, as a way of obtaining nationally recognized training certification while they are concurrently enrolled in the Marine Propulsion program at the college.

Florida Keys Community College is one of two community colleges in the entire United States which offers an Associate in Science in Marine Propulsion Technology. The other college is located in the state of Washington.

Contact:
Joseph Carbonell, Coordinator
(305) 296-9081, ext. 206

Florida Keys Community College
5901 West College Road
Key West, FL 33040
Total headcount enrollment-Credit: 5,363; Non-Credit: 4,385
Campuses/sites: 3; Full-time faculty: 32

GULF COAST COMMUNITY COLLEGE

HONORS PROGRAM

Courses are taught through symposium in a physical setting designed to promote discussion and debate

The Gulf Coast Community College Honors Program provides superior students a core of courses designed to fit every transfer program the college offers. Regardless of whether the student intends to major in English or engineering, mathematics or music, the honors program provides the student with at least 16 hours of core general education and majors courses in the honors setting, and adds only one credit hour to the student's curriculum. Courses for which credit could be acquired through CLEP, advanced placement and dual enrollment were eliminated. The remaining general education core courses are grouped to provide each participant a broad spectrum of course requirements with a variety of delivery systems.

Participants are expected to take at least one course from each of the following divisions with the exception of Division III (from which two courses must be selected):

I) Honors Symposium (1 credit);

II) Understanding the Arts, Freshman College Chemistry, or Zoology;

III) General Psychology, American National Government, or Western Civilization I;

IV) Literature or Ethics; and

V) course in the major area.

Symposium, literature and ethics are designed to develop critical and creative thinking skills. These, as well as the psychology, government and history courses, are taught through symposium in a physical setting designed to promote discussion and debate. The art course centers around a major group production that promotes the need for study of form and style, and the execution of which involves development of group problem-solving skills. Chemistry stresses development of problem-solving skills through a series of lab projects rather than the traditional cookbook laboratory experiments. Zoology addresses similar skills through study of systems evolution. Each of these courses is taught in a specifically designated honors section reserved for honors students.

Any course in the major field may be made honors if the student contracts with a professor who will direct special assignments, individual research or in-depth papers in lieu of some portion of the regular assignments. Contracts have been let with great success in such courses as Calculus III, Creative Writing, Organic Chemistry, Constitutional Law, and Engineering Physics, to name a few. Students who graduate from the honors program will have completed at least one course in which opportunities for one-on-one work with a professor are established through the completion of an honors contract.

Students must have a 3.5 GPA from either high school

Continues on Page 142

or 15 hours of college work to gain admission to the program and must maintain a minimum 3.0 GPA to participate. Only those who complete the program with a cumulative 3.5 are designated as honors program graduates with the accompanying awards and recognitions.

An advisory committee composed of representatives from the major academic divisions as well as student interest areas oversees the honors program as it continues to evolve. Additional funding for special activities are provided by local businesses and individuals and are disseminated through the College Foundation.

Contact:
Sandra Y. Etheridge, Project Coordinator
(904) 872-3848

Gulf Coast Community College
5230 West Highway 98
Panama City, FL 32401
Total headcount enrollment-Credit: 7,500; Non-Credit: 10,000
Campuses/sites: 1; Full-time faculty: 100

CULINARY MANAGEMENT

The program relies on a balance of management and culinary skills courses

The growth of employment opportunities in the hospitality industry both in Florida and the nation over the past several years is well-documented. With this trend expected to continue, Gulf Coast Community College, through the availability of a Federal Title III Grant and with its own resources, has developed a Culinary Management program tailored to meet regional employers' needs for management.

Philosophy instilled into culinary management graduates can be summarized in four points: 1) expansion of culinary skills equivalent to a nationally established certification level; 2) development of communication skills; 3) understanding of fundamentals of management, as accepted by today's industry; and 4) development of professionalism and individual growth for leadership in a conducive environment.

Each of the preceding points is implemented through the total curriculum that relies on a balance of management and culinary skill courses. The input provided by the local area advisory committee is most valuable in setting and maintaining this balance. Careful selection of staff and the maintenance of low student-teacher ratios also have led to program success.

Throughout the brief tenure of this program, which started in 1988, numerous success stories have evolved. From its highly successful gourmet dinner series to the string of gold medals earned at the National Vocational Industrial Clubs of America (VICA) skills and leadership competitions, program capabilities have exceeded all expectations. Students are not just graduating from the program; they also are graduating with individual honors, such as being listed in Who's Who in American Community Colleges. A recent graduating student was selected to sit as student representative on the State of Florida Council for Vocational Education. Others are emerging as leaders within the state VICA organization, most notably are two Gulf Coast Community College culinary management students currently holding the offices of president and historian. On the culinary side, last year students traveled out of state to Alabama to claim the "Best of the Show-Student Category" at the Montgomery Culinary Salon. Additional successes include the annual fundraising projects that have been initiated by the program. The Bay Culinary Classic, now in its sixth year, has generated funds in excess of $30,000 in scholarship seed monies. The annual Pasta Challenge recently completed its third year and again was an enormous success.

In just four years, the Culinary Management Program has grown to be one of the premiere programs in the state, if not the country. The program recently was accredited by the American Culinary Federation Education Institute Accrediting Commission, striving to be selected among only 50-plus programs currently achieving that status.

Contact:
Travis Herr, Coordinator
(904) 872-3850

Gulf Coast Community College
5230 West Highway 98
Panama City, FL 32401
Total headcount enrollment-Credit: 7,500; Non-Credit: 10,000
Campuses/sites: 1; Full-time faculty: 100

AUTOMOTIVE STUDENT SERVICE EDUCATIONAL TRAINING (ASSET)

The program combines automotive technical training with college general education and management courses

Prospective students seeking management positions in the automotive services field may take advantage of the new co-sponsored Automotive Student Service Educational Training (ASSET) program at Hillsborough Community College. This project is the result of joint commitments of HCC, the Ford Motor company, Brewster Technical Center, and local Ford-Lincoln-Mercury dealerships. It is a two-year college program leading to an Associate in Science degree in Industrial Management.

By combining automotive technical training with college general education and management courses, graduates will be prepared to work as automotive technicians and to advance in their careers after gaining experience.

The ASSET curriculum includes sophisticated technical training on Ford vehicles and components in such areas as engine, transmission and brake repair combined with the on-the-job training and general college courses. Automotive training is provided by Brewster Technical

Center, college courses are taken at HCC, and the on-the-job training is provided by local sponsoring dealerships. Importantly, students are paid by the sponsoring dealerships while employees during a five- to nine-week period of full-time work that alternates with six to nine weeks of classroom instruction.

Becoming a student in the program requires being at least 18 years of age, having a high school diploma or equivalent, college level scores on either the MAPS, ACT or SAT tests, and sponsorship by a local Ford dealership.

Tuition for the program is $2,430 the first year. This includes the purchase of hand tools, but not application and student fees. Costs for the second year are about $1,000 in addition to the fees. Financial aid is available for students in this program

Twenty-five students are expected to enroll in this program each fall, resulting in a steady production of highly trained automotive managers contributing to the community.

Contact:
Sherry Kersey, Associate Vice President for Technical Programs
(813) 253-7055

Hillsborough Community College
PO Box 31127
Tampa, FL 33631-3127
Total head count enrollment-Credit: 31,480; Non-Credit: 11,832
Campuses/sites: 4; Full-time faculty: 241

COLLEGE-MILITARY EDUCATIONAL CENTER

Courses taught at the base have made it easier for military personnel, their dependents and base employees to pursue degrees

Hillsborough Community College and the educational administration at MacDill Air Force Base have joined forces to forge an innovative educational partnership enabling military personnel, dependents, civilians and other government employees to be degree-seeking on a unique MacDill-based calendar of courses.

The offering of particular credit classes is based on educational needs of students with some 60 sessions per semester, serving approximately 800 students. These year-round sessions are housed in the newly completed MacDill

Education Center, with staffing being a joint effort of HCC and MacDill.

Since HCC came to MacDill more than 13,000 students have taken courses at the base facility. Through the fall 1992 semester, 863 courses had been taught. From its inception, about 2,500 students new to college have enrolled in this special location.

For those non-military students taking courses at the site, a MacDill AFB pass is required with information there about obtained through the HCC Education Center at MacDill.

Contact:
Diana Fernandez, Dean of Dual Enrollment and MacDill AFB
(813) 253-7000

Hillsborough Community College
PO Box 31127
Tampa, FL 33631-3127
Total headcount enrollment-Credit: 31,480; Non-Credit: 11,832
Campuses/sites: 4; Full-time faculty: 241

MOBILE LEARNING UNITS

*⬚ For residents in remote areas without any transportation, the only way to get ⬚
a college education is through specially equipped vans that come to them*

Indian River Community College serves a large four-county area that includes lower-income and remote communities not served by public transportation. Without a personal vehicle, many residents are unable to reach one of the college's centers. Strongly believing in the importance of educational accessibility for all, IRCC has put three mobile learning vehicles on the road to bring education to convenient community locations.

In 1984, the first mobile learning unit, a computer van, was introduced. Equipped with 14 computer stations, the van has enabled 3,152 students to learn computer skills since the program's inception. Classes range from introduction to computer usage to more advanced examinations of disk operating systems and word processing packages.

Funded by the college at a cost of $80,000, the mobile computer lab was a novel approach that proved so successful that two other mobile units have since been introduced.

The mobile agricultural computer lab is designed to transfer advances in computer technology from the research lab to the field. Underwritten by a $175,000 state grant awarded to IRCC and South Florida Community College (SFCC) in cooperation with the University of Florida's Institute of Food and Agricultural Services, the lab has, since 1990, brought training in agricultural software to groves, farms and ranches. Participants may begin with an introductory seminar in agricultural software or may complete courses required for the AS degree program in agriculture.

Ideas for the agricultural unit were solicited from IRCC's Agricultural Advisory Committee, comprised of college administrators and area agricultural leaders.

The latest addition to the IRCC educational fleet is a learning center for basic skills in reading, math, English and GED preparation. The school on wheels, Project MODEM, is supported in part by a grant from the Department of Education in cooperation with the Department of Health and Rehabilitative Services.

Contact:
Tom Deal, Vice President, Instructional Services
(407) 462-4704

Indian River Community College
3209 Virginia Avenue
Fort Pierce, FL 34981
Total headcount enrollment-Credit: 21,000; Non-Credit: 28,000
Campuses/sites: 7; Full-time faculty: 150

HOSPITAL PARTNERSHIP
FOR ALLIED HEALTH TRAINING

*⬚ Hospitals agreed to redirect some of their recruiting money ⬚
toward the college's nursing program and scholarships*

Increasing demand coupled with shrinking supply has resulted in a national shortage of qualified nurses and other health care providers. The problem is particularly acute in Florida where rapid population growth and a high percent age of older residents tax existing health care facilities.

In 1989, Indian River Community College joined with seven local hospitals to combat the area's critical nursing shortage through an innovative partnership. Administrators of the seven hospitals agreed to provide financial support by re-directing a portion of the funds they normally spend in recruiting nurses outside the area. In 1992-93, the hospitals pledged to provide more than $173,000 to support IRCC's nursing program and fund nursing scholarships.

This support has enabled IRCC to increase the size of its two-year Associate Degree Nursing program to 120 students, a 50 percent increase over pre-program capacity. The hospitals have underwritten direct costs for IRCC to add four full-time nursing instructors, convert classrooms to a lab, and purchase additional training equipment. The Nursing Challenge Grant established by the Florida Legislature in 1989 provides additional monies for the program.

As a result of the scholarships and publicity generated regarding the hospitals' contributions, IRCC has attracted particularly qualified applicants; IRCC ADN graduates typically achieve 100 percent passing rates on state and national licensure exams.

In 1990, a respiratory therapy program partnership was formed linking a state training grant, the College and five area hospitals that in 1992-93 will provide $93,270 in support. Program participants complete 900 clinical hours in affiliated hospitals, and the first seven graduates earned their degrees in May 1992.

Mutually beneficial partnerships, the programs have enabled the college to provide a well-trained pool of allied health graduates who have local ties and are likely to remain in the area.

Contact:
R. Isenburg, Vice President, Applied Science and Technology
(407) 462-4783

Indian River Community College
3209 Virginia Avenue
Fort Pierce, FL 34981
Total headcount enrollment-Credit: 21,000; Non-Credit: 28,000
Campuses/sites: 7; Full-time faculty: 150

LAKE CITY COMMUNITY COLLEGE

GOLF COURSE OPERATIONS PROGRAM

A unique part of the program is the first year of equipment and shop management in the college's Turf Equipment Technology building

The Golf Course Operations Program at Lake City Community College prepares tomorrow's golf course superintendents to be progressive managers.

The Golf Course Operations Program began in 1967 as a direct response to industry needs. There were no schools effectively training students to become golf course superintendents. The college identified this industry need and formed an industry advisory committee to assist in curriculum development.

The program began as a two-year AS degree program, but in 1976, a unique golf course equipment and shop management module was added, creating the three-year format.

The students take general education courses, general horticulture courses, and courses dealing specifically with golf course situations. Some of the specific courses include: Control of Insect and Nematode Pests, Control of Disease and Weed Pests, Golf Course Irrigation, Golf course Maintenance Systems, Golf Course Organization and Administration, Landscape Design for Golf Courses and Golf Course Seminar.

The first year of equipment and shop management in the college's modern, 15,000-square-foot Turf Equipment Technology building involves four instructors. Managing the expensive, sophisticated golf course equipment is an important part of the golf course superintendent's job, and the Lake City students are well-trained in this area.

The two summers of required field training are an important part of the training success of Golf Course Operations. The students receive 12 credits for each summer of on-the-job training (OJT) done within a 500-mile radius of Lake City. Students work for 12 weeks and must keep a daily log book and write an extensive report. The employer fills out an evaluation form indicating the student's work habits, attitudes, and proficiencies, goes over the evaluation with the student, and the student sends this evaluation to the school along with the log book and report. Each student is visited twice by division faculty, each time it is a different instructor. The instructors evaluate the student's progress and submit a written report. All these factors are used in determining the student's grade.

Students may go beyond the 500-mile radius range if granted special permission by the Division chair. In the summer of 1992, there were 106 Golf Course Operations students at sites in 21 states and two foreign countries – although most were in Florida. One student was in Indonesia working with a LCCC graduate who is the Golf Course Superintendent at the Bali Golf Club. Two students were in Finland at the Vierumaki Club under LCCC graduate Bruce Chestnutt. The summer of 1992 makes the fourth summer of OJT students in Finland, with all expenses paid by the Finnish Sports Institute.

The summer OJT program does much more than help train students. It also provides essential "back to industry" training for the division faculty, recruiting opportunities and excellent public relations. Getting the Lake City students and faculty "out and about" spreads the word about this unique program at small, rural Lake City Community College in the midst of the north Florida pine forests.

The Golf Course Operations program exemplifies what can be done with industry and education working together. In the mechanics module alone, more than $500,000 of new turf equipment is loaned to the program every year so the students can learn on the latest models. Industry support comes in the way of equipment loans, technical seminars, product donations, and scholarship support. The school could not provide the current level of training without the important industry partners.

Continues on Page 146

More than 850 Lake City Community College Golf Course Operations graduates are throughout the southeast U.S., the rest of the U.S., and in Bali and Jakarta, Indonesia, Singapore, Thailand, the United Arab Emirates, and Finland. The tremendous success of this program has been a rewarding experience for everyone involved.

In summary, the three-year, 117 credit hour, AS degree program:
1) enrolls 150 students;
2) accepts 45 to 50 new students every fall;
3) has eight full-time faculty, division chair, and secretary involved in division, which includes Golf Course Operations, Landscape Technology and Turf Equipment Management;
4) boasts 100 percent job placement, usually as assistant golf course superintendent;
5) requires one-year work experience before acceptance;
6) requires two summers of internship; and
7) has strong industry support.

Contact:
John Piersol, Chairperson
(904) 752-1822 ext.

Lake City Community College
Route 3, Box 7
225 Lake City, FL 32055
Total Head Count: Not Provided
Number of campuses/sites: 1 Full-time faculty: 69

PROJECT SECOND CHANCE

The project aims to increase enrollment and retention of African-American and Hispanic male students

There has been a well-documented decline in the enrollment of African-American and Hispanic males in post secondary education. Although Florida's State Board of Community Colleges mandated that each college develop and initiate a program to address the devastating issue of African-American male enrollment in post secondary education, Lake-Sumter Community College felt a need to also address the issue of Hispanic male enrollment in post secondary education.

Project Second Chance was designed as a true model of a transition program. Criteria to participate include:
1) student must be of African-American or Hispanic descent;
2) student must be a high school drop-out, college drop-out or a first-generation college student; and
3) the student must have a desire to commit to earning a GED and/or a college degree.

Once selected for participation, students attend an orientation session conducted by the Associate Dean of Students and the Assistant to the President. During this session, students are introduced to the staff of the Learning Center and given a tour of the facility. Monthly meetings are conducted for these students that include such issues as self-esteem, financial aid and short- and long-range planning.

The college's commitment to the project includes the waiver of all application and admission fees for the participants. These young men are afforded the same academic counseling and other services as every other student.

The success of Phase I of the program has been phenomenal. The initial enrollment in Fall Term 1992 was 27, with 15 completing the program by earning grade point averages ranging from 1.5 to 3.8. These students are still enrolled at the college.

In the Fall Term 1993, the program accepted seven more male students. To date, only one of these young men has withdrawn from classes. It is anticipated that by Fall Term 1994, there will be a need to make sure all these males receive full financial aid so that another group of students can benefit from Phase II of Project Second Chance. When the current participants are on financial aid, they will be encouraged to work on campus, which is Phase II of Project Second Chance.

As a result of the success of this project, African-American student enrollment has increased by 30 percent.

Contact:
Beverly J. Robinson, Assistant to the President/Equity
(904) 365-3531

Lake-Sumter Community College
9501 U.S. Highway 441
Leesburg, FL 34788-8751
Total enrollment headcount: 2,715
Campuses/sites: 3; Full-time faculty: 41

YOUTH LEADERSHIP

The program prepares today's students to be tomorrow's local, state and national leaders

High school students in rural communities, particularly those students who are considered student leaders and/or scholars, when they graduate, very seldom return to their communities. But Lake-Sumter Community College, as the only institution of higher learning in the "heart" of Central Florida, feels strongly that it should play a vital role in the future growth of the communities it serves and has, therefore, initiated a Youth Leadership Program.

The Youth Leadership Program strives to change two common patterns students from rural communities follow: 1) only 10 to 20 percent will attend a community college, especially if that college is in the area; and 2) upon completion of post secondary education, they either move away, or (if they went away to college) do not return to their communities.

The Youth Leadership Program identifies high school students who have demonstrated leadership in Lake County and Sumter County schools and communities, and prepares them for constructive leadership, committed involvement in local issues, and responsible participation in the future of their communities. Thirty high school juniors from 11 public and independent schools in the two-county area, who represent a cross section of the community in terms of gender race and neighborhoods are the participants in the program. The advantage of conducting this program for high school juniors is that, when they become seniors and have one more year of high school, they will have opportunities to become involved with a community activity related to their program experience. The ultimate goal is to make such an impact on these youth leaders that they will choose to pursue leadership roles at the local, state or national levels; as well as serve as role-models for their peers and younger youth.

To be eligible, students must:

1) attend a public, independent or private school in Lake or Sumter County that is accredited by the Southern Association of Colleges and Schools;
2) be a current junior;
3) be approved by the high school principal;
4) demonstrate leadership in school and/or community activities; and
5) be academically sound (a grade point average of "B" or better) because they will miss one day of classes each month for five months in order to attend the Youth Leadership Program.

Even though the college is the sponsor of this program, its unique feature is that it is operated completely by a Community Advisory Board, which selects each year's class from the applications received, plans each month's activities, and provides the resources needed (transportation, food, money, etc.) to assure the program's success.

The five program days in which the students are involved include: Education Day, Inside the System (Criminal Justice System), Dollars and Cents (Local Economy), Are We Our Brother's Keeper (Poverty and Cultural Diversity), and Local Health Care Issues.

Contact:
Beverly J. Robinson, Assistant to the President/Equity
(904) 365-3531

Lake-Sumter Community College
9501 U.S. Highway 441,
Leesburg, FL 34788-8751
Total enrollment headcount: 2,715
Campuses/sites: 3; Full-time faculty: 41

ANATOMY AND PHYSIOLOGY MICROBIOLOGY RESOURCE CENTER

With enrollments growing at more than 30 percent in vocational health science courses, the Center has become a central support structure

Tailored for health science students who have little or no science background, the Anatomy and Physiology / Microbiology Resource Center supports more than 300 students each semester taking Anatomy & Physiology, and Microbiology on the Bradenton Campus. The Center was established in the fall of 1991 in preparation for the implementation of new science curricula, designed for AS health science students (Nursing, Respiratory Therapy and Radiography). With contributions of a dedicated faculty and the efficient use of existing systems and supplies, the APMRC has made the difference between success and failure for hundreds of vocational students.

Prior to 1991, health science vocational students would

Continues on Page 148

take various prerequisite science courses before beginning the study of Anatomy & Physiology and/or Microbiology. Due to guidelines set by the Natural League of Nursing, the MCC Nursing Program had to reduce the number of semester hours in the programs (including required prerequisite courses). Hence, the science courses (Anatomy & Physiology and Microbiology) were revised somewhat so they could be offered with no science prerequisites. Because only students who had successfully completed the prerequisites ever took the AS health science courses, the faculty were greatly concerned about the "new" students (those without any science background). The concern was for their welfare, that they would continue to succeed in their study of the science courses. The decision was reached to create the APMRC to serve our students' needs.

The creation of the APMRC was a joint effort of several areas on campus: the SAIL Center director (George Silvanic), the Health Science Division (chaired by Dr. Carol Singer), the Division Office (Mike Mears, chair of the Division of Mathematics,. Science and Technology), and the Department of Natural Science (primarily the biology faculty: Dr. Ellen Cover, Cathy Oliver, John Wilson and Sandra Wilson). While the above shows a broad-based support of this venture, the vast majority of the contributions have come from the SAIL Center, which houses the Resource Center, and the biology faculty, who have helped the Center evolve into an outstanding, invaluable resource at our college.

The following is a partial list of some of the developments that have occurred to enhance student success:

- a complete set of microscope slides representing all of the prepared slides used in the laboratories, plus four microscopes, lens cleaner and lens paper for use with scopes were transferred to the Center;
- a copy of the Instructor Manuals to accompany the Anatomy & Physiology texts were added so students can read the additional information by the author and use the tests created by the publisher for review purposes;
- microbiology reference textbooks were placed in the Center;
- file of copies of old tests are maintained for student use;
- additional instructor notes created for their students were filed; videotapes of various topics dealing with Anatomy & Physiology made by the biology faculty and media services at MCC (they are available for viewing and/or duplication in the Center);
- file copies of previous students' anatomy notes are maintained for current students' use;
- models of various body parts (skull, torso, etc.) were donated by the Nursing Department and the Department of Natural Science;
- tutorial help available by instructors and student assistants;
- a television monitor and VCR area available for viewing the skeleton while examining models;
- memory tools and charts are available for organic molecules and related information; and
- the Learning Styles Inventory is given at the beginning of the course and graded by the SAIL Center staff (this helps both the students and instructor utilize the most effective learning style).

The Anatomy & Physiology/Microbiology Resource Center has grown into an invaluable resource for the vocational health science students. With enrollments growing at more than 30 percent in these courses, and with the change in prerequisites occurring during the same period, the Resource Center has become the central support structure for hundreds of these students. This has been a reasonably low-cost venture, with the emphasis on cooperation among varied units in the college, and could be duplicated at other community colleges and technical schools.

Contact:
Mike Mears, Division Chair
(813) 755-1511, ext. 4267

Manatee Community College
PO Box 1849
Bradenton, FL 34206
Total headcount enrollment-Credit: 8,144
Campuses/sites: 2; Full-time faculty: 137

PROJECT STEP
(SKILLS AND TRAINING FOR EMPLOYEE PROGRESS)

Ninety-eight percent of the participants are female, 80 percent are black, 33 percent quit high school and 57 percent are single parents

Project STEP is an exciting, non-traditional three-step program that provides job-related literacy/basic skills training to 250 direct-care workers employed at Sunrise Community, a private, non-profit organization. Sunrise provides education, health care and training in a residential setting to children and adults with severe to profound developmental disabilities.

Demographically, participants in Project STEP are characterized by a limited educational experience, low literacy levels, low-paying jobs, limited financial resources, dependence on public assistance programs and low self-esteem. With an average age of 35, 98 percent are female, 80 percent are black, 33 percent have not completed high school, and 57 percent are single with dependents.

Project STEP has a strong motivational component that addresses improving confidence and self-esteem in adult workers. Project STEP also uses innovative educational training methods, interactive classrooms and employee-developed case studies. All classes are taught at the work site in mobile classrooms dedicated to the Project. As of August 1992, Miami-Dade delivered approximately 19,000 student hours of functional literacy and basic skills training.

Phase One provides direct-care workers with 40 classroom hours of instruction in the literacy and basic skills necessary to perform their current jobs. It focuses on reading comprehension, written and oral communication, and basic math.

Phase Two prepares employees to meet the increasing skill requirements resulting from their changing workplace as the residents they work with move to group homes in the community. Providing an additional 40 hours of instruction, the curriculum focuses on critical thinking and problem solving and continues basic skills and literacy training.

Phase Three is literacy/basic skills training for supervisors. Involving an additional 20 hours of classroom instruction, it is required for all employees in supervisory positions and is available for those employees who desire or who are recommended for career advancement.

Funded by a U.S. Department of Education workplace literacy grant, curricula and other project materials will be made available in a Planning Guide in order to encourage replication in intermediate care facilities for the developmentally disabled, as well as in other types of long term health care facilities.

Contact:
Regina A. Guaraldi, Director, Project STEP
(305) 237-2878

Miami-Dade Community College-Kendall Campus
11011 SW 104th Street
Miami, FL 33176
Total headcount enrollment-Credit: 55,539; Non-Credit: 16,527
Campuses/sites: 5; Full-time faculty: 913

MIAMI-DADE COMMUNITY COLLEGE-KENDALL CAMPUS

VISUAL ARTS TEACHING GALLERY

Originally conceived to serve Visual Arts and Humanities courses, the gallery now is a resource for such varied programs as Fashion Design and Psychology

Interest in the Visual Arts increased extraordinarily beginning in the late 1960's. To serve that interest, Miami-Dade Community College created a Teaching Gallery at its Kendall Campus in 1970. At a time when there were no other forums for Contemporary Art in the Miami area, students were able to view actual works and conduct dialogues with important artists who frequently accompanied their exhibitions. The program provided a model for other art facilities that followed and continues as a pre-eminent venue for the presentation of art exhibitions and lectures in the community.

Prior to the existence of the Teaching Gallery, students taking Humanities courses (an AA requirement) or Art History could be exposed to art images only in the form of textbook illustrations or projected slides. Since no reproductions of art works convey the actual color, scale or texture of the original, students graduated with approximately the same experience they could get by reading recipes and lists of ingredients without an opportunity to taste the actual food.

Although originally conceived as a tool to serve Visual Arts courses and Humanities, the Teaching Gallery has become a popular resource for Fashion Design, Architecture, Psychology, English, Honors and virtually every course requiring inspiration, material and the development of critical thinking for written assignments. Classes of all ages are bused to the facility by Dade County Public Schools, and a variety of community organizations and art interested individuals make regular use of the frequently changing exhibitions.

A Permanent Collection of art objects also was begun in 1970. Because the Teaching Gallery initially was set up as a Learning Laboratory facility, substantial savings of instructional expenses were effected. A portion of those savings were utilized for art rental and purchase funds and the growing Permanent Collection quickly attracted the attention and assistance of sympathetic art dealers and collectors. There are now 579 objects in the collection - approximately half of them were acquired as gifts. Unlike virtually all other purchases made by the college, the art objects have not eventually become used up, worn out, obsolete or depreciated in any way. Instead, they have appreciated to an average of several times their original value- the most dramatic example to 4,800 percent of its purchase price.

Having existed in recycled classrooms and a vacated cafeteria site, the Teaching Gallery is scheduled to move

Continues on Page 150

into a space designed to house, protect and display its Permanent Collection to better advantage alongside temporary exhibitions. A historical perspective will then be provided continuously for the largely contemporary work shown. Students interested in pursuing museum and gallery professions will receive enhanced practical experience, and studio art courses will have access to examples of professional art works in all mediums at all times.

Another aspect of the program is a printmaking subscription series which generates income for special projects while providing more student access to professional artists and their works.

Contact:
Robert J. Sindelir, Director
(305) 237-2322

Miami-Dade CommunityCollege-Kendall Campus
11011 SW 104th Street
Miami, FL 33176
Total headcount enrollment-Credit: 55,539; Non-Credit: 16,527
Campuses/sites: 5; Full-time faculty: 913

CHILD DEVELOPMENT AND EDUCATION

The major sites for students' field experience include the North Campus Pre-School Laboratory and some community early childhood centers

Since 1967, Miami-Dade Community College-North Campus, through its Pre-School Laboratory, has maintained a model Early Childhood program. Today, the program has expanded into the Child Development and Educational Program, which specializes in education and training for students who desire entry into the field of Early Childhood Education and those working in pre-school programs, day care centers, Head Start centers and public and private elementary schools.

The Child Development and Education program is a dual-degree program leading to both an Associate of Science degree and an Associate of Arts degree, after the completion of 62 hours. Students may also select the option of completing four core courses in early childhood education meeting requirements for a "Specialized Training Award." Competencies mandated for child-care training by the Florida State Department of Health and Rehabilitative Services is addressed in the curriculum of the four Early Childhood Education Core courses.

The goal of the program is to design and develop an educational program based on developmental principles, programmatic research, parental values, and the needs and interests of children. The program is further committed to an action-oriented approach to teaching and learning based on concrete experiences that are developmentally appropriate for young children. The curriculum of the Child Development and Education program combines instruction with intensive field experience. Students are, therefore, provided an opportunity to integrate theory with practical experiences within a culturally diverse environment. The major site for field experience is the North Campus Pre-School Laboratory and selected community early childhood centers, public school pre-k, kindergarten and primary grades. The commitment of the program to serve the college and community has advanced the development of outstanding college and community resources and fosters collaborative arrangements between the college, other community agencies, and the Dade County School System. Major components of the program include the Pre-School Laboratory, the Satellite Learning Center and the Children's Resource Center.

The Pre-School Laboratory, a model educational program that serves as a major training facility for early childhood and elementary education majors, child care providers, private and public school teachers, early childhood professionals and paraprofessionals in the community. The laboratory school implements a quality developmentally appropriate program for children from three to five years of age on a sliding fee scale. In 1987, the Pre-School lab was awarded the Florida State Board of Community College Commitment to Education Award. Mainstreaming of handicapped children is a part of the Pre-School Lab program in a cooperative venture with the Dade County Public School Pre-Kindergarten Exceptional Education Program.

Satellite Learning Center is a cooperative program in conjunction with Dade County Public Schools. Established to help alleviate the overcrowding of public schools, the Satellite Learning Center enables children of faculty, staff and students to attend kindergarten through second grade at the North Campus. Children receive instruction from Dade County Public School teachers. MDCC-N provides classroom facilities located adjacent to the Pre-School Lab.

The Children's Resource Center serves as a centralized information resource and community-based program that supports the Early Childhood academic program as well as professionals in the community through professional development programs. The professional training offered on the North Campus consists of credit and non-credit early childhood training courses. The Children's Resource Center provides conferences, mini-conferences, seminars and workshops for students and community educators.

Conferences address issues significant to teachers and administrators in the Dade County Public Schools. Consequently, attendance and participation by members of the school system are substantial and favorably received. Training mandated by the Florida State Department of Health and Rehabilitative Services (HRS) is coordinated through the Children's Resource Center for child care providers. Approximately 60 percent of HRS Training for certification in Dade County (about 3,000 child care providers and/or staff) is provided by the Center. The total number of participants for the Center's professional calendar is approximately 5,500 yearly. In 1991, the Center obtained contracts with Metro-Dade, Child Development Services to provide Child Care Resource and Referral to Dade County.

Recognition of the Child Development and Education program has been received through the continued funding support provided by the College, United Way, Metro-Dade Child Development Services, Title XX and Head Start. Grants have been awarded from the Florida Department of Education, Food and Nutrition Management Division, and Florida Bureau of Exceptional Education for Training of Paraprofessionals working with Handicapped 3, 4, and 5 year old pre-kindergarten children. The Children's Resource Center receives additional funding through private membership and donations. The Director's position, clerical support, instructional and operational costs are funded by MDCC. Additional costs incurred are reimbursed through contracts and grants from other community and governmental agencies.

Contact:
Carolyn Wright, Coordinator, (305) 237-1164
Muriel W. Lundgren, Director, Children Resource Cntr, (305) 237-1451

Miami-Dade Community College-North Campus
11380 NW 27 Avenue
Miami. FL 33167-3495
Total headcount enrollment-Credit: 23,000; Non-Credit: 15,000
Campuses/sites: 5; Full-time faculty: 263

REGIONAL TEST CENTER

The Center implements the latest advances in statistical methodology and computer technology

Miami-Dade Community College-North Campus is committed to responding to the needs of its students and serving the multi-ethnic South Florida community. This commitment requires flexibility, innovation and a dedication to excellence, values reflected in the operation of the Regional Test Center at Miami-Dade-North.

The Regional Test Center implements the latest advances in statistical methodology and computer technology. Testing at Miami-Dade is comprehensive, employing numerous formats and currently serving approximately 25,000 examinees per year, including those with special needs. Standardized multiple-choice tests are just a small part of an array of educational measurement techniques employed by the Regional Test Center.

A cadre of tests are offered to Miami-Dade students, including Computerized Placement Test, English Placement Test, Tests of Adult Basic Education, Correspondence Exams, College Level Academic skills Test, and Wonderlic Personnel Test. In addition we offer a host of external exams (State and National programs). These exams include computer based tests as well as paper/pencil tests.

The Regional Test Center is currently equipped with a dedicated file server networking 45 computer stations. A modem, located in the control room, allows for data transmission to Testing Agencies on a regular basis. The Center is also equipped with a "state-of-the art" security system that includes motion detectors, restricted access via key pad entry and key locks, data safe disk drive locks, and mirrors that allow staff to monitor candidates from all vantage points. The control room is adjacent to the computer testing rooms, separated by a glass wall that allows for constant monitoring.

The Center is designed so that multiple computer-based tests are offered simultaneously in each of the two computer testing rooms. A third room is used for paper/pencil testing. The third room is designed with an adjacent room equipped with scanning equipment. Since today's equipment and methods rapidly become obsolete, we are constantly upgrading equipment, increasing security and implementing new procedures.

The Center cooperates with the Educational Testing Service and the College Board in piloting computer based tests. We are among a select few colleges across the nation to have participated in the pilot projects for the computer-based tests of the College Level Examination Program (CLEP), Graduate Record Examination Program (GRE), and the new version of the National Teacher's Examination (PRAXIS).

The Center currently holds several contractual agreements with testing agencies. The following tests are

Continues on Page 152

administered via contractual agreements: State of Florida Insurance Licensure Exams, Computer Adaptive Test for CLAST (CAT-CLAST) and Pilot Testing for several different exams through the Educational Testing Service. We are one of a few sites across the country selected by ETS to offer the official computer based version of the GRE and PRAXIS beginning in the fall of 1992.

The design of the Center allows us to offer special services to the clients we serve. Those candidates who pass the State of Florida Insurance Licensure Exam are photographed and issued an official insurance license on site. Candidates who take the CAT-CLAST are issued an unofficial test score and then receive their official scores within two weeks. They no longer have to wait six weeks for feedback regarding their performance on the test.

The CLAST is an exam that is required by all Florida public colleges and universities for obtaining the Associate in Arts degree or for attaining junior status. The test is also a requirement for Florida Teacher Certification candidates. The CAT-CLAST is the computer adaptive version of CLAST, which is available for candidates needing to retake the English Language Skills, Reading and or Math subtests of the exam. The test is offered several times per week. We have a schedule that is flexible in meeting the needs of our students and other candidates needing the service.

The test is in great demand and our ability to meet the needs of so many people has resulted in candidates traveling from around the state and even from out of state to sit for the test at the Regional Test Center. Candidates can take the CAT-CLAST at our center, which is one of three sites in Florida chosen to offer the test, and receive immediate feedback in the form of an unofficial score upon completion of the exam. The immediate feedback provided to candidates is an added benefit to computer adaptive testing.

The Regional Test Center continues to be recognized by the Educational Testing Service and other testing agencies for presenting an outstanding program. The Center has been deemed a national model for the delivery of services in a "state of the art" mode.

Contact:
Sherie Goldstein, Coordinator of Testing, (305) 237-1015
John Greb, Associate Dean, Student Services, (305) 237-1056

Miami-Dade Community College-North Campus
11380 NW 27 Avenue
Miami, FL 33167-3495
Total headcount enrollment-Credit: 23,000; Non-Credit: 15,000
Campuses/sites: 5; Full-time faculty: 263

MIAMI-DADE COMMUNITY COLLEGE-WOLFSON CAMPUS

CENTER FOR ECONOMIC EDUCATION

※ *The Center provides in-service teacher training develops programs* ※
for adults and serves K-12 schools

In August 1987, the Wolfson Campus of Miami-Dade Community College became the nation's first community college to establish a Center for Economic Education. The M-DCC Center is one of eight Centers of Economic Education located throughout Florida at various universities.

The M-DCC Wolfson Center for Economic Education is affiliated with the Florida Council on Economic Education and is one of 250 Centers belonging to the National Council on Economic Education (formerly known as the Joint Council on Economic Education).

The Center's mission has been to service both private and public schools, K-12 in Dade and Monroe counties to enhance their economic education. The Center, additionally, develops programs and materials for the adult community.

To foster the basic goals of the Center several innovative curriculum methods have been instituted. The "Stock Market Game" (a simulation of investment), the Chicago Board of Trade's "Commodity Challenge" (a student-oriented research project), the *Wall Street Journal's* Education Edition for area high schools, and curriculum materials to accompany the Florida Chamber of Commerce video, "Small Business Enterprises," have all provided significant learning experiences for students in the program.

In addition to providing a variety of nationally and state-produced programs, the MDCC Wolfson Center has created four different credit courses accepted by the state's Department of Education for teacher recertification. Two of the four credit courses are for elementary teachers and the other two apply to middle school and high school educators. For each area of instruction (elementary or secondary) the two courses offered cover micro economics and macro economics, with appropriate instructional strategies and materials for their student populations.

In each year since its inception, the Center has seen teachers from these credit courses win state and national awards for their work in their classrooms. Teachers attending the Center's re-certification classes have won *Business Week* magazine's national competition for innovative teaching. Center students have also been consistent winners in the state of Florida's "Commodity Challenge" program, which awards an all-expenses paid trip to Chicago for the winning student and teacher.

In-service programs have been a vital component in achieving the Center's mission. Such programs, varying in length of time from several hours to a full-day or weekend experience have been delivered on the following topics: Personal Financial Planning; Energy and Economics; Middle School Economic Instruction; Global Education; The Gulf War: Its Impact on the U.S.; The Economics of the Stanford Achievement Test; Community Resources; Advanced Placement Economics; The Stock Market; The Commodity Challenge; and "Ecoverde–Environment and Economics."

These in-service programs have involved community business and professional leadership in their development and delivery.

One of the most unique programs offered by the Center is the "Business Dialogue." In this special forum, teachers and selected area professionals come together to discuss selected topics including the Savings and Loan Crisis, International Trade, Free Trade Zones, and Personal Investment for the 90's. The Miami-Dade Center has been

responsible for establishing an Economic and Business Awards Competition at the local county fair. This enables classrooms to compete for prize money and stock certificates based on the quality of Economics and Business projects submitted. The Dade County Youth Fair is the largest county fair in the state, therefore an excellent means of showcasing the quality of economic education developed within the Miami-Dade service area.

The Center has worked closely with Dade and Monroe county school administrators to develop programs and materials appropriate for their curriculum. The Center created a curriculum guide and video that highlighted the importance of "Tourism and Development" for Monroe County.

Although the M-DCC Wolfson Center is the newest center in the State's network and the only one located at a community college, it has been recognized as a leader within the state and at the national level. The staff of the Miami-Dade Wolfson Center consistently presents programs at the state and national conventions and serves on state and national organizations and commissions.

Contact:
Gail A. Hawks, Director
(305) 237-3233

Miami-Dade Community College-Wolfson Campus
300 NE Second Avenue
Miami, FL 33132
Total headcount enrollment-Credit: 16,860; Non-Credit: 3,195
Campuses/sites: 5; Full-time faculty: 169

MIAMI-DADE COMMUNITY COLLEGE-WOLFSON CAMPUS

INTERAMERICAN CENTER

The Center offers courses and program using a progressive curriculum that relies on a unique bilingual method of instruction

Considered one of the largest maintenance bilingual (English/Spanish) programs at the post-secondary level in the U.S., the Wolfson Campus's InterAmerican Center (IAC) has served the educational needs of its community for more than two decades. Miami's location as a gateway to the Caribbean, Central America and South America has resulted in its development as an international cultural and financial center.

From its inception, this model program has served as a catalyst in bilingual education at the college level in this region of the U.S. The bilingual (English/Spanish) instructional mode in which courses are offered at IAC is one of the ways M-DCC fulfills its mission and commitment to provide alternative student learning opportunities. Bilingualism is viewed not as a transitory stage in students' educational development, but rather as an asset to be capitalized on throughout the academic experience. This option is offered to all who attend the InterAmerican Center – Hispanics as well as the growing number of non-Hispanics. In terms of mission, the Center has always viewed bilingualism and biculturalism as definite assets to

be cultivated within the Dade County area.

Started as a small-scale, evening off-campus academic venture in 1972, the bilingual outreach center and, subsequently, the bilingual program (as it was then called) offered two evening courses at a neighborhood center, only three miles from the main campus. Its initial enrollment was 60 students. Today, it has nearly 4,000 students. In terms of enrollment, it is equal to and larger than two of M-DCC's Campuses and six of the 28 community colleges in the state of Florida.

The InterAmerican Center offers courses and programs to anyone wishing to earn college credits through a progressive curriculum that relies on a unique bilingual method of instruction. Five academic departments provide the leadership for making comprehensive programs available in business and computer studies: English communications, social and natural sciences, humanities, mathematics, and foreign languages (including translation/interpretation studies as well as language training in English as a second language). IAC students may

Continues on Page 154

choose from a wide variety of programs and courses leading to a two-year Associate degree in academic areas.

Short-term training programs are offered as well.

The InterAmerican Center is well-known for the kind of personalized services rendered to students. Special academic support in virtually every discipline is available to all students needing individualized attention and instruction.

The faculty, as teachers and facilitators, possess those unique qualities that enhance teaching and learning, motivating students to reach their highest potential. Students enjoy an ongoing dialogue with professors and seek opportunities to discover their strengths through formal and informal meetings. Faculty are intensely involved in promoting academic excellence and demanding the personal best of each student in class.

The uniqueness of Miami's Latin Quarter (Latin Havana) is an ideal background for community and cultural programs sponsored by Miami-Dade Community College's Wolfson Campus and the InterAmerican Center. Annual festivals such as Miami Book Fair International serve to enrich the academic and cultural life of students, the campus and community. In addition to major events, the InterAmerican Center sponsors monthly art exhibits, film series, workshops, concerts and special events of interest to a wide variety of community groups. Conferences, seminars and group meetings are held in the Center's community conference suite in conjunction with special community organizations.

In summary, the Center's philosophy is simple: teaching and learning in a multicultural environment where students and faculty are the center of an ongoing academic exchange .

Contact:
Jose Vicente, Dean
(305) 237-3822

Miami-Dade Community College-Wolfson Campus
300 NE Second Avenue
Miami, FL 33132
Total headcount enrollment-Credit: 16,860; Non-Credit: 3,195
Campuses/sites: 5; Full-time faculty: 169

NORTH FLORIDA JUNIOR COLLEGE

PROGRAM FOR THE HEARING IMPAIRED

By providing students with knowledge about non-educational topics, energies before expended on daily living crises can be applied to academics

North Florida Junior College's Program for the Hearing Impaired is a unique program that challenges and trains hearing-impaired students from all over Florida and the Southeast to be prepared for the 21st Century. Vital reasons for its success are its setting in a rural area and the program design. The holistic model considers education more than just the academic or vocational classroom by encouraging the development of each student to his/her full potential. The various components of the program, begun in 1985, are designed to meet this overall objective.

To be successful, the hearing-impaired individual must learn to live independently in a hearing world. This training begins with a summer program that facilitates the transition from secondary to post secondary education and continues throughout the year with monthly seminars. By providing the students with a knowledge base pertaining to non-educational topics, energies previously expended on daily living crises can be transferred to the academic areas.

Because both the vocational and associate degree tracks are available at the same institution, students may choose or change tracks. Within the vocational track students choose drafting, masonry, building maintenance technol-

ogy or office technology. Employability skills training and an internship program prepare students for the transition to the world of work.

To be truly independent, the hearing-impaired student must be able to communicate with a hearing employer. Hearing-impaired vocational students enroll in special sections of non-credit developmental skills courses in reading, English and mathematics. In the English class, students learn about their own language (American Sign Language) and how to transfer ASL to English.

Inherent in any mainstreamed program is the need for qualified personnel, including tutors, note-takers, counselors and personnel who can help foster personal and social growth on the part of the students. NFJC's program provides these support services. In fact, an outgrowth of the program is an interpreter training program.

National awards include the AACJC/J.C. Penney Award in 1988 and the 1990 National Rural and Small Schools Consortium Exemplary Program Award. The program director is the author of a textbook, *Orientation to Deafness*, and an innovator of deaf education strategies.

Contact:
Dr. Nanci Scheetz, Director, Program for the Hearing Impaired
(904) 973-2288 or TTY (904) 973-2284

North Florida Junior College
1000 Turner Davis Drive
Madison, FL 32340-1698
Total headcount enrollment-Credit: 1,228; Non-Credit: 905
Campuses/sites: 1; Full-time faculty: 29

CURRICULUM INNOVATIVE COMMUNICATION NETWORK

The state-wide network makes curriculum innovations throughout the state accessible to all interested Florida community colleges

The Florida Association of Community Colleges, Curriculum and Instruction Commission, together with the Florida Information Resource Network (FIRN), have developed a system that electronically accesses abstracts of the best Florida Community College curriculum innovations. The abstracts are developed after the yearly state-wide Curriculum and Instruction competition and are input into GROUP CONFERENCING within FIRN MAIL. Library Learning Resource Centers and individuals or departments that have modems or access to the mainframe computer can call up the curriculum abstracts. The project is four years old and contains twenty-seven abstracts.

The goal of the FACC project is to make excellent curriculum innovations that occur in the Florida community college system accessible to all those interested in knowing about the community college curriculum.

The project has been presented to the National Council of Institutional Administrators, which collects curriculum innovations nationwide and presents abstracts in book form. The FACC project is unique because it is accessible statewide on a computer network.

Contact:
George Matsoukas, Grants Coordinator, (407) 439-8201
Jeannine Burgess, FIRN Tech. Education Consultant, (407) 439-8295

Palm Beach Community College
4200 Congress Avenue
Lake Worth, FL 33461
Total head count enrollment-Credit: 30,664; Non-Credit: 16,912
Campuses/sites: 4; Full-time faculty: 193

PALM BEACH COUNTY DISTANCE LEARNING NETWORK

The project enables the college to offer and receive courses spanning the entire county that would not otherwise be available

As a result of a partnership between Palm Beach Community College, Southern Bell and the Palm Beach County School System, students and faculty have had access to a completely interactive telecommunications network for the purpose of conducting classes, lectures, in-service training and sharing video resources. This project has enabled the college to offer and receive courses spanning the length and breadth of the entire county that would not otherwise have been available. It has enabled the college to meet the increased demands for available resources and requests for student accountability.

The Palm Beach County Distance Learning Network links eight sites across the county and is paid for by Southern Bell of Florida. Because of the two-way interactive nature of this network students are exposed to a wider range of educational resources.

In addition to the fact that master teachers in specialized fields are available and the learning process is more exciting, benefits for:
- students include library materials are available and accessed by way of this system;
- teachers include the sharing of instructional materials, expertise, teaching strategies;
- the college include the fact that specialized teachers in calculus and foreign languages are available to a much greater degree, library materials are more widely dispersed, and the network is providing an equitable education to all students in the district regardless of location.

The range of services this network encompasses is an array of equipment and applications, ranging from the ordinary telephone to the more advanced technologies of fiber optics that deliver multimedia, interactive instruction. In all locations the classrooms of this network are located in the Library Learning Resource or Media centers.

Contact:
Brian Kelley
(407) 439-8114

Palm Beach Community College
4200 Congress Avenue
Lake Worth, FL 33461
Total headcount enrollment-Credit: 30,664; Non-Credit: 16,912
Campuses/sites: 4; Full-time faculty: 193

COMMUNITY PARTNERSHIP TO BEGIN A DENTAL HYGIENE PROGRAM

The local dental society pledged cash, equipment and provided input into curriculum development

Stymied by the state's inability to fund new program start-up costs, both the District Board of Trustees and the Board of Directors of the foundation at Pasco-Hernando Community College (P-HCC) have placed major emphasis on business/educational partnerships to develop or enhance many of the college's high-cost curricula. One such partnership emerged with the local dental society as a result of a need for a dental hygiene program to serve the college's two-county district.

Acting on this need, college staff initiated contact with other dental hygiene programs in the state to investigate the feasibility of developing partnerships with existing programs at other community colleges. These efforts were not successful, primarily because of the distance students would be required to travel and the lack of space for sufficient numbers of P-HCC students in these other programs. Thus, this avenue did not appear to be a long-term solution that would provide a consistent supply of skilled hygienists for Pasco and Hernando counties.

College staff then began to investigate the possibility of starting a dental hygiene program at P-HCC. Both needs assessment data and community interest strongly supported this need. However, it was readily apparent that the institution, the fastest-growing public community college in Florida, did not have sufficient resources to undertake this expensive program, particularly during a difficult economic period.

Although committed to the idea of this program, college staff reported to the dental society that sufficient monies for this program would not be available for at least five years, the earliest possible time before a state-funded Allied Health Programs Building would be constructed. The dental society responded by pledging $140,000 in cash, in addition to the donation of major laboratory equipment. The dental society also volunteered to appoint a committee to provide input into curriculum development, to assist with the intricacies of the dental accreditation process, and to aid college personnel with technical expertise.

With these commitments from the dental society, the college agreed to move forward with the program. Nevertheless, there was still a major hurdle to overcome: the college had neither the space nor the resources to provide an on-campus dental clinic. However, Pasco County was in the process of building a health clinic, less than five miles from campus, that would include a dental clinic to serve county clients. In fact, there was no money to staff the clinic with a dentist. Here was another opportunity for a symbiotic, cost-effective partnership. The college would be able to utilize the space for training and the students, under the supervision of college program dentists, would be able to provide some services.

In the fall of 1991, about four years after the process began, P-HCC admitted its first class of six dental hygiene students. A second class was admitted in 1992. The program is accredited by the Commission on Accreditation of the American Dental Association. The success of this endeavor illustrates that there are cooperative means to begin needed programs, even in times of financial exigency.

Contact:
Harry Albertson, Executive Director, P-HCC Foundation, Inc.
(904) 567-6701

Pasco-Hernando Community College
36727 Blanton Road
Dade City, FL 33525-7599
Total head count enrollment-Credit: 10,2003; Non-Credit: 7,300
Campuses/sites: 6; Full-time faculty: 68

A SHORT COURSE IN BLACK STUDENT SUCCESS

A continuing education program is designed to increase opportunities for black students through understanding of their cultural diversity

As part of ongoing efforts to help personnel serve the needs of potential and currently enrolled black students, college staff at P-HCC developed a continuing education program, "Black Student Success," for faculty and staff from all campuses. This program was designed to increase the opportunities for achievement of black students through enhanced understanding of their cultural diversity and holistic needs. This four-hour program contained short units on:

1) a review of black history as a basis for understand-

ing current philosophies and behaviors in American society;

2) an exploration of how current environments and lifestyles influence the behaviors of black students;

3) a review of the effects of self perception on confidence, perseverance, and initiative in entering and continuing post secondary education;

4) an exploration of strategies to assist black students in getting started in post secondary education, e.g., evaluating the student's current academic standing, advising students into courses that will help assure academic success, and encouraging their participation in college activities;

5) a review of ways to reach black male students to encourage post secondary education;

6) a review of the importance of learning "the basics" in English and mathematics, and strategies to ensure initial and ongoing success in these activities;

7) an exploration of the philosophies of expecting the most from black students so they will be challenged appropriately and assisting them in setting goals that will help them achieve at the highest level possible;

8) an exploration with students of the assistance, the programs, and the activities that helped them most in pursuing their college education; and

9) a challenge to the participants to use the information from the seminar to assist in increasing the opportunities for black student success in post secondary education.

Faculty, staff, and students from P-HCC as well as personnel from the two-county public school system, served as presenters. The program was well-attended and received high evaluations from participants. The program was videotaped for those who could not take part. In conjunction with this program, college staff developed a *Directory of African-American Speakers* to aid faculty in scheduling classroom speakers. This directory also includes a partial bibliography of African-American titles available in the college's libraries. As another measure of the success of this endeavor, this program was chosen for inclusion in a national conference on diversity, "Valuing Diversities: Building Healthy Attitudes in Diverse Communities," in Jacksonville, Florida in February 1993.

Contact:
Sylvia Thomasson, Dean of Student Services, (813) 847-2727
Imani Asukile, Equity Officer/Minority Recruiter, (904) 567-6701

Pasco-Hernando Community College
36727 Blanton Road
Dade City, FL 33525-7599
Total head count enrollment-Credit: 10,2003; Non-Credit: 7,300
Campuses/sites: 6; Full-time faculty: 68

LIFE CENTER
(LIFESTYLE IMPROVEMENT AND FITNESS EDUCATION)

Each campus center offer programs to students, college employees, community members, and both government and private-sector employees

As the perceived value of preventive medicine increases business and industry are developing wellness programs for their employees, and hospitals are opening wellness clinics for healthy people who want to learn how to stay healthy. And now, so is Pensacola Junior College. One of the college's newest facilities, the LIFE (Lifestyle Improvement and Fitness Education) Center emphasizes the total wellness of the student. At Pensacola Junior College, the LIFE Center programs fall into the category of preventive medicine and participants are effectively learning to improve their lifestyles. The LIFE Centers offer programs and classes to many distinct populations including: students, faculty/staff, community members, employees of large corporations, and, through joint ventures, municipal government and local hospitals. It is a satellite operation, with a LIFE Center on each of the college's three campuses.

All students and/or community members who enroll in Concepts of Life Fitness, a three-credit-hour course, are eligible to use the LIFE Centers. This course, which is one of the college's general education requirement course choices, emphasizes the importance of a healthy lifestyle and how to make positive lifestyle changes. It is a combination of classroom lectures, health assessments and equipment instruction. The comprehensive fitness assessments include: determination of cardiovascular fitness, pulmonary function, body composition, nutrition, muscular strength and endurance, and flexibility. The participants have the choice of a variety of exercise equipment that meet the needs of any exercise program and include: Nautilus strength-training machines, bicycles, rowers, stair-stepping machines, treadmills, upper body exercisers and cross-country ski machines. Anyone who successfully completes Concepts of Life Fitness, either through credit or audit, can register in subsequent terms for

Continues on Page 158

Recreation/Fitness Lab, a continuing education course that allows the use of the LIFE Centers during open hours. Supervision is provided by professional exercise specialists who design and monitor personalized programs as well as instruct participants in the use of all equipment.

Although the LIFE Center concept itself is well-established, the addition of supplementary programs, especially the Cardiac Rehabilitation component, is an innovation that distinguishes the Pensacola Junior College LIFE Centers from other similar programs. The community-oriented, physician referred, Medically Supervised Cardiac Rehabilitation Program is a scientifically and medically sound exercise and education program for cardiac patients and those at high risk for heart disease. The Cardiac Maintenance Class constitutes the second level of the rehabilitation program.

Additional programs offered in the LIFE Centers include a free Nutrition Counseling Program where PJC dietetic technician students, under the supervision of their instructor, provide counseling for PJC students, faculty and staff. Special programs and scheduling are provided for federal government personnel and local branches of large corporations who enroll their employees as part of their company's health benefit package. In addition, a program entitled "Fit Check" has been developed for members of the City of Pensacola Fire Department. This program provides annual health/fitness assessments and rehabilitation for all members of the department. An Internship Program, in cooperation with The University of West Florida, provides baccalaureate degree candidates in their last semester of study and graduate students in the areas of health, physical education, and exercise science experiential learning in their chosen career fields.

The existing LIFE Center programs continue to grow in enrollment and new programs are developed as the need arises. All programs are evaluated by faculty and administration on an annual basis to insure that they are meeting their goals and objectives.

Contact:
Terry Dillon, Department Head
(904) 484-1314

Pensacola Junior College
1000 College Boulevard
Pensacola, FL 32504
Total headcount enrollment-Credit: 12,503; Non-Credit:17,594
Campuses/sites: 5; Full-time faculty: 233

PROFESSIONAL DEVELOPMENT

Each employee prepares a professional development plan that is reviewed, updated and approved during the annual performance evaluation conference

Committed to the concept that professional development activities benefit the entire college community by promoting academic excellence and refreshing staff skills and spirits, Pensacola Junior College has developed a comprehensive, professional development program with the following goals: 1) to provide a comprehensive new employee orientation and faculty qualification/credentialing system; 2) to provide opportunities for formal in-field educational experience including undergraduate and graduate course work; 3) to provide opportunities for informal in-field educational experiences through in-service events conducted by the college, as well as out-of-district conferences and workshops; 4) to provide non-traditional opportunities for growth, including job exchange programs, sabbaticals, educational leave, retraining and research programs; and 5) to recognize the value of professional growth by including it as one of the criteria for selection of teaching award recipients, for determining faculty promotions in rank, and for merit pay increases for administrative staff.

The operation of the program is relatively simple. Each employee prepares a professional development plan that is reviewed, updated and approved during the annual performance evaluation conference with his or her supervisor. The plan is forwarded to the College In-service Office, which maintains a database of professional development information that can tell an individual employee details about all of the in-service activities he or she has attended, his or her plan expiration date, the types of activities considered in-field for the individual, and other similar information. The program is conducted in five-year cycles, so that each person has sufficient time in which to complete his or her planned activities. Each year the college budgets special funds to support both individual and district activities; at least once in the five-year cycle, each employee is entitled to use a specific amount of college funds to pursue approved development activities individually. These funds can be used for items such as course fees, conference registration and travel.

Contact:
Jill White, Associate Vice President
Marcia Williams, Director, In-service and Staff Development
(904) 484-1773

Pensacola Junior College
1000 College Boulevard
Pensacola, FL 32504
Total headcount enrollment-Credit: 12,503; Non-Credit:17,594
Campuses/sites: 5; Full-time faculty: 233

LEARNING RESOURCE CENTERS

▓ *The centers assist students in all facets of the college's academic* ▓
and vocational programs

A dedication to the success of each Polk Community College student led to the combining of academic support with the leading edge of computer technology in the establishment of Teaching/Learning/Computing Centers (TLCC) on each of the college's campuses. The centers assist students in all facets of the college's academic and vocational programs.

Each TLCC provides networked computers for student use in such activities as: preparing papers; writing computer programs; producing computer graphics; remediation in writing, reading, and mathematics; and computer-assisted drafting. A Novell network connects the computers in each TLCC with four computer classrooms on each campus. The two campuses are connected by a fiber-optic link.

Instructional materials in support of the curriculum are available in each TLCC. These include anatomical models, microscopes, specialized biological equipment, video and audio tapes, 35 mm slides, filmstrips and computer software.

Specialized services are provided in the TLCCs to meet the unique needs of each student. Tutoring is regularly available in mathematics and English, while many other subjects are supported as needed. The staff utilizes adaptive computer technology to provide for the special needs of disabled students. In addition, make-up tests and many other required tests are administered in the centers.

The TLCCs and the faculty enjoy a close, cooperative working relationship. The faculty encourage students to use the services of the TLCC's, where they find a friendly atmosphere conducive to learning and supportive of instruction. Through the Teaching/Learning/Computing Centers, students are given the opportunity to achieve their individual educational goals.

Contact:
Ken Webber, Coordinator, Learning Support Services
(813) 297-1044

Polk Community College
999 Avenue H Northeast.
Winter Haven, FL 33881-4299
Total headcount enrollment-Credit: 16,940; Non-Credit: 19,794
Campuses/sites: 2; Full-time faculty: 106

CRIMINAL JUSTICE TRAINING:
LAW ENFORCEMENT-ACADEMY TRACK

▓ *This route not only prepares students for a career in law enforcement,* ▓
but also integrates program objectives with a two-year AS degree

Polk Community College was the pilot location for Florida's first agency-driven Criminal Justice program, with objectives directly integrated with a two-year Associate of Science degree. The program was developed after years of a somewhat frustrating situation for graduates of academic criminal justice programs. Regardless of the level of the degree they earned, they were not eligible for Florida certification as an officer until completion of a certification academy program. These academy programs, which are offered throughout the State of Florida in 40 training centers, are lengthy and costly.

This prompted the Florida Department of Law Enforcement (FDLE) and the Department of Education (DOE) to carefully study and review Florida's criminal justice training and educational delivery system. A group of sheriffs, police chiefs, correctional administrators and educators joined with FDLE, DOE and the Department of Corrections to initiate the Criminal Justice Training Program Improvement Grant.

The grant's task force members agreed that an integrated, agency-driven delivery system would be the most efficient delivery system to best ensure that Florida's officers have the competence needed to meet current challenges, as well as those of the 21st Century. Their recommended delivery system became known as the Enhanced Criminal Justice Training and Education Delivery System.

Pioneered at Polk Community College, the Law Enforcement-Academy Track makes students who complete the degree program eligible to take the Criminal Justice Standards and Training Commission (CJSTC) certi-

Continues on Page 160

fication examinations for police and/or corrections officer.

These students attend certification courses that parallel their academic studies. The certification courses have been enhanced to provoke research and project work comparable to other college level studies.

Criminal justice employers are very interested in these students and their placement future looks good. Numerous other community colleges throughout the state are preparing "mirror" programs of PCC's.

Contact:
Don Shattler, Manager, Criminal Justice Training
(813) 297-1030

Polk Community College
999 Avenue H Northeast
Winter Haven, FL 33881-4299
Total headcount enrollment-Credit: 16,940; Non-Credit: 19,794
Campuses/sites: 2; Full-time faculty: 106

STRATEGIES FOR CRITICAL THINKING AND TEACHING EXCELLENCE

*⊠ In the thinking workshops, participants are taught to move from concrete examples ⊠
to abstract ones, from the familiar to the unfamiliar*

When Santa Fe Community College implemented a program that invited faculty in all disciplines to participate in a series of workshops, they found that by emphasizing the process of thinking and learning, the quality of the papers improved. Since these workshops focused on the craft of writing, it was clear that the next series of workshops should emphasize the art of thinking.

The college wanted to find a way to make the transition smoothly from writing strategies to thinking strategies. In July 1991, the college collaborated with Educational Testing Service to modify and test a product that ETS has successfully used for K-12 teachers, entitled "Strategies for Critical Thinking Across the Curriculum." We knew our faculty were teaching these skills but were unaware of the pedagogy. The workshops clarified the process and allowed them to consciously plan lectures and lab experiences with the specific goals in mind.

In the thinking workshops, the participants are taught to move from concrete examples to abstract ones and from the familiar to the unfamiliar. Thus when teaching a discipline concept, one would first give a familiar example that students could physically or mentally manipulate. Then

move to the abstract, unfamiliar concept. The students generalize from the familiar to the unfamiliar, from concrete to abstract.

The workshops have stimulated the faculty to rethink their course objectives and methods, reaffirmed the student/teacher relationship in the learning process, and challenged them to experiment with new ideas and techniques. Two workshops are conducted each academic year, in the fall and spring semesters, and 20 faculty participate in each workshop.

The program costs were minimal due to the experimental agreement we had with ETS, and the results met both our needs. Faculty are trained to conduct the workshops in-house. The workshop sessions are spread over six weeks, thus our faculty can participate in the program with minimal disruption to their course commitments.

The results of this program were presented at the October 1993 League for Innovation conference in Orlando. ETS has taken the revisions and suggestions made by our faculty and is offering a version of "Strategies for Critical thinking Across the Curriculum" for community colleges nationally.

Contact:
Heijia Wheeler, Dean, Arts and Sciences
(904) 395-5061

Santa Fe Community College
3000 NW 83rd Street
Gainesville, FL 32606
Total head count enrollment-Credit: 12,000; Non-Credit: 22,000
Campuses/sites: 3; Full-time faculty: 241

ENTRY-LEVEL ASSESSMENT:
USING COMPUTER-ADAPTIVE TESTING

*The student's test score is produced on the screen immediately
following the test, taken on the microcomputer*

Because community colleges with open-door admission policies attract student populations with varied levels of academic preparedness, quick and effective assessment is key to providing students a quality educational experience. At Santa Fe Community College (SFCC), the Computerized Placement Tests (CPTs) thrust basic-skills assessment into a new era while providing effective and efficient assessment.

The CPTs computer-adaptive test battery, developed by the college board, was designed for the primary purpose of assessing entry-level skills to provide appropriate course placement. Computer-adaptive testing is a new concept that uses microcomputers to administer the test and report final scores. The test battery consists of four untimed subtests: reading comprehension, sentence skills, arithmetic and algebra. Items in each test are selected from an extensive item test bank of varying difficulty and content. The student's test score is produced on the screen immediately following completion of the test.

In 1986, SFCC began a project to investigate the effectiveness of the CPTs for entry-level assessment. Two years of exploration and research indicated that the CPTs were effective in placing students in appropriate courses, while providing many benefits over traditional paper/pencil tests. In 1989, the CPTs test battery was accepted as one of the state-approved assessment tests; SFCC adopted the CPTs as the on-site assessment instrument. Continued research findings provided valuable information for student advisement and curriculum revision. Current students are focusing on the CPTs for special student populations, including students with learning disabilities and students for whom English is a second language (ESL).

Research findings regarding the use of new technology to address the critical assessment issue have been shared through publications, presentations and personal communications on local, state and national levels - helping many colleges implement solutions to their assessment problems. The League for Innovation in the Community College has acknowledged the CPTs project, accomplished through partnerships with the College Board, IBM and community colleges, as a significant achievement.

Contact:
Pat Smittle, Chairman, Learning Labs and Development Studies
(904) 395-5384

Santa Fe Community College
3000 NW 83rd Street
Gainesville, FL 32606
Total head count enrollment-Credit: 12,000; Non-Credit: 22,000
Campuses/sites: 3; Full-time faculty: 241

COMPUTER ASSISTED WRITING

*Technical writing, creative writing, and journalism courses
use the computers as an integral part of instruction*

At Seminole Community College computers are used to enhance such processes as brainstorming, note-taking, drafting, revising, documenting and editing. This integration of microcomputer word-processing and the writing process has been going on since 1983. Through Computer Assisted Writing (CAW), the goals are to admit how difficult the tasks involved in writing are; to show how microcomputers can assist a working writer in accomplishing those tasks; and to enhance integral writing processes.

Two new courses (ENC 2270, Computer Assisted Writing I, and ENC 2271, Computer Assisted Writing II) are taught entirely on microcomputers in the English Macintosh Classroom. The first focuses on learning how to use microcomputers and word processing software integrally with the various writing processes. The second teaches Desktop Publishing, while maintaining the rigors of fine writing. The traditional course offerings now incorporate orientations to and assignments accomplished in the Writing Center. The two college preparatory courses require one extra hour in the Writing Center each week. During that hour students work with language and computer tutors. The English I and English II courses formally incorporate the Macintoshes and the Writing Center to the degree desired by the individual instructor, but records indicate that the majority of English I and English II students use the facility extensively. Technical writing, creative writing and journalism courses use the micros as an integral part of instruction. The advent

Continues on Page 162

of desktop publishing has attracted numerous new users from other disciplines, as writing across the curriculum efforts are extended.

Faculty who teach writing with the assistance of computers have realized that the natural end-product of writing is publication and/or presentation of information – rather than merely the creation of documents in manuscript form. Thus, desktop publishing fits into the department's Computer Assisted Writing curriculum. Therefore, the second course in this sequence, CAW II, focuses on publication and presentation.

In varied formats, ENC 2271 has been offered to area K-12 instructors and to high school honor students. The first effort was an exciting one-week "forced march" which met during the Summer Term. Each K-12 teacher selected assignments appropriate to actual teaching needs. The class started on a Wednesday afternoon, and by the following Wednesday afternoon, the students had produced fine and exciting works. Contact is maintained with these teachers to inform them of improved equipment and to invite them to return to the Writing Center. A good relationship has been established and additional workshops will be offered each year.

The second special version of ENC 2271 was a four-week program funded by the Governor's Summer Program for high school honor students, and was an integral part of an exciting interdisciplinary program including philosophy and ethnographic research which focuses on the history of Seminole County.

Students enrolled in arts and sciences courses are encouraged to use the Writing Center on a walk-in basis. Most students, and many of our faculty and staff members, have done so. A true sense of collaboration among the writers has created a highly supportive environment. The facility is literally a center, not a lab, and is staffed with dedicated instructors and tutors who offer as much one-on-one instruction as possible. Students are proud of the quality of the papers they submit to instructors and the state of Florida and FACC have seen fit to grant awards of excellence for curricular and instructional innovations based on the use of microcomputers in English composition courses.

Contact:
Bruce Aufhammer
(407) 323-1450, ext 414

Seminole Community College
100 Weldon Boulevard
Sanford, FL 32773
Total headcount enrollment-Credit: 19,523; Non-Credit: 9,187
Campuses/sites: 2; Full-time faculty: 131

DIVERSIFIED COOPERATIVE TRAINING (DCT)

The program provides special-needs, unemployed adults with selected occupational skills

The Diversified Cooperative Training (DCT) Program at Seminole Community College is the only program of its kind in a Florida community college setting. Since 1988, it has helped hundreds of unemployed adults, ages 16 to 60, become employable, productive, contributing members of society.

Unlike DCT programs at the high school level that work with younger students with little or no work experience, the DCT Program at SCC works with unemployed adults who have suffered emotional or physical traumas or other circumstances that have interfered with their ability to transition into employment.

The primary objective of this program is to provide special-needs, unemployed adults with selected occupational skills through employment-related instruction and concurrent, paid, supervised on-the-job training.

By forming cooperative agreements with area employers and combining resources with community agencies, the DCT Program has been able to link the best of rehabilitation and education into a cost effective, timeline-based set of activities that lead to employment.

During fiscal year 1991-1992 alone, a staff of 15 part-time and full-time employees provided instruction to 555 students in one or more components of the DCT Program. The program maintains a success rate of between 85 and 100 percent per class.

The program budget includes support from the college, the Carl D. Perkins Amendments, the JTPA, and contracts from Health & Rehabilitative Services (HRS) and the Private Industry Council of Seminole County/Vocational Rehabilitation (PIC/VR).

Besides monetary recognition in the form of grants and contracts, the DCT Program has been recognized for its success at the state and local levels. Numerous presentations on the program have been given at state and regional conferences, and the program was cited in the 1991 edition of *Community Colleges' Exemplary Instructional* *Programs*, a publication sponsored by the Council of Instructional Affairs.

Contact:
Linda Ley-Siemer
(407) 323-1450, ext.536

Seminole Community College
100 Weldon Boulevard
Sanford, FL 32773
Total head count enrollment-Credit: 19,523; Non-Credit: 9,187
Campuses/sites: 2; Full-time faculty: 131

INDUSTRY SERVICE - LESCO, INC.

The college has a full-time faculty member at the company and has developed specialized as well as general education credit instruction

What began as a three-year skills training program at a local business became a symbiotic relationship of such benefit that South Florida Community College now has a full-time faculty member at Lesco, Incorporated.

The association with Lesco, Incorporated, formally began in 1986 with a Florida's Sunshine State Skills program, which was initiated to assist community colleges in working with new business and industry. The partnership began with a skills training program set up at the Lesco site to train machinists and other metal workers. The program was the only Sunshine State Skills project funded for three consecutive years, due to the continued expansion of the company and to the continued need for increased and diversified skill training.

When the grant ended, the relationship did not. Since the beginning of the relationship the program at Lesco has grown from skill training in machining and metalworking to other skill areas, such as forklift safety, quality control training, drafting, computer numerical controlled machining and drafting and design, supervisory training, and basic skills instruction.

To meet the needs of the growing company, the college has developed specialized, as well as general education college credit instruction, leading to degree completion. In addition, the college is now beginning formal training in interaction management and Total Quality Management within the company.

The company has dedicated classroom and office space for the college's use and considers the college as a permanent part of the company. Company management gladly flex the schedules of their employees to encourage regular and ongoing education, both at the company site and on the college campus. Since the relationship with South Florida Community College began in 1986, education has become a major employee benefit at Lesco, Inc.

Contact:
Michelle Roberts, Dean, Vocational/Technical Education
(813) 453-6661, ext. 165

South Florida Community College
600 West College Drive
Avon Park, FL 33825
Total headcount enrollment-Credit: 5,299; Non-Credit : 10,820
Campuses/sites: 5; Full-time faculty: 36

ACADEMIC DUAL ENROLLMENT

⊞ Not only does the program allow students to complete college courses early, ⊞
it also prepares them better for other aspects of college life

Besides dual enrollment classes taught in person to high school students, South Florida Community College now offers telecourses, an innovation that benefits Highlands County students who had their offerings restricted due to the reduction of the school day from seven to six periods. These students study the telecourse tapes and materials in supervised study periods, under the auspices of a college-certified instructor.

The particular goals of the dual enrollment program are: 1) to provide accelerated learning opportunities for college-qualified high school students; 2) to enhance community college and high school communications; and 3) to establish closer high school and community college articulation regarding numerous academic transfer issues.

The program has resulted in thousands of college-credit hours being awarded to hundreds of students. (One high school student actually amassed enough college credits to receive her Associate in Arts degree on the same night she received her high school diploma!) The dual enrollment program has also benefited enrollment at SFCC by providing significant first contact with many students who later became full-time SFCC students. Moreover, the programs' impact is obvious in regard to the many students who were better prepared for college life and work as a result of their dual enrollment experiences.

The dual enrollment program is structurally implemented in the following manner: 1)agreements are negotiated and approved with the three county school boards; 2) administrative steps to determine course and instructor selection, instructor certification, and program review and evaluation as detailed in a procedures Manual; and 3) the SFCC instructional staff evaluation instruments (administrative evaluation and student evaluation) are applied equally to dual enrollment staff.

The academic dual enrollment program at SFCC has received the continued and enthusiastic support and cooperation of the Highlands, Hardee and DeSoto County school boards. Public reactions have been positive as indicated by the steady increases in dual enrollment enrollments, and the high school counselors have reported numerous endorsements of the program from parents.

Contact:
Robert Fitzgerald, Dean, Arts & Sciences
(813) 453-6661, ext. 329

South Florida Community College
600 West College Drive
Avon Park, FL 33825
Total head count enrollment-Credit: 5,299; Non-Credit : 10,820
Campuses/sites: 5; Full-time faculty: 36

SECONDARY SCHOOL TEACHER
BIOTECHNOLOGY TRAINING

⊞ The program helps secondary science educators gain conceptual understanding ⊞
of gene cloning and its impact on society

Secondary science educators gain conceptual understanding of gene cloning and its impact on society through the Biotechnology Training program at St. Johns River Community College. This is especially important today, when the impact of biotechnology is becoming increasingly apparent. Noted biotechnologists say that biotechnology will have more impact on human health in the next 25 years than antibiotics had in the last 25 years. Biotechnology will also help solve food shortage problems and provide us with the capability to diagnose and treat diseases such as cancer and AIDS.

Participants in the training program are involved in hands-on laboratory experiences revolving around extracting DNA from bacteria, separating the fragments, and inserting the DNA fragments into other bacteria. Lecture-discussion sessions include such topics as DNA fingerprinting and diagnosis of some genetic diseases. Participants perform preparatory activities required to instruct recombinant DNA laboratories. Upon completion of the training program, participants have gained a basic knowledge of recombinant DNA technology and are able to instruct secondary science students in these techniques.

The training program, which is conducted in cooperation with the Interdisciplinary Center for Biotechnology Research at the University of Florida, carries three college credits. The program is currently offered in a one-week summer session for approximately 21 participants. Instruction is provided cooperatively by the biological science faculty at SJRCC, who have undergone extensive training at the University of Florida to prepare them to teach secondary school teachers, and by researchers from the University of Florida. SJRCC is one of few community colleges in the state to offer the program.

The textbook for the course is *DNA Science* by D. Micklos and G. Freyer. This is the first year SJRCC has offered the training program. Expansion is planned for the future. All participants completed the program successfully.

Contact:
Shirley Kennedy, Dean of General Education
(904) 328-1571

St. Johns River Community College
5001 St. Johns Avenue
Palatka, FL 32177-3897
Total head count enrollment-Credit: 5,537; Non-Credit: 837
Campuses/sites: 3; Full-time faculty: 71

FLORIDA SCHOOL OF THE ARTS (FLOARTS)

Admission to the school, which has five program areas,
is by audition and/or portfolio review

The first state-supported arts school for high school and college students in Florida, the Florida School of the Arts at St. Johns River Community College has continued to grow as its curriculum has expanded.

The Florida School of the Arts, which serves the entire state, has five program areas: visual arts (fine arts and graphic design); dance (modern and ballet); musical theatre; production/design- technical theatre and costume design; and theater. Programs in each of the disciplines are structured such that students receive an interrelated, well-rounded arts education. Admission is by audition and/or portfolio review.

The academic component of the degree desired is fulfilled by St. Johns River Community College. The Associate in Arts degree is geared toward students who want to continue their training at a four-year university. This degree is based upon completion of a minimum of semester hours in both general education and the Florida School of the Arts foundation program. FloArts awards the Associate in Arts degree with specializations in Visual Art, Dance, Theatre-Acting, and Theatre Production/Design. The Associate in Science degree is geared toward students who want to go from the School directly into the arts profession. This degree requires completion of the arts foundation courses, a concentrated arts major, and semester hours in both general education and business courses. FloArts awards the Associate in Science degree in Visual Arts With a specialization in Fine Art and Graphic Design, and the Associate in Science degree in Performing Arts with a specialization in Ballet, Modern Dance, Theatre Production/Design, Acting, and Musical Theatre.

FloArts has been granted the authority by the State Board of Education to award the high school diploma. The high school program requires the completion of all state secondary education requirements while enrolled at the School. Students may be admitted in the 11th grade.

Within the framework of a supportive, interrelated academic community, FloArts seeks to offer quality training in the visual and performing arts to aspiring artists who exhibit outstanding talent or potential. The school, whose faculty, administration and programs are continually evaluated by the Florida School of the Arts Advisory Council, operates on the premise that intense, individualized instruction and practical hands-on experience are essential to the full development of creative abilities.

Contact:
Gayle Kassing, Dean of the Florida School of the Arts
(904) 328-1571

St. Johns River Community College
5001 St. Johns Avenue
Palatka, FL 32177-3897
Total head count enrollment-Credit: 5,537; Non-Credit: 837
Campuses/sites: 3; Full-time faculty: 71

APPLIED ETHICS

The course, which is required, replaced one that had a strong philosophical bent and had gone untaught due to lack of student interest

There has been a well-documented decline in ethical behavior and human values during the last 30 years, triggering an enormous resurgence of interest in ethics. Believing American schools and colleges should be a starting place for morality in our nation, St. Petersburg Junior College designed an ethics course to address real-life situations. Since 1985, the revised course has been required of all students seeking Associate in Arts degrees and of students in selected Associate in Science disciplines.

Applied Ethics is designed to ensure that SPJC graduates:

1) understand the historical development of ethics;
2) demonstrate the nature of ethical issues when confronted with examples of situations containing such issues;
3) understand the relationship between the foundational values of a society and the quality and mode of life in that society; and
4) apply consistent and logical reasoning processes to resolve ethical issues.

Applied Ethics replaced a course that had a strong philosophical bent and had gone untaught due to lack of student interest. To make sure the course objectives and scope strongly reflect community and societal values, a Community Advisory Committee comprising leaders and decision-makers from diverse backgrounds provided the review and direction needed to implement the course. In addition, the course is continually evaluated by students and observers such as the Ethics Advisory Committee. Before his death, the course was routinely evaluated by Dr. Paul N. Ylvisaker, former dean of Harvard University's Graduate School of Education.

The course reviews the historical development of ethics, examines a variety of ethical dilemmas and gives students practice resolving such dilemmas through the use of statutory and professional codes as well as through ethical reasoning. Emphasis is placed on logical analysis and responsible decision-making. The Honors Applied Ethics course, which is by invitation only, emphasizes critical analysis of issues in order to generate options and determine choices for resolving dilemmas. Emphasis is on verbalization of concepts. Both are three-hour, freshmen-level courses.

A textbook, *Ethics Applied*, penned in part by national contributors, has been compiled.

In seven years, the Applied Ethics programs have grown to include six full-time instructors and several adjuncts from various professional backgrounds. SPJC also has used the course as a springboard to ethics seminars for public officials and members of the Florida Bar.

Contact:
Emily Baker, Instructor-in-Charge
(813) 341-4313

St. Petersburg Junior College
PO Box 13489
St. Petersburg, FL 33733
Total headcount enrollment-Credit: 34,000; Non-Credit: 19,000
Campuses/sites: 5; Full-time faculty: 292

PROJECT FLAMINGO

The multi-million dollar project calls for networking the college's sites and instructional and administrative personnel within each site

In 1989, the District Board of Trustees of SPJC launched a multi-million dollar initiative dubbed "Project Flamingo." The project was a response to the vision of a college-wide technology network that addresses multiple goals. SPJC sought to:

1) foster communication by sharing messages and complete files and reports electronically within a college that spans the county with seven separate sites, and having widespread availability of the wealth of external information in national databases;
2) strengthen administrative management by providing easy access to institutional information, developing an executive information system, and saving personnel time and money through electronic reporting and document processing;
3) improve student services especially in the areas of advising, counseling, and orientation; and, most importantly,
4) promote excellence in teaching and learning both by enhancing classroom instruction and encouraging student involvement.

Project Flamingo calls for networking the college's sites and instructional and administrative personnel within each site. The plan is to connect Unisys, DEC and Apple technologies so that information can be shared by individuals. The project also incorporates Macintosh technology directly into the curriculum and classroom to enhance student learning outcomes. Eventually, SPJC envisions transmitting voice, data and video through a fiber optic network, integrating all three elements into classroom multi-media experiences.

The college has installed faculty development centers and student labs at each of its campuses. Graduate courses are offered through the neighboring University of South Florida to assist faculty in developing instructional applications. Macintosh computers have been provided to faculty and staff at the college's Clearwater campus, District Office and selected sites. The first inter-site networking occurred during 1990 as those two sites were connected, with additional faculty and staff at those sites provided Macintosh computers and training. These actions enabled the college to enter into a pilot phase, testing communication between those sites, data analysis and retrieval, and shared access to external databases. At the same time, faculty will be able to use the tools for curriculum develop-

ment and students will discover applications that enhance classroom learning. In 1991, the college's Allstate Center (with its emphasis on criminal justice and corporate training activities) was brought into the network. Later, as more cabling, equipment and applications are added to the network, college faculty will be able to access knowledge bases and files anywhere within the college's computer system. As departments or sites are brought into the network, end-users will be trained and provided with equipment.

This project is being made possible by many financial partnerships between the college and members of the private sector, including Apple, DEC and Unisys Corporations. Local members of the private sector will be offered the opportunity to participate in raising an additional $3-million for Project Flamingo.

Project Flamingo has been recognized in a chapter of the *EDUCOM* book *Transforming Teaching With Technology*, in an article in *T.H.E. Journal*, and in *The Chronicle of Higher Education*. In addition, an SPJC-produced video features Ted Koppell of ABC and Don Harrison of CNN talking about the project.

Contact:
James Olliver, Vice President, Institutional and Program Planning
(813) 341-3316

St. Petersburg Junior College
PO Box 13489
St. Petersburg, FL 33733
Total head count enrollment-Credit: 34,000; Non-Credit: 19,000
Campuses/sites: 5; Full-time faculty: 292

COLLEGE REACH-OUT

The college reaches out to at-risk students in grades 6 through 12
to encourage them in their studies and to later pursue college

The Minority Out-Reach Education (MORE) Program at Tallahassee Community College identifies assists, motivates and prepares at-risk/disadvantaged students of the district of Leon, Gadsden and Wakulla Counties for post secondary education.

In an effort to accomplish the objectives and goals set forth in the program, the students are identified by the Counselor Associates at the 11 school sites in the district. An outstanding cooperative relationship exists between the superintendents, principals, counselors and other staff members in each county and TCC. These identified students are tracked through middle, high school and into college as part of the evaluative process of the effectiveness of the Reach-Out Programs across the state.

The MORE Program, which has received annual state grants since 1984, is composed of various components which are implemented on an ongoing basis. Each year activities are identified to encourage academic interests in counseling the students to realize the value of post secondary education. Many role models are provided during these activities to help the students realize the posi-

tive relationship between good learning skills and economic and social mobility. The MORE Program can be credited with outstanding programs and activities designed to enhance student's self-esteem and self-worth.

Components are:
1) The TCC Middle College Program at the Gadsden Center. During the Fall of 1990, the Gadsden County School District, TCC and the Florida Institute of Education formed a partnership and implemented the concept of the Middle College Centre. A total of 25 high-risk students entered into the program at the ninth-grade level and will be encouraged to remain until graduation. The student successes have been contributed to the small student/teacher ratio, exposure to peer role models and tutors, mentors and cultural enrichment.

2) The school instructional component based in three middle schools of Leon, Gadsden and Wakulla Counties are taught by outstanding role models on

Continues on Page 168

a daily basis.

3) Student/Parent Orientations are held each semester at TCC to provide financial aid counseling, career assessments, motivational speakers, tours of the campus.

4) ACT Preparation Workshops. An ACT Preparation Workshop is offered for eight weeks during the Fall and Spring semesters for those students in Leon and Gadsden Counties who are seeking to satisfy college entrance admission requirements.

5) Tutorial Support Component. During February 1991, the TCC Volunteers organization was formed on campus. It is composed of college students who volunteer one semester to tutor the MORE students in Leon County during and immediately after school hours. As a result of this additional tutorial support, we have seen a marked improvement in their grades as well as their overall attitude toward learning.

6) Cultural Enrichment. Numerous activities are conducted at TCC in observance of Black History Month. All of the MORE students at the 11 sites are invited to participate in a Black History Brain Bowl Competition, thereby providing exposure to a college setting and cultural awareness of African American contributions to society. Additionally, a Black History Convocation is held which features a distinguished speaker from the local community.

Significant Program Achievements:

1) Several students from the program had an opportunity to speak before the State Board of Education as well as the EA/EO Committee for the Division of Community Colleges.

2) The MORE Program was presented as an entry for the 16th Annual Exemplary Practice Award sponsored by the Student Development Commission of the Florida Association of Community Colleges.

3) Ninety percent of the MORE seniors in the eight high schools of Leon and Gadsden Counties graduated during the 1990-91 calendar year. Fifty-four percent of these graduates enrolled in colleges.

4) The MORE students who participated during the Fall 1992 ACT Preparation Workshop showed 85 percent improvement from the pre to the post tests.

Making computers an integral tool in the chemistry lab without having to turn students into computer experts is a goal of Tallahassee Community College

The College recognizes that with low-cost, yet powerful microcomputers, the science educator has a reasonable means of exposing students to computer technology in a scientific context. In particular, microcomputers are capable of giving students experiences in the areas of:

1) complex, quantitative analysis of scientific data via spreadsheets;

2) direct data acquisition from laboratory instruments and analysis thereof;

3) simulations of chemical processes and/or laboratory experiences which would be too costly or dangerous to justify under a traditional laboratory setting; and

4) exploration of chemical databases including graphical and interactive videodisc formats.

Contact:
Debra McCray, Enrollment Services
(904) 539-8334

Tailahassee Community College
444 Appleyard Drive
Tallahassee, FL 32304-2895
Total head count enrollment-Credit: 13,644; Non-Credit: 1,013
Campuses/sites: 2; Full-time faculty: 130

COMPUTERS IN FRESHMAN CHEMISTRY

Students in the General Chemistry course for science/engineering majors are introduced to computer technology as used in "real world" environments

In 1989, Tallahassee Community College was awarded a National Science Foundation Grant for Instrumentation and Laboratory Improvement (ILI) to implement computer technology into the Freshman Chemistry Laboratories. Both IBM and Macintosh computer systems were introduced into the Freshman Chemistry Laboratory curriculum. The IBM machines are used for direct data acquisition (DDA) through IBM's Personal Science Laboratory (PSL) system; while the Macintosh systems are used for HyperCard simulations and interactive exploration of chemical databases. Both systems are utilized for spreadsheet analysis of collected data and simulations. With a dual system approach, a wider choice of educational software could be utilized.

To accomplish this goal of using the computer as an integral tool in the science laboratory without having to turn students into computer experts or programmers, both systems were required to have a similar operating environment. Thus, Windows is employed to provide an icon based-interface like the Macintosh, Excel is the spreadsheet used in both environments, and all programs are menu-driven. Students learn more involved programs in a progressive fashion on a "need to know" basis. Using spreadsheets as an example, students progress from simply entering data and printing charts and graphs early in the first semester lab to writing the spreadsheet formulas by the end of the second semester.

All students in the General Chemistry course for science/engineering majors are thus being introduced to computer technology as utilized in "real world" environments. The use of computers in laboratory situations is being extended into the other chemistry laboratory courses. Integration and extension of computer use into these courses required SPD funds one summer to develop the basic structure of the courses and requires continuing evaluation and updating of materials by instructors.

In addition, the investigators were selected to speak at Macademia Southeast '91 Conference and at the NSF-Catalyzed Innovations in the Undergraduate Laboratory Session of the 204th ACS National Meeting (1992).

Contact:
Carol O. Zimmerman, Science/Math Division
(904) 488-0462

Tallahassee Community College
444 Appleyard Drive
Tallahassee, FL 32304-2895
Total head count enrollment-Credit: 13,644; Non-Credit: 1,013
Campuses/sites: 2; Full-time faculty: 130

COMPUTER INTEGRATED MANUFACTURING

The CIM lab not only serves students but also is available for use by professional groups, manufacturers and others using business-related software

A $1-million Computer Integrated Manufacturing (CIM) laboratory is the centerpiece of a Valencia Community College program serving students, professional groups and manufacturers.

The CIM program trains electronics specialists in areas such as programmable controllers, industrial computers and automated systems, and is tailored for those first entering the job market as well as those workers who wish to upgrade their skills. Students learn to evaluate performance of automated production-line equipment, to modify operational characteristics of production-line equipment (either by software modifications of computers or controllers, or by hardware modifications), and to use instrumentation to evaluate malfunctioning equipment.

The students receive instruction in a manufacturing demonstration laboratory that is designed as a "teaching factory." This laboratory demonstrates software used for production planning, computer-assisted design and quality control. Students can also perform applied research and problem solving that is necessary to the high technology workplace of today.

The CIM laboratory, on Valencia's West Campus, is available for use by virtually any organization using business-related software. Knowledge gained by students in areas such as printing, manufacturing, inventory control, food processing, entertainment ride controls and software systems can help industries become more productive, thereby contributing to economic development of this region.

The instructional program leading to the Associate in Science Degree includes courses in: Automation Systems, Programmable Controls, Electromechanical Components and Mechanisms, Systems Instrumentation, Computer Assisted Design, Automated Test Equipment, Manufacturing Resources Planning (MRP), Shop Floor Data Collection, and Quality Control. Over the past three years many of these courses have been offered on campus and on-site with industries. More than 2,600 employees from Central Florida businesses have taken one or more of these courses during the past three years to upgrade job skills.

The Florida High Technology and Industry Council designated Valencia as a Center of Specialization in Computer Integrated Manufacturing in 1987. In 1990, the Valencia Community College CIM Program was selected as the Outstanding Vocational Program in the Southeast by the U.S. Department of Education. In addition, the U.S. Department of Commerce has designated the Valencia CIM Laboratory as a "Shared Manufacturing Facility." This will provide local manufacturers an opportunity to have "hands on experience" with modern manufacturing productivity tools in support of training, product design, manufacturing process planning, and evaluation of systems for possible use at their facility.

The Computer Integrated Manufacturing (CIM) Facility at Valencia Community College supports advanced manufacturing technology transfer and education. Recently expanded to accommodate automated assembly of printed wiring boards with both surface-mounted and insertion components, this facility incorporates flexible robotics work cells, automated material handling, bar code systems for data gathering, and automated test equipment. The automated assembly facility is linked by a Token Ring Network to the Valencia Computer Laboratory to interface with Manufacturing Resource Planning (MRP) and Statistical Process Control (SPC) software programs.

This facility promotes competencies of U.S. workers in

Continues on Page 170

the global marketplace, supporting the preparation of the "knowledge-based" work force needed in the 1990's. It also has the potential for becoming a Manufacturing Productivity Institute of regional and national significance. Center memberships include the National Coalition of Advanced Technology Centers, the Alliance for Manufacturing Productivity, and the National Coalition for Advanced Manufacturing.

The Computer Integrated Manufacturing Facility at Valencia has been supported by a number of local manufacturers and suppliers of manufacturing productivity tools, including IBM, Seimens Stromberg-Carlson, Martin Marietta, Gould-Modicon, Bridgeport, and others. Suppliers are encouraged to use this facility for demonstration of software and hardware systems for productivity improvements.

Contact:
Hugh Rogers, Chairman, Computer & Engineering Tech. Programs
(407) 299-5000, ext. 1290

Valencia Community College
PO Box 3028
Orlando, FL 32802
Total head count enrollment-Credit: 36,800; Non-Credit: 26,140
Campuses/sites: 6; Full-time faculty: 244

COMPUTER PROGRAMMER TRAINING FOR THE DISABLED

The hallmark of the program is the successful partnership among the business, education and rehabilitation sectors, benefiting all involved

Computer Programmer Training for the Disabled at Valencia Community College serves individuals with severe disabilities by providing training, supportive services and job placement in the field of computer programming. The hallmark of the program is the successful partnership among business, education and rehabilitation, benefiting all involved. Community leaders are involved in the program, and not in name only. The program is directed by a Business Advisory Council (BAC) comprising executives from a variety of different industries and representatives of collaborating agencies. The direct involvement of these partners in the program's operation ensures that the training provided is responsive to the employment needs of the Central Florida business community and the training needs of individuals with disabilities in Central Florida.

The Business Advisory Council members interview and select applicants, design the curriculum, evaluate the students' progress and develop and place students in internships and jobs. These members contribute thousands of hours, serving as counselors, evaluators, lecturers and role models.

Computer Programmer Training for the Disabled represents an innovative approach to the provision of vocational training for severely disabled persons. The training provides short-term, intensive, high-quality training in the high-tech, high-demand field of computer programming, delivered in a mainstream educational setting, on Valencia Community College's East Campus rather than in the segregated setting found in a rehabilitation center. In addi-

tion, the content of the training responds to needs identified in local labor market analyses and is geared to meet the demands of local business and industry.

Because the program exists solely for the purpose of providing job training and job placement in competitive employment for individuals who are severely disabled, there is a comprehensive and all-pervasive effort on the part of the program staff and Business Advisory Council members to develop and nurture each students' employability. Formal presentations by BAC members on topics such as time management and telephone etiquette, Business Advisory Council evaluations, class meetings and committees, open houses, corporate visits and eight-week internships are all designed to reinforce the development of skills necessary for students to be hired and to remain successfully employed for many years.

Each year, with the guidance and support of its Business Advisory Council, the program graduates another class of programmers. However, graduation is not the primary goal, placement is. Over the nine year life of the program we have achieved a 95 percent placement ratio.

Because many members of the target population are not served by community agencies because of the severity of their disabilities, the program's staff must be aggressive and creative in their outreach activities to develop referrals to the program. Many individuals who are severely disabled are marginally involved in society because they do not work and have, in many cases, been told their disabilities are too severe to allow them to work. To ensure these individuals have an opportunity to learn new careers, the program works through physicians' offices, physical therapy departments in clinics and hospitals, exceptional education centers, Vocational Rehabilitation, Private Industry Council, Job Services and food stamps offices, churches, and community agencies serving individuals with disabilities.

Contact:
Deborah Clark, Center Director, High-Tech Training for the Disabled
(407) 299-5000, ext. 2222

Valencia Community College
PO Box 3028
Orlando, FL 32802
Total head count enrollment-Credit: 36,800; Non-Credit: 26,140
Campuses/sites: 6; Full-time faculty: 244

WILDLIFE TECHNOLOGY

Students enjoy an intense field-oriented program during the summer term,
when field trips cover all of Georgia's physiographic regions

The Wildlife Technology program at Abraham Baldwin Agricultural College is the largest two-year program of its kind in the United States and the only one in Georgia.

Initiated in 1968, it is fully accredited by the North American Wildlife Technology Association. Graduates receive an Associate in Applied Science degree in Wildlife Technology. They find jobs as land managers or in collecting data in a research project. They may also find positions in a shooting preserve or in large land management situations where they will work under the direction of wildlife biologists. Other sources of employment include the state and federal wildlife conservation agencies and private businesses.

Students take classes in Power Equipment, Forest Measurements I, Introduction to Mapping, Forest Surveying I, Dendrology, Natural Resource conservation, Forest Wildlife Management, Forest Safety, Conservation Law Enforcement, Forest Game Management, Aquatic Resource Management, Forest Soils, Microcomputers in Forest Resources, Advanced Wildlife Technology, Wildlife Seminar, Silviculture and Principles of Supervision. The basic studies requirement includes English composition, Business Communications, Speech, Technical Mathematics, American History, American Government, Biology and Criminal Justice.

In addition to time in the classroom, students enjoy an intense field-oriented program during the summer term. Field trips cover all of Georgia's physiographic regions, with emphasis on the diversity of habitat types, wildlife species present and associated management procedures. During these visits, students participate in a variety of wildlife management practices conducted under the supervision of Georgia Department of Natural Resources Wildlife Management personnel.

Two full-time faculty members administer the program with the assistance of another full-time faculty member who works with the program during the summer. Two technicians also serve the program in addition to other duties. For his efforts with the program and with conservation statewide, Associate Professor of Wildlife Dick Payne was recently selected as Wildlife Conservationist of the Year by the Georgia Wildlife Federation and the Sears Roebuck Company.

A new addition to the program focuses on non-game wildlife including habitat, birds, wildflowers and other subjects.

Contact:
Dick Payne, Associate Professor
(912) 386-3508

Abraham Baldwin Agricultural College
ABAC 9, 2802 Moore Highway
Tifton, GA 31794
Total head count enrollment-Credit: 2,667; Non-Credit: 4, 412
Campuses/sites: 1; Full-time faculty: 98

INCENTIVE PROGRAM

More than half the grant recipients have chosen to return for at least one more quarter
of college work at their own expense

Incentive grants, which give students a no-obligation taste of college, result in more than half of the recipients continuing with their studies at Abraham Baldwin Agricultural College.

The Incentive Program began during the winter quarter of 1987 in an attempt to allow students to enter or re-enter the college classroom at no financial risk. A total of 50 Incentive Grants were offered for students who met the following criteria:

1) have been out of high school for at least five years before applying to this program;
2) high school graduates or must have successfully completed the GED examination (the GED can have been completed at any time as long as the potential student has been out of high school for a minimum of five years);
3) legal residents of Georgia;
4) must not have attended college within the last five years, nor have earned more than 20 hours of college credit;
5) must complete an Abraham Baldwin application and medical form; and
6) will be limited to a minimum of up to one five-hour credit course for fall quarter.

However, students with access to an employer reimbursement program will not be eligible for the Incentive

Program.

The Incentive Grant covers the tuition, application fee and parking sticker at an approximate cost of $140 per person. The cost is picked up by the ABAC Foundation, which encourages faculty and staff members to contribute to the Foundation for the specific purpose of funding Incentive Grants. In years past, well more than half the Incentive Grants have been funded by the faculty and staff of Baldwin.

During the time the Incentive Grant has been offered, more than half the students choose to return for at least one more quarter of college work at their expense. Several of the students who began in the Incentive Grant Program have graduated from the institution – one of them graduated with honors. The program has been very successful, and plans are to continue the program one quarter per year in the future.

Contact:
Garth Webb, Director of Admissions
(912) 386-3230

Abraham Baldwin Agricultural College
ABAC 9, 2802 Moore Highway
Tifton, GA 31794
Total head count enrollment-Credit: 2,667; Non-Credit: 4, 412
Campuses/sites: 1; Full-time faculty: 98

ANDREW COLLEGE

LEADERSHIP DEVELOPMENT COURSE

The course is designed to, among other things, help participants develop an awareness of the moral and ethical responsibilities of leadership

Where have all our great leaders gone? This seems to be the rallying cry of today's society. In fact, it would appear that the trust and credibility of our leaders is at the lowest level ever. This critical situation brings us to an inescapable conclusion: the education and development of better leaders must be one of the nation's most urgent priorities. The proper setting for this education is this country's college campuses.

Andrew College, in coordination with Phi Theta Kappa, is offering a course in leadership development. Under the premise that leadership abilities are necessary at all levels and facets of community life, the course provides a basic understanding of leadership theory and assists the participants in developing a personal philosophy of leadership. To accomplish this task, the course is designed to help participants develop an awareness of the moral and ethical responsibilities of leadership, their personal style of leadership, and essential leadership skills.

This course is designed to serve not only the leadership development needs of the college student but also members of the community-at-large. There is a demonstrable need for leadership training among existing and emerging leaders in civic organizations, local governing boards, and various not-for-profit and for-profit institutions. With few modifications, the materials and teaching methods of the Leadership Development Course may be used to serve the community.

The Leadership Development Course is offered at Andrew College as a humanities seminar for two quarter credit hours. The course is open to all students.

Contact:
Karan Berryman
(912) 732-2171

Andrew College
College Street
Cuthbert, GA 31740
Total head count enrollment-Credit: 300
Campuses/sites: 1; Full-time faculty: 15

ATHENS AREA TECHNICAL INSTITUTE

RESEARCH LABORATORY TECHNOLOGY

The program curricula mirrors that of the Biotechnology associate degree program for the first year

The Research Laboratory Technology program at Athens Area Technical Institute is the only one of its kind in the state and is nationally unique among chemical technology programs in that it also focuses on microbiological techniques. The curriculum covers the basic principles of chemistry, biology and microbiology; analytical laboratory techniques; laboratory instrumentation; growth, isolation

Continues on Page 174

and characterization of microorganisms; histologic techniques and immunological techniques. This prepares skilled technicians to work in research laboratories.

Graduates can receive either a diploma or Associate of Applied Technology degree upon completion of the curriculum requirements. The associate degree program is designed to extend the competencies of graduates in the areas of general chemistry and biology. The general studies component of the associate degree program is added to develop written, oral and computational skills and to provide breadth to the curriculum in the areas of humanities, behavioral sciences and mathematics. The program began in 1966 in cooperation with the University of Georgia.

Both the associate degree and diploma programs are designed to prepare graduates to perform as skilled technicians in various types of research, service and quality assurance laboratories. These types of laboratories are engaged in a wide range of activities such as quality control; food, water, soil and product testing; and research and development of new products and processes.

During the mid-1980's, the university began a concerted effort to attract biotechnology industries to Athens by setting up a biotechnology center. To facilitate the needs of these new industries, an Associate of Applied Technology degree in Biotechnology was added in 1989. The curricula for both the Research Laboratory Technology and the Biotechnology associate degree programs are the same for the first year in order to provide students with an opportunity to make an informed decision about which major to pursue.

The Biotechnology curriculum covers basic theories of chemistry, biochemistry, microbiology and biotechnology and their practical applications, and graduates are qualified to serve as laboratory technicians in the biotechnology laboratories. These types of laboratories are involved in activities such as the manipulation of plants for increased food production and disease resistance; the mass production of organic chemicals, vitamins, antibiotics, hormones and pesticides by living organisms; the mass production of fermented food products; and the manipulation of microorganisms for product modification or for the production of new products.

An advisory committee composed of local industry leaders provides faculty with information to ensure that the program is responsive to the needs of area employers. Furthermore, a state technical committee composed of leading scientists from the Georgia Institute of Technology, the University of Georgia, the U.S. Environmental Protection Agency, the U.S. Department of Agriculture and several private industries reviewed the programs' curricula to validate their content.

Two full-time faculty members, along with two part-time instructors and three laboratory assistants, are employed to provide the instructional components of this program. The institution received a major equipment grant from the Georgia Department of Technical and Adult Education to purchase the laboratory equipment needed to implement the Biotechnology program. Currently, the institution maintains an inventory of equipment valued at more than $500,000 to operate this program.

The program was recently featured in *NCTI*, the newsletter published by the American Chemical Society Division of Analytical Chemistry.

Contact:
Carol White, Program Director
(706) 542-8050

Athens Area Technical Institute
U.S. Highway 29 North
Athens, GA 30610-0399
Total head count enrollment-Credit: 2,023; Non-Credit: 6,859
Campuses/sites: 1; Full-time faculty: 68

THE CENTER FOR CONTINUOUS IMPROVEMENT

⚏ Companies that become charter members can take an active role ⚏
in identifying and developing workshops and seminars

The Center for Continuous Improvement at Athens Area Technical Institute represents an innovative partnership between a public, two-year post secondary technical institute and business and industry located within a 12-county area of northeast Georgia.

Dedicated on June 24, 1991, the fundamental purpose of the Center is to readily translate into action a manager's desire to empower his or her employees with the knowledge and skills needed to maintain their competitive posture in today's global economy. Any organization, regardless of its size, is eligible to participate in the "total quality" training and consulting services provided under the auspices of the center.

Initial operating funds for the various Center-sponsored activities were generated through private endowments by various organizations interested in the continued economic prosperity of the region, as well as from the charter membership fees paid by the businesses and industries who realized the importance of this resource. Since its founding, 14 area companies have elected to become charter members including: ABB Power T&D Company Inc., Athens; Alcan Recycling, Greensboro; Athens Regional Medical Center, Athens; Athens Regional Carrier Transicold, Athens; CertainTeed Corporation, Athens; Del Mar Window Coverings, Athens; Denon Digital Industries, Madison; E.I. duPont De Nemours and Company, Athens; Fowler Products Company, Athens; General Time Corporation, Athens; Johnson and Johnson Consumer Products Company, Royston; NORAMCO, Inc., Athens; Reliance Electric Company, Athens; and St. Mary's Hospital, Athens. Each charter member contributed a minimum of $10,000 to become actively involved in the Center.

Charter membership status provides company representatives the opportunity to take an active role in identifying and developing workshops and seminars to improve product quality and customer satisfaction. These representatives serve on the Center's advisory board and are responsible for identifying pressing training needs and then developing training agendas that fit the philosophy of the new culture being implemented within each organization. The diversity of the firms represented in the charter membership provides a broad perspective to monthly discussions on how to shape the training agenda. These representatives share a commitment to world class quality, share each other's experiences in the implementation of these concepts and offer advice on how to avoid some of the pitfalls encountered in the implementation process.

Enlightened plant managers agree that the best training investment is the one that buys tailor-made instruction. For that reason, the majority of the seminars and the hands-on workshops offered through the center are not generic, commercial, "programmed" packages. Rather, these seminars incorporate only the skills and knowledge as specified by the charter members. The emphasis of each workshop or seminar is altered for each subsequent session according to the feedback received from the workshop participants. Though developed according to the specifications of the charter membership, these workshops and seminars are made available to non-members who find a need for a specific topic.

One strategic advantage provided by the Center for Continuous Improvement lies in the fact that it provides multiple services at one local source that until now were available at multiple sources and only in northeastern and western states. By participating in the center-sponsored programs, companies have been able to trim the employee development costs while still maintaining the quality and level of training needed to ensure the long-term future of not only the employees but also the business or industry involved. No longer are expensive trips to distant workshops required.

The collective monies of the charter membership make it possible to bring in outside sources when appropriate. Individually, these organizations would not be able to afford such training. Partnerships established by the Center for Continuous Improvement with Kepner-Tregoe in New Jersey and the J-I-T Institute of Technology in Colorado make it possible for these prestigious companies to bring their training to Athens. The Kepner-Tregoe workshops have helped plant and production managers increase productivity by providing employees with a systematic approach to isolating the causes of problems, determining the best way to correct them, and preventing new problems from occurring. Workshop participants are given the opportunity to address on-the-job applications in order to develop their problem-solving skills.

Training is only one of the services provided through the Center for Continuous Improvement. The Center also conducts a monthly tour program of a facility known to have achieved success or progress in the implementation of total quality management practices. On-site consulting services have also been provided to a number of organizations.

Contact:
Sherrie Ford, Vice President, Business and Industry Services
(706) 369-5763

Athens Area Technical Institute
U.S. Highway 29 North
Athens, GA 30610-0399
Total head count enrollment-Credit: 2,023; Non-Credit: 6,859
Campuses/sites: 1; Full-time faculty: 68

CARDIOVASCULAR TECHNOLOGY

*✺ Students can take advantage of resources from both the college ✺
and University Hospital, which work in partnership with ATI*

Heart disease is the number one killer affecting society today. Through early diagnosis and treatment, people can continue to live normal, active lives. With the increased technology now available, the scheduling of cardiovascular diagnostic tests and treatments is increasing rapidly—but, there also is a decreasing number of qualified personnel to perform these procedures. Augusta Technical Institute has one of the few cardiovascular technology programs in the United States. The program, the result of a contract between Augusta Technology Institute and University Hospital in July, 1992, utilizes the strengths and facilities of both parties to provide a cardiovascular program. Although graduates from this programs and other allied health programs are overwhelmed with offers of employment, it remains difficult to recruit students.

University Hospital provides two full-time cardiovascular technology instructors, classrooms, clinical facilities, supplies and equipment for the cardiovascular technology courses. Augusta Technical Institute provides liability insurance for the cardiovascular students, processes financial aid applications, and provides classrooms, instructors, supplies and equipment for the core courses (English, Math, Psychology, Chemistry, Biology, and Anatomy and Physiology). Augusta Technical Institute will also grant an Associate Degree in Cardiovascular Technology to graduates of this program.

The purpose of the program is to prepare students for employment within a hospital, physician's office, medical clinic or mobile outreach laboratory to work with physicians to evaluate, diagnose and treat heart patients. Graduates of the program will be able to perform examinations at the request or direction of a physician, be proficient in the use of analytical equipment, and provide a foundation of data from which a correct anatomic and physiologic diagnosis may be made. Procedures performed by the cardiovascular technologist include, but are not limited to, cardiac catheterization, collection of arterial blood gas specimens, echocardiography, exercise stress tests and doppler ultrasound.

Augusta Technical Institute and University Hospital work together for quality patient care and optimum student learning. Accreditation is being sought for the cardiovascular program from the Division of Allied Health Education and Accreditation of the American Medical Association. The cardiovascular program is designed to ensure that graduates will take the Cardiovascular Credentialing International/National Board for Cardiovascular Testing to become a Registered Technologist.

Contact:
Alice Frye, Dean, Allied Health
(706) 771-4180

Augusta Technical Institute
3116 Deans Bridge Road
Augusta, GA 30906
Total head count enrollment-Credit: 3,832; Non-Credit: 6,013
Campuses/sites: 2; Full-time faculty: 84

CENTER FOR ADVANCED TECHNOLOGIES TRANSFER

*✺ The program translates information-age technologies and ✺
global competitive pressures into practical applications*

Technology is advancing more rapidly than ever before, with organizational operational/management philosophies moving at a more reluctant, subtle pace. Business and industry along with education and government are faced with difficulties and challenges that are a direct result from these two movements of our times. In 1983 a team of faculty and managers at Augusta Technical Institute recognized these challenges. The team established a new applied research program that could translate the imminent onslaught of information-age technologies and global

competitive pressures into practical applications at the factory/business floor.

Today, the Center for Advanced Technologies Transfer (AMTEC) is a viable contributor in the transfer of new and leading technologies to businesses and industries in its service region. AMTEC's role has expanded from its original role (technology transfer to small and medium-size manufacturers) to a broader scope of program development and technical services offerings. An example of a broader range of offerings is in current organizational philosophies such as Total Quality (TQ) and Total Quality Management (TQM).

International quality standards are also a significant influence on AMTEC offerings. ISO 9000 is a set of international quality standards which have been adopted in Europe and soon will be standard practice in the USA. The net result is that any company that now wants to do business with the European Common Market must be ISO 9000-registered. This is an example of a global pressure that impacts AMTEC's response to aid its business service community with an action process. A process that created an AMTEC Quality Management Advisory Team. This team is selected from quality managers, quality engineers, scientists, and AMTEC staff. This highly qualified team serves as advisors, program developers, and in many instances, as instructors. The foremost goal of AMTEC in its ISO 9000 training series is to provide local companies the "complete avenue" that enables them to become ISO registered.

AMTEC is recognized across the USA as an innovative leader in applied technology transfer activities. This recognition has come from a series of successful technical offerings in computer aided drafting (CAD). AMTEC, as an Authorized Autodesk Training Center has advanced from offering basic Autocad to advanced offerings in AutoLISP (a graphics programming language), Autocad Customizing, Solids Modeling, and Multi-Media.

Manufacturing technologies such as Geometric Dimensioning and Tolerancing (GD&T) is a superior methodology for achieving today's quality standards. It is another example of applied research activities that is essential for manufactures to achieve and maintain competitive quality in a worldwide market place. Along with GD&T AMTEC offers Computer Aided Manufacturing (SMART-CAM) and a full range of Programmable Logic Controller (PLC) courses.

As a matter of repeat and regular course offerings, AMTEC provides a wide array of computer applications and computer programming courses. "C" programming and "UNIX" operating systems, along with computer basic are routinely offered and available on a seven-day-week basis.

AMTEC developed an Adaptive Computer Technologies program for handicapped individuals. These innovative offerings include physically challenged individuals who are hearing impaired or totally deaf, blind persons, and individuals who have special mobility handicapping conditions. This program provides the trainee an opportunity to learn at a faster pace and to a higher level that has heretofore been unattainable. The computer has made this program possible and highly effective. For the first time handicapped persons are competing in the open job market with parity competitive job skills. An example of this fact is in an AMTEC job initiative that is training twelve handicapped individuals to become loan processors and professional associates for employment in a local bank.

AMTEC's future is an exciting and optimistic venture as it grows with emerging technologies and seeks fungible methods to apply them to the needs and best interests of business, industry, education, government and the community it serves.

Contact:
Jim Weaver, Director
(706) 771-4000

Augusta Technical Institute
3116 Deans Bridge Road
Augusta, GA 30906
Total head count enrollment-Credit: 3,832; Non-Credit: 6,013
Campuses/sites: 2; Full-time faculty: 84

BAINBRIDGE COLLEGE

SCHOOL-COLLEGE PARTNERSHIP FAIRS

The fairs, involving teachers and students from a six- to eight-county region, have increased articulation between area schools and the college

Sometimes all it takes is a little exposure to college to whet a once-unmotivated student's appetite for education after a high school diploma. Bainbridge College has done just that since its founding in 1973.

As early as 1979 the Humanities Division of the college initiated International Night, which focused upon international cuisine, films and customs. Since that time, the Humanities Division and two other divisions, the Social Science and Science/Mathematics Divisions, have expanded the college's partnership activities. The list of annual activities now includes an essay competition for high school seniors, a foreign language fair, elementary and secondary science fairs, and a social science fair. Each of these competitive activities involves teachers and students from a six- to eight-county area of southwest Georgia.

While the goals of the individual partnerships vary, they have shared goals as follows:

1) to use the activity as a teaching tool to help promote study in the discipline;
2) to promote articulation between area schools and the college;
3) to provide educational and enrichment opportuni-

Continues on Page 178

ties for students who may not otherwise receive them;

4) to help students to be more competitive in larger fairs or related activities; and

5) to enhance public relations and provide recruitment for Bainbridge College.

The impact of these partnerships has been diverse. Participation has greatly increased. The number of contestants has increased tenfold in several of the fairs. Projects have improved and competition has become more keen. Many of the local students have won state-level competition. Articulation between the college and area schools has increased. Many individuals (approximately 1,300 faculty, students and community people) annually come onto the campus to observe and participate in these activities.

Capital resources required to underwrite the expenses of each fair average approximately $350. The human resources involve volunteer faculty from the college and the area schools and the community. Sometimes more than 35 volunteers are involved in carrying out a single fair.

The partnerships are fostered by oral and written communication with teachers of the various disciplines, by making presentations to areas students and teachers, and by attendance at state-sponsored meetings to keep abreast of rules and regulations relating to the activities. Many of the college faculty annually visit each of the service area schools through their involvement with the partnerships, judge the local school competition, and coordinate the articulation between campus winners and the next level of competition.

All of the activities have received excellent coverage in local newspapers. Additionally, the partnerships of the Humanities Division have been given special recognition by the Chancellor of the University System of Georgia. The partnerships of the Mathematics/Science Division also have been the topic of a mini workshop for the Association of Biological Laboratory Education and presented in the September/October 1990 issue of *The Journal of a College Science Teaching*.

Contact:
Margaret Smith, Vice President, Academic Affairs
(912) 248-2515

Bainbridge College
U.S. Highway 84 East
Bainbridge, GA 31717
Total head count enrollment-Credit: 1,023; Non-credit: 4,300
Campuses/sites: 1; Full-time faculty: 45

ENGLISH AS A SECOND LANGUAGE (ESL)

The college took the program to area migrant workers through a converted Winnebago camper

Bainbridge College took its English as a Second Language (ESL) program to area migrant workers through a converted Winnebago camper in an attempt to teach them basic survival English.

The college's initiative to pilot an English as a Second Language Program was an outgrowth of the institution's Fiscal Year 92 strategic planning process. Input from faculty and staff reflected a heightened awareness of the growing migrant population, their link to the strong agricultural economy of the service area, and the need for them to know English as a second language.

In early spring 1992, college officials communicated with service area citizens and organizations to research the breath of the outreach activities to the Hispanic population. The feedback gleaned was that area migrant workers could benefit by the college's involvement, especially if it could be instrumental in taking the classes to the camps where the population resided.

The college administration concluded its findings from the investigatory research warranted the college's underwriting a pilot program. Besides teaching migrants survival English, another instructional goal was to teach the students to ask for and understand directions to places

such as the police station, hospital and health department. This included enabling each student to understand and respond to requests for his/her name, address, location and date of birth, marital status, number of children, name of employer, names of parents, etc. It also included numbers, days, months and colors.

The college's converted Winnebago camper was used as the traveling headquarters for the ESL program. Approximately $200 worth of gasoline was used in travel and to run the generators for air conditioning the vehicle and using the lights, computers, and listening stations. The cost of instructional materials, a cassette tape and two accompanying ESL booklets was $100. Four instructors were used — three paid and the fourth a volunteer. The instructors' salaries came to approximately $700. Five cassette listening stations, two Apple computers, an ESL software program, one table, 25 to 30 chairs, and one portable outdoor light were also provided by the college. Additionally, substantial office support was provided by the Department of Continuing Education to coordinate the program, contact and contract with instructors, copy tapes and booklets, and provide other assistance.

Sixty-one participants were served. Most could speak

PAGE 178 • GEORGIA

and read no or little English. Program outcomes were to be evaluated using a simple pre- and post-test. This test, consisting of simple questions written in English, was administered at the first class. Unfortunately, almost all of the students moved to Virginia prior to the end of the course, making it impossible to administer the post-test. Prior to the last session observation revealed that students who spoke no English initially responded in English to simple questions delivered in English. Whether the 12-session program has any lasting effect depends in part on the students' ability to practice what they learned. For that reason, students were given two ESL booklets and cassette tapes for use in any location they might reside.

Contact:
Mark Pelton, Director, Continuing Education
(912) 248-2516

Bainbridge College
U.S. Highway 84 East
Bainbridge, GA 31717
Total head count enrollment-Credit: 1,023; Non-credit: 4,300
Campuses/sites: 1; Full-time faculty: 45

BRUNSWICK COLLEGE

MULTI-TRACK CERTIFICATE PROGRAM

Three allied health programs share instructors for the first quarter, then divide into different tracks

Brunswick College has developed a unique multi-track certificate program for three occupational areas in its Allied Health Department: Practical Nursing, Surgical Technology and Nursing Technician. There is an increasing need for allied health personnel in the Southeast region of Georgia because several hospitals are enlarging their surgical suites and will require the employment of additional nursing and surgical staff

The multi-track program begins with Practical Nursing, Surgical Technology and Nursing Technician students enrolled together during the Fall Quarter. These three programs have similar courses in the didactic areas anatomy and physiology, interpersonal relations, basic pharmacology, and beginning clinical skills. The three programs share instructors for the first quarter, with each instructor teaching the component for which they are best qualified. At the end of the first quarter, the three programs divide, with each program taking a different track.

The Practical Nursing and Surgical Technology programs require three additional quarters, while the Nursing Technician program requires only one additional quarter. At the end of the first quarter, students who, because of grades not high enough to continue in Practical Nursing or Surgical Technology, or because of personal choice, have the option to continue one additional quarter and receive a certificate as a Nursing Technician. Therefore, the Nursing Technician program provides an early exit point for students.

The Practical Nursing/Nursing Technician programs utilize a team approach to oversee both the didactic and clinical components of both programs. The Surgical Technology program utilizes a single instructor. Practical Nursing students who receive clinical instruction in the surgical area (including pre-anesthesia holding, surgery, post-anesthesia recovery, outpatient surgery, and endoscopic room) are supervised by the Surgical Technology instructor. Students are scheduled so no more than 12 students are supervised by an instructor at any one time.

Because funds for new programs were not readily available, Brunswick College was challenged to develop a plan whereby the need could be met with the least expenditure of limited funds. The Southeast Georgia Regional Medical Center is very supportive of the multi-track program concept and provides financial support. The College determined that by increasing the average enrollment from 26 to 36 students, the new multi-track program could be justified while maintaining a low enrollment in Surgical Technology to prevent saturating the job market.

Since the inception of the program, graduates of Practical Nursing have a 95 percent or higher pass rate on the national certifying examination, with one group of graduates ranked first in the nation based on the results of the graduates' performance of the national licensure examination. The Surgical Technology graduates have a pass rate of 100 percent, with a job placement rate of 100 percent for all graduates.

Contact:
Julia Dent, Instructor-in-Charge
(912) 264-7251

Brunswick College
Altama at Fourth Street
Brunswick, GA 31523
Total head count enrollment-Credit: 2,586; Non-Credit: 2,571
Campuses/sites: 1; Full-time faculty: 50

HONORS PROGRAM

Students are expected to analyze topics and engage in participatory learning experiences, including class discussions and research

As a community college, Darton College serves an array of students who need remediation and other academic support systems. But in doing so, Darton realized that the needs of its best students had been largely ignored. Thus, in 1990, the Darton College Honors Program was created. It is designed to challenge our best students academically and also to help them see themselves as college, career and community leaders, while developing the professional leadership skills they need to go with the self image. Twenty-nine freshmen are accepted into the program each year.

By providing academic classes for Honors Program participants in all areas of the core curriculum and by focusing on current issues in these classes, students become aware of challenges that must be confronted. They are expected to analyze topics and engage in participatory learning experiences, including class discussions and out-of-class research and projects. The honors courses offered and the faculty selected are chosen with program goals in mind. Hence we have a program, not just disconnected honors courses.

To complement the academic side of the program,

Honors Program participants enroll in a quarterly seminar that focuses on personal development. The purpose of these seminars is to make students aware of workplace issues and challenges so that they will be able to cope and lead others effectively. Professional behavior is learned and practiced in seminars and role plays with friends rather than on the job where errors are costly. The leadership development materials developed by Phi Theta Kappa have been incorporated into two quarters of the six-quarter program. Other seminars are developed by the Honors Program Coordinator. Some portions of the honors seminars were adapted for use with other college groups in 1992/93.

The program is a partnership of the college and the private sector. Administrative costs and academic courses are funded by the college, while seminars, awards and special excursions are funded by private gifts to the college foundation. Individuals from the community and the faculty teach the seminars and academic courses.

The Darton College Honors Program has been recognized in area newspapers and in the Georgia Honors Council newsletter.

Contact:
Ann T. Engram, Program Coordinator
(912) 888-8810

Darton College
2400 Gillionville Road
Albany, GA 31707
Total head count enrollment-Credit: 2,400
Campuses/sites: 1;Full-time faculty: 75

COMMUNITY SERVICE FOR SCHOOL STUDENTS AND TEACHERS

Boosting test scores while making science and math fun for middle school and high school students is the goal of this program

Southwest Georgia students test below the state norms in science and mathematics. In an attempt to remedy the problem, the following components were developed to increase the students interests in science and mathematics.

The Adventures in Science unit is designed for middle and elementary students. This unit includes chemistry components, a reptile collection, physics, ecological activities, a nature trail and two mammalian skin and skull collections, of which one circulates from school to school throughout Southwest Georgia. The unit is modifiable so that it can be taken to the students or students can come to the campus. This adventures program is funded by the

division. The mammal collection-preparation component was funded in part by a Georgia department of Education, Title II grant. Enrollment in 1991-1992 was 2,000.

The Regional Science Fair is affiliated with the state and international fairs. It encourages middle and high school students to do minor research and present it through the fair system. Workshops are provided for students and teacher-supervisors. Two hundred and ten students participated in the 1992 Fair. The Fair is funded by the Merck Company Foundation and the Darton College Foundation.

The Mathematics Tournament is designed to encourage and recognize outstanding high school mathematics students. The competition is for individuals and teams. Two hundred and thirty participated in the 1992 Math Tournament. The Mathematics Tournament is funded by the Georgia Power Foundation and the Darton College Foundation.

The *Science/Math Newsletter* is published quarterly by the division to keep the teachers of this region informed of opportunities, examples of lab exercises, trends in the fields, and listings of tournament and fair winners. The Newsletter is funded by the Division.

The Program has served primary-elementary, middle school, and senior high school students. It has provided teachers with supplements to their curricula as well as continuing education workshops. Additional components are being added to the Adventures in Science portfolio to offer variety for those students who participate a second or third time.

Contact:
Melvin C. Bowling, Chairman, Science/Mathematics Division
(912) 888-8830

Darton College
2400 Gillionville Road
Albany, GA 31707
Total head count enrollment-Credit: 2,400
Campuses/sites: 1;Full-time faculty: 75

College/University Core Curriculum

*▓ This unified curriculum is an effort to address problems related to transferring credits ▓
to the University System of Georgia*

The Core Curriculum is an outgrowth of the philosophy of providing a curriculum at DeKalb College common to all institutions during the first two years of college.

The University System of Georgia, of which DeKalb College is a member, proclaims its Core Curriculum to be one of the most important aspects of the overall philosophy as a system of public higher education. The system core curriculum was established in 1966 for the general purpose of aiding and facilitating the educational progress of students as they pursue baccalaureate degrees within and among the units of the university system. This unified Core Curriculum represents an effort to deal effectively with the increasing curricular problems of students that result from increased enrollments in the state's two-year colleges, increased mobility of student population, increased number and complexity of major fields of studies offered by senior units, and increased problems related to transfer of credit among units of the University System of Georgia.

The Core Curriculum provides the following four areas of study: Humanities and Fine Arts (20 quarter hours); Mathematics and the natural sciences (20 quarter hours); Social sciences (20 quarter hours); and courses appropriate to the major field 30 quarter hours

The designated academic areas of study within the 60-hour portion of the Core Curriculum comprise broad fields of study and are limited to specific courses of a general education nature. Each institution has the latitude of curricular development within this flexible plan.

This curriculum, as an essential feature of the University System has three primary purposes:

1) it establishes the principle that general education is the foundation of all baccalaureate degree programs;

2) the Core encourages each institution to develop a superior program of general education, reflecting its mission; the guidelines of the Core require demonstrated achievement in some specific areas, but also allow for the inclusion of other areas of achievement deemed desirable by each institution; and

3) the Core guarantees students and their parents that full credit for courses satisfactorily completed at one institution will be accepted by all other System institutions; this guarantee affirms the integrity of credits offered throughout the university system.

Contact:
Martha Nesbitt, Vice President, Academic Affairs
(404) 244-2370

DeKalb College
3251 Panthersville Road
Decatur, GA 30034
Total head count enrollment-Credit: 15,976; Non-Credit: 6,267
Campuses/sites: 24; Full-time faculty: 320

Interpreter Training

Strong emphasis is placed on students and faculty involvement, interaction and contribution to the deaf and interpreting communities

DeKalb College's Interpreter Training Program was one of the first such programs in the country and remains the only college-level program in Georgia teaching advanced American Sign Language (ASL) and interpreting.

Founded in 1977, its primary goals is to prepare individuals to become qualified, highly skilled Interpreters. Graduates of the Interpreter Training Program are employed as educational interpreters (elementary, high school and college), freelance interpreters (education, legal, medical, religious, vocational and business), and as sign language instructors.

The demand for trained, qualified interpreters greatly exceeds current supply, due in part to federal laws regarding the rights of people who are disabled. These persons must have equal access to education, employment opportunities and services in the government and private sectors. The interpreting profession makes it possible for individuals who are deaf or hard-of-hearing to overcome many barriers and to bridge the communication gap.

American Sign Language has gained respect and dignity as a rich, beautiful and unique foreign language. A wide variety of individuals seek out our program in order to become fluent ASL communicators as well as interpreters. In 1991-92, the department enrolled approximately 110 students per quarter in the basic sign language courses and 50 students in the interpreter program itself. Enrollment continues to increase each year. Courses are taught by the program coordinator, a full-time instructor and up to 12 adjunct faculty with experience in interpreting and working with Deaf communities. Courses are highly inter-

active and use new advances in video technology to enhance instruction and feedback in the visual language of signs.

After completing three prerequisite ASL courses and/or demonstrating conversational proficiency, students are admitted into a six-quarter sequence of knowledge and competency building courses leading to either an Award of Completion or an AAS degree in Interpreting for the Deaf. The program includes courses addressing:

1) receptive and expressive skills development in American Sign Language;
2) an orientation to deafness;
3) American Deaf culture, community and history;
4) the interpreting Code of Ethics and its application in various interpreting settings;
5) the process of interpreting and transliterating;
6) specialized interpreting situations; and
7) field experiences. Strong emphasis is placed on student and faculty involvement, interaction and contribution to the deaf and interpreting communities.

The Interpreter Training Program at DeKalb College works closely with the Georgia Registry of Interpreters for the Deaf (GRID), the Georgia Interpreting Services Network (GISN) and the University of Tennessee-Knoxville. These four institutions have cooperated to establish the program, maintain its high standards, offer continuing education opportunities, and provide practicum sites and job placement.

Contact:
Christine A. Smith, Coordinator
(404) 299-4360

DeKalb College
3251 Panthersville Road
Decatur, GA 30034
Total head count enrollment-Credit: 15,976; Non-Credit: 6,267
Campuses/sites: 24; Full-time faculty: 320

New Connections

The project serves unmarried persons with custody of a minor child and homemakers with diminished income

Special services for single parents, displaced homemakers and single pregnant women has become an issue of great importance in efforts to build a world-class work force that includes all segments of the population. This is no less so at DeKalb Technical Institute, where the New Connections Project recognizes that the typical single parent, displaced homemaker and single pregnant woman

suffers from low self-esteem, from insufficient education or from too little training to become employable - not to mention myriad survival problems that require special attention. Even those who are employed are oftentimes under-employed and in need of assistance.

New Connections provides services to unmarried or legally separated persons who have custody of a minor child or children and to homemakers who for specific reasons have a diminished income. The project prepares people to be more competitive in the job market and to be more useful, functional citizens in the community. New Connections provides a wide variety of counseling and educational activities that include life management topics, job search skills, occupational training and support services. It networks with 28 community agencies such as the Department of Family and Children Services, the DeKalb YWCA, and The Task Force of the Homeless, which refer their clients to enroll in education and training that remove them from welfare support. It utilizes workshops that focus on self-esteem, assertiveness training, and stress management.

Since 1984, the Project has served increasing numbers each year with many graduating to obtain lucrative employment. This has been accomplished by concentrating on:
1) participant recruitment;
2) identifying individual needs and developing an individual plan of action;
3) enrollment in occupational training; and

4) job placement assistance.

New Connection services begin with a group information session conducted with prospective participants. After enrollment in the project each participant's needs are assessed, the TABE Test is administered for academic review purposes, and an individual Plan of Action is prescribed for each participant in the areas of pre-employment training, program/course enrollment in technical education, and support services such as child care assistance and public transportation.

An intense schedule of activity-oriented workshops and seminars are held quarterly to provide:
1) 60 hours of job readiness skills, life management skills, motivational topics, career awareness, and self-acceptance/self-confidence skills;
2) 18 hours of information on coping with domestic violence, parenting, drug awareness, and human sexuality;
3) remedial education where needed for occupational training; and
4) activities that encourage enrollment in high-paying non-traditional occupational programs.

Contact:
Joretta Clement, Coordinator
(404) 297-9522 ext. 108

DeKalb Technical Institute
495 North Indian Creek Drive
Clarkston, GA 30021
Total enrollment head count-Credit: 4,897; Non-Credit: 19,909
Campuses/sites: 4; Full-time faculty: 118

GAINESVILLE COLLEGE

COMPUTING ACROSS THE CURRICULUM

Bringing computers to all facets of academic life has resulted in a seemingly endless demand for student access to computers

Offering computing across the curriculum, not just requiring a computer course, is the way to make students computer literate, Gainesville College decided in the mid-1980's. Since then, computing across the curriculum strategy, coupled with effective computing and administrative support, has resulted in a tremendous upsurge in personal-computer usage.

For instance, in the Business Division, in addition to the usual Introduction to Computers applications course, the Accounting classes and Business Communications also now require extensive use of computers. There are study guides, tutorials and simulations available to students of Economics. In Humanities all English 101 classes meet in one of the computer classrooms. Other English classes, ranging from developmental to literature courses, regularly require computer usage. Also in Humanities, a Macintosh computer lab allows the incorporation of computerized graphics into the art curriculum, and foreign Language students must now spend several hours per week using computer-assisted instruction in a computer lab devoted solely to foreign languages.

This pervasiveness of computers happened only with the close involvement of interested faculty and staff. Initial allocation of computing resources was determined by the Director of Computer Services with the advice of the Academic Computing Advisory Committee, which was composed of computer-interested faculty and staff from across campus.

For the past few years most of the mathematics classes have used a computer in class for demonstration purposes. For access to tutorials and other mathematics software, the mathematics division has had its own computer lab, which has resulted in a dramatic increase in Math computer usage. In the sciences, physics has successfully incorporated computers in laboratory experiments. Another large user group for the new math computer lab will be Computer Science students who, in the past, have mainly used the drop-in or library computers.

All of the above computers, except for the art lab, are now connected to the campus computer network, which recently joined state and world-wide networks .

Continues on Page 184

The future of academic computing at Gainesville College considerably brightened recently when the State Legislature approved funding for a new building. A part of the new building, which should be occupied in fall 1994, will be the Academic Computing Center. Having this new facility will allow the upgrading and consolidation of the business computer classroom, the mathematics computer lab, the drop-in lab, and the library student computers into one area. This will enable increased computer access since the Academic Computing Center will be a separate part of the new building with its own controlled entrances.

The computing across the curriculum strategy has been so successful that it has resulted in a seemingly endless demand for student access to computers. The new Academic Computing Center is going to arrive at exactly the right time.

Students responding to the "Sophomore Survey" continue to reflect growing comfort with the adequacy of their preparation to enter an increasingly computer-oriented world.

Contact:
Byron Drew, Coordinator, Academic Computing
(404) 535-6281

Gainesville College
PO Box 1358
Gainesville, GA 30503
Total head count enrollment-Credit: 2,900; Non-Credit: 10,000
Campuses/sites: 1; Full-time faculty: 85

INTEGRATED STUDENT DEVELOPMENT

Student leaders are receiving regular training experiences to support their work, and the Student Center is more inviting

Integrating student development programming has had dramatic and positive effects on the Gainesville College student body: the number of student organizations has increased by one-fourth, the Intramural Program is garnering widespread recognition, and the performing arts have produced nationally competitive groups.

But for most of the first 25 years of the college's history, students were not nearly so involved.

Then, developing faculty support, the retirement of two administrators, and the impetus of the self-study process supported the realignment of responsibilities, the creation of a chief student affairs officer position, and the development of this new division for student development programming from an integrated perspective.

A representative steering committee to assist in planning for the area was established. A plan was developed with three stages. The first stage was the development of a program model that would guide future planning for the new division. Mission and goal statements were created using both student development and wellness concepts. The second stage of the plan focused upon organizational adjustments that embraced the "development of the whole student concept" from admissions assistance to transfer support and/or job placement. The final stage of the plan was facility renovation, which included renovation of the Student Center to produce a "warm" environment conducive to a sense of community and development of plans for expansion of the facility to accommodate for future growth.

The division was assigned the responsibility for new student orientation and for the delivery of Gainesville College 101, a course provided to support the transition to college process. Students are encouraged in both of these programs to become involved in the out-of-class opportunities at the institution. Special attention is given also to the needs of the non-traditional students and those taking advantage of the evening programs. Every effort is being made to guard against the development of a "P-C-P" ("Parking Lot-Classroom-Parking Lot") experience for our students. Real progress in providing the students with a comprehensive educational experience is apparent as the plan is being carried out.

The number of student organizations has increased by 25 percent to 25. Student leaders are receiving regular training experiences to support their work. Students are finding the Student Center more comfortable and inviting with the change of a few colors and the addition of more comfortable lounge furniture. The Intramural Program is receiving state and national recognition, including two consecutive second-place finishes in the National Flag Football Tournament. Members of the Delta Epsilon Chi organization have received state, regional and national awards. The Anchor student newspaper is an award-winning publication as are two literary magazines produced through student leadership. The performing arts, including art, drama and instrumental and choral music, are amply supported and have produced regionally and nationally competitive groups.

Valuable financial support for these programs is provided by the Gainesville College Foundation through tuition scholarships for students in the several areas of student activities and clubs and organizational leadership. Student activities are also supported by the College's developing Alumni Association, which considers the linkage a key element in generating future allegiance of students with their "First Alma Mater." This allegiance with its former students must be secured by two-year colleges if they are to be viable in the increasingly competitive fund-raising environment that faces all educational institutions.

The Personal, Academic, and Career Exploration (PACE) Center (formerly the Guidance Center) is working toward greater professionalization by supporting the counselors in gaining the Licensed Professional Counselor credential. Students are being exposed to and encouraged to think about such issues as abortion, sexually transmitted diseases, the war on drugs, multicultural diversity, and the addictive personality. All of these efforts are helping Gainesville College to produce students who are well-rounded adults ready to become contributing members of society. Career planning and educational decision-making, a need of a majority of our entering students, is being addressed effectively also.

Contact:
Tom G . Walter, Vice President, Student Development
(404) 535-6377

Gainesville College
PO Box 1358
Gainesville, GA 30503
Total head count enrollment-Credit: 2,900; Non-Credit: 10,000
Campuses/sites: 1; Full-time faculty: 85

MIDDLE GEORGIA COLLEGE

REGENTS ENGINEERING TRANSFER PROGRAM

▨ *The college can design an engineering course of study for a student* ▨
who might wish to transfer to any Georgia senior college

Middle Georgia College has such a variety of freshmen- and sophomore-level engineering courses - 30 of them - that it can design a program of study for a student majoring in any field of engineering or engineering technology. Its large assortment of engineering and engineering-support courses is so complete, in fact, that a student can take courses at MGC that are equivalent to the first two years at Georgia Institute of Technology. Because Middle Georgia College also offers additional technical and liberal arts courses, the typical engineering student elects to stay at MGC for more than six quarters.

This variety is possible because of the Regents Engineering Transfer Program, in which qualified students who are seeking a four-year degree in engineering may begin their college studies at Middle Georgia College. Upon successful completion of the pre-engineering curriculum, students may transfer to Georgia Tech to complete the degree requirements.

There are three different methods for admission to the Regents Engineering Transfer Program at Middle Georgia College:
1) Entering freshmen must have achieved at least a 550 on the mathematics portion of the SAT, a 450 on the verbal portion of the SAT, and a 3.0 high school grade-point average.
2) Entering freshman students who might not meet the above requirements, but have been accepted for admission to an Engineering Program at Georgia Tech.

3) Students who do not meet the requirements of either of the above methods may be admitted at the end of their freshman year, if they meet all the following requirements:
   a. completion of Calculus I and Calculus II, with grades of at least "B"
   b. completion of General Chemistry I and General Chemistry II, with grades of at least "B"; and
   c. Middle Georgia College grade-point average of at least 3.0.

Regents Engineering Transfer Program students who satisfactorily complete the pre-engineering curriculum and apply for transfer will be accepted to Georgia Tech. However, admission to the most popular majors at Georgia Tech will be based upon overall grade-point average, performance in the required prerequisite courses, and availability of student spaces.

Students who do not meet the specific qualifications of the Regents Engineering Transfer Program may still enroll in our pre-engineering program, and take courses that will prepare them to enter the junior year at Georgia Tech or some other senior college that offers baccalaureate programs in engineering. (Admission to senior college will be based upon the student's academic performance at Middle Georgia College.)

The college's engineering department works closely with several other schools, so that Middle Georgia College can design a course of study for a student who might wish to

Continues on Page 186

transfer to a senior college besides Georgia Tech and major in either engineering or engineering technology. Middle Georgia College knows which of its transfer courses will be accepted by the University of Georgia, Auburn University, Mercer University, Southern College of Technology, and Georgia Southern University.

Contact:
J. Hardwick Butler
(912) 934-3055

Middle Georgia College
Cochran, GA 31014
Total head count enrollment-Credit: 1,878
Campuses: 2; Full-time faculty: 70

CAMPUS COMMUNITY ISSUES FORUM

The forum topics range from freedom of speech to the Holocaust and to energy conservation

An ongoing series of issue-oriented programs involving faculty, students, staff and community, has prompted dialogues involving the background of the war for the liberation of Kuwait, the boundaries of free speech, genocide and the Holocaust, and energy conservation strategy alternatives.

Some were based on the National Issues Forum guidelines. Others were held in response to perceived needs of the students and community.

Each session lectures by Dr. John Ricks, Chair of the Social Science and Education Division, begins with a brief introduction to the topic, sometimes with a pertinent video. This is followed by a variety of opinions or approaches to the subject presented by a panel of professors and knowledgeable community members. At this point the leader and/or the panel take questions and comments from the audience, which comprises students, faculty, staff and the general public. In each case the formal part of the program lasted an hour, but animated discussion filled a second hour and sometimes longer.

Prior to each session, the social science professors prepare their students for the programs and appropriate publicity measures target all the intended audiences. These have been held at a variety of times and in a variety of formats to try to get maximum participation. Programs such as these, along with our Options speakers bureau on international affairs and other parts of town-gown interface, help us realize the "community" in community college.

Contact:
John Ricks
(912) 934-3063

Middle Georgia College
Cochran, GA 31014
Total head count enrollment-Credit: 1,878
Campuses: 2; Full-time faculty: 70

BRIGHTER FUTURE CAREER PROGRAM

The program targets public school students seeking self-improvement and career opportunities, but were held back by "life" circumstances

The Brighter Futures Career Program at Savannah Technical Institute aims to help students acquire a GED and to give them a chance to attain a post-secondary diploma or degree. This program targets those public school students who were seeking self-improvement and career opportunities, but due to their "life" circumstances, were unable to attain those things.

Students desiring entry into this program must meet the program criteria, which include the following features: age requirement, counselor or principal referral, and parental consent.

Developed out of the collaborative efforts of such sources as Savannah Technical Institute, local high schools and the Adult Education Center, the program was designed with five phases:

1) student recommendations from secondary schools;
2) screening interviews with student candidate and parents/ guardians;
3) assessing the student in areas of reading and math;
4) program orientation after acceptance; and
5) program participation in GED and career classes.

Students involved in this program are provided support services as their individual needs dictate.

This program is implemented through the financial partnership of Savannah Technical Institute and the Savannah-Chatham County Board of Public Education. The funds allow selected students to waive tuition costs and to receive course books and tools.

Contact:
Jerome Huff, Program Liaison
(912) 315-4509

Savannah Technical Institute
5717 White Bluff Road
Savannah, GA 31499
Total head count enrollment-Credit: 3,748; Non-Credit: 3,357
Campuses/sites: 5; Full-time faculty: 70

CAREER ASSISTANCE

The program is a minimum of three years, with the first year consisting of classroom lab and instruction, the last two working for a local company

Helping students become self-sufficient means more at Savannah Technical Institute than just providing the academic foundation for students who have encountered economic hardships, it also means employment in their chosen career. Such help, through the Career Assistance Program was possible through the concerted efforts of three resources: Savannah Technical Institute, local businesses and industries, and private citizens.

The Career Assistance Program provides selected students with: financial support by paying 75 percent of their tuition and providing a living stipend, and on-site training employment by paying the students' salary while employed for one full year, after completing their program of study.

This program also encourages local companies to provide on-site training, and to permanently employ students into career positions within their organization.

The program is a minimum of three years with the first year consisting of classroom and lab instruction at Savannah Technical Institute. The second year includes a full year of employment at a selected local company. The students' salary would be equal to that paid to other entry-level company workers for that particular job classification. The students' salary is paid solely from funds donated by the private citizens.

The students who are placed at the various companies would be considered full-time employees with all rights and privileges as other employees. The company will agree to rotate the training assignments to maximize the student's education and skills, and maximize the students' worth to the company. A company site supervisor is assigned to evaluate the student's progress quarterly. The third year of the program entails the agreement of the company to defray the entire cost of the student's salary for a minimum of two years.

The program is funded solely by the generous contributions of two concerned private citizens. Their donation of $205,000 served as the financial base upon which this program was built.

Contact:
Verlene Lanpley, Recruiter/Admissions Coordinator
(912) 351-4499

Savannah Technical Institute
5717 White Bluff Road
Savannah, GA 31499
Total head count enrollment-Credit: 3,748; Non-Credit: 3,357
Campuses/sites: 5; Full-time faculty: 70

ELDERHOSTEL

▩ The economic impact of Elderhostel programs ▩
on local businesses has been significant

Elderhostel, an educational program for adults older than age 60 offers inexpensive, short-term academic programs hosted by educational institutions around the world. It also offers economic gains for the colleges and communities in which it thrives.

A non-profit educational organization, Elderhostel began in 1975 linking the European hosteling concept with the residential emphasis of the Scandinavian Folk Schools. From a modest New England beginning, there now exists an international network of more than 1,800 participating institutions.

A typical, campus-based program includes six nights (Sunday evening Saturday morning), three academic courses that meet for 12 hours each week day, and simple but comfortable dormitory accommodations. The classes are all offered for non-credit and no specific prior educational experience or background is required.

Demand for Elderhostel programs has grown so rapidly that many institutions now utilize sites such as retreat centers, conference centers and hotels. In these cases, programs normally run for five nights rather than six, but classroom hours remain the same.

It should be noted that while Elderhostel is a "people-oriented" program, the focus is on academics. Courses are developed on campus, class descriptions written, and then cleared through the state Elderhostel office prior to submission to national for inclusion in the catalog.

South Georgia College has placed its emphasis on the development of off-campus sites for a variety of reasons. First, despite the fact that Elderhostel is primarily an academic program, travel to the site is a consideration since Elderhostel attracts people from all 50 states and foreign countries. Access to interstate highways, airports and rental car facilities are considerations. Second consideration is the fact that because the client group does travel great distances to arrive at an Elderhostel site, commercial facilities offer some advantages, i.e., private baths, in-room

phones and television, more elegant dining, and classroom space more conducive to older adult learning styles than do campus-based programs. Finally, there should be some commitment to the economic development of a region or state from educational institutions. While Georgia is blessed with a row of barrier islands (St. Simons, Jekyll, Sea Island, Tybee Island) which contain resort, beach front hotels and motels, this is a seasonal economy which has some tremendous "down times." The economic impact of Elderhostel programs offered during these times is extremely beneficial to the welfare of these commercial properties, their employees, and this region of the state. While Elderhostel participants are students first, they are also tourists with money to spend in a local economy.

As a result of this philosophy, the Elderhostel program at South Georgia College has become one of the largest programs in the nation. During the 1991-92 academic year, the college offered 57 program weeks at off-campus locations which enrolled more than 2,700 people. The college has identified a cadre of more than 30 part-time instructors which are supplemented with faculty from the campus when possible. Together, this corps of instruction has developed over 45 separate courses which are offered through this program.

The program is administered through a full-time staff position for off-campus Elderhostel programs who is on-site each week of program operation. He is assisted in this process by "house parents" — former Elderhostel attendees who are given tuition, room and board for the week in return for their assistance and for being on-call for emergencies 24 hours a day.

The program has been recognized by the state director for Elderhostel as the largest program in the state of Georgia, has been featured in several newspaper and magazine articles, and has resulted in the program coordinator being recognized as the Outstanding Adult Educator of the Year by the state adult education association.

Contact:
Richard Cotton, Director, Continuing Education and Public Service
(912) 383-4213

South Georgia College
100 West College Park Dr
Douglas, GA 31533-5098
Total head count enrollment-Credit: 2,000; Non-Credit: 5,000
Campuses/sites: 1; Full-time faculty: 52

EXPLORING SELF POTENTIAL (ESP)

The program's objective is to interest and prepare certain public school students to attend college

The primary objective of South Georgia College's Exploring Self Potential (ESP) program is to interest and prepare selected Coffee County public school students to attend college. These students would not likely develop the motivation or academic preparation to enroll in college without the special assistance provided by the program.

Exploring Self Potential activities center around computer sessions held on the SGC campus where the students focus on building math, reading and English skills. The sessions are so popular that their frequency was increased from once a month to twice a month at the students' request. The program also utilizes the services of SGC students who visit the public schools one afternoon each week to work with ESP students as tutor/mentors. Public school personnel and SGC faculty help each ESP student to explore career options and review academic strengths and weaknesses. The capstone of the 1991-92 ESP experience was a six day cultural/historical trip to Washington, D.C.

The effectiveness of the ESP program is assessed through group sessions, questionnaires, student essays, student speeches, scores on standardized tests and grades in school. Students and their teachers report that ESP students' grades improved during the school year. Individualized help provided by SGC tutor/mentors, test-taking skills sessions taught by SGC faculty, and personal attention all contributed to the improvement of the students' grades.

One of the three high school seniors in the ESP program graduated from Coffee High School in June with honors and entered South Georgia College in the fall. A second graduate attended SGC during the summer and exempted all developmental studies courses. The third ESP senior opted to join the Armed Forces immediately after graduation but plans to continue her education while in the service.

In its four years of operation, SGC's Early Intervention Program has touched the lives of many Coffee County public school students and their families. The hard work of Program Director Dr. Wilma Lott and her associates Ms. Marlene Bush and Dr. Grace James has made a positive difference in our community.

Contact:
Wilma Lott, Program Director
(912) 383-4316

South Georgia College
100 West College Park Drive
Douglas, GA 31533-5098
Total head count enrollment-Credit: 2,000; Non-Credit: 5,000
Campuses/sites: 1; Full-time faculty: 52

JOURNALISM

The curriculum is timely, broadening students' knowledge and experience about the powerful mass media

An integrated approach to journalism training has resulted in Windward Community College's students winning internships in statewide competition, becoming editors at university and community publications, and establishing themselves in the journalism community.

The journalism courses at Windward Community College are part of the campus's growing emphasis on writing as an area of excellence. At a time when the mass media play such a vital part in our lives, these courses strive to:

1) help students become more informed consumers of news;
2) provide a practical, professional approach to journalism training;
3) give students – even non-journalism pre-majors – opportunities for publication;
4) build skills in critical thinking, writing, editing, and accurate language usage; an
5) foster a sense of ethics and responsibility in reporting news.

Four types of courses are offered:

1) a three-credit basic news writing class for pre-majors or those fulfilling a communications requirement;
2) a one to three variable credit lab that produces the campus newspaper *Ka 'Ohana*;
3) a one-credit grammar and usage class that builds language awareness; and
4) an independent study option in which advanced students can pursue more specialized training in writing/editing, graphic design, advertising, public relations, print or broadcast journalism.

These students are encouraged to seek internships, write for community publications or design projects that give them training opportunities they wouldn't get in an ordinary classroom situation.

The student newspaper has won a national first-place award for three straight years from the American Scholastic Press Association for community colleges of its size. The program also has forged links with the working press in Hawaii. These professionals serve as speakers and sometimes mentors on student projects, helping to bridge the gap between the classroom and the "real world." They also assist with job placement and help build a professional network of which WCC's students can become a part.

Contact:
Elizabeth Young, Instructor
(808) 235-0077/7333

Windward Community College
45-720 Keaahala Road
Kaneohe, HI 96744
Total head count enrollment-Credit: 1,850; Non-Credit: 20,000+
Campuses/sites: 1; Full-time faculty: 46

COMPUTER ASSISTED INSTRUCTION IN WRITING

▦ The computer-assisted classroom provides the ideal setting ▦
to use writing as a tool while maximizing technology

Windward Community College's Language Arts Department integrates computer-assisted instruction, including networking technology, into the Freshman Writing Program on campus.

This dramatic change began in 1989, when the Language Arts Department commenced planning, designing and launching an $80,000 Computers and Composition Project for Windward Community College's first fully equipped Computer Assisted Instruction (CAI) Writing classroom facility.

CAI English 100 writing instructors were provided training through workshops to prepare them to integrate computer technology into their writing classes. A major goal for this project is to promote excellence in teaching and learning both by enhancing classroom instruction and encouraging student involvement both in and out of the classroom and lab facilities.

The Computers and Composition project called for network conversion of a language arts classroom. The new classroom, equipped with 20 student Macintosh computer stations and an instructor's station, with networked SE File Server and a specialized Data Show overhead, provide students with the technology needed to complete all stages of the writing process with efficiency and ease. Various collaborative writing, grammar and mechanics textbook software augment CAI instruction.

The computer enhanced technology for English 100 writing classes has enriched the teaching methods of the language arts curriculum. This pedagogical emphasis derives partly from education and composition research that demonstrates how well computer-assisted and networked collaborative technology enhances the writing process. The college computer-assisted composition classroom provides the ideal environment to learn how to use writing as a tool while maximizing on current technology.

To facilitate this project's goals, two supporting facilities, the campus' Learning Center and Library, were equipped with networked Macintosh computers and printers. These facilities house textbook grammar and mechanics enrichment software to provide students the opportunity to complete CAI writing assignments.

This Project's merits have been recognized in a May 1992 presentation at the "Computers Across the Curriculum: A Conference on Technology in the Freshman Year," sponsored by the City University of York, The National Project on Computers and College Writing and the National Network in Writing.

Contact:
Frank Mattos, Coordinator
(808) 235-0077

Windward Community College
45-720 Keaahala Road
Kaneohe, HI 96744
Total head count enrollment-Credit: 1,850; Non-Credit: 20,000+
Campuses/sites: 1; Full-time faculty: 46

FISHERIES TECHNOLOGY

The program's success has been based upon students operating the college rainbow trout hatchery

With 80 percent of the commercially produced trout in the United States coming from the Snake River area in south central Idaho, the initiation of the Fish Technology Program at the College of Southern Idaho in 1977 was a natural. The program was established with the assistance of local industry, primarily to train workers for the commercial fish industry. Its success has been based upon students operating the college fish hatchery, which has an inventory of 500,000 Rainbow Trout. Students also receive hands-on experience at area private fish farms, along with cooperation and advisory help from private industry, state and federal hatcheries.

This nine-month program is a unique vocationally oriented aquaculture course. Students finish with an Associate of Applied Science certificate. Past students have come from as far away as Pakistan, France, England, Columbia and many parts of the U.S.. due to the uniqueness of the program. Some have already earned degrees, but want hands-on management experience. The competency-based curriculum is divided into four distinct areas:

1) Fish Management;
2) Disease of Fish I and II;
3) Fish Nutrition; and
4) Practicum that includes Operation of the Hatchery.

The program was named the 1989 Idaho Post Secondary Vocational Education Program of the Year, and Professor Terry Patterson was named the college's Top Vocational Educator in 1990. Industry also provides many scholarships to the students, with two $500 scholarships and a $1,500 grant from feed dealers. Fish tech students have also been involved in research and in 1988 had the first successful spawning of a Snake River White Sturgeon in captivity. This was a cooperative venture with the Idaho Fish and Game Department and private industry. Graduates of the program are employed in the area for which they are trained. Approximately 80 percent of the graduates work in the industry. They are employed in private fish hatcheries, as well as with state and federal game departments.

Contact:
Terry Patterson, Instructor-in-Charge
(208) 733-3972

College of Southern Idaho
PO Box 1238
Twin Falls, ID 83303-1238
Total head count enrollment-Credit: 3,915; Non-Credit: 4,575
Campuses/sites: 4; Full-time faculty: 100

RADIATION SAFETY TECHNOLOGY

Graduates are employed at nuclear installations throughout the United States

Radiation Safety Technology (RST) was initiated at Eastern Idaho Technical College in 1970. From its meager beginning of four students housed in a rented facility, RST has grown into a nationally known program serving the Department of Energy, service contractors and the nuclear power industry. Radiation Safety Technology offers two avenues for students to meet their vocational needs:

• A nine-month preparatory program offers a Certificate of Applied Science in Radiation Safety Technology. This program offers, to the successful student, an opportunity to join the work force at the entry level of Operational Health Physics.

• An Associate of Applied Science Degree in Radiation Safety Technology. This program requires a two-year commitment (18 months). This avenue not only aids the successful graduate to begin at the entry level of Operational Health

Physics but also it creates a path for a health physics technician to enter the professional status of Radiological Engineering, ALARA Engineering, Environmental Surveillance, etc.

Required course work for both paths is criterion referenced to such military regulating organizations as the U.S. Department of Energy, the Institute of Nuclear Power Operations, and the American National Standards Institute. The curriculum is validated by a local advisory council made up of individuals from local nuclear operations contractors. The curriculum is reviewed on an annual basis and upgraded to meet governmental and local demands.

The goal of Radiation Safety Technology is to provide the nuclear industry with the most technically competent graduates possible. Because of this objective, the training departments of the contractors at the Idaho National

Engineering Laboratory (INEL) work closely with Instructors at EITC to achieve this goal. Equipment and expertise is traded between INEL and EITC. Program costs are locally administered with an allocation of two full-time faculty.

A Supervised Work Experience (SWE) is completed at the Idaho National Engineering Laboratory under the guidance of EITC instructors and in cooperation with supervisors and lead technicians from three contractors - EG&G Idaho, Argonne National Laboratory-West, and Westinghouse Idaho Nuclear Corporation. Each student is provided with a SWE checklist which spells out specific tasks to be accomplished while performing in-plant training. Students are allowed to perform these tasks in support of the largest test reactor in the world and they are also incorporated into the most modern reprocessing plant in the United States. This type of cooperation is invaluable to students and, ultimately, the nation, by providing the best experience for the dollars spent. Graduates of Radiation

Safety Technology are employed at nuclear installations throughout the continental United States, including: Idaho National Engineering Laboratory; EG&G Idaho; Westinghouse Idaho Nuclear Corporation; Westinghouse Electric Corporation-Naval Reactor Facility; Babcock & Wilcox; Argonne National Laboratories-West; Westinghouse; Batelle Northwest; United Nuclear Corporation; Los Alamos, New Mexico; Science Applications International Corporation; Martin Marietta Oak Ridge National Laboratories; Knolls Atomic Laboratory; Bartlett Nuclear Corporation; Power Systems; Numanco; and Afftrex, Limited.

In addition, the Radiation Safety Technology program offers upgrade training to employed health physics technicians by offering an evening course to enable them to sit for the National Registry of Radiation Protection Technologists examination. EITC hosts this annual examination and is the testing center for Idaho and Utah.

Contact:
Student Services
(208) 524-3000 or (800) 662-0261

Eastern Idaho Technical College
1600 S 2500 E.
Idaho Falls, ID 83404
Total head count enrollment-Credit: 460; Non-Credit: 5,973
Campuses/sites: 1; Full-time faculty: 30

HAZARDOUS MATERIALS TECHNOLOGY

▓ *The program prepares students who can meet industry needs for people* ▓
with knowledge of complex hazardous materials regulations

During the past quarter century Americans have become increasingly aware of the potential danger posed to human populations by the use and transport of hazardous materials and the disposal of industrial waste. As environmental laws to address this have become more complex, industry has expressed a need to hire competent personnel knowledgeable of hazardous materials regulations and trained to properly identify, monitor, store, transport, track and dispose of its hazardous materials.

Eastern Idaho Technical College has responded to that need by creating its Hazardous Materials Technology Program. The Hazardous materials Technology Program is designed to produce trained technicians, with special knowledge of hazardous materials, for employment by industry. Students enrolled in the program take courses in the following areas of instruction:

1) Hazardous Materials and Environmental Laws & Regulations;
2) Chemical and Physical Properties of Hazardous Material;
3) Biological and Health Effects of Hazardous Materials;
4) Hazardous Materials Clean-up and Emergency

Response Procedures; and
5) Management of Hazardous Materials.

In addition to the above-listed areas, students are required to take general studies courses, including written and oral communications, computer usage, and math.

Hazardous Materials Technology is an Associate of Applied Science degree program. The Hazardous Materials Technology Program at EITC began in the fall of 1990. Graduates of the program are employed in a number of industries and consulting firms. They perform duties as varied as asbestos removal, sampling of Department of Defense Facilities, employee training, and hot cell clean-up at nuclear reactors.

An integral part of the EITC curriculum includes a Supervised Work Experience. Students are placed off campus, in industry or government, and gain "hands on" experience by actually working with individuals involved with hazardous materials or related practices and issues. The location of Eastern Idaho Technical College near the Idaho National Engineering Laboratory provides a unique opportunity for students to gain experience with radioactive and/or mixed waste. Many students perform their

Continues on Page 194

Supervised Work Experience at this Department of Energy (DOE) Facility. Recognizing the need for trained technicians to help in the clean-up of DOE facilities, the Department of Energy has targeted two-year, post secondary schools as a potential source of the thousands of technicians DOE will require for its clean-up activities.

Eastern Idaho Technical College has taken a leading role in organizing a consortium of schools in the Pacific Northwest to respond to the need expressed by DOE. In addition, faculty involved with the development of the program at EITC, are working with DOE and faculty from colleges representing other areas of the country, to develop a core curriculum that will be used to train Hazardous Materials Technicians nationwide.

Contact:
Student Services
(208) 524-3000 or (800) 662-0261

Eastern Idaho Technical College
1600 S 2500 E.
Idaho Falls, ID 83404
Total head count enrollment-Credit: 460; Non-Credit: 5,973
Campuses/sites: 1; Full-time faculty: 30

PROJECT PAVE

*▦ PAVE helps participants discover such things as personal aptitudes ▦
and attributes and possible options in light of that personal insight*

More than 90 percent of adults in transition, armed with confidence from Project PAVE at Black Hawk College, are completing courses and more than half are re-enrolling. PAVE (Preparing for Academic/Vocational Excellence), begun in 1988, is designed to facilitate and promote college accessibility, decision-making strategies and expand personal options. This is achieved through a class that provides the student with information about themselves and the options available, plus support and encouragement throughout the decision making and planning process.

PAVE targets under-served populations – potential reentry adults – who face real or imagined barriers to achieving more in their lives. They lack the skills and knowledge to explore their options and do not know where to go for help. The content of the PAVE class at Black Hawk College - East Campus provides the participant with self-knowledge in the areas of career interest, aptitudes, personal attributes and academic achievement levels, as well as information about options available to the participant in light of that personal information. The less obvious, but essential ingredients in the PAVE program are the development of self-confidence in the participants, as well as a feeling of comfort in an academic setting.

The original projected return to Black Hawk College on an investment of $12,000 each year, for a four-year period, was $61,000. Preliminary figures indicate that after four years, the return is more than $64,000.

While the return to Black Hawk College in terms of increased credit hours and funds is most gratifying, the numbers cannot reflect the success Project PAVE is in the minds of the students. The goodwill generated by PAVE is immeasurable. Evaluations of the course have been positive and enthusiastic: "We're on our way. Thanks much, it began with your class;" "It helped me to make a decision about what course of action to take and how to do it;" and "It gave me the courage to attend college."

Contact:
Mary E. Vermeulen, Associate Professor and Counselor
(309) 852-5671, ext. 226

Black Hawk College
6600 34th Avenue
Moline, IL 61265
Total head count enrollment-Credit: 14,641; Non-Credit: 1,589
Campuses/sites: 2;Full-time faculty: 165

TRADITIONAL ENGLISH AS A SECOND LANGUAGE

*▦ The program serves immigrants who are highly educated professionals ▦
needing ESL training before entering college-level classes*

Black Hawk College revised its Traditional English as a Second Language (ESL) program to serve a new group of immigrants, highly educated professionals seeking college education, careers and personal enrichment. The college had quickly recognized the need for change as the new group of immigrants arrived in the Quad Cities. This group was not able to fit into the Adult Basic Education (ABE) classes, but because of the language barrier, neither were they able to access college-level classes. A transitional ESL program was needed.

The development and the execution of the transitional ESL program make it unique. A collaborative effort of the ABE and main campus faculty, the program itself functions with a seamless curriculum tightly tied at one end to ABE and at the other end to the academic program.

The Transitional ESL program is overseen by a committee composed of the Dean of Liberal Arts, Business, and Public Services, the Director of ABE, the ESL Coordinator, the Department Chair of ABE-ESL, and a member of the Counseling Department, and the Director of the Academic Services Center. This committee meets about three times each semester to ensure that the inter-departmental systems are running smoothly, to exchange information on program effectiveness, and to set future program directions. The committee keeps in sync the three main pieces of the program – the ABE/Transitional level one, the level two and three of transitional ESL classes, and the counseling program.

The curriculum design for the program follows the NAFSA guidelines for Academic ESL programs. It is a three-level program that focuses on the four language skill areas of listening, speaking, reading and writing. The program also incorporates study skills and uses materials that acquaint students with the concerns of the U.S. society and the world. The level one transitional program is housed at the Outreach Center, and run under Adult Basic Education. However, to enter this program students must

Continues on Page 196

achieve a specified score on the Michigan Test of English Language Proficiency and commit themselves to daily class attendance and homework. The Department Chair of ABE-ESL gives the test each semester. ESL students from all Outreach programs are invited to take it. The ABE-Transitional level one has been crucial to helping the less confident student build the courage needed to face the "complex" world of the main campus. Once in level one, students make frequent trips as a class to the main campus to learn how to use the library. They meet with students in levels two and three. The listening comprehension tapes for level one are on reserve in the Independent Learning Center, so students make visits on the weekends to the main campus.

At mid-term time a counselor from the main campus visits the level one class to help students prepare their schedules and their financial aid papers for the transition to level two and to the transitional main campus ESL program.

Once the students are in levels two and three, the transition to their next step begins. While learning English, students take the Discover program, a computer aided career orientation program and meet with counselors to map out their plans after ESL. At the end of the program, the students take an exit paragraph test, given and graded by the English Department faculty, to ensure that the students are competent enough in English to be successful in the university parallel program or their career program.

The design of this program is like a web that facilitates movement of students from one segment of the curriculum to another. The execution of this program is in the hands of a team whose frequent communication assures that the students can move through the web without getting stuck. The originality of this program lies not in the individual pieces, but in the way they work together to serve the students.

Contact:
Anne Bollati, Program Coordinator
(309) 796-1311, ext. 1128

Black Hawk College
6600 34th Avenue
Moline, IL 61265
Total head count enrollment-Credit: 14,641; Non-Credit: 1,589
Campuses/sites: 2; Full-time faculty: 165

PROFESSIONAL TRUCK DRIVING

The program, a cooperative venture between the college and a transportation firm, helps fill a need for professional drivers

Carl Sandburg College and a national transportation firm located within the college district collaborated to establish a four-week comprehensive course focused on the trucking industry and structured for today's rigorous standards of highway safety. Because trucking is an important part of the economy and one of the nation's fastest-growing industries, this is an especially vital program.

Students have the advantage of hands-on experience with state-of-the-art, late model equipment. Basic driving skills, transportation fundamentals, qualifications for Commercial Drivers Licensing, along with attitudes for success are presented by certified instructors.

Extensive screening of applicants is completed by the transportation firm prior to enrolling students. Only those with the greatest likelihood of success are accepted into the comprehensive four-week program. A combination of classroom and driving range instruction, including highway, city and night driving along with Commercial Driver Licensing are provided at the college facility. Following the satisfactory completion of the first four weeks, a student will be placed with a Certified Driver

Trainer for approximately five weeks of: driving over-the-road; making pick-up and delivery appointments; loading and unloading freight; and preparing paperwork, including daily driver logs and assorted tasks and routines necessary to prepare students as a professional truck driver.

During the five weeks over-the-road experience, students will receive pay as a trainee driver, which will follow with guaranteed employment for successful completion of the entire program. This cooperative program between the college and Munson Transportation meets a distinct need of this trucking firm, as there is a severe shortage of qualified drivers within the industry. It also provides a short-term vocational program with 100 percent placement potential for dedicated students. A special student-loan agreement with a local bank allows qualified individuals to borrow the minimal program cost and then repay the loan on a payroll deduction plan, once employed with Munson Transportation. Equipment and instructors are provided by the trucking firm, with classroom and administrative assistance from the college. Nearly 1,200 individuals have expressed an interest in the program that is designed to accommodate 60 people each month.

Contact:
Sherry L. Berg, Dean, Community and Extension Services
(309) 344-2518, ext. 250

Carl Sandburg College
2232 South Lake Storey Road
Galesburg, IL 61401
Total head count enrollment-Credit: 15,684; Non-Credit: 8,313
Campuses/sites: 3; Full-time faculty: 57

LIMITED RADIOGRAPHY

▨ The nine-month certificate program uses interactive videos to prepare ▨
"limited permittee" radiographers for this high-demand field

The first of its kind in Illinois, the Limited Radiography program at Carl Sandburg College incorporates interactive video disc technology. Such a program is crucial because over the past decade advances in the field of medical imaging have created manpower demands that cannot be adequately met by the current supply of individuals who perform a limited scope of radiographic examinations.

During the 1990-91 academic year, the State of Illinois enacted legislation to allow "limited permittee" radiographers to perform chest, extremity, spine, and/or skull and sinuses examinations. Seeing the need for a formal educational program to train these individuals, Carl Sandburg College embarked on the development of a nine-month, certificate program in Limited Radiography. The curriculum covers radiation protection, equipment operation and maintenance, image production and evaluation, patient care and management, and anatomy and radiographic positioning appropriate to each of Illinois' four limited permittee categories. Graduates are eligible to take the Illinois Department of Nuclear Safety licensing examination in any or all of the categories.

The program was implemented fall semester 1992 at the college's Carthage Extension Center. The course content and sequence were designed to closely parallel the first year of the associate degree Radiologic Technology program now offered at the Galesburg campus. With this structure the program can provide competent personnel for employment in the private offices and clinics of Illinois physicians, as well as offer articulation with the two-year program for those graduates who wish to pursue full certification by the American Registry of Radiologic Technology.

The Limited Radiography program also has enjoyed partial funding through a Title III, federal grant. Grant funds have been used to purchase modern radiographic equipment, which enables students to simulate patient positioning and the selection of exposure factors in a laboratory setting. In addition, the program uses the video disc technology Macintosh and IBM computers that are compatible with Level III video disc programs currently available for radiologic technology.

Contact:
Elaine Long, Program Coordinator
(309) 344-2518, ext. 311

Carl Sandburg College
2232 South Lake Storey Road
Galesburg, IL 61401
Total head count enrollment-Credit: 15,684; Non-Credit: 8,313
Campuses/sites: 3; Full-time faculty: 57

PROJECT LEAP
(LIFESKILLS EMPLOYMENT AWARENESS PROGRAM)

▨ The program reduces recidivism by helping ex-offenders ▨
re-integrate into society and careers

Designed to keep ex-offenders from returning to prison, a Chicago City-Wide College program provides mentoring and job placement assistance for 90 former inmates returning to Chicago.

Project LEAP (Lifeskills Employment Awareness Program) begins for each offender 90 days before release. During this time, inmates selected for their participation in academic and vocational training while incarcerated are enrolled in classes to learn resume writing, job interviewing and job search skills. They also are given lifeskills courses in stress management, conflict resolution, budgeting and self-awareness. Such orientation is needed, because in Illinois the recidivism rate reaches 65 percent.

Classes are conducted by Project LEAP instructors

located at the community college, where the prison is located. There are three prisons involved in Project LEAP: Hill Correction Center, served by Carl Sandburg College; and Vienna Correction Center and Shawnee Correction Center, both served by Southeastern College.

While the inmates are attending LEAP classes, a team of mentors from Chicago City-Wide College make two to three trips to the prisons to provide activities designed to establish rapport between the inmates and themselves. The activities include an orientation session to describe what they can expect upon their return to the city. The Chicago team also dispenses news about Chicago, about sports teams, job trends and answers questions from the class.

Continues on Page 198

They usually bring magazines and Chicago papers, as well as motivational videos for the men. Then they sit down, one-on-one with each inmate to do any assessment of their background in terms of skills and employment history, family status, survival needs (such as housing and clothing) and possible substance-abuse history. During these sessions, the participants often talk about feelings and misgivings about their ability to re-integrate to society.

Contact:
Chicago City-Wide College
(312) 553-5900

Chicago City-Wide College
226 West Jackson
Chicago, IL 60606
Total head count enrollment-Credit: 3,365; Non-Credit: 9,004
Campuses/sites: 2; Full-time faculty: 25

PROJECT OPPORTUNITIES

This welfare-to-work program includes intensive interaction in goal-setting, self-awareness and career planning

Getting people off federal aid and into paying careers is the goal of opportunities, an intensive program at Chicago City-Wide College. The program, a model for other Illinois colleges, is a result of collaboration with the Illinois Department of Public Aid, the Illinois Community College Board and 10 community colleges across the state.

It is designed to facilitate school attendance by Aid to Families with Dependent Children (AFDC) recipients. The program came about because state legislature had determined that case management responsibilities for some participants should be transferred from the Department of Public Aid to 10 selected colleges. A successful assessment and mentoring project, funded by IDPA and conducted by Chicago City-Wide College, was used as the model for the new program, called Opportunities.

The program includes a two-week assessment of careers and basic skills, combined with exposing students to occupations and training of programs available to them. Intensive interaction in goal-setting, self-awareness and career-planning takes place as well. The original program was designed for men receiving general assistance benefits. The mentoring and other supportive services help this "at risk" population succeed in fulfilling their goal of self-sufficiency.

With minor adjusting, the program is working well to enroll, retain and support 916 AFDC women in the City Colleges of Chicago in 20 hours of instruction and related activity.

There are four campuses of our district where the Opportunities students are enrolled: Malcolm X College, Kennedy King College, Chicago City-Wide College and Olive-Harvey College.

As part of the collaboration, the Illinois Department of Public Aid has provided four full-day training sessions for the college's Opportunities staff on forms and procedures. They have also provided two full-time (IDPA) administrators to work on-site for crisis intervention and problem-solving.

Contact:
Chicago City-Wide College
(312) 553-5900

Chicago City-Wide College
226 West Jackson
Chicago, IL 60606
Total head count enrollment-Credit: 3,365; Non-Credit: 9,004
Campuses/sites: 2; Full-time faculty: 25

REDUCING COSTS SAVINGS FUND

✖ Employees have suggested some innovative and effective ways ✖
to both save the college money and generate revenue

At College of DuPage, any employee may write a cost-saving proposal for a project that nets payback to the college. The money saved is banked for future projects.

This has led to some fascinating and innovative cost savings, with the money being paid back to the college and banked for future projects. The resolution establishing the fund states that $150,000 be used exclusively for innovative cost-savings projects, and that the fund shall be reimbursed up to the operating amount of $150,000 from savings generated by the implementation of such projects.

The major outcome of the establishment of this fund has been the development of a mentality of cost saving/avoidance by everyone. Even though a particular project may not get support from the fund, staff may devise another way to fund it because of its merit. Any member of the college community can propose a cost-reduction project.

Three examples of the many major projects implemented in the past few years through this fund include a Fitness Center, Arts Center Programming and Computer Aided Drafting and Design.

The Fitness Center accommodates the full range of community college populations. It is available to students and the public 72 hours per week, and is operated as an open lab requiring one professional to be on duty during operating hours. The equipment for the center was purchased with $62,000 from the Reducing Costs Savings Fund. The fund was repaid this amount in 2-1/2 years. The $15 course fee generates $32,000 per year, which is placed back in the Physical Education Center account for operating the Center and replacing equipment. The equivalent of one instructor is used, saving the college two full-time equivalent professional salaries per year – approximately $80,000, plus fringe benefits of $9,000. Total annual savings: $121,000.

In the fall of 1986, the college's Arts Center opened with the goal of being the cultural center for the college's district – and breaking even in the process. As a result of the efforts of the Center's director and staff, the Center provides direct support toward salaries of 10 people at a total cost of $145,000. In addition, the rental of the facility to community organizations generates approximately $90,000 per year – 80 percent of the total operation of the Arts Center. Attracting big-name shows and artists to the campus has had numerous benefits in terms of public relations and providing quality programs to members of the community. In addition, the college is able to provide academic classes with special workshops conducted by performing artists. If the institution were to contract with visiting artists for classrooms, it would cost about $30,000 per year. Over three years, the estimated annual savings were $145,000 in salary expenses that do not require support from the operating fund, plus $30,000 that would be needed to contract with visiting artists for classroom presentation, or a total of $175,000 annually. Overall, with income from rentals, the Arts Center has generated a total annual return to the college of $265,000.

Computer-Aided Drafting and Design was initiated because the demand for highly sophisticated computer equipment is rising in every discipline (although the level of sophistication varies from program to program). We devised a way to meet the diverse needs of such programs as art, fashion design, drafting, architecture, hotel management, electronics, manufacturing, horticulture, interior design, commercial art and air conditioning – without spending dollars on expensive software and hardware for each program. We established one large, versatile laboratory equipped with state-of-the-art equipment, staffed by a professional to support each of the aforementioned programs. Instructors in these programs assign projects to be completed in this versatile CADD lab. The lab is available 15 hours per day and on weekends. To accomplish the objectives of the various programs mentioned in the traditional method of delivery would have required 14 more CADD stations, at a cost of $105,000 and another full-time instructor at an annual cost of $42,000.

Contact:
Kenneth Kolbet, Vice President, Administrative Affairs
(708) 858-2800, ext. 2218, or (708) 858-9078

College of DuPage
22nd Street and Lambert Road
Glen Ellyn, IL 60137
Total head count enrollment-Credit: 31,625; Non-Credit: 4,490
Campuses/sites: 2; Full-time faculty: 292

FACULTY DEVELOPMENT

*⬚ With financial backing and management support from the Teaching Center, ⬚
faculty can develop projects that lead to instructional innovation*

The College of DuPage provides two programs aimed at faculty development: the Office of Instructional Design and the Teaching Center. Each office provides a different type and level of service to faculty, and both work together to cover all faculty development concepts.

Full- and part-time faculty at College of DuPage have access to the Office of Instructional Design and Educational Telecommunications. With financial backing and management support from the office, college faculty are able to develop projects which lead to instructional innovation and the development of instructional software, video and print materials for use by their students. The service has evolved from an ad hoc, faculty self-help organization to a full-service support office, which annually supports more than 65 faculty assignments, and generated nearly 400 projects over the 5-1/2 years. Approximately $175,000 is available in direct salary support for faculty. The office maintains a faculty-centered approach to its operations, offering all necessary support in a "one stop" service package.

Faculty have won awards for work done under office auspices, and a number of their instructional products have won recognition in a national marketplace. Faculty interested in financial and/or management support for their ideas apply to the office. A committee of two provosts, two deans and the director of the Office of Instructional Design considers the quality of the projects and suitable awards are made. The office provides funding for faculty projects from its own budgets or will broker support for projects from other campus offices. Additionally the office supports the project clerically and managerially by providing typing, project structure, timelines and materials. Finally, the office provides expertise – either in-house or from outside consultants – on things ranging from instructional strategies to video production and systems design.

One project will serve as an example of how the process works. In this case, members of the nursing faculty wanted to develop software to teach their students charting skills. Since no adequate product was on the market, the office funded their work. The nursing faculty members, with systems design consulting from the office, programmed the software. A consultant refined their computer code to enable it to run on a network. The Office of Instructional Design worked with graphic artists to design and produce suitable documentation. Deemed worthy enough to market, their software product, ChartSmart, is now earning money for the school and the nursing faculty, through sales to other colleges across the nation.

College faculty have developed nearly 400 instructional design projects, including:

- development of courses in creativity and critical thinking;
- computer simulations to teach radiation technology students how to interface patients and equipment;
- a video to teach signing techniques for hearing impaired; a computer/video game and simulation, *Hinderclay*, to teach feudalism in western civilization courses;
- interactive video disks for earth science and child care;
- CAD applications across the curricula;
- a college-wide style manual for composition; and
- video formative tests in histology.

Additionally, the College of DuPage formally opened the Teaching Center in September 1992 as a resource for its full-time and part-time faculty. The Center's activities are led by a half-time coordinator who is a member of the college faculty and supported by a 10-member faculty advisory committee. The college provides appropriate clerical support. The Center has two spaces which can be used for all activities from solitary research through group discussion. The Teaching Center is working in three directions

1) outreach to individuals to support their teaching in as personal and unique a manner as possible;
2) efforts to define and communicate institutional resources to faculty; and
3) initiatives to support and involve faculty in implementing college goals.

To summarize each of these:

The first purpose of the newly created Center is to work hand-in-hand with its dedicated teaching faculty to improve instruction. In outreach to them, the Center is striving to create a climate of discussion, an open-door policy where personal teaching concerns are paramount. For example, the Center conducts "Shoptalk," a weekly, informal, wide-ranging lunchtime discussion group on teaching. The coordinator is available to all faculty to aid them in their personal assessment of the teaching styles and strategies. The Center will seek to create partnerships between new and more experienced faculty.

Secondly, because the college is a mature and complex institution with a rich environment for support of faculty, the Center will become a major point for college faculty to access these services. Among these services are financial support/release time for instructional design, staff development, research, grant writing, team teaching, interdisciplinary course development and teaching, and a variety of other options. At the core of the task of apprising faculty of college services is information-gathering and dissemination. Among the tasks under consideration is development of a detailed, computerized staff directory detailing all full- and part-time faculty interests and expertise. The Center will assist in coordination and promotion of staff development courses, workshops, brown-bag discussions and forums.

Thirdly, the Center seeks to help faculty address institution-wide instructional commitments and policy. Examples include the college commitment to use instructional telecommunications technology, to build international awareness among its students, to meet state mandates on teaching of human relations and to infuse developmental methodologies.

Contact:
Joe Barillari, Director, Instructional Design, (708) 858-2800, ext. 2490
Frances Fitch, Coordinator, Teaching Center, (708) 858-2800, ext. 2793

College of DuPage
22nd Street and Lambert Road
2793 Glen Ellyn, IL 60137
Total head count enrollment-Credit: 31,625; Non-Credit: 4,490
Campuses/sites: 2; Full-time faculty: 292

VISION QUEST: A FACULTY DEVELOPMENT PROJECT

Classical literature is used to strengthen humanities instruction across disciplines

Faculty suggestions that there be more interdisciplinary teaching and an honors program resulted in Vision Quest at Danville Area Community College.

The concerns that prompted the development of the Vision Quest project are familiar ones to Illinois community colleges, and the project's successful format is applicable to other colleges as well. DACC, like others in Illinois, has a diverse student body, a large number of part-time students, a steadily increasing enrollment, and a curriculum which includes baccalaureate, occupational, developmental, adult basic, and non-credit courses. Integrating the curriculum to better meet needs of this diverse student body is a constant concern, as is faculty development. The full-time faculty's heavy teaching load and separation by discipline leave little time for intellectual pursuits or for interaction, particularly across campus. The Vision Quest project has been a successful effort to meet these curriculum and development concerns.

Also applicable to other colleges' experiences were the strengths of DACC in undertaking this project. Strong administrative support and the evolution of a long-range plan for the college which emphasized ongoing curriculum examination and faculty development were necessary components for success of the Vision Quest project. Faculty who voluntarily worked on committees to plan the long-term future of our college had recommended a greater attention to interdisciplinary teaching, writing and reading across the curriculum, more and better training for full-time and part-time faculty, and faculty training to develop an honors program to attract the better students from our area high schools. The Vision Quest project addressed all of those needs.

The purpose of Vision Quest was to strengthen humanities instruction across the disciplines at Danville Area Community College by engaging faculty and students in studying classical literature on the theme of the quest. Quest literature encompassed questions and patterns that will enrich not only literature courses but also other humanities and non-humanities offerings across the curriculum. A "Vision Quest" capstone course completed the emphasis.

The objectives of Vision Quest were faculty development, strengthening the DACC library's holdings in the classics, application of the quest motif and quest literature to classroom teaching across the curriculum, and development of a Vision Quest capstone course for students in the projected DACC honors program.

Vision Quest brought together faculty from all disciplines of the college to investigate master works with a quest motif. The project began with a pre-seminar session in April 1991, when a visiting scholar, Robert Kilmer, helped 23 DACC faculty members define "quest" and begin exploration of primary sources. During Intersession 1991, faculty members participated in an intensive seminar which met four days a week. Master works studied during the seminar, under the guidance of visiting scholars, included Dante's *Inferno*, Milton's *Paradise Lost*, Eliot's *The Waste Land*, and Lessing's *The Four-Gated City*. In addition to readings, lectures and discussions of these master works and related secondary sources, the seminar included museum tours and a concert on the quest theme.

From August 1991 through March 1992, participating faculty presented monthly or bi-monthly Friday afternoon workshops to show how they integrated quest motifs into teaching and intellectual exploration in their own disciplines.

On April 24, 1992, visiting scholar Robert Kilmer

Continues on Page 202

returned again to guide participants in assessing their experience and planning for the future.

The college president and other administrators have supported the project enthusiastically and submitted the project to the state's community college board as DACC's nominee for innovative faculty development. They are pleased about the projected activities described above, all volunteered by Vision Quest participants at little or no cost to the college.

Contact:
Jan Cornelius, Liberal Arts Instruction
(217)443-8841

Danville Area Community College
2000 East Main Street
Danville, IL 61832
Total head count enrollment-Credit: 3,284; Non-Credit: 259
Campuses/sites: 1; Full-time faculty: 62

DANVILLE AREA COMMUNITY COLLEGE

WORKFORCE CHALLENGE 2000

The goal is to prepare and maintain a qualified, adaptable workforce for the region

In response to manufacturers' concerns that too few people were qualified to replace future retirees, Danville Area Community College pulled together diverse sectors of the community to form Workforce 2000.

Representatives of area industries had told Danville Area Community College President Harry Braun in 1989 that about 40 percent of the manufacturing work force in Vermilion County will be eligible for retirement within the next decade. Under Dr. Braun's leadership, from spring 1990 through the end of that year, a 25-person steering committee developed plans. Led by joint chairs Braun, Illinois Power regional manager Jesse Price and General Motors Central Foundry plant manager Al Scargall, the committee determined Workforce Challenge 2000's mission: to plan and implement a program to prepare and maintain a qualified, adaptable work force for Vermilion County and the area served by Danville Area Community College.

In January 1991, the effort expanded, with more than 200 people from different sectors of the community exploring ways to achieve that mission. In committees and subcommittees, participants brainstormed, studied, took surveys and consulted with employers, labor representatives, parents, teachers, students, counselors, administrators and others. In June, chairs of each committee and subcommittee presented their ideas and the ideas they had gathered from the community. Other participants made suggestions, asked questions and developed recommendations. From that process, participants reached a consensus on how to address a number of inter-related local work force concerns.

The result is a plan to:

1) change education to make sure students gain the skills they need for the work force of the future;
2) have area public schools and Danville Area Community College work together to share ideas, programs and educational resources;
3) help students discover their career interests and determine what preparation they need to pursue those interests;
4) provide more in-service training and resources for teachers, counselors and administrators, helping them become more effective;
5) improve students' self-esteem, helping them realize they are capable of succeeding in school and, later, work;
6) develop and implement innovative and non-traditional ideas for improving education;
7) increase cooperation between business/industry and education;
8) increase parents' participation in their children's education;
9) provide more training to keep workers up-to-date with current and changing work force needs;
10) help both functionally unemployed and newly displaced workers to return to the work force as productive employees;
11) provide better human services to workers, helping them solve or reduce personal problems that affect their jobs;
12) make sure more people with personal problems voluntarily seek help from human service agencies;
13) reach more troubled youth and very troubled youth with improved human service programs – enabling more to overcome personal barriers to developing good job skills; and
14) better inform the community about current and future work force needs.

Through Workforce Challenge 2000, the Danville area has recognized its work force problems and has taken the first steps toward resolving them. Already, simply by joining forces on Workforce Challenge, various sectors of the community have met the goal of increasing cooperation. Publicity about Workforce Challenge 2000 has increased the community's awareness of the work force needs of the future. An education summit held in

February 1991 brought together 1,000 junior high and high school teachers and administrators to talk about how education must change to meet the needs of a changing world. A second education summit for all area educators was held in October 1991.

Many who worked on the early stages of Workforce Challenge 2000 have volunteered to see their plans through the next stages. The full text of committee and subcommittee ideas – a compilation of nearly 200 pages – is available for guidance. Still, more people must contribute their efforts and creativity. Workforce Challenge 2000 carries no governmental imperative; its success or failure depends on individual schools, businesses, industries, human service agencies and others carrying the ideas forward. Workforce Challenge 2000 is succeeding with the help of the entire community.

Contact:
Mary Lou Meader, Coordinator
(217)443-8586

Danville Area Community College
2000 East Main Street
Danville, IL 61832
Total head count enrollment-Credit: 3,284; Non-Credit: 259
Campuses/sites: 1; Full-time faculty: 62

STUDENT ASSISTANCE PROGRAM

The program offers such varied services as legal advocacy, family planning and debt management

The Student Assistance Program at Elgin Community College does everything from identifying and helping troubled students to offering parenting classes and pre-retirement counseling. The program provides the following general services:

1) a hotline number to receive 24-hour, seven-day-a-week assessment and referral for a personal problem;
2) referral to a professionally, certified specialist in the area in which the student has been assessed to be having a problem;
3) an educational environment, free from the abuse of alcohol, drugs or domestic unrest;
4) promotion and reinforcement of healthy, responsible living; the individual's responsibility within the community; and the intellectual, social, emotional, spiritual or ethical, and physical well-being of students;
5) immediate response to the student so that long-term therapy or treatment can take place for the student and their family; and
6) in-service training by professional health care specialists in the community for faculty and staff to help in identifying troubled students in the classroom.

Specifically, the Student Assistance Program offers:
1) 24-hour, in-person assessment of emotional difficulties;

2) assessment and referral for substance-abuse-related problems;
3) consumer credit counseling and debt management;
4) legal advocacy and related services for victims of domestic violence;
5) assessment of Premenstrual Syndrome;
6) assessment and referral for children who may benefit from weight-reduction programs;
7) assessment of emotional difficulties, including initial psychological testing;
8) pre-retirement counseling;
9) injury prevention through the teaching of proper body mechanics;
10) pre-marital Physician's Certificates;
11) parenting classes;
12) classes dealing with children's health and lead poisoning;
13) family planning services;
14) temporary emergency shelter and emergency assistance (food, clothing and financial aid);
15) hearing screenings, developmental screenings for children ages 0-3, and scoliosis screenings for young family members;
16) respite services for eligible families of children with developmental disabilities; and
17) use of fitness game fields for the disabled and non-disabled, under the instruction of a fitness specialist.

Contact:
Gayle Saunders, Director of Counseling
(708) 697-1000, ext.

Elgin Community College
1700 Spartan Drive
7422 Elgin, IL 60123
Total head count enrollment-Credit: 10,000; Non-Credit: 4,000
Campuses/sites: 2; Full-time faculty: 110

INTERNATIONAL STUDIES

The program promotes diverse activities, including a Sister City initiative, Model United Nations and a Global Insights Luncheon Series

A Sister City initiative, Model United Nations and a Global Insights Luncheon Series are among several activities of the Elgin Community College International Studies Planning Group (ISPG). In addition, this group has provided leadership resulting the following complex set of activities that together comprise international studies at this college:

- International Visiting Scholar Program;
- World Maps Project;
- Student Study Abroad Program;
- International Faculty Exchange Program;
- Foreign Student College Employment Program;
- Foreign Student Internship Program;

- International Students Achievement Program;
- International Events Series;
- Culinary Arts Students International Program;
- International Student's Flags' Display;
- European Community Quality Assurance Standards Program;
- Illinois Word Trade Center Association membership;
- International Students Admissions Program;
- International Advising and Counseling Program;
- Organization of Latin American Students;
- International Student Ambassadors Program;
- Black Students Association; and
- United States of All Cultures.

Contact:
Gayle Saunders, Director of Counseling/Career Services
(708) 697-1000, ext.

Elgin Community College
1700 Spartan Drive
7950 Elgin, IL 60123
Total head count enrollment-Credit: 10,000; Non-Credit: 4,000
Campuses/sites: 2; Full-time faculty: 110

EMERGENCY DISASTER SERVICES TECHNOLOGY

The program helps the general public and emergency responders protect themselves and others in times of disaster

The state-of-the-art Emergency Disaster Services Technology program at Frontier Community College is especially crucial for the region, which is located near an earthquake fault and also is known as "tornado alley."

This district-wide program covers approximately 3,000 square miles. Formerly called the Emergency Preparedness Program, it began offering classes in the winter of 1970. The program is designed to help the general public and emergency responders protect themselves and others during time of disaster.

Currently, the EDST program offers a general Emergency Disaster Services Technology Certificate. In addition, certificates are also offered in Emergency Preparedness Auxiliary Police, Emergency Preparedness Emergency Medical Technician-Ambulance, Emergency Preparedness Volunteer Firefighter II, Emergency Preparedness Government/Industry, Emergency Preparedness SCUBA, Emergency Preparedness Personnel, and Emergency Preparedness Paramedic.

The strength of this program is evident in its flexibility. The program offers one central provider of services. These services are offered in a non-traditional manner making it possible to provide on-site training, off-sequence instruction on an "as needed" basis and maintain flexible

beginning dates for situations involving emergency training demands. These qualities are imperative in order to meet the emergency training demands of the communities this program serves.

In addition to offering credit courses to the emergency response community, the EDST program offers a wide variety of in-service/seminar type instruction through on-site delivery. Examples of class locations include ambulance services, hospitals, sheriff's departments, Emergency Services Disaster Agency headquarters, Ruritan meeting halls, churches, fire departments and college campuses.

The program is designed to train and prepare emergency responders to meet a wide variety of emergency situations. Areas of training generally include firefighting, auxiliary police, emergency planning and mitigation (civil defense) radiological response, hazardous material response, and emergency medical response. Frontier community College makes every possible attempt to keep the costs of this program to a minimum because many of the emergency responders in this area are volunteers, and receive no monetary support.

There are 72 courses offered within the EDST certificate. The first quarter of instruction began in the winter of

1970 with 60 students enrolled. The fall semester of 1991 recorded an initial enrollment of 1,223 students, generating 1,936 semester hours. The fall 1991 enrollment also reflected approximately 160 classes being offered at 55 locations. During FY91, the EDST program generated 17 percent of the total college enrollment.

A high quality of instruction is maintained through several avenues. A majority of the instructors delivering education to the local emergency responders are directly involved in the field in which they teach. Most bring many years of experience to their classrooms. Teacher training is also incorporated within this program to ensure instructors are kept current in their fields.

Statistics on the number of lives saved and value of diminished property losses as a result of the training received in this program are not readily available. Nonetheless, in the end, this program is about people helping other people. Preparedness is the key. A majority of the students are currently involved, on a daily basis, in meeting the emergency response needs of their communities. Whether classified as a civilian or an active emergency response professional, the students who have taken Frontier Community College's EDST Program, when called upon to apply emergency lifesaving knowledge and skills, are prepared to respond.

Contact:
Wesley Weber
(618) 842-3711

Frontier Community College
Lot #2, Frontier Drive
Fairfield, IL 62837
Total head count enrollment-Credit: 8,308; Non-Credit: 1,246
Campuses/sites: 1; Full-time faculty: 3

HIGHLAND COMMUNITY COLLEGE

RETIRED SENIOR VOLUNTEER PROGRAM

The program provides volunteers who help 47 not-for-profit agencies in four northwest counties of Illinois

Retired seniors help Highland Community College (HCC) and numerous community and civic groups through volunteer efforts that enrich both the seniors and those they serve. Founded by HCC in 1973, the Retired Senior Volunteer Program (RSVP) provides a variety of opportunities for retired persons aged 60 or older.

The RSVP provides volunteers to the four northwest counties of Illinois, and these volunteers provide a variety of services to 47 not-for-profit agencies. In 1991, RSVP volunteers generated more than 50,000 hours of community service. RSVP volunteers assist with bulk mailing for the college, nursing home friendly-visitor programs, hospital volunteer programs, delivering Meals on Wheels, and they also act as museum assistants. RSVP volunteers are also utilized to transport elderly clients to and from congregate meal sites. RSVP volunteers began four years ago to assist in area grade schools by tutoring individual students in math and reading. Volunteers also assist in the grade school libraries, helping with special programs and craft projects. The RSVP school volunteer program has been recognized on a state level through the Illinois

Intergenerational Initiative. RSVP also has two signing groups that perform regularly in area nursing homes and community events.

In addition, RSVP utilizes volunteers to assist in fund raising activities. The volunteers meet regularly to quilt for the public, and to create quilts that are raffled each year. Furthermore, the RSVP also sponsors a local arts and crafts show for senior citizens to sell merchandise that they have made. In addition to the above activities, in the fall of 1992, RSVP began placing volunteers in eight Head Start classrooms. The volunteers assist by reading to the students, helping with meal and snack times, supervising playground activities, accompanying classes on field trips, and working with parents and students on make-it or take-it craft projects. Other volunteers function outside the classroom by making hats and mittens, quiet books, tote bags for crayons, books and other things for the children.

Initially, RSVP was authorized in 1969 under Title VI, Part A of the Older Americans Act, as amended. Today RSVP operates under Title II, Part A, Section 201, of this act, as amended.

Contact:
Michael J. Shore, Director
(815) 235-6121, ext. 290

Highland Community College
2998 West Pearl City Road
Freeport, IL 61032
Total head count, enrollment-Credit/Non-Credit: 4,000
Campuses/sites: 1; Full-time faculty: 45

PARENTS AS TEACHERS (PAT)

The program prepares parents to become more effective teachers of their pre-school age children

An intergenerational program at Highland Community College (HCC) helps parents build a foundation of support, self-confidence and basic academic skills to enable their family to function in today's society.

Begun in 1988 by Head Start and HCC's Adult Education program, the Parents As Teachers (PAT) project has been very successful and continues to grow. Committed to the philosophy that parents can and do make a difference in their child's education, the primary goal of the PAT program is to prepare parents to become more effective teachers of their pre-school age children.

The program is housed in the Adult Education building on the HCC campus. The primary funding sources have been grants from the Secretary of State office and the Illinois State Board of Education. Recruitment is done entirely through agency referrals, primarily Head Start, Public Aid, Township and other organizations. Parents who sign a form indicating their interest in PAT are contacted through a home visit by PAT teachers. Thereafter, if a parent decides to participate, barriers to attendance are discussed and resolved to enable the parent(s) and children to attend.

The program consists of separate classes for parents and children. The Parent Program includes several components. In the "Make and Take" section, parents create an activity in class that reinforces or teaches school readiness and learn how to work with their children in making the project at home. In the "parent sharing" component, parents air concerns about family life and discuss solutions with other parents in a non-threatening, informal environment. One day each week free counseling is available through the Family Life Center. In addition, free transportation to and from the program site is available for parents and children.

The Child Program is provided for all 2- to 5-year-old children who have a parent in the program. Program goals for the children are primarily physical, social and emotional rather than academic. Included are experiences that promote following instructions, sharing, listening, and gross and fine motor development.

As a result of the success of the project at its Freeport location, the HCC PAT program has expanded its activities to include a pilot site in an additional city, Mt. Morris. Although HCC did not have the additional funds to support this project, it was agreed that the college would supply the staff and offer technical assistance if Mt. Morris would provide a site, child care, transportation, supplies and materials. Several organizations stepped forward to offer their services and the Mt. Morris PAT program, a truly cooperative effort, began in early 1992.

The HCC PAT program continues to look forward to the future. Plans include initiating more cooperative efforts such as that with Mt. Morris, expanding the PAT program to include school-age children, and offering Parent Program classes on-site in area businesses during lunch hours to enable more parents to participate in the program.

Contact:
Sandy Feaver, Adult Education Director
(815) 235-6121, ext. 254

Highland Community College
2998 West Pearl City Road
Freeport, IL 61032
Total head count enrollment-Credit/Non-Credit: 4,000
Campuses/sites: 1; Full-time faculty: 45

QUEST
(QUALITY EDUCATION FOR UNDERGRADUATE TRANSFER STUDENTS)

QUEST, a model transfer program, integrates knowledge into a more coherent curriculum

QUEST at Illinois Central College contains more hours of general education, more interdisciplinary courses and more "open-ended" assignments than the standard transfer program. Perhaps more importantly, it creates a "Community of Learning."

QUEST (Quality Education for Undergraduate Transfer Students) was developed in response to the 1985 national report, *Involvement in Learning*. QUEST, a model transfer program that now enrolls about 400 students:

1) provides a greater breadth of skills and knowledge
2) integrates that knowledge into a more coherent curriculum

3) promotes in the classroom more active modes of teaching; and

4) creates a sense of group belonging and social integration.

Based upon 15 identified core competencies, the QUEST curriculum not only contains more hours of general education than the standard transfer program at ICC, but also more of the courses are prescribed. The competencies are consciously reinforced across the curriculum through regular meetings of the instructors to coordinate their courses and reinforce the connections between them. The curriculum is also more integrated through interdisciplinary courses and team-teaching. The Survey of Social Sciences, for example, has four faculty in the class at the same time to interact and show the relationships between their disciplines of history, geography, economics and sociology.

The teaching methods used in the program are designed to engage the student's active participation: small group work, study groups, independent study, tests that call upon the student to connect pieces of information and to generalize from them. The "open-ended" kinds of assignments include those whose outcomes are less predicted and whose means and direction are left to the responsibility of the student.

The "Community of Learning" creates a sense of belonging to a group, a collegiality among students and faculty. Students not only share common experiences within the same classes but also they participate with the faculty in a number of cultural events, field trips and other activities outside the classroom. Free tickets to college and community concerts, plays, films and lectures are given to the QUESTers and the faculty who accompany them. A student advisory board selects and plans the social events. The QUEST students also have their own "common room" in which to study, gather between classes or meet for special programs. For better communication, each student has a mail slot in the common room, and a weekly newsletter keeps everyone informed of the achievements, celebratory events, and goings and doings of QUESTers.

Conceived as a total program from recruitment, counseling, social activities and instruction, QUEST has been given the Teaching and Learning Excellence Award by the Illinois Community College Board, and it is one of the exemplary programs being studied by John and Suanne Roueche as part of the Community College Leadership program.

Contact:
Ronald Holohan, Dean
(309) 694-5301

Illinois Central College
One College Drive
East Peoria, IL 61635
Total head count enrollment-Credit: 12,853; Non-Credit: 1,428
Campuses/sites: 2; Full-time faculty: 186

SELF-EMPLOYMENT TRAINING (SET)

The program helps low-income and/or unemployed persons – particularly minorities and women – establish and operate successful businesses

An economic development program at Illinois Central College that assists low-income and/or unemployed persons establish and operate micro-businesses has been a huge success. In only two years, the Self-Employment Training (SET) Program assisted in the development of more than 53 new businesses, and the creation of more than 127 news jobs in a five-county Central Illinois area. The attendant savings is more than $400,000 in government entitlements (i.e. public aid, unemployment benefits, etc.). The success of this program is based on the focusing, coordination and utilization of existing community, governmental, educational and private sector economic development programs and services. Special emphasis is placed on recruiting minority and female participants.

The tuition-free SET Program consists of five components:

1) the Business Training Component, consisting of at least 78 classroom hours focused on the development of a viable business plan while creating an awareness of the circumstances which lead to a successful business endeavor;

2) the Management Consulting Support, which provides individualized support for SET graduates on an annually renewable basis; during this phase, the SET graduate is taught how to independently handle typical small business management issues and problems; areas of assistance include marketing plan refinement, accounting practices, personnel management, bidding and estimating, collective bargaining and related union matters, legal issues, utilization of existing resources, risk management and bonding, operational efficiency, etc.;

3) the SET Workshop Series addresses the general educational needs of program participants while emphasizing continued business skill enhancement and state-of-the-art trends;

4) the SETnet Micro-Business Network is an organi-

Continues on Page 208

zation of graduates and program participants who share talents, experiences and provide mutual support while participating in the shaping of future educational programs, assisting in creating public awareness of micro-business issues, and in helping recruit potential SET participants; and

5) the SET Revolving Loan Funds, which provide direct loans or commercial loan guarantees to SET graduates who demonstrate a "need;" the use of funds is coordinated by the SET program while the funds are appropriated and administered specifically for certified SET graduates, by city and county governments, and community action agencies.

This program was originally funded by Illinois Central College through the Illinois Community College Board's Economic Development Grant, the State of Illinois Department of Commerce and Community Affairs, and the Economic Development Council for the Peoria Area, Inc. Annual program budget is less than $40,000, or $665 per participant, while saving more than $3,300 per participant in government entitlements.

The SET Program received a 1992 National Association of Counties Achievement Award; has been recognized in the Illinois Community College Board's publication, *EXCEL*, the Illinois Department of Commerce and Community Affairs publications, the U.S. House of Representatives *Congressional Record*, many regional publications, radio and television programs; and has selected to conduct presentations for the American Association of Community and Junior Colleges, Illinois Association of Community College Administrators, the National Conference of Community Services and Continuing Education.

Contact:
Michael F. Kuhns, Program Coordinator
(309) 676-7500

Illinois Central College
One College Drive
East Peoria, IL 61635
Total head count enrollment-Credit: 12,853; Non-Credit: 1,428
Campuses/sites: 2; Full-time faculty: 186

COAL MINING TECHNOLOGY

Short-term courses serve nearly 5,000 students each semester, helping meet immediate industry needs

Illinois Eastern Community Colleges launched the Coal Mining Technology program 20 years ago when the coal mining industry in Southern Illinois was at its peak. When the market for Southern Illinois coal began to decline, it appeared that the program might be dropped. Instead, the program today - in a dramatically different form - is strong and growing rapidly, enrolling nearly 5,000 students per semester in short-term courses.

The health of the Coal Mining program can be credited to initiative, flexibility, and creativity in meeting the needs of industry. Although IECC still offers the standard two-year Associate Degree program in Coal Mining Technology, most of the FTE from the coal mining program now is derived from short courses, which include everything from Mining Accident Prevention and Advanced First Aid to Roof Bolter Hydraulic Systems and High Voltage Electrical Retraining.

With the approval of the Illinois Community College Board, the courses are marketed statewide and in Indiana by a staff which works at nights, on weekends, or on any schedule that fits the requirements of the mining industry.

The 15-member staff is supervised by the Associate Dean of Industrial Technology and includes full-time instructors and part-time instructors. Cooperative agreements have been arranged with seven other community colleges throughout the state so that students in those college districts can have access to this specialized training. The Illinois Department of Mines and Minerals, the U.S. Bureau of Mines, MHSA, the United Mine Workers of American and companies of the coal industry have worked very closely with the college in the development of the program.

Job opportunities for graduates include maintenance foreman, repairman, miner and various mine technician positions. Machinery repair, welding, hydraulics and electrical skills achieved in this program are transferable to occupations outside the mining industry to any heavy-industry occupation that requires these skills. In addition, the credits received in the Coal Mining Technology Program transfer into the Capstone Industrial Vocational Education and Mining Engineering Technology Program at Southern Illinois University at Carbondale.

Contact:
George Woods
(618) 985-3741, ext. 371

Illinois Eastern Community Colleges
233 East Chestnut Street
Olney, IL 62450
Total head count enrollment-Credit: 25,610; Non-Credit: 1,600
Campuses/sites: 4; Full-time faculty: 150

TELECOMMUNICATIONS

▦ The program's clients includes such major players as GTE, AT&T, ▦
the U.S. Naval Weapons Center and the University of Illinois

The Telecommunications Program at Illinois Eastern Community Colleges took a dramatic leap in enrollment with the growth of fiber optic networking, and the divestiture of the phone system, but the increased enrollment is also tied to a savvy understanding of program marketing.

IECC's telecommunications program was launched in 1975, when rotary dial telephones were the standard of the day. The early program enrolled a few dozen students and was geared to short-term training only. As the demand for training and the sophistication of the training increased, IECC developed a two-year, Associate Degree program in Telecommunications, and obtained approval from the Illinois Community College Board to offer it statewide. (Such statewide approval is unusual in Illinois; in most cases, community college districts may only offer programs within their geographic boundaries.) IECC also developed short-term training programs, custom-tailored to fit industry's needs.

Since the mid-1980's, the Telecommunications program has increasingly expanded its list of clients, with the roster now including such major players in the telecommunications field as GTE; AT&T; the U.S. Naval Surface Weapons Center in Crane, Indiana; and the University of Illinois.

The staff includes a director, who also serves as an instructor; a program assistant; five full-time faculty, and five to six part-time faculty. The degree program enrolls about 70 students per year, while the short-term training programs have enrolled more than 1,000 student/employees in the past three years. This growth has been produced in a rural community in Southern Illinois which is more generally known for its abundant production of corn and soybeans.

Instead of focusing on theory, or strictly on new, high technology systems, the IECC Telecommunications program provides a wide range of training. Courses offered through this program not only include the basics, such as pole climbing, phone installation, and cable splicing, but also cover the high technology end, such as digital switching, fiber optics and networking, and microwave and satellite communication. Since there are thousands of old telephone systems still in existence, there is still a pressing need for employees who can repair and maintain these systems. Meanwhile, IECC has supported the program by investing in professional development and purchasing new state-of-the-art equipment, factors that have helped the IECC Telecommunications program attract a diversity of clients.

Although the Telecommunications program has its colorful brochures and marketing strategies, its promotion has centered primarily on one-to-one contact with the people in the trade. Training requests most frequently come "by word of mouth." Staff members serve as speakers at state telephone conventions, set up booths at telecommunications trade shows, and heed the advice of their advisory council.

The Telecommunications staff is currently participating in a new delivery system - transmission of instruction over long distances through two-way interactive video. This instant instructional delivery system has tremendous potential for rural areas, such as Southern Illinois, which are constantly exploring new ways to bridge distances and use new technologies to revitalize their economies.

Contact:
John Highhouse, Lincoln Trail College
(618) 544-8252

Illinois Eastern Community Colleges
233 East Chestnut Street
Olney, IL 62450
Total head count enrollment-Credit: 25,610; Non-Credit: 1,600
Campuses/sites: 4; Full-time faculty: 150

EVALUATING FOR EXCELLENCE: EFFECTIVE FACULTY EVALUATION

▨ *The evaluation form has been praised by faculty for being open-ended* ▨
and for requiring that specific observations be written

Praised both by faculty and administrators, an in-class faculty evaluation system provides formative assistance and leads to the process of probation and progressive remediation for those unable or unwilling to show improvements at Illinois Valley Community College.

The "evaluating for excellence" program led to removal of 12 ineffective tenured faculty members through due process procedures. The evaluation process allowed the college to tenure more than 35 new faculty members while denying tenure to 14 persons during a 12-year period beginning in 1980, when it was approved by the Illinois Valley Community College Board of Trustees.

Illinois Valley's evaluation system has been written up in two nationally publicized books, *Evaluating for Excellence* and *Merit in Education*, written by the college's dean of instruction.

Faculty leaders see the evaluation system as being "fair, provided us with input, provides for remediation for those persons needing it, and is trying to help those persons in need." They laud the fact that in-class evaluators must spend the full classroom period observing, provide written and oral responses to the faculty member and allow for discussion of the points made. The evaluation form is also praised by faculty as being open-ended and requiring specific observations to be written for both meritorious and improvement comments. In short, the evaluator must be clear as to what observations were made and specific in presenting them to the faculty member.

The college has become a leader in providing outstanding graduates at the transfer universities in the state of Illinois and ranks 1, 2 and 3 at most universities reporting success of graduates.

"Evaluating for Excellence" has become nationally known and has the respect of the AACC, Illinois Community College Board and the ACCT, as all of them have utilized speakers from IVCC at state and national conferences.

Contact:
Hans A. Andrews, Dean of Instruction
(815) 224-2720

Illinois Valley Community College
578 East 350th Road
Oglesby, IL 61348-1099
Total head count enrollment-Credit: 4,550; Non-Credit: 6,500
Campuses/sites: 1; Full-time faculty: 76

FACULTY QUALIFICATIONS AND COMPETENCIES

▨ *The administration set up a process that provides for a thorough review* ▨
and annual update of each faculty member's experience

In 1989, the Illinois Valley Community College board of trustees accepted the fifth *Qualifications and Competencies Handbook* for faculty. The system has continually been updated and improved since its initial development in 1981.

The Illinois legislature passed a tenure law for community college faculty in 1980, and provided for tenure and seniority based upon such terms as qualified, competent, competent to render, etc.

The faculty and administration at IVCC worked for a year to develop the minimum qualifications that should be required for all faculty positions by subject and discipline. Faculty who were to be hired would be considered as "qualified" if they met the minimal qualifications listed in the board-approved handbook. Competency would be granted for those courses prepared for, taught and evalu-

ated through in-class supervisory evaluators. The qualifications were consistent for both full-time and part-time faculty.

The administration was directed to maintain a listing of competencies and qualifications for all full-time faculty and academic support personnel. The administration made it clear that minimum qualifications would not be compromised to "protect" all of the existing personnel who did not fit the published minimum qualifications. The administration set up a process that provided for a thorough review of each faculty and academic support member's experience at the college. Each faculty member now has a yearly updated "competency and qualification" sheet in his/her personnel folder.

The early fears quickly dissipated and the system has given the college a systematic, fair responsible and legally defensible system of determining faculty qualifications and competencies.

The college has published two articles on the system in a nationally distributed professional journal and has had calls for copies of the handbook from dozens of colleges around the country. In addition, college personnel have spoken at state and national conventions about the system.

Contact:
Hans A. Andrews, Dean of Instruction
(815) 224-2720

Illinois Valley Community College
2578 East 350th Road
Oglesby, IL 61348-1099
Total head count enrollment-Credit: 4,550; Non-Credit: 6,500
Campuses/sites: 1; Full-time faculty: 76

COMPUTER INTEGRATED MANUFACTURING (CIM)

A hi-tech center utilizes state-of-the art equipment, including three robots as well as vision, conveyer and retrieval systems

At John A. Logan College, a High-Tech Center is completely dedicated to a state-of-the-art Computer Integrated Manufacturing (CIM) program that gives students practical experience in integrating the manufacturing processes from initial design to the finished product.

Through a series of two federal grants, this rural community college established the CIM curriculum. CIM is the utilization of modern computers by the science of manufacturing to manage all the technologies used to operate a manufacturing business and to increase overall efficiency and productivity in manufacturing. The concern is for how the product is manufactured, distributed, documented and supported. The following are included in the study of CIM: robotics, CAD, CAM, CAD-CAM, PLCS, materials handling, storage and retrieval, payroll, invoicing, receiving, bid specs, production scheduling, record keeping, order entry, and inventory control.

Both a two-year associate degree and a one-year certificate program are offered. The degree programs are designed to prepare men and women for a variety of positions in computer integrated manufacturing. The student is exposed to the total CIM environment and to a broad knowledge of the basic aspects of CIM.

John A. Logan College CIM facilities are housed in the High-Tech Center at the college and utilize state-of-the-art equipment. The CIM cell is composed of an automated storage and retrieval system, a conveyer system, three different robots, two CMC machining centers, a vision system, a bar code reader system, and all necessary software to make the cell functional.

The student who graduates from the CIM program has practical experience in integrating the manufacturing processes from initial design to the finished product.

Contact:
Paul McInturff, Career Dean
(618) 985-3741

John A. Logan College
Route 2, Box 145
Carterville, IL 62918-9900
Total head count enrollment-Credit: 5,786; Non-Credit: 747
Campuses/sites: 1; Full-time faculty: 83

TECH PREP

The program has been expanded to include junior high/middle school and elementary levels

Selected as one of the original Illinois colleges to implement a Tech Prep Program in 1990, John A. Logan College quickly expanded Tech Prep to include junior high/middle school and elementary levels.
The concept has been infused into the secondary schools in two ways:
1) stand-alone classes in applied mathematics, applied communications, principles of technology, and applied biology/chemistry; and
2) integration of applied methods in traditional mathematics, science, and communications classes.

In addition to the integration of applied methods, the infusion of employability skills and interpersonal skills into

Continues on Page 212

existing courses has been highly successful.

Graduates of secondary and post secondary institutions who have completed Tech Prep requirements will receive Tech Prep certification in addition to certificates and degrees. These certificates will signify to prospective employers that "certified students" have the academic, vocational/technical, interpersonal, and employability skills they are demanding; and therefore, should be given preference when hiring.

Contact:
Paul McInturff, Career Dean
(518) 985-3741

John A. Logan College
Route 2, Box 145
Carterville, IL 62918-9900
Total head count enrollment-Credit: 5,786; Non-Credit: 747
Campuses/sites: 1; Full-time faculty: 83

SWINE MANAGEMENT PROGRAM

▨ *The goals include increasing efficient pork production* ▨
and producing a higher quality product

Developed to meet existing local needs, the Swine Management Program at John Wood community college boasts near 100 percent placement of all graduates.

It began in 1980 with an instructional philosophy encompassing the specialized knowledge and skill development associated with swine production and related agribusiness. Emphasis is placed on agriculture leadership development through active and successful participation in the JWCC Agriculture Club. Average enrollment has been 25 full-time students besides an active evening class schedule.

This program was developed in response to existing local needs and growing statewide demand for swine managers, as verified by employers within the swine production industry. The curriculum was developed and is monitored by an active advisory committee, including local pork producers. In this manner, students are assured of an education which meets today's needs while keeping abreast of technological developments. Each John Wood Swine Management student participates in an eight-week, four-credit-hour internship with a pork producer in a Swine Management operation. As a result, each student receives valuable on-the-job training while receiving wages during this internship experience. The program is the only one in the state of Illinois with a swine teaching laboratory and classroom under one roof. The agriculture staff has given seminars at the American Vocational Association Conference in New Orleans and Atlanta on this unique, innovative educational program.

Basic purposes of this program are to increase efficient pork production, increase employability of students, promote cost-effective operations, produce a higher quality product within a better production environment and promote efficiency of the pork production business. These objectives have been accomplished, which can be directly attested to by the regional, state and national recognition given to this program.

This program was identified as the best Agricultural Technology Instructional Program in the United States in 1987, as decided by the National Association of State Departments of Agriculture. This organization comprises all the Commissioners, Secretaries and Directors of Agriculture who are elected or appointed in each of the 50 states within the United States.

The Swine Management Program at JWCC received the Best Instructional Program Award within the 12-state Midwest region in 1987 (won by Ohio State University in 1986). Subsequently, competition at the national level with the other three regional winners selected JWCC Swine Management Program as the Best Instructional Program in the country. (This recognition was given to California State University in 1986). Each of these two awards carried a monetary recognition of $7,000. The college endowed the $14,000 in the John Wood Community College Foundation and is awarding student scholarships each year, based upon the interest earned.

The program employs a distinctive specialized curriculum in a creative combination of classroom instruction, laboratory work, occupational internships and Work/Study opportunities. Upon graduation, the students have averaged three to five job opportunities each, at an average salary of $20,000.

The program is housed in a facility which seats 25 people comfortably within the classroom and houses a 72-sow farrow-to-feeder pig operation which produces more than 1,200 feeder pigs annually within the classroom/production facility. Since the facility was constructed under the guidance of the subcommittee of the JWCC Agriculture Advisory Council, it was done in direct and close cooperation with the agriculture business community. Consequently, the agribusiness community has consistently recognized this as a "model" program, linking education and business.

The John Wood Swine Management facility was constructed from blueprints designed by members of the Swine Subcommittee of the JWCC Agriculture Advisory

Council. The curriculum was designed by members of the Adams and the Pike County Pork Producers, in concert with the Board of Directors of the Illinois Pork Producers, a commodity organization working directly with pork production in Illinois. The instructor, a proven animal husbandryman and educator, was selected through cooperative efforts of members of the swine production industry and administrative staff at John Wood Community College. The primary instructor has been identified as recipient of the Outstanding Educator Award by the Illinois pork producers organization, in addition to the two primary instructors receiving the Outstanding Instructor Award at John Wood Community College.

John Wood Community College is committed to students by maintaining low tuition and fee costs ($44 per credit hour), offering talent scholarships to agriculture students totaling more than $12,000, helping students in finding part-time employment and actively employing work/study students.

The Swine Management Program prepares students to make significant contributions to agriculture by improving their knowledge and skills in pork production. To those in agriculture, the result is a competitive advantage by increasing the efficiency of pork production. To the consumer, the result is a better quality product, both in nutrition and taste.

Contact:
Larry Fischer, Director, Agricultural Programs
(217) 236-5711

John Wood Community College
150 South 48th Street
Quincy, IL 62301
Total head count enrollment-Credit: 5,912; Non-Credit: 5,446
Campuses/sites: 5; Full-time faculty: 36

BROADCAST ELECTRONICS TECHNOLOGY

Because it is difficult to keep faculty and equipment current within existing budgets,
this program is taught in partnership with Harris Corporation

One of the challenges facing community college electronics programs today is how to keep faculty and equipment current, while remaining within budgetary constraints. John Wood Community College solved both problems by creating a partnership with Harris Corporation.

The Broadcast Electronics Technology program is taught by Harris Corporation for John Wood Community College through an educational services contract. Under the agreement, Harris Corporation staff members teach all of the technical courses in the Broadcast Electronics program. Harris also supplies most of the equipment to be used for student training. In return, JWCC reimburses Harris Corporation on a per credit hour basis. All general education courses are supplied directly by JWCC. Students are registered by JWCC, where they pay tuition and receive grades and transcripts.

Available as a 43-semester-hour certificate or a 64-semester-hour AAS degree, the Broadcast Electronics

Technology Program has several distinctive advantages for students, businesses, and JWCC. For the student, the program offers faculty with extensive and recent "real-world" experience, state-of-the-art equipment, low JWCC tuition rates, and extensive support services available through JWCC. For Harris Corporation and other local electronics companies, the benefits include a local labor pool trained by practitioners in the field of electronics on current equipment, thereby reducing the expense of recruiting technicians to the area. For JWCC, the principal advantage of the program is access to faculty and equipment that are traditionally beyond the reach of a small rural community college.

Since its beginning in 1979, the Broadcast Electronics Technology program has graduated more than 150 technicians. Placement for the program is strong (more than 90 percent), and starting salaries are excellent. Graduates of the program are automatically eligible for certification by the Society of Broadcast Engineers.

Contact:
John T. Drea, Assistant Dean of Instruction
(217) 224-6500, ext. 169

John Wood Community College
150 South 48th Street
Quincy, IL 62301
Total head count enrollment-Credit: 5,912; Non-Credit: 5,446
Campuses/sites: 5; Full-time faculty: 36

COMPUTER LANDSCAPE DESIGN

Offered as part of a Certificate of Achievement in landscaping, Computer Landscape Design provides students with unique technological training

Joliet Junior College's Computer Landscape Design (CLD) provides both current and future landscapers a unique opportunity to learn a technology which has quickly become a standard in the green industry. Through this and other landscape classes, the JCC horticulture program enrolls students from a dozen Illinois community college districts.

Computer landscape design provides landscapers or land use planners with tools to create an original drawing in far less time than conventional board-based techniques, allowing a designer to dedicate more time to refining drawings and exploring options. Using CLD, a designer can quickly illustrate multiple options within a design scheme, or make changes at a client's request. CLD software also provides for cost-estimating and billing.

JJC landscape instructor Mark Kuster utilizes computer work stations in JJC's popular mechanical design technology lab to teach LANDCADD, the industry standard design software. Each semester, certified landscape architects make up the majority of Kuster's 10-person evening CLD class. Kuster is the only certified LANDCADD trainer among Illinois community colleges and possibly the first community college educator in the nation to be certified.

Computer landscape design is offered as part of a Certificate of Achievement in landscaping. Students must first take courses in board-based drawing and computer-aided design.

Kuster emphasizes site planning, land development, and use of the cost-estimating features in his classes. Kuster, whose experimentation with computer assisted design software began in 1980, was invited to address the Community College Consortium's Winter 1992 Institute. He also has introduced a course in computer videoscaping, which will allow a landscape designer to create a photo-like image to illustrate plant and landscape choices for a particular commercial or residential site.

Contact:
Mark Kuster, Instructor, Agricultural and Horticultural Sciences
(815) 729-9020, ext. 2400

Joliet Junior College
1216 Houbolt Avenue
Joliet, IL 60436-9352
Total head count enrollment-Credit: 10,427; Non-Credit: 913
Campuses/sites: 4; Full-time faculty: 146

SUPPLEMENTAL INSTRUCTION

Students meet with supplemental instructors after each class to review material and also are encouraged to meet for individual tutoring

From one year to the next, Supplemental Instruction in one class at Joliet Junior College increased the retention rate from 58 percent to 83 percent, a testament to collaborative learning.

Joliet introduced Supplemental Instruction as a pilot program in the summer of 1991 for at-risk students and students in at-risk courses. Supplemental instruction is designed to explain and clarify concepts presented in the target course and to review and reinforce related study skills through small group discussions, activities and assignments. The Supplemental Instruction program includes lessons in note-taking, study skills, reading, test preparation, memory enhancement, time management and similar topics.

Supplemental instructors at JJC are students with majors or minors in the field, with a minimum 3.0 grade point average in the content area. Preference is given to students who earned an "A" in the target class.

In addition to regularly attending the target class, the supplemental instructors meet with students immediately after each class session to review material and to explore related topics. Students are also encouraged to meet with the supplemental instructors for individual tutoring and to use the resources of the Academic Skills Center.

Supplemental instructors work approximately 20 hours each week. The instructors are paid to attend a tutor training session, hold office hours in the Academic Skills Center and to prepare materials .

Supplemental instruction has been used for three classes at JJC: anatomy and physiology, introduction to psychology, and introduction to Spanish. Retention in the 49-student anatomy and physiology class rose from 58 percent to 83 percent compared with the same class one year earlier. The completion rate for the class was 40 percent higher. There was a 12 percent increase in "A"s, 7 percent increase in "B"s, 2 percent more "C"s, 8 percent fewer "D"s, 10 percent fewer "E"s and 14 percent fewer withdrawals. A trial with another 49-student anatomy and physiology class, revealed that the 30 SI students received an average grade of 2.96 (4.0), while non-supplemental students earned an average grade of 2.39. The retention rate during the second trial was 54 percent for SI students, and 50 percent for non-supplemental students. The program will be extended to a rhetoric class and an introductory accounting class.

Contact:
Charlene Wagner, Instructor, Academic Skills Center
(815) 729-9020, ext. 2284

Joliet Junior College
1216 Houbolt Avenue
Joliet, IL 60436-9352
Total head count enrollment-Credit: 10,427; Non-Credit: 913
Campuses/sites: 4; Full-time faculty: 146

RADIOGRAPHY

*By introducing the program to applicants' friends and families,
the college boosted recruiting and retention efforts*

A successful tool for recruiting and retaining student in Kankakee Community College's Radiography Program has been to invite the applicant's parents, spouses and friends to an informational meeting about the program.

At the meeting, the college explains in detail about the program, pointing out not only the positive aspects of the program but also the areas that can cause the student some concerns (time involved, commitment, patient-related issues). Any interested person is offered the opportunity to spend some time in the Radiography Department at one of the clinical sites to get a better idea of what this career is all about.

Approximately 70 people attended one meeting, when we knew our acceptance into the 1990 class would be 17. This gave us the opportunity to direct the other potential students to become better prepared for acceptance the following year. Those other students who were not accepted in previous years could have been lost to us completely. We surveyed our present students as to their feelings about the meeting and received very positive responses.

Associated costs: Time, but no money.

Personnel requirements: Director of Program and Instructor/Clinical Coordinator.

Key concepts for success:
1) have faculty members directly involved in this program;
2) balance out the negative and positive aspects of the program;
3) give students plenty of time for questions and answers; and
4) have the family and friends "buy into" the program.

Contact:
Ed Viglia, Director
(815) 933-0278

Kankakee Community College
PO Box 888 River Road
Kankakee, IL 60901-0888
Total head count enrollment-Credit: 3,824; Non-Credit: 1,811
Campuses/sites: 1; Full-time faculty: 20

CELEBRATION OF LEARNING

*The program helps break the cycle of under-education by giving children a good beginning
and helping their parents improve themselves through education*

The Kankakee area has a high rate of unemployment, a high number of Public Aid recipients, a high percentage of high school dropouts and a high number of undereducated adults. Bringing hope through this hopelessness means breaking the intergenerational cycle of under-education. Kankakee Community College and the local public school district tried to do just that, by giving "at risk" children a good educational beginning. In addition, the college and school district help parents improve themselves through education and by enticing them to become partners in their children's education.

Continues on Page 216

The goal of the cooperative effort was to make parents aware of how important the education of their children and themselves is by celebrating it. The plan entailed inviting the parents of 50 of the Head Start and Bright Beginnings students to a free "celebration" dinner on the KCC campus. Their hosts were KCC's Vice President for Academic Affairs, the Dean of Continuing Education, a vocational-technical instructor, a health careers instructor and the founder of KCC's nationally recognized Parenting Program. These hosts greeted the parents as they arrived, visited with them during a relaxed, laughter-filled dinner and spoke about the celebration of education.

A key goal of the project was to expose the parents in a non-threatening, informal manner to the opportunities available to them at KCC. The KCC hosts provided tours of the campus and answered the parents questions about the college's offerings as they would for any prospective students. The informal celebration atmosphere made the information very palatable and the fact that they were on the KCC campus made it all very tangible. They could see how KCC might be their chance for a new beginning that would lead to a better job and, more importantly, a better and brighter future for their families and the community.

To make this "evening out" possible for the parents, the local public school district provided free child care for their children and free transportation to the college. The local school district picked up the tab for those expenses (about $200), while the college and school district split the cost of the $256 dinner tab.

And to make it feel like a true celebration – and keep KCC on the parents' minds - everyone went home with gifts, including KCC t-shirts, notebooks and baseball caps, plus free tickets to a KCC men's basketball game.

Contact:
Merikay Gilmore, KCC Special Populations Coordinator
(815) 933-0323

Kankakee Community College
PO Box 888 River Road
Kankakee, IL 60901-0888
Total head count enrollment-Credit: 3,824; Non-Credit: 1,811
Campuses/sites: 1; Full-time faculty: 20

STUDENT VOLUNTEER CORPS

The corps has placed student volunteers in various positions serving the disadvantaged, elderly, young and illiterate

Because compassion and respect are lessons just as important as English and Math, Kaskasia College District #501 created a Student Volunteer Corps that placed student volunteers in various positions serving the disadvantaged, elderly, young and illiterate.

Kaskaskia College developed the Student Volunteer Corps in cooperation with the Governor's Office of Voluntary Action. The Task Force which guided the establishment of the program was comprised of representatives from various community constituencies including schools, businesses, government, nonprofit associations, social service agencies and philanthropies.

Volunteerism is seen as a giving of time and talents with no direct financial compensation expected nor received. A part-time employee directs the program, interviewing students and agencies to match locations and interests, and documents volunteer hours. Students may obtain either academic credit and/or transcript documentation for volunteer work completed.

The program benefits the students, the community and the college. It allows students to gain meaningful experience relating to their major and to be much more competitive in the job and college transfer market. It teaches compassion and respect. The community benefits from the infusion of idealistic, energetic college students willing to labor for the experience. College classes and programs become more relevant as the program puts student learning skills to immediate use.

Contact:
Evelyn Stover
(618) 532-1981

Kaskaskia College District #501
27210 College Road
Centralia, IL 62801
Total head count enrollment-Credit: 3,900
Campuses/sites: 1; Full-time faculty: 67

FAMILY LEARNING CENTER

*▨ The Center houses traditional classrooms, a computer center ▨
for students to use, a lending library and a child care center*

Economically disadvantaged students often want an education but cannot get to campus for lack of transportation, lack of affordable child care or lack of knowledge about opportunities. Kaskaskia College District #501 addressed all these issues by literally taking education to them.

The Family Learning Center in Centralia, a section of the community that has a high minority population as well as a greater number of unemployed and undereducated residents, is accessible to students who are most in need of Basic Skills, GED Life Skills, Parenting Skills or Job-Seeking Skills provided by the Human Resources Development Specialist office but have a major transportation problem.

Site selection also took into consideration possible collaboration with the local Head Start program, housed next to these facilities. Every effort has been made to establish a positive learning atmosphere for remediating educational deficiencies and for encouraging and preparing for entry into post secondary classes at Kaskaskia College main campus or other extension center sites.

This facility houses traditional classrooms, a computer center for students to use to enhance their classroom instruction, and a lending library consisting of fiction, children's books, textbooks and work books as well as a variety of magazines. Child care services are provided on site for the children of students while the students are attending classes. In addition, tutoring rooms are available for use by volunteer tutors and learners who are participants in the college-administered literacy program, The Reading Link. To ensure students have access to complete services, the Vocational Special Needs Counselor at Kaskaskia College is available at the site on a scheduled basis to provide career and personal counseling for the students. This also establishes a contact for students when they enroll and attend classes at the college's main campus. Since its inception, more than 275 students have enrolled and generated 2,754 hours of credit. In addition to the classes, parenting workshops are provided and have served 867 adults and 191 children. Topics for these workshops have included Read To Your Child, Family and Parenting Skill Topics, and Intergenerational Activities.

The facility continues to provide a location for students to broaden their education, as well as a site for community interagency meetings. The program has been received in such a positive manner that the local food pantry has chosen to locate on the basement level. A program sponsored by Head Start and "The Reading Link" provides learning opportunities for families.

All services are provided free of charge and are under the development and direction of the College's Adult Education and Literacy Office.

Contact:
Marilyn Schmidt, (618) 532-1981, ext. 259
Bess Wesling, (618) 532-1981, ext. 258

Kaskaskia College District #501
27210 College Road
Centralia, IL 62801
Total head count enrollment-Credit: 3,900
Campuses/sites: 1 Full-time faculty: 67

MORAINE VALLEY COMMUNITY COLLEGE

CONSOLIDATION AND ENHANCEMENT OF ACADEMIC COMPUTING SERVICES

*▨ The consolidation reduced downtime, centralized lab operations, ▨
increased lab accessibility and modernized hardware*

At Moraine Valley Community College, the consolidation of Academic Computing Services has had dramatic impact: efficient lab scheduling has slowed the need for additional hardware, despite a 103 percent increase in the number of class sessions served; annual funds expended for supplies have not increased, even though there has been extensive growth in lab utilization; and shared use of software has also resulted in cost avoidance by limiting the number of copies required.

With the addition of a computer repair technician and a parts inventory, downtime due to repair was significantly reduced, and no additional dollars for repair have been required. Overall, the consolidation and enhancement of academic computing services has resulted in increased delivery of computerized instruction, more efficient operations, while demonstrating significant cost avoidance totaling more than $400,000.

Continues on Page 218

This is in sharp contrast to the spring of 1987, when academic computing consisted of a few departmentally controlled labs and three general-use labs housed within the Learning Resource Center (LRC) that were scheduled by a part-time lab supervisor. Little or no coordination and planning existed between departments using computer based instruction. Scheduling conflicts and under-utilization problems coexisted as users competed for peak times. In some areas, computers were repaired on site by repair-service companies charging hourly fees in excess of $60, while in others, expensive maintenance contracts were purchased. Much of the hardware was rapidly becoming dated, and software usage was not controlled or shared.

With the opening of the Center for Contemporary Technology (CCT) scheduled for the fall of 1988, the need to address academic computing concerns took on a sense or urgency. The Academic Computing Committee (a voluntary membership committee of faculty, staff and administrators) was charged with the task of establishing future direction for the delivery of computerized instruction throughout the campus. The goals identified were:

1) to consolidate and centralize lab operations;
2) to limit the number of departmentally "owned" labs, thus increasing accessibility and utilization;
3) to reduce downtime and repair costs;

4) to increase the quantity and modernize the hardware available; and
5) to encourage curricular experimentation with computers.

The Academic Computing Committee recommended that the LRC address the first three goals, while the committee would address the other two. Budgeted funds in the amount of $135,046 were identified in 36 departmental accounts and transferred to the LRC to initiate implementation.

In addition to relocating a majority of the hardware to the Learning and Computing Center (LCC) in the new CCT building, the committee recommended the purchase of new hardware, networks, and a fiber optic link to the administrative mainframe to address the goal of increasing and modernizing available hardware, and the administration found innovative methods to fund these requests.

For meeting these goals, Moraine Valley received the 1992 Illinois Community College Board Cost Effectiveness/Cost Reduction Award.

Although duplication of the LCC itself may not be possible at other community colleges, the establishment of an Academic Computing Committee with a goal of sharing resources across the college is a model any institution can follow.

Contact:
Diane Grund, Associate Dean, Learning Resources
(708) 974-5290

Moraine Valley Community College
10900 South 88th Avenue
Palos Hills, IL 60465
Total head count enrollment-Credit: 13,938; Non-Credit: 3,953
Campuses/sites: 1; Full-time faculty: 184

PROJECT SUCCES (SCIENCE UNDERGRADUATE CORE CURRICULUM EVALUATION SYSTEM)

The curricula targeted for review and change included Anatomy & Physiology, Engineering Physics, Environmental Science, Biology and Chemistry

At Moraine Valley Community College, developing a competency-based curriculum in the biological and natural/physical sciences was predicated upon five major issues identified by the vice president for academic affairs in 1989:

1) the need for science programs to keep pace with the changing impact of technology;
2) the requirement that all students attaining the AA-degree or AS-degree would be required to take eight hours of lab science as part of general education;
3) the dramatic decrease in state-funding for higher education in Illinois since 1986;
4) the need to maintain adequate staff development opportunities for full-time science faculty; and
5) the forthcoming re-accreditation standards to be

met by the college, and the revised expectations of four-year colleges and universities regarding articulation and transfer requirements.

The curriculum modification and development system used to address these issues was called SUCCES – Science Undergraduate Core Curriculum Evaluation System. The paradigm for SUCCES relied heavily on the DACUM (Developing a Curriculum) process which was pioneered at Ohio State in the early 1970's for occupational programs, but which has not been extensively applied to science areas. The extension, however, seemed practical, since "sciences" deal directly with well-defined competencies which students must master before four-year college matriculation or employment.

The seven curricula targeted for competency-based review and modification were: Anatomy & Physiology,

Engineering Physics, Environmental Science, General Biology, General Chemistry, Microbiology, and Organic Chemistry.

The SUCCES model, as funded by DOE, authorized a three-year budget of $330,448 – a 75 percent DOE, and 25 percent college appropriation. Expenditures included $14,566 for faculty development, $262,216 for equipment to support the revised curricula, and $12,860 for consultants.

Highlights of this project have been recombinant DNA and photo-microscopy experiments in Microbiology, human cadaver lab in Anatomy & Physiology, departmental finals in General Chemistry, complete revision of the two-semester courses in Environmental Science and General Biology, and the addition of FT-IR to Organic Chemistry.

Contact:
James Fraites, Dean, Liberal Arts & Sciences
(708)974-5236

Moraine Valley Community College
10900 South 88th Avenue
Palos Hills, IL 60465
Total head count enrollment-Credit: 13,938; Non-Credit: 3,953
Campuses/sites: 1; Full-time faculty: 184

OAKTON COMMUNITY COLLEGE

STUDY SKILLS IN THE DISCIPLINES SEMINAR

*▨ The seminar guides faculty in developing strategies and assignments ▨
for teaching basic study skills for specific disciplines*

Assuming relatively few students can transport skills learned in developmental courses to more traditional classes, the Study Skills Seminar at Oakton Community College prompts faculty to think specifically about what kinds of processes are required for learning in their own disciplines. The seminar guides faculty in developing strategies and assignments for teaching students the basic study skills required for those disciplines.

Two faculty members, Marilee McGowan (English/reading) and William Taylor (political science) designed and teach the seminar, which received the 1990 Bright Idea Award from the Illinois Community College Administrators Association.

The seminar is based on the premise that most courses teaching study skills are developmental courses taken by relatively few students; even students who do take the courses often are unable to transport skills learned in those classes to the more traditional class whose focus is the subject matter of a discipline. McGowan and Taylor believe that if math or English or history instructors work consciously to model effective learning behavior for their disciplines, and if they purposely design their assignments to lead students through a series of steps leading to mastery, then they will be giving their students an important opportunity to learn to perform successfully.

The seminar itself comprises 11, 30-minute sessions, and has been offered each semester since the spring of 1990. Full- and part-time faculty from a variety of vocational and baccalaureate disciplines participate. Seminar participants:
•review both theoretical and practical information on the learning process and the roles that reading, writing, listening and retention play in student learning;
•analyze learning strategies to determine which ones are most appropriate to their disciplines;
•design assignments and test questions that will serve as learning tools for both themselves and their students; and
•evaluate the effectiveness of those strategies in their classroom settings.

Central to the seminar is the question of the study skills required for particular disciplines. Students who major in a given subject usually don't have to stop and think about how to learn the material in their courses; it comes naturally to them. But the chemistry major who takes a literature course is often bewildered, at least at first, by the necessity of reading assignments and writing papers in a way wholly different from what s/he is used to in chemistry courses. For the student whose study skills are marginal, the challenge and frustration of moving across disciplines is even greater.

To date, more than 70 Oakton faculty members have participated in the Study Skills Seminar. The most critical resource supporting the seminar is the creative energy and leadership of the two faculty members who developed it. Modest allocations of alternate time (the equivalent of a three-credit course for the seminar leaders and one-credit for participants) have been the only direct costs. The continuing encouragement of administrators is an important though non-quantifiable resource as well.

Contact:
Richard Storinger, Dean of Communications
(708) 635-1952

Oakton Community College
1600 East Golf Road
Des Plaines, IL 60016
Total head count enrollment-Credit: 11,250; Non-credit: 14,000
Campuses/sites: 2; Full-time faculty: 145

CRITICAL LITERACY PROJECT

The project includes faculty seminars, a national conference and a faculty-training institute

Originated by faculty who wanted to design a seminar to teach themselves way to teach critical thinking, the Critical Literacy Project (CLP) at Oakton Community College has revitalized instructors.

Under the sustained leadership of five program initiators, the program has grown to include several components:

- faculty seminars that have been offered in a variety of formats (weekly for a semester, intensively during the summer, in targeted workshops);
- follow-up seminars that focus on the development and application of classroom assignments to foster critical thinking;
- an annual national conference that brings together more than 300 participants;
- an institute for training faculty from other institutions who wish to promote similar activities at their campuses; and
- numerous in-service professional development programs presented by CLP leaders.

To date more than half of Oakton's full-time faculty members, a large number of part-time faculty members, and several staff members have participated formally in components of the CLP. Through departmental meetings and discussions, program content and critical thinking teaching strategies have been disseminated to many more instructors. Presentations have been made to more than 50 different colleges and universities throughout the nation, further expanding the impact of the CLP.

The CLP has received state and national recognition. Last year Oakton was designated a Beacon College through the AACC program. The Beacon College project brought together teams of faculty from 10 participating institutions in an intensive, residential seminar that trained them in the basic concepts, principles and strategies of the CLP; they, in turn, will serve as in-house experts to train their colleagues. In the spring of 1992, the Illinois Community College Board presented Oakton its Award for Excellence in Teaching and Learning for the CLP. Articles about the project and about teaching strategies acquired as a result of participation in the seminar or related workshops have been published in a variety of journals. The number of presentations noted above further illustrates the recognition accorded to the program.

The CLP requires a variety of resources. Most important, it requires knowledgeable, dedicated, energetic faculty members. Oakton CLP participants have been compensated in a variety of ways: the FIPSE grant and college funds have been used for direct stipends, alternate time, and to offset salaries of part-time faculty members teaching courses that would otherwise have been taught by full-time faculty. The Beacon College grant subsidized costs for the residential seminar described above. Administrative and staff support has been provided, generally without charging the project directly, through many offices, including Staff Development, Curriculum and Instruction, and the Division of Communications. More recently, in lieu of other incentives, participation in the CLP may be used by faculty to meet certain criteria for promotion and for salary advancement. The continuing vigorous encouragement for faculty to be involved in the CLP is a crucial resource, albeit one that is difficult to measure quantitatively.

At Oakton, the Critical Literacy Project is perceived as an exemplary professional development project, one that has been a model for other projects in the institution, that has enabled them both to sharpen their teaching skills and to gain professional recognition outside the institution for their expertise, and that has solidified the commitment of the college to professional development activities.

Contact:
Richard Storinger, Dean of Communications
(708) 635-1952

Oakton Community College
1600 East Golf Road
Des Plaines, IL 60016
Total head count enrollment-Credit: 11,250; Non-credit: 14,000
Campuses/sites: 2; Full-time faculty: 145

VETERINARY TECHNOLOGY

A strong cooperative relationship with the University of Illinois and the humane society and solid financial backing contribute to the program's success

Veterinary Technology students at Parkland College receive experience through medical rotations at the University of Illinois college of Veterinary Medicine and by working at the humane society. This and other factors contribute to the 90-plus percent pass rate of graduates on licensure exams.

Primary and secondary objectives of the program, which began in 1974, are to:

1) provide a broad scope of knowledge concerning veterinary technology and related disciplines that is adequate for enabling students to understand the significance and ramifications of procedures which they perform;

2) equip students to perform safely, effectively, efficiently, and to demonstrate professional responsibility and accountability;

3) encourage students' recognition of the need for continued professional growth following graduation, through active organizational and vocational involvement;

4) foster communication skill development, so that graduates are able to form positive working relationships with veterinarians, lay personnel, and clients, as well as to respond equally to the needs of animals and owners;

5) emphasize guidance and counseling support so that students will develop self-confidence and a professional image, in addition to an awareness of their potential occupational opportunities and contributions to their profession, community, Parkland College, and society; and

6) prepare students for state certification examinations by assisting them to attain a broad-based understanding of veterinary medicine practice.

The instructional sequence is in keeping with these objectives. The first year is designed to provide basic skills in surgery, anesthesia, clinical pathology, nursing, pharmacology, radiology, and handling, in preparation for the required externship, which must be completed in the state of Illinois between the first and second year. The externship allows the student to acquire extensive practical experience while working with veterinarians in a variety of facilities (e.g., small animal and large animal practices; drug manufacturing firms; research institutions; universities). In the second year, students enhance their proficiency in the basic skills, and acquire more specialized knowledge. They receive valuable experience through medical rotations in small animal medicine, ophthalmology, surgery, clinical pathology, large and small animal radiology, necropsy, food animal medicine, and equine medicine at the University of Illinois College of Veterinary Medicine. In addition to the rotations and classroom instruction, students work at the Champaign County Humane Society, and may take the American Association of Animal Laboratory Sciences (AALAS) Laboratory Animal Technician Examination.

Currently, 34 students are enrolled in the Veterinary Technology Program each year. The graduation rate ranged between 63 percent and 88 percent for the period 1986-1991. Until 1991, the State of Illinois did not release information regarding licensure examination pass rates; in 1991 and 1992, the pass rate was 100 percent. It is estimated that, for previous years, student pass rates have exceeded 90 percent.

In its latest accreditation report to the AVMA, Parkland's Veterinary Technology Program cited its major strengths:

1) a dedicated faculty;
2) excellent facilities;
3) strong cooperative relationships with the University of Illinois College of Veterinary Medicine and the Champaign County Humane Society;
4) adequate financial backing to maintain exemplary quality;
5) support resources within the college, including counseling, library, learning laboratory, and placement services;
6) summer practicum;
7) extensive admissions criteria; and
8) advisory committee.

The curriculum has been fully accredited by the North Central Association of Colleges and Secondary Schools since 1976. Concurrent accreditation by the American Veterinary Medical Association (AVMA), since 1976, has enhanced and ensured stability and positive recognition for the curriculum. In addition, the Illinois Community College Board (ICCB) and the Illinois Board of Higher Education (IBHE) have approved the instructional sequence.

The program received the 1988 U.S. Department of Education Secretary's Award for Outstanding Vocational Education Programs, and the Veterinary Technology student organization was named Parkland College's Club of the Year for 1987, 1988, 1989, 1991 and 1992.

Contact:
Paul Franklin Cook, Program Director, (217) 351-2382
Susan Maurer, Department Chair, (217) 351-2383

Parkland College
2400 West Bradley Avenue
Champaign, IL 61821-1899
Total head count enrollment-Credit: 9,577; Non-Credit: 181
Campuses/sites: 1; Full-time faculty: 147

VISUALIZATION COMPUTER GRAPHICS SPECIALIST

▦ *The program resulted from a collaboration with the National Center* ▦
for Supercomputing Applications at the University of Illinois

The Visualization Computer Graphics Specialist program at Parkland College is one-of-a-kind, resulting from a collaboration with the National Center of Supercomputing Applications at the University of Illinois.

Curriculum development was initiated as a response to an awareness of need for technicians trained in performing scientific visualization functions on a computer graphics workstation. Individuals who were engaged in this activity had been completely self-taught and self-motivated. No training programs for this specialty had been established in the United States. The technological applications of 2-D and 3-D computer graphics workstations had moved rapidly into the workplace, far surpassing the available number of qualified users. This shortage of qualified technicians has continued, both locally and nationwide.

The Visualization Computer Graphics Specialist program originated, and was funded, as a grant proposal to the U.S. Department of Education (DOE). A certificate was approved by the Illinois Board of Higher Education (IBHE) in 1989; in 1991, IBHE approved expansion of the sequence, with the replacement of the certificate program by an AAS curriculum.

Objectives of the 61-hour AAS curriculum are to:

1) train students to fully utilize computer graphics workstations;

2) provide a well-rounded combination of skills, supplementing technical coursework with general-education courses (computer ethics, English composition, social science, humanities);

3) equip students with a working knowledge of key components of computer graphics visualization work (mathematics, numerical analysis, data structures, FORTRAN or PASCAL, C programming language, the UNIX operating system, scientific visualization, art, technical communications);

4) establish internships which enable students to work with actual scientific, mathematical, and engineering graphics visualization applications, executed on high-performance computer graphics workstations, in an environment that replicates the workplace; and

5) generate employment referrals for graduates of the program, and develop individual placements after students complete their internships.

The two Computer Graphics courses, which are the core of the curriculum, are taught in the Renaissance Education Laboratory (REL) at the University of Illinois's Beckman Institute; this facility contains high-performance Silicon Graphics workstations and software valued at more than $1 million. Additionally, Parkland contributes its own computer facilities, particularly the UNIX laboratory. Implementation of the program was not costly to Parkland, since existing classrooms, laboratories, academic support service, and faculty were utilized. The major drawback to replication is that access must be gained to workstations. Parkland recommends that other institutions considering implementation of a comparable program contact businesses and/or research firms to determine the feasibility of accessing scientific visualization workstations during evening hours when the facilities are not in use.

The program received an award of a DOE Cooperative Demonstration Grant, entitled Advanced Certification Program for Computer Graphics Specialists (January 1989 to August 1990); Nomination for the 1992 (DOE) Secretary's Award for Outstanding Vocational-Technical Education Programs (one of two Illinois post secondary programs submitted).

Contact:
Dick Bennett, Program Director, (217) 351-2549
LaVerne McFadden, Department Chair, (217) 351-2583

Parkland College
2400 West Bradley Avenue
Champaign, IL 61821-1899
Total head count enrollment-Credit: 9,577; Non-Credit: 181
Campuses/sites: 1; Full-time faculty: 147

EDUCATIONAL GUARANTEE PLAN

▦ *Students who earn AA or AS degrees are guaranteed that they* ▦
are properly prepared for entry into their chosen fields

Illinois is the first state in the nation to offer a comprehensive educational guarantee to college graduates, and Prairie State College is the first Illinois community college to adopt the guarantee policy.

The college, following the Illinois Community College Board (ICCB) stand behind the skills and competencies of graduates, has established standards the graduates can expect to attain, with guaranteed skills incorporated into revised curricula and course descriptions. The guarantee covers both transfer and technical programs. According to Harry L. Crisp II, ICCB chairman, Prairie State will serve as a pilot program for implementing the state's guarantee initiative.

Prairie State College students who complete an Associate in Arts or Associate in Science degree will be guaranteed that they will be properly prepared for entry into their chosen fields. According to PSC President E. Timothy Lightfield, if Prairie State courses don't transfer, the college will refund the tuition paid for the non-transferring course credits. And, for a graduate of an AAS degree or certificate who is judged by his or her employer to be lacking in the technical or the general educational skills necessary for entry to the position, Prairie State will provide up to nine tuition-free credit hours of additional skill training in the program.

The AA-degree or AS-degree classes must have been taken at PSC no earlier than two years before attempting to transfer, and any refund request must be made within two years after graduation. An AAS degree graduate or certificate recipient must have earned the degree or certificate no earlier than one year prior to the beginning date of employment and be employed full-time in a position related to the program of study. The employer must certify in writing that the graduate is lacking entry-level skills within 90 days of the graduate's initial date of employment.

Contact:
Denise Czuprynski, Director, Community Relations
(708) 709-3636

Prairie State College
202 South Halsted Street
Chicago Heights, IL 60411
Total head count enrollment-Credit: 5,299; Non-Credit: 549
Campuses/sites: 3; Full-time faculty: 90

3-D (DEVELOPMENT, DIPLOMA, DEGREE): A MODEL FOR WORKPLACE LITERACY

A cooperative program with Governors State University and local businesses, it offers on-site education and training from basic skills to a master's degree

Prairie State College, Governors State University and local businesses have joined to offer on-site education and training from basic skills to an associate's, bachelor's or master's degree to employees in area companies.

The "development" portion includes PSC's literacy and English as a Second Language (ESL) program. Begun in 1985, the South Suburban Literacy Institute confronts the problem of adult illiteracy in the southern Chicago suburbs by providing one-on-one tutors for adults in District 515. Volunteer tutors, who have successfully completed 16 hours of training, assist adults at least 16 years of age who read at or below a sixth grade reading level. The South Suburban Literacy Institute at Prairie State College has served more than 680 students since its inception, with more than 450 active volunteers aiding adult learners.

English as a Second Language is open to those 16 years old and older whose native language is not English. Students enrolled in the ESL program develop skills in speaking, reading, writing and listening to English.

The "diploma" component consists of PSC's pre-General Education Development (GED) and GED programs. The GED classes help students review and prepare before taking the high school equivalency exam. The learning areas covered and tested are English, social studies, science, reading and math skills. Preparation and testing for the Illinois and Federal Constitutions are also included.

Upon successful completion of the high school equivalency exam, a student may pursue completion of a certificate program or of a two-year associates' degree program, part of the "degree" portion of this program. A student may also earn college credit through PSC's "Portfolio Development" course, designed to award credits for life learning and career experiences.

After successful completion of a two-year degree program, students may pursue undergraduate and graduate studies through Governors State University, which awards BA, BS MA and MS degrees.

Contact:
Charles Jenrich, Director, Corporate and Professional Education
(708) 709-3795

Prairie State College
202 South Halsted Street
Chicago Heights, IL 60411
Total head count enrollment-Credit: 5,299; Non-Credit: 549
Campuses/sites: 3; Full-time faculty: 90

PRINCIPLES OF EFFECTIVE SPEAKING

Students may evaluate themselves through computer-assisted writing, presentation ancillaries and hands-on usage of video tape

Surveys of employers time and time again report that communication skills are one of the priorities desired in prospective employees. But communicating in today's electronic-dominated world requires more than the rhetoric learned in standard speech courses. To that end, Rend Lake College (RLC) has designed the basic public speaking course that addresses the old and the new in communication.

Through a regimen of model replication speaking assignments, the course incorporates computer-assisted writing presentation ancillaries and finally hands-on usage of video tape in the self-evaluation component.

First, the students are presented with four different models for building an effective speech. They are subdivided into two areas of concentration – information speaking and persuasion speaking. The students are presented outline models of these two areas using MacWrite on a pre-formatted Macintosh disk of their own. In the first weeks of the course each section is taken to the RLC computer lab and instructed on the basics of computer usage. During the initial speaking assignment period, the open lab is staffed during operating hours by the speech instructional staff so that any speech student in need of additional assistance has access to an instructor (though it may not be their own). Additionally, all sections of Composition classes at RLC use the Macintosh Lab so students often will receive double the exposure and assistance in this component. The students are required to use the computer to generate four outlines and self-critiques. At the option of the instructor students may present these materials on disk for evaluation, leading to a paper-less and thus more environmentally sound education.

Second, the students are required to use ancillaries during their speaking presentations. This is accomplished in many ways. The students are presented with examples by their instructors of effective poster chart overhead projector and video tape usage during speaking situations. Usage of RLC's satellite system allows both students and instructional staff to create pertinent video materials by accessing such cable channels as C-SPAN (Cable-Satellite Public Affairs Network). C-SPAN is beamed on an ongoing basis to the speech classrooms where specific assignments have been tailored by the instructional staff to help the student become aware of how communication works in today's world. Additionally, RLC has acquired Aldus Persuasion and CA-Cricket Presents software that is made available to the students. These two prógrams, linked with RLC's state-of-the-art scanners and laser printers, are especially applicable to teachers and business majors as they are in the forefront of making winning presentations in the current marketplace. These programs will create all of the aforementioned materials plus have the added option to produce them as color slides for a presentation. Exposure to these and other computer software makes the student more prepared to enter the work force equipped to compete and satisfy their employer. The instructional staff constantly is reviewing and attending computer seminars that are aimed at the current business market, rather than at education, so that RLC may give their students the cutting edge.

Finally, all of the student speaking assignments are recorded on video tape as a personal library of their work in the course. Early assignments in the course expose the students in a non-threatening way to the video camera so that when they present their speeches it does not introduce an added anxiety. The student is required to view each speech and then write a self-critique using a set criteria. Before this takes place the instructor will critique several examples of student speeches on video tape using the criteria to help direct the student in the correct way for accomplishing this component.

The future of the basic course at Rend Lake College will continue to expand as technology evolves. Future proposals to equip the instructional staff with portable computers programmed with Macro commands linked with classrooms equipped with CD-ROM Cameras will make the evaluation of the students' work more consistent and effective. This technology when available will enable the student and instructor to coordinate presentation and evaluation to pinpoint more precisely those areas upon which improvement can be made.

Contact:
Stephen B. Tietz, Vice President
(618) 437-5321

Rend Lake College
Route 1
Ina, IL 62846
Total head count enrollment-Credit: 7,600; Non-Credit: 2,500
Campuses/sites: 1; Full-time faculty: 59

MUELLER TRAINING

The college and Mueller Company together provide the company's employees with worker assessment and basic skills enhancement

Richland Community College and Mueller Company combined resources and personnel to give the company comprehensive, tailored training. Mueller Company, a leading manufacturer of gas and water control valves, approached Richland's Center for Business and Community Development about the time it planned to invest several million dollars to upgrade its Decatur facility. Mueller wanted a comprehensive training program to prepare the work force of more than 600 employees to meet the upcoming changes. This program included worker assessment, basic skills enhancement and GED classes, and technical skill training modules.

The first phase began with an assessment of plant personnel, using the Test of Adult Basic Education (TABE). Following the assessment of 288 employees, educational counseling was provided to all who participated. If employees met the minimum reading and math requirements (8.9 grade level), they advanced to the technical skill training modules.

Those who did not meet reading and math requirements were referred to basic skills enhancement classes. The classes' curriculum corresponded with the employee's reading level, providing instruction that allowed the employee to sequentially attain the skills necessary for future training modules. Forty-eight employees reached an 8.9 reading and/or math level. Their average reading and math gain was 3 years and 5 months with 60 hours of instruction. To date, six self-contained enrollment classes and four open-entry study skills classes have been conducted at the company.

The second phase began with Mueller's list of essential competency skills for employees, which assisted in the development of "Module I - Fundamentals of Machining" and "Module II - Computerized Numerical Controls" (which could only be taken after successful completion of Module I). Extensive testing instruments were piloted on management and supervisory teams. After refinement, a 100-question test resulted for each module. These instruments serve as both pre- and post-tests.

The first hour of the first class session is devoted to taking the pre-test. If an individual scores 70 percent or higher, that student is given the option to either proficiency the module or remain in the class. The remaining 20 hours of the class are made up of lecture and demonstrations, concluding with the pre-test, now administered as a post-test.

At least 172 supervisors and hourly workers have taken Module I and 139 have taken Module II. The program is voluntary.

The company has since requested "Module III - Advanced Machining" and "Module IV - Advanced Computerized Numerical Controls." These hands-on programs conclude with a project demonstrating the competency-based objectives set forth initially. (Written quizzes throughout the classes also ensure knowledge of objectives.) The first session of Module III is currently being offered to 42 individuals. Upon successful completion, these people will have the opportunity to take Module IV.

Modules I, II, III and IV will be offered until all employees (or as many as desire to) have completed this program.

The process of combining internal resources and personnel at Richland to package "comprehensive training" for Mueller is something that can be replicated by any community college. The collaborative approach taken by the company and the college promoted and strengthened existing ties between the two, strengthened relationships among the participating departments within the organizations, and successfully met training goals for the personal and professional development of Mueller employees.

Contact:
Nancy Cooper, Director, Center for Business & Community Development
(217) 875-7200, ext. 223

Richland Community College
One College Park
Decatur, IL 62521
Total head count enrollment-Credit: 10,700; Non-Credit: 1,200
Campuses/sites: 2; Full-time faculty: 46

PROJECT STUDENT RETENTION AND STUDENT SUCCESS

One aspect of the project is a comprehensive student tracking system, which augments assessment and orientation

Faced with a declining population, Sauk Valley Community College developed a retention program that emphasizes a student-centered environment.

Recognizing that retention is everyone's responsibility, a college-wide retention task force was formulated. The college began by contracting with the Noel/Levitz Center for Institutional Effectiveness to conduct an Institutional Service Audit to assess the present degree of a student centered climate. Recommendations from the audit served as a basis for a college-wide retention program.

The first component of the plan was to create a student-centered environment. A series of staff development workshops aimed at creating a climate of commitment and caring for students was developed using the Noel/Levitz CONNECTIONS Program. This program is currently being conducted for administrators, support staff and faculty. The goal is an improved student-centered and service-oriented climate.

The second component of the new retention strategy was to develop a college-wide assessment and placement program. The Retention Committee proposed, and the Board of Trustees approved, an Assessment and Placement Policy. This policy provided for mandatory assessment of all students in writing, reading and math skills, and mandatory placement in reading courses, if needed. A year-long evaluation of testing standards and assessment research was conducted prior to development of the policy. In addition to the systematic assessment of abilities was the identification of those student needs that must be addressed to facilitate positive development.

The third, and a major component of the project, was the development of an extended orientation course that interlocks with the college intake and assessment services

and provides an environment to address student's special needs at the beginning of their college experience. Students earn one semester hour of credit in the class, which meets twice a week for eight weeks. More than 300 freshman were enrolled for the fall of 1992, and in 1993 all new students participated. The course is being taught by student services staff and selected faculty members who are committed to providing a positive and success oriented environment for new students. The ultimate goal of the extended orientation is to assist a greater number of students develop more effective ways of achieving success and persisting toward their unique, stated goals.

A final component of the retention program is the creation of a comprehensive student tracking system. For the new assessment and orientation programs to be successful, a means of tracking individual student progress is needed. Although this component is only in the second year of a four-year development plan, students already are being identified on the basis of their individual goals, determined in the assessment and orientation process. It is planned to use the data for a variety of support service interventions, including academic advising, career counseling and learning skills assistance. This is based on the premise that early assistance and supportive direction for students having difficulty will improve their performance. A Director of Student Research has been employed to conduct student outcomes research, to measure the degree to which the college is meeting the goals of its retention project.

In addition to college resources, the retention initiative is funded by a Title III Strengthening Institutions Grant. The program has been recognized by the Noel/Levitz Center for Institutional Effectiveness.

Contact:
John Sagmoe, Vice President, Student Services
(815) 288-5511

Sauk Valley Community College
73 Illinois Route #2
Dixon, IL 61021
Total head count enrollment-Credit: 2,900; Non-Credit: 1,600
Campuses/sites: 1; Full-time faculty: 59

ELECTRONICS TECHNOLOGY

Through long-range planning, courses are modified and new courses are added to allow for continued development of the curriculum

Sauk Valley Community College students may utilize block scheduling in the Electronics Technology program, which is flexibly designed to allow course modifications and continued curriculum development.

Although the Electronics Technology Program has the two-fold purpose of preparing students to enter today's work force and to further their education by transferring to a senior college or university, the primary objective is to give students the knowledge and skills to become electronics technicians or to enter other related areas of electronics. The key ingredients in the success of this program have been the commitment by the instructors to actively market and recruit for the program, to continuously update the curriculum and to aggressively seek the financial resources necessary to accomplish this.

In recent years the need for staff in the Electronics Technology Program has grown from one instructor to three full-time staff equivalents; classes are frequently filled months before classes begin.

Through long-range planning, existing courses are modified and new courses are added to allow for continued development of the curriculum. The instructors believe that almost every area of technology and manufacturing has some connection with electronics. To meet the variety of applications, three areas of instruction have been developed: industrial applications, microprocessor and computer concepts, and AM and FM radio communications. Many industries in the immediate area, such as Borg Warner, General Electric, Northwestern Steel, National Manufacturing, Wahl Corporation, and Donaldson Corporation, utilize electronics technicians in at least one of these three areas. The staff is committed to addressing and implementing the specific areas of training recommended by the advisory committee comprised of local industrial representatives. A series of three courses dealing with programmable controllers has been developed over

the past four years to respond to industry need. Data acquisition equipment, computers, and programmable controllers of the same type used by local industries allow students to experience state-of-the-art applications in their labs.

An innovative approach utilized in the electronics program is block scheduling. Instead of presenting individual classes over a 16-week semester, many classes are presented in four-week blocks. Classes are taken consecutively instead of concurrently. This provides better use of lab time, students can concentrate on one area at a time for total absorption of the material presented, thus allowing employers to send employees to school for one specific course, and not have them tied up for a whole semester. Student and employer needs are also met by the use of flexible scheduling for swing shifts.

In addition to basic program funding through the regular college budget, donations from the electronic instrument companies, local industry and the College Foundation have been essential in maintaining an up-to-date curriculum.

Sauk Valley Community College has articulated an agreement with area high schools so that students who have a basic background in electronics may enter the program with credit given for the training already received. The program also actively pursues agreements with senior institutions which will allow students the option of continuing their education.

Contact:
Zollie W. Hall, Dean, (815) 288-5511, ext. 356
J.L. Cogdall, Professor of Electronics, ext. 296

Sauk Valley Community College
73 Illinois Route #2
Dixon, IL 61021
Total head count enrollment-Credit: 2,900; Non-Credit: 1,600
Campuses/sites: 1; Full-time faculty: 59

SOUTHEASTERN ILLINOIS COLLEGE

ADULT BASIC EDUCATION

▨ A computer-managed instructional system has improved implementation ▨
and assessment of adult basic education

A computer-managed instructional system at Southeastern Illinois College helps educators and learners deal with difficulties of the Adult Basic Education (ABE) and General Education Development (GED) systems.

This technology is crucial at Southeastern Illinois College, which has been the principal Adult Basic Education and GED instructional provider in the region of southeastern Illinois for several years. As a single provider, the Office of Adult Education at the college has diligently served all five rural counties of its district. For the past few years, the college has been working toward creating Developmental Learning Resource Centers (DLRC's) in each of the counties, whereby individual learners, and part-time teachers in the program could access materials appropriate to any individual learner's performance level.

In 1991 Illinois mandated that all state adult education programs implement the Test of Adult Education (TABE). This computer-managed instructional (CMI) system is a response to the need for improved implementation, and assessment of the TABE and the Illinois Adult Basic Education system.

Southeastern has been awarded three consecutive grants for this special project, which were conducted under provision of Section 353 of the Federal Education Act. During the first grant of fiscal year 1991, a Computer-Managed Instructional (CMI) system, entitled Individualized Educational Instruction Plan (IEIP), was developed. This instructional system links individual pre-assessment to three basic academic skill areas of English, reading and

Continues on Page 228

mathematics, creating an electronic prescriptive educational curricula planning program. During FY 1992, the project was expanded, refined and pilot tested. The pilot sites included urban, rural and incarcerated populations in Illinois. This was done to validate the potential use of the computer technology as a versatile and easy-to-use instructional component that enhances the efficiency and effectiveness of the ABE/GED process by providing administration, staff and students with assessment-driven IEIP's that help organize and direct the instructional process. During FY 1993, the project expanded to include more adult education programs located throughout Illinois. It produces a self-contained teacher staff development package and an ongoing self-assessment plan for the instructional evaluation process.

The computer-managed instructional system was developed to help educators and learners deal with difficulties of the Adult Basic Education (ABE) and General Education Development (GED) systems. This computer-managed instructional system will not solve all the problems, but it could serve as a positive step toward resolving basic academic skill deficiencies for each individual involved in an ABE/GED program. It could help provide a standardized approach in alleviating key basic skills weaknesses and thereby assist adult learners to acquire basic knowledge and gain confidence, which serve as preliminary steps to a life of continued growth and expansion. This CMI system links diagnostic input taken from each student's TABE diagnostic results with specific assessment determined cognitive objectives, suggested activities, and a directory of resources. The curricula synthesizes the informational data from the Illinois Community College Board's (ICCB) 310 Project of 1984. The directory of resources includes preferred major adult education printed and computer-aided instructional materials that Illinois adult education programs already own. Additionally, it is flexible and open-ended, which allows for updates and additions of resources, objectives and suggested activities. It enables the part-time ABE/GED faculty, learning laboratory facilitators and adult learners to obtain Individualized Educational Instruction Plans (IEIP) on an immediate and personalized basis.

The project employs two computer programs from CTB MacMillan/McGraw-Hill:
1) an assessment coordinating program called "TABE on Testmate," which links the student Test of Adult Basic Education (TABE) results and produces a selection of hardcopy (paper) reports, such as the Class Grouping and the Individual Prescriptive Reports; and
2) a "shell" program called "Lesson Builder," which generates the individualized student prescriptions.

The two programs, when implemented together, achieve a basic skills curricula that is assessment-driven. The electronic curriculum, unlike so many paper format-ted curricula, is effectively and efficiently usable by teachers, students and learning laboratory facilitators. The computer linkage of the learner's pre-assessment or diagnostic test results from the TABE on Testmate and the curriculum bank in Lesson Builder allows the IEIP to enhance the instructional process. This effectively pinpoints the focus of competency-based instruction, according to the educational level of each student in a program which is largely conducted by part-time faculty. The advancement brings Southeastern Illinois College and the state of Illinois to the forefront of those implementing the United States Secretary of Labor's Commission on Achieving necessary Skills (SCANS) principles.

From its inception, the system has had continuous feedback from all members of the Southeastern's adult education program. During the developmental stage, interaction from the instructors helped shaped the design and content of the curricula. Throughout the pilot testing, on-going suggestions and feedback from the instructors and the students resulted in modifications which have enhanced the system. The results of the pilot testing indicated an overall +.6 to +1.2 grade equivalent increase in basic academic skills knowledge by students using the computer-managed instructional system above those of students not using the system. Additionally, all of the participants reported that they found the system beneficial. Evidence of the flexibility of the CMI system is illustrated by the varied and individualized implementation strategies, as each teacher used their ingenuity and expertise in the implementation of the IEIP prescriptions.

The five basic steps of Southeastern's Computer-Managed Individualized Educational Instruction Plan (IEIP) implementation process are:
1) Each student is given the TABE battery of tests (either level E, M, D or A) as appropriate according to the TABE Locator Test.
2) The instructor takes the TABE answer sheets to a computer that is connected to an optical scanner.
3) The answer sheets are scanned, the software programs (i.e., TABE on Testmate and Lesson Builder) implement their "seamless interface."
4) The instructor pins reports. (There is a selection of reports available, according to the needs of student, instructor, resource person or administrator).
5) The instructor and student(s) are provided the quality curricular materials they end to enhance the instructional phase of the adult education system. Simultaneously, the administrate has the reporting data it needs to ensure that each student will receive the maximum benefits from the educational program.

This five-step process illustrates the ease and efficiency

of the computer-managed instructional system that is serving rural, urban and incarcerated members of the state's adult population, and provides a unique example of how computers can play a critical role in the instructional development process.

Contact:
Richard Hagan, Dean of Adult and Continuing Education
(618) 252-6376

Southeastern Illinois College
3575 College Road
Harrisburg, IL 62946-4925
Total head count enrollment-Credit : 3,665; Non-Credit: 238
Campuses/sites: 6; Full-time faculty: 125

SPOON RIVER COLLEGE

AFRICAN AWARENESS WEEK

The week includes art displays and presentations by nationally acclaimed African writers and performers

The brain child of students and their African Literature instructor, African Awareness Week at Spoon River College includes performances, lectures and art displays.

As the name implies, the purpose of the project is to expand the knowledge and appreciation of the African culture for SRC students and people of all ages within the college district by bringing to the college's Canton Campus a variety of African artists, artifacts, exhibits, and experiences, almost all of which are free and open to the public.

Presented annually since 1990, African Awareness Week includes performances on the campus by nationally acclaimed African writers and performers, lectures by scholars of the African experience, as well as first-hand accounts of people who lived in various African countries. It features displays of African art and artifacts and special video presentations on aspects of African art such as The Metropolitan Museum's videotape entitled "The Art of the Dogon" shown in 1992. A highlight of the week-long event is an authentic African dinner served at the college. The cost is minimal, and participants are invited to wear African attire to heighten the authenticity of the affair.

Through such diversity, African Awareness Week offers a learning experience to people of all ages. Because the public is invited to participate in all of the festivities, the events are attended by a cross-section of the population within the college district. Moreover, students in the African Literature class this year provided a learning opportunity to young children by presenting African stories and games to the children in SRC's daycare department.

In addition to the obvious knowledge of the African culture afforded students of English 216, African Awareness Week allows them the opportunity to develop organizational and leadership skills as well as heightens their sense of community awareness and interaction. All the various tasks needed to implement the project are committee assignments for the literature students: everything from publicity to programming is the responsibility of the students.

Funding for African Awareness Week is provided by Spoon River College, the Student and Cultural Affairs Committee, and the Illinois Arts Council.

Contact:
Martha Strode, Instructor
(309) 647-4645

Spoon River College
Rural Route #1
Canton, IL 61520
Total head count enrollment-Credit: 2,612; Non-Credit: 323
Campuses/sites: 4; Full-time faculty: 34

SPOON RIVER COLLEGE

DIESEL TRACTOR TECHNOLOGY

Instructors visit shop foremen and businesses to coordinate training and establish credibility with those who make hiring decisions

Spoon River college has implemented "time scheduling" into Diesel Tractor Technology instructors' teaching assignments, whereby blocks of time are set aside for field work off campus. This enables the current staff of two instructors to visit shop foremen and businesses to coordinate training and establish credibility with those who make the hiring decisions in the agricultural equipment industry.

Continues on Page 230

Since the program began in the 1960s, through the spring of 1992, there were a total of 663 DITEC students in the SRC program; and the instructors placed in jobs more than 90 percent of those who completed the program in jobs, proof that the program's many accolades are deserved.

In its early years, SRC modeled the program after existing company training programs and relied on a well-rounded advisory council. SRC launched its program with four instructors and 48 students. With the use of modular scheduling, the program flourished. The teaching emphasis was three-fold:

1) instruction in the basics;
2) hands-on experience in the shop; and
3) on-the-job-training to serve as a realistic bridge to the work force.

With specific general education requirements as a part of the curriculum, SRC's DITEC program not only prepares its students as mechanics, servicemen and parts men, but offers some managerial background as well.

Since its inception, the DITEC program at SRC has emerged as a state and national leader in diesel technology training. Its success is due in large part to the program's advisory council, which has been an integral part of program updating and revision. Moreover, a staff of dedicated instructors highly trained in basic applied science concepts has taught classes and helped individuals in "one-on-one" situations.

Recognition comes in the form of an abundance of state and national awards consistently won by SRC DITEC students in various competitions. At the 1992 Illinois PAS Agricultural Equipment Diagnostic Skills Contest, SRC's DITEC students captured 16 of 32 awards, including the first place individual award and the second place team award. The Spoon River College student with the highest individual ranking and his partner went on to win the first place team at the National PAS Contest in March sponsored by Deere & Company. They succeed a long list of national winners from SRC. In 1991 and 1988 SRC students won both the first place team and first place individual awards, and in 1986 SRC won the second place team award.

In addition, Spoon River College's DITEC program is a hallmark in agricultural and industrial mechanics technology and has served as a model for other technical programs around the country.

Contact:
Brian Telander, Instructor
(390) 647-4645

Spoon River College
Rural Route #1
Canton, IL 61520
Total head count enrollment-Credit: 2,612; Non-Credit: 323
Campuses/sites: 4; Full-time faculty: 34

TRUMAN COLLEGE, HARRY S.

VENTURES IN SCIENCE

The program targets Hispanic high school students with limited English language proficiency and works with them throughout high school

Because education, and particularly science and math education, is the key to economic competitiveness in today's global marketplace, Truman College developed a program that identifies minority high school students, particularly Hispanic students who have a limited language proficiency in English, and provides academic preparation and motivation for these students.

Truman College acts as the coordinator for a series of activities undertaken by the program's "partners." These partners include Motorola corporation, the Chicago Public Schools, the University of Illinois at Chicago and Argonne National Laboratory.

The merit of the project is based on a number of factors. First, Ventures in Science provides a long-term approach which follows each student throughout his or her high school years. This consistent encouragement and support is essential for meaningful results. Another is the emphasis on the roles of teachers and parents. Through the University of Illinois at Chicago and Truman College, teachers receive staff development and parents meet to discuss student progress. The bilingual track is a third characteristic of the project which has substantial merit. Through this approach, not only will English speaking minorities be reached, but Hispanic students with limited language proficiency in English. This approach leads to an expansion of the math/science/engineering pipeline.

Other technical factors leading to merit are: the use of the team-teaching approach, with a high school teacher and college professor combining to present the lessons to the students; reaching "average" students; the use of many resources through the program's "partner;" and linkages with the Chicago Teachers' Academy and the Young Scholars program.

In 1990, Truman College, through its Vice President for Faculty and Instruction, began searching for partners in order to design and implement Ventures in Science. Full-scale implementation began in the summer of 1992 when 40 minority students who had just graduated from eighth grade began a six-week summer program. Funding was provided by the Department of Energy.

Students received a full day of instruction which included 1-1/2 hours of integrated math and science, 1-1/2 hours of English/ESL, 1 hour of counseling and 1 hour of physical education. The program was delivered by five professionals from Truman College, the Chicago Public Schools, and the Math and Science Teachers Academy. The theme of the entire program was the Ecosystem of Chicago. Field trips were included that complemented the theme, and provided ample discussion among the participants. Motorola Incorporated contributed a small stipend to cover lunch and transportation costs for students.

The summer participants will continue with the program on Saturdays during the regular school year throughout high school. A new class will begin each summer.

Contact:
Elena Mulcahy, Director
(312) 907-4097

Truman College, Harry S.
1145 West Wilson Avenue
Chicago, IL 60640
Total head count enrollment-Credit/Non-Credit: 16,962
Campuses/sites: 42; Full-time faculty: 152

COMPUTER TRAINING

"At risk" students enrolled in the program are expected to earn 31 credits and receive a certificate within 12 months

The Truman College/Association House Computer Training Program is a collaborative venture that brings together the resources of a community college, a social service agency, and major corporations for the purpose of converting "at risk" students into academic achievers and skilled workers.

Candidates selected for the program are required to have a high school education (diploma or GED), be highly motivated to participate in a demanding, but supportive, educational/training program and belong to an economically disadvantaged group. A profile of the 90 students currently enrolled indicates that 70 percent are Hispanic and 15 percent are black, 40 percent are on public aid, 20 percent hold full-time or part-time jobs, 10 percent are married, and 30 percent are single parents. Their average age is 25, although the age range is from 18 to 55.

Students enrolled in the Computer Training Program are expected to earn 31 college credits and receive an "Advanced Certificate in Computer Operations" within a 12-month period. The curriculum, which was developed jointly by Association House Staff, Truman College faculty and business leaders, includes mathematics, English, business and computer operations courses, as well as a one credit course on personal and career skills development. Students are given placement tests to determine their proficiency in mathematics and English and placed in appropriate level courses in those disciplines. They are required to pass English 100 and Mathematics 100 before receiving the Advanced Certificate.

Highly qualified program staff, most of whom are Hispanic, provide on-going personal, academic and career counseling. The publication of a quarterly newsletter and fundraising activities teach students organizational and team work skills. Discipline and a sense of responsibility are stressed throughout the program and are reinforced through the Student Standards Committee which advises staff on disciplinary matters.

This program addresses the following important recommendations put forth in Building Communities: that community colleges develop an aggressive outreach plan for disadvantaged students; that they give more attention to student retention; and that the reading, writing and computational ability of all first-time community college students be addressed when they enroll.

The seed money for establishment of the program was given by the Mac Arthur Foundation, which funded it for four years, an exception to their policy of funding new programs for only one year. The success of the program has stimulated other major corporations and foundations to support it with money, technical expertise, steering committee membership, and/or employing graduates.

Seventy-six percent of the at-risk students who started the program since its beginning have earned their certificates. Approximately 16 percent of the completers have chosen to continue studying full- or part-time toward a college degree.

Contact:
Melenne Mosquera, Program Director
(312) 989-6297

Truman College, Harry S.
1145 West Wilson Avenue
Chicago, IL 60640
Total head count enrollment-Credit/Non-Credit: 16,962
Campuses/sites: 42; Full-time faculty: 152

PRINCIPLES OF TECHNOLOGY FOR STUDENTS AT A CORPORATE SITE AND INTERCONNECTIONS '90s

*▣ Chemical Waster Management, Inc. provides a laboratory, mentors and instructional ▣
assistance for this cooperative effort of business and education*

Although the Principles of Technology program is coordinated by Waubonsee Community College, it is a cooperative effort of school districts, colleges and businesses. It is open to all interested high schools. Those who participate can enjoy the use of a $250,00 laboratory dedicated by Chemical Waste Management, Inc., expressly for the students.

Principles of Technology (PT) is the applied physics program developed by the Center for Occupational Research and Development (CORD) that has now been implemented in a substantial number of sites across the country. It provides students with a solid foundation in the principles of all technology rather than the specifics of one particular technology. The course is two semesters and runs 1-1/2 hours per day.

Besides Waubonsee Community College and Chemical Waste Management, specific school districts involved include Batavia, Geneva, Aurora and St. Charles, in addition to the Corridor Partnership for Excellence in Education.

Waubonsee Community College serves as the administrative and fiscal agent for the program. The college, in cooperation with the PT Advisory Committee, sets the annual tuition, determines session times and class size, and manages other operational details as necessary. The college collects tuition from participating districts and pays all expenses incurred in the operation of the program.

Chemical Waste Management, in addition to providing the laboratory site for the PT program, will:

• match up professional staff as mentors to individual students or small groups of students; mentors will take personal interest in their charges, assist them with the PT work and will help them develop a positive work ethic, an awareness of career opportunities and an awareness of the professional and corporate culture that exists at the Research Center;

• identify staff who will assist the regular PT instructor; assistance can be in the form of subject matter consultation, help with set-up and demonstrations, guest lectures, etc.;

• identify staff who will visit each participating school at least once a year to present a recruitment workshop; and

• host an informational meeting for guidance counselors from participating or interested schools at least once annually.

In addition, during the summer, the Corridor Partnership for Excellence in Education and the college provides for 120 teachers, counselors and principals, six days of hands-on related experiences in industry to better acquaint them with the work force needs. Participant companies include the following: AT&T Bell Laboratories; Amoco Research Center; Caterpillar, Inc.; Chemical Waste Management; George J. Ball, Inc.; Furnas Electric Co.; and Motorola, Inc.

Both of these programs have received significant attention nationwide because of the unique partnership.

Contact:
Kenneth W. Allen, Assistant VP, Research & Community Programs
(708) 466-4811, ext. 404

Waubonsee Community College
Route 47 at Harter Road
Sugar Grove, IL 60554
Total head count enrollment-Credit: 9,731; Non-Credit: 1,300
Campuses/sites: 2; Full-time faculty: 68

TELECOMMUNICATIONS INSTRUCTIONAL CONSORTIUM (TIC)

*▣ The system delivers credit college programming to high school students ▣
studying German, Japanese, Calculus, Advanced Geometry and Physics*

Bringing college courses to more people via a two-way, interactive microwave system makes a Waubonsee Community College education more accessible to those at remote sites, while still enabling the instructor and students to see and hear each other.

Waubonsee Community College began this system in

the fall of 1988. Currently the system links the main Sugar Grove campus with downtown Aurora campus and with campuses at Waubonsee Valley High School, Plano High School, Oswego High School, Kaneland High School, and the Illinois Mathematics and Science Academy (IMSA). Waubonsee, IMSA, and the participating high schools form the Telecommunications Instructional Consortium, better known as "TIC."

The goal of the consortium has been to provide expanded opportunities to district-wide locations and area high school students.

During the day, the college uses the TIC system to deliver credit programming between the Sugar Grove and Aurora campuses. In the evening the high school sites become extension sites for the delivery of college credit courses. At the college level, the TIC experience has been very successful:

- More than 5,000 students have participated in college credit courses.
- An average of 30 college credit courses in all disciplines are offered each semester.
- 89 faculty members have taken advantage of in-

service training for teaching on the TIC system and 46 have taught classes on the TIC system.

- Expansion plans call for the system to connect Waubonsee Community College with two neighboring community colleges.

At the high school level, the TIC system has allowed area high school students to take classes in German, Japanese, Calculus, Advanced Geometry and Physics. The Illinois Mathematics and Science Academy has shared courses in astrophysics, advanced geometry, and topics in modern physics over the TIC system.

A recent research study funded by the Illinois Board of Higher Education found that students who participated in courses over the TIC system were as successful as those students who took the course in the traditional manner.

Contact:
Lynn Blakesley, Dean, Learning Resources & Instructional Technology
(708) 466-4811, ext

Waubonsee Community College
Route 47 at Harter rd.
378 Sugar Grove, IL 60554
Total head count enrollment-Credit: 9,731; Non-Credit: 1,300
Campuses/sites: 2; Full-time faculty: 68

WILLIAM RAINEY HARPER COLLEGE

BASIC ACADEMIC SKILLS FOR EMPLOYEE DEVELOPMENT (BASED)

The program includes employee assessment, job/literacy task analysis, instruction, materials, counseling and evaluation services

Literacy partnerships between William Rainey Harper College and business and industry have resulted in significant upgrade of workers' academic skills and productivity. Such improvement is critical for American business and industry to compete in a global marketplace with the existing work force.

Harper College's Adult Educational Development (AED) Department began the special workplace effort in 1987, through the Basic Academic Skills for Employee Development (BASED) program. More than 5,800 on-site enrollments have been taken since then. This has generated more than 9,600 credit hours (140,250 hours of instruction, at least half on company time).

Employees have significantly improved reading levels, usually in eight weeks with a functional context curriculum and materials, or have mastered basic arithmetic skills in eight to 16 weeks of instruction. Most employees have passed industrial reading and mathematics tests and have kept or upgraded their jobs.

Other documented outcomes include new product success, improved supervisor or performance ratings, reduced product cycle time, less materials waste, fewer customer complaints, and fewer accidents. Affective employee changes include better communication with supervisors and peers, improved attendance and punctual-

ity, increased understanding of job duties or company policies and procedures, greater profitability, and better morale.

The main objective of the BASED program is to improve employee academic skills by offering customized programs, utilizing a model of planning, employee assessment, job/literacy task analysis, instruction, materials, counseling, and evaluation services. Adult education concepts utilized include voluntary employee participation, collaboration with on-site business staff, customized instruction using employer materials, nontraditional method of demonstrating employee progress, and shared time. Variable course credit has allowed a flexible year-round schedule. Some unique elements have been action research (e.g., examination of employee assessment instruments), multiple partnerships, corporate commitment, or design (e.g., integration of instruction, group/individual team building/problem solving, and factory production).

A fee structure has been based on tuition rate plus 25 percent to 30 percent to cover costs of program development, customized instruction, and on-site liaison. The BASED program is implemented by the AED chair and two staff members in cooperation with the College Director of Corporate Services and business partners.

Continues on Page 234

Companies have contributed expertise in planning and research, employee recruitment, employee salaries during class time, on-site liaison, orientation of instructors to business operations, job-related materials, employee and instructor recognition activities, classroom space and equipment, and other fee-based services such as tutoring and interpreters for the deaf.

The quality and scope of the BASED program have contributed to recognition of Harper College by a 1992 resolution in the State of Illinois General Assembly, by Illinois Community College Board in 1992 as a first recipient of the Work Force Preparation Award, by an evaluation team of the Illinois State Board of Education in 1990, by AACJC in the 1989 "Keeping America Working" Award program, and by the U.S. Department of Education in 1988 by naming the AED Department as one of two outstanding community college adult education programs in the nation. The program has been featured in the *New York Times* and *Wall Street Journal* and has been featured on CBS and CNN.

Contact:
Patricia Mulcrone, Professor/Chair, Adult Educational Development
(708) 397-3000, ext.

William Rainey Harper College
1200 West Algonquin Road
2223 Palatine, IL 60067
Total head count enrollment-Credit: 15,418; Non-Credit: 11,051
Campuses/sites: 27; Full-time faculty: 213

WILLIAM RAINEY HARPER COLLEGE

CAREER TRANSITION SERVICES

The Center helps individuals seeking a career change as well as businesses needing outplacement services for employees

Today more than ever, as workers find themselves on the sidelines of the marketplace in jobs lost to downsizing and restructuring, there is increased demand for assistance in helping individuals to manage their careers. But career direction and job search assistance has, for the most part, been reserved for the college student just starting a career or for the high-level executive who has been afforded handsome severance packages (which include extensive outplacement assistance).

Harper College and the Private Industry Council of Northern Cook County therefore developed a comprehensive, self-supporting, full-service Career Transition Center.

The aim in establishing the Career Transition Center was dual-purposed:

1) to address the job and career issues of the individual who have established careers and who either lost their jobs or were seeking a career change; and

2) to offer assistance to the many local companies that were looking to provide high quality outplacement services to employees at a reasonable cost.

Envisioned was a "one-stop-shopping" service delivery system through our center for programs, guidance, assistance and support to those experiencing a career transition.

Today, the Career Transition Center offers myriad programs, including: outplacement and career management programs for companies; group seminars on career assessment, career options, job search strategies, resume preparation, interviewing skills and personal effectiveness strategies program; and individual career counseling, resume production service, and support group activities.

The objectives of the Career Transition Center are to service companies that are downsizing or restructuring and wish to provide assistance to those they must let go; assist companies in providing career management programs for current employees in order to facilitate them in "taking charge of their careers;" and offer workshops for community members who have lost their jobs, are entering or re-entering the work force, making a career change, or are exploring career options.

The program is set up as an auxiliary program of the college and, therefore, must be self-supporting. All programs are fee-based with the exception of the Career Transition Center, which is opened to the public at no cost. These resources include: computers with various software programs, phones, resource directories, periodicals, newspapers, books, job opportunity listings, a copy machine and a laser printer, as well as individual cubicles.

The Center has assisted more than 2,000 community residents and 25 companies have taken advantage of our outplacement services.

Career Transition Services is the recipient of the 1992 "Bright Idea Award" by the Illinois Council of Community College Administrators.

Contact:
Mary Ann Jirak, Coordinator
(708) 459-8233

William Rainey Harper College
1200 West Algonquin Road
Palatine, IL 60067
Total head count enrollment-Credit: 15,418; Non-Credit: 11,051
Campuses/sites: 27; Full-time faculty: 213

ANDERSON WORK FORCE DEVELOPMENT: COMPUTER NUMERICAL CONTROL

▣ Students gain self-confidence through the program by actually ▣ producing a "real" product in the final learning phase

The Computer Numerical Computer Control project at Ivy Tech of Anderson has become so popular that the college has been named a National Training Center for Smart Cam Software and students come from all over the United States for training in state-of-the-art Cad-Cam fundamentals. Ivy Tech Anderson recognized the need for training in CNC (Computer Numerical Control) technology in the early 1980's. In conjunction with local industries, the college established a training center for this purpose. The state of Indiana awarded grants to the program in excess of $500,000, used only for the purchase of equipment (computers, plotters, printers, CNC machines). A state-of-the-art Cad-Cam lab was created. Local industries provided instructors, who developed and instructed classes. More than 1,000 employees have received training in programming of CNC machines.

While meeting the training needs of local industries, the center also serves as a resource and provides assistance to other outside businesses and industries.

The students are instructed on how to use the software,

how to construct geometry, and how to write CNC programs. After the students complete the programming phase, they go to the machine tool and manufacture their design. The progressive learning procedures develop and teach the process of engineering, designing and manufacturing a product through CNC. The students gain self-confidence through the process by actually producing a "real" product in the final learning phase.

The lab equipment consists of 11 IBM work stations, two trainer CNC machines, one full-size three-axis CNC machine, and one full-size CNC lathe. The program has one full-time instructor with more than 25 years of toolmaking experience and 15 years of CNC experience. The college is continuously upgrading the equipment to stay current with the state-of-the-art Cad-Cam industry.

This project, made possible through the cooperation of Industry, Ivy Tech and the state of Indiana, "demonstrates the partnership between the state and private industry in helping to retrain our Hoosier work force to meet the demands of world competition," said Governor Bayh.

Contact:
Anderson Shane Wilson, Business and Industry Coordinator
(317) 643-7133

Indiana Vocational Technical College–Anderson
104 West 53rd Street
Anderson, IN 46013
Total head count enrollment-Credit: 710
Campuses/sites: 1; Full-time faculty: 10

INDIANA VOCATIONAL TECHNICAL COLLEGE-EAST CENTRAL DISTRICT

LEADERS PROGRAM

▣ The program inspires college employees to provide leadership for the betterment ▣ of the district, its civic communities and society

Believing its employees should be leaders both on and off campus, Indiana Vocational Technical College-East Central District developed a year-long leadership development program. With its roots in the district's mission, the program includes a commitment to the development of human resources and to contribute to the needs of its civic communities, the college and society.

The Leaders Program is designed to develop the leadership talents of its employees, to enable and inspire them to provide leadership for the betterment of the district, its civic communities, the college as a whole and to society. The training enables them to function as effective leaders, provides them with access to information useful in leading, and connects them with leaders through a series of experiences. The focus is on leadership in general rather than on

management/administration in two-year colleges.

The five content tracks are developed across 10 half-day sessions. Additional activities outside these sessions included public speaking workshops, a personal interview with two program advisory board members, small group discussions of readings, and a focus group to evaluate the program upon its completion. Sessions were held in places of interest; e.g., board and training rooms of local industries, municipal meeting rooms, on the campuses of private colleges. Content tracks developed were:

1) cognitive development related to leadership; e.g., paradigm shift, change, characteristics of effective leaders;
2) leadership skills; public speaking, team building,

Continues on Page 236

conducting meetings; group decision making, strategic planning;

3) networking with people who model effective leadership;

4) opportunities to apply what they were learning; and

5) personal growth in preparation for leadership.

The average cost per participant was $250; this could be reduced considerably by increasing the number of participants because most of the costs were for session presenters. Costs were covered by the college; participants were encouraged to buy their own copies of some paperbacks (but even this was not required as multiple copies were on reserve in the campus libraries).

Written evaluations were completed immediately following each session. The entire program was evaluated in writing and in focus groups a few weeks after its completion. Among the findings: increased self confidence; an obvious increase in the number, scope, and variety of leadership activities of participants; and interest of non-participating employees in the readings. Long term follow up evaluations are planned.

First-year participants have indicated a strong desire to continue leadership development activities and to extend their relationship to the program. Accordingly they will be involved in site selection, advisory board membership, publishing a newsletter featuring leadership activities, case study development, small group facilitation, etc.

Materials available upon request: Session agendas, reading list.

Contact:
Judith Redwine, Vice President/Chancellor
(317) 966-2656

Indiana Vocational Technical College-East Central District
2325 Chester Boulevard
Richmond, IN 47374
Total head count enrollment-Credit: 4,518; Non-Credit: 596
Campuses/sites: 3; Full-time faculty: 70

BASIC SKILLS ADVANCEMENT PROJECT

In addition to standard services, the project also includes specific accommodations
– such as note-taking and special testing - to individuals with disabilities

Consistently recognized as one of the most effective in the state, the Basic Skills Advancement Project of Ivy Tech Region 05 serves a widely disparate population.

Based in Kokomo with additional delivery sites in Logansport, Wabash, and Grisson Air Force Base, Ivy Tech Region 05 serves a six-county delivery area and provides a two-year technical education in 13 occupational program areas. As an open-door institution, it serves a varied student population ranging from recent high school graduates to returning adult students.

To assist students in improving these skill levels, the Basic Skills Advancement Project was funded in 1985 with monies from a basic state grant available through the Carl D. Perkins Vocational Education Act. The Basic Skills Advancement Project Department is responsible for assessment, course placement, course delivery and any additional assistance students may require to successfully complete their educational goals. Targeted populations include those persons who are academically and/or economically disadvantaged, disabled or of limited English proficiency.

This process of assistance begins with the assessment of basic skills using a standardized assessment instrument. Following the administration of the assessment and subsequent individual counseling about results, the student is placed in recommended courses to improve skills in reading, writing and mathematics. Students are strongly advised, at this Region, to take all courses recommended based on the assessment results before proceeding with occupational courses.

Developmental level courses include instruction in reading comprehension and vocabulary, English grammar and composition, mathematical computation, algebra, study skills, critical thinking, and basic computer literacy and keyboarding skills. Computer-assisted instruction and traditional classroom instruction allow students to schedule courses more conveniently. The department's instructors and technicians provide individual and group tutoring in all general academic areas to any student who requests such assistance.

Additionally, the department provides specific services to individuals with disabilities that might form barriers to their success. These services include note-taking, special testing arrangements, and taped lectures and books. A disabled employee acts as an advocate for all disabled persons in the Region and as liaison to community and external agencies. Another staff member communicates with hearing disable students in the Region.

Two of its faculty have been honored in the last three years with the President's Award for Outstanding Instruction. Its program plan was presented at the Indiana Vocational Association Special Needs Division Conference in 1990.

Contact:
Pam Lewis, Department Head
(317) 457-4520

Indiana Vocational Technical College-Kokomo Region 05
PO Box 1373,
Kokomo, IN 46903-1373
Total head count enrollment: 2,179
Campuses/sites: 2;Full-time faculty: 26

INTERIOR DESIGN TECHNOLOGY

Students work on community projects involving realistic budgets and challenging client requirements

When Ivy Tech Interior Design students graduate, they are ready to compete in the job market with graduates of four-year programs. By meeting minimal standards of both NASAD and FIDER, the curriculum offers all courses necessary to meet competencies required of entry-level interior designers.

Students in the program work on community projects involving realistic budgets and challenging client requirements. By evaluating information gained through extensive client interviews, the interior design student learns critical problem solving skills. These skills are further enhanced by the enforcement of the limited budgets required by most clients. The program further fosters real-world applications through its emphasis on computer-assisted drafting, product awareness and problem-solving skills.

Participation in state-wide student design competitions is expected of all students prior to graduation. These competitions are sponsored and juried by the Institute of Business Designers and participated in by students from four universities throughout Indiana as well as Ivy Tech. Design problems are solved by the students working in teams, which encourages cooperative problem solving .

Additionally, all students in the Interior Design program are required to present their finished design solutions to a jury of professional architects and designers at the end of each semester.

Students travel to the Merchandise Mart in Chicago each spring to participate in the National Remodeling and Redecorating Conference. They are able to attend a multitude of seminars and workshops as well as tour showrooms of manufacturers and suppliers. Additionally, each fall the program participants travel to southern Indiana to tour the architectural showpieces in Columbus and the international furniture factories located in the Jasper area.

The interior design students range in age from 18 to 60, all sharing a common passion for creating functional, aesthetically pleasing interior environments.

Contact:
Denise Hagelskamp, Program Coordinator
(317) 459-0561

Indiana Vocational Technical College-Kokomo Region 05
PO Box 1373,
Kokomo, IN 46903-1373
Total head count enrollment: 2,179
Campuses/sites: 2;Full-time faculty: 26

GENERATIONS TOGETHER

The program prepares persons 55 and older to enter the child care profession at the skilled-entry level

Due to the expanding need for child care and the rising number of citizens living longer, the Generations Together Program was created to bring those two populations into a mutually beneficial relationship. The program is a one-of-a-kind employment training curriculum designed to prepare persons 55 and older to enter the child care profession at the skilled-entry level. Generations Together originated with the University of Pittsburgh Center for Social and Urban Research and became available as of fall 1992. The curriculum contains child development information, job search skills, practicum experience, and the

Continues on Page 238

program involves recruitment, orientation, maintenance and evaluation.

The collaboration of the Job Training Partnership Act, Green Thumb (Job Placement for Older Workers) and Indiana Vocational Technical College provided this program for local citizens to meet a local need of training and employment for older workers. Local child care centers were eager for these workers due to their reliability and life experiences, as well as the fact that they were being trained in child care skills. The program consisted of child development information, job search skills and practicum experience. The training program has been officially approved by the Council for Early Childhood Professional Recognition, satisfying eligibility for the Child Development Associate Certification.

The first step of the program involved recruitment, which was conducted by JTPA. The potential worker needed to pass a physical examination as well as a screening interview to assess their interest and availability. Appropriate staff to provide the training modules was also part of this step.

The second step involved orientation so that the older adult could become familiar with the expectations of the training, receive counseling for returning to school, study assistance, and placement in a local child care facility for on-the-job experience.

The maintenance portion of the program facilitates the working relationship between the participating organizations and the ongoing program supervisors at the job placement as well as the knowledge and skill development provided in the classroom.

Finally, evaluation was conducted to assess the skill development of the students, the acceptance of the program by the local child care sites, and the trainees evaluation of their own experiences.

The participants in the program were women ages 55 to 65 years old, including those of Caucasian, Black and Mexican heritage. They were quite hesitant about returning to the educational experience, but blossomed during the 13-week training period. A rise in self esteem and confidence was experienced and evidenced by their self-statements at the conclusion of the program as well as by statements from the instructors and practicum directors of the program. Their eagerness to gain employment as a result of the training also was evident.

This program was offered at the Anderson campus of IVTC Region 06. Plans for expansion to the other community sites in the region are in progress, as is a repetition at the original site. An advisory committee that includes a wider base of community agencies is planned. Also, as a result of the program evaluation, opportunity for the participants to experience various practicum sites is being planned.

Contact:
Nancy Hoffman, Child Development Program Chair
(317) 289-2291, ext. 407

Indiana Vocational Technical College-Muncie Region 06
4301 South Cowan Road, PO Box 3100
Muncie, IN 47307
Total head count enrollment-Credit: 2,242
Campuses/sites: 3; Full-time faculty: 40

INDIANA VOCATIONAL TECHNICAL COLLEGE-NORTH CENTRAL REGION

PACT (PARENTS AND CHILDREN TOGETHER)

Parent-child teams attend 14 two-hour sessions, divided equally between computer labs and personal development/career exploration workshops

Can parental involvement enhance the academic achievement of at-risk students and improve their attitude toward school? PACT (Parents and Children Together), a program for junior high students and their parents offered at Indiana Vocational Technical College (Ivy Tech), is testimony that it can.

The success of the PACT programming is a result of the combined efforts of two agencies. Parent-child teams are recruited through the effort of the Indiana Department of Work Force Development services (WDS). Ivy Tech provides the expertise of its basic skills staff and the use of its Learning Laboratory with computer-assisted instruction. The costs of offering the program are shared equally by IVY Tech and WDS.

The two major criteria for the program are to:

1) involve parents and their children in a learning situation in which they are both students; and
2) offer studies that feature interesting, useful subjects for both groups.

Eighth- and ninth-grade students are targeted as ideal participants because they are old enough to take the lead occasionally in interaction with their parents, but young enough to benefit from projected long-term results.

Parent-child teams attend 14 two-hour sessions at Ivy Tech. The time is divided equally between the computer lab classes and the personal development/career exploration workshops. Based on school records and achievement test scores, the instructors develop individual lesson plans for each student designed to strengthen skills in reading, writing, and/or math through computer-assisted instructional software during the computer portion of the program. Additionally, computer literacy including computer operation, basic word processing and spreadsheets, have proven to be beneficial for both parents and children.

The second half of the program focuses on personal development. During the workshops, parents and children identify personal assets and abilities, learn how to set goals, establish the importance of a positive self-image, and learn about approaches to work and career choice. Computer simulations develop critical thinking skills and help individuals handle timely issues, pressures and situations. In addition, community field trips increase awareness of career options.

The PACT program has grown from five parent-child teams in 1989 to 26 teams in 1991. The children have benefited from a more positive self-image, improvement in basic skill levels, and raised level of expectation resulting from participation in a college environment. The parental and family benefits include better communication with the children, a special quality time set aside weekly, computer awareness and literacy, and motivation to return to school to further their education.

As an incentive for parents to participate, IVY Tech offers a free college course to all parents who complete the PACT program. Many parents not only have taken advantage of this offer but also have continued their education at the college. One of the parents who accepted this offer says she is now a positive role model for her daughter to stay in school and further her education.

Contact:
Grace Rodgers, Program Coordinator
(219) 289-7001

Indiana Vocational Technical College-North Central Region
534 West Sample Street
South Bend, IN 46619
Total head count enrollment-Credit: 2,906; Non-Credit: 753
Campuses/sites: 3;Full-time faculty: 54

INDIANA VOCATIONAL TECHNICAL COLLEGE-WABASH VALLEY

PLASTICS PRODUCTIVITY TRAINING CENTER

The college is meeting the needs of area business by graduating qualified potential employees and updating current employees' skills

As the Terre Haute and West Central Indiana Area evolved into a major plastics manufacturing area over the past several decades, the Wabash Valley Region of Indiana Vocational Technical College saw the need for a Plastics Productivity Training Center. Working with local economic development officials, plastics manufacturers, and government officials, such a center was developed in conjunction with a new Associate in Applied Science Degree Program in Plastics Technology.

The Plastics Productivity Training Center works with local industries to:

1) provide the training in the newest concepts in plastics productivity;

2) provide training to the employees of the plastics industries in West Central Indiana;

3) operate a training laboratory that demonstrates the technology in the local plastics industry;

4) operate a technology transfer center through a laboratory that represents the applications of the newest technology in the plastics field; and

5) coordinate efforts with other regions and agencies to promote the plastics industry as a major factor in the economic development strategy for the state of Indiana.

The Center began operations in the summer of 1991, and has had extraordinary success at working with the local plastics industry. It was partially funded by the state of Indiana with a $250,000 Strategic Development Fund Grant.

The Plastics Technology Program was approved by the Indiana Commission for Higher Education in December of 1990, and began its first classes in the fall of 1991. The two-year program offers a technical core focusing on molding and processing, extrusion, strength of materials, manufacturing, product and mold design, and CAD/CAM applications. The technical support core includes related technologies such as CAD drafting/design, fluid power, machining, programmable controllers, and the manufacturing production and operation process, including quality control.

The link between the Plastics Productivity Training Center and the Plastics Technology Program serves a dual purpose. The two-year program ensures local industries that they will have a steady stream of well-qualified graduates entering the work force. Conversely, students in the program can be confident in the knowledge that, due to the close relationship with local employers, the technologies they are learning will be applicable upon graduation.

Since the inception of the Plastics Productivity Training Center and the Associate Degree Program, response has been overwhelming. Larger facilities for the Center now

Continues on Page 240

are being renovated so the service to industry and students can continue expanding. The Center also has served as testimony to what can be accomplished when public education and private industry combine forces to ensure quality of training.

Contact:
Don Nalon, Center Coordinator/Program Advisor
(812) 299-1121

Indiana Vocational Technical College-Wabash Valley
7999 U.S. Highway 41 South
Terre Haute, IN 47802-4898
Total head count enrollment-Credit: 2,500; Non-Credit: 4,200
Campuses/sites: 2; Full-time faculty: 62

AIRCRAFT SUPPORT INDUSTRIES PRODUCTIVITY TRAINING

An Applied Technology Center is expected to be instrumental in attracting aviation-related firms to the Terre Haute region

The Aircraft Support Industries Productivity Training and Applied Technology Center at IVTC-Terre Haute is a unique partnership of public education with government officials to ensure the economic development of an area through education. The "Airport Project" combines traditional two-year college programs at the same facility where specialized industrial training is taking place. Since the instructional programs housed at the Center are those directly related to the aviation industry, there is a synergy resulting from the specialized services provided to the areas growing aviation companies and the programs.

The project was a joint effort of IVTC-Terre Haute, the City of Terre Haute, Hulman Regional Airport, and the Alliance for Growth and Progress (a local economic development group). Providing long-term economic security, comprehensive economic development resources, and business and industry assistance are the predominate goals of the Center. These goals will be fulfilled through a variety of programs located in a facility operated by Ivy Tech on the grounds of Hulman Regional Airport.

Two new instructional programs were developed by the college to address the needs of the aviation industry. A Technical Certificate in Avionics focuses on the electronic components needed in modern aircraft. The Associate in Applied Science Degree in Aircraft Maintenance Technology allows students to choose between specialties in Avionics or Airframe & Powerplant. Students who complete the AAS with a specialty in Airframe and Powerplant are prepared to sit for FAA Certification.

Those who specialize in Avionics can qualify for FCC as well as FAA Certification. The combination of these programs will help to fill a nationwide demand for aircraft technicians that is expected to grow significantly throughout the next decade.

The Productivity Training and Applied Technology Center works with new and existing aviation companies to improve their competitiveness. Experts consult with companies to improve processes as well as test the implementation of new technologies prior to actual production. These resources are expected to be instrumental in attracting aviation-related firms to the Terre Haute area.

In addition to the instructional programs and Productivity Training and Applied Technology Services, the College's Office of Business and Industry Training is located on-site at the airport facility. At this location it continues to provide specialized training services to the area's business community, as well as offering workshops appropriate for the aviation industry. Total Quality Management, Participative Management, OSHA Certification, and Hazardous Materials are a few of the many topics available for workshops.

With all of the components included in the "Airport Project," the Terre Haute area has acquired a comprehensive training and economic development asset that will provide the community with many rewards. The partnership that created the Center has placed Terre Haute in a position to grow and prosper as the aviation industry grows in Indiana.

Contact:
Ed Hornback, Director
(812) 299-1121

Indiana Vocational Technical College-Wabash Valley
7999 U.S. Highway 41 South
Terre Haute, IN 47802-4898
Total head count enrollment-Credit: 2,500; Non-Credit: 4,200
Campuses/sites: 2; Full-time faculty: 62

STUDENT TRANSITION INTO EDUCATIONAL PROGRAMS

*▨ The program is designed to give learning disabled students the chance to develop ▨
their own abilities and achieve their highest academic potential*

Vincennes University offers a unique academic support program for college-bound learning disabled students. STEP (Student Transition into Educational Programs) provides comprehensive services for LD students as they make the transition from high school into the learning/living environment of a college campus.

Founded by Jane Kavanaugh and Susan Laue in the fall semester of 1991, STEP accepts 24 to 40 students, both fall and spring semesters.

With adequate support services, Vincennes University believes that LD college students can be successful. In STEP, student strengths rather than deficits are the emphasis. Compensatory techniques rather than remediation are the thrust. Using the STEP support services, students learn to capitalize on their strengths and compensate for their deficits.

STEP is designed to give LD students the opportunity to develop their own unique abilities and to achieve their highest academic potential. Students develop a sense of self worth as well as the skills needed to function and to learn independently in college. By developing their own capabilities and independence, students are more successful as they make the transition from high school into college.

There are some unique opportunities available to STEP students. Specialized classes have been designed to support the students and to help them be more successful. Coping In College, a four-semester class, addresses topics that college LD students face.

The first semester focuses on self-advocacy and learning to verbalize strengths, weaknesses and needed accommodation. Speakers address such issues as stress and self-esteem. Together, the students develop STEP strategies and basic study skills.

The second semester focuses on learning strategies, organizational skills and interpersonal skills. During the third semester students develop self-realization skills and begin a mentorship program linking them with first-semester STEP students.

The final semester addresses job-readiness skills and reinforces the students' previous learning through teaching second-semester students.

Other classes available only to STEP students are an English word processing/beginning keyboarding class paired with a Fundamentals of Writing class that is taught using the computer; a specially trained faculty member teaches both classes. For students with severe reading problems, a multi-sensory remedial reading class with a maximum class size of three is also available. Finally, trained LD professionals provide many other benefits to the students including tutoring, IEP's, weekly academic progress monitoring, consultation, and assistance with alternative testing or program accommodation.

As a participant of STEP, students have responsibilities such as attending classes, maintain a C average, and attending assigned weekly tutoring and study sessions. Students are expected to take a Study Skills class during their first year at VU. As they become more proficient, students are expected to assume more responsibility for the practice of self-advocacy and self-monitoring, by initiating contact with teachers, demonstrating competency skills and requesting accommodations.

Admission to STEP is based on determination of student eligibility, space remaining and completion of the application process, which includes submission of a STEP application, a separate VU admissions application, a recent psychological evaluation which includes documentation of a learning disability, and confidential letters of recommendation from an LD teacher and a regular teacher or guidance counselor. The STEP fee is $250 per semester in addition to VU tuition. Since space is limited, students are encouraged to apply early.

Contact:
Jane Kavanaugh or Susan Laue, Co-Directors
(812) 885-4209

Vincennes University
1002 North First Street
Vincennes, IN 47591
Total head count enrollment-Credit: 6,610; Non-Credit: 949
Campuses/sites: 5; Full-time faculty: 383

BOWLING LANES MANAGEMENT AND TECHNOLOGY

*The program has received financial and academic support
from several major companies in the industry*

Known throughout the bowling industry as a respected, effective program, the Bowling Lanes Management and Technology program at Vincennes University has a very simple yet far-reaching goal: to provide both the corporate and private sectors of the industry with a centralized location where they can recruit fresh, innovative minds that have been trained and exposed to all facets of bowling operations.

The program was developed in the late 1960's and early 1970's through a desperate need for qualified technicians and managers in a rapidly growing industry. The first few students were primarily focused on the technological side of maintaining and repairing the many types of sophisticated equipment used in bowling centers. As the industry developed and prospered, a need for well-trained, energetic managers also surfaced. To accommodate that need, in 1973 the management curriculum was added to the technology program. From its early days in the 1970's of averaging six to eight students, the two-year associate degree program has grown to an enrollment of 34 students.

The program has received the support both financially and academically from several major companies within the bowling industry. In excess of $100,000 of equipment has been added to the program through a joint funding effort of Vincennes University and several of these companies. In addition, the corporate leaders have recognized the importance of the academic side by developing and donating both written materials and educational video programs to the University for use in the Bowling Management curriculum.

As a result of this cooperation, is the initial stages of planning and development of a *Bowling Lanes Management Workbook & Guide*. This will provide for the first time in the industry a written format for not only students to follow, but those already on the job wishing to improve their skills.

Two of the bowling industry's leading trade magazines, *Bowlers Journal* and *Bowling Digest* have highlighted the management program at Vincennes University several times. Each has sought to inform the industry through articles and letters of the need to have highly trained, specialized individuals operating our bowling centers. The program was also selected to provide a two-week management training seminar for the United States Air Force European operations in the fall of 1991. In 1988, the program was awarded the honor of being recipient of the Indiana Vocational Education Award for Excellence.

Contact:
Gary Sparks, Instructor
(812) 885-4428

Vincennes University
1002 North First Street
Vincennes, IN 47591
Total head count enrollment-Credit: 6,610; Non-Credit: 949
Campuses/sites: 5; Full-time faculty: 383

FURNITURE PRODUCTION TECHNOLOGY

*The program, which emphasizes computer-assisted drafting, includes
a heavy concentration of math and physics technology*

In a local labor market where 87 percent of the local industry is or relates to furniture manufacturing, Vincennes University-Jasper Center offers a Furniture Production Technology curriculum designed to produce students with the employability, academic and technical skills needed by industry.

The program evolved from a Workplace Learning Pilot Program sponsored by the Indiana Commission on Vocational and Technical Education. Extensive research by university personnel and business leaders concluded the viability of this program. The curriculum is based on industry-established standards which give the students the expertise necessary to succeed in a furniture production occupation as well as providing local business and industry with an educated labor pool.

Vincennes University-Jasper Center established a cooperative arrangement with area high schools and local furniture manufacturers. The program, which emphasizes computer-assisted drafting, interpersonal and teaming skills, can begin in the local high schools. Many of the skills learned through classroom instruction are transferred to the industry where students participate in workplace learning experiences. The program also includes a heavy concentration of mathematics and physics technology.

Included in this curriculum is a computer-assisted drafting certificate that can be completed outside of the Furniture Production Technology Program.

This program produced its first graduates in December 1992 and shows great promise for the future.

Contact:
Bob Reeves, Coordinator
(812) 482-3030

Vincennes University-Jasper Center
850 College Avenue
Jasper, IN 47546
Total head count enrollment-Credit: 3,302; Non-Credit: 1,025
Campuses/sites: 1;Full-time faculty: 17

MEDICAL ASSISTANT PROGRAM

▓ Program graduates consistently score among the top ▓
10 percent of one- and two-year programs nationwide

From the start, the Medical Assistant Program at Des Moines Area Community College was recognized for its high standards. It was one of the first programs established when the college was founded in 1966 and one of the first one-year programs accredited by the American Association of Medical Assistants and The American Medical Association in 1977. There was no criteria for one-year program accreditation prior to that time.

Since the beginning, this program has been meeting the needs of the health care community in the urban and rural areas of Iowa. Placement is nearly 100 percent and frequently there are more available positions than there are graduates seeking employment. This high placement rate reflects the educational program at DMACC that incorporates classroom knowledge with laboratory experience in Human Body in Health and Disease, Medical Terminology, Medical Office Procedures, Medical Laboratory Procedures, Professional Development, Medical Office Management, and Diagnostic Radiography. This learning is reinforced during 10 weeks of clinical experience under the supervision of a physician and staff members in an office setting, dealing with actual patients.

Upon completion of the program, the graduate is well-qualified to perform as an efficient, safe, multi-skilled health practitioner. The need for this type of personnel in health has never been greater than it is at the present time. Federal and state regulations continue to influence the type of care provided in an out-patient setting, requiring quality assurance in all aspects of care.

Graduates of the Medical Assistant Program consistently score among the top 10 percent of programs in the nation when compared with graduates from both one- and two-year medical assistant programs. Most importantly, the physician/employers know that a DMACC graduate is well-prepared to step into a position and be productive and cost-effective after a short orientation period.

The Medical Assistant Program encourages students to become actively involved in community health needs through participation in food and clothing drives, blood screening in cooperation with the Red Cross, taking electrocardiograms for participants in the Polk County Elderly Program, and participation in various other activities. Active involvement in the professional organization, the American Association of Medical Assistants, is also encouraged to raise the awareness of the lifelong educational experience that is essential for a medical assistant working in a rapidly changing and expanding profession.

The program has two full-time instructors with expertise in various aspects of their profession, and a Radiographic Technologist to teach the Diagnostic Radiography course.

Health care delivery continues to change rapidly. New procedures, enhanced testing techniques, increased regulations, increased outpatient procedures and a constant concern for patient welfare all provide a challenge as the Medical Assistant Program changes to meet these diverse needs.

Contact:
Pam Van Ast
(515) 964-6200

Des Moines Area Community College
2006 South Ankeny Boulevard
Ankeny, IA 50021
Total head count enrollment-Credit: 11,214; Non-Credit: 48,666
Campuses/sites: 4;Full-time faculty: 245

AUTOMOTIVE TECHNOLOGY

▓ Course work incorporate technical skills with courses in communications, ▓
human relations, technical math and technical physics

Students who enter the Des Moines Area Community College's (DMACC) Automotive Technology program, are virtually assured of rewarding careers. Thanks both to a curriculum that has won many awards and to extensive support from auto manufacturers, the Ankeny Iowa program has placed more than 95 per cent of its graduates in recent years.

In addition to the Automotive Technology program, DMACC is the only community college in Iowa to offer the General Motors Automotive Service Educational Program (ASEP) and the Ford Automotive Student Service Educational Training Program (ASSET). These programs are designed to educate and train individuals for careers as GM or Ford dealership service technicians. The three programs are fully certified by the National Automotive Technical Education Foundation (NATEF), the program certification arm of the National Institute for Automotive Service Excellence (ASE) which provides ASE certification for technicians. The ASEP and ASSET programs involve classroom lectures and laboratory activities. Unlike conventional programs where the student goes to college and then seeks a job, the ASEP and ASSET student, with DMACC's assistance, secures an employer/sponsor before starting their program. Half of the student's time is spent attending classes at DMACC with the remaining time spent as a paid intern in the sponsoring dealership. Each specialized subject is taught in DMACC classrooms and labs, followed by related work experience at the dealership.

DMACC's three Automotive Technology degree programs are delivered in 22 courses per program, totaling 73 semester hours per program. The programs are 100 percent competency-based using the high priority tasks identified by NATEF as the standard base from which the curricula were developed. Course work in the three programs incorporate technical skills with courses in communications, human relations, technical math, and technical physics in an effort to develop the skills needed to accurately diagnose and repair the automobiles of today and tomorrow. Quality communications and human relations skills are stressed. The outcome of this approach has been noticed and praised by employers.

Automotive manufacturers are both beneficiaries of and benefactors to the automotive programs at DMACC. More than 70 late-model cars and light trucks, donated by vehicle manufacturers are used to let students practice their skills. The school has also received dozens of engines, transmissions and other components for training purposes.

DMACC is one of six colleges in the nation to offer the Ford Phase II program where contracted training is provided on a full-time basis for Ford dealership technicians. DMACC is also a General Motors, Service Technology Group remote training site, where two service training classrooms are staffed to provide the service train-

ing needs of GM dealers in Iowa. In addition, use of the automotive facilities is regularly provided for remote dealer service training for Chrysler, Mazda, Isuzu, PPG Industries, Dupont, State Farm Insurance and other corporations doing automotive-related training.

The 16 faculty and staff members forming the DMACC Automotive Technology programs instructional team include 12 faculty members, one administrator, a counselor, a full-time parts clerk, a secretary and a custodian. All of the faculty are ASE certified master technicians and between them represent 156 years of industrial experience and 117 years of teaching at DMACC.

Because of the partnerships with the manufacturers enjoyed by the Automotive Department, the faculty have current model year training available on site. Each faculty member is expected to attend a minimum of 10 days of Ford and GM training at the on-site training centers each year, along with as much other manufacturer-based training as possible. Release time and substitutes are freely offered to make this level of faculty in-service training possible. Several of the faculty members are on nine-month contract and spend their summer working in industry to keep current with what is happening in the industry.

DMACC's Automotive Technology Department has produced 10 of the last 12 Iowa Vocational Industrial Clubs of America (VICA) post secondary automotive champions, along with a second-place national winner in 1985 and a third-place national winner in 1986. In 1988 and 1989, the program placed second in the Motor Vehicle Manufacturers Association/AVA Industry Planning Council's competition. In 1990, DMACC placed first in the nation in this prestigious competition. In 1992, the Automotive Programs received the Secretary's Award for Outstanding Vocational-Technical Education Programs from then-U.S. Secretary of Education, LaMar Alexander.

Contact:
Chuck McFarlin
(515) 964-6200

Des Moines Area Community College
2006 South Ankeny Boulevard
Ankeny, IA 50021
Total head count enrollment-Credit: 11,214; Non-Credit: 48,666
Campuses/sites: 4;Full-time faculty: 245

EASTERN IOWA COMMUNITY COLLEGE DISTRICT

ENGLISH AS A SECOND LANGUAGE (ESL)

The program includes six levels of courses, each with its own set of classes, texts and materials, and teaching strategies

As the Eastern Iowa Community College District saw more and more students with limited English proficiency, it developed an ESL (English as a Second Language) program to help them make the transition to college-level work. In 1988, the credit ESL program was implemented on the Scott campus. During the 1991-92 academic year, the program was evaluated, revised and expanded to the other two college campuses. A district-wide task force was appointed to carry out the evaluation process. The membership of this committee included credit and non-credit ESL faculty from the three campuses, the academic deans and the assistant dean of international students.

The ESL program is a multi-level program of intensive

Continues on Page 246

and semi-intensive instruction that is administered within the Division of Academic Affairs. The program is being considered for foreign language credit to be used in satisfying credit requirements toward earning an associate in arts degree. The program consists of intensive (18 to 20 hours per week for eight weeks) and semi-intensive (eight to 10 hours per week for 16 weeks) instruction. There are six levels of courses each with its own set of classes, texts and materials, and teaching strategies. The standardized Michigan Test Battery is administered to students for initial placement in the ESL courses.

Competencies and skill levels are identified for each course and course level, building on the previous level. The Michigan Test is also used as a post-assessment of progress in proficiency.

With competencies clearly defined for level of the credit courses, the task force members decided to revise the non-credit ESL program. This program would also be defined in levels with competency and skill level. This would allow for a smooth transition from non-credit courses to credit courses. The student would not lose valuable time or experience duplication in course study. Both programs are on-going year round, allowing the students to progress from one level to another without unduly long breaks in their ESL study.

The credit ESL program consists of intensive and semi-intensive instruction. The Intensive ESL program (Levels 1-3) offers an average of 18 hours of instruction per week for each eight-week session, which is considered full-time course of study. The Advanced ESL program (Levels 4-6) offers an average of nine hours of instruction per week for a 16-week semester, allowing the student to enroll in other college credit courses under the advisement of the ESL faculty. The faculty and advisors assess, advise, and provide ongoing support services to these students in an effort to acquaint them with campus and community life, and the expectations of academic study in college.

Most of the students are adults with high school diplomas who plan to pursue a degree at the community college for the purpose of employment or transfer to a four-year college to complete a bachelors degree.

The multi-level credit and non-credit ESL program has been successfully implemented at the three colleges of the EICCD and is available for duplication at other institutions.

Contact:
Norma Papik, Dean of the College, Clinton Community College
(319) 242-6841

Eastern Iowa Community College District
306 West River Drive
Davenport, IA 52801-1221
Total head count enrollment-Credit: 8,148; Non-Credit: 46,839
Colleges/centers: 6; Full-time faculty: 155

ENVIRONMENTAL SCANNING PROCESS

The environmental scanning process creates an awareness of the external environment and its impact on the college

Since 1986, the Board of Directors of the Eastern Iowa Community College District has annually formulated Points of Focus – priorities that have become the themes of resource development efforts, new program initiatives and staff development activities. During each annual retreat, the directors reaffirm existing points and add, but never delete, new points. Between 1986 and 1989 the list grew to 10 priorities.

But just as involvement is key to learning, involvement is key to change, a philosophy that prompted the EICCD Board of Directors to move to a broader base of participation in determining district priorities and using information regarding the external environment in its planning efforts.

In 1989, the EICCD initiated a process of environmental scanning whose intent was to create an awareness of the external environment and its impact on the community college, and to foster a receptivity to change. Environmental scanning had been used by the board in the determination of its Points of Focus, scanning had given the district the competitive advantage in the pursuit of funds from external sources, and it had provided the impetus for new program exploration and development.

After environmental scanning was integrated into the EICCD Strategic Planning Process, Vision 2020 – a 122-page environmental scan document, summarizing major trends and projections in the following five categories – was distributed to all EICCD employees, directors and some community members:

1) the changing population and demographics;
2) the workforce/workplace;
3) political, societal and ecological changes;
4) the changing technologies and information explosion; and
5) the global economy.

Statements of Impact of these external trends on the future of the EICCD were formulated and are reflected in 32 Vision Statements for the EICCD. The Mission of the EICCD was revised, and new goals and objectives formulated.

An environmental scanning process was established

which systematically collects and monitors information describing changes in the external environment, in order to continue our identification and assessment of emerging developments, trends and precursor events that may affect the strategic and tactical objectives of the EICCD.

A two-step staff development program was developed for administrators, faculty and support staff to gain their participation as members of the EICCD Environmental Scanning Team. The first component presents an overview of environmental scanning, its importance and benefit to an organization, the definition of terms, and activities on how to scan. All participants are requested to serve as scanners for the district; information regarding the external environment is submitted on an abstract form. This information is utilized in the compilation of a monthly newsletter, *An Environmental Scan Update*. This newsletter summarizes major events, trends and projections in an area crucial to the institution's long-term planning efforts. The update includes factual information as well as questions regarding the impact of these events and trends on the EICCD and its service area.

The second component of the staff development program is a follow-up to the first. The scanners identify those trends which may be important to the future of the EICCD and which are monitored through the environmental scanning process. These trends are then linked directly to the planning process, program and curriculum development and improvement, resource development, and staff development of faculty and staff.

Contact:
Jan Friedel, Associate Vice Chancellor, Academic Affairs & Planning
(319) 322-5015

Eastern Iowa Community College District
306 West River Drive
Davenport, IA 52801-1221
Total head count enrollment-Credit: 8,148; Non-Credit: 46,839
Colleges/centers: 6;Full-time faculty: 155

REGISTERED NURSE FIRST ASSISTANT

The training program includes didactic instruction and related independent clinical internship

Seeing a need, especially rural Iowa, for Registered Nurse First Assistants (RNFA), Hawkeye Community College developed a training program with input from the nursing and medical professions.

During a surgical procedure, the RNFA carries out functions that will assist the surgeon in performing a safe operation with optimal results for the patient. Nursing diagnosis is used as the defining guide in planning and implementing patient care, (pre-op and post-op), and expanded functions are stressed and elaborated as the nurse is prepared to assume responsibility in scrubbing, draping, retracting, exposing, clamping, ligating and suturing under the direct supervision of a licensed physician.

The program includes didactic instruction and related independent clinical internship to prepare nurses to provide perioperative assessment, intraoperative intervention and post operative evaluation for patients.

Utilization of RN First Assistants in the operating rooms of health facilities in Iowa has been approved by the Iowa Nurses' Association, the Iowa Medical Society, Iowa Chapters of the Association of Operating Room Nurses, Inc., and reviewed by the Iowa Board of Nursing.

The RNFA applicant must be a graduate of an accredited school of nursing, licensed in the state in which his or her clinical internship will be accomplished. He/she must have had at least four years OR experience or be certified (CNOR), and a letter of reference from his/her OR supervisor. The student will need the agreement (signed letter) of a Board Certified General Surgeon for the associated clinical internship.

The instructors for the didactic portion of the program are a Board Certified General Surgeon and a registered nurse who currently teaches and works in the OR and who has a MSN degree.

Contact:
Carol Brobst, Department Chair, Health Sciences
Barbara Steen, Program Coordinator
(319) 296-2320

Hawkeye Community College
1501 East Orange Road, PO Box 8015
Waterloo, IA 50704
Total head count enrollment-Credit: 2,467 ; Non-Credit: 50,319
Campuses/sites: 1; Full-time faculty: 111

GENERAL TECHNOLOGY

*▦ The program is applicable for people from a variety of backgrounds, ▦
including law enforcement, business, human sciences and sales*

For a number of years, post secondary colleges have struggled with how to grant academic credit for skills and competencies that individuals have acquired by way of the work force. In 1983, Hawkeye Community College found a way through the General Technology program, designed for individuals who have reached journeyman or equivalent proficiency in their trade or occupation.

The General Technology program – for people wanting an Associate in Applied Science Degree for job advancement or just personal satisfaction – is applicable to those with skills and competencies in a wide variety of occupations, including law enforcement, fire science, business, management, secretarial, health, sales, social or human sciences and industrial. It is the intent of the General Technology program to provide occupationally competent students the opportunity to complement their skills through courses that are relevant to their identified career goals.

The student starts the program by taking a Portfolio Design course. The requirement for the course is a portfolio, consisting of the following elements: goal statements, plan for future course work, chronological time line, auto-biography, competency statements, verification documents, and transfer credit documents. The portfolio is assessed at the end of the term. The assessment provides the following information to the student:

1) the number of academic credits granted for experiential learning;
2) previous academic course work transferred to their program of study; and
3) required and recommended courses needed to complete their individual program of study.

The minimum credits that must be completed to earn the Associate in Applied Science degree is 60 semester credits. The maximum credits allowed for experiential learning is 30 credits. Students are required to meet the college's residency requirement and complete a minimum of 12 credits in general education. Students pay a nominal fee for credit assessed through the portfolio process and normal tuition for all academic courses. Students can proceed through their program of study at their own pace. The Department Chair works with each student after their portfolio assessment, and is viewed as a student advisor.

Contact:
John W. Sorenson, Department Chair
(319) 296-2320

Hawkeye Community College
1501 East Orange Road, PO Box 8015
Waterloo, IA 50704
Total head count enrollment-Credit: 2,467; Non-Credit: 50,319
Campuses/sites: 1; Full-time faculty: 111

PHYSICAL THERAPIST ASSISTANT PROGRAM

*▦ A unique aspect of the program is the use of competency labels, ▦
placed in a computerized format, for courses*

In response to a critical lack of physical therapist assistants (PTA) in Iowa (there were only six in 1988), Indian Hills Community College launched the state's first PTA program in the fall of 1989.

The PTA program curriculum integrates technical, arts and science, and clinical courses sequentially to provide competency-based learning. Program goals were established based on the knowledge and technical skills graduates will be required to utilize throughout their career.

A PTA graduating from IHCC shall be able to: provide physical therapy services as specified in the plan of care developed by the physical therapist; demonstrate competency in patient preparation and treatments that may include the use of exercise, appropriate modalities and functional activities; respond to acute changes in physiological state; teach other health care providers, patients and families to perform selected treatment procedures and functional activities; communicate in an effective manner verbally, non-verbally and through documentation; understand basic concepts related to the health care system, including multi-disciplinary team approach, quality care, governmental agencies, private sector, role of other health care providers, health care facilities, issues and problems; and demonstrate safe, ethical and legal practice in patient care.

One unique aspect of this program is the use of competency labels. Technical courses have defined competencies. These competencies have been placed in a computerized format and are given to the students to carry to their clinical sites. Clinical supervisors observe a skill being provided to a patient at least three times without assisting the student physically or verbally. Once a student is able to show they can perform a procedure with independent consistency, the clinical supervisor signs and dates the computer competency label and the student returns it to the program director for documentation. In this way, measurement of knowledge and application skills is done twice for each competency, once by academic faculty and again by clinical faculty for assurance of meeting program goals and documenting student achievement. This system was highly praised by the national accreditation team for its uniqueness and its assurance of quality instruction.

The PTA Program was accredited by the Commission on Accreditation in Physical Therapy Education of the American Physical Therapy Association in April 1991. The Iowa Legislature passed a licensure bill for PTA's on June 1, 1991.

Program statistics are excellent. Placement is 100 percent, and all of our graduates have passed the National Licensure examination.

The quality of IHCC's PTA program has been acknowledged by the American Physical Therapist Association (APTA), as it has been recommended as a model for other colleges to emulate. As a result of this recommendation, IHCC has been contacted by colleges in several states to share curriculum, competencies, and clinical evaluation methods. In addition, programs based in states that do not currently have state licensure for PTAs are seeking information regarding the strategies that resulted in state legislation to allow licensure for PTAs in Iowa.

The Physical Therapist Assistant program has a staff of a part-time program director, who also teaches some courses, and one part-time instructor.

Contact:
M. Ann Aulwes, Department Chair, Health Occupations
(515) 683-5164

Indian Hills Community College
525 Grandview
Ottumwa, IA 52501
Total head count enrollment-Credit: 4,761; Non-Credit: 31,752
Campuses/sites: 2 ;Full-time faculty: 125

LASER/ELECTRO-OPTICS TECHNOLOGY

The college articulates with high schools and colleges, so that both entering and graduating students have a wide choice of options

The Indian Hills Laser/Electro-Optics Technology program features a competency-based curriculum rich in hands-on experiences that meshes with the other technologies offered in a beautiful, new 131,000-square-foot, $7.1-million Advanced Technology Center.

Initiated in August 1985 with the aspiration of providing a new program for an emerging technology, the program has grown commensurably with the burgeoning field of lasers. Today's laser electro-optics technician must possess a diverse knowledge extending from the procedures and principles of scientific, industrial and medical lasers to the processes and techniques of the various systems to which laser technology is applicable. Further, laser technicians can typically expect to enter their field in capacities ranging from construction and installation to operation and maintenance. Technologies featured at the Center include Robotics/Automation, Electronics/Telecommunications, Computer Systems/Networks, and Machine Technology. Students working toward their Associate of Applied Science degrees enter their "major" field after completing a thorough four-term Core program, which emphasizes proficiency in electronics, computer basic and research skills.

In order to minimize extraneous vibrations, the laser laboratory was built on a separate foundation from the remainder of the building. The lab has a large central work space from which smaller project and supply areas radiate, thus accommodating a wide variety of student activity simultaneously. Not only are the facilities state-of-the-art but also the array of laser equipment is extremely diverse. Indian Hills was selected to host the 1992 National Laser/Electro-Optics Instructors Conference, sponsored by the Center for Occupational Research and Development (CORD).

Much of the success of the program is attributed to the close working relationship both the college and the laser department maintain with industry advisors. This has helped keep the program current, resulted in equipment donations exceeding $300,000, and provided the opportunity for laboratory visits and classroom lectures by industry representatives.

Accessibility and availability are key components in the delivery of the program across both traditional and non-traditional populations. Indian Hills offers articulation with high schools and colleges so that both entering and graduating students have a wide choice of educational and work options from which to choose. The students' Laser Club is affiliated nationally with the Laser Institute of America, and sets an annual goal of attending the National Conference of Lasers. The laser program has been a part of two federally-funded Cooperative Demonstration

Continues on Page 250

Projects, which were designed to provide laser proficiency to electricians and to provide non-traditional female students with the opportunity to complete a technical major.

The Laser/Electro-Optics Technology program has one full-time instructor/coordinator. In addition, several other advanced technology instructors teach specified courses.

Contact:
Stan Vittetoe, Dept Chair, Advanced Tech Conventional Program
(515) 683-5280

Indian Hills Community College
525 Grandview
Ottumwa, IA 52501
Total head count enrollment-Credit: 4,761; Non-Credit: 31,752
Campuses/sites: 2;Full-time faculty: 125

IOWA CENTRAL COMMUNITY COLLEGE

THE INTERNATIONAL AWARENESS SEMESTER

Each spring semester is designated Iowa Central's International Awareness Semester, with themes ranging from "Germany" to "Iowa and the Pacific Rim"

An annual International Awareness Semester has not only fostered an international climate for Iowa Central Community College students and area residents, but also it has enhanced the college's image. Foreign students find they are readily accepted within the student body. International delegations increasingly visit this very rural area of Iowa with projects in mind.

Iowa Central always had recognized the effects of the many changes in technology on our world and the ever-increasing need to understand the people and cultures of other nations. But not until the spring semester of 1989 was there a concentrated effort to provide continuity to the college's programming or to broaden it to a larger audience. That is, there was no organized plan for developing a campus climate for global awareness. Students received small doses of global information and experience which did not create an understanding of other cultures.

In 1989, Iowa Central began working with other Iowa community colleges to develop the International Awareness and a series of programs which would emphasize one country or area of the world. That year the group decided to focus on U.S./Soviet Relations. With the help of an Iowa Humanities Board grant they were able to bring Soviet scholar/journalist David Shipler to each of the five community colleges. In addition to this event a Russian family spent a week in residence at Iowa Central, the humanities department presented a program entitled "An Evening of Russian Art, Music, and Dance," and a group of students and Area V residents traveled to the Soviet Union.

The multiple programming provided the continuity necessary for students as well as area residents to develop a broader awareness of U.S./Soviet relations. Public radio interviews and newspaper articles had an impact on individuals unable to attend the actual events. Through these efforts the goal to foster global awareness began to be realized.

Since 1989, each spring semester has been designated Iowa Central's international awareness semester. The annual themes have included Iowa and the Pacific Rim, Japan, Germany and Mexico. Each year interest grows, along with the volunteer force of college employees, students and representatives from supporting agencies. A steering committee decides the theme and oversees the programming, while other volunteers prepare the integral details of one event.

When possible, Iowa Central works with the other community colleges and/or other agencies to enhance the offerings available through group efforts. These external groups may change from year to year depending on common interests. For example, five community colleges worked together on Germany and received a grant to bring two scholars from Schleswig-Holstein for week-long stays at each campus. Another year Iowa Central teamed up with the University of Iowa, the Iowa Sister States Organization, and the Japan External Trade Organization (JETRO) in developing "Japan: The Floating World" theme. Because of these efforts, Iowa Central is developing a long-term plan for a sister school relationship with a Japanese university.

The steering committee makes a concerted effort to serve a variety of audiences. The calendar of events usually includes one festive family event, several programs aimed at students, one seminar for business and industry, a program of the arts, and a study tour. Funding for this endeavor comes from a number of sources, including the Iowa Central Foundation, Buena Vista College, the Greater Fort Dodge Area Chamber of Commerce, Fort Dodge Rotary International, as well as the Iowa Humanities Board and the Iowa Arts Council.

Contact:
Mary Sula Linney, Chairperson
(515) 576-7201, ext. 2624

Iowa Central Community College
330 Avenue M
Fort Dodge, IA 50501
Total head count enrollment-Credit: 4,619; Non-Credit: 32,523
Campuses/sites: 4; Full-time faculty: 90

INDIVIDUALIZED COLLEGE EDUCATION

*A wide spectrum of support services and flexible programming
helps meet the needs of students with disabilities*

Each Iowa Central student with disabilities who needs flexibility in his/her education may work with program coordinators to tailor an individual plan. The Individual College Education program was introduced in 1983 as a support service on the Fort Dodge campus. The program began operation with an enrollment of 10 students, one coordinator and one tutor.

The typical ICE student profile is one of a student who has had difficulty with the conventional school curriculum and may have been in special programs at the high school level. Most of these students have been diagnosed as disabled at some point in their educational experiences. Ensuring accessibility to students with special needs means providing a wide spectrum of support services, all or part of which the individual student may need to utilize.

Services begin during the intake process following the student's request for help. During the intake period, the coordinator of the program assists each student in an evaluation and assessment of his/her academic and vocational strengths and barriers. A plan is then developed between the student and program coordinator to specify what types of academic support services and/or accommodations will best help the student accomplish his/her educational goal.

The primary service utilized by the students include one-to-one tutoring in the content area. Other strategies and accommodations include: computer use, study skills, time management, organizational skills, note-taking, proofreading, taped textbooks, taped lectures, library assistance, reduced course loads, testing accommodations, academic advising and advocacy. Student progress is monitored throughout the semester in order to detect the need for modifications.

The ultimate goal of the program is to aid the student in identifying an appropriate job choice and then to prepare him/her for that job by encouraging enrollment in related courses from which the student has an ability to benefit. Over the years the program has consistently surpassed the annual objective of 80 percent of the students enrolled to achieve one of the following goals:

- graduate and/or obtain employment;
- continue her/his educational program at ICCC;
- transfer to another accredited educational institution; and
- participate in another appropriate vocational or rehabilitation program.

Legislation such as Section 504 of the Rehabilitation Act of 1973 and the American with Disabilities Act has helped to expand post secondary educational opportunities and career choices for people with disabilities. The ICE program has helped to increase awareness of the rights of the students with special needs at Iowa Central. Today ICE serves approximately 50 disabled students enrolled in traditional college programs on all four campuses. The program employs two coordinators and 10 tutors. ICE is widely supported by faculty and staff campus-wide, with teachers, advisors and counselors referring students for service on a regular basis. Through the ICE program Iowa Central allows qualified disabled students to obtain educational and vocational training after high school.

Contact:
Barb McClannahan, Program Coordinator
(515) 576-7201, ext. 2501

Iowa Central Community College
330 Avenue M
Fort Dodge, IA 50501
Total head count enrollment-Credit: 4,619; Non-Credit: 32,523
Campuses/sites: 4; Full-time faculty: 90

HAZARDOUS MATERIALS TRAINING AND RESEARCH INSTITUTE

*To deliver state-of-the-art student and staff development programs,
the Institute has a strong industrial training program with businesses*

Since its inception in 1987, the Hazardous Materials Training and Research Institute (HMTRI) has served thousands of workers and hundreds of businesses and colleges with hazardous materials training and curricular materials. The Institute was established as a non-profit organization by the far-sighted presidents of two neighboring community colleges that have long been leaders in environmental worker training.

Kirkwood Community College was designated in 1975 as the first EPA 104(g) Water/Wastewater training facility in the nation. It has graduated 500 students from this program and delivers upgrade training and consultant assistance to 2,000 water/wastewater plants and operators

Continues on Page 252

throughout Iowa annually. Kirkwood's industrial wastewater pre-treatment training led to its role as the premier college in Iowa offering short-term, non-credit hazardous materials training serving local industry through open enrollment and customized contract training.

The Eastern Iowa Community College District (EICCD), headquartered in Davenport, Iowa, received a multi-million dollar EPA grant in 1985 to develop the first Hazardous Materials Technology program for credit students in the nation, and was one of the first colleges certified to provide asbestos training by EPA. EICCD is supported by curriculum developers with demonstrated ability in DACUM, competency-based education, program evaluation and testing.

The presidents of Kirkwood and EICCD envisioned a collaborative, non-competitive approach to environmental/health and safety training for their colleges when they established HMTRI in 1987. The institutions agree not to duplicate services. They share equipment, instructors and designate specific courses to be delivered by one or the other of the colleges. While EICCD focuses its resources on the development of credit programming, Kirkwood takes responsibility for OSHA 1910.120 short-term non-credit health and safety training, landfill and incinerator operator training, recycling, and compost training, water and wastewater training.

Other purposes of the Institute are to market the curricula developed by the two colleges and prepare other community colleges nationwide to collaboratively respond to the hazardous materials training needs in their respective states.

HMTRI has organized national and regional hazardous materials training workshops for other community colleges, and delivered these in Texas, California, Oregon, Michigan, Illinois and Iowa. Intensive trainer institutes for instructors are scheduled each year in Iowa.

To deliver state-of-the-art student and staff development programs for educational institutions, HMTRI maintains a strong industrial training program of its own contracting with businesses throughout the nation to deliver training on-site.

Recently, HMTRI developed a community college affiliate program which has grown in number to more than 50 member colleges/trainers, representing more than 30 states and Canada. HMTRI works with our affiliates to initiate credit and non-credit hazardous materials training programs on their campuses. Most use HMTRI curriculum and avail themselves of the Institute's marketing and technical assistance.

One of the objectives of the affiliate program is to prepare other community colleges and their instructors through train-the-trainer and on-the-job training programs. Through its OJT program, HMTRI contracts with colleges to do short-term haz mat health and safety training on their campus, providing a lead instructor, equipment, and an equipment technician. The affiliate college provides support instructors who observe and assist HMTRI's lead instructor in delivering training. The final objective is to develop a self-sufficient program at the affiliate college. HMTRI has helped Salt Lake Community College, Utah; Casper College in Wyoming; Faulkner State Junior College, Alabama; Amarillo Community College, Texas; and Crowder College, Missouri, to initiate short-term haz mat health and safety training.

Through its direct contact with industry, workers and educators, HMTRI recognizes the tremendous demand for hazardous materials health and safety training that is needed locally, at reasonable cost, and oriented to worker learning styles. Accessible, affordable, adult, technical and hands-on education is the forte of the two-year college.

Contact:
Pat Berntsen, Director
(319) 398-5677

Kirkwood Community College
6301 Kirkwood Boulevard SW, PO Box 2068
Cedar Rapids, IA 52406
Total head count enrollment-Credit: 9,612; Non-Credit: 65,445
Campuses/sites: 7; Full-time faculty: 189

TELECOMMUNICATION SYSTEM

▨ Kirkwood classes, supplemental educational and community service ▨
programs may all be transmitted nationally or internationally

Kirkwood Community College, serving a seven-county area encompassing more than 4,300 square miles, began distance learning as a means of reaching its sprawling student population in the late 1970's.

With the assistance of a grant from the Public Telecommunications Facilities Program of the National Telecommunication Information Administration, in the early 1980's the college designed and installed a comprehensive interactive video system that assured that no one in the Kirkwood service area lived more than 30 minutes from a Kirkwood classroom. The resulting system, called the Kirkwood Telecommunication System (KTS), utilizes several technologies to provide five discreet educational networks.

The primary KTS network is called Telelink. It consists of two-way video/two-way audio microwave interconnections that link origination classrooms on the Kirkwood campus with classrooms in each of our county learning centers and the Iowa City Campus. This network carries more than 30 credit classes each semester. In addition to the live/interactive classes, this network also carries additional voice/data lines for telephone, fax and data interconnects with the main campus. The other four networks are based on ITFS technology, which is one-way video and two-way audio. The first of these networks, called the Secondary School Network, interconnects the Kirkwood campus to 20 high schools. This network carries shared high school classes, selected college credit classes for high school students, special events and, during the evening hours, college credit classes and continuing education classes for adults living in the area. Also included is the Urban Network, which interconnects school facilities of the Cedar Rapids School District, and the Business and Industrial Training Network (which provides selected programs to area business locations). The fifth network is the KTS Cable Network. This network provides a cable service which is carried on the basic tier of cable service in 21 communities and reaches over 70,000 households. Programming consists of telecourses and selected educational and informational programs.

Starting in 1980, with two classes reaching 30 students,

KTS has grown steadily each year. Currently the system provides more than 30 credit classes each semester, reaching more than 1,400 student registrations. The networks also carry a variety of supplemental educational activities as well as community service programs. During the mid-1980's the college added self-paced Open Learning Labs, utilizing pre-recorded telecourses, audio and computer courses at the county learning center locations. These labs, along with cable television, now number an additional 1,400 registrations each semester.

In 1990, the college added a satellite uplink, allowing programs and classes originating at Kirkwood or any of the learning center locations to be transmitted nationally or internationally. The college currently works with a variety of educational and business clients utilizing satellite teleconferencing for education and training. The college will also serve as a regional switching center for the state-wide Iowa Educational Telecommunications Network, a high capacity, full motion, fiber optic network targeted to have begun initial service during 1993.

The Kirkwood Telecommunications System continues to receive hundreds of visitors from around the country each year. As a trailblazer in the field of distance learning, Kirkwood and KTS have been featured in a variety of national and international publications.

Contact:
Rich Gross, Dean
(319) 398-5481

Kirkwood Community College
6301 Kirkwood Boulevard SW, PO Box 2068
Cedar Rapids, IA 52406
Total head count enrollment-Credit: 9,612; Non-Credit: 65,445
Campuses/sites: 7; Full-time faculty: 189

SURGICAL TECHNOLOGY

The curriculum now includes a Medical Terminology course, a special First Aid course and the linking of clinical experience to a classroom course

Although the Surgical Technology program has been part of the Marshalltown Community College curriculum for approximately 20 years, shifts in health care funding, training of RNs, and state requirements caused dramatic enrollment fluctuations – until recently.

Through the leadership of the instructor, Kathy Balmer, enrollment has increased annually as the curriculum has been upgraded to include additional time for a Medical Terminology course, a First Aid course tailored for Surg Tech students, and linking clinical experience directly to a classroom course for grading.

As enrollment increased a concerted effort was made to place students in hospitals with a variety of surgical facilities and staffs. Students now take clinical experience in eight different hospitals located in Central Iowa.

With increased visibility for the program, job placement has been excellent. Successful graduates are now sending new students to the program.

For the future, plans are being made to offer a second year in the program with additional general education courses. This would qualify the student for an Associate in Science degree.

Contact:
Kathy Balmer, Instructor
(515) 752-7106, ext. 290

Marshalltown Community College
3700 South Center Street, PO Box 430
Marshalltown, IA 50158
Total head count enrollment-Credit: 1,314
Campuses/sites: 1; Full-time faculty: 45

DRAFTING AND DESIGN TECHNOLOGY

▨ An active advisory committee has helped the college maintain ▨
state-of-the-art software and hardware

The Drafting and Design Program has evolved from a drafting-board oriented program into a highly technical computer assisted drawing/computer assisted manufacturing program (CAD-CAM). Auto-CAD is used extensively in the drafting courses.

An active advisory committee has worked with the college to maintain state-of-the-art software and hardware. The program has maintained close relationships with area

industries. This has aided in job placement for graduates and a continual flow of ideas for upgrading the program.

During the 1991-92 year, several local high schools worked with the program coordinator to articulate parts of high school Industrial Technology programs into the college program. Through a combination of credit and advanced standing high school students are able to graduate sooner or take more advanced courses.

Contact:
Jerry Turner, Instructor
(515) 752-7106, ext. 230

Marshalltown Community College
3700 South Center Street, PO Box 430
Marshalltown, IA 50158
Total head count enrollment-Credit: 1,314
Campuses/sites: 1; Full-time faculty: 45

NO-TILL FARMING

▨ Approximately 100 acres of no-till corn and beans have been dedicated ▨
to the project for a five-year demonstration

Because Iowa top soil quality is rapidly eroding, North Iowa Area Community College is teaching no-till farming, an alternative that would keep farm productivity as well as the state's economy from diminishing.

To test and demonstrate the latest techniques in no-till farming, NIACC and BASF partnered to operate a farm using long-term, large-scale techniques appropriate to no-till farming. Approximately 100 acres of no-till corn and beans have been dedicated to the no-till project for a five-year demonstration that began in the spring of 1992.

A mutual goal of NIACC and BASF is to enhance and provide no-till development demonstrations, and training. No-till education is provided for students, farmers and other people interested in no-till farming practices. In addition, effects of no-till farming practices on farming productivity, costs, and soil and water quality in the North Iowa region will be demonstrated.

Iowa top soil quality is eroding rapidly. If soil erosion continues at the current rate, it will be difficult to maintain farm productivity. Samples of soil taken from the middle of a field compared to soil samples in the fence row, where the soil is not tilled, reveal that tillage is not necessarily good for the land. In no-till, the only time the soil is disturbed is when the farmer opens up a slot to put the seed in. No-till farming is planting directly into plant

residue, formerly plowed under as "trash." Farmers must learn to manage residue, leaving as much on the surface as possible to conserve moisture and improve soil. No-till farming is a way for farmers to conserve soil and water, be environmentally sound, and use safe farm chemicals. It is believed farmers can reduce money spent on chemical control with the no-till system and proper education and management. The number of no-till acres in Iowa grew by nearly one-third to almost 1-million acres in 1991, according to statistics kept by the Conservation Technology Information Center (CTIC) in West Lafayette, Indiana. In fact, no-till farming may eventually be the primary farming system in the Corn Belt.

NIACC's no-till demonstration project, located on campus, helps promote the use of no-till by providing an opportunity for farmers to witness the benefits first-hand. The site gives students a chance to learn about no-till operations, to use agronomy skills in real-life settings and to learn about chemicals and their use. NIACC facilities and personnel assist farmers as they take advantage of this new resource. Scheduled tours, conferences and workshops are held to demonstrate the latest no-till techniques and innovations. More than 500 visitors from several states have participated in work shops and toured the NIACC facilities since spring.

Contact:
Larry Eichmeier, Instructor/Program Leader, Agricultural Technology
(515) 421-4225

North Iowa Area Community College
500 College Drive
Mason City, IA 50401
Total head count enrollment-Credit: 3,074; Non-Credit: 70,000
Campuses/sites: 1; Full-time faculty: 84

HYPERWRITER FOR INSTITUTIONAL EFFECTIVENESS

*▓ Through technology, decentralized data-gathering leads to on-site ▓
quality improvement, while still supporting a central repository*

At North Iowa Area Community College, an interactive computer program promotes use by faculty and staff, thereby encouraging broad-based involvement in creating and watching quality efforts. North Iowa Area Community College adopted the interactive computer program in 1990, while engaged in a self-study process. It stores and displays institutional effectiveness information. There were four reasons for this decision:

1) to centralize previously scattered data;
2) to broaden the use of analytical data to improve quality;
3) to raise the level of visibility for and participation in the institutional effectiveness effort; and
4) to develop a communication tool for internal and external audiences.

Historically, North Iowa Area Community College created institution-wide change through a broadly participative strategic planning process. But it also wished to use analytical data to continually improve quality in the daily, goal-driven operations of the college. Decentralized data gathering efforts seemed likely to lead directly to quality improvements; staff could make immediate incremental changes indicated by on-site analysis. Choosing a central repository for this data, Hyperwriter!, minimized the customary hazards of decentralized data collection: inconsistent data definitions, duplicated data, unavailable data. In addition, the centralized location of the program solves an administrative need to use cross-divisional data for grant and report writing.

The program has a colorful, user-friendly branching characteristic. High visibility of the data encourages data reporters' attention to accuracy, completeness and thoughtful analysis. The program feature that allows users to build files containing only audience-appropriate documents simplifies communication sharing in presentations to internal and external constituencies.

Contact:
Tucki Folkers, Director, Developmental Education
(515) 421-4293

North Iowa Area Community College
500 College Drive
Mason City, IA 50401
Total head count enrollment-Credit: 3,074; Non-Credit: 70,000
Campuses/sites: 1; Full-time faculty: 84

JOHN DEERE AG TECH PROGRAM

*▓ The privately sponsored program provides classroom lecture and lab experiences ▓
on John Deere products and a program at a John Deere dealership*

The John Deere Ag Tech program at Northeast Iowa Community College is a privately sponsored program that provides classroom lecture and lab experiences on John Deere products and experience at a John Deere dealership. Designed to upgrade the technical competence and professional level of the incoming farm equipment dealership technician, the program is sponsored by John Deere Company, Kansas City Branch, and operated by Northeast Iowa Community College, Calmar Campus.

The total program is completed in four semesters and one summer term or approximately 21 months. Each specialized subject is studied in the classroom and laboratory on campus and then followed by related work experience in the dealership. For example, the first semester involves 16 weeks of courses, followed by the second semester of the first year with 16 weeks at the dealership. The work experience at the dealership relates as much as possible to the course work just completed at the college. Classroom instruction covers the basics, as well as the latest developments in all John Deere agricultural and consumer products.

Since considerable time is spent at the dealership, the program requires the student to have a sponsoring John Deere dealer. Each of the participants in this cooperative endeavor – the college, the John Deere Company, a John Deere dealership and the student – has specific responsibilities. These were identified prior to the start of class and have continued to be the guidelines by which this program is maintained and operated.

The major responsibilities of the college include:
1) maintain a current curriculum approved by the John Deere Corporation;
2) provide a dedicated classroom and laboratory;
3) provide a John Deere trained instructor;
4) provide equipment and necessary tools; and
5) conduct student visitations during cooperative

Continues on Page 256

work experience and work with the dealership training coordinator and provide the customary services to these students that are part of a community college setting, such as counseling, testing and placement.

The John Deere Corporation responsibilities include:
1) encourage dealer cooperation and support;
2) provide special training for John Deere Ag Tech instructor;
3) furnish college with John Deere training equipment; and
4) provide college with essential training materials.

The John Deere dealership responsibilities include:
1) interview and select students who the dealership will sponsor throughout the entire program;
2) appoint an in-dealership coordinator to assist the college's John Deere Ag Tech instructor in planning and monitoring the cooperative work experience;
3) provide appropriate paid work experiences that will assist the student in utilizing the theory and lab activities from the previous semester while in the dealership; and
4) participate in orientation meetings at the college and/or act as a member of the program advisory committee.

The student responsibilities include:
1) obtain and maintain a sponsorship with a John Deere dealership;
2) maintain academic standards, a 2.0 GPA on a 4.0 scale, and adhere to academic policies of the college;
3) wear uniforms and safety glasses while on campus and during cooperative work experience at the dealership;
4) participate in all learning activities at the scheduled times; and
5) be responsible for program cost, including tuition, fees, books and tools.

In summary, for the program, which started in the fall of 1989, there have been 27 graduates, 26 of whom remained employed at John Deere dealerships. Forty students are now enrolled in either the first or second year of the program.

Contact:
Robert Maxson, Business, Agriculture & Communications Dept Chair
(319) 562-3263

Northeast Iowa Community College
PO Box 400
Calmar, IA 52132
Total head count enrollment-Credit: 3,114; Non-Credit: 54,001
Campuses/sites: 2;Full-time faculty: 98

NON-DESTRUCTIVE TESTING TECHNOLOGY

This open-entry program trains technicians to non-destructively test materials, parts and products for such industries as automotive, air craft and construction

With the only Non-destructive Testing Technology program in Iowa and one of very few in the nation, Northeast Iowa Community College draws students from throughout the nation and world.

Non-destructive evaluation or testing, whichever you choose to call it, is a developing technology of vital importance to the future of American industry. One only has to consider the societal impact of recent catastrophic failures in aerospace, transportation, energy and infrastructure industries to realize that significant change will need to occur in our education if American industry is to prosper.

This unique, individualized, open-entry program was initiated to train technicians to non-destructively test materials, parts and products for a wide variety of industries including automotive, air craft and construction. Students are taught to test metal, concrete and composite material by any one or more of the five basic testing methods (namely x-ray, ultrasound, eddy current, magnetic particle and liquid penetrant testing). Northeast Iowa Community College offers a diploma with options in x-ray and ultrasound, an Associate in Applied Science degree, and an Associate of Arts. This latest degree allows easier transfer of Non-destructive Testing Technician credits into Iowa State University's Engineering Science program, where graduates receive an engineering degree with an emphasis in non-destructive evaluation. The articulation with Iowa State University was born out of a push from the American Society for Non-destructive Testing (ASNT) and initial funding from the National Science Foundation, so this five-year integrated program could begin immediately to produce and meet the demands for engineers.

The non-destructive testing program has 16 students enrolled with a projected enrollment cap of no more than 24 students, as NICC facilities and projected equipment will only accommodate that count. The program recently completed its fourth year of operation and there have been

16 graduates. Thirteen are working full time in directly related employment and three are going on to further education, with one of the three being the first recipient of the scholarship made available by the National Science Foundation to transfer into engineering at ISU.

Contact:
Arnold Prosch, Instructor
(319) 556-5110 or (800) 728-7367

Northeast Iowa Community College
PO Box 400
Calmar, IA 52132
Total head count enrollment-Credit: 3,114; Non-Credit: 54,001
Campuses/sites: 2;Full-time faculty: 98

LONG-TERM CARE FACILITIES STAFF DEVELOPMENT PROJECT

The college provides a variety services at-cost to area nursing facilities, which feel genuine ownership of the program

In the fall of 1989, Northwest Iowa Community College quickly addressed a need within the nursing home industry for assistance with staff development/in-service programming. The ongoing project that since has evolved includes the following objectives:

1) assist area nursing homes in developing quality staff development/in-service programs;
2) identify consultants and trainers to meet the identified training needs of the nursing homes;
3) provide educational consultation to nursing homes where qualified staff development personnel are not available;
4) strengthen the image of the college as a provider of quality continuing education in the merged area; and
5) involve at least 50 percent of the total number of nursing facilities in the merged area in this program.

Each year the Health Occupations Coordinator meets one-on-one with the Director of Nursing at each nursing facility involved in the project. Together they identify training needs and identify possibilities for appropriate speakers/trainers for the upcoming year. Since nursing staff is the largest segment of the population of employees at a nursing home, training pertinent to nursing is given priority. Other segments of the employee population are also served, but to a lesser degree. Classes deemed to be appropriate content are assigned professional continuing education credit. The Health Occupations Coordinator is responsible for matching up facilities and speakers and for scheduling the program each month.

These services are provided on an at-cost basis to the nursing facilities. Participants are enrolled as continuing education students and attendance records are kept on permanent file at the college. Currently, nine of the 16 nursing facilities in the service area are totally involved in the project. Three more facilities participate, but on a limited basis. When the project began, only five facilities participated. In addition, one residential care facility participates in the total program. Each year, additional facilities have taken advantage of the program. There has been no attrition.

Annual evaluation of the program has identified strengths and weaknesses, which have been enhanced or corrected respectively. The nursing facilities definitely reflect a genuine feeling of ownership of the program and reliance on the college to continue to provide them with this service.

Contact:
Marilyn Lofflin, Health Occupations Coordinator
(712) 324-5061, ext. 143

Northwest Iowa Community College
603 West Park Street
Sheldon, IA 51201
Total head count enrollment-Credit: 746; Non-Credit: 25,403
Campuses/sites: 1; Full-time faculty: 40

ELECTRICAL CODE TRAINING

*A "buffet" of study modules allows access to more than 10
different related electrical occupations*

Distance learning is the centerpiece of a project to provide educational opportunities to people in the electrical industry who otherwise could not take time away from a job to retrain or update skills. Initiated in 1987, the innovative project at Northwest Iowa Community College was spurred by representatives from the electrical industry who wanted educational materials that offer electrical technicians located in remote locations the opportunity to upgrade electrical skills and knowledge. The electrical industry continued to advise NCC on necessary topics for the materials and possible revisions.

A survey of the electrical industry showed a need for a "buffet" of study modules. This flexibility allows access to more than 10 different related electrical occupations and allows the student to select subject areas and to progress at his/her own learning speed.

A national marketing survey returned more than 900 inquiries. The inquiries were received from more than 10 foreign countries. Currently students are enrolled in the program from 12 different states and from outside the continental United States.

The college is successfully working with electrical state associations in various cities and states for approval and adoption of the program to meet apprenticeship training and journeyman apprentices.

Students enrolled in the self-directed electrical study program benefit in many ways. Enrollees in related electrical fields such as electrical draftsmen and engineers are able to select modules of specific subject areas that are related to the enrollees' fields of expertise. This allows enrollees to increase knowledge and expertise in the National Electrical Code and associated electrical theory and practices. Often, electrical personnel require access to the theory portion of an apprenticeship training program. These student enrollees generally pursue a certificate program that requires two to three years for completion. In addition, experienced electrical personnel are often required to pursue continuing education hours to maintain licensing in their respective states, due to updating of the National Electrical Code every three years. Several states have approved the college's self-directed program for their continuing education hours.

The college has utilized authors outside the college expertise to strengthen and broaden the scope of the program. Currently the program is serviced with part-time staff. It is anticipated that a full-time secretary and instructor will be required as the program continues to grow.

Contact:
Robert De Zeeuw, Manager, Business/Industry Training Institute
(712) 324-5061

Northwest Iowa Community College
603 West Park Street
Sheldon, IA 51201
Total head count enrollment-Credit: 746; Non-Credit: 25,403
Campuses/sites: 1; Full-time faculty: 40

MEDICAL LABORATORY TECHNOLOGY

*A joint program with Scott Community College has served
as a model for similar programs in three states*

The developmental leader in the state of Iowa for cooperative educational ventures in medical laboratory technology, Southeastern Community College has served as a model for three such programs in the state.

Establishing Southeastern's Medical Laboratory Technology program as a joint venture between Southeastern and Scott Community College greatly reduced start-up costs and allowed both colleges to make more efficient use of facilities, equipment and faculty.

It began during the spring of 1989, when Southeastern was contacted by a local hospital with a request to explore additional health-related-training programs. Hospital personnel indicated there was a serious problem developing in the recruitment of trained health technicians. Following a series of meetings with health care providers and educational institutions in eastern Iowa and western Illinois, it was decided that a program in Medical Laboratory Technician would best meet local needs. It was also decided that due to the initial start-up cost and the limited number of enrollees anticipated, this program would work best as a joint effort between Southeastern and Scott Community Colleges. A joint agreement between the two institutions was instituted in the fall of 1989.

Of the six-semester AAS degree program (four semesters and two summer terms), three-semesters and one-summer term are offered at both colleges. All students are required to attend classes only taught at Scott for the remaining one semester and one summer term. Some related courses are also available on Southeastern's South Campus in Keokuk, Iowa. One component of the program is 12 semester hours of clinical practicum, which provides students with hands-on experiences in a hospital setting. Because of the cooperative nature of the agreement, students receive their training in a wide range of hospital settings throughout southeastern Iowa.

The response to this program by students and health care providers has been very positive. It has provided students at Southeastern with an educational opportunity that Southeastern could not have offered without the joint effort with its northern neighbor, Scott Community College.

Contact:
Ed Schiefer, Dean of Instruction
(319) 752-2731

Southeastern Community College
1015 South Gear Avenue, Drawer F
West Burlington, IA 52655-0605
Total head count enrollment-Credit: 3,555; Non-Credit: 24,881
Campuses/sites: 2; Full-time faculty: 82

SOUTHEASTERN COMMUNITY COLLEGE

EMERGENCY MEDICAL TECHNICIAN-PARAMEDIC

The program is designed for either full- or part-time students, allowing emergency caregivers the chance to earn higher certification

The Emergency Medical Technician-Paramedic Program at Southeastern Community College was the first EMT program in the state of Iowa to provide its students with the opportunity to earn a college degree in this field.

The EMT-Paramedic curriculum awards college credit to students enrolling in any of the three levels of EMT training, and awards credit to currently certified EMT and paramedics for past training. It also provides students with the opportunity to take selected arts and sciences courses, eventually culminating with an Associate of Applied Science Degree. The arts and sciences courses are related to the EMT-Paramedic field and will provide the student with a broad base upon which to make reasoned decisions when giving emergency care.

The program is an outgrowth of courses offered through the Adult and Continuing Education Division of Southeastern Community College in West Burlington, Iowa. It is established as either a full-time or a part-time program, which allows currently employed emergency caregivers an opportunity to attend classes and earn higher certification. One of the important component of the program is an intensive clinical and field experience portion. This provides numerous opportunities for students to experience hands-on training.

Contact:
Ed Schiefer, Dean of Instruction
(319) 752-2731

Southeastern Community College
1015 South Gear Avenue, Drawer F
West Burlington, IA 52655-0605
Total head count enrollment-Credit: 3,555; Non-Credit: 24,881
Campuses/sites: 2; Full-time faculty: 82

WALDORF COLLEGE

HONORS PROGRAM

A Philosophy course, the centerpiece of the program, is designed to foster critical thinking skills and expose students to ideas of the West

Because Waldorf College recognizes that different students have different needs and specializes in meeting those needs, honors students receive individualized instruction from some of the college's best faculty as well as:
1) take small seminar-type courses centered on the world of ideas;
2) engage in independent learning and research activ-

ities rarely available to freshmen and sophomores at larger institutions;
3) participate in special events on campus; and
4) travel to concerts, plays, seminars and museums.

Waldorf College holds memberships in both the National Collegiate Honors Council and the Upper Midwest Honors Council. The college's Beta Lambda

Continues on Page 260

chapter of Phi Theta Kappa, the international honors society for two-year colleges, is one of the oldest in the nation. Honors Program students provide leadership for the extensive activities sponsored by these organizations.

The Honors Program is open to first-semester freshmen with a minimum composite ACT score of 26 and a high school cumulative grade point average of 3.6. Other outstanding students may become involved in the program at almost any time during their Waldorf career. Full-time students with an established Waldorf grade point average of 3.0 may take Honors Program courses, but students must have a 3.5 grade point average to be full members of the Honors Program, and be considered Waldorf Scholars at graduation.

Students participating in the program must enroll for Philosophy 200, 289, 290, and three additional credits of honors courses. PHL 200 is the centerpiece of the program and is designed to foster critical thinking skills and to offer the student a survey of ideas of the West through primary texts. PHL 289 and 290 are honors seminar courses which are offered each semester and deal with a variety of selected topics. Other courses available to honors students include a two-semester English/History course, independent study and honors contract courses.

Waldorf College offers an overseas "capstone" experience to students successfully completing the Honors Program. Students who wish to be a part of the overseas experience must enroll in an independent study during the second semester of their sophomore year, and make a public, scholarly presentation of this work during the college's annual Inquirer Week. Inquirer Week is a multi-faceted program which, in many ways, is the academic climax of each year. As part of this program students are given the opportunity to present their scholarly papers and to have them published. Those students who are qualified and chose to participate in the overseas trip will work together with the program director to plan the itinerary, and a schedule of study to prepare for the journey.

Contact:
Laird Edman, Director
(515) 582-8221

Waldorf College
106 South Sixth Street
Forest City, IA 50436
Total head count enrollment-Credit: 593
Campuses/sites: 1; Full-time faculty: 34

ACADEMIC ACHIEVEMENT CENTER

The Center serves all students and faculty and sponsors workshops on faculty professional development

The Academic Achievement Center helps both at-risk students and honor students at Waldorf College maximize their learning and its impact.

Located in the heart of the Waldorf College campus, the Center serves all students who desire to improve or enhance their learning skills and/or their academic performance. It provides seminar rooms for individual or group study, a variety of technologies to support courses (including interactive video), and adjoins The Atrium IBM Computer Lab. It is the home of the Learning Disabilities Program, the Academic Support Program and the English as a Second Language Program.

The Center's staff of part-time peer and professional tutors provides assistance with many of the college's classes. Full-time Center staff members provide comprehensive assistance for students to: improve study skills; make a successful transition to the academic demands of college; and help them to understand, expand, and effectively work with their individual learning styles.

The Center works closely with faculty and other departments such as the Registrar, Admission, Academic Affairs and Student Services offices to identify students having academic problems, and to plan and provide assistance. In addition to working with students, the center's staff assists Waldorf's faculty with using technology in their classes and in support of their professional activities. The Center also sponsors workshops on faculty professional development.

The Academic Support Program is designed to enable a limited number of students, who have earned below a 2.0 GPA (on a 4.0 scale) in high school, or who have low ACT scores, to become successful in college. It offers developmental courses for areas of academic weakness (such as reading and math), as well as special monitoring, academic counseling, and tutoring services to support standard college courses (such as biology and English). The goals of the program are to provide students with the academic skills, knowledge, and motivation needed to graduate from Waldorf and be successful at a four-year college or university.

The Learning Disabilities Program is learning-strategies based, and students are accepted with the potential to succeed in college. Students in the Learning Disabilities Program participate fully in college life, experience academic success, and many graduate as honors students.

The intensive ESL Program includes a nine-week summer course that offers a variety of language and cultural experiences. Additional ESL follow-up course work and support occurs during the academic year. The program focuses on the essential skills of language learning: listening, speaking, grammar, reading and writing. Enrollment in the course is limited to ensure the students receive the individual attention language requires. The students also have the opportunity to broaden their understanding of American culture by participating in a variety of outdoor and cultural activities.

Contact:
Paulette Church, Director
(515) 582-8208

Waldorf College
106 South Sixth Street
Forest City, IA 50436
Total head count enrollment-Credit: 593
Campuses/sites: 1; Full-time faculty: 34

ASSOCIATE DEGREE COMPLETION IN NURSING

A collaboration with another college resulted in the establishment of this one-year program

Western Iowa Tech Community College and Northwest Iowa Technical College responded to a severe nursing shortage by forming a unique partnership that resulted in a one-year Associate Degree Nursing Completion program. To help fill the need for more such programs, the collaboration linked the Western Iowa Associate Degree in Nursing to Northwest Iowa's practical nursing Program and began delivering this training in the city of Sheldon.

The joint program, particularly aimed at providing rural areas with health care workers, was prompted by the Final Report of the Iowa Health Professional Shortage Committee. The need for additional training for registered nurses becomes acute when coupled with the fact that Iowa has the highest 85 year and older per capita in the nation.

Although there are associate degree nursing programs throughout the state of Iowa; opportunities in the northwest corner of the state remain limited. The Final Report identified only two programs in the northwest tier of 12 counties. At the time, Northwest Iowa Technical College (in Sheldon, Iowa) was the only institution offering a Practical Nursing Program without an Associate Degree Nursing Completion program.

The opportunity for Northwest Iowa's LPN program graduates to complete an Associate Degree also provided Western Iowa the opportunity to offer an additional section of the current Associate Degree Nursing Program, without significantly increasing financial commitment. This collaborative program began in the fall of 1990 and began its third year with an enrollment of 24 students in FY 1992. Nursing classes are taught by Western Iowa nursing faculty at the Northwest Iowa site. General Education and support courses are taught by Northwest Iowa faculty. The college of record is Western Iowa in Sioux City, Iowa.

The Iowa Department of Education is fully supportive of this concept and has encouraged expanding this innovative delivery concept to include other programs. Other allied health programs are currently being explored in cooperation with three other community colleges in Northwest Iowa. Major benefits to the state of Iowa, community colleges and students include the reduction of program duplication, increased cost effectiveness and efficiency, and assessable training opportunities for students in Northwest Iowa.

Contact:
JoAnn Erickson
(712) 274-6400

Western Iowa Tech Community College
4647 Stone Avenue, PO Box 265
Sioux City, IA 51102-0265
Total head count enrollment-Credit: 2,578; Non-Credit: 45,593
Campuses/sites: 7; Full-time faculty: 82

LIBERAL ARTS AND TRANSFER EDUCATION

Drawing upon concepts in competency-based vocational education, faculty designed a curriculum development process for arts and sciences courses

Western Iowa Tech Community college faculty designed and implemented a seven-objective, competency-based curriculum for arts and sciences that soon will be used for all curricula.

This change dates back to 1987, when Western Iowa Tech Community College (WITCC) was granted authorization by the Iowa Department of Education to offer freshman and sophomore liberal arts and sciences courses paralleling the first two years of university education. The primary goal of the college was to develop curricula leading to an Associate of Science and Associate in Arts degrees that would enable student to succeed in future personal, educational and social endeavors. Optimum transfer of credits was also a major concern.

Believing that students who complete studies in the arts and sciences should possess certain fundamental competencies relating to particular disciplines, WITCC began its curriculum development process by searching for successful curriculum design models that incorporated the identification of student outcomes. While current literature regarding competency-based or outcome-based education is replete for career and occupational education, it was discovered that there was a void of similar information for academic course and program development. Drawing upon concepts that worked well in competency-based vocational education, the WITCC faculty designed and implemented a unique curriculum development process for arts and sciences courses. To help fund this project, the college applied for and was awarded a five-year grant totaling more than $2-million.

The curriculum development process that was agreed upon had seven objectives:

1) identify freshman and sophomore courses that support each of the major disciplines of study (natural sciences, mathematics, social sciences, humanities and communication skills);
2) identify course content and sequence;
3) establish course objectives;
4) validate student outcomes;
5) identify support resource materials for each course, i.e., test, references, equipment;
6) develop assurances that courses transfer to senior institutions; and
7) establish an appraisal process to determine the effectiveness of each course developed.

Western Iowa Tech instructional staff, with the assistance of a broad-based steering committee, was responsible for meeting each objective.

What distinguished the curriculum development process as unique and effective was the curriculum committee responsible for each course. Committee members were faculty and/or administrators representing their respective discipline. They were employed at private and public four-year colleges and universities to which WITCC students would most likely transfer. Ten colleges from three states (Iowa, Nebraska and South Dakota) participated. During intensive two-day sessions, a facilitator worked with each committee to assure that the participants reached consensus on course descriptions, objectives, student outcomes, course content, sequence and supporting resource material. This process allowed for comprehensive discussion and interaction on all aspects of a specific course. Additionally, each of the representatives agreed to act as a liaison for WITCC to articulate the newly developed courses with comparable course at their home institutions.

As of the spring of 1992, 61 faculty from visiting colleges helped develop 27 courses in five disciplines. By the fall of 1994 nearly all of WITCC's curricula will be developed using this model. Benefits of this project resulted in the following:

1) enhanced professional relationships between WITCC faculty and the faculty from participating institutions;
2) an increased sense of confidence by WITCC students in knowing they have appropriate education for transfer of credits and successful continuation of study at a receiving college; and
3) a sense of ownership in WITCC's curriculum by colleges participating in the project.

Recognition: NCA Review Team, Iowa Annual Visit Report.

Contact:
Douglas Kanaly
(712) 274-8733, ext. 1233

Western Iowa Tech Community College
4647 Stone Avenue, PO 265
Sioux City, IA 51102-0265
Total head count enrollment-Credit: 2,578; Non-Credit: 45,593
Campuses/sites: 7; Full-time faculty: 82

COMPREHENSIVE SCHOLARSHIPS

 Scholarships have boosted enrollment growth of the college
at a time when enrollment at other institutions is declining

Because federal grant and loan programs exclude many capable students who do not qualify or do not apply, Butler County Community College provides endowed scholarships through selection into activity programs such as music, theater, academic challenge, leadership and livestock judging.

The Board of Trustees has placed an emphasis on raising scholarship dollars through the endowment association. At the beginning of the 1991-92 academic term there were 101 endowed scholarship funds. These endowed scholarships produced $99,190 for scholarships.

The distribution of the scholarships is diversified through various programs in the financial aid office. The students may earn scholarships through selection into activity programs. In addition, a wide range of academic scholarships are provided for high school valedictorians, salutatorians, faculty dependents and senior citizens.

A specific scholarship that has encouraged many adults to return to college is the Adult Re-Entry Scholarship. It is a tuition scholarship provided to individuals who have been out of school and want an opportunity to return to school and prove their capabilities. The scholarship is provided for one semester with few limits on eligibility.

These scholarships along with vocational scholarships, traditional athletic scholarships and a diversified assortment of academic scholarships have been a big boost to the growth of Butler County Community College. In the last five years the college has grown 56 percent. The last year alone saw an 18 percent growth in enrollment at a time when many colleges were showing enrollment declines.

This program of scholarships has been successful because of the wide support of the Board of Trustees, administrators, staff, faculty and the community. The team work and effort has been a big boost to the college.

Contact:
Jan Green, Director, Financial Aid
(316) 321-2222, ext. 122

Butler County Community College
901 South Haverhill
El Dorado, KS 67042
Total headcount enrollment-Credit: 7,151; Non-Credit: 2,903
Campuses/sites: 23; Full-time faculty: 103

HONORS PROGRAM

 The program includes an eight-hour core curriculum that includes
honors seminars and an independent study project

Designed to enrich and expand educational opportunities, the Honors Program at Butler County Community College helps students develop as individuals, as college students and as members of the community. The honors curriculum enables students seeking an academic or creative challenge not available in a traditional classroom setting to receive recognition of their efforts. The Honors Program is open to all BCCC students, but to graduate from the Honors Program a student must have an overall 3.5 GPA and successfully complete the core curriculum of the program: an honors English Composition II, two Honors Seminars, and an Honors Independent Study project – for a total of eight credit hours.

The Honors Program began at Butler County Community College in 1987. In the summer of 1988, the first activity sponsored was the Summer Enrichment Program in English for Composition I for high school seniors. The Southwest Program, which took the place of the Summer Enrichment Program in 1991, is an expense-paid, week-long study tour of the Southwest. Not only do

the students learn about the diverse and rich cultural history of the area, but they also learn about the environment and camping.

Honors Seminars have taken place for the past four years. They provide an interdisciplinary approach to specific topics. Seminars have included: "Arts in the Community," highlighting local museums, concerts and theater productions; "The Election Year," discussions from various perspectives of local and state officials and politicians; "Environmental Issues," featuring a prominent member of Green Peace, an international environmental group; "History from the People Who Spoke It," first-person presentations of historical personages; "Issues in Health Care," a visit to the state legislature and presentations by noted health care officials; and "Travels in Kansas Prairie History, extended field trips to historic areas in Kansas."

There are two options available for the development of individual projects: an Honors Option with a regular class

Continues on Page 264

and an Honors Independent Study with a faculty mentor. Projects have included: an experiment on recombinant genetics; an experiment determining the source of particular odor in the carnivorous grasshopper mouse; a research project with emotionally disturbed children, a musical composition of a song; a creative writing project in short story; and computer-illustrated children's book.

Contact:
Bill Langley, Director
(316) 321-2222, ext. 139

Butler County Community College
901 South Haverhill
El Dorado, KS 67042
Total headcount enrollment-Credit: 7,151; Non-Credit: 2,903
Campuses/sites: 23; Full-time faculty: 103

UNITED STATES HISTORY SEMINAR

Through hands-on experiences, such as re-enactments, terrain walks and historical restoration projects, students become physically and emotionally involved in history

Through innovative living history techniques that complement existing traditional methods of teaching, Coffeyville Community College has revived interest in United States history – particularly regarding the Civil War. This revival was critical, after 40 years of declining student interest toward the field of history and a consequent lack of exposure to the many values that have nurtured the pioneer spirit of Americans.

The United States History Seminar Program was designed to:

1) develop the students' appreciation of past historical values;

2) enable students to use their own values and lifestyles when evaluating historical events;

3) show students the relevancy of history and the opportunity to use lessons learned in their own lives;

4) appeal to the total student population, history and non-history majors; and

5) show the students the importance of community service and the personal rewards of helping others.

Originating in 1970, the program has blended both traditional and non-traditional teaching strategies. Students continue to write research papers, conduct oral reports and negotiate reading lists. However, using the concept of living history, students are asked to use all of their senses to master Civil War history. Through hands-on experiences, such as Civil War re-enactments, terrain walks and historical restoration projects, students become physically and emotionally involved in the nation's history.

The United States History Seminar Program received state and national exposure for coordinating the resources of the states of Kansas and Connecticut during a dedication ceremony honoring the life and achievements of Prudence Crandall, a white educator from Connecticut who established the state's first school for black girls. Driven out of Connecticut for violating the "Black Laws," she settled in Elk Falls, Kansas, where she lived out the rest of her life. As a part of the Elk Falls project, the Seminar Class also restored an 1893 Pratt Truss Bridge, which spans the Elk River. Dr. Raymond Powers, Director of the Kansas Historical Museum, Topeka, Kansas, has recently nominated the restored bridge for publication in the Kansas Historical Register.

Since 1970, the United States History Seminar Program has received both state and national recognition for its many Civil War re-enactments and historical restoration projects, helping many small communities in Kansas develop tourism programs of their own. In addition, the program has generated 17 career United States military officer B-23 public school history instructors, five college history professors, two National Military park historians, and three museum curators. A video tape is available through Coffeyville Community College explaining this unique three-hour class.

Contact:
Frank Ortolani, Instructor-in-Charge
(316) 251-7700, ext. 2062

Coffeyville Community College
11th and Willow Streets
Coffeyville, KS 67337
Total head count enrollment-Credit: 2,008
Campuses/sites: 1; Full-time faculty: 72

RADIO BROADCASTING

Program graduates can write commercials, produce copy and news, work both a rotary board and slide board, and understand radio programming

Because no lecture or lab is better than the real thing, Colby Community College Radio Broadcasting students begin working with the department's state-of-the-art equipment immediately upon entering the program.

The philosophy of the department is that an education in broadcasting must contain both theory and practice. CCC utilizes lecture and the classroom experience to teach the theories of broadcasting. The department uses KTCC, 91.9 FM, to teach students the various skills and techniques they will need as members of the broadcasting industry.

The study of broadcasting is very exact and precise. Students who pursue such a career are expected to dedicate themselves to the discipline of working long hours and to use self-motivation to excel. The Radio Broadcasting program at CCC is centered around the working aspects of a radio station. The student graduating from CCC's Radio Broadcasting Department will be able to write commercials, produce copy and news, work both a rotary board and slide board, and understand the programming of a radio station.

The Radio Broadcasting Program at CCC is specifically designed for entry into the industry after graduation. The previous six years have granted CCC Radio students 100 percent placement. However, should a student wish to transfer to a four-year school, he/she may do so at various institutions throughout the state. It is recommended that the student know which school he/she plans on attending after graduation, and work up an articulation agreement to assure transferability of courses.

Contact:
Jon Burlew, Director
(913) 462-3984, ext. 282

Colby Community College
255 South Range
Colby, KS 67701
Total headcount enrollment-Credit: 2,628
Campuses/sites: 1; Full-time faculty: 70

PHYSICAL THERAPIST ASSISTANT PROGRAM

The curriculum is designed to be completed in four semesters and a summer

Students in the Physical Therapist Assistant Program at Colby Community College get clinical experience in health care facilities in Kansas and neighboring states. Such experience, coupled with other stringent requirements and a huge demand for PTAs, contributes to an enviable 100 percent placement rate of graduates.

The physical therapist assistant is required to work under the direction and supervision of the physical therapist. The physical therapist assistant may perform physical therapy procedures and related tasks that have been selected and delegated by the supervising physical therapist. Where permitted by law, the physical therapist assistant may also carry out routine operational functions, including supervision of the physical therapy aide or equivalent, and documentation of treatment progress. The ability of the physical therapist assistant to perform the selected and delegated tasks shall be assessed on an ongoing basis by the supervising physical therapist.

The Physical Therapist Assistant curriculum is designed to be completed in four semesters and a summer. All general courses are scheduled the first year (two semesters). Satisfactory completion of these courses is a prerequisite to being accepted for the second year. The second year is devoted entirely to professional courses. These two semesters are a mixture of lecture and laboratory sessions on campus and supervised clinical experiences. After completion of the fourth semester, an additional 12 weeks (mid-May to early August) of supervised clinical experience is required. A brief seminar class follows the summer clinicals.

Contact:
Pat Erickson, Director
(913) 462-3984, ext. 325

Colby Community College
255 South Range
Colby, KS 67701
Total headcount enrollment-Credit: 2,628
Campuses/sites: 1; Full-time faculty: 70

NON-DESTRUCTIVE TESTING

The program spans the technical aspect of Total Quality Assurance by teaching how to examine without affecting serviceability of a part

In the fall of 1992, Cowley County Community College and Area Vocational-Technical School implemented the state's first Non-destructive Testing associate degree program, a program that spans the technical aspect of Total Quality Assurance. Simply stated, a Non-destructive Testing (NDT) inspector examines a manufactured product without affecting the serviceability of the part. The NDT curriculum is designed to acquaint the student with the six major non-destructive testing disciplines:

1) radiography, the use of penetrating x or gamma radiation;
2) ultrasonic, the transmission of high-frequency sound waves;
3) eddy currents, electromagnetic testing using electrical currents;
4) magnetic particle, inducing a magnetic field within the test part;
5) liquid penetrate, coating the test part with a visible or fluorescent dye solution; and
6) visual examination, including the use of precision measuring instruments.

Cowley County Community College and Area Vocational-Technical School received $200,000 from the State of Kansas to implement the NDT program. Prior to program's establishment, Kansas businesses and industries recruited NDT inspectors from outside the state or trained them internally. In addition to the grant monies, Kansas businesses and industries donated well over $300,000 of technical equipment for use in the program.

The steering committee for the Non-destructive Testing program primarily comprises Level II and Level III NDT inspectors from the following companies: Beech Aircraft Corporation, The Boeing Company, Cessna Aircraft Company, GEC Precision, General Electric, Gordon-Piatt Energy Group, Grief Brothers, Rubbermaid, Total Petroleum, and the Air Capital Society of Non-destructive Testing. To ensure the integrity of the Non-destructive Testing program, committee members had direct input in curriculum development and equipment acquisitions.

The Non-destructive Testing curriculum is offered as an associate degree of applied science program, and requires the completion of 72 credit hours in the following areas: technical core courses, 27 credit hours; technical-related courses, 24 credit hours; integrated academic courses, 21 credit hours. The NDT curriculum is a two-year program designed to provide entry-level employment or transfer credit – or the courses can merge directly into other Industrial Technology programs such as Aircraft Airframe and Powerplant, Machine Tool Technology, Welding Technology, or the Quality Processes Improvement program.

Contact:
Charles White, Associate Dean, Vocational Education
(316) 442-0430, or (800) 592-CCCC

Cowley County Community College and Area Vocational-Technical School
25 South Second
Arkansas City, KS 67005
Total headcount enrollment-Credit: 3,200 Non-Credit: 400
Campuses/sites: 2 Full-time faculty: 46

TOTAL QUALITY MANAGEMENT/CONTINUOUS IMPROVEMENT

The college's rural setting has fostered a strong connection with the private sector and a more cooperative mindset throughout the community

Although some rural community colleges believe a lack of funds and equipment means they are not capable of all the wonderful programs and ideas presented in educational circles, Cowley County Community College and Area Vocational-Technical School uses its rural setting as an opportunity – an opportunity to integrate academic and technical programs. Additionally, new and strong connections between business/industry, government, retail and education have been established.

In 1991, a local industry leader came to share with Cowley County Community College's administration and faculty about the needs and desires of his industry. The concept of Total Quality Management/Continuous Improvement (TQM/CI) was mentioned. Discussions with business and industry ensued, resulting in the development of courses and programs to be offered. These were presented and approved by local business/industry, the college and State Board of Education.

During the same time frame, local business/industry and educational leaders began to establish a group referred to as a "Deming Users Group." The vision of this group was to share TQM/CI with the community, resulting in the development of a "world-class" work force and "world-class" communities. The college's desire is to touch every aspect of society with this concept, including one-person businesses, industries employing hundreds of workers, educational institutions and government agencies. Out of these beginnings a solid group of leaders from various parts of society has developed. They are now referred to as the TRQIN, Two Rivers Quality Improvement Network.

The unique thing is the community-wide commitment. There must be major changes in both the "attitude" and the "structure" of the organization or community to be able to implement and build ownership. Those changes are occurring through the TRQIN and the college's TQM/CI program. An area-wide endeavor toward a more cooperative, interactive mindset is developing. Cowley County Community College and a four-year private college 10 miles away share in hosting the monthly meetings. These breakfast meetings are attended by an average of 60 or more area leaders. The chair of the TRQIN is an instructor from Cowley County Community College.

The TRQIN works closely with the college's TQM/CI program. This allows for a constant interaction with many and various element of society to more quickly help meet the needs of this area. New lines of communication and a new spirit of cooperation have developed. The success of the TRQIN and the TQM/CI program has created interest from the executive branch of the state government. There is desire to implement the same approach in their offices.

The TQM/CI program has two sides. First is the structural side, which includes the tools and statistical applications. This allows the tracking and identification of process functioning. All technical programs include some aspect of this. A second and more difficult is the attitudinal side. Included are: human development, attitude development, critical thinking and problem-solving, teamwork, ethics, responsibility, and learning to be a thinking, functioning, "empowered" human being. The TQM/CI program addresses both of these areas. It is truly an integrated approach and requires constant crossing of the boundaries between academic and technical programs.

The rural setting has allowed a "cross functional" type approach to addressing possibilities for this school and area. This is beneficial to each person involved as well as to the entire area being served. The community and school have developed a more cooperative, interactive mindset. "Total Quality Management/Continuous Improvement" has become the approach to educational and area-wide opportunities.

Contact:
Jim Miesner, Instructor-in-Charge
(316) 442-8124/6925 or (800) 592-CCCC

Cowley County Community College and Area Vocational-Technical School
25 South Second
Arkansas City, KS 67005
Total headcount enrollment-Credit: 3,200 Non-Credit: 400
Campuses/sites: 2 Full-time faculty: 46

DONNELLY COLLEGE

ENTREPRENEUR TRAINING

⊠ *The program is designed to increase entrepreneurial capabilities of the poor* ⊠
and minorities and to improve potential for business development

During the past 15 to 20 years, small business development in America increased approximately 25 percent; during the same period, minority small business ownership decreased more than 60 percent. Lack of expertise, experience and access to start-up capital are seen as primary reasons for this disparity in growth patterns.

The Entrepreneur Training Program (ETP) at Donnelly College was designed to stimulate an increase in small business development through appropriate training, experience and support. More specifically, the goals of ETP are:

1) to provide minorities with the opportunity to develop skills in management, operations, sales marketing and other technologies required for successful business;

2) to organize and mobilize the human, technical and financial resource necessary to establish revenue-generating enterprise in which the participants are part owner; and

3) to organize a comprehensive support system (personal, academic, administrative, managerial) to "shelter" or incubate the enterprise during start-up and growth phase.

The program is designed to impact economic growth by increasing the entrepreneurial capabilities of the poor and minorities and improving the potential for new business development in the community. Students must complete academic requirement for an Associate in Applied Science Degree, learn business terminology, business development techniques and business operations concepts. Students learn to apply that knowledge in several steps:

1) During their first semester, they develop a business plan for an initial venture, a low-overhead, labor-intensive operation. The student operates the venture for eight weeks, after which the student

Continues on Page 268

and instructor complete a spot operation analysis to evaluate key result areas, i.e., goal and objectives, marketing, record keeping, experience, etc.

2) By the end of second semester, the student develops a complete plan for the actual "primary business" to operate after graduation.

3) Applications for funding start-up costs are made during the third semester.

After acquiring funding, they may start operations and run the venture from the program's small business incubator for the remaining year. Tutoring and academic support is provided, when needed, by Student Support Services of Donnelly College. Money to fund the student's initial venture start-up during the first semester is provided by Capital Investment Fund. The Venture Capital Assistance Fund provides support to help start a student's primary business. Profits from student's initial venture are maintained in this fund until needed.

The Small Business Incubator serves students enrolled in the program who are operating their initial and primary venture. The incubator provides a desk, phone, filing space, receptionist service, typewriter and computer use, fax service and business consultation service by instructor. In June 1989, Citicorp Financial Service contributed $1,000 to establish the Entrepreneur Training Program's Capital Investment Fund. In 1991, the Entrepreneur Training Program received an Economic Excellence Grant of $5,000 from Southwestern Bell Foundation to help train lower-income persons. The program has been spotlighted on several radio and television shows willing to inform the public through their media: "KC Concerns" on KCMO Radio, "Live Line" on KCXL Radio, and "Kansas City Live" on American Cablevision. Numerous articles and editorials have been written about the program; most notable was an editorial in the *Kansas City Kansan* praising the program. Jerome Toson, Director of the program, was recently featured in *Ingrams*, a highly regarded Kansas City business magazine.

Contact:
Jerome Toson
(913) 621 6070

Donnelly College
608 North 18th Street
Kansas City, KS 66102
Total headcount enrollment-Credit: 542; Non-Credit: 427
Campuses/sites: 1; Full-time faculty: 35

POVERTY INTERVENTION

The program helps students gain interview and assessment skills through courses and various social agencies

In cooperation with local churches, Donnelly College developed the Poverty Intervention program, which provides practical experience for students to learn how to understand and use the resources of an urban area in assisting low-income families. It consists of hands-on experience with low-income households emphasizing:

1) their interaction with "systems" in the city (employment, housing, legal, health care, utilities);

2) their use of "help" offered by churches, agencies and individuals; and

3) their potential for self-development.

The student will gain interview and assessment skills through preparation courses as well as access to the services of various social agencies (governmental, private and church-based), knowledge of unique resources of particular neighborhoods and churches, and methods of linking the poor with supportive "communities."

The course in Poverty Intervention utilizes a "seminar" approach. Primary content is generated by the student' presentations of case studies and verbatims from their home-visit and follow-up work with low-income households. Developing a supportive group dynamic and a high level of personal initiative and interaction is essential. Instruction in process and in content is included.

Class activities include: home visits verbatim and self-development case studies. Community resource people meet with the class to discuss how their agency or business operates relative to low-income persons. These include utility company customer service personnel, government-assistance providers, social agency staff, consumer credit counselors, and others dictated by issues raised in the class.

The program was developed in cooperation with local churches under the direction of the Foundation for Clinical Pastoral Education, a non-profit corporation founded to bring assistance to members of the community identified as being in need of self-help. Now in its infancy, the program has received limited acclaim except among local agencies and churches. Students who have an interest in social work find the program beneficial and rewarding.

Contact:
Terry Woodbury
(913) 621-6070

Donnelly College
608 North 18th Street
Kansas City, KS 66102
Total head count enrollment-Credit: 542; Non-Credit: 427
Campuses/sites: 1; Full-time faculty: 35

MUSIC PROGRAM

*▨ Voice and instrument students study in top facilities, give several ▨
performances annually and excel at competions*

Hutchinson Community College students enjoy significant community support, making it one of the strongest music programs in the state and, possibly, the nation. The music program is among the college's oldest programs and today includes choral music, concert and pep band and jazz.. There are four factors that account for the success of the HCC music program:

1) the quality of the instruction and directors of the various programs;
2) the quality of the facilities;
3) the amount of money raised for scholarships; and
4) the number of performances given each year by the groups.

The choral music program at Hutchinson Community College has been in existence for more than 60 years. There are three ensembles which make up the Choral Music Program. They are the Concert Choir (60 students), the Chamber Choir (24 students), and the Vocal Jazz Ensemble (15 students). Combined, these groups perform a total of 50 annual performances. In 1992, the Concert Choir was selected to perform at the Kansas Music Educators Association state convention, being the first community college concert choir to perform there in nearly 21 years.

The bands of HCC are a source of great pride for the prestigious universities in the Midwest. In 1992, the HCC band program placed more students in the Kansas All Community College Honor Band than any other Kansas community college. HCC band students are also well-represented each year in the Kansas Intercollegiate Band at the Kansas Bandmasters Convention, placing more students than most four-year universities. The bands are their own best recruiters, as they perform for local area high schools on a regular basis. The band membership is about 60 for each band. The HCC pep band is one of the largest and most recognized groups of all the ensembles, performing for more than 100,000 sport fans each year. All band students (as well as faculty) play in the Pep Band and receive scholarship money for their efforts.

The Hutchinson Community College Jazz Program was started in 1975 and began its 19th year during the 1993-94 school year under Jazz Studies Director, Mr. Bryce Luty. Mr. Luty has been responsible for the program since its inception and during his tenure, has raised the program to national prominence. The Number One Jazz Ensemble has been invited to perform at several national and international events. In 1977 the band was invited to perform at the Southwest/Northcentral Division of Music Education National conference in Kansas City; in 1978 performed at the National MENC Conference in Chicago; and in 1991 was invited to perform as the community college representative at the International Association of Jazz Educators Conference in Washington, D.C.

The Number One Jazz Ensemble makes from 25 to 30 performances each school year. Included in their concert schedule are a fall and spring tour to high schools throughout the state, various business and service club performances at the local, state and national level, and three formal concerts (fall, winter and spring) on the campus of HCC. Guest artists of national and international fame are invited to participate with the jazz groups on the formal concerts given on the HCC campus. Some of these artists performing in concert with the HCC Jazz Ensembles include Louie Bellson, Bob Brookmeyer, Pete Christlieb, Buddy DeFranco, Jon Faddis, The Four Freshmen, Urbie Green, Rich Matteson, Don Menza, Ed Shaughnessy, Bobby Show, Lew Soloff, Clark Terry (on three different occasions), and a host of other well-known artists in the jazz world.

The community supports this program very well and each year raises around $8,000 to provide $400 scholarships to 20 young musicians who audition and are selected to perform in the Number One Jazz Ensemble.

Contact:
Dee Connett
(316) 665-3500

Hutchinson Community College
1300 North Plum
Hutchinson, KS 67501
Total head count enrollment-Credit: 4,508; Non-Credit: 53
Campuses/sites: 1; Full-time faculty: 100

LEARNING STRATEGIES PROGRAM

Students earned better grades in the courses to which they applied strategies than did non-strategies students

Initially designed to meet the needs of special learners, the Learning Strategies Program proved so successful it was redesigned for the entire Johnson County Community College student population.

It began in the early 1980's grounded in the Learning Strategies Program developed at the Kansas University Institute for Research on Learning Disabilities. The program initially included one instructor and a small number of students who had received academic support services in high school. The results of the initial effort were noteworthy enough to attract the attention of college administrators, who asked that a pilot study be conducted to determine the effectiveness of Learning Strategies for the general student population. The results of the pilot were encouraging and a formal evaluation study was conducted in 1985-86. Again the results were positive: students who took Learning Strategies courses earned a letter grade higher in the courses to which they applied strategies and had GPAs averaging one grade point higher than non-strategies students. This GPA difference was maintained during the subsequent semesters that the students remained at JCCC.

Learning Strategies courses offer students the opportunity to learn and master cognitive and metacognitive skills through practice with feedback on relevant content material. A total of eight different courses are offered: College Learning Methods (3 credits), Strategic Learning System, Memory Strategies, Exam Strategies, Learning Strategies for Math, Textbook Strategies, Lecture Notes Strategies, and Learning Strategies for Career Programs (1 credit each). All of these courses count for credit toward the Associates degree offered at JCCC. The program maintains a research component for regular assessment of its effectiveness; revisions are made as needed.

The instructional methodology used in Learning Strategies courses consists of an eight-step process:

1) assessment of student study practices;
2-3) description and modeling of the strategy;
4) evaluation of learner comprehension of the strategy;
5) guided group practice;
6) independent practice with individual feedback;
7-8) mastery and generalization of the strategy.

Learning Strategies classes frequently are paired with "content" classes (such as psychology or history) so that students can take a Learning Strategies course geared specifically to that content; this facilitates a higher level of thinking in class discussion and group practice.

The Learning Strategies Program has grown to include two full-time and six adjunct instructors who teach approximately 600 students in the various Learning Strategies courses offered each semester. It has received local and national recognition, including being named in 1988 by the League for Innovation in the Community College as one of the most innovative programs identified in that organization's 20-year history.

Contact:
Dick Scott, Program Director, Speech, Lang. & Academic Enhancement
(913) 469-8500, ext. 3904

Johnson County Community College
12345 College Boulevard
Overland Park, KS 66210
Total headcount enrollment-Credit: 15,710; Non-Credit: 20,000
Campuses/sites: 1; Full-time faculty: 256

FIRE SCIENCE

The program addresses real-world needs of employed and aspiring fire service personnel and represents a model for interagency cooperation

Much of the Fire Science curriculum at Johnson County Community College has been made available on a self-paced study and telecourse basis to accommodate already-employed fire service personnel, serving as a model for a variety of career programs. The Fire Science program provides pre-employment training for men and women seeking careers in the fire service field, specialized study leading to required professional certifications, and an Associate of Arts degree that supports fire agencies' educational incentive plans and standards for promotion.

Developed in cooperation with fire departments, certification boards and other regional educational providers, this comprehensive program addresses real-world needs of employed and aspiring fire service personnel and represents a model for interagency planning and cooperation. Using full-time faculty to teach both the credit and non-credit courses, the program places equal weight on career preparation and continuing professional education.

At the entry level, aspiring fire service candidates complete a Firefighter I non-credit certificate program consisting of an Essentials of Firefighting course that results in Firefighter I level certification recognized by the Kansas Fire Safety Training Authority, and an EMS First Responder course that prepares them for the Kansas Board of EMS examination and certification – a credential required of all personnel who staff ambulance or rescue vehicles. Additionally, they must complete three courses on recognition of, properties of and response to hazardous materials. These courses satisfy National Fire Protection Administration requirements and yield Kansas State Emergency Response Council certification. Firefighter I certificate holders thus bring to their applications for fire service jobs the requisite training that departments otherwise would have to provide early on in their tenure. Thus, program graduates are greatly advantaged in the selection process.

While the Firefighter I certificate courses are given in non-credit formats primarily to service the entire Kansas City area, they can be credited as technical electives in the Associate of Arts Fire Service Administration degree through the college's advanced standing process. The focus of this degree is on education for management and command rather than duplicative "hose and ladder" training provided by fire departments. The curriculum emphasizes management principles, fire administration, codes and law, tactics and strategies, as well as a strong general education component that supports pursuance of a baccalaureate degree. The Johnson County Fire Chiefs Association had a major role in shaping the curriculum, and its members have agreed to integrate the degree into their educational incentive plans and standards for promotion. Technical electives can also be satisfied through courses available under a cooperative agreement between area college's fire science programs.

This is truly a program designed with the needs of fire science personnel and agencies in mind and it could well serve as a model for a variety of career programs.

Contact:
Bill Benjamin, Instructor
(913) 469-8500, ext. 3360

Johnson County Community College
12345 College Boulevard
Overland Park, KS 66210
Total head count enrollment-Credit: 15,710; Non-Credit: 20,000
Campuses/sites: 1; Full-time faculty: 256

PRATT COMMUNITY COLLEGE/AREA VOCATIONAL SCHOOL

CAREER MOBILITY LP-AD NURSING

Program facilities include a large lecture room, skills laboratories equipped with mannequins and simulators as well as computers with state-of-the-art software

The Career Mobility LP-AD Nursing Program at Pratt Community College/Area Vocational School is a bi-level program that prepares students for the nursing profession at the licensed practical or registered nurse (AD) level.

The program, which consistently has had a waiting list of students from a seven-county area, was both initiated and accredited by the Kansas State Board of Nursing in 1982. A decade later, it was accredited by the National League for Nursing, which selected it to be the state test site for one of the league's newest computer programs.

The college prepares nurses who provide services that vary in scope and complexity accourting to the educational and clinical experiences of the practitioner. The services provided by nurses vary in scope and complexity according to the educational preparation and clinical experience of the practitioner. The LPN is prepared to give supportive and restorative care under the direction of a registered nurse or a person licensed to practice medicine or dentistry. LPNs generally function in acute care or long-term facilities. They can perform nursing tasks with precision, safety and efficiency. On entry into practice, the AD Registered Nurse is capable of performing safely and effectively in a specific role. The AD nurse is prepared to give skilled bedside nursing care to patients with common and recurring (chronic) general conditions within the framework of established and structured acute and/or long-term care settings.

The purpose of the program at PCC/AVS is to academically and clinically prepare those individuals who are capable of a career as an LPN or as an RN at the Associate Degree level. The nursing faculty is dedicated to providing a high-quality, comprehensive nursing program designed to serve the educational needs of the college's service area and to provide high-quality, well-educated nurses for health-care facilities.

The graduate of the Associate of Applied Science in Nursing will: function as a safe, knowledgeable, competent provider of nursing care; use appropriate communication with and about patients, families and other health care personnel; teach patients and families appropriate information concerning wellness and illness; manage patient care for a group of patients in an acute or long-term care facility; and demonstrate behaviors which show an awareness of being a member of the nursing profession.

The nursing program at PCC/AVS offers the student

Continues on Page 272

several opportunities to complete his/her nursing education. A student may choose to complete one year of nursing classes, which results in eligibility to sit for the NCLEX-PN exams in October. Upon completion of the summer LPN option class, the student may choose to complete the second year of nursing education classes and receive the Associate Degree of Applied Science in Nursing, taking the NCLEX-RN exams in July or elect to complete the first two semesters of nursing classes, skip the summer LPN course, and continue the next fall and spring semesters to complete the associate degree. A qualified student who is already an LPN may also enter the second year of nursing classes to obtain the associate degree.

The practical nurse program includes two 10-credit-hour and one four-credit-hour nursing classes which consist of 244 theory clock hours and 456 lab/clinical clock hours. In addition to these classes, the student must take the required general education classes, which include an additional 22 credit hours (306 theory hours and 136 lab hours).

The associate degree program includes four 10-credit-hour nursing classes which consist of 408 theory clock hours and 768 lab/clinical clock hours. The general education courses required for the associate degree include an additional 29 credit hours which comprise 423 theory hours and 136 lab hours. For those students who are LPNs entering the second year of nursing classes, an additional three credit hour (45 theory hours) "bridge" course is required the summer prior to entrance.

The facilities for the nursing program include a large lecture room, three skills laboratories equipped with mannequins and up-to-date simulators as well as student computers with state-of-the-art software. The students also utilize the community's hospital and long-term care facilities as well as St. Francis Regional Medical Center and HCA Wesley Medical Center in Wichita, Kansas, for their clinical rotations.

The Kansas State Board of Nursing allows this program to enroll a maximum of 30 freshmen and 30 sophomore students each year. The majority of students are from the seven-county area that the college services, but a few have been from out of state (including one student from Hawaii).

Since its implementation, at least 75 students have completed the Practical Nursing Program. A 100 percent passage rate has been obtained by the students who have taken their state board exams.

At least 157 students have completed the Associate Degree Nursing Program. The overall passing percentage rate (including those who repeated the exam) on the NCLEX-RN boards for the Pratt Community College/Area Vocational School ADN program is 99 percent.

The LP-AD Nursing Program can boast of a 100 percent placement rate. The average starting salary of the 1991 graduates is $12.25 per hour. Many of our graduates are employed in the seven-county area serviced by the college, but several are on staff at major health care facilities in large, metropolitan areas across the United States.

Contact:
Carolyn Banks, Director
(316) 672-5641, ext. 233

Pratt Community College/Area Vocational School
Highway 61
Pratt, KS 67124
Total head count enrollment-Credit: 3,476
Campuses/sites: 5; Full-time faculty: 43

PRATT COMMUNITY COLLEGE/AREA VOCATIONAL SCHOOL

ELECTRIC POWER DISTRIBUTION

Several industry representatives serve on the program advisory committee and help provide new equipment and instructional materials

The Electric Power Distribution program at Pratt Community College/Area Vocational School has developed a sound reputation across Kansas and surrounding states, drawing students from as far as Alaska. Successful placement with employers and constant demand for graduates have resulted in a two-year waiting list of students interested in entering the program.

Such a program might have been difficult to implement before 1983, when Pratt Community College was formally approved as an Area Vocational School. The unique combination of a community college and AVS provides students flexibility in obtaining career goals. Designated occupational programs are designed to allow a student an

opportunity to receive an occupational certificate or an associate degree. The employment potential, student interest and industry support are essential for the success and continuation of the program.

In 1984, PCC/AVS established a program for students to receive training in electric power distribution. The program is one of only two in Kansas and has been a success in providing trained line workers for rural electric cooperatives, municipalities and major utility providers.

The instructional program consists of 32 credit hours of on-campus training and a 10-credit-hour occupational work experience block. The on-campus curriculum includes specific skill training in setting, framing and staking poles; installation and maintenance of lines, meters and transformers; climbing poles; and digger and basket truck operations and rescues. Instruction in electrical theory, system design, and first aid and personal safety is integrated with a mathematics, industrial relations and communications curriculum. Upon successful completion of the 42-credit-hour program the student is awarded an occupational certificate. Successful completion of 22 additional hours in general education degree requirements and coursework in electronics, computer-aided drafting and business entitle the student to an associate of applied science degree.

Since the implementation of the program more than 150 students have successfully obtained the certificate, and more than 400 additional utility workers have participated in workshops and seminars held on the campus and training centers. A placement rate exceeding 95 percent is consistent within the graduating class. The 1991 graduates obtained an average starting salary of $8.50 per hour.

Facilities include a lecture classroom, indoor shop, a 15-acre outdoor training center, a digger truck, trencher and a basket truck. Several industry representatives serve on the program advisory committee and regularly assist in providing new instructional materials, demonstration equipment, employment leads and other means of support.

Contact:
Mike Brooks, Instructor
(316) 672-5641, ext. 119

Pratt Community College/Area Vocational School
Highway 61
Pratt, KS 67124
Total head count enrollment-Credit: 3,476
Campuses/sites: 5; Full-time faculty: 43

SEWARD COUNTY COMMUNITY COLLEGE

GLASSBLOWING IN A COMMUNITY COLLEGE: A COOPERATIVE APPROACH

The impact on students is significant as they experience one of the great historic art forms that, unfortunately, is dying out

A Glassblowing program has served as a bridge of cooperation between Seward County College and Liberal High School and is helping preserve a waning art form.

The program was conceived in the spring of 1991, when Mike Stearman, art instructor at Seward County Community College, and Chuck Watson, an art instructor at Liberal High School, began developing and implementing a college-level course in glassblowing. Since the college did not have equipment necessary to offer the class but the high school did, the course would have to be taught on the high school campus. Stearman and Watson approached the appropriate administrators at both sites concerning their proposal and received hearty support. That summer the course was submitted to the Academic Affairs Council of Seward County Community College and to the Kansas State Department of Education for approval, which was soon granted. A contract was drawn up between the two educational entities, granting compensation to the high school at the rate of $10 per credit hour to cover the cost of fuel and consumable materials and setting forth other significant parameters. The course was offered in the fall of 1991 and again in the spring of 1992, with approximately seven students enrolled in each of the two semesters. Mr. Watson, the resident expert in glassblowing, served as the teacher.

At present the impact of the program is limited and hard to assess. Certainly the program may be a beginning point for further cooperation. SCCC may be the only community college that offers a class in glass blowing, and only one of the regent schools in Kansas (Emporia State) offers the class. Of course the impact on students must be significant as they experience "up close and hot" one of the great historic art forms that, unfortunately, is dying out.

The course has two goals:

1) to enable students to understand the chemical properties of glass, its historic uses and its properties as a creative medium; and

2) after lecture, demonstration and actual experimentation, to afford students the opportunity to plan and produce functional and/or nonfunctional art works from molten glass, using ancient handling methods and decorative techniques.

The course was implemented through the creative dialogue of two artists and the cooperative spirit of community college and high school administrators.

Expenses occurred for the class are partially covered by a $30-per-student supply fee along with the usual tuition fees for college classes at SCCC.

Human and academic resources are most valuable to the program. Liberal is fortunate to have such gifted artists as Chuck Watson and Mike Stearman, who are both willing to

Continues on Page 274

share their talents and to work together. Chuck has developed a high school blown glass program, which is one of only two in the state of Kansas (the other is offered by Emporia High School.) Liberal is also fortunate to have a school system and a college that are willing to work together in ways the mutually enhance their perspective programs.

The blown glass program has received local recognition, being highlighted in the local paper, the *Southwest Daily Times*, soon after the class was implemented.

Contact:
Michael Stearman
(316) 624-1951, ext. 685

Seward County Community College
Box 1137
Liberal, KS 67905-1137
Total headcount enrollment-Credit: 1,519
Campuses/sites: 1;Full-time faculty: 48

SWINE MANAGEMENT COOPERATIVE PROGRAM

Graduates could be employed in a wide array of swine production positions, including swine herdsman and swine farm manager

Hands-on experience helps give Seward County Community College students an edge in the fast-growing swine management industry, which needs qualified personnel with the latest technology and management skills. Students are required to take an "internship" in a swine confinement unit to have a realistic perspective of the day-to-day responsibilities of swine production.

The swine management program grew out of a business/industry need of DEKALB Swine Breeders, Inc., located at Plains, Kansas. SCCC and DEKALB Swine Breeders, Inc., worked together to develop a career training option to the Agriculture program that is designed to develop personnel for entry into supervisory and production positions in the swine industry.

A special admission process is required of students because of the nature of the program. In addition, all students accepted into the program are provided a full scholarship (room/board/tuition/fees/books) by DEKALB Swine Breeders, Inc.

The students spend the first week of the first semester in orientation to the program.

The curriculum is designed to develop a student's management and production skills and the ability to utilize the latest technological skills available in the swine industry. This is accomplished by providing classes with "hands-on" experiences in a modern swine confinement operation. The program teaches current technology in animal science, livestock nutrition, swine anatomy, health and production, and agricultural economics essential to swine production.

The students are required to complete 64 credit hours – 18 credit hours of general education for an Associate in Applied Science degree; 28 credit hours of required swine management courses; 18 credit hours of agriculture electives from a designated list.

Students who complete the program could be employed in a wide array of swine production positions, including swine herdsman and swine farm manager.

The swine management instructors at SCCC are provided to the college by DEKALB. DEKALB has assigned two full-time employees to the responsibility of teaching the courses scheduled at DEKALB. In addition, the college's agriculture program coordinator assists in the teaching of this program on campus. First-year students are on campus during the morning and spend the afternoon at DEKALB. Second-year students will spend the morning at the "lab" at DEKALB and the afternoon and evening on campus.

The program enrollment can accommodate only 24 students (12 in the first year class and 12 in the second year class). The program has not required any major investment due to the "living lab" at DEKALB.

The program has been featured in the major pork industry periodicals as well as trade shows, including the World Pork Expo at Des Moines, IA.

Contact:
Michael Schwab
(316) 624-1951, ext. 637

Seward County Community College
Box 1137
Liberal, KS 67905-1137
Total headcount enrollment-Credit: 1,519
Campuses/sites:1; Full-time faculty: 48

RE-ENTRY PROGRAM

An applied Life Skills Lab provides special population students with sequential structuring of occupational choice and applied learning techniques

The Re-Entry Program at Ashland Community College prepares displaced homemakers, single parents, students with disabilities and the disadvantaged for college and employment.

Transitional preparatory services, funded through Single Parent/Homemaker set-asides in the Carl D. Perkins Act of 1990, include career assessment and guidance, counseling, and special programs implemented to meet specific needs in areas such as pre-enrollment/pre-employment skills, study skills/test anxiety, and non-traditional career paths. The Re-Entry Program also sponsors O.A.S.I.S. (Once Again Students in School), a student organization, and a variety of gender-equity seminars. An outreach component takes these services throughout ACC's five-county service area. Mileage and child care reimbursements are available to eligible participants.

Services for all students pursuing technical majors are funded by Perkins Act grants for support of special populations in post-secondary education, with emphasis on ensuring gender equity and the equitable integration of vocational and academic education. Recently, an applied Life Skills Lab has been developed to provide special population students with sequential structuring of occupational choice and applied learning techniques.

Re-Entry Program funding through JTPA and JOBS grants as well as the Carl D. Perkins Act totaled nearly $500,000 for the 1991-92 academic year, a 51 percent increase over the previous year. Special populations funding provided services for 1,572 students, including direct support to more than 200 handicapped students, and also provided for microcomputer laboratory equipment, instructional materials, and faculty development activities related to the support of special populations in post secondary education.

Through the Re-Entry Program, disadvantaged students have a variety of opportunities to develop academic and occupational skills needed to become more competitive, and more successful, in both the college setting and the work force of the future.

Contact:
Louise Shytle Program Coordinator
(606) 329-2999, ext. 301

Ashland Community College
1400 College Drive,
Ashland, KY 41101
Total head count enrollment-Credit: 3,267; Non-Credit: 1,546
Campuses/sites: 5; Full-time faculty: 70

ACADEMIC SUCCESS PROGRAM

Main components are required participation, enhancement of skills and development of a faculty/counseling Academic Success Team

The Academic Success Program at Ashland Community College is a multi-step effort to improve student retention and achievement. This is done by strengthening ACC's system of assessment, placement and support for all students, especially those with skills deficiencies, and by providing ongoing program assessment and evaluation.

Initiated in 1991, the program's main components are:

1) required participation in assessment and placement for first-time students;

2) consolidation and enhancement of the existing developmental skills services and facilities; and

3) development of a faculty/counseling Academic Success Team.

All first-time degree-seeking students are now required to participate in ASSET screening for college readiness in mathematics, English composition and other disciplines, and ASSET or Nelson-Denny testing of reading proficiency. Students whose assessment scores indicate weaknesses in one or more basic skills areas or whose reading levels below a 12th-grade equivalent are assigned to the Academic Success Program for advising, placement in developmental courses as indicated, career planning assistance, referral to other resources, and ongoing counseling and support. Faculty are encouraged to refer other students who might benefit from the program, with Success Program staff providing faculty with feedback on the outcomes of their referrals.

Operating out of new classrooms and labs in the Learning Resources Center, the Academic Success Program has a core staff of four developmental English/Reading instructors, a developmental mathematics instructor and a counselor. This "Academic Success Team" works with an advisory network of additional faculty,

Continues on Page 276

representatives from all academic divisions, and the Coordinators of the JTPA/Re-Entry and the Student Support Services programs to establish additional services as needed.

In addition to providing a screening method, ASSET results will permit comparison of student entry skills and achievement levels with a large, national community college sample. Reassessment of skills at the point each student is ready to proceed into college level courses will be a part of the institution's evaluation of the Academic Success Program's impact on academic achievement.

By creating an inter-divisional support network and by consolidating and relocating existing mathematics and English/reading laboratories, the Academic Success Program strengthens ACC's ability to serve students with basic skills deficits. While some of these components are not new, organization into a operational unit will allow better tracking of students enrolling with basic skill deficits and increase the likelihood of the institution meeting their unique academic needs.

Contact:
Barbara Nicholls, Program Coordinator, (606) 329-2999, ext. 571
Louise Shytle, Program Coordinator, (606) 329-2999, ext. 301

Ashland Community College
1400 College Drive,
Ashland, KY 41101
Total head count enrollment-Credit: 3,267; Non-Credit: 1,546
Campuses/sites: 5;Full-time faculty: 70

WORK FORCE TRAINING

Local, statewide and national training has been delivered, helping to grow award-winning local plants

The growing global economy and our customers' increasing demands for quality of goods and services have brought about high levels of demand for work force training – demands that Elizabethtown Community College is eager and prepared to meet. The college's Office of Business & Industry grows partnerships with business and serves as a center for economic development in this rural section of Central Kentucky.

In the fall of 1986, the funded full-time position of Business & Industry Liaison was created in an otherwise self-funded department. From its beginning with Basic Supervision and Statistical Process Control, the department has grown to more than 30 training curriculums in the Total Quality area. The department has grown non-credit classes to meet the training requests of employers. Non-credit classes include, but are not limited to:
•Statistical Process Control;
•Just In Time;
•Quick Changeover;
•Materials Requirement Planning;
•Design of Experiments;
•Coaching Skills;
•Performance Management;
•Quality Interpersonal Communications;

•Implementing Total Quality;
•Changing Roles of Managers; and
•Team Development.

New curriculums are quickly added as needs and competencies are identified.

During the first semester of service, two companies and approximately 200 trainees were served. Today more than 3,500 participants and more than 70 companies are provided a wide range of services each year. Beginning with basic skills assessments and the design of skills development programs, through training to consulting in organizational culture change, the college has grown curriculums and personnel to meet the challenge. Local, state-wide and national training has been delivered, helping to grow award-winning local plants, recognized as the benchmark in their field.

The faculty are both adjunct and from the credit program. The college's structure and reporting system have fostered this blend, which has subsequently developed support from the faculty for new credit programs in Total Quality. While individual classes have existed for several years, a full two-year curriculum in Quality is in development.

Contact:
Shannon Whelan, Business & Industry Liaison
(502) 769-2371

Elizabethtown Community College
600 College Street Road
Elizabethtown, KY 42701
Total head count enrollment-Credit: 4,316; Non-Credit: 1,145
Campuses/sites: 5;Full-time faculty: 68

VENTURE PROGRAM

Designed to ease a new faculty member's transition, the year-long program includes mentoring and exposure to the Appalachian culture

Hazard Community College experienced a 300 percent growth in students since 1986 and a similar growth of its faculty ranks. But given the college's philosophy to advertise nationally in order to hire the best and brightest instructors, many faculty arrive to this Appalachian campus and region with scant knowledge of the area, its culture and the college. So Ron Reed, Assistant Professor of English, was charged to create a program which would inculcate faculty into the college arena.

Integral to this orientation/learning process was an emphasis upon five areas:

1) a system that relied heavily on mentoring from veteran faculty;

2) a program that increased self-awareness on the part of new faculty;

3) a process that would lead to a smoother transition into the region and the college;

4) a procedure that promoted more extensive knowledge and a growing appreciation for the Appalachian culture; and

5) a program that was year-long in scope. Support for the program was given by the Community College System, the administration, and the faculty.

A mission statement was created, mentors were selected, and a semester-long program was put in place. Several workshops on planning, teaching, the college's goals and effectiveness were conducted. New faculty were taken on a tour of the area, including lunch provided by the new ARH Hospital. The Myers-Briggs Personality Indicator was used to pair veteran faculty with new faculty. Both groups participated in a full day's workshop on the Myers-Briggs Inventory.

A mentoring workshop was held to provide mentors with guidelines for their upcoming meetings. It was decided that the September meeting would focus on the new faculty member's adjustment to the area. The October meeting would focus on the faculty member's work with students. The November meeting would concentrate on faculty evaluation, and the December meeting be scheduled as a summary of the first semester's experience. The mentors also decided to put together a pot-luck Thanksgiving luncheon for their partners the Tuesday before Thanksgiving.

A third component of the Venture Program was the emphasis on social gatherings. Venture participants were taken to a nearby mountain-top retreat where they were taught square dancing by the local people. An October retreat to Natural Bridge State Park occupied one Saturday. In October as well the group was taken to see *As You Like It*, as performed by the North Carolina Repertory Company. All these social occasions were planned as ways for entire families to meet and enjoy each other. Free Family memberships to the Performing Arts Series were given to each mentor and earner. During the second semester several informal teas and discussions served as ways to bring the new faculty together for a few moments away from their harried schedules.

The mentors and their partners turned in each month very brief summations of their meetings. These summations indicated that the partners felt very comfortable with one another and that the mentoring relationship was a positive learning influence. At year end, when the faculty (both mentor and partner) summed up the program, they spoke of how much they had learned during the year.

All the Venture faculty were given much to read. Passed out and discussed over the course of the year were excerpts from *Night Comes to the Cumberlands*; *The Southern Highlander and His Homestead*; *A Report of the Shakertown Roundtable Conference*; *Building Communities: A Vision for a New Century*; *A Summary of Selected National Data Pertaining to Community, Technical, and Junior Colleges*; Scott Willis' article "The Complex Art of Motivating Students;" a *Lexington Herald Leader* guide to Kentucky's Fall Festivals; and a faculty inventory titled *Seven Principles for Good Practice in Undergraduate Education*.

The Venture Program, then, started out as a method for orienting new faculty by providing mentoring, social occasions, and various seminars and workshops. Very little money was used in the program, so the program is financially feasible in most any college. The key concepts - mentoring, increased self-awareness of teaching and learning, socializing with care for both the new faculty member and her or his family, and seminars devoted to providing information in an efficient manner - underscore the success of this program. As a result of Venture, no turnover in faculty among mentors or new faculty occurred. Faculty report they were glad to know that someone cared specifically about them and their success. Families quickly became immersed into the local culture and felt comfortable sooner. Students received the benefit of learning from scholars who were more at ease.

Contact:
Ron Reed, Program Coordinator/Assistant Professor of English
(606) 436-5721

Hazard Community College
1 Community College Drive
Hazard, KY 4l701-2402
Total head count enrollment-Credit: 1,776; Non-Credit: 10,000
Campuses/sites: 5;Full-time faculty: 67

THE 50 MILE CLUB: A PROGRAM FOR WELLNESS

The object of the employee wellness program is to accumulate at least 50 miles of exercise – including walking, biking and aerobics – over a 50-day period

From the White House and Fortune 500 companies to industry and through academics an overwhelming amount of responsible research has demonstrated the need to make individual health a priority. Numerous and successful are institutional wellness programs that promote health activities.

As educators, we devote considerable time to our respective occupational skills. While we reflect on accomplishments in our fields, what of our individual time is centered around health activities? Armed with the documented studies from business and university alike, it is overtly apparent that we should be concerned about high blood pressure, heart disease, sodium intake and calorie counting.

In a concerted effort to promote a program of wellness (while having some fun) Hazard Community College has instituted an effective wellness program entitled "The 50 Mile Club." The object is to accumulate 50 (or more) miles over a 50-day period. How the 50 or more miles is attained is up to the participant. Activities such as biking, jogging or walking are calculated in true miles. Other events such as aerobics, tennis, weight training or racquetball are converted from a 1/2-hour to one mile equivalent. For example, playing 1-1/2 hours of tennis would equal 2-1/2 miles earned.

Each participant charts his or her progress on their own and turns in their mile sheets by 5 p.m. on the final day. Those participants completing at least 50 miles are recognized at an end of-semester awards ceremony with a T-shirt. Additionally, the man and woman accumulating the most miles will be awarded a plaque which reads: "HCC's Outstanding Athlete - Wellness Champ 19__"

The 50 Mile Club is open to all employees at the college, and the participation and results have been very impressive. One woman, a regular smoker, began walking an average of 3-1/2 miles a day. She won the women's division by racking up 162 miles!

Hazard Community College opens up its 50 Mile Club during each semester. We truly believe this self-paced program is a fun way of promoting health awareness while reaffirming that enthusiasm for one's existing activity – so it is our motto: "Come out, join the 50 Mile Club, and complement that strong mind with a healthy body!"

Contact:
Reid Mackin, Instructor of Speech and Communications
(606) 436-5721

Hazard Community College
1 Community College Drive
Hazard, KY 4l701-2402
Total head count enrollment-Credit: 1,776; Non-Credit: 10,000
Campuses/sites: 5;Full-time faculty: 6

EDUCATIONAL ENRICHMENT

This work force training program for business and industry includes union, management and a newly formed Labor Management Committee

The Henderson Community College Adult Learning Center (ALC), besides providing adult basic education, also offers work place classes that have served as a model for the rest of the state. The classes provided through the Educational Enrichment Program for business and industry are a true partnership with union, management, a newly formed Labor Management Committee and HCC.

The financial obligation for this program is divided among the union, management and Labor Management Committee; the ALC provides the expertise and instruction. All classes are held at union halls or plant sites. Approximately 410 employees have been at eight plant locations. The ALC opened in 1987, with money provided through a grant from the Kentucky Department of Education, Henderson Community College (HCC), which is a part of the University of Kentucky Community College System. Besides the work place literacy and adult basic education, the Center provides GED, upgraded skills, literacy and English As a Second Language (ESL) to adults in the community who are lacking basic skills or high school credentials. The ALC serves more than 1,100 students each year; the staff has grown from two instructors in 1987 to 12 part-time and full-time employees today. Services are provided in 14 off-campus locations; the Center on campus is open 50-1/2-hours each week.

The Educational Enrichment Program has received the

following awards: the Kentucky Association for Adult and Continuing Education presented the college awards for "Outstanding Supervisor in Adult Education" and "Outstanding Coordinator of Continuing Education" and the Kentucky Office of Adult Education Services awarded the program at Alcan Aluminum Company the "Outstanding Adult Education Workplace Program."

Contact:
Sandra Walters, Supervisor, Adult Learning Center
(502) 827-1867, ext. 270

Henderson Community College
2660 South Green Street
Henderson, KY 42420
Total head count enrollment-Credit: 1,462; Non-Credit: 1,685
Campuses/sites: 1;Full-time faculty: 48

JEFFERSON COMMUNITY COLLEGE

RECRUITMENT AND RETENTION PROJECT

A unified approach to retention covers everything from pre-enrollment to the post-class phase

In the spring of 1978, Jefferson Community College faced the possibility of a decline in enrollment. While this decline was short-term (Jefferson increases enrollment by approximately 10 percent each year), the possibility of a decline forced the college to begin discussing issues of retention from the students' point of view. The resulting student-based Recruitment and Retention Project has four major components:

1) pre-enrollment phase, which includes examination of the college's image, a review of public relations efforts, an examination of recruitment activities, and an analysis of campus appearances;

2) campus enrollment phase, which focuses on improving and extending orientation practices and advising programs, streamlining registration processes, and determining processes whereby the college can reduce its "no-show" rates;

3) class attendance phase, which focuses on classroom policies and procedures for clarity and student understanding, the reasons why students do not complete courses for which they enroll, and the improvement of teaching techniques; and

4) post-class phase, which focuses on ways to bring students back to the college each semester and on appropriate support for students on probation or suspension.

This approach to retention efforts has provided the college with a unified structure with which to examine each segment of the college in terms of its contribution to student retention and its inter-relatedness to other segments.

In the spring of 1988, the college marked its first 10 years with the Recruitment and Retention project in operation. Results of the project include:

1) improved classroom teaching;
2) improved semester-to-semester retention rates;
3) more course completions;
4) expanded developmental course selections;
5) needs-based faculty/staff development;
6) more efficient orientation, advising, counseling and registration;
7) improved administration and management;
8) improved public relations and image;
9) substantial cost savings; and
10) campus beautification.

Contact:
Ronald J. Horvath, President
(502) 584-0181, ext. 121

Jefferson Community College
109 East Broadway,
Louisville, KY 40202
Total head count enrollment-Credit: 11,800; Non-Credit: 15,000
Campuses/sites: 3; Full-time faculty: 250

INSTITUTIONAL VALUES

Faculty and staff compiled a publication outlining Jefferson Community College's key institutional values

Jefferson Community College faculty and staff worked to compile a publication that helps them focus on common goals and beliefs in the midst of countless college rules and regulations. The process of re-focusing on the institution identity and mission was initiated through the "Institutional Values Project" during the spring of 1982.

The college's project began with the president's review of excellence literature. From this literature, he developed a single simple question for all college personnel: "What do JCC employees believe about themselves and the students they serve?"

The next step in the project was handled by the college's staff development office. The office staff formulated mini-groups comprised of several faculty and staff members in combinations that brought people together who ordinarily do not work closely. The staff development office assigned a leader and a record to each group and set meeting times. All group leaders presented the key question noted above to their groups. Recorders listed all comments and discussion points, then sent summaries of meetings to the president. He compiled and edited all comments and submitted them to focus groups of faculty and staff for reactions. After several revisions of these value statements, focus group participants were asked to identify behaviors that reflect each value.

From this process a publication emerged entitled "Institutional Values," This document lists the following as key values at Jefferson Community College:
1) quality instruction with college-level standards must be maintained at all times;
2) the college exists in a dynamic environment which promotes self-evaluation and encourages innova-

tion;
3) the preservation of the college in pursuit of its mission must take priority over individual concerns while safeguarding the rights of faculty, staff, or students;
4) academic freedom and the free exchange of ideas are essential elements of the college;
5) students can grow toward their full academic potential as they experience the jobs of discovery and participate in the rigors of academic study;
6) students possess personal abilities which can be further refined and developed;
7) students have a right to enroll in classes appropriate to their ability levels;
8) students must be responsible for taking an active role in their own learning to make their educational experiences significant and meaningful;
9) faculty and staff must develop and maintain a strong interest in the growth of students and the community we serve;
10) faculty and staff are responsible and accountable for their personal and professional actions as they carry outtheir assignments;
11) effective communication and cooperation among faculty and staff are necessary to fulfill the mission of the college;
12) the college is responsible for providing professional development activities for faculty and staff; and
13) faculty and staff must be treated fairly and in accordance with these value statements.

Contact:
Ronald J. Horvath, President
(502) 584-0181, ext. 121

Jefferson Community College
109 East Broadway
Louisville, KY 40202
Total head count enrollment-Credit: 11,800; Non-Credit: 15,000
Campuses/sites: 3; Full-time faculty: 250

TEACHING CONSULTATION PROGRAM

Faculty who want to analyze their teaching work with consultants, who are recognized by their peers as outstanding instructors

One of the most effective and popular faculty development programs offered in the University of Kentucky Community College System (UKCCS) is the Teaching Consultation Program (TCP). Basically, TCP provides a consulting service to faculty who want to analyze their

teaching and to make changes in their teaching behavior. Faculty members who are recognized by their colleagues as outstanding teachers and who have attended a teaching consultant's workshop serve as consultants. Teaching consultants work with one or two instructors each semester and are released from one three-hour class to do so. In the 1992 spring semester, 27 teaching consultants worked with 41 faculty clients at the 14 colleges.

Using TCP, consultants follow a set of procedures developed in the School of Education at the University of Massachusetts at Amherst in the early 1970's. These procedures, which Bergquist and Phillips describe in Volume 2 of *A Handbook for Faculty Development* (1977), are designed to help faculty recognize and consciously develop instructional behaviors most appropriate for themselves and their students. The key stages of the program are initial interviews, data collection, data review and analyses, planning and implementing changes, and evaluation.

One of the key components of TCP is the Teaching Analysis by Students (TABS) Questionnaire, which is used in the data collection stages. Based upon the extensive research of Robert Wilson and others at the University of California at Berkeley, this questionnaire was developed originally at the University of Massachusetts at Amherst and revised by UKCCS teaching consultants. The questionnaire contains 33 items describing instructional behaviors, five items describing teaching emphasis, and 12 items describing student characteristics. Students respond to the items on TABS using opscan sheets, which consultants send to the program coordinator for scanning and analysis.

In UKCCS, a multi-campus system with 14 colleges dispersed throughout Kentucky, the coordinator for Faculty/Staff and Program Development (a member of the Chancellor's staff) schedules the TCP calendar, handles computer logistics, develops and coordinates workshops and prepares reports. College presidents recruit teaching consultants and provide them with travel appropriations and release time. Since the Consultation Program was implemented in 1977, more than 500 UKCCS faculty have participated in the program. Participants have consistently given it excellent ratings. In addition, research by Rozeman and Kerwin that was reported in the 1991 winter issue of *The Journal of Staff, Program, and Organization Development* (pp. 223-230) indicates that the program improves student ratings of participants' teaching behavior and that students perceive the improvements in the semester after the faculty participate in the program.

Program implementation requires the availability of certain computer equipment to process the TABS questionnaire and the willingness of faculty to learn how to use the materials and procedures of TCP. In UKCCS, providing the release time is the major program cost. Hearing the compliments that faculty and students have given TCP has convinced college presidents that the program is well worth the cost.

Contact:
Michael Kerwin, Faculty and Program Development Coordinator
(606) 257-1539

Kentucky Community College System, University of
Brekenridge Hall
Lexington, KY 40506-0056
Total head count enrollment-Credit: 46,000 ; Non-Credit: 300,000
Campuses/sites: 29; Full-time faculty: 1,179

KENTUCKY COMMUNITY COLLEGE SYSTEM, UNIVERSITY OF

LEADERSHIP ACADEMY

▨ *Goals include increasing the number of women and minorities in leadership* ▨
roles and developing a training model others can use

The Leadership Academy is the Kentucky Community College System's response to the complex challenge of developing leaders for a state-wide system from the ranks of faculty and staff. The need to prepare the next generation of leaders was addressed on a national basis by the Commission on the Future of Community Colleges, sponsored by the American Association of Community Colleges (AACC) in 1988. Additionally, the Commission on the Future of the Kentucky Community College System recommended in its report in 1989 that the Kentucky System implement leadership development activities.

Dr. Allen Edwards, President of the Lexington Community College (one of 14 colleges in the system) first presented the idea for the Leadership Academy in a concept paper submitted to the Kentucky Futures Commission. The paper was later developed into a grant proposal, which was accepted by AACJC as one of 11 initial Beacon College projects funded by the Kellogg Foundation. The Kentucky Community College System agreed to provide additional funding for the Academy, and the Leadership Academy was formally established in July 1990. The Community College System is currently sponsoring the second annual Leadership Academy.

The goals for the Academy continue to be:
1) to develop leaders for the state-wide system from the ranks of faculty and staff;
2) to increase the number of women and minorities in leadership roles; and
3) to develop a model of leadership training and networking which can be used in other states.

Academy participants and alternates are selected from each of the 14 colleges through selection processes developed by the college presidents. The Academy Advisory

Continues on Page 282

Board accepts the colleges' first choices of candidates and then chooses from among the alternates in order to achieve gender and racial balance in each class. Academy activities are designed to complete a cycle of experiences, reflective observation, abstract conceptualization and active experimentation.

The Academy includes a Summer Institute which focuses on state and national issues in education, business, and government, and on personal growth and development. Following the Summer Institute, participants develop and complete a semester internship at their college under the mentorship of the college president. During the internships, two retreats are held to reveal the economic, geographic, cultural and political diversity of Kentucky. A critical part of the Academy is the writing component which requires that participants submit to the Academy director evaluation reports on Academy activities and on their personal development and growth.

One of the presidents of the 14 colleges serves as the Academy Director, and all of the presidents are involved in presenting and conducting the Academy. Their total commitment and involvement in the Academy ensures its success. Capital resources needed for the Academy amount to approximately $200,000 for the initial year (includes the purchase of laptop computers for participants), and $100,000 thereafter.

It is too soon to determine the results of the Academy which still is relatively new, but two participants from the first Academy have moved into the role of academic dean at their colleges. It will take at least five years for the success of the Academy to be measured, but the short-term evaluations from participants and presidents have been excellent. The real measure will be in the success of bringing minorities and women into leadership positions in Kentucky's community colleges. At least now there is a highly visible and well-supported effort to do that.

Contact:
Allen Edwards, College President/Director, Leadership Academy
(606) 257-4831

Kentucky Community College System, University of
University of Breckinridge Hall
Lexington, KY 40506-0056
Total head count enrollment-Credit: 46, 000; Non-Credit: 300,000
Colleges/campuses: 29; Full-time faculty: 1,179

CROSS-DISCIPLINARY CLUSTERS °

Students and faculty have a greater awareness of how various disciplines view and approach similar material

Since the fall of 1989, Lexington Community College has been developing a series of courses that encourage faculty and students to work together across academic disciplines. Using the traditional American, European and British history and literature survey courses, the two programs reached across division boundaries to create "Cross-Disciplinary Clusters." The purpose of these 12-hour combinations of history and literature is twofold:

1) to provide students with an opportunity to explore the different ways in which individual disciplines frame questions, develop and test hypotheses, investigate materials and reach conclusions on a common base of knowledge; and

2) to help students appreciate the fact that knowledge generated by one discipline can enhance and clarify knowledge generated by another.

By pairing disciplines in a structured way we have learned that students discover some of the links between different areas of inquiry and transfer their analytical and synthetic skills from one discipline to another. Students and teachers have become more conscious of what is learned in each of the traditional courses alone, even as the instructors show them some of the connections between the two disciplines. Certainly, this approach has made teaching more satisfying because instructors assume that

certain relevant questions, prescribed in the planning stages of the clustering process, will be covered in the related courses – and students come to class with a richer background than would otherwise be the case.

Evidence of heightened awareness by both students and faculty abounds. From the very first semester of implementation, students were not tracked into the clusters but could take the related courses anytime before they graduated or transferred to the University of Kentucky. Yet the original writers of the clusters told each other stories of students who brought what they learned from one class to another – and sometimes argued with the second instructor that "that's not how I learned it before!" Discussion would ensue for the whole class as to the differences and similarities of the two disciplines' approach to the very same materials. This environment seemed perfect for the team-teaching approach, which had never before been attempted by these two programs.

As part of a National Endowment of the Humanities two-year grant, two faculty members collaborated on developing the course content and teaching methodologies necessary for a team-taught, six credit hour class for the American Studies Cluster. The results were astonishing. One of the faculty members was a veteran of the community college system and was ready to give this experiment the one last chance to keep her committed to teaching – the excitement and inherent rewards of each class period seemed to give her new life. In their evaluations of the experimental class, the students demanded that they needed more time – and when asked to describe what part of the course needed to be expanded, the answers were as varied as the different course topics! The journals they wrote each week to describe what they observed to be evidence of the cross-disciplinary experience were as enlightening to the faculty teaching the course as they were to the students writing them.

Another group of faculty worked together on a grant that funded the purchase of videos for the Early European history and literature classes. Using the cross-disciplinary themes as a guide, they purchased $1,000 of films such as *Oedipus Rex*, *Jesus Today*, *Dante* and *Hamlet*. The group met to analyze the films and develop questions that might help provide the grant writers with evidence of student enrichment. For example, for the theme on Ancient Origins of Western Civilization, "War, Heroes and Civilization," the following question was asked and counted as half of unit exams in both the literature and history classes: "Was Oedipus Rex a hero? Focus on his role as a leader in the Hellenic Age, comparing and contrasting him with other individuals studied in this course so far." As part of their self-evaluation of this cross-disciplinary part of their exams, students responded easily as to the clarity of the links between the courses in their analysis of the theme through the video of the play, *Oedipus Rex*, e.g., Oedipus' blindness and his leadership within classical Greek ideology.

More cross-disciplinary courses are being developed by an expanding group of faculty who see the inherent value of the collaborative learning process. And since both associate degree and pre-baccalaureate students take these courses, it has been clear to all of us here at LCC how this form of educational innovation can benefit all.

Contact:
Peggy Allen
(606) 257-4831

Lexington Community College
209 Oswald Building, Cooper Drive
Lexington, KY 40506-0235
Total head count enrollment-Credit: 4,863; Non-Credit: 4,400
Campuses/sites: 2;Faculty: 121

CALCULUS

The typical Calculus I class visits the computer lab six to 10 times per semester

Calculus courses at Lexington Community College are supplemented by graphing activities using microcomputers in a laboratory. A pilot course several years ago was funded by a Title III Institution Strengthening grant, and the laboratory set-up and full implementation was made possible by a National Science Foundation Instrumentation and Laboratory Improvement grant the following year.

Laboratory exercises are an integral part of each of the courses in the calculus sequence. Each class visits the laboratory frequently during the semester to do graphing activities appropriate to the topics currently being studied. These activities are not interactive, and are not intended to replace traditional classroom instruction, rather to supplement and enhance it. Several software packages are available, but the one used almost exclusively, both for class discussions and assignments, is MPP, the Mathematics Plotting Program, and MPP3D, both of which are shareware written by a mathematics professor at the U.S. Naval Academy. MPP is extremely easy to use and was written to support calculus courses, so it is appropriate and streamlined. We also have a site license for MicroCalc, and it is available on the computers in the laboratory, but we use it very little for classroom activities, as we feel it does too much for the student. It also has many more options and several levels, and is simply not as straightforward to use. The amount laboratory activity varies with course and instructor. The typical Calculus I class visits the laboratory six to 10 times per semester, and is required to hand in as many written laboratory assignments.

Other mathematics courses use the laboratory also, but on a more limited basis: elementary calculus, finite mathematics, statistics, and trigonometry. These classes tend to be fully subscribed with 35 students, many of whose computer literacy is minimal. These courses typically visit the laboratory two to six times during a semester.

The principal investigator in this project has been invited to make presentations about it at state meetings,

Continues on Page 284

and to organize a workshop at the national AMATYC meeting. Two of the faculty members involved in the project, Ms. Crowley and Mr. Ott, were also invited to write a review of three dimensional graphing software. This appeared in the January 1992 issue of the *College Mathematics Journal*.

Contact:
Lillie Crowley, (606) 257-6148
Steve Ott, (606) 257-6113

Lexington Community College
209 Oswald Building, Cooper Drive
Lexington, KY 40506-0235
Total head count enrollment-Credit: 4,863; Non-Credit: 4,400
Campuses/sites: 2; Faculty: 121

MAYSVILLE COMMUNITY COLLEGE

ENVIRONMENTAL SCIENCE

*▨ Courses prepare students to sample and analyze air, water and soil, and ▨
stress application of scientific principles to pollution control problems*

Although most every corporation, company or business of any size has had to conform to an increasing number of state and federal environmental regulations, there had been no environmental science program to prepare students for technical positions in our region. To answer this need, the faculty of Maysville Community College has worked closely with representatives from industry as well as state and local government to develop 10 new Environmental Science courses.

These Environmental Science courses have been designed to provide individuals the background necessary for understanding the ecological relationships of the environment. The various courses will prepare individuals to sample and analyze air, water and soil in accordance with state and federal regulations through emphasis on practical lab and field experiences. The coursework also stresses the application of scientific principles to pollution control

problems in accordance with state and federal regulations. Environmental Science courses are applicable towards fulfillment of the requirements of an Associate in Science degree.

Graduates in this field will be qualified to be employed as technicians by federal, state and local governmental units as well as utilities, private industry, and environmental engineering consulting firms. The various Environmental Science courses place emphasis on developing the student's ability to function effectively in a variety of job situations. Environmental technicians may be responsible for such duties as air pollution surveillance, analysis or water and wastewater samples, ground water and surface water assessment, field sampling, data interpretation and other support services to engineering and science professionals.

Contact:
Sharon Wilson, Associate Professor, Biology
(606) 759-7141

Maysville Community College
1755 U.S. Highway 68
Maysville, KY 41056
Total head count enrollment-Credit: 1,328; Non-Credit: 1,684
Campus/sites: 6; Full-time faculty: 43

OWENSBORO COMMUNITY COLLEGE

ARCHEOLOGY

*▨ The program operates closely with the state archaeological community and maintains ▨
a community advisory committee that includes Native Americans*

For the past 50 years, archaeological sites in western Kentucky have been irreversibly damaged by illicit digging for artifacts. To discourage the pillaging of such sites and build a sense of community pride in its Native American heritage, Owensboro Community College has developed an academic program in archaeological studies.

The program is designed to ensure that students:
1) recognize the value of scientific methodology in approaching the study of such sites;

2) develop a sense of empathy for the Native American community with regards to such investigative studies;
3) promote the development of dialogue between the archaeological and Native American communities; and
4) understand the vital importance of such cross-cultural research and dialogue.

In order to ensure that its responsibilities to both the

scientific and Native American communities are maintained at a professional level, the program operates closely with the state archaeological community and maintains a community advisory committee which includes active Native American participation. It has gained the respect of both groups.

Besides an introductory course, the program offers focused archaeological studies in both old world and new world civilizations. The program offers a field trip each semester to outstanding museums and during the summer of 1992 conducted an international field trip to the Mayan region of Mexico. The program also maintains an ongoing archaeological field school where current excavations give students field experience and develop their laboratory analytical skills. In 1993, the program is moving into new facilities which will include state-of-the-art archaeology/earth science laboratories and display areas. All courses taught in the program are transferable to baccalaureate programs.

This program has developed in the short span of four years, and while many of its objectives involve long-term attitudinal adjustments, all indications suggest the program is well on its way to accomplishing its goals.

Contact:
Bruce Beck, Associate Professor, Anthropology
(502) 686-4400

Owensboro Community College
4800 New Hartford Road
Owensboro, KY 42303
Enrollment head count-Credit: 2,650; Non-Credit: 5,000
Campuses/sites: 3; Full-time faculty: 5

OWENSBORO COMMUNITY COLLEGE

BUILDING COMMUNITIES: A STRATEGIC PLAN

The plan addresses such topics as instruction, campus life, community partnerships, institutional effectiveness and leadership

In 1989, Owensboro Community College initiated a strategic planning process to develop a strategic plan for OCC and a model strategic planning process that might guide other community colleges in strategic planning efforts. With support from the BellSouth Foundation through the Owensboro Citizens Committee on Education, a local education advocacy group, a consultant team of three national community college leaders – Dr. R. Jan LeCroy, Dr. Kay McClenney and Dr. Nancy Armes LeCroy – was selected. Its results included the development of *Building Communities: A Strategic Plan for Owensboro Community College in Partnership with its Community* and the AACJC publication *Building Communities Through Strategic Planning*.

The National Commission on the Future of Community Colleges' report, *Building Communities: A Vision for the New Century*, provided the framework for the OCC strategic plan. The process emphasized the building of communities throughout its recommendations. Community was viewed in the same sense as it was defined in the national report as "not only as a region to be served, but also as a climate to be created." The plan addressed the major topics included in the national report: students and faculty, curriculum, instruction, campus life, community partnerships, institutional effectiveness and assessment and leadership. Recommendations were developed under each topics for both the college and the community it serves.

The "building communities" theme also guided the steps in the strategic planning process: the review of the college's mission, articulation of its shared values, assessment of its internal and external environment, identification of its strategic direction, and statement and approval of the plan itself.

To maintain the currency of the strategic plan as a road map for the future of the college, the Planning Council undertook a thorough review of the plan and the progress made in addressing its initial recommendations during the 1991-92 academic year. As a result of this review, the college revised its statement of values and reaffirmed it commitment to building communities.

Contact:
John M. McGuire, President
(502) 686-4400

Owensboro Community College
4800 New Hartford Road
Owensboro, KY 42303
Enrollment head count-Credit: 2,650; Non-Credit: 5,000
Campuses/sites: 3; Full-time faculty: 5

ENGLISH VIA COMPUTER MODEM

A student may access a bulletin board, upload an essay and even confer with an instructor via computer

Many people who would like to take college courses but are restricted by physical limitations, work schedules, family responsibilities or distance now can attend Paducah Community College English classes via computer modem. The instructor maintains a host computer and creates the materials, tutorials, assignments and grading techniques necessary to make this course equal to that of an on-campus class. English 101 and 102 first were offered through this medium in spring 1992.

The student accesses a bulletin board and uploads an essay into the system. The teacher retrieves the essay, grades it, makes comments, and puts it back into the computer. The student then downloads the essay for revision. Teaching effectiveness is enhanced by this method because the teacher and student have one-on-one working conditions. A greater number of individual contacts are reported by teachers involved in similar projects as instruction is via computer interchange. This means that the teacher and student communicate with one another over chat lines within the computer or through the message board on the computer where very specific questions and answers may be exchanged. Learning is enhanced as students have the sole attention of the instructor during this interchange. A combined total of 27 students were enrolled in English 101 and English 102 modem course at the college. The student learns in a self-paced, individualized, independent manner.

Student/teacher conferences continue to be important and are in person, over the phone, or via chat lines in the computer link. The instructor has developed materials for this project, and some published materials are free and available for student use. A grammar tutorial called PEER comes with the Beacon Handbook which is required with the particular English class. PEER is a self-paced grammar tutorial which each student can use as they need in their area of weakness. The instructor can also make a free word processor software package available to any student who does not have one. Modem costs start around $40.

Contact:
William Wade, Associate Professor, English
(502) 554-9200

Paducah Community College
PO Box 7380
Paducah, KY 42002-7380
Total head count enrollment-Credit: 3,200; Non-Credit: 1,650
Campuses/sites: 5; Full-time faculty: 70

INTERACTIVE TELEVISION

The technology enables real-time interaction between two remote sites and provides a high level of security

The Tennessee Valley Authority and South Central Bell support a distance learning project in western Kentucky that utilizes compressed video for interactive television. This technology is the same employed by business for video teleconferencing, but it suits the specific needs of many distance learning settings equally well.

The project connects three local districts in Hickman and Fulton counties. Paducah Community College and Murray State University, 50 miles apart, are linked to each other and the three districts by Tl telephone lines. These high-quality phone lines, the equivalent to 24 regular phone lines in terms of message-carrying capacity, are also capable of supporting interactive voice and data traffic.

One classroom at Murray and one at Paducah serve as the distance learning sites. These rooms are equipped with multiple cameras one is trained on the students; one is on the teacher, and one points down at a copy stand to shoot transparencies, books and other printed material. Codecs, special pieces of hardware, take the analog signals (comprising both video and audio) from the cameras, digitize and compress them, then send them over the Tl lines. A code at the other end decompresses and reconverts the information into analog form for display. A fax machine was also placed in each room to transmit hard copy.

The main instructional highlight of this technology is it enables real-time interaction to take place between the two remote sites. Students and the instructor can see and hear each other as if they were all in the same room. Another benefit is the high level of security afforded by this approach. If the signal is put up on a satellite, anyone with the proper equipment can beam it down to their own site. By using codes and phone lines, only the intended receivers have access.

And the combination of security and interactivity affects the behavior of participants. For example, it was observed at PCC that students were much more willing to "stay after" class to discuss with the teacher a particular problem, to ask questions or to go over a returned test. They could put their returned homework on the copy stand under the graphics camera and discuss a point in detail without the inhibition of knowing other students were watching and listening.

Contact:
Steve Patton, Coordinator, Telecommunications
(502) 554-9200

Paducah Community College
PO Box 7380
Paducah, KY 42002-7380
Total head count enrollment-Credit: 3,200; Non-Credit: 1,650
Campuses/sites: 5; Full-time faculty: 70

PRESTONSBURG COMMUNITY COLLEGE

COLLEGE COLLOQUIUM

The Colloquium serves the dual purpose of provoking thought while promoting interaction across divisions and departments

Prestonsburg Community College countered the loss of cohesiveness that accompanies dramatic growth with a faculty development program that showcases faculty talents and promotes sharing.

Such a program was slow in coming, however, because for years the overall college growth was slow. This pattern of growth changed for Prestonsburg Community College (as it did for many others throughout the nation) when, in the mid-1980's, a great surge of what we now call "non-traditional students" began to dramatically increase enrollment figures. Prestonsburg, a small, rural college located in Central Appalachia that serves a five-county area in eastern Kentucky, then saw its need for more faculty surge as well.

Increasingly, the divisions (Humanities, Physical Sciences, Biological Sciences and Social Sciences, each with its related technologies) became entities unto themselves; the community of faculty, staff and administration which had previously enjoyed and taken for granted the luxury of close acquaintanceship and easy communication, now began to feel the effects of a 50 percent increase in faculty and staff size within a five-year period. From a student body of approximately 1,500 in the fall of 1986 and faculty and staff of 75, Prestonsburg Community College in the fall of 1991 had a student body of almost 3,000 and a faculty and staff of 145.

A dilemma often confronts a college as it grows from a relatively small, closely-knit faculty and staff to one that is larger and more diverse. While the effects of growth are generally positive, negative ones can also accrue. Faculties can lose some of the cohesiveness that once characterized them, and this loss can result in lowered morale with a lessening of overall effectiveness. Prestonsburg Community College has countered this problem imple-

menting a component of faculty/staff development called The College Colloquium. The College Colloquium is a faculty development program that showcases the talents of faculty and helps promote cohesiveness and sharing.

The Prestonsburg Community College Colloquium provides a one-hour forum for faculty and staff to present programs related to their areas of expertise or interest. The Colloquium serves the dual purpose of informing, entertaining or provoking thought, while at the same time promoting a meeting ground of social and intellectual interaction across divisions and departments.

Examples of programs presented illustrate their diversity. The division of physical sciences and related technologies has been represented by such topics as "Some Remarks and Questions in Essential Mathematics," "Off and On: Computer Literacy," and "Engineering Computer Graphics: Past, Present and Future Trends." The division of social sciences and related technologies has given presentations on "The History of Fundamentalism in America," "Breadmaking: A Hands-On Approach," "Student Outcomes: Student Evaluations," and "Hero Archetypes in Human Development." The division of humanities and related technologies has contributed such presentations as "Plastics: The Aesthetic Nuisance," "Microbiology: Its Effects on the Outcomes of Major Historic Battles," and "Stress Management Techniques." While the content of the programs tends to be discipline-specific, they are presented in a manner that can be enjoyed and understood by faculty and staff participants from all divisions and departments.

Because the programs are short, they require relatively little time of preparation, thus alleviating a problem which confronts most faculty and precludes their "taking on"

Continues on Page 288

KENTUCKY • PAGE 287

extra projects. The programs are presented in an early morning (8 a.m. to 9 a.m.) time frame, when few classes are scheduled. Specifically, the time format of the colloquium consists of the presentation itself, from 8 a.m. to 8:40 a.m. The last 20 minutes, 8:40 a.m. to 9 a.m., are reserved for discussion and questions and answers. In most cases the presenter brings handouts which further explain or enhance the topic of the presentation. Coffee and doughnuts are available, and the informality of the atmosphere allows participants to serve themselves without fear of disrupting the flow of the program.

Contact:
Laura T. Weddle, Faculty/Staff Development Coordinator
(606) 886-3863

Prestonsburg Community College
1 Bert T. Combs Drive
Prestonsburg, KY 41653
Total head count enrollment-Credit: 2,886; Non-Credit: 22,015
Campuses/sites: 2

MINE TRAINING INSTITUTE

Students may participate in short-term and long-term courses training sessions, workshops and seminars

With Eastern Kentucky's economy heavily dependent upon the coal mining industry, Southeast Community College has placed a special emphasis on helping the industry develop to its fullest potential.

Through its Mine Training Institute, the college is working to make coal produced in Appalachia competitive in domestic and world markets. To accomplish this, the industry needs to implement cost-reduction measures such as upgrading the knowledge and skills of employees.

At the Institute, students can participate in a program of training and services that include both short-term and long-term courses, training sessions, workshops and seminars. The program is designed to meet the ongoing training needs of coal mining employees and focuses primarily on the areas of mine maintenance, engineering technology, safety and mine laws.

The Institute opened in the fall of 1992, complementing the college's two-year degree program of mining technology already in place. Under the degree program, students can earn an associate in applied science degree in mining technology which prepares them for employment as supervisors, surveyors, assistants to engineers, mechanics and mid-management positions.

Courses offered at the Institute cover such categories as electricity, hydraulics, programmable logic control and computer aided drafting. The Institute also provides training designed to meet state and federal certification requirements. Mining employees can take advantage of programs in new miner training, electrical training and underground and surface mine foreman training.

All programs offered at the Institute are approved by the Mine Safety and Health Administration and the Kentucky Department of Mines and Minerals. All training is conducted by state and federally certified instructors with several years mining experience.

Since the Institute began to serve the coal mining community, hundreds of miners have completed training programs, and coal companies throughout the region have come to rely on the college to meet their training needs.

Contact:
Edward D. Wright, Director
(606) 589-2145

Southeast Community College
300 College Road
Cumberland, KY 40823
Total head count enrollment-Credit: 2,453; Non-Credit: 1,881
Campuses/sites: 3; Full-time faculty: 58

PROJECT GENESYS

A college-wide computer network links three campuses and creates an atmosphere of computer awareness and literacy

Begun in 1988, Project GENESYS (General Education System) has established a computer network at Southeast Community College that is recognized as the most advanced and innovative in the University of Kentucky's Community College System.

The computer network serves as a vital link with the university and allows for effective communication between the three campuses operated by Southeast. Its myriad administrative and academic applications has created a college-wide atmosphere of computer awareness and literacy.

Project GENESYS required the integration of microcomputers with mini and main frame systems based primarily on existing equipment. Development of the system included the purchase of a number of micro computers used both in academic labs and administrative offices.

The administrative feature provides full access to registration, admissions, financial aid, libraries, business offices and bookstores. The services are available at all three campuses and at one remote site, allowing creative student record processing with the University of Kentucky. The system also makes it possible to provide temporary registration locations within a five-county area with access to central student records for admission and registration.

The record processing techniques, aid processing, fee assessment and student accounts programs are being considered for implementation throughout the university's community college system, which includes 14 colleges.

The project has included installation of computer labs at all three campuses with open access to the student body, faculty and local communities. Each lab features 20 stand-alone micro computers with each facility modeled after a central lab allowing easy movement from one location to another.

In addition, restricted access computer labs were established for nursing, off-campus administration and mining technology. Interactive learning materials on subjects including biology, English, computer science and mathematics were also included in the project.

Project GENESYS has enhanced classroom instruction, improved the implementation of administrative procedures and provided a comprehensive network to meet the needs of the college, its students and the local communities.

Contact:
Paul Adams, Computer Manager
(606) 589-2145

Southeast Community College
300 College Road
Cumberland, KY 40823
Total head count enrollment-Credit: 2,453; Non-Credit: 1,881
Campuses/sites: 3; Full-time faculty: 58

CULINARY ARTS

*※ The program includes an apprenticeship, a certificate in food service ※
careers and a management development diploma*

In less than three years, Delgado's Culinary Arts Program went from being a program that seemed destined for deletion to one that is drawing students from all over the United States and even from foreign countries. In fact, last spring semester, a student from Iceland entered. The Icelandic government, which is paying the student's tuition, chose Delgado Culinary Arts Program after examining culinary programs across the United States.

Three years prior, this program was unaccredited and was losing students. Today it is one of only 27 culinary programs in the United States that has been accredited by the American Culinary Federation. Moreover, not only is the program growing but also a new Certificate Program in Culinary Arts has gone into effect.

The Delgado Community College Culinary Arts Department has three programs. These programs are designed to produce trained cooks for the culinary industry. The following academic areas are available in the program:

1) The Culinary Apprenticeship Program, which is a three-year Associate Degree program awarding students: Diploma, Associate of Applied Science; Certificate, Department of Labor for Apprenticeship; Certificate, Completion as a Journeyman Cook from the American Culinary Federation (ACF); and Certificate, Certification as a cook with the ACF. The Apprenticeship program follows the tradition of European Culinary training programs in that it provides the students with practical work experience under the supervision of an executive chef in hotels and restaurants in the metropolitan New Orleans areas. During the three years of the apprenticeship program, students are required to complete a minimum 6,000 hours of on-the-job training under the supervision of an executive chef and 900 hours of related classroom instruction under the direction of culinary arts faculty. Classroom instruction includes basic food preparation, ice carving techniques, garde-manger

skills and actual gourmet luncheon preparation. The culinary apprenticeship program admits two classes each fall semester and has a special application procedure. All applications are reviewed by a culinary panel; students are selected on the basis of personal interviews and Delgado College placement exams.

2) Recently approved by the State of Louisiana's Board of Regents, the second program grants a certificate in Food Service Careers. This program mirrors the first year of the Culinary Apprenticeship Program.

3) Management Development Diploma Program offered by the Education Foundation of the National Restaurant Association. This program consists of a series of comprehensive courses designed to provide food service managers and hospitality program students with training they need to assist in their success in the industry. A certificate will be issued through the NRA upon completion of the courses.

Delgado's Culinary Arts Program has gained widespread recognition. It has been featured in area newspapers and on local television programs. Students have participated in local and state American Culinary Federation and American Restaurant conventions and their achievements in various culinary competitions have been outstanding.

One special aspect of the Culinary Arts Program is the Friday luncheons prepared by the students taking CULA 217-Culinary Practicum. These luncheons are open not only to Delgado faculty and staff but also the public as well. Under the supervision of a faculty chef, students plan each menu, prepare all courses and serve in all capacities from waiter to maitre d's, to head chef. Each semester these students are placed in leading area restaurants where they work a 40-hour week. Underscoring the program's success is the fact that upon graduation most students remain in the restaurant where they apprenticed.

Contact:
Iva Bergeron, Program Director
(504) 483-4208

Delgado Community College
615 City Park Avenue
New Orleans, LA 70119-4399
Total head count enrollment-Credit: 22,414
Campuses/sites: 6;Full-time faculty: 750

SINGLE PARENT PROGRAM

*This institution combats feminization of poverty by providing opportunities
for economic and psychological independence*

The major goal for participants in the Single Parent Program at Louisiana State University at Eunice is to learn marketable skills that would improve their economic status. This objective is critical for participants, most of whom are from low-income backgrounds. Prior educational achievement level of most single parents is extremely low, partially due to the fact that secondary schools either have no programs or very limited programs in place to assure retention. As a result, many applicants have obtained neither a high school diploma nor a grade equivalency diploma (GED). This program is an outreach effort to assure such students of their potential to successfully complete their curriculum with a marketable skill.

The Single Parent Program is funded in part by the Carl D. Perkins Vocational and Applied Technology Education Act Amendments of 1990 (Perkins II) and administered by the Louisiana State Department of Education.

Many former participants are currently enrolled and receive federal financial aid. Additionally, many have completed associate degree programs, while others have enrolled in (and some have completed) bachelor's or advanced degree programs. This institution has successfully combated feminization of poverty by providing low-income single parents with the opportunity to become gainfully employed as well as psychologically and economically self-sufficient. Through prior counseling and testing to allay fears associated with entering college, approxi-

mately 50 applicants were enrolled in the Single Parent Program during the first week in June, 1993. Some of the objectives established to attain this goal are:

1) Students will improve basic skills as a result of attending a minimum of four to six skills-building workshops related to improving self-esteem, career exploration, stress reduction, planning and time management, and success in college (study skills and test taking).

2) Through pre/post ACT testing participants will demonstrate improved skills in English, mathematics, natural sciences and reading as measured by a minimum increase of four points on the composite score.

3) Seventy percent of participants will demonstrate mastery of the curriculum-based academic and vocational courses in which they are enrolled by earning a grade of "C" or better at the conclusion of the summer semester 1993.

Program personnel work in teams to assist participants in achieving program goals. Administrators, faculty, counselors and past project participants work together to ensure logical and non-duplicative services. Personnel are dedicated to the series of successful projects which have created a source of pride and accomplishment for participants.

Contact:
Delmar D. Bentley, Coordinator of Counseling
(318) 457-7311

Louisiana State University at Eunice
PO Box 1129
Eunice, LA 70535
Total head count enrollment-Credit: 2,861; Non-Credit: 10
Campuses/sites: 1; Founded: 1967

FIRE SCIENCE

*The program prepares students for a variety of occupations
as well as offers classes for professional development*

The LSUE fire science program is a cooperative effort between the Fireman Training Program at Louisiana State University (Baton Rouge) and Louisiana State University at Eunice. Administrative control is exercised by LSUE, which grants the associate degree. The Fireman Training Program provides physical facilities and shares personnel resources located throughout the state. Continuing education training provided at the Baton Rouge complex correlates to components of the LSUE associate degree curriculum.

The associate degree program is designed to prepare persons for one or more of the following occupations: industrial fire prevention specialist, insurance inspector/investigator, fire codes enforcement officers, fire administrator, fire equipment sales representative, fire department officer and firefighter. The program offers a broad scope of courses in general education and fire science for firefighters seeking professional development as well as for individuals serving industry in the various fire

Continues on Page 292

protection areas.

Courses of instruction include basic fire-fighting skills, fire codes/prevention, fire department management, inspection, industrial fire protection, hazardous materials, personnel training, building construction, fire and arson investigation and public fire education.

Contact:
David Fultz, Coordinator
(318) 457-7311

Louisiana State University at Eunice
PO Box 1129
Eunice, LA 70535
Total head count enrollment-Credit: 2,861; Non-Credit: 10
Campuses/sites: 1; Founded: 1967

MAINE CENTER FOR OCCUPATIONAL HEALTH AND SAFETY

▨ The Center addresses Maine's high rate ▨
of work-related injuries

For the past decade, Maine has experienced one of the highest rates of recorded work-related illness and injury in the country. At the same time, rates for workers' compensation insurance and costs associated with workers' compensation claims were among the highest in the nation. While debate about the probable causes and possible cures for this situation raged in the State Legislature and the press, CMTC responded by developing the Center for Occupational Health and Safety.

The Center began operations in October 1988 with the goal of making work in Maine a safer, healthier and more productive experience by offering training and education to Maine workers and their employers. In 1989, the Center began offering courses leading to a Certificate (30 credit hours) and an Associate in Applied Science Degree (64 credit hours) in Occupational Health and Safety. These were, and still are, the only academic credentials in Occupational Health and Safety available in Maine.

The program was one of the first at the college developed specifically for non-traditional, part-time students. During the 1991-92 school year, 40 students were matriculated in the program. About one-third of these were full-time students; many were dislocated workers who were taking advantage of the slow economy in New England to move into a more rewarding profession; several were injured workers for whom a career as a health and safety professional offered an opportunity to return to the work force committed to reducing the hazards to which other workers are exposed.

Staff of the Center has grown to include a part-time manager, two full-time instructors and a part-time secretary. In May 1992, the first two Associated Degrees in Occupational Health and Safety were awarded by CMTC. Both graduates are employed in occupational health and safety programs in manufacturing firms.

In addition to the academic programs, the Center provides continuing education programs as well as contract training for business and industry. In FY '92, the Center delivered more than 5,000 contact hours of training through seminars, workshops, on-site training and over the University of Maine's Interactive Television Network.

Funding for the Center has come from a variety of grants from the public and private sectors and from program revenues. Among the more significant sources of support have been grants from two area manufacturers that were cited for violations by the Occupational Safety and Health Administration (OSHA). As part of their settlements, the companies and the agency agreed that substantial support for the efforts of the Center would be an appropriate offset against some of the assessed fine.

These grants, totaling $225,000 over four years, in addition to a voluntary contribution from Bath Iron Works, an appropriation from the State Occupational Safety Training and Education Fund, and a grant under the Training Grants Program of the National Institute for Occupational Safety and Health (NIOSH), have provided the majority of operating funds for the Center. It is the intention of the Maine Technical College System to incorporate the academic activities of the Center into the General Fund operations of the college; the continuing education efforts will remain self-supporting.

Contact:
Annee Tara, Center Manager
(207) 784-2385

Central Maine Technical College
1250 Turner Street
Auburn, ME 04210
Total head count enrollment-Credit: 1,500 Non-credit: 511
Campuses/sites: 1; Full-time faculty: 42

TECHNOLOGY AND SOCIETY

▨ Literature and film give students a peek ▨
at the impact of advancing technology

In the emerging world society and global economy it is becoming ever more important that skilled technicians both understand and are able to deal with change. Former Harvard Professor and Economist, Robert Reich, has said: "...[I]t is not enough to produce a cadre of young people with skill. If our enterprises are to be the scenes of collective entrepreneurship – as they must be – experts must have the ability to broadly share their skills and transform them into organizational achievement; and others must be prepared to learn from them."

With this in mind, the Communication and Social

Continues on Page 294

Science Department of Central Maine Technical College has designed the Technology and Society course to be relevant to the technical curriculum and meet transfer standards for social science credit at the senior institutions within the state of Maine and the New England Region.

Students study the literature and film of the 20th Century to identify the effect of advancing technology on our society. The object of their study is to understand the way that technological innovations have transformed our society and culture and shaped our views on such issues as work, medical care, mass media, warfare, family life and the environment.

It is hoped that through the study of technology as it has been reported in both fiction and non-fiction literature, poetry, film and other media sources, the student will gain a better understanding of the society and the importance of technological change to the development of social institutions.

The course depends heavily on in-class discussion of the assigned reading and media. Students are encouraged to participate and share differing viewpoints on important societal issues.

Three hours of credit are awarded upon successful completion.

Contact:
William Frayer, Chairperson, Communication & Social Science Dept.
(207) 784-2385

Central Maine Technical College
1250 Turner Street
Auburn, ME 04210
Total head count enrollment-Credit: 1,500 Non-credit: 511
Campuses/sites: 1; Full-time faculty: 42

ENVIRONMENTAL TECHNOLOGY

The program prepares students for entry-level employment in a burgeoning field

In response to heightened awareness of ecological crises facing New England and the critical shortage of skilled technicians available to deal with environmental issues, Southern Maine Technical College developed and implemented a program in Environmental Technology. This AAS degree program, begun in 1989, in cooperation with the New England Interstate Environmental Training Center, aims to provide students with the fundamental skills required for entry-level employment in a variety of existing and emerging careers in the environmental sciences/disciplines.

The curriculum was developed with the assistance of an advisory committee composed of representatives from environmental service companies, engineering firms, water districts, pollution-abatement facilities, state environmental agencies and industries which employ skilled environmental technicians. The program of study emphasizes the basic sciences (chemistry, biology, physics, math, geology) and includes technical courses covering water and wastewater treatment, hazardous waste management, emergency response, air pollution, solid waste management, and environmental laws and regulations. The environmental courses are taught by two full-time faculty, and the science, general education and other support courses are delivered by the appropriate departments.

In addition to traditional classroom, field and laboratory instruction, students are required to complete an internship or extensive special project. The internship experience usually occurs in the summer between the first and second years, and is designed to prepare students for employment in specialized fields by providing an opportunity to acquire information and skills in the workplace. In many instances, the work-based learning enhances the student's abilities beyond the scope or capabilities of the academic program and provides an opportunity to refine career objectives. The internship component of the program was developed as a work-based learning demonstration project with a grant from the National Alliance of Business.

Most graduates have been successful in finding employment and some have transferred to other colleges to pursue higher degrees in environmental or related science fields.

Contact:
Robert E. Goode, Program Chairman
(207) 767-9540

Southern Maine Technical College
Fort Road
South Portland, ME 04106
Total head count enrollment-Credit: 2,400 Non-Credit: 7,000
Campuses/sites: 1; Full-time faculty: 91

PLANT AND SOIL TECHNOLOGY

*▩ Program graduates are entering a field of unprecedented growth, ▩
particularly in the service sector*

Southern Maine Technical College's Plant and Soil Technology program remains strong, thanks to faculty members who are acknowledged leaders in the green industry. The plant and Soil Technology Program, established in 1972 to meet the needs of green industry employers by educating their future and present employees, originally was a one-year certificate program in cooperation with the University of Maine at Orono. There still is reciprocity for purposes of transfer with University of Maine, but for the past few years students have been able to obtain an associate degree at SMTC. Since the degree has been offered, the one-year certificate program has phased itself out because most students attend for two years.

Not only are faculty leaders in the green industry, but also are many graduates. Graduates include the current and past presidents of the New England Nurserymen's Association, Maine Nurserymen's Association, Maine Golf Course Superintendents Association, and the Maine Arborists' Association. And PST graduate Terry Skillin is president of Skillin's Greenhouses and was listed in 1990 by *Nursery Management* magazine in the nation's top 100 garden centers. Many graduates of the program are sole proprietors running businesses, which contribute to an industry with annual revenues in Maine in excess of $65-million (source - Maine Department of Agriculture, latest figures 1985).

The certification examination for the green industry is sponsored by the Maine Nurserymen's Association and upon successful completion of this examination one receives the designation Maine Certified Nurseryman. There are 84 individuals holding MCN status, of these 46 are PST graduates.

The green industry has enjoyed unprecedented growth in the past two decades. The demand for graduates will continue to increase particularly in the service sector. Graduates of the program are employed in the following areas: landscape contracting, landscape maintenance, golf course management, municipal park departments, greenhouse management, flower shop management, retail garden center management, wholesale nursery operations, arboriculture, teaching, and estate grounds management.

The department was given $130,000 in 1984 by an anonymous donor with the express purpose of providing funding for horticultural education where state funding was not available. The fund has a value in excess of $200,000 at this time. The funds have been used to provide full tuition scholarships for more than 60 students, week-long field trips twice a year for more than 60 students, week-long field trips twice a year for students, computer and video equipment for the department, and a distinguished lecture series. This series has been held each winter since 1985 and has had a total attendance of more than 500 individuals for the four or five lecture series each year. Leaders in horticulture from around the world have been speakers, including Dr. Marc Cathey (Director U.S. National Arboretum), Dr. Alex Shigo (USDA), Dr. Michael Dirr (University of Georgia), Dr. Stephen Spongburg (The Arnold Arboretum), Ian Baldwin (Great Britain), Dr. Carl Whitcomb (Oklahoma State University), and Dr. Elton Smith (Ohio State University).

A strength of the program is the emphasis on practical applications in the curriculum. There are eight part-time faculty and one full-time program coordinator/professor.

Program Chair Richard Churchill has been the Executive Secretary of the Maine Landscape and Nursery Association since 1976, giving SMTC great recognition through this involvement. He has served as a director of the Maine Arborists' Association for the past decade and is the president-elect. The governor appointed him to the Maine Arborists' Examining Board in 1986. In 1992 he was appointed to the Maine Urban Forest Council by the state commissioner of conservation. Membership is held in several other associations.

The Plant and Soil Department has a long tradition of providing service to our surrounding neighbors. The Department has provided studies, conducted by students, for the municipalities of South Portland, Portland, Westbrook and Saco. Philanthropic activities in the form of plantings have been extended to churches and such organizations as the YMCA and Ronald McDonald House. The department chair designed, and with students, planted the Longfellow Arboretum in Portland in 1976. The department chair provides his services as a volunteer naturalist with the Appalachian Mountain Club. The department has provided a horticultural therapy program at the Maine Medical Center for more than 10 years. The department serves as the resource for the Forest Diversity Project. More than 50,000 packets of seeds and seedlings have been distributed in Maine during the past three years.

Contact:
Richard Churchill, Program Chair
(207) 767-9500

Southern Maine Technical College
Fort Road
South Portland, ME 04106
Total head count enrollment-Credit: 2,400 Non-Credit: 7,000
Campuses/sites: 1; Full-time faculty: 91

THE EDUCATION NETWORK OF MAINE

⋇ *Interactive television brings far-flung* ⋇
students close to their professors

The Education Network of Maine combines current telecommunications technology with the human resources of the University of Maine System to produce a distance education network designed to make education more accessible to people of Maine.

Barriers of geography, cost and time had restricted access to education in Maine for generations. The Education Network of Maine was designed to address these barriers of access for people living in Maine's remote communities.

The network was developed by the University of Maine at Augusta (UMA) in consultation with Maine's Technical College System, Maine Maritime Academy, other university campuses, Maine Public Broadcasting System, New England Telephone and the Maine Department of Education.

The interactive television system (ITV) was designed and built for UMA by the Maine Public Broadcasting System in 1988. A two-way audio and video fiber-optic spine, leased from New England Telephone, connects electronic classrooms located at each of the University of Maine System campuses. At each of these campuses, the classroom signal is broadcast via ITFS from one transmitter to multiple receive antennae a the various receive sites. The signal can be transmitted from each campus throughout its own geographic region or throughout the entire state.

Students in remote ITV classrooms are taught by a professor who is simultaneously teaching to a classroom of students on campus. In this electronic classroom, one camera focuses on the instructor while another scans charts, diagrams or other visual materials. The instructor and visual images are electronically "transmitted" to the remote sites where the students can see and hear the instructor on television monitors. An audio talk-back system permits students in these distant locations to interact with the instructor and with other students.

The Education Network of Maine delivers courses primarily through the medium of interactive television, but a supporting network of other information technologies provides students and faculty with additional opportunities to communicate. Computer conferencing, for example, allows students and faculty to correspond about course issues regardless of time and distance.

Eleven university off-campus centers and 50 high school sites located throughout the state serve the bulk of the students enrolled in courses on the Education Network of Maine. Off-campus centers coordinate registration, academic advising, admissions, financial aid, counseling and other services for students at the centers and at the high school sites in their region. A toll-free number (1-800-696-6000) is available for use by students, faculty or anyone in Maine who would like information about the network's courses and services.

Materials are distributed to students and faculty through UMA's Office of Distance Education Technologies. All course materials, including syllabi, handouts, quizzes and exams are sent to this central office for copying, collating and dissemination to all locations. Classes are videotaped and can be viewed at a later time should a student miss a class or wish to review before an exam.

Students at university campuses and at all off-campus centers and sites have access to URSUS, the university's computerized public-access library catalog. This database lists the book holdings, periodicals and state and federal documents of the University of Maine System. URSUS also contains collections of the Maine State Library and the Law and Legislative Reference Library at the Statehouse and allows students to search the collections of Colby, Bates and Bowdoin Colleges. Journal articles may be searched through CARL, the Colorado Alliance of Research Libraries, or through INFOTRAC, which includes an expanded index of academic, business and health journals. Students may order materials from their computer terminal and have them sent directly to a specified location.

The Education Network of Maine serves students of every age and in every region of the state, but it is Maine's rural women who make greatest use of the network's services. Surveys of these students show that the majority are over the age of 30 (55 percent), female (74 percent), and typically travel 11 miles to the ITV classroom, compared with the 28 miles it would have taken to commute to the nearest university campus. Studies document that these students do as well or better academically as their on-campus peers.

Since the fall 1992 semester, students may earn UMA associate degrees in General Studies, Business, Social Services and Liberal Arts through the Education Network of Maine. A range of innovative, challenging courses allow students to earn required credits in areas such as lab science, foreign language and college writing without requiring them to travel to a college campus.

These advances in course design are primarily the result of a grant from the Annenberg/CPB Project, which has enabled UMA to fund faculty and staff proposals aimed at upgrading curricula and support services for distant students. This program of faculty and staff development is supported by the Center for Distance Education at UMA, which serves as a national model for development and training in the educational uses of information technology.

As the community college of the University of Maine System, UMA has primary responsibility for off-campus associate degree education. As such, UMA selects and schedules the courses and faculty for associate-level degree programs offered on the network. The other campuses of the University of Maine System schedule their baccalaureate and graduate programming on the Education Network of Maine through UMA's Office of Enrollment and Information Services. The Education Network of Maine Academic Advisory Council, with representatives from each University of Maine System campus, is responsible for the long-range academic planning of courses and programs at all academic levels.

Because of the statewide enrollment possibilities, network-delivered courses are rarely canceled for lack of sufficient enrollment, allowing small communities, for the first time, to offer their populations a full-range of college courses. A total of 67 courses were broadcast over the Education Network of Maine in the fall 1992 semester. Of the 2,177 course sections offered during this semester, 2,108 were scheduled at off-campus locations.

Contact:
W. Clark Ketcham, Director of Enrollment Services
(207) 621-3000

University of Maine at Augusta
University Heights
Augusta, ME 04330-9410
Total head count enrollment-Credit: 2,791 Non-Credit: 1,896
Campuses/sites: 8 Full-time faculty: 71

FACULTY-BASED ASSESSMENT MODEL

The model makes sure student outcomes are supported through courses, programs and activities

Faculty are given broad input into all aspects of the education process at Allegany Community College. But the input doesn't end there. The community and employers also provide input, keeping education up-to-date and relevant.

The objectives of the Faculty-Based General Education Integration and Assessment Model are:

1) to identify the outcomes/competencies that the faculty believes are important for the ACC graduate to achieve by graduation;
2) to name the courses, programs and activities that will provide the outcomes;
3) to teach those outcomes in all ACC curricula; and
4) to have all faculty determine if these general education outcomes are being achieved.

All full-time and part-time faculty in the four general education divisions were individually interviewed by division chairmen to learn what they believe is important for a quality general education. Division-wide meetings were held to share ideas with faculty colleagues and a list of outcomes was made. The four objectives lists were combined and an unduplicated college-wide listing was made. ACC's definition of general education now includes eight major categories of student learning.

A grant proposal that was made to the Maryland Assessment Resource Center for funds resulted in a grant of $3,600, with the college contributing a matching amount for a total of $7,200. Also, Perkins funds were used to consider the priority of integrating academic and vocational education. Some of this money was used to hire consultants from the Maryland DACUM Resource Center who helped a faculty panel define and do "breakouts" of the list of outcomes. The faculty panel included faculty from both liberal arts and career programs. In the Spring of 1992, this faculty panel held lengthy meetings in the evening hours to complete "breakouts" of two of the eight categories of general education outcomes. Although the Vice President for Instructional Affairs and the Director of Institutional Research and Planning attended the meetings, only the faculty panel provided input. The paid consultants were the facilitators. The faculty members dedicated their time and energy without pay.

In the fall of 1992, a two-day faculty workshop was held and full-time faculty divided into six work groups that were asked: 1) to complete the "breakouts" of the remaining six general education categories; and 2) to begin "mapping" the courses/activities in which the various outcomes were introduced, reinforced, or measured by the instructors.

Part-time faculty received information on the full-time faculty meetings.

The results of these faculty work groups were combined into a "mapping chart" that listed all competencies/outcomes and corresponding "breakouts." The next step in the process was to have faculty "complete" the mapping charts – i.e., rate the extent to which each competency and "breakout" is addressed in each course.

Following a division chairmen and program directors meeting at which faculty panel members explained the process of completing the mapping charts, another faculty workshop was held at the beginning of the Spring 1993 semester.

Following an explanation by faculty panel members, all faculty divided into their respective departments to complete the mapping charts for each credit course within that department. The instructor who taught the course completed the mapping chart. In multiple section courses, it was required that a consensus be reached and only one mapping chart be completed. Although many of the mapping charts were completed the day of the workshop, faculty were given additional time to complete mapping charts if needed. By February 1993, a mapping chart had been completed for every credit course offered at ACC.

The next step is to enter the collected information from the mapping charts into a database that will allow for analyses. Ultimately, the faculty panel will be able to compare course requirements in the various programs offered by the college and identify "gaps"– i.e., programs in which students "miss" certain competencies by virtue of the existing course content and/or course mix in that program. Eventually, course content will be changed and/or program requirements altered to assure that every graduate is taught the identified competencies, regardless of his/her program of study.

The faculty panel will invite representatives who serve on each of ACC's program advisory committees to a meeting(s) to explain the project and to gather relative input from these important community resources. This link to the community and the employers of ACC graduates will strengthen the general education integration project by providing feedback on what the community leaders and advisory representatives feel is important to the general education of ACC students.

FY 94 will be devoted to the assessment phase of the project. This phase of the project will include faculty training and pilot assessment projects.

Contact:
Gene Hall, Vice President, Instructional Affairs
(301) 724-7700, ext. 288

Allegany Community College
Willowbrook Road
Cumberland, MD 21502
Total head count enrollment-Credit: 2,915; Non-Credit: 9,900
Campuses/sites: 1; Full-time faculty: 81

CENTER FOR THE STUDY OF LOCAL ISSUES

*A centerpiece of the Center's work has been
a twice-yearly survey of residents' attitudes*

It's unusual to find a community college engaged in research, but it makes a great deal of sense when it's "community" research. That's the case at the Center for the Study of Local Issues, established in 1978 by the Social Sciences division at Anne Arundel Community College. The Center is an extension of the community service mission of the college.

The Center has a twofold purpose:

1) to allow students and faculty to apply social science research methods to community issues; and

2) to bring the college and the community together, for a better understanding of local issues.

Its objectives are:

1) to provide an effective, low-cost method for collecting and analyzing information needed for decision making by government, business and community agencies serving Anne Arundel County citizens;

2) to provide ways for students and faculty to develop applied research skills; and

3) to bring recognized authorities to the community for discussion of issues and for information exchange.

Through the Center's student intern program, participants learn to craft research questions, discuss client needs, gather data, write computer programs, analyze results and present their findings to a client. Students also are enlisted to conduct telephone surveys.

Over the years, the Center has sponsored a diversity of projects which allow students and faculty to use their social science training in innovative and imaginative ways. In a 1983 project, people learned first-hand the difficulties of being physically handicapped. For a day on campus, volun-

teers were blindfolded or placed in wheelchairs. They then tried to carry out their regular daily activities. This study resulted in a pamphlet entitled "Go Anywhere, Do Anything," which won the outstanding project award of the Mary and chapter of the American Association of Planners for 1985.

Central to the Center's activities has been survey research. Twice a year, it conducts telephone interviews of county residents to determine citizen attitudes toward major local and national topics of interest. Questions measure attitudes toward the economy, perceptions of the most important problem facing the county as well as reactions to local, state and national issues.

The Center has conducted survey research for clients such as the Anne Arundel Trade Council and the county executive's office, assessing citizen perceptions of the county's economic health. It also helped the Anne Arundel Medical Center evaluate how effectively it meets its mission of community service.

In past years, the Center operated as an educational clearinghouse, linking professional expertise with locally identified community problems. The Center has hosted community workshops to focus discussion on topics including youth and sexuality, the family, gun control, futuristic thinking for the 21st Century and stereotyping.

Also, the Center has hosted workshops around the country to share information on community-based applied research. The workshops are tailored to meet requests for training faculty and refreshing their research skills. Workshop sites have included Honolulu, Michigan, New Jersey and Florida. Topics included applied sampling techniques, questionnaire design, how to use computer-based statistical packages and data analysis.

Contact:
Director of the Center for the Study of Local Issues
(410) 541-2230

Anne Arundel Community College
101 College Parkway
Arnold, MD 21012-1895
Total head count enrollment-Credit: 17,884; Non-Credit: 20,523
Number of campuses/sites: 1 campus/240 sites; Full-time faculty: 194

ENVIRONMENTAL CENTER

*Many students who interned at the Center have entered careers
monitoring and regulating environmental activities*

Anne Arundel Community College is situated on the Broadneck peninsula, surrounded by wetlands and Chesapeake Bay tributaries, a perfect site for the college's Environmental Center. Established in 1980, the Center

provides professional growth for faculty and hands-on academic experience for students through applied research on environmental problems facing local and state govern-

Continues on Page 300

ments.

Its priority objectives are shoreline stabilization to curtail erosion in high-energy environments; storm water management to improve water quality; the control of undesirable marsh vegetation to create better habitat for aquatic wildlife; monitoring water quality to help devise appropriate solutions to wetlands problems; and enhancement of fisheries to maintain an ecological balance.

The Center has employed more than 100 student interns and more than 20 college faculty and staff members to conduct research and apply solutions. Many of the students are now employed by government agencies that monitor and regulate environmental activities.

Since its inception, the Center has been a partner with government agencies, community groups, environmental organizations, businesses and industries. Staff members field more than 700 phone calls annually from various groups.

The Center has been involved in nearly 40 research projects since 1980. Clients include the Chesapeake Bay Trust, Nevamar Corporation, U.S. Fish and Wildlife Service, the Maryland Department of Natural Resources, the Environmental Protection Agency, U.S. Navy, the Maryland State Highway Administration, the Magothy River Association and the Severn River Association.

For example, the Center helped the Chesapeake Bay Trust produce an educational how-to video to teach the public about water quality monitoring in local waterways.

For Nevamar Corporation, the Center cut the temperature of discharge water entering a local waterway by creating cooling pools; it then used the warm pools as an aquatic nursery to germinate native marsh grass seeds. The Center uses the plants for marsh restoration, sediment control and shoreline erosion control in other projects.

This summer, the Center earned national recognition from U.S. environmental leaders. It won a 1992 Special Merit Award for helping Nevamar set up the wetlands nursery and for using the Providence Center for disabled adults to grow the plants used in various Center projects.

Another award-winning project is the SeaBee Beach marsh grass project, which began in 1988. The Center designed and coordinated the project with the help of numerous partners, including the U.S. Navy, Nevamar, Providence Center and community volunteers.

The project involved creating a continuous tidal marsh along 1,800 feet of shoreline, controlling an invasion of the undesirable Phragmites plant, hand-planting 20,000 marsh grass seedlings and improving aquatic resources of on-site impoundments. Maryland's governor gave the project his "Salute of Excellence" award in 1989.

Projects involving citizen volunteers include water quality monitoring, fisheries enhancement and studies of the effects of recreational water use on water quality. The Center has worked with more than 1,000 volunteers in its projects.

Contact:
Stephen Ailstock, Center Director
(410) 541-2230

Anne Arundel Community College
101 College Parkway
Arnold, MD 21012-1895
Total head count enrollment-Credit: 17,884; Non-Credit: 20,523
Number of campuses/sites: 1 campus/240 sites; Full-time faculty: 194

BALTIMORE CITY COMMUNITY COLLEGE

COLLEGE SUCCESS SEMINAR

The seminar is an elective that covers such topics as choosing goals and building support networks

Like many community colleges, a significant part of the mission of Baltimore City Community College is to provide "...basic skills and success strategies for under prepared students." In addition to operating a large, aggressive and creative Academic Development Program to assist the under-prepared and at-risk students to become independent, self-confident learners, Baltimore City Community College offers a unique three-credit course called the College Success Seminar.

The College Success Seminar is an elective that provides an opportunity for Baltimore City Community College students to learn and apply the attitudes and behaviors that lead to success in both college and in life. Topics covered in the course include choosing meaningful goals, creating effective action plans, building support networks, believing

in oneself (self-esteem), accepting personal responsibility and maximizing learning.

Students meet once a week in a large-group seminar and twice a week in a small-group workshop. The approach of the course is twofold: to offer our students a supportive community as they confront their challenges; and to teach them attitudes and behaviors essential to vaulting the barriers that lie between them and their goals.

The college supports an aggressive training program conducted by the seminar coordinator, Dr. Skip Downing, for the faculty who teach the College Success Seminar. One of the instructors wrote the following about her experience: "The College Success Seminar instructors meet together weekly. There is a carefully built sense of camaraderie in those faculty meetings. Each meeting is carefully structured and yet we have ample opportunity to learn from one another, discuss common problems and develop strategies to solve them."

Dr. Downing was recognized for his contribution to student success when he received the ACCT Northeast Regional Faculty Member Award in 1992. Here's what one students said at semester's end: "I know that if I had not had this class it would have been a struggle for me this semester. I really don't think I would have done as well as I did in my other classes if it wasn't for this class. I've learned so much about myself and life."

Contact:
Skip Downing, Seminar Coordinator
(410) 333-5411

Baltimore City Community College
2901 Liberty Heights Avenue
Baltimore, MD 21215
Total head count enrollment-Credit: 5,198; Non-Credit: 13,513
Campuses/sites: 2; Full-time faculty: 122

INSTITUTE FOR INTER-CULTURAL UNDERSTANDING

The Institute helps increase sensitivities to ethnic and racial groups in the metro area

One of the new initiatives at Baltimore City Community College is the Institute for Inter-Cultural Understanding (IIU).

The IIU is a formal effort to increase sensitivities to ethnic and racial groups in the Baltimore Metropolitan area. While cities across the nation are experiencing the sting of racial/cultural diversities, Baltimore City Community College intends to provide a leadership role in developing strategies and programs to help foster the inclusion of groups into an increasingly multi-cultural society. An important role for the institute is the examination of ideas and attitudes that contribute to positive inter-cultural group understandings.

The IIU was conceived by faculty in the Social and Behavioral Sciences Department. They successfully promoted their concept for inclusion in the college's TransCentury Plan, a comprehensive package of 16 initiatives designed to prepare students for the challenges of the 21st Century. For initial funding the faculty won a competitive, in-house grant of $15,000.

In its first year of existence, the IIU moved to a position of influence and respect at the college. The IIU has attracted 34 members from the college community, representing diverse cultural backgrounds. It is organized into six working committees, and its members have developed a mission statement and a set of goals for the organization. The IIU has been highly visible through its participation in the college's 1991 Holiday Party, the Colloquium on the West Indies, the presentation of Bill Demby, and the recent winning of one of eight Beacon Grants, which were awarded at the AACJC National Convention. The Beacon Grant will fund an effort to develop and nourish a strong source of community among a consortium of seven culturally diverse community college populations in the Baltimore-Washington metropolitan area. Baltimore City Community College will serve as a Beacon College and assume a leadership role in this prestigious program.

Contact:
Richard Bucher, Institute Chair
(410) 333-5458

Baltimore City Community College
2901 Liberty Heights Avenue
Baltimore, MD 21215
Total head count enrollment-Credit: 5,198; Non-Credit: 13,513
Campuses/sites: 2; Full-time faculty: 122

CENTER FOR TEACHING EXCELLENCE

Teaching improvement through the Center is fostered in a non-evaluative context that encourages voluntary participation

Teaching is the central and essential activity at Catonsville Community College, where the establishment of the Center for Teaching Excellence reminded us that without quality teaching and the learning which accompanies it, a college is meaningless.

The goals of the Center for Teaching Excellence include improving, enhancing and expressing the quality of teaching at CCC. For many years, these goals had been addressed in a variety of uncoordinated ways. To highlight and organize ongoing and new efforts and activities related to the institutional and national focus on the quality of teaching, Catonsville Community College established the Center for Teaching Excellence in 1985. It has expanded its services, programs and participants each year, and in 1989 the Center received the Maryland Association of Higher Education Distinguished Program Award.

The formal establishment of the Center for Teaching Excellence had the full support of administrators at the college, and was a combination of "top-down" encouragement and "bottom-up" initiative. On this subject, faculty and administration came together beautifully; the faculty knew they were supported and the administration knew the college benefited.

The Center for Teaching Excellence has established a working group of teaching faculty to share successful strategies and explore new teaching techniques, and to tap into creative ways of faculty enrichment in their professional assignments. This group of "Master Teachers" (called the Teaching Corps) are faculty who have received public recognition of the quality of their teaching through various internal and external awards. The Center has conducted a survey of the Teaching Corps to determine the characteristics, motivations and philosophies of the excellent teachers chosen for the Corps. These have been translated into an inventory for excellence in teaching, available to all faculty. The Corps members volunteer their time to work with colleagues for improved teaching. A Directory of Corps members available for peer assistance is published annually for all faculty.

Research indicates that very few colleges have centers that aim at teaching improvement and enhancement in a non-evaluative context, encouraging faculty to assess their own performance and seek assistance on a voluntary basis. Even fewer use excellent teachers as voluntary peer tutors for other faculty. These are features of Catonsville's Center for Teaching Excellence. A current project of the Center is "Teaching Dialogues," where faculty pairs work together on their teaching skills and discuss their teaching philosophies for a semester. The Dialogues program is now being extended to include adjunct faculty.

Following a survey of all faculty, an extensive Faculty Development program has been developed offering a wide variety of topics related to teaching. Annually the Center sponsors a two-day Teaching conference that all faculty attend prior to the beginning of the academic year. A two-week Summer Institute on the Art and Craft of Teaching is offered each summer for all teachers, including elementary and secondary school faculty, and their attendance is awarded in-service credit by the State Department of Education.

Most programs are videotaped for future use. In addition, the Center has videotaped some of CCC's excellent teachers in classroom settings. These tapes reflect various teaching styles, and are part of the Center's permanent collection, which also includes bibliographies, books, magazines, articles and films directly related to teaching. The Center also provides video support for faculty who wish to review their own teaching or experiment with new teaching styles.

The Center for Teaching Excellence encourages improved evaluation of teaching as professional assignment, and improved measurement of student outcomes as validation that good teaching results in good learning. It also encourages faculty to explore new educational technologies, and has established a Multi-media Center for faculty to experiment with state-of-the-art equipment and instructional materials.

CCC's Center for Teaching Excellence has contributed to the education of both students and faculty, and to the level of discourse about the educational process. Faculty have become learners again, exploring new ideas in a collegian way. Although well-educated in the content and methods of their disciplines, community college faculty are rarely trained as teachers. The Center is enabling them to address this need in their professional development and performance. In reaffirming its commitment to quality teaching, the college has focused on its educational mission. Faculty renewal and accomplishments contributing to teaching excellence have led to more lively learning for students.

Contact:
Leroy Giles, Center Coordinator
(410) 455-4363

Catonsville Community College
800 South Rolling Road
Catonsville, MD 21228
Total head count enrollment-Credit: 25,624; Non-Credit: 21,000
Campuses/sites: 4; Full-time faculty: 200

JANUARY TERM INSTITUTE

▦ By temporarily immersing students in college residential life, Catonsville ▦
encourages articulation elsewhere after graduation

The January Term Institute provides selected Catonsville Community College students with a unique and intensive liberal arts college transfer exploration, by a temporary but total immersion in the academic, social and residential life of Western Maryland College, a private liberal arts college.

The purpose of JTI, which takes place during Western Maryland's three-week January Term, is to encourage students to seriously consider transfer after receiving their AA degree, and to include residential liberal arts colleges in their options.

The objectives of the January Term Institute include offering a unique transfer experience at no cost to the students, allowing students to become members of a residential learning community for an intensive three-week period, proving to community college students that they can succeed in the academic environment of a residential liberal arts college, targeting students who statistics say are least likely to continue their education at a four-year college, and highlighting both the transfer mission of CCC and the transfer goals of WMC. All these objectives have been achieved during the annual institutes, which are continuing.

Students are chosen for one-time participation in JTI based on their accumulated credits (a minimum of 24 completed, including English 101), grade point average (a minimum of 3.0), and curriculum interest. The institute can currently accommodate up to 20 students annually, due to funding limits. Fifty-five percent of the class are non-traditional transfer students, including returning adults and racial and ethnic minorities. All participants are fully funded through scholarships contributed by the partner institutions. The January Term Institute has enrolled 47 students to date, of whom 29 were non-traditional transfer students. Of the total participants, 15 were men and 32 were women. Ninety percent of those completing the institute received grades of B or better in their courses. Eight CCC student leaders have participated, including several presidents of the Student Government Association. All courses the students completed transferred back to CCC as meeting curricular requirements or electives.

January Term Institute was implemented by the careful planning, financial commitment and good will of the partner schools. All qualified students are personally invited to apply for the institute, and applications are reviewed by a faculty panel. Selected students attend a special orientation and registration session in October, and commit to the terms of the scholarship, one of which requires residence at WMC during the institute. Students are fully integrated into the academic and social life of the college as WMC students. An events coordinator is assigned to work with JTI students to assure this happens, and to plan special events for them, such as financial and counseling, group discussions, parties, and both an initial reception and a final banquet.

Students, faculty and administration regularly evaluate the JTI program and recommended revisions as needed. In the third year, the evaluations were 100 percent positive, with no recommendations for improvement cited, demonstrating that responses to earlier recommendations resulted in achieving the highest quality program. This assessment was recently confirmed when the January Term Institute received the Maryland Association of Higher Education's Distinguished Program Award of Merit.

Contact:
Mary Hines, Associate Dean, Instruction
(410) 455-4250

Catonsville Community College
800 South Rolling Road
Catonsville, MD 21228
Total head count enrollment-Credit: 25,624; Non-Credit: 21,000
Campuses/sites: 4; Full-time faculty: 200

FAMILY SUPPORT AND EDUCATION CENTER

▦ On-site support services include substance abuse counseling ▦
and quarterly development screening for all children

Cecil Community College's Family Support Center provides comprehensive, supportive services to teen and young parents 25 years of age or younger to promote self-sufficiency through education and training. The core services are offered on-site at no charge to participants and include adult and parent education, child development activities, home visiting, employment and training assistance, health education, recreation and counseling.

Funded in July 1988 by a grant from the Maryland State Department of Education, the program is housed in the middle of a low-income housing project, making services accessible to those in greatest need. The Center provides van transportation to many participants who reside in other townships within the county. Transportation and child care appear to be the major obstacles for adults requiring education and training. The Center offers 750 instructional hours per year of adult education classes by providing these services to young parents who have dropped out of school.

These educational services are supplemented with career counseling and financial resources to enable the high school completer to enroll in credit and non-credit courses. A highly successful component of the Center is the STAR program which provides non-traditional training programs for their gender. STAR parents have enrolled in degree programs in the fields of accounting. chemical laboratory technician, computer programming and electricity. These women have established goals of higher wage earning jobs to enable them to leave the welfare system and support themselves and their children.

On-site support services such as substance abuse coun-

seling, case management workers, family planning clinic, and quarterly developmental screening for all children birth through four years of age help ensure a stronger family unit, leading to program completion and success.

The Family Support and Education Center presently maintains eight full-time employees and nine part-time staff. Many faculty and administrative staff from the Community College provide in-kind contributions of their time and resources as well. Approximately $335,500 in grants have been received for FY 93. The FSEC is equipped with two classrooms, computers for student use, a health clinic, full-service kitchen and dining room, and infant and toddler rooms.

The Family Support and Education Center has been visited and studied by Harvard University, John F. Kennedy School of Government, National Center for Children in Poverty. and the Children's Defense Fund. A national award from the Ford Foundation for Innovations in State and Local Government was given to the Family Support Center network in Maryland, with Cecil Community College's Center recognized as a leader in quality service delivery.

Contact:
Angie Barnett, Director
(410) 392-9272

Cecil Community College
1000 North East Road
North East, MD 21901
Total head count enrollment-Credit: 2,239; Non-Credit: 2,645
Campuses/sites: 3; Full-time faculty: 54

CECIL COMMUNITY COLLEGE

ADULT LITERACY / GED PROGRAM

⌘ *This program arms homeless people with education and support* ⌘
to become economically self-sufficient

Cecil Community College aims to help homeless people become economically self-sufficient through Project MEET (Mentoring, Education, Employability, Training).

During fiscal year 1990 and 1991, Cecil Community College's Adult Literacy/GED Program implemented the project in conjunction with the Maryland State Department of Education. The goal of this project is to assist homeless victims of domestic violence, homeless alcoholic men and homeless single parents by helping each individual develop an educational, employability and mentoring plan of action.

The college received a very positive evaluation from MSDE for exceeding all enrollment and educational goals during the first year of implementation. The college joined with local shelters such as the Cecil County Domestic Violence Shelter, Meeting Ground, and Wayfarers House, to recruit, retain and assist students in meeting all goals.

In addition, Adult Literacy/GED Program staff wrote a special projects grant proposal for fiscal year 1992 to expand services for homeless individuals as well as single

parents. Project HOME, Helping Others through Mentoring and Education, was funded by the Maryland State Department of Education to serve 45 single parents and homeless individuals. The college expanded student support services in conjunction with the college's Family Support and Education Center. Project staff also utilized the center's facilities to conduct three semesters of evening Adult Basic Education classes. Project mentors were hired to assist students with meeting personal needs such as finding housing employment and child care. While the project is not yet over, staff have exceeded anticipated enrollment goals.

The Adult Literacy GED Program operates a total of seven projects serving students included in, but not limited to, the federal and state priority target groups outlined in the Adult Education Act as amended by the National Literacy Act. The college's program serves undereducated adults, institutionalized adults, homeless adults, employed adults with basic skills deficiencies, non-English speaking adults, public assistance recipients, adults with disabilities, and adults whose lack of basic skills reduces their ability to improve the literacy level of their families.

Since 1988, the college's Adult Literacy/GED Program has significantly increased student enrollment by 40 percent. This growth can be attributed to the strengths that the program exhibits: a solid and strong foundation in the county, a committed and qualified staff, and a solid foundation of procedures and methods for collecting data and completing goals and objectives.

The Maryland State Department of Education conducted the college's Adult Literacy GED Program quadrennial ABE evaluation in October 1991. As a result of the evaluation, the Branch Chief for Adult and Community Education nominated Cecil Community College's Adult Literacy/GED Program for the United States Secretary of Education's Outstanding Adult Education Program Award. Cecil's Adult Literacy GED Program was recognized by MSDE representatives as an outstanding program for its administration, staffing, and accountability system.

Contact:
Joseph Rose, Director
(410) 392-3366

Cecil Community College
1000 North East Road
North East, MD 21901
Total head count enrollment-Credit: 2,239; Non-Credit: 2,645
Campuses/sites: 3; Full-time faculty: 54

TOPS 2000 (TRAINING OPPORTUNITY SERVICES)

Partnerships with agencies have been enhanced by connecting businesses with agencies that provide work force development

It has been widely-noted that there will be a disastrous work force/skills gap by the year 2000, unless corrective steps are taken. In response to this call to action, Charles County Community College launched the TOPS 2000 (Training Opportunity Services) program in 1990. The college's Continuing Education and Community Services Division had as its main objective the creation of an arm of the institution outwardly focused on the community, which would identify the needs of the community and translate those needs into workable solutions within the college's mission.

As a result of this objective, the college examined its infrastructure and its ability to deliver a variety of training in a relatively short turnaround time and through non-traditional means of delivery. Changes included a restructuring of the administrative body into functional areas such as marketing, training services and operations.

The program has significantly contributed to the college's partnerships with state agencies, the business community, local and state government, end-users (students) and internally. Partnerships with state agencies have been enhanced through helping to connect businesses with agencies that provide assistance for work force development. Strong business connections have lead to joint training programs and the donation of needed equipment.

An increasing reliance on the college as a provider of training has been noted. Through its proactive stance, the TOPS 2000 program has learned a great deal about the needs of the business community and has been involved in dialogue, planning and training during times of significant employee layoffs, influxes of technology and in other instances to serve not only as a training service, but as a partner in solving county/regional problems.

Contact:
Audrey Ware, Dean of Continuing Education & Community Services
(301) 934-2251, ext. 446

Charles County Community College
Mitchell Road, PO Box 910
La Plata, MD 20646-0910
Total head count enrollment-Credit: 5,800; Non-Credit: 13,279
Campuses/sites: 4; Full-time faculty: 70

COLLEGE PREPARATION PROGRAM

*⊞ The college, county schools and local communities jointly ⊞
oversee and advise the project for disadvantaged students*

The Southern Maryland Early Intervention, College Preparation Program is part of a state-wide initiative, composed of five regional components, designed to assist environmentally and economically disadvantaged students in grades six, seven and eight.

The primary goal of this enterprise is to enable these students to achieve at above-average academic levels through their middle and high school years and to make post-secondary education on either the community college or four-year college level a viable reality.

The Southern Maryland group, one of the five regional constituents, is composed of six collaborating sectors, which include three county-wide public school systems (Calvert, Charles and St. Mary's counties) and three institutions of higher education (Charles County Community College, St. Mary's College and the University of Maryland, College Park). The program is overseen by a governance committee made up of personnel from each of the county schools and the colleges. In addition, representatives from the local communities assist with advice and direction of the project as members of an advisory committee.

Funded through a grant from the Maryland Higher Education Commission, the Early Intervention Program is a three-year pilot study intended to form the basis for a more permanent and pervasive program to ensure that the necessary support is made available throughout the state to students in this targeted population.

Through this arrangement, the targeted middle school students (now followed into their ninth and tenth grade high school years), their parents, teachers and counselors have the opportunity to become familiar with three very distinct post-secondary institution types, ranging from Charles County Community College (a two-year institution) to St. Mary's College (a four-year liberal arts college) to University of Maryland at College Park (a large, research-oriented university).

Although each institution was given the initial flexibility to design programs that maintain a distinct identity. Similar student-oriented activities common to all three colleges include tutoring, mentoring programs, a lecture series featuring role models, college campus visits, scholarships for summer enrichment programs and continuing education, dialogues with college faculty, phone-a-thons with college and university students, weekly student meetings, college preparation/financial aid nights, technological-cultural field trips and parent meetings.

Participation in the program, as of 1992, included a total of 296 students; 133 students from Charles County, 113 students from St. Mary's County, and 50 Calvert County students.

Project recognition has come in the form of local media publicity and through national speaking engagements. In February 1991, SMIP organizers were asked to present an historic overview of the program at the Middle States Regional Meeting of the College Board. In September 1992, the project director spoke at the national COMBASE conference on the partnership aspects of SMIP.

The 1992-93 academic year was the final year of the pilot study. SMIP hopes to obtain additional funding through state, federal, or private resources in order to continue the project.

Contact:
Robert R. St. Pierre, Project Director
(301) 934-2251, ext. 524

Charles County Community College
Mitchell Road, PO Box 910
La Plata, MD 20646-0910
Total head count enrollment-Credit: 5,800; Non-Credit: 13,279
Campuses/sites: 4; Full-time faculty: 70

EARLY CHILDHOOD DEVELOPMENT

*⊞ Graduates are prepared to work in preschools, schools, day care centers ⊞
and institutions working with exceptional children*

The Early Childhood Program at Essex Community College is unique in offering more than one area of training in the field of child care. The Associate in Arts Degree is awarded to students completing studies in Preschool Elementary School Aide, Program Management, and Special Education Aide. Within these options, students have the flexibility, and are encouraged, to be prepared for the varying needs of the job market by fulfilling the requirements of more than one option.

In addition, the program, implemented in 1976, offers a

variety of innovative courses to accommodate people already working in the field. For example, the Infant Curriculum course, which includes infants, their parents and the students, is scheduled on Saturday mornings and the Day Care Management courses are offered on weekends during the winter session. The overall purpose of the Early Childhood Development program is to train care-givers who will function competently in a variety of settings. Graduates of this program are prepared to function as teacher aides in the elementary school, program directors in day care centers, teachers of preschool children, or as aides and assistants in institutions dealing with exceptional children.

The Early Childhood Development program is supported by two learning centers, the Early Childhood Learning Center and the Hourly Preschool Center. Both centers are housed in one on-campus building. In addition, the program is supported by three full-time faculty members, as well as four administrators/teachers for the two learning centers. The Learning Center is designed as a model day care program to serve the needs of the children and parents in the community. The program operates under the philosophy shared by the Education Department that children learn best by exploration and "doing." The program seeks to meet the physical, social, emotional and intellectual needs of each child through a rich learning environment. The Center is licensed by the Baltimore County Health Department for children ages three, four and five. The Hourly Preschool Center is designed to assist students by providing a stimulating

program for their children. The program also supports a Children's Developmental Clinic that helps children with developmental problems. Activities are provided by the volunteer services of trained students and community clinicians. A Saturday morning program meets 10 Saturdays each college semester.

In cooperation with local businesses, community members and other organizations, the program supports three major initiatives, an Annual Update for Child Care Personnel, a program advisory committee and an internship program. The annual update is a one-day workshop that provides care-givers an opportunity to upgrade their knowledge in the field. Faculty and child care professionals from the community, such as the National Association for the Education of Young children, join together in this endeavor.

Members of the department, in cooperation with the program coordinator of the Mental Health/Human Services program, developed a Sexual Assault Prevention Program model to address sexual child abuse. It is the largest preschool sexual abuse prevention program in the nation, having trained more than 650 teachers in six states and serving more than 5,000 children, ages three through six.

In 1991, the Early Childhood Development program received the Maryland's "Award of Excellence" for the outstanding post secondary program in the state, presented by the Maryland State Department of Education, Division of Career and Technology Education.

Contact:
Donna Jacobs, Program Coordinator
(410) 780-6574

Essex Community College
7201 Rossville Boulevard
Baltimore, MD 21237
Total head count enrollment-Credit: 11,475; Non-Credit: 12,000
Campuses/sites: 1; Full-time faculty: 172

ESSEX COMMUNITY COLLEGE

ARTIFACTS OF CULTURE

This humanities program, geared toward adults returning to college, inverts the traditional pyramid of learning

The Artifacts of Culture program is designed to be of special interest to adults returning to college primarily for purposes of ongoing personal enrichment, intellectual stimulation and lifelong learning, as well as to provide transfer electives in humanities. The program uses a team-taught interdisciplinary care-study approach to the humanities through a series of one-credit course modules. Each module is devoted to the intensive study of a single masterpiece, theme of movement of world art, music, literature, architecture or other humanities discipline.

The program was created in direct consequence of participation in the 1977 American Association for Higher Education conference, "New Directions in Humanities."

A team of faculty developed an alternative to the introductory/survey approaches to the humanities disciplines. The first year (1978-79) of the program was made possible by a pilot grant from the National Endowment for the Humanities.

Program objectives were to develop and deliver a continuing, ongoing, innovative and exemplary model program of higher education in humanities for adults. The program was designed to elucidate the encounter between the mature student and a given cultural artifact, strengthen the humanities regionally and locally, and provide a model exemplary program for dissemination in other institutions

Continues on Page 308

of higher education locally, regionally and nationally.

The uniqueness of the program is inherent in a design that inverts the traditional pyramidal model of learning, in which "broad foundations" are laid in introductory courses and then successively narrower foci are introduced in succeeding electives. In contrast, by introducing students to the intensive case-study of selected artifacts, the program demonstrates that a student with no particular assumed background can in fact achieve a competent level of discourse in analysis and criticism in the humanities.

The 14-year-old program has experienced a continuous growth in enrollment, as well as increased recognition among humanities programs in higher education, both locally and nationally. It has generated 120 course modules in humanities education for adults and has had an enormous impact on the intellectual lives of the students who have taken courses and the teachers who have taught in the program. As a direct result of the Artifacts program, Essex Community College has recently generated two major NEH grants, one a Study Group for 25 teachers from the Baltimore County Community College system (1990) on the Encounter of Cultures in the New World, and the other a national NEH Institute (one of only 18 offered nationally in 1992) on the same subject, open to 25 faculty from two-year and four-year colleges selected

nationally. The program has also recruited two successive Fulbright-Scholars-in-Residence at Essex, for the 91-92 and 92-93 academic years. These activities are unusual for any college, but are unprecedented for a community college.

In 1986, the Maryland State Board for Community Colleges listed the Artifacts program in its Honor Roll of Outstanding Achievements. Also in 1985-86, Essex Community College was selected as one of 13 nationally selected mentor exemplary programs in the Johns Hopkins/NEH "Exemplary Humanities Programs for Adults" project. Presentations of the Artifacts program have been made at meetings sponsored by the National Endowment for the Humanities, The Johns Hopkins University School of Continuing Studies, the George Mason Conference on Non-Traditional and Interdisciplinary Programs, the Community College Humanities Association, the Annual International Conference on Programs, the Community College Humanities Association, the Annual International Conference on Teaching Excellence (National Institute of Staff and Professional Organization), the National Master Teacher seminars in Orlando, and the Maryland State Board for Community Colleges.

Contact:
George Scheper, Instructor-in-charge
(410) 780-6539

Essex Community College
7201 Rossville Boulevard
Baltimore, MD 21237
Total head count enrollment-Credit: 11,475; Non-Credit: 12,000
Campuses/sites: 1; Full-time faculty: 172

GARRETT COMMUNITY COLLEGE

STUDENT ASSISTANCE CENTER

The Center centralizes such things as admissions, financial aid, advising and course schedules

The Student Assistance Center at Garrett Community College provides a one-stop shop for a variety of student assistance.

This contrasts with many colleges, where new students are sent to various offices such as: admission information, application, financial aid, placement testing/evaluation, academic advising, course schedules, catalogs. The purpose of the SAC is to centralize these services. Unless an inquiry to the college's phone switchboard requests a specific office, most phone calls are channeled to the SAC, where staff listen to the request and usually handle the situation without switching to another office. Staff know the intricate workings of the college and usually provide sufficient information to take care of a variety of needs. If necessary, the caller is given a name for referral and is immediately transferred to the extension where more detailed assistance can be given.

The central feature of the SAC is the experience for the

new student coming to the college for the first time. The student comes to one office for application, placement testing/evaluation, and academic advising leading to student matriculation. This one-stop-shop provides continuity and lessens frustration and the feeling of "where do I go?" which is prominent in the mind and experience of all new students. The SAC assigns an academic advisor to the student, usually based on the intended major the student wishes to pursue. However, all academic advisors are trained to be generalist advisors for all GCC programs. When the student has completed the placement testing in English, reading and math, the student meets with an academic advisor for about 90 minutes. During this session the student is greeted and welcomed to the college, and in a structured but informal way taken through a check list of items, including a review of the application, placement test review, request for the high school transcript, college program review and selection, information about transfer opportunities, transfer credit evaluation, non-traditional credit evaluation, the financial aid application, career planning, housing needs, college policies and procedures, course selection, registration preparation, and review of the student packet.

Such personal attention acquaints the student with one person who will assist with diverse needs during the course of the college experience.

This service is directly in line with the Garrett Community College mission, which states: "Garrett Community College believes it can best overcome barriers to seeking a higher education by respecting and caring for students as individuals, by defining their strengths and needs, by starting where they are ready to begin, by providing them with supportive programs and services, and by motivating and encouraging them to achieve standards of personal and academic excellence. GCC seeks to make itself known as a friendly, open, warm, and supportive college that makes every student feel welcome and that supports each individual's aspirations for a better life."

Contact:
Manning L. Smith, Director, Student Services
(301) 387-3011

Garrett Community College
PO Box 151
McHenry, MD 21541
Total head count enrollment-Credit: 700; Non-Credit: 3,000
Campuses/sites: 1; Full-time faculty: 14

LEARNING ENHANCEMENT AND ASSISTANCE PROGRAM

The assistance program for under-prepared students has maintained an 80 percent success rate in all subject areas

Some students may enter Garrett Community College under-prepared for its academic rigors, but most of those who turn to the Learning Enhancement and Assistance Program (LEAP) become well-prepared for college studies. LEAP was designed to serve as a broad umbrella of assistance to make the institution more user-friendly. Its scope and sequence is comprehensive of the needs of the entire student community.

LEAP'S establishment can be traced to 1989, when the Learning Enhancement Council of Garrett Community College responded to the need for a separate developmental center on campus. As the concept emerged, it became obvious that the needs of students included:

1) assistance with learning skills in general;
2) specialized testing;
3) individual learning program;
4) support to the mainstream curriculum; and
5) opportunities for honors programs.

LEAP facilitates:

1) accurate placement and supplemental testing;
2) appropriate curriculum;
3) individual learning plans for special students;
4) referral services for mainstream students having difficulty;
5) peer tutoring;
6) orientation to college courses;
7) mastery learning; and
8) referral to external professionals as needed.

The college installed a program director with a tests and measurements background, a writing lab coordinator, a coordinator for the mathematics program, and assistance in reading, mathematics and English. Simultaneously, placement testing divided students into four categories based on scores and apportioned them as remedial, developmental, mainstream or honors. Curriculum was delivered by a faculty trained for the task in special summer in-service clinics. Unlike some collegiate instructional models, these professionals were trained to provide a warm, supportive environment conducive to success while maintaining rigorous exit criteria based on mastery learning. The delivery system was expanded to deliver developmental courses in tandem through credit and non-credit modalities. This configuration allowed the college the opportunity to provide refresher seminars and "gap clinics" for students to refresh skills once attained. Refreshed students could exit test to the next level.

On the developmental level, the program has maintained an 80 percent success rate in all subject areas while delivering students to the mainstream college curriculum. Feedback from professors confirms that students are readied for the college experience by the education LEAP has delivered.

Among mainstream students, the LEAP has created new opportunities for peer tutoring of others, access to an honors fraternity and honors courses. Students now share a

Continues on Page 310

general feeling that academic weaknesses may be remedied without shame. Perhaps most important, students are able to see a "ladder for success" – a much-needed commodity in the new and different world called college.

Contact:
George McDowell, Director
(301) 387-6666

Garrett Community College
PO Box 151
McHenry, MD 21541
Total head count enrollment-Credit: 700; Non-Credit: 3,000
Campuses/sites: 1; Full-time faculty: 14

HUMAN SERVICES TECHNOLOGY

The program is articulated with a local branch campus of Frostburg State University

The Human Services Technician Program at Hagerstown Junior College is one of the three fastest-growing career and technology education programs at the college. The program serves three distinct clienteles.

First, there are approximately 100 students enrolled in the program who are preparing for employment in the human or social services field and for possible transfer to a baccalaureate degree program.

Second, the instructor in charge, working closely with the college's dean of instruction and the director of training for the Maryland Department of Social Services, established a career ladder program for employees of the local Department of Social Services.

Third, the college offers a substance-abuse option, which results in completion of either a certificate or an associate degree along with partial completion of the certification process for becoming a substance-abuse counselor by the Maryland Office of Education and Training for Addiction Services.

As a result of this diversified curriculum, the Human Services Technician Program is recognized as an important career entry or career development strategy within the college's service area.

The program is articulated with the local branch campus of Frostburg State University. Graduates of the program transfer to Frostburg with no loss of credit. This articulation agreement functions as the second step in a career ladder designed to professionalize the human and social services community in the college's district.

During academic year 1991-92 the Human Services Technician Program participated as a pilot program for the development of a tech prep 2 + 2 agreement. The instructor in charge, in cooperation with faculty from the local vocational high school, the local business college, and Frostburg State University developed an integrated curriculum and procedures for articulation that allow expanded professionalization of a series of high school and business college programs.

Finally, the program has a very active student organization. Representatives of the Human Services Club cooperate with colleagues from community colleges in the middle Atlantic region, the Mid-Atlantic Consortium for Human Services. Students have the opportunity to attend an annual conference and participate in training that is directly relevant to their role as entry-level human services workers.

In five years the human services program has grown from approximately two dozen students to a comprehensive, multi-focused career development opportunity for a diverse group of community residents.

Contact:
Nan Ottenritter, Instructor in Charge
(301) 790-2800, ext. 273

Hagerstown Junior College
1400 Robinwood Drive
Hagerstown, MD 21742-6590
Total head count enrollment-Credit: 3,300; Non-Credit: 5,000
Campuses/sites: 1; Full-time faculty: 53

ADMINISTRATION OF JUSTICE PROGRAM

*▦ The program allows students to emphasize in either ▦
police services or correctional services*

In addition to its diversified curriculum, the Administration of Justice Program at Hagerstown Junior College conducts community research activities and reaches out to diverse clients. Its comprehensive career and technology education offering leads to either the associate degree or certificate with an emphasis in either police services or correctional services.

The program enrolls approximately 130 regular students who are preparing for employment as either police or correctional officers and for possible transfer to a baccalaureate degree program. The instructor in charge has developed a close working relationship with the Western Maryland Police Training Academy. In cooperation with the training officer of the academy, he teaches part of each recruit class and conducts an orientation regarding articulation between the program and the academy.

A military base is located in the college's district. The instructor in charge works closely with the provost marshal and the company commander of the military police company. Courses are offered on the base so that military police personnel can upgrade their professional training and prepare for promotion in the military.

The program is designed to provide credit for training done under the auspices of the Maryland Correctional Academy. The instructor in charge cooperates with the correctional training staff to help students understand the nature of the articulation between the correctional academy and the program.

The program provides a structure for the college's Center for Public Policy Studies. The center provides non-credit workshops and seminars, conducts field research projects, and assists with data collection and analysis on public policy issues. The instructor in charge, in cooperation with other social science faculty and the dean of instruction, has received grants from the Maryland Humanities Council, City of Hagerstown, and Washington County to conduct research projects and provide public awareness activities regarding results of the research.

Finally, the program has a very active student organization. Representatives of the 5-14 Club plan and conduct field trips, public awareness activities and forums for discussion of issues relevant to the law enforcement community. For instance, the students have coordinated visits to the Department of State, headquarters of the Maryland Police Training Commission, and the national headquarters of the FBI in Washington, DC.

Contact:
Steve Zabetakis, Instructor in Charge
(301) 790-2800, ext. 223

Hagerstown Junior College
1400 Robinwood Drive
Hagerstown, MD 21742-6590
Total head count enrollment-Credit: 3,300; Non-Credit: 5,000
Campuses/sites: 1; Full-time faculty: 53

REVITALIZATION: A PRESCRIPTION FOR CHANGE

*▦ Each June, administrator retreats are held to discuss ▦
successes, failures and fallacies of revitalization*

Montgomery College, Maryland, approaches its 50th anniversary with a long-standing reputation among students and the community for providing excellent education and delivering quality services. But Montgomery College will not ride complacently into its 50th year on past accomplishments. Instead, the president of the college chose to take a hard, honest look at the institution and the ways the college conceived, executed and delivered its educational program and student-related services.

A 1987 self-study concluded that the community and student perception of Montgomery College was generally excellent. However, the study also revealed that its structure was not as effective as it could be and the college needed to recapture some of the enthusiasm, momentum and flexibility inherent in younger institutions. In response to the study and with a deliberate intent to invigorate the existing internal organization, President Robert Parilla launched his "Revitalization" campaign.

According to Dr. Parilla, "Revitalization grew out of an effort to reaffirm the college commitment to teaching and learning within a framework that promoted personal initiative, involvement and empowerment; emphasized quality; eschewed bureaucratic barriers; and encouraged a culture of community teamwork and mutual support."

Revitalization comprises a number of values and precepts designed to break up the traditional hierarchical way of thinking about an organization. Typical vertical

Continues on Page 312

structures for information flow and accountability are called upon to be both compressed then expanded horizontally: The pyramid is inverted; the customers, not the CEO, are at the apex. Issues such as poor communication, conflicting priorities, and other "turf" concerns are removed and replaced by a team approach which crosses functional categories and espouses a unified institutional perspective.

And how is the college faring in its revitalizition? "We've come a long way and have a long way to go," is the general consensus among the college community. Central administration is reduced in size, becoming a more fit and streamlined operation. The college moved from three vice presidents to one chief administrative officer and eliminated associate directors and other middle management positions, which spread the planning and implementation responsibilities among the provosts, deans, faculty and staff throughout the three campus institution.

However, change by nature means shifting course, and while much has been accomplished, the road between old and new thinking is sometimes bumpy. Yet Dr. Parilla is committed to the revitalization process, and he and other leaders in the college are determined to see it through to maturity.

Each year in June, administrator retreats are held to inspire lively discussion of the strengths, weaknesses, successes, failures, fallacies and triumphs of revitalization. Administrators are asked: "What's working well? What's not? How can I improve?" Much of the time is devoted to small group discussions, with each group team expanding upon the focus questions. Recommendations range from ways to more effectively reallocate time, funds and staff to more personal measures that call for changes in administrative behavior encouraging greater interaction with students and staff.

What's next? In the continued spirit of revitalization, related philosophies will gradually permeate the new college climate. Already, Total Quality Management (TQM) and other successful corporate strategies are finding a place in the new structure of Montgomery College.

For some, change is unsettling, but for Montgomery College revitalization is recognized and welcomed as a healthy and innovative process. Most importantly, it is improving services to students and to the community.

Contact:
Linda Johnson, Marketing Services Coordinator
(301) 279-5310

Montgomery College
900 Hungerford Drive, Suite 140
Rockville, MD 20850
Total head count enrollment-Credit: 23,000; Non-Credit: 21,000
Campuses/sites: 3; Full-time faculty: 394

TECHNICAL EDUCATION

The programs are turning out skilled technicians ready to fill an increasing number of employment positions

Montgomery County, Maryland, is among the growing number of communities faced with an alarming problem: How do we fill the increasing number of technically challenging jobs in the modern work force when the pool of qualified workers is drying up? The issue of comprehensive technical education for employees is fast becoming the focus of corporate agendas across the globe and is likely to be one of the most critical challenges of the 21st Century.

Montgomery College has responded to the crisis by making technical education a priority. With a mission to serve both the citizens and businesses in Montgomery County, the college has introduced new programs and expanded others to train people for more rewarding, well-paying technical careers. At the same time it helps satisfy the business community's demand for qualified technicians.

More than 50 high-standard technical career programs are offered emphasizing general education and specific technical skill areas. Students completing the program are awarded the associate in arts degree. The college also offers a number of one-year certificate programs. In addition, the Homer S. Gudelsky Institute for Technical Education houses state-of-the-art centers for Apprenticeship and Technical Trades, Automotive Technology, Building Trades Technology and Printing Management Technology.

The College Preparation Technical Program, "Imagine Your Tomorrow," begins in the junior year of high school and leads to the completion of an associate in arts degree in Electromechanical Technology, Computer-aided Drafting and Design, Biotechnology, and other technical fields. For those already working in the field, Corporate Employee Training, offered through the Office of Continuing Education, provides excellent technical and management training and education tailored to the needs of individual businesses. Both those considering a career in technical trades and senior-level tradespeople are brought together through the Skilled Worker Emeritus Program through which tradespeople mentor students.

Students are further alerted to increasing technical

career opportunities through the Survey of Technical Careers, a course that explores a variety of technical occupations.

The Division of Career and Technology Education, Maryland State Department of Education, administers federal funds provided under the Carl Perkins Act in support of the college's efforts to educate students in technical fields through cooperative programs and by providing instructional equipment and materials, guidance and counseling, and supplemental services to special populations.

Also, the Cooperative Education Program allows students to complement classroom experience with on-the-job training. The work done through this program relates directly to the student's academic major or career goals. Co-op students are among those studying accounting, computer science, child care, biotechnology and many other curricula.

Additionally, Health Care Career program coordinators, in cooperation with five Montgomery County hospitals, are vigorously recruiting students and providing them extra career preparation and financial assistance through a grant from the state of Maryland.

Finally, the Work Force Evaluation Project, coordinated through Continuing Education and the Assessment Center, provides employee testing services for businesses and government agencies.

Contact:
Linda Johnson, Marketing Services Coordinator
(301) 279-5310

Montgomery College
900 Hungerford Drive, Suite 140
Rockville, MD 20850
Total head count enrollment-Credit: 23,000; Non-Credit: 21,000
Campuses/sites: 3; Full-time faculty: 394

FUND RAISING AND FRIEND RAISING

Outreach resource centers have developed new and alternative sources of funding in a time of otherwise shrinking budgets

Discipline-related outreach resource centers at Prince George's Community College encouraged faculty to become academic entrepreneurs in designing programs and obtaining funding that provide opportunities for academic enrichment, professional growth and service to the college and to the community. In an era of diminishing funds from traditional state and county funding sources, the college's outreach resource centers have developed new and alternative sources of funding for their affiliated divisions and departments.

Since its initial $25,000 summer science institute grant in 1987, the college's first center, the Science and Technology Resource Center, now attracts an average of $500,000 annually in grants and gifts to support science, mathematics, engineering and health technology programs and services. The Humanities Resource Center, created in 1990, raised more than $320,000 in 1992-93 to support humanities, fine and performing arts, social sciences and English studies programming.

Funding sources for the Science and Technology Resource Center's activities include five grants from the National Science Foundation: Eisenhower Title II monies through the Maryland Higher Education Commission; the Chesapeake Bay Trust; private foundations; professional societies; and local business and industry. The Humanities Resource Center has received four grants from the National Endowment for the Humanities, seven from the Maryland Humanities Council, one from the Department of Education, and various funds from state and local arts councils, professional societies and private contributions.

Contact:
Patricia A. Cunnif, Director, Sci. & Tech Resource Ctr, (301) 322-0432
Lyle E. Linville, Director, Humanities Resources Ctr, (301) 322-0600

Prince George's Community College
301 Largo Road
Largo, MD 20772
Total headcount enrollment-Credit: 17,000; Non-Credit: 19,000
Campuses/sites: 1; Full-time faculty: 206

UNDERSTANDING CULTURAL PLURALISM

*▨ The course on cultural pluralism is a graduate-level seminar ▨
that includes several guest lecturers*

Although national trends point to the need to respond to an increasing diverse student population, the skills necessary to do so sometimes need to be cultivated in faculty. So the course "Understanding Cultural Pluralism" was created.

This followed the president's appointment of a Cross-Cultural Education Advisory Council (CCEAC). The council is co-chaired by Robert C. Hardwick, Executive Assistant to the president, and Alonia C. Sharps, Assistant to the President for Minority Affairs and Affirmative Action Programs. The council, which recommended the new course, is mandated to make recommendations to the president regarding cross-cultural education initiatives, particularly in the area of instruction.

Robin Hailstorks and Paul Van Cleef, members of the council, were asked to develop a course on cultural plurality. A description of the course is as follows: An examination of the concepts of cultural diversity, cultural pluralism, multi-culturalism, inter-ethnic relations, and cross-cultural and global perspectives. The concepts of race, gender, culture, ethnicity, nationality, and minority and majority group status will be discussed from the perspective of how these categories influence our behavior toward people who are different from us. Emphasis will be placed on developing strategies that encourage cultural pluralism. Factors that encourage mono-culturalism will be identified.

The course objectives are to:

1) define the concepts of cultural pluralism, multi-culturalism, inter-ethnic relations, cross-cultural and global perspectives;

2) discuss the concepts of race, gender, ethnicity, culture, nationality, and minority and majority group status in relation to how these conceptualizations influence behavior, as well as how culture influences our thinking, perception and modes of communication;

3) identify factors that influence our thinking and behavior toward persons who are like us or unlike us, identify strategies for enhancing our awareness and acceptance of cultural diversity and strategies for bridging our understanding of cultural differences;

4) discuss some of the myths and realities of ethnic minorities who reside in the United States; and

5) develop strategies for implementing a multicultural curriculum and for diversifying the work setting.

This course is a graduate-level seminar and includes a number of guest lecturers, in-class exercises, and audiovisual material. Each participant is required to keep a journal, complete structured exercises, and to submit a plan for diversifying his/her work setting. Approximately 20 participants enroll in the course each semester. The course was pilot-tested by the CCEAC for the Fall 1992 Semester. This course will ultimately be offered to county residents and to the local business community. Administrators from the County Public School System have attended this course. A student version of this course was to be offered for the Spring 1994 Semester.

Funding for this course was secured through a grant from the U.S. Office of Education, Title III Program.

Contact:
Robin Hailstork, (301) 322-0539
Paul Van Cleef, (302) 322-0653

Prince George's Community College
301 Largo Road
Largo, MD 20772
Total headcount enrollment-Credit: 17,000; Non-Credit: 19,000
Campuses/sites: 1; Full-time faculty: 206

CHEMICAL DEPENDENCY COUNSELING

*▨ The program, unique on the entire Eastern Shore of Maryland, prepares trained ▨
professionals for various understaffed counseling specialties*

The steadily increasing population on the Eastern Shore of Maryland brought with it a disproportionate increase in the number of chemically dependent residents. Few trained professional counselors were available for hire to work in the treatment centers assigned to help this disadvantaged population. In response to the critical necessity

to curtail the ever-increasing incidence of drug and alcohol abuse in Maryland, Wor-Wic implemented a program to train chemical dependency counselors.

To start, the DACUM (Developing a Curriculum) model of analyzing training needs was adopted to design a curriculum suited to our unique set of circumstances. The

DACUM method operates under the premise that skilled workers are better able to describe their occupation than anyone else. In 1986, a panel of practicing counselors and agency administrators was convened under the auspices of Wor-Wic. The panel's task was to draw on its collective experience and produce not only a list of skills the trained counselor should possess and tools and equipment needed to foster those skills, but also identify traits and attitudes the needed prospective counselor should exhibit. A DACUM matrix of occupational competencies was drawn up and a precise curriculum to satisfy the identified needs developed.

A constant monitoring of the alignment of our courses with the level courses required by the Office of Education and Training for Addiction Services (OETAS) took place to ensure that our offerings would be within the certification requirements of the Maryland Department of Health and Mental Hygiene.

Wor-Wic's completed program was submitted for approval to the Maryland State Board of Community Colleges. Approval was granted, and our program began in September, 1988. For continued guidance, a Program Advisory Committee (PAC) composed of faculty, students and practicing professionals was formed and still serves as an invaluable source of vital input.

The program stands unique in the fact that it is the only one of its kind on the entire Eastern Shore of Maryland and has targeted its availability, not only to traditional but also to non-traditional students. The program's uniqueness is further demonstrated by being one of only two in the entire state leading to an Associate of Arts Degree in this specialty.

The Chemical Dependency program is designed to prepare students to work as paraprofessionals in chemical dependency programs in institutions and private and state agencies. Program graduates can qualify for employment in county addictions programs as addiction counselors after successfully completing six core courses. The flexibility of this program allows students to enter the job market or transfer to a four-year college or university and work toward an advanced degree.

Student learning at Wor-Wic is effectively achieved through a combination of classroom instruction, which establishes a firm theoretical base, and real life simulation, which allows the student to turn theory into practice. In the classroom, formal lecture and group discussion of current trends in counseling procedures and client behavior are applied by means of role playing in simulated group and one-on-one therapy sessions. Many of these sessions are video-taped or audio-taped, reviewed and critiqued by the students, thus providing an open forum for the exchange of ideas.

In another phase of the program, actual case histories are used as the basis for hands-on experience and student orientation to procedural matters. Further orientation is provided through the use of sample materials acquired from state and private counseling agencies. These materials include actual client case histories and documentation of counseling sessions. From these sample documents, students have the opportunity to write treatment plans which include behavioral goals and objectives; develop psychological profiles; and write discharge summaries. Throughout the curricula, research papers are required for the majority of courses offered and close attention to current professional journals is demanded as a basis for scholarly investigation. The student is also required to attend and critique community self-help groups.

In the last two semesters, the student is required to participate in two 200-hour supervised practical experiences in the real world. Active participation in these agencies' programs affords the students the opportunity to apply their theoretical knowledge in a practical setting using two of the most common treatment modalities, i.e., in-patient and out-patient therapy.

The teaching staff, both full-time and part-time, are highly competent and include practicing psychologists, licensed social workers and certified chemical dependency counselors, all of whom draw heavily upon their extensive field experience in the performance of their instructional duties.

The program has gained state-wide recognition for its excellence. The Office of Education and Training for Addiction Services (OETAS) has endorsed it as one which not only meets, but also surpasses its standards for counselor training. Additionally, in 1990, the Maryland State Department of Education presented the Chemical Dependency Counseling program with an Award of Excellence. The steady growth of the program and the positive feedback from graduates as to their preparedness attests to the impact on the community and inspires the college to make even greater strides in our future endeavors.

Contact:
Diane Lesser, General Studies Department Head
(410) 749-6030

Wor-Wic Community College
1409 Wesley Drive
Salisbury, MD 21801
Total headcount enrollment-Credit: 4,066; Non-Credit: 5,938
Campuses/sites: 4; Full-time faculty: 30

EASTERN SHORE CRIMINAL JUSTICE ACADEMY

The academy serves as a regional police training center
for all eight Eastern Shore counties

More than 40 criminal justice agencies turn to the Eastern Shore Criminal Justice Academy for training.

The Academy grew out of a need for a regional police academy to serve law enforcement agencies on Maryland's Eastern Shore. In the fall of 1978, co-sponsored by the Ocean City Police Department, Salisbury Police Department, and the Criminal Justice credit program at Wor-Wic Community College, the Eastern Shore Police Training Center (ESPTC) emerged. Following two pilot entrance-level courses, the Maryland Police and Correctional Training Commissions certified the ESPTC as the 15th police academy in the state of Maryland. This certification issued in June of 1979, was the first to authorize a community college to operate a full-time police academy.

By 1980, the Criminal Justice Department at the college had assumed full responsibility for the operation of the ESPTC and course offerings were expanded to include in-service police training, administrative and supervisor training and special interest courses. Although the college service area included only Wicomico and Worcester counties, the ESPTC served as the regional police training center for all eight Eastern Shore counties. In 1982 at the request of corrections institutions in the area, the college undertook the lengthy process of seeking state certification to operate an academy for jail and correctional personnel. In 1983, the Maryland Correctional Training Commission

certified the ESPTC as a correctional academy, making it the first institution in the state to receive dual certification. Following this dual certification, the name was changed to the Eastern Shore Criminal Justice Academy (ESCJA).

The Program Advisory Committee (PAC) of the Criminal Justice Credit Program helps guide the academy on its mission to provide mandatory training for law enforcement and correctional personnel in three basic areas: entrance-level, annual in-service, and supervisor training. This committee, which consists of 30 representatives from various federal, state and local police and correctional agencies, also helps select the technical and specialized courses of training offered throughout the year.

The academy now offers more than 3,000 hours of instruction annually to more than 1,200 criminal justice practitioners throughout the state. All instruction is approved and inspected by the Maryland Police and Correctional Training Commissions (MPCTC) and instructors meet their stringent certification requirements.

The ESCJA functions as a cooperative effort between the college and the criminal justice community. Almost half of all the instruction offered is provided gratis by federal, state and local agencies. This interaction has resulted in reduced operational costs and reduced fees to participating agencies. Entry-level students successfully completing these courses are also afforded the opportunity to earn college credits at the same time.

Contact:
Michael D. Gray, Criminal Justice Department Head
(410) 543-2712

Wor-Wic Community College
1409 Wesley Drive
Salisbury, MD 21801
Total headcount enrollment-Credit: 4,066; Non-Credit: 5,938
Campuses/sites: 4; Full-time faculty: 30

ASPECTS OF FREEDOM

▓ *Students in this humanities course are exposed to important philosophical,* ▓
artistic and literary documents about freedom

Berkshire Community College Aspects of Freedom is a unique humanities course that examines freedom through works of philosophy, art and literature. It offers students at Berkshire Community College an opportunity to think and to write critically about areas of human experience not usually included in their generally career-oriented curriculums. Students in the course are exposed to important philosophical, artistic and literary documents about freedom, they are asked to examine these documents analytically and they are encouraged to relate them in creative and useful ways to their own experiences. In addition to this, emphasis is placed on accepting ambiguity, on learning to see that often two or more very different positions on an issue may be successfully defended.

Aspects of Freedom (HUM 121) grew out of a national conference in the spring of 1990 that was sponsored by the National Endowment for the Humanities and the American Association of Community and Junior Colleges. Entitled "Advancing the Humanities," the conference gathered community and junior college teachers from various regions in the country and encouraged them to develop new humanities courses aimed primarily toward students in occupational programs, but by no means limited to them.

The course was designed to examine such issues as Freedom of Speech, Freedoms and Limitations in Families and Relationships, Freedom Over One's Body, Freedom of Education, Freedom and Repressive Forces in Culture, and Escapes from Freedom. As some of these titles suggest, conditioning, custom and other forces limiting our freedoms are explored.

In addition to reading historical, philosophical and other types of expository writing, students read literature (novels, stories and poetry), look at some visual art and watch videos. They are encouraged to participate in class discussions, semi-formal debates, and small group study.

We function as secretaries, nurses, accountants, technicians and business people of various sorts, but we also function as human beings apart from, yet related to, all our vocational and career skills. It is this specifically human dimension of our lives which Aspects of Freedom addresses. The humanities, specifically literature, present life-like representations of people struggling with problems, conflicts of all sorts, and trying to resolve them. This course in particular explores people's attempts to become free and to realize their human potential in a number of different contexts.

Contact:
Mario Caluori, English Professor
(413) 499-4660, ext. 305

Berkshire Community College
350 West Street
Pittsfield, MA 01201
Total head count enrollment-Credit: 1,870; Non-Credit: 1,902
Campuses/sites: 2; Full-time faculty: 75

NURSING AND ALLIED HEALTH
ANNUAL LABOR MARKET SURVEY

▓ *The annual survey helps the college and health care workers* ▓
keep a pulse on the profession

When the Division of Nursing and Allied Health at Berkshire Community College conducted its first annual labor market assessment several years ago and then responded to the needs identified in that survey, it quickly became the health care employer's best friend.

Now, instead of recruiting out of town, area hospitals, nursing homes and home care agencies call the division when they need workers. The division, in turn, calls health care providers each spring for what has become an annual survey of labor demands.

As a result, Berkshire Community College offers a full

continuum of nursing and allied health programs which go well beyond the traditional range of community colleges.

When new laws required nursing homes to hire certified nursing assistants, the college launched a seven-week program to turn out trained workers. Grants and private agreements with providers allowed most of the students to be trained at no cost to them.

When area hospitals bemoaned the lack of registered nurses with bachelor's degrees, BCC developed a part-time bachelor's program in conjunction with the University

Continues on Page 318

of Massachusetts at Amherst.

Nurses interested in obtaining a graduate degree can also take selected core courses for the MSN at BCC.

The annual survey has also been used to avoid flooding the market with unnecessary graduates. For example, when the division measured the demand for physical therapy assistants, it found that it made sense to only offer the program every other two years.

The division's Health Education Center uses the survey to provide access to health education programs NOT offered at BCC, but for which the survey indicated a need. The center accomplishes this through advisement and the identification of support courses that can be taken at BCC and then transferred to a degree or certificate granting institution.

Contact:
Joan Johnston, Division Chair
(413) 499-4660, ext. 266

Berkshire Community College
350 West Street
Pittsfield, MA 01201
Total head count enrollment-Credit: 1,870; Non-Credit: 1,902
Campuses/sites: 2; Full-time faculty: 75

PC LAN TECHNICAL SPECIALIST TRAINING

The program combines the three leading areas of operating systems, programming and networking

In 1991, Bristol Community College became the first community college in the region to offer high-tech PCLAN Technical Specialist Training.

BCC translated industry's need for skilled network administrators into a PCLAN Technical Specialist Program. This training program is designed to develop and enhance the skills necessary to effectively use, manage and service computer technologies. BCC's PCLAN Program includes three components: Introduction to UNIX/C Programming; Advanced UNIX/C Programming; and Novell Certified NetWare Engineer (CNE). Each component is comprised of 160 hours of instructor-led course time along with optional available lab time. By offering a program combining the three leading areas of operating systems, programming and networking, BCC captured the leading edge in the computer technology environment.

To offer the program's Novell CNE component, BCC became a certified Novell Technology Institute (NTI) Affiliate and is the first college in the region to offer the complete CNE training. As an NTI Affiliate BCC must maintain the ability to provide the highest quality of Novell

education and must meet Novell's stringent education standards by teaching Novell-developed courses using Certified Novell NetWare Instructors (CNIs). CNIs qualify themselves through intensive Train-The-Trainer programs conducted by Novell and keep current with the latest Novell course developments through periodic updates. With continued training, CNIs maintain the knowledge and network expertise that are the core of the NTI Affiliate program.

To support the PCLAN Specialist Training Program BCC put together a complete Novell NetWare LAN with workstations for students and one UNIX server. This laboratory has become an important resource for educating students in many of the college's degree and non-credit courses.

BCC has found that the key to success is not only training students for the technologies that are here today, but also anticipating the technologies emerging on the horizon. This foresight has enabled Bristol Community College to grow and better meet community needs for a better trained, effective work force.

Contact:
Francine Fink, Director, Center for Business and Industry
(508) 678-2811, ext. 2154

Bristol Community College
777 Elsbree Street
Fall River, MA 02720
Total head count enrollment-Credit: 4,972; Non-Credit: 4,203
Campuses/sites: 5; Full-time faculty: 95

TECH PREP / TWO PLUS TWO

The college and 13 schools have developed a pioneering strategy to serve students

Since 1988, Bristol Community College has established itself as a pioneer in the development of Tech Prep/Two Plus Two programs. The college, in conjunction with eight comprehensive and five regional vocational technical high schools, has developed a strategy to design a challenging and systematic program of study for high school students whose career choices do not likely require a bachelor's degree. The prime focus on the project has been to address the need for a rigorous and focused program of study for those students not enrolled in college preparatory programs. The initiation of collaborative agreements by Bristol Community College with participating school districts placed emphasis on the development of academic and technical core courses at the high school level that would ensure a logical progression to the community college and eventually to the workplace.

For the past five years, staff members of Bristol Community College and the participating school districts have met regularly to oversee and direct the Tech Prep/Two Plus Two Program. Over the past two years a formal consortium has developed under the direction of a Tech Prep Task Force. The task force is composed of the college president and 13 school superintendents; it meets biannually to review and sign articulation agreements, and to review Tech Prep project activities. Specific consortium-sponsored staff development and curriculum development activities are carried out under the direction of a 17-person Implementation Committee.

Under the aegis of the general articulation agreements, a series of cluster articulation agreements have been developed in the areas of Business Technologies, Engineering Technologies, Computer Information Systems and Office Administration.

Over the 1992-93 academic year, the Tech Prep program expanded to include newly articulated programs in Child Care, Culinary Arts and Health Technologies.

This program was developed under grants from the Massachusetts Board of Regents from 1987-1990, and from the Massachusetts Division of Occupational Education for 1991 and 1992.

Contact:
Frank Llamas, Coordinator
(508) 678-2811, ext. 2339

Bristol Communit
777 Elsbree Street,y College
Fall River, MA 02720
Total head count enrollment-Credit: 4,972; Non-Credit: 4,203
Campuses/sites: 5; Full-time faculty: 95

COACH / MENTORS PROGRAM

The program builds academic skills through individual tutoring and counseling

Coach/Mentors is a uniquely designed student support program for students who are academically disadvantaged and/or handicapped vocational educational students and who are enrolled in the following Associate of Science degree programs: Early Childhood Education, Office Technologies, Criminal Justice, Accounting, Computer Information Systems, and Management (Hotel and Restaurant Retail or General). Students who participate in the Coach/Mentors program have an opportunity to enhance their success rate by utilizing a variety of services not normally offered to all Cape Cod Community College students. Among them are:

- individual tutorial assistance by highly qualified professionals;
- instruction in word processing;
- participation in on-going orientation and career workshops; and
- individual academic and career counseling.

The Coach/Mentors Program identifies individuals and then guides them through a semester of skill-building techniques which are combined with intensive tutorial and counseling support. The intention of the program is to noticeably increase the chances of these students remaining in college and completing an Associate's Degree in a collegiate technical career program.

The college administers the College Board Computerized Placement Tests in Sentence Skills, Reading Comprehension, Basic Mathematics, Elementary Algebra and College Level Mathematics to the students before they register for classes. Physically challenged students are identified from traditional college recruitment sources and from instructor's recommendations. The college's learning specialist and 504 coordinator also refer

Continues on Page 320

eligible students for this program.

During the second week of each semester, students are invited to participate in a comprehensive orientation program. At this time, students meet the project staff (coordinator, counselor and two basic skill tutors) and also learn more of the support services available to them through participation in Coach/Mentors.

Students are then assigned Coach/Mentors (or tutors) and meet on a regular basis for at least one hour per week in the Academic Development Center. Drop-in time is also available to students who are in need of additional assistance.

The project coordinator, counselors, instructors and tutors work closely in a team collaboration. The tutors communicate with the student's instructors and focus their tutorial sessions based on specific recommendations. Student files are maintained to reflect progress, problems and strategies for success. The project coordinator provides on-going progress reports to the students' instructors and weekly meetings are held with project staff to discuss students' progress and program evaluation.

Students supplement their tutoring by learning to use the IBM-PC word processing programs: WordPerfect and

Correct Grammar. Both provide the student with an opportunity for writing and revising and an immediate printout of their work. Correct Grammar adds the dimension of a superior grammar and spelling checker. Students further strengthen their tutoring with the computerized tutorial programs: Skills Bank, a series that builds basic skills in English and mathematics.

Disabled student's special needs are assessed on a regular basis and appropriate accommodations are provided. Access mediums are coordinated through Coach/Mentors and include texts on tape, print enlargements, reading exams, proctoring un-timed tests, providing readers/note takers, and coordinating interpreters. Individual student files are maintained to assess progress and problems encountered by these students. The project coordinator provides ongoing progress reports to the students' instructors to evaluate the success of the support services and accommodations given to physically challenged students.

The Coach/Mentors Program was recently designated as an Outstanding Program by the Division of Occupational Education and the Carl D. Perkins Vocational Act.

Contact:
Carol Dubay
(508) 362-2131

Cape Cod Community College
Route 132
West Barnstable, MA 02668
Total head count enrollment-Credit: 4,000; Non-Credit: 900
Campuses/sites: 1; Full-time faculty: 88

HOTEL / RESTAURANT MANAGEMENT

A cross-section of hospitality industry practitioners comprise the faculty

With more than 20-million Americans employed in the food service and lodging industries, careers in both hotel and restaurant management are among the fastest-growing professions in the United States. Beyond that simple fact, they also have the potential of career growth and worldwide employment opportunities in the years ahead.

Thousands of men and women are joining the ranks of hospitality management each year. They face the dynamic challenge of pleasing their guests by leading and inspiring employees by their best efforts. As in all professions, success comes to those who are properly prepared and Cape Cod Community College invites its students to challenge themselves by exploring the opportunities for hospitality education, industry experience and professional growth at the college.

Cape Cod Community College faculty represents a broad range of hospitality industry practitioners who provide our students with a practical, up-to-date education. Cape Cod Community College students have the opportunity to gain industry work experience either on

Cape Cod or at other exciting locations such as Disney World, Florida, or Vail, Colorado. Among the many field trips scheduled each year are those to the hotel and restaurant shows in New York and Boston. Extensive industry contact is available through guest speakers, alumni and such professional associations such as the Massachusetts Restaurant Association and the American Culinary Federation.

Students have the opportunity to practice their skills by catering various functions at the college's fully-equipped food service laboratory. The Innkeepers Club also sponsors many social and educational events where students can polish their all-important people skills.

Hotel/Restaurant graduates are prepared for entry-level management positions in the following areas: Front Office Management, Hotel and Catering Sales, Kitchen Management, Food and Beverage Control, Beverage Operations, Dining Room Management, Conference Planning, Purchasing, Housekeeping, and Innkeeping.

Cape Cod Community College offers an extensive

program of precollege instruction, tutoring and refresher courses. Many industry-sponsored scholarships are distributed each year to those eligible students.

The Hotel/Restaurant Management Program is the designated Center of Excellence at Cape Cod Community College.

Contact:
Robert Johnson
(508) 362-2131

Cape Cod Community College
Route 132
West Barnstable, MA 02668
Total head count enrollment-Credit: 4,000; Non-Credit: 900
Campuses/sites: 1; Full-time faculty: 88

THE MATH CONNECTION

This fast-paced television program is designed to stimulate interest in math

The Math Connection is a public-access cable mathematics television program aimed at students in grades four through seven. The show stimulates students' interest and exposure to mathematics by involving students and teachers in the production of the show.

A *Math Connection* planning council consists of teachers from several area communities and the Greenfield Community College mathematics faculty. This group plans and implements the show.

The program has three main segments: an interview with a guest from the community who uses math in his or her profession or hobby; "Ask the Student," a feature where students demonstrate how they solve open-ended problems; and "Challenge Corner," where groups of kids demonstrate problem-solving projects they have completed in their classrooms.

Additional features of the show include "Zingers," which are interesting math facts presented with computer graphics; "Stepping Out," which highlights how math is used in area businesses and special projects in classrooms; and a "Johnny No Math" character played by a local comedian, who demonstrates what can happen in the world if you don't know math.

The Math Connection has completed three seasons and produces about 16 half-hour shows each year. Some segments of the program are produced in the college's television studio, and feature the work of a number of media students. The balance of the program, hosted by Linda Cavanaugh, chair of the mathematics department, airs live from the Greenfield station.

Produced by Greenfield Community College and cablecast on Greenfield Community Television and stations in the neighboring towns of Amherst and Shelburne Falls, funding for the project comes from the Dwight D. Eisenhower Grant, Title II, through the Massachusetts Higher Education Coordinating Council.

The Math Connection was selected for inclusion in the American Association of Community and Junior Colleges handbook of Exemplary Programs and Services in small and rural colleges in 1991. The Massachusetts Higher Education Coordinating Council (then known as the Board of Regents) named *The Math Connection* an "exemplary program" in 1991 as well. *The Math Connection* has also completed a mathematics training manual for school teachers with an accompanying video.

Contact:
Linda Cavanaugh
(413) 774-3131, ext. 324

Greenfield Community College
One College Drive
Greenfield, MA 01301
Total head count enrollment-Credit: 2,317; Non-Credit: 655
Campuses/sites: 1; Full-time faculty: 58

AUTOMOTIVE TECHNOLOGY T-TEN
(TOYOTA TECHNICAL EDUCATION)

The program is geared toward the incoming dealership technician

Exemplifying the community college tradition, Massachusetts Bay Community College (MBCC) has extended the threshold of the campus into the community, encouraging partnerships with business and industry that promote both excellence and employment. One prime example is in the automotive service field, where today's automotive service field requires comprehensively-trained technicians who possess not only the specific skills needed in their field, but also the ability to continue to adapt their knowledge as technological and industrial advances continue. In order to meet these demands, the college has merged tradition with technology.

The Toyota T-Ten Program is a two-year automotive program designed to upgrade the technical competence and professional level of the incoming dealership technician. The curriculum, which has received national accreditation by ASE/NATEF, was collaboratively designed by Toyota Motor sales, USA (Toyota) and MBCC, and leads to an Associate in Science Degree in Automotive Technology. The program involves classroom lectures and laboratory classes of Toyota products, with a cooperative experience integrated into the curriculum. In addition, students achieve college competencies in critical thinking, reading, writing and math that add to their potential for life-long learning and professional growth.

MBCC was the first community college in the nation to develop a partnership with Toyota Motors. The T-Ten curriculum is now used by more than 30 institutions in 28 states as well as in Japan, Africa and other places where Toyota sells cars. The automotive electronics service program is the basis for training the new technicians needed for the next generation of automobiles – and beyond. Toyota supplies not only the equipment and vehicles students use in the program, but has also donated several additional vehicles for use in various school activities, including more than $40,000 in financial and tool scholarships as well as some of the most sophisticated learning materials available.

The national recognition received by the program has been outstanding. In 1988, the MBCC/Toyota partnership won the state's Exemplary Program Award for Outstanding Collaborative Training in the Commonwealth. The United States Department of Education recognized the program as one of 10 such exemplary programs in the entire country. The program was featured at the 1989 convention of the American Association of Community and Junior Colleges as one of the outstanding training programs of its type in the nation.

A cooperative experience provides an opportunity to apply technical skills and to gain an understanding of the technician's role in customer satisfaction. Students receive feedback from both their work supervisor and their teachers during placement, with an emphasis on developing independent problem-solving abilities. Graduates of this program have been placed in dealerships throughout the state, often working as paid employees at their cooperative work site. This program provides a pool of proven, qualified and talented commitment to customer satisfaction, everybody wins – the customer, the dealership, the community, Toyota, and most importantly, the student.

Contact:
George Luoto, Dean
(617) 237-1100, ext. 157

Massachusetts Bay Community College
50 Oakland Street
Wellesley, MA 02181
Total head count enrollment-Credit: 4,861; Non-Credit: 500
Campuses/sites: 2; Full-time faculty: 97

THE COLLEGE INTEGRATION PROJECT FOR STUDENTS WITH LEARNING DISABILITIES

The program helps students with disabilities make the transition from high school to college

Although some students with learning disabilities graduate from high school with the necessary skills to succeed in college, still others come from segregated programs or courses that did not prepare them to enter into more competitive settings.

The College Integration Project (CIP), offers comprehensive support for these students in making the transition from high school to college. Their difficult adjustment is due not only to weak course preparation, but also to their inexperience in advocating for themselves in the educational mainstream and a lack of understanding of what is expected of them in a more integrated setting.

CIP offers a set of activities during the first semester designed to help under-prepared students with learning disabilities to develop the skills to function independently in a post secondary setting. It enlists support from nearly every key aspect of the student's environment in working toward this goal. Outreach to area high schools makes students and teachers aware of the project. Assessment and evaluation provides information about the student's first-semester focus on how parents can support their child while encouraging increased independence. Faculty training helps integrate students by improving faculty

awareness and ability to teach to different learning styles. Finally, mentor tutors meet with students regularly and co-facilitate self advocacy groups designed to foster student independence. They serve as role models for success.

The project is supported by the Fund for the Improvement of Post Secondary Education, U.S. Department of Education. Goals are to:

1) increase the success and retention of these high risk students;

2) reduce the amount of specialized assistance usually required for these students outside the classroom;

3) integrate students into the social mainstream; and

4) ensure that independent learning behaviors are being reinforced both in the classroom and at home through work with faculty and parents.

A publication was disseminated in the fall of 1992 explaining the overall structure of the project for replication by other institutions. It includes a training curriculum for parents, a series of student publications developed by the self-advocacy groups, a faculty publication describing their experiences working with these students, and a tutoring manual compiled by the mentor tutors. This project has been presented at local and national conferences.

Contact:
Gail Hammond
(617) 237-1100, ext. 251

Massachusetts Bay Community College
50 Oakland Street
Wellesley, MA 02181
Total head count enrollment-Credit: 4,861; Non-Credit: 500
Campuses/sites: 2; Full-time faculty: 97

PEOPLES' REPUBLIC OF CHINA PROJECT

Massasoit is trying to help Peking University build a computer network of library catalogs

Massasoit Community College is helping Peking University Library automate its own card catalog and build an automated computer network of university and college library catalogs in the Beijing area as well as to other institutions in China.

This project is deemed to be imperative to the rapid modernization of China and the growth of democratic institutions there. It is particularly important that Peking University, China's oldest university, assume the initiative in the construction of this automated library network. It is vital that the influence of universities and colleges be expanded through library networking throughout China

and become less culturally isolated from the mass of the Chinese people. This is essential to peaceful growth. It is a project that has necessitated cooperation with Digital Equipment Corporation, whose equipment is used by Peking University Library. Digital Corporation is engaged with Massasoit in the initial planning of the project.

Massasoit Community College is involved with Peking University through the final phases of a Fulbright project that began in 1990. Initiating a consortium of Southeastern Massachusetts colleges, Massasoit sought to enhance China studies in school systems and colleges in the area.

Continues on Page 324

Twenty-one faculty from the area underwent intensive studies in Chinese language and culture for three months in the spring of 1990 in preparation for summer studies in Beijing and other cities of China during the summer of 1990. The second phase of the project included preparations for a "Grand China Conference" in April 1991, attended by more than 200 educators from schools and colleges in Southeastern Massachusetts. The third phase of the project was the fulfillment of those contracts by the Fulbrights and dissemination of their acquired China expertise throughout Southeastern Massachusetts' schools and colleges.

Besides Peking University, the host institutions in China include Beijing Foreign Languages Normal College and Beijing Union University. More than 1,000 books and video tapes have been gathered and sent to the libraries of these institutions to strengthen their collections in American Studies. In addition, funds were raised to support graduate study in the United States for one of our young academic hosts from Beijing Foreign Languages

Normal College. He is studying for a master's degree in communications at Bridgewater State College.

In April 1992, a group of four Chinese university presidents and administrators were hosted by Massasoit Community College during their visit to the United States. They are representatives of the External Scholarly Exchange Committee of the Beijing Municipal Bureau of Higher Education. The Chinese educators visited educational institutions in Boston, New York, and Washington, D.C. They were particularly interested in learning about operations in community colleges which focus upon technical and professional education. The delegation was scheduled to host an exchange delegation of staff from Massasoit in October 1993. There is apparently a need to expand access to higher education, which is associated with the drive toward modernization. The American community college seems to be a model which is attractive because it is particularly responsive in its curricula and programs to market demands.

Contact:
James P. Yess or Richard V. Rapacz
(508) 588-9100

Massasoit Community College
One Massasoit Boulevard
Brockton, MA 02402
Total head count enrollment-Credit: 6,421; Non-Credit: 1,010
Campuses/sites: 2; Full-time faculty: 160

MASSASOIT COMMUNITY COLLEGE

RUSSIAN AND UKRAINIAN PROJECTS

*▓ Faculty and staff exchanges for the purposes of teaching ▓
and staff training are central to the project*

What began as an agreement to help the Soviet Union develop community colleges after the Iron Curtain's fall led to specific work with Russia and Ukraine. The efforts date back to the Spring of 1990, when faculty and staff of Massasoit Community College visited the Soviet Academy of Pedagogical Sciences in Moscow and met with Dr. Zoya Malkova, Director of the Academy's Institute of General Education. Dr. Malkova made a reciprocal visit to the Massasoit campus in the Spring of 1991 when she studied the operations of community colleges in the commonwealth for several weeks. At the conclusion of this visit in 1991, Dr. Malkova and Dr. Burke negotiated and signed an agreement in behalf of the Soviet Academy and Massasoit Community College to jointly undertake the development of community colleges in the Soviet Union. The Academy concluded that community colleges would be important to the creation and operations of a market economy and in producing technical and managerial expertise for businesses, factories, hospitals, stores, commercial and agricultural enterprises, and other social entities. The skills necessary for these institutions to function in a market economy had to be developed in the Soviet Union.

The political upheaval of 1991 culminated in the

collapse of the Soviet Union and the ultimate formation of the independent republics of Russia and Ukraine. Dr. Malkova and Dr. Burke both agreed that the need for community colleges was still present, if not greater, in the new republics. Plans for a visit to institutions in St. Petersburg, Moscow, Kaluga and Vladimir in Russia were developed. Also planned was a visit to Kherson in Ukraine. Kaluga is about 100 miles southwest of Moscow. Vladimir is about 100 miles northeast of Moscow. Kherson is about 100 miles east of Odessa, on the Dnieper River, near the river's mouth at the Black Sea. All the planned visits took place between May 12, and May 25, 1992. Agreements were signed in all locations to cooperate in the development of community colleges.

Faculty and staff exchanges for purposes of teaching and staff training are central components of each of the institutions. Programmatically, the greatest demand for cooperative activities is at present in business areas, including marketing and small business management. A consortium of sister colleges – including Bridgewater State College and Cape Cod Community College – has been formed to better meet the conditions of the agreements. Massasoit Community College is seeking support from public and private institutions to underwrite the costs of transportation, communication and logistics in this project. Although the great industrial powers have recently agreed to provide technical assistance in the development of the Soviet Union, the financing and form of that effort still remains undefined. Massasoit is moving ahead with this project in anticipation that those sources will be available to support the potential growth of our initiative.

Contacts with appropriate divisions of the United States Information Agency and the Agency for International Development have been made. Projects in Russia and Ukraine have been targeted for increased funding in the United States Information Agency. Preliminary discussions with both agencies are presently underway prior to the writing of formal proposals. The consortium is prepared to act immediately upon funding, and so are our Russian and Ukrainian colleagues.

Contact:
James P. Yess or Richard V. Rapacz
(508) 588-9100

Massasoit Community College
One Massasoit Boulevard
Brockton, MA 02402
Total head count enrollment-Credit: 6,421; Non-Credit: 1,010
Campuses/sites: 2; Full-time faculty: 160

ACTIVATING LEARNING IN THE CLASSROOM

🏵 *The program was conceived, organized and is taught* 🏵
by faculty for faculty

Middlesex Community College is facing the challenges of an increasingly diverse student population, a rapidly growing number of adjunct faculty, and an expanding curriculum. Each of these changes requires the faculty to reconsider their course content, their methods of teaching, and the experience of the classroom. Activating Learning in the Classroom (ALC) began in 1989, to meet this need for a forum and to create a teaching community to discuss the scholarship of teaching.

One of the unique qualities of the ALC Program is that it is an instructional and development program conceived, organized and taught by faculty for the faculty. The two coordinators are faculty members – a professor of psychology and a professor of humanities. They are each given 50 percent release time; the other 50 percent of their time is spent practicing what they preach in their own classrooms. Colleagues, therefore, meet and discuss with colleagues. The faculty participants stress the importance of this colleague exchange and commented on a recent external program evaluation that the ALC Program is a "splendid interdisciplinary opportunity to learn from each other, (and) be affirmed as professionals who continue to develop."

As the needs of the college have evolved, the ALC program has changed and evolved. Initially, eight full-time professors from across the disciplines met together in a semester-long seminar to discuss the process of teaching and learning and to create a Course Guide that reflected these discussions. As the number of part-time faculty has increased dramatically, the ALC Program expanded to include Community Mentoring, a series of paired seminars incorporating 24 part-time and full-time faculty from across the disciplines in a collaborative curriculum development program.

Each seminar pair addresses a specific skill or strategy - the development of an extended syllabus, collaborative learning and learning styles, assessment of student learning. All participating faculty are engaged first in a theoretical session, next in the development of curriculum materials, and finally in both a peer and a student evaluation process as well as a review of their newly-developed materials by the program coordinators. These materials are kept by each faculty member in a teaching portfolio that includes their ALC work, the comments of their colleagues and students, and their own future revisions. By sharing this common experience of the teaching portfolio, the full-time and part-time faculty engage in an ongoing, non-threatening exchange that breaks down some of the isolation of teaching, supports the less experienced members, enhances the materials of the more experienced members, incorporates student feedback, and creates an interdisciplinary community of scholars, comfortable with each other.

The ALC Seminars have directly involved 51 faculty members, while individual workshops, run throughout the semesters by the ALC Coordinators, have included more than 70 participants new to the program. Initially funded by a Title III grant, ALC is now funded by the college through the Division of Staff, Program and Resource Development.

The ALC Program has been highlighted at NISOD,

Continues on Page 326

NCSPOD, and ACAFAD Conferences, as well as in professional days at other colleges. In October 1991, the coordinators presented the program at the Moscow State Pedagogical University in Russia. A description of the program has been published in the *Journal of Staff, Program, and Organization Development* and in *Innovation Abstracts*.

Contact:
Janet Jones, Humanities Professor, (617) 275-8910, ext. 4679
Donna Duffy, Social Sciences Professor, (617) 275-8910, ext. 4510

Middlesex Community College
Springs Road
Bedford, MA 01730
Total head count enrollment-Credit: 12,976; Non-Credit: 1,960
Campuses/sites: 5; Full-time faculty: 122

MIDDLESEX COMMUNITY COLLEGE

ASIAN STUDIES FACULTY DEVELOPMENT

Course modules with Asian content and perspectives have been added to a variety of courses

Course modules with Asian content have been added to such courses as psychology, nursing, business and art following the creation of an Asian Studies Faculty Development program.

The program began in the summer of 1990, when MCC President Carole Cowan participated in a colloquium of college presidents at the East-West Center in Honolulu, Hawaii. Together, college presidents and Asian Studies experts created an international Asian Studies curriculum development project which would aid faculty in colleges throughout the country in introducing Asian Studies into their curricula. The following year, Middlesex was chosen to send two faculty and an administrator to participate in the East-West Center's first Asian Studies Development Program's three-week summer institute.

The team returned from this institute and concentrated its efforts on assisting faculty in infusing course modules with Asian content and perspectives into already established courses. This effort was bolstered by the administration's commitment to purchase more than $4,000 worth of supporting library and audio-visual materials, and the successful submission of a $9,000 Japan Foundation Library Support grant. This year our Asian Studies program received the Exemplary Program award from the National Council of Instructional Administrators.

On February 7, 1992, the East-West Center designated Middlesex as a Regional Center for Asian Studies Development in the northeast region of the United States. As a result, Middlesex has begun to serve as the mentor for other institutions that share our goal of infusing courses, curriculum and campus life with an appreciation for Asian traditions. In 1992, the college formed a Regional Asian Studies Group composed of 10 faculty from seven community colleges in the state of Massachusetts. During an 18-month period, this group, composed of faculty with specialties ranging from gerontology to early childhood education, will infuse course modules with Asian content and materials into one of the courses they already teach.

A major feature of professional development at Middlesex Community College has been its link with course and curriculum development and internationalizing already established courses. We have been fortunate enough to receive a National Endowment for the Humanities (NEH) grant that allowed us to run a 1993 four-week summer institute for 20 faculty on the cultures of mainland Southeast Asia. We have also received a Department of Education Title VI grant that enabled us to run a 1992 three-week summer institute for eight faculty on East Asia. The guiding idea behind these institutes has been the improvement of teaching by expanding the faculty's knowledge of the content in their subject area, that is, professional development by learning about the works, ideas, and values that originate in other cultures.

Other initiatives that are part of our Asian Studies Development Program include:
- a teaching exchange with the Beijing Institute of Management in the People's Republic of China;
- a three-week study tour to Beijing and Shandong province taken by 12 students and two faculty escorts;
- the opening of a branch campus (Middlesex China Institute) in Jinan, Shandong Province to provide non-credit courses, taught by Middlesex faculty, for business and government officials;
- tentative student and faculty exchange agreements with the Chinese Academy of Sciences and Shanghai International University;
- a Korean Visiting Scholar from the Fulbright

Scholar-in-Residence Program who assisted business faculty in the development of international business modules for business courses; and
•plans to host a Japanese Visiting Scholar from the

Fulbright Program to do course and curriculum development in humanities and social science courses.

Contact:
Julien Farland, Humanities Professor
(617) 275-8910, ext. 4680/6584

Middlesex Community College
Springs Road
Bedford, MA 01730
Total head count enrollment-Credit: 12,976; Non-Credit: 1,960
Campuses/sites: 5; Full-time faculty: 122

AVIATION SCIENCE

▨ *The program accepts students with no aviation background* ▨
and turns them into pilots and flight instructors

North Shore Community College Aviation Science program, which focuses on professional pilot training, is the only such associate degree program offered by a community college in the six New England states. In 1992, this program expanded to include an option for pre- air traffic controller training. It too is the only community college program of its kind in New England. This dual track combination is most unusual at the community college level.

This open-admission program has accepted students with no prior aviation background and has graduated them as commercial pilots and flight instructors within a two-year period. Graduates are employed world-wide by major airlines, regional carriers, corporations, the FAA and the military. Graduates are encouraged to further their education to the baccalaureate level. Transfer is facilitated through a two-plus-two agreement.

The program director is an FAA-approved chief instructor and personally advises each aviation student. Courses are offered day and evening. Flight training is provided by independent flight schools chosen by the student. Student progress is monitored by the chief instructor.

The air traffic control option will offer a unique internship experience in cooperation with the FAA. Students will observe controllers on site in FAA control towers, regional radar centers and administrative headquarters.

The two programs have a combined enrollment of approximately 80 students. One full-time coordinator/professor is assigned to this program supplemented by part time faculty as needed.

The Aviation Program at NSCC is an institutional member of the University Aviation Association and of MAAC (the National Consortium of two-year Aviation Colleges). The pilot ground school courses are approved by the FAA under part 141 of the Federal Air Regulations. The college was chosen in 1990 to be the 25th Aviation Resource Center in the nation and houses an extensive library of aviation information. In 1992, the college received a grant from the FAA to host an Aviation Career Education summer camp for children ages seven to 12. In 1989, the coordinator received a regional award from the FAA as best aviation educator at the community college level. Graduates have won the prestigious Aero Club of New England scholarships twice in the last five years.

Contact:
Robert S. Finkelstein, Program Director
(508) 762-4000

North Shore Community College
1 Ferncroft Road
Danvers, MA 01923
Total head count enrollment-Credit: 8,000; Non-Credit: 2,000
Campuses/sites: 3; Full-time faculty: 130

PROJECT INTERLOCK

*The program aims to increase minority student access
to engineering and technology fields*

For minority students, Project Interlock opens the door of opportunity to engineering sciences and technology that may have otherwise remained closed. Students successfully completing this program are assured of junior-year status in engineering programs at the University of Massachusetts (Lowell), as well as at several additional independent and public institutions including historical black colleges.

Funds provided by grants from industry, our foundation, and individuals are available to cover tuition, text books and other college fees for the students selected for this program. Every student is carefully evaluated to assure that his or her academic needs are adequately met. Among these assurances are small classes and extensive use of successful minority engineers as role models, tutors and mentors.

At least 100 students have participated in Project Interlock since its inception. More than 25 of these students are enrolled in a four-year college and/or university science and engineering program. In 1990, one of our Interlock graduates received the first baccalaureate degree awarded with its roots in our program. In the past two years, five additional students have joined the baccalaureate ranks with many others standing on the threshold of graduation. The outstanding quality of this program is evidenced in that our Interlock graduates receive significant scholarship awards from the four-year institutions to which they transfer.

Contact:
Karen Laing-Hughes, Project Coordinator
(508) 762-4000

North Shore Community College
1 Ferncroft Road
Danvers, MA 01923
Total head count enrollment-Credit: 8,000; Non-Credit: 2,000
Campuses/sites: 3; Full-time faculty: 130

BED AND BREAKFAST SEMINARS

*The one-week seminars help Eastern Europeans learn
to rebuild their economy*

Since the spring of 1991, Northern Essex Community College has been aggressively seeking federal money which has been made available to help foster economic development in Eastern Europe.

The college's efforts were successful in the winter of 1991/1992 when it, in collaboration with the University of Nitra in Czechoslovakia, received a $24,064 grant from the United States Department of Labor to develop two seminars for Czechoslovakians hoping to establish bed and breakfasts in their country.

The one-week seminars were held in late February and early April in the Tatra Mountain Region of Slovakia, one of two main ethnic regions of Czechoslovakia, located near the Austrian border. The Tatra Mountain Region offers beautiful scenery, a rich history, cultural opportunities and fine Czechoslovakian products such as crystal, leather, tile, wood furniture and woolen goods.

Under Communist rule, the area was never allowed to develop its potential for tourism. Now that Communist rule has ended, the country is planning to move in this direction with help from the United States.

Teaching the seminars were Northern Essex business instructors Kevin Fitzgibbon, who teaches in the Hotel and Restaurant Management Program, and Ted Wroblewski, owner of the Bernerhof Inn in Glen, NH. The seminars covered the fundamentals of the hospitality field and how to set up and run a bed and breakfast. Presentations were offered with the help of an interpreter and technicians.

Eighty people, including local Slovak business people, representatives from the American Consulate and regional Slovak ministers of travel and tourism, attended the seminars. Since the seminars were offered two participants have opened businesses, including a bed and breakfast inn and a wine store, and a Slovakian Tourism Association has been formed.

The college has continued its contact with Czechoslovakia working with the University of Nitra on plans to develop training in other areas, including small business management, accounting, marketing/management, banking, and health and sanitation. The two institutions are also hoping to arrange faculty/student exchanges. Other areas of training which may be needed in the future include English as a Second-Language, computerization, office technology and training of senior managers.

Contact:
Jean Poth, Chairperson, Business Division
(508) 374-3624

Northern Essex Community College
Elliott Way
Haverhill, MA 01830
Total head count enrollment-Credit: 6,949; Non-Credit: 2,911
Campuses/sites: 7; Full-time faculty: 130

CREATIVE TEACHER ENRICHMENT ACTIVITIES IN SCIENCE

The college and local public school systems together offer teachers continued support

Northern Essex Community College Creative Teacher Enrichment Activities in Science project and local school systems together offer teachers in-service training in the areas of the earth and physical sciences at the elementary and middle/junior high school level.

The finalized after-school and in-school Teacher Enrichment Activities (TEA's) are developed in conjunction with teacher input from each participating school system as determined in "Focus Group Meetings" that occur throughout the year. Funded through a Higher Education Coordinating Council Title II Dwight D. Eisenhower Mathematics and Science Program Grant, the Creative Teacher Enrichment Activities in Science Project (C-TEAS) was developed through collaborative planning between Northern Essex Community College and the Lawrence and Haverhill Public School Systems.

The project includes provisions for continued contact between the teacher participants and the TEA subject-matter specialist through a Collaborative Mentor Service and provides a source of Conference Pool Funds to support increased attendance at professional meetings by Massachusetts teachers.

The project objectives are:

1) to improve and expand the knowledge of the teacher of science in a particular subject area;
2) to give the teacher of science some practical applications through "hands-on" laboratory exercises that relate to key concepts in the earth and physical sciences;
3) to provide the participants with a collection of laboratory materials and aids for integration into their science curriculum;
4) to encourage participants in the development of creative materials which emphasize the experimental process;
5) to provide participants with continued support in curriculum development; and
6) to provide a source of funds to support increased attendance at professional meetings by Massachusetts teachers.

Contact:
Edward DeSchuytner, Project Director
(508) 374-3891

Northern Essex Community College
Elliott Way
Haverhill, MA 01830
Total head count enrollment-Credit: 6,949; Non-Credit: 2,911
Campuses/sites: 7; Full-time faculty: 130

EDWARD T. SULLIVAN LABOR-MANAGEMENT CENTER

Courses are designed to give unions and managers insight into the needs of both sides

In recent years concerns have grown about the decline in American competitiveness and job security. In light of the partnership which exists in other countries between business, labor and government, some unions have come to question the traditional, adversarial approach to labor-management relations in this country.

At Quincy College in Massachusetts a center has been

Continues on Page 330

established to promote new thinking in this area, in cooperation with Local 254 of the Service Employees International Union. The Edward T. Sullivan Center is advised by a Council of prominent business, government and union leaders, including Boston University President John Silber, Massachusetts Labor Secretary Christine Morris, and White House staffer Ronald Kaufman, a Quincy College graduate.

In its first year the Sullivan Center established a research library and sponsored a conference and seminar series. More than 250 attended a statewide conference on Labor Issues in Public Education. The Presidents of the Boston and Massachusetts Teachers Unions joined a panel discussion on such topics and teacher testing and tenure reform. Mark Roosevelt, Chair of the legislature's Joint Education Committee, and a leading advocate of reform, provided the keynote speech. During the spring a seminar was offered to union members on "win-win" strategies in labor negotiations. Members also heard a Japanese business executive delivering his perspective on management and productivity.

In the fall of 1992 the college began a labor-management concentration in its business degree program. New courses include: Labor Economics; Labor Law; Collective Bargaining and Trade Unionism; and Labor History. This program will be offered at the main campus, south of Boston, and at a satellite campus in western Massachusetts. Courses are designed to provide union members and potential managers with insights into the legitimate needs of both sides. Plans are also underway to recruit fellows to undertake research projects on the New England economy.

With more than 17,000 members, Local 254 is the largest union local in New England. Its President, Edward T. Sullivan, has been active in union affairs since the administration of Franklin Roosevelt. In addition to Local 254, the center is supported by individual, union and corporate memberships. It will reflect Mr. Sullivan's philosophy that "a contract is not worth the paper it's written on if the company goes out of business."

Contact:
0. Clayton Johnson, President
(617) 984-1776

Quincy College
34 Coddington Street
Quincy, MA 02169
Total head count enrollment-Credit: 4,700; Non-Credit: 1,475
Campuses/sites: 7; Full-time faculty: 51

SPRINGFIELD TECHNICAL COMMUNITY COLLEGE

MANUFACTURING TECHNOLOGIES

The program serves traditional students and local industry employees

Springfield Technical Community College is helping manufacturers regain ground lost in recent years because of their inability to manufacture quality products in competitive, cost-effective fashion. Computer Integrated Manufacturing (CIM) at STCC represents a holistic, computerized manufacturing training program that uses integrated, automated systems from managerial courses through to CAD, CAM and robotic shop floor hands-on production of goods.

CIM at STCC recently has been advanced through partnership with IBM that has resulted in a multi-million dollar laboratory training facility, used not only to train STCC's manufacturing and business majors, but also to educate local manufacturers on the uses of these new workplace technologies. STCC's training capacity includes authorized training in SMART CAM, AutoCAD and IBM-CIM.

The use of computer technology is now being increasingly integrated into the production and management functions employed by internationally competitive manufacturers to minimize waste, reduce costly inventories, reduce order/delivery turn-around time, as well as to improve the quality of products. However, automation of not only manufacturing and business functions but also of service-sector kinds of activities has led to a work environment that is increasingly networked and where new uses of fiber optics, lasers and holography enhance manufacturing processes. STCC's Laser Electro Optics curriculum and a National Science Foundation Instrumentation grant have led to the development of a non-destructive holographic laboratory for students training in this specialized field.

Not the least of the manufacturing technologies included in the curricula are those that support the coexistence of manufacturing activities and ecosystems. Industrial Wastewater Treatment Technology and Environmental Technology at STCC consist of courses and laboratory exercises that train technicians to treat manufacturing waste to government standards and to safely handle the hazardous by-products of today's manufacturing processes.

The design of the curricula of STCC's cutting-edge manufacturing technologies lead students to completion of AS degrees and certificates in a half-dozen specialized manufacturing-related areas. In addition, through the college's Center for Business and Industry Development, the college's state-of-the-art manufacturing facilities and highly trained faculty provide contract training to local industry employees designed to expedite the transfer of modern manufacturing technologies into local companies and to assist in stemming the further erosion of American manufacturing to overseas competitors.

In total, more than 1,250 individuals receive training in manufacturing technologies at STCC each year. A dozen full-time instructors and more than 50 part-time instructors meet the needs of the students and the companies who are trained.

Contact:
Dick Warner, Chair, Engineering Technologies, (413) 781-7822, ext. 3501
Tom Holland, Dean, Business Development, (413) 781-7822, ext. 3864

Springfield Technical Community College
One Armory Square
Springfield, MA 01105
Total head count enrollment-Credit: 5,880; Non-Credit: 322
Campuses/sites: 1; Full-time faculty: 173

MASSACHUSETTS REGISTRY OF MOTOR VEHICLES / COMMUNITY COLLEGE PARTNERSHIP

The college is one of many institutions working with the state to implement the program

Springfield Technical Community College coordinates all colleges in the state that administer a test to commercial drivers. The need for such testing follows the Commercial Motor Vehicle Safety Act of 1986, which requires that all commercial operators obtain a Commercial Drivers License (CDL) in order to drive commercial vehicles after April 1, 1992. It has been the responsibility of each state to design and administer a test to commercial drivers in order to comply with the federal regulations.

During the winter of 1991, Registry of Motor Vehicle (RMV) officials began a discussion with Springfield Technical Community College (STCC) Center for Business and Industry Development staff members concerning the possibility of using the community college facilities in the Commonwealth as testing sites. Massachusetts has 15 community colleges geographically spread throughout the state. In was anticipated that there would be a need to test nearly 200,000 drivers before the April 1992 deadline.

In April 1991, the Community College Directors of Business and Industry met with the Director of Driver Licensing for the RMV to discuss plans for the implementation of the testing program in which 13 of the 15 colleges agreed to participate in the program.

A contract was signed between the RMV and STCC for 27 weeks of testing, ending on January 4, 1992. STCC entered into sub-agreements with the other participating schools for testing. The community colleges were compensated by the RMV for the services of proctors at each test session as well as administrative costs. All billing was handled by the coordinating college, STCC. In addition to the testing component, the contract provided for administrative, coordinating and public relations services of STCC as well as computer scanning of all tests to determine pass or fail scores. The contract was extended on December 31, 1991, until March 28, 1992, to accommodate the large number of drivers needing testing. During the extension of the contract, an oral test was introduced for those who had difficulty reading and was administered at each of the community college sites. In addition, the majority of colleges participating in the testing program contracted with private consulting agencies or individuals to offer training programs for drivers in preparation for the CDL test.

The CDL testing project was one of the first projects in the Commonwealth that utilized the facilities and expertise of such a large number of community colleges working as a group. The program also was unique in that it was a cooperative project between two Commonwealth agencies. Although the contract has ended, the RMV officials responsible for the project are involved in ongoing discussions with STCC staff regarding future programs. Additionally, Business and Industry Directors throughout the state are discussing other areas where the cooperation of the colleges working with outside agencies might strengthen the colleges and provide much-needed services, using the model of the Massachusetts RMV/Community College Partnership.

Contact:
Ann Dunphy, Center for Business/Industry Relations
(413) 781-7822, ext. 3842

Springfield Technical Community College
One Armory Square
Springfield, MA 01105
Total head count enrollment-Credit: 5,880; Non-Credit: 322
Campuses/sites: 1; Full-time faculty: 173

WORKPLACE PARTNERSHIP PROJECT (WPP)

▣ Keys to the programs' success have been the inclusion of employers ▣
and unions, as well as respect for adult learners

A workplace literacy project of Alpena Community College has significant union involvement, giving it more credence than had it been assembled only by the college and area employers.

The project grew from a 1990 assessments of reading, math and communication skills among employees at several local companies that were planning substantial investments to upgrade production equipment. Employers needed to know if workers would be able to effectively use the new technology that was about to change the way they did their jobs. When a critical need was revealed to invest not only in upgrading equipment but also to advance the skills level of their employees as well, the Alpena Workplace Partnership Project (WPP) was conceived.

Receipt of a $200,000 U.S. Department of Education demonstration grant in May 1991 allowed the college, in cooperation with Penn State University's national literacy center, to create a model for delivering meaningful instruction in the workplace.

One key to the success of the program has been the partners assembled. Employers, of course, were included, but perhaps the most significant factor in gaining credibility, acceptance and voluntary participation among employees was having the local council of unions as an initiator of the project. Another key is respect for adult learners. Years of solid technical experience on the job make them important sources of information regarding their learning needs. They are already extremely capable employees, and by helping them become better communicators, independent thinkers, resourceful team players and competent problem solvers, the WPP enhances their value

in a changing workplace.

With a goal of providing competency-based, job-related basic skills classes, the instructional team uses a holistic approach that includes:

1) a well-structured assessment/evaluation plan inviting the student to chart learning progress based on personal goals;
2) courses in which the students initiate specific and relevant activities within the content area based upon workplace needs;
3) encouraging and empowering the adult learner to connect the global value of the content areas of reading, writing and math to professional and personal learning intentions;
4) deriving classroom materials from authentic workplace documents, communications issues or math problems relevant to a particular site;
5) shared team responsibility for workplace curriculum planning, decision-making and on-going evaluation of the instructional process; and
6) clear communication between employers, employees and the college and community regarding the workplace project.

Four employers thus far have joined the project, providing on-site space and release time for about 150 employees who have voluntarily participated. The staff includes the project director, three instructors and a secretary. Alpena WPP was selected for a Public Broadcasting Service feature on national workplace literacy initiatives and for presentations at several conferences, including the 1992 National Rural Education Association Convention.

Contact:
Don MacMaster, Project Director
(517) 356-9021, ext. 344

Alpena Community College
666 Johnson Street,
Alpena, MI 49707-1495
Total head count enrollment-Credit/Non-Credit: 2,718
Campuses/sites: 2; Full-time faculty: 60

ALPENA VOLUNTEER CENTER

▣ An inter-organizational group fosters communication, cooperation ▣
and observance of National Volunteer Week

Alpena Community College has a far-reaching, positive effect on its community through the Alpena Volunteer Center, which assists human services agencies and matches the skills and interests of volunteers with requests for volunteer help. Established in 1977 at the request of local human service agencies, the Center remains true to its

original mission while evolving into a respected wellspring of activity for the common good. Working so actively within the community has resulted in four additional Volunteer Center goals:

1) serving as a clearinghouse for information on community services and providing that information

through directories and handouts;
2) responding to community needs;
3) assisting human services agencies, organizations and schools by offering resources, training, networking and consulting services as needed; and
4) and promoting activities related to "people helping people" and community improvement.

Success with volunteers is due to a well-defined process that includes personal contact in potential sites and individual interviews with all prospective volunteers, handbooks for those supervising and those volunteering, active recruitment, formal application and orientation, and a system to track and evaluate all placements. An estimated 25,000 hours of service valued at more than $195,000 is donated yearly through the Volunteer Center to agencies, civic groups and community special events. The Volunteer Center coordinates Alpena Community College's internship program, provides a volunteer component to the college's student leadership program, operates a VolunTEEN program involving nearly 100 high school students, and handles court-referrals of first-time offenders in non-violent crimes who are sentenced to community service. Maintaining mailing lists and providing labels and bulk mailing for non-profit groups are popular services, along with organizing the annual Christmas Wish List, through which people who wish to give time, gifts or money are matched with requests. The Volunteer Center has established an inter-organizational group, called Leaders of Volunteer Efforts, to foster communication, cooperation and observance of National Volunteer Week. The group has become a partner in such successful initiatives as the city beautification project and board training

activities. It was the catalyst for Alpena's participation in the Kettering Foundation's National Issues Forums, and formation of a broadly representative community child care steering committee.

Concepts key to the longevity and success of The Volunteer Center include:
1) follow professional standards of confidentiality, performance and integrity;
2) call on agencies and organizations before recruiting volunteers to determine the need for volunteer help;
3) avoid turf battles, by meeting with people who might feel you are infringing and asking how you can help their efforts, being prepared to change direction if necessary;
4) start projects on a small scale, learn from mistakes and build on successes;
5) give priority to the help that is requested rather than to start other projects; and
6) don't lose sight of the main goal of helping the community.

The college provides 54 percent of the $70,000 budget; 38 percent comes in philanthropic funding from the local Besser Foundation, and another 8 percent is derived from local sources. A three-quarter time director, three half-time coordinators, five volunteers and additional support as needed from college staff accomplish the organizational work of The Alpena Volunteer Center. Recognition has come from the Keep Michigan Beautiful Foundation, the League for Innovation in the Community College, and the State of Michigan, which named the center's director to the state community services commission.

Contact:
Vernie Nethercut, Center Director
(517) 356-9021, ext. 335

Alpena Community College
666 Johnson Street,
Alpena, MI 49707-1495
Total head count enrollment-Credit/Non-Credit: 2,718
Campuses/sites: 2; Full-time faculty: 60

WATER PURIFICATION TECHNOLOGY

For more than 20 years, this was the only program of its kind in the state, and one of only a few such programs in the nation

Sciences, mathematics and even civics are incorporated into Bay de Noc Community College's Water Purification Technology program. It's an appropriate program for Bay College. Located in the small city of Escanaba on the northwest shore of Lake Michigan; this vast but sparsely populated Upper Peninsula of Michigan boasts natural resources of lakes, rivers and forests.

Protecting and managing these natural resources requires dedicated, trained professionals. This need was recognized and, in 1969, Bay College implemented its Water Purification Technology program. For more than 20

years, it was the only program of its kind in the state, and one of only a few associate degree programs in the nation to provide education and training for operations and management personnel in the water/waste water treatment industry.

Today, the program enrolls an average of 58 students per semester, and graduates 20 to 25 annually: 85 percent enter the workplace as operators of industrial and municipal water utilities, operations specialists for consulting engineering firms, technicians in chemical laboratories,

Continues on Page 334

and research and sales personnel for chemical and equipment manufacturers and distributors. The additional 15 percent of graduates continue their education to the bachelors degree level and beyond.

It is an interdisciplinary program incorporating segments of several sciences – biology, chemistry, physics and mathematics. It includes the basics of civics, sanitary, environmental, and chemical engineering, and it includes specialized training in electronics, mechanics, hydraulics and computer sciences.

In addition to her full-time teaching responsibilities, the program's instructor/coordinator, Ms. Barbara Hauser, manages a full-time, two-month co-op required of all program students; develops and operates regional training seminars for operations personnel; and conducts specialized on-site training courses for waste treatment facility operators.

Her published text, *Practical Hydraulics Handbook*, (CRC Press), and two unpublished texts, *Water Chemistry*, and *Water Utility Management*, have been developed for use in the Water Purification Technology classes. Ms. Hauser was named Outstanding Occupational Educator for 1991 by the Michigan Occupational Dean's Council.

Contact:
Chuck Gold, Dean, Technology and Industrial Training
(906) 786-5802

Bay de Noc Community College
2001 North Lincoln Road
Escanaba, MI 49829-2511
Total head count enrollment-Credit: 2,352; Non-Credit: 372
Campuses/sites: 3;Full-time faculty: 43

PULP AND PAPER TECHNOLOGY

A paper technology lab simulates technical processes in the paper industry environment

With the only Pulp and Paper Technology associate degree program in the state of Michigan and one of only seven in the U.S. and Canada, Bay de Noc provides current and future paper manufacturing employees with the high-tech and high-touch skills needed to meet the demands of the work environment. The program began in fall 1989, following a year of planning and a $206,000 grant from the state of Michigan to help equip a paper technology lab. The lab equipment simulates technical processes in the paper industry environment, allowing students to make paper and also test the quality of the paper for strength, texture and durability. In addition to the lab, the program includes courses in electronics, instrumentation, mechanical operations, math, chemistry, manufacturing and environmental concerns.

There are seven pulp and paper manufacturers within a 60-mile radius of Bay College. The Upper Peninsula paper industry, like numerous manufacturing and business concerns across the nation, retooled to high technology processes to increase productivity and remain globally competitive.

Working in partnership with industry representatives, Bay College personnel developed a 73-credit-hour program, which provides students with options of an Associate of Applied Science degree, or transfer to Western Michigan University or University of Wisconsin-Stevens Point for baccalaureate degrees in Paper Science or Paper Engineering. The program enrolls 20 to 25 students annually, and placement rates are averaging 80 percent. The program receives wide support from area industries such as equipment, teaching materials/supplies, advisory participation, guest lecturing and summer co-op positions for students.

Contact:
Chuck Gold, Dean, Technology and Industrial Training
(906) 786-5802

Bay de Noc Community College
2001 North Lincoln Road
Escanaba, MI 49829-2511
Total head count enrollment-Credit: 2,352; Non-Credit: 372
Campuses/sites: 3;Full-time faculty: 43

Associate Degree / Practical Nursing

The program makes it easier for high school seniors to be dually enrolled in their high school and the nursing program

High school seniors may be dually enrolled in their high school and the C.S. Mott Community College Associate Degree/Practical Nursing program, thanks to just one of many aspects of a monumental program revision. Before embarking on such changes, however, faculty in 1990 reviewed many different curricular models. None fit the framework that was envisioned. Hence, the faculty, using Bloom's Taxonomy, developed a "ladder continuum concept" called the Cognitive Skills Ladder for Nursing Practice." This concept became the constant throughout each component of the curriculum from entry into and exit from the program. It was the first program overhaul since 1973.

The program's conceptual framework is a Meta paradigm of man (person), environment, health and nursing on a continuum from simple to complex, tied together by the nursing process. Placed on the cognitive skills ladder, these appear as vertical threads of the curriculum and are reflected in the level competencies as well as in the totality of the terminal competencies.

The faculty's first major decision in keeping with the ladder concept constant was to combine the ADN and the PN programs, requiring all entering students to be grouped as one class during the first year of the program. Students declared their major by the second semester of the program, with those students declaring PN graduating after the first calendar year and those students declaring ADN graduating after completing the second calendar year.

The faculty, using the revised program philosophy and conceptual framework, placed ADN and PN students on a grid along the ladder continuum based on competencies at each of the six identified levels of the program. Expectations were clearly delineated for the six levels of the programs. On the ladder continuum, the dual-enrollment students enter the second level of the ADN/PN program. Moreover, the new program framework simplified entry for LPN already employed in the field.

The returning LPN enter the program at level four on the ladder continuum. Further, articulation with the University of Michigan-Flint is enhanced with delineated expectations and leveling as shown on the ladder continuum.

The ADN/PN program is designed to ensure that MCC graduates are:

1) competent entry level practitioners;
2) safe, contributing members of the nursing care delivery team; and
3) educationally prepared to make critical decisions regarding their continuing education, growth and development.

The program has been approved by the College Professional Studies Committee, The Michigan State Board of Nursing, and is accredited by the National League for Nursing (NLN). Additionally, the program received a grant from the Helene Fuld Foundations to fund interactive video hardware for the New Nursing Learning Center. With this added technology, students have an additional experiential dimension in their skills practice.

Contact:
Mamie Howard, Dean of Health Sciences
Elizabeth Petrella, Coordinator, ADN/PN Program
(313) 762-0318

C.S. Mott Community College
1401 East Court Street
Flint, MI 48503
Total head count enrollment-Credit: 10,858; Non-Credit: 9,390
Campuses/sites: 2;Full-time faculty: 174

Magazines by Telephone for the Visually Impaired

The college, a high school and a non-profit group sponsor Volunteer Voices, a telephone reading service for visually impaired residents

There is a widely voiced concern that college students today may not be adequately committed to community service, to civic responsibility and to the habit of helping others. But community college students in particular may feel the necessity of working in order to pay for college expenses, loans and fees, and to reduce debt burdens. These obligations often preclude serious commitment to

community service. For them, Mott Community College initiated Volunteer Voices, a project that provides tuition credit in return for community services.

In 1991, Mott combined resources with the Mott Middle College, an on-campus alternative high school, and Newspapers for the Blind, a non-profit organization spon-

Continues on Page 336

soring a telephone reading program, to provide a volunteer reading service for visually impaired residents. In exchange for educational services and financial assistance intended to reduce student debt and increase student retention, honors students each semester serve as editors and mentors in oral reading for Middle College students. They provide five weekly magazines by telephone for 800 visually impaired residents in the community.

To reduce debt burden, 15 honors students each semester receive free tuition for 12 credit hours in return for reading newspapers and weekly magazines, via telephone, as well as mentoring 20 at-risk high school students and monitoring their progress in reading for the blind. Students are selected based on need, interest, and leadership potential to serve as volunteer studio staff for 10 hours a week. They report an increase in self-esteem and leadership skills as well as gaining an appreciation of the value of community service. As mentors, they are responsible for rehearsing the readings with the high school students so that the final product is of recordable quality. High school students are gaining poise in reading aloud, additional reading skills, and a greater awareness of world events. Because Newspapers for the Blind needs qualified,

competent volunteer readers to provide consistent access to daily newspapers and weekly magazines, all of the participants agree that Volunteer Voices is a win-win project.

Honors students in community colleges frequently fall through the cracks when it comes to receiving financial assistance. While sometimes not qualifying for Pell grants or other needs grants and assistance, they nevertheless have a difficult time providing a living and staying in school. A project like this could find wide application in other colleges because it provides assistance for at-risk students, a worthwhile community service for visually impaired residents, and also provides a means for high achieving students to stay in school.

The project has been funded by the U.S. Department of Education's Fund for Improvement of Post Secondary Education (FIPSE) as an innovative project for student community service. Plans to expand the program are being explored through the Merit network and on several college campuses. Students involved in the project made presentations at both the Phi Theta Kappa Michigan regional convention and at the Phi Theta Kappa national convention, held in Dallas in April, 1993.

Contact:
Gail Knapp, Honors Program Director
(313) 762-0350

C.S. Mott Community College
1401 East Court Street
Flint, MI 48503
Total head count enrollment-Credit: 10,858; Non-Credit: 9,390
Campuses/sites: 2;Full-time faculty: 174

GLEN OAKS COMMUNITY COLLEGE

SPEAKERS PROGRAM

The program, begun by a former student, has featured such notable speakers as Carl Sagan and Sir David Attenborough

Despite its small size and rural location, Glen Oaks Community College has had such noted lecturers as Carl Sagan, Steven J. Gould, Sir David Attenborough, James Burke, David Macaulay and Jean-Michel Cousteau (son of Jacques Cousteau) and Galen Rowell, noted National Geographic photographer and explorer.

How does a rural college in southern Michigan attract such renowned people? Through the enthusiasm, dedication, and persuasive skills of a former student. Vicki Copeland began the Speakers Program almost three years ago. Ms. Copeland was working on a science project, "The Evolution of Flightlessness in Birds," and decided to try to personally contact Dr. Gould, a noted authority on evolution for references to resources. During their conversation, Ms. Copeland asked Dr. Gould if he would come to Glen Oaks to help stimulate science studies at the college. He generously consented to give one of his few public appearance lectures at the college during the winter of 1989. Since then, the program has continued to grow and flourish.

The Glen Oaks Speakers Program operates mainly on donations from area individuals, businesses, and the college's progressive Foundation. Also, an important factor in fundraising is a "Patron's Dinner," hosted in the home of one of the enthusiastic supporters of the program prior to the evening lecture. Between 100 and 125 people pay $50 to attend the dinner, the major portion of which helps support the cost of the Speakers Program. The featured speaker is the guest of honor at the dinner.

All seating in the balcony of a local auditorium is given free of charge to area high school students. The high school science instructors identify students to attend. The program helps build bridges to area K-12 schools for the college's science program. Often, the speaker visits the Glen Oaks campus the next day and visits with students or presents a workshop.

The key factor to the success of the Glen Oaks Speakers Program is an interested and dedicated coordinator. Also important is a professional agent willing to take the time to understand the local needs and to grasp the programming philosophy. Additional factors include: personal contact with faculty, area schools, and businesses to promote; a solid, dependable cadre of volunteers; offering free seating for approximately one-sixth of the auditorium to area high school students; and a very supportive president and College Foundation.

Contact:
Vicki Copeland, Program Coordinator
Dennis McCarthy, Dean of Community Services
(616) 467-9945

Glen Oaks Community College
62249 Shimmel Road
Centreville, MI 49032-9719
Total head count enrollment-Credit: 2,038; Non-Credit: 1,170
Campuses/sites: 1;Full-time faculty: 33

CENTER FOR BUSINESS SERVICES

The Center offers seminars and customized training, as well as extensive research on regional business trends

Glen Oaks Community College offers a unique combination of services to area businesses that goes beyond seminars, workshops and counseling. Glen Oaks also does extensive research on business trends in the college's service area, resulting in two publications helpful to area economic development practitioners, banks, real estate offices, social service agencies and many other organizations. These publications are:

1) *St. Joseph County Business Outlook*, published quarterly and providing information about employment, industrial strength, as well as leading economic indicators that can be compared from quarter-to-quarter and year-to-year; and

2) *Wage Survey of Manufacturing*, which gives area employers an indication of what is occurring with wages in a wide variety of manufacturing job categories (published semi-annually and enables employers to monitor wage trends geographically and over time).

In addition to the publication services, the Center offers a wide variety of seminars and customized training. About half of these programs are on-campus and half on-location at area businesses. Also provided is one-to-one counseling for current business owners and a special course in "How to Start a Business in Michigan." Importantly, the college has taken a lead role in creating a regional Forum for Economic Development, where citizens interested in improving the climate for doing business meet and share their concerns and ideas on how to better use resources and do cooperative efforts.

A key factor in the success of the Center for Business Services is the expertise of the director, who has more than 20 years teaching experience and more than 20 years of business experience. Also, the business community is contacted frequently through personal visits and telephone inquiries. Target mailings with personal letters are also a major technique for promotion. The Center director is conscientious in providing information that is accurate and presented in such a way that it is understandable and useful. The Center follows a research format for economic analysis that was developed by the Upjohn Institute, a leader in employment and economics research in the Midwest. An advisory committee (The Forum for Economic Development) composed of area economic development practitioners, business people and area chambers of commerce representatives helps ensure for regular communication and community support.

Contact:
Jack Mann, Center Director
Dennis McCarthy, Dean of Community Services
(616) 467-9945

Glen Oaks Community College
62249 Shimmel Road
Centreville, MI 49032-9719
Total head count enrollment-Credit: 2,038; Non-Credit: 1,170
Campuses/sites: 1;Full-time faculty: 33

CULINARY ARTS

*▣ The Culinary Arts program has food service and banquet responsibility ▣
for local civic functions and college foundation events*

The high degree of professionalism found in Grand Rapids Community College Culinary Arts students is evident, considering the program has food service and banquet responsibility for local civic functions and important college foundation events, which always must be just right. GRCC started the program in 1980 to meet the needs of this expanding hospitality industry. Michigan's number one industry today is tourism. It generates billions of dollars in sales and employs thousands of individuals. Nationwide, by the year 2000, it is estimated that there will be 2-million unfilled job opportunities in the industry.

The two-year Associate degree program in Culinary Arts started in a renovated college kitchen with two full-time instructors and 21 students. In 1981, the program moved into new facilities with a new kitchen, a 65-seat restaurant, a take-out deli/bakery and banquet space for 200 guests. The program gained an additional kitchen in the renovated 1893 Victoria style home that houses the Grand Rapids Community College Foundation. With the addition of five full-time chef instructors, the Culinary Arts program was given the food service and banquet responsibility for local civic group functions and for GRCC Foundation fund raising events. The GRCC Foundation's financial resources have grown from its 1981 level of $398,000 to $4.5-million today, partly due to the many social events prepared by the students of the Culinary Arts Department.

In 1991, the program expanded to accommodate the 300 students currently in the program by moving into the college's new Applied Technology Center. The additional 30,000 square feet of space houses five kitchens, a restaurant, an executive dining room, a beverage and mixology laboratory, a bistro, four banquet rooms, two class rooms, a culinary arts library, and an office complex. Of the total $1.4-million in kitchen equipment purchased, $500,000 were donated by equipment manufacturers and local busi-

nesses to make this facility the state-of-the-art culinary teaching facility in the country.

Professional contributions by the staff of 14 full-time and six part-time instructors are broad and far reaching. Commitment to the food service industry is demonstrated on both the local and national level. Locally, faculty serve on the advisory committees of three area vocational food programs. They have served in executive positions in local chapters of national and state food service associations and groups. National involvement includes positions on the national boards and committees of the American Culinary Federation, National Restaurant Association and the Council on Hotel Restaurant and Institutional Education.

The instructional staff remains student-centered, by volunteering their time and services for many extracurricular student events. These extra educational opportunities range from department fund-raising events to state-wide student competitions to yearly visits to each high school in the community college district.

The Department feels strongly that the students be exposed to the many cross-cultural influences on cooking. This is accomplished in two ways:

1) the department, in cooperation with the local chefs association, sponsors a monthly visiting chef series that brings nationally acclaimed chef's to the campus; and

2) the department, since 1984, has sponsored foreign travel opportunities. Past student cultural trips have been to Germany, Great Britain and France. Future cultural trips are planned to Australia, Japan and China.

Of the numerous local, state and national awards and recognition given to GRCC Culinary Art's program, the best reward is its record of 99 percent placement rate among its graduates and their ensuing success.

Contact:
Robert Garlough, Chairperson, Hospitality Education Division
(616) 771-3690

Grand Rapids Community College
143 Bostwick Northeast
Grand Rapids, MI 49503
Total head count enrollment-Credit: 22,410; Non-Credit: 3,867
Campuses/sites: 2;Full-time faculty: 242

BUSINESS AND TECHNICAL TRAINING

*Educational programs serve more than 200 companies
and 3,000 people annually*

The Business and Technical Training Department of Grand Rapids Community College provides customized training for industry. This training is designed to give employees the skills necessary to upgrade and enrich their jobs. The staff is available to meet with company representatives to access their companies training needs, design custom curriculums, implement tailor-made programs and evaluate the program's success. Educational programs are serving more than 200 companies and organizations while serving more than 3,000 people annually. The Business and Technical Training Department provides training in the following fields:

1) Micro Computer Training
   - Introduction to Computers
   - DOS
   - Microsoft Windows
   - Word Perfect 5.1
   - MS Word for Windows
   - MS Excel for Windows
   - Pagemaker
   - Lotus
   - Quattro Pro
   - FoxPro;
2) CAD and CAD/CAM
   - AutoCAD (Rel. 11 and 12)
   - AutoCAD for Windows
   - AutoCAD Certification Exam
   - AutoSketch
   - AutoLISP Programming
   - AutoCAD 3D
   - AutoCAD Customization
   - AutoDesk Multimedia Products
   - Bridgeport EZ Surf
   - Bridgeport EZ CAM
   - CadKey
   - MicroStation
   - SmartCAM;
3) SPC/Quality
   - Statistical Process Control (SPC)
   - Experimental Design (DOE)
   - Problem Solving
   - Blueprint Reading
   - Geometric Dimensioning and Tolerancing
   - Technical Math
   - Quality Assurance
   - ISO 9000 Training
   - Coordinate Measuring Machine (CMM)
   - Advanced Quality Systems Training - Boeing
   - Supervisory Training; and
4) Plastics
   - Injection Molding Machine Operator Training.

Contact:
Donald R. Boyer
(313) 771-3600

Grand Rapids Community College
143 Bostwick Northeast
Grand Rapids, MI 49503
Total head count enrollment-Credit: 22,410; Non-Credit: 3,867
Campuses/sites: 2; Full-time faculty: 242

GUARANTEE FOR CREDIT TRANSFER AND JOB COMPETENCY

*The guarantee lowers faculty resistance to accountability
for educational outcomes*

In 1986, the faculty, administration and Board of Henry Ford Community College approved a guarantee for credit transfer and for job competency that many colleges have since used as a model. That approval followed a full year of intensive review of the proposal that involved faculty and local business leaders.

While the faculty was initially skeptical of guaranteeing course transfer and job competency, the impact over five years has been to significantly validate the high quality of education that HFCC offers. The guarantees have also served to reduce resistance to accountability for educational outcomes.

The guarantees are important components of the annual marketing campaigns, and HFCC has received numerous calls from all around the country about its guarantees.

There is a minimal commitment of human resources to the project. Literature is provided from the Office of College Relations, and counselors share four-year college transfer program plans with interested students.

Here are HFCC's guarantees:
- Henry Ford Community College will refund the

Continues on Page 340

tuition of any HFCC graduate for any course passed at HFCC with at least a "C" grade, if that earned course credit does not transfer to a college or university within two years of graduation from HFCC. Such classes must be listed as transferable on the transfer institution's official curriculum guide sheets, dated 1986 or thereafter, on file in the office of the HFCC Counseling Division.

•Any graduate of an associate degree program in occupational studies who is judged by his/her employer as lacking in technical job skills normally expected of a job-entry level employee will be provided further skill training of up to 16 semester credit hours by HFCC without charge.

Contact:
Randall Miller, Vice President, College Relations
(313) 845-9649

Henry Ford Community College
5101 Evergreen Road
Dearborn, MI 48128-1495
Total head count enrollment-Credit: 15,511; Non-Credit: 373
Campuses/sites: 3;Full-time faculty: 213

TUITION FREEZE GUARANTEE

The guarantee requires that a student graduates from the college within four years

Effective summer 1989, for new students, Henry Ford Community College guarantees that tuition rates will be frozen for students who graduate from HFCC within four years. Any tuition increase levied by the college during those four years will be refunded to the student upon graduation.

To qualify for the tuition freeze program, a student must complete all course work at HFCC, graduate within four successive years of enrollment and apply for a tuition rebate after graduation. Students who receive financial aid, except for loans, are not eligible for the program.

Contact:
Randall Miller, Vice President, College Relations
(313) 845-9649

Henry Ford Community College
5101 Evergreen Road
Dearborn, MI 48128-1495
Total head count enrollment-Credit: 15,511; Non-Credit: 373
Campuses/sites: 3;Full-time faculty: 213

ACHIEVEMENT PLUS PROJECT

The project is rooted in the theory that 95 percent of any student population can master any body of knowledge

The Achievement Plus Project (A+) gives at-risk students learning experiences that enhance their academic and personal growth at Kalamazoo Valley Community College.

The guiding principles of Achievement Plus have theoretical roots in the research of Benjamin S. Bloom and John B. Carroll, whose research led them to conclude that 95 percent of any population of students can master any body of knowledge provided that three factors are in place:

•Cognitive Entry Behaviors, which refer to the pool of information and skills students bring to a particular learning task and to their ability to transfer that base of information to new situations, including reading comprehension, arithmetic processing, language development, writing ability, and logical processing.

•Affective Entry Characteristics, which refer to a complex compound of interests, attitudes, and self-views unique to each learner, frequently termed motivation but also inclusive of perseverance, aptitude, previous success in subject, feelings about the subject.

•Quality of Instruction, which refers to the instructional design decisions that teachers make in the presentation, explanation and ordering of the elements of the learning tasks; i.e., sequence and nature of learning task, procedures, clarity of objectives, adequacy of directions, quality of materials, quantity and quality of examples, etc.

These factors provide the organizing principles for the Achievement Plus Project.

The Cognitive domain is addressed through coursework

in developmental English, reading and two levels of mathematics. The English courses, offered in the Macintosh Lab, provide students with computer instruction as well as language skill-building.

The experiences to enhance growth and development in the Affective domain include adventure activities such as team spirit, adversity training and communication skill-building at off-campus retreat sites, coursework in study and college survival skills, and participation in the A+ Mentoring Project. In addition, the Achievement Plus Project provides students with a full-time counselor to offer support and guidance in decision-making and problem-solving as well as course and program selection.

The third factor, Quality of Instruction, is addressed through careful selection and training of those instructors who have shown an interest in working with the Achievement Plus student population. The program's director provides the A+ philosophy and training so that all staff and faculty are functioning under the same premise. Both director and assistant director offer maintenance of the principles and practices through day-to-day interactions and formal meetings.

In the fall of 1993, the A+ Project entered its sixth year of operation. With only some minor changes in curriculum, the purpose of the A+ mission has not changed: providing students with the strategies and academic preparation to enter and successfully complete college-level courses.

Contact:
John Corbin, Director, (616) 372-5375
Carol Head, Assistant Director, (616) 372-5492

Kalamazoo Valley Community College
6767 West "O" Avenue
Kalamazoo, MI 49009
Total head count enrollment-Credit: 15,929; Non-Credit: 1,777
Full-time faculty: 112

KALAMAZOO VALLEY COMMUNITY COLLEGE

INTERNATIONAL STUDIES

Faculty, staff and students have been active in participating and presenting on a variety of forums on international/global/multicultural issues

More than 100 sections of internationalized courses across 19 disciplines, as well as 40 to 50 sections of international and foreign language courses, are the annual manifestation of an aggressive and acclaimed International Studies program at Kalamazoo Valley Community College.

Born in the late 1980's as a concerted effort by a number of KVCC administrators and faculty, the program used a five-year plan as the blueprint. A two-year grant by the U.S. Department of Education, under Title VI (Undergraduate International Studies and Foreign Language Program), provided crucial outside funding that supplemented internal resources that allowed the development of international curriculum, co-curriculum activities, the establishment of the International Studies program and provided opportunities for professional growth for faculty and staff.

Since then, five additional projects were partially funded by outside sources (i.e. AACJC-Kellogg Foundation, U.S. Department of Education, European Community Studies Association) that allowed the undertaking of further curriculum, co-curriculum and other professional activities relating to international/global/multicultural areas.

Today, the International Studies program enrolls about 170 students and offers an Associate in Arts and Certificate degrees.

Sixty-one faculty have developed more than 30 international modules and several international courses and teach regularly the aforementioned internationalized, international and foreign language courses. Furthermore many of them are instrumental in supporting co-curriculum international activities for KVCC students, faculty, staff and the community, such as International Week, Earth Day, World Food Day, Hispanic Month, Black History Month, Women's History Month and a number of international colloquia, workshops and luncheons.

KVCC faculty, staff and students have been active in participating and presenting on a variety of regional or national forums on international/global/multicultural issues, and are always enthusiastic in sharing curriculum works, experiences and expertise. The KVCC International Studies program has the laudatory reputation of eagerness in sharing resources, networking and collaborating with colleges and individuals in Michigan and across the country. Such an attitude has proved very successful in supporting noteworthy joint projects, in nurturing enthusiasm, leadership and accomplishments, and in bringing outside recognition.

Contact:
Theo S. Sypris, Program Director
(616) 372-5283

Kalamazoo Valley Community College
6767 West "O" Avenue
Kalamazoo, MI 49009
Total head count enrollment-Credit: 15,929; Non-Credit: 1,777
Full-time faculty: 112

MICHIGAN • PAGE 341

2 + 3 PROGRAM

The program, for engineering students, features cooperative education along with usual classroom work

Kellogg Community College and GMI Engineering and Management Institute of Flint are engaged in a 2+3 Program for engineering students that has become a model for subsequent relationships GMI has developed with both Jackson and Lansing Community Colleges in Michigan. Long a respected engineering school, GMI has a unique program that features a cooperative education aspect along with the usual engineering classroom work.

KCC students opting for the 2+3 receive 320 hours of hands-on, paid work experience while they are completing their first two years of study at Kellogg Community College. They also receive counseling in how to interview through the college's Placement office, and attend an orientation session where there is a GMI representative to respond to their specific concerns.

Co-op sites in the KCC district are developed through the joint efforts of a faculty coordinator and the college's Business and Industrial Services director, who has ongoing contact with companies that can provide co-op experiences.

Contact:
Kathy Tarr, Director, Public Relations
(616) 965-3931

Kellogg Community College
450 North Avenue
Battle Creek, MI 49017-3397
Total head count enrollment-Credit/Non-Credit: 19,000
Campuses/sites: 1;Full-time faculty: 100

REGIONAL MANUFACTURING TECHNOLOGY CENTER

The Center's specialty is training for skilled trades and maintenance positions in manufacturing

Training is flexible at Kellogg Community College's Regional Manufacturing Technology Center, where people may start at any time and choose their own attendance schedules.

The successful result of the combined efforts of industry, education and government, the Center's construction was financed jointly by the State of Michigan and the W.K. Kellogg Foundation. It is operated as a joint venture by the college and the city of Battle Creek.

The Center was located at the Ft. Custer Industrial Park in order to bring customized trades training to the center of industrial activity in the Battle Creek area. Some students have only to "cross the street" to get to classes.

The Center's specialty is training for skilled trades and maintenance positions in manufacturing. The staff can also provide a wide variety of customized training to fit the specific needs of an individual employer.

Training at the Center is delivered in a flexible format. Programs are self-paced, guided by journeyman instructors who emphasize hands-on learning. With the "open entry/open exit" admissions policy, students may opt for a certificate or an associate degree or take only as many hours of training as they require to fit their specific needs.

Programming at the Center is continuously monitored by advisory committees from industry who know the dynamics of manufacturing and how its change should be reflected in the Center's curriculum content. These same manufacturers, including Nippondenso and the Kellogg Company, were among the many local businesses contributing nearly $1-million to provide the Center with state-of-the-art equipment. So satisfied has the Kellogg Company been with the training of its employees that the company has halted its own internal training program in favor of the Center's program.

Eighty percent of the Center's students are company-sponsored, so job placement hasn't been a major issue. Of the non-sponsored students, about 85 percent are placed following completion of their training. The measure of success for the Center is the number of companies served, the number of students served, and the number of companies who bring repeat business to the Center. Currently 54 companies are represented, with nearly 700 students enrolled.

Because the training is individualized, student retention is near the 95 percent mark in the competency-based programs. As others have seen the success enjoyed by the trades programs, adaptations have been implemented in the developmental curriculum on campus and the office information systems (secretarial) program.

Recognition of the program has included the Exemplary

Program designation of the National Council for Instructional Administrators as well as articles in *Technical/Skills Training* from the American Society for Training and Development, and *Focus*, the newsletter for the National Center for Manufacturing Sciences.

Contact:
Dennis Bona
(616) 965-4137

Kellogg Community College
450 North Avenue
Battle Creek, MI 49017-3397
Total head count enrollment-Credit/Non-Credit: 19,000
Campuses/sites: 1;Full-time faculty: 100

LAKE MICHIGAN COLLEGE

WINNER WITHIN

The college "adopts" students in sixth grade and promises full two-year scholarships upon high school graduation

The Winner Within program for at-risk students earned Lake Michigan College the Beacon Award from the American Association of Community Colleges in 1990, to help other colleges implement similar programs in their communities. Through the Winner Within, 76 students were "adopted" by the college in 1987 when they were in the sixth grade, and promised full two-year scholarships upon their high school graduations. The students are 90 percent minority, and most are eligible for federal assistance programs. Many parents have not earned high school diplomas, and only one has achieved advanced education (an associate degree). The name of the program was selected because, rather than seeking to identify students who are already "winners," its goal is to develop the "winner within" all children. In addition, college staff and interested community members become mentors for individual students, with the responsibility of contacting their assigned student on at least a monthly basis. Sponsors serve as mentors who model adult success and positive qualities that often differ from the student's experiences, helping to broaden the student's options. Now in the 11th grade, the students have attended a variety of special activities at the college, such as plays, art exhibits, sporting events and social gatherings. The students also receive a monthly newsletter. The students' graduation rates and academic success will be compared with a control group upon their high school graduations.

The scholarships are funded by an annual "Winner's Circle" auction, which has raised nearly $500,000 in the five years it has been held. In addition to funding the scholarships, this event has served as an important conscience-raiser for Lake Michigan College, and is a much-anticipated social event for the community. Additional funding has been received from grants from the Whirlpool Foundation, Michigan Council for the Arts, Michigan Council for the Humanities, private businesses and individuals.

Contact:
Charmaine Kibler, Director of Grants
(616) 927-8155

Lake Michigan College
2755 East Napier Avenue
Benton Harbor, MI 49022-1899
Total head count enrollment-Credit/Non-Credit: 7,819
Campuses/sites: 6;Full-time faculty: 72

LAKE MICHIGAN COLLEGE

TRAINING PARTNERSHIP

The partnership with Whirlpool helps strengthen economic and work force development

When Whirlpool Corporation began evaluating 350 sites across the United States to build and expand its Consumer Assistance Center in 1990, Lake Michigan College's Corporate & Community Development Division and the Cornerstone Alliance submitted a competitive training proposal focusing on customer service. Whirlpool liked what it saw and Benton Harbor, Michigan, along with Knoxville, Tennessee, was selected as expansion site.

A part of the college's mission is to strengthen regional economic development through work force development

Continues on Page 344

and quality training. To serve Whirlpool Corporation, the college is focusing on two major goals:
1) transitional technical training; and
2) strategic long-term product-related, job skills, and continuous improvement training.

The Business & Industry Training Department works with Whirlpool to redesign the existing Consumer Assistance Representative training. The expansion of the Consumer Assistance Center will allow Whirlpool to handle about 9 million consumer inquiries annually with state-of-the-art computer technology and artificial intelligence equipment. The training is focused on technical job skills, product-related training, continuous improvement and supervision training. It is estimated that it will take approximately 12,300 to 16,000 training hours to implement the Consumer Assistance Center business objectives.

To accomplish the objectives, training workbooks and video-based programs are designed for specific training modules to reinforce the training of Consumer Assistance Center employees. In addition, a video was produced to emphasize "world-class service telephone behaviors" with interactive exercises. The division provides a Training Project Manager to develop the training programs in collaboration with Whirlpool staff. Lake Michigan College has provided the following training services:
1) developed 22 skill-based training modules with self-paced employee workbooks and leader's guides;
2) designed tests to measure competency of knowledge and skills based upon the training modules;
3) completed five video-based training programs by providing assistance in technical writing, video script writing and video production capabilities for Consumer service and Technical Field Representatives;
4) edited and updated 17 training videos with new training materials/graphics; and
5) trained more than 115 existing employees.

As a result, Lake Michigan College continues to serve as a strategic training partner in developing other Whirlpool Corporation training delivery system projects. In three years, the bottom line is that more than 100 new employees have been hired and trained using these training materials, which benefits economic revitalization of our community. A two-year strategic training plan is being developed for 1993-95. This training project is supported by several financial partnerships between the college, Whirlpool Corporation, Michigan Department of Education, and the Cornerstone Alliance. Approximately $2.5-million has been budgeted to implement the training project, including $92,223 grant award from the Michigan Economic Development Job Training program. The training programs designed will impact an additional 450 factory technicians and 6,900 independent service dealers.

Contact:
Jack N. Wismer, Vice President, Corporate & Community Development
(616) 927-8100

Lake Michigan College
2755 East Napier Avenue
Benton Harbor, MI 49022-1899
Total head count enrollment-Credit/Non-Credit: 7,819
Campuses/sites: 6;Full-time faculty: 72

MACOMB COMMUNITY COLLEGE

AUTO SERVICES TRAINING

The 80-credit hour program combines technical and liberal arts classes

In an effort to help automobile technicians become more service-oriented, Macomb Community College has joined with the Big 3 auto companies – General Motors, Ford Motor Co. and Chrysler Corp. – to teach humanities to auto tech students.

The Auto Service Training Program, which began in 1985, combines technical and liberal arts classes. When students complete the 80-credit hour program, they receive Associate Degrees in Applied Science.

The Big 3, which were interested in adding the humanities aspect to the auto tech program, believed that auto technicians trained in customer relations and human values would enhance a dealership's service, which would positively impact sales. A trained technician, as envisioned in this program, would lead to greater customer satisfaction.

Chrysler and Macomb Community College joined together to form such a program, where students would be taught sensitivity to the importance of the auto to the buyer. The Auto Services Training Program was later implemented by General Motors and Ford.

Students, who must go through a rigorous selection process before entering the program, are sponsored by dealerships, who either pay half the training costs or promise the students a job upon completion of the program. The almost 300 students that have gone through the Auto Services Training Program spend eight weeks in the classroom and eight weeks working for the automobile dealership. Upon completion of the program, the students enter the field as service technicians.

The featured liberal arts course in the program, "Humanities 292: The Automobile in American Culture," incorporates textbooks, lectures and field trips centered around the automobiles impact on American life, arts and societal changes.

The course examines how the automobile effected the decentralization of cities, creation of metropolitan areas, development of a highway system and broadening of rural citizens' lifestyles. Also, it looks at the automobiles effect on art – how artists learned to use the auto as a subject and how they learned to use speed and motion in their work.

"The Automobile in American Culture," which is based in the elements and terminology of a traditional humanities class, also includes field trips to historical museums, city areas affected by the advent of the auto, antique car museums, assembly lines and automobile design shops.

Students are required to take other general education classes, which all are specialized for the automobile. For example, an environmental science class discusses the automobiles effect on the atmosphere, common work-based chemicals and the disposal of chemicals.

The Auto Services Training Program helps students grow in knowledge, skills and potential in servicing products, and the completion of the general education courses adds a balance of qualities vital to working in today's service industry.

Dealers who have participated in the program have indicated that students become effective employees, who have a well-rounded perspective on their relationship with the automobile, the automobile industry and its influence on society.

Contact:
Dana Anderson, Director, Center for Automotive Educ. & Training
(313) 445-7007

Macomb Community College
14500 Twelve Mile Rd
Warren, MI 48093
Total head count enrollment-Credit: 38,748; Non-Credit: 10,930
Campuses/sites: 3;Full-time faculty: 320

COMPUTERIZED PROGRAM ADVISING SYSTEM (CPAS)

The computerized system provides a seamless transition through enrollment, registration, academic advising and credit transfer

A computerized system leads Macomb Community College students through enrollment, registration, academic advising and credit transfer – and even reminds them when to call a counselor. The Computerized Program Advising System (CPAS), on-line since 1987, provides students and faculty with a timely and accurate measure of each student's progress toward his or her academic objective. The requirements of associate degree and certificate programs offered by Macomb Community College are entered into the college's Enrollment Information System (EIS) data base by the Business and Public Service, Applied Technology, and Arts and Sciences divisions. The Employment and Transfer Assistance Department supplements Macomb program data with the transfer requirements of 24 four-year colleges and universities. This information is then interfaced on the college's mainframe computer with each student's selection of a program and transfer plans, as supplied by the Counseling Department. The entire process is overseen by the Enrollment Office.

After a student's first semester at Macomb, the student begins receiving a computer-generated Student Program Plan (SPP) prior to the registration period for fall and spring terms. The SPP denotes courses completed, courses and credits left to take and grade point averages. If a student has not declared a major, the SPP reminds a student to do so as soon as possible and provides the telephone number to call to make an appointment with a counselor. Since the program's inception in 1987, nearly 20,000 SPPs have been mailed.

The outcome of CPAS and the SPP is a seamless transition, leading students through enrollment, registration, academic advising and credit transfer with minimal confusion. The Academic Standards Committee is also considering expanding CPAS' functions to include long-term monitoring. This would require the addition of such data as student course withdrawals and final semester grades.

CPAS has no specific budget. Funding for the implementation and operation of CPAS has been divided among several college divisions and departments. The computer software and hardware used for CPAS is also used for several other programs and purposes.

Contact:
Salvatore Evangelista, Associate Dean, Student Development Svcs.
(313) 445-7183

Macomb Community College
14500 Twelve Mile Road
Warren, MI 48093
Total head count enrollment-Credit: 38,748; Non-Credit: 10,930
Campuses/sites: 3;Full-time faculty: 320

WRITING ACROSS THE CURRICULUM

▓ Instructors who otherwise would not have felt comfortable with ▓
writing-intensive assignments, have lauded the program

Advanced Composition students at Monroe County Community College become "Writing Fellows" and help their peers improve their communication skills through a non-threatening critique of writing assignments. This system is designed to help offset the nationwide decline in students' writing abilities.

On the college level, the popularity of Writing-Across-the-Curriculum and related programs ("Writing-Across-the-Disciplines," process writing, Writing-Intensive courses) bears witness to the concern about the need to teach writing in English courses and the concomitant need to assign writing in other disciplines as well. After a two-year research survey, begun in 1986, of Michigan community colleges and several out-of-state programs, Dr. John Holladay of Monroe County Community College set up our Writing-Across-the-Curriculum program, which began in the fall of 1988, and which was unique for Michigan in that it focused upon the training and use of "Writing Fellows," for its viability.

The program has been working successfully at Monroe County Community College ever since. A select group, the "Writing Fellows," is trained in the Advanced Composition class, then assigned to various instructors in all the disciplines – instructors who have volunteered to participate in the program and who have restructured their classes to make them more writing intensive by assigning several papers, or reports or journal assignments. The fellows read and comment on all rough drafts of writing assignments, documenting their critiques and advising the students about high-level concerns: whether the paper has carried out the assignment, whether the writing is clear, if it makes its points, etc. Fellows are indoctrinated not to be editors, not to focus on lower-level aspects such as spelling and punctuation. When papers are discussed by peers, all the positives of peer tutoring enter in: a non-threatening, often caring environment that enables the student to discuss and clarify as he or she learns to express ideas in writing to a fellow student.

The "Writing Fellows" have a camaraderie that is special. Since they were selected for their superior academic traits, it's an honor for them to be asked to be a "fellow," and what results is a true "fellowship." At the semester's end, they gather for picnics and lunches to celebrate their success. In addition to the advanced composition class they attend, there's a $250 stipend for each fellow. There is a WAC budget and a WAC coordinator, Dr. Holladay, who began the project, received recognition from several articles he wrote for nationwide circulation. He has succeeded by Sue Zwayer, who has been active in WAC and peer tutoring conferences.

The ENGL 254 Advanced Composition course not only concentrates on how to criticize a fellow student's written work, but also gives the students advanced training in discriminating between good and poor writing and the chance to keep journals to monitor their own writing progress. For the first time this year, an advanced composition class will be taught each full semester, fall and winter. Both the former and the present WAC coordinators assert that having Writing Fellows is the key to making a Writing-Across-the-Curriculum program a success. The institution, by providing a WAC budget and by promoting across-the disciplines subscription, has proved its support for the program. Instructors who would otherwise not have felt comfortable with writing-intensive assignments, have lauded the program as well.

This program is coordinated by one faculty member as two-fifths of her load, in addition to the actual teaching of the advanced composition course. It includes up to 50 writing fellows in any given semester at a cost of $250 per writing fellow for the semester.

Contact:
Sue Zwayer, Coordinator
(313) 242-7300, ext. 423

Monroe County Community College
1555 South Raisinville Road
Monroe, MI 48161
Total head count enrollment-Credit: 3,668; Non-Credit: 1,639
Campuses/sites: 3; Full-time faculty: 60

PAYBACK FOR EDUCATION

The program is designed to treat eighth- and tenth-graders special and to stress the importance of a college education

Fog and a two-hour school starting delay for some students did not keep county 8th- and 10th-graders from participating in the third annual Payback for Education. The event was held at Monroe County Community College, on March 26, 1992, and by all indications was another huge success. The goal at each of these programs is to treat the students special for a day. The students are asked to dress accordingly for a conference situation.

The theme that year stressed the importance of attitude to present and future achievements. It is not always your aptitude that determines your achievements; it is your attitude. The conference and workshops emphasized this theme. In today's world attitude is very important. For all of us, attitude toward school, work, friends, parents, teachers, future education, employers and life is the key to success. Even more important is the attitude we hold about ourselves.

Each Payback for Education also has a recurring theme that stresses the importance of students to set their sights on a two-year goal of education at the community college. Eighty percent of the jobs in the near future will require two-years beyond high school, while only 20 percent of the jobs will require a bachelor's degree.

The program begins with the major sponsors welcoming the students. MCC honored the students in 1991 by inviting the governor of Michigan to be the featured speaker. In 1990, the featured speaker was a local television personality. In 1992, a motivational speaker from the State Department encouraged the students to set their sights high and to be determined to achieve any goals they set. They need to believe it and not let day-to-day problems get in the way.

After the introduction, which lasted approximately 45 minutes, the students were off to their workshops. The workshops were presented by the college counselors and individuals from business and education who volunteered their time and talents.

The luncheon was a favorite with the students. The Monroe County Community College's Culinary Arts class prepared a gourmet luncheon for the students and the business representatives. This was a relaxed period in which the business representatives talked with the students. For a nominal fee each business purchased one table that seats seven students.

After lunch a Buzz Session was held. Each luncheon table was given a business or related-theme problem and as a team they were asked to give the best solution. They were given 40 minutes to Buzz on the problem. This was businesses favorite part of the program. They enjoyed hearing the solutions that the students had. The winners received a Monroe County Community College-Payback for Education t-shirt.

As an assignment, the students were requested to write an essay on their day at Monroe County Community College. When we received these comments, we printed a newsletter and sent this along with a Certificate of Participation to the students home. Some students have received summer jobs due to their luncheon with the businesses.

Detroit Edison donated a 20-minute professional video tape of the 1991 program. The college and each participating school received a copy of the tape. Each school was encouraged to create their own mini-Payback for Education workshops reaching the many students that were unable to attend.

This review of the program is but a glimpse of a very involved and valuable experience for the 300 students that attend.

Contact:
David McKay, Business Division Chair
(313) 242-7300

Monroe County Community College
1555 South Raisinville Road
Monroe, MI 48161
Total head count enrollment-Credit: 3,668; Non-Credit: 1,639
Campuses/sites: 3; Full-time faculty: 60

PERSONALIZED ACHIEVEMENT LABORATORY (PALAB)

Most PALab courses are taught on a one-to-one basis, with assignments tailored to the pace of each student

The Personalized Achievement Laboratory (PALab) at Muskegon Community College has successfully removed much of the stigma and threat of remedial courses. An open-lab center that offers individualized credit courses in reading, writing and basic math, PALab enrollment in writing and math courses consists of a mixture of students seeking elective credit and those placed by mandatory testing. Most reading students enroll voluntarily. An essential contributor to MCC's "Open Door Policy," the PALab develops skills and attitudes needed for success. A former English instructor, Beverley Turner, said it best: "The Personalized Achievement Laboratory at Muskegon Community College is a warm and welcoming place." Testimony to the PALab's mission of providing a non-threatening atmosphere is the growing enrollment. Another example of success exists in the grades of students who take PALab courses. Tracking shows that there is a close relationship to student success with PALab students who come to college poorly prepared academically.

Most PALab courses are taught on a one-to-one basis, and assignments are tailored to the pace of each student. Weekly scheduled conferences with instructors and paraprofessionals provides constant monitoring of the students'

skill development, allowing for assignments to be adjusted accordingly. The PALab is open at least 60 hours each week, providing ample time for students to spend their free time upgrading basic skills. Peer tutoring also is available.

The PALab works closely with the Diagnostic Testing Center, better enabling student skill levels to be properly assessed. In addition to its one-on-one teaching efforts, the PALab also conducts seminars, short continuing-education courses and on-site industrial classes, thus meeting community educational needs as they emerge. Created in 1972, the PALab has indeed evolved into a key center of learning within a larger center of learning, a primary resource for educational growth that has earned broad acceptance in the community.

The PALab employs seven full-time persons, including a department coordinator, three instructors and three para-professionals. Additionally, there are approximately 20 part-time instructors and paraprofessionals, and 35 to 45 peer tutors. Out of a total student headcount of 5,500, more than 800 students each semester enroll in PALab courses and tutoring services.

Contact:
Donald Goodman, Coordinator
(616) 777-0331

Muskegon Community College
221 South Quarterline Road
Muskegon, MI 49442
Total head count enrollment-Credit: 5,500; Non-Credit: 3,000
Campuses/sites: 1;Full-time faculty: 98

CHILD DEVELOPMENT ASSOCIATE (CDA) PROGRAM

The program provides credentials to qualified care givers who work with children from birth to age 5

Because one of the key concerns of working parents is the quality of care their young children receive from day care providers, Muskegon Community College offers area residents opportunities to acquire education specific to the care of children.

The Child Development Associate (CDA) Program in the Education Department at MCC represents local efforts to provide competency- and performance-based professional preparation for workers in early childhood education. In doing so, the program has played a major role in upgrading the skills of area employees. This program is affiliated with national efforts and provides credentials to qualified care givers who work with children from birth to age 5. A significant portion of program

requirements involves field work, which allows students to quickly apply the excitement and interest in what they learn in the classroom.

MCC has co-opted the national "competency goals" in attempting to provide students the finest child care education available in West Michigan. Students are expected to learn how:
1) to establish and maintain a safe, healthy learning environment;
2) to advance physical and intellectual competence;
3) to support social and emotional development and provide positive guidance;
4) to establish positive and productive relationships with families;

5) to ensure a well-run purposeful program responsive to participant needs; and

6) to maintain a commitment to professionalism.

College advisors work on-site with students and child care staff utilizing hands-on materials to directly reinforce learned theory and principles. Because of this, students acquire a sense of ownership of the CDA Program. This one-on-one approach helps the student acquire new ideas, appropriate developmental practices, and innovations in early childhood education, thus contributing to keeping area child care center staff up-to-date, current and fresh.

CDA Certificate holders may follow the "ladder approach" to career development by later working to earn their AA degree, and eventually a bachelor's degree in education. Many graduates go directly into the work force as lead teachers in day care centers, nursery schools and pre-schools. Students may choose to focus on "center-based" employment or emphasize "family day care" skills. Currently under development are "infant-toddler" and "home visitor" CDA programs. Enrollment in CDA programs at Muskegon Community College generally reaches 150 students annually.

The Education/Child Development Department employs one full-time instructor/coordinator and 15 adjunct instructors. Information on MCC's CDA Program has been provided requesters from Japan, Europe, Latin America and Hawaii.

Contact:
Harry Robinson, Education Coordinator
(616) 777-0277

Muskegon Community College
221 South Quarterline Road
Muskegon, MI 49442
Total head count enrollment-Credit: 5,500; Non-Credit: 3,000
Campuses/sites: 1;Full-time faculty: 98

HOSPITALITY PARTNERSHIP

More classes are being transitioned from campus locations into a recently renovated downtown hotel for "real-world experiences"

A recently renovated downtown hotel serves as a training center for Northwestern Michigan College students and as an economic boost for the area. Through a partnership between Northwestern Michigan College and the Rotary Center of Traverse City, the landmark Traverse City Hotel was acquired, renovated and then reopened in July 1991.

Since then, more than 2,000 learners have been engaged in a variety of learning experiences at the hotel. College students are enrolled for internships (focused work experiences), practica (rotating, observational experiences), and traditional courses such as Introduction to the Hospitality Industry and Baking. In the introductory course, students learn firsthand about hotel operations through meetings with supervisors and employees. Each unit is complemented by presentations by hotel staff. In the bakery class, small groups of students work under the guidance of the pastry chef to produce baked goods used in the hotel food outlets. More classes are being transitioned from campus locations into the hotel for "real-world experiences."

Area elementary, junior high and high school students participate in a learning series designed to support the Michigan Public Act 25 Core Curriculum in what are known as "Real World Encounters." Thousands of school children from throughout the region have toured the hotel, made breads, practiced customer service skills, observed people at work and more in a field experience that complements their current studies. Counselors' and area teachers' meetings are hosted with tourism leaders to discuss opportunities for careers.

Organizations which provide services to disadvantaged and disabled citizens work with the hotel and college staffs to integrate individuals into both learning and employment experiences. Other community-based organizations are also meaningfully engaged in a variety of learning activities.

Leadership for this community-wide effort is provided by a Resort Management department chair, whose salary is paid by the hotel and whose other expenses (including benefits) are paid by the college. His office is at the hotel. Guidance for the development of this community venture is provided by an Education Committee comprising Rotarians, college staff and hotel management. Hotel oversight is provided by a Board of Directors, primarily comprising Rotary members plus one college representative, who are updated monthly on the educational partnership.

Prior to development of this program, most other nationally recognized programs were either reviewed or visited. This approach was clearly unique – destined to become "world class."

Contact:
Roberta Teahen, Dean of Occupational Studies
(616) 922-1151

Northwestern Michigan College
1701 East Front Street
Traverse City, MI 49684
Total head count enrollment-Credit: 6,547 Non-Credit: 5,817
Campuses/sites: 5; f ull-time faculty: 101

COMPUTER INFORMATION SYSTEMS

Students learn the latest technology, while professionals in the field receive cutting-edge retraining

A Computer Information Systems (CIS) degree program may be centered at the Orchard Ridge Campus of Oakland Community College, but most of the curriculum is available at the other three college campuses as well. This program is unique because of the planning system involved, the quality and currency of the courses and its impact on students. The plan was put together very systematically by the dean with the faculty from all four campuses. By doing this, the impact on students of the major change in the curriculum was quite minimal in the transition.

Three years were spent on the planning and implementation process for the development of the present program. The challenge was to take a program that was meeting some of the needs of the business community and develop it to meet the rapidly developing high technology in the field.

The Strategic Plan began with an IBM Application Transfer Study in 1987 which involved all levels of staff throughout the college. In 1988-89 a Needs Assessment was done deeply involving the business community. In spring 1990 the faculty completed the Curriculum Plan, and the CIS Hardware Plan was finished in September 1990. The Board of Trustees endorsed the plan, and approved the first wave of equipment for $227,000 for winter 1991, together with a commitment of $225,000 for a second wave of equipment in fall l991, and a Third Wave of $225,000 in fall 1992. OCC implemented the plan by providing students state-of-the-art work stations, which are usually only found in engineering or high technology programs. The college has been teaching advanced technology for the last three years. Incoming, students are served because they are learning the latest technology, while professionals in the field are coming for re-training because of the higher technology and more thorough training available at the college.

The planned program led to the use of the new technology of UNIX stations and the Sun RISC processor technology. The three-year plan enabled OCC to standardize computer hardware and software across our multi-campus college. Students can take a course on one campus and transfer to another without a change in the learning process. This smooth transition is important to our community where a large number of students elect to move from campus to campus. Students also know that they can easily go to the advanced courses realizing that they all have received the same background when they enroll in the advanced courses at Orchard Ridge.

The other side of the CIS curriculum is the microcomputer area which has continued to grow. Using a Local Area Network (LAN) system we are providing instruction utilizing Windows technology, and productivity tools such as word processing, spread sheets, database and communications.

Thorough planning made the impact on the students of the major curriculum change minimal. Students report great satisfaction with the program; it is growing dramatically and has been well received by the business community. Enrollment and comments from both beginning students and professionals in the field are extraordinarily positive.

Contact:
Bruce Martin
(313) 471-7223

Oakland Community College – Orchard Ridge Campus
27055 Orchard Lake Road
Farmington Hills, MI 48334-4579
Total head count enrollment-Credit: 44,036; Non-Credit: 8,369
Campuses/sites: 9;Full-time faculty: 292

OAKLAND COMMUNITY COLLEGE

MENTAL HEALTH / SOCIAL WORK ASSOCIATE DEGREE

The curriculum facilitates college transfers, as well as provides training for associate level careers

The Mental Health/Social Work Associate Degree Program regularly produces more Oakland Community College graduates than most any other career program, giving the community much-needed practitioners. Centered at the Auburn Hills Campus, for about 20 years it has reached out to the students and community of Oakland County and the greater Detroit and Pontiac metropolitan area. The program places 135 students per year in more than 70 different internship sites. It has consistently had full enrollments. Graduates work in psychiatric hospitals, crisis centers, social service agencies, schools, courts, substance abuses centers, geriatric facilities, developmental centers and other human services agencies. Seventy percent of the graduates also transfer to bachelor degree programs through 2+2 arrangements in the fields of social work, special education, etc. More than half of the students are of "nontraditional" age and backgrounds, many are in transition from the household or from other careers. Twenty percent are already employed in the field and enroll in the program to upgrade their skills or increase their employability.

There are several unique features of the program. Characteristics address many of the recommendations put forth in Building Communities, the report of the AACJC Commission on the Future of Community Colleges. These unique characteristics include:

1) The curriculum is designed to facilitate college transfer as well as provide training for associate level careers. We combine the "liberal" and "useful" arts. Because of skill classes and 460 hours of field training, our students automatically qualify for Social Work Technician certification from the state, and yet because of the large number of liberal arts and social science components, more than eight different universities accept the program

in 2+2 arrangements.

2) The coordinators of the program have made an effort to use as many field placements as possible to acquaint potential employers with the program and the students. The strategy has worked, because many have hired program graduates. In addition, several employers have contracted with us to educate or update their current staffs. As an example, the entire program was taught on site at a local psychiatric hospital to upgrade skills and credential 18 employees. These liaisons have created an external recognition for us. Agencies call us to ask for interns, or for potential job applicants.

3) We have also received external recognition because of our efforts to reach out to the community through our "Community Awareness Institute." Low-cost workshops and non-credit courses that draw on the resources of our program are offered to professionals and general citizenry. Nationally known authorities are brought in annually to speak on topics of mental health and social concern. This branch of our program is a resource and a service to our general community.

Contact:
Melvin B. Chudnof
(313) 340-6579

Oakland Community College – Orchard Ridge Campus
27055 Orchard Lake Road
Farmington Hills, MI 48334-4579
Total head count enrollment-Credit: 44,036; Non-Credit: 8,369
Campuses/sites: 9;Full-time faculty: 292

SCHOOLCRAFT COLLEGE

HUMAN RESOURCE DEVELOPMENT

The initiative includes a faculty database with such information as education, professional organizations, licenses, publications and sabbaticals

A Human Resource Database puts everything from a Schoolcraft College faculty member's certifications to his publication at one's fingertips, and strict committee-developed guidelines keep faculty hirings in check. These and other initiatives resulted from the 1984 establishment of the Human Resource Development Committee. The committee, created by the Vice President of Instruction, was a response to the vision of a college-wide faculty development program. The committee's charge was to:

1) catalog the skills of the instructional staff;
2) develop a program for professional development of the teaching faculty;
3) develop a schedule for the replacement or non-replacement of faculty as they retire; and
4) recommend new staff where needed. The database was developed through the use of a questionnaire.

The college now can retrieve information about its faculty on educational background and training, certifications, licenses, external expertise, external work experiences, professional organizations, community service

work, presentations, publications, honors/awards, college committees, sabbatical leaves, retraining, release time, leaves of absence, grants and a miscellaneous category which allows the college to get information not gathered through any one of the previous areas identified.

The college has in place guidelines for professional development through two sources: State Fast Track, which is a 50 percent matching fund, and the Human Resource Development Committee. The funds are intended for:

1) unplanned professional growth activities targeted to provide direct change, revision, or expansion of the program curriculum;
2) the alteration and upgrading of knowledge of the faculty and skills directed toward discipline content;
3) the needs of the faculty members in an extemporaneous fashion to assimilate information related to cognitive methods, systems, and devices and processes; and
4) attendance at national/state general or professional

Continues on Page 352

conferences/conventions.

The committee has also developed a paradigm for hiring or not hiring new faculty. This instrument requires the use of supplemental data which consists of:

1) a list of new and projected programs;
2) enrollment trends and projections for all departments in the college;
3) program evaluations as prepared by the Office of Instructional Research as well as summaries of the respective departments' Five-Year Plans;
4) written recommendations from assistant deans pertaining to which departments in their estimation are in need of new faculty;
5) a list of faculty being retrained;
6) a list of retirements and other imminent vacancies; and
7) a list of all departments with their respective ratios of credit hours taught by full-time faculty compared to total credit hours generated.

Because the instrument has weighted factors attached to it, the final recommendation to hire or not to hire is well-substantiated.

The committee also has meaningful input in sabbatical leave requests, retraining proposals, release time and grant requests that have come from the faculty.

The final training project that the committee has been a part of is the Michigan Colleges' Consortium for Faculty Development. The Faculty Development series, a collection of videotapes on important education topics, can provide quality training for beginning instructors. The consortium also finds it works as review material for more experienced teachers. The modules provide an easy method for on-site faculty development.

The topics covered include: course goals and objectives, the first day, planning the lesson, planning instruction for higher levels of thought, cultural communications, test design and grading, assessment as a process, and teaching and learning styles.

The goals are being made possible by State Matching Funds, by the financial partnership of the Michigan Colleges' Consortium for Faculty Development and by the college's financial commitment to the Human Resource Development Committee.

Contact:
Louis A. Reibling, Dean of Instruction
(313) 462-4451

Schoolcraft College
18600 Haggerty Road
Livonia, MI 48152
Total head count enrollment-Credit: 14,097; Non-Credit: 13,551
Campuses/sites: 5;Full-time faculty: 133

SOUTHWESTERN MICHIGAN COLLEGE

RESULTS-VERIFIED TRAINING

Employers are recognizing that the most important competitive advantage their firms possess is skilled and experienced employees

Manufacturers, literacy councils and a school district are among those cooperating in region-wide work force training led by Southwestern Michigan College. More than 20 manufacturers/processors, a Private Industry Council, a vocation/technical center, literacy councils, adult education centers, an intermediate school district, local governmental agencies, and economic development groups are cooperating in this project will prepare area workers for changing responsibilities and technologies.

Assisting employers in the process of changing culture is the major thrust of the jointed developed training packages facilitated by Southwestern Michigan College. Moving from perceptions of manufactured components as being the end product, to acceptance of both internal and external customer satisfaction as an end product, is the foundation of the changes taking place.

Having strong, competitive businesses in our area is the impetus for training. Southwestern Michigan College joined with area manufactures and processors in planning for the needed change. Transferring some problem-solving from managers to plant floor personnel, developing

communication and analysis skills necessary to accomplish that end, and improving the product quality and a faster delivery of goods to the customer, are dictating more involvement of first-line employees.

The growing global orientation of business has produced a fundamental change in attitude toward training. Capital, raw material and equipment are all easily duplicated by competitors. Employers are beginning to recognize that the most important competitive advantage their firm possesses is their skilled and experienced employees. Through the ingenuity and resourcefulness of employees, firms attempt to set apart their products and services from those of their competition. To tap these potentials, a human resource strategy must be developed to help people adapt to changing market expectations. Business is now committing to this concept of continual improvement in employee skills, as well as customer service.

Wesley Muth, SMC Corporate Services Dean, relates that the college uses the same team approach in designing training with industry representatives that is stressed in the training content presented. The industrial leader and his or her staff share a vision that must be addressed by training content. After determining which issues create training needs, employee skill assessments pinpoint appropriate levels of training content. Then an industry steering committee works with the college in formulating objectives and expected outcomes of the training. Just as the organization is asked to concentrate on meeting or exceeding their customer expectations, Southwestern Michigan College follows suit by targeting the customer goals that must be attained for successful training outcomes.

Most training programs conclude where the SMC training packages begin. It is the practical application and follow-up of the training content that enables Southwestern to guarantee the promised benefits of training. In the model espousing the conceptual circle of "Plan, Do, Analyze, Act," much training involves only the first two elements of planning and implementing, without regard to the other two key components. After preparing objectives and desired outcomes with industrial clients, applications of training concepts and behavioral change is specified for client validation. The emphasis then shifts from the testing of knowledge gained in training to monitoring the use of this knowledge in improving productivity, quality and safety in the workplace. Application of concepts to improve processes is the critical factor in making the training relevant and beneficial.

Working in partnership with community-based constituencies, Southwestern Michigan College garnered the $500,000 state grant which supports a million-dollar training project. The participating corporate needs served as a basis for preparation of the grant request. This funding provides match incentive awards for the 20 firms engaged in training over a 12-month period that began in January 1993.

Contact:
Wesley Muth
(616) 782-5113

Southwestern Michigan College
58900 Cherry Grove Road
Dowagiac, MI 49047
Total head count enrollment-Credit/Non-Credit: 5,491
Campuses/sites: 7;Full-time faculty: 46

ST. CLAIR COUNTY COMMUNITY COLLEGE

PLASTICS INDUSTRY INSTITUTE

The college leases lab space for research and development to a company,
which in turn provides specialized training to the college

With the proximity of the automotive industry and access to international markets, plastics has become a major industry and employer in the Blue Water area of Michigan. But until recently the college's Plastics Technology program did not meet all the needs of the fast-growing industry. Meetings between three major plastics firms' CEOs and college personnel forged a closer relationship between industry and education that led to the creation of the Plastics Industry Institute.

The CEOs, along with college President R. Ernest Dear, chartered the Institute in the spring of 1991 with the primary goal being "to provide joint technical, problem solving, team building, supervisory, and basic academic skill training for an existing and expanding work force."

A director and an operations group were appointed to determine areas of training that would be pursued. A survey of 15 area plants determined that supervisory training was needed. The team came up with a list of 26 training areas in which supervisors wanted training. These ranged from communications skills to problem-solving techniques to motivation and team-building. Eighteen instruction modules were developed and 19 supervisors began training spring of 1992. Certificates were awarded for the completion of each training cluster with the Certified Supervisor Diploma issued at the end of the 100-hour program.

Tentatively planned is training as a Certified Operator, and in Technical Processing and Material Handling, along with seminars on materials. In the fall of 1993, training was opened up to some 35 other plastics and plastics-related companies in the Blue Water area.

Two spin-offs of the Plastics Institute have been the development of a Plastics Processing Technician Program, the only one of its kind in the U.S., and leasing of college laboratory space for research and development by one of the companies. That company is also providing training on a new 200-ton machine located at the college .

A key factor in the success of the Institute has been the cooperation among area companies involved.

Contact:
John P. Borris, Director
(313) 984-3881

St. Clair County Community College
323 Erie Street, PO Box 5015
Port Huron, MI 48061-5015
Total head count enrollment-Credit: 4,634; Non-Credit: 2,217
Campuses/sites: 6;Full-time faculty: 95

TWINNING RELATIONSHIP

The arrangement benefits both Canadian and American college students

Two colleges serving diverse populations have bridged international waters to provide higher education to a much larger area than originally possible, all at a fraction of the cost. Lambton College of Applied Arts and Technology, located in Sarnia, Ontario, Canada, and St. Clair County Community College, Port Huron, Michigan, established a cooperative twinning relationship in 1988.

Lambton serves residents of the Province of Ontario, while St. Clair serves its county. The two colleges each offer various programs not offered by the other. For many years residents from each college's district have demonstrated interest in the educational offerings available at the other college.

With the thought in mind of meeting the needs of as many students from the area as possible, the two colleges reached an agreement encompassing the following points:

1) Each college will admit as students, into as wide a range of programs as possible, residents from the other college's district, on payment of the same tuition fees as would apply to local residents, ensuring that the numbers so admitted will be approximately equal.
2) The two colleges will assist each other in marketing their unique programs in the others district.
3) Transfer arrangements between appropriate programs will be established.
4) The colleges will share information and work together in any areas which may be beneficial to their respective student bodies and employees, including such matters as curriculum development, placements, community programming, and program rationalization.
5) Whenever possible, in-service and professional development opportunities on campus will be opened to faculty and staff of each college.
6) From time to time, the two colleges will implement faculty and staff exchanges.
7) The two colleges will cooperate in ancillary enterprises such as international education projects.

The Twinning Relationship has lead to some 75 students a year participating in the agreement.

Contact:
Judy Morris, Dean of Student Services
(313) 989-5560

St. Clair County Community College
323 Erie Street, PO Box 5015
Port Huron, MI 48061-5015
Total head count enrollment-Credit: 4,634; Non-Credit: 2,217
Campuses/sites: 6;Full-time faculty: 95

ETHICAL DECISION-MAKING (EDM)

This one-credit course has been required of all freshmen since 1986

In 1985, aware of the growing national concern regarding moral education, Suomi College began exploring alternative models for teaching applied ethics. As a result, a required one-credit ethical decision-making course for freshmen was instituted in 1986. The course has been taught since then by a group of approximately 14 faculty from across departments.

Rooted in the work of Lawrence Kohlberg, EDM engages students in structured discussions of moral dilemmas. Other aspects of the course have included journal writing, class projects and group building activities. The goal of EDM has been to increase student awareness of ethical dimensions of life, enhancing their ability to reflect on and discuss ethical issues.

Faculty teaching the course have regularly evaluated its content and revised the course in response to their experiences in teaching and their reading in the field. This regular evaluative process has facilitated inter-disciplinary conversation about teaching in general and ethics in particular.

The course has also spawned experiments in residential hiring. It is hoped that the course will eventually lead to a broad integration of ethical discussion into the entire life of the campus.

Contact:
Kurt Keljo, Dean of the College and Faculty
(906) 487-7232

Suomi College
601 Quincy Street
Hancock, MI 49930
Total head count enrollment-Credit: 535; Non-Credit: 5
Campuses/sites: 2;Full-time faculty: 23

FINNISH STUDIES

*▨ Suomi, the only college in the country founded by Finns, ▨
has extensive research facilities available for Finnish study*

As the only college in the United States founded by Finns, Suomi College maintains a commitment to Finnish Studies. The program is designed to give students a competency in the Finnish language and an understanding of both Finnish and Finnish-American cultures. Students planning to transfer to a baccalaureate program will have a solid general education, along with expertise in Finnish language and culture. The program is also suited to persons who wish to develop the skills to read, write and speak Finnish at the level required for use and enjoyment of Finnish periodicals and conversation.

Along with its rich Finnish history, Suomi has extensive research facilities available for Finnish study. Located on the campus is the Finnish-American Historical Archives. The Archives collection includes hundreds of oral histories, manuscripts, books, newspapers, photographs and artifacts containing valuable historical information. Students are able to utilize the archives, developing a thorough knowledge of the Finnish-American culture, as well as archival research skills.

Another feature that is unique to the program is that students at Suomi can study Finnish-American culture as well as Finnish culture in an area of intense Finnish settlement. The Finnish immigrants who came to the U.S. in the late 1800's and early 1900's, and their 650,000 descendants have developed a distinct culture. The local area was historically one of the centers for Finnish immigration and today retains its Finnish flavor and its Finnish-American heritage.

Suomi is one of only a few institutions of higher learning in America where one can study the Finnish language and culture. The college's rich history and largely Finnish community setting are the perfect context for the Finnish Studies Program.

Students are given the opportunity to begin their studies in the Finnish language and culture. The Finnish American Heritage Center at Suomi provides a unique resource for students interested in this field of study.

Contact:
Daniel Maki, Social Science Instructor
(906) 487-7257

Suomi College
601 Quincy Street
Hancock, MI 49930
Total head count enrollment-Credit: 535; Non-Credit: 5
Campuses/sites: 2;Full-time faculty: 23

TECH PREP

*▨ All students at schools involved in the program create first-draft ▨
career plans while in the eighth grade*

Because of its rural setting in northern Michigan, West Shore Community College is one of the state's smallest community colleges. Yet its Technical Preparation Partnership with area schools has become a national model.

Due to the sparse population of this rural area, establishing a Technical Preparation Partnership made a lot of sense to area school superintendents and college officials. In fact, discussions on establishing a partnership began even before the term "Technical Preparation Partnership" meant anything.

Inspired by Dale Parnell's book *The Forgotten Half*, in the mid-1980's, West Shore Community College officials approached the Mason-Lake Intermediate School District, which was looking into ways to expand its vocational-technical offerings.

Since then virtually all the 1988 plans for the Technical Preparation Partnership have become realities:

1) The voters of the Mason-Lake Intermediate School District approved a 1 mill tax levy for perpetual support of vocational education and the Technical Preparation Partnership.

2) Five Tech Prep programs are offered at WSCC. They are Computer Aided Drafting, Electronics, Medical Skills, Restaurant/Food Service Management, and Welding. Other Tech Prep programs are available to students at high school sites in Auto Technology, Office Practices, Computer Accounting, Graphic Arts, Machine Trades, Marketing, Data Processing, and Building Trades.

3) All the high schools in WSCC's service area are involved with the Technical Preparation Partnership, including those in Manistee and Oceana counties.

Continues on Page 356

4) Students are better able to move from high school technical training to advanced occupational studies at WSCC. Some 55 of WSCC's current students came through the Tech Prep program.

5) Career planning has become a major thrust. All students at the schools involved in Tech Prep create first-draft career plans when they are in the eighth grade and write an educational development plan that will prepare them for their career field. They follow and update this plan through their high school years. All students, not just the college prep students, now have a plan for their future.

6) Funding for the expansion of WSCC's Technical Center, which will house many of the Tech Prep programs, was more easily acquired because of the attractiveness of the cooperative venture – creating a training facility to be utilized by high school students, college students, and adults.

Also, funding for vocational education equipment is coordinated between the area high schools and WSCC. For example, neither WSCC nor the area schools could have acquired equipment to teach Computer Aided Design, but together it was possible and now both the Technical Preparation Partnership and WSCC offer this specialty. WSCC and Mason-Lake ISD officials have been giving presentations on the development of the local Technical Preparation Partnership throughout Michigan as well as at conferences in San Diego, Dallas, Chicago and for the group of Indiana Vocational Technical Colleges.

"We have a strong partnership between the college, Mason-Lake and Manistee Intermediate School Districts, and area high schools; we've acquired equipment; and we've built a building; but the most important thing is that we have a brand new, innovative curriculum ready for our students," said Dr. Terry E. Luxford, WSCC Dean of Occupational Curricula.

"Our Technical Preparation Partnership benefits the students and also the taxpayers," said James L. Pinkerton, Mason-Lake ISD Administrative Assistant for Vocational Education. "Because we're pooling resources, together we have better equipment and facilities than if we were separate entities and the total cost is much lower. There are more programs available to the students of the area and we've been able to qualify for more grant funds to develop the programs and pay for equipment and facilities."

Pinkerton added that the level of cooperation between the schools, college, and ISD has been very high, which has led to a current enrollment of about 400 students in the Tech Prep programs. "Currently we're stressing the importance of early career counseling and educational preparation so that when our students are juniors and seniors they will have the background they need to make the most of their occupational studies."

The objectives of the Technical Preparation Program are to:

1) provide clear, concise information to students and parents on the preparation needed for high school graduates to enter the world of work or to continue their education;

2) ensure that every technical preparation student has an educational plan with career goals and the necessary preparation to reach those goals;

3) assure that every technical preparation student graduates from high school with a marketable skill;

4) increase the number of high school graduates who continue their education at the community college level;

5) increase the number of community college students who receive their associate degrees in career and technical programs and who may continue their education in four-year colleges; and

6) provide the labor market with highly skilled workers who possess advanced academic, technical, and critical thinking skills.

Contact:
Terry Luxford
(616) 845-6211

West Shore Community College
PO Box 277
Scottville, MI 49454-0277
Total head count enrollment-Credit: 1,400; Non-Credit: 600
Campuses/sites: 1; Full-time faculty: 26

GENERAL AQUACULTURE

▓ This growing aspect of fish husbandry is taught under working ▓
farm conditions in cooperation with private growers

Alexandria Technical College is meeting the need of the expanding fish farming industry by providing technicians trained in all aspects of fish husbandry. A quick review of indusry data demonstrates how timely is this program. Worldwide, fish farming produces about 110 species of fish, 13 species of shrimps, prawns and crayfish, and a wide variety of shellfish and marine plants. Of the approximately 215-billion pounds of fish consumed, fish farming accounted for about 25-billion pounds, or about 12 percent. Economists at the Food and Agriculture Organization (FAO) forecast a shortage of 20 percent of the fish and seafood needed to meet the worldwide demand by the year 2000.

Aquaculture has been the fastest-growing agricultural industry in the United States in the last 20 years, growing at the rate of 20 percent per year. This is in spite of the fact that Americans consume little fish and seafood compared to the rest of the world. However, changing consumer attitudes toward the health of various animal proteins have caused a shift in demand toward fish and seafood. Now, aquacrops are seen as an important part of diets designed to address two major dietary problems of Americans: high cholesterol levels and obesity.

Worldwide aquaculture provides only 18 percent of the total U.S. supply of fish and seafood. Specifically, U.S. aquaculture provides only 5 percent of our needs. Thus, the future for aquaculture is promising. As demand for fish continues to grow, and the oceans continue to be depleted of their reserves, more and more of our fish needs will need to be met by fish farming.

The demand for farmed fish will serve to stimulate rural economies by utilizing land which is marginal for tradi-

tional dry-land crop production, as well as create new jobs and an infrastructure of related skills and services.

All of the above will require technicians to take aquaculture into the 21st Century. Course materials provide for a wide range of hands-on training, including fish harvesting and hauling, egg-taking, egg incubation, larval feeding, pond seining, water chemistry monitoring, pond fertilization, plankton monitoring, facility disinfection, fish processing, hatchery design and maintenance, and fish health diagnosis and treatment. All aspects of training are performed under working farm conditions in cooperation with private growers as well as in facilities developed by the college. Students are shown "how" and "why" a task is to be performed, and must demonstrate competence in actually "performing" the specific task. In addition, all students must complete a 10-week internship at a fish production facility.

To keep pace with current technology, students spend considerable time working with commercial-size recirculating production systems for Tilapia and Walleye. Students help design and construct recirculating systems and maintain an active role in maintenance and modification based on fish response.

The first group of graduates were available to the work force in spring of 1992; 90 percent were placed in fish production facilities prior to graduation. Graduates leave the program knowing what is expected of them in the workplace, and they understand the importance of consistency and reliability when dealing with live organisms. They are taught to anticipate problems and understand the consequences of their actions.

Contact:
Larry Belusz, Instructor-in-Charge
(612) 762-0221

Alexandria Technical College
1601 Jefferson Street
Alexandria, MN 56308
Total head count enrollment-Credit: 2,450; Non-Credit: 23,000
Campuses/sites: 1;Full-time faculty: 102

ORAL HISTORY RESEARCH PROJECT

▓ Students wrote histories of the city's buildings, people, places and events ▓
as seen through the eyes and ears of those they interviewed

An Oral History Research Project at Anoka-Ramsey Community College helped students become interested in history while developing a rapport with a group of older community residents. This unique writing project consumed several freshman English composition classes

during the 1991-92 academic year at the college's Coon Rapids campus. Students interviewed senior citizens and others in the area about their recollections of early Coon Rapids. They then wrote their own histories of the city's

Continues on Page 358

buildings, people, places and events as seen through the eyes and ears of those they interviewed. The final result will be a published book of student writing.

The project is a collaborative effort, created out of a conversation over Little League games as a member of the Coon Rapids Historical Commission and a member of the college's English Department, Elizabeth Nist, cheered their children's teams. Nist believed the project would help students develop an interest in history and what it truly represents to younger people today, as well as giving them an audience and reason to write, edit and revise. The commission sees it as a way to document history of the city, which, at a population of more than 50,000, is one of the largest suburbs in the Minneapolis/St. Paul area, and to give an opportunity to audiotape people who have been part of that history for many years.

The Composition I students re-enrolled into Composition II to finish their projects. An advanced expository writing class the fall of 1992 had many of the same students completing the final book, planned for publication in late 1993. More than 200 students were involved in the project during the 1991-92 year, working in small groups which acted as their own editing boards. A newsletter for their peers is also published regularly to report the status of the project.

The project grew over the course of the year and drew the interest of the country's historical society and other nearby cities, as well as the state Minnesota Historical Society.

Nist's application of contemporary theories of teaching writing (developed through the National Writing Project and the Minnesota Writing Project) has led to other advantages in addition to improved student motivation to write and to learn. There is now a large group of older community residents who have a personal relationship and rapport with a large group of mostly younger college students – a community relations benefit no one could have planned!

Contact:
Elizabeth Nist, English Department
(612) 422-3308

Anoka-Ramsey Community College
11200 Mississippi Boulevard NW
Coon Rapids, MN 55433
Total head count enrollment-Credit: 11,200; Non-Credit: 4,800
Campuses/sites: 2; Full-time faculty: 104

MATH DEPARTMENT CALCULATOR PROJECT

One classroom has 45 calculators and a projector, which allows students and the instructor to simultaneously see keystrokes and results of calculations

The Mathematics Department at Anoka-Ramsey Community College introduced graphing calculators as an integral part of classroom learning and teaching during Fall Quarter 1992. Although calculators have been used for years, this project allows each student in the class to access the same graphing calculator, a Texas Instruments TI-81, as used by the instructor.

The instructor uses a projector which projects a full-screen image of the calculations and/or graphs resulting from the formulas presented. The students and the instructor can see, at the same time, with the same calculator keystrokes, the results of their calculations and revise their computations accordingly.

One classroom is equipped with 45 calculators and the projector.

Courses with heavy emphasis on formula graphing in math and science have first access. If the project proves successful, it is anticipated that instructors could adapt the process to other courses as well.

Contact:
Ron Davis, Dean of Academic Affairs
(612) 422-3330

Anoka-Ramsey Community College
11200 Mississippi Boulevard NW
Coon Rapids, MN 55433
Total head count enrollment-Credit: 11,200; Non-Credit: 4,800
Campuses/sites: 2; Full-time faculty: 104

SERVICES TO INDIAN PEOPLE PROGRAM (STIPP)

STIPP's professional American Indian staff provides a support network for Indian students at all seven campuses

An American Indian staff provides a complete support network for Indian students at each of the Arrowhead Community College's (ACC) campuses, which serve 55 percent of the state's American Indians attending Minnesota's community colleges. The Services to Indian People Program (STIPP) is the unique "parent" program for the Region's Indian education efforts and reflects ACC's commitment to the Indian community and students. It was instituted in ACC in 1982. ACC Indian enrollment in 1981 was 74; it grew to 130 in 1982. Fall quarter enrollments (1991) were 441, or 6 percent of the ACC student population. American Indians constitute 3 percent of the region's population, and are the only significant minority group in the ACC service area.

STIPP serves as a bridge between those at seven of Minnesota's 11 Indian Reservations and the achievement of their educational and career goals. The program provides essential support needed by Indian students to overcome major barriers to success in college (e.g., low income, cultural differences, lack of college preparation, personal/family problems).

STIPP's professional American Indian staff provides a complete support network for Indian students at each of ACC's seven campuses. Activities include: student recruitment at more than 150 area high schools; assistance in academic advising and registration; tutoring; support services, including follow-up and intense mentoring; Indian Student Associations; Indian cultural events, Indian Studies courses; and, if needed, referrals to developmental courses or to social service agencies.

Regular regional meetings bring together student support staff, including STIPP, enrollment management, counseling, and basic skills. STIPP's personal approach has served as the model for several subsequent student support programs. STIPP-sponsored activities such as holiday gatherings and pow wows welcome Indian students, families, and the larger Indian community to the campuses. Indian administrators and faculty serve as role models within the community, which encourages aspira-

tions for higher education. STIPP reflects ACC's commitment to supporting American Indian students as they "learn both roads" – respect for their traditional culture and language, coupled with the opportunities for the future which an education affords.

STIPP was created for American Indian students residing on and off the reservations in the large, mostly-rural ACC service area. The tribal group served is largely Ojibwe (Chippewa). Any American Indian person who self-identifies as being Indian is served by STIPP. Persons served range from those who have retained the Ojibwe language and culture, to many who have had little exposure to their heritage. Initially funded by a foundation grant, the program was incorporated into the annual college budget at the end of the grant period, in 1986-87. In 1983, there was a single Indian staff member in ACC. Now there are three Indian full-time administrators, five full-time minority faculty, 17 part-time faculty each quarter, and 19 staff members.

Professional development activities to credential Indian staff include special grants and sabbaticals, as well as workshops and Indian education conferences, and other assistance. ACC STIPP staff have regularly received honors from the Minnesota Indian Education Association. Several STIPP staff members have participated in a series of Ford Foundation Diversity Project seminars for ACC and Bemidji State University faculty on cultural diversity in the curriculum, and have subsequently received curriculum development grants for projects such as development of an oral Ojibwe language lab. In 1991, ACC's STIPP program was selected as one of six programs nationwide to receive a Minority Student Success Award from the AACC. Finally, in the long list of ACC Indian education efforts, one is unique in the U.S.: the unprecedented state-tribal relationship at ACC's Fond du Lac Community College. It is the only tribally controlled college in the U.S. that receives both federal and state funds; the other 23 tribal colleges are funded solely by the federal government.

Contact:
Anne M. Erickson, Public Information Director
(218) 327-4380

Arrowhead Community Colleges
1855 East Highway 169
Grand Rapids, MN 55744
Total headcount enrollment-Credit: 6,733
Campuses/sites: 7; Full-time faculty: 163

ARTIST-IN-RESIDENCE

The program helps to raise the level of artistic awareness of residents in this largely-rural region

Arrowhead Community Colleges reach out to the community through an Artist-in-Residence program that creates a chance for residents to experience original works of creative artists. The program "exemplifies the kind of programming our performing Arts Touring Program was created to support," according to Arts Midwest Senior Program Director Susan Chandler.

The extended three- to four-week Residency Program occurs in the seven ACC campus communities, located in Northeastern Minnesota. The campuses are Hibbing, Itasca, Mesabi, Rainy River and Vermilion Community Colleges and the Duluth and Fond du Lac Community College Centers. The artists are selected for their excellence, and for their experience in presenting formal and informal performances, master classes and workshops. Accessible, high-caliber performing arts events are offered to community groups free-of-charge (there is a minimal fee for formal performances). The artist spends an average of two to three days in each community, offering informal presentations which are conducive to dialogue with the audiences. This aids in bridging the gap between artist and audience.

Groups served include community/civic groups, professional organizations, churches, senior citizens, public and tribal schools, disabled persons, college students at ACC campuses, and local artists/arts groups. Presentations are adjusted to all age groups; community groups select a program tailored to audience interests/needs. Collaborations often occur during the residency. Recently, specific portions of the residency were co-sponsored by a county Historical Society and by a community-based FM radio station.

The Residency Program helps to raise the level of artistic awareness in this largely-rural region. Artistically adventurous performers from the Midwest are often selected. The colleges are seen as cultural focal-points in their communities; for this reason, providing access to cultural enrichment and diversity is identified as a major Residency Program goal. The 1992 residency featured jazz musician Richard Davis, creating an opportunity to honor the enormous contributions African Americans have made to American music. Past residency artists include a marimbist, guitarist, actor, performance artist/mime and two dance companies.

A Residency Program director coordinates and oversees the entire project, including negations with the artist; writing grant proposals; setting up the general schedule; preparing news releases and other publicity materials; and developing an evaluation process for the entire project (including host group, artist, and campus coordinator evaluation forms). Campus coordinators are responsible for scheduling residency activities in their respective communities and for handling publicity at the local level. Campus coordinators are generally the college's Continuing Education directors or other individuals who have developed good contacts within many and diverse community groups, and are therefore able to identify and work well with host organizations.

Funding for the Residency Program has been provided each year by the USX Foundation, ACC and its campuses. Additional support for the 1992 project has been obtained from the Arrowhead Regional Arts Council, Arts Midwest, Meet the Composer-Midwest, and the U.S. West Foundation.

Contact:
Anne M. Erickson, Residency Program Director
(218) 327-4380

Arrowhead Community Colleges
1855 East Highway 169
Grand Rapids, MN 55744
Total headcount enrollment-Credit: 6,733
Campuses/sites: 7; Full-time faculty: 163

GERITOL FROLICS

This show has had such an impact on the lives of the people involved that it was funded by the Sears Roebuck Foundation for replication

The Geritol Frolics is a fast-paced, Las Vegas-style musical, dance and comedy review put on each year by approximately 100 adults 55 years and older. The Frolics has performed for the National Conference on Aging and has been featured on ABC Television

The first Geritol Frolics started at BCC in 1987. It is based on a belief that senior citizens need creative outlets for their mental and physical health. The Geritol Frolics involve approximately 100 senior citizens each year from the service area of the college as creators, writers and performers (singers, dancers and actors) in a professional quality variety show. The quality is vital as it gives validity and encourages the self-respect of the performer. The same or superior production values are given to this show involving the older adult as is given to any of the shows in the college theatre season.

This show has had such an impact on the lives of the people involved, that it was funded by the Sears Roebuck Foundation for replication in three pilot sites to show that it can work in diverse areas of the United States. The pilot sites were in Fresno, California; Dallas, Texas; and Baltimore, Maryland. In addition to the 24 performances staged annually in Brainerd, the group has added performances at the Orpheum Theatre in Minneapolis, the St. Paul Civic Auditorium, and the Duluth Convention and Entertainment Center. Each year the Geritol Frolics staff writes a new script and performs a new show. The main run of the show is 16 performances in the spring, with a rerun of the same show for another 16 performances in the fall. Then a new show is written, set, staged and performed again for the next spring. The 32-plus performances given annually in Brainerd are normally sold out the first day tickets are on sale.

In January 1993, the entire Geritol Frolics cast and crew went to Las Vegas and the first National Senior Theatre Festival at the University of Nevada at Las Vegas.

Associated costs are estimated at $20,000 with an income from the show at $47,000. There is a $25,000 net profit built into the show. Personnel requirements include a producer/director, technical director, designer and a choreographer. The remaining personnel are Geritol Frolics volunteers.

The Frolics succeed because Brainerd Community College treats the senior citizen as a first-class citizen. The college does not skimp on those technical things which make a show look professional! The show has professional-quality leadership in dance, music, acting and in all phases of the production.

Contact:
Bob Dryden or Dennis Lamberson
(218) 828-2525

Brainerd Community College
501 West College Drive,
Brainerd, MN 56401
Total head count enrollment-Credit: 1,823
Campuses/sites: 1; Full-time faculty: 45

EURO-CAMPUS

Participants are kept off the typical tourist motor coaches and instead use trains and subways, as ordinary natives would

When Brainerd Community College began its study-travel program in 1986, foreign travel was a relatively rare activity for its students, area residents and even faculty. Since then, the college's study-travel program has raised the international consciousness of this land-locked part of North America. The college has guided more than 300 students, community participants and faculty through an intense, highly individualized travel experience in the United Kingdom. Participants have ranged in age from 18 to 86, and former Minnesota Governor C. Elmer Anderson, traveling as a community participant, celebrated his 80th birthday by attending a session of Parliament.

While there is nothing particularly new about a college-sponsored trip with an academic focus, this trip from the outset was promoted as special in the sense that participants themselves would be directly involved in planning their own itineraries built around personal interests and selections from a rich menu of academic course offerings.

The trip itself is scheduled for 12 days during the college's spring quarter break and is carefully integrated with a winter quarter course of each participant's choosing. Approximately 100 recent participants, for example, were able to develop personal itineraries built around any one of five or six courses, including Culture of Great Britain, Women's Issues (focused on female writers and gender issues in the United Kingdom), London theater, art history, and an innovative British geology course whose laboratory content was partially derived from an investigation of London building stones. In all these courses, students and community participants met together beforehand and traveled together, and instructors report many cases in which community members, having simply signed up for the program as a tour, became enthusiastically engaged in its course content.

Participants are kept off the typical tourist motor coaches that are so much a part of the European travel scene. Instead, with the guidance of program staff, they use the British trains and subways and are involved as much as possible in traveling as ordinary British folk would.

A project goal is that all participants learn enough about the country to be able to travel completely on their own should they ever return. Many have returned – on their own or with a subsequent college travel group. Oddly, for many Brainerd-area people, London is now a more familiar city than Minneapolis-St. Paul, the nearest metropolitan area, approximately 100 miles away.

Continues on Page 362

Meanwhile, Brainerd merchants report significantly increased interest in British and European merchandise among local shoppers.

Word of the success of this program has spread to faculty on other campuses in the Minnesota Community College System. Brainerd's staff has provided opportunities for interested faculty from other community colleges to travel with its groups and experience the program first-hand. Such efforts in part have been funded by Bush Staff Development grants from the MCCS. So far similar programs have thus been successfully launched at both Austin and Itaska Community colleges.

The next program, while still based in England, for the first time offered three-night side trips to either Dublin or Paris.

Contact:
James T. Casper, Dean of Instruction
(218) 828-2525

Brainerd Community College
501 West College Drive,
Brainerd, MN 56401
Total head count enrollment-Credit: 1,823
Campuses/sites: 1; Full-time faculty: 45

FERGUS FALLS COMMUNITY COLLEGE

SPARTAN BASKETBALL BUDDIES

The program introduces and develops basketball skills while promoting a positive attitude toward the game and the college

The Spartan Basketball Buddies program provides greater visibility for Fergus Falls Community College and introduces many to the campus and its varsity basketball program. Introduced in the fall of 1988, the program's goal is to introduce and develop basketball skills and promote fun, positive attitudes toward the game in the young people of Fergus Falls and surrounding communities.

The Basketball Buddy Program features the Spartan men's basketball team, in uniform or warm-ups, demonstrating and teaching basketball fundamentals. No competitive games of any type are played. The clinic is held on four Saturday mornings in November and December. Girls and boys, grades 1-6, may sign up for any of three 45-minute sessions, starting at 9:15 a.m. on each Saturday. The Spartan men's basketball team, under Coach Dave Retzlaff, directs youngsters in fundamental areas including shooting, passing, ball handling, dribbling, defense and lay-ups. Squad members are assigned two to a station and have five minutes with each of the five groups of young people to demonstrate and teach their assigned skills. After five minutes, a whistle sounds and the players move to the next group.

A typical session would include:
9:15 - on-the-floor shooting with music with varsity players;
9:25 - Coach Retzlaff greets, gives brief message for the day;
9:30 - quickly split youngsters into five arbitrary groups (height works quickest) and commence with the five, five-minute teaching stations;
9:55 - drawing for girl and boy "Game Buddy;" and
10:00 - second session promptly enters and begins.
The first two Saturdays follow the above schedule. The third Saturday is devoted to practicing for two half-time performances during a regular-season Spartan basketball

game. The children are assigned to one of two games where they demonstrate learned ball handling skills (approximately 16 to 18 skills, 30 seconds each) with the help of upbeat music and a student manager leader. The fourth and final Saturday features Tanya Crevier, "World's Finest Female Basketball Handler," who entertains and directs all clinic sessions that morning. Later that same afternoon or evening, she performs at half-time of one of our regular season games.

Each participant is charged a $10 fee, with our local Coca-Cola Company helping to cover the remaining cost, usually in the form of providing t-shirts.
Participants enjoy:
•receiving a buddy t-shirt with printing on the front and back which they must wear to each session;
•receiving a colorful size five Buddy basketball, printing on three panels, which they are asked to bring to each session;
•learning basketball fundamentals;
•associating with Spartan men's basketball team;
•receiving an 8x10 poster (third Saturday) with schedule and varsity players' pictures (an autograph time at the end of this session is a highlight for youngsters and Spartan players);
•a candy treat on the second Saturday and Coca-Cola for each participant on the fourth Saturday;
•free admission to all Spartan basketball games by wearing their buddy shirts to the game;
•a "Game Buddy" drawing for each session, one girl and one boy, to match the total number of Spartan women's and men's home games (winner drawn will be in the locker room for pre-game talks, run onto the floor with the team, be introduced with the team during spotlight introductions, and "high five" his/her favorite Spartan player mid-court);

- seeing and visiting Tanya Crevier; and
- a fun, positive experience and relationship with the game of basketball, Spartan players, and Fergus Falls Community College.

Parents enjoy:
- watching their children from bleacher sections, often visiting or video taping their youngsters; and
- free coffee, cookies, rolls and newspapers provided by the Buddy Basketball Program.

The "Spartan Basketball Buddy Program" idea originated with former North Dakota State University head basketball Coach Erv Inniger. Our first attempt with this program was in 1988, when we made 180 spots available. These were filled within three days! With our limited space for participants and spectators, we are now at our maximum of 100 children per session, which means we involve 280 to 300 young people from Fergus Falls (popu-

lation 12,500) and five neighboring communities.

The Basketball Buddy Program has been a tremendous success – to the point where 15 to 20 parents will hand-deliver registration slips to us the day their children bring them home from school to assure the session they want. The young people love it because they get a shirt, ball, treats, time with our players and they have fun with no winners or losers. Parents rave about the Buddies because it is a positive, non-threatening situation for their children to learn and get excited about the game. No competition between participants! Fergus Falls Community College receives tremendous exposure with the community service area, attracting many people who have never been on our campus. The Spartan men's basketball team promotes their program and provides a fun, relaxed environment to relate to and work with area young people as role models.

Contact:
Dave Retzlaff
(218) 739-7538

Fergus Falls Community College
1414 College Way, Fergus Falls,
MN 56537
Total headcount enrollment-Credit: 1,300 Non-Credit: 950
Campuses/sites: 1; Full-time faculty: 33

SIFE (STUDENTS IN FREE ENTERPRISE)

This business organization for students gives a role in teaching others about a market economy

A Fergus Falls Community College student business organization – the only such group at any of Minnesota's community colleges – gives members a better understanding of the free enterprise system and a role in teaching others about a market economy. SIFE (Students in Free Enterprise) was conceived by a Texas businessman in the mid-1970's to combat the negative attitudes exhibited toward business entrepreneurs and the free enterprise system. Knowing that those negative attitudes can be the result of lack of understanding and education, SIFE was established as a student organization at the college level. Established in 1989, FFCC's SIFE team develops year-long educational projects. One year's projects carried them from garbage to government. Following represents some of their efforts:
- sponsored its second annual science and invention fair to increase young students' interest in those careers (the number of participants increased by 64 percent, from 35 students in 1991 to 55 in 1992);
- created a business mentor program in which FFCC students received hands-on experience at an area business of their choice;
- presented a character education lesson, "Are you brave enough to be a chicken?" to a local 4-H club and trained FLA members at the high school to teach the lesson to three elementary classes;

- printed 1,000 litter bags advertising free enterprise with the cooperation of Pat's and Doug's Amoco stations in Alexandria and Fergus Falls;
- erected six billboards in three major communities within a lOO-mile radius to promote education and free enterprise;
- wrote news releases to area newspapers regarding the national deficit and spending; and
- appeared on local radio and TV shows to create community awareness of SIFE and its projects and to promote free enterprise.

The SIFE team is advised by two FFCC business faculty members. The organization meets weekly. The limited resources needed to support trips by the team to regional and national competitions have been supported by the Fergus Area College Foundation and local business mentors.

The FFCC SIFE teams have distinguished themselves since their inception. Each year they have traveled to the regional competition in Chicago where they have competed mostly against four-year institutions. The team organizes a presentation summarizing the year's projects and efforts. Their presentations are made to a panel of business executives and entrepreneurs. (This competition was created in 1984 by Wal-Mart's Sam Walton.) Since

Continues on Page 364

there are well over 2,500 SIFE teams across the country, the FFCC SIFE teams have gained a strong reputation with the following honors: in 1989 the SIFE team won the "Rookie Team of the Year" trophy in Chicago at regional competition; in 1990 the SIFE team not only won at regional competition in Chicago but also advanced to

international competition in Kansas City where they met international business experts H. Ross Perot and Sam Walton; in 1991 the SIFE team received a $500 award at the Chicago competition; and in 1992 the SIFE team won at regionals and advanced to compete at the international competition.

Contact:
Kristi Lausch
(218) 739-7535

Fergus Falls Community College
1414 College Way
Fergus Falls, MN 56537
Total headcount enrollment-Credit: 1,300Non-Credit: 950
Campuses/sites: 1;Full-time faculty: 33

COMPUTER-AIDED DRAFTING AND DESIGN

By installing computers in the drafting program, Hibbing was among the first to bring computers into the community college

Hibbing Community College, a pioneer in computers in the classroom, prepares students for virtually any drafting field through its Computer-Aided Drafting and Design (CAD) program. This highly successful program has, in recent years, developed into one of the finest pre-engineering departments in the Midwest.

By installing computers in the drafting program in March 1984, HCC was among the first to bring computers into the community college. Since that time the program has been updated annually, so that students are now studying on micro-computers and the large Hewelett-Packard Apollo stations, along with a variety of the latest in drafting software, including AutoCAD, VersaCAD/VANCE and UltiMap.

Advances in the department were first made possible by a federal Title III grant, allowing the installation of state-of-the-art computer drafting systems with updated software. All the IBM compatible systems have been replaced with new 486 systems.

Using the CAD workstations and software, student drafters can "draw" and modify shapes instantly on their screens. For example, students supply the computer with a center point, and a radius and a circle appears. A student who once took a week to complete three drawings can typically produce nine to 15 during the same amount of time using a CAD system.

Such attractive productivity gains caused the number of

CAD terminals in operation to increase from 246,100 in 1986, to 980,400 in 1990.

The enrollment limit at Hibbing is 28 students per year, with night classes arranged according to interest and demand. A typical class includes both men and women, ranging from age 19 to age 52, as well as professionals and employees who work in CAD. A complete two-year sequence of pre-engineering courses is also available for pre-engineering students who transfer on to a four-year college.

"A student has to be willing to devote a lot of time to the program," said Instructor Earl Willmarth. "But the outcome is rewarding."

Students who complete the program can work in almost any drafting field; architecture, electrical, mechanical and structural engineering, and, most likely, will be doing a predominance of their work on computers. Few graduates are "board operators" any longer..

After completing an Associate Degree in CAD at Hibbing, two-year students have found that placement is excellent, especially if the graduates are willing to relocate (e.g. Minneapolis area), Willmarth said.

The Hibbing CAD program has been modernized by Willmarth and consists of one other full-time instructor and one lab technician. They produce a business-like environment, and assignments for students that are realistic and workable.

Contact:
Earl Willmarth, Instructor-in-Charge
(218) 262-6700

Hibbing Community College
1515 East 25th Street
Hibbing, MN 55746
Total head count enrollment-Credit: 1,175; Non-Credit: 1,119
Campuses/sites: 1; Full-time faculty: 65

NURSING

*⊠ Alternative teaching methods incorporating writing ⊠
have made nursing process theory less of a drudgery*

Inver Hills/Lakewood Community College nursing faculty have alternative methods of teaching nursing process theory through writing assignments that are unique, comprehensible and enjoyable. This is a striking difference from the traditional methods of teaching nursing process theory (i.e. column format and steps of nursing process), many faculty and most students perceived teaching or learning of nursing process content to be a real drudgery. Nursing process theory is an analytical problem-solving process that teaches critical thinking skills. Successful applications of this theory in written nursing process assignments generally correlates with clinical competence in caring for patients. During the period from 1990-1992, the nursing faculty evaluated the nursing curriculum and associated nursing process theory assignment and to design new writing assignments. The following outcomes were achieved over this two year period:

1) written assignments related to nursing process theory were leveled and sequenced over the duration of the two year nursing degree program
2) Bloom's (Taxonomy of Educational Objectives) and Perry's (Intellectual Development) theories were integrated into nursing process theory writing assignments; and
3) new methods and tools were developed to teach the written nursing process theory.

The process that was used to evaluate the nursing curriculum and the actual writing assignments which were developed were presented at the International Conference on Teaching Excellence, May 24, 1992, in Austin, Texas. This project was supported by the Minnesota Community College System Writing Across the Curriculum Bush Grant Workshops. All nursing faculty participate in the integration of this content across the nursing curriculum.

Contact:
Lee Ann Joy, Director
(612) 450-8598

Inver Hills Community College
8445 College Trail,
Inver Grove Heights, MN 55076
Total head count enrollment-Credit: 5,500; Non-Credit: 2,100
Campuses/sites: 1;Full-time faculty: 90

LITERACY IN BASIC BIOLOGY THROUGH MULTI-MEDIA

*⊠ Students may view the course on videos at their own pace, ⊠
which helps improve the attrition rate*

With an unacceptably high attrition rate in Inver Hills Community College introductory biology courses and the realization that many students were arriving very unprepared, the college developed a multi-media teaching approach to try to turn the tide.

Empowered with grants, plans were developed for a new course intended for under-prepared students. Biology 96, Basic Concepts in Biology, was designed around a video format so that students would have some control over the pace of their learning. Twelve units have been completed to date. Each unit covers a topic traditionally covered in an introductory biology course. The sequence of topics follows Biology 100 and is intended to provide preparation as well as self-confidence for students before they enroll in that upper level course.

The tapes which provide the focus for each unit have been produced locally during the summer months in cooperation with our AV department. We are currently running approximately 60 students a year through the course and those that move on to the 100-level course are demonstrat-

ing a high degree of success. We are convinced that the visual medium in the form of the tapes has been the most significant element in success of the students. The next logical step in the ongoing evolution of the course will be to convert all of the units to interactive, multimedia.

In November of 1991 the college purchased an IBM Advanced Academic System and work began to convert the entire course to multimedia. The units are being generated in a windows environment utilizing Toolbook from Asymetrix as the authoring system. Four units have been completed to date and they were incorporated into the course during the Fall quarter of 1992. The topics were selected for production based on the availability of good quality laserdiscs to support the visual components. During the 1992-93 academic year, the AV department worked with the biology department to prepare a master tape of selected clips from the video tapes produced during phase one of the development. A laserdisc is being pressed from the master tape and the clips can be selected for incorpo-

Continues on Page 366

ration into additional multimedia units. It is anticipated that the entire course will be converted to interactive multimedia by the Fall quarter of 1994.

Grant support from the Bush Foundation, National Science Foundation and Minnesota Community College System provided a total of $40,000. System Student Success funds supported a $6,600 IBM Advanced Academic System. Four biology instructors rotate teaching responsibility. This program has been nationally recognized by the American Association of Higher Education's Faculty Recognition Program, 1989.

Contact:
Dennis J. O'Melia, Biology Professor
(612) 450-8606

Inver Hills Community College
8445 College Trail,
Inver Grove Heights, MN 55076
Total head count enrollment-Credit: 5,500; Non-Credit: 2,100
Campuses/sites: 1;Full-time faculty: 90

NON-PROFIT CENTER SERVING PEOPLE OF COLOR

The Center was developed, organized and administered by people representative of the various ethnic groups being served

Minneapolis Community College, with a three-year grant from the Saint Paul Companies, has established a Non-Profit Center serving Communities of Color. The uniqueness of this program is that it was developed, organized and administered by people representative of the various ethnic groups being served. It is culturally authentic and shaped by the communities of color.

The Center provides technical assistance, leadership training, the development of mediation services, and planning time related to public policy issues and concerns. The targeted clientele are people of color involved or interested in non-profit agencies. Specifically, the communities sought for participation are African American, Hispanic, Native American and Asian. Part of the learning process will be the sharing of language, purposes, and issues among different communities, cultures and groups. The training ranges from how to organize a non-profit group, to board/staff relationships. Services began in the fall of 1992.

Contact:
Nick J. Maras
(612) 341-7023

Minneapolis Community College
1501 Hennepin Avenue
Minneapolis, MN 55403
Total head count enrollment-Credit: 6,511; Non-Credit: 4,500
Campuses/sites: 5;Full-time faculty: 86

A CELEBRATION OF DIVERSITY

Children in the summer program learn from instructors who come from or have experience in the culture they represent

Minneapolis Community College offers a week-long children's diversity program entitled "A Celebration of Diversity." The session, which runs twice each summer, offers children between the ages of four and 12 an opportunity to learn about and experience different cultures first-hand. Each day a different culture is celebrated through art, music, dance, games, stories, customs and food. Children learn from instructors who come from or have experience in the culture they represent.A recent addition to the program is the Disabilities Day where children learned to develop awareness of and sensitivity to various disabilities. This innovative program, which also highlights the cultures of Africa, India, South America and Native Americans, has filled to capacity each year, and response continues to grow. It is one program that has brought the college media attention from the local papers.

Contact:
Sue Moyer
(612) 349-2596

Minneapolis Community College
1501 Hennepin Avenue,
Minneapolis, MN 55403
Total head count enrollment-Credit: 6,511; Non-Credit: 4,500
Campuses/sites: 5;Full-time faculty: 86

DESIGNING EDUCATIONAL EXPERIENCES FOR DISABLED STUDENTS

▓ Three classes were designed; one focuses on support available ▓
while the other two are paired with English courses

A Normandale Community College program enables students with disabilities to both receive and provide assistance to other students. The DEEDS (Designing Educational Experiences for Disabled Students) program began in 1981 as a result of Federal Title I funding. The program was a response to the recognized need for services to students with physical disabilities, hearing disabilities, vision disabilities, learning disabilities, etc.

The program served an average of 243 students per quarter during the 1991-92 academic year. Based on student need and instructor/student/DEEDS staff consultation the following accommodations were provided as appropriate:
- building orientation (elevators, accessible routes, restrooms, etc.);
- student support for coping with a disability in college;
- alternative testing (this may include extended time, tape recorded tests, proofreading, writing assistance, interpreted tests for hearing impaired students);
- proofreading of written assignments;
- assistance with faculty contacts concerning accommodation of disabilities in the classroom and/or lab, testing situations, etc.;
- individual assistance-organizational planning, time management;
- referral for taped textbooks through a national recording agency (RFB) and a state agency;
- orientation to adaptive computer equipment;
- referral to appropriate outside agencies for additional support;
- sign language/oral interpreting; and
- note-taking.

Three three-credit classes for DEEDS students (PDEV 70, 71, 72: DEEDS) were designed for students with disabilities. The first course focuses on providing group support, campus orientation information, self-advocacy skills training, disability accommodation information, and training in adaptive computer technology. The second and third courses are paired with related English composition courses and utilize computer assistance to review grammar and develop paragraph writing skills.

The DEEDS program is located within the Independent Learning Center, which provides testing services, peer tutoring, and academic support materials, including computers, for the use of the entire college community. In this setting, students may be both receivers and providers of assistance to other students. The staff for the DEEDS program includes a coordinator, one or more interpreters, college laboratory assistants, secretarial support, and college and community volunteers as well as the coordinated support of the Independent Learning Center.

Initially funded by Title I funding, the DEEDS program has received ongoing support though the college's general funds, Minnesota Community College System support, grants, and community service organizations, such as, the Bloomington Rotary Club, the Kaiser Roll Foundation and the Bush Foundation.

A 1990 Bush Foundation-supported review by outside evaluators said of the DEEDS program: "Evaluation is a term used with great regularity in post secondary institutions. The reality however is that few individuals or programs are truly willing to put themselves under the microscope of critical review. An often seen irony is that these teachers, administrators or programs which do initiate this activity are generally those in least need of such review! The DEEDS program is in this category."

Contact:
Mary Jibben, Coordinator
(612) 832-6422

Normandale Community College
9700 France Avenue South
Bloomington, MN 55431
Total headcount enrollment-Credit: 9,317; Non-Credit: 1,078
Campuses/sites: 1; Full-time faculty: 169

HEALTH WELLNESS

✵ The Wellness Committee strives to meet staff and student needs ✵
with a variety of integrated events throughout the school year

The Wellness Task Force of Normandale Community College has helped create an environment that encourages and supports all students, staff and community in the development and maintenance of a positive and healthy lifestyle. Initial activities promoted by the task force (formed in 1988) included:

1) a survey of all staff on the need for wellness support and encouragement;

2) a health risk questionnaire for all interested staff; the results of individual assessments were given to participants and college scoring shared with all; and

3) a three-day staff wellness workshop was held that included activities with an intellectual, professional, physical, social and emotional wellness emphasis.

Feedback from faculty and the Wellness Task Force led to a building remodeling project that created a fitness center and a wellness resource center to accommodate staff and students in new coursework. Highlights include:

1) a Wellness for Life course taught by an interdisciplinary team that includes health and nutrition information (after self-assessment, students develop a plan for their total wellness that includes physical exercise);

2) a Wellness Resource Center set up and maintained by students/staff involved in the wellness courses;

3) a Fitness for Life course that involves individual health/physical fitness assessment, a plan for improvement and an evaluation (students and staff may take the credit course, which includes open lab access, day, evening and weekends; upon completion of the course, students may workout in the fitness center for a fee; after an orientation session, staff may also use the center);

4) a Walking Fitness course with special appeal for older returning female students; and

5) the redesign of physical education coursework to emphasize courses in total wellness: i.e., conditioning, nutrition and exercise, personal fitness.

The Wellness Committee members strive to meet staff and student needs with a variety of integrated events/activities throughout the school year, such as: brown bag seminars and lectures on nutrition; healthy cooking; stress management; posture assessment; weight loss; acupuncture; bio-feedback; aerobics; Tai Chi; individual exercise planning; CPR classes (refresher or certification); and "fitness weeks" (which include rollerblading, fitness walks, body composition testing, step classes and massage class).

"Heart Healthy" continuing education classes are offered for staff and community members.

The Wellness/Physical Education staff recently implemented an older adult wellness program funded through a Minnesota Community College Faculty Development Grant. The program was marketed to older residents in the local communities as well as Normandale Community College staff. The program provided fitness assessment of body fat composition, and the level of cardiovascular, flexibility and strength components. This enabled both instructors and participants to set appropriate goals. The program was designed to meet each individual's personal needs and limitations. Activities such as fitness walking, strength training, Tai Chi, weight management, relaxation and stretching were all provided. This ongoing program will be provided early in the morning on a quarterly basis and aims to assist participants in taking charge of their lifestyles while having fun. The Sunrise Wellness Program was highlighted in the local newspaper with quotes from pleased participants and staff.

All of these health promotion programs have been offered on a voluntary basis, with minimal college funding.

Contact:
Geneva Middleton, Associate Dean
(612) 832-6339

Normandale Community College
9700 France Avenue South
Bloomington, MN 55431
Total headcount enrollment-Credit: 9,317; Non-Credit: 1,078
Campuses/sites: 1; Full-time faculty: 169

STUDENT SUCCESS PROGRAM

*▓ Student success falls within four areas: curriculum, physical environment, ▓
supportive contacts and student life*

A Student Success Program at North Hennepin Community College is well-rounded, assuming student success results from academic, social, personal and institutional involvement by students. Its formation dates prior to the 1989-90 budget planning cycle, when the administration and faculty of North Hennepin Community College decided to emphasize our goal of supporting student success by allocating $50,000 to fund projects that would contribute to that effort. Faculty, staff or administrators could submit proposals to their respective deans with the final decision on funding made by the Cabinet (President, two deans, financial officer). Projects ranged from seed money to establish a Center for Writing to the purchase of two sets of video disk players, color monitors and interactive math tutorial video disks, allowing the math faculty to provide another approach to the learning of mathematics at the basic level.

The following year, student success became an important initiative in the Minnesota Community College System and was supported by an allocation to each college. At North Hennepin rather than rush into spending the allocation, a Student Success Committee was formed to clarify what was meant by "Student Success" within our college.

After considerable work, a North Hennepin model was developed. The college believes student success is created by four types of student involvement: academic, social, personal and institutional. All this falls within four areas of the college: curriculum, physical environment, supportive contacts and student life. This model is represented by a 4-by-4 grid. In each of the 16 cells, the committee developed examples of projects which could contribute to the integra-tion of a commitment to Student Success within the college.

The committee then moved in two directions using both existing and new structures. A letter and a copy of the student success grid was sent to all standing committees on campus. Each committee was encouraged to use the grid and to let Student Success provide the focus for their decision making. The Facilities Committee has been particularly involved in funding projects in the physical environment area while the Student Life Committee has used its funds to develop new ventures which support the theme.

In order to encourage new thrusts, the committee developed an RFP and sent the application form and the Student Success grid to all faculty and staff on campus. Fifty-seven proposals were received and 33 were funded, including four from students, two from the secretarial staff and the rest from faculty and counselors. Release credit for a Student Success Coordinator also was funded to ensure projects are completed in a timely manner.

The impact of the funded projects on the curriculum and supportive contacts areas has been particularly great. (Information on the specific projects is available from the coordinator.) The major accomplishment beyond the individual projects is the integration throughout the campus of the notion of Student Success as a guiding principle. Whether one is in the College Learning Center, Diversity Program office, Counseling, Registration, a Curriculum Committee meeting or in budget hearings, "Student Success" is a phrase often heard at North Hennepin Community College.

Contact:
Kathy O'Connell
(612) 424-0743

North Hennepin Community College
7411 85th Avenue North
Brooklyn Park, MN 55445
Total head count enrollment-Credit: 5,932; Non-Credit: 8,000
Campuses/sites: 2; Full-time faculty: 117

PROBLEM SOLVING

*▓ The five-credit, quarter-long course is team-taught, ▓
and rarely do any of the sections have unfilled seats*

In 1985, equipped with a $45,000 grant from EXXON Corporation, 10 faculty members from Philosophy, Physics, Accounting, Business, Architectural Technology, Art, English, Math, Psychology and Sociology gathered to begin developing a course on effective thinking. It was a unique enterprise since no academic area "owned" the content of the curriculum. Indeed, in the beginning no one knew what the content should be. Nevertheless, the goal was to have a course ready for Spring Quarter 1986.

The result: a five-credit, quarter-long course that is team-taught and rarely has any unfilled seats. The term

Continues on Page 370

"problem solving" was selected for the course over the more widely used term "critical thinking" because problem solving is doing, involves clarification of goals, prizes creativity, is comprehensive, is positive and covers non-verbal as well as verbal contexts. In addition, it lends itself to cross disciplinary examples of exercises and consists of skills which can be taught.

The course is taught by a team of three people – usually one new instructor with two experienced ones – all from different disciplines. The maximum class size is 70 and rarely are there vacant seats in any of the four sections taught each year. Generally, a week-long unit consists of a faculty presentation, small group work, a wrap-up discussion and a test. Students also must write their reflections and proposed applications for each unit presented.

The course starts with problems that look simple, problems which are almost perceptual: patterns. From there the course goes on to study patterns which are more hypothetical and require controlled testing: casual patterns. The third unit focuses on the stages in the problem-solving process where generating alternatives is crucial.

The middle four units of the course shift from emphasis on structures of specific types of problems to emphasis on development of general techniques important for all problem-solving: heuristics, creativity, diagramming and critical thinking.

The final four units concentrate on the most difficult and complex types of problem solving: decision-making, values conflicts, and problems only solvable by double-loop thinking, which calls all assumptions into question.

A full-page picture story about the course appeared in the *Minneapolis Star Tribune*. Workshops on effective thinking have been given to Minnesota Community College administrators and faculty. In addition, the course was used as a basis for a nearly $1-million Thinking Across the Curriculum grant, funded for three years by the Bush Foundation. The lead instructor is now the director of the project which includes faculty at all 21 campuses of the Minnesota Community College System.

Contact:
Joel Peterson
(612) 297-5546

North Hennepin Community College
7411 85th Avenue North
Brooklyn Park, MN 55445
Total head count enrollment-Credit: 5,932; Non-Credit: 8,000
Campuses/sites: 2; Full-time faculty: 117

NORTHLAND COMMUNITY COLLEGE

INDIAN IMAGES MONTH

▩ *The month-long celebration helped unite students,* ▩
faculty staff and the community

In April 1992, Northland Community College hosted its second annual Indian Images Month. The "All Nations Club" at Northland Community College worked extremely hard to put together a fine group of entertainers, artists, speakers and workshops. Their efforts have helped in bringing together students, faculty, staff and community, to show these groups the beauty of Native American Culture.

Some of the scheduled events included:
- Portrait of the Chippewa Exhibit: Photographs by Charles Brill. An exhibit of 100 contemporary photographs of the Red Lake Indian Reservation.
- Kevin Locke: A Lakota of the Standing Rock Reservation, a past recipient of the National heritage Fellowship from the National Endowment for the Arts. Mr. Locke is recognized for his preeminence as a player of traditional flute music, and is a performer of the Lakota hoop dance.
- Lee Cook: Assistant to the President for Diversity at Augsburg College in Minneapolis, Mr. Cook was a guest speaker. Mr. Cook spoke to an audience of students, faculty, staff and concerned citizens on the topic of cultural sensitivity and the changes in Indian education over the 25 years. Mr. Cook is a member of the Red Lake Band of Chippewa Indians and has held many positions in higher education in the state of Minnesota.
- Lorenzo Blacklance: An artist from Low Brule, South Dakota, who displayed his abilities in the Northland lobby with an original painting. Mr. Blacklance donated his work to the All Nations Club, which in turn gave the painting as a gift to the Northland Community College library for all to enjoy.
- A Taste of Indian Culture and Silent Auction: On April 22 samples of Native American food were served to students and staff by All Nations Club. They were also given a chance to bid on art work

donated to the club.
- Seven Feather Dance Club: A group of elementary children from Grand Forks, North Dakota, ranging in age from 6 to 13 years old, performed in front of a full house in the NCC theater.

Contact:
Sue Minnick, Vice Provost
(218) 681-2181 or (800) 628-9918

Northland Community College
Highway 1101 East
Thief River Falls, MN 56701
Total head count enrollment-Credit: 1,373; Non-Credit: 350
Campuses/sites: 1;Full-time faculty: 24

NORTHWEST REGIONAL TRAINING FOR POLICE

Classes are held in 13 training sites throughout the 12-county regions, making it convenient for all officers to participate

Since its inception in 1990, Northland Community College's Northwest Regional Training for Police (NRT) has become a model for regional law enforcement training, according to Minnesota state officials who oversee such programs. The quality and quantity of law enforcement training offered is vital because Minnesota requires 48 hours of continuing education every three years for their officers. In the beginning, NRT met with the department heads of 40 law enforcement agencies covering 12 counties in northwest Minnesota. An agreement was made that NRT would offer 360 hours of continuing education in a nine-month school-year. Departments could join for $195 per officer. With approximately 200 officers in the training area, NRT has an annual budget of $40,000.

Training is managed through NCC personnel, but the actual training is done through a variety of local, state and national training experts. The classes are held in 13 train-ing sites throughout the 12-county region, making it convenient for all officers to participate.

Several goals were set by area department heads, which NRT has successfully met. They are:
1) convenient training, by offering the classes in a variety of sites throughout the 12 counties;
2) quality training using only qualified experts in the field;
3) relevant training, because course topics are selected by an eight-member committee; and
4) reasonable prices.

NRT averages 60 classes per training year. Each officer in the region averages nearly 20 hours of training per year. In 1991-92, NRT officers attended 3,728 hours of training. Annual surveys confirm the fact that NRT is reaching its desired goals.

Contact:
Kevin L. Stuckey, Coordinator
(218) 681-2181

Northland Community College
Highway 1101 East
Thief River Falls, MN 56701
Total head count enrollment-Credit: 1,373; Non-Credit: 350
Campuses/sites: 1;Full-time faculty: 24

GREATER ROCHESTER AREA UNIVERSITY CENTER

While each of the eight involved institution independently grant degrees, every effort is made to minimize duplication of program offerings

In an environment where higher education institutions have found themselves having to do more with less, Rochester-area educational and civic leaders have banded together to provide area residents with a potent arsenal of higher education opportunities.

Higher education was a topic of concern addressed in a 1986 community-wide needs assessment entitled *Future Scan 2000*. The *Future Scan 2000* report generated a number of recommendations for Rochester higher education, from which sprang the Greater Rochester Area University Center (GRAUC) Board of Providers and GRAUC Board of Directors.

The Board of Providers is comprised of the top executive officers from eight higher education providers: Mayo Foundation, Minnesota Bible College, Minnesota

Continues on Page 372

Riverland Technical College, Rochester Community College, Saint Mary's College of Minnesota-Rochester Center and Winona State University-Rochester Center. The board formulates policy and coordinates educational programs, student services efforts and public information initiatives. The first chairperson of the Board of Providers, former Rochester Community College President Geraldine A. Evans, is now chancellor of the Minnesota Community College System.

The Board of Directors is comprised of Rochester area civic, business and governmental leaders. Its purpose is to promote efforts to provide information about educational resources, to determine emerging needs and methods to meet those needs and to seek support for higher education. The first chairperson of the board of Directors, A.M. "Sandy" Keith, is chief justice of the Minnesota Supreme Court.

The two boards worked together to gain funding approval from the 1990 Minnesota Legislature for construction of a joint educational facility on the RCC campus. Called the University Center Rochester, the $17-million building is being shared by RCC, the University of Minnesota Rochester Center and Winona State University-Rochester Center. Already completed and occupied, the center will provide new science and computer labs, student services areas, interactive television classrooms, additional library space and faculty and administrative offices.

While each of the eight GRAUC institutions independently grants degrees, every effort is made to minimize duplication of program offerings. Taken as a whole, the schools offer more than 150 programs, ranging from one-year certificates to Ph.D.-level degrees. More than 20 programs are collaborative efforts between schools.

Additional areas of cooperation involving at least two of the institutions include library, bookstore, child care, duplicating and audio-visual services, as well as joint use of facilities. In addition, a marketing committee under the direction of the Board of Providers has received approximately $100,000 in funding to jointly promote Rochester-area higher education opportunities in the past four years. Marketing funds have been provided by the Board of Directors, the Rochester Area Foundation and service organizations.

Rochester Community College has had a strong background in educational cooperation during the 1980's and into the 1990's. Evans guided the college in a number of successful cooperative efforts. These initiatives included a "2 plus 2" program with Winona State University, joint health-related programs with the Mayo Foundation, cooperative programs with Minnesota Riverland Technical College (MRTC) and a Tech Prep program involving RCC, MRTC and local school district.

Contact:
Dr. Karen Nagle, President
(507) 285-7215

Rochester Community College
851 30th Avenue SE
Rochester, MN 55904
Total head count enrollment-Credit: 3,987; Non-Credit: 9,405
Campuses/sites: 1; Full-time faculty: 85

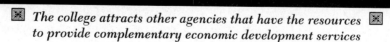

BUSINESS / INDUSTRY OUTREACH

The college attracts other agencies that have the resources to provide complementary economic development services

A key component of Rochester Community College's mission is to serve business and industry, as well as to enhance the economic development potential of the college's service area. RCC accomplishes these goals by directly offering services and by attracting other agencies to provide complementary economic development services.

The college offers a wide variety of video conferences in the state-of-the-art Coffman Continuing Education Center. RCC offers technical conferences which are heavily attended by employees of Rochester's IBM plant.

The college also offers video conferences covering such topics as leadership, team-building, contract negotiation and other management issues. Furthermore, RCC periodically provides video conferences and seminars concerning educational topics such as Tech Prep. The college is an active member of the Rochester Area Quality Council, which has members from business, industry and educational institutions. In addition, RCC offers business and industry customized training. Topics may be specific, such as classes for medical transcriptionists or training on WordPerfect software, or may be more general in nature, such as courses to develop effective writing skills or for supervisory management.

Another service is the Rochester Small Business Development Center (SBDC), for persons who either plan to start a small business or who currently operate a small business. The Center provides training opportunities on a wide range of business topics, makes available basic and applied research, provides one-on-one counseling free of charge to the small business owner and refers clients to other existing business programs. Located on the RCC campus, the Center is partially funded by Rochester Community College, Winona State University and the U.S. Small Business Administration. The SBDC is also involved in a new project called Small Business 2020, a cooperative effort with the Rochester Area Chamber of Commerce to provide long-term training to small business owners.

In addition, the Strategic Financial Analysis Project, a cooperative effort with Rochester lenders, will provide one-on-one comprehensive strategic financial analysis for 20 small businesses. Partially funded by the Southeastern Minnesota Initiative Fund, this SBDC's successful projects is the Minnesota Women's Network for Entrepreneurial Training (MWNET). The program matches established women business owners with protégés who either plan to

start a business or who own a fledgling business. Ellen Nelson, co-director of the Rochester SBDC, was named 1992 Minnesota Women in Business Advocate by the U.S. SBDC for her work in directing the Rochester area MWNET program. Also, the college has attracted and provides space on the RCC campus for three business/industry outreach programs, and Minnesota Project Innovation helps small technology and manufacturing companies take advantage of federal funding, procurement and technology transfer opportunities.

Finally, Minnesota Technology, Inc., provides consulting services and technology-based seminars to area business and industry.

Contact:
Ellen Nelson
(507) 285-7536

Rochester Community College
851 30th Avenue SE
Rochester, MN 55904
Total head count enrollment-Credit: 3,987; Non-Credit: 9,405
Campuses/sites: 1; Full-time faculty: 85

ENVIRONMENTAL STUDIES

The program employs an experiential, hands-on approach that makes students more aware of the state's wildlife habitats

An experiential, hands-on approach that actively involves students in broadening their ecological awareness of the state's wildlife habitats is the cornerstone of the Environmental Studies program at Vermilion Community College.

The program was first funded in 1989, when the Minnesota Legislature granted Vermilion Community College $50,000 per year for two years (later renewed) to conduct educational programs for the International Wolf Center. The International Wolf Center is a combination of private, public and professional groups concerned with wolf education.

Vermilion, together with the Educational Committee of the International Wolf Center, began to work toward the following objectives: to promote public education about wolves and their environment through an integrated program that includes the Science Museum of Minnesota Wolves & Humans Exhibit, field programs, a speaker's bureau, outreach, information clearinghouse, live wolf exhibit and other educational activities.

The college, in conjunction with the International Wolf Center education committee, has developed programs that appeal to a diverse national and international audience, from preschoolers to senior citizens. The credit programs

developed include week-long research expeditions, backpacking trips to study wolves on Isle Royale of Lake Superior, and the most popular program, a Wolf Weekend.

During the Winter Wolf Weekend students ski, snowshoe, dogsled and fly into wolf country to examine a kill site and other wolf signs as they study predator/prey relationships of the timberwolf. Participants also get first-hand experience with the radio telemetry equipment, learning about the 30-plus years of research involving the wild wolf population of the Superior National Forest. Through their wolf education programs Vermilion discovered that there is a growing interest in environmental studies. In response to that interest, an Environmental Studies program was created in 1991. These courses employ an experiential, hands-on approach which actively involves students in broadening their ecological awareness and appreciation of northern Minnesota's forest environment and wildlife inhabitants. In addition to those wolf topics, some of the courses now being offered are Boreal Forest Ecology, Eagle and Osprey Surveys, and Black Bear Ecology.

The Environmental Studies program has grown from one part-time administrator/part-time instructor to include an educational coordinator, primary instructor and several adjunct faculty.

Contact:
Susan Meisner, Educational Coordinator
(800) 657-3609, ext. 7286

Vermilion Community College
1900 East Camp Street
Ely, MN 55731
Total head count enrollment-Credit: 1,278; Non-Credit: 2,609.92
Campuses/sites: 1;Full-time faculty: 22

LABORATORY IN INTRODUCTORY PSYCHOLOGY

Many labs include computer-simulation experiments that develop students'
computer literacy while demonstrating their use in research

At Willmar Community College, a course gives first- and second-year psychology majors a chance to be introduced to computer functions often reserved for upper-division course work. The course resulted from the desire of psychology faculty to give students the opportunity to participate in a "hands-on" lab experience in general psychology that would introduce them to the basic features of sound research design, ethical considerations in research, problems in interpreting research data, as well as acquaint them with apparatus used to demonstrate important principles affecting human behavior.

The course carries one credit and follows a programmed learning format. The lab is staffed by college work-study students majoring in the behavioral sciences and supervised by psychology department faculty. There are eight lab units completed by students over an approximate 11-week quarter. Many of the labs include computer-simulation experiments and activities which assist in the development of students' computer literacy while demonstrating the utility of computers in facilitating research work.

Lab activities are presented in physiological psychology, sensation, perception, learning, memory, motivation/emotion, testing, and abnormal behavior. Students practice writing up experimental results, interpreting data, critiquing methodology, searching for extraneous variables and considering ethical problems in conducting experimentation. This course is an outstanding opportunity for first-year and second-year students majoring in psychology to be introduced to computer functions often reserved for upper division course work in psychology.

The lab is housed in a new behavioral science/human service teaching center and is equipped with both IBM and Macintosh computers as well as basic laboratory apparatus for demonstrating principles underlying human behavior. The lab course is offered each academic quarter and can accommodate up to 12 students per term.

Contact:
Charles Gander, Instructor-in-Charge
(612) 231-5129

Willmar Community College
PO Box 797
Willmar, MN 56201
Total head count enrollment-Credit: 1,339; Non-Credit: 2,000
Campuses/sites: 1; Full-time faculty: 39

NATIVE AMERICAN AWARENESS GATHERING

The Gathering increases an appreciation of America's native people
and has become a powerful lifetime force for those involved

An annual Native American Awareness Gathering at Willmar community College is an opportunity for the campus and community to confront lingering stereotypes and prejudices in today's society. The Native American Awareness Gathering, one of two educational activities that emphasize Native American issues, involves faculty, both Native American and non-Native American students, and a variety of community and Native American resource persons.

An annual Native American Awareness Gathering, first held in 1986, has become a focus of the efforts to increase cross-cultural understanding. The 1992 Native American Awareness Gathering focused on the goal of cross-cultural understanding and various topics were addressed through keynote and small group sessions. Some of the topics presented include: clarification of history regarding the 500th anniversary of Columbus; Spirituality; Red Road Recovery; The Sacred Pipe; Intercultural Relationships;

Native American Gaming; Economic Development; Cultural Sensitivity; Racism; and the 1862 Uprising in Western Minnesota. An art and craft show is also presented along with a Pow Wow and feast. About 3,000 people from the community attended.

A core group of 35 individuals (including Willmar Community College students, faculty and native Americans from four states) serve on an advisory committee for this event. The budget is met through various agencies such as institutional funding, committee fund raising activities, community agencies, the Lower Sioux Agency, and grants from the Southwest Minnesota Arts and Humanities Council and the Southwest Minnesota Initiative Fund.

With the lingering stereotypes and prejudices in our society today, Willmar Community College views cultural sensitivity education as a vital component of the college experience. The Native American Awareness Gathering increases not only understanding but also an appreciation of America's native people with the goal of incorporating this experience into the value system that students will take with them to their communities, places of employment and family settings. This has become a powerful lifetime force and experience for those involved.

Willmar Community College has also developed an educational field trip that involves direct on-site immersion of students enrolled in Racial and Cultural Minorities and Cultural Anthropology classes. This immersion includes Amish, Hutterites, and Native Americans with a particularly strong focus on Native Americans. The students travel 2,000 miles in three states and spend several days involved in living in the reservation environment.

Both programs have received recognition from fellow educators, the community, Native American elders and tribal leaders.

Contact:
Dennis Waskul, Instructor-in-Charge
(612) 231-5123

Willmar Community College
PO Box 797
Willmar, MN 56201
Total head count enrollment-Credit: 1,339; Non-Credit: 2,000
Campuses/sites: 1; Full-time faculty: 39

LANDSCAPE ARCHITECTURE

▩ *Much-needed campus renovation is underway through a partnership* ▩
with a university and the National Park Service

Coahoma Community College, believing in working with business, industry and participating agencies in providing quality education, recently entered a working partnership with a university and the U.S. Department of Interior's National Park Service in a campus renovation project.

Coahoma Community College and Agricultural High School (CCC-AHS is one of two college campuses in Mississippi that still house a high school) are in great need of renovations to landscaping, traffic flow and security measures. With the help of Mississippi State University's Department of Landscape Architecture and the National Park Service, CCC now has the renovation plans needed.

Founded in 1949 as an outgrowth of Coahoma County Agricultural High School, CCC's heritage was established in 1924 as the first county in Mississippi to provide an agricultural high school for Negroes under the then existing "separate but equal" doctrine of education. That tradition has survived at CCC-AHS as has three of the original buildings of the early campus.

The National Park Service, in trying to supervise the restoration and maintenance of those three original buildings, agreed to work with MSU's Department of Landscape Architecture to devise three workable plans. CCC officials then could choose one of these three renovation options.

Twenty-three fifth-year landscape architecture students from MSU made a three-day on-site visit, researching Mississippi Delta and Coahoma County tradition, history, culture, etc. as well as doing topographical studies. The National Park Service consulted with the students, and in November 1992, three final plans were presented to CCC officials.

CCC plans to use the three plans in both short-term and long-term campus renovation. Community involvement with CCC-AHS will provide fund-raising efforts as well as donations of materials, equipment, labor, etc., in order that the plans can be carried out to beautify the historical landmark.

Contact:
Freddie Caswell
(601) 627-2571

Coahoma Community College
3240 Friars Point Road
Clarksdale, MS 38614-9722
Total head count enrollment-Credit: 1,423; Non-Credit: 239
Campuses/sites: 4; Full-time faculty: 57

GRAPHIC, PRINT AND REPROGRAPHICS LABORATORY

▩ *Xerox Corp. agreed to help establish the lab because it was impressed* ▩
with services already established at the college

Coahoma Community College has entered into a three-way partnership with the U.S. Department of Interior and the Xerox Corp. in establishing a Graphic, Print, and Reprographics Laboratory on the CCC campus.
CCC's program has five establish curriculums:
1) vocational, which involves one-year training in printing and job placement;
2) technical print graphics with two-year training and transfer to a four-year institution;
3) technical print graphics, which involves two-year print graphics technical training and job placement;
4) technical print service maintenance is a two-year program with job placement in maintaining and repairing printing equipment; and
5) academic print management program for two-year training and transfers credits to a four-year institution for further study in upper management

training.
The three-way partnership was made possible by the executive branch directive for Historically Black Colleges and Universities Programs. Located in the economically disadvantaged Mississippi Delta, the printing curriculum at CCC will bring one of the top five manufacturing industries to the heart of the Delta to provide productive careers for Mississippians.

Xerox Corp. signed on because it was impressed with CCC's Single Parent Program, a program which allows single mothers to live on campus with their children while attending classes; the children are even placed in college-supported day care systems so they can be close to their mothers.

CCC provides the instructors and the student work force to be trained; Xerox supplies much of the state-of-the-art equipment; and The Interior oversees the project and will eventually have its own printing duplicated on the CCC campus.

Initiated in 1989 through a Memorandum of Understanding, the partners proceeded with assessment of curriculum, course variables, equipment needs, etc. After 18 months of labor and student construction (carpentry, masonry and electrical work), the laboratory was dedicated in January 1991, and the course curriculum is now underway.

Contact:
Sheila Portia-Mapp
(601) 627-2571

Coahoma Community College
3240 Friars Point Road
Clarksdale, MS 38614-9722
Total head count enrollment-Credit: 1,423; Non-Credit: 239
Campuses/sites: 4; Full-time faculty: 57

EAST CENTRAL COMMUNITY COLLEGE

ADVISEMENT INTERVENTION

The advisement program includes an "early alert" system that notifies both students and advisors of absentee and/or academic problems

In addition to providing full-time academic and vocational-technical counselors, East Central Community College in 1985 implemented an advisement-intervention program whereby faculty members also serve as academic advisors in their respective fields of study.

As part of the advisement-intervention process, advisors are selected from the teaching faculty according to their respective programs of study and are thus well-qualified to assist students in their career planning. Frequent meetings are held between the students and their advisors on matters pertaining to their educational or vocational careers. Students also pick up midterm grades from their advisors. During this meeting students carefully track their progress by recording their mid-semester and prior grades on a locally developed check list. This procedure helps ensure that students meet their graduation, personal improvement or transfer goals without any surprises. With careful planning, students can find and pursue the course of study that will be most helpful in their chosen profession. Each student is thus aided in choosing a vocation and pursuing the curriculum which is best suited for that purpose.

There are two additional aspects of the advisement program. First, counseling services are being offered during evening hours on the Decatur campus and at various locations throughout the five-county district where the courses are offered. Secondly, an "early alert" system is in place which notifies, by form letter, both students and advisors of absentee and/or academic problems. These communications are made before midterm and help to solve student problems before they become magnified.

The successful implementation of the advising system involved four factors:
1) the total commitment of the college president;
2) faculty involvement in program planning;
3) a student-centered environment; and
4) a strong case showing the positive relationship between advisement intervention and recruiting/retention.

The human and capital resources necessary for successful implementation include:
1) faculty commitment and time;
2) a designated advisement coordinator; and
3) postage and supplies.

In 1991, East Central's Advisement-Intervention System was recognized by The American Association of Community and Junior Colleges "Small/Rural Community College Commission" as an exemplary program. Furthermore, in 1992, an article entitled "Advisement Intervention, A Key Strategy for a New Age - Student Consumerism," which described, in detail, East Central's Advisement system, was published by the Clearinghouse on Rural Education and Small Schools (CRESS) in the ERIC Database.

Contact:
H. Greggory Jefcoat
(601) 635-2111

East Central Community College
PO Box 129
Decatur, MS 39327-0129
Total head count enrollment-Credit: 1,395; Non-Credit: 226
Campuses/sites: 2; Full-time faculty: 48

STRATEGIC PLANNING AND EVALUATION

▦ *People from all areas and functions of the college* ▦
are involved in the planning process

East Central Community College defines strategic planning as the general process for determining institutional purpose, direction and priorities. The college developed its first formal Strategic Plan during the 1985-86 year. This plan is a five-year, rollover plan that is revised and extended for an additional year on an annual basis. The process used in its development is broad-based and comprehensive, providing sufficient structure to assess institutional effectiveness.

The planning process involves projecting assumptions over the planning period and adopting a plan of action in response to the projected assumptions. This process helps the faculty and the administration gain a common understanding of the support parameters in which the college exists and in which it is expected to perform its mission. The process also assists the faculty and the administration in developing strategies for reaching goals and objectives and for evaluating results.

All goals and objectives of the Strategic Plan are stated in terms of specific outcomes to be accomplished. Time frames, revenue/resource requirements, strategies, and evaluative criteria are listed for each of the objectives in the plan. These objectives are listed under the following sections: Administrative/ Management, Fiscal Management, Instructional Support, Staff Development, and Student Services.

The committees involved in the planning process are representative of all areas and functions of the college. The same broad-based involvement that was emphasized in its initial development is built into the continuous revision and evaluation of the Strategic Plan. In order to facilitate communication among faculty, administration and other constituents concerning the various aspects of the planning process, the college publishes the *East Central Community College Strategic Plan* and the *East Central Community College Policies and Procedures Manual.*

The strategic planning process addresses each of the goals of the institution to assure that they are implemented and evaluated for their effectiveness. The Strategic Plan lists strategies for each of the objectives, and it lists evaluative criteria to assess the achievement of the individual objectives. This guarantees that the goals and objectives are evaluated annually. As a result of the evaluation process, conclusions are reached concerning the status of the various programs of the college. The various strategic planning committees annually review the results and revise the strategic plans in order to ensure the fulfillment of the goals and, thereby, the fulfillment of the mission of East Central Community College.

Contact:
Eddie M. Smith, President
(601) 635-2111

East Central Community College
PO Box 129
Decatur, MS 39327-0129
Total head count enrollment-Credit: 1,395; Non-Credit: 226
Campuses/sites: 2; Full-time faculty: 48

RESOURCE AND COORDINATING UNIT FOR ECONOMIC DEVELOPMENT

▦ *The RCU has developed excellent working relationships with* ▦
county and state officials, economic developers and industry

The Resource & Coordinating Unit for Economic Development (RCU) has had a positive and significant impact on the state's economic development since Hinds Community College District President Dr. Clyde Muse initiated it in 1988. Major goals and objectives include:
- Adult Basic Education, which provides basic skills training for adults throughout the community;
- Industry Basic Education, which provides on-site basic skills training to enhance employee skills;
- Job-Specific Customized Training, which provides

Literacy Task Analysis (LTA) and develop appropriate curriculum and instructional materials to provide customized training to business and industry;
- In-Service Training for Vocational and Technical Instructors, which provides assistance to instructors to enhance teaching skills and utilize the current practices used by business and industry;
- Customized Computer Training, which provides short term intensive workshops on current software

application packages to business and industry;

- Business and Government Services, which assist companies in achieving positive results through its employees by providing staff development activities;
- Industrial Services, which provide customized training for new and expanding industry;
- Small Business Development Center (SBDC), which provides one-to-one confidential counseling and training assistance in all aspects of small business management; and
- International Trade Center (ITC), which provides training and assistance in all aspects of international trade.

In FY'89, the RCU began operation with a director, secretary, industrial services coordinator, business & government coordinator, computer specialist instructor, and two basic education instructors. In four years, full-time employees have increased from seven to 18 and part-time employees have increased from two to 45. In the first year of operation, the RCU served 2,700 individuals. In FY'92 in excess of 8,400 individuals were served through one of 14 areas directed by the RCU.

The first year of operation one industry was being served with on-site basic skills training. Today, three sites exist, each with a computer lab valued in excess of $60,000. The district also is serving 18 other industries with basic skills training through the use of two 28-foot motor homes. Each unit provides K-12 customized training and is valued in excess of $100,000.

The RCU has developed excellent working relationships with county and state officials, economic developers and the existing business and industries through the district. This has resulted in numerous partnerships and alliances that have allowed for substantial growth.

This project was initiated by the president and the board because of their commitment to having a significant input on the economic development of the state. The initial financial commitment was in excess of $280,000. The FY'92 budget was just under $1-million dollars. The first year of operation, the RCU generated revenues of 44 percent of the budget. In FY'92, after four years of operation, the RCU generated revenues in excess of 110 percent of the budget.

The RCU has been recognized in the *Bureau of National Affairs Employee Weekly*, the *Atlantic*, the *Mississippi Business Journal*, numerous employer publications, by local Chambers of Commerce, the Mississippi National Guard, and the governor of Mississippi. In October 1991, the RCU received the "Exemplary Training Award" from the Mississippi Chapter of the American Society for Training and Development (ASTD).

Contact:
Bob Mullins, Director, District
(601) 857-3312

Hinds Community College
PO Box 1263
Raymond, MS 39154-9799
Total head count enrollment-Credit: 8,806; Non-Credit: 2,413
Campuses/sites: 7; Full-time faculty: 372

HINDS COMMUNITY COLLEGE DISTRICT

SERVICES FOR THE DEAF AND HARD OF HEARING

Students are not only mainstreamed into college classes, but they also are integrated into the campus community

In 1986, a landmark post secondary program for deaf and hard of hearing students was established at Hinds Community College, Raymond Campus, through a joint agreement with the Mississippi Department of Rehabilitation Services, Division of Vocational Rehabilitation. Prior to the program at Hinds, deaf and hard of hearing students in Mississippi had to compete with hearing students with only minimal accommodation or travel to another state for post secondary training. No comprehensive program with a full line of support services was available within a four-state area. Unemployment and under-employment of deaf and hard of hearing students were rampant.

During that same year Hinds Community College, Raymond Campus was chosen as the sixth affiliate of the Post Secondary Education Consortium (PEC) whose central office is located at the University of Tennessee, Knoxville. PEC provides monitoring and funds to programs in the Southeast region to enhance the learning environment for deaf and hard of hearing students and to provide outreach services to non-affiliate programs.

Support services provide equal opportunity to enter and succeed in any of the college's existing academic, technical or vocational fields of study on the Raymond Campus. These services include but are not limited to:

1) qualified interpreters for classes, tutorial sessions, and college events;
2) career, personal/social and scholastic counseling;
3) tutors and note-takers;
4) in-service orientation and training to faculty and staff;
5) fully accessible dorms with loaner telecommunication devices (TTD's) for phone calls, televisions

Continues on Page 380

with built-in closed captioned decoders, and flashing fire alarms and doorbells;

6) loaner assistive listening devices (ALDs) such as personal FM systems, portable amplified phone handsets, and flashing/vibrating alarm clocks;

7) a one-week Summer Orientation Program for entering freshmen; and

8) a special class for transition to work or to another college.

Students are not only mainstreamed into college classes, but they are also integrated into the campus community by the provision of support services. They participate and often become leaders in extracurricular activities such as clubs, sports and special interest groups.

Services are provided to 40 to 50 deaf and hard of hearing students each semester from Mississippi, Louisiana and Arkansas. The service personnel includes a PEC administrator, a full-time coordinator, three full-time interpreters, a program counselor, a secretary, 15 part-time interpreters and a student worker. Student Support Services coordinates the provision of trained note-takers and professional tutors.

The program is funded by state monies through Vocational Rehabilitation, a grant from the Post Secondary Education Consortium and a special budget from Hinds Community College. Contributions from individuals and community organizations assist with the purchase of assistive listening/alerting devices.

The Services for the Deaf and Hard of Hearing Program has received excellent commendations in the PEC Peer Processing Evaluations. The program has been recognized in *College & Career Programs for Deaf Students*, *National On-Campus Report*, *Clarion Ledger*, and the *Disability and Rehabilitation Journal*.

Contact:
Carol Kelley, Coordinator, District
(601) 857-3310

Hinds Community College
PO Box 1263
Raymond, MS 39154-9799
Total head count enrollment-Credit: 8,806; Non-Credit: 2,413
Campuses/sites: 7; Full-time faculty: 372

TOYOTA-TECHNICAL EDUCATION NETWORK (T-TEN)

Toyota picked the college as the best venue for training entry-level technicians

In 1987, Holmes Community College, Toyota, USA, and Gulf States Toyota, Inc. formed a partnership to provide state-of-the-art automotive education. The Toyota Technical Education Network (TTEN), a new wave of automotive education, consists of Toyota dealerships, leading educational institutions and exceptional students across the nation who recognize the need for state-of-the-art automotive education. This recognition, coupled with extensive Toyota support (special service tools, equipment, vehicles, technical publications, the most advanced curricula in the industry, and financial assistance) results in an unbeatable program that is breaking new ground in automotive technology and vocational training.

Students are trained on Toyota products, with advanced automotive theory, practical classroom application and direct dealership experience working alongside a Toyota Technician. Students are pre-qualified by the school for their technical skills and problem-solving abilities. These young men and women then receive training and assistance that can help them on their way to rewarding and profitable careers within a Toyota dealership.

As technology advances, Toyota will continue to be the leader in adapting new technologies for the benefit of its customers. T-TEN provides a pool of proven, qualified and talented entry-level technicians trained to meet the growing demands of Toyota dealerships service departments. With this commitment to customer satisfaction, everyone wins – the customer, the dealership, the community, Toyota and, most importantly, the student!

Holmes Community College was selected as a training center through a process of evaluating schools for the establishment of T-TEN programs. The purpose of the process was to determine the best possible school and location to meet the needs of Toyota dealerships for entry-level technicians. The training center is one of four in the Gulf States region consisting of Oklahoma, Texas, Louisiana, Arkansas and Mississippi.

The Toyota-Specific Instructional Staff consists of instructors who are identified by the school to teach the Toyota Master Training Courses and TEAM Curriculum. These instructors have met minimum requirements as established by Toyota and are ASE certified in the areas that they teach. Toyota Training for the Specific Instructional Staff is provided by the Region/PD, and can the obtained at satellite training facilities or at the Region/PD.

The purpose of a Toyota-Specific Instructional Staff is to provide T-TEN students with instructors who are qualified to teach Toyota Master Training courses and the specific curriculum. The specific curriculum provides students with the latest automotive technical training to prepare them for employment at a Toyota dealership.

The curriculum supports the school in providing entry-level technicians trained in Toyota technology for employment at Toyota dealerships.

Computer networking will allow for nationwide communications to enhance and supplement the curriculum. Students are enrolled in the T-TEN program based on their ability to meet entrance criteria. Leadership skills are developed through the Vocational Industrial Clubs of America (VICA). VICA is an active student organization that emphasizes total quality at work, superior occupational skills, high ethical standards and pride in a job well done. Toyota recognizes VICA as the organization that will give T-TEN students an edge in gaining employment and in developing technical and interpersonal skills necessary to provide total customer satisfaction.

Contact:
Jimmy Rigby, Instructor
(601) 472-2312

Holmes Community College
PO Box 369
Goodman, MS 39079
Total head count enrollment-Credit: 3,760; Non-Credit: 2,348
Campuses/sites: 3; Full-time faculty: l05

ASTRONOMY

Major emphasis is placed on photoelectric photometry
– a relatively easy technique – of suspected visible stars

The major goal of science education is to teach the student to "do" science. This is best achieved by providing the student with the opportunity to use the scientific method on a real problem. The science of astronomy provides a wealth of research problems that are scientifically important but within the abilities of beginning students.

The astronomy course at Holmes Community College is designed to provide students with:

1) an introduction to the basic concepts of astronomy;
2) familiarity with the tools and methods of observational astronomy; and
3) the opportunity to use this knowledge to make observations of real scientific value.

The college observatory is central to the success of our astronomy program. The observatory houses a 0.35-meter Schmidt-Cassegrain telescope. The telescope is equipped to make photometric and astrometric observations of celestial objects. The observatory instrumentation includes a photodiode photometer, PMT photometer, spectrograph, filar micrometer, CCD camera and computer. The observatory instrumentation was funded, in part, by a grant from the National Science Foundation (ILI Grant #USE-9151141).

The observatory instruments are used by astronomy students to learn proper observational techniques and to obtain data on astronomical objects. Astronomy students contribute to a number of research projects at the observatory. However, major emphasis is placed on photoelectric photometry of suspected variable stars. Photoelectric photometry is a relatively easy technique to learn and observations of this type on suspected variable stars are of considerable scientific value.

The data obtained from these student observations are provided to research institutions and to organizations such as the American Association of Variable Star Observers and the Association of Lunar and Planetary Observers. A few students have presented reports of their findings at amateur astronomical society meetings. Some student projects will probably result in student publications in astronomical journals.

Contact:
Michael Burchfield, Instructor
(601) 472-2312

Holmes Community College
PO Box 369
Goodman, MS 39079
Total head count enrollment-Credit: 3,760; Non-Credit: 2,348
Campuses/sites: 3; Full-time faculty: l05

COMPUTER PROGRAMMING TECHNOLOGY

The program features state-of-the-art equipment and participates in co-op agreements with private industry

Jones County Junior College is remaining on the cutting edge of computer technology while contributing a large number of Computer Programming Technology graduates to the ranks of area employers.

Keeping up with the technology, however, can be challenging. The computer industry with hardware and software emphasis has been making dramatic changes. The availability of many different programming languages and massive changes in hardware caused many junior/community college programs to reduce the funds allocated to the program, or allow the program to cease to exist with no state-of-the-art equipment. This was due to three factors: cost of continuously changing software, cost of hardware and training/retraining competent instructors. But the Computer Programming Technology Program has shown its ability to exist in a very competitive environment. This program has developed from having one teacher, 22 freshmen, two sophomore and a very small placement in 1974, to a state-of-the-art program today. This program has five teachers, 90 freshmen, 25 sophomores and a 90 percent average placement for two-year graduates.

The largest employer in our area has more than 1,650 employees and a MIS staff of 27 with 19 MIS employees from JCJC. This firm is three blocks from a major state university. More than 80 percent of the 130 computer installations in the service area have at least one MIS professional from JCJC. The largest computer consultant in a three-state area has 75 programmer/consultants. Five of the programmer/consultants are junior college graduates and all are from JCJC. We have participated in training/re-training employees in computer utilization in more than 75 industries in our area.

JCJC Administrative MIS Director is a JCJC graduate, as are the two programmers. All on-campus software (except library applications) is written in-house. Some of the applications have been developed by students in the Systems Design classes. A group of students developed and implemented an Individual Curriculum Planning System for all vocational-technical students. This included state and federal reports. A student in this group was hired by the school and this application will be developed for the entire student body.

This program participates in co-op agreements with private industry. A firm will employ a student for a semester of co-op and then hire that student as a full-time programmer; however, this is not a requirement.

The students have the opportunity to participate in Phi Beta Lambda (PBL), a national business organization for junior/community and senior college students. JCJC Computer Programming Technology students have partic-ipated in Data Processing competitions from 1975 to the present. Students have placed in the top three in Mississippi competition for 14 years and in the top 10 nationally for four years. In addition, a 1991 graduate was recognized by *USA Today*/AACJC as one of the top 30 graduates in the nation based on her activities at JCJC and her GPA achievements.

Three program instructors were instrumental in the development of a state-wide model curriculum. This program served as a pilot school in the successful implementation of this curriculum, which all junior/community colleges must implement by 1994. The program and faculty are continuously receiving awards for excellence. The program has been recognized as a leader in curriculum, hardware, software and placement of students. It has received the Outstanding Post-Secondary Award in 1987 and in 1992. Individual faculty members have been recognized as: Jones County Outstanding Young Woman by BPW in 1988, Outstanding Business Educator for Mississippi in 1987, Outstanding Mississippian by the Jackson, MS Chapter of DPMA.

Faculty members have served or are serving as: president of the State Business Education Association, membership director in the regional business association, local county school board member, Alternative School Organization Board and as officers in DPMA, a national professional organization. In addition, instructors have served on the State Summer Conference Planning Board since its inception in 1980 and have been presenters at the conference each of those years. One faculty member has made presentations on the state, regional and national level for professional associations. All five faculty members have extensive industry experience and continue to work in private industry. Four of the five faculty members have masters degrees and meet Southern Association of Schools and Colleges(SACS) Certification for teaching computer science. This is the largest group of junior/community college SACS qualified computer technology instructors in the state.

The cost of high technology programs with state-of-the-art hardware staffed by competent qualified faculty is extremely high. A program cannot lose enrollment if they expect to continue. JCJC has maintained the same basic enrollment for the past five years while many of the other Computer Technology Programs in the state were losing enrollment. This program has maintained its profitability to the local institution and inherent value to the professional community by its willingness to change with new computer developments, a "big" ear to private industry with regard to what they want in a computer employee, and the faculty's interest in the student and the programs academic excellence. A program is only as good as the support given by the local administration and the state vocational-technical leaders. This program has received total support from these administrative leaders.

Contact:
Robert S. Landrum
(601) 477-4080

Jones County Junior College
900 South Court Street
Ellisville, MS 39437
Total head count enrollment-Credit: 4,391; Non-Credit: 630
Campuses/sites: 1; Full-time faculty: 160

AQUACULTURE PRODUCTION TECHNOLOGY

Students may enter a 12-month or a 24-month program, and each track includes hands-on instruction on three ponds

Aquaculture and especially ponding operations (the growing of food fish in above-ground ponds) has exploded across certain areas of the nation, and nowhere is that more evident than in Mississippi's Delta region bordering the Mississippi River. In 1991, a total of 300-million pounds of pond-raised, grain-fed catfish were produced on 100,000 acres of ponds, creating $300-million in revenue.

This aquaculture explosion has created a growing demand for people trained in all aspects of this relatively new industry. To fill this need, Mississippi Delta Community College developed its Aquaculture Production Technology program in 1990.

This two-tiered program provides classroom and laboratory instruction in commercial catfish culture and harvesting. Included in this is instruction in feeding, culturing, protecting and propagating commercially produced catfish.

Graduates of the Aquaculture Production Technology program at the 12-month level are awarded a Certificate of Aquaculture Production. Those who complete the 24-month program are awarded an Associate of Applied Science Degree. Employment opportunities for graduates of the certificate program exist as skilled laborers in the catfish production area and graduates of the technical program qualify as technicians or managers in this area. The program is coordinated by one full-time instructor who has several years of experience in the aquaculture area. The hands-on instruction takes place on three ponds (two five-acre, one 10-acre) with a natural biofiltration pond developed by NASA's John C. Stennis Space Center. This system allows wastewater from the producing ponds to be purified and reused.

In addition, MDCC is one of 16 Aquaculture Learning Centers in the nation. This program, funded through a USDA grant, makes the college a focal point in training post-secondary teachers from across the nation in the field of aquaculture. The college has also recently completed a partnership with Mississippi Power & Light Co. in which catfish were raised in indoor tanks using heat pump technology.

MDCC is participating in a project funded by the Mississippi Department of Energy and Transportation in which new aquaculture products and procedures can be demonstrated under actual pond conditions.

Contact:
John Park Taylor, Instructor
(601) 246-5631

Mississippi Delta Community College
PO Box 668
Moorhead, MS 38761
Total head count enrollment-Credit: 2,48; Non-Credit: 1,533
Campuses/sites: 2; Full-time faculty: 160

APPLIED TECHNOLOGY AND DEVELOPMENT CENTER

⬜ The private sector not only helped start the Center, ⬜
but also continues to remain active in its operation

Education and industry's mutual commitment to the economic development of the Mississippi Gulf Coast is clearly demonstrated at the Mississippi Gulf Coast Applied Technology and Development Center.

The education and training facility opened in 1991 and is a cooperative venture between Mississippi Gulf Coast Community College (MGCCC), Mississippi Power Company and the Harrison County Development Commission. The project epitomizes a meeting of the minds and money as state and local education, local government and private industry pooled resources to assemble a model method and facility for enhancing the development of area businesses.

The 40,000-square-foot, $2.2-million facility was funded with $1.5-million from Mississippi Power Company, $340,000 from Mississippi Gulf Coast Community College, and an equal amount from the Vocational Division of the State Department of Education. An additional $550,000 for equipment was funded by the vocational Division of the State Department of Education. Land for the Center and $50,000 for site preparation was donated by the Harrison County Development commission.

Perhaps what makes the Applied Technology and Development Center initiative different from other public and private partnerships is the fact that all entities remain actively engaged in the partnership.

The Center is owned and operated by the college; however, operating expenses are shared by the college and Mississippi Power Company. The operation of the facility is monitored by an advisory committee of representatives from the college, the state, Mississippi Power and the development commission.

The college conducts vocational skills training classes at the Center and works with the Harrison County Development Commission to provide employee training for new and existing businesses. Since opening, the college has coordinated, conducted or assisted with training for more than 50 local industries and several thousand local employees.

Mississippi Power uses the Center to conduct all employee training, from management seminars to line crews.

The Mississippi Legislature has also supported new and existing businesses by approving a 25 percent tax credit on all training dollars spent through local community colleges. The Harrison County Development Commission promotes the facility and this incentive while recruiting new industry to the area.

In addition, the Vocational Division of the State Department of Education continues to provide funds for approved industrial start-up training projects at the Center.

Contact:
Barry L. Mellinger, President
(601) 928-6380

Mississippi Gulf Coast Community College
PO Box 67
Perkinston,MS 39573
Total head count enrollment-Credit: 8,721; Non-Credit: 3,102
Campuses/sites: 7; Full-time faculty: 323

COLLEGE LITERACY PLAN

⬜ The literacy programs, once operated individually, ⬜
now are part of a coordinated effort

When the state's community and junior college's inherited the responsibility for literacy program without receiving more money to implement them, Mississippi Gulf Coast Community College decided radical change was due. College President Dr. Barry L. Mellinger sought a college literacy plan that would organize the literacy efforts of the college, generate funds for operation and meet the needs of a diverse community population. This came after at least 10 years of operating such programs as separate entities.

In 1992, a college literacy plan was developed and

approved. A Campus Literacy Manager (CLM) was placed at each main campus. CLMs coordinate the college's literacy programs with community-based organizations who serve clients in need of instruction (such as human services and youth courts) or who operate literacy programs. The CLMs search for ways that the college literacy programs can work with the local community to solve specific needs such as English as a Second Language classes. The CLM is responsible for assessing and placing the student in a appropriate program. The plan also includes a district director of literacy and adult basic skills instruction who coordinates securing grants to operate the college's literacy program.

The literacy programs have evolved into three programs: JOBS, ABE/GED and QuickStart Plus. The college operates ABE/GED classes in 10 sites over the four-county district. The ABE/GED programs include a family literacy program and a corrections program. The college is the provider of the educational component of the JOBS program for AFDC recipients. This program works closely with the New Horizons, the college's single parent/displaced homemaker program. New Horizons adds a life skills segment to the education component of the JOBS program. Through a JPTA grant, the QuickStart Plus program is serving high school drop-outs, ages 16 to 21. Located at four sites, QuickStart Plus offers seven choices for participants, including the GED, plus additional training or work experience.

In the college's service area, one-fourth of the population over 25 years of age does not have a high school diploma. The college literacy program was expected to serve about 2,000 students during 1993-94. Using $150,000 in local money (salaries and mach funds), more than $900,000 has been brought in via grants to operate the literacy programs.

After completing the literacy programs, students have continued their education by entering every kind of program the college offers. In fall 1992, 4,879 GED graduates were enrolled in Mississippi's 15 community colleges; 1,197 of those students were enrolled at Mississippi Gulf Coast Community College.

Contact:
Elizabeth Nelms
(601) 897-4371

Mississippi Gulf Coast Community College
PO Box 67
Perkinston, MS 39573
Total head count enrollment-Credit: 8,721; Non-Credit: 3,102
Campuses/sites: 7; Full-time faculty: 323

SOUTHWEST MISSISSIPPI COMMUNITY COLLEGE

VOCATIONAL ROTARY DRILLING

The program offers extensive practical training, which includes hands-on experience with drilling rigs

In 1972, plans began for the Vocational Rotary Drilling program at SMCC, and five years later the first drilling equipment was purchased. At the time, there were only three drilling programs in the nation. SMCC instructors examined these programs, patterning their own after them. The initial class was scheduled an additional six years later, with the first class graduating in 1985. At the present time, SMCC is the only public institution in the nation that offers a drilling program.

The Rotary Drilling program offers extensive practical training in water well technology as well as instruction in rig operations. In the last few years, the program has expanded to include environmental concerns. SMCC now has the equipment and resources to perform soil sampling and other environmental investigations. Students get hands-on experience with several types of drilling rigs. The majority of rotary drilling graduates are now finding employment in environmental testing areas.

Contact:
Charles Sterling, Assistant Vocational Director
(601) 276-3719

Southwest Mississippi Community College
College Drive
Summit, MS 39666
Total head count enrollment-Credit: 1,562; Non-Credit: 46
Campuses/sites: 1; Full-time faculty: 71

WATER / WASTEWATER & HAZARDOUS MATERIALS TECHNOLOGIES

▦ Program training sites range from the college campus to treatment plants ▦
throughout Missouri and other states

As our understanding of the world has grown, we have become increasingly aware of the environmental consequences of technological advances – and the need for qualified technicians who can minimize the effects of pollution and hazardous wastes. Crowder College, a training leader in this field, is preparing such people through the college's privately operated water/wastewater training facility. This facility, acquired more than a decade ago, and its training efforts have expanded to house an Environmental Resource Center.

The Center prepares students for environmental careers and assists those currently in the field to improve their technical skills. The vast array of training and consultative services currently provided through the Center encompass: water treatment, wastewater treatment, water quality, and hazardous materials handling. Training sites range from the college campus to treatment plants throughout the state of Missouri to several other states across the country.

Two degree programs in Environmental Health Technology are offered on the college campus, the Associate in Applied Science and the Associate in Arts. In addition, a vocational certificate program option is available for students who wish to pursue three semesters (12 months) of intensive training in water/wastewater treatment. Students participating in these program options receive a unique blend of academic training and practical experiences which prepare them for immediate employment. For students who are already working in the field but who want to upgrade their job skills, the training program is customized to meet their special needs. The Resource Center is in the process of establishing a degree program option in hazardous materials.

The Environmental Resource Center's Water/Wastewater Treatment training program has been designated as the only full-time, permanent training program in the state, and as such it has been developed to provide in-service and continuing education courses which meet the needs of the 5,000 certified operators in Missouri. The resulting courses range in length from one day to 10 weeks and focus upon practical operational techniques relating to specific training processes. New courses are added to the curriculum as technologies emerge or when new laboratory monitoring is required. The most recent additions to the training include a two-day biomonitoring and an industrial pre-treatment course.

Specialized training for industry, consulting engineers and municipalities is provided on a contractual basis. The specialized training projects are designed to meet the specific needs of the businesses, industries or governmental entities, and training programs are customized to the experience and educational levels of the students, the technologies in operation, and the applicable federal regulations. Training has been delivered for many companies, including the Chrysler Motor Company, Union Electric, and EFCO Industries. In addition, the ERC has provided training for 10 new treatment facilities and compliance training in more than 100 wastewater facilities through grants from the Environmental Protection Agency.

The seven-member faculty is as diverse as the training programs which are offered through the Center. They come from a variety of academic backgrounds, and all have experience in the environmental field. Thus, they incorporate first-hand knowledge from the real work-world into their classroom teaching, presenting realistic and invaluable examples and training simulations for their students.

Crowder College's Environmental Resource Center has been recognized by the Missouri Department of Natural Resources for its training efforts and has received the designation as the state's water/wastewater training program. In addition, the Environmental Protection Agency has awarded annual contract work to the center in more than 12 states. Other awards and recognitions include membership in the National Small Flows Clearing House Advisory Committee, receipt of the 1990 Environmental Education Award presented by the National Environmental Training Association, and special recognition by the Missouri Water Wastewater Association and the Region VII Environmental Protection Agency for instructional excellence.

Contact:
Lorene Lindsay, Environmental Resource Center Director
(417) 451-4700

Crowder College
601 Laclede
Neosho, MO 64850
Total head count enrollment-Credit: 1,632; Non-Credit: 1,500
Campuses/sites: 1;Full-time faculty: 68

MISSOURI ALTERNATIVE AND RENEWABLE ENERGY TECHNOLOGY CENTER

In addition to providing a unique alternative energy transfer curriculum, the Center sponsors and annual summer institute for high school juniors and seniors

All levels of society must answer the call to alleviate the escalating concerns associated with the status of today's environment. Crowder College is doing that by creating first-hand opportunities for its students to explore the effects of alternative sources of energy. These opportunities not only have led the students to develop a deeper understanding of environmental issues and potential solutions but also have enabled them to study and communicate with other people from across the nation and the world.

Based upon the college's endeavors in the area of alternative energy, the governor of Missouri has signed a bill which designates Crowder College as the Missouri Alternative and Renewable Energy Technology (MARET) Center. This designation has paved the way for the college to expand its extracurricular focus beyond solar technology through the introduction of a formal program of instruction in multiple alternative energy sources. The program has been developed after consulting with several resources, including the Engineering Program Transfer Coordinator at the University of Missouri at Rolla, area industry representatives, and governmental agencies such as the Department of Energy and the Department of Natural Resources. A review of employment opportunities and national trends completed another phase within the curriculum development activities.

Since the planning process highlighted the strengths of providing hands-on, project-oriented learning opportunities, the curriculum was structured to include one applied research course each semester. Each of these courses has been organized to enhance the computational, analytical, and problem solving skills of the students and to provide an avenue for continuous self assessment. The remainder of the alternative energy curriculum includes mathematics, science and general education courses.

In addition to providing a unique alternative energy transfer curriculum, the Missouri Alternative and Renewable Energy Technology (MARET) Center sponsors

an annual Alternative Energy Summer Institute for high school juniors and seniors. To date, the institute has attracted students from across Missouri, and plans include opening the program to students from other states. The Center also engages in cooperative applied research projects with area industries and serves as a clearing house for the dissemination of energy information. Another focus of the Center includes the provision of educational outreach services to the Missouri public schools, through which the college's solar car has traveled to schools all over the state.

Resources which have acted as the catalyst for the college's alternative energy focus have included several full-time faculty and high-level administrators. Through their vision and creativity, the college has aggressively pursued and secured a number of public and private grants which have provided the necessary supplies and equipment to move the alternative energy program forward.

The visibility gained through the development of Crowder College's three solar cars (the first became the first vehicle to cross the country using only sunlight for energy; the second was the first to race across a continent and placed second among American competitors in an Australian race; and the third car competed not only in the GM SunRayce from Orlando to Detroit, placing fifth out of 32 college and university entries, but also raced in the second Australian World Solar Challenge, taking second in its class) has led to a recent invitation to participate in an international road rally sponsored by the Japanese government. The college's selection was based upon a recommendation from the U.S. Department of Energy, which cited excellence in design and level of educational activities in the field of alternative sources of energy as the basis for the recommendation. Further recognition has come in the form of a planning grant from the Environmental Improvement and Energy Resources Authority to design a facility which models the latest developments in energy efficient technologies.

Contact:
Arthur Boyt, Program Director
(417) 451-4700

Crowder College
601 Laclede
Neosho, MO 64850
Total head count enrollment-Credit: 1,632; Non-Credit: 1,500
Campuses/sites: 1;Full-time faculty: 68

SCIENCE CENTER

The Center has more than 60 demonstrations and experiments that are loaned to elementary and secondary science teachers to use in their classrooms

To increase science teachers' effectiveness and improve student achievement, East Central College formed a Science Center for elementary and secondary teachers in 1990. Specific factors that influenced the development of the Center were:

1) low test scores on standardized science tests;
2) limited amounts of science equipment in all schools;
3) teachers who are very uncomfortable teaching; and
4) most science curricula are not stimulating, thus making it difficult to teach science.

East Central College's Science Center, funded through three separate Eisenhower Grants, has more than 60 demonstrations and experiments that are loaned without charge to teachers for use in their classrooms. Most of these demonstrations and experiments are either too expensive for the individual schools to purchase, or they represent materials that are not readily available through ordinary science suppliers. To enhance their understand-

ing of the experiments, teachers have participated in 16-week workshops in which they have assisted in constructing and assembling the equipment. Besides the teachers participating in these workshops, advanced secondary science students and undergraduates interested in pursuing teaching also assisted in constructing and assembling the materials. The reason for having students participate in these workshops with the teachers was to stimulate interest in careers in science and teaching and to provide closer interactions between students and teachers.

As interest in the loan program quickly increased, teachers requested the assistance from undergraduate students to assist them in presenting materials in their classrooms. During a 16-week workshop, East Central College under graduates provided 1,100 hours of assistance to science teachers. Teachers were better able to teach science, while undergraduates were able to receive valuable teaching experience. Since the inception of the Science Center, the scores on standardized tests have significantly increased among participating teachers.

Contact:
Patrick Woolley, Science Department Manager
(314) 583-5195

East Central College
PO Box 529
Union, MO 63084
Total head count enrollment-Credit: 4,881; Non-Credit: 1,500
Campuses/sites: 3;Full-time faculty: 59

DENTAL ASSISTING OPEN-ENTRY / EXIT

Non-traditional students make up at least half of the enrollment, thanks to a flexibly scheduled program

An open entry/open exit format has nearly doubled enrollment in a once-declining Dental Assisting Program at East Central College. Besides increasing enrollment – and literally saving the program from extinction – the format change:

1) attracts the non-traditional student such as the adults wishing to re-enter school and/or the work force;
2) better serves the dental community and community at large by allowing students to enter on any day of any week, choosing their own pace for completion, therefore graduating at different times of the year; and
3) prepares more students with the knowledge and skills to become certified dental assistants by working more closely with the student on a one-to-one basis.

The program was patterned after the Dental Assisting Program at Pinellas Technical Education Center in St. Petersburg, Florida. However, since their entire school operates on this concept and it is a vocational program, many changes and decisions had to be made by our administration and faculty to fit this one program into a traditional junior college setting.

Classes are not structured (lecture/lab) – the student works at their own pace by studying from self-instructional materials. This self-paced learning creates less frustration as the student is working at their own speed; and they are competing with no one but themselves. Also, they work with the instructors individually, which helps them better understand how to perform the skills necessary to a dental assistant.

The new open entry/exit program has attracted not only the young traditional students but also the non-traditional students, who make up at least half of the enrollment. The flexibility of the program attracts those who are working, mothers with young children, as well as mature adults. Those students who are full-time have completed the certificate program in 8-1/2 to 11 months (11 months being the normal time to complete). Those who are part-time students have up to two years to complete. In addition, a student has the option of completing 20 more credit hours of general education to receive an AAS degree in Dental Assisting.

The new program cut the faculty from two full-time, two part-time faculty to two full-time faculty, with the proviso that should enrollment increase beyond a 1:12 ratio, part-time faculty would again be engaged.

This type of program required more audio/visual aids than a traditional type. Monies for the needed equipment and learning resources were provided by the Carl Perkins Act with matching funds from the college.

The program has been well received by the public and the dental community. Enthusiasm for the program seems to be growing, people being a good source of publicity. The open-entry/exit program has been recognized by feature articles in the local newspapers.

Contact:
Jacqueline Hartz, Director, Allied Health
(314) 583-5193

East Central College
PO Box 529
Union, MO 63084
Total head count enrollment-Credit: 4,881; Non-Credit: 1,500
Campuses/sites: 3;Full-time faculty: 59

VETERINARY TECHNOLOGY

Adjacent to the college are 305 acres of pastureland with outbuildings and pens used for the care and studies of large animals

Jefferson College is located with a unique relationship to St. Louis that allows exposure to all aspects of veterinary biochemical industries and provides excellent opportunities for experience in farm animal technology.

The curriculum for the Veterinary Technology program was developed with the assistance of St. Louis area veterinarians under the guidance of the program director (a licensed veterinarian with 20-plus years of experience in laboratory animal care, specializing in experimental surgery as well as extensive mixed-animal practice).

The program is housed in a college facility that was specifically designed for clinical training and is equipped with modern state-of-the-art veterinary equipment. Adjacent to the college are 305 acres of pastureland with outbuildings and pens used for the care and studies of large animals.

Students successfully completing the two-year program in Veterinary Technology, including a required summer internship, are awarded the Associate of Applied Science degree. The program provides for the combined study of college-level general education courses and extensive coursework in science and veterinary technology theory and practice. Both the Missouri and American Veterinary Medical Associations have committees that promote rigid guidelines for accreditation of veterinary technology programs to ensure high-quality training in both the academic and practical instruction. The Jefferson College program, begun in 1976, has been accredited by both of these associations. Qualified technicians are registered with the state of Missouri after successfully completing their state board examinations. Students graduating from the program are also encouraged to apply for the American Association of Animal Science Certification.

The program, one of two certified programs in the state of Missouri and one of 68 nationwide, offers the student a wide range of career paths in the veterinary technology career field. The Jefferson College graduate may be employed by veterinarians, research farms, research hospitals, universities, drug companies or the federal government. A considerable number of graduates continue on with their education and complete a DVM. Typically, job placement after successful completion of the program is about 100 percent with the majority of the students taking positions as laboratory and veterinary assistants.

The Veterinary Technology program at Jefferson College has an active advisory committee that has been responsible for helping to initiate the program, change the curriculum, donate equipment, and provide tours, speakers and job placement information.

Contact:
Joe White, Chair, Occupations Division
(314) 789-3951

Jefferson College
1000 Viking Drive
Hillsboro, MO 63050
Total head count enrollment-Credit: 4,129; Non-Credit: 4,450
Campuses/sites: 2;Full-time faculty: 105

LASER-ELECTRO-OPTICS TECHNOLOGY

*▓ Each lab is equipped with a closed-circuit camera and intercom to aid ▓
in monitoring student progress and to ensure safety rules are enforced*

In the mid-to-late 1980's, when few institutions offered a two-year Associate of Applied Science degree in Laser Electro-Optics Technology, Jefferson College stepped forward with its own program.

The need for such programs had been a growing since the laser was invented more than 30 years ago. Over the years a number of four-year college curriculums have been developed to train individuals in the engineering and research disciplines that have been needed to advance laser technology. But as lasers left the research stage to be used in practical applications, such as in the manufacturing and medical fields, the need for those with technician skills has been building. There has been a demand for people who can build, modify, install, operate, troubleshoot and repair lasers.

The two-year program is also unique in that it provides a good deal of hands-on experience for the student in five well-equipped laboratories. Each lab is equipped with a closed-circuit camera and an intercom to aid in monitoring student progress and to ensure that safety rules are enforced. This laboratory complex includes the following laser types: Helium Neon; Dye; Argon Ion; Carbon Dioxide; Copper Vapor; Diode; Nd: YAG, CW; and Pulsed.

One goal of the program is to provide realistic laboratory experiences for 50 percent of the total time available. This lab/lecture balance has aided in student placement.

The curriculum consists of seven laser electro-optics courses, six electronics courses, as well as math, physics and general education courses. Graduates of the program are prepared to immediately enter the job market because of skills obtained in the areas of laser safety, laser operation procedures, optical alignments, optical system integration, electro-optical device modulation, beam parameter measurements and component quality analysis.

The Laser Electro-Optics program at Jefferson College has an active advisory committee that has been responsible for helping to initiate the program, change the curriculum, donate equipment and provide tours, speakers and job placement information. In May 1988, the first Laser Electro-Optics students graduated. At the present time, it is the only full two-year Laser Electro-Optics program in Missouri.

Contact:
Fred Thies, Chair, Technology Division
(314) 789-3951

Jefferson College
1000 Viking Drive
Hillsboro, MO 63050
Total head count enrollment-Credit: 4,129; Non-Credit: 4,450
Campuses/sites: 2;Full-time faculty: 105

AUTOMOTIVE TECHNOLOGY

*▓ The centerpiece of the college's automotive program is its ▓
34,000-square-foot High Technology Building*

The nationally acclaimed Automotive Technology program at Longview Community College (one of the Metropolitan Community Colleges of Kansas City, Missouri) trains competent people for positions in the automotive industry, upgrades existing personnel and responds to the industry's training needs. The centerpiece of Longview's automotive program is its 34,000-square-foot High Technology Building. The facility has four large dedicated laboratories with the latest in diagnostic equipment, well-equipped classrooms, a well-stocked parts room and a library of reference and repair manuals. And the demand for technical training is growing as the sophistication of automobiles increases.

A major component of the program's success is the strong, formal partnerships Longview has developed with General Motors Corporation, Ford Motor Company and Toyota. These corporate partners provide much of the diagnostic equipment, cars, reference and repair manuals and in-service training for Longview instructors. All instructors are certified by the National Automotive Technician Education Foundation. The company partners, along with their dealerships from across the region, look upon Longview as their training partner for current and future employees.

Students can elect specialized automotive technology courses that train them to work as General Motors, Ford or Toyota automotive service technicians. Automotive Technology students earn the Associate in Applied Science degree, or a certificate of proficiency. The program offers students other choices as well. Areas of study include auto mechanics, automotive merchandising (sales, service management and customer relations) or heavy equipment (trucks, buses, stationary engines and equipment for construction, excavation and mining).

Unlike many vocational programs, Longview automotive students spend about two-thirds of the time working in the program and about one-third in regular liberal arts courses. Technical students learn communication skills, consumer attitudes, computer skills, work ethic and attitude as a part of a total education package.

Where the Automotive program doesn't have formal partnerships, it has proactively sought to provide both facilities and expertise to companies such as Nissan Motors, Hyundai and other auto makers to train service personnel. These companies also have contributed cars, equipment and reference materials for their various models. The program received the Motor Vehicle Manufacturers Association's "Award for Excellence" for post-secondary education in 1988. Two years later, the Automotive Technology program was named one of the nation's 10 best vocational programs by then-U.S. Secretary of Education Lauro Cavazos, for "achieving the highest standards of excellence in vocational education."

Contact:
William H. Fairbanks, (816) 672-2061
Donald V. Loegering, (816) 672-2295

Longview Community College
500 SW Longview Road
Lee's Summit, MO 64081
Total head count enrollment-Credit: 15,439; Non-Credit: 3,659
Campuses/sites: 2;Full-time faculty: 100

PROGRAM FOR ADULT COLLEGE EDUCATION (PACE)

An integrated approach to instruction is a significant reason for the program's success

The story of PACE as a nationally credible model for serving working adults is well-established. The secret of that success is flexible evening and weekend scheduling and a curriculum of intense academic clusters or "blocks." Since 1979, this flexibility has provided a means for working adults with busy schedules to take college classes and earn an associate's degree in just two years. PACE students attend one weeknight class (usually for four hours) at a convenient location of their choice, watch a video tape course at home (four 1/2-hour tapes each week), and attend a weekend conference (Friday evening and a full day Saturday and Sunday) once a month. Students can complete a liberal arts program in two years if they go to summer school and earn either an Associate in Arts transfer degree, or an associate's degree with a business emphasis.

Each block equals 12 credit hours. Five blocks plus two credit hours comprise the 62 credits needed to graduate. In each cluster the courses are related to each other by theme. The academic blocks include ethics and social science, English and humanities, philosophy and social science, advanced humanities, and science and math. Students welcome the assurance as adults that they will be in the company of other working adults in small classes with personalized instruction. Usually they are responsible to only one teacher for all three courses in a block, which reduces stress and further integrates learning.

Team teaching on the weekends is another critical component of PACE. PACE instructors and their integrated approach to instruction are largely responsible for its success. Working together, multiple instructors are utilized to create a reinforced learning experience. Characterized as an "eclectic" group, they are dedicated and caring, experienced and enthusiastic. A certain camaraderie exists among both instructors and students. PACE students have access to all student services available at Longview Community College, including child care, career and personal counseling library, services for handicapped and more. They are the only students who enjoy the convenience of telephone enrollment.

More than 1,000 students enroll in Longview's PACE each semester. Because the convenience of PACE is one of the hallmarks of its remarkable success, PACE has expanded to more than a dozen learning sites around the Kansas City metropolitan area. The program has been so successful over the years that the University of Missouri-Kansas City adopted the model for junior-level and senior-level course work. It is now possible to transfer from Longview's PACE to the university's PACE and earn a bachelor's degree.

PACE has grown to about 12 percent of Longview's total enrollment. At the same time, PACE students constitute al most 25 percent of the graduating class. In the words of one student, "PACE showed me college wasn't learning *what* to think but *how* to think."

Contact:
Sarah A. Hopkins, Program Director
(816) 672-2215

Longview Community College
500 SW Longview Road
Lee's Summit, MO 64081
Total head count enrollment-Credit: 15,439; Non-Credit: 3,659
Campuses/sites: 2;Full-time faculty: 100

PRIVATE-SECTOR EMPLOYEE TRAINING

※ *Companies involved must be engaged in manufacturing, research* ※
and development, or provide services in interstate commerce

Maple Woods Community College joined with Wilcox Electric, Inc., in launching an employee training program that is the first in Missouri to take advantage of a state law aimed at helping growing companies expand and train new workers.

The law, passed in 1990 by the Missouri General Assembly, evolved from legislation introduced under House Bill 1364, known as the Missouri Community College New Jobs Training Program. The bill is designed to assist not only companies that want to relocate to Missouri but also to help existing businesses expand.

In taking advantage of the new law, Wilcox officials implemented a company-wide "shared leadership" program to train new workers for their expanding work force. Under the program, Wilcox workers make recommendations for ensuring employee work quality and productivity. The program was implemented with the help of the Metropolitan Community Colleges District of Kansas City, which includes Maple Woods.

Wilcox manufactures electronic navigational systems, primarily for aircraft. The training program is offered at the company's 320,000-square-foot manufacturing plant in Kansas City North.

The new law works like this: Companies that are interested in starting an employee training program can collaborate with a Missouri community college to create a training program. The state Department of Economic Development must approve the plan. Then the community college issues "training certificates" (similar to bonds), for the amount of money needed to pay for the training. Companies in the program may guarantee the certificates or they may be publicly sold. Part of the new workers' state income tax is earmarked to repay the certificate. The company does not get cash or tax credits from the state. It's the workers' income tax that pays for their training.

Companies that are eligible to participate in the state program must be engaged in manufacturing, research and development, or provide services in interstate commerce. Types of training eligible for funding include customized training, adult basic education, on-the-job training or occupational skills training.

Wilcox has hired about 200 employees under its training program and was to hire about 50 more through 1993. The Metropolitan Community Colleges sold about $850,000 in training certificates to finance the Wilcox program. For the first 100 employees hired under the program, 2.5 percent of their state income tax will go to retire the training certificates. For any additional employees, 1.5 percent goes to the certificate fund. The remainder of the income tax, up to a maximum of 6 percent, goes to the general fund.

Contact:
Stephen R. Brainard
(816) 437-3044

Maple Woods Community College
2601 NE Barry Road
Kansas City, MO 64156
Total head count enrollment-Credit: 4,959; Non-Credit: 1,381
Campuses/sites: 2;Full-time faculty: 60

PROJECT SUCCESS

※ *Students may participate in individual counseling to address specific areas* ※
that serve as barriers to personal and professional growth

The Project Success program at Moberly Area Community college tries to help at-risk female students improve their financial lot through a career and life skills class, individual counseling, mentoring and internships. This project is a joint effort between the Job Training and Partnership Act, the Missouri Council on Women's Economic Development and Training and Moberly Area Community College.

Twenty women who are eligible for JTPA funding, have been selected to be participants in the program. An additional 20 women have been asked to participate in a control group, which consists of taking the evaluation measures only.

Phase 1 consists of the Life and Career Skills class, which provides experiences and group support in developing self-esteem, self-awareness healthy coping styles, assertive communication, healthy relationships and vocational exploration. Students also have the opportunity to participate in individual counseling to address specific areas which serve as barriers to their personal and professional growth.

Phase 2 will focus on the refinement and application of personal and professional attitudes, skills and behaviors. Specific interventions will include a professional mentoring program, internship opportunities and a weekly seminar to provide continued support and guidance.

At the end of the project, the control and treatment groups will be compared to determine the effectiveness of the educational interventions in the hopes of providing this as a working model for other educational institutions.

Contact:
Ruth Ann Finck, Dean, Vocational Education
(816) 263-4110

Moberly Area Community College
College Avenue and Rollins Street
Moberly, MO 65270
Total head count enrollment-Credit: 1,653
Campuses/sites: 1;Full-time faculty: 40

STAFF DEVELOPMENT AND LITERACY RESOURCE CENTER

The Center provides the necessary tools and services to produce a well-trained, competent force of adult educators

The Missouri ABE Staff Development and Literacy Resource Center trains teachers, literacy coordinators, ABE directors and staff through workshops and practical training. The Center, at Moberly Area Community College, specifically offers training and staff development that includes Teacher Certification Workshops, Literacy Coordinator training, technology training and specialized in-service workshops.

Teacher Certification Workshops are offered as two- or three-day workshops and are held monthly at Moberly Area Community College. All beginning teachers are required to attend a certification workshop in order to teach Adult Basic Education in Missouri. Experienced ABE teachers are required to attend at least every other year. During the summer months, certification workshops are held on university or community college campuses across the state. College credit is granted for the workshops and applies toward the requirements for a Missouri five-year ABE certificate. The coordination and arrangements for all the certification workshops are handled by the Missouri ABE Staff Development and Literacy Resource Center.

Literacy coordinator training is also offered. This workshop is designed to acquaint new literacy coordinators with the state and federal guidelines for the use of literacy funds, with methods of training tutors, and ways to facilitate tutors and new adult readers. It also addresses the important issues of confidentiality, goal-setting, coordination, and management of tutor training materials. All literacy coordinators associated with Missouri's Adult Basic Education programs are required to attend this training.

In addition, the Department of Elementary & Secondary Education, ABE teachers, and ABE directors are very interested in using technology to reach the new adult reader, as well as other adult learners who could benefit from adult Basic Education. New hardware and software designed for adults is frequently evaluated by the ABE Staff Development and Literacy Resource Center. As new technology becomes available to Missouri's ABE programs, the purchase, dissemination and training are also provided by the Center.

Specialized in-service training may consist of small in-services or two- to three- day workshops. The topics are those that are requested by the state's Adult Basic Education teachers and directors or by the state director of Missouri Adult Basic Education. Contributing to the in-service effort is a lending library of tapes, videos, books and other materials that directors and teachers may borrow at any time.

The goal of the ABE Staff Development and Literacy Resource Center is to provide the necessary tools and services to produce a well-trained, competent force of adult educators for the state of Missouri.

Contact:
Evelyn Jorgenson, Director
(816) 263-4110

Moberly Area Community College
College Avenue and Rollins Street
Moberly, MO 65270
Total head count enrollment-Credit: 1,653
Campuses/sites: 1;Full-time faculty: 40

FRANCIS CHILD DEVELOPMENT INSTITUTE

The Institute brings together four major child care training components under one umbrella for an effective and efficient operation

When the Francis Child Development Institute began in 1990 as the Francis Child Development Resource Center, it was one of the first of its kind in the nation. The program provided free, on-site services to child care center staff and home care providers. Its goal was to reduce the risk of problem students in the inner city later on by teaching child care workers to deliver high quality, comprehensive services to children and families. Through its programs the Francis Center sought to promote the healthy growth and development of children. The Francis Center met its objectives by reaching out to child care centers and family day care providers in the central city, helping them to provide comprehensive child development services to children in their care and their families. Services included: early childhood education; nutrition; dental and medical screenings; social services; high quality child care; and parent education and involvement.

The Francis Center expanded to the Institute in 1991 and began to offer more opportunities for child-care training and education. The Institute provides a model continuum of traditional and innovative training options, for career-seeking students and for existing personnel in the early childhood care and education field. The program is now a unique organization that brings together four major child care training components under one umbrella for an effective and efficient operation – the Child Development Center, a Resource Center, an Early Childhood Academic program, and a Pre-service/In-service Program.

Penn Valley maintained a Child Development Center for 20 years that served students, employees and the community. The Center has also been a resource for field placements for child growth and development, psychology and nursing students at Penn Valley. In 1990 the Center was replaced with a state-of-the-art facility that serves as a laboratory in which students and care providers can observe an excellent developmentally appropriate early childhood environment in action. The lab is staffed by early childhood trained personnel and students, and includes three well-equipped classrooms, an outdoor play space, a multi-cultural library, and a computer for each classroom. Staff: one coordinator, two teachers, students.

The Resource Center services have remained essentially the same since its inception. Recently the Center entered into collaboration with the Kansas City, Missouri, School District and the KCMC Child Development Corporation and has screened more than 500 inner-city children. Staff: one coordinator, three resource specialists.

The Early Childhood Academic Program is offered through Penn Valley's Human Science and Education Division and includes a variety of courses such as Child Growth and Development, Health and Safety, Nutrition, Literature, and Issues and Theories. Students can earn a certificate in Child Growth and Development either on or off campus. The field-based program is competency- and performance-based contractual education. Students may also choose to pursue an Associate in Applied Science degree by combining the certificate coursework with additional college requirements. An Associate in Arts degree also can be earned.

The staff includes one full-time faculty member, a Child Development Associate (CDA) coordinator and 60+ faculty advisors.

The Pre-service/In-service Program offers CDA training and technical assistance related to early childhood care and education at a number of sites in Greater Kansas City. Through the expanded program, providers can receive in-service and on-the-job training that helps prepare them to pursue a CDA credential.

Recently, Institute services have expanded and include:

1) adding a research technician to collect and analyze data;
2) adding a resource specialist to focus on improved child care services to children with special needs;
3) creating incentives for provider participation in training;
4) developing a school-age child care program and curriculum; and
5) upgrading the skills of Institute staff.

This program was funded initially through a multi-year grant from the Francis Families Foundation administered through the Greater Kansas City Community Foundation and Affiliated Trusts. It is made possible through a unique public-private partnership with Penn Valley and KCMC Child Development Corporation, the local Head Start sponsor which provides consulting and technical assistance for program development. Approximately $1-million in grants and contributions have been received from the Francis Families Foundation, the Metropolitan Community College District, Penn Valley, AT&T, the Vocational funds of the Missouri Department of Elementary and Secondary Education, the George L. and Dolly F. LaRue Trust of the Greater Kansas City Community Foundation and Affiliated Trusts, reimbursements from the Child and Adult Care Food Program and the Missouri Division of Family Services, and student and parents' fees

A major strength of the Francis Child Development Institute is that it is a model of a true public/private partnership. Key partners were not only involved in the initial conception of the Institute, but they remain actively involved in its financial support and in its program implementation and policy oversight. The Institute's director also holds the position of Associate Dean of Instructional Services in order to ensure that the Institute, as a comprehensive entity, is fully integrated into Penn Valley's organizational structure

The Francis Child Development Institute was cited in *Child Care Challenge*, a report issued by the Select Committee on Children, Youth, and Families of the U.S. House of Representatives. The publication highlighted child care centers nationwide that provide working families with innovative and creative services

---

Contact:
Carole L. Ellison, Associate Dean, Instructional Services
(816) 759-4352

Penn Valley Community College
3201 Southwest Trafficway
Kansas City, MO 64111
Total headcount enrollment-Credit: 5,842; Non-Credit: 17,500
Campuses/sites: 3; Full-time faculty: 98

PENN VALLEY COMMUNITY COLLEGE

PRE-APPRENTICE LINEWORKER TRAINING

Students receive hands-on training in all facets of power line construction and maintenance by a veteran lineworker instructor

A Pre-Apprentice Lineworker Training Program Task Force was formed in 1989 to explore the prospect of developing a local program to be a source of screened, trained helpers to bid into lineworker apprentice positions with area utilities. The following problems were identified:

1) the lack of women and minorities employed as lineworkers or apprentices;

2) the selection of unsuitable employees and their later elimination from the program because of an inability to climb poles;

3) the investment of training dollars on employees who leave the program to return to the remote geographical areas from which they were recruited; and

4) the lack of community involvement (i.e. very few Kansas City area applicants).

Penn Valley (representing the Metropolitan Community College District) and the Kansas City Power & Light Company (KCPL) collaborated to develop the Pre-Apprentice Lineworker Training Program, which was designed to accomplish the following goals:

1) provide a pool of pre-tested, drug-screened, qualified applicants for helper and apprentice positions with area utilities;

2) provide a qualified pool of minority and female applicants for lineworker apprentice positions;

3) provide qualified employees for lineworker apprentice positions who exhibit the least probability of leaving a company and/or the program prematurely because of an inability to climb poles; and

4) aggressively obtain placement slots for each trainee who successfully completes the program.

The unique partnership was launched in October 1990, with 17 students enrolled in the 32-week program. Women and minorities were especially targeted in recruitment efforts, and applicants were subject to substance screenings upon entering and completing training. Because KCPL and Penn Valley wanted to eliminate financial barriers that would discourage qualified applicants from enrolling, KCPL pledged grants to Penn Valley for aid to students whose financial need would otherwise prevent them from entering the program. More than 120 applicants underwent a battery of physical and academic tests to be considered for admission. Students received hands-on training in all facets of power line construction and maintenance by a veteran KCPL lineworker instructor.

Both the training and academic requirements were completed at Penn Valley's Pioneer Campus. Two specially designed pole fields were set up, at the Pioneer Campus and at an additional site within blocks of the Pioneer Campus, to facilitate lineworkers' training. Program instruction is divided between classroom lecture and lab work, with most of the lab time spent outdoors. Students gained experience in building overhead and underground power lines while they dealt with the full range of weather conditions.

Hands-on training provided all facets of power line construction and maintenance, including climbing; framing and setting of poles; hanging, connecting and banking of transformers; stringing overhead, underground, primary, secondary and service wires; and driving, maintaining and operating a backhoe, trencher, and various digger trucks. Graduates also received completion cards in the American Red Cross MultiMedia First Aid Course and the American Heart Association Cardiac-Pulmonary Resuscitation Course.

Twelve participants successfully completed the program in the first year (May, 1991) and were hired as Helpers by KCPL, and to date, seven of them are in KCPL's Lineman/Splicer Apprentice Program (KCPL is committed to hiring at least 14 graduates per year for three years). Fifteen students successfully completed the second class and 14 were recently hired by KCPL. One student was referred to other utilities.

The program has been expanded to include students from the Illinois Electric Company in Peoria, and KCPL has expressed an interest in further developing the training to serve as a hiring pool for all labor/trade classifications.

Continues on Page 396

Program funding has been provided by KCPL in the form of scholarships ($70,000 per year less $35,000 reimbursement for instructor); initial vehicles ($18,000 in-kind); the initial program instructor; and personal equipment ($7,000). Penn Valley has provided its Pioneer Campus for academic classes and vehicle storage; one training field; academic program development; maintenance and upkeep of building and grounds; maintenance of equipment; and program administration. The City of Kansas City, Missouri, provided fenced land and temporary buildings for the off-campus training field; water and electrical hookups for the training field; and interaction in and liaison with the local community for support.

The Pre-Apprentice Lineworker Training Program has been featured on local television newscasts as well as in the June 20, 1991, edition of *The Kansas City Star* newspaper.

Contact:
Jack Bitzenburg, Dean, Continuing Education
(816) 759-4055

Penn Valley Community College
3201 Southwest Trafficway
Kansas City, MO 64111
Total headcount enrollment-Credit: 5,842; Non-Credit: 17,500
Campuses/sites: 3; Full-time faculty: 98

ST. CHARLES COUNTY COMMUNITY COLLEGE

INSTRUCTIONAL RESOURCES

✦ *Because the entire campus is wired with EtherNet, faculty and staff may use* ✦
their personal computers to search for information in the library

When the future looks toward a virtual library without walls, when the collection itself is not as important as the ability to get information, when articles can be delivered on demand in 24 hours so that ownership is not as important as being able to deliver information in a timely fashion – when all this is true, how do you design a library building?

St. Charles County Community College is a new community college which moved to a permanent campus in January 1992. The first phase of construction included four buildings: academic/administration, instructional resources center, student center and physical services. All four buildings and offices and classrooms within these buildings are wired for voice (telephone), data (EtherNet), and video (RF distribution) to provide maximum access to all means of communication.

The Instructional Resources Center (IRC) houses the minicomputer used for the library automation system. The computer is connected directly to the EtherNet backbone. Also on the EtherNet in the library is a Novell network with WordPerfect and other utility programs. All workstations in the library are personal computers rather than "dumb" terminals. They are connected to the EtherNet and either access the Novell fileserver or pass through the Novell to the minicomputer. Thus staff members have powerful workstations with access to the integrated automation system, word processing, a database manager, and the ability to use CD-ROM readers. Students have on-line public access workstations, which will eventually allow them to download information to a disk or take advantage of a graphic user interface.

To maximize access and minimize response time for automated periodical indexes, selected periodical indexes will be loaded on the mini-computer with the library automation system. An interface with the library automation system allows access to the periodical indexes using the same search strategy as the catalog. A patron at any public access workstation can choose to search either the on-line catalog or periodical indexes. For those databases available only on CD-ROM, a CD-ROM tower is connected to the EtherNet backbone to allow access from every workstation.

A leased line to Internet via the Missouri Research and Education Network is attached to the EtherNet backbone allowing every workstation connected to EtherNet access to library catalogs and remote databases throughout the world. In addition, a gateway on the library automation system gives any designated workstation the ability to dial out. Staff members can dial out to order books electronically, to use OCLC for cataloging or interlibrary loan, or to access local library catalogs. Patrons can dial in to the library system as well.

Since the entire campus is wired with EtherNet, faculty and staff can use their personal computers from their offices in other buildings to search for information in the library. Library staff members can also access the administrative computer to place flags on the records of students with outstanding fines. While it is necessary to build a library with walls, present technology allows these walls to define a space without limiting access to resources beyond these walls.

Contact:
Joan Clarke
(314) 922-8470

St. Charles County Community College
4601 Mid Rivers Mall Drive
St. Peters, MO 63376-0975
Total head count enrollment-Credit: 4,631; Non-Credit: 5,576
Campuses/sites: 1; Full-time faculty: 55

DEAF COMMUNICATIONS STUDIES

Besides teaching American Sign Language, courses also make students aware of such things as the interpreters codes of ethics and deaf culture

There is a growing awareness and sensitivity to the educational needs of disabled students. Recent requirements of the Americans with Disabilities Act have increased expectations of accommodation and service to the disabled – in the classroom, workplace or out in the community.

St. Louis Community College at Florissant Valley has long offered an array of programs designed to assist those who work with the disabled and impaired, ranging from sign language workshops, American Sign Language courses (ASL), "Silent Weekend" encounters, and sessions on deaf culture and communication. In 1982, the campus developed a Deaf Communications Studies emphasis to its associate degree in communications arts.

DCS primarily stresses mastery of ASL, but also includes courses to make students aware of the interpreters code of ethics, deaf culture and variations in signing and interpretation, and the importance of flexibility and creativity. DCS students learn an entirely new language (ASL), as well as how to effectively communicate that language to others. Students learn to interpret meaning rather than merely translate words.

The program makes extensive use of college labs. Interpreting sessions are taped for review and a special signing lab provides students extensive interpreting experience. In addition, each student is required to complete 50 hours of interpreting practicum at a local business, agency, school or office. They also develop interpreting skills by working with deaf students on campus.

DCS meets the needs of a variety of students. In addition to those looking for a career in the rapidly growing field, it provides formal instruction for those with skills but no training.

An increasing number of DCS students are professionals who wish to communicate directly with their impaired clients or patients. Florissant Valley also is a member of a six-school consortium, headed by Johnson County (KS) Community College, that provides up-to-date interpreting skills training for those employed in the field.

DCS is one part of a network of related programs for disabled and hearing impaired. The college sponsors the Florissant Valley Theatre of the Deaf, and the campus theatre was the first in St. Louis to sign performances.

Contact:
Geneva Shearburn, Program Coordinator
(314) 595-2025

St. Louis Community College at Florissant Valley
400 Pershall Road
St. Louis, MO 63135-1499
Total head count enrollment-Credit: 10,405; Non-Credit: 6,896
Campuses/sites: 1;Full-time faculty: 138

HYPERTEXT COLLEGE CATALOG

An on-disk college catalog similar to this one should be easy for most colleges to create because the contents probably exist on disk in some form

Using a program for IBM compatible PCs, St. Louis Community College has developed an on-disk, hypertext college catalog. The on-disk catalog efficiently cross-references a huge volume of text, providing rapid access to hundreds of files.

The HyPlus hypertext program from Maxthink© (which may be distributed without paying royalty fees) is easy for both developers and users. While graphics may be included, HyPlus and its associated utilities are particularly well-suited to projects that involve large amounts of text. The program does not require a mouse and users must learn only a very few keyboard commands.

The on-disk college catalog was created because:

1) First and foremost, the on-disk college catalog is a tool for students, counselors and advisors. A system of menus (in levels from broad to specific) quickly takes a user to the information he or she wants. All other data remain available, but users only deal with what is needed.

2) The on-disk catalog is fast, particularly on a hard drive. With a printed catalog, users must flip back and forth. With the on-disk catalog and after just a few minutes of experimenting, the same user can instantly call up information about degree programs, course descriptions, graduation requirements, fees, financial aid, phone numbers, etc., with just a few keyboard strokes. Virtually all catalog information is cross-referenced on the disk. In addition, the program provides users a

Continues on Page 398

glossary of unfamiliar terms, abbreviations and explanations. Attached to a laser printer, the hypertext program prints hard copy of a curriculum or an admissions form faster than you could take the printed version to a copying machine.

3) The cost of printing a traditional college catalog continues to increase. This year, the printed catalog is offered to students through bookstores for $3. In the future, the on-disk version should cost half that amount.

4) The on-disk catalog is easy to update. Any word processor can be used to search and replace calendar dates, names, telephone numbers, etc. The good news for anyone interested in an on-disk college catalog is that much of the most laborious work has already been done. No matter the size of the printed catalog, the contents probably exist on a disk in some form. After in-house computer experts help convert the files into ASCII text, you are ready to start arranging it under some logical menuing scheme with hypertext.

Contact:
Charles Rock, Professor, Media Services
(314) 595-4496

St. Louis Community College at Florissant Valley
400 Pershall Road
St. Louis, MO 63135-1499
Total head count enrollment-Credit: 10,405; Non-Credit: 6,896
Campuses/sites: 1;Full-time faculty: 138

RESPIRATORY THERAPY PATHWAY AND DISTANCE LEARNING

Participants may take up to six credit hours at once and must complete all coursework within five years

Enrollments were down in the Respiratory Therapy program in the mid-1980's; consequently, area hospitals had difficulty recruiting trained respiratory therapists. St. Louis Community College at Forest Park looked at two solutions to address these problems: partnership or pathway programs with neighboring community colleges, and a distance learner program for out-of-district students.

The first pathway program was developed with St. Charles County Community College (SCCCC) in 1989 after a St. Charles hospital contacted Forest Park for training. The hospital had initially contacted SCCCC. However, SCCCC is prohibited by the state coordinating board from offering a duplicate respiratory therapy program, because of SCCCC's proximity to Forest Park.

The three-year, Pre-Respiratory Therapy Pathway program was designed so that St. Charles residents could start their first year of training at SCCCC, and finish their last two years at Forest Park. All general education and science courses are taken in St. Charles; all respiratory therapy coursework is completed at Forest Park. Total credit hours are 78 to 79; graduates earn the Associate in Applied Science degree and are eligible for the registry exam.

A similar partnership agreement was signed with neighboring Jefferson College in 1990. Since then, three students from Jefferson and seven students from St. Charles have enrolled at Forest Park to finish their Respiratory Therapy training.

The Distance Learner program allows respiratory technicians from around the state to take courses by mail to up grade their skills and earn their registry credentials. It was designed to help the working technician who can't attend school or who may not live near a Respiratory Therapy program.

Participants can take up to six credit hours at one time and must complete all coursework within five years. However, the student must drive to Forest Park for a written exam after completing each course. Clinical requirements are satisfied at the person's place of employment. The student also is evaluated at a clinical site in St. Louis at the time of the written exam. Since the Distance Learner program was introduced in January 1988, three students have graduated and eight are currently in the program.

The faculty who developed both programs, Tom Anderson and Jim Brennan, were recognized as Innovator of the Year by the League for Innovation in 1990.

Contact:
Jim Brennan, Associate Professor
(314) 644-9266

St. Louis Community College at Forest Park
5600 Oakland Avenue
St. Louis, MO 63110
Total enrollment head count-Credit: 7,564; Non-Credit: 4,937
Campuses/sites: 1; Full-time faculty: 225

HUMAN SERVICES DEVELOPMENTAL DISABILITIES OPTION

The program targets entry-level workers as well as those who want to upgrade their skills or who need more specialized work

Landmark federal legislation is dramatically changing the way services are offered to individuals with developmental disabilities. As the community integration movement grows, practices of segregation and institutionalization are disappearing. With community integration comes a critical need for more qualified providers to work with persons with developmental disabilities.

St. Louis Community College at Forest Park is helping fill that need through a pre-service associate degree program in developmental disabilities, one of about 20 programs nationwide and the only one offered in Missouri and Illinois.

Before receiving a $98,000, three-year grant to establish the program in 1990, the community college had been offering non-credit coursework targeted to the different levels of employee groups with the Productive Living Board.

The PLB wanted a more formalized educational program to address the shortage of trained paraprofessionals in the St. Louis area. The PLB recognized that with the new federal legislation comes a need to fill such jobs as classroom aides, integration facilitators, transition planners, developmental aides, personal assistants, respite care providers, job coaches in integrated employment settings, sheltered workshop employees, integrated assistants in day care and head start programs, etc.

The 64-credit-hour AAS program and certificate are targeted not only to entry-level workers but also to people already working in the field who want to upgrade their skills, degreed people whose career goals require more specialized work in developmental disabilities, and people whose jobs require them to have knowledge of current programs and legislation in the field of developmental disabilities. The faculty coordinator, Dr. Mary Ann Price, has been asked to be the technical assistant to the states of Missouri and Illinois under a federal grant from the Paraprofessional Resource Network out of the City University of New York. Price, who is an appointee to the Education Committee of the Missouri Governor's Alliance for the Prevention of Disabilities, already has served as consultant to the University of Missouri-Kansas City in replicating the Forest Park program. UMKC's program started up in the fall of 1993.

Contact:
Mary Ann Price, Faculty Coordinator
(314) 644-9657

St. Louis Community College at Forest Park
5600 Oakland Avenue
St. Louis, MO 63110
Total enrollment head count-Credit: 7,564; Non-Credit: 4,937
Campuses/sites: 1; Full-time faculty: 225

COMPUTER-DELIVERED MATHEMATICS INSTRUCTION

Students complete all work on-line, with off-line packets of practice tests that are completed out of class

St. Louis Community College at Meramec uses a computer-based system to deliver instruction in its Mathematics Lab, where enrollment in the lab is approximately 1,000 students per semester. Three-credit-hour courses in Basic Math, Elementary Algebra and Trigonometry are available. Students in these courses choose between the computer aided instruction (CAI) lab or traditional classroom sections. In the lab students work at their own pace in a mastery learning environment with supervision by lab staff.

Courseware is delivered on 84 TICCIT (Timeshared Interactive Computer Controlled Instructional Television, sold by Loreal Copra) workstations on a dedicated system. TICCIT is also available for stand-alone systems. Courseware was specifically designed for adult learners, and because source code is available, material could be tailored to our curriculum. Three faculty members have done extensive courseware authoring. The extensive record-keeping capacity of TICCIT tracks student time on task and records student progress, grading all on-line assignments and tests, and averaging student grades.

Students and staff find TICCIT to be extremely user-friendly. Introductory lessons explain lab policies and procedures, and the TICCIT keyboard includes learner control keys. Staff members act as tutors and study skills instructors, intervening when students need help.

Students complete all work on-line, with off-line packets of practice tests which are completed outside of class. Students spend an average of 50 hours on-line to complete Basic Math or Elementary Algebra, and 75 hours on-line to complete Trigonometry.

Continues on Page 400

Fontbonne College is regularly involved in our computer-based lab, using the lab for site visits by students, in their graduate program in computer education. As part of the Fontbonne College program, staff at Meramec gathered data relating to the effectiveness of the lab's computer based instruction.

We have found CAI to be an effective tool for instructing large numbers of adult learners in self-paced learning situations. Students receive immediate, consistent feedback. A great deal of our success is due to the support of administrators, and the dedication and innovative attitude of the staff in the lab.

Meramec's TICCIT lab was recently chosen as one of the 100 Joe Wyatt Challenge Success Stories (recognition given for innovative use of technology in the classroom).

Contact:
Laurie McManus or Lillian Seese
(314) 984-7500

St. Louis Community College at Meramec
11333 Big Bend Boulevard
St. Louis, MO 63122
Total head count enrollment-Credit: 14,867; Non-Credit: 10,142
Campuses/sites: 3;Full-time faculty: 167

REAL-TIME TRANSLATION FOR STUDENTS WITH DISABILITIES

The college has helped at least 54 other institutions start similar programs, which benefit both the disabled and court reporting students

For students with disabilities, a court reporter writes in real time the teacher's lecture, which translates into English and appears on a computer screen – thus giving students with disabilities equal access in the classroom and court reporting students valuable experience. A grant from the Southwestern Bell Foundation in 1991 enabled St. Louis Community College to adopt this practice, which helped the college balance tight budget restrictions with student needs. In the classroom, after the court reporter's translation appears on a computer screen, the court reporter prints out a copy of the lecture notes at the completion of the class so that the student may use them to study for the next day's class. The court reporter learns to perfect this skill of writing for real time and therefore makes them even more employable. It is a win/win situation because both students gain from this experience, and it is nice to see students helping students become successful.

With the passage of the Americans with Disabilities Act, it is imperative that St. Louis Community College keeps abreast of the impact that this act will have on this college as well as the community. The program has been able to help more than 60 students both on the Meramec and the Florissant Valley campuses by providing a real-time writer/note-taker for their classroom. Statistics have proven that the students have been successful in these classes. The college has assisted 54 other institutions to start similar programs and has received numerous awards as well as recognitions for this innovative program.

Contact:
Judy Larson
(314) 984-7500

St. Louis Community College at Meramec
11333 Big Bend Boulevard
St. Louis, MO 63122
Total head count enrollment-Credit: 14,867; Non-Credit: 10,142
Campuses/sites: 3;Full-time faculty: 167

INTERACTIVE TELEVISION PROGRAMMING

*A fiber optic network links the college, local schools,
health care facilities and community service groups*

Dawson Community College in Glendive, Montana, has embarked on a major project that will dramatically improve the level of services it offers to the smaller communities in its eastern Montana service area: the construction of a fiber optic network for the transmission of interactive television programming between DCC, local schools, health care facilities and other community service organizations. The network will allow citizens in any of the network communities to participate in classes, conferences or presentations originating in one of the other network communities.

The potential applications of this technology are virtually unlimited. They include:

- transmission of college-level classes between DCC and area communities, without the added expense and difficulties of students or instructors traveling between sites; both students and instructors could be located at any point along the network, making a wider range of courses available in communities other than Glendive, and allowing DCC to draw on the additional teaching resources available in those communities;
- training in nursing and allied health occupations for residents of surrounding rural communities;
- provision of enhanced medical care, through the collaboration of area physicians and specialists with technicians in rural health care facilities;
- provision of college-level classes to advanced students at area high schools, without removing those students from the high school location for part of the day;
- provision of courses for personal enrichment and for professional continuing education to residents of area communities at their home locations; and
- facilities for meetings and conferences for area community service agencies, eliminating the expenses of travel to a central location.

The wide range of applications for this technology represent a significant potential for improving the quality of life in the isolated rural communities of eastern Montana.

The interactive television (ITV) network has been developed in close collaboration with the local telephone cooperative. It represents the latest technology in full-motion interactive video, adapted for the special requirements of classroom instruction and community service. In the ITV system which has been developed for use at DCC, the instructor plays a central and critical role. The system has been designed to enable complete interaction between the instructor and students at all sites. The objective is to provide students at distant sites with the same quality of instruction as those at the instructing site. The ITV studio and transmission equipment have been designed to allow the instructor to attain this objective without the assistance of additional production technicians and personnel. Instructors will receive training in methods of ITV teaching, to help them adapt their instructional styles and make full use of the technological capabilities of the system. DCC is extremely proud of its role as a leader in educational telecommunications for the region.

This interactive television project is a unique cooperative effort among educational institutions, health care providers and private sector telecommunications firms. The initial impetus for the project was to address a critical shortage of registered nurses in the region; this brought together instructors and students from Miles City, Glendive and Sidney, along with Glendive and Sidney hospitals as clinical training sites.

Courses in nursing were first transmitted over the ITV system in spring 1992, and the first graduates of the program received their degrees in spring 1993. In addition to the nursing courses, the ITV system will allow DCC to expand its course offerings in the town of Sidney, some 50 miles away. Previously, courses at the Sidney Center were offered only in the evenings, as the majority were taught by DCC instructors who made the 100-mile round trip once a week. That travel is no longer necessary, as the ITV system allows instructors literally to be in two places at once!

Demand for ITV courses is expected to grow rapidly. Initial planning sessions have already been held with area high schools to identify courses of interest to their students and the citizens in their communities. The technology may very well enable DCC finally to fulfill its mission of providing higher education and lifelong learning opportunities to all the communities of eastern Montana.

Contact:
John W. Curtis, Institutional Research and Development
(406) 365-3396

Dawson Community College
PO Box 421
Glendive, MT 59330
Total head count enrollment-Credit: 700
Campuses/sites: 2; Full-time faculty: 28

LAW ENFORCEMENT

For students who want more than a two-year degree, the program includes enough general electives for them to articulate

The Dawson Community College program in law enforcement is unique in the state of Montana, where it is the only two-year degree program specifically focused on law enforcement.

Students completing the two-year program receive an Associate of Applied Science Degree in Law Enforcement. The program provides the initial training a future peace officer needs to be productive at the entry level in local, state or federal agencies, correctional facilities or private law enforcement agencies. The program also provides a broad technical training that, together with experience, should enable students to advance to positions of increasing responsibility. Further, while DCC's program is designed to prepare graduates for immediate employment, it is also planned for maximum transferability. The curriculum provides a foundation broad enough to allow the graduate to pursue further study at the baccalaureate or graduate level in law enforcement, criminology, penology or police administration.

The basic law enforcement core consists of courses consistent with curriculum recommendations of the AACJC, and was approved by the Montana Association of Criminal Justice Educators. The student planning on entering the career field can select, in addition to the four required law enforcement courses, up to 18 credit hours of electives from a variety of technical law enforcement skill courses. Because students in Montana may have to wait up to one year before they can attend the Montana Law Enforcement Academy, specialized courses such as firearms training, traffic accident investigation, criminal investigation and police patrol procedure are highly valuable for immediate job performance. Students already employed in law enforcement may continue their education through a program of independent study courses. Most law enforcement and related courses, with the exception of technical skill courses, are available through independent study; experiential learning credit is also available. Several DCC students who were employed before completing the program are finishing their degrees in this manner.

For students who wish to continue their training beyond the two-year degree, the program is flexible enough to include 18 credits of general electives in science, math, computer applications and humanities. The required communications and social science courses already exceed the general education requirements for the AA degree in those core areas. DCC's accreditation by the Northwest Association of Schools and Colleges assures that courses taken here will be accepted for transfer at other institutions. Law enforcement transfer students have done very well at their new colleges: students who have continued their education beyond the Associate degree have earned bachelor's, master's and law degrees, and two are completing doctorates. In-state transfers are primarily to Montana State University or the College of Great Falls, and most out-of-state transfer students go to Minot State University in North Dakota. The DCC program has been designed to articulate closely with the programs offered at these transfer institutions, and students have experienced little difficulty in pursuing further degrees. Other out-of-state transfer destinations include Lewis-Clark State College (Idaho), Metropolitan State College and the University of Denver (Colorado), Sam Houston State University (Texas), University of Delaware, University of South Dakota and the University of Arizona.

Career opportunities in law enforcement are promising, and the program at DCC prepares both men and women for careers in this challenging and rewarding field. Opportunities are expanding for law enforcement personnel in both the public and private sectors. Every community in the United States requires police protection service, and there are an additional 15,000 federal and state jurisdictions and agencies which employ law enforcement officers. In recent years economic conditions in Montana have resulted in the elimination of some positions, however jobs continue to become available in the state. For example, a grant application by the Montana Board of Crime Control in the late 1970's to the Law Enforcement Assistance Administration included an attrition survey of all Montana law enforcement agencies. This report indicated an average attrition rate of 18 percent among approximately 1,500 employees. An informal study of the local police department indicated the average annual attrition rate over a 25-year period was 20 percent. In the private security sector, a 1985 report by Hallcrest Systems for the National Institute of Criminal Justice Research indicated a 10 percent annual growth rate for the decade. Indications are that the annual growth rate has exceeded that projection, as there are approximately three times as many private security personnel as public law enforcement personnel employed. In addition to the general law enforcement degree, DCC's program offers a private security option.

DCC law enforcement graduates are also employed in many states other than Montana, including Wyoming, North and South Dakota, Colorado, California, Alaska, Virginia and Florida. While most are employed with local governments, city police and county sheriff departments, graduates are also employed by a wide variety of state and federal agencies. Alumni have been very successful in finding employment in the field after graduation. A five-year study completed by DCC in 1985 indicated that 82 percent of program graduates were employed or had been employed full-time in law enforcement since graduation.

Most of the balance were either in the military or attending college. The 1990 study indicated that 73 percent of graduates were employed or had been employed full-time in law enforcement, 10 percent were employed part-time in private security, and the rest were either in the military or enrolled in further education.

Contact:
Holly Dershem-Bruce, Program Director
(406) 365-3396

Dawson Community College
PO Box 421
Glendive, MT 59330
Total head count enrollment-Credit: 700
Campuses/sites: 2; Full-time faculty: 28

FLATHEAD VALLEY COMMUNITY COLLEGE

FOREST TECHNOLOGY

⊞ Students have a forest area where they conduct experimental harvesting ⊞ operations and conduct laboratory classes

One of the programs for which Flathead Valley Community College is best known is its Forest Technology Program. Situated in the center of the Flathead National Forest – with more than 3-million acres of forest lands available for use, study and recreation – the college launched this program early in its history.

Since that time the program has evolved to accommodate changes in technology such as the use of computers in land management decisions, and changes in philosophy such as the shift in training employees for the U.S. Forest Service to training them to successfully contract with the Forest Service and other agencies.

The program is one of only 22 programs in the United States and Canada which is recognized and fully accredited by the Society of American Foresters. It is the only Forest Technology program available within the eight-state region which includes Idaho, Montana, North and South Dakota, Wyoming, Utah and Colorado, and thereby attracts students from across the country.

Flathead Valley Community College works with numerous agencies and organizations to provide a better education for Forest Technology students and to assist the organization with their mission, including the U.S. Forest Service, Flathead National Forest, Montana Department of State Lands, private timber companies, and the U.S. Soil Conservation Service. In exchange for laboratory sites, the Forest Technology students frequently conduct projects and provide needed services to the organizations, such as timber inventory, timber cruising, tree planting, snow surveys, etc.

One of the most innovative partnerships which has been recognized nationally was with private timber companies. Through Carl Perkins grant funding and a local match by the Western Wood Products Association, a four-year Sawyer Safety Program was established in an effort to lower worker compensation rates for woods workers. In-service safety evaluations of working timber sawyers and timber-falling short courses have successfully reduced the rates, and the program has now been assumed by the Montana Logging Association.

To assist Forest Technology students in competency, field classes are oriented to simulate actual working conditions of typical employing organizations. Mensuration, Cruising Systems and Advanced Mensuration are designed to teach necessary techniques and to simulate actual working conditions by having full-day schedules of work with appropriate job assignments.

The college also has a cooperative lease agreement with private individuals, which allows the Forest Technology program students to use a specific portion of their property as the FVCC Experimental Forest. Under the agreement, the students manage the unit and conduct experimental harvesting operations. The Experimental Forest is also used to conduct laboratory classes and to study basic mensuration and surveying techniques, varying habitat and timber types, timber conditions and terrain.

Many of the Forest Technology students are involved in the FVCC Logger Sports Team, the only intercollegiate athletic team on campus. Team members have consistently demonstrated their skills, taking first place for four consecutive years at the western state conclave by defeating teams from many large, four-year universities. In 1987, the team was the first representing a two-year college to win the competition. In addition to annual competition, the team is best known on campus and in the community for its willingness to facilitate the needs of the community.

Dr. Robert Beall, a Forest Technology instructor and coach of the team, says, "The most important benefit is the building of character through activities." These have included many community service activities, including the raising of funds for scholarships, victims of the California earthquake, and community residents with special needs.

One event the team sponsors each year is an annual Family Forestry Expo. In 1990, a local mill donated 40 acres of timberland, and students built trails and demonstration stations on the area. While each May the public is invited to two days of talks and demonstrations, the focus is

Continues on Page 404

primarily on approximately 1,500 fifth-grade schoolchildren who participate in the event.

To address the increasing demand for women in forestry, federal grant funds have provided the means to recruit women to the Forest Technology program. Consequently, 92 percent of this year's sophomore class are women.

The FVCC Forest Technology Program has been given formal recognition by the American Society of Foresters, and it has received a Montana Gender Equity Award for exceptional efforts in career counseling, classroom attention and employment assistance for young women. The Sawyer Safety Program has attracted national attention.

Contact:
Robert Beall, Forest Technology Instructor
(406) 756-3898

Flathead Valley Community College
777 Grandview Drive
Kalispell, MT 59901
Total head count enrollment-Credit: 2,000; Non-Credit: 4,100
Campuses/sites: 2; Full-time faculty: 63 FTE

SURVEYING

Students use state-of-the-art equipment, thanks to a loaner program sponsored by the Topcon Company

Unlike many large institutions which perceive surveying as adjunct to much larger programs, the emphasis that Flathead Valley Community College places on surveying as a program in its own right is important to its image as the best in the state. It has a long history as a solid, effective program that prepares students for careers as Professional Surveyors and Surveying Technicians. Moreover, it is the only program in Montana which emphasizes land surveying.

In spite of its longevity, the program is expected to continue to grow to keep up with the demand for surveyors in the region. There is a steady influx of population and growth in western Montana, particularly in the scenic Flathead Valley, which is being widely publicized as "the last best place."

Students in the FVCC surveying program are provided an appropriate balance between basic surveying skills for entry-level employment in the profession and the more in-depth study of the technical and legal concepts required for examination and registration as a professional land surveyor. Although the program credits are transferable to a four-year college or university, many students opt to receive an AAS degree.

Montana is a leader in state registration requirements; its exams are recognized by the National Council of Engineering Examiners (NCEE). The courses offered in the FVCC surveying program meet the educational part of the State Board of Registration's requirement for licensure as a Professional Land Surveyor. (The alternative route for students to obtain professional recognition would be to attend an ABET accredited four-year surveying program, of which there are only three in the Northwest.) The program also meets state requirements to allow an applicant to automatically qualify to take the Land Surveyor in Training (LSIT) examination.

To meet the rapidly changing advances in technology, modern, state-of-the-art surveying equipment has been obtained through an innovative loaner program sponsored by Topcon Company. Flathead Valley Community College was the first school in the nation selected by Topcon to participate in the program, which has provided the college with two total stations, two data collectors, and associated software. While the college is responsible for the maintenance and insurance of the equipment, Topcon updates it each year with its newest models. This partnership, along with the addition of new microcomputers, has allowed FVCC's surveying students to be exposed to the types of equipment they will encounter in the everyday working world.

The Montana Association of Registered Land Surveyors (MARLS) is a staunch advocate of the program, providing scholarships to second-year FVCC surveying students.

Contact:
Dave Dorsett, Surveying Instructor
(406) 756-3913

Flathead Valley Community College
777 Grandview Drive
Kalispell, MT 59901
Total head count enrollment-Credit: 2,000; Non-Credit: 4,100
Campuses/sites: 2; Full-time faculty: 63 FTE

INTERACTIVE FIBER-OPTIC TELECOMMUNICATIONS

The network delivers the Associate Degree Registered Nursing program to two rural communities

Through a joint venture with another community college and several community health care agencies, Miles Community College delivers an Associate Degree Registered Nursing program to two communities in rural eastern Montana via fully interactive fiber-optic telecommunications.

Miles Community College delivers the lecture portion of the Nursing program from Miles City, Montana, over the fiber-optic telecommunications system and provides on-site clinical instruction to students in Glendive, Montana (home of Dawson Community College), and in Sidney, Montana; the two distance sites are 82 and 132 miles from Miles City, respectively. Dawson Community College delivers the general education support courses to the students, with those living in Sidney receiving some of the courses via the telecommunications system. Clinical instruction is provided by Miles Community College instructors on-site in health care agencies in Glendive and Sidney.

While the Nursing program is the pilot project for use of the new system, numerous other educational products are provided and planned for delivery over the system. Some of the general education courses provided by DCC are given over the system, while numerous other courses, workshops and seminars are planned for delivery. Required continuing education for nurses will be one of the primary deliveries, and specialized programs or courses offered by either of the two community college will be prime options for delivery to the community of the other college.

Other possible uses of the system include usage by public schools or other community agencies on a time-rental basis. Liaisons to create these possible usages are underway.

The system is fully interactive with the instructor controlling the camera selections (including pan, zoom and tilt), a camera-in-camera option, and with instruction that can be delivered from any one of the three sites. The instruction is fully supported with electronic bulletin board transmissions and cooperative library and financial aid agreements.

Contact:
Frank Williams
(406) 232-3031

Miles Community College
2715 Dickinson
Miles City, MT 59301
Total head count enrollment-Credit: 742; Non-Credit: 200
Campuses/sites: 1; Full-time faculty: 24

COOPERATIVE VENTURES

Because the college serves such a vast region, partnerships are necessary to adequately serve its students

Eastern Montana has the most rural, remote communities in the lower 48 states. To serve the 110,000 people living in the 43,000-square-mile area – a slightly larger area than New York State-Miles Community College looks to partnerships with a variety of entities.

The college's Interactive Fiber-Optic Telecommunications project, critiqued elsewhere, is a working/contracted arrangement among nine entities including: our sister institution, Dawson Community College; Mid-Rivers Telephone Cooperative; U.S. West Communications; two community hospitals and two nursing homes at Sidney and Glendive; and the High School of Richland County. All nine entities are involved daily during the instruction of nursing students. Hospitals have provided permanent classroom space within the hospital complexes; Dawson Community College and the high school have provided

ITV classrooms; and the phone cooperative has supplied incentive funding, technical expertise, and special pricing of services for signal transmission.

Formulating this complex partnership is a direct result of earlier work with Montana Power Company and the creation of a Power Plant Technology program (PPT). The PPT program helped to train staff for a 700 Mega-Watt coal-fired generation plant within our service area, some 90 miles off campus. It is a mission of this college to train people across the service area so that individuals can stay with the land and within the community. The partnership with MPC allowed Miles Community College to tap industry for assistance with the training processes saving industry the expense of bringing a permanent work force in from out-of-state.

Continues on Page 406

Negotiations are under way to bring about the next major partnership venture. In order to improve the placement of secondary and post-secondary graduates, we seek to link the two community colleges, the state Job Service and Social and Rehabilitative Services (SRS) Offices from three districts, 10 high school districts, three telephone cooperatives, a community-based organization, JTPA and welfare programs from 10 counties. Our optimism of being able to bring this group together is based on our campus-based JOBS Coordinating Committee. Made up of all programs which feature job placement as any part of their program, the college, Job Service, community-based organizations and other agencies meet monthly to coordinate training needs and recruitment efforts, and to make sure that individuals with needs are having those needs met. The coordination helps to facilitate client services, smoothing the transition from one program to another for clients, students and graduates. Our larger service area partnership will feature more than 43 entities seeking to meet the needs of clients and our graduates.

Contact:
Fred McKee, Director of Development
(406) 232-3031

Miles Community College
2715 Dickinson
Miles City, MT 59301
Total head count enrollment-Credit: 742; Non-Credit: 200
Campuses/sites: 1; Full-time faculty: 24

ASSOCIATE DEGREE IN NURSING

Most students come from small towns, wherein they plan to practice upon graduation – which is helping offset a shortage of nurses in rural communities

When Nebraska's current community college system was established in the early 1970's, the community colleges became responsible for most associate degree programs - with nursing education one of the few exceptions. But by the late 1980's, after state universities eliminated Associate Degree in Nursing (ADN) programs, the community colleges finally inherited the responsibility. Central Community College developed an ADN program and admitted its first class for the 1989 fall semester, just in time to try to meet a critical need for nurses in rural communities.

The goal was to develop a high-quality ADN program that:

1) would have sufficient flexibility to serve students drawn largely from small rural communities; and

2) provide a career mobility ladder to facilitate transfer of licensed practical nurses into the ADN program and transfer of ADN graduates into BSN programs offered by four-year colleges.

Central Community College has practical nursing (PN) programs in Kearney and at its Platte Campus in Columbus. In developing the ADN curriculum, the PN curricula were completely revised to assure a seamless articulation process. Currently the first two semesters of study in the PN programs are identical to the first two semesters of study in the ADN program. Although the ADN class roster fills quickly, PN graduates form a ready pool to fill any last-minute vacancies which might occur in the second-year ADN class. In addition, the college has articulation agreements with all BSN programs in Nebraska.

The ADN curriculum includes 18 semester-hours of general education courses, which students can complete on any of CCC's three campuses or through off-campus learning centers operated in more than 30 communities. Further accessibility is provided by offering an option for students to complete the program in three years instead of two.

Popularity of both the PN and ADN programs remains high, with the college receiving more than 1,000 inquiries a year from people interested in enrolling. ADN classes are predominately non-traditional, with the average age of students somewhere in the mid-30's. A majority of students come from small towns where they plan to remain and practice after graduation. They typically are highly dedicated, motivated and focused on their profession.

The ADN program has proven effective in serving the needs of rural communities in central Nebraska. The inaugural ADN class graduated in the spring of 1991 and had a 97.5 percent success rate in passing the registered nurse examination the first time taken, ranking the class first among all registered nurse education programs in the state for that testing period. A total of 36 out of the 39 original graduates are practicing in rural Nebraska, and all of the 1992 graduates are working in rural communities.

Contact:
Mary Lou Holmberg, Associate Dean
(308) 384-5220

Central Community College-Grand Island Campus
PO Box 4903
Grand Island, NE 68802-4903
Total head count enrollment-Credit/Non-Credit: 8,030
Campuses/sites: 3; Full-time faculty: 32

NATURAL GAS EMPLOYEE TRAINING

The college trains a utility company's employees in everything from basic classes in gas piping to advanced courses in energy utilization

KN Energy is a fully integrated natural gas utility with operations in seven states ranging from the well-head to use by the consumer. When the company's natural gas service division in the early 1970's recognized the need for a comprehensive training program to meet the needs of its service technicians, KN approached Central Community College-Hastings Campus. The result is a training partnership which received AACJC recognition in 1982 and completed its second decade in 1992.

The program, linked with the already-established Heating, Air conditioning and Refrigeration program, is designed to provide KN Energy service technicians:

1) training in basic skills as they begin their careers;

2) advanced training as they gain experience; and

3) training on emerging technologies which affect the natural gas appliance service industry.

The Hastings Campus provides a full-time instructor

Continues on Page 408

dedicated solely to the natural gas training program. KN Energy also provides an instructor who teaches courses focused specifically on company policies and operating procedures. The two instructors work together to continuously plan and develop curriculum which reflect changing technology.

Courses offered through the program range from basic classes in venting, gas piping and electricity to advanced courses in high efficiency appliances and energy utilization, as well as classes on specific types of appliances. Hastings Campus courses in first aid and cardiopulmonary resuscitation also are included.

About 200 KN Energy service technicians attend the Hastings Campus program for one week each year, with average attendance at seven to eight people a week. A key component of the program is the flexibility in scheduling offered by the self-paced individualized system of instruction which is predominant on the Hastings Campus.

Because students work individually under the supervision of an instructor, KN Energy can assign each technician to the level of training appropriate for their experience and ability. As a consequence, eight people can be enrolled in the program the same week, with each person taking a different course of study.

The program includes 20 separate week-long courses, so even long-term employees have the opportunity for continuous training and career development. Experienced technicians also might repeat courses taken years before in order keep up with changes in technology that have been incorporated into the curriculum.

Employee evaluations of the training are reviewed annually and suggestions are considered in developing new material for the program. KN Energy also has been active in encouraging other natural gas companies to take advantage of the program.

Contact:
Wayne Foster, Instructor
(402) 463-9811

Central Community College-Hastings Campus
PO Box 1024
Hastings, NE 68902-1024
Total head count enrollment-Credit/Non-Credit: 6,630
Campuses/sites: 3 Full-time faculty: 62

CENTRAL COMMUNITY COLLEGE-PLATTE CAMPUS

OFF-CAMPUS LEARNING CENTERS

*The individualized format of the courses makes it possible to offer variable credit,
enabling students to enroll for individual units*

The Central Community College-Platte Camps Community Education Office offers curriculum courses to its 10-county service area on an individualized basis through 30 learning center sites. In most cases the learning centers are established at the local school through an affiliation agreement. Centers typically are open one or more nights per week, and some centers also schedule daytime hours.

Central Community College uses individualized instruction in a majority of its programs and courses and as a consequence has developed self-paced study packets using a variety of media including print, slide-tape, film strips and videotape. By their nature these materials are highly portable and are designed for use by students on an individualized basis. Goals in establishing the off-campus learning center program were to:

1) extend the regular campus curriculum as much as feasible to sites distant enough from a campus to make commuting unfeasible or unattractive; while 2) providing adequate access to campus faculty; with 3) adequate local supervision to assure that quality of the curriculum and instructional delivery is maintained.

More than 80 individualized courses are offered, drawn from both academic transfer and vocational-technical programs. The individualized format of the courses also

makes it possible to offer the flexibility of variable credit. Courses typically are organized into one-semester-hour units. Students unable to make large commitments of their time can enroll for individual units.

Each site has a Learning Center Manager hired on a part-time basis to assist students in their course work, proctor tests and serve as a contact between the student and the campus faculty who write the curriculum and grade the course work. Because students work independently, there is no minimum enrollment requirement for a given course. In a sparsely populate rural area, this provides great flexibility in meeting individual needs.

Because students work individually, it isn't necessary that they start and end courses at the same time. A student who isn't able to begin a course the week the learning center opens for a semester can begin when he or she is ready. However, ending dates for the fall and spring semesters correspond with ending dates for the campus.

The first learning center opened in January 1980, in Albion, NE, with approximately 30 people enrolled. In 1991-92, about 500 people enrolled in the learning centers each semester, generating more than 2,000 registrations. Students who enroll for enough credits during a semester are eligible for financial aid programs. Depending on the major area of study, students can complete between one-half and three-fourths of the requirements for an associate degree through their local learning center, saving time and reducing travel costs. The learning center program has accounted for the major share of growth in the campus Community Education operation over the last 10 years.

Contact:
Ron Kluck, Associate Dean, Community Education
(402) 564-7132

Central Community College-Platte Campus
PO Box 1027
Columbus, NE 68602-1027
Total head count enrollment-Credit/Non-Credit: 7,080
Campuses/sites: 3; Full-time faculty: 35

ENVIRONMENTAL LABORATORY TECHNOLOGY

Students receive comprehensive training in the basic techniques and instrumentation found in a modern chemical analysis laboratory

Although the need for trained, entry-level, chemistry-based laboratory workers is well-known, some institutions haven't always successfully delivered. The major problem has been too low an enrollment to justify personnel costs and supply and equipment expenditures. That low enrollment is likely due to the narrow focus of these programs on pure chemical technology, while ignoring other sciences that appeal to the general public and also present significant and interesting employment opportunities for the graduate.

At Southeast Community College, a program called Environmental Laboratory Technology offers the traditional analytical chemistry required of a chemistry-based technician training program but also offers laboratory oriented course sequences in water and wastewater technology, microbiology, and biochemistry/biotechnology. All of these are important in a world concerned with water quality, bacterial and chemical pollution, and the application of chemical and biological data to the quality of man's environment.

The program includes course work in basic chemistry, biology, microbiology, physics, communications, math and computers during the first year. The second year focuses on analytical chemistry, applied microbiology, biochemistry and water/waste water plant operations and laboratory. Thus the students receive comprehensive training in the basic techniques and instrumentation found in a modern chemical analysis laboratory. They receive training in the procedures used to isolate and identify potential microbial pathogens. They receive the background needed to successfully pass the state certification examination for water and waste water treatment plants. They also become trained in the techniques used to isolate and study biomolecules.

The Environmental Laboratory Technology program has been recognized nationwide for its quality and innovation. In 1990, it won a National Science Teachers Association Ohaus award for innovation. A textbook written for the analytical chemistry course sequence was published in 1988 and has been widely adopted by training programs that are evolving in other locations. Instructors in the program have been presented a number of teaching awards reflecting their dedication and the quality of their instruction. These awards include two local awards as well as a national award sponsored by the Chemical Manufacturers Association based in Washington, D.C. A two-year, $10,000 grant from the New York-based Sandoz Foundation was presented to the program in 1990 for student scholarships. Indications are that this grant will be renewed in 1992.

This program was evolved over a period of 20 years in Lincoln, Nebraska, and has been supported and well-received by the industrial and government laboratories in Lincoln and the surrounding area. Enrollment has been good and job placement has been 100 percent since 1987.

Contact:
John Kenkel, Program Chair
(402) 437-2485

Southeast Community College-Lincoln Campus
8800 "O" Street
Lincoln, NE 68520
Total head count enrollment-Credit: 4,000; Non-Credit: 12,000
Campuses/sites: 1 Full-time faculty: 125

CHILD DEVELOPMENT SERVICE

An on-campus Child Development Lab, adjacent to the instructional classrooms,
provides hands-on, well-supervised training for students

Quality child care is one of the most urgent needs of our nation today. Families, businesses, towns, cities, states and the entire country are being affected by the lack of quality, dependable and affordable care for infant through school-age children. Southeast Community College has been making every effort to address this pertinent issue by training quality child care providers since 1975. The college also provides affordable, quality, developmentally appropriate on-campus child care in a new Child Development Center built in 1989 for students and staff.

The Child Development Services Program trains students to be child care providers in a wide variety of settings, from large daycare centers to preschools, family daycare homes, group homes, private family care (nannies), recreational camps and playgrounds, and para-professionals in public school settings. Students choose to complete a four-quarter program for which they earn a diploma, or a six-quarter program for which they earn an Associate of Applied Science Degree. The AAS option provides additional training in administration and business management skills with employment opportunities as a director, assistant director or owner of a child care business.

The on-campus Child Development Lab is adjacent to the instructional classrooms. The Child Development Center is licensed to care for 118 children from six weeks through 11 years of age. Operating expenses are paid by revenues received from client payments for Child Care. Students in the Child Development Services Program are assigned to work in a different age-level room for each of the quarters they are in the program. Students spend a minimum of eight hours per week in the Lab during their first quarter to 17 hours per week during their last two quarters. If students prefer to build upon the option of being a professional nanny, they take additional nanny classes which includes a practicum with a private family.

By the end of six quarters, students have completed a minimum of 924 clock hours of hands-on-experience with children of all ages. New students can determine if child care is the correct profession for them by having immediate opportunities to work with and plan activities for children. Because of this positive, successful exposure to children, many students choose to further their education after graduating from SCC by becoming public school teachers, special education teachers, children psychologists, etc.

The true success of this program can be attributed to the unique correlation of the instructional program with the expectations and assignments given the students while they are assigned to the lab. Each instructor designs his/her curriculum around the developmentally appropriate practices being modeled in the Child Development Center. The students are taught the theory and course content in the classroom and go immediately into the lab where they see the theories in action or can practice and try them out for themselves. The instructional staff and the staff at the Child Development Lab are excellent examples of employer-sponsored child care providers of the future.

The true winners in this arrangement are the students and staff at Southeast Community College who are assured of having quality, developmentally appropriate child care for their children from 6 a.m. to 10 p.m. In 1991 the Child Development Center was recognized by the Nebraska Department of Labor for its "Contribution to the Prosperity, Welfare and Economic Stability of Nebraska." In addition, for the last four years the Child Development Center staff has received the Nebraska Department of Social Services "Certificate of Appreciation for Successful Work with Children." The Child Development Center is nearing completion of Accreditation by the National Association of Education of Young Children.

Contact:
Jeanette Volker, Dean
(402) 437-2449

Southeast Community College-Lincoln Campus
8800 "O" Street
Lincoln, NE 68520
Total head count enrollment-Credit: 4,000; Non-Credit: 12,000
Campuses/sites: 1 Full-time faculty: 125

COMPUTER AIDED DRAFTING

An automated AutoCAD Training Center laboratory serves both business/industry and the college

An automated AutoCAD Training Center laboratory serving business and industry also has become a primary source of instruction for SCC-Milford Campus faculty seeking proficiency in Computer Aided Drafting.

The Center evolved along with the CAD program, which began during the 1983-84 academic year. Initially an IBM Fast Draft system with two work stations was purchased and an instructor designated to be the lead person for the development of Computer Aided Drafting on Campus.

The original goal was to provide Computer Aided Drafting to students in the Architectural Technology, Manufacturing Engineering Technology and Surveying and Drafting Technology programs. These three programs enroll approximately 120 majors each year.

In 1985-86, a change was made from the IBM Fast Draft hardware to IBM Microcomputers using AutoCAD software. This facilitated establishing a laboratory with 20 machines. This change made it possible to provide instruction on a class basis and thus provide more students with more time on the CAD stations.

From the beginning in 1983-84, the demand for CAD instruction has increased significantly in the three original programs and eight other programs are currently including some CAD instruction in their curriculum. Since the fall of 1992, the college has had five CAD laboratories with 80 student stations, using 386 and 486 machines.

The three original programs (with name changes) are Architectural Technology, Manufacturing Engineering and CAD Technology, and Surveying & CAD Technology. Each has a CAD laboratory designated for their primary use. In addition, a general CAD laboratory is shared by students from Machine Tool Technology, Commercial Art, Electromechanical, Electrical, Electronic Engineering, Electronic Servicing, Welding and Metallurgy and Non-destructive Testing.

A second step forward was also made in 1985-86 with the college negotiating an agreement with AutoDESK, the manufacturer of AutoCAD software to implement the CAD Training Center. Under the Agreement, the college provides basic and advanced CAD classes for existing business/industry technicians and the college received a special rate on software purchases.

The demand from business/industry has continued to grow and now utilizes the majority of the time available in an automated AutoCAD Training Center laboratory. The Training Center has served both business/industry and the college. AutoDESK and Southeast Community College have also expanded the original Training Center to include certification to be a Multi-Media Training Center.

Placement of graduates from the three programs with a major emphasis in CAD (students receive more than 200 clock hours of instruction) has been excellent, with 94 to 96 percent placement in their field of training. The Training Center has been recognized by AutoDESK over the past four years as the top Training Center world-wide in the area of curriculum, facilities and instruction.

Contact:
Thomas C. Stone, Campus President
(402) 761-2131, ext. 221

Southeast Community College-Milford Campus
Rural Route #2, Box D
Milford, NE 68405
Total head count enrollment-Credit: 1,350; Non-Credit: 185
Campuses/sites: 3; Full-time faculty: 85

INDUSTRY LINKAGES

Advisory committees, industry co-sponsors of programs and of training centers have kept campus linkages strong with the private sector

The Milford Campus, since its beginning in 1941, has striven to maintain a close working and communication linkage with business and industry. Today these linkages involve:
1) a comprehensive advisory committee for each program;
2) industry co-sponsors of Associate Degree programs; and
3) industry sponsorship of on-campus training centers

for existing industry technicians.

Each AAS and diploma program has a separate advisory committee. The campus-wide administration and supervisors of the advisory committee are under the direction of the Placement/Advisory Committee/Safety Office. This office provides guidance and assistance for each program chair in developing the agenda for meetings, contacting advisory members, operation of the meetings, follow-up

Continues on Page 412

after meetings and committee membership. The office has also developed an Advisory Committee handbook to assist both the program chairs and the advisory committee membership.

The major priority of the committee is to review programs on an annual basis and make recommendations for change that will keep the program in tune with current and future changes. Secondary benefits to the programs include: instructor in-service assistance, equipment material donations, student field trips and access to job opportunities.

Each committee has 15 to 22 members who represent the various diversities of the technical jobs that the program prepares students to enter.

The close linkages with business and industry have evolved into four associate degree programs that are co-sponsored by industry. These programs are: General Motors Automotive Service Educational Program; John Deere Ag Tech; John Deere Ag Parts Management; and Building Materials Merchandising. The John Deere programs are both the first programs of this type in the nation co-sponsored by John Deere. The John Deere Ag Tech program has been replicated at eight other locations in the U.S. and Canada. The John Deere Ag Parts

Management is one of two programs co-sponsored by John Deere in North America.

All four programs receive significant industry support in materials, equipment, special tools, training mock-ups, recruiting assistance, and cooperative education placement.

The second type of educational programming which is sponsored by business and industry is the technician training centers for technician update training. The three on-campus centers are: GM Training Center, John Deere Pro Tech Training Center and AutoDESK AutoCAD Training Center. These are operated at no cost to the college. The trainers are college employees who are kept updated on the latest technology by the respective firm. They also provide an on-campus training center for college faculty. The three training centers have the potential for helping to keep 85 percent to 90 percent of the regular AAS programs updated.

The AutoCAD Training Center has been recognized by AutoDESK for excellence in the areas of Curriculum, Instruction and Facilities as compared to other training centers worldwide. The John Deere AAS programs have been recognized and featured in several Ag industry journals.

Contact:
Thomas C. Stone, Campus President
(402) 761-2131, ext. 221

Southeast Community College-Milford Campus
Rural Route #2, Box D
Milford, NE 68405
Total head count enrollment-Credit: 1,350; Non-Credit: 185
Campuses/sites: 3; Full-time faculty: 85

FUEL FIRE SAFETY

The program teaches employees how to use a fire extinguisher during the first minutes of a blaze

Responding to the training needs of business and industry continues to be a vital role for community colleges. In 1991, Western Nebraska Community College was approached by a local gas and pipeline industry to provide Fuel Fire Safety for their employees.

The Fuel Fire Safety Program was developed in a cooperative effort between the college and gas industry, with assistance from an Advisory Committee. The program provides a comprehensive one-day training program designed to give employees the knowledge and confidence they need in the use of a fire extinguisher during the first two or three minutes of a fire.

A 20-acre training site, with more than 20 different simulations, provides class members with hands-on experience in using a variety of extinguishers, from 20-pound hand-held portables to 350-pound wheeled units. Gasoline, propane and natural gas are used in the simulated fuel fires. Students begin with basic fire situations, and as their skills develop, move on to more demanding fire problems. Simulations include fires at pump seals, flange leaks and a severed natural gas main. Training in extinguisher recharging and maintenance is also included.

The course is for employees working in industries that handle hazardous materials, including natural gas and propane. It includes both classroom and fire field instruction and is offered as a 1/2-credit college course.

A program brochure and an eight-minute videotape are used to describe more completely what is covered in the course and are available upon request.

Contact:
Jeff Sprenger, Program Coordinator
(308) 254-5450

Western Nebraska Community College
1601 East 27th Street
Scottsbluff, NE 69361
Total head count enrollment-Credit: 2,169; Non-Credit: 2,684
Campuses/sites: 2; Full-time faculty: 69

OVERCOMING BARRIERS

A Multicultural Assistance Center is just one of a series of strategies to serve the needs of the multicultural constituency

To help the growing Hispanic and Native American student populations overcome barriers to higher education, Western Nebraska Community College (WNCC) created a Multicultural Assistance Center that is developing services to:
1) inform targeted populations of educational and employment opportunities;
2) ease the transition into the community college, four-year institutions and work force;
3) provide parental education assistance;
4) provide a transfer bridge;
5) offer peer mentoring;
6) create support groups;
7) promote mother/daughter enrichment;
8) offer a cultural diversity segment in the Student Orientation prior to each semester; and
9) create a Leadership Institute that will provide the critical decision-making skills and support necessary to be successful in a college environment.

The Center and these goals are rooted in the 1989 update of the WNCC Board of Governors Strategic Plan. The board discovered that while WNCC enrollment had remained flat, Hispanic and Native American registrations had nearly tripled, reflecting the changes in regional population demography.

Generally the regional multicultural population is characterized by lower test scores, higher basic skills needs, increased financial assistance needs, and a need for unique special services. Historically, Hispanic and Native American students who had attended WNCC had not fit this generalization. Thus, lack of needed programs had gone unnoticed.

In response to this changing student clientele, WNCC developed the Multicultural Assistance Center as one of a series of strategies to serve the needs of the multicultural constituency. With the reduction of barriers, it expected that these activities will result in improved services for multicultural students, lower attrition and expanded enrollments. The Multicultural Assistance Center utilizes input from a Hispanic Advisory Committee and committees composed of leaders from the multicultural community.

The program director and staff have successfully begun an ongoing dialogue with the Hispanic and Native American communities and have reviewed census, demographic, enrollment and educational data. The data has been analyzed and translated into a comprehensive plan aimed at serving the multicultural constituency. The year 2000 will need the services of an educated population, and the Multicultural Assistance Center is designed to ensure that students from all walks of life have the opportunity to succeed and fully participate.

Contact:
Rodolfo J. Flores, Director, Multicultural Assistance Center
(308) 635-6154

Western Nebraska Community College
1601 East 27th Street
Scottsbluff, NE 69361
Total head count enrollment-Credit: 2,169; Non-Credit: 2,684
Campuses/sites: 2; Full-time faculty: 69

MACHINE TOOL TECHNOLOGY

The college has state-of-the-art facilities that include destructive and non-destructive testing laboratories

State government represents the largest payroll in Carson City, the Nevada State Capitol. The next-largest payroll is manufacturing, which Western Nevada Community College supports and promotes through an exemplary Machine Tool Technology program.

The college has the finest Machine Shop training facilities on the West Coast, thanks in large part to legislative and private support.

First, a local metal building manufacturer donated the building. In order to construct the building, voluntary support was provided by the Associated General Contractors. The resulting 5,000-square-foot building houses the Machine Tool Technology program, including

approximately $500,000 of equipment appropriated by the Legislature. This includes a destructive and non-destructive testing laboratory. The equipment is state-of-the-art, including a CNC drilling machine. A private company has also donated a CNC lathe. Several other pieces of equipment have been donated including four industrial robots.

In addition to teaching the Machine Tool Technology classes leading to the Associate in Applied Science Degree, special classes are customized for local companies.

The program has been recognized in publications of the Nevada Manufacturing Association and the State Council on Economic Development.

Contact:
Rick Van Ausdal, Instructor, (702) 887-3076
Jerry Barbee, Assoc. Dean, Applied Science & Technology, (702) 887-3038

Western Nevada Community College
2201 West Nye Lane
Carson City, NV 89703
Total head count enrollment-Credit: 5,061; Non-Credit: 1,034
Campuses/sites: 9; Full-time faculty: 68

CRIMINAL JUSTICE

Students may pursue specializations in law enforcement, corrections and juvenile justice

In only one year, Western Nevada Community College Criminal Justice program grew from suffering a lack of instructional staff to one of the college's largest occupational programs.

The turnaround began in the spring of 1991, when WNCC made a commitment to the criminal justice industry in Northern Nevada to employ a full-time coordinator/instructor.

Today there are three areas of emphasis that a student can pursue in this Associate of Applied Sciences degree program: law enforcement, corrections and juvenile justice. A fourth area of emphasis is being developed to provide students an opportunity to pursue a career in probation and parole.

Criminal Justice training is based totally on competency-based instruction, which was developed under the direction of the Criminal Justice instructor and the WNCC curriculum coordinator. By the fall 1992 semester, students in the criminal justice program were being evaluated and their skill attainment electronically recorded. This information is electronically available to the Associate Dean of Applied Science and Technology, Job Placement

Center, Curriculum Coordinator and others for reporting purposes. By making the information available to the Job Placement Center, the Center can develop placement folders (hard copies and/or electronically) for all potential employees of the criminal justice industry.

The Criminal Justice program has been on the leading edge for the implementation of Tech Prep in the state of Nevada. Even though to become employed in some fields of the criminal justice a student is required to be of certain age, the WNCC program has worked with local school districts to allow students an opportunity to receive release time from the high schools to pursue criminal justice training at the college. WNCC is currently working with the school districts and the State Department of Education to allow certain criminal justice courses to meet some high school graduation requirements.

WNCC works very closely with the Police Officers Standards and Training Department as well as the Department of Corrections and the Nevada Highway Patrol. Through a comparison process that identifies competencies taught through the academies and the competencies required for criminal justice course credit, the college accredits the academy programs and provides college credit to students who have completed the training programs through each academy.

Western Nevada Community College is committed to providing the best possible training available to meet the needs of the criminal justice work force. The college is dedicated to the concept of providing quality instruction, which is only possible through a cooperative working relationship with the criminal justice industry. The college's commitment and dedication is the results of many hours of listening to the needs of the industry and surrounding communities.

Contact:
Richard Finn
(702) 887-3143

Western Nevada Community College
2201 West Nye Lane
Carson City, NV 89703
Total head count enrollment-Credit: 5,061; Non-Credit: 1,034
Campuses/sites: 9; Full-time faculty: 68

PROJECT REDIRECTION

Single parents and displaced homemakers get strong encouragement from the program

Financially disadvantaged single parents and displaced homemakers who normally could not afford college get a chance at New Hampshire Technical College, where they don't have to bear alone the tuition and fees, books and supplies, child care and transportation. This outreach, thanks to Project Redirection, is funded through the Carl Perkins Vocational Education Act.

Project Redirection began in July 1985 to provide single parents and displaced homemakers with a career development educational program that will enable them to find employment in non-traditional areas and new and emerging technologies, thus achieving financial independence. Project Redirection started with a handful of students and has evolved to support (fall 1992 semester) 52 single parent/displaced homemaker students. In addition to offering financial support, a variety of academic and personal supports are also available through this program.

In addition to achieving financial independence and removal from AFDC/Welfare, the long-term benefits of this project are extraordinary. Including the graduating class of 1993, more than 100 students have graduated with Project Redirection assistance. Students completing the program enjoy personal satisfaction and financial independence as well as a new feeling of importance as contributing members in their community. Cash flow within the community as well as tax revenues generated by this group can make a significant contribution to the area.

These students become role models for their children leading the way in breaking the cycle of poverty.

Project Redirection is implemented through a response (proposal) to an RFP from the NH Department of Education and competes for single parent/displaced homemaker funds from the Perkins Act. The Project Director recruits, interviews, and accepts appropriate candidates who have been accepted to New Hampshire Technical College, Nashua.

Project Redirection is one of the oldest single parent programs in the country and has been recognized in newspapers, radio, TV, National Displaced Homemakers Network and the U.S. Department of Labor Women's Bureau.

Contact:
Mary Gillette, Director
(603) 882-6923

New Hampshire Technical College
505 Amherst Street
Nashua, NH 03061-2052
Total head count enrollment-Credit: 551
Campuses/sites: 2; Full-time faculty: 3

PROJECT CORE

Financially needy women get a push toward higher-paying technology careers

Project CORE (Counseling, Outreach, Retention, Education) provides financially needy women on a career path with higher salaries and more opportunities for advancement.

Education will be in the form of an Associate degree or certificate in Machine Tool Technology, Telecommunications, Computer Networking, Computer & Electronics Technology, Drafting (CADD), Electronic/Mechanical Technology (Robotics), Automotive Technology and Aviation Technology. Project CORE also provides financial, academic and personal support to women who are enrolled.

Project CORE, a federally funded (through the Carl Perkins Vocational Education Act) program, began in July 1991 to give women the support needed to ensure successful completion of their technical programs and to give survival techniques for successful job placement in a male environment.

"Women Exploring Technology," a two-week summer seminar is also available to give women a hands-on experience, to get a realistic look at the world of technology and to assist with career choice.

Project CORE has been in operation for two years. Due to its success, women are now enrolled in every technical program offered at this college and are entering the work force in technical careers with starting salaries of $30,000. Recruitment strategy information provided to career counselors and social service agencies are making more women aware of technical career options.

Project CORE is implemented through a response (proposal) to an RFP from the NH Department of Education and competes for sex-equity funds from the

Perkins Act. The Project Director recruits, interviews, and accepts appropriate candidates who have been accepted to New Hampshire Technical College, Nashua.

Project CORE has been recognized in newspapers, radio, the National Displaced Homemakers Network and the U.S. Department of Labor Women's Bureau.

Contact:
Mary Gillette, Director
(603) 882-6923

New Hampshire Technical College
505 Amherst Street
Nashua, NH 03061-2052
Total head count enrollment-Credit: 551
Campuses/sites: 2; Full-time faculty: 35

PRE-TECH FOR THE LEARNING DISABLED

Faculty have been specially trained to provide appropriate measures

Learning disabled students have for several years succeeded in the technical programs at the New Hampshire Technical College at Laconia, as a result of a variety of special kinds of assistance that the college has made available – coupled with lots of effort expended by the students. Many students have earned honors and have transferred their earned credits to other degree-granting colleges and universities.

Students who acknowledge that they have a learning disability or students who wish to be tested are directed to a trained learning disabilities specialist for determination of the proper modification or remediation. Faculty have been trained to work with students and provide appropriate measures and have done so with considerable success.

Learning disabled students and others are also encouraged to utilize the college's tutorial staff, some of whom are students who have demonstrated strength in subject areas and who can communicate with and assist other students.

For learning disabled and other students, a battery of other aids is available. These include computer programs to assist students to learn in specialized areas, instruction in compensatory techniques, development of learning plans where indicated, etc.

In addition, the college provides developmental education in a program called "Pre-Tech," which is constituted of small classes in developmental math, developmental reading and writing, and principles of technology. Pre-tech courses are taught by teachers who monitor the progress of each student on a weekly basis, consult with each student in a team format, teach the courses utilizing collaborative teaching techniques, who have succeeded in building a very high retention rate.

This team effort has resulted in a retention of more than 90 percent of students who entered the program.

Contact:
Neil Steiger
(603) 524-3207

New Hampshire Technical College–Laconia
Route 106
Prescott Hill, Laconia, NH 03246
Total head count enrollment-Credit: 1,078; Non-Credit: 862
Campuses/sites: 1; Full-time faculty: 25

COLLEGE SUCCESS MANAGEMENT

This required course provides an academic and social introduction to college life

Positive and meaningful interaction between the individual student and the academic and social systems of the college can strengthen the students' goals and commitments to maintain persistence. The lack of it can lead to various forms of dropout.

So New Hampshire Technical College-Manchester developed College Success Management, a one-credit, required course that provides an introduction to the academic, social and interpersonal environment of college life. Students participate in a variety of experiences to review and determine individual academic, career and personal goals. They are encouraged to accept responsibility for their own success and to develop an awareness of and

Continues on Page 418

appreciation for diversity. The college provides a supportive environment for student interaction and discussion.

College Success Management replaces a course that was taught in a structured environment and allowed students no choice in adapting the course to meet their individual needs. The student population on our campus is diverse, including a large number of ESL students, single parents, older students in need of retraining, as well as students directly out of high school.

The course places an emphasis on the diverse needs of the student population. The first part is based in a traditional classroom setting. Faculty/staff facilitate standard lessons in: College and Community Resources, Learning Styles Assessment, Study Skills, Time Management, Values Clarification and Community Development.

The second part of the course begins with a standard competency-based examination and conferences between the faculty and the individual student. Students contract to attend college sponsored workshops and seminars designed to address a variety of needs. Workshops and seminars are offered in the following topic areas: Critical Thinking, Public Speaking, Research Techniques, Communication Skills, Conflict Resolution, Human Sexuality, Money Management, Nutrition, Advanced Study Skills, Career Development, Chemical/Drug Dependent, Depression, Diversity, Resume Writing, Interview Skills, Eating Disorders, Math Anxiety, Parenting Skills, Stress Management, Health and Wellness, AIDS, Birth Control and issues of Aging. As our student body changes, the topics for workshops and seminars will also change.

In special circumstances, a student may choose an alternative to the seminars. Instead the student may volunteer his/her time in a community service project that has been prearranged and approved by the faculty member and community agency.

During the final part of the course, students again meet individually with their faculty member to review progress throughout the semester, evaluate their activities and workshops and receive their final grade. The format of the College Success Management course is supported and accepted by all constituents of the college. The variety of topics and alternatives allows each student to meet his/her needs to achieve personal and academic success.

Contact:
Joan Acorace, Assistant Dean, Academic Affairs
(603) 668-6706

New Hampshire Technical College-Manchester
1066 Front Street
Manchester, NH 03102
Total head count enrollment-Credit: 2,000; Non-Credit: 700
Campuses/sites: 1; Full-time faculty: 55

INTERNATIONAL CAST THEATRE

*Acting helps foreign students learn unique American English sounds,
vocabulary, idioms, phrasing and intonations*

Each fall semester the Theatre at Bergen Community College presents a production with an "International Cast." Each play has actors cast from our diverse student body, involving students from many countries, including the USA. The primary purpose of the production is to involve foreign students in an activity which enhances classroom learning, introduces cultural discussion, and creates an atmosphere where international and American students must work together toward the creation of the art of theatre.

The productions are "produced" by the Social Sciences/Communication Arts Division, and are directed by a faculty member teaching in the Speech for International Students area.

Participation in the performing arts is proving to be of great value to our foreign students. The college's American Language Program (ESL) provides extensive classroom training in speech, grammar, reading and writing. The speaking and listening skills taught in speech classes are greatly utilized during the rehearsal and performing stages of production. These student-actors must speak the American English language with all of its unique sounds, vocabulary, idioms, phrasing and intonations. They are memorizing an example of how to speak the language; and, they concentrate on listening to others speaking the same sounds over and over.

This is particularly valuable to those students who return to their homes and neighborhoods where only their native language is spoken.

If the play is a good American play, all the better to increase cultural awareness. Our country's attitudes concerning age, sex, death, ancestry, independence, nutrition, etc. may be different from other's. The students relish pointing out these differences, and similarities, to each other.

Many, many of our international students are professionals back home, but are now treated as unskilled laborers here because of differences in professional guidelines. They are spoken to as if they are children or not intelligent – loudly, with lots of gestures. There are, on the stage and behind, great opportunities to display innate talents which may otherwise go unnoticed and unappreciated - acting, singing, dancing, painting, lighting, costuming, designing, constructing, creating.

Material is selected with a language-culture learning point of view. The plays reflect American society. Interesting vocabulary and well-chosen words for speaking are considerations. Plays with good, straightforward narrative work best. Characters that are easy for non-actors to become involved with will make acting less self-conscious for some students. Scripts allow for diversity in casting. Future plans include scripts that may utilize more mature performers, thus involving community and campus involvement.

Scripts staged thus far include: *The Firebugs* by Max Frisch, *The Zoo Story* by Edward Albee, *Diary of Adam & Eve* by Mark Twain, and *The Girls in 509* by Howard Teischman

---

Contact:
Ken Bonnaffons, Director
(201) 447-7143

Bergen Community College
400 Paramus Road
Paramus, NJ 07652-1595
Total head count enrollment-Credit: 12,333; Non-Credit: 15,651
Campuses/sites: 1; Full-time faculty: 214

THE ANNUAL YOUNG PLAYWRIGHTS' FESTIVAL

*Students, ages 8 to 18, may see their original works come to life
on the college stage*

The Young Playwrights Festival of Bergen County is an annual play writing competition open to students ages eight through eighteen in the Bergen County school system. Sponsored by Bergen Community College, the John Harms Center for the Performing Arts, The Bergen County Superintendent of Schools and the Bergen 2000 Partnership, the project offers an excellent opportunity for community outreach. Its goal includes:

1) development of writing skills, specifically for the theatre;
2) the nurturing of young playwrights who may someday contribute to the American professional theatre;
3) the artistic growth of the college acting students who experience play development first hand; and

Continues on Page 420

4) the creation of a continuing partnership between the college and the community which is dedicated to the fine arts.

Open to any student in the Bergen County school system, the competition is broken down into three categories: elementary (grades three through five); middle school (grades six through eight); high school (grades nine through 12). Students may submit either simple sketches or fully developed one-act plays (no longer than 30 pages). Unity of time and place is encouraged in the structure of the plays, although this is not a rigid criterion for selection by a reading committee consisting of college professors, high school drama teachers and theatre professionals. There is one winning play from each category. (In the past, however, two high school plays were selected because of their equal merit.) In addition to the winning plays, there are three runners-up who are also honored in a ceremony prior to the performance.

After the selections have been made, the plays are cast utilizing the talent of the advanced acting students at Bergen Community College. After the first read-through of the plays, the director, who is a professor at BCC, meets privately with the student playwrights and their individual teachers in order to discuss rewrites. Each playwright then has approximately three weeks to make the changes, if necessary. (The elementary grades have usually been exempt from this rewriting process with only minor changes made.) Although artistic freedom is respected, the rewriting process is a requirement for participation in this project. During the rewriting, the playwright, the director and each teacher are in frequent communication.

A month after the first read-through, the cast begins an intense two-week rehearsal period with what are essentially second drafts of the plays. Playwrights are asked to attend at least three rehearsals in order to make any changes they may deem necessary. This is probably the most exciting part of the process, in which the creative talents of the playwright, the actors and the director all begin to play a part in the development of the new play.

Rehearsals take place at the college. On the day of the performance, the BCC cast and crew pack up and travel to the John Harms Center where they do a technical and dress rehearsal of the plays. This is a marvelous experience for the BCC actors.

That evening, prior to the performance, the County Executive of Bergen County presents the winning playwrights and the runners-up with awards and certificates. The plays are then performed as staged readings, just as it is done in the professional theatre. This means that although the actors carry script in hand, the plays are fully staged with lighting, costumes, make-up and a suggestion of props and sets. This stage in play/development provides the playwright with the opportunity to see how their plays work "up on their feet" prior to a full production. This is exactly what is done in the professional theatre as new plays are readied for full production.

Initiated in 1991, the Festival drew an audience of more than 200 people the first year. The second year, attendance more than doubled. The Young Playwrights Festival of Bergen County represents an exciting and unique collaboration between young writers, student actors, educators and the professional theatre.

Contact:
Mary Clifford, Project Director
(201) 447-7143

Bergen Community College
400 Paramus Road
Paramus, NJ 07652-1595
Total head count enrollment-Credit: 12,333; Non-Credit: 15,651
Campuses/sites: 1; Full-time faculty: 214

COLLEGE-WIDE COMPUTERS

※ *One of the 30 discipline-specific labs is the Electronic Music Studio,* ※
equipped with synthesizers and samplers

Brookdale Community College offers students the use of more than 700 computers in 35 campus computer labs (five are open, 30 are discipline-specific). Several labs have LANs and are connected to the main campus network.

An Adaptive Equipment Lab at Brookdale makes computer skills available to students with disabilities. Adaptive dimensions include such hardware and software as voice-activated keyboards, screen readers, keyboard filters, image enlargers, voice synthesizers, subscriber services, and more. Also located at Brookdale is the grant-funded New Jersey State Resource Center for Adaptive Aids for the Blind and Visually Impaired.

Brookdale was also selected in 1990 by IBM as one of only six regional training sites to provide training in the AS-400 system. Twenty terminals provide specialized instruction in this mid-size business system and provide hands-on opportunities to students and area business people.

Brookdale, through membership in the Northern Computer Integrated Manufacturing Systems and working with the New Jersey Institute of Technology and the Center for Manufacturing Systems, is able to offer students training in the latest manufacturing processes. Instruction in the Robotics Lab, Computer Aided Design

Lab, Fluids/Hydraulics Lab, and Silicon Graphics Computer Center gives students a realistic look at their 21st Century workplace.

The Electronic Music Studio at Brookdale (called MIDI, for Musical Instrument Digital Interface) is one of the finest in the country, with 15 student workstations. MIDI studio equipment such as synthesizers and samplers are used in teaching and training sessions, collaborative projects, and original music composition for advertising, soundtracks and other commercial applications.

The college's Audio Studio offers an ultramodern 24-track recording, mixing and editing facility; students learn digital audio tape mastering on a 320 Mb hard disk digital workstation, with post production audio sweetening equipment ready to layover narration and sound effects. Brookdale music technology graduates may walk into any recording house from LA to London and go right to work in the latest technologies.

More than 60 percent of Brookdale faculty have their own computers at their desks, with which they preview and create software, communicate with other computers around campus, and communicate via InterNet with faculty around the country. Professors at Brookdale have developed several multi-media applications in art, biology, psychology and reading. Representatives from Brookdale are often among those offering presentations and demonstrations at conferences around the country, including the annual League for Innovation conference.

Brookdale was the only community college to win an EDUCOM NCRIPTAL Higher Education Software Award in the 1987-1990 competition: the Distinguished Curriculum Innovation Award was presented to Brookdale faculty Sandra Varone and Karen D'Agostino for their "Making Word Processing Work" implementation on the IBM PS/2 Model 30. The approach teaches basic writing to the under prepared student, using the computer every step of the way.

Brookdale was also selected twice in 1991's Joe Wyatt Challenge: "101 Success Stories of Information Technologies in Higher Education." Brookdale's MIDI Studio and the mathematics computer classroom application, "Using Software in the Teaching of Mathematics," were chosen from hundreds of entries from such prestigious institutions as Rennselaer Polytechnic, MIT, Cornell, and Stevens Institute of Technology.

Many of the computers at Brookdale were provided for under a New Jersey Department of Higher Education grant program entitled "Computers in the Curricula." Other sources of funding include the College's Foundation, the Monmouth County Board of Chosen Freeholders, and corporate gifts from such New Jersey neighbors as AT&T and IBM/ROLM.

Computer usage at Brookdale has proved a resounding success. All Brookdale degree students who choose to benefit from the college's computer orientation and offerings leave Brookdale with sound, up-to-date computer skills that are immediately applicable to their chosen field of employment and/or study.

Contact:
Joanne Levey, Director, Academic Computing
(908) 224-2739

Brookdale Community College
Newman Springs Road
Lincroft, NJ 07738
Total head count enrollment-Credit: 19,765; Non-Credit: 20,000
Campuses/sites: 5; Full-time faculty: 211

NURSING USING INTERACTIVE VIDEODISC SIMULATIONS

Interactive videodisc simulations allow nursing students to work with the same "patient"

Interactive videodisc technology in Burlington County College's Associate of Applied Science degree program in Nursing exposes students to realistic simulations of patient care before the students begin their clinical internships at hospitals.

Burlington County College has invested in Level III interactive videodisc systems which, through the marriage of personal computers and laser discs, allow for these accurate portrayals of the contextual aspects of patient care. There is rapid access to information in both visual and auditory form. The extensive BCC software collection includes laser disc programs in cardiac care, the suicidal adolescent, medication administration, prevention of occupational exposure to AIDS, intravenous therapy, mechanical ventilators, therapeutic communications and emergency simulation.

Interactive videodisc simulations enable each student to work with the same "patient" and to observe the consequences of their clinical decisions without exposing a live patient to risk. Faculty members have noticed that students who use these simulations will often explore various treatment options.

This 70-credit Nursing Program uses its interactive videodisc systems in several modes: in a large group setting with a special video projector and custom-built screen, in small groups clustered around videodisc work stations in the nursing practice lab, and with individual students. The

Continues on Page 422

advantage of this technology, especially in the individual student setting, has been the accuracy, consistency, and replicability experienced by each student. In the classroom setting, following a presentation of didactic material, a panel of three students is often chosen to make clinical decisions as the interactive videodisc simulation unfolds. As the consequences of the students' decisions are viewed, the entire class offers comments on their peers' actions.

Based on Burlington's experiences with the Nursing Program, interactive videodisc simulations have been expanded to include programs in hospitality management, mathematics, workplace literacy and biology.

Burlington's use of interactive video in nursing instruction was demonstrated at the Community College Consortium's 1992 Winter Institute on Community College Effectiveness and Student Success in Jacksonville, Florida, and was demonstrated at the League for Innovation in the Community College's 1992 technology conference in Orlando, Florida.

Contact:
Colleen Glavin-Spiehs, (609) 894-9311, ext. 408
Richard J. Pokrass, (609) 894-9311, ext. 331

Burlington County College
County Route 530
Pemberton, NJ 08068-1599
Total head count enrollment-Credit: 7,116; Non-Credit: 7,834
Campuses/sites: 13; Full-time faculty: 91

LEARNING INSTITUTE FOR ELDERS (LIFE)

*Senior adult institute members plan their own curriculum
and recruit their own instructors*

The Burlington County College Learning Institute for Elders (LIFE) provides senior adults with opportunities to keep their minds active and become an integral part of college life.

The program was born when College President Robert C. Messina, Jr., brought together interested citizens, representatives of Elderhostel and members of the college staff, to explore ways the college could do more to work with the retired residents of the community. The resulting program has been an outstanding asset to the college.

LIFE offers adults 55 years and older the opportunity to define and pursue their own educational goals. The program focuses on expanded horizons and enhanced personal development for its participants. Members plan their own curriculum and recruit their own instructors, often tapping the wealth of expertise in their midst. Membership the first year totaled 50 people, and has since grown to more than 150. For a nominal annual fee the members can participate in as many LIFE activities as they wish.

Recent course offerings have included Meet the Media, Photography, Introduction to Major World Religions, Line Dancing, Fibers and Fabrics, Genealogy, Conversational Spanish, Aqua Exercise, Computer Basics, Chess for Beginners, and Day Trips to Places of Interest.

Of major importance to the college has been the willingness of LIFE members to also assist in other endeavors. LIFE members currently work with the regular student body as volunteer tutors, serve on various college committees to offer an independent community perspective on a variety of issues, and even helped set up a new robotics lab.

LIFE participants have also gained significant campus and community awareness for some recent achievements. A team of LIFE members won the campus-wide College Bowl academic competition in 1991, and other LIFE teams won the countywide corporate spelling bee in 1991 and finished second in 1992.

LIFE operates with an independent board of directors, consisting mostly of retired corporate executives and educators. The college provides a variety of support services.

Contact:
Linda Bennett
(609) 894-9311, ext. 498

Burlington County College
County Route 530
Pemberton, NJ 08068-1599
Total head count enrollment-Credit: 7,116; Non-Credit: 7,834
Campuses/sites: 13; Full-time faculty: 91

THE MID ATLANTIC POST-SECONDARY CENTER FOR THE DEAF AND HEARING IMPAIRED

*⚿ The center comprehensively prepares students ⚿
for independent living*

The Mid Atlantic Post-Secondary Center for the Deaf and Hearing Impaired comprehensively prepares Camden County College students for independent living.

The Center offers comprehensive programs and services for deaf and hearing impaired students. Technical and vocational certificates and degree programs are offered to deaf and hearing impaired students whose hearing loss would prevent them from succeeding in college level courses without additional support services. Students who choose career-track certificate and degree programs receive job readiness training. In addition, the Center's focus is to prepare students who have not had experience in independent living to live independently in the community. Thus, the Center's main objective is to prepare deaf and hearing impaired students to become independent members of society. This is accomplished through its comprehensive programs and services.

The main components of the Center's program are:

- the summer Preparatory Program, an orientation to college life; career exploration is conducted along with life planning and intensive independent living training; an evaluation and assessment of each student is performed to assure appropriate placement.
- the Bridge Program, an academic skills component that utilizes specialized language and communication instruction and provides pre-vocational skills training;
- college programs, including degree and certificate programs offered; the Center also offers certificate programs designed to meet the needs of their students in Word Processing, Personal Computer Specialist, Computer Operations and Computer Aided Design/Computer Aided Manufacturing;

- Academic Support Services, which include the provision of interpreters, tutors, note-takers and counseling;
- a Career & Life Planning component that includes courses in Career and Life Planning and Cooperative Education and counseling;
- Independent Living, which is ongoing training that begins during the Summer Preparatory Program and continues throughout the students' enrollment in the program to develop the students ability to live independently in the community; also, the Center provides specialized equipment and assistive devices that are technological devices to enhance accessibility and education;
- the Faculty Development and Support Program, which prepares faculty to work with deaf and impaired students and provides a resource for ongoing support; and
- the Community Service Center on Deafness and Hearing Impairments, which provides deaf and hearing impaired students with advocacy and interpreting services in the community.

Established in 1986, the Center for the Deaf and Hearing Impaired currently serves 94 students from the Northeast and Mid Atlantic states.

Funding for the Center is provided by the college, Camden County and the New Jersey Department of Higher Education. Approximately $650,000 is realized from these sources to support the center's budget. The center has received the "Golden Hands Award" from the National Association of the Deaf and a certificate of Dedicated Service by the New Jersey Association of the Deaf.

Contact:
Terry Osborne, Center Director
(609) 227-7200, ext. 506

Camden County College
PO Box 200
Blackwood, NJ 08012
Total head count enrollment-Credit: 15,713; Non-Credit: 3,000
Campuses/sites: 2; Full-time faculty: 117

SCHOOL / COLLEGE PARTNERSHIP

❋ *The core of the partnership is the Faculty Development Institute* ❋
for high school faculty

The School/College Partnership Program has led to Camden County College and public schools sharing some fiscal, programmatic and human resources.

Initiated in 1988, the program with the county's 21 public high schools was meant to develop a close relationship with the county's school districts. Three projects were implemented that achieved this objective:

1) the creation of a Faculty Development Institute (FDI) for high school faculty;

2) the implementation of dual credit courses in 21 public high schools; and

3) the development of 2+2 Tech-Prep articulation agreements between the high schools and the college in advanced technologies.

The success of this program has established a unique working partnership between the college and county school districts to cooperatively prepare students for future careers in allied health, advanced technology, business and social services. As a result of this program, the early stages have been completed for the establishment of an Advanced Technology high school on the college's campus to integrate the academic preparation of students for careers in CIM, CAD, computer and laser technologies.

The core of the School/College Partnership Program is the Faculty Development Institute. The institute is composed of high school faculty, college faculty and technical staff and representatives of business and industry. The objective of the institute is to transfer advanced technology knowledge to high school programs through training programs for high school teachers. The institute provides training in laser, computer integrated manufacturing and computer-aided design technologies, while business and industry have provided a realistic view of the industrial needs in these fields

The Faculty Development Institute has motivated school district educators to modify curricula, purchase new equipment and upgrade their knowledge abases in the new technologies. This has resulted in the establishment of 35 Tech-Prep articulation agreements with the county's high schools. The Tech-Prep project is designed to make clear and concrete the practical applications of math and science in the technologies for students in grades eight through 12 who are not historically college-bound or science-oriented. College faculty have reviewed the syllabi of the high school science math courses and made recommendations that would make the courses more technically and practically oriented. As a result, a "Technical Awareness" course for the eighth grade has been developed and an "Introduction to Technology" and Technical Math course for ninth grade. Students completing the Tech-Prep requirements take technology courses at the college in the 12th grade. Thus, they have been academically prepared and have accumulated college credits for a smooth transfer into the college's technology curricula when they graduate from high school.

The third project of the School/College Partnership Program is the dual credit project. College faculty and high school faculty have worked together on course syllabi in languages, English, mathematics and the sciences to certify the college credits can be given for the courses taught in the high school. All 21 of the county's public high schools participate in the project and more than 3,800 students have received college credits in the past four years.

This project is fully funded by the college. Fifteen full-time faculty coordinate and evaluate the dual credit courses at the high schools, for which they are compensated at a total annual cost to the institution of $15,000. This project has been publicized in *Linkages*.

Contact:
Edward McDonnell, Dean, Community Education
(609) 227-7200

Camden County College
PO Box 200
Blackwood, NJ 08012
Total head count enrollment-Credit: 15,713; Non-Credit: 3,000
Campuses/sites: 2; Full-time faculty: 117

THE MATH AND WRITING CENTER

❋ *Students who use the Center show increased retention* ❋
and higher grades

Because colleges have allowed under-prepared students to enroll, the institutions' job is to prevent failure, frustration and high attrition rates, and to provide friendly

environments. At County College of Morris, a Math and Writing Center does just that.

With the help of a three-year New Jersey Challenge

Grant, the Center was established in 1989 to work with a specifically defined target population: minorities (Blacks, Latinos and American Indians), under-prepared students, the learning disabled, and the physically handicapped.

The Center employs three types of tutors: faculty members, paraprofessionals, and student (peer) tutors. Tutors work with students on a one-on-one and small-group basis.

College faculty members have enthusiastically supported the Center. They have also presented workshops, review sessions and, on occasion, brought their classes to the Center. In general, they encourage students to take full advantage of its services.

A variety of instructional audio and video equipment is available to the students in the Center. Audio tapes have not proven to be popular, but video cassettes obtained from textbooks and publishers, as well as tapes prepared by the college's own faculty are well-liked and effective. Interactive videodisc workstations are being introduced in the Math Center.

Although the Center is relatively new, initial indications are that it is highly successful. By its second year, almost 80 percent of the minority students who were enrolled in a math or math-related course or an English composition course used the Math and Writing Center; data show that there was a significantly higher retention rate (about 20 percent) for students who used the Center than for students who didn't.

Grades also improved. For example, about 50 percent of the pre-calculus students who did not use the Center did not pass the course, which is typical nationwide. But, only about 30 percent of the pre-calculus students who did receive help in the Math Center withdrew from the course or failed it.

County College of Morris' Math and Writing Center reaches out to students at all levels of ability and preparation, which has made it possible not only to attract but also to retain a greater population of students than ever before.

Contact:
Diane Zitek, Coordinator, College Relations
(201) 328-5052

County College of Morris
214 Center Grove Road
Randolph, NJ 07869
Total head count enrollment-Credit: 10,568; Non-Credit: 9,000
Campuses/sites: 8; Full-time faculty: 196

COUNTY COLLEGE OF MORRIS

HUMANITIES / INTERNATIONAL STUDIES

This liberal arts transfer program offers a heavy dose of language, including Chinese and Hebrew

Americans are hearing daily that the world is getting smaller, that we are living in a global village. Satellites bring us news from around the world in seconds and nearly every large American corporation is actually an international corporation.

To introduce students to this new world perspective, the County College of Morris has designed the Humanities/International Studies Option, a liberal arts transfer program in the Associate in Arts Degree.

Two major components of the program focused on international students and international studies. As the number of international students grew to more than 800, the college recognized the need to offer them new support services and thus created an International Students Club. Attendance at weekly meetings mushroomed, and members quickly surfaced as some of the most active and energetic on campus.

With an active social organization now in place to complement the strong academic programs, the college pursued formal exchange programs and eventually hosted two German students and 15 Latin American students under the Cooperative Association of States for Scholarship – better known as the CASS program.

But internationalizing a campus goes beyond international students. CCM's American students needed to broaden their perspectives as well. The college first plunged into the area of language by expanding its offerings to include four semesters each of: Spanish, French, German, Italian, Russian, Chinese, Japanese and Hebrew. The enrollment response was outstanding.

CCM's second goal was establishing an International Studies curriculum with foreign language as its core. New classes in cultural geography and intercultural communication also filled quickly.

Perhaps the most interesting accomplishment was in developmental studies. New Jersey students take a statewide test after their admission to college and must remediate any academic weakness through non-credit courses. With a small state grant, eight CCM faculty developed an anthology of intercultural readings with low reading level, but high interest level articles.

Articles on traditions, global problems, roles of men and women, and folk tales, just to name a few, were included. Now, instead of seeing remedial courses as a rehash of their high school English classes, students emerge from a semester of remediation knowing much more about the rest of the world than many of their fellow freshmen.

Continues on Page 426

CCM also provides study abroad opportunities for students through two consortia, the College Consortium for International Studies and Partnerships for Service Learning. Through these programs, students may enroll in U.S.-supervised low-cost programs in 19 countries and still remain students of the college. CCM has sent at least 30 students to seven different countries in recent years.

Another outstanding aspect of this program is that it has cost the college very little. Most of the grants were small and the college judiciously decided not to join professional organizations with high membership fees. Instead, CCM networked and joined a statewide council to further global education. As a result of these efforts, CCM has made the international attitude prevail on campus.

Contact:
Diane Zitek, Coordinator, College Relations
(201) 328-5052

County College of Morris
214 Center Grove Road
Randolph, NJ 07869
Total head count enrollment-Credit: 10,568; Non-Credit: 9,000
Campuses/sites: 8; Full-time faculty: 196

LEGAL ASSISTANT TRAINING

The curriculum is designed to provide students with courses that will help them in general law or a specialty area

In 1970, Cumberland County College became the first college to offer a college degree program for paralegals. It continues to be strong today.

This program was proposed by the Cumberland County Bar Association in response to a study conducted by the association's Education Committee. That study determined that legal assistants could relieve practicing lawyers of routine tasks, while assisting in providing cost-efficient legal services to clients. While the New Jersey State Bar Association and the American Bar Association were strongly advocating increased reliance on paralegals, little was being done to formalize the training necessary to assume such functions. As the paralegal field grew over the years, educational standards became necessary, and the American Bar Association through the Standing Committee on Legal Assistants established voluntary accreditation criteria for paralegal education programs.

The Legal Assistant Program at Cumberland County College is accredited by the American Bar Association as well as the New Jersey Department of Higher Education and is a member of the American Association of Paralegal Education.

The curriculum of the Legal Assistant Program is designed to provide students with paralegal courses that will assist them in a general law practice or a specialty area of the law. The courses include: Introduction to the Legal System; Introduction to Legal Research and Writing; Advanced Legal Research and Writing; Mechanics of Property Transactions; Family Law, Wills and Estates; Law Office Management; Business Law; and Civil Litigation.

At the conclusion of their studies, students complete the Legal Assistant Practicum which requires students to perform 90 hours of paralegal work under the direct supervision of an attorney in a law office, with the courts or with a government agency. To provide students with a simulated trial experience, the Legal Assistant students participate in the New Jersey Bar Foundation's Intercollegiate Mock Trial Competition. The focus of each paralegal class assignment is practical application of the material to prepare students for the workplace and to ensure that the original and continuing objectives of the Bar Association are met.

Among the college library's significant holdings is an extensive collection of law books including the *New Jersey Statutes*, the *United States Code*, the *New Jersey Law Reporters*, *Corpus Juris Secundun*, and the *Shepard's Citation* series.

Students are required to utilize these books in their course work. Additionally, on the three computer terminals in the library dedicated to the Legal Assistant Program, students can access Westlaw, an on-line computerized legal research system; complete WESTrain, an off-line legal research training program; and prepare their assignments on WordPerfect.

The success of the Legal Assistant Program can be measured by the placement of its graduates. Alumni can be found in law firms in Cumberland County as well as the surrounding counties and Philadelphia.

Contact:
Mary Herlihy Fay, Program Director
(609) 691-8600

Cumberland County College
PO Box 517
Vineland, NJ 08360
Total head count enrollment-Credit: 3,600; Non-Credit: 1,100
Campuses/sites: 1; Full-time faculty: 45

ADDICTIONS STUDIES

The program serves a region ranking among the highest in rates of addiction and HIV

The main campus of ECC is located centrally in the urban core of northern New Jersey. This region ranks among the highest in rates of addiction, HIV, and related social problems, the college enhanced its Human and Social Sciences degree program by adding a third option, drug and alcohol counselor certification, to the existing concentrations in social work and mental health.

Courses were submitted to the state addictions certification board, and approval was granted in July 1981. Initially, the program consisted of a basic addictions and pharmacology course, a counseling and treatment course, an internship seminar and field placement, and the core human services and social science requirements.

In response to the creation of a new, entry-level certification, a new course in case management was developed. This allowed the college to meet all the requirements for this certificate. Students are also prepared for the national standardized oral and written case presentation. This is the only undergraduate addictions degree program in New Jersey.

The program has been recognized for its leadership in this area and has received grant funding for new activities. The following grants have been received:

1) State grant for a student and employee addictions program in 1985;

2) Department of Education/Fund for the Improvement of Secondary Education (DOE/FIPSE) grant for peer facilitation of drug prevention 1987-89;
3) DOE/FIPSE grant for a regional campus drug prevention consortium in 1989-91; and
4) Center for Substance Abuse Treatment/U.S. Substance Abuse and Mental Health Science Administration, to be one of 30 regional providers of the national Project for Addiction Counselor Training (PACT) in 1992.

The college is one of only five colleges in the country to be a PACT provider. A subcommittee of the state certification board was formed to advise the PACT program and minority addictions counselor training, coordinated by ECC. The board includes local agency directors and program graduates. Staff are involved in the national core instrument task force of FIPSE, and in the training of new prevention consortia staff of FIPSE. The program has also hosted and coordinated an annual in-service training conference for agency staff and volunteers for the last seven years.

More than 60 graduates of the program are employed in the field, including five agency directors and a member of the state certification board.

Contact:
Peter Myers, Program Coordinator
(201) 877-3254

Essex County College
303 University Avenue
Newark, NJ 07102
Total head count enrollment-Credit: 10,532;
Campuses/sites: 2; Full-time faculty: 153

CENTER FOR TECHNOLOGY

The college is expanding and developing programs in emerging technological fields

With its student body consisting of a 75 percent minority population, Essex County College is committed to encouraging and providing support to minority students interested in pursuing studies and careers in the high growth area of the sciences and technology industries. Thus, the development of a Center for Technology is a high priority for funding for physical facilities, programs and academic support services.

In the present structure, classroom space and laboratory space that is used for the liberal arts and natural sciences has been reconfigured into computer, electronics and robotics laboratories and architectural studio space. Over

the next two years, subject to budgetary conditions and to the changing needs of our service area, the college is expanding and developing programs in the emerging and exploding technological fields. These programs will be housed in a new comprehensive Technological Center. This Center is to provide new resources of space and equipment specifically designed to meet the needs of the expanding technology career opportunities. As a comprehensive technological Center, programs housed in the Center will contribute to the educational achievements and potential success of previously disadvantaged college

Continues on Page 428

students of science and engineering.

The Center will allow ECC to expand and embellish its current multiple goals that include Tech Prep Technology, AAS degrees and Continuing Education programs.

Tech Prep addresses the challenge to our profession to begin to articulate the nature and value of technology in the education of our younger students. It is necessary to intervene early. The 2+2+2 initiative serves as a model for bringing a continuous exposure to the sciences and mathematics. Seminars for both high school faculty and students are held to demonstrate the ever-changing technology in the business and industrial marketplace. Juniors and seniors will take college credit courses at the Center. A well-organized level of support for these students by both high school and college faculty is expected to significantly improve the success rate of students in the engineering related programs.

Among the strong AAS offerings are the programs leading to opportunities for careers in the fields of architecture, engineering, computer engineering, computer integrated manufacturing, mechanical and electrical engineering technologies. Architectural technology is both innovative and professional on the community college level. Both first and second year students' projects are judged each semester by practicing professional architects. The new space will allow the "showing" of the students' designs and construction of their full scale projects.

Although present Continuing Education facilities are limited, ECC is a MASTER CAM Authorized Training Center. Our goal is to empower employers to advance the job skills of their employees. We are seeing a dramatically changing work force in today's competitive economy. With the expansion of our space and resources we will develop programs tailored to the specific needs of companies, agencies and community based organization.

Contact:
Helen Kuruc, Dean, Science and Technology
(201) 877-3194

Essex County College
303 University Avenue
Newark, NJ 07102
Total head count enrollment-Credit: 10,532
Campuses/sites: 2; Full-time faculty: 153

HUDSON COUNTY COMMUNITY COLLEGE

THE BLUEPRINT PROJECT

Subtitled "A Guide to Becoming a Comprehensive Urban Community College," the project report has more than 200 recommendations

In spring 1992, the State Department of Higher Education sent a team to visit the college, after the fourth president in three years resigned unexpectedly and there were assertions of "political interference" in the college. The team raised questions about the renewal of the institution's operation license.

A group of leading citizens was appointed to the Hudson County Community College Task Force by the County Executive and with the approval of the State Department of Education. The group was charged with reviewing the status of the college and making recommendations for the future. Upon completion of this group's work, the Hudson County Board of Chosen Freeholders approved the appointment of the Blueprint Project leadership with a six-month time line to devise a plan that would guide Hudson County Community College to become a "comprehensive, urban community college."

The *Blueprint Project Report* contains 139 pages of recommendations in detail, documentation and appendices. There are more than 200 major recommendations for action between 1992-93 and 1997-98.

Under Academic Issues, the report calls for new direction of the mission of the college as a provider of a comprehensive liberal arts program and community service. Degree programs are to increase from 20 to 32 as well as certificate program expansion to 16, specifically in allied health, nursing, business, hospitality management, public and human services, science and technology, along with expansion of liberal arts and sciences transfer programs.

The college will need to provide career education, job training and retraining, and upgrading of skills in keeping with the priorities of county employers. The general education preparation must develop workplace-ready citizens. Honors programs, incentives to high school GED completers to continue education, expansion of English as a Second Language offerings, and new curricula to serve students who do not progress to college level study are some of the direction provided by the report.

Cooperative relationships with secondary schools and senior higher education institutions must be enhanced and extended. Library collections and services must provide adequate space for books and increase links with local, regional and national library networks.

The college needs to investigate the possibility of becoming a regional center for education and service to the impaired and learning disabled persons.

In the area of Continuing Education/Community

Services, the college needs to provide education on business sites and at the college. A Small Business Development Center in North Hudson is recommended, as is the provision of additional educational programs to the incarcerated and recipients of Aid to Families With Dependent Children, along with educational counseling to adults.

Cultural functions with the many ethnic communities, older adult activities, single parent opportunities are recommended as part of the community services component.

The preparation of unemployed and underemployed workers through the Job Training Partnership Act agency needs to continue. Services for precollege students through a Four College Consortium and with Rutgers Center for Management Development are recommended.

In the faculty area, the number of full-time and part-time faculty needs to be increased. More course sections need be taught by full-time faculty. The college needs to hire additional qualified minority faculty as role models for the diverse student body. All teaching of Hudson County Community College students need be provided by its own faculty as appropriate facilities become available.

Enrollment of head count degree and certificate students needs to increase from 3,076 to 6,337, resulting in a full-time equivalent student growth from 2,227 to 4,524. The number of students served each year by the Continuing Education/Community Services must increase from 1,649 to 10,420.

Course offerings are to be extended in specific areas of the county and instruction on company sites and in community neighborhoods is to be provided.

In the area of Student Services, a broad spectrum of student services needs to be made available. Retention needs to be increased. Assessment and developmental services, career counseling and placement services were given high priority. Financial aid and registration functions need automating with, ultimately, a telephone touch tone registration system installed for convenience and efficiency.

The infrastructure of the college administration needs strengthening with recommendation coming in the area of personnel procedures, organizational reporting relationships, staff development and more. The principle of Total Quality Management must embody every activity. Advisory groups, alumni relationships and student mentors are all mentioned in the recommendations to develop enhanced relationships with the college and students.

Physical facilities and additional space for auditorium, exhibition space, community and student activities are encompassed in the consolidating of functions from several rented buildings to a purchased one as a permanent site in the Journal Square area of Jersey City. The future plans recommend a move to the development of a principal campus with new construction at the Hudson County waterfront by the fall of 1996. Facilities in North Hudson also need to be renovated or purchased.

Schedules and calendars need to be reworked so that more opportunities would be available for students who may not be able to enroll at traditional times.

The final recommendations came in the area of Finance. Emphasis was placed on the recommendation of seeking special state capital and operating appropriations.

Contact:
Office of the President
(201) 714-2100

Hudson County Community College
901 Bergen Avenue
Jersey City, NJ 07306
Total head count enrollment-Credit: 4,140; Non-Credit: 1,008
Campuses/sites: 1; Full-time faculty: 44

HUDSON COUNTY COMMUNITY COLLEGE

DEVELOPMENT OF THE COLLEGE MISSION

Several hundred people from the college and community participated in a forum to help refine the college's mission

A fully developed plan for the operation of a comprehensive urban community college in Hudson County was the recommendation of a Blue Ribbon Panel empowered to review the status of Hudson County Community College in May 1992. The establishment of the Blueprint Project followed, and its report was completed and released in March 1993.

First among the more than 200 recommendations of the project report was the development of a mission statement which reflects Hudson County Community College as a comprehensive urban community college.

During the latter part of the Blueprint Project preparation, the college began identifying constituencies and gathering information about which functions, programs and services the college should undertake.

Through the HCCC Office of Planning and Institutional Research several preliminary activities were completed and compiled in a document named, "Background Documents for the February 27, 1993 Forum to Consider Issues Related to the Mission of HCCC as an Urban Comprehensive Community College." These documents

Continues on Page 430

were a draft revised mission statement resolution passed by the HCCC Board of Trustees in September 1992; Missions, Goals and Objectives.

Statement from *Characteristics of Excellence in Higher Education* (1982); *A Comprehensive Urban Community College: A Vision for the Future*; The philosophy, mission and goal statement from *Hudson County Community College, Master Plan 1986-1991*; An Overview of National Samples of 67 Mission Statements from Comprehensive Community Colleges (1993); and HCCC mission survey results (1993). These survey results included comments from the college community, as well as comments from the external community.

A Mission Forum was set up to take place in a large hotel facility within the county. The president of the college invited several hundred interested individuals to participate in the forum. The invited participants were drawn from faculty, staff, students, alumni, trustees and community leaders. Prior to the actual event, participants received the above documents and a copy of the draft of the *Blueprint Project Report*, which had been completed but not fully printed and accepted by the end of February.

The forum opened with a presentation by Louis Bender, Ph.D., retired, Florida State University. Dr. Bender defined the mission as a declaration of the purpose and intent of an organization that sets the boundary for accreditation. He further defined the words urban, comprehensive, accessible and affordable (all setting the tone for further examination by the participants in the individual discussion groups).

Each discussion group consisted of 10 to 12 participants with a cross-section of trustees, students, community leaders, staff and alumni. The group was led by a facilitator and resource person. In the two-hour small group setting, each group addressed two issues. In some cases, the same issue appeared before more than one small group. A recorder summarized in writing the main points of discussion in each group. At the wrap up session, each group presented the main point summary to the larger gathering of participants. As a follow-up to the forum, the summaries were shared in writing with the participants and were used to further refine the new mission statement for the revitalized urban comprehensive Hudson County Community College.

Discussion topics included:
- How can an understanding of the role of HCCC as a comprehensive urban community college be developed in the general community? Among college staff?
- How can the mission of a comprehensive urban community college be implemented at the North Hudson Center in West New York?
- What specific obligations does HCCC have as a higher education service provider to a population that includes large numbers of persons for whom English is not a first language?
- How can the role of the college be implemented with regard to economic development and to business and industry?
- What should HCCC do to assure that it meets its responsibilities to provide accessible educational opportunities to those who desire them and can benefit from them?
- What does HCCC need to do to meet its responsibilities as a transfer college?
- What obligations does HCCC have with regard to those who seek a college education but do not possess the requisite skills (e.g., language or math) to successfully complete college-level work?
- What are the responsibilities of HCCC with regard to not-for-credit programming and activities in the context of its mission as a comprehensive community college?
- How can student personnel support services help HCCC meet its mission as a comprehensive urban community college?
- What does HCCC need to do with regard to vocational/occupational/career education in the context of its mission as a comprehensive urban community college?

Contact:
Office of the President
(201) 714-2100

Hudson County Community College
901 Bergen Avenue
Jersey City, NJ 07306
Total head count enrollment-Credit: 4,140; Non-Credit: 1,008
Campuses/sites: 1; Full-time faculty: 44

MERCER COUNTY COMMUNITY COLLEGE

PARTNERS IN LEARNING

At any time, between one-fourth and one-third of Mercer's full-time faculty are active participants in the program

As implemented at Mercer, New Jersey's Partners in Learning faculty development model has helped reduce faculty isolation, improve faculty-student communication, create greater collegiality among faculty and generally improve the campus educational environment.

This profoundly simple, adaptable and self-sustaining approach was originally conceived by the late Dr. Joseph Katz as the New Jersey Master Faculty Program. With encouragement and funding from the state Department of Higher Education, it has been adopted at 20 colleges through the New Jersey Institute of Collegiate Teaching and Learning (NJICTL). Program components include:

- faculty pairs attending each other's classes and interviewing each other's students, with a focus on how students learn;
- monthly gatherings of participants, for unguarded discussion and sharing of concerns as teachers; and
- individual writing and sharing of an essay about each semester's experience.

What results is a focus for professional bonding and sharing which is distinct from, but not in conflict with, the faculty union or equivalent framework for addressing terms and conditions of employment. The focus is on teaching well, but the process is not evaluative. Suggestions and ideas emerge frequently and unpredictably; participants observe their teaching improving incrementally and gain confidence in what they do. At any given time, between one-quarter and one-third of Mercer's full-time faculty members are active Partners in Learning participants.

The program serves as an almost magic well for the improvement of teaching at Mercer. Faculty members can draw out of it whatever they wish. They can dip in for a bit of refreshment or plunge in and emerge mightily revitalized. For the institution, it serves as an ongoing source of creative attention to good teaching, driven by the natural desire of faculty members to belong to a vital professional community. Its contribution is far more lasting than occasional "quick fix" seminars.

The critical role of administration is to keep hands off. Each semester, a faculty member receives a small workload adjustment to coordinate program activities. Through college-wide distribution of the coordinator's notes from each monthly meeting, the entire faculty keeps informed and feels connected.

A Mercer professor (Marilyn Dietrich) serves as southern NJ coordinator for NJICTL's Partners in Learning efforts. She observes that the concept finds different successes at different campuses, depending on the composition and character of the faculty and the nature of their programs.

Contact:
Thomas N. Wilfrid, Acting Dean, Academic Affairs
(609) 586-4800, ext. 330

Mercer County Community College
200 Old Trenton Road
Trenton, NJ 08690
Total head count enrollment-Credit: 12,502; Non-Credit: 18,000
Campuses/sites: 2; Full-time faculty: 122

MERCER COUNTY COMMUNITY COLLEGE

NETWORK FOR OCCUPATIONAL TRAINING AND EDUCATION

The network strengthens economic development through the sharing of resources

Mercer County Community College facilitates a network of 19 colleges sharing resources and expertise. This Network for Occupational Training and Education (NOTE) strengthens economic development throughout the state by utilizing the shared resources and expertise of the state's community colleges.

The Network was conceived in 1990 by New Jersey's Department of Higher Education, which solicited proposals for the formation and operation of the network through the leadership of a single community college in the state. Mercer County Community College's proposal, which emphasized collegiality and consensus, a clear regard for each institution's autonomy and a governance structure involving the participation of all Network members, was chosen. The college has facilitated the operation of the network since its inception.

The membership of NOTE consists of one representative from each of the state's 19 community colleges. In addition, NOTE includes one non-voting representative from the DHE Office of Community Colleges and one from the New Jersey Council of County Colleges.

The work of the Network is carried out by four committees: Governance, Marketing, Database Management and Strategic Planning. Each NOTE representative serves on one of the committees and shares in the responsibility of specific network functions.

During its first two years, NOTE adopted an overall mission statement and goals, established an on-line catalog of courses, programs and services, and carried out a variety of marketing activities.

The NOTE membership has established a model agreement through which the 19 community colleges can serve statewide employers and has piloted it's use with one employer. In addition, representatives from the Departments of Commerce and Labor have met with NOTE members to discuss how their agencies might work with community colleges to better serve the state's business community.

During the third year of NOTE, the colleges participated in the state's innovative Workforce Development Partnership Program (WDPP) legislation, which provides new funds for job training. Having developed ways in which to work together, and having established a connec-

Continues on Page 432

tion with state agencies, NOTE will utilize its consortium capabilities to help implement WDPP during this coming year. WDPP-funded projects involving cooperative working arrangements include providing uniform needs assessment and counseling for WDPP applicants and providing statewide training for the health care industry.

NOTE is funded through a grant from the New Jersey Department of Higher Education using federal Vocational Education Title IIB funds for Program Development, Modernization and Expansion (PDME).

Contact:
Linda Milstein, Assist. to the Dean for Corporate & Cmty Programs
(609) 586-4800

Mercer County Community College
200 Old Trenton Road
Trenton, NJ 08690
Total head count enrollment-Credit: 12,502; Non-Credit: 18,000
Campuses/sites: 2 Full-time faculty: 122

PROJECT ACADEMIC SKILLS SUPPORT (PASS)

Program activities help learning disabled students enhance their social and decision-making skills

Project Academic Skills Support (PASS) features activities designed to help learning disabled students at Ocean County College develop an awareness of their individual learning styles.

Designed to assist students with documented learning disabilities to succeed academically and socially at the college level, PASS is open to full-time students as well as to part-time students who are involved in at least one basic skills or college-level course.

PASS program activities are designed to help learning disabled students develop an awareness of their individual learning styles, arrange for accommodations to allow for academic success and enhance social and decision-making skills required for a satisfactory performance in a college environment. Students are tested by Learning Disabilities Teacher/Consultants who familiarize students with the facts about their particular learning strengths and weaknesses. At this time, the need for specific accommodations is clarified.

A series of four Academic Skills Support classes, taught by PASS staff, is organized to teach strategies to increase a student's ability to acquire, retain and express content area information. Skills in the time management, note-taking, test preparation and test-taking are emphasized.

Weekly group counseling sessions are scheduled for PASS students, and PASS staff counsels students on an individual basis including providing academic advisement. Counseling is directed toward increasing the social and behavior skills used in managing daily responsibilities and difficulties. Incoming PASS students participate in a summer orientation program which helps students become familiar with the campus while sampling college-level lectures and materials.

PASS, a regional New Jersey center, serves a four-county area including Ocean, Monmouth, Burlington and Camden counties. Individual students or other institutions may arrange for student assessment for learning disabilities on a fee basis. PASS staff organize and participate in regional and state workshops for promoting awareness of and information about techniques for working successfully with learning disabled students at the college level.

The PASS Center is committed to the philosophy that self-awareness, improved social skills and a better knowledge of learning strategies will increase the learning disabled student's opportunities for success in college. Accommodation, not academic exemption, is emphasized. This project has been made possible through a multi-year grant from the State of New Jersey.

Contact:
Maureen Renstle, Project Director
(908) 255-0400

Ocean County College
College Drive
Toms River, NJ 08754-2001
Total head count enrollment-Credit: 8,353; Non-Credit: 8,000
Campuses/sites: 1; Full-time faculty: 121

CHALLENGE GRANT PROJECT

▨ The planning grant helped the college strengthen minority ▨
student recruitment and retention

To recruit and retain minority students, Raritan Valley community college has five primary goals:

1) Multicultural Sensitivity and Awareness: To create an environment on campus that is sensitive to and respectful of the diverse needs of members of minority and multicultural groups and promote the development of harmonious interaction between minority and non-minority populations.

2) College and Career Success Program: To bridge the gap between students' expectations of college life and college expectations of student performance. To increase minority and academically high risk RVCC students' specific educational and career planning skills resulting in their increased rates of graduation from college, successful transfer to four-year institutions, and/or transition into the labor force.

3) Reading and Writing Enhancement: To increase retention among students who score in the lowest quartiles of the NJCBSPT in reading and/or writing, and improve retention of students who test into the lowest 10 percent of English I.

4) Career and Educational Awareness of Minority Middle School Students: To establish a system of partnership and collaboration between the college and Somerville Middle School. To provide tutorial assistance and basic skills instruction to minority middle school students and to provide career and educational effectiveness training to their parents.

5) Career Guidance Services for Minority Secondary School Students: To establish a system of high school and college partnership and collaboration in order to increase 9th through 11th grade minority students' specific educational and career planning skills resulting in their increased rates of high school graduation and enrollment in appropriate post secondary institutions.

Meeting those goals is possible through the college's Challenge Grant Project addressed "The Minority Initiatives" priority of the 1989 New Jersey State Department of Higher Education (DHE) Challenge Grant program.

RVCC manages the project through the existing organizational structure. The Vice President for Academic and Student Affairs serves as the Project Director. For purposes of responsibility and accountability within the project, a project manager reports directly to the vice president, and serves as the day-to-day operations supervisor. A system of management based on attainment of objectives is utilized to administer the project and to coordinate the efforts of those staff members involved. Through this process of objective preparation and review, each staff member is fully cognizant of his/her role as a staff participant and contributor, and of how each operational portion of the project coordinates with and supports all related activities.

In order to adequately carry out the activities in the project, the institution added four new positions to the organization, three additional counselors and one Learning Disabilities Specialist. In addition, the Office of Student Affairs agreed to commit a substantial portion of the Directors of Career Planning and Placement's time to assist in carrying out project related activities. Similarly, the Office of Instruction agreed to allow a professor of Sociology release time to chair one of the project components, the multicultural component. The team of people that have been assemble to carry out this project over the next three years is called the "Success Group."

The project was funded through a grant from the New Jersey State Department of Higher Education for $1-million to be used over a three year period. Various components of the project have been written about in the local papers as well as the major paper in the state, *The Star Ledger*. In addition, the project was listed as one of the outstanding project funded by the state in the Chancellor Annual Report to the State Board of Higher Education. The college made a major presentation at the national convention of the American Counseling Association (ACA).

Contact:
Thomas L. Green, Vice President, Academic and Student Affairs
(908) 526-1200

Raritan Valley Community College
P.O. Box 3300
Somerville, NJ 08876
Total head count enrollment-Credit: 5,650; Non-Credit: 3,300
Campuses/sites: 1; Full-time faculty: 88

CENTER FOR INTERNATIONAL BUSINESS AND EDUCATION

▦ The Center conducts a monthly round table to meet the needs ▦
of local businesses in the global market

Raritan Valley Community College, in cooperation with public, private and state agencies, has established the Center for International Business and Education to promote and develop a comprehensive International Business Education Program.

The Center provides international business training to expand and develop the global market awareness needed to be competitive in the area of international trade for local businesses, industries and college students. In addition, the Center conducts monthly International Trade Round Tables, export seminars, conferences, and offers 10 different conversational language courses as well as free counseling service for newly established and potential exporters.

The purpose of the International Education Program is to develop, implement and promote international-related activities which would contribute to promoting global understanding among faculty, students and the local community and stimulate interest in international studies.

In order to promote the international program, the college has been sponsoring faculty development workshops, seminars and cultural activities that focus on international curriculum colloquia, ethnic art expositions, seminars on international social-political issues, and study abroad opportunities since 1984. The college has hosted business seminars co-sponsored by the local Chambers of Commerce and other local and state government agencies.

The Center conducts the monthly International Trade Round Table to meet the needs of local businesses to network and exchange information on global market and trade issues. There are more than 75 companies who are members of the Round Table, and that number is growing.

In order to develop linkages with the business community, the college established an International Business Advisory Board in 1988. This Board consists of prominent local business members and local industry representatives, as well as representatives from local Chambers of Commerce, the NJ Commerce Department-International Trade Division, the U.S. Small Business Administration, and the U.S. Commerce Department. This Advisory Board is responsible for providing information related to the local businesses' needs and current business trends. The Advisory Board has also passed the five-year strategic plan to further develop and implement the International Education Program here at the college.

The college is committed to helping newly established local small businesses develop international trade skills and business awareness to promote international business, which will benefit both the business community and the college's students.

Today, business people, government leaders and educators are all in agreement that internalizing our curriculum is one way to help maintain the United States' competitive position in the world economy. Globalizing the curriculum, however, cannot be limited to social studies, languages and literature. All curriculum, especially business education, must have a global perspective. By enlarging the scope of business education to include international concerns, we can prepare students for world citizenship and full membership in the international work force. International business education enables students to develop an understanding of basic business concepts as well as the culture, political structure, legal systems and business practices of other nations.

The business advisory members and the college believes that our economic survival as a nation will depend largely on our businesses being able to compete effectively in the world economy. But the playing field has been altered dramatically.

In order to prepare our students to be global citizens, we have already started working with our business community to utilize them as resources. The international business community has been helping to serve as members of the Advisory Board, as well as serving as guest speakers.

For our effort in promoting International Business program, the Center was awarded a two-year grant from the U.S. Department of Education, International Education, Title VI, Part B. The Center also received the 1992 Mentor Award from the New Jersey Commerce Department and also the New Jersey World Trade Council's Educational Award for our program.

Contact:
Tulsi Maharjan, Director
(908) 526-1200, ext. 8312

Raritan Valley Community College
P.O. Box 3300
Somerville, NJ 08876
Total head count enrollment-Credit: 5,650; Non-Credit: 3,300
Campuses/sites: 1; Full-time faculty: 88

INSTITUTE FOR INTENSIVE ENGLISH

The ESL program, originally funded with grant money, has become profit-making

At Union County College, where the English as a Second Language (ESL) student population represents more than 56 nationalities, the Institute for Intensive English provides quality ESL instruction and American cultural orientation.

The program was begun in 1975 to serve the ever-increasing population of immigrants and new citizens, as well as a limited number of foreign (I-20 visa) students, whose goals are threefold: academic, vocational and social. The institute has grown to serve more than 1,200 full-time students and offers classes at all college locations. The student population, which is reflective of the local demographics, is diverse. Many students work full time out of necessity and attend school full time also. More than 65 percent receive financial aid; a growing number of employers subsidize students' tuition.

The curriculum is designed to integrate ESL instruction in listening, speaking, reading and writing skills and to incorporate various aspects of American culture. There are six progressive levels of instruction, from beginning to advanced, as well as ESL electives such as Pronunciation and Advanced Conversation. In addition, a special two-semester sequence of freshman composition is offered in lieu of ENG 101 and is reserved for ESL students. Two very successful bridge courses are offered: ESL/Math and ESL/Biology; these are taught cooperatively by ESL and content area faculty. An important part of the program is a computer-aided-instruction curriculum component, which has become a national model.

Each student enters the program at a level which is determined by a mandatory in-house placement test. After successful completion of level 6, a certificate is awarded, and academic-bound students continue their studies in mainstream courses.

While the program was originally funded by grant monies, it quickly became self-supporting and for the past several years has been profit-making. Three main factors have enhanced program success: a growing local population of limited English speakers, enthusiastic support of the administration, and a very strong professional faculty. Currently the full-time tenured/tenure track faculty number 21, and there are over 40 adjunct faculty. All have masters degrees in TESOL (Teaching English to Speakers of Other Languages); several have doctoral degrees. Many, both full-time and part-time, have been with the program for more than 10 years.

In addition to the intensive program, ESL classes are offered at corporate sites and on weekends through the Continuing Education program and at senior citizen centers through the LIFE program. The JTPA program at the college also offers ESL/Secretarial training and ESL/Adult Basic Ed.

The combination of these programs provides comprehensive ESL instruction in the area served by Union County College.

Contact:
Helen Aron, Institute Director
(908) 965-6030

Union County College
1033 Springfield Avenue
Cranford, NJ 07016
Total head count enrollment-Credit: 10,476; Non-Credit: 9,500
Campuses/sites: 3; Full-time faculty: 190

COLLEGE FOR KIDS

The program provides diverse enrichment activities for youth ages 2 through 17

College for Kids caters to a variety of interests, including sports, science and math, drama, journalism and computers.

It began at Union County College with a handful of courses for youngsters 8 to 12 years old. In the summer of 1985 there were eight courses offered for youngsters with an enrollment of 60 children participating in arts and crafts activities. Since 1985, College for Kids has grown,

expanded its offerings and provides for the enrichment and enhancement of youth ages 2 through 17.

Each year Saturday programs are conducted during the fall and spring semesters and the Summer program now offers more than 50 programs with enrollments of more than 1,600 kids. College for Kids now gives our kids the opportunity to choose a sports camp (soccer, baseball,

Continues on Page 436

tennis, basic martial arts or basketball); experience science and math through courses in astronomy, rocketry, chemical magic and math; enhance their creative and thinking skills through courses in musical theatre, painting and drawing; learn to be a journalist in Newscamp; develop their computer skills; or travel through history in the medieval ages; or take an ocean adventure at the Jersey shore.

The College for Kids Program teachers are as diverse as our children. They are regular college faculty, elementary school teachers from surrounding towns, coordinators of gifted and talented programs in local districts, and the head coaches of our college sports teams.

The College for Kids brochure has received two awards, one from the National association of LERN (Learning Resources Network) in 1988 and a second award in 1991 from the New Jersey Association of Lifelong Learning. In 1992, the Union County College College for Kids program was awarded the Point of Excellence Award from Kappa Delta Pi for distinguished contribution to the field of education.

Contact:
Robert Schipa
(908) 709-7603

Union County College
1033 Springfield Avenue
Cranford, NJ O7016
Total head count enrollment-Credit: 10,476; Non-Credit: 9,500
Campuses/sites: 3; Full-time faculty: 190

WARREN COUNTY COMMUNITY COLLEGE

GOVERNOR'S CHALLENGE GRANT

The grant prompted creation of a work force training program featuring flexible scheduling and quality instruction

In answer to a challenge to be a contributor to the regional economic stability, Warren County Community College creatively designed work force training programs that have a variety of tuition sponsorships.

Training programs developed and offered included Human Behavior in the Workplace; Handling the Difficult Employee; Medical Office Management; Certified Medical Assistant; Office Systems; Certified Nursing Assistant; Certified Homemaker Home Health Aide; Group Home Counselors/Aides, etc.

The college also researched labor demand occupations and business training needs (in some cases free training was offered as an incentive for businesses to begin or continue training); consulted with experts in the field for development of courses (job skills and equipment necessary, employment opportunities); cultivated partnerships with agencies such as the Private Industry Council, Department of Labor, etc. to sponsor individuals for training.

Funds support development of courses, including consulting and planning; administrative and clerical support; instructional supplies and equipment as required by the program such as computers, software, medical (hospital bed, EKG machine, etc.)

Key factors in success were:
1) flexible program design;
2) adaptability to special needs and changing community needs;
3) up-to-date, practical, relevant and immediate application of skills learned;
4) quality instruction; and
5) funds for initial development.

Contact:
Nancy Laudenslager, Director of Business & Community Programs
(908) 689-7613

Warren County Community College
Route 57 West
Washington, NJ 07782
Total head count enrollment-Credit: 961; Non-Credit: 1,937
Campuses/sites: 1; Full-time faculty: 12

PROCUREMENT AND ACQUISITION

▩ The program's curriculum responds to needs ▩
in private industry and government

At the request of officials at Cannon Air Force Base and with the encouragement of fiscal personnel of other area public sector agencies, Clovis Community College has developed a two-year Associate degree program in Procurement and Acquisition.

The curriculum is designed to respond to the need in both private industry and government for formal academic preparation specific to the field of purchasing and contract management.

The program is essentially a business administration degree adapted to the special needs of public sector procurement/purchasing officers. In addition to a strong general education component, the degree plan includes related requirements in accounting, statistics, business law, economics and management, as well as courses in procurement and acquisition.

The major requirement provides instruction in concepts of procurement and acquisition, contract law, cost and price analysis, and contract negotiation. Students may choose from several restricted electives in procurement and acquisition to complete the major. Degree plans may vary depending on the intended career of the student: federal, state and local, or private sector.

The program is structured as an in-service degree, in anticipation of a large response by persons already employed full-time in procurement and related functions. Some of the required coursework is offered on a weekend format, and with consideration given to award of college credit for documented non-college training corresponding to established course requirements. A cooperative education option and a variable "topics" course provide for employment-based education and for flexible response to specialized needs

The program was developed by an advisory committee consisting of Clovis Community College personnel, Cannon AFB personnel and representatives of other public sector agencies. Municipalities, counties, state and federal agencies, hospitals, school districts and other private and public entities offer employment opportunities in this field, and are numerous in New Mexico and in the Clovis Community College service area.

Contact:
Jim Turner, Vice President, Administration and Finance, (505) 769-4030
David Caffey, Dean of Instruction,(505) 769-4011

Clovis Community College
417 Schepps Boulevard
Clovis, NM 88101
Total head count enrollment-Credit: 3,674; Non-Credit: 237
Campuses/sites: 2; Full-time faculty: 44

MULTICULTURAL MOTIVATIONAL WORKSHOP

▩ The program encourages students in junior and senior high ▩
to consider college as part of their future

Growing out of a strong concern for minority drop-out rates, low enrollment on post secondary education and a need for positive role models, the Motivational Workshop was started by the Adult Re-Entry Program in January 1992. The program was designed to prompt junior high and high school students to think about their futures. Although it was offered and had a positive message for all, it primarily targeted minority groups.

This was accomplished by providing a panel of community role models with whom students could identify. The program began with a keynote motivational speaker and then continued with the panel. The strong message given by all was that we do have choices in life, that despite obstacles, we can succeed, but we need to think about what it is that we want and make "good" decisions. Education was emphasized as the way to have a success-ful future. The panel members discussed their early lives, the obstacles they faced, and the short and long term goals that they set which enabled them to reach their goals. The panel comprised attorneys, police officers, educators, homemakers, counselors, and Air Force personnel, all of whom honestly told of their childhood experiences and how they reached their goals. All panel members and the keynote speaker volunteered their time.

Between March 1992 and May 1992, this workshop was presented four times and heard by more than 200 students. The program was considered successful and the students' response was extremely positive. Students were given a booklet of "The M&M's of Motivation" and a pamphlet, "Yes, I Can," which contains biographies of the

Continues on Page 438

panel members. The workshop was given both at Clovis Community College (in conjunction with a career fair and a tour) and at a church for a Senior Confirmation Class.

We hope to expand the program to all junior high and high school students.

Contact:
Barbara Martinez, Coordinator, Adult Re-Entry Program, (505) 769-4087
Lovina Mack, Director of Student Services,(505) 769-4085

Clovis Community College
417 Schepps Boulevard,
Clovis, NM 88101
Total head count enrollment-Credit: 3,674; Non-Credit: 237
Campuses/sites: 2; Full-time faculty: 44

DONA ANA BRANCH COMMUNITY COLLEGE

NANNY TRAINING

The curriculum includes instruction relating to such things as managing family resources and improving family dynamics

Acknowledging that children are one of our country's greatest resources, Dona Ana Branch Community College designed a program that emphasizes child care in the home. The Nanny Training Program was started in 1989 with funds from a Carl Perkins grant. The nanny curriculum serves as a pilot program in the state of New Mexico and has provided information to other schools starting a nanny program.

The nanny program provides training for approximately 20 students each year. The curriculum includes instruction relating to managing family resources, managing responsibilities, improving family dynamics, strengthening parenting skills and applying homemaker education skills to a career. The nanny students learn how to provide more functional family management in their personal circumstances affording a stronger basis for job seeking and job keeping in their individual careers. Disabled students who may lack technical facility have the opportunity to acquire interpersonal skills that lead to independence and economic self-sufficiency as a child care provider.

The nanny classes prepare child care specialists who are trained in child development, cultural awareness, etiquette, family dynamics, nutrition, defensive driving, safety and first aid. The program at Dona Ana Branch Community College is designed to provide basic educational background plus practical hands-on experiences in child care. A nanny must be prepared to plan and carry out activities that promote a child's overall development.

The training provided at Dona Ana Branch Community College prepares a nanny to adapt to a variety of environments, such as homes in rural and urban settings, and families with different social, cultural and religious backgrounds. Students learn infant and child care by applying information in a practical setting.

The program consists of eight courses that are three credits each. The classes taught are Child Development in Applied Settings, Child Management, Infant and Toddler Care, Child Nutrition, Child Health and Safety, Activities for Children, Professional Development, and Field Experience. Emphasis is placed on functional skills and responsible decision-making, with students practicing analytical thinking skills in a variety of settings.

One of the most important components of the program is a 200-contact-hour field experience where the students practice skills and knowledge gained in coursework. The Dona Ana Branch Community College program is taught by one full-time and one part-time instructor.

To ensure that the course objectives and scope provide appropriate training needed for quality care of children, an Advisory Committee comprising nannies, employers, educators and health care providers meets regularly. The diverse backgrounds provided by the committee contributes to a broad based program. In addition, the program is continuously evaluated by students, faculty and administrators.

Ninety-three percent of the graduates work in a child care position in the state of New Mexico. Graduates of the nanny program have an average of eight positions, generally located in homes, to select from. Approximately 36 percent of the graduates continue their education, often while working in a position which utilizes the skills that they learned in the nanny program.

Contact:
Garlene Petersen, Child Care Coordinator
(505) 527-7629

Dona Ana Branch Community College
3400 South Espina, Box 30001 – Department 3DA
Las Cruces, NM 88003
Total headcount enrollment-Credit: 3,405; Non-Credit: 3,232
Campuses/sites: 3; Full-time faculty: 49

TUTORIAL SERVICES

The program includes peer tutors who motivate, inspire and provide instructional support

Tutorial Services at Dona Ana Branch Community College were developed to help meet the personal and academic challenges of the under-prepared adult learner. The services are unique in the ability to facilitate the adult learner from the adult basic level through the community college and first-year college level.

The need for such expanded student services resulted in part from the Developmental Studies program. Committed to providing quality educational opportunities emphasizing student success, DABCC in partnership with the Adult Basic Education, and Educational Success and Disabled Student Services developed Tutorial Services.

The goals of DABCC Tutorial Services are to mentor and tutor our students keeping in mind their many responsibilities of work, family and school. Peer tutors are used as role models to motivate, inspire, provide instructional support, and help build realistic plans to accomplish their academic endeavors. Attempts are made to assess academic strengths and weaknesses, help students to recognize their learning skills, improve study methods and techniques, instill academic responsibility, and eliminate the barriers of academic frustration and anxiety.

Tutorial Services seeks to effectively serve the learner by providing tutoring in a variety of modes, media and locations. Two drop-in labs are available for extended daily hours: Quintana Learning Center (QLC), providing adult basic education and basic skills; and the Tutor Center for developmental math, English, reading, and study skills and weekend tutoring.

Additional tutorial support is provided through computer-aided, video, and audio-cassette instruction available through the QLC. Peer tutors facilitate drop-in or individual appointments, study groups, workshops and review sessions throughout the semester. They also provide instructional support by offering class workshops, lab tutoring, and teaching specialized units at the instructors' requests. Academic tutorial support is now given in: developmental studies; computer technology, computer-aided drafting; secretarial administration (bookkeeping); water technology, heating, air conditioning and refrigeration; adult basic education; and soon to expand to the adult health and paralegal programs.

Tutorial assistants are solicited from academically qualified New Mexico State University and second year DABCC work/study applicants who demonstrate a sincere interest in "making a difference" in the lives of our students. Tutors for our specialized technical courses may be hired through the Student Employment Service. Intensive tutor training is provided at the beginning and throughout the semester covering such topics as: study skills; time management; college survival skills; critical thinking skills; stress management; learning sales; mentoring the adult learner; tutoring the limited English deficient, learning and physically disabled, and the testing/math anxious.

Because of the institution's strong commitment to student success, funding for Tutorial Services comes in part from the Carl Perkins Grant for Disadvantaged Students administered by the Educational Success and Disabled Student Services and other institutional monies. Additional institutional support includes administrative support, office and work space, resources, and staff expertise for tutor training, counseling and advisement.

Contact:
Esther Enriquez-Weatherley, Tutor Coordinator
(505) 527-7632

Dona Ana Branch Community College
3400 South Espina, Box 30001 – Dept. 3DA,
Las Cruces, NM 88003
Total headcount enrollment-Credit: 3,405; Non-Credit: 3,232
Campuses/sites: 3; Full-time faculty: 49

AVIATION MAINTENANCE TECHNOLOGY

Former program graduates are employed as mechanics from Alaska to Florida, from New Jersey to California

Since the Aviation Maintenance Technology Program at ENMU-Roswell began in 1968, it has developed into one of the nation's best training programs for careers in aviation maintenance.

The philosophical basis of the program is to provide students with the highest quality of instruction including actual hands-on work with a wide variety of operating aircraft. To this end, the Aviation Maintenance Technology Program provides in-depth training in the maintenance of all types of aircraft. The variety of aircraft provides students the opportunity to receive hands-on training in

Continues on Page 440

applying the latest techniques to actual aircraft. For example, the newly acquired MU-2D pressurized project allows students to gain experience in pressurized systems, bleed-air environment control, reverse thrust capability, and auto-start computers. The curriculum is the only one approved by the Federal Aviation Agency in the state of New Mexico.

There is a national shortage of trained aviation maintenance technicians. The Aviation Maintenance Technology Program at ENMU-Roswell is providing trained aviation maintenance technicians to address this critical shortage. The program has an excellent record of placing graduates. Former graduates are employed as mechanics at locations ranging from Alaska to Florida and New Jersey to

California. Graduates are employed as mechanics working on corporate jets, turbo props, and turbo-charged twin and high performance all-weather single engine aircraft.

The Aviation Maintenance Technology Program is housed in a modern facility adjacent to the Roswell, New Mexico airport. The 23,000-square-foot facility containing a hanger and classrooms was constructed in 1978 at a cost of $1.1-million. There are eight operational aircraft used in the instructional program along with a wide variety of support equipment. All program faculty maintain FAA airframe and power plant ratings as well as maintaining ratings as pilots. The program is recognized by the New Mexico Commission on Higher Education as a Program of Technical Excellence. The program

Contact:
Bob Cates, Associate Dean of Vocational Education
(505) 624-7000

Eastern New Mexico University-Roswell
PO Box 6000
Roswell, NM 88202-6000
Total head count enrollment-Credit: 2,072; Non-Credit: 450
Campuses/sites: 3; Full-time faculty: 52

PETROLEUM TECHNOLOGY

The college has a 14-acre outdoor lab where students may apply classroom knowledge

The Petroleum Technology Program at ENMU-Roswell is unique not only to New Mexico, but also from a national perspective. Like some other programs, the Petroleum Technology Program provides instruction in all phases of the petroleum industry. However, this program differs from others of its kind in its special emphasis on the application of classroom instruction.

The outdoor lab area provides students an opportunity to apply knowledge gained through classroom instruction. About 60 percent of instructional time is devoted to teaching petroleum engineering principles. While the balance of the time is devoted to utilizing actual oil field equipment in the 14-acre outdoor lab. No other program offers such a wealth of petroleum equipment for hands-on learning experiences.

While there has been a decline in recent years of people

employed in the petroleum industry, there is still a strong demand for students trained at the Petroleum Technology Program, which began in 1975. For many years, the petroleum program has been offering certificate and associate degree programs in petroleum technology.

In addition to traditional courses, the Petroleum Technology Program offers a number of non-traditional approaches to meet educational demand. For example, petroleum seminars are offered as refresher courses for industry personnel. Several university petroleum engineering programs send students to the Petroleum Technology Program at ENMU-Roswell to provide their students with hands-on experience. The program is recognized by the New Mexico Commission on Higher Education as a Program of Technical Excellence.

Contact:
Bob Cates, Associate Dean of Vocational Education
(505) 624-7000

Eastern New Mexico University-Roswell
PO Box 6000
Roswell, NM 88202-6000
Total head count enrollment-Credit: 2,072; Non-Credit: 450
Campuses/sites: 3; Full-time faculty: 52

ARMY EARLY COMMISSIONING

*▨ Young people can take advantage of a no-strings-attached ▨
summer introduction to military life*

A six-week summer camp at New Mexico Military Institute gives young people just out of high school a taste of the Army, without any obligation to join NMMI or the Army.

This program allows recently graduated students to attend free the summer camp at Fort Knox, KY, if they have a 2.0 or higher GPA, an ACT score of 19 or higher or an SAT score of 850 or higher and are able to pass an Army physical. Transportation, room and board are all paid by the Army. At the end of the summer camp the student will receive $650 for attending. The student can also try for Army ROTC scholarships while at the camp.

After attending the summer camp the student may attend NMMI and if they wish join the Advanced ROTC program. This allows them to complete their first two years of college and at the same time become a second lieu-

tenant in the Army Guard or Reserves.

During this time they are paid $100 per month and given a $1,000 uniform allowance. The student can then attend the college of their choice and complete their baccalaureate degree. During the last two years of college the student will affiliate with a Guard or Reserve unit as a second lieutenant and go to drill once a month. These two years count for time and grade and puts the student two years ahead of the four-year ROTC student.

After graduation the student can choose to go active duty as a second lieutenant with two years experience or get a job and maintain their status in the Guard or Reserves. Students wishing to go active duty usually have a better chance of getting an active duty slot by going through the two-year program.

Contact:
Admissions Office
(800) 421-5376

New Mexico Military Institute
101 West College
Roswell, NM 88201
Total headcount enrollment-Credit: 950
Campuses/sites: 1; Full-time faculty: 75

SERVICE ACADEMY PREP

*▨ The institute models its academics after the nation's military ▨
academies and has a Corps of Cadets*

New Mexico Military Institute offers one of the best Service Academy Prep Programs in the country. In one recent year, 57 NMMI students were appointed to the Air Force, Naval, West Point and Merchant Marine academies.

More proof of the success of NMMI's outstanding academic preparation in preparing students for the academies is the large number of students sent to NMMI by the Academy Foundations. In 1992-93, the Falcon and Naval Foundations and the Association of Graduates for West Point sent 68 students for preparation.

Although attending NMMI does enhance the chances

for an appointment, it does not make an academy appointment automatic. Because NMMI is modeled after the academies academically and has a Corps of Cadets, a student who succeeds at NMMI shows he is the caliber of student who can do well at the academy.

The academy prep program follows a pre-engineering track. The first semester students usually take Calculus I, English Composition, Physics or Chemistry and an elective such as U.S. History, Speech or Foreign Language. If the student does not get accepted to an academy, these courses are transferable should the student wish to continue his education at another college.

Contact:
Admissions Office
(800) 421-5376

New Mexico Military Institute
101 West College
Roswell, NM 88201
Total headcount enrollment-Credit: 950
Campuses/sites: 1; Full-time faculty: 75

EARLY CHILDHOOD TRAINING

The college's Child Development Center includes a college classroom, preschool classrooms and observation rooms

San Juan College recognizes pressing state and regional needs to increase the quantity and improve the quality of professionals who work with young children. The college's service area (San Juan County) includes geographically isolated rural areas and the county has the third-highest percentage of economically disadvantaged children in New Mexico.

So in 1986, San Juan college initiated its Early Childhood Program to fulfill the need for qualified child-care givers, preschool, and Head Start teachers in the country and surrounding remote areas. In addition, the program provides training for public school paraprofessionals as mandated by the 1990 New Mexico State Department of Education licensure standards.

Credentials offered by the program include the Child Development Associate certificate (a national, vocational certificate required by Head Start), a one-year certificate, and an AA degree (both of which complement the three levels of paraprofessional licensure).

In January of 1990, the college completed a state of the art $750,000 Child Development Center, which included a college classroom and two preschool classrooms with adjoining observation rooms equipped with sound and one-way mirrors. The Center serves as a model practicum site as well as a site for more than 1,000 observations per year. The program at the Center is one of six in New Mexico accredited by the National Academy of Early Childhood Programs, and is the only two-year institution in the state to have such a program as a training facility. The availability of the Center has enabled the program to institute a high quality practicum-based program for early childhood professionals.

In addition to our on-campus facilities, the program offers off-campus courses on the Navajo, Jicarilla Apache, Ute Mountain Ute, and Southern Ute reservations, and has provided CDA advising in 27 rural Native American Communities.

Finally, San Juan College is the recipient of a Kellogg Foundation grant to serve as a "BEACON" institution. As part of this grant the Early Childhood Education Program will develop a series of seminars and dissemination materials for other community college personnel who are training paraprofessionals in AA degree or CDA credential programs.

As an example, in 1986, the Shiprock Agency of the division of Navajo Development, which serves as the grantee for Indian Head Start Services in San Juan County, indicated a need for training in early childhood education. The Shiprock Agency is one of five agencies under the Division of Navajo Child Development and serves between 600 and 700 children each year in 19 preschool centers and 13 Homebase Programs. Many of these centers are located in very remote reservation areas, and their needs for information training and support were great.

Now, National Head Start requirements for CDA credentialing and the current federal appropriation increase to double the number of children served in Head Start programs, which vastly increases the demand for training in early childhood education.

An additional need in our geographic area is for trained paraprofessionals to work as teacher assistants in area public schools. A December 1990 survey of paraprofessionals in four area school districts (Aztec, Bloomfield, Central and Farmington) indicated that roughly 75 percent of those responding had no formal training in education at all, and only 3 percent have an AA degree.

With the October 1990, New Mexico State Department of Education regulation, which requires licensure for "educational assistants," San Juan College is in a position to provide training for the large percentage of the areas' 300 paraprofessionals who meet only minimal licensure requirements.

Contact:
Betty Chester
(505) 599-0246

San Juan College
4601 College Boulevard
Farmington, NM 87402
Total head count enrollment-Credit: 3,960; Non-Credit: 6,000
Campuses/sites: 3; Full-time faculty: 65

PROFESSIONAL PILOT TRAINING

Not only does this program provide job opportunities, but also it attracts new residents who come to work for Mesa Airlines

San Juan College and Mesa Airlines, Inc., jointly operate a flight school and degree program to train and recruit pilots to the airline. This venture is the only comprehensive pilot training and degree program in New Mexico which is designed to meet the needs of a local airline.

Mesa Airlines is a regional airline that provides service to 68 cities in New Mexico, Colorado, Wyoming, Arizona, Texas, Nebraska and South Dakota. The carrier has experienced a continual growth since 1982 when it began its operation in Farmington. Because of its growth, there has been a constant need to hire additional employees. This need, coupled with a shortage of qualified pilots, set the stage for the college-airline agreement to train pilots.

In addition to an Associate of Applied Science Degree in Aviation Technology, the student earns his/her private license, instrument, commercial, and multi-engine ratings. For those individuals who want to qualify as air transport pilots, this program provides them with a unique opportunity found nowhere else in New Mexico and in very few places throughout the United States. In order to fly for Mesa Airlines, an individual must have 1,500 hours of flight time, with 200 of those hours being multi-engine. By going through the San Juan Pilot Training Program, an individual can fly with Mesa with 300 to 400 flight hours. If

the pilot is employed by Mesa Airlines after graduation from San Juan College, that individual could expect to obtain his/her ATP (Air Transport Pilot) within a couple of years.

Not only does this program provide job opportunities for people in New Mexico, but also it brings in permanent residents from outlying areas who become students and then employees with Mesa Airlines.

This program demonstrates San Juan College's commitment to meet the needs of our community and the State of New Mexico. In order to provide quality education, we must listen and respond to the needs of companies such as Mesa Airlines.

Mesa Airlines began its operation in 1982 with three employees and one airplane flying between Farmington and Albuquerque. Today, the company has 24 aircraft valued at $64-million, serves 68 cities, and employs more than 400 people. Skyway Airlines is also a wholly owned subsidiary of Mesa Inc., based out of Milwaukee. On April 1, 1990, Mesa Inc. entered into a five-year agreement with United Airlines and now operates United Express routes. With this type of growth, it is obvious that there is an ongoing need for highly trained personnel.

Contact:
Charlie Houghten
(505) 599-0339

San Juan College
4601 College Boulevard
Farmington, NM 87402
Total head count enrollment-Credit: 3,960; Non-Credit: 6,000
Campuses/sites: 3; Full-time faculty: 65

STUDENT OUTCOMES MODEL

Student outcomes assessment is separate from staff or faculty performance evaluations

Santa Fe Community College (SFCC) initiated a student outcomes assessment process in 1986 to evaluate and improve its educational programs. The assessment methods are relevant to student goals and the educational mission of the college. The model has become a valuable tool for internal quality control, continuous program improvement and reporting to external agencies.
Specifically, the Student Outcomes Model is designed to:
1) identify what the college wants to teach
2) measure the degree to which the college is doing it; and
3) collect information to help do it better.
In reality, the SFCC outcomes studies are an ongoing

series of brief, practical, issues-oriented reports with applications to specific instructional practices or programs. The studies (and subsequent reports) reflect the continuous attention to program improvement and instructional enhancement. The process properly places student outcomes as an integral function of the college's total quality control system.

The studies – conducted annually – are simple and relevant and provide usable information. The format and procedures meet the standards of formal research to establish validity and reliability but remain simple to carry out. The simplicity encourages faculty and staff to conduct

Continues on Page 444

issues-oriented studies under the coordination of a college-wide Student Outcomes Committee.

Among the annual studies are:

- Correlation Study - Final Exams and Acquired Competencies;
- Licensure Exams Success Rates;
- Student Opinion Surveys;
- Graduate Follow-up Study;
- Employer Follow-up Study;
- College Transfer Study; and
- Course Success and Completion Rates Study.

Critical to the success of measuring effectiveness is a commitment to separate student outcomes assessment from staff or faculty performance evaluations. Outcomes work is most successful when faculty and staff enthusiastically seek out opportunities to participate.

Since 1986, the outcomes model also has proven to be useful for meeting agency reporting requirements. As a measure of institutional effectiveness, the studies have been used in the accreditation and self-study process. Seen as measures of academic gain, the studies are incorporated into the federal vocational reporting standards. The studies are also a vital component of the consumer information made available to new and prospective students.

Contact:
Anthony Garcia, Dean of Students
(505) 438-1262

Santa Fe Community College
PO Box 4187
Santa Fe, NM 87502-4187
Total headcount enrollment-Credit: 3,600; Non-Credit: 3,600
Campuses/sites: 1; Full-time faculty: 35

STAFF AND ORGANIZATIONAL DEVELOPMENT

A key part of the program is the Professional Development Plan, required of all faculty

The Staff and Organizational Development Program at Santa Fe Community College is heavily oriented toward promoting learning opportunities for faculty and staff that improve work effectiveness, support productivity, increase leadership skills and promote high morale. The program has been uniquely successful in integrating faculty evaluations into a comprehensive professional development program.

There are four components to SFCC's program:

1) Planning. Staff development activities are developed in a yearly cycle. To determine which activities are most appropriate, full- and part-time instructors and division heads are surveyed, the college's deans and president are consulted, and faculty evaluations from peers and students are used to identify areas for strengthening teaching performance.

2) Programming. In a given academic year, the staff development director typically designs and implements 75 to 100 different workshops and programs for faculty and staff, all of which are designed to promote effective teaching and build a positive attitude toward student success.

3) Disseminating Information. Articles and books on current topics of interest, along with announcements of special educational conferences, are regularly distributed to faculty. *Innovation Abstracts*, a weekly publication of the National Institute for Staff and Organizational Development, is sent to both full- and part-time faculty. In the Learning Resource Center, a special section has been set aside with professional development books, periodicals, videotapes and related educational materials.

4) Evaluating. Full- and part-time faculty are evaluated each semester by their peers and by students. Full-time faculty are also evaluated each year by their immediate supervisors. Each of the staff development activities is evaluated by participants. An annual survey of all faculty and staff is also used to evaluate the effectiveness of the staff development program as a whole.

An integral part of SFCC's Staff Development Program is the Professional Development Plan (PDP), required of all full- and part-time faculty. The objective is to promote quality instruction and reward instructors who commit themselves to a professional growth plan. Part-time faculty may earn incremental salary increases by taking part.

Faculty may choose among 14 different activities to earn PDP credit. For example, they may have a class session videotaped and evaluated by an experienced faculty member; they may attend SFCC-sponsored professional development activities (some are required); they may undertake independent reading projects; they may complete a self-assessment inventory; or they may create their own plan to meet their unique needs.

One of the most popular PDP activities is the "Faculty Forum," a regularly scheduled program that brings full- and part-time faculty together to discuss educational issues, share ideas and promote group problem-solving. One new faculty member commented, "As always, the opportunity to share problems and concerns with other faculty members helps to dispel some of the feelings of isolation which are an occupational hazard."

Perhaps the most unique aspect of SFCC's Staff Development Program is that faculty evaluations have been effectively integrated into a comprehensive professional development plan so that the evaluation process is seen as an opportunity to improve teaching. Full-time faculty agree it is a way for them to learn new teaching strategies; part-time faculty feel less isolated and a more

integral part of the college. Whereas research in faculty evaluation processes generally concludes that they are often ineffective, the SFCC program demonstrates that this does not necessarily have to be – especially if the fundamental purpose is professional growth rather than evaluation. A recent climate survey conducted at SFCC revealed that 93 percent of the full-time faculty feel that the evaluation procedures used by their supervisors, peers and students are fair and effective.

Contact:
Beatrice Davis, Director, Staff and Organizational Development
(505) 438-1312

Santa Fe Community College
PO Box 4187
Santa Fe, NM 87502-4187
Total headcount enrollment-Credit: 3,600; Non-Credit: 3,600
Campuses/sites: 1; Full-time faculty: 35

UNIVERSITY OF NEW MEXICO-LOS ALAMOS

ENVIROMENTAL SCIENCE / ENVIRONMENTAL AND OCCUPATIONAL SAFETY

✳ *The Environmental Science and the Environmental and Occupational Safety* ✳
programs include cooperative education phases

For the University of New Mexico-Los Alamos, training students to address the growing concern about the environment was a natural expansion of the traditional course material in science and engineering.

A tentative program was first put together and discussions were held with the Engineering College of the parent institution in Albuquerque, NM. By the fall of 1990 the programs at the Branch College were in place. Currently there are two: Environmental Science and Environmental and Occupational Safety.

The Associate of Science in Environmental Science degree program is designed to introduce students to the field, and to provide a basic science education at freshman and sophomore level in chemistry, physics and biology. The curriculum emphasizes mathematical and scientific principles that prepare a student to understand and assist in problem-solving. Students also are introduced to the fundamentals of hazardous materials and hazardous waste management. The curriculum allows a student to explore the field of environmental science from the perspectives of both regulation and engineering. Students may continue toward a baccalaureate program or, after completing the associate degree, acquire an entry-level position as a technician in the field. A total of 67 credit hours with a GPA of 2.0 or better is required for graduation. A Certificate in Environmental Science may be earned by completing 32

credit hours of selective courses of study with a GPA of 2.0 or better.

The Associate of Applied Science in Environmental and Occupational Safety degree program is designed to introduce students to the field of environmental technology, and health and occupational safety. The curriculum emphasizes fundamentals of environmental science, hazardous materials, electronics, instrumentation and computer programming. A basic mathematics and science education, and hands-on experience are also provided that prepare a student to understand and assist in problem-solving, and to provide quality technical support in a wide variety of environmental science and occupational health and safety areas.

Although the program is considered to be a terminal degree program, many of the courses articulate with baccalaureate programs at four-year universities. A total of 67 credit hours with a minimum GPA of 2.0 is required for graduation. No certificate is available in this field of study.

An unusual aspect of these programs is the Cooperative Education phases that may be used towards the degree for a maximum of three credit hours. UNM-LA has an office that is quite successful in placing students in part-time paid employment in their fields of study with local scientific and engineering establishments.

Contact:
Robert Dinegar, Science Coordinator
(505) 662-5919, ext. 408

University of New Mexico-Los Alamos
4000 University Drive
Los Alamos, NM 87544
Total head count enrollment-Credit: 2,522; Non-Credit: 170
Campuses/sites: 1; Full-time faculty: 0

PROFESSIONAL NANNY TRAINING

▓ Local day care centers provide sites for practicum observations ▓
and a local restaurant provides a "hands-on" etiquette exam

The Professional Nanny Training program, recognized nationwide for its high quality, has a nearly non-existent drop-out rate, and a virtual guarantee that graduates will be employed. It started at the University of New Mexico-Los Alamos with a $34,000 grant from the New Mexico Department of Vocational Education to pilot a program for training professional nannies. The project was in response to:

1) the need for professional-level child care for families not served by existing, traditional child care services; and

2) to provide a short-term, intensive program of college-level instruction for students seeking employment in a child care field.

In designing the program, UNM-LA staff consulted with the American Council of Nanny Schools, the International Nanny Association, numerous nannies and nanny placement agencies throughout the U.S., a local advisory committee and families seeking in-home child care. The one-semester training (18 university credits) consists of Child Growth and Development, Family Studies; Child Health, Safety and Nutrition (including First Aid, CPR, Defensive Driving and Boat Safety and Water Rescue); Activities and Community Resources for Children; Professionalism for Nannies; and 100 hours of practicum. Offered twice yearly during the summer and fall semesters, the summer training meets Monday through Friday, 8 a.m. to 5 p.m., and attracts mostly recent high school graduates and college-age students. The fall training meets weekends, all day Saturday and noon to 6 p.m. on Sunday. The weekend program meets the needs of a greater number of non-traditional students and those who need to work full-time while completing the training.

Students in the program represent wide-ranging diversity: ages 18-57, educational backgrounds from a GED to a master's degree, and ethnic origins including American Indians, Anglos, Asians and Hispanics. Two male students have also completed the program. The drop-out rate for the program is nearly non-existent, with 96 percent of students registered completing the training.

The program has received nationwide publicity, including articles in the *New York Times* and *Chicago Tribune*, features on radio talk shows in Florida and New Mexico, two statewide TV features and numerous items in local media. As a result, graduates have been much sought after, with employment opportunities within New Mexico and across the country. In addition to working as traditional live-in nannies, graduates of Professional Nanny Training are also working in day care centers, pre-schools, Head Start Programs, as public school classroom aides and provide child care for resort facilities. Single parent graduates have obtained positions which allow their own children to accompany them to work. UNM-LA has more than 400 requests from families wishing to hire the 44 graduates to date.

Salaries for graduates have exceeded expectations for child care providers. Those employed in live-out positions are earning $5 to $12 per hour. Those in live-in positions earn $200 to $350 per week, plus room and board, and often enjoy such perks as travel and club memberships. Cost of the training is $395 tuition and fees, plus approximately $100 for books and supplies.

Community involvement in the program is high: local day care centers provide sites for practicum observations, police and fire departments make presentations on home safety and fire prevention, youngsters from the community participate in on-campus art and literature activities with nanny students, and a local restaurant provides a "hands-on" etiquette exam.

The UNM-LA Professional Nanny Program includes five part-time instructors, numerous individual workshop consultants and a full-time program director. The training emphasizes the career ladder for child care professionals and is integrated into a variety of degree programs within the university system.

Contact:
Vann Atwater, Program Director
(505) 662-5919

University of New Mexico-Los Alamos
4000 University Drive
Los Alamos, NM 87544
Total headcount enrollment-Credit: 2,522; Non-Credit: 170
Campuses/sites: 1; Full-time faculty: 0

HUMANITIES CORE CURRICULUM

The premise of the program is to connect key courses such as English, History and Science with a common theme

Believing that the general education requirement should emphasize the commonality rather than the disparity among disciplines, Adirondack Community College created a Humanities Core Curriculum that links key courses with a common thematic thread.

This replaced the pervasive form of the general education requirement for the associate degree that can be characterized as a prescribed distribution requirement. Under that format, students select from short lists of courses in specified disciplines, and supplement these with free electives. This approach often results from political negotiation aimed at protecting divisional turf rather than a coherent educational philosophy, thus leaving the student with the impression that the disciplines covered are in no way interrelated.

It was a significant experiment to move at least a portion of Adirondack Community College's general education requirement away from the segregated and toward the integrated humanities core curriculum. Early examples of this included sections of freshman English, U.S. History from 1866, and a science course (Man and His Environment), using environmental issues as a thematic link. The English course used environmental readings and writing assignments, while the history course gave special emphasis to the environmental movements, both complementing and supplementing materials covered in the Man and His Environment course. Course work was supplemented with field trips, guest lecturers, and informal seminars in the homes of instructors. Fund-raising activities were also undertaken to support activities.

During the fall 1992 semester, the theme was our Greek heritage. The linked courses include History of Western Civilization to 1500, Introduction to Archaeology, and English. Again, fund-raising activities helped underwrite a spring field trip to Greece.

The program has been enthusiastically received by the students. The results from assessment questionnaires are extremely positive. Many of the students lauded not only the educational value of program – particularly its coherency – but also its social value. Study groups formed, friendships were forged, and a sense of place, often lacking on a commuting campus, emerged.

The faculty are satisfied not only with the educational impact the program has had on the students, but also its renewing effect on them.

Contact:
Pat Duncan
(518) 793-4491, ext. 408

Adirondack Community College
Bay Road
Queensbury, NY 12804
Total head count enrollment-Credit: 3,550; Non-Credit: 5,500
Campuses/sites: 2; Full-time faculty: 94

THE FRESHMAN EXPERIENCE

First-semester success is easier for new students who learn how to choose classes and relate to staff

A significant step toward reversing the trend of declining retention was to help first-semester freshmen learn how to choose classes and relate to staff. The Freshman Experience is the result of eight years of putting several ideas into practice.

The program is made up of several components focusing on first semester success. They include appropriate placement in first-semester classes, the development of a significant relationship between each first-time full-time student with a staff member, an early warning system, and the improvement of overall academic advisement.

The process begins with Individualized Placement, where each incoming student meets one-on-one with a counselor during the summer, and Prescriptive Admissions, which attempts to place first-time full-time students into the Freshman Experience Program that best meets their needs. ACC's in-house research indicated that, despite mass testing of all incoming full-time freshman, the best predictor of student success is the high school transcript, carefully studied. Full-time admission is prescribed into one of four programs offered during the first semester. The programs are Freshman Seminar, College Survival, Honors Seminar and Developmental Studies.

The Freshman Seminar, the largest program, is a one-credit pass/fail course designed to introduce the student to the college experience. The course is taught by a faculty or staff member who then serves as the academic advisor to

Continues on Page 448

the fifteen students in the seminar. The course is designed by the instructor to best utilize his or her skills in helping the students develop survival skills such as note-taking, test-taking, and time management, as well as making them aware of campus resources and activities. We have found that one of the most important factors in this option is the development of the relationship between instructor and student.

The College Survival program is designed to serve the student who in the past was at high risk of dropping out. The student is enrolled in a core of first-semester courses which both challenge and support, as well as one course from his or her major. The main course is a four-credit graded course which helps students take a look at their skills, and through academic assignments, to begin to develop survival habits. Team-teaching and group interaction are key to this option's success. Students who enter college lacking self-esteem and academic skills develop a sense of power and confidence as they work hard to meet new challenges.

TheHonors Seminar, modeled on the strengths of the College Survival Program, is a three-credit graded liberal arts course designed to challenge our strongest students. The course is team-taught by distinguished faculty from different divisions, and combines academic disciplines to stretch the intellectual capacity of its participants. The seminar is the beginning course of a 15-credit honors program which offers students options from various divisions.

Developmental Studies, the newest option in the Freshman Experience is a pre-college, non-credit set of courses designed to bring weak students to college level. Students are team-taught by an English and a Math instructor and work with 15 other students on study strategy and skill development. This program aims at preparing its participants for college course work after one semester.

In each of the four Freshman Experience options academic advisement is stressed, and the student receives the message from the college that he is important and that the college cares about his success. Academic advisement has been significantly augmented to assist with these efforts. Statistics indicate that the first semester of college is predictive of future success and, clearly, an important place to focus our attention.

In addition to the first-semester seminars and improved advisement, our Early Warning System encourages all faculty to contact Student Services if a student is not attending class or failing to perform satisfactorily in the first several weeks of each semester. Student Services personnel then follow-up on the student, attempting to help him solve problems which might interfere with his continued enrollment.

ACC's Freshman Experience Program has dramatically affected our retention (it has been raised over 10 percent in six years), and has received much recognition. Much of our burgeoning enrollment is a result of these retention efforts. ACC staff have traveled extensively to train other colleges to develop and teach Freshman Seminar, and an article has been published on the program's development. Last year, Noel and Levitz recognized the program in their national awards competition.

Contact:
Robbin Esser, Coordinator
(518) 793-4491, ext. 202

Adirondack Community College
Bay Road
Queensbury, NY 12804
Total head count enrollment-Credit: 3,550; Non-Credit: 5,500
Campuses/sites: 2; Full-time faculty: 94

BOROUGH OF MANHATTAN COMMUNITY COLLEGE

EVENING / WEEKEND NURSING

Designed for working adults, the curriculum is identical to the day program – although completion takes a year longer

Borough of Manhattan Community College (BMCC), in collaboration with two local unions, has established an Evening/Weekend Nursing Program designed specifically for working adults.

District Council 37, an affiliate of the AFL-CIO (which represents 130,000 New York City employees) and Local 1199 (representing hospital employees) worked with BMCC and The City University of New York in order to give their members an opportunity to pursue a degree in Nursing on a part-time basis. The University recognized the need to serve this population as well as the need to assist in addressing the nursing shortage in New York City.

Unlike the College's day Nursing Program, which was conceived as a traditional two-year curriculum, the evening program is designed to be completed in three years, strictly on a part-time basis. Students in both programs graduate with an Associate in Applied Science degree and are eligible to take the New York State Licensure Examination for Registered Nursing (RN). The partnership between the unions and the college has led to the establishment of a series of support mechanisms, all of which are geared to enhance success for our working students.

While the Evening/Weekend Program is open to any

qualified BMCC student, special recruitment and academic support plans were developed in conjunction with the two unions to inform, guide and assist the union membership in completing the application process, facilitating registration and increasing academic success. Curriculum requirements are identical to the day program but limit evening students to 11 credits per semester. The special mechanisms used within the program include:

1) a mandatory college-wide basic skills assessment program, the requirements of which must be completed before admission to the Nursing Program;

2) a pre-freshman program which provides students who have remediation requirements an opportunity to satisfy those requirements before enrolling in their first semester;

3) special group orientation sessions, assessment testing sessions, admissions appointments and registration dates for union members;

4) a full-time college counselor/advisor who is available evenings and Saturdays for nursing students and is responsible for tracking student progress and maintaining personal contact with students and instructors; the counselor plays a vital role in an academic early warning system, linking students with tutorial and other counseling assistance for union members, the counselor serves as liaison with union representatives;

5) a union counselor available evenings and Saturdays for union students who serves as a liaison with college staff;

6) a non-credit pre-chemistry course designed to prepare students for first semester chemistry, historically the most difficult of the Pre-Nursing courses; this is supplemented by an innovative science tutoring program, with a tutor attending class sessions to forge a closer link to the tutoring that occurs outside the classroom;

7) peer tutoring in the Nursing Tutorial Lab to reinforce knowledge of nursing concepts and prepare students for examinations; while tutoring is available to all nursing students, attendance is required of those who fail a first examination in a nursing course;

8) basic skills classes for union students requiring remediation, offered on site at union headquarters by the college; and

9) monthly meetings between college and union administrative staff to review the progress of the program and its students.

The Evening/Weekend Nursing program has yielded outstanding results in terms of student success and retention. Beginning with an initial enrollment in Fall 1989 of 26 students (all union), the program has grown to a current enrollment of 636, of which 318 are union members. Of the 636 enrolled in fall 1992, 588 successfully completed their remedial, pre-nursing or clinical nursing courses, representing a retention rate of 93 percent.

The Evening/Weekend Nursing Program has been recognized by various agencies within the State of New York for its innovative and effective means of addressing New York City work force needs and is being used as a model for the development of similar programs within The City University of New York.

Contact:
Barbara Tacinelli, Nursing Department
(212) 346-8700

Borough of Manhattan Community College
City University of New York, 199 Chambers Street
New York, NY 10007
Total head count enrollment-Credit: 15,766;
Full-time faculty: 284

COLLABORATIVE COMPUTER CALCULUS

The Mathematics Department reformed the techniques used in teaching calculus

As a result of innovations in the teaching of calculus, mathematics faculty have been able to increase the success rate of students in calculus classes from 55 percent to 75 percent and have, at the same time, doubled the number of students completing the calculus sequence. The strong foundation in calculus has also led more students to enroll in upper-level mathematics courses at Borough of Manhattan Community College (BMCC) of The City University of New York.

This is of particular note at BMCC, which serves groups often under-represented in fields associated with science and mathematics. Located near the financial district in New York City, BMCC serves a diverse student population consisting of 55 percent African-American, 28 percent Hispanic, 8 percent Asian and 9 percent other; A large number of students are also nontraditional, many returning to school after a long absence and many single parents. Seventy-two percent of the students are female.

With the help of a grant from the National Science Foundation, the Mathematics Department undertook the task of reforming the techniques used in teaching calculus.

Continues on Page 450

The Mathematics Department currently has two computer classrooms and an open-access mathematics laboratory. Students participating in the Collaborative Calculus Project make use of Macintosh, Apple IIe and IBM personal computers and have used Maple, Derive, True Basic Calculus, Milo, Master Grapher and Anugraph software in completing their projects. Students work in small, mixed-ability groups and are responsible for learning the material as well as for helping their teammates learn. Classes are structured to begin with concrete activities that allow the less-prepared students in the collaborative group to make a contribution and to end with open questioning that allows the well-prepared students to be challenged.

Students are expected to complete a portfolio, including a summary essay describing the projects and how the software was used for each project. Students use desktop publishing software to help make their final reports look professional. Typical projects assigned include the projectile problem to find the angle at which the range of the projectile is maximized, and problems requiring that students find a curve for which Simpson's rule for estimating the area under the curve is not the best method for estimation. Faculty have noted the persistence and resourcefulness of students in solving the problems and found that the students examined additional cases to determine if their conclusions remained valid. Mathematics faculty are continually challenging students and are planning assignments to create animated mathematics projects.

Contact:
Patricia Wilkinson
Lawrence Sher, Mathematics Department
(212) 346-8530

Borough of Manhattan Community College
City University of New York, 199 Chambers Street
New York, NY 10007
Total head count enrollment-Credit: 15,766
Full-time faculty: 284

PASS (PERSONAL AND ACADEMIC SUPPORT SERVICES)

The Center serves hundreds of students yet provides individual assistance

While serving between 600 and 800 students per year, the PASS (Personal and Academic Support Services) PASS Center at Bronx Community College still manages to provide a comprehensive array of specialized services on an individual basis to its participants.

The academic needs of students enrolled in the PASS Center are assessed and referrals are made to appropriate specialists who offer: professional tutoring in reading, writing, English as a Second Language, and study skills; consultation and academic support for students with learning disabilities; peer tutoring primarily in business, science and mathematics courses.

The college, recognizing the complex personal and social challenges facing its students, has joined with the DOE in contributing funds to the project. This has enabled the program to offer the services of an attorney for legal advice and referral and a psychologist to provide counseling. A transfer counselor and a social service counselor, paid by funds from the Student Support Services grant, are also part of the staff of five full-time and five part-time professionals and 35 peer tutors. These individuals, working together as a team, are qualified to provide comprehensive support services to participants, enabling many to persevere in the face of overwhelming obstacles while in pursuit of a college education.

The retention rates for program enrolled students with special learning problems were 80 percent in 1991, and 87 percent in 1990. Approximately 67 percent of all enrolled students who receive tutoring earn grades of C or better in related courses. The program is currently one of 20 Student Support Service programs in a nationwide study sponsored by the DOE and conducted by WESTAT, a research firm based in Rockville, Maryland. The PASS Center receives visits from educators who are touring the college from out-of-state and other countries.

Originally funded by the U.S. Department of Education in 1970, its reputation has enabled it to gain additional funding under Title III from the DOE and through the Carl D. Perkins Vocational and Applied Technology Education Act from the New York State Education Department, to develop and conduct an innovative tutor training project. One of the objectives of the project will be to enable tutors to qualify for level one of certification as outlined by the College Reading and Learning Association.

A fundamental dynamic of the PASS Center is that it works because students, faculty and administration of the college believe in its goals and give it their support. It is a source of pride for which many can take a share of credit.

Contact:
Ingrid De Cicco, Director
(212) 220-6106/6107

Bronx Community College
West 181st Street and University Avenue
Bronx, NY 10453
Total head count enrollment-Credit: 6,769; Non-Credit: 17,195

EVOLUTION OF A RETENTION PLAN

*▒ Faculty were asked to establish remedial courses as prerequisite ▒
for entry-level courses*

In the spring of 1980, 19 percent of the students enrolled at Bronx Community College were suspended for academic reasons, mostly a low grade point average. Why? Although the entering freshman class was tested and placed into either remedial or college level courses, a majority of the students ignored the remedial placement and attempted college courses. One of the college core courses had a success rate of 1 percent for misplaced students.

Faculty were asked to establish remedial courses as prerequisites for the entry-level courses. In an open and frank discussion in the College Curriculum Committee, prerequisites were established. As one would suspect, some courses emphasized writing preparation, some reading and others mathematics.

To implement the prerequisites, which were really skills levels, the following scheme was developed. Tests in writing, reading and mathematics were converted to remedial placements. A student was assumed to need all remedial courses to encourage participation in the testing.

Test data removed remedial placements from the students record. The resulting placement record was then programmed into an on-line registration system which compared the college level freshman course prerequisites with the students placement record. The program would not permit registration of under-prepared students in the courses that demanded greater skills development. The student would receive an RR (remediation required) message. This assured that students would get off on the right track.

Having assured a good start, the college had to be prepared to assist students with a mid-course correction. Students entering academic probation were told to register for a nationally recognized Learning to Learn course that the college faculty had altered to meet local needs. The course produced statistically significant and permanently improved grade point averages and persistence.

The result of this approach was to reduce the 19 percent suspension rate to 9 percent in the spring of 1992.

Contact:
Carl J. Polowczyk, Dean of Academic Affairs
(212) 220-6185

Bronx Community College
West 181st Street and University Avenue
Bronx, NY 10453
Total head count enrollment-Credit: 6,769; Non-Credit: 17,195

APPLIED TECHNOLOGY FOR UNIVERSAL INSTRUMENTS

*▒ The Tech Prep model has been applied to a program for industrial employees ▒
without college degrees*

Broome Community College has taken the Tech Prep model and applied it to a program for industrial employees without college degrees. This innovation resulted from a partnership formed by Broome Community College with industry, and is a non-credit Certificate Program in Applied Technology offered in cooperation with Universal Instruments.

Universal, a subsidiary of Dover Electronics, manufactures automation equipment for electronics manufacturing assembly and testing of electronic circuits, software and computer-controlled electronics manufacturing equipment.

The pilot program initially targeted Universal employees, without college degrees, holding technical positions in manufacturing, fabrication and engineering. Successful completion of the six-course program (in math, principles of technology, communication and problem-solving) will prepare the employees to enter one of several Associate in Technology degree programs at Broome Community College.

The pilot program is based on the Tech Prep model developed by Dale Parnell in his book *Tech Prep Associate Degree, A Win/Win Experience*. In that publication, Parnell discusses the use of "applied academics" as an alternate to teaching math and science to "concrete learners." This model was primarily developed to improve the skills of middle quartile high school students and has effectively been used in many states such as North Carolina, Texas and Oregon.

Realizing that these employees probably fit the target group of the Tech Prep model, a special math test was prepared to assess math skills of 134 workers who volunteered to be a part of this new certificate program. As a

Continues on Page 452

result of this test, 20 employees were chosen to start Applied Math I and 16 employees were chosen to start Principles of Academics" for the teaching mode. Videotapes, hands-on experience, and considerable laboratory experience replaceed the traditional lecture method of instruction. The instructors were specially trained for this teaching method by Tony Marinez form Lander High School in Austin, Texas. Lander High School has been involved in Tech Prep and applied academics for over six years.

Both courses use material developed by the Center of Occupational Research and Development (CORD) whose home is in Waco, Texas. Due to the required hands-on experience and strong laboratory exercises required, a new "classroom" had to be developed on site at Universal to create this new teaching technique. Thousands of dollars have been invested by Universal to create this new teaching environment and to purchase necessary laboratory equipment.

What is unique about this program is the adoption of the Tech-Prep model to retrain America's work force. Student feedback has been very positive, and employees involved in this Tech Prep industrial model will have the skills to remain competitive in a global economy.

Contact:
Bill Beston, Dean of Technologies, Engineering and Computing
(607) 778-5014

Broome Community College
PO Box 1017
Binghamton, NY 13902
Total head count enrollment-Credit: 6,785; Non Credit: 8,500
Campuses/sites: 1; Full-time faculty:

THE TEACHING RESOURCE CENTER (TRC)

The Center provides physical space and a variety of forums for faculty to confer

The Teaching Resource Center at Broome Community College connects human resources, sponsors faculty learning, coordinates educational resources, provides publishing opportunities and promotes classroom research.

In addition, the Center provides physical space and a variety of forums for faculty to confer on pedagogical issues. Cross-campus peer interaction and mentoring also are encouraged and scheduled through the Center. The Center provides workshops, mini-courses and other learning activities requested by faculty to foster teaching excellence. In a recent year, 27 topics were offered, the majority of which were developed and presented (pro bono) by Broome Community College faculty.

Also available through the TRC are instructional materials such as model course outlines, exams, and classroom visuals, available to faculty campus-wide. The TRC educates faculty about, and connects them with, existing campus resources. A Faculty Handbook and a faculty orientation program were developed through the Center.

Professional literature on teaching and educational theory are housed in the TRC and key publications are distributed. The Teaching Resource newsletter, Center Stage, written and published by faculty, is devoted to a specific theme each month.

The Teaching Resource Center supports and encourages faculty-initiated research in teaching. Mini-grants were provided last year for faculty interested in researching classroom assessment. Also each year the college adopts a campus-wide theme and each instructor is asked to incorporate the theme into their courses. Workshops and activities which focus on infusion are also offered through the Teaching Resource Center.

The Center is directed by a faculty member on full release time, who confers with a Teaching Center Board comprising faculty representatives from each division, Coordinator of Professional Development, an adjunct faculty member, a non-classroom faculty member and a representative from the Learning Assistance Center.

Contact:
Alice McNeely, Center Coordinator
(607) 778-5354

Broome Community College
PO Box 1017
Binghamton, NY 13902
Total head count enrollment-Credit: 6,785; Non Credit: 8,500
Campuses/sites: 1; Full-time faculty:

TELECOMMUNICATIONS STUDIES

The program offers two degree options: Radio and TV Broadcasting or Radio and TV Technology

Cayuga Community College's Telecommunications programs keep on the pulse of the industry and keep up with the interests of the community. The telecommunications department produces *Cayuga Showcase*, an entertainment program featuring musicians performing at the college and *Cayuga Forums*, a talk-show format program focusing on issues of interest to the college community and the general public. Additionally, the college produces special programs, including selected city council meetings, for area broadcast. All programs are broadcast over the local cable channel.

The college's successful foray into telecommunications began in 1971, when the AAS degree in Telecommunications was introduced at Cayuga (then, Auburn) Community College.

The program's development resulted from research which revealed an increasing demand for trained television and radio technicians. This need extended beyond the field of broadcasting to educational institutions having/developing television installations and instructional media centers.

At the time of the program's introduction, Cayuga had already developed a Television Resource Center. The center, which featured a television studio with three cameras, master control and distribution center, was responsible for producing special programs for classroom instruction and handling distribution of video tape materials for use by every college department. Broadcasting over two closed circuit channels, the center expanded in the spring of 1971 to include a weekly news broadcast.

In 1979, the Telecommunications program "evolved" into two separate degree options:
1) Telecommunications: Radio and Television Broadcasting; and
2) Telecommunications: Radio and Television Technology.

The change in curriculum was the result of ongoing curriculum review to assure that programs were meeting current needs.

The Radio and Television Broadcasting degree option offers students training in radio and television production, performance, management, lighting, audio and directing. In a professional environment, student work on television and radio productions is emphasized. Cayuga's facilities include a broadcast-quality color television station which serves 11,500 households via cable, editing suites, portable field units, and an FM/stereo radio station telecommunications area that holds their interest. The program prepares students for employment in a variety of broadcasting positions, including camera operators, technical directors, video editors, industrial video specialists, electronic news gathering specialists, newspersons, disc jockeys and management personnel. It is also appropriate for students who wish to transfer to an upper-division college or university upon graduation.

The Radio and Television Technology degree option provides practical training in broadcast engineering, maintenance and operation procedures. Students work on production, engineering and operations projects in a professional environment which includes several television studio diagnostic stations and a fully operation radio lab utilized for technical instruction. Program graduates are eligible to receive certification as Broadcast Technologists from the Society of Broadcast Engineers. In fact, Cayuga's program was the first two-year program in New York State to receive official accreditation from the Society of Broadcast Engineers. Program graduates find employment as radio, television, audio and cable engineers and technicians.

In 1991-92, Cayuga's telecommunications department received a national award for Cayuga Showcase, winning best entertainment program in the Association for Education, Communication & Technology/Community College Association for Instruction & Technology National Video Competition. *Cayuga Showcase* also was a finalist in the 1992-93 national competition.

Contact:
Steven Keeler, Assistant Professor, Humanities
(315) 255-1743

Cayuga Community College
197 Franklin Street
Auburn, NY 13021-3099
Total head count enrollment-Credit: 3,521
Campuses/sites: 5; Full-time faculty: 73

BIOLOGICAL FIELD STATION

*▨ The field station, also open to children, arouses interest in ecology ▨
and the environment*

The Livingston Oak-Hill Biological Field Station, serving college students and grade-school children, is on a rustic two-acre site along the Hudson River. In addition, the station has been used as a laboratory annex for General Ecology, Hudson River Ecology and Environmental Studies classes on campus.

When established by Columbia-Greene Community College in 1991, the purpose of the Livingston Oak-Hill Biological Field Station was fourfold:

1) expand the laboratory resources and teaching capabilities of the Scientific Studies Division;

2) provide extracurricular study opportunities for area grade- and secondary-school students through the Institute of Natural History;

3) establish a river research facility for grant-funded projects; and

4) provide an ecological study and research center to help support efforts to improve the environment of the Hudson River.

Jon Powell, a technical assistant at the college and an instructor in the college's Institute of Natural History, was instrumental in acquiring the lease agreement to the site from Henry Livingston of Livingston, NY. The college also has access to Livingston lands adjacent to the station. With a small budget and much donated time and equipment,

members of the science faculty renovated a century-old former freight station and boat house located on the site.

In addition, groups of grade-school children have experienced day-long workshops introducing them to species in and around the waterway. During the workshops, Powell and his assistants use seine nets to catch pumpkin-seed sun fish, darters and other river inhabitants for display. The workshops also serve as a primer on Hudson River history and include a tour of the remains of a 19th Century iron-smelting operation.

In terms of research, the river station project has undertaken a contract-funded study of a zebra mussel encroachment on the Hudson. With a $30,000 grant from the Water Research Laboratory of Vicksburg, Miss. (in conjunction with the U.S. Army Corps of Engineers), Powell and C-GCC professors Peter Ambrose and William Cook have employed water chemistry, Bentic organism sampling and controlled method experiments to study the impact of the immigration.

The work of the river station, including the zebra mussel study, has been covered widely in the area media, helping to raise the awareness of the Hudson River environment throughout the region. The station is available to the faculty and staff of other institutions for research purposes.

Contact:
Jon Powell, Director
(518) 828-4181

Columbia-Greene Community College
Box 1000
Hudson, NY 12534
Total head count enrollment-Credit: 1,770; Non-Credit: 7,471
Campuses/sites: 1; Full-time faculty: 49

HONORS PROGRAM

*▨ Honors projects have ranged from poetry and prose ▨
to building robots and offering music recitals*

Corning Community College has a unique Honors Program in that there is no separate honors curriculum, series of honors courses or honors section that a student must take to earn an honors degree. Rather, all academic courses the college offers may be taken at an advanced or honors level by any qualified student in any academic program offered by the college.

This design was prompted by Faculty Association concerns that the "honors" students should not be segregated from the general student body. That done, the program was designed to be interdisciplinary and to give honors students control and responsibility for their own

learning and discovery, which very seldom occurs in traditional courses

A student who has a GPA of 3.5 or better and who is curious as well as highly motivated may take any course at an advanced or honors level by developing an honors project for that course. The honors project or topic to be explored is mutually agreed upon by the student and his/her mentor who is usually the instructor of that course. The mentor serves as a guide for the honors student who bears complete responsibility for his/her own discovery and project. Upon successful completion of his/her honors project, the faculty mentor awards "H" (Honors designation) for the relevant course.

The types of honors projects have included the writing of short stories and poems, building and repair of robots, offering of music recitals, as well as the more traditional research projects. Several students have had their honors projects published in professional journals of their chosen field.

An integral part of Corning Community College's Honors Program is the Honors Forum which is a three-credit-hour interdisciplinary seminar. The Forum is more similar to a graduate seminar than a community college course. The average size of the Forum is 12 students and three faculty representing the Social Sciences, Humanities and the Sciences. The Forum faculty members function as guides as well as participants, learning along with the students. The Honors Forum serves several vital functions:

1) the Forum provides honors students with a venue for the exchange and testing of ideas and theories derived from their honors projects

2) the Forum provides students with the opportunity to analyze and synthesize information from

students representing a wide variety of disciplines; and

3) the Forum allows the students to develop critical thinking, argumentative, and oral presentation skills usually reserved for upperclassmen or even graduate students.

Upon successful completion of 12 credit hours of honors level work, which usually entails two or three honors projects as well as Honors Forum and a cumulative GPA of 3.5, the student qualifies for an Honors diploma from Corning Community College.

Corning Community College's flexible and interdisciplinary Honors Program has received statewide and national recognition. A study through the office of Dr. Kenneth Hall, Assistant Vice Chancellor for Academic Programs, selected Corning Community College's programs as model honors program in the State University of New York system. The National Collegiate Honors Council has also highlighted Corning Community College's honors program as a model program for community colleges in its publication *Honors in the Two-Year College*.

Contact:
Joseph J. Hanak, Program Coordinator
(607) 962-9208

Corning Community College
1 Academic Drive
Corning, NY 14830
Total head count enrollment-Credit: 3,900; Non-Credit: 1,300
Campuses/sites: 4; Full-time faculty: 119

DUTCHESS COMMUNITY COLLEGE

LIFE SCIENCE PROBLEM-SOLVING INSTITUTE FOR ELEMENTARY TEACHERS

The program is for teachers desiring experimental learning leading to increased self-confidence and expertise

In order to enrich under-represented and under-served elementary school students, Dutchess Community College developed the Life Science Problem-Solving Institute for Elementary Teachers, which shows in-service teacher/participants how to employ problem-solving skills in life science curriculum, and to enhance curriculum through the introduction of and use of regional life science resources.

Begun in 1989, the program emphasizes self-esteem building and cooperative rather than competitive or individualistic social interaction. These skills employed in the classroom will be significant in encouraging the success of students, particularly historically under-represented students, as they approach learning life science through group problem solving.

The program takes place at Dutchess Community College's Norrie Point Environmental Center, a life science resource in itself. It consists of a three-week summer session and three one-day return sessions the following October, January and March. The program is

designed to accommodate 45 teacher participants each year.

Components of the summer program include:

1) a refresher lecture/field activity series to increase self-confidence in life science instruction, increase understanding of life science principles contained in the New York State Elementary Science Syllabus, and increase awareness and use of life science resources in the region;

2) trust building and group problem-solving activities stressing cooperative interactions and instruction strategies;

3) problem-solving process instruction activities;

4) the construction of life science problem-solving units and strategies for use in the classroom during the academic year;

5) field activities; and

6) interaction with life science and curriculum development specialists.

Continues on Page 456

The three return sessions will provide continued stimulation, the opportunity to compare results and to network and plan future activities. The project will be managed by Dutchess Community College personnel with the support of an established Advisory Group composed of teachers and administrators from several school districts who participated in the three preceding institutes.

The program is offered to Dutchess County elementary teachers desiring experimental learning leading to increased self-confidence and expertise for teaching life sciences topics at levels I, II or III (NYED Elementary Science Syllabus) and to facilitate the problem-solving process in the classroom. It is designed to meet the following in-service training needs:

1) to increase participants' personal understanding of life science principles and topics (instruction will focus on: plant and animal needs and dependencies; offspring production among plants and animals; species dependencies and community; and mutual impacts of living things and their environment, and environmental influences on population size);

2) to increase participants' demonstration skills so that they may help students solve problems effectively and easily, and apply those skills in a manner which supports the development of positive science attitudes among students;

3) to increase personal knowledge of and use of available area resources for life science instruction; the program will introduce participants to many of these resources, both people and places, such as nature centers, parks and organizations;

4) to develop problem-solving activities for classroom use during the 1992/93 academic year;

5) to establish an electronic communication network among teachers throughout the county who are integrating problem-solving approaches into their curriculum plans for life science instruction; and

6) to familiarize participants with proposals for improving results in the 1990's, presented in the Commissioner's "New Compact for Learning."

The program includes networking among educators at Dutchess Community College, Dutchess County BOCES, and Dutchess County school districts, along with representatives of Dutchess County business and industry organizations. Networking is carried out through the Dutchess County (BOCES) Science Advisory Council.

The program is made available by federal funds of the Dwight David Eisenhower Title IIA incentive administered through the New York State Department of Education. Approximately $125,000 in grant funds have been provided for 140 teacher-participants during the four years of its administration.

Contact:
Arthur Pritchard, Professor, Allied Health and Biological Sciences
(914) 471-4500, ext. 3003

Dutchess Community College
53 Pendell Road
Poughkeepsie, NY 12601
Total head count enrollment-Credit: 7,509; Non-Credit: 4,721
Campuses/sites: 5; Full-time faculty: 143

DUTCHESS COMMUNITY COLLEGE

STUDENT DEVELOPMENT SEMINAR

The seminar assumes student personal and social growth is as important as academic development

Because the assessment and facilitation of student personal growth and development should be given equal consideration with academic progress, Dutchess Community College instituted the Student Development Seminar (SDS) in the spring 1991 semester. This program has continued and grown each subsequent semester.

Following extensive review of the student development literature, six developmental dimensions were outlined as the basis of the SDS program:

1) Academic Involvement and Autonomy. Develop the skills to utilize campus resources, manage time effectively and maximize academic performance.

2) Career Awareness and Planning. Possess an awareness of the world of work and the decision-making skills required to be successful in career/job selec-

tion and advancement.

3) Social and Peer Interactions and Relationships. Be comfortable in relationships with others, while developing social skills needed to communicate.

4) Cultural Awareness And Participation. Become aware of cultural and artistic resources in our society, while developing the skills to make informed choices.

5) Wellness & Health Behaviors/Lifestyles. Develop a lifestyle of good health practices and wellness.

6) Acceptance of Others. Enhance his/her own value system which facilitates the acceptance and respect for individuals of different backgrounds, cultures, races and beliefs.

All full-time freshmen at DCC are required to register

for SDS. Students must attend and participate in at least six events/activities, one in each dimension listed above. Each student is provided with an extensive listing of the events and activities under each of the six dimensions at the beginning of the semester.

In addition, attendance and participation is assessed by completion of an evaluation form at the conclusion of each activity or event. The students academic transcript reflects the results of their attendance or non-attendance at the six required events.

The SDS responds to the realization that colleges need to proactively facilitate student personal and social development. Colleges, employers and society in general have become increasingly aware of the importance of personal and social skills in the success and well-being of individu-als. Many of our personal and societal ills – substance abuse, sexism, racism, intolerance, poor health and stress-related illnesses – can be linked to a lack of decision-making skills, avoidance of self-responsibility for action, and lack of knowledge and respect of other individuals and groups in our society.

The SDS Program requires extensive coordination by several members of the Department of Student Personnel Services. In addition, all members of the department offer events or activities that students attend.

The SDS Program has been recognized via presentations at the National NASPA Conference in March 1992 and by publication in *Colleague*, an annual collection of articles on academic and administrative issues published by the State University of New York.

Contact:
Howard Himelstein, Associate Dean, Student Personnel Services
(914) 471-4500

Dutchess Community College
53 Pendell Road
Poughkeepsie, NY 12601
Total head count enrollment-Credit: 7,509; Non-Credit: 4,721
Campuses/sites: 5; Full-time faculty: 143

CULTURAL DIVERSITY

Infusing into curriculum an awareness of cultural, religious, gender and economic diversity broadens students' world view

Six mini-grants led some Erie Community College faculty to rewrite course outlines and syllabi to infuse historical perspective and awareness of traditions and cultures.

At the end of the spring 1992 semester, the grants were in various stages of completion. However, in the case of the BI-105 course (Biology – "Man and His World"), the infusion of aspects of cultural diversity had proceeded from the organization/planning stage to implementation and assessment. Information gained as a result of assessing has become the basis for reorganization and development of alternative teaching strategies to be piloted in the course. This process should, therefore, be ongoing.

The purpose of the "Man and His World" course is to examine (from a global perspective) impending issues such as the condition of the environment and overpopulation. The objective is to increase awareness of the influence of factors such as nationality, religion, gender and economic class. The resultant affective goals include the development of an increased sensitivity to issues and the development of greater tolerance for a variety of opinions. The course is not recall-focused, but is driven towards analysis and evaluation, and, therefore, has the potential to impact on the basic value system of the individual. Students have the opportunity to develop several general education competencies that include writing effectively, organizing material, and analyzing data in order to form reasoned value judgments.

The assessment process included both summative and formative components. The summative was the usual end-of-topic examinations, however, each included an opinion essay on a relevant issue of a complex moral and ethical nature. The essay was graded on the supporting facts not on the position taken. A tallying of class opinion on these essays was then utilized for further class discussion.

The formative component employed a number of techniques suggested by Cross & Angelo, the "Minute Paper," for example. Typical questions were, "Has anyone in the class affected the way you feel about the issue being discussed? Have you impacted on how others view the issue under investigation?" Again, to "go full circle," the information gathered from these Minute Papers became the basis for continued dialogue and analysis. The instructor kept a journal describing each class meeting. This journal included a record of student comments and level of involvement, a list of objectives (cognitive and affective), a description of teaching strategies employed and a personal commentary on the events that occurred in the classroom. The journal became the significant source of data that later

Continues on Page 458

was used to complete five case studies. The case studies encompass components of the organization, implementation and assessment phases, and will be presented in a series of workshops offered by the Teacher Resource Center.

Contact:
Robert Sackett, Assessment Coordinator, (716) 851-1428
Paulette Snyder, Associate Professor, Biology, (716) 851-1376

Erie Community College
6205 Main Street
Williamsville, NY 14221-7095
Total head count enrollment-Credit: 15,000
Campuses/sites: 3; Full-time faculty: 500

DISABLED STUDENT SERVICES

Direct services include tutors, note-takers, alternative testing arrangements and adaptive equipment

Not satisfied with merely serving Erie Community College students with disabilities, the college also reaches out to area residents with disabilities in a variety of ways. This commitment started with the Disabled Student Resource Center at South Campus, established in 1983 with VEA funds to hire a Coordinator of Special Services to provide services for three students in wheelchairs and for eight who were deaf.

By 1991-92, the Disabled Student Services department comprised a full-time coordinator, three counselors – two full time, one part time – a full-time technical assistant, a part-time professional tutor and a part-time secretary who provide services for more than 500 disabled students on three campuses.

Direct services to students, as mandated by the Rehabilitation Act of 1973, Section 504, include tutors, note-takers, alternative testing arrangements, availability of specialized equipment such as telephone Devices for the Deaf (TDD), adaptive computer accessibility, etc.

Staff participation on college and campus committees ensures that the needs of disabled individuals will be considered in long- and short-term planning, campus activities, facilities accessibility etc. Department staff and activities are funded through a combination of college budget and VATEA funds amounting to more than $200,000 annually.

Staff members of Erie's Disabled Student Services department extend the college's commitment to serve disabled individuals in the community. ECC was instrumental in establishing, and continues to chair WNY Collegiate Consortium of Disability Advocates (CCDA), a coalition of post secondary, secondary and agency personnel, which is proactive in addressing the needs of disabled high school students who are interested in attending college. The consortium has served as a model for establishing similar groups state-wide. Activities include annual training programs for secondary and post secondary faculty and staff; annual college night program for disabled individuals; and a speakers bureau on topics related to transition, advocacy and the rights of disabled persons under the law.

Other ECC activities include a recent award to establish a regional Transition Coordination site at the college; development of a job coach training program; participation on the State Education Department's Committee on Interpreter Services; technical assistance to other colleges; and programs and frequent presentations at conferences.

Awards and recognitions include excellent evaluations by the Middle States Association of Colleges and the NYS Education Department; the Coordinator and Technical Assistant have both been ECC President's Award recipients; and the Coordinator of Special Services is a 1993 recipient of the State University of New York (SUNY) Chancellor's Award for Excellence in Professional Service.

Contact:
Kathy Hoffman, Coordinator of Special Services
(716) 851-1832

Erie Community College
6205 Main Street
Williamsville, NY 14221-7095
Total head count enrollment-Credit: 15,000
Campuses/sites: 3; Full-time faculty: 500

CLASSROOM ASSESSMENT TEACHING PROJECT

▦ Faculty use student feedback to adjust instruction ▦
and, ultimately, improve learning

In 1992, Finger Lakes Community College began a project designed to encourage faculty to systematically introduce Cross and Angelo's (1988) classroom assessment techniques into their teaching. As used by Cross and Angelo, "classroom assessment techniques" (CATs) refers to a variety of ways in which faculty can solicit feedback from all members of a class about the learning that occurs following instruction. The feedback is used to adjust instruction. Typically CATs are not graded. The Classroom Assessment Techniques Project sought to:

1) provide a link between institutional assessment activities and classroom teaching;

2) develop a series of case studies of classroom teaching that could be used as starting points for discussions of teaching and learning at FLCC; and

3) systematically investigate the impact of CATs on retention and student learning at FLCC.

Eight faculty from eight disciplines were invited to participate in the project. They received $300 per semester for participation. Another faculty member received a course load reduction to serve as project director. Faculty agreed to try various CATs at least eight times the first semester, to meet regularly to discuss their experience with CATs, to develop case studies of classrooms that could be printed in-house for the benefit of other faculty, and to share their experience with college community by presenting a workshop during the days set aside for professional development at the beginning of the spring semester. The project began in fall 1992; faculty voted to continue it into spring 1993, citing its value to their teaching.

All faculty believe the use of CATs improved their teaching; students surveyed in these classes believe CATs improved their learning. Some faculty believed the use of CATs encouraged students to come to class better prepared. Most faculty found they had to adjust specific assessment techniques to their classes. Retention in classrooms examined was equal or above the retention of comparable classes from the previous fall semester. The panel discussion of CATs was well-received by colleagues in January 1993 workshop. The written case studies are in progress.

Contact:
Leonard Malinowski, Department of Mathematics
(716) 394-3500

Finger Lakes Community College
4355 Lake Shore Drive
Canandaigua, NY 14424
Total head count enrollment-Credit: 4,002; Non-Credit: 2,204
Campuses/sites: 4; Full-time faculty: 98

CENTER FOR TEACHING EXCELLENCE

▦ Workshops, teleconferences and brown bag sharing sessions ▦
open the door to new instructional techniques

Through the College Center for Teaching Excellence, full-time faculty mentor other full-time and part-time faculty at Finger Lakes Community College. Established in 1991, the Teaching Center strives to encourage instructional innovation, and to facilitate the continuing improvement and development of instruction at Finger Lakes.

From 1991 to 1993, the Teaching Center has sponsored workshops, teleconferences and brown bag sharing sessions through which faculty explore new instructional techniques and issues related to student learning. Faculty and "outside" experts present at workshops. The Teaching Center has a library of books, journals and media on pedagogy for faculty use. The Teaching Center makes available small awards to faculty who wish to pursue classroom research projects.

The Teaching Center has a coordinator and a planning board made up of the coordinator, seven teaching faculty, and representatives from audio visual services, adjunct faculty and the community. The Director of Instruction attends ex-officio. There is an Advisory Board of community educators.

Programming is the responsibility of the Teaching Center Board. Initial programming was preceded by a

Continues on Page 460

needs assessment of the faculty which will be repeated biannually.

The Teaching Center budget is approximately $6,000.

Part of this support comes from the FLCC Foundation, and part from the budget of the Executive Dean of Educational Services.

Contact:
Henry Maus, Teaching Center Coordinator
(716) 394-3500

Finger Lakes Community College
4355 Lake Shore Drive
Canandaigua, NY 14424
Total head count enrollment-Credit: 4,002; Non-Credit: 2,204
Campuses/sites: 4; Full-time faculty: 98

INDIVIDUAL STUDIES / COLLABORATIVE CAREER LEARNING

The certificate program focuses on minorities, women, the limited English proficient and people with disabilities

In our increasingly technological society, career training programs often inadequately serve women, minorities, limited English proficient, and handicapped individuals. Since 1984, Fulton Montgomery Community College has been righting that situation through a unique one-year certificate program. Individual Studies/Collaborative Career Learning (COCAL).

Individual Studies/COCAL is patterned after a similar effort successfully designed and implemented by Bay de Noc Community College, a small college in northern Michigan. Adapted to meet New York State education requirements, it is designed to reflect the needs of the local job market by providing educational training in occupations in which employment needs are significant, yet not great enough to justify a full-time program.

The COCAL model provides students with two semesters of hands-on learning in a professional setting. By following competency-based objectives students are assured of an optimum learning experience in fields in which jobs are available. Their performance is monitored and evaluated for the total 16 credits (8 each semester) which are earned. Concurrently, students register for an additional six to nine credit hours from existing college course offerings. Graduates are awarded a state accredited Individual Studies Certificate.

The current individual Studies/COCAL catalog lists 33 occupational titles, from administrative aide to veterinary hospital attendant. Most recently, with the growth in the health field, COCAL is working primarily in hospitals and medical offices to provide training in such job-marketable areas as medical assistant, EKG technician, phlebotomist, bio-med repair and physical therapy aide.

Individual Studies/COCAL is a cost-effective method of providing additional career training on an individual need basis. Business and industry are paid $360 for each student ($1 per hour) as an added incentive for training. Additional costs are salaries for the director, two assistant directors and a secretary. Mileage is paid for training development and monitoring at the training sites.

In its nine-year history, Individual Studies/COCAL has grown from five students to its current level of 47 students. A 1992 survey indicates that 91 percent of the graduates have obtained employment, the primary goal of the program. Its most recent impact has been on the large dislocated worker population in the two county area.

By responding to their need for short-term retraining, partnerships have been established between the college, the Department of Labor and local Private Industry Councils. In addition, students are referred to the program from Vocational Education Services for Individuals With Disabilities (VESID) and the college's English as a Second Language (ESL) and Displaced Homemaker programs. Its contributions to the special populations it serves and the community at large has been written about in local trade publications.

Contact:
Judy Campbell, Director
(518) 762-4651, ext. 315

Fulton-Montgomery Community College
Route 67
Johnstown, NY 12095
Total head count enrollment-Credit: 2,692; Non-Credit: 3,880
Campuses/sites: 1; Full-time faculty: 81

EARLY ADMISSION

▩ *Students may fulfill high school graduation requirements* ▩
while receiving college credits

Because limited funds and limited personnel prohibit many high schools in rural communities from offering advanced courses for seniors, Fulton-Montgomery Community College created the Early Admission Program. Students who rank among the top 50 percent in their class may study full time at the college. This allows the student to fulfill high school graduation requirements and receive college credits simultaneously.

Under the Early Admission Program:

1) students who apply meet with the director of admissions to schedule and register for classes

2) full-time early admits are eligible to apply for New York State Tuition Assistance Program (TAP) and campus-based scholarships such as the Presidential and All-County Scholarships (Early Admission students are not eligible for Federal Title IV funds)

3) participants' grades are reviewed at mid-term and those with below a "C" in any class must meet with the director of admissions

4) full-time early admits any also obtain assistance in completing college transfer applications, scholarship essays and admission essays from the Admissions staff; and

5) the progress of each student is reported to their high school guidance counselor.

Currently, Fulton-Montgomery Community College enrolls 36 full- and part-time Early Admission students, an increase of 30 percent since 1988. Approximately 70 percent of Early Admit students complete the associate degree at FMCC before transferring to a baccalaureate institution.

Associated Costs: College promotional items such as brochures, view books and catalogs.

Personnel Requirements: Director of Admissions, Admissions secretary, Admissions staff and Financial aid staff.

Keys to success:

1) students can experience college by enrolling in challenging courses during their senior year of high school

2) the program allows qualified students to attend college full-time and complete high school graduation requirements simultaneously

3) the program shortens time span of completing baccalaureate degree; and

4) the student's progress is monitored by the Director of Admissions in order to guide those who need assistance with the transition from high school to college.

Contact:
C. Campbell Baker, Director of Admissions
(800) 721-3622, ext. 200

Fulton-Montgomery Community College
Route 67
Johnstown, NY 12095
Total head count enrollment-Credit: 2,692; Non-Credit: 3,880
Campuses/sites: 1; Full-time faculty: 81

INMATE HIGHER EDUCATION

▩ *The program, among the oldest in country, has been shown* ▩
to lower recidivism among participating offenders

Genesee Community College started its inmate education program at Attica Correctional Facility in 1973, making it one of the oldest programs in the country. In the past 20 years, the college has served approximately 3,000 inmate students and lowered recidivism at the same time.

The college operates in five walled prisons in western New York, serving approximately 300 inmate students enrolled in full-time college study. Students, typically members of minority groups, attend classes during the evening hours. Several years ago the college installed computer laboratories in each facility.

The faculty in the program include full-time and part-

time instructors from Genesee Community College. Each facility has a full-time college coordinator supervised by the director of inmate education.

There are several sources of financial assistance for inmate students including PELL and New York State Tuition Assistance Program (TAP). Almost all students receive PELL and TAP.

Correctional officials enthusiastically support the inmate education program as it provides meaningful and productive programming for inmates. Offenders who gain a college education while incarcerated return to prison at

Continues on Page 462

significantly lower rates than other inmates.

The inmate education program has been recognized by New York's Department of Correctional Services for helping to lower offender recidivism. The college was also instrumental in helping to form the first inmate higher education professional association in the state of New York.

Contact:
Pam Sterling, Director
(716) 343-0055

Genesee Community College
College Road
Batavia, NY 14020
Total head count enrollment-Credit: 4,000; Non-Credit: 8,000
Campuses/sites: 11; Full-time faculty: 80

STUDENT INFORMATION MONITOR

SIMON is touch-screen based and allows students to access and print out data in college administrative systems

Technology permeates Genesee Community College, where students may obtain a personal demographic, schedule, transcript, degree audit, financial aid and billing information from SIMON (Student Information Monitor).

Since 1989, SIMON has provided an inviting, graphic-oriented, touch-screen-based, real-time window that allows students to view and obtain printed copies of information contained in the college's administrative systems.

SIMON was physically designed to resemble a bank Automated Teller Machine (ATM). Students have controlled access to the real-time environment, which provides them with pre-defined and directed query capability to information stored in college databases on a digital VAX mainframe computer. While utilizing an IBM touch screen that displays Macintosh-like icons with a Zenith personal computer, it relies on test, computer graphics and digitized audio to convey the information. In addition to allowing access to personalized information, SIMON also answers questions about the college, both static information (such as building locations and a staff directory) and changing data (such as the schedule of campus events).

Contact:
Eileen Partise, Assistant Dean, Academic Support Services
(716) 343-0055

Genesee Community College
College Road
Batavia, NY 14020
Total head count enrollment-Credit: 4,000; Non-Credit: 8,000
Campuses/sites: 11; Full-time faculty: 80

PHYSICAL THERAPIST ASSISTANT

Statistics show very promising employment prospects for graduates of the program

The Physical Therapist Assistant, Associate in Applied Science degree program at Herkimer County Community College is preparing physical therapist assistants for a rigorous but rewarding career.

In 1987, the program began with a determination of need, a projection of demand, and a preliminary survey of anticipated employment opportunities. The need for allied health practitioners is great throughout the country. A variety of reasons, including turnover within the field, stressful work conditions, low salaries, longer life expectancies, and highly technological approaches to addressing the nation's medical needs, contribute to the shortage of practitioners.

A need was also established statewide and in the college's regional community. Demand for a program of this type was researched. The college has had applicants to the program whose numbers have far exceeded the established limits. Employment opportunities were an additional researched factor. Statistics obtained showed very promising employment prospects for graduates of the Physical Therapist Assistant program. The first graduating class (1992) of physical therapist assistants have all been successful in obtaining employment in their chosen career field.

The goals of the program are to:

1) provide for a sound theoretical and practical base for physical therapy;
2) provide a broad general education background;
3) provide the skills to utilize the scientific principles, as a means to treat or prevent disability, injury, disease or other health related conditions;
4) provide adequate laboratory experience to use the problem-solving process of physical therapy in dealing with a variety of patients/clients;
5) provide quality clinical education to enhance skills gained in the classroom and laboratory; and
6) graduate a qualified technical health care practitioner, who carries out patient care functions under the supervision of the physical therapist.

The physical therapist assistant carries out the treatment which has been designed by the physical therapist, after evaluation of the patient record, personal interview, and physical assessment of the patient. The physical therapist assistant communicates any observed changes in the patient's condition which may require a reassessment of the patient by the Physical Therapist and therefore, a change in treatment.

The implementation of the goals stated above comes through a comprehensive curriculum plan that includes an organized and sequential series of integrated student-oriented learning experiences, designed to enhance the attainment of the terminal competencies of the physical therapist assistant.

The human resources required for the implementation of a program of this nature include a full-time program director/instructor, a full-time academic clinical coordinator of education/instructor, and a part-time instructor. A multitude of clinical faculty are also required to assure that the fieldwork aspect of the comprehensive curriculum plan is met.

An initial commitment of $70,000 was required to set up the existing physical therapist assistant clinical procedures lab on campus. As technology continues to move forward, a continued commitment is required to maintain the necessary high level of quality.

The Physical Therapist Assistant program at Herkimer County Community College has received accreditation from the Commission on Accreditation in Physical Therapy Education of the American Physical Therapy Association. The program is also approved by the New York State Board of Regents.

Contact:
David Champoux, Chair, Telecommunications and Applied Sciences
(315) 866-0300 or (800) 947-4432, ext. 230

Herkimer County Community College
Reservoir Road
Herkimer, NY 13350
Total head count enrollment-Credit: 3,046; Non-Credit: 3,362
Campuses/sites: 1; Full-time faculty: 87

CRIMINAL JUSTICE

The program prepares students for careers in federal, state, county and local law enforcement

Criminal Justice students need more than labs – even those that simulate reality – to prepare them for work on the street. That's why Herkimer County Community College students work with members of the New York City Police Department and take field trips to the New York State Police Academy crime laboratory in Albany, NY.

The Associate in Applied Science degree program in Criminal Justice at Herkimer County Community College was introduced in 1975. Initially, the program was a one-plus-one program in which students completed one-year at HCCC and one year at Hudson Valley Community College, which granted the degree. The program was designed to prepare students for careers in federal, state, county and local law enforcement organizations including private and public security agencies.

In 1984, HCCC introduced a two-year program in Criminal Justice. The curriculum was designed to develop occupational competence for entry into criminal justice

agencies as a paraprofessional in community corrections, criminal investigation, protective services, probation and similar fields. The program also incorporated a practicum course which provides students with an understanding of the operation of a criminal justice agency through specialized practical daily experience working with professionals in the field. Students have completed practicums with law enforcement agencies, probation departments, private security agencies, the U.S. Marshall's service, the State Attorney General's Office, and the New York State Division for Youth.

In 1986, the AAS degree program in Criminal Justice: Security was introduced due to anticipated demand for trained personnel in this field. The program prepares students for entry into security positions in business and industry, and upgrades skills of those already in the field. In addition to the AAS degree programs, students can opt

Continues on Page 464

to earn an AA degree in Social Science with a Criminal Justice emphasis. The college is in the process of establishing an AS degree in Criminal Justice. This program will prepare students for transfer to four-year institutions.

In addition to the two-year programs, the college offers a one-year Certificate in Law Enforcement and a Certificate in Corrections. These certificates are designed primarily for those already in the criminal justice field to upgrade skills and knowledge, and to prepare others for entry-level positions in law enforcement and corrections.

The college recently opened a Criminal Justice Laboratory, utilized in unique courses including Criminal Investigation and Forensic Science. The Criminal Justice Educators Association of New York State has commended the courses which we offer in our programs.

Students in criminal justice programs at HCCC are active in a variety of community projects, including serving as volunteer firefighters and emergency medical technicians. Also, the Criminal Justice Club is an integral part of the Criminal Justice programs. Students tour area prisons and regional state police headquarters as part of club activities.

Currently, there are three full-time faculty members for the criminal justice program. Faculty members work closely with students in selecting appropriate programs and courses to meet individual career goals. The program has an advisory board of area professionals who provide input into the curricula.

Contact:
Joseph DeLorenzo, Chairperson, Humanities/Social Science
(315) 866-0300 or (800) 947-4432, ext. 200

Herkimer County Community College
Reservoir Road
Herkimer, NY 13350
Total head count enrollment-Credit: 3,046; Non-Credit: 3,362
Campuses/sites: 1; Full-time faculty: 87

HUDSON VALLEY COMMUNITY COLLEGE

CULTURAL DIVERSITY: A CLASSROOM EXPERIENCE

The course, according to a survey of students, successfully broke down negative cultural stereotypes

A new course entitled "Cultural Pluralism in American Society" focuses on an analysis of a wide spectrum of selected minority groups and to investigate their relationship to the dominant society. The goals of the course, first taught in the fall semester of 1991, are:

1) to enhance cross-cultural awareness by examining the influence of racial and ethnic identity upon the psychological and social dynamics of interactions among individuals from diverse backgrounds;

2) to define and describe minority status and its implications for minority group members;

3) to discover why ethnic and racial distinctions continue to survive regardless of the homogenizing pressures of complex urban societies;

4) to determine the consequences of cultural pluralism in American society and how it continues to affect our cultural and social institutions; and

5) to make students more sensitive to the issues and negative consequences of discrimination, racism, including institutionalized racism, with the goal that awareness will lead to understanding and understanding will lead to a diminishing of these practices.

In an attempt to assess whether or not these goals were achieved, a research instrument entitled "Survey of Cross/Cultural and Gender Attitudes" was developed and administered the very first day of class. Careful analysis of the data demonstrated that negative stereotypes were most strongly held against African-Americans, Jewish-Americans and Italian-Americans. During the last week of classes, students were again asked to complete another attitude survey specifically on the three above-mentioned groups. The results demonstrated that many of the negative stereotypes lessened as a result of class material and open discussions. The results of the pre-test and the post-test were validated by use of a control group, which in this case was not only a different class, but also a totally different subject area.

Since the inception of the course, two sections have been offered and filled to capacity each semester. Due to the growing demand, three sections will be offered on campus this fall and one section will be taught at a state employee facility off campus. The New York State Employee Training Program, in conjunction with Hudson Valley Community College's "Life Plus One" program, specifically requested this course be taught to New York State employees enrolled in this unique program. State employees will hopefully gain valuable information from this course as well as be provided with the opportunity to earn college credit.

The original course proposal was supported by a State University of New York/Hudson Mohawk Consortium Grant. More recently, the actual course and its resulting research were selected by the SUNY Faculty-Senate-Student Life committee as a program that "Enhances the Spirit of Campus Community" and will be included in a catalog of such programs, which will be distributed to all of the campuses of the State University of New York.

Contact:
Dennis L. Nagi
(518) 283-1100

Hudson Valley Community College
Vandenburgh Avenue
Troy, NY 12180
Total head count enrollment-Credit: 4,262; Non-Credit: 8,362
Campuses/sites: 1; Full-time faculty: 248

JEFFERSON COMMUNITY COLLEGE

JUNIOR VISITATION DAY: A TOUCH OF CLASS

The program promotes higher education to high school juniors from 15 area schools

Inviting more than 500 high school juniors to a college campus for one day can be fun, exciting and, at Jefferson Community College, it can be rather "classy." "A Touch of Class" gives high schools junior in the neighboring tri-county area the opportunity to discover more about college life by exploring both academics and student life.

The program was initiated in 1978 when JCC Admission was examining ways of promoting higher education opportunities to the small rural high school population in the area. Most high school seniors had never been on a college campus and, therefore, held reservations concerning the "fit" for them. Admissions counselors felt that visitation held the key.

The college is so committed to the program that classes are canceled so that every member of the college community can participate. JCC students are trained as tour guides, and act as club representatives and lunch servers. Faculty present mini-sessions and greet buses. Staff support the activity by preparing name tags, room assignments and schedules. JCC students guide groups of 10 to 12 juniors through a schedule of activities which feature:

1) a series of "mini-sessions" conducted by each of the four college divisions and presented by faculty (titles such as "Academic Survival," "Doing the Right Thing," "Inter-collegiate Sports," "Rock Music and Social Censorship," "Is Psychology More Than A Rat in a Box?" provide insight, information, and humor);

2) the Phil Donohue Show, hosted by JCC's own "Phil," and his or her panel of faculty, students and staff who informally provide an informative question/answer show relating to issues which are important to prospective college students;

3) a tour to familiarize juniors with the campus and introduce them to the JCC clubs and organizations, which are represented at various sites along the tour route; and

4) lunch and light entertainment (usually a comedian).

This project is a minimal cost to the college and the benefits are many. Most important, the college serves the local community by promoting higher education to juniors from 15 high schools.

Comments from counselors include: "You've developed an outstanding program;" "For many of our students, it was the first time they have set foot on a college campus so it was a positive experience. Keep up the good work;" "Every student I talked to was very positive!"

Junior visitation Day "A Touch of Class" has been recognized by the American Association of Community and Junior Colleges Small/Rural Community College Commission as an Exemplary Program.

Contact:
Rosanne N. Weir, Director of Admissions
(315) 786-2408

Jefferson Community College
Outer Coffeen Street
Watertown, NY 13601
Total head count enrollment-Credit: 2,746; Non-Credit: 304
Campuses/sites: 6; Full-time faculty: 85

COLLEGE CONSORTIUM

⌗ Consortium members offer degrees at the associate, baccalaureate ⌗
and master's level to both military and civilian populations

Three diverse but significant elements precipitated the creation of an educational consortium: the Army's decision to locate its newly activated 10th Mountain Division at nearby Fort Drum, local demand for additional educational services, and a task force study regarding the need to establish a four-year college in Watertown.

Funded through the State University of New York, the consortium, referred to as the SUNY Colleges in the North Country, began operation in the spring of 1985 with eight member colleges offering degrees at the associate, baccalaureate and master's level.

Goals of the organization are to:

1) promote and support existing programs;
2) develop new degree programs to better meet the needs of the area;
3) maintain a cooperative relationship with Fort Drum and member campuses;
4) provide a positive atmosphere in which students are offered encouragement and help in their educational endeavors; and
5) create more effective methods of marketing the consortium.

At the consortium office, located on the Fort Drum military installation, an executive director attends to the daily operation of the office. Full-time, on-site coordinator/instructors representing Jefferson Community College and three other four-year institutions provide coordination, student advisement and continuity of instruction.

As a founding member of the organization, Jefferson Community College offers extension courses at three separate sites in the area as well as supports the lower-level requirements of the members offering baccalaureate degrees. In addition to the 15 associate degree and six certificate programs on its main campus, JCC also is a leader in flexible scheduling, offering condensed eight-week terms and providing special request classes designed to fit into a particular unit or group's training calendar.

Consortium colleges participate in the Service Members' Opportunity College. This network allows military students and their family members to obtain degrees from member colleges with a minimum number of courses completed at the host campus. At the associate level, more than 1,100 SOCAD agreements have been processed with Jefferson Community College since the consortium's inception.

In its ninth year of operation, the consortium has shown continued growth both in enrollment and in number of courses offered. From 1985 to 1992, enrollment in credit courses as well as the number of credit-bearing courses quadrupled.

In summary, the consortium has proven to be a very successful endeavor. Flexibility in scheduling and a spirit of cooperation have enabled campuses such as Jefferson Community College to better meet the higher educational needs of its military as well as civilian populations.

Contact:
Wanda R. Lancaster, Exec. Dir., SUNY Colleges in the North Country
(315) 773-9007

Jefferson Community College
Outer Coffeen Street
Watertown, NY 13601
Total head count enrollment-Credit: 2,746; Non-Credit: 304
Campuses/sites: 6; Full-time faculty: 85

ENTERPRISE AT LaGUARDIA COMMUNITY

⌗ The program helps students see thematic connections across disciplines ⌗
and helps them develop collaborative skills

An innovative use of learning communities has netted improved student success at LaGuardia Community College.

"Enterprise," a grant-funded program within the Division for Academic Affairs, supports curricular and pedagogical innovations in the business career areas of study. Enterprise's offerings assist students in seeing the thematic connections across disciplines, developing skills in working collaboratively and in using effective learning

strategies, and establishing supportive relationships with peers, faculty and counselors to facilitate early intervention when personal and academic problems arise.

Enterprise supports academic innovation through:

1) the training of faculty in active learning and collaborative learning strategies, including extensive use of group work and case studies; and
2) the development of thematically linked multi-disciplinary learning communities and enhanced

sections of high-risk courses using student-led study groups. Currently, among Enterprise's offerings are clusters/pairs which connect basic skills and college-level courses as well as others which link general education courses to career content courses.

Enterprise offered its first set of course clusters, pairs and special sections of "high risk" courses enhanced with student-led study groups, in the fall 1990 academic quarter. Each academic quarter since, Enterprise has offered five to six clusters, pairs or enhanced sections with study groups, serving 130 to 150 students. Its latest innovations include course pairs in which students with limited English proficiency but high math skills are permitted to enter college-level introductory computer accounting courses while they attend special ESL classes to improve skills in reading and understanding technical content.

A full-time director, reporting to the associate dean for academic affairs, administers Enterprise in collaboration with the faculty and chairs of the participating departments. Grant funding supports the clerical, printing and postage expenses involved in student recruitment and registration as well as special advisement and career development services.

Evaluations have shown that participating faculty and students view their experiences in Enterprise offerings as very positive. Students have enthusiastically reported that they enjoyed the classes and particularly identified the establishment of a student community as a positive aspect of their experience. Enterprise students have generally achieved higher levels of academic success than non-participating students. In some cases, the differences are dramatic: for example, 76 percent of students taking Economics I as part of the Enterprise Business Cluster earned a C or higher, compared to 45 percent of the students who took regular sections of the same course.

Enterprise was recognized nationally in February 1992 when its director was selected as one of 12 "Outstanding Freshman Advocates" in a competition sponsored by the National Conference on the Freshman Year Experience. Enterprise was cited as a model for the implementation of course cluster/pairs in "A Time to Every Purpose: Integrating Academic and Occupational Education in Community Colleges and Technical Institutes," by W. Norton Grubb for the National Center for Research in Vocational Education, July 1992.

Contact:
Meryl Sussman, Program Director
(718) 482-5408

LaGuardia Community College
31-10 Thomson Avenue
Long Island City, NY 11101
Total head count enrollment-Credit: 9,398 Non-Credit: 23,990
Campuses/sites: 2; Full-time faculty: 200

LaGuardia Community College

New Student House

⌘ This "immersion experience" is designed to create an appetite for education ⌘
among the 75 entering students annually enrolled

New Student House is a first-term "immersion experience" designed to foster both a sense of intellectual community and a realization of the importance of foundational knowledge to subsequent education. By utilizing a teaching team, a collaborative approach to both planning and instruction, and common course theme ("Relationships"), the project supplies a full roster of tightly integrated courses for entering students.

Each term of operation, the project enrolls 75 students (in sections of 25) at several levels of competence in basic skills and creates a tailored program of study for each.

Under a grant from New York State Vocational Education, this project is creating, testing, modifying and integrating into the curriculum a thoroughgoing "coordinated studies" program of basic skills courses in reading, writing and speech. Modeled on successful nationwide experiments with "learning communities" and an earlier project at the college (Super cluster), this project purposefully restructures the curriculum, to break down traditional, often rigid, barriers between disciplines and to emphasize (and so utilize) learning as an integrated, social process.

The project aims to improve students' ability to fulfill their basic skills requirements quickly and effectively, then to move on to the regular curriculum. In sum, it works to improve significantly the course completion, retention and progress rates for these traditionally "at-risk" students.

The reading, writing and speech instructors each teach three courses (a full term's roster for all but the speech instructor) within the project and devise the integrated curriculum.

A counseling component is a major part of the project: a project counselor not only teaches adapted versions of the "New Student Seminar" required of all incoming students, but also works in all project classrooms to help students improve necessary "learning tools" such as study skills. A project director oversees and coordinates are planning, scheduling and curriculum development, and serves as liaison to the many college offices involved in administer-

Continues on Page 468

ing the project. Computers also play a vital part in the writing and reading components of the project (and a lesser role in the speech component), thereby taking advantage of LaGuardia's considerable strength in developing an effective computer-based pedagogy. LaGuardia's extensive work in collaborative learning, students learning from each other through carefully organized small-group tasks, is another major feature of the project.

Contact:
Brian Gallagher, Director
(718) 482-5670

LaGuardia Community College
31-10 Thomson Avenue
Long Island City, NY 11101
Total head count enrollment-Credit: 9,398 Non-Credit: 23,990
Campuses/sites: 2; Full-time faculty: 200

INSTITUTE FOR QUALITY IMPROVEMENT

The Institute trains employees of area business how to improve processes and create a positive work culture

The Institute for Quality Improvement at Mohawk Valley Community College is dedicated to promoting the adoption of Total Quality principles in all segments of business, industry and education in the Mohawk Valley.

The IQI has developed a core curricula of 25 modules tailored to meet the specific needs of manufacturing, health care, service industries and the education community. More than 25 area professionals are certified in the use of the curricula. Training as well as continuous support and consulting services are available from the Institute through the college's Office of Corporate Programs. IQI has access to many area businesses who are currently involved in Total Quality, trained professionals for on-site consultation, a library of Total Quality videos, and various grant programs for funding of long-term training.

The IQI assists businesses and educational institutions in developing a support structure and role clarity for employees in organizations. Employees are trained to understand and use the practical skills and effective tools to build commitment, change behavior, assess and improve processes and create a positive participative culture. The purpose of the training is to have employees master the principles of continuous process improvement and take ownership of their successes. The training process and coaching services encourage self-sufficiency and help to build management commitment, implementation design, quality awareness and statistical skills necessary for long-term, organization-wide success.

Mohawk Valley's Office of Corporate Programs has been providing training programs since 1983. The IQI has taken the lead in providing affordable Total Quality training. The Institute provides a system of assessment, development and training as well as continued consulting and evaluation support from certified professionals and follow-up and referral through its association with organizations such as the Mohawk Valley Quality Improvement Council (MVQIC) and the ASQC Central Mohawk Valley Chapter.

More than 25 area business, industry and education professionals have received more than 120 hours of detailed training in order to qualify for IQI Instructor Certification. Teams of instructors are available for tailored training in manufacturing, health care, banking and insurance and other service organizations as well as educational institutions. Instructors can train all employees or train key personnel in "train-the-trainer" programs. The Institute provides consulting services as well as continued support from the Office of Corporate Programs.

The IQI Partnership Plan between the IQI and contracting organizations is designed to provide employees with the necessary training and support to implement the process of total quality improvement. Training is available in the following areas: Senior Management Workshops, Quality Assessments, assistance in the creation of a Quality Council, Middle Management Workshops, Process Action Team implementation, Management Skills training, Union Awareness Briefings, Resource Personnel Workshops, and Train-the-Trainer programs.

The IQI has been so successful that an additional 25 instructors have been or are currently being trained to meet the requests for instruction in Total Quality.

Contact:
Regina M. Clark, Director, Dept of Corporate & Community Programs
(315) 792-5524

Mohawk Valley Community College
1101 Sherman Drive
Utica, NY 13501
Total head count enrollment-Credit: 6,273; Non-Credit: 1,176
Campuses/sites: 2; Full-time faculty: 183

THE ARTS AND THE HUMAN CONDITION

▓ *Designed for nursing students, the interdisciplinary Humanities course* ▓
ties literature, music and art with nursing

Developed for nursing students, an interdisciplinary Humanities course provides a context other than clinical for examining subjects such as anatomy; healers; disease, disability, and madness; and the cycle of life. It covers what literature, music and art might have to tell nursing students about these subjects. Prior to this course, the Humanities Department had no course designed for students in a specific curriculum.

As part of the National Endowment for the Humanities/American Association for Community and Junior College's Developing Regional Humanities Networks Project, it was created by Professors Steven J. Mocko and Carolyn West Pace, with Sandra A. Engel, Head, Humanities Department

Professors Pace and Mocko received a modest amount of released time in fall of 1991 to complete the necessary research and to design the course. In spring of 1992, two sections ran, both on the Utica campus, and in fall 1992, again two sections ran, this time one on the Rome campus and one in a correctional facility. The college expanded its library and media holdings appropriately.

The readings for the team-taught course included Susan Sontag's *Illness as Metaphor* and *AIDS as Metaphor*, Camus' *Plague*, Tolstoy's *Death of Ivan Illych*, May Sarton's *As We Are Now*, and Lytton Strachey's essay on Florence Nightingale from *Eminent Victorians*. Students purchased a package of university prints, including Coles' "Voyage of Life" series, Goya's "Old Age," Caravaggio's "Death of the Virgin," and Greek and Roman images. They examined the images of medicine in *Frankenstein*,

Flatliners and *Dune*; the music for the course included Philip Glass' *Einstein on the Beach*, and selections from Handel and Mozart.

Field trips were organized to the Munson-Williams-Proctor Institute and to an art exhibit on AIDS at Hamilton College. Students kept a journal, took exams and completed projects of their own choosing. Subjects for the student projects included pet therapy, music therapy, analysis of images of nurses in film, and an analysis of drawings of a 7-year-old child.

NEH/AACJC provided MVCC with a mentor, Professor James von Schilling of Northampton Community College in Bethlehem, PA., who had experience designing an interdisciplinary course. Professors Mocko, Pace and Engel met with Nursing faculty and the Nursing Program Advisory Board and gave presentations at the Nursing Executives in Education of the Mohawk Valley (NEXES), and at the College's Board of Trustees meeting. Professors Pace and Mocko gave a presentation entitled "Healers in the Arts" to the honors nursing students at SUNY-Morrisville, and they later gave a presentation on the course at the Community College Humanities Association in Baltimore in November 1992. The course was featured in the December 1992 *Advancing the Humanities News*.

Student evaluations indicated that students were pleased but thought the work was too extensive. Therefore, slight adjustments have been made. In fall 1993 two other instructors team-taught the course in the distance learning program.

Contact:
Sandra Engel
(315) 792-5450

Mohawk Valley Community College
1101 Sherman Drive
Utica, NY 13501
Total head count enrollment-Credit: 6,273; Non-Credit: 1,176
Campuses/sites: 2; Full-time faculty: 183

WRITING ACROSS THE CURRICULUM

▓ *Critical thinking skills are challenged when writing-intensive assignments* ▓
come from courses throughout the college

The Monroe Community College (MCC) Writing Across the Curriculum (WAC) Program is a grass-roots educational movement which received administrative support from its inception. By incorporating writing-intensive assignments in courses throughout the college, a student's analytical and critical thinking skills are challenged, maximizing the student's learning.

Goals of the program are: enhanced learning through writing; improved methods of teaching; development of critical thinking skills; experience in content-articulation; better communication skills; and continuing professional development.

The ultimate goal of the MCC WAC Program is excel-
Continues on Page 470

lence in education.

In 1984, through the Professional Development Committee, the MCC faculty chose to experiment informally with WAC. In 1988, the positive results of the first four years prompted formal commitment of the college to WAC through two consecutive MCC Foundation grants. In 1990, the WAC Program became an integral expenditure in the college budget.

The program is guided by a faculty committee and a WAC administrator. The committee is chaired by the WAC program coordinator, a teaching faculty member with partial release time. The WAC Committee organizes faculty WAC workshops, three to five per year, and calls for writing-intensive course proposals. The proposals are evaluated by the WAC Committee and $300 stipends are awarded for committee-approved proposals. An additional incentive has been conference travel money available to the WAC Program participants.

By fall 1992, the MCC WAC Program listed 111 faculty participants (out of 297 full time teachers) who taught 405 writing-intensive sections across the disciplines. These benefited more than half of the students enrolled at MCC.

The MCC WAC Program is bursting with growth and innovation. There are informal WAC Talks during faculty pizza lunches; WAC "All Write" T-shirts; *WAC Notes*, a faculty newsletter; promotional WAC videotape; formal WAC workshops, both general and discipline-specific. The most innovative is a prospective Writing-Intensive Degree of Choice in any discipline, which the WAC committee is currently researching and defining.

At the core of success of the MCC WAC Program is the volunteer approach in the program promotion, and positive, often enthusiastic participant response which encourages others to join.

Contact:
Stasia J. Callan, English Professor/Program Coordinator
(716) 292-3370

Monroe Community College
1000 East Henrietta Road
Rochester, NY 14623-5780
Total head count enrollment-Credit: 14,123; Non-Credit: 6,033
Campuses/sites: 27; Full-time faculty: 293

MONROE COMMUNITY COLLEGE

DAMON CITY CENTER: MAJOR URBAN INITIATIVE

The Center in downtown Rochester reaches under-served populations such as women and minorities

Monroe Community College's Damon City Center, built to cater to an under-served population in the city of Rochester, is enjoying enrollment beyond initial projections

The state's third-largest community college, MCC established the new urban center in January of 1992. The project was more than three years in the making. A formalized community interest survey indicated there was considerable support from the business community-based organizations to establish a presence of Monroe Community College in downtown Rochester. Former Monroe County Executive Tom Frey and MCC President Dr. Peter A. Spina commissioned a feasibility task force that unanimously recommended the development of a city campus.

College officials entered a year-long planning phase which examined local facilities, potential academic programs, necessary student support services and budget requirements for the project. In 1991, the Board of Trustees authorized the renovation of the upper floors of a large, vacant downtown department store for the purposes of initiating a college campus within the inner city.

The Damon City Center began operation in January 1992, and attracted more than 2,000 registrants in its first semester. The student population represented a healthy balance of city residents and employees of downtown businesses. Demographically, 65 percent of the students were women, the minority mix was 48 percent and the average age exceeded 30.

The Damon City Center now offers three associate degree programs. Soon the college will identify academic programs to be relocated from the main campus. The five-year enrollment projection calls for an enrollment of more than 6,000 students; current registrations are running ahead of schedule.

A consortium of colleges is currently being formed that will offer bachelor- and graduate-level programs at the Damon City Center. The Rochester City School District has begun planning for the development of an Alternative High School within the building.

Negotiations are proceeding with the large public library in the City of Rochester to establish a branch library at the Damon City Center that will serve student and faculty needs as well as the general public. This model establishes a complete educational center with courses and programs at several levels and sets forth a continuation of education, which city residents and employees can enter based upon current skills and progress to the desired level.

Monroe Community College has recently been asked to join a Ford Foundation project under the auspices of the National Center for Urban Partnerships, which will focus

Continues on Page 471

on strategies to improve minority completion of the baccalaureate degree. The Damon City Center will serve as the lead institution in this regard and will involve representatives of other educational institutions, area businesses, government representatives and leaders from community-based organizations.

The Damon City Center has recently been recognized by the Rochester Downtown Development Corporation and the Rochester Coalition for Downtown for bringing educational opportunity to the city, promoting diversity and advancing human relations.

Contact:
Floyd (Bud) Amann, Center Administrator
(710) 262-1610

Monroe Community College
1000 East Henrietta Road
Rochester, NY 14623-5780
Total head count enrollment-Credit: 14,123; Non-Credit: 6,033
Campuses/sites: 27; Full-time faculty: 293

HONORS PROGRAM

Honors students are offered personalized experiences to meet their academic and emotional needs

The Nassau Community College Honors Program addresses the academic, social and economic profile of gifted students who are unable to afford four-year institutions that offer courses of study of comparable quality and rigor. Many of these students are also younger or more indecisive about their academic goals than their peers and benefit from the personal guidance the program offers.

Because students often must work to meet tuition and living expenses, the program accommodates their personal schedules by offering multiple sections of honors classes, day and evening, thus enabling eligible students to retain full honors status. To achieve this flexibility in scheduling, honors classes are often specially designated, highly enriched sections of regular courses, as opposed to the more standard model of special seminars offered only once a semester at a single time period. This mechanism also gives students more options for fulfilling honors requirements and guarantees full transferability.

A variety of advisement patterns geared toward full applicability to varying associate degree requirements provides further flexibility and ensures that students can graduate after a two-year course of study without spending additional time and money. Day and evening summer honors courses are, however, offered for students who work full time and wish to retain full honors status.

In general, NCC honors students are offered very personalized experiences to meet their academic and emotional needs. The program prides itself on an informal, family-like atmosphere to ease students through a smooth transition from high school to college and to nurture self-confidence as they explore academic options. Often this process begins when students are still in high school through their exposure to Honors at NCC through two special outreach components, the Honors Connection and the Selected Scholars Programs. These programs invite bright high school students to take honors classes and participate in honors activities while in their junior and senior years.

Classes are small, in some cases limited to 10 to 12 students, to create a seminar environment, fostering an excellent rapport between students and instructors. Students are individually advised by the Honors Coordinator, who has detailed records on each participant and can generally offset the confusion and constraints of general registration. The engaging and personal atmosphere is further maintained for students through various program activities such as an Honors Club, opportunities to publish in the *Honors Journal*, and the receipt of certificates of merit and letters of commendation. NCC Honors graduates routinely transfer to and flourish at first-rank baccalaureate institutions.

Contact:
James Gulli, Dean of Instruction, Continuing Ed. and Extended Day
(818) 914-8562

Nassau Community College
1 Education Drive
Garden City, NY 11530
Total head count enrollment-Credit: 21,552; Non-Credit: 4,047
Campuses/sites: 1; Full-time faculty: 520

MULTI-DISCIPLINARY COURSES

▦ Students see it is impossible to understand Picasso's Cubism ▦
without a sense of the ideas of Darwin and Einstein

Responding to the perception that change is the only constant in our modern world, Nassau Community College has initiated a series of reforms designed to give focus and relevance to the diverse perspectives of course offerings.

The multi-disciplinary courses MDC 101 and MDC 102, supported in formation and implementation by a grant from the National Endowment for the Humanities, have been the watershed of curriculum innovation at the college. The multi-disciplinary approach to contemporary issues has led faculty to revise their ideas about their own disciplines and to design strategies which examine the relationship of issues, providing students with the opportunity to use their disciplinary knowledge as well as contemporary culture and experience.

Both MDC 101 and MDC 102 study the monumental changes in the perceptions of nature, human nature, society, and the universe in the course of the 20th Century, MDC 101 from a science and social science orientation, MDC 102 from a humanities and artistic orientation. The courses may be taken in any sequence and because of the parallel structure of the courses students are encourage to take both. They see it is impossible to understand Picasso's Cubism without a sense of what the ideas of Darwin and Einstein did to shape modern thought, or to grasp literary language, even simple narrative and dialogue, without looking at the ideas of Nietzsche and Freud. The scope of

the courses, the "modern mind" and beyond, coincide with students' interests, and the format of the courses, starting with a central human figure wrestling with modern problems, has kept the ideas alive and relevant. The courses have allowed students to think and write about problems of their own, and to realize the sources of their predicaments.

The central figures which serve as springboards to the discussion of complex issues in MDC 101 are Darwin, Marx, Freud and Einstein. Students read primary sources and explore various approaches to ideas of evolution, human motivation, social conflict and physical theory. In MDC 102 the central figures are Picasso, Kafka, Camus, and Frank Lloyd Wright, with extensive readings of Virginia Woolf, James Baldwin, the music of Stravinsky and Berg, and much contemporary film and art.

By fall 1992, 70 faculty members, from more than 20 disciplines, had attended Faculty Seminars which provide time to read the material, discuss pedagogy, and prepare to teach the courses. Recently, courses have been scheduled in the evening and at off-campus sites in addition to four day sections of each course per semester. Students taking MDC courses have participated in Learning Communities in which MDC course material is coordinated with, for example, their English, Sociology, Economics, or History courses. A two-volume textbook published by Ginn Press, written and edited by MDC faculty, is available.

Contact:
Joan Sevick, Program Director
(516) 222-7185

Nassau Community College
1 Education Drive
Garden City, NY 11530
Total head count enrollment-Credit: 21,552; Non-Credit: 4,047
Campuses/sites: 1; Full-time faculty: 520

ACCESS CENTER

▦ The Center is an outreach to a minority, disadvantaged and inner-city ▦
populations seeking education and training

In an effort to better serve its major urban contingency, Niagara County Community College in 1989 opened an extension center in the city of Niagara Falls. The ACCESS (Adult Center for Comprehensive Education Support Services) provides a "one-stop shopping" service to people seeking education, training and other related support services.

Co-located in the ACCESS Center is a consortium of agencies including The County Departments of Social Services, Education and Training, Cooperative Extension, Speech and Hearing, Health and Mental Health. The

Center, initially funded by New York State, houses several unique programs serving the originally intended urban population. These programs include the Center for Educational Opportunity Support Services (CEOSC), the Structured Educational Support Program (SESP), New Ventures and Options.

CEOSC is a Department of Social Services-funded project which provides welfare mothers with a special orientation to college prior to enrolling in credit programs at the college's main campus. This highly successful program currently enrolls between 200 and 400 single mothers each year and provides day care, transportation, educational expenses and counseling support.

SESP is a high school drop-out prevention program operated in cooperation with the City of Niagara Falls Board of Education. It's an after-school program serving at-risk youth and provides remedial education, counseling and career education in an effort to build basic skills, self-esteem and motivation for continued high school success and graduation. Skills for Life and Career Program. This program provides assistance to adult welfare recipients helping them to build self-esteem and job readiness skills leading to increased employment opportunities.

New Ventures is a state-funded program providing training in non-traditional careers for women.

Finally, the Options program provides training in self-esteem and career direction to youths who are first-time criminal offenders and who are enrolled by the courts in this program as an alternative to incarceration.

In addition to these special programs, the college offers credit and non-credit courses, career planning services including counseling, computerized career interest assessments and a career information library. All of the special programs offered at the ACCESS Center are based on the case management process. Most directors of special programs serve as case managers or utilize case management staff to work on an individual basis with clients enrolled in their programs. The center also houses a licensed Childcare Center, serving infants through grade 4, and an after-school latchkey program.

Contact:
Tony Tullio, Chairman, Trott Extension Site
(716) 278-8150

Niagara County Community College
3111 Saunders Settlement Road
Sanborn, NY 14132
Total head count enrollment-Credit: 11,842; Non-Credit: 20,000
Campuses/sites: 5; Full-time faculty: 242

NIAGARA COUNTY COMMUNITY COLLEGE

"NCCC... IN YOUR NEIGHBORHOOD"

College employees got to know the people they serve through various outreach efforts

"NCCC... In Your Neighborhood" is a major, two-year college-wide community relations effort. Primarily, it consisted of visits of one to two months in each community the college serves.

Events are varied, ranging in size and impact from a haunted house (involving hundreds of college students and local school children) that raised more than $6,000, to faculty, staff and students visiting nursing homes or reading to children in area libraries. It truly allows college employees to get to know the people they serve in their community and, at the same time, gives local residents the opportunity to be more aware of the college and its resources.

The individual visits have been accomplished through committees composed of Institutional Advancement staff, employees and students from those communities being visited – and eventually residents of the communities. First staff, employees and students meet to discuss what their community is like, how we might learn more about the community, and how they might learn more about us.

Together we prepare a list of community persons who should be invited to a meeting. This meeting could be a breakfast or lunch or it could be in the evening on campus or in their community. These meetings have included cookies and coffee at the Village Hall, breakfast at NCCC and a summer continental brunch on the porch of a town's historic tavern. At these meetings, the personality, goals, problems, and the heart and soul of the community are shared, and ideas are generated on how we and the community can get to know each other better.

From these ideas have come several items, including:
- recognition of the local school teachers who our students say have had major impact on their lives, of outstanding alumni and of families whose members have had many and varied relationships with the college;
- a major event, often a fund-raiser, to assist a community project;
- several small events to get to know various community groups.

Outreach has been with representation of the entire community elected officials, school personnel, historical groups, athletic organizations, hospitals, senior citizen groups, small and large businesses and industry, children's and parents groups, and general citizenry who attend the events.

Beyond the initial outlay accomplished through end-of-the-year surplus funds, financial resources have included NCCC College Association Inc., the NCCC Foundation, Inc., and Institutional Advancement/Public Relations budget (money spent in this area is generally part of another project, i.e. Arts Calendar, Community Education Tabloid). As the state and county financial resources became more strained over the past year and a half, businesses also have donated food, prizes, etc.

Continues on Page 474

The Dean of Institutional Advancement heads the project with the Director of Community Services as coordinator of special events and a part-time staff member to handle the correspondence and follow through activities. The majority of activities are held evenings and weekends, and most of the help is volunteer.

The "NCCC... In Your Neighborhood" program has generated a positive reaction in the county as seen through articles in the newspapers, editorials, letters to the editor, and letters to the college. It also won the State SUNY-CUAD award for Community Relations in 1991, and a CASE gold for Community Relations in 1992.

The program ended in October 1992, with the entire county invited to our community (NCCC campus) for a Scholarship Dinner and an all-day Family Fun and Fitness Fair. Our "N-Triple-Scene" cable show and student Community Service Volunteer program, both developed as an extension of the program, will continue.

Contact:
Jane N. Haenle, Dean, Institutional Advancement
(716) 731-3271, ext. 184

Niagara County Community College
3111 Saunders Settlement Road
Sanborn, NY 14132
Total head count enrollment-Credit: 11,842; Non-Credit: 20,000
Campuses/sites: 5; Full-time faculty: 242

HYPERCARD STACKS IN ANATOMY AND PHYSIOLOGY

The "stacks" include animation, graphics and quiz questions to pique student interest

The traditional classroom milieu places constraints upon an instructor who tries to provide information to students in a concise and interesting way. This is especially true in a community college setting where great heterogeneity exists in each classroom.

At NCCC, Anatomy and Physiology is required for students in Nursing and Radiologic Technology. Many students find the course demanding, even overwhelming; others find the pace to be tedious. Efforts to deal with this dilemma have culminated in an ongoing "HyperCard stack" development project started in 1990.

The Hypercard application for Macintosh computers supports the development of these "HyperCard stacks." They can be viewed as a computerized stack of index cards. The user can move from any "card" to any other, anywhere in the "stack" with speed and flexibility. There is no set beginning or end. One has at his/her fingertips a data file on a given topic. "Stacks" can utilize photographs, video, voice and music, and can access information on videodisks and compact discs. Once created, "stacks" can be coupled and altered as needed.

The "stacks" developed at NCCC include animation, graphics and quiz questions to pique the students' interest. The design allows the user to move from topic to topic at his/her own speed, to choose the depth of presentation and the amount of repetition. Some "stacks" are interactive; students can manipulate variables and interpret results. Students who enjoy working independently can do so. The "stacks" are tailored to address students' weaknesses and are designed to tie in with the text in use.

Funding for the purchase of computers and instructor time for development was provided by URTER and NCCC. The "stacks" are utilized both in labs and on an independent basis. Approximately 80 to 100 students take "R and P" each semester; lab sections are limited to 20 students.

The Biology lab on the Saranac Lake campus is equipped with four Macintoshes, containing all of the available "stacks" on their hard drives. A single, similarly equipped, Macintosh is available in the Learning Lab on the Saranac Lake campus. The long-term goal is to provide each of the three campuses with Macintoshes and all of the "stacks".

Students have responded very positively. More than 500 hours were "logged" by students during the first semester of record-keeping on two Macintoshes, in one lab, utilizing the first two "stacks" developed. Future plans include the development of similar HyperCard "stacks" for use in College Biology and Human Biology on all NCCC's campuses.

Contact:
Beth Johnson, Associate Professor, Biology
(518) 891-2915

North Country Community College
PO Box 89, 20 Winona Avenue
Saranac Lake, NY 12983
Total head count enrollment-Credit: 1,643; Non-Credit: 2,200
Campuses/sites: 3; Full-time faculty: 38

EASY (EQUAL ACCESS SYSTEM)

 Distant Learning uses a high-grade voice microphone
and a computer with a writing tablet

NCCC serves the largest and most rural part of New York State, an area of mountainous terrain and long winters. In an effort to reduce staff travel, and to share quality instruction among our three campuses, Distant Learning (DL) was instituted in 1987. Audio graphics was judged the most cost-effective ($9,000 per site) and practical method to bring two-way interactive instruction between the three campuses.

How does the system work? A high-grade voice microphone is combined with a computer with a writing tablet. The signals from both are combined and sent out over a single, standard telephone line. At the remote site the signal is split; the voice is delivered to a speaker, and the computer signal to a 25-inch TV which acts as an electronic blackboard. Beforehand, many of the instructors prepare graphic screens, which can be displayed at the appropriate moment and then brought alive by adding additional notes. A microphone is provided for every two students so they can respond and question the instructor. The entire system is backed up with fax machines to transmit tests and materials. To make the system more humanistic, DL assistants work the system and generally act as the eyes of the instructors at the remote site.

Instructors generally transmit from the remote site at least every two weeks.

Nursing was the first class to go on line. The following semester College Chemistry and a Mental Health went DL. This was then followed by Hematology, Criminal Justice, Pharmacology, College Chemistry II, Organic Chemistry, and Introduction to Art. In each case the instructor was given release time from one class to prepare materials, graphics and train on EASY.

There have been several side benefits. DL telephone costs led to a review of the college's overall telephone operation. This led to a buy-out of the leased telephone system, the acquisition of cheaper telephone lines (FX and Watts lines), and the reduction of inter-campus cost to an average of $4 per hour. A telephone conference room was established to conduct college administrative and committee work between the three campuses.

The most memorable moment occurred when a former nursing student drove out of the bush of Uganda to a pay phone in order to speak to our current nursing students about the joys and realities of humanitarian work in Africa and we were able to share her comments (via DL) across all campuses.

Contact:
Peter Biddle, (original) Director
(518) 891-2915

North Country Community College
PO Box 89, 20 Winona Avenue
Saranac Lake, NY 12983
Total head count enrollment-Credit: 1,643; Non-Credit: 2,200
Campuses/sites: 3; Full-time faculty: 38

ENG 250 VOICES OF DIVERSITY

This English course studies the pride and prejudice experienced
by minority groups and expressed in literature and film

"Multi-culturalism," "Diversity," and "The New Demographics" are not merely 1990's buzz words – they reflect a growing awareness of the need in our society to nurture the humanistic values of tolerance, acceptance and inclusion of those that are different. Thus a new English course, Voices of Diversity, was developed recently at OCC, augmenting previously existing courses in Women's and Afro-American Literature.

Studies of the pride and the prejudice experienced by minority groups in American culture, as expressed in literature and film. Many of the following "Voices," their songs and their outcries, will be heard each semester: The Gay and Lesbian Voice; and New-Immigrant Voice; the Native American Voice; the Voices of the Homeless, the Drugged,

the Disenfranchised, the Disabled, and the Socially Alienated.

Course goals include:

1) to become familiar with selected examples of minority articulation in America;
2) to develop sensitivity to multicultural diversity, its social problems, and its verbal, formal and thematic variety of expression;
3) to encourage sound critical judgment and aesthetic appreciation of multi-cultural artistic expression; and
4) to discourage stereotyping and prejudice through detailed textual examination of individualized

Continues on Page 476

human stories and songs.

Although the content of Voices is occasionally, and perhaps inevitably, controversial, and the diversity of forms of expression (fiction, drama, poetry and film) challenging, this new offering is rapidly growing in popularity; a discussion of expansion towards a Multicultural Concentration is currently being considered.

Contact:
Thomas McKague, Instructor
(315) 469-2613

Onondaga Community College
Syracuse, NY 13215
Total head count enrollment-Credit: 8,512; Non-Credit: 13,890
Campuses/sites: 13; Full-time faculty: 224

ENG 201 SELECTED TOPICS IN POETRY

▓ *The course is designed around an independent study program,* ▓
with infrequent class meetings

In an attempt to adapt to the diverse scheduling needs as well as academic needs of our adult student population, Onondaga Community College has inaugurated telecourse programming in conjunction with the local educational TV channel (WCNY).

One such telecourse conjunction is the nationally acclaimed Voices and Visions series, which is a three-credit college sophomore level course in American Poetry based on the public television series of the same name. The course is designed around a structured independent study program with infrequent (six to seven per semester) class meetings, focusing on eight major American poets, from Whitman to Dickinson to Plath.

Course goals include:

1) to introduce the life and work of eight American Poets (selected from the 13 presented in the whole program) in their historical and cultural contexts so that the distinctiveness of each poet as well as their connections may be seen;

2) to read a diversity of poetic voices and styles;

3) to provide the critical terminology to explore the poet's craft;

4) to encourage the reading of more poems by these and other poets;

5) to encourage responses to a variety of poets and to explain what the poems elicit in both discussion and writing; and

6) to fully comprehend the wide-ranging significance of linguistic eloquence to culture in general.

It is the conviction of the OCC English Department that that which was perhaps "oft thought" but "ne'er so well expressed" will continue to have relevance, even well into the "Computer Age," because human feeling will always require expression.

Thus, Voices and Visions was inaugurated especially for those self-motivated students who otherwise "simply can't schedule." Another telecourse, The Story of English, is also offered, and the department plans further telecourses, including a sequence in required Freshman English, to better serve our increasingly expansive student population.

Contact:
Thomas McKague, Instructor
(315) 469-2613

Onondaga Community College
Syracuse, NY 13215
Total head count enrollment-Credit: 8,512; Non-Credit: 13,890
Campuses/sites: 13; Full-time faculty: 224

WRITING CONSULTANCY PROJECT

▓ *The interdisciplinary project primarily serves those in the technical* ▓
and allied health programs

The Writing Consultancy Project (WCP) is an innovative, non-traditional interdisciplinary approach to upgrading thinking and communication through writing. Though the project offers its services to all content areas, its principal clients have been, and continue to be, the technical and allied health programs because documentation in these areas is recognized as professionally, legally and ethically interrelated with performance and accountability.

In the WCP English Department, "writing consultants" accept invitations from content area faculty, departments and degree programs. They work with individual departments and instructors to develop practical strategies for improving student writing in the specific academic and professional arena (Nursing, Occupational Therapy, Physical Therapy, Medical Laboratory Technology, Electrical Technology, Dental Hygiene, Business/Person-nel Management).

The writing consultant and instructor then work as a team with the students through:

1) A credit bearing course, 11160-11161: Technical Writing Module. This 1-1/2 credit module is a co-requisite of designated content courses, i.e. Electricity I, Principles of Physical Therapy II, Clinical Training. The writing consultant teaches with the content instructor; they utilize time within the original course, individual conferences, required supervised writing in the computer-equipped Technical/Medical Writing Lab. They develop specific lessons and materials that show how a writing skills (logical organization) is applied to Laboratory Summaries or Nurse's Notes. The writing consultant also confers with the student on the rough drafts; the consultant and instructor grade and finalize drafts. Those grades count for both the Technical Writing Module and the content course grade.

2) A series of workshops/lessons integrated into the content course. Using the same techniques as above, the writing consultant and instructor team-teach.

3) A guest workshop or lesson. This "one-shot" experience focuses on one particular writing need, like "answering an essay exam question."

4) Individual consultation session(s) with instructor. In these, the writing consultant will help the instructor analyze the specific writing demands and needs; they will develop strategies (including) materials) which the instructor will then use.

Funded during its evolution by federal, state and area grants, the WCP also utilizes its award-winning Technical-Medical Writing Lab in which students do the writing and revising of their content area assignments; they also acquire basic computer and word processing literacy.

Employer and graduate surveys indicate WCP students perform as well as professional/occupational writers. College-wide and department-specific reaccreditation have also singled out the WCP for individual commendation.

Contact:
Christine Godwin, Chair, Dept. of English/Foreign Lang., (914) 341-4035
Betsy Reape, Project Coordinator, (914) 431-4014

Orange County Community College
115 South Street
Middletown, NY 10940
Total head count enrollment-Credit: 6,027; Non-Credit: 2,500
Campuses/sites: 7; Full-time faculty: 155

ORANGE COUNTY COMMUNITY COLLEGE

PROFESSIONAL DEVELOPMENT

The program integrates professional development needs perceived by administrators and by faculty and staff

The result of a nine-year evolution, Orange County Community College's Professional Development Program is built on an exciting dynamic that integrates the professional development needs perceived by top and mid-level administration as well as the "grass-roots" faculty and staff.

Its main goals are to help faculty and staff:

1) maintain college-wide and individual professional currency

2) strengthen and encourage professional and personal vitality; and

3) transfer and apply these to our educational programs and situations.

To meet these goals, specific development opportunities are available at each level. These include:

1) All-College In-Service Workshops (August, January and June) that focus on professional concerns such as Learning Styles with Dr. Anthony Gregorc; Assessment Strategies; Wellness; Cultural Diversification;

2) a New Faculty/Staff Orientation Program (two semesters); this program includes workshops such as Academic Support Services, the Learning Resource Center Student Development Staff and Services, Academic Advising with Computers, Ethics, The College Yesterday and Tomorrow: History & Grant History and Grant Possibilities, and Roundtable with the President and Academic Vice-President;

3) a Course & Faculty Mentoring Program (two semesters); tenured faculty serve as mentors for new and adjunct faculty teaching multi-section core courses such as Basic Writing, Freshman English and Mathematics;

4) a Sabbatical Program (year-round);

5) Individual Conference, Course Work, Mini-grant and Special Project Opportunities (year-round); through the Faculty and Staff Development Committee, individuals may propose specific

Continues on Page 478

projects and receive funding support through college budgeted funds and SUNY Tuition Reimbursement Program; and

6) a Wellness Program (year-round), developed by F&SD Committee and its Wellness Sub-committee; it includes all-college wellness and ongoing short-term workshops and events.

To assess, plan for, offer and evaluate the Professional Development Program, the present administration has created and supported a dynamic top-down, bottom-up governing process. Major administration offices, academic departments and the Faculty and Staff Development Committee contribute to the overall activity. They are assisted by the Professional Development Facilitator, who helps to plan, coordinate and publicize activities from all areas. The Office of the President handles the sabbatical and SUNY Tuition Reimbursement Programs. The Office of the Academic Affairs Vice-President oversees the All-College Workshops, the Course Mentoring program, and New Faculty/Staff Orientation Workshops. The Human Resources Officer is in charge of civil service training. Each instructional department may also plan and implement its own targeted "grass-roots" member.

With elected members from academic areas, support services, administrative affairs and civil service, the committee submits its sub-formal proposals for the yearly planning cycle; to complete this task, it relies heavily on an annual survey of faculty and staff. The committee has its own budget to supplement department monies, and, in addition to the activities listed above, funds the Faculty and Staff Development Newsletter and the Colleagues' Corner series.

Contact:
Sandra F. Mark, Vice President, Academic Affairs
John H. Whiting, Associate Dean for Instruction
(914) 344-6222

Orange County Community College
115 South Street
Middletown, NY 10940
Total head count enrollment-Credit: 6,027; Non-Credit: 2,500
Campuses/sites: 7; Full-time faculty: 155

ROCKLAND COMMUNITY COLLEGE

INTERNATIONAL STUDENT ACTIVITIES

Activities include an International Students' Thanksgiving Dinner and short-term study abroad

International Student Activities at Rockland Community College involve a variety of offices, ethnic groups and projects on campus. Seven of these activities are:

1) Practicum in Cross Cultural Issues is a Life Skills and Psychology Course which pairs first semester International Students with "Veteran" students. The pairing encourages a structured relationship for sojourners who have the task of developing new friendships in an unfamiliar environment. Class time is used to train the veterans in cross-cultural adjustment, communication and the helping relationship.

2) The International Students' Thanksgiving Dinner offers international students a way to learn about American culture as they enjoy a typical holiday meal. Local organizations and restaurants donate food and the college community volunteers time and talents to make this the Intercultural highlight of the fall semester.

3) The Intercultural Festival held each spring turns the table so that our International students teach Americans about their foods, cultures and values.

4) Short-term Study Abroad experiences provide opportunities for Rockland students to learn about other cultures through travel to these destinations and encourages students from overseas to study at the Rockland campus. Two of several study abroad experiences include exchanges with Chile and Croatia.

5) The Incoming International Student Orientation is a four-day series of lectures, meetings and tours to help integrate students who arrive from overseas.

6) Hispanic Heritage Month includes an awards ceremony, presentations, lectures and performing arts which represent the outstanding contributions of the Spanish-speaking world. This month focuses on both local and international accomplishments of Latino's.

7) African American History Month is a series of presentations and activities to heighten awareness of the important contributions of persons of African descent. These activities reinforce the idea that all cultures have contributed to who we are as human beings – and all of us benefit as a result of this diversity.

Contact:
Terence P. Hannigan, Coordinator
(914) 574-4269

Rockland Community College
145 College Road
Suffern, NY 10901-3699
Total head count enrollment-Credit: 12,523; Non-Credit: 9,559
Campuses/sites: 7; Full-time faculty: 192

ACADEMIC INTERVENTIONS

An intake and assessment process addresses students' study habits and attitudes, career goals and learning styles

Faculty members play an important role in Rockland Community College's Academic Interventions Program, which provides preventive advising to students encountering academic difficulty early in their college career.

Faculty are asked to take note if students miss classes, tests or assignments, or have difficulty making reasonable progress. They are encouraged to look for early warning signs prior to the fifth week of class and to initiate contact with students to clarify the situation. If this is not possible, they may complete a referral form and send it to the Coordinator of the Academic Interventions Program. The coordinator then contacts the students and meets individually with them to create an appropriate action plan, which may involve work on study skills, time management, stress reduction, direct communication with their instructors, withdrawing from the class, or working with a counselor. The coordinator provides written follow-up to the referring faculty, and often in-person or telephone consultation. During the 1991-92 year, faculty members referred 651 students to the program.

A second component involves mandatory participation in the program for students placed on Academic Warning or Academic Probation. Students are required to complete an intake and assessment process which addresses their study habits and attitudes, career decidedness, learning styles and barriers to success. Individualized plans are then developed, which may involve regular check-in sessions or ongoing counseling. During the 1991-92 year, 636 students met with staff in 1,293 individual counseling appointments (an increase of 42 percent over those served the previous year).

For a sample of 253 students on probation who participated in the program, the mean grade point average increased from 1.12 to 1.68 between spring 1991 and spring 1992. The ratio of credits completed to credits attempted improved from 64 percent to 75 percent.

The most frequently mentioned concerns expressed by students on probation were:
- personal problems, 20.4 percent;
- time management, 18.4 percent;
- work hours, 16.2 percent;
- poor study skills, 17.7 percent;
- undecided about career/curriculum, 15.8 percent;
- lack of motivation or interest, 11.3 percent;
- test anxiety, 9.1 percent.

The most frequent suggested interventions were:
- expunge failures, 41.5 percent;
- biweekly check-in, 11.9 percent;
- register for Study Skills/Test-taking workshop, 11.0 percent; and
- change curriculum at Records Office, 9.7 percent

Contact:
Linda Reisser, Dean of Student Services, (914) 574-4206
Cleta Ciulla, Coordinator, Academic Interventions Prog., (914) 574-4357

Rockland Community College
145 College Road
Suffern, NY 10901-3699
Total head count enrollment-Credit: 12,523; Non-Credit: 9,559
Campuses/sites: 7; Full-time faculty: 192

STATEWIDE TELECOURSE INSTRUCTION IN MATH/SCIENCE

A studio audience participates and an 800 number is provided for call-in questions in this course for teachers

With budgetary restraints a fact of life today, many public and non-public teachers are finding themselves teaching outside their primary areas of expertise. Additionally, school districts are finding it very costly to provide in-service programming in new or "cutting edge" teaching techniques. But thanks to a collaboration of Schenectady County Community College and the New York Network/SUNYSAT and the regional vocational center (Albany, Schenectady, Schoharie BOCES), a series of workshops offers a wide range of topics. to teachers.

Institute programs focus on expanding the curricular planning options for teachers through developing strategies by which teachers can include family members, new classroom technologies, interdisciplinary teaming, and students themselves into the entire learning environment. Recent topics have included Constructive Geometry, Cooperative Learning, Gender Equity, Family Mathematics, Interdisciplinary Mid-Level Studies, and video Production in Math Instruction.

Workshops are telecast live to down-link sites throughout the state. Some regional cable systems also broadcast the workshops over their public-access channel. A studio audience is utilized as active participants and an 800

Continues on Page 480

number is provided so that site participants can call in with questions regarding the presentation. Taped copies are also available for those school districts or locations who choose to utilize professional workshop days for the delivery of the workshops. Depending upon the topic, workshops range in length form one to six two-hour sessions scheduled after school from 3:45 p.m. to 5:45 p.m.

Evaluative feedback is sought from program participants to obtain suggestions for new topics.

Contact:
Thomas Nelson, Coordinator
(518) 346-6211, ext. 118

Schenectady County Community College
78 Washington Avenue
Schenectady, NY 12305
Total head count enrollment-Credit: 3,467; Non-Credit: 684
Campuses/sites: 1; Full-time faculty: 292

STATE UNIVERSITY OF NEW YORK COLLEGE OF AGRICULTURE & TECHNOLOGY AT MORRISVILLE

JOURNALISM

Students work on the campus newspaper, radio station and literary magazine and participate in media internships

The Journalism program at SUNY Morrisville prepares students for entry-level jobs as reporters in the news media, and increasingly, for transfer to four-year colleges and universities. When they transfer, students continue their studies in journalism, communications, public relations, graphic design, photography, technical writing and several other disciplines linked to the communication industry.

The curriculum emphasizes the foundations of good journalism: developing and writing a news story; shooting, processing and printing photographs; editing and laying out a weekly newspaper; and operating under deadline pressure.

Students learn their profession through participation on the *CHIMES* newspaper, at the campus radio station, WCVM; on the campus literary magazine, *The Image*; and through internships on campus and with business and media settings that stress hands-on learning. The intensive two-year program has yielded two Pulitzer Prize nominees in photography, a national press award winner in television news, several international correspondents, most recently in the Persian Gulf War, and numerous public relations officers, including the general manager of a professional baseball team.

First and foremost, the program stresses basic news-writing skills. Graduates are able to communicate news stories clearly and succinctly, and carry these abilities across whatever form of writing their jobs require.

At the same time, they are exposed to state-of-the-art technologies in computerized pagination, desktop publishing, radio broadcasting, and black-and-white photography.

This program celebrated its 25th anniversary in the 1992-93 academic year. Graduates are among the most loyal alumni of the college, and remark constantly that their professional success is due in large part to the skills in communication they learned at Morrisville. They return to campus as members of the program's advisory committee, which serves to keep the program up-to-date with the demands of the work place.

Contact:
Gerald A. Leone, Chairman
(315) 684-6169

State University of New York
College of Agriculture & Technology at Morrisville
Morrisville, NY 13408
Total head count enrollment-Credit: 3,200;
Campuses/sites: 2; Full-time faculty: 130

STATE UNIVERSITY OF NEW YORK COLLEGE OF AGRICULTURE & TECHNOLOGY AT MORRISVILLE

EQUINE STUDIES

The program features outstanding facilities, including an indoor riding arena and turn-out paddocks

Students in the Equine Studies Department at SUNY Morrisville learn by doing. Each student is responsible for the total care of one or more of the more than 100 horses boarded at the college. The Morrisville College Foundation, Inc., the college's independent gift-receiving organization, owns many of the horses that are used in both equine programs.

The Department features outstanding programs in

Equine Science and Management (Saddle Horse Management) and Equine Racing Management/Harness Racing or Thoroughbred Racing) as well as a developing program in thoroughbred management.

The Saddle Horse program, begun more than 25 years ago, teaches students all facets of the care and handling of different breeds of saddle horse. The college offers boarding opportunities for privately owned horses, and many owners send their animals to Morrisville for breaking and training. All such tasks are handled by students under the watchful eyes of expert faculty members who bring years of industry experience to their classes.

The saddle horse program offers both a Career Program and an Equestrian Studies program, both at the AAS level. Students who choose the Career Program find work after graduation as grooms, trainers, riding instructors, or managers with stables, arenas, and race tracks. While both programs require courses in math and science, students who choose the Equestrian Studies Program take more of those courses and are prepared to transfer after graduation to a four-year college or university, where they may pursue careers in equine management, veterinary science, or other fields related to the horse industry.

The Equine Racing Management Program features instruction for the Standard-bred industry that is as fine as one will find anywhere in the United States. Graduates find work throughout the country as grooms, trainers, managers, and drivers in the harness racing industry.

Horses owned by the Morrisville College Foundation and trained at the college have competed successfully in parimutuel events such as The Meadowlands, Pompano Race track, Vernon Downs and others.

The college sponsors an annual Standard-bred Auction, which features fine yearlings and race horses offered by consignors throughout New York State and the Northeast.

The auction is the largest of its kind in the state.

The Standard-bred program features a half-mile harness racing track, the only one of its kind on a college campus in the country. Students who perform well in their first-year studies in the Standard-bred program may qualify for a summer program between their freshman and senior years. In this program, they are responsible for the care and feeding of two to three race horses, and race the animals at county fairs, parimutuel tracks, or Sire Stakes races.

Many students work with the college's nationally recognized team of Belgian mares at draft horse shows throughout the country. The team is among the college's more visible marketing tools, making dozens of appearances each year at horse shows and other celebrations.

The college's riding team, which competes in Region II of the Intercollegiate Horse Show Association (IHSA), has had great success against two- and four-year colleges and universities. Most recently, the team won fourth-place team stock seat honors at the 1992 IHSA championships.

The Equine Studies Program at Morrisville features outstanding facilities, including a 90-by-280-foot indoor riding arena, complete with an attached classroom; breaking and training facilities; stables; and turn-out paddocks.

The college is establishing a Thoroughbred Program that would complete its Equine Racing offerings. Preliminary plans call for thoroughbred breeding and training facilities adjacent to the college's current Equine Facility. Students are preparing two thoroughbreds, including a two-year old in training and a yearling; in the fall of 1992, five more Thoroughbreds began training for sale and for racing in the spring semester.

Morrisville currently stands two stallions commercially, and students maintain the extensive thoroughbred breeding program as part of their work in the college's breeding and artificial insemination courses.

Contact:
William Madison, Animal Science Chairman
(315) 684-6083

State University of New York
College of Agriculture & Technology at Morrisville
Morrisville, NY 13408
Total head count enrollment-Credit: 3,200;
Campuses/sites: 2; Full-time faculty: 130

STATE UNIVERSITY OF NEW YORK – COLLEGE OF TECHNOLOGY AT DELHI

HOSPITALITY MANAGEMENT

An on-site hospitality center features a full cocktail lounge, specialized kitchen facilities and conference rooms

An outstanding feature of the Hospitality Management program at State University of New York College of Technology at Delhi, is the new state-of-the-art Alumni Hall Hospitality Center. This 5,000-square-foot facility provides a hospitality laboratory center housing every major product line and profit center found in today's dynamic hospitality industry.

Some of the facilities and academic technologies available to Delhi students include: front desk training facility; sleeping room suites provided by Marriott and Sheraton; conference and meeting rooms; a full cocktail lounge; banquet and catering center and full-service restaurant, both with specialized kitchen facilities; and classrooms capable of satellite video transmissions

The Alumni Hall Hospitality Center was a joint financial

Continues on Page 482

effort between the State of New York, Delhi Hospitality Alumni and the hospitality industry.

These facilities are part of a program that was among the first two-year Hotel and Restaurant programs in the country. The origins of the department date back to the first programs offered by the original institute in the early 1900's, when the Domestic Food Science curriculum was created.

The current hospitality programs began to take shape in the mid 1950's, with the creation of the Hotel and Restaurant Technology programs. These original programs have evolved into a modern curriculum utilizing the newest concepts and facilities available in today's hospitality and travel industries.

The faculty of 10 offer a diversity of degrees and indus-try expertise to the students of Delhi's programs. Faculty hold graduate degrees from Michigan State, Rochester Institute of Technology, Cornell University, New York University, Florida International University and the University of Maryland. Faculty industry experience ranges from the leading hotel chains, to national food service companies, to corporate travel management.

Delhi also maintains a unique relationship directly with today's hospitality industry. Due to the longevity of Delhi's programs, more than 4,000 Delhi Hospitality alumni are working in some aspect of the industry. This creates an industry network directing potential employers and the newest industry innovations to the Delhi campus and its programs.

Contact:
Robert Seibert, Assistant Professor/Department Chair
(607) 746-4189/4122

State University of New York College of Technology at Delhi
Main Street
Delhi, NY 13753
Total head count enrollment-Credit: 2,046; Non-Credit: 873
Campuses/sites: 1; Full-time faculty: 109

STATE UNIVERSITY OF NEW YORK COLLEGE OF TECHNOLOGY AT DELHI

VETERINARY SCIENCE TECHNOLOGY

A building is dedicated to the program, housing 10 species of animals, a surgical suite and various laboratories

Established in 1961 as the first of its kind in the U.S., the Veterinary Science Technology program at State University of New York, College of Technology at Delhi, has developed into a dynamic, nationally recognized program of study, fully accredited by the American Veterinary Medical Association (AVMA).

The extensive laboratory facilities and hands-on experiences with companion, laboratory, farm and exotic animals are major assets of the program. Graduates of the Veterinary Science Technology curriculum can pursue a variety of careers or transfer to a four-year institution to obtain a bachelor's degree in a related field.

Program options are Animal Health Technician and Laboratory Animal Technician. Graduates completing the Animal Health Technician (AHT) professional licensing examinations (AHT's) are employed by veterinarians in small, large and mixed animal practices. The AHT's role is comparable to that of the registered nurse and other medical technicians. Their professional duties may include surgical and medical nursing, laboratory testing and performing radiographic procedures under the supervision of a licensed veterinarian. Graduates may also work in zoos, public health, government and other related fields.

Laboratory Animal Technicians are employed by the pharmaceutical industry, medical, dental and veterinary colleges; breeders of laboratory animals; and diagnostic and testing laboratories. Under the direction of veterinarians or research scientists, technicians may perform animal husbandry, pharmaceutical testing, administrative and related duties. Those graduates who complete advanced laboratory animal courses are qualified to take the American Association for Laboratory Animal Science Registry examination at the Laboratory Animal Technician level.

A required practicum, or preceptorship, in an animal hospital, veterinary practice or animal research facility enhances the student's skills and employment potential.

A major building of the Delhi campus, the animal and plant sciences building (Farnsworth Hall), offers excellent research and clinical facilities. Specialized housing for 10 species of animals, a large surgical suite, and laboratories for anatomy, radiography, clinical technology and research are included.

A special feature of the program is the Delhi-Cornell Connection. Transfer opportunities for those students that are considering becoming veterinarians are available at Cornell University after successful completion of a special 70-credit-hour program at Delhi.

Contact:
Dominic Morales, Chair, Animal and Plant Sciences Department
(607) 746-4349

State University of New York College of Technology at Delhi
Main Street
Delhi, NY 13753
Total head count enrollment-Credit: 2,046; Non-Credit: 873
Campuses/sites: 1; Full-time faculty: 109

TechniCenter

*▨ The Center offers tailored training, from communications ▨
to computers, to employers of the Long Island area*

Advanced technology, increased skill requirements and changing demographics have forced both business and institutions of higher education to meet the challenges of providing a more productive work force. In order to remain competitive, employers have realized that they must assume the primary responsibility in assisting their employees to improve their basic skills and gain new ones.

In response to this need, Suffolk Community College opened its TechniCenter, located in the Hauppauge Industrial Park, in 1985. Since then, it has been meeting the needs of Long Island employers by providing low-cost quality training through contract courses and grant-funded programs.

The success of the TechniCenter lies in its ability to offer employer-specific training tailored to a company's unique individual needs. In 1987, for example, a group of SCC faculty designed a course for Arrow Electronics and traveled to the company's Virginia facility to teach it. This innovative venture was so successful that Arrow invited the same team of professors to teach the course in Canada the following summer.

Other TechniCenter training programs have included communication skills, computer applications, entrepreneurship, management/supervision, and office technology. It has also conducted seminar series specifically for women and minorities in business. To date, more than 150 companies and 3,000 students have received training at the TechniCenter.

The TechniCenter has been chosen by the New York State Department of Economic Development to play an integral role in a regional consortium of industry, economic developers, and local educators to take the concept of Total Quality Management from the seminar stage to the company-specific phase. Through a state grant of $40,000, the TechniCenter will help local companies to determine how they can benefit from TQM, develop and implement a specific plan, and provide customized training for their employees.

The TechniCenter has established a TQM committee for members of the Hauppauge Industrial Association, some of which are small companies who would like to implement a TQM program but do not know where to start. In addition, the TechniCenter holds an annual TQM conference.

Most recently, the TechniCenter began offering programs in international business. In November of 1991, it held a conference on global quality and followed up with a series of seminars on topics such as ISO 9000, applying for the Baldrige and Excelsior Awards, a TQM overview, and statistical process control. In conjunction with the Hauppauge Industrial Association, it also hosts monthly breakfast meetings on the topic of exporting. Because of increasing demand, the TechniCenter now offers courses in English as a Second Language.

In addition, the TechniCenter offers a JTPA 8 percent Basic Skills Program for economically disadvantaged students, funded by the Department of Labor. It includes 360 hours of reading, writing, math, GED preparation and keyboarding. A Computer Skills Program, also funded by the DOL, includes word processing, Lotus 1-2-3, keyboarding, d-base, data entry, and job readiness.

Contact:
John Webb Barham, Provost, Open Campus
(516) 434-1080

Suffolk Community College
533 College Road
Selden, NY 11784
Total head count enrollment-Credit: 21,000; Non-Credit: 14,000
Campuses/sites: 4; Full-time faculty: 524

Opinion Research

*▨ The results of a year-long polling exercise were covered ▨
by the local media, including TV news*

A group of students at the Eastern Campus of Suffolk Community College in a special topics course embarked on a year-long polling exercise that was covered by the local media, including TV news.

For the fall semester these students, in the course on methods of public opinion polling, received training by a retired executive vice president of the Roper Organization, a leading opinion research company, on the techniques and methods of telephone interviewing. On the break between the fall and spring semesters of the 1991-92 academic year, students interviewed by telephone 500 randomly selected residents of eastern Long Island. The respondents were asked a series of questions covering

Continues on Page 484

social, political and economic attitudes.

During the spring semester the data collected from these telephone interviews were used to explore and develop statistical concepts in a special section of the college's statistics course. Each student was required to develop a hypothesis based upon the questionnaire, test the hypothesis and, finally, produce a report from the data gathered through the study.

At the end of the semester, students presented their findings to the college community. These presentations were covered by local media, including a local cable TV news program.

The purpose of this year-long experience was to provide students training in public opinion polling techniques and to use this information to explore and apply the principles of statistics that summarize and analyze opinion data. As a by-product, the college provided the local community valuable information through the investigation of local attitudes on a variety of topics. It is a long-term goal of this program to develop a community research center which would serve the region for a variety of public interest, non-profit and business survey needs.

Contact:
Steven Kenny, Provost, Eastern Campus
(516) 548-2564

Suffolk Community College
533 College Road
Selden, NY 11784
Total head count enrollment-Credit: 21,000; Non-Credit: 14,000
Campuses/sites: 4; Full-time faculty: 524

ALCOHOLISM AND DRUG ABUSE CURRICULUM

The program has been viewed as the model curriculum for the state of New York

The Alcoholism and Drug Abuse program at Sullivan County Community College's Loch Sheldrake campus enjoys one of the lowest attrition rates in the college, thanks to the creative use of the college's study center and tutorial services by the ADA staff. Its successes are responsible for the program being considered a model for the state.

The program, established in 1973 by Social and Behavioral professor Richard Dunn, trains students to become counselors who will work with drug addicts and alcoholics.

When the program began at Sullivan, it was the first academic accredited degree program in Alcoholism and Drug Abuse in America. For all practical purposes the ADA program was created from nothing. There was no model to follow and no texts available 19 years ago, so Dr. Dunn wrote and developed much of the material that was used and distributed in each ADA course.

Since its inception, the ADA program has grown from 14 to more than 185 full- and part-time students per semester.

Other schools have consulted Dr. Dunn and his faculty and look to him as a leader in this field. The program is unique, requiring people with unusual talents, training and abilities.

The field placement and training opportunities are exceptional because Sullivan County has some of the best rehabilitation facilities in the country. Our ADA graduates work all over the East Coast in treatment facilities of every description and they've earned a good reputation.

Dr. Dunn's interest has led to his involvement in international ADA programs. He is a member of a unique group representing thirteen countries, which is funded by the World Health Organization of the United Nations, the Vatican and by the Communist Party in Italy. This group trains European drug counselors.

Because of these international ties, Dr. Dunn and members of Sullivan's alumni were part of a group of 100 attending the first American-Soviet Conference on Alcoholism. Out of that conference grew a unique exchange program between the United States and Russia, and in January 1990, a group of Soviet experts on alcoholism visited SCCC and began training in the "American Model" of alcoholism counseling. The Russians attended ADA classes at Sullivan and received academic instruction in the American approach to the disease under the supervision of Dr. Dunn and the ADA staff. During the summer of that same year, a group of Sullivan ADA students and alumni accompanied several American experts to Russia to help establish a treatment center there based on the American model.

Contact:
Dr. Richard B. Dunn, Division of Social and Behavioral Science
(914) 434-5750

Sullivan County Community College
PO Box 4002
Loch Sheldrake, NY 12759-4002
Total head count enrollment-Credit: 2,578; Non-Credit: 696
Campuses/sites: 11; Full-time faculty: 63

TOYAMA JAPAN EXCHANGE PROGRAM

American students and Japanese students study business in the others' country

In 1989, Sullivan County Community College formed a unique exchange program with the Toyama Business School, a private two-year college located in the Town of Kosugi in the Prefecture of Toyama, Japan.

It operates in a $3-million school building, financed and built by the Japanese, called Sullivan County Community College Toyama. The complex contains classrooms and a library/study center. The program reports to Saul Whynman, associate dean of faculty, Office of External Programs at the Loch Sheldrake Campus.

Sullivan offers a full Associate in Science (AS) curriculum in Business Administration at Toyama. In addition, students may choose courses from the Humanities, and Social and Behavioral Sciences. All classes are taught in English by Sullivan County Community College Faculty.

The exchange program allows Japanese students to study business for three semesters with Sullivan professors at the Toyama campus. Toyama students then travel to the United States and spend their last semester on the Loch Sheldrake campus where, upon successful completion of the program, they receive their American degree in business administration while also receiving a Japanese credential.

The program in Japan follows Sullivan's business administration curriculum, although certain of the courses were adapted to Japanese business (e.g. both Japanese and American Business Law are taught).

American students and other English-speaking students are also offered the opportunity to enroll in the Japan Studies Program at Sullivan's Toyama campus and study for a semester or more in Japan. The program allows for intensive or casual study of Japanese, depending on the student's interest. In addition to Japanese Language, Conversation, Reading and Writing, other courses specific to that part of the world are taught. For example, Japanese Business and Political Systems, Asian Studies, Japanese History and Japanese Literature, Music and Art are offered.

Since its inception about 23 American students have taken advantage of the opportunity to study in Japan and 87 Toyama students have graduated from Sullivan County Community College Toyama.

Dr. Jeffrey B. Willens, president of Sullivan County Community College, believes the exchange program has been "vitally important for the future of both countries, and an opportunity for two cultures to exchange cultural ideas."

Contact:
Saul J. Whynman, Associate Dean of Faculty for External Programs
(914) 434-5750

Sullivan County Community College
PO Box 4002
Loch Sheldrake, NY 12759-4002
Total head count enrollment-Credit: 2,578; Non-Credit: 696
Campuses/sites: 11; Full-time faculty: 63

COLLEGE TEACHING CENTER

The Center supports a variety of services offering potential for faculty growth and development

The College Center (CTC) at Tompkins Cortland Community College provides innovative professional development services, including roundtables and needs assessment, to faculty.

Developed from recommendations of a faculty task force, the CTC is staffed by a part-time coordinator selected from faculty ranks and is governed by an Advisory Board consisting of seven elected faculty members, the Instructional Software Specialist, the Division Head for Instructional and Learning Resources (ex officio), and two external members.

The Board guides and directs the activities of the Center, functions independently of college administration and controls its own budget expenditures. Maximum effort is made to reinforce the staff-centered nature and philosophy of the CTC. The CTC is conveniently located in the heart of the college's single-building campus, adjacent to other instructional support services, including the library and media services.

The CTC supports a variety of services that offer opportunity for faculty growth and development:
- individual consultations on matters related to classroom teaching;
- centralized clearinghouse of resources and materials related to instruction;

Continues on Page 486

- ongoing series of workshops, panel discussions and presentations (recent topics have included information literacy, bias and student achievement, writing across the curriculum, diversity and the curriculum, self-esteem and learning, holistic processing and math education);
- incentive awards for innovative classroom teaching projects;
- training programs on instructional computer applications and other areas of instructional technology;
- noon-time roundtable discussions;
- individualized self-assessment program; and
- faculty needs assessments related to teaching.

In 1990-91, Tompkins Cortland was awarded a three-year grant from the Fund for the Improvement of Post-Secondary Education (FIPSE) for the purpose of extending the services of the college Teaching Center to the college's adjunct faculty. The goal of the FIPSE initiative is to "introduce a multidimensional program that would work with part-time/adjunct faculty to build teaching effectiveness, increase participation in professional activity, and instill a sense of confidence and understanding in their teaching roles."

Among the activities specifically supported by the FIPSE Program are:
- an expanded teaching-centered adjunct orientation program;
- a master Teacher Certification Program for adjuncts;
- a mentoring program, which pairs new adjuncts with senior full-time or adjunct faculty members;
- workshops and individualized training in new instructional technologies for classroom support;
- Board of Trustees Adjunct Excellence in Teaching Award; and
- a newsletter targeted specifically to adjunct faculty.

With a relatively modest institutional investment, Tompkins Cortland Community College has reaped significant benefits from the CTC and FIPSE initiatives. Approximately 80 percent of full-time faculty have participated in CTC-sponsored programs and activities, many as presenters sharing their particular expertise.

The FIPSE program has given adjunct faculty a greater sense of participation in the academic life of the college. Thirty-seven adjunct/senior faculty mentoring pairs were established in 1991-92, and 12 adjunct faculty received Master Teacher Certification Awards in spring 1992.

The College Teaching Center and the FIPSE Program have been featured in regional and national presentations, including the Annual Colloquium on Undergraduate Teaching/Learning at Massachusetts Bay Community College, the Annual FIPSE Directors meeting, and the spring 1992 AACJC Conference in Phoenix.

Contact:
Bill Demo, Division Head, Instructional and Learning Resources
(607) 844-8211, ext. 4354

Tompkins Cortland Community College
170 North Street, PO Box 139
Dryden, NY 13053-0139
Total head count enrollment-Credit: 2,904; Non-Credit: 3,000
Campuses/sites: 3; Full-time faculty: 64

TROCAIRE COLLEGE

HUMANITIES COURSE

⊞ *The required course enables students to relate specific works* ⊞
to the historical milieu from which they emerged

A Trocaire College Humanities course challenges freshmen to explore relationships between literary genres, music and art, and in so doing, breaks down the stereotype that two-year colleges merely provide technical training.

Since 1973, the college's English department has been offering a required course, EN 102, that challenges all freshmen students to explore the connections among various literary genres, music and art. Such exploration leads students to an enriched understanding of human values, needs and aspirations.

The Humanities course is designed to ensure that every student who receives an associate degree from Trocaire College is:
1) enabled to develop his/her ability to understand fiction, drama, poetry, music and art;
2) given opportunities to enjoy these humanistic expressions;
3) enabled to explore relationships among the arts;
4) led to relate specific works of literature and the fine arts to the historical milieu from which they emerged; and
5) exposed to works from as many cultures as possible.

To ensure that the Humanities course achieves its desired goals, the course is periodically evaluated by the Dean of Liberal Arts, the Chairperson and faculty of the English Department. End-of-semester student evaluations are also given serious consideration. As a result of these evaluation procedures, in the Spring Semester of 1992, the Humanities course was significantly revised to include a broader range of authors, artists and musicians to better reflect the multicultural realities of the present time.

The one-semester course includes selections from the oral tradition: fable, folklore and myth; short stories, poetry, drama, music and art. Students are required to read assigned material and to submit papers related to the readings. Students are also required to attend one live concert (classic, authentic jazz or Gospel), make one visit to an art gallery and, if possible, to attend one live drama. Four lecture demos presented by guest lecturers, artists and musicians are woven into the course.

A textbook, *Literature: An Introduction to Fiction, Poetry and Drama*, X.J. Kennedy, Harper Collins, 1991, is used in the revised Humanities course.

The Humanities course includes three full-time instructors, one part-time instructor, two adjunct instructors and several guest lecturers. During the 1992 fall semester, the three full-time instructors were invited to make a presentation of this innovative course at the 27th Annual Northeast Regional Conference on English in the Two-Year College, held in Boston.

Contact:
Lynn Sullivan, Chairperson, Humanities Division
(716) 826-1200, ext. 255

Trocaire College
110 Red Jacket Parkway
Buffalo, NY 14220
Total head count enrollment-Credit: 1,300; Non-Credit: 790
Campuses/sites: 1; Full-time faculty: 46

HEALTH CARE OFFICE MANAGEMENT

The program, designed with the help of health care office managers, focuses on competencies ranging from accounting to medical transcription

There is an increasing need for persons trained to specifically manage the health care office. As the health care field evolves from single practices to group practices, the medical profession has become more specialized. Group practices have formed to efficiently fill the needs of the patients and the doctors, with group insurance plans contributing to the trend. With this growth, the need for record-keeping and business offices have also grown.

Because no area college offers such a program for the health care office manager, Trocaire College developed the Health Care Office Management concentration. The program has been designed with the assistance of health care office managers. The curriculum focuses on medical office competencies including medical terminology, medical transcription, medical coding, medical accounting with third-party reimbursements, and management theory. Graduates of the program will find employment in large health-care groups, as well as private offices.

Members of the Advisory Group enthusiastically say the program fills a community need, as well as promotes the professional status of medical office managers. Student interest has been high in this unique program.

Contact:
Irene Cuddihy, Chairperson, Business Program
(716) 826-1200, ext. 270

Trocaire College
110 Red Jacket Parkway
Buffalo, NY 14220
Total head count enrollment-Credit: 1,300; Non-Credit: 790
Campuses/sites: 1; Full-time faculty: 46

NURSING

The program is kept small to enhance learning and encourage discussion

Attractive salaries for Registered Nurses and the track record of Ulster's nursing program have increased enrollment and even forced it to be capped, at least temporarily.

The program is kept small to enhance learning and to encourage discussion between students and faculty. Students take only one nursing course at a time. After their first semester, each course is an intensive seven-week block. During the final seven-week course students explore professional trends and issues, analyze the problem of managing care of a group of patients, and synthesize knowledge and skills acquired in previous courses. This course requires students to be in hospital clinical labs for seven hours per day, three days per week, for four weeks experiencing different roles as primary care givers, delegators and medication nurses.

Goals of the program are to:
1) develop a basic core of knowledge and skills

Continues on Page 488

needed to provide nursing care in a variety of settings;

2) encourage personal growth and development by including general education courses which provide a supportive framework for nursing science; and

3) prepare graduates to pass the National Council Licensure Exam.

The program relies on well-defined assessment methodology including academic requirements, college lab requirements, and hospital clinical laboratory performance expectations.

A course may be repeated only once, and if a student is not successful the second time, may not continue in the program. No more than two nursing courses may be repeated, and the nursing course sequence must be completed within five years.

A minimum grade of C must be achieved in all nursing and science courses to progress in the program.

Fall of 1992 marked the largest number of students (110) ever enrolled in the nursing program. Completion of the program leads to an AS degree, with all courses transferable to baccalaureate programs.

For the last six semesters the percentage of Ulster's nursing graduates who have passed the national licensure exam for Registered Nurses has been significantly above the state and national averages of 88 and 92 percent.

Recent donations by several Northeast manufacturers and hospitals have included equipment valued at more than $10,000. Local health care organizations, who value graduates of the program, provide tuition assistance to students who agree to work at their institutions after graduation.

To accommodate increased enrollment, the department requires one full-time department chairperson, six full-time and seven to 14 part-time faculty, and one instructional assistant in the nursing skills laboratory.

Contact:
Shirley Krembs, Professor/Department Chair
(914) 687-5234

Ulster County Community College
Stone Ridge, NY 12484
Total head count enrollment-Credit: 6,540; Non-Credit: 620
Campuses/sites: 1; Full-time faculty: 75

ENVIRONMENTAL CONTROL / HAZARDOUS WASTE

The curriculum has been a prototype for similar programs and courses worldwide

Ulster County Community College's program in Environmental Control/Hazardous Waste occasionally allows students to conduct research projects for community groups concerned with water supplies and to make recommendations to safeguard these supplies. In one instance, the students' water study saved a local homeowners group $10,000 in research fees.

Such hands-on opportunities have been part of the program since it was developed in 1975 with funding from the U.S. Environmental Protection Agency and the New York State Department of Environmental Conservation. The curriculum proved to be a prototype for similar programs and courses throughout the United States and other nations.

The Associate in Applied Science program offers students two paths:

1) to enter the work force upon graduation; or

2) to transfer to a four-year college or university to pursue the baccalaureate degree.

While students have transferred to a variety of colleges,

Ulster has designed specific transfer agreements in Environmental Engineering Technology with Penn State University and in Environmental Science with the State University of New York College at Plattsburgh.

Through lecture and lab work on campus, the goals of the program are to:

1) develop a solid foundation of environmental control concepts and training in all aspects of water chemistry;

2) provide hands-on experience in the safety practices needed to work with hazardous materials;

3) teach lab analyses interpretation; and

4) develop an extensive understanding of environmental law and practice.

In the summer of 1992, the United States Department of Energy designated the College's program as a participating college for its Energy Environmental Restoration Waste Management Undergraduate Scholarship Program. For each participating scholar, the college receives tuition, fees and an academic allowance from the program's contractor, Oak Ridge Associated Universities. The scholar also receives a stipend and summer employment/practicum.

Faculty include two full-time and four part-time; state-of-the-art laboratory equipment and materials have been purchased through EPA, NSF and VEA grants.

Contact:
Theodore Skaar, Professor/Department Chair
(914) 687-5173

Ulster County Community College
Stone Ridge, NY 12484
Total head count enrollment-Credit: 6,540; Non-Credit: 620
Campuses/sites: 1; Full-time faculty: 75

WESTCHESTER COMMUNITY COLLEGE

MOMS ON THE MOVE

Students in the program have done as well as or better than other WCC students

Moms on the Move (MOMS) is a cooperative effort between Westchester Community College and the County Department of Social Services that breaks the cycle of dependence on public assistance. The program provides the education and training necessary for people to enter the job market and earn sufficient salaries (at least $25,000) to become independent.

With the strong support of the Westchester County Executive, the County's Commissioner of Social Services and WCC President Joseph N. Hankin, the program began in 1990, after administration of a basic educational skills test to welfare mothers revealed that 42 percent were college ready. That fall, 210 of them began working on associate degrees or certificates at the college, utilizing programs already in place as well as some which were especially created or expanded to accommodate the MOMS participants.

By fall of 1991, the program had enlarged to include 460 students, more than meeting the target goals set for the new academic year; by the spring semester their numbers had grown to 531. In May 1992, 17 of these welfare mothers marched in WCC's commencement procession, crossing the stage to receive associate degrees or certificates in a variety of health care and office technology fields, areas in which there is a demand for workers in Westchester. At least 100 additional students graduated during 1992-93.

Along the way to graduation, participants in the Moms on the Move program are assisted by the many existing and newly enhanced support services at WCC. A pre-freshman program funded by the U.S. Department of Education helps those who need remedial reading, writing and math skills prior to actually entering college programs. English as a Second Language immersion courses help non-English speaking welfare mothers learn English well enough to keep up with college-level teaching. A specially designed science course enables students to succeed in the advanced sciences necessary for the health care professions. Counseling, tutoring and support teams have been put in place particularly for the MOMS population.

Funding for the MOMS program has come from more than $2.5-million in grants from the Department of Social Services, 75 percent of which comes from the federal and state governments. Existing grants and in-kind services from the college have come to another $1.5-million. More than $3.2-million in state and federal grants for tuition, for which public assistance recipients automatically are eligible, were initially secured. The cost per student has been approximately $3,818 annually.

Academically, Moms on the Move participants have done at least as well as, and sometimes better than, other WCC students. For instance, in the fall 1991 semester, 15 percent of all WCC's full-time students earned a 3.0 average; 22 percent of the Moms on the Move students earned such averages. In the 1992-93 academic year, the president of Phi Theta Kappa, the college's liberal arts honor society, was a MOMS mother. In March 1992, one of the participants was awarded a $2,000 scholarship from the Avon Foundation to continue her education. Students have received many other scholarships both to continue their education and to move on to four-year programs.

The Moms on the Move program is achieving its goal, which is to give those on welfare, who have the ability and potential, the means and the confidence to further their education and secure a better future for themselves and their children. By assembling the package of federal, state and county funds and by utilizing the community college's expertise and resources, it is a program replicable around New York State and the nation.

Contact:
Margaret Olson, Director, Special Student Services
(914) 785-6966

Westchester Community College
75 Grasslands Road
Valhalla, NY 10595
Total head count enrollment-Credit: 11,847; Non-Credit: 8,000
Campuses/sites: 13; Full-time faculty: 212

PALS / MPALS LIBRARY AUTOMATION PROJECT

The user can search one library database or the databases of all network libraries, which include universities, school districts and government archives

A library automation project that began with Westchester Community College and the Information Services Department of Westchester County Government has evolved into a consortium with a combined 4.5-million records available.

The PALS/MPALS project began in 1983 and provides a user-friendly system that helps students and other library users to develop information literacy skills and to reach out far beyond the confines of the campus.

The PALS/MPALS (Project for Automated Library Systems and Multi-Project for Automated Library Systems) at first only had an opac (on-line public access catalog) available. Then a circulation module was added, making WCC the first academic library in the county to have an automated catalog and circulation system.

The success of the project at WCC encouraged other academic libraries to consider PALS/MPALS, prompting the creation of WALDO (The Westchester Academic Library Directors' Organization). That consortium now has more than 25 colleges and universities, three school districts, one public library, and the county archives as members, all of them networked through PALS/MPALS.

WALDO has committees of librarians and information systems professionals who work together to improve the software, to develop instructional materials, and to recommend new databases for the consortium. Preparations are underway to add modules for serials, authority control, acquisitions, and editing functions. Connections with the on-line public access catalog used by most of the public libraries in the county are being discussed.

In addition to books, databases now available to any member of the consortium include ERIC, a local news index, the Government Printing Office Manual, Library of Congress Subject headings, a periodicals holdings list, Peterson's college guides in full text, and databases produced by University Microfilm, including Periodical Abstracts, Newspaper Abstracts, and ABI/Inform. By 1992-93, MedLine was expected to be available as well.

The beauty of the system is that the user is able to access every available database using one simple command language. Thus at any terminal the student can navigate from one database to another, choosing articles and books, checking local newspapers or national ones, reading abstracts, and locating resources available throughout the area.

The user can search one library or all libraries. The system is available on campus at more than 25 terminals in the Learning Resource Center (library), in virtually every office, and via dial access to faculty and students. Bibliographic instruction at WCC is done in a classroom equipped with an on-line overhead projection system.

In essence, students, faculty members, administrator or county residents who use the WCC Learning Resource Center have at their fingertips access to most library information within the county and its nearby environs. Since the system is also available in several public schools, those students can develop information literacy skills early, and have them strengthened as they go on to college.

Because approximately 50 percent of WCC students transfer to continue their education, often at other colleges in the area, the information literacy skills they develop at the Learning Resource Center are easily transferable. Thus users who learn the PALS/MPALS system can meet the information needs for lifelong learning, can access information relating to their businesses and careers, and can answer questions which permit them to be productive citizens in an information laden society.

PALS/MPALS has won a National Association of Counties (NACo) award and has been mentioned in the book *Information Literacy* by Patricia Senn Breivik and E. Gordon Gee (Mac Millian) in the chapter, "Enhancing Service to the Community."

Contact:
Rosanne Kalick, Director, Library Service
(914) 785-6962

Westchester Community College
75 Grasslands Road
Valhalla, NY 10595
Total head count enrollment-Credit: 11,847; Non-Credit: 8,000
Campuses/sites: 13; Full-time faculty: 212

ANIMAL CARE AND MANAGEMENT

Because so many classes are on the weekend, numerous professionals in the field are able to serve as adjunct faculty

Alamance Community College's Animal Care and Management program is the only such two-year curriculum in North Carolina and, perhaps, the nation. This uniqueness, along with the flexibility of a weekend college, makes the program quite appealing on a statewide and even regional basis.

In 1986, ACC initiated its Animal Care and Management curriculum in response to documented needs of employers in the field and expressed interest from individuals currently employed or aspiring to careers in Animal Care and Management. From the beginning, the program was designed to provide both in-service training for existing employees and pre-service education for those wishing to enter the animal care field. To accommodate the schedules of students with full-time or part-time jobs, ACC set up the major courses in the curriculum through its weekend college. Related course requirements closely parallel those in the law enforcement option of the criminal justice curriculum and are therefore available at a wider variety of times. Students also have the option of completing these related courses at other institutions and transferring them to ACC. This was considered particularly important for a degree program intended to serve the entire state.

Since the program's inception, an advisory committee of professionals and civic leaders concerned about Animal Care and Management has played a vital role in structuring the curriculum. Because of the weekend scheduling of the classes, the college has access to numerous professionals in the field who serve as adjunct faculty. These practicing professionals bring their extensive experience to the classroom along with access to area facilities and equipment to enhance student learning.

Contact:
Michael H. Meredith
(919) 578-2002, ext. 2144

Alamance Community College
PO Box 8000
Graham, NC 27253
Total head count enrollment-Credit: 3,548; Non-Credit: 4,288
Campuses/sites: 2;Full-time faculty: 78

COMMUNITY SERVICES DIVISION

A single phone call from the community results in a comprehensive proposal of service and training

The Community Services Division of Anson Community College is truly responsive to the community. The division is structured so that a single phone call from the community results in a comprehensive proposal of service and training, whether the college is the provider or the broker.

Generally, proposals are more comprehensive in scope than requested because expertise in all facets of community education can participate in its development. This provides customer satisfaction. Designed by the second president of the college, its responsibility was to offer all non-degree/diploma programs and to provide a comprehensive range of services for the community.

Within the division are the following programs and services: Literacy Education, Continuing Education, Business and Industry Services, the Small Business Center, Protective Service Education, Human Resources Development, and Arts Council programming.

In 1979, the Trustees of Anson Community College determined to move the Community Services Division from its location close to the Polkton campus to the main street of the county seat, Wadesboro. The relocation was in response to the vision of one of its board members who felt that the move would:

1) create more opportunities for service;
2) make the division that served the public highly visible;
3) link the main campus located on the western edge of the county with the largest block of population;
4) make the college a part of downtown vitalization; and
5) bring education to main street.

The result of the move was greater than anticipated. For instance:
- enrollment in educational programs doubled;
- people feel comfortable and secure at the downtown location;
- the college's economic development activities increased;
- not only does the college know the changes and

Continues on Page 492

opportunities within the community as they occur, the leadership is there to address the situation immediately;

- the college's Small Business Center works cooperatively with the Chamber of Commerce in sponsoring training programs, in recruiting new small businesses, in counseling with potential investors and entrepreneurs;
- networking with all county agencies located in the county seat became a reality;
- the college conference room became a center of decision-making; and

- today, the college through its Community Services Division, is the leader in the community's economic development.

Community Services Division has twice received commendations from the Southern Association of Colleges and Schools. Cited were the division's location and the organizational structure. Educators with responsibility for all facets of service can come together at a moment's notice to address any issue.

The facility for the division and supplemental funding is being provided by a local foundation.

Contact:
Lois Crumpler, Dean, Community Services Division
(704) 272-7635, ext. 64

Anson Community College
PO Box 126
Polkton, NC 28135
Total head count enrollment-Credit: 1,671; Non-Credit: 4,738
Campuses/sites: 4;Full-time faculty: 37

INSTITUTIONAL EFFECTIVENESS PLANNING

Evaluation begins with each employee and moves up through the department and division and, ultimately, to the entire institution

The Comprehensive Development Plan for Anson Community College is sure not to become a shelf ornament. It's dynamism is assured because: modifications to the plan and the budget are made four times a year (updating is simplified by the use of worksheets and three-ring binders); and changes are made on the computer and a new worksheet printed and distributed to update the planning notebooks.

The plan was developed in 1988-89, when the college engaged the services of an educational planning consultant. The resulting plan not only helped secure a Title III grant for the college but also provided the foundation of the current institutional effectiveness planning process.

A 15-member planning committee leads the college through the process. Members represent every aspect of college operations, every employment level as well as the president of the student association. From there, the planning cycle moves down through the divisions to the departments and culminates with the individual employee's personal plan. Evaluation begins with each employee's evaluation of his or her effectiveness and moves up

through the department to the division, and ultimately, to the institution as a whole.

At every level the planning steps are repeated, always narrowing the focus. The basic steps of the cycle are:

1) identification of challenges and opportunities, study of data about the service area, and review of evaluations of the previous year's accomplishments;
2) establishment of goals and objectives with performance indicators to describe what will exist to prove success and when this should happen;
3) strategies or activities that will be done to meet the objectives; and
4) the resources needed (in the early spring, preliminary budget allocations are made based on the plans).

Institutional Effectiveness Planning at Anson Community College is a process, not an event. Commended by the Southern Association of Colleges and Schools, this process is a work-in-progress. It is constantly being enhanced and amended to increase its effectiveness and efficiency.

Contact:
Judith Smith, Dean, Planning and Development
(704) 272-7635, ext. 41

Anson Community College
PO Box 126
Polkton, NC 28135
Total head count enrollment-Credit: 1,671; Non-Credit: 4,738
Campuses/sites: 4;Full-time faculty: 37

CENTER FOR LIFELONG LEARNING

Among other things, the Center was designed to provide an opportunity for older learners to pursue current intellectual interests

At the Blue Ridge Community College Center for Lifelong Learning, older learners not only pursue current intellectual interest, return to neglected educational activities and explore new areas of learning, but also they help create their own educational activities – including lectures, courses, field trips, discussions, concerts and cultural events.

Patterned after a model developed during the Institute Movement of the 1960's, the Center opened in 1990 and operates under by-laws, with officers elected annually in June. All paid members (a $25 lifetime membership fee is charged) have voting rights. A small fee is also charged for most courses and workshops. Non-members pay an addi-

tional fee if space allows outside enrollment. A Curriculum Committee, headed by the Vice President for Curriculum, creates and plans courses.

A sampling of courses that have been offered include The Romance of Musical Instruments, Backstage with the Orchestra, Sports in America, The World We Live In, Power Words and Word Power, and many others of a similar nature. Judges, former ambassadors and generals are among the experts who have been presenters.

By June 1993, the Center had more than 700 members. It is coordinated by the college's Office for Continuing Education and has become a very positive connection between the college and active seniors in its service area.

Contact:
Martha Sneed, Coordinator, Community Services
(704) 692-3572, ext. 260

Blue Ridge Community College
College Drive
Flat Rock, NC 28731
Total head count enrollment-Credit: 2,223; Non-Credit: 12,127
Campuses/sites: 2; Full-time faculty: 50

TECHNICAL INSTRUMENTATION LABORATORY

Four associate degree programs integrate lab experience with classroom studies

The Technical Instrumentation Laboratory on the Blue Ridge Community College campus is an asset both to the college and industry. It resulted from cooperative efforts by industry, faculty and administration.

Industry representatives on program advisory committees had recommended establishment of a laboratory that would:

1) support and enhance classroom work; and
2) respond to training needs created by technical advances in local industry.

Such a laboratory became an urgent goal for a senior instructor in BRCC's engineering technology program, an MIT graduate whose background included 30 years in industrial management.

That instructor convinced the president that a commitment from the college would enable him to approach local industries that would benefit from such an instructional resource. Other instructors of courses that would incorporate laboratory work joined in helping to plan space requirements, identify equipment needed, prepare a comprehensive budget and identify additional industries that might contribute funding. Staff members with industry contacts, trustees and Foundation Directors were further involved in planning and executing the funding

campaign. One trustee, a retired plant manager of a major local industry, volunteered to direct the campaign.

Blue Ridge Community College also approached the National Science Foundation, basing that appeal on the experience of other community colleges in the Southeast and assurance from the National Council on Resource Development that NSF would consider a well-considered proposal from a community college. The outcome was a $50,000 grant, matching an equal commitment from the college. Gifts from local industries in response to a well-structured campaign enabled the college to hold a dedication open house just 18 months after the president responded to the instructor's enthusiastic proposal of August 1988.

Four associate degree programs integrate laboratory experience with classroom studies: Drafting and Design Engineering Technology, Electromechanical Technology, Electronics Engineering Technology, and Industrial Engineering Technology.

The Technical Instrumentation Laboratory is divided essentially into two sections. One includes Computer Aided Design (CAD) and Computer Aided Manufacturing (CAM), and the other is devoted to computer numerical

Continues on Page 494

control (CNC). Both sections focus upon the planning and development of engineering specifications through the use of microcomputers. In the automatic control section students learn how electronics can be combined with mechanical, hydraulic or pneumatic systems to achieve automatic programmable control.

The Technical Instrumentation Laboratory will also be available for scheduled industry seminars on theory and applications of automatic control and CAD / CAM equipment.

Contact:
John Hnatow, Associate Dean, Applied Technology
(704) 692-3572, ext. 226

Blue Ridge Community College
College Drive
Flat Rock, NC 28731
Total head count enrollment-Credit: 2,223; Non-Credit: 12,127
Campuses/sites: 2; Full-time faculty: 50

FUTURES CURRICULUM

⌘ *The curriculum modules are designed to be used as enrichment* ⌘
lessons either collectively or as individual seminars

For 18 months, five community colleges in North Carolina worked with the 21st Century Futures Corporation to develop a Futures curriculum for instructional use within each college. The Futures curriculum modules are designed to be used as an enrichment lesson, collectively in a semester/yearly course, or as a set of individual seminars.

Instructor strategies are designed for: a seminar classroom environment; practicing group or team learning; promoting individualized relevant exercises for learners; and developing additional modules created by the learners.

Learner strategies are designed to: meet the learners' needs based on interests, job, organization and citizen involvement; practice the art of futurism and forecasting; use a variety of resources for expanding the learner's knowledge; motivate for lifelong learning; and provide practical applications for everyday living.

The learning environment should be: conducive to examining a broad range of ideas; conducive to building consensus; rich in the use of multimedia resources; designed for access to on-line data bases and CD Rom Libraries; able to access C-Span, interactive public television and other teleconferencing activities.

Evaluation techniques are used to: demonstrate that the learner understands the basic concepts of the goals and objectives of the modules; develop the learners' capacities to use their knowledge, skills, and processes for relevant issues; and build a data base of learning modules designed and developed by the learners in the Futures curriculum.

Supporting resources are: a comprehensive bibliography; handouts of articles and other materials; transparency masters to support the basic concepts; slides of trends and demographic data designed by Gayle; and a revised *Citizen Knowledge of the Future.*

Futures Curriculum, Modules (M. Gayle, 1992) Copyright @ 1992 by 21st Century Futures Corporation.

Contact:
Johnnie Simpson, Vice President for Instruction
(919) 754-6900

Brunswick Community College
PO Box 30
Supply, NC 28462
Total head count enrollment-Credit: 1,578; Non-Credit: 4,149
Campuses/sites: 3; Full-time faculty: 24

BRUNSWICK INTERAGENCY PROGRAM

⌘ *The college hosts an interagency program for educating adults* ⌘
with developmental disabilities

The Brunswick Interagency Program for educating adults with developmental disabilities was developed after key local citizens saw a need for a community program correlating cognitive development and vocational training for adults with developmental disabilities.

But there was one significant problem: Brunswick County is a large and rural, with no public transportation. So the campus of Brunswick Community College was selected for its central location, and the partners in the project decided to provide transportation Monday through

Friday, 12 months a year. Those partners – the college, Southeastern Mental Health, Advocates for Retarded Citizens, and Brunswick County Public Schools – initially housed the program in mobile units. Then in 1989, they moved it into a new 8,500-square-foot building on the new Brunswick Community College campus. This facility includes classrooms and an apartment, as well as an adjacent woodworking shop and a greenhouse.

Brunswick Community College provides compensatory education, which is a curriculum of task-analyzed lessons and activities in the following domains: Language, Math, Social Science, Consumer Education, Community Living and Health. Southeastern Mental Health provides an Adult Developmental Activity Program which provides the training in activities of daily living, vocational evaluation and work activity training. In 1989, Supported Employment, Job Coach Model, was added through a grant from North Carolina Department of Vocational Rehabilitation. A job coach assesses students, locates jobs and trains students one-on-one, enabling them to become gainfully employed. This program has been expanded this year through a grant from the North Carolina Council on Developmental Disabled to include a mobile grounds-keeping crew, a custodial crew and food service enclave.

Brunswick Interagency Program, based on students individual needs, provides a continuum of educational programs that enables them to develop to their ultimate potential and to achieve some level of independence. Brunswick Interagency Program received the Governor's Award for Excellence in Education in 1987 and is supported by the community and recognized as a state-of-the-art program. In seven years, the program has grown to a staff of 20.

Contact:
Anita White, Program Director
(919) 754-6900

Brunswick Community College
PO Box 30
Supply, NC 28462
Total head count enrollment-Credit: 1,578; Non-Credit: 4,149
Campuses/sites: 3; Full-time faculty: 24

CALDWELL COMMUNITY COLLEGE AND TECHNICAL INSTITUTE

WRITERS SYMPOSIUM

The symposium provides a valuable educational experience for the citizens of this relatively isolated and deprived area

Since the spring of 1989, Caldwell Community College and Technical Institute has presented an annual writers symposium for students, public school teachers and general adult audiences.

When presented in conjunction with additional course work (scheduled in two-hour meetings over a five-week period), the writers symposia provides curriculum students the opportunity to earn two quarter hours of humanities credit. Public school teachers may earn one unit of continuing education credit. The general public may attend for personal enrichment and interest.

The topics and writers featured during the annual symposia follow:
1) a Symposium of North Carolina Writers, featuring Maya Angelou, Michael McFee, Doris Betts and Clyde Edgerton;
2) a Symposium of Writers from the Southern Appalachian Region, featuring Nikki Giovanni Wilma Dykeman, Sue Ellen Bridgers, George Ella Lyon and Jim Wayne Miller;
3) an Evening with Ernest Gaines;
4) Young Women Writers of the Carolinas, featuring Kaye Gibbons, Marianne Gingher, Dori Sanders and Lucinda MacKethan;
5) an Evening with Peter Turchi; and
6) Native Sons: Coming Home, featuring Gary Hawkins, Don Secreast, Michael McFee and Robert Morgan.

Like most predominately rural areas, Caldwell and Watauga counties (the institution's service area) enjoy limited cultural and educational experiences.

Only 9 percent of the Caldwell County adult population are college graduates, compared to the state average of 18 percent. A recent state report indicated that Caldwell County, with its 30 percent dropout rate over the four high school years, leads the state in secondary school dropout percentages. The area is also economically disadvantaged – with average per capita income that is only about 75 percent of the state average. The symposium provides a valuable educational experience for the citizens of this relatively isolated and deprived area.

Continues on Page 496

Benefits of the writers symposia are numerous and significant. These conference encourage reading, stimulate the study of literature and humanistic issues, and bring together diverse groups of people who share a love of writing and learning.

Contact:
Laurette LePrevost, Instructor-in-Charge
(704) 726-2338

Caldwell Community College and Technical Institute
1000 Hickory Boulevard
Hudson, NC 28638
Total head count enrollment-Credit: 5,000; Non-Credit: 9,000
Campuses/sites: 2; Full-time faculty: 65

CALDWELL COMMUNITY COLLEGE AND TECHNICAL INSTITUTE

VISITING ARTIST CULTURE FOR A RURAL AREA

Visiting artists stay in the community for one to two years and act as "art ambassadors"

Caldwell Community College and Technical Institute has used a state Visiting Artist Program to build long-lasting projects. This unique approach means each of CCC and TI's Visiting Artists not only have contributed to the high quality of arts in the foothills of western North Carolina, but also most of them have created arts programs which are continuing long after their tenure expires.

The North Carolina Arts Council has co-sponsored the Visiting Artist Program with the Department of Community Colleges since 1974. Artists in a variety of disciplines – music, folk arts, visual and design arts, literary arts, theater, dance and interdisciplinary arts – spend a residency of one to two years in the community. Acting as an "arts ambassador," the artist's activities typically include demonstrations, performances, lectures, workshops, classroom appearances, exhibitions, and/or organization of community events. The program has been under the supervision of the Dean of Arts and Sciences, which has given the program a continuity in planning.

In 1974, CCC and TI's first visiting artist, David Ariel, designed a 120-seat theater in what was formerly a student lounge. The theater recently has been renovated and is the site of the college's theatrical and musical events as well as community theater productions.

The next Visiting Artist, Bill Wilson, whose residency began in 1976, organized Foothills Performing Arts, Inc., a community theater now presenting the 16th season. Each season consists of five shows and one summer presentation for children (attendance exceeds 5,000 annually). Foothills Performing Arts uses the college as its base for performances. The organization provides staff for the theater.

In 1979, Visiting Artists Robert and Andrea Rosen worked closely with local retired public and school band directors to form the Caldwell-Lenoir Community Band. Now in its 13th year, the band performed at the 1982 World's Fair in Knoxville, Tennessee, and appears regularly at college and community events. Students in the music program at CCC and TI perform with the community band for performing ensemble credit.

Bill Jones, the Visiting Artist from 1981 to 1983, created a Concert Series which featured local and regional musical talent. The series was expanded in 1987 and was retitled the Performing Artist Series to reflect more accurately the programming of dance and theater acts in addition to both folk and chamber music.

During his tenure as Visiting Artist, Bill Jones proposed a music program, which was established in 1984 and which offers an Associate in Fine Arts degree. Students study music theory and history, private applied lessons, and are offered performance opportunities which transfer to four-year institutions.

The Unifour Jazz Ensemble was founded by Visiting Artist Tom Smith in 1984. The 22-member big band recorded two albums, performed at Musicfest, USA in 1987, and was recognized that year by *DownBeat* magazine as the finest community jazz ensemble in the nation. Its sister organization, the Unifour Jazz Society, promotes jazz functions throughout the area. CCC and TI still assist the CCC Swing Band, which performs big band music from the 1930's and 1940's.

In the last five seasons, under the direction of Director of Music Kay S. Crouch, the series has featured international chamber musicians (the Ten-Strings Duo from Switzerland and Magenta Music from Ireland), internationally known folk musicians (David Holt, New Grass Revival, Odetta), national dance troupes (the African-American Dance Ensemble, American Dance Festival), and national tours of theatrical presentations (*Mark Twain on Tour, Oh, Mr. Faulkner, Do you Write?*) in addition to regionally known artists.

Contact:
Kay Crouch, Instructor-in-Charge
(704) 726-2326

Caldwell Community College and Technical Institute
1000 Hickory Boulevard
Hudson, NC 28638
Total head count enrollment-Credit: 5,000; Non-Credit: 9,000
Campuses/sites: 2; Full-time faculty: 65

BASIC LAW ENFORCEMENT TRAINING

As a rule, 100 percent of the students have passed the final state exam

As the program facilities for Basic Law Enforcement Training have developed from donated used trailers with holes in the well-worn floors, to the currently used building with state-of-the-art equipment, so has the program itself seen such progress.

When law enforcement training was developed at CCC in 1973, students took a 160-hour course. Over the years, that changed to 240 hours and then to the current 556 hours, exceeding the 464-hour state requirement. Carteret Community College requires the extra hours in order to include more hours than the state dictates in physical training, firearms, law enforcement driver training and defensive tactics. The students must show competence and proficiency in 34 topics of instruction.

The program's building has classrooms and exercise rooms. Specialized rooms for "shoot-don't shoot" decision-making practice and crime scene investigation were built by the college's Light Construction curriculum students and decorated by the Interior Design curriculum students and Basic Law Enforcement Training students with donated furnishings. An outdoor obstacle course, a separate firearms range and a driving range are also part of the facilities used in training.

The primary goal of North Carolina's and Carteret Community College's Basic Law Enforcement Training program is to improve the overall law enforcement profession in the community. The success of the program is evidenced by the support of the law enforcement agencies in the surrounding areas. With only one full-time director/instructor, local officers are depended upon as part-time instructors. Their dedication involves having to take time to be certified as instructors by the state of North Carolina through classes, examinations and evaluations. Their loyalty to the Basic Law Enforcement Training program has been shown by their equipping trainees with uniforms and required leather equipment.

The commitment and devotion of the instructors and trainees is demonstrated by the caliber of the graduates. As a rule, 100 percent of the students have passed the final state exam and gone on to do a fine job protecting our citizens. Don Richards, the Basic Law Enforcement Training director, coordinates the five-month program two times a year and supervises the approximately 15 part-time faculty members and 30 students.

Contact:
Donald R. Richards
(919) 247-6000

Carteret Community College
3505 Arendell Street
Morehead City, NC 28557
Total head count enrollment-Credit: 2,363; Non-Credit: 5,407
Campuses/sites: 1; Full-time faculty: 45

HOSIERY TECHNOLOGY

Rapidly advancing technology in the hosiery industry significantly impacts this region, with more than 120 mills in a 50-mile radius

The Hosiery Technology Center of Catawba Valley Community College sits in a state that produces more than 60 percent of the nation's hosiery and a region that produces 35 percent of that. There are more than 120 hosiery mills within a 50-mile radius of CVCC. These mills generate more than $600-million in annual sales, exclusive of sales of secondary suppliers such as yarns, machine parts, etc.

The Center, a technology transfer center, was established in the spring of 1990 on the CVCC campus with privately donated funds from Catawba Valley Hosiery Association (a regional trade association) totaling $10,000, along with start-up grants totaling $75,000 in each of two years from the State of North Carolina and Catawba County.

The Center's mission is obvious: Keep the region at the fore of the industry. The impact of rapidly advancing technology on the hosiery industry is substantial. Computerized knitting equipment, complex dyeing procedures, increased sophistication in finishing and increasingly complex merchandising programs demand improved efficiency and productivity. Since its inception, Center activities have included:
- 25 workshops and seminars with 618 attendees;
- 46 classes with 186 attendees;
- acquisition of 19 pieces of equipment for training through donation and purchase;
- hiring one full-time hosiery industry professional as Center Director, along with a full-time secretary;
- organizing a volunteer Advisory Committee with 24 members drawn from the hosiery industry in

Continues on Page 498

western North Carolina; and

- renovating a 2,760-square-foot area on the CVCC campus for use as demonstration, training, classroom, display and office area.

Growth of the program will continue in the immediate future. The Hosiery Technology Center's physical space will expand when it occupies a portion of a recently purchased 100,000-square-foot building adjacent to the

college campus. The Hosiery Center will join other college activities housed in the new Center for Advancing Technologies, benefiting from shared classroom and seminar space.

Expanded floor area will give the Hosiery Technology Center the opportunity to add significant state-of-the-art equipment that will enhance the training available to the work force.

Contact:
Dan St. Louis, Center Director
(704) 327-7000

Catawba Valley Community College
2550 Highway 70 SE
Hickory, NC 28602-9699
Total head count enrollment-Credit: 5,550; Non-Credit: 28,044
Campuses/sites: 1; Full-time faculty: 97

NORTH CAROLINA QUALITY CENTER

The Center focuses on teaching the nuances of Total Quality Management to business and industry

Catawba Valley Community College has been designated as the Quality & Productivity Center for the 58-member North Carolina Community College System. The designation, which was made fall 1991, includes a three-year grant totaling $225,000.

The North Carolina Quality Center (NCQC) provides a springboard for initiatives in Q&P throughout the state by giving each community college the knowledge and skills necessary to train business and industry in their service areas. The new NCQC promotes the value of TQM, creates and disseminates instructional modules that can be used by each community college, involves volunteer leadership through the creation of a state-wide Advisory Team of business and education leaders, and thoroughly evaluates the materials and delivery of instruction.

Over the three years of the grant, the project provides the following to the participants from the community colleges: two state-wide meetings promoting TQM; 18 regional train-the-trainer workshops providing TQM theory and skills building; six regional TQM Success Forums assisting community colleges in continuous improvement of their quality programs; and individual consulting with the participating community colleges by the NCQC Director and local management team.

CVCC is uniquely qualified within the North Carolina

Community College system to implement the system-wide Q&P effort. The college staff was among the first on the system to receive training in total quality management and has built an enviable track record in the dissemination of training to area industry. Since 1987, four college faculty and staff members have received certification as TAI Trainers and one faculty member has completed 50 percent of the work needed to be certified as a TQ Master Trainer.

Approximately 300 people have been exposed to TQM instruction delivered by CVCC through: 21 seminars, workshops and telecasts (representing 94 hours of instruction to 1,070 attendees, including a four-day live downlink of a seminar by Dr. Deming in September 1991); 22 short courses delivered to 15 companies and organizations (representing 275 hours of instruction to 634 enrollees); and 25 sections of a TQM curriculum course delivered to 14 companies and organizations (representing 1,265 hours of instruction to 397 enrollees).

The NCQC for North Carolina Community Colleges is an exciting initiative for both CVCC and the system. It provides an opportunity for the community colleges to provide the education and training that is required by the state's business and industry to maintain the competitive edge in the global marketplace.

Contact:
John Ellis, Center Director
(704) 327-7000

Catawba Valley Community College
2550 Highway 70 SE
Hickory, NC 28602-9699
Total head count enrollment-Credit: 5,550; Non-Credit: 28,044
Campuses/sites: 1; Full-time faculty: 97

FOOD SERVICE MANAGEMENT (CHEFS TRAINING)

Students are so successful, it is nearly impossible to visit an area restaurant or club without having your meal prepared by a program graduate

In 1986, Central Piedmont Community College recognized a need to expand its Food Service Management Program to prepare graduates to fill an increasing demand in the Charlotte area for individuals trained in the field. The result of that institutional commitment is a program nationally recognized for its quality – quality demonstrated by the excellence of its students, success of its graduates, caliber of its faculty and strength of its public sector partnerships.

The program serves about 1,000 individuals annually, and these students have earned at least 57 culinary competition medals. Graduates enjoy 97 percent placement in the region, state and nation. The number of executive chefs in Charlotte and Mecklenburg County hotels, country clubs and restaurants who are graduates continues to increase. It is, for example, almost impossible to visit an area restaurant or club without having your meal prepared by a CPCC graduate.

The present 25,000-square-foot instructional facility and its program equipment are state-of-the-art. Recently, some $250,000 in equipment has been donated by Piedmont Natural Gas Company and Duke Power Company. These generous donations have provided for the addition of a "small quantity" lab and demonstration kitchen. This area enables instructors to provide learning and practice experiences that incorporate the latest industry techniques and products. This kitchen is also used for video production for instruction and community involvement.

An industry demand for bakers currently challenges the program. The college is seeking resources to add additional space for a dedicated baking lab.

The program has three full-time and 18 part-time instructors. These adjunct faculty are all working chefs and bring their industry experience to the classroom. The National Institute for Staff and Organizational Development (NISOD), in conjunction with the University of Texas's celebration of community college teachers, awarded the program its 1992 Excellence Award. In 1987, the North Carolina State Award for Excellence, in conjunction with North Carolina Restaurant Association and the Vocational Association, presented the program its Excellence in Post Secondary Food Services Education Training award.

In addition to the program's partnerships with area businesses, the chefs training program staff and faculty work closely with the Charlotte Chapter of the American Culinary Federation and the Charlotte/Mecklenburg and North Carolina Restaurant Associations

---

Contact:
James Cannon, Department Chair
(704) 342-6721

Central Piedmont Community College
PO Box 35009
Charlotte, NC 28235
Total head count enrollment-Credit: 29,964; Non-Credit: 29,278
Campuses/sites: 4; Full-time faculty: 219

ABLE (ADULT BASIC LITERACY EDUCATION)

An aggressive publicity campaign resulted in significant donations to help fund the literacy program

CPCC initiated a unique literacy program in 1983 to teach adults basic literacy skills. The uniqueness of the ABLE program is its use of technology to teach basic reading, writing and math skills in neighborhood centers, allowing adults learning opportunities during hours convenient to them and providing an opportunity to increase their literacy levels at a faster rate than traditional literacy programs. The goals of ABLE are to:

1) provide learning experiences for students to improve reading, writing and math skills to a GED level more quickly than could be expected in traditional programs;

2) attract adults who might not otherwise enroll in a literacy program;

3) retain adults in the program to a greater extent than traditional programs; and

4) provide support, referral and instruction which will assist adults in meeting life-goals such as continuing education, getting a job or becoming more effective parents.

In mid-1982, CPCC produced a 13-minute videotape, *The Economic Time Bomb*, which addressed how illiteracy was negatively affecting the Charlotte-Mecklenburg

Continues on Page 500

community. Presented to civic clubs, church groups, Mecklenburg legislators, County Commissioners and industry/business leaders, this video increased community awareness and support of the project. The Mecklenburg County Commissioners voted to allocate $100,000 to CPCC for the ABLE project if the college could raise the balance of $203,000 for the total start-up costs. The Philip L. Van Every Foundation of Charlotte and the Knight Foundation each donated $25,000. First Union Bank contributed $10,000, and the additional funds were donated by other businesses and individuals.

ABLE has incorporated a variety of instructional methods, including individualized instruction by computer, audio and videotape, television, print materials and one-to-one tutoring using volunteers. Research and development in curricula are ongoing. More than 7,000 adults have enrolled in ABLE since the first center opened in a shopping mall in 1983. Today, approximately 600 adults are served quarterly in the ABLE centers housed in a shopping center, a YMCA and a neighborhood community center. ABLE is funded as a component of the Adult Basic Education department at CPCC.

Assessment and placement procedures have ensured proper placement in the program, resulting in better retention due to immediate success. Student success rates continue to improve. For example, students in the lower reading level (0 to 4) complete a skillbook in an average of 34.2 hours. Upper-level reading students (5 to 8) increase a grade level in an average of 29.4 hours. Students in the math curriculum increase a grade level in an average of nine hours. Pre-GED instruction is also available using computer software.

ABLE program faculty and staff continue to research and develop new and innovative methods for teaching basic literacy skills to adults. Developed with a FIPSE grant from the U.S. Department of Education, the Learning Styles Survey interactive videodisc has allowed the assessment of the preferred learning styles of low-literate adults. The READY Course, a reading comprehension instructional program with digitized audio, and the NEW READER Bookstore, a phonics-based beginning reading program, have been developed and are used across the nation. The ABLE program has been replicated at community colleges in North Carolina with funds from First Union Bank and at other educational institutions across the nation.

ABLE has been recognized in numerous journals and newsletters such as *T.H.E. Journal*, *The Chronicle of Higher Education*, *Business Council for Effective Literacy*, *Adult Literacy and Technology Newsletter*, and the *Wall Street Journal*. ABLE was also the recipient of the U.S. Department of Education Secretary's Award for Outstanding Adult Education Programs in 1989 and of the local Golden Book Award from ReadUp Charlotte in 1991. ABLE was nominated for the 1987 President's Volunteer Action Award and for the 1992 President's Annual 1,000 Points of Light Award. In 1987, Barbara Bush visited to recognize the 350 volunteers tutoring in the program, and again visited in 1988 at her own initiative. Hillary Clinton visited in April of 1992. One of the ABLE students was recognized as a National Adult Learner of the Year in 1989.

Contact:
Cynthia Johnston, Department Head
(704) 342-6716

Central Piedmont Community College
PO Box 35009
Charlotte, NC 28235
Total head count enrollment-Credit: 29,964; Non-Credit: 29,278
Campuses/sites: 4; Full-time faculty: 219

CRAVEN COMMUNITY COLLEGE

ACTIVITIES FOR SCHOOL-AGED CHILDREN (SERVICE PROJECT)

Weekend training sessions are held for parents to learn such things as building a child's self-esteem and activities to do at home

During the spring of 1992, the Craven County School System received a "Comer" grant to provide in-service training to a designated school serving "at risk" children. The Department Chair of the Early Childhood curriculum at Craven Community College was invited to participate in the parent involvement component of the grant, called "Weekend College."

During a four-month period a number of parent training sessions were held on these topics: Understanding Child Development, Building Self-Esteem, and Activities to Do at Home with Your Children. Approximately 80 to 100 parents participated. The training sessions were culmi-

nated with a special dinner where the parents were given certificates recognizing their involvement and course completion. Evaluations completed by the participants indicated that they had gained many parenting skills that would make their home environment more conducive to learning. In addition, the school climate showed significant improvement because of the staff involvement in the planning and implementation of the project.

As a continuation of the "Comer" project into the next school year, the school staff requested that there be another joint venture between the college and Bridgeton Elementary School, where the previous training sessions had been held. However, their request was not for further assistance in parent training, but for assistance in another way: developing instructional materials to be used with children in the classroom. This request came at a time in the school year during which a course, "Activities for School-Aged Children," was being taught. The instructor of the course had a planning session with the teachers in the elementary school; as a result, they developed a plan which involved the college students enrolled in the course.

Six class periods were designated in the calendar, during which the students developed instructional materials for each grade level in the school. Prior to each class, the college instructor and the elementary teachers considered the raw materials needed, ideas to be utilized and the time period allotted for the activities. During these designated work sessions, the college students made games and activities from various curriculum areas that were later used with the children at that school. Not only did this service project aid the school-aged children, but also the college students gained knowledge in the instructional areas of reading, math, science, language and social studies as they developed their own resource files to be used later when they were employed in the schools as teacher assistants.

Contact:
Betty Quinn, Instructor-in-Charge
(919) 638-7343

Craven Community College
PO Box 885
New Bern, NC 28563-0885
Total head count enrollment-Credit: 4,085; Non-Credit: 7,131
Campuses/sites: 2; Full-time faculty: 61

STUDENT ORIENTATION AND STUDY SKILLS

✻ *The 97 percent retention rate demonstrates that the study skills class* ✻
is making a difference

Since 1975, an orientation and study skills class has been required of all graduates – but for the first decade it didn't seem to do much good. Then dramatic changes begat dramatic results: a 97 percent retention rate.

The humble beginning was ORI-101, offered one day a week for 11 weeks of the quarter. Initially, it was taught by any instructor who needed some extra hours. The students perceived the class as unimportant and often took the class the last quarter before graduation. In the late 1970's, a Special Services grant to support disadvantaged students led to the creation of an additional course, ORI-100, a 22-hour course for students who tested into developmental classes. But the retention rate in orientation at both levels was low in spite of efforts to make the content relevant.

Changes started taking place in 1986, when more specific study skills were added and only instructors who elected to teach orientation did so. The library work was upgraded to introduce the MLA format for research papers and to include an introduction to the computer labs. However, the problems of low retention and lack of importance continued.

Then, a few years ago several unique solutions, some suggested by students during course evaluations, were initiated. First, orientation became the responsibility of the Division of Developmental Studies. This structure encourages linkage to support services offered by the division through the Academic Skills Center such as tutoring, counseling, career advising, academic software and parallel reading classes. This also offers a location where the college's large population of non-traditional students continue to seek advice and support after the orientation class has ended.

Next, the accelerated orientation course was moved to the first 11 days of the quarter instead of being spread out over an entire 11-week period. Now all the important information about policies, procedures, personnel, library work and study skills is presented at the beginning of the quarter. The students know where to go for answers and how to solve some of the problems they encounter. *Writer's INC.*, the text, became an invaluable teaching tool which students are encouraged to keep as a reference source.

Finally, the orientation and study skills class for students who test into developmental classes was extended to 33 hours. The content of the course includes orientation to the college, study skills and library work, which results in higher GPAs and, consequently, an enhanced self-image. Students share their successes and fears about making the transition into college and bond with other students in similar life situations. The study skills component consists of outlining, note-taking, memory techniques, test-taking, instructor expectations, and organizational skills. Additionally, students learn to engage in self-evaluation for continuous improvement. The text for this longer course is the *Master Student*.

The 97 percent retention rate reflects the success of the new structure. Students stay in the classes because the

Continues on Page 502

course answers their needs. When students have the study skills they need to survive and a firm belief in their own self-worth, they persist in school. Research validates that our students will graduate if they persist – and that we can make a difference.

Contact:
Catherine Hewlette, Dean of Developmental Studies
(919) 638-7284

Craven Community College
PO Box 885
New Bern, NC 28563-0885
Total head count enrollment-Credit: 4,085; Non-Credit: 7,131
Campuses/sites: 2; Full-time faculty: 61

ALTERNATIVE HIGH SCHOOL PROGRAM FOR TEEN PARENTS

The program is housed on the college campus and child care is provided at the college's Child Development Center

Nationally, a staggering 80 percent of teen-age parents drop out of high school as they face the responsibility of feeding, clothing and nurturing a child when they are barely out of childhood themselves. Many of these young families depend on public assistance to survive. The Alternative High School Program for Teen Parents, offered on the campus of Davidson County Community College in cooperation with area public school systems, is experiencing a high success rate in keeping these young parents in school and helping them obtain the skills needed to become good parents and good citizens.

The primary objectives of the program are to:

1) provide a sound educational curriculum that encourages the young parents to complete their high school education and seek additional training and education after graduation;

2) provide employability skills and vocational training in order that the students will be able to achieve financial independence in the future and experience a more productive life for their family and themselves;

3) improve parenting skills of the teen parents by providing sessions on prenatal care, parenting and child development; and

4) enable young parents to gain self-confidence and control over the direction of their lives.

The Teen Parent program has served 273 teen-age parents ages 12 to 20 since its inception in 1986, with a dropout rate of 14.8 percent. The program is housed in a large, self-contained classroom on the college campus with a number of educational resources, including computers, a video cassette recorder and monitor. Child care services are provided by the college's state-approved Child Development Center. The students also have access to and are encouraged to use the college's Learning Resources Center with a library and variety of support services including tutorial services, computerized instructional services and skills labs. Each student participates in an academic curriculum designed for his/her appropriate grade level. Although many of the students return to their respective high schools after a year in the program to complete their high school careers, students also have the option of enrolling in the Adult High School and General Educational Development programs at the college. Eighty percent of the students age 16 and older are also enrolled in one or more college-level classes.

The Teen Parent program continually seeks to maintain communication and support from individuals, agencies and businesses in the community. Some of the students are employed by businesses in the Industrial Cooperative Training Program. Health professionals, former students, and representatives from the Agricultural Extension office, domestic violence services, social services, health department, legal services and mental health department regularly speak in the classes.

The program participates in the North Carolina Coalition of Adolescent Pregnancy and received the 1992 Governor's Award for Employment, Education, and Training Excellence.

The participating public school systems share the expenses of the program and provide a principal, counselor and two instructors. Home-bound instruction is provided for new mothers during postpartum recovery. The community college pays the part-time salary of its advisor/coordinator to the program and provides a classroom, daycare facilities, promotional and other materials, custodial services, and office and classroom supplies. Assistance also comes from foundation grants.

Contact:
Janie Carter, Program Coordinator
(704) 249-8186

Davidson County Community College
PO Box 1287
Lexington, NC 27293-1287
Total head count enrollment-Credit: 3,594; Non-Credit: 10,989
Campuses/sites: 1; Full-time faculty: 80

MULTIMEDIA COMPUTER-ASSISTED PRESENTATIONS

Multimedia computing allows the instructor to actively link video, illustrations and audio with lecture

Associate Degree Nursing classes at Davidson County Community College broke away from traditional lecture presentations during the 1992-93 academic year and entered an exciting new era in the classroom for both faculty and students as multimedia computer-assisted classroom presentations made their debut.

Multimedia computing is an interactive environment that combines computer technology and audio/visual technology in the classroom. Instructors have the option of combining audio, video, graphics and motion in their classroom presentations. Although now in use only in the nursing program, the technology is available to all curriculum programs and is expected to spread to classrooms across campus as additional faculty members become familiar with the system.

DCCC purchased two software starter systems after a significant number of faculty indicated an interest in adding multimedia technology to the instructional resources available to them. One system is mobile and is available for use in classrooms. The second is stationed in the Learning Resources Center for use in actual development of presentations and individual viewing of programs. The equipment includes a computer screen, CD Rom and video cassette recorder. The image on the computer screen is projected onto a larger screen in the classroom, in effect creating an electronic blackboard.

Multimedia computing allows the instructor to actively link video, illustrations and audio with a lecture. All this can be accomplished without turning several machines on and off. Scanning equipment allows the instructor to use illustrations from publications such as books, newspapers and magazines. In the Pharmacy 100 Calculating and Administering Medications class, the instructor has used the scanner to capture the images on bottles of medication to show as examples to students. Instructors may use music, sound that accompanies video clips, or record their own voices into the presentations. With the click of a computer mouse, they may switch from video to still photo images and text to graphics. In addition to graphics provided through commercially prepared software packages, instructors may also create their own illustrations.

While the system is being used primarily in classroom presentations, programs are also being developed for individual use by students. Instructors may develop exercises for students to complete in reviewing course materials and make presentations available as a tutoring service. The nursing program is also working toward a presentation that will assist students in preparing for the nursing licensure examination following graduation.

DCCC's Health and Human Services Division adopted the development of computer-assisted classroom instruction as a primary goal during the 1992-93 academic year. Faculty have adopted development of multimedia presentations as part of their professional development plan. They have attended seminars to prepare them for using the system and will share their knowledge with other faculty members interested in applying this technology in their classrooms.

Contact:
John Thomas, Dean, Learning Resources
(704) 249-8186

Davidson County Community College
PO Box 1287
Lexington, NC 27293-1287
Total head count enrollment-Credit: 3,594; Non-Credit: 10,989
Campuses/sites: 1; Full-time faculty: 80

CRITICAL READING

The course, designed for those entering Respiratory Care, allows students to read at the level required for working respiratory therapists

To meet the needs of Developmental Studies students entering the Respiratory Care Program, the program directors of these two areas designed and implemented a new critical reading course. It addresses the need for higher thinking skills and more technical critical reading skills. This new approach for under-prepared students enhances the chances of their success as they enter a highly specialized field.

To make the course relevant to the student's future studies, the course design uses technical reading materials in Respiratory Care to teach concepts such as note-taking, annotation, critique and research. This innovative solution to improving student performance also allows the student to practice reading skills at the level required of the working respiratory therapist. To further this concept,

Continues on Page 504

actual respiratory devices and their accompanying literature are demonstrated and discussed in class. A field trip to a local medical library is team-taught to provide instruction on medical research and retrieval that allows for student in-service and medical term paper development.

An evaluation of the course first taught in the spring of 1992 showed that all students from the respiratory critical reading course have maintained at least a "B" average for courses related to respiratory care. The attrition rate for former Developmental Studies students in the Respiratory Care Program dropped from 60 percent (fall '91) to 0 percent (fall '92).

The two program directors who designed and implemented this course were recognized by Durham Tech's President for their innovative solution to a recognized problem. They were awarded the college's first Effective Innovation in Instruction Award. Already the course is being used as a model for other programs, such as the Business Technologies Program, which now offers its own critical reading course.

Contact:
Richard D. Miller, Program Director, Respiratory Care
Mary Anne F. Grabarek, Program Director, Developmental Studies
(919) 598-9374

Durham Technical Community College
1637 Lawson Street
Durham, NC 27703
Total head count enrollment-Credit: 8,068; Non-Credit: 23,909
Campuses/sites: 6; Full-time faculty: 225

OPTICIANRY

Students help run an optical clinic on campus, where eye glass orders are filled and minor repairs are done

Durham Tech offers the only Opticianry program in North Carolina. The program attracts students from across the state and prepares them to become opticians, optical salespersons, ophthalmic assistants and contact lens technicians.

The accredited, comprehensive program gives students hands-on training in surfacing (blocking, fining, polishing and inspecting both plastic and glass single-vision and multifocal lenses); benchwork (which includes hand beveling, safety beveling, heat treating, chemical tempering, tinting, mounting and framing lenses); and dispensing (measuring, adapting and fitting eyeglasses and contact lenses).

In preparation for their future opticianry careers, Durham Tech's Opticianry students get much more than textbook knowledge. The program features practice that gets students out in the field, adjusting and repairing eyeglasses at medical centers and senior citizens centers.

Likewise, the program gives its students regular contact with the public, as they help run the program's optical clinic on campus, where they fill eyeglass orders and provide minor repairs and adjustments of eyeglasses.

The program is also state-of-the-art. Students are trained to use the newest software equipment found in commercial labs. They learn to keep inventory, maintain patient records and generate receipts and orders on the computer. They discover how the software can be used as a selling tool, to demonstrate the weight, thickness, and materials of a particular order for glasses.

As a result of the program's design, 97 percent of the program's graduates are employed in the opticianry field. The program is accredited by the Commission on Opticianry Accreditation and approved by the North Carolina State Board of Opticians. It is a seven-quarter day-time program that awards the Associate in Applied Science degree.

Contact:
Richard V. Dukes, Program Director
(919) 598-9374

Durham Technical Community College
1637 Lawson Street
Durham, NC 27703
Total head count enrollment-Credit: 8,068; Non-Credit: 23,909
Campuses/sites: 6; Full-time faculty: 225

EASTERN FIRE SEMINAR

*⊞ During training, students must battle heavy smoke and intense ⊞
heat to satisfy performance objectives*

It has been proven that fire service personnel who have been trained using real equipment in realistic situations have a much better chance of promptly extinguishing a fire when an actual emergency occurs. The situation can also be stabilized more quickly when personnel are well-trained. Fayetteville Technical Community College provides such training through the Eastern Fire Seminar. By utilizing classroom situations, local ponds, drill towers, and other structures, the Eastern Fire Seminar provides firefighters with a wide variety of practical experiences.

An annual event hosted by Fayetteville Technical Community College in conjunction with the Cumberland County Fire Chiefs and Firefighters Associations, the seminar consists of 34, 12-hour courses ranging from classroom lectures to practical classes, including live fire training and other hands-on exercises.

Each year, the challenge in developing the Eastern Fire Seminar is to design a training program that closely simulates those emergency situations which firefighters and other Emergency Services personnel will actually face on their jobs. For example, one of the 34 courses offered is implemented during the response to a fire. The highlight of this class occurs on the second day when an actual structure is burned. Students perform fireground skills, such as

Ventilation Practices, Fire Streams, Self-Contained Breathing Apparatus, etc., during the live burn to further complement their training.

During training, students must battle the disorienting effects of heavy smoke and intense heat to satisfy required performance objectives. Practical training situations such as these maintain high interest from participants and build confidence and teamwork that cannot be accomplished in a classroom setting. The realistic training offered in this seminar also helps firefighters and other Emergency Services personnel comply with state and federal mandates. These regulations require performance-based skills for training and education in addition to a required number of training hours to complete different objectives.

Over the years, the Eastern Fire Seminar has continued to grow. In 1992, the seminar drew more than 1,000 students from more than six states. Instructors for the course are selected from candidates throughout the United States based on their areas of specialty.

The Eastern Fire Seminar will continue to play a major role in preparing firefighters for the future and in introducing new and more sophisticated technology that can save lives and property.

Contact:
Robert Atkinson, Director, Emergency Services/Continuing Education
(919) 678-8430

Fayetteville Technical Community College
PO Box 35236
Fayetteville, NC 28303
Total head count enrollment-Credit: 11,549; Non-Credit: 29,247
Campuses/sites: 1; Full-time faculty: 192

WESTOVER COMMUNITY EDUCATION PARTNERSHIP

*⊞ The program allows visitations between high school and college faculty, ⊞
to exchange ideas and identify resources to share*

A Partnership Program ties the high school, community college, local business and industry, and the entire Westover community together in a cooperative effort to identify common needs and better educate high school students.

The partnerships, initiated by Fayetteville Technical Community College and Westover Senior High School, prepare students for college, additional technical education or direct entry into the work force. Equipment and resources in the high schools, at FTCC, and in business and industry are shared to provide the greatest benefit for all students. Additionally, the partnership provides opportunities for faculty interaction, mentoring programs,

college and career counseling for the high school students, and increased community and business involvement in the educational process.

The Partnership Program, available through the county school system, allows visitations between high school and FTCC faculty. Visitations are designed for the exchange of ideas, teaching strategies, and identification of cross-utilization of equipment and training devices. For example, a Westover chemistry teacher might meet with an FTCC chemistry instructor to discuss the level of instruction necessary to prepare students for college chemistry courses.

Continues on Page 506

The mentoring system benefits high school as well as FTCC students and staff. The system allows high school students in the Tech Prep program to visit a college faculty member and to observe and participate in hands-on training in the student's chosen career field. Selected FTCC students become mentors to the high schoolers and provide information on how the subject matter is applied in their career fields. Additionally, dual enrollment in both high school and the community college is planned for some high school students to gain advanced skills. This opportunity allows students to observe how college instruction differs from high school instruction and thus develop better studying and researching skills. The high school guidance and career counselors share ideas and strategies with FTCC counselors and, in turn, become familiar with the campus Career Center, further easing the transition for high school students.

Another component of the Partnership Program, the connection with business and industry, is vital. The business partners share business and industry training needs and provide information on new business practices. Additionally, they provide guidance in changing career field objectives, job interviewing techniques, and prerequi-

sites for their particular fields. The Westover Senior High School principal and his staff were instrumental in drawing this partnership together. They identified business leaders who are firmly committed to the principles of the Partnership Program.

Community involvement will be expanded by increasing the number of business partners in the program, and parents are encouraged to volunteer as coordinators and chaperones. They will be invited to tour business and industry locations with their children to view operations in specific career fields on a first-hand basis.

In June 1992, eight teachers, two students, one parent (all from Westover High School), and one chemical engineer from DuPont Corporation (one of the industry partners) met for a three-day workshop at Fayetteville Tech. The focus of the workshop was to identify goals, objectives and strategies to be implemented by the high school, FTCC and business/industry as part of their partnership. The resulting ideas are innovative and easily implemented at minimal expense. Community Education Partnership is the missing link that connects the parents, businesses, educational institutions and, most importantly, the students to focus on common goals and direction.

Contact:
Ed Jackson, Dean, General and Service Programs
(919) 678-8244

Fayetteville Technical Community College
PO Box 35236
Fayetteville, NC 28303
Total head count enrollment-Credit: 11,549; Non-Credit: 29,247
Campuses/sites: 1; Full-time faculty: 192

CUSTOMER SERVICE TECHNOLOGY

▓ *The program is a direct response to industry requests for employees* ▓
trained in customer service

The Customer Service Technology program, established at Guilford Technical Community College in August 1987, was the first program of its kind in the United States. It was developed in direct response to requests from industries seeking to locate in the area who needed a source of trained employees.

Students in this program study a comprehensive curriculum that covers all facets of customer service, from the operation of computers to the psychology of dealing with the various types of customers within the business environment.

Customer service skills are unique in that they apply to all businesses, regardless of type or function. The CST program prepares students for employment with business, industry and government organizations that interact with customers in a value-added manner. These employees will represent the organization to the customer in a variety of functions such as credit service; retail sales and order entry; credit, collection and authorization services; and

fraud control. The CST program uses state-of-the-art technology to train students for entry into the customer service field.

The Customer Service Technology Advisory Committee consists of representatives of various industries in the surrounding area. This committee meets on a monthly basis to review the progress of the program and to provide valuable input from industries' point of view. The committee reviews curriculum offerings and gives support to the administration. The committee's primary functions are to make the community more aware of the CST program and to help the business community realize the value of a prospective employee with this training. Also, the committee has established a Customer Service Technology scholarship fund with scholarships awarded to outstanding second-year students.

The Customer Service Technology program has one full-time instructor and several adjuncts from various professional backgrounds.

In 1989, this curriculum was awarded first place as an Exemplary Community College Instructional Program by the National Council of Instructional Administrators. This was in competition with 600 programs from more than 1,300 community colleges nationwide.

Contact:
Lynda Hodge, Department Chair, (919) 334-4822, ext. 2611
Jane Cassady, Administrative Secretary, (919) 334-4822, ext. 2603

Guilford Technical Community College
PO Box 309
Jamestown, NC 27282
Total head count enrollment-Credit: 10,882; Non-Credit: 23,935
Campuses/sites: 5;Full-time faculty: 175

INDUSTRY / EDUCATION PARTNERSHIP

The partnership provides the college with a full-time faculty member and on-call support for local industries

A partnership between Haywood Community's Regional High Technology Center and two large, local industries (2,500 total employees) has resulted in on-call support services focused on the training and retraining needs of industrial employees who work on, around or in the maintenance of specific automation control systems within each plant.

Prior to the partnership with HCC, the two industries were contracting privately as needed with independent consultants for services on automation control equipment made and installed by the same manufacturer. The college recognized a need to provide training in these areas, but lacked the funds to employ a technical specialist with the capabilities to meet the industries' expectations. Through this program, the industrial partners provide financial grants to HCC for the services of the specialist(s) and for the use of the High Technology Center. These grants allow the college to employ a faculty member with a highly technical educational employment background. Without sharing the costs of such an individual with the industrial partners, the college would not be able to meet the salary requirements of the position.

Through this partnership the industries receive the on-call support of a world-class and plant-floor experienced training specialist(s) for the automation control systems areas of their production operations. The partnership provides Haywood Community College with a full-time faculty member for engineering technologies curricula and for outreach services to local industries. Additional industry/education partnerships have been developed since 1986 with other companies within western North Carolina, with similar benefits for all parties involved.

Contact:
Sam Wiggins, Director, Regional High Technology Center
(704) 452-1411

Haywood Community College
1 Freedlander Drive
Clyde, NC 28721
Total enrollment head count-Credit: 4,500; Non-Credit: 6,000
Campuses/sites: 1; Full-time faculty: 57

ACADEMIC ADVISING

Advisors may register students any time, because multi-term registration is available under an annual schedule of classes

Since 1989, the advising process at Isothermal Community College has been an ongoing, decentralized process that can be managed effectively at the individual faculty advisor level. This change from a model of advising that was limited to course selection recommendations during a central registration period allows students to make informed choices and decisions regarding educational, career and life goals.

Each advisor is assigned students as part of the admissions process. From that point forward, advisors set student appointments at their discretion. Personal computers have been provided to all faculty advisors in support of the advising process. Advisors can access student records, including placement scores, transcripts, program progress data and graduation readiness data. In addition, advisors have the ability to register students at any time. Multi-term registration is possible because an annual schedule of

Continues on Page 508

classes has been developed.

This advising model has resulted in many positive impacts. Advisors provide accurate up-to-date information incorporating the latest changes in program requirements. Student retention has improved, and student satisfaction with the advising process is strong. Because registration now occurs over an extended period, deans are able to monitor enrollment patterns and modify course schedules accordingly. The present goal is to expand the system to include academic alert and intervention features that will allow the advisor to assist students at the point a problem arises rather than at the end of instructional periods, when little or no remedy is possible.

Achieving this advising model has required a substantial investment of time and physical resources. A series of professional development meetings and workshops were essential in sensitizing faculty to the expanded role of the advising function. Capital resources were required for acquiring and networking computer support. Hours of planning and preparation were essential in redefining policies and procedures associated with admissions, scheduling and registration. These expenditures in time and resources were essential, however, in the commitment to a student centered environment.

The Isothermal Community College academic advising model was officially recognized in 1991 by the North Carolina Department of Community Colleges as one of three exemplary programs in North Carolina.

Contact:
Robert E. Harrison, Vice President, Academic and Student Affairs
(704) 286-3636

Isothermal Community College
PO Box 804
Spindale, NC 28160
Total head count enrollment-Credit: 1,700; Non-Credit: 15,475
Campuses/sites: 2; Full-time faculty: 54

SPECIAL TOPICS COURSES

Special Topics courses have focused on a variety of subjects, including the South in literature, the Appalachian culture and film history

A fairly typical generic listing in many college catalogs begins with the phrase "Special Topics in..." This listing is usually there as a catch-all for any experimental course some instructor proposes teaching. It is an option that may be rarely used – or it can be a dynamic outlet that generates interest not only for students but for faculty as well. At Isothermal Community College, the "Special Topics" listing has been used over the years to bring a variety of very challenging courses to campus.

Faculty in the English Department have offered Special Topics courses covering such themes as the brilliant future of man; the American dream in the American novel; the religious theme in British poetry; the South in literature; Black American literature; North Carolina writers; and Appalachian culture. All of these courses have been team-taught. All have used an interdisciplinary approach, and all have utilized resources beyond the scope of the department. A grant from the North Carolina Humanities Committee assisted greatly with the Appalachian Culture course – one of the most comprehensive as well as one of the most popular courses offered.

In addition to Special Topics in English courses, Isothermal Community College has offered others in Humanities and is preparing for one in Sociology. One of the best humanities courses the college has offered was called – for lack of a better term – "Modern American Culture." In it the college dealt with each decade from the 1950's to the present and looked at every aspect of popular culture we possibly could – everything from political concerns and general attitudes to fashions and furniture. When students studied the 50's, they danced the shag. They staged a war protest for the 60's, a rock concert for the 70's, etc.

In another popular Special Topics course students ventured into Middle Earth on a J.R.R. Tolkein excursion. In another, students studied the history of film. The course planned for 1992-93 addressed the more serious concern of family violence. Designed for students in the social sciences and criminal justice, the course featured outside speakers and served as a forum for discussing ways of bringing this social ill under control.

There is no long-range plan in effect for what may be taught under a "Special Topics" listing or when a course may be taught. As popular as the courses have been, none has been repeated. They give instructors a chance to deal with a timely issue or a special interest. As such they have been excellent sources of professional development for the teachers. They have also provided an opportunity for students to take something different.

Isothermal Community College has received some recognition for the Special Topics courses. The Religious Themes in British Poetry course won the national Phi Theta Kappa award in 1988 for the best use of the honors theme for that year. Three of the English faculty were featured in 1988 at a regional meeting of the Community College Humanities Association to discuss the Appalachian Culture course, and a brief article on the courses was included in the 1988 NCIA publication, *Exemplary Academic Programs at the Community College.*

Contact:
Nancy H. Womack, College Transfer Division Dean
(704) 286-3636, ext. 306

Isothermal Community College
PO Box 804
Spindale, NC 28160
Total head count enrollment-Credit: 1,700; Non-Credit: 15,475
Campuses/sites: 2;Full-time faculty: 54

JAMES SPRUNT COMMUNITY COLLEGE

SWINE MANAGEMENT TECHNOLOGY

Intense marketing and recruitment campaigns have effectively shown young students the possibilities of a career in agribusiness

The Swine Management Technology program at James Sprunt Community College is proving to be a successful model of community-based programming and cooperation between local industry and community college education. This unique two-year program is one of a very few in the United States and the only community college program east of the Mississippi.

The 1993-94 academic year marked the fifth year of operation for the associate degree program, which was created in response to the local swine industries' growing need for trained mid-management personnel. Following an extensive needs analysis of eastern North Carolina in 1988, a special grant from the Department of Community Colleges provided start-up funding for the program.

From inception to implementation, the Swine Management Technology program has profited from industry input. In addition to providing significant funding assistance, local industries and growers serve on a program advisory committee, reviewing program organization and course content and assisting with marketing and recruitment.

The program's principal goal is to provide well-trained personnel to help fill the growing industry needs for mid-management and other supervisory positions without having to recruit outside the state. The two-year degree program, as well as diploma and certificate programs which have evolved from it, is already doing a good job of achieving this objective: so far every graduate has been placed in a management or manager-trainee position before final graduation.

Also being met are companion goals of strengthening the community college/industry partnership, preparing local citizens for local jobs, and changing the image of agriculture as a career choice from negative to positive.

Intensive marketing and recruitment campaigns, using brochures and videotapes developed by the college in area high school and middle school career classes, are proving effective in educating young students about the "modern" career opportunities in the swine industry and other areas of agribusiness.

The success of James Sprunt's Swine Management Technology program has illustrated that the local community college and local industry can work effectively in partnership to achieve common goals. Its success has brought about more understanding between the college and industry. Most importantly, the training provided is helping industry meet its need for skilled employees and the students' need for marketable employment skills.

Perhaps the greatest impact of the Swine Management program's success is its example that similar community-based, cooperative efforts can achieve the same results.

Contact:
Mary Wood, Dean, Academic and Student Services
(919) 296-2422

James Sprunt Community College
PO Box 39
Kenansville, NC 28349-0398
Total head count enrollment-Credit: 1,500; Non-Credit: 2,400
Campuses/sites: 18; Full-time faculty: 40

HUMANITIES COURSES

In addition to traditional lectures, the courses incorporate hands-on experience and the use of primary source material

Even during James Sprunt Community College's early years as a technical institute, its leaders recognized that occupational education must provide training for living as well as for earning a living. With the help of the National Endowment for the Humanities, courses were developed to complement career-oriented classes by teaching the value and relevance of the humanities and humanistic thought.

In 1978, the college received a $49,221 pilot grant from NEH to develop three interdisciplinary humanities courses for students in two-year technical programs. These courses – The Nature of Man, The Nature of America, and The Future of Man – have since been offered as electives in all two-year technical programs. Textbooks are not used, and the courses stress critical thinking and communications skills rather than mastery of factual material.

Student response to these courses has been good. In evaluating the courses, some students said their whole outlook on life had changed. Others said they had reevaluated opinions and values.

In 1981, JSCC received a $113,914 grant from NEH to develop and implement additional humanities courses and to revise the existing ones to reflect a more humanistic perspective. Called "Learning for Living," this three-year project resulted in five new courses: Politics, Economics and Human Values; The Black Experience; The Individual and Society; Southern Culture; and Humanities for Vocational Students. The first four are now offered as humanities or social science electives for technical students. The fifth may be substituted for the required Human Relations course for vocational students.

In 1986, JSCC added a two-year college transfer program, and three years later NEH provided a grant of $52,588 to develop a humanities core studies program for those students. The purpose of these courses is to enhance the "cultural literacy" of college transfer students through the study of the history, literature and art of the ancient, medieval and modern world.

To facilitate transferability, the courses were developed as separate three-quarter sequences in Western Civilization, World Literature, and History of the Fine Arts. (They have since been changed to two-quarter sequences of five-credit-hour courses.) The courses were coordinated chronologically. Students are encouraged to take all three related courses in the same quarter.

In addition to the traditional lecture approach, these courses incorporate hands-on experiences and the use of primary source materials, as well as joint field trips. The courses have been popular, and they have proven to be especially beneficial to students who take all three subjects in the same quarter.

In 1991, the instructors of the core humanities program also began co-editing *Wellspring*, a magazine of literature and the arts, with an interdisciplinary approach. Work was solicited from students in commercial art and creative writing classes, evaluated by student volunteers from the World Literature class, and transferred to computer disks by typing students. Layout and design was done by commercial art students. *Wellspring* was named the best literary journal in the southeastern region by the Community College Humanities Association.

JSCC continues to offer these classes with its regular full-time and adjunct faculty members. Team-teaching, which was originally used for many of the courses, has been largely abandoned because of budgetary pressures, but the interdisciplinary approach is still used and the courses still prepare students to live fuller, richer lives.

Contact:
Mary Wood, Dean, Academic and Student Services
(919) 296-2422

James Sprunt Community College
PO Box 39
Kenansville, NC 28349-0398
Total head count enrollment-Credit: 1,500; Non-Credit: 2,400
Campuses/sites: 18; Full-time faculty: 40

EQUINE TECHNOLOGY

▦ Before graduation, each student completes an internship on a farm ▦
that specializes in the student's area of interest

Providing transportation and invaluable field labor, the horse played an integral role in the development of our United States. Today, as a viable component of agriculture, sports, entertainment and recreational activities, the horse is at the center of a $15.2-billion industry. In 1983, recognizing a need for trained individuals in the equine industry, Martin Community College established the Equine Technology program, the only program of its kind in the state of North Carolina.

With the primary objective to prepare students for entry-level positions in all facets of the horse industry, the following curriculum options are available to highly motivated students:

1) a two-year Associate of Applied Science degree in Equine Technology;
2) a 12-month Diploma in Equine Management; and
3) a nine-month Certificate in Horse Husbandry.

A strong science curriculum combined with extensive "hands-on" laboratories is designed to prepare students to make sound management decisions based on scientific principles. Graduates of the Equine Technology program are employed as grooms, assistant farm and breeding managers, exercise riders, trainers, wranglers, riding instructors, and veterinary assistants, while others work for various breed registries. An integral aspect of the curriculum is the internship that each student completes prior to

graduation. Internships are completed on farms that specialize in the student's area of interest and frequently result in post-graduation employment.

To ensure that the curriculum would provide relevant instruction and opportunity, an advisory committee consisting of equine industry leaders was established. The Equine Technology Advisory Committee meets semi-annually to review program policy, assist with hiring instructional personnel, and to provide support as needed.

MCC boasts facilities that provide an optimum environment for the educational process. The new Martin Arena-Equine Facility includes a 140-foot-by-220-foot indoor riding arena and allows continuation of classes regardless of weather. This unique facility is the site of horse shows and other events that enable students to gain valuable experience. Available to private individuals and organizations wishing to host various horse and non-horse related events, Martin Arena is also home to the Annual Stampede In The Park Rodeo. Proceeds from this event are distributed through the college's Foundation as scholarships to MCC students enrolled in one of the colleges 17 curriculum programs.

In addition to local students, individuals from 12 states and Canada have enrolled in the Equine Technology program. Their contribution to the eastern North Carolina community continues to be highly valued.

Contact:
Michael J. Yoder, Director
(919) 792-1521

Martin Community College
Kehukee Park Road
Williamston, NC 27892-9988
Total head count enrollment-Credit: 840; Non-Credit: 1,618
Campuses/sites: 3; Full-time faculty: 28

ALLIED HEALTH CONSORTIUM

▦ The consortium has enabled the expansion of class offerings ▦
and led to cooperative transfer programs

In order to prevent a critical shortfall of health care workers, Mitchell Community College, the Mooresville Graded School District, and Lake Norman Regional Medical Center formed the Allied Health Consortium. This tri-agency coordination of resources, funded by the Lowrance Hospital Fund, is designed to meet the training and service needs for the allied health field in the Mooresville-South Iredell area.

The three-year, $450,000 grant is designed to meet the allied health training and service needs of local residents; employ personnel to expand health care training, educa-

tion, and services; modify facilities; and purchase equipment. The Allied Health Extension Center is located at Mitchell Community College Mooresville Center and interfaces with the Tech-Prep program at Mooresville High School. A Coordinator of Allied Health Services oversees the planned instruction and community programs. A monthly newsletter facilitates communication among consortium members and the community.

In continuing education, classes for nursing assistants have been upgraded and expanded. A full range of classes

Continues on Page 512

is now offered in First Aid, CPR and Emergency Medical Services, along with courses to meet the continuing education and re-certification needs of area health professionals. Forums on health care issues are offered to the community-at-large. Additional classes and seminars are planned for the public which will focus on health and wellness, and on the care of elderly and disabled family members at home.

At the curriculum level, two new courses now are offered: Medical Assisting and Nursing Assistant/Home Health Care. This latter course is intended for those students who view nursing assistant training as an entry-level training position that will ultimately lead to a higher-level career in the allied health field. It is designed to appeal to students who are uncertain about a career in professional nursing or who need to make up academic deficiencies to qualify for the Associate Degree Nursing Program at Mitchell Community College. It should also appeal to students who are interested in the allied health field in general, and who would benefit from the clinical experiences as well as the other related courses and career guidance available.

In order to provide career choices yet avoid the high start-up costs of many programs, cooperative transfer programs are being developed with neighboring community colleges in: Medical Records, Radiology, Respiratory Care, Physical Therapy and Occupational Therapy. Clinical experiences will primarily be in local hospitals. A scholarship fund has been established; scholarship students will commit to working in local facilities as graduates.

Contact:
Maureen Slonim, Coordinator
(704) 663-1923

Mitchell Community College
500 West Broad Street
Statesville, NC 28677
Total head count enrollment-Credit: 1,443; Non-Credit: 3,077
Campuses/sites: 2; Full-time faculty: 48

LITERACY THROUGH THE NEWSPAPER

*A joint initiative with the local newspaper involved
12 GED preparation lessons, published weekly*

Increasingly, literacy is defined as having a high school diploma. Almost 1.7 million North Carolinians, 40 percent of adults age 16 or older, fail to meet this standard of literacy. More specifically, approximately 25,000, or nearly 50 percent of the adult population of Iredell County, do not meet this standard. So in an innovative approach to delivery of basic skills education, Mitchell Community College and *The Statesville Record and Landmark* formed a rather non-traditional partnership to increase the accessibility of basic skills instruction within the college's service area.

The target population for this effort included those individuals who desired to earn a GED but were unable to attend traditional classes due to various reasons including, but not limited to, child care problems, transportation problems, physical disabilities, and personal and/or work schedules. On September 15, 1992, the GED newspaper preparation program began.

Each partner made major commitments in terms of time, money and expertise. The newspaper agreed to provide 12 full pages of space over a 12-week period. They also committed their publicity and marketing expertise to this project. The college agreed to provide a coordinator, instructors, materials, supplies and facilities to carry out the project. Logistically, the program provided 12 individual GED preparation lessons, published weekly in the local newspaper. These lessons were designed to be completed at home and mailed to Mitchell Community College for grading and evaluation. The lessons were then mailed back to the student. The college offered supplemental classes for those students who wished to participate. Tutoring by telephone was also available.

This program was so successful that it was replicated in *The Mooresville Tribune*, a weekly newspaper within the same service area, beginning in April of 1992.

Four-hundred-fifty persons were officially involved in the program. Many of these students enrolled in the more traditional basic skills classes upon completion of the 12-week program. More than 80 of these individuals earned a high school credential within the academic year.
Positive outcomes of this program include:
- increased educational attainment level of population of Iredell County, due to increased accessibility of instruction;
- increased visibility and credibility of basic skills program within the area;
- increased awareness of the problem and possible solutions among the college constituents; and
- increased access to the college by those who were previously deterred by barriers such as child care problems, transportation problems, scheduling

problems or physical disabilities.

This program provided a service to all segments of the local community and therefore marked the newspapers and the college as leaders in community-based education.

Contact:
Carol Johnson, Coordinator
(704) 878-3221

Mitchell Community College
500 West Broad Street
Statesville, NC 28677
Total head count enrollment-Credit: 1,443; Non-Credit: 3,077
Campuses/sites: 2; Full-time faculty: 48

TAXIDERMY MINI-COURSE

Attendees now number more than 500 and come from throughout the United States, Canada and Mexico

Piedmont Community College began a specialized taxidermy program in the early 1970's that celebrated its 20th anniversary in April 1994. PCC serves a very rural community with a rich history of outdoor activities (such as hunting and fishing) that has made the specialized taxidermy program a natural for this area.

The first Taxidermy Mini-Course was developed in response to local taxidermists' and the college's full-time taxidermy students' requests for information to help transition their trade from a hobby into a viable business. They wanted to learn new technology and have the opportunity to learn from skilled taxidermists from outside the immediate college service area.

At the first Taxidermy Mini-Course, three well-known taxidermists, two from Virginia and one from Louisiana, were employed by the college to instruct six, three-hour mini-courses on taxidermy techniques that had made them successful. Sixty-six students from throughout the Eastern Seaboard – Maine to Florida – attended the first Taxidermy Mini-Course, a one-day program, which was held during a February snow storm. The next mini-course was held in July of the same year in the midst of a heat wave, when 90 students attended. Each year since, the Taxidermy Mini-Course has been held the last weekend in April, with continued growth.

The 20th Taxidermy Mini-Course was scheduled to be held in April 1994, when 44 three-hour courses were scheduled to be taught by 24 nationally recognized taxidermists. Also planned was a taxidermy competition judged by professional taxidermists, suppliers exhibits and an auction to support the college's full-time taxidermy program

Each year since the Taxidermy Mini-Course was moved to the college's campus in 1979, there have been increasing numbers of attendees camping on campus to cut their attendance cost. Many family members now accompany the Mini Course attendees and shop in the area or just relax – a family vacation! Attendees now come from throughout the United States, Canada and Mexico, and enrollment of students has surpassed the 500-student level. Total participation, including exhibitors, instructors, students and family members has consistently been in excess of 600 persons.

The Piedmont Community College Taxidermy Mini-Course has helped bring a hobby into a lucrative small business utilizing modern technology and business techniques. A key to the success of this unique program has been the college's consistent commitment to quality. Attendees' suggestions for quality improvements are reviewed and implemented as appropriate. The college has continually improved the delivery of the program and has developed a staff of support personnel who look forward to the "spring migration" of taxidermists to this rural community.

The college's full-time taxidermy program has continued to grow, draw positive national interest and is noted as a premier taxidermy program. Donations to the taxidermy program and publicity of the college's taxidermy program have been side benefits of this annual continuing education program.

Contact:
Phyllis Gentry, Continuing Education Coordinator
(910) 599-1181

Piedmont Community College
PO Box 1197
Roxboro, NC 27573
Total enrollment head count-Credit: 1,974; Non-credit: 4,882
Campuses/sites: 2; Full-time faculty: 53

CERTIFIED FLORIST DESIGN AND DAILY SHOP OPERATIONS

The courses, delivered annually, were developed in partnership with members of the state florist association

Piedmont Community College supports and promotes economic growth of the florist trade through a partnership between its Continuing Education Division and members of the North Carolina State Florist Association's Educational Committee. Since 1985, the college has worked with the association to develop educational courses to prepare florists to sit for an exam to be administered by the association, which would certify each successful completers as a North Carolina Certified Professional Florist.

The two educational courses developed and delivered annually are: Certified Florist Design and Daily Shop Operations.

These courses are conducted in a back-to-back arrangement for 10 days Flowers have been provided by the North Carolina Florist Association, with the college and the asso-

ciation sharing in the cost of the instructional program. The program has continually utilized off-campus conference center locations for hosting the program where learning continues even when class is not in session. Great networking has been established within the florist trade as a result of this arrangement.

The college has utilized floral designers and other instructors from Texas A & M University and the Texas State Florist Association. Many of the course textbooks and tests were developed and published by the Texas Association.

This partnership has benefited from continuous input from Florist Association members, attendees, graduates of courses, instructors and college staff. The end result is higher quality floral products for North Carolina residents and a more successful florist trade in North Carolina.

Contact:
Phyllis Gentry, Continuing Education Coordinator
(910) 599-1181

Piedmont Community College
PO Box 1197
Roxboro, NC 27573
Total enrollment head count-Credit: 1,974; Non-credit: 4,882
Campuses/sites: 2; Full-time faculty: 53

INDUSTRIAL CONSTRUCTION TECHNOLOGY

Local construction industries helped fund, market and identify tasks and course content

Pitt Community College piloted for other North Carolina community colleges a comprehensive construction training program for the region, designed to offset shortages of skilled manpower for future capital industrial construction in eastern North Carolina. The program, which trains industrial construction workers as well as future craft supervisors, project managers, etc., resulted from a partnership between business, industry and educators.

Representatives from local industries took a leadership role in funding, marketing and identifying tasks and course content. The first Industrial Construction Technology (ICT) class started in September 1992, utilizing the college's existing facilities, instructional personnel and equipment from other ongoing industrial programs. One

additional faculty member was employed to teach/coordinate the program. As the program progresses, additional full-time or part-time staff will be needed. Plans are underway to construct a dedicated industrial construction training facility where students will acquire real on-site skills, working with materials and machinery used in industry.

The primary goal of the program is for students to graduate with an AAS degree in Industrial Construction Technology. The first year is structured to balance general education and industrial courses. Through their choices of technical electives, students may concentrate on pipefitting, millwright and electrical/instrumentation courses. With this curriculum format, the students will not only gain technical construction skills but also the important related skills necessary for them to assume leadership roles in the industries where they work. A secondary goal is to provide upgrade training in the various skills areas for industrial employees already working in one of the construction crafts.

Contact:
James E. Fulcher, Division Director
(919) 355-4428

Pitt Community College
Highway 11 South, PO Drawer 7007
Greenville, NC 27835-7007
Total head count enrollment-Credit: 6,433; Non-Credit: 7,172
Campuses/sites: 1; Full-time faculty: 120

RETRAINING OLDER WORKERS FOR HEALTH CARE CAREERS

The program offers training for older people who want to become phlebotomists or medical clerk/guest attendants

Along with a continuously grave shortage of skilled health care personnel in eastern North Carolina is an ever-aging population. A Pitt Community College program addresses both by tapping the pool of mature and stable individuals who desire to work.

Pitt Community College, University Medical Center of Eastern North Carolina Pitt County, and the Eastern Area Health Education Center collaborated on a project to "Retrain Older Adults for Health Care Careers." The program offers scholarships and specialized training to high school graduates in the 55-and-older age group from Pitt County who would like to train to become phlebotomists or complete courses for medical clerk/guest attendant positions.

The program is based on the premise that there are many older workers who desire to continue productive employment and have the interpersonal skills and life experiences that help them cope with the types of situations found in health care. On the other hand, there are health care positions such as in phlebotomy where there is a definite shortage of qualified workers. This premise is supported by data from the Employment Security Commission, which has identified more than 2,000 people age 55 and older who are seeking employment through offices in Pitt and four adjacent counties.

Grant funds have been secured from the James J. and Mamie Richardson Perkins Trust for the scholarships offered to older students. An implementation grant was obtained form the Kate B. Reynolds Charitable Trust. The Reynolds Health Care Trust is a private foundation in Winston-Salem, North Carolina, created in 1946 through provisions in the will of Mrs. William N. Reynolds to improve health care in North Carolina.

The phlebotomy program educates individuals to draw blood from patients for testing. The classroom portion of the program is conducted on campus and the clinical education component occurs at University Medical Center of Eastern North Carolina-Pitt County and at several other community hospitals, doctors offices and clinics. An on-campus cholesterol screening provides students with the necessary number of microcollections needed to meet the requirements for graduation from the program. The program received initial approval for four years from the National Accrediting Agency for Clinical Laboratory Sciences (NAACLS). Students are eligible to sit for national certification examinations as a result of the NAACLS approval.

Older workers interested in the medical clerk/guest attendant positions in health care agencies enroll in a program, which provides them with a certificate in medical assisting. The courses in the Medical Assisting certificate program include medical terminology, computer applications, filing and oral communications. Students completing this program have the skills necessary for a variety of clerical and receptionists jobs in health care settings.

Many industries have found that older workers make positive contributions to the workplace, including providing commitment, loyalty, stability, experience, maturity, knowledge and people skills. The older workers also benefit from increased self esteem, camaraderie, a more structured life style and the chance to increase a fixed income. Younger employees gain a stable mature role model. In other words, everyone benefits!

Contact:
Judith W. Kuykendall, Health Sciences Division Director
(919) 355-4309

Pitt Community College
Highway 11 South, PO Drawer 7007
Greenville, NC 27835-7007
Total head count enrollment-Credit: 6,433; Non-Credit: 7,172
Campuses/sites: 1; Full-time faculty: 120

TECH PREP

Since the advent of Tech Prep, the drop-out rate is lower, SAT scores are higher and more students are attending college

When Joe Grimsley arrived as the president of Richmond Community College, the remedial courses were disturbingly overflowing. After visiting with several faculty members, he was convinced that high school students needed a more challenging and rigorous program, particularly in the areas of mathematics and communication skills. At the same time, the superintendent of Richmond County Schools was looking for a way to motivate students to stay in school and maximize their educational opportunities.

Inspired by Dale Parnell's book, *The Neglected Majority*, the two men saw Tech Prep as a means of motivating and serving the students about whom they were concerned. They both felt that Parnell's suggested model of "2+2" did not provide the needed intervention early enough. To remedy the situation, they added two more years and developed a "4+2" version, with students starting Tech Prep in their freshman years in high school.

The Richmond County Tech Prep model includes three courses of study: Business; Health and Human Services; and Engineering (Electrical, Industrial and Mechanical). A set of required and recommended academic and vocational courses are provided for each of the three. All require that students take Algebra I and progress through a math sequence of courses leading to Algebra II. Science courses related to the specific field of interest (anatomy and chemistry for nursing, for example) are outlined and recommended.

The Richmond County Tech Prep effort has become a model for many school districts and community colleges throughout the country. Thousands of people from all over the United States have traveled to the Richmond County and attended one of the monthly on-site visitations at Richmond Senior High School. The visitations include short presentations by the team of leaders (school superintendent, college president, college admissions director, junior and high school principals, vocational director, business and industry leaders, etc.) and a tour of the building to observe classes and facilities.

Not only has Tech Prep significantly altered the face of education in Richmond County (drop-out rate cut by more than half, higher SAT scores, more students going on to college, etc.), but also it has had an impact on the whole state. By 1996, for example, all North Carolina school districts will be expected to have Tech Prep courses of study available for their students. Richmond Community College and Richmond County Schools have received recognition and awards for their combined efforts. The United States Department of Education recently announced that the program will receive funds to be one of the eight national demonstration sites for Tech Prep.

Contact:
Myrtle Stogner, Director, Tech Prep Leadership Development Center
(919) 582-7187

Richmond Community College
PO Box 1189
Hamlet, NC 28345
Total head count enrollment-Credit: 1,695; Non-Credit: 6,900
Campuses/sites: 4; Founded: 1964

TECH PREP EXECUTIVE LEADERSHIP

The leadership program enlightens educational and business leaders across the country about Tech Prep

In 1986, Joe Grimsley, the President of Richmond Community College, and Doug James, the Superintendent of Richmond County Schools, joined forces and initiated a "4+2" version of Dale Parnell's Tech Prep. Since then, Tech Prep in Richmond County has grown and matured and become a model for hundreds of other school districts and community colleges throughout the nation. Its success was directly related to the joint resolution from the North Carolina State Board of Community Colleges and the North Carolina State Board of Education directing all North Carolina school districts to have Tech Prep programs operational by the year 1996.

One of the critical factors leading to the success of Tech Prep in Richmond County has been the collaborative leadership of Doug James and Joe Grimsley. Since the initiation of Tech Prep, the two have continued to work closely on Tech Prep and on other educational issues. Both tend to look at the two institutions as one system, in which students can progress with ease and with minimal interference. The educational process in Richmond County is almost seen as a 15-year process (K-12+2 years of college).

Realizing the strength of collaborative leadership and its power to impact Tech Prep so positively, the Kellogg Foundation of Battle Creek, Michigan, awarded a grant to

Richmond Community College to promote the concept of collaborative leadership as it applies to Tech Prep. To this end, a two-day seminar has been developed and presented in a number of sites throughout the country. The basic seminar format (which changes according to the needs of each specific audience) is a blend of information acquisition and skill development. Educational and business leaders, participating in teams of three to six persons, gain knowledge about Tech Prep, leadership and collaboration.

The majority of the seminar is devoted to time in which the teams work together to develop and/or refine their Tech Prep programs, while strengthening their collaboration skills.

In addition to the seminar experiences, the grant has provided funding to publish a quarterly newsletter (*Collaboratively Yours*) and develop a manual on collaborative leadership and Tech Prep.

Contact:
Anne B. Crabbe, Director, Executive Leadership Program
(919) 582-7182

Richmond Community College
PO Box 1189
Hamlet, NC 28345
Total head count enrollment-Credit: 1,695; Non-Credit: 6,900
Campuses/sites: 4; Founded: 1964

FINE AND CREATIVE WOODWORKING

The program emphasizes the design and construction of find quality custom furniture

The Fine and Creative Woodworking program at Rockingham Community College is the only curriculum program of its type offered in North Carolina, and one of only a handful offered in the United States. Rockingham began the two-year program in 1987, the culmination of the college's effort to develop a program that would:

1) operate on a high curriculum and instructional standard;
2) have a low tuition; and
3) be unique to RCC so it would attract students from outside its local county and, indeed, on a national level.

The program emphasizes the design and construction of fine quality custom pieces of furniture. The curriculum includes design of period styles and creative work. Students are challenged with in-depth study and practical experience in many aspects of woodworking. Students first develop basic skills in using hand tools and machinery to construct items using basic joinery. They progress to the study of wood, wood properties, drying, treating and bending.

Students acquire knowledge and skills related to woodworking such as design as well as the interpretation of design; computer-assisted drafting; the use of appropriate tools; construction techniques; and equipment use, maintenance and repair. Also covered are shop organization and layout, business operations and management, and production processes. Graduates receive an Associate of Applied Science degree.

"Our program is very flexible," says lead instructor David Kenealy. "We're able not only to advance the knowledge and skills of a novice woodworker, but also to refine the work of an experienced craftsperson."

Instruction is tailored for individuals interested in starting their own businesses. Students also are prepared for employment opportunities in the furniture manufacturing industry and cabinet and custom furniture shops. RCC is located 50 miles north of High Point, NC, the furniture production capital of the nation.

The program's facilities encompass more than 10,000 square feet. Included are four individual work areas, designated as the drafting/design lab, finishing lab, bench room, and machine shop. All machinery meets top-quality, industrial standards.

The program has attracted students from Europe, Alaska, Washington state, and the Midwest, as well as the East. They design and craft both traditional and contemporary pieces such as grandfather clocks, lowboys, cabinets, workbenches, desks, tables, chairs, dulcimers, banjos and even a canoe. Their work has been exhibited at the International Woodworking Show in Atlanta, the NC State Fair, the Rockingham County Folk Festival, and in Chapel Hill. The program has been featured in two publications, *Woodshop News* and *Better Homes & Gardens Wood*.

In addition to the curriculum program, the college has been able to offer several woodworking workshops such as "Routers, Jigs and Fixtures" and "Making Bent-Wood Shaker-Style Nesting Boxes."

Contact:
David Kenealy
(919) 342-4261, ext. 178

Rockingham Community College
PO Box 38
Wentworth, NC 27375-0038
Total head count enrollment-Credit: 6,925; Non-Credit: 7,121
Campuses/sites: 1; Full-time faculty: 52

COMPREHENSIVE ADULT STUDENT ASSESSMENT SYSTEM (CASAS)

*Various types of learning styles and rates of learning are accommodated,
as each student has an individual learning plan*

Because the traditional academic program was not applicable to the adult learner needs, Rockingham Community College gradually implemented a competency-based literacy program. The established goals for this new, innovative approach were to:

1) increase student retention;
2) better meet business and industry needs;
3) increase facilitator skills; and
4) deliver basic skills instruction in an applied functional context.

When fully in place in 1990, this new innovative literacy approach called the Adult Enrichment Program replaced the traditional academic program, which had resulted in poor student and facilitator retention. A change in program philosophy, curriculum and technique was required to implement such a new approach. To ensure quality programming, students and facilitators are given opportunities to constantly evaluate program implementation, content, management, and to develop curriculum and participate in regular staff development.

The Adult Enrichment Program utilizes the Comprehensive Adult Student Assessment System (CASAS) as the vehicle to implement a true competency-based program. Skills covered include, but are not limited to, listening, reading, computation, writing, oral and written communication, problem solving and critical thinking.

Instruction is student-driven instead of instructor-driven. Instruction is adjusted to accommodate the diversity found in adult populations. Various types of learning styles and rates of learning are accommodated, with each student having an individualized learning plan. Progress is marked at various levels within each broad literacy level to document student mastery and ensure quality of instructional content and delivery. Utilizing the CASAS system, RCC has been able to access tools to customize programs for workplace literacy. RCC has the ability to assess worker skills, analyze jobs for skills needed, and customize curriculum to meet specific worker and workplace needs. RCC has been very successful in providing specific competency-based instruction for business and industry.

The Adult Enrichment Program employs 30 part-time facilitators, three part-time staff members and two full-time staff members. During the program year 1992-1993 the college operated a budget of more than $335,000. The success of the Adult Enrichment Program has been validated by recognition throughout the state. RCC was the first community college in North Carolina to implement a competency-based program utilizing CASAS. RCC has been used as a model for other community colleges and for state and national businesses that wish to implement a progressive, successful competency based program for adult learners.

Contact:
Sabrina Garrett, Coordinator, Literacy Programs
(919) 342-4261, ext. 305

Rockingham Community College
PO Box 38
Wentworth, NC 27375-0038
Total head count enrollment-Credit: 6,925; Non-Credit: 7,121
Campuses/sites: 1; Full-time faculty: 52

PROJECT EAGLE

*The program helps indigent people improve
their standard of living through education*

Sampson Community College's Project Eagle began in 1989 as an experiment to determine if, when barriers that block the indigent from furthering their education and seeking self-reliance were removed, they would voluntarily strive to improve their standard of living through a commitment to education. Over one four-year period, 296 unduplicated participants were served through Project Eagle.

Through the cooperative efforts of the local Private Industry Council, the Department of Social Services, and the college, funds were secured to implement the program. Buses were obtained through private support from the Sampson Community College Foundation in order to address one of the main barriers, transportation. Initially, 50 participants were targeted in 1989-90, but 1,218 were served. Returning and new enrollees totaled

186 in 1990-91, 120 in 1991-92, and 90 in 1992-93.

Project Eagle was a proactive response to the forthcoming Welfare Reform JOBS Program which was implemented in 1990-91. Because of the foresight that went into creating Project Eagle, the college was positioned favorably to meet the challenge of new mandates to provide educational services and employability skills training to public assistance recipients.

Positioned, but inadequately funded to support the many needs of a high-risk population, the college received a grant of $30,000 from Z. Smith Reynolds to augment the program. The grant enabled the college to meet the needs of all participants during the 1990-92 school years. The funds were used to provide support services, to increase recruiting, and to provide day care coordination, counseling and follow-up. An additional $28,000 was awarded to the Project in 1992 and has been used to purchase a 14-passenger van, to fund part-time clerical support, and to match JOBS funding for an on-site social worker.

Students success measures show that Project Eagle is accomplishing its goal. During the 1992-93 project year, 19 students obtained unsubsidized employment, nine students obtained their GED's or Adult High School Diplomas, 37 students passed one or more tests of GED or earned one or more credits toward high school diploma requirements, two students entered a college curriculum program, 11 students attained employability competencies, and one student returned to high school full-time.

Growth in basic skills attainment averages a 1-1/2 grade level increase over a nine-month period. Measurements during the fall of the 1992-93 quarter revealed 35 percent of the project participants functioning below the 6th grade reading level as compared to 40 percent during 1991-92 and 58 percent during the initial 1989-90 year. At the end of the project year, the functioning level percentages reveal that the number of participants functioning below the 6th-grade level dropped 19 percent. Delivery of basic skills training includes structured classroom presentations, one-on-one tutorial assistance and interactive computerized learning system available to all participants.

The Eagle program is unique in that there is a special effort to meet a variety of training needs for each individual. Both academic and employability competencies are taught in response to specific deficiencies. In addition to this training, a community-wide effort to bring the resources of local agencies, business and service organizations to this population is in operation through special seminars.

Seminars address the expressed needs of participants and present avenues for barrier removal. The seminar program is a volunteer effort made available through local business leaders and agency personnel. Since 1989, there have been approximately 50 volunteer presenters as seminar guests. Some of the topics presented during the 1992-93 year included: Employment and Training Opportunities, Crisis Intervention, Coping with Children, Discipline, Positive Thinking, Values Clarification, Health Care Opportunities, AIDS, Decision-Making, Abuse, Wellness, Relationships, Self-Motivation, Alcohol and Drug Awareness.

Under a contractual agreement utilizing JOBS funding, the college conducts an Employability Skills Seminar for JOBS/JTPA participants to provide job seeking and job readiness skills. Areas addressed include self-esteem building, application completion, interviewing techniques, resumes, worker trait expectations, using labor market information, and making career decisions. Forty-nine participants enrolled in the Employability seminar during 1992-93.

Job development and placement assistance is available for Employability seminar participants. Other avenues for job training include the Sampson County Employment and Training program and participation in the annual Sampson County Job Opportunities Convention. Participants completing their educational program and earning their GED, high school diploma, or degree program also have access to services from ESC, JOBS and Employment and Training.

Monitoring visits for all program years have been very positive. The project consistently served a greater number than funded until recently requested to limit participants. The major emphasis of the project, to remove barriers to preparation for the work force or advanced training, has been substantially supported by numerous funding sources that augment these efforts. Progress is steady, faster than through traditional avenues – and with the numerous collaborative support services Eagle provides, almost free of barriers.

Contact:
Billie Crawford Eure
(919) 592-7176

Sampson Community College
PO Box 318
Clinton, NC 28321
Total head count enrollment-Credit: 1,630; Non-Credit: 4,160
Campuses/sites: 1; Full-time faculty: 48

KOLLEGE FOR KIDS

*▨ This enrichment program for children ages 7 to 12 ▨
emphasizes stimulating intellectual curiosity*

With the emphasis on year-round schooling, Southeastern Community College took the initiative to bring that concept to Southeastern North Carolina with the establishment of the first annual Kollege for Kids in 1991. Sponsored by SCC's Community Services Program, the following objectives were developed to:

1) create excitement for learning;
2) have fun, with a purpose;
3) introduce students to new ideas and subjects; and
4) build a learning foundation for future use.

Kollege for Kids is an enrichment program for children ages 7 to 12. The emphasis of the program is creating an environment that stimulates intellectual curiosity. Volunteer college faculty devote their time to instruct future "SCC" students in a variety of subjects such as Rocketry (using principles of electronics) Double Bubble (learn the scientific process through the making of bubble gum), Making Music (Music Department faculty assists students in writing, producing and staging a musical Production), Video Production (EDU-Cable Director turns a TV studio over to eager youngsters who learn all phases of TV production), and many other programs. All these programs are designed to give students the opportunity to enrich their horizons in a college setting. By 1992, the second year for SCC's Kollege for Kids, it had grown from 120 to 180 participants. Students had to be turned away because of class size limitations. Plans are underway to expand the program in the future.

Contact:
Beverlee Nance, Director of Continuing Education
(919) 642-7141

Southeastern Community College
PO Box 151
Whiteville, NC 28472
Total head count enrollment-Credit: 2,456; Non-Credit: 4,200
Campuses/sites: 1; Full-time faculty: 53

INMATE EDUCATION

*▨ The college, with help from local and state officials, ▨
developed a re-structured plan for prison education*

By legislative mandate, prison education in North Carolina is the responsibility of the community college system. Over the years, community colleges have provided educational opportunities for inmates with mixed results.

With an emphasis on accountability in all phases of educational offerings, especially vocational education for prison inmates, it is necessary that colleges develop prison education programs that meet local, state and SACS accreditation standards. In the past, it was extremely difficult to get program completers in vocational programs in a prison setting. The primary reason for this was that the programs were usually either too long, fragmented, or not relevant to the job market. To remedy these and other obstacles to quality programs, Southeastern Community College staff, in cooperation with North Carolina Department of Community College staff and North Carolina Department of Corrections officials, embarked on a mission to address the issue of quality in prison educational programs.

The solution was actually quite simple. The first step was to evaluate existing programs at the prison unit for effectiveness, job potential, adequateness of resources and interest. Based on these findings, the college, with assistance from local and state department of correction personnel, as well as department of community college staff, developed a plan for prison education. Several programs were eliminated (because of ineffectiveness and lack of employment potential) and an additional one was re-structured.

Using Employment Security Commission data, the college identified three occupations with potential for employment through the year 2000. Armed with that information, college staff created four vocational programs that meet SACS and DCC curriculum standards. Each program is a certificate program approved under DCC curriculum standards, 11 weeks in length.

To fund instruction, assistance was obtained from Carl Perkins Vocational Education Funds and the Department of Corrections purchased supplies and equipment from the inmate welfare fund. College staff also received assurance from the Department of Corrections to limit transfer of inmates to give them the chance to complete the programs in which they are enrolled.

Inmates are not allowed to repeat a program once they have successfully completed it. However, given the structure of the programs, it is possible that within one academic year an inmate can complete as many as four occupational programs, all of which prepare the inmate for an entry-level position in a specific vocation.

Before this program was implemented, the rate of program completion was less than 10 percent. Within a year the completion rate has risen to 47 percent, and it is anticipated that a completion rate of 85 percent or better will be achieved and maintained by the next evaluation.

Contact:
Harry Foley
(919) 642-7141

Southeastern Community College
PO Box 151
Whiteville, NC 28472
Total head count enrollment-Credit: 2,456; Non-Credit: 4,200
Campuses/sites: 1; Full-time faculty: 53

ELECTRONEURODIAGNOSTICS

An integral part of the four-quarter program is clinical work experience at hospitals and clinics

Southwestern Community College has become a regional allied health training center for 14 Western North Carolina counties.

The concept was endorsed by the North Carolina Department of Community Colleges and special funding for the project was provided by the General Assembly shortly after President Norman K. Myers and the SCC Board of Trustees developed the plan in 1983. In 1985, construction began on the 72,000-square-foot WNC Regional Allied Health and Geriatric Training Center.

Opened in September 1988, the facility now houses 10 instructional programs representing a wide range of health care fields. Of the 10 programs, one is unique to North Carolina's system of 58 community colleges. Electroneurodiagnostics, a one-year diploma program offered exclusively at Southwestern Community College, involves recording and studying the electrical activity of the brain, spinal cord and nervous system.

Originally designed with a major focus on administering the EKG test (which records brain and heart activity), the program was entitled Electrodiagnostics. However, when instructor Fay Tyner was employed during the 1989-90 academic year, she modified the curriculum to focus upon the nervous system (brain and spinal cord) and changed the name to Electroneurodiagnostics.

Currently, the curriculum is designed to provide students with the knowledge and skills necessary to obtain recordings of brain functions through the use of electroencephalographic (EEG) equipment and other electrophysiological devices. In addition, students develop skills in taking and abstracting histories, documenting the clinical condition of patients and preparing descriptive reports of recorded electrical activity for neurologists and other physicians.

An integral part of the four-quarter program is the clinical work experience that students receive at hospitals and clinics throughout North Carolina and South Carolina and Georgia. Tyner has expanded the clinical sites to more than 10 locations.

Co-author of the first textbook in the electroneurodiagnostics field written at the technologies level, Tyner is never without a professional challenge. With the curriculum modification in place, her next goal for the program is to achieve national accreditation. According to Tyner, there are only 14 or 15 accredited training programs nationwide. The accreditation process has been initiated and a self-study of the Southwestern Community College program is underway.

Contact:
Fay Tyner, Program Director
(704) 586-4091, ext. 309

Southwestern Community College
275 Webster Road
Sylva, NC 28779
Total head count enrollment-Credit: 2,151; Non-Credit: 6,434
Campuses/sites: 3;Faculty: 48

SEASONAL RANGER LAW ENFORCEMENT TRAINING

The program is designed to prepare a seasonal park ranger for law enforcement duties

Established in 1976, as an elective component of Southwestern Community College's Criminal Justice program, the National Park Service Seasonal Ranger Law Enforcement Training program is recognized nationwide. Students come from all across the United States to attend the intensive 10-week (460-hour) training sessions that are offered annually during the fall and spring quarters.

Designed to prepare a seasonal park ranger to perform law enforcement in areas administered by the National Park Service, program graduates are eligible to receive a Level II law enforcement commission. The commission enables rangers to carry firearms and perform such duties as make arrests, investigate motor vehicle accidents (excluding facilities), take initial reports on felonies and fatalities, and assist in follow-up investigations under the supervision and direction of a Level I law enforcement authority.

Employment opportunities for graduates of the training program are available at one of the more than 300 parks, monuments and other facilities of the National Park Service in the contiguous 48 states, Alaska, Hawaii, Puerto Rico, the Virgin Islands and Guam.

Southwestern Community College is one of approximately 20 colleges nationwide currently offering law enforcement training for seasonal rangers. The instructional format includes lecture, laboratory exercises and practical exercise. Laboratory exercises are non-evaluated training situations in which students practice a law enforcement skill under the guidance of an instructor. A practical exercise is a training/evaluation situation in which students, under the direction of an instructor, participate in a law enforcement related scenario or perform a law enforcement related skill which is graded and must be satisfactorily performed to receive a graduation certificate (i.e., firearms or emergency vehicle operation).

The program consists of 39 topics of study, including constitutional and criminal law, courtroom testimony and procedure, search and seizure, human relations, ethics and conduct, crime scene management, photography, narcotics and dangerous drugs, basic accident investigation, defensive tactics, defensive tactics, firearms training, the history, philosophy and objectives of National Park Service Law Enforcement, and National Park Service Law Enforcement Policies and Guidelines.

Contact:
Susan McCaskill, Director, Continuing Education/Public Safety Training
(704) 369-7331

Southwestern Community College
275 Webster Road
Sylva, NC 28779
Total head count enrollment-Credit: 2,151; Non-Credit: 6,434
Campuses/sites: 3; Faculty: 48

ENGLISH AS A SECOND LANGUAGE

One ESL program is designed for those wanting an American higher education and another for those needing survival skills to function in English-speaking environs

Because all students whose native language is not English are not academically equal, Wake Technical Community College offers two distinct programs through its ESL department.

The first is an intensive English program that meets on the main campus and offers classroom instruction on four levels of proficiency in reading, composition, grammar and conversation. These classes are designed for students who wish to study at the college and university level in the United States. The classes meet the requirements for those students who have a student visa. Tuition for these classes is the same as for any other curriculum class offered at the college.

The second is a competency-based English language program with an emphasis on survival skills and improving a student's ability to function in an English-speaking environment. Classes, offered on beginning, intermediate and advanced levels, are held daily during the week on the main campus, and in church, high schools and other sites throughout the community in the day and evening.

Both programs are supplemented by the campus ESL lab, where there are materials for self-study. These multi-level materials focus on listening comprehension, pronunciation and writing. Students also have access to the Learning Center, which includes a computer lab, a math lab, a writing lab and a reading lab.

The ESL Department also offers a Test of English as a Foreign Language (TOEFL) preparation class through continuing education. This class meets twice a week on the main campus.

Off-campus classes focus on conversational communication skills and are offered on beginning, intermediate and advanced levels of proficiency.

Persons 18 years and older who are non-native speakers of English can enroll in ESL classes. Students must first take an English Proficiency Test to determine appropriate placement.

Contact:
Nancy Blount, Director
(919) 772-0551

Wake Technical Community College
9101 Fayetteville Road
Raleigh, NC 27603
Total head count enrollment-Credit: 12,232; Non-Credit: 27,742
Campuses/sites: 3;Full-time faculty: 205

SCIENTIFIC VISUALIZATION
COMPUTER GRAPHICS TECHNOLOGY

Students in the program learn to transform abstract, numerical concepts and data into concrete images

Wake Tech is offering a new two-year program in Scientific Visualization Computer Graphics Technology. The program is funded in part by a grant from the National Science Foundation. Students learn the process of transforming abstract, numerical concepts and data sets into concrete, multi-dimensional images that give a new perspective and understanding.

Computer graphics, computer art and visualization are an integral part of the curriculum. Graduates find jobs in fields such as aerospace, automotive, computer-aided engineering, film/video animation, robotics and medicine.

Contact:
Martin Clark, Dean, Engineering Technology
Vincent Revels, Vice President for Curriculum Services
(919) 772-0551

Wake Technical Community College
9101 Fayetteville Road
Raleigh, NC 27603
Total head count enrollment-Credit: 12,232; Non-Credit: 27,742
Campuses/sites: 3;Full-time faculty: 205

PROJECT ENABLE

The main goal of the project is to demonstrate an effective approach to meeting the basic workplace needs of employees of small firms

To prepare today's workers for tomorrow's jobs, basic skills training for the workplace is essential. As new technologies change the nature of work and create or alter existing jobs, the unskilled worker will be at a disadvantage. Jobs of the future will require higher and higher levels of skills; employers will find it more and more important to upgrade the skills of their employees if they are to compete in a developing global economy.

Wayne Community College, in response to this challenge, designed an innovative two-year pilot program for delivering workplace basic skills training to small business employees in rural North Carolina. Funded with a $250,000 grant from the R.J. Reynolds Tobacco Company, the college operates a centralized computer-assisted open entry, open exit program supplemented by individualized instruction. In addition, it employs a unique service outreach marketing strategy.

The NC Rural Economic Development Center acts as a fiscal agent and provides general oversight for the project. The Department of Community Colleges provides technical assistance and assists the Rural Center in monitoring the project's activities.

The major goal of the project is to demonstrate an effective approach to meeting the basic workplace needs of employees of small firms. The Workplace Curriculum includes basic academic skills in reading, math and language arts, along with problem-solving, communications, interpersonal skills and career development.

Advisory committees which assist with program deci-

Continues on Page 524

sion-making and evaluation include a local group composed of area small business representatives, and a state committee whose role is project evaluation. Since its inception in March 1991, Project ENABLE has been continuously monitored and evaluated by a Third Party Evaluation Team.

More than 200 small business employees have taken advantage of this program, which is free of charge.

Contact:
Marsellette Morgan, Program Coordinator
(919) 735-5151

Wayne Community College
Caller Box 8002
Goldsboro, NC 27533-8002
Total head count enrollment-Credit: 3,944; Non-Credit: 8,722
Campuses/sites: 3; Full-time faculty: 88

AVIATION MAINTENANCE TRAINING

Training, some of it computer-based, is constantly being upgraded to meet industry demands

Responding to requests from the local Air Force base and aviation-related enterprises, Wayne Community College began the Aviation Technology Program in 1969. The program was designed to answer a local demand for training in airframe and powerplant (A&P) maintenance, leading to Federal Aviation Agency certification of its program graduates. The program was offered in the technical Associate of Applied Science and vocational-diploma curriculums.

The program began with three instructors and a department chairman with a maximum enrollment of 60 students. When it began to produce technically competent and highly motivated "A&P" technicians for the aviation community, students began to come from all over the state, filling to capacity and forcing waiting lists to be formed for the few slots the graduates created. After adding more space and upgraded equipment, the program was authorized by the FAA to expand its enrollment to 100 students in 1988.

With the program at its 100-student capacity, the goals are still the same as when it first began – to produce technicians who will be well-prepared to maintain aircraft that are complex and ever-changing.

Students undergo more than 2,200 contact hours of aviation maintenance training in eight quarters in addition to the required related courses applicable to their program selection.

Training is constantly being upgraded to meet industry demands. Computer-Based Training is being implemented to allow students to interact with the programs and to become comfortable interfacing with a computer which is becoming a common form of troubleshooting on aircraft. Composite technology is replacing older subjects to reflect changing technology of aircraft airframes.

Strict instructor/student ratios and expensive equipment makes this a high cost/FTE program. Only an institution that is committed to offering high quality, and technically challenging programs that offer excellent employment potential for its graduates should undertake this curriculum.

Outside assessment of the program is ongoing by FAA inspections every six months for compliance of regulations and maintenance of training standards. Program assessment through an advisory committee and surveys of graduates and employers aid the department in planning and implementing changes as required.

Contact:
Harry Blanchard, Department Head
(919) 735-5151

Wayne Community College
Caller Box 8002
Goldsboro, NC 27533-8002
Total head count enrollment-Credit: 3,944; Non-Credit: 8,722
Campuses/sites: 3; Full-time faculty: 88

POWER/PROCESS PLANT TECHNOLOGY

Students in the program learn all aspects of the operation of modern, fossil-fueled power plants

A request by the energy industry for trained power plant operators prompted Bismarck State College to initiate a one-of-a-kind Power Plant Technology program in 1976. A similar program in Process Plant Technology began in 1982.

To BSC's knowledge these programs are the only ones of their kind in the country. The programs are becoming well-known in the industry and graduates are in demand, finding employment nationwide. For instance, one year 15 graduates began work at the same time at a power plant in New Hampshire. Placement is almost 100 percent for the approximately 75 graduates each year. The program is constantly at capacity and there is usually a one-year wait for acceptance.

Department Chairperson John Lamontagne receives calls every week from around the nation, requesting interviews with students or asking for help in setting up training programs. Fina Oil in Hot Springs, Texas, recently hired six graduates. Fina Oil has also contracted with BSC to write a three- to four-hour comprehensive exam of the 45-week course for use as a screening device in hiring employees.

The Power Plant Technology program provides students with entry-level job skills to become power plant operators in coal-fired power generating stations and as boiler operators for institutions. Students learn all aspects of the operation of modern, fossil-fueled power plants. Power plant operators are responsible for starting up, operating, repairing and maintaining all equipment used in power plant operations. An advisory committee of industry representatives from a four-state region provided recommendations on the program's goals and curriculum,

and continues to advise the program.

Process Plant Technology students are prepared for employment in coal gasification, and chemical or petro-chemical plants. They learn skills equipping them to work in all sorts of plants that use a distillation process, such as oil refineries, ethanol plants, natural gas plants and fertilizer processing plants.

The two programs are almost identical for 39 of the 45 weeks. Theoretical and practical training in mechanical and chemical technology make it possible for graduates to apply their knowledge to related industrial operations, including water treatment plants, sewage treatment plants, water turbine plants and other large institutions.

A certificate is awarded upon successful completion of the programs. Additional course work may lead to an Associate in Applied Science degree.

Beginning with eight students and two faculty, the programs now enroll 112 students with five faculty. Since the start, more than 600 students have successfully completed the curriculum.

The program began with $20,000, but a similar program is getting started this year with $400,000. Equipment and materials are constantly upgraded to keep the program current.

The Process Plant Technology program was a 1985 national finalist in the U.S. Department of Education Secretary's Award for Outstanding Vocational Education Program in the United States. In 1990, the North Dakota State Board of Vocational Education named the Power Plant advisory board as the Outstanding Advisory Committee of the Year.

Contact:
John Lamontagne, Department Chairperson/Assistant Professor
(701) 224-5489

Bismarck State College
1500 Edwards Avenue
Bismarck, ND 58501
Total headcount enrollment-Credit: 2,472; Non-Credit: 9,100
Campuses/sites: 1; Full-time faculty: 85

BISMARCK STATE COLLEGE

JAZZ CELEBRATION

The primary goal of the celebration is to provide students and the community with an appreciation of live jazz performance

Bismarck State College has sponsored a Jazz Celebration each year since 1974-75, bringing the "cream of the crop" among professional jazz artists to the Bismarck area. What makes BSC's Jazz Celebrations unique is that all-star performing artists come to the campus, whereas most colleges that sponsor jazz festivals bring jazz clinicians to

work with students from several high schools and/or colleges.

Bismarck State College is not aware of another community college in a rural setting that sponsors a jazz celebration similar to this.

Continues on Page 526

The celebration has grown from one guest the first two years (pianist Jaki Byard and trumpeter Clark Terry) to celebrations that feature up to six jazz greats. Byard, a jazz educator, composer and recording artist from the Boston area, has become the "dean" of BSC's Jazz Celebrations through his participation in all except one of these three-to four-day events.

A partial list of other guest artists includes Nat Adderley, Cat Anderson, Gary Burton, Doc Cheatham, Richie Cole, Richard Davis, Alan Dawson, Herb Ellis, Chuck Florence, Dizzy Gillespie, Major Holley, Barney Kessel, James Moody, David "Fathead" Newman, Charli Persip, Butch Thompson, Ernie Wilkins, Joe Williams and Phil Woods.

Several of the artists have performed at more than one BSC Jazz Celebration. Jazz critic Gary Giddins has participated as a lecturer.

The celebrations include a wide range of clinics, lectures and films, but the main emphasis is the presentation of major jazz artists in recitals and concerts. The format also includes performances by some of the visiting artists with BSC's Jazz Band.

In addition to blues singer Joe Williams, other vocal jazz artists have been featured and, in recent years, have conducted clinics for BSC's vocal jazz ensemble.

People of all ages throughout the area have come in contact with these jazz greats through performances at elementary and high schools and at senior citizen centers in Bismarck and neighboring small towns.

The primary goal of the jazz celebrations is to provide our students and community with an appreciation of live jazz performance. A secondary benefit is the cultural diversity the African-American musicians bring to a campus and community whose population is primarily Anglo-Saxon in heritage.

The BSC Jazz Celebration, one of the community's musical highlights of the year, was initiated by Dr. Lloyd Anderson, Vice President of Instruction. He continues to coordinate the celebrations with the assistance of Erv Ely, associate professor of music. Funding has come from a variety of sources, including grants from the National Endowment for the Arts and the Bismarck State College Foundation.

The celebrations have been noted in these well-known jazz publications: *Down Beat*, *Cadence*, *Billboard*, *Gene Lee's Jazzletter*, and Leonard Feather's *Encyclopedia of Jazz in the '70s*.

Contact:
Lloyd Anderson, Vice President, Instruction
(701) 224-5440

Bismarck State College
1500 Edwards Avenue
Bismarck, ND 58501
Total headcount enrollment-Credit: 2,472; Non-Credit: 9,100
Campuses/sites: 1; Full-time faculty: 85

URBAN FORESTRY

Bottineau, located near the forested rolling hills known as the Turtle Mountains, is ideally situated for forestry studies

As cities have become more aware of the "green industry" and general environment needs, the demand for urban foresters has increased. Statements such as the following are typical of the comments received from tree expert companies about the program and North Dakota State University-Bottineau: "I would be willing to enthusiastically support your program as I believe wholeheartedly in what you are doing. The tree industry needs a program such as the one you offer."

Since 1907, NDSU-Bottineau (then called School of Forestry) has been dedicated to educating foresters to care for the region's forests. Over the years the training program has changed to keep pace with industry's needs, and today is responding to the need to train urban foresters.

The current training program produces a forest technician who has a good working and philosophical knowledge of these changes and understands what can be done to help re-balance nature. These will be the field people who can make the administrative decisions work. The instructor responsible for the training is an ISA certified arborist. The curriculum blends urban and traditional forestry into a solid basis for students' success.

Bottineau is ideally situated for forestry studies. The institution is located near the forested rolling hills known as the Turtle Mountains. The North Dakota Forest Service, located on the campus of NDSU-Bottineau, provides an excellent resource for the program. A nursery owned and operated by the Forest Service provides excellent outdoor laboratory opportunities for the students as well as a cooperative learning work site.

The students in the program have received recognition in 1991 and 1992 by the Governor of North Dakota and the Centennial Tree Commission for tree-planting projects they have conducted. People associated with the program have been active in the Society of American foresters. In 1988 and 1989, the North Dakota State Highway Department contracted with this training program to inventory the maintenance requirements of public rest areas along major roadways and to prune and maintain the areas as well.

The objectives of the Urban Forestry training program are to:

1) give a solid foundation of technical courses which provide the student with marketable skills
2) assist the student in adapting to technological changes in the workplace; and
3) provide a course of study which can be articulated into a baccalaureate degree program.

Job placement for the urban forestry student has been enhanced because of federal legislation appropriating funds to cities to support the "green industry."

Contact:
Robert Underwood
(701) 228-5434

North Dakota State University-Bottineau
First and Simrall Boulevard
Bottineau, ND 58318
Total headcount enrollment-Credit: 410
Campuses/sites: 1; Full-time faculty: 21

WILDLIFE MANAGEMENT / PARKS AND RECREATION

Among several courses is one in which students visit a wildlife refuge for hands-on training in such things as food analysis and census-taking

Uniqueness and originality are two trademarks of the North Dakota State University-Bottineau two-year natural resource curriculums. Bottineau is ideally located for natural resource studies near the Turtle Mountains and their recreational areas nestled in forested rolling hills. The J. Clark Salyer Wildlife Refuge, Lake Metigoshe State Park, and many other natural features provide a superb outdoor environmental laboratory.

Several natural resources training courses are available to students who enjoy the outdoors. Students actually look forward to their 5 a.m. field trip to the Wildlife Refuge. There, under the guidance of the instructor, they assist refuge personnel and receive valuable practical training. Classroom, lab and fieldwork are combined to make this one of the finest fish and game management programs in the region. Hands-on training in the areas of specimen preservation, food analysis, waterfowl banding, census-taking and trapping are provided.

Field trips to state and national parks, such as the Theodore Roosevelt National Park and the Lewis and Clark State Park, highlight the parks and technology student training program. Students work in city, state and national park systems or in related recreational areas.

The Associated Press wire service has carried the wildlife portion of the natural resource curriculum in a press feature. The uniqueness of the training involves classroom instruction and practical experience combined to provide students with training relevant to the workplace. The curriculum requirements integrate general education with vocational education competencies to allow the programs to be, in part, transferable. This mixture of course work ensures that the student will possess flexibility, should he or she decide later to pursue a baccalaureate degree.

The objectives of the programs are to:

1) give a solid foundation of technical courses which provide the student with marketable skills
2) assist the student in adapting to technological change in the workplace; and
3) provide a course of study which can be articulated into a baccalaureate degree program.

Documented are 20 years of producing graduates, many who are permanently employed in the field and certified according to the criteria established by the Wildlife Society. The Society, as well as the North Dakota Wildlife Federation, rate the programs as outstanding and provide scholarship support. Five Canadian provinces and 43 states, including Hawaii, have been represented in the Natural Resource programs. The majority of North Dakota Park Managers are graduates from the programs as well.

The instructors are professionals who have been employed with the Texas Game, Fish, and Parks Department; the North Dakota Parks and Recreation Department; the North Dakota Forest Service; and the U.S. Wildlife Service as park rangers, park managers, nursery managers, researchers and consultants. For the past eight years, the wildlife instructor has served as Regional Vice President for the Wildlife Federation.

Contact:
Alan Aufforth, (701) 228-5463
Paula Berg, (701) 228-5470

North Dakota State University-Bottineau
First and Simrall Boulevard
Bottineau, ND 58318
Total headcount enrollment-Credit: 410
Campuses/sites: 1; Full-time faculty: 21

TELEMARKETING OPTION

Training services have been enthusiastically received, fostering a growing commitment to telemarketing, telesales and teleservice

Students in the Telemarketing Trainingprogram at University of North Dakota-Lake Region practice in a 10-station telemarketing laboratory, which creates a business-like atmosphere for learning. This practical experience is one reason graduates are prepared not only to work in telemarketing but also to manage a telemarketing department.

The telemarketing option falls within the two-year AAS-degree Marketing Program. The Telemarketing Training Program serves the needs of campus-based students as well as the needs of diverse constituent groups, including owner/managers of businesses seeking to expand and/or enhance sales and customer service capabilities; telesales representatives and customer service staff working in businesses; and work force training for telemarketing firms.

A unique two-week, on-campus program has also been developed for individuals seeking certification as a Telemarketing Sales Representative. This program was delivered to a class of physically challenged individuals seeking a career option compatible with their disabled condition. As a result, a telemarketing company, Abilities United, has been established in North Dakota employing physically disabled people.

The telemarketing lab is equipped with IBM PC's, networked with Novel, installed with Salemaker Plus Telemarketing Database software, Microsoft Works, Word Perfect and Harvard Graphics. Tape recorders and telephones with five outbound lines complete the lab.

Students begin to develop telephone skills by calling each other. The conversations are recorded, played back and evaluated. As their skills develop, students are introduced to live-work projects. A number of local charities and businesses have contracted with the Telemarketing Program for telemarketing services carried out as live-work exercises by students. At graduation they are prepared to manage or establish a telemarketing department for their employers.

The Marketing Department staff members have "suit-cased" their training services and traveled the state offering workshops for business owner/managers and/or sales staffs. The workshop entitled "Telemarketing Application to Marketing/Management" is designed for business owners/managers and/or interested in expanding their marketing approach to include telemarketing. Another workshop entitled "Training the Telesales Professional" is for individuals seeking to develop skill as a Telephone Sales Representative (TSR).

Several larger businesses have contracted with program staff to provide telemarketing training "customized" to fit their own specific training needs. A two-day workshop has also been developed for businesses seeking to utilize an automated tracking system in their telemarketing efforts. Training on the use of a software system, Salemaker Plus, is provided, along with assistance customizing the database.

A video library has been developed for the department to include the entire Telephone Doctor Series, "90 Telemarketing Skills in 90 Minutes" by Stan Blu and several videos on customer service.

Nadji Teharani, editor of *Telemarketing Magazine*, donated the Telemarketing Magazine periodical series to the library, from the beginning issue published in 1982, along with an index by topic for the series.

Training services have been enthusiastically received, fostering a growing commitment to telemarketing, telesales and teleservice and improving the odds of individual success through the practical, hands-on approach to learning customer service, sales and marketing skills. The results of an informal survey of alumni of UND-Lake Region telemarketing training indicates a growth in sales directly attributable to effectively applied telemarketing.

Contact:
Karen Liere, Instructor-in-Charge
(800) 443-1313

University of North Dakota-Lake Region
1801 College Drive North
Devils Lake, ND 58301
Total headcount enrollment-Credit: 2,011; Non-Credit: 697
Campuses/sites: 2; Full-time faculty: 25

FLIGHT SIMULATOR MAINTENANCE

Many students enter the program with little or no electronics experience, yet graduate with an internship under their belts

As technology has progressed, the lines between what is reality and fantasy have become extremely blurred. Today, technology promotes simulation of our wildest fantasy without the associated hazards. And at University of North Dakota-Lake Region, the fantasy of flight is indulged.

With two A-10 simulators obtained from the military, students are trained in the concept of flight simulation operation and maintenance.

This program, which was started in the fall of 1989, is the only program of its kind in the nation. Prior to UND-Lake Region's entry into flight simulation maintenance training, all training was conducted by the military. Retiring or separating military personnel would then go on to work for the major airlines and other flight simulator users.

Simulation use has increased dramatically due to the degree of sophistication, realism and cost-effectiveness of training. This increased use requires qualified, competent and knowledgeable technicians to service these complicated machines, but the shrinking pool of trained technicians was becoming a cause of concern by simulation users within the simulation defense contract agencies.

UND-Lake Region was asked to consider conducting flight simulation maintenance training and, after much research, began accepting students for training in this specialty.

Students who enter the simulation maintenance program tend to have little or no prior experience in electronics. The program's immediate goals for these students is to teach them basic electronics, then progress onto more advanced electronics, while teaching the concepts of flight and simulation. Students graduate from the program after completing an internship period of two to three months at a simulation site.

Coursework covered in this program equip students to become journey-man/woman level technicians in simulation. In addition, the electronic courses taught here also opens a broad range of other electronic career opportunities.

Feedback from industry has been very positive and supportive of what we are doing here at UND-Lake Region. It is our intent to continue working closely with our industry partners to ensure relevancy and currency of coursework.

Contact:
David Yearwood, Instructor
(800) 443-1313

University of North Dakota-Lake Region
1801 College Drive North
Devils Lake, ND 58301
Total headcount enrollment-Credit: 2,011; Non-Credit: 697
Campuses/sites: 2; Full-time faculty: 25

COOPERATIVE EDUCATION

*By alternating students between the classroom and the work place,
essentially two students are enrolled for every classroom seat*

All of the Cincinnati Technical College's 45 associate degree curricula include alternating terms of cooperative work or clinical practice with academic study – and enjoy a 98 percent placement rate.

CTC was founded on cooperative education, the educational philosophy that combines classroom and laboratory learning with paid related work experience. Because of this, an unusual academic calendar was adopted. Each academic year consists of five 10-week terms. A typical full-time student graduates in two years with an associate degree and nearly one year of work experience.

In 1990-91, CTC had 3,000 co-op student job placements with 600 employers. Students earned $6-million. Students can test their preliminary career choices against the reality of working in the career.

Co-op vastly improves students' prospects for securing jobs after graduation. Co-op enables students to pay for a significant portion of their college expenses through earnings made on the co-op job. Co-op teaches students valuable job search skills. The work component and contributions from co-op earnings are major factors in encouraging first-generation college students to pursue a college degree.

The alternating term co-op program and five-term calendar allows the physical facility to be fully utilized. By alternating students between the classroom and the workplace, essentially two students are enrolled for every classroom seat.

Co-op also is a recruitment and retention tool. Cooperative education builds a strong and positive relationship between the college and the local business community. Co-op graduates are an excellent source for new employees, especially since employers can use on-the-job performance as a basis for selection. Employers have access to a pool of minority workers, important for affirmative action efforts. Hiring co-op graduates is cost-effective in terms of recruitment and training. Research has shown that former co-ops are retained as employees longer.

Contact:
John Wagner
(513) 861-7700

Cincinnati Technical College
3520 Central Parkway
Cincinnati, OH 45223
Total head count enrollment-Credit: 9, 412; Non-Credit: 2,000
Campuses/sites: 1; Full-time faculty: 130

DEVELOPMENTAL EDUCATION

*Students may need from one to five developmental education courses
in language and math skills*

Because two-year colleges are the access institutions to higher education for many Americans, community and technical colleges are facing the challenge of preparing students for college-level studies. At Cincinnati Technical College, nearly 40 percent of entering degree students need some type of developmental education. The developmental education prescription may involve as little as one course to as many as five courses in areas such as reading, math, grammar and writing.

Students in developmental education at CTC are of three types: recent high school graduates who are unprepared for technical coursework, adults who did not take prerequisite coursework in high school, and adults who have not used previously learned skills (such as algebra) in several years.

Readiness for technical coursework is determined during the admissions process through the ASSET test of the American College Testing Service. ASSET test scores are related to skill levels in basic first-term courses in CTC's curricula. Students whose scores show skill levels below those needed to master first-term coursework are referred to academic counselors in each academic division.

Division counselors work with the students to prepare a pre-technical sequence of courses. Some students may require assistance in several areas while others may require help in only one area. Counselors may hold special workshops on study skills or note-taking for their students. They are advocates for the students, help them find assistance if special needs are determined, and monitor progress.

The Developmental Education Department offers the remedial coursework. Classes may be individualized or held in the traditional lecture setting. CTC has a separate developmental education laboratory where students may work in group settings, with tutors, or with adaptive learning environments such as computers, audiotapes, videotapes, etc. Diagnostic techniques are used to measure progress. Competency rates of 80 percent are required before a student may continue on in any area of study.

Contact:
James Marcotte
(513) 569-1618

Cincinnati Technical College
3520 Central Parkway
Cincinnati, OH 45223
Total head count enrollment-Credit: 9, 412; Non-Credit: 2, 000
Campuses/sites: 1; Full-time faculty: 130

COURT REPORTING

Because Court Reporting is a language-based technology, emphasis is placed on English and vocabulary development

Court reporting students train in a mock-courtroom classroom in which computer-integrated systems are available at Clark State Community College, Ohio's first state-assisted institution to offer such a program.

The court reporting courses, first offered in 1971, lead to an Associate Degree in Business. The program earned National Court Reporters' Association (NCRA) approval in 1976 and has maintained this approval continuously. It includes courses in machine shorthand, anatomy and physiology, psychology, office management, law and legal terminology, typing, business communications, and general studies consisting of the humanities and social sciences. Because CRT is a language-based technology, emphasis is placed on English and vocabulary development. To provide students with on-the-job experience, an internship is required.

In 1989 faculty members of the CRT program applied for and won a Program Excellence grant of $150,000. Funds from this grant enabled faculty to design the mock-courtroom classroom with computer-integrated systems. In this state-of-the-art facility, students practice simulated courtroom activities. For example, students record court proceedings on their steno machines which are linked to microcomputers. A software program translates these machine notes into English for display on monitors. These real-time activities give immediate feedback to the student-reporters on their progress. This courtroom setting, coupled with a special computer system, provides special challenges and opportunities to students preparing for the court reporting profession.

In more than two decades, the Court Reporting program has grown and been recognized as a program of excellence. The major facilitation for the program's success was, and continues to be, Kay Frazier, who has nurtured the program from a dream to a reality. Frazier has achieved the status of Certified Reporting Instructor (CRI) and has been invited to sit on the NCRA's Task Force on Student Education Standard, a national committee charged with the task of mapping out a blueprint to implement the long-range plans for the NCRA.

Contact:
Kay Frazier, Business Technologies
(513) 328-6037

Clark State Community College
PO Box 570
Springfield, OH 45501
Total head count enrollment-Credit: 2,859; Non-Credit: 4,674
Campuses/sites: 1; Full-time faculty: 59

STARTING POINT

This welfare-to-work program includes seminars on how to succeed in the classroom and step-by-step assistance in interviewing

The Starting Point program at Clark State Community College offers a comprehensive package of education, social and pre-employment services to help individuals make the transition from welfare to the work force.

The program was established by Title II of the Family Support Act of 1988, through an inter-agency agreement between the Ohio Department of Human Services and the Ohio Board of Regents. Clark State was one of five institutions selected to pilot the JOBS (Jobs Opportunities and

Continues on Page 532

Basic Skills) Student Retention Program. More than 300 students receiving Aid to Families with Dependent Children (AFDC) have been assisted by the program.

Services include: assessment of vocational preference and aptitude; assessment of employability; seminars on how to succeed in the classroom; personal and academic counseling throughout training; step-by-step assistance in resume writing/interviewing skills; and job placement. Interfacing with area social services, employment, and counseling agencies is also handled in the client's best interest. The program's staff prepares the client for education, provides a support system during training, and develops the skills necessary to secure employment after graduation.

Contact:
Kandyce Meo
(513) 328-6024

Clark State Community College
PO Box 570
Springfield, OH 45501
Total head count enrollment-Credit: 2,859; Non-Credit: 4,674
Campuses/sites: 1; Full-time faculty: 59

SITE (STUDENT INFORMATION TERMINALS)

Terminals in six campus buildings provide students with such things as transcripts, schedules and instructors' office hours

Providing students with timely and accurate information is an important retention and student success strategy. With the advent of the information age, more and more information needed by students is stored electronically. For Columbus State Community College students, that information is only a keystroke away.

SITE (Student Information Terminals) affords students access to selected components of their educational record and other college information that is stored on the college's mainframe computer. Through this project, dedicated SITE computer terminals are placed in the lobby areas of six buildings on the campus. Through SITE, students have access to:

1) a transcript of their grades;
2) their schedule of classes;
3) campus phone numbers and office hours for instructors;
4) the degree audit program; and
5) the master schedule of classes, listing seating capacities and course status (open, filled, etc.) along with registration and fee payment deadlines.

To access the SITE program, students enter their personal identification number and date of birth. A number of security safeguards prevent unauthorized release of the student's educational record, including an automatic log-off after 30 seconds without a keyboard response. The program is menu-driven, and users select the information they wish to see.

With one exception, degree audit, students may only view the information that appears on screen. With degree audit, students may elect to see an audit report based on their current major areas of study or engage in "what if?" questioning by entering any one of the college's degree program codes. Degree audit then compares the degree program requirements with the student's transcript and registration files and identifies the extent that degree requirements are met. Students who use the degree audit option may request, via the SITE terminal, a printed copy of the audit report which will be available in the college's records office the following morning. When the student leaves the program, the audit program defaults to the student's declared major; no record can be changed via the SITE program.

Operational since September 1991, SITE is popular with students. Frequently requested services include the grade transcript and Degree Audit programs. Future enhancements may include: a calendar of events; personalized job placement listings; student-to-student E-Mail; and a list of required text books for courses.

The SITE project was developed by a team of students enrolled in the Computer Science program's final project class, a capstone course for computer science majors.

Contact:
Mike Leymaster, Vice President, Student Services
(614) 227-2455

Columbus State Community College
550 East Spring Street
Columbus, OH 43215
Total head count enrollment-Credit: 16,510; Non-Credit: 3,610
Campuses/sites: 5; Full-time faculty: 184

PROCESS FOR VALIDATING A TECHNICAL PROGRAM

▨ Curricula Program validation is a continual process that must include ▨
those responsible for and those affected by the program

Columbus State Community College's Engineering Technologies Division has developed an effective and relatively quick way of externally validating technical program curricula utilizing industry expertise. This process can also be used to develop new programs.

The philosophy that underlies this process is that program validation is a continual process, requires commitment, and must include those persons responsible for the program and those affected by the program.

The process was piloted in the Mechanical Engineering Technology (MET). Since then, it has been employed by other departments in the division. It is currently undergoing minor revision. If possible, department faculty members should be actively involved in all steps of the process. The process consists of:

1) selecting a validation committee; appoint a program advisory committee or ask a currently appointed committee to be involved in the validation process; the committee should comprise industry representatives, who should meet monthly during the process;

2) preparing a program validation survey; collect information to send to industry reviewers; this includes outcomes for the program, general education, and each course (written in competency-based language) and a six-quarter course sequence; respondents are asked to describe these outcomes by marking "agree," "modify," or "delete;"

3) conducting a representative industry survey; respondents receive the survey packet, including a cover letter signed by all of the department's full-time faculty and a general questionnaire about the companies' hiring expectations and future needs; during the brief interview, each company representative is informed of the project's significance and an appointment is scheduled for picking up the survey in two weeks; when the surveys are picked up, faculty members have an opportunity to discuss the program in detail with respondents and to collect as much information as possible;

4) collecting additional information by conducting a DACUM to better define the skills needed by workers of the occupation being reviewed, inviting an external accreditation group to evaluate and provide feedback on program operations (if appropriate) and visiting similar programs at other institutions (if possible); and

5) modifying existing curriculum; all faculty and the department chairperson need to spend uninterrupted time reviewing and discussing the recommended changes and deciding how to implement them; this can best be done in a retreat setting; results should be shared with the program advisory committee; sometimes, only minor modifications are needed; other times, total rethinking of content, how it is taught, what students should be able to do at the end of the program, and how student performance is assessed is required.

Collectively, the industry survey, the DACUM profile and the advisory committee review provide valuable input for curriculum validation and improvement. In order to continually review the program to identify areas needing improvement, the process should be repeated every three years.

Many benefits have resulted from the validation process, including: assurance that all program and course outcomes were written in competency-based language; improvement of teamwork and morale among faculty because they were an integral part of the validation process; confirmation that the curriculum currently in place conformed to regional and industry needs; increased visibility and credibility for the program within the industry; and key companies and individuals who were potential recruiters and program promoters were identified.

Contact:
Engineering Technologies Division
(614) 227-2575

Columbus State Community College
550 East Spring Street
Columbus, OH 43215
Total head count enrollment-Credit: 16,510; Non-Credit: 3,610
Campuses/sites: 5; Full-time faculty: 184

DENTAL HYGIENE

Inner-city residents represent more than 35 percent of the recall patients who visit the college's clinic every two to six month

Cuyahoga Community College dental hygiene students serve more than 4,000 patients annually, including many inner-city resident. This outreach, combined with the most current technological advancements available, gives graduates a bright future in the field.

The program was founded in 1964 as one of the original health career curriculums. Since that time it has graduated more than 800 dental hygienists who have gone on to become licensed dental hygiene professionals.

In 1975, CCC's dental hygiene program initiated 2+2 agreements with area colleges to enable their graduates to obtain a bachelor's degree in allied health sciences, technical education or advanced training in dental hygiene. The transfer agreement with Baldwin Wallace College for a BS in Allied Health Technology has since expanded to include acceptance of technical credits from six additional health career programs at CCC, including Physician's Assistant, Surgeon's Assisting, Respiratory Care, Radiology, Physical Therapist Assisting and Occupational Therapy Assistant programs. This was as a result of the documentation of successful completion of the Baldwin Wallace curriculum by many dental hygiene students. Today, graduates of the Dental Hygiene program can select from the following institutions for degree completion: Baldwin Wallace College, Ohio State University, University of Akron and Lake Erie College. Currently, a career ladder concept within the dental profession is developing with CCC and Case Western Reserve Dental School for an auxiliary to prepare and enter dental school leading to the DDS degree.

Students working in the on-campus dental training laboratory render preventive dental health services, including medical/dental histories, patient education, cleaning and polishing of teeth (oral prophylaxis), radiographs, pit and fissure sealants, amalgam polishing, nutritional counseling within the scope of dental health and fluoride treatments. The cost for adults and children is under $5, with a maximum fee of $15 per family. Inner-city residents represent more than 35 percent of the recall patients who visit the clinic every two to six months.

The dental hygiene program at CCC, anticipating a decline in the demographics of available high-school-aged applicants, set the pace with innovative recruitment strategies. Each phone call or letter requesting information about dental hygiene is handled by the Director of Dental Hygiene and a Health Career Enrollment Center. Interested students are encouraged to schedule an academic advising appointment with a full-time faculty member of the dental hygiene department. The one-on-one session discusses the individual needs of each prospective student, gives them a tour of the facility and allows them to interact with students in the program. Several open house and career days are held each academic year, with specific invitations mailed to area dental assisting programs. A CCC faculty representative also visits vocational high school programs each year to share admission/enrollment details about the dental hygiene program. The dental hygiene student head count has remained at nearly 100 percent or its projected FTE for the past 10 years.

The dental hygiene curriculum has been updated periodically to remain abreast of the technological advancements in the field of dentistry. Specific lecture/laboratory courses have been developed in the basic and dental sciences whereby the lecture provides general content and the laboratory is geared entirely toward the dental or oral application of the material, i.e., microbiology. In addition, lecture manuals have been written by the dental hygiene faculty for each of the dental science courses. An extensive clinic manual and student workbook is currently in its fifth revision since 1967. An infection control handbook, representing all current OSHA standards is utilized and updated quarterly for every student.

Upon completion of the dental hygiene program, the students complete board examinations leading to licensure. The dental hygiene program developed a two-day intensive and comprehensive board review course offered by the continuing education department. This course is held in June each year and enjoys statewide attendance by graduates from the other eight schools of dental hygiene in Ohio. A strong curriculum and clinical preparedness enable CCC dental hygiene students to continue the 98 to 100 percent successful passing record on the Dental Hygiene National Board.

Contact:
Donna M.F. Homenko
(216) 987-4410

Cuyahoga Community College
2900 Community College Avenue
Cleveland, OH 44115
Total head count enrollment-Credit: 24,300; Non-Credit: 5,241
Campuses/sites: 3; Full-time faculty: 381

CUSTOMER SERVICE

The program sensitizes all employees to the needs of external and internal customers through improved communications

The Customer Service program at Edison Community College originated in a desire to re-orient the entire college culture toward the needs of students. The college has had links for years with a Deming user group and saw such a program as an element in total quality management. It also is rooted in the belief that students, co-workers, supervisors and employees are valuable human beings who deserve the best possible service from each one of us.

The goals of the program are to sensitize all employees to the needs of external and internal customers and, through improved communications, better serve all customers.

Customer service training began in 1990 with the purchase of the Noel Levitz program, Connections, designed specifically for support staff in higher education. A staff member led groups of 10 in four sessions spaced over four months, thus giving time for discussion and reinforcement. So much was learned in Connections training about college problems and behaviors that training was extended to supervisors and non-supervising professionals.

The trainer designed customized sessions as well as follow-up training for all of the original Connections participants.

The communications component has been developed through regular meetings of the front-line staff who deal daily with students – people from the bookstore, admissions, faculty support offices, etc. By coming together across unit lines and through having shared communications training in Connections, they increasingly solve their own problems. A *Customer Service Update* is published daily by 9 a.m., informing the college community of meetings, policy and procedure changes and general news. Other communication initiatives include regular student focus groups, graduate interviews and open conversation hours with the dean.

The program is improving service for students but it also is improving efficiency. As people communicate more openly, problems are solved more quickly. Students say the college is friendly, hassle-free and inviting.

Interest in the program has been expressed by several other colleges.

Contact:
Sharon Coady, Dean, Academic and Student Affairs
(513) 778-8600

Edison Community College
1973 Edison Drive
Piqua, OH 45356
Total head count enrollment-Credit: 10,285; Non-Credit: 3,699
Campuses/sites: 2; Full-time faculty: 41

CORE VALUES

Certain core values are integrated into every course, which do not require new staff or any investment beyond normal professional development

In the spring of 1991, the faculty of Edison Community College decided that certain core values were so important to a student's development and education that they should be addressed in every course offered at the college. These values have been validated though a needs assessment of local employers and through the SCANS report for American 2000. The values are: communication skills, both oral and written; critical thinking; cultural diversity; ethics; inquiry/respect for learning; and interpersonal and team skills.

During the following academic year, faculty committees began defining each core value as it would be operationalized at Edison. Several tasks still lie ahead. The faculty are developing suggested strategies for incorporating each core value into different kinds of courses in order to provide guidance to new full-time and adjunct faculty

members. Some strategies will be curriculum-based while many will be instructionally based. The committees also will deal with assessment, since the core values are considered an integral part of general education.

In a student's two-year experience at Edison, the core values will be introduced in first-year general studies and technical courses. Then the skills can be built upon and enhanced as the student advances through his or her two-year transfer or technical degree program. A final assessment, such as a capstone course or a portfolio, will be developed for each program to give students the opportunity to integrate information from their technical and general studies courses and to demonstrate the core values that are fundamental to an Edison graduate.

The program will require considerable thought and

Continues on Page 536

some time as it is implemented over several years. But it does not require new staff or any investment beyond normal professional development. As a new program, it has not yet received outside recognition nor has its impact been determined.

Contact:
Mary O'Neil, Associate Dean, Business and Advanced Technology
(513) 778-8600

Edison Community College
1973 Edison Drive
Piqua, OH 45356
Total head count enrollment-Credit: 10,285; Non-Credit: 3,699
Campuses/sites: 2; Full-time faculty: 41

FIRELANDS COLLEGE-BOWLING GREEN STATE UNIVERSITY

MENTORSHIP WORK / STUDY PROGRAM

The program is not a "quick fix," but a long-term commitment to increasing the number of minority teachers in classrooms

Like school districts across the nation, the Sandusky City School System was experiencing difficulty in recruiting and retaining minority teachers for their classrooms. Time and money was spent traveling to teacher recruitment fairs around the country in order to attract potential candidates for the system, only to see those hired return to their homes after a few years.

Faced with increasing pressure from the minority community of Sandusky to hire more teachers of color, the Sandusky City Schools, the College of Education and Allied Professions at Bowling Green State University, and Firelands College developed a long-term plan to recruit and develop a group of potential students to enroll in teacher education programs. These students would be assisted financially to attend the local branch campus of Bowling Green State University, Firelands College, and then to transfer to the senior institution to complete their education degrees.

This program, hardly the "quick fix" technique employed earlier, strives to support local individuals with the desire to attend a major university in order to become certified to teach in the state of Ohio. It is hoped that since these people are community members in the city of Sandusky, they will be more committed to the city and will teach in Sandusky for a much greater length of time. Coupled with the major goal of merely increasing the number of minority teachers in the Sandusky region, the program seeks to increase the number of recent high school minority graduates (particularly males) who enter teacher education preparation programs.

MIND is a no-frills program which utilizes its funding to directly assist the students with the cost of their tuition. Each student is required to apply for financial aid before receiving grant funding through a local subsidiary of the General Motors Corporation. The cost of administering the program is borne by Firelands College and the Sandusky City Schools, who provide a total of three administrators to oversee the project.

As the program progresses, Firelands College has become the primary agent in the management of the program and development of the private grant funds. The vital contact with Firelands and BGSU students alike is maintained by Firelands College through the Associate Director of Academic Services (who is the academic advisor and program director for the group) and the Director of Enrollment services (who oversees the bursar accounts).

The impact of the MIND program has had far-reaching consequences, not the least of which is the more than 200 percent increase in the minority student population at the Firelands College due to MIND student enrollments. Prior to this program, minority students numbered less than 15 in a student body of approximately 1,200.

MIND students take an active interest in college life and are pleased and proud to participate in events for the college and the community. Examples of this are:
- organization of the spring Gospel festival, 1992;
- presentations to interested new adult students at evening program, "Taking the Next Step;" appearances in the college video and press promotional ads;
- liaison work with area school and community groups to encourage young children to complete their education and go to college;
- representation of student body on committees at the college to plan and promote activities; and
- volunteer work during new student orientation.

Most MIND students are typical returning adults (the average age is approximately 31) with multiple responsibilities. Nearly all work at least part-time and have families to care for. They take school very seriously and are dedicated to their studies. Conversations with them reveal their lifelong goal to continue their education, and the joy and empowerment they feel now as they are finally making progress toward that goal.

The community involvement in the development of the program coupled with the collaboration between the local college and the Sandusky City Schools has created a spirit of cooperation among the participants. The students' loyalty to Firelands College and Sandusky schools is especially heartening as we hope to see positive outcomes in the employment of these students in the area upon the completion of their degree.

The MIND Program received Honorable Mention in

Recognition of Program Development in Teacher Education from the Association of Teacher Educators at their national conference in New Orleans, February 1991.

Contact:
Penny L. Nemitz, Director, Academic Services
Kim Campbell, Associate Director, Academic Services
(419) 433-5560

Firelands College-Bowling Green State University
901 Rye Beach Road
Huron, OH 44839
Total head count enrollment-Credit: 1,405; Non-Credit: 1,183
Campuses/sites: 1; Full-time faculty: 35

FIRELANDS COLLEGE-BOWLING GREEN STATE UNIVERSITY

"DON'T VEG... PRE REG" A RETENTION PROGRAM

The program is promoted via direct mail, posters, faculty announcements, a video urging pre-registration and direct phone calls to students

In the fall of 1988, an enrollment management team was put together to take a hard look at why Firelands College had experienced four straight years of deficits and declining budgets. The initial assumption was that this college was going to have to beef up its promotional activity and otherwise attract greater numbers to campus. Upon analyzing the enrollment data, it became apparent to the team members that retention was an even greater challenge.

A plan of action was formulated by the Academic Services Office which focused on the challenge of getting current students to make a commitment to continue their education at Firelands College. "Don't Veg... Pre-Reg" was an expression thought to be just catchy enough to attract attention and just nebulous enough to get people to wonder what it meant.

Firelands College, like many small campuses, is too small to relegate student retention to something "those people over there do." If the program was to work, it was necessary to mobilize the entire college community. The Director of Academic Services was named coordinator of the student retention effort. From the start, her main job was to gain support of the other administrative offices and, most particularly, the faculty.

The promotional facet of the program included a direct mail campaign, posters, faculty announcements in class about new course offerings, and the development of a promotional video urging students to pre-register for the next semester's classes. The promotional video capitalized upon a closed-circuit television capability that has been developed on campus. Each classroom has a monitor that is controlled through a central office. From 50 minutes past the hour until the professor started class, the promotional video, featuring testimonials by successful students as well as the most respected professors and the dean urging students to make a commitment to continue their education, appeared on the classroom monitor. The repeti-

tion impacted the students while some of the testimonials spurred comments by professors before they started class. This lent credibility to the effort.

In conjunction with the promotional campaign, in-service meetings for faculty academic advisors were conducted. The importance of student retention was stressed as well as the methods for moving students from mere class scheduling to academic program planning. This provided a sense of teamwork on the part of the faculty advisors and allowed the Director of Academic Services to assume a distinct leadership role in the effort.

Another effort that was mounted concerned the use of the college receptionists in the day and in the evening to better communicate with students. Many of the Firelands College students suffer from the "butterfly" syndrome which results in them being oblivious to many types of more traditional student activity promotion. Instead of waiting for phone calls to come into the campus, the receptionists were trained to make outgoing calls to students to remind them of pre-registration dates and to urge their participation. Those students who indicated that they were unsure of their ability or willingness to continue were identified. Those names were given to the Academic Services staff who compiled an advising background on each and then called them to provide suggestions as to how they could best continue their education.

There were also social events scheduling during pre-registration periods to help build an enthusiasm and build a rallying point. The Dean held forums with students aimed at motivating them to peak performance in there upcoming exams as well as plans for the next semester. Enrollment Services (Registration and Financial Aid) and College Relations were all heavily involved in the planning and implementation of the plan to insure that the publicity would be backed up by responsive administrative procedures when a student did decide to pre-register.

Continues on Page 538

The program has been working. In fact, fall to spring retention rates placed Firelands well above the national average for two-year colleges ("National Dropout Rates," ACT National Center for APE 1989).

Benefits to the college include stabilization of financial position, better workload analysis for faculty, positive press coverage, and increase in faculty and staff morale.

The cost for program was relatively minimal: $2,000 for video, equipment, etc., already in place. Posters, flyers and other promotional materials were all done on college's publishing system.

The program won the Noel-Levitz 1990 Retention Excellence Award, with Noel-Levitz stating that this program is a "finesse" retention effort which shows the vital link between course registration and retention. In 1991 ACT/NACADA voted this program the Certificate of Merit in recognition of Innovative and Exemplary Practices in the Academic Advising of Students.

Contact:
Penny L. Nemitz, Director, Academic Services
(419) 433-5560

Firelands College-Bowling Green State University
901 Rye Beach Road
Huron, OH 44839
Total head count enrollment-Credit: 1,405; Non-Credit: 1,183
Campuses/sites: 1; Full-time faculty: 35

DISTANCE LEARNING/INTERACTIVE TELEVISION NETWORK

With ITV, teachers can see the expressions of their students and answer their questions as if they were in the same classroom

A county-wide interactive television (ITV) network, the first ITV system in Ohio to link public schools and a university, was dedicated at Kent Ashtabula in the fall of 1991.

With ITV, smaller, rural schools can offer more courses without incurring additional expense, and students at smaller, rural schools can take language, math and science courses usually only available to larger, urban schools.

The idea for the distance learning system was conceived in 1989, when members of the Civic Development Corporation of Ashtabula County (CDC), superintendents of seven school districts, representatives of the Ashtabula County Joint Vocational School, and administrators of Kent Ashtabula formed an ITV task force.

Following a CDC feasibility study and the unanimous agreement of area school boards and teachers associations, a $1.2-million fundraising campaign began. A CDC fund drive netted $500,000 from excited area residents, businesses and industries. To that amount was added a $250,000 line-item grant from the Ohio General Assembly, and $45,000 from the Martha Holden Jennings Foundation of Cleveland. In addition, a federal Excellence in Education grant, administered by the State Department of Education, awarded $25,000 to each of seven school districts and the vocational school. The $20,000 needed to equip the Kent Ashtabula ITV classroom was supplied by the Ashtabula Area College Committee, Inc.

In May 1990, a 29-member Ashtabula County Interactive Television Network (ACITN) Council was formed, comprising the Ashtabula Campus dean, school superintendents, teachers and representatives of the private sector. An ITV coordinator was hired in October 1990.

ITV classrooms in eight area high schools, the Ashtabula County Joint Vocational School, and Kent Ashtabula are linked by fiber optic cable, which is leased from and maintained by four telephone companies in Ashtabula County. Each of the school districts owns and maintains its own ITV classroom equipment, which includes two sets of three monitors (one set for the instructor to view the students at three off-campus sites, and one set for the students to view each other); an additional monitor for students to view the instructor or demonstration materials; three cameras to transmit the live images to the monitor screens; a VCR; and a fax machine.

Any one of the 10 classrooms can serve as the "originating" site, and can link up with three other sites simultaneously. Persons in all of the four classrooms can see, hear and converse with each other. Consequently, teachers can see the expressions of their students and answer their questions as if they were in the same classroom. Also, instructors can distribute and collect quizzes or exams via the fax machine.

Another capability of the ITV system is broadcasting one-way to all 10 sites at the same time. Kent Ashtabula students are able to enroll in university courses but attend class at ITV classrooms throughout the county. Area teachers, for example, are able to sign up for graduate education courses, but can save driving 20 or 30 miles to the campus by attending the classes in their home school's ITV classroom.Continuing education courses and literacy volunteer training classes are also conducted over ITV.

Plans for additional programming include adult basic education classes, in-service training, community meetings, staff development programs with area industries and special events.

Contact:
John K. Mahan, Dean
(216) 964-4211

Kent State University-Ashtabula Campus
3325 West 13th Street, Ashtabula
OH 44004
Total head count enrollment-Credit: 1,020; Non-Credit: 113
Campuses/sites: 1; Full-time faculty: 30

NURSING

First-year students provide direct patient care such as administering medicine and second-year students provide care to patients with complex needs

Although Nursing students are educated to care for patients of all ages, the projected rise in the elderly population prompted Kent State University-Ashtabula Campus to focus on the older adult patient.

The program, with a 95 percent to 100 percent annual passage rate on the National Council Licensure Examination for registered nurses, enjoys a reputation for excellence. Considered as one program by the National League for Nursing, the Associate of Science Degree in Nursing is conferred at three of Kent's seven regional campuses: Ashtabula, East Liverpool and Tuscarawas.

Reasons identified for the program's outstanding success are:

1) a selective admissions policy which requires applicants to have a high school grade point average of 2.5 or better in 16 units of college preparatory math, sciences and humanities, and a minimum ACT score of 21 or SAT of 900;

2) demanding and caring faculty experienced in nursing and holding masters degrees and above;

3) strong support from a nursing advisory committee, area health care providers and agencies, individual campus deans and the university; and

4) regular follow-up studies of graduates and their employers that provide statistics and information for maintaining program excellence.

The nursing program's curriculum is balanced between nursing courses and liberal education requirements, and totals 70 semester hours of credit. All of the nursing courses include both lecture and clinical experience in hospitals and nursing homes. For example, first-year students provide direct patient care such as administering medicines and giving baths, and second-year students provide nursing care to patients with complex needs.

Another component of each nursing course is computer-assisted instruction (CAI). A 12-station computer lab, staffed with a full-time lab manager, and interactive video programs, which allow students to "participate" in nursing situations and decision-making, provide students with the latest advances in nursing education technology. Fully equipped skills labs, with complete patient bed units and a skills lab instructor, also help the associate degree nursing students to excel in the clinical setting.

Currently, a committee which includes well-known associate degree nursing consultant Verle Waters from California, is working to convert the curriculum from a social/psychological basis to a nursing theorist model. This new curriculum method is based on the nursing theory of Dorothea E. Orem.

The result of the University's efforts is a high demand for Kent's associate degree nurses, who enjoy a 100 percent employment rate.

Contact:
Jeanne Novotny, Program Director
(216) 964-4234

Kent State University-Ashtabula Campus
3325 West 13th Street
Ashtabula,OH 44004
Total head count enrollment-Credit: 1,020; Non-Credit: 113
Campuses/sites: 1; Full-time faculty: 30

BIOMEDICAL ELECTRONICS TECHNOLOGY PROGRAM

Graduates are frequently called upon to share their knowledge and experience as they assist in the training of other health care professionals

The Biomedical Electronics Technology program at Kettering Medical Center works with Kettering's shared clinical engineering service, which helps students and training staff keep up with developments in the field.

The professional services of well-trained Biomedical Electronics Technicians (BMETs) are continually in demand. BMETs have an understanding of the theory of operation, the underlying physiological principles, and the safe practical, clinical application of biomedical equipment. Due to widespread usage and the continual development of new and more complex systems, the BMET is a vital part of the modern medical team. Graduate BMETs are employed in hospitals, shared clinical engineering services, research laboratories, bioequipment industries, and other health care facilities.

The daily activities of BMET graduates as they deal with an extensive variety of biomedical equipment systems typically include: inspection, safety testing, calibration, installation, preventive maintenance modification and repair. They may also be expected to perform in specialized areas such as managing programs of biomedical equipment control or replacement parts inventories, checking on code compliance, and making product evaluations. In addition, they are frequently called upon to share their knowledge and experience as they assist in the training of other health care professionals.

The program is designed to give diligent students the opportunity to gain the necessary knowledge, needed skills practical experience, professional status and confidence they need to function as BMETs. At the conclusion of the program, it is expected that they will be able to successfully complete the written certification examination, find positions as entry-level BMETs, gain the required two years of experience, and be fully certified Biomedical Electronic Technicians. Students are able to get practical experience working with the biomedical electronics systems routinely in use at the Medical Center and other Dayton-area hospitals.

The practicum at the end of the study program provides the students with the opportunity to sample full-time positions in several types of BMET employment situations and allows students to demonstrate their abilities to prospective employers.

The BMET program operates under the college's accreditation by the North Central Association of Colleges and Schools. There is no professional body that accredits BMET programs. The students' professional qualification to work in their field is demonstrated by their certification by the International Certification Commission for Clinical Engineering and Biomedical Technology.

Contact:
David Unger, Chairperson
(513) 296-7201

Kettering College of Medical Arts
3737 Southern Boulevard
Kettering, OH 45429
Total head count enrollment-Credit: 725
Campuses/sites:1; Full-time faculty: 65

PHYSICIAN ASSISTANT

Successful completion of rotations in emergency medicine, pediatrics, surgery, mental health, obstetrics/gynecology, and internal medicine is required

Kettering Medical Center and Kettering College of Medical Arts share a commitment to excellence in patient care and a Christian concern for spiritual as well as physical and mental well being. Coursework and clinical experiences in the Physical Assistant program are designed to support and enhance that commitment.

The Essentials and Guidelines for an Accredited Educational Program for the Physician Assistant defines a physician assistant as a health care provider who "...is academically and clinically prepared to provide health care services with the direction and responsible supervision of a doctor of medicine or osteopathy. The functioning of the physician assistant includes performing diagnostic, therapeutic, preventive and health maintenance services in any setting in which the physician renders care..."

Kettering prepares students to meet those standards through four 16-week semesters and two 10-week summer terms. Patient contact begins in the latter half of the first semester, as students develop skill in taking the medical history and performing the physical examination. Clinical involvement increases steadily as students progress through the program. The second semester of the first year, students spend two full days per week in an office practice. During the second year, they have rotations in a variety of clinical settings, including hospital inpatient services, emergency departments, physician offices, ambulatory care centers, and other kinds of health care facilities.

Successful completion of rotations in emergency medicine, pediatrics, surgery, mental health, obstetrics/gynecology, and internal medicine is required for graduation. Students are introduced to the range of health care services in the community, to prepare them for rapidly expanding employment opportunities for physician assistants.

KCMA physician assistant students complete their preparation with a full-time clinical clerkship during the final 10-week summer term. The department strongly encourages students to divide the experience into two five-week experiences in two different practice settings; one of these must be in family practice, internal medicine, pediatrics, or emergency medicine. This is done to optimize students' preparation for the national certifying examination which is normally taken in October following graduation. Students have responsibility for arranging these clerkships, with the assistance and approval of the department. Many of these experiences lead to employ-ment.

In the interest of student success and well-being, as well as in response to recommendations of the accrediting agency, all student work programs during the academic year must be approved. With department approval, students may be permitted to work up to 10 hours per week. Students are advised that, during the second year, some clinical rotations are likely to conflict with a work schedule. If conflict occurs, the students' responsibility is to the rotations arranged for him/her. During the final summer clerkship, students are not permitted to work.

Each physician assistant student must have dependable transportation for travel to rotation sites. Some sites are more distant than others, with distances as far as 50 miles from the college. When possible, the department tries to arrange sites in the vicinity of students' homes, provided that the clinical experience is not compromised. The clinical coordinator works closely with each student to arrange a mutually satisfactory series of clinical experiences; even so, students must be aware that the wishes of each student cannot be accommodated on all rotations.

Contact:
L. Delyte Morris, Chairperson
(513) 296-7201

Kettering College of Medical Arts
3737 Southern Boulevard
Kettering, OH 45429
Total head count enrollment-Credit: 725
Campuses/sites:1; Full-time faculty: 65

LIMA TECHNICAL COLLEGE

OFFICE ADMINISTRATION: SELF-PACED OPTION

A student may enter a self-paced course at any point and is given one year to complete the work

While other business areas had little difficulty filling evening sections of courses, such sections in the Office Administration program at Lima Technical College were frequently canceled due to insufficient enrollment – until a self-paced option was created.

Self-paced instruction, which continues to evolve, is an alternative to traditional classroom instruction but is not intended to replace it. Each course developed into a self-paced format maintains the same content, evaluation procedures, expected learning outcomes, and credit earned as its traditionally taught counterpart. The only differences are the method of instructional delivery and the time allowed to complete the course.

A handbook is prepared for each self-paced course that directs the student through the course and offers supplementary explanations of text material. Audio-visual and computer-aided materials are also used to enhance the student's learning process. Twenty-five to 35 hours per week are designated as self-paced instructor hours, when a teacher is on duty in the lab. These are the hours during which students may ask for assistance, take exams and turn in assignments. Because the course is self-paced, the student asks for an exam, when he or she feels prepared for it. However, the student may not retake an exam.

A student may enter a self-paced course at any point in time and is given one year from date of registration to complete the work. However, the course handbook provides the student with a schedule of weekly activities that will allow the course to be completed in the regular 10-week quarter. A student must meet all designated prerequisites for each course just as her or his traditional counterpart must.

Students who enroll in a traditional section may transfer to a self-paced section if they so desire. During the quarter of registration, a student in a self-paced section may transfer to a traditional section if one is currently being offered, and the student is at an appropriate point for entry. Students may take one or more courses in the self-paced format at the same time they are taking other courses in the traditional format.

Approval was given to develop the first set of courses

Continues on Page 542

during the summer of 1990, and the first courses were offered during the fall quarter of 1990. A part-time instructor was hired to oversee the self-paced lab during the specified hours. During the second quarter of operation a second part-time person was added. After one year of operation and a better-than-expected response to the program, a full-time faculty position was added to the Office Administration program, with the primary responsibility of the individual to be the teaching and management of the self-paced program. Course registrations in the spring quarter of 1992 reached 73, an increase of 508 percent from the first quarter of the program (fall 1990).

The introduction of the self-paced option for many of the Office Administration courses is clearly meeting a variety of needs of students in the college's service area. Among the reasons students give for signing for one or more self-paced courses are:

1) the flexibility of time that allows them to meet family, job, and personal commitments;
2) the opportunity to work in a non-structured environment;
3) the ability to move at their own pace – faster or slower than in the traditional classroom;
4) the opportunity to begin the program and/or a course during an "off quarter" or at any point in time; and
5) the chance to work with a concept as long as necessary before being evaluated.

Additional courses have been targeted for development into a self-paced format. Eventually, all Office Administration courses will be available in the self-paced format. As the college expands its media development capabilities and use of alternative learning strategies, the self-paced program will evolve to include the utilization of multimedia technology and distance learning.

Contact:
Jane Cape, Coordinator
Lynn Child, Director
(419) 221-1112

Lima Technical College
4240 Campus Drive
Lima, OH 45804
Total head count enrollment-Credit: 2,633; Non-Credit: 422
Campuses/sites: 1; Full-time faculty: 85

LORAIN COUNTY COMMUNITY COLLEGE

LORAIN COUNTY EDUCATION / TRAINING CONSORTIUM

Six consortium partners serve large-scale industrial training needs in the region

The Lorain County Education/Training Consortium (LCE/TC) is a non-profit, self-funded organization serving large-scale industrial training needs in Lorain County and adjacent area. The six partners comprising the consortium are the Lorain County Community College, Lorain County Joint Vocational School, Lorain City Schools, Ohio Industrial Training Program, Private Industry Council and the Ohio Technical Transfer Organization.

The consortium partnership was formed to accomplish training goals that go beyond normal individual institution capabilities. The LCE/TC considers itself to be the "one-stop shop" in technical and non-technical training needs for business and industry.
Specific advantages include:
- complete training services from remediation to high-tech;
- will train on "any shift," on- or off-site
- train-the-trainer and curriculum development services;
- a professional HRD and non-technical training staff;
- training capabilities for all employees, including production workers, apprenticeship craft and maintenance personnel, and supervisory and management;
- all training programs are custom-designed for the client;
- complete assessment services;
- convenience of single-source invoicing; and
- a full-time consortium coordinator maintaining close contact with both clients and training, ensuring efficient and effective quality of services provided.

The consortium has been highly successful in achieving its goals. Currently, it holds ongoing contracts with such companies as Ford Motor, USS/Kobe Steel and York International. LCE/TC continues to strive to improve itself by increased emphasis on collaboration of its members. Growth is assured by continuous examination of market needs and matching those needs to institutional capabilities. Individual partners are now realizing benefits not previously obtained; and the effort of a collaborative partnership has produced the synergy necessary to successfully serve the training needs of business and industry.

Contact:
Robert Grundy, Consortium Coordinator
(216) 365-5222, ext. 7702

Lorain County Community College
1005 North Abbe Road
Elyria, OH 44035
Total head count enrollment-Credit: 8,000; Non-Credit: 6,000
Campuses/sites: 1; Full-time faculty: 114

PUBLIC SERVICE INSTITUTE

The Institute helps bring about positive change in the economic, social an cultural conditions in Lorain County

Lorain County Community College's Public Service Institute (PSI) works with local governments, non-profits and civic leadership in helping to solve community problems.

Created through a collaborative effort by local foundations, assistance includes direct and brokered connections to professional experts, organizing and conducting workshops and seminars, and assisting in the development and marketing of appropriate professional education courses. The Institute was designed as part of a series of efforts to bring about positive change in the economic, social and cultural conditions in Lorain County.

The mission of PSI is to utilize the resources of higher education to:

- assist in the development of a sense of community in Lorain County;
- assist in the enrichment of the experience of serving on non-profit boards;
- assist in the enhancement of the experience of service as a public official;
- assist in improving communication between the public and governmental and non-profit officials;
- assist in making education and training resources available to governmental and non-profit officials;

- assist in providing cross-institutional problem-solving capacity of governments and non-profits; and
- provide access to quality research information.

The Institute pursues its mission in collaboration with a number of other institutions. Foremost among those is the Urban University Program of the Ohio Board of Regents, chiefly the Cleveland State University College of Urban Affairs and the Urban Center at the University of Akron. The Institute has also utilized resources from Kent State, Wright State and Youngstown State universities. Collaboration in providing courses and seminars has chiefly been with Cleveland State University, as has development of public official training programs. Work in developing survey research capacity has chiefly been with the University of Akron.

The Institutes also has worked closely with the Lorain County Chamber of Commerce, the Lorain County Community Foundation, the United Way and other community-wide organizations. Its work has been organized into the following areas: Board Mentoring, Council Mentoring, Policy Research, Crosshairs Targeting Economic Analysis, The Politics of Excellence, Internship Program and Public Service Careers.

Contact:
Daryl Tukufu, Executive Director
(216) 365-5222

Lorain County Community College
1005 North Abbe Road
Elyria, OH 44035
Total head count enrollment-Credit: 8,000; Non-Credit: 6,000
Campuses/sites: 1; Full-time faculty: 114

TRANSFORMATIONS: TRAINING FOR TECHNOLOGY

The program is an effective economic tool that generates a knowledgeable work force at no cost to industry

Transformations: Training for Technology is an innovative program designed and implemented at Lorain County Community College that combines broad-based education with specialized technical skills. This 18-week, 640-hour program offers flexibility in areas of manufacturing as well as other areas of education/training.

Originally designed through a $237,000 grant from the U.S. Department of Education for dislocated (laid-off) workers, industry has become very excited about the

model for upgrading the current work force. The model is customized to meet the skill and competency level required for specific applications, and can be offered for credit, non-credit or combinations of both. This is also a very effective economic development tool, generating a knowledgeable work force at no cost to industry.

The Transformations program takes a holistic approach to education and training, including assessment, counsel-

Continues on Page 544

ing and job placement. Advisory committees are formed from local industry to identify specific job needs in areas of manufacturing, and the model is designed around those

needs. The program, generating 29 to 31 college credits, has a 94 percent job placement rate.

Contact:
Sandra Everett, Technology Project and Training Manager
(216) 365-5222, ext. 7035

Lorain County Community College
1005 North Abbe Road
Elyria, OH 44035
Total head count enrollment-Credit: 8,000; Non-Credit: 6,000
Campuses/sites: 1; Full-time faculty: 114

MUSKINGUM AREA TECHNICAL COLLEGE

KEYS, ACCESS AND TECH LEARNING CENTER

Professional and peer tutoring programs and a lab for a computer-aided instruction
help students reinforce and practice skills presented in class

Muskingum Area Technical College uses an integrated approach to developmental education: Keys, Access and Tech Learning Center (TLC). The philosophy behind MATC's three developmental programs is that underprepared and disadvantaged students need more than academic assistance to become successful college students.

Recognizing the needs of returning adults students, the college used Carl Perkins grants to create the Access Program in 1985. A more comprehensive developmental program, the Tech Learning Center, began with the 1988 receipt of a $500,000 Title III grant. In 1990, due to the implementation of the Ohio Human Services JOBS Program, the college developed the Keys Program with a grant from that agency. Assessment testing indicates that 78 percent of entering students require services from at least one of these programs.

The Keys Program serves Human Services clients who lack the survival skills and social preparation necessary for academic success by providing a bridge to the college's culture. Also a non-quarter based program, Keys uses a workshop and collaborative learning approach. Topics addressed include: expectations of family and friends; stress reduction strategies; time management; budgeting; goal-setting; problem-solving; decision-making; appropriate behavior with instructors; and developing a work ethic. Keys also includes individualized occupational assessment and intervention services which provide referrals to community agencies for child care, counseling or other needs. The goal of the Keys program is provide effective coping and networking strategies to encourage persistence.

The Access Program minimizes institutional barriers for adult students, many of whom are referred to Muskingum Tech via federal job training programs, rehabilitation services, workers' compensation, or human services agencies. To provide flexibility in scheduling, Access enrolls students any time during the quarter and allows them to set their own weekly course schedules. To encourage a sense of control, Access lets students work at their own

pace in a lab setting, with individualized instructor assistance as needed. To alleviate financial hardship, Access waives fees for those students ineligible for financial aid. To assist students with non-academic problems, Access utilizes the services of an intervention aide. The goal of the Access Program is to give returning adult students flexibility as they add "student" to their other life roles.

Research has shown that developmental or remedial services alone are insufficient to ensure student success. Therefore, in addition to offering a curriculum of seven basic skills courses, the TLC includes a significant academic advising component. Professional and peer tutoring programs and a lab for computer-assisted instruction help students reinforce and practice skills presented in the classroom. All of these services, along with the assessment testing program for new students, are coordinated in one location – the Tech Learning Center – improving communication, cooperation and program quality. The goal of the program is to enable students initially identified as underprepared to progress to college-level classes with the personal development and academic skills needed to accomplish their educational goals.

The primary differences in these programs are the delivery systems and domain emphasis. Keys utilizes an open-entry workshop format, Access offers non-quarter-based individualized self-paced learning, and the TLC offers quarter-based classroom instruction. Keys develops affective skills, while the TLC and Access Programs focus on cognitive and academic processes. Students may participate concurrently or sequentially in any of the programs as appropriate. Muskingum Tech is committed to addressing the needs of the whole person by implementing this integrated approach to developmental education.

Indicators of the programs' success include these facts: 25 percent of those recognized at the annual academic honors program started with developmental education, 31 percent of 1992 graduates began their careers in developmental education, and 80 percent to 100 percent of students surveyed over a three-year period were highly satisfied with their developmental classes. These programs, Access, Keys, and TLC, have empowered under-prepared and disadvantaged students.

Contact:
Debra Stockwell, Program Coordinator, (614) 454-2501
Lisa Butler, Cambridge Access/Keys Coordinator, (614) 432-6568

Muskingum Area Technical College
1555 Newark Road
Zanesville, OH 43701
Total head count enrollment-Credit: 2,403
Campus/sites: 2; Full-time faculty: 47

LOCAL EARLY ADMISSION PROGRAM (LEAP)

Allowing high school students to take college courses eases the transition to college work and increases the number of high school graduates who pursue higher education

The primary goal of Northwest Technical College's Local Early Admission Program (LEAP) is to bridge the "leap of faith" between high school and college. Specifically, objectives are to:

1) ease the transition from high school to college work;
2) increase the participation rate of high school graduates who pursue higher education;
3) enhance high school curricula by providing advanced coursework;
4) promote transfer of college credits;
5) acquaint students with costs of higher education; and
6) expand program offerings at Northwest Technical College.

In the beginning, the LEAP coordinator discussed program details with area school superintendents and presented the project to their boards of education. Upon approval of the school board and local superintendent, the LEAP coordinator met with high school guidance counselors to select college courses to be offered and to identify a schedule of class meetings. Building principals were consulted to determine an available classroom. High school juniors or seniors with at least a 3.0 grade point average were allowed to register for the college course.

The primary instructor for LEAP classes is a full-time faculty member of Northwest Technical College who is granted released time to teach at the high school sites. Other faculty are appointed by the college to teach LEAP courses as needed. The LEAP coordinator is also a full-time member of NTC, with released time to facilitate meetings with school boards, superintendents, guidance counselors, students, parents and community leaders.

Costs of personnel to teach and coordinate the LEAP project are funded by NTC. Classroom sites are provided by local high schools. Scholarships are sponsored by local businesses and civic groups to contribute one-half of the student's share of tuition and fees.

The Local Early Admission Program is expanding to additional schools interested in the project. One school was selected for a pilot program in the fall of 1991. Three schools participated during the 1992-93 year and four others are in the planning stages. The LEAP project has received letters of support from school administrators, parents and students.

Contact:
Lawrence J. Zachrich, Coordinator
(419) 267-5511

Northwest Technical College
Box 246-A, 22-600 State Road 34
Archbold, OH 43502
Total head count enrollment-Credit: 1,833; Non-Credit: 1,162
Campuses/sites: 1; Full-time faculty: 39

COMPUTER PROGRAMMING TECHNOLOGY

⊠ The Novell Network was established in an open lab for use by all students using ⊠ application software in support of the courses and all degree programs

When faced with a growing problem of maintaining computers and software for use by students, staff and faculty, Northwest Technical College developed the Novell Networking Project, designed to:

1) provide for consistency of computer software on a college-wide basis;
2) improve the control of log in and access to computer software on a college-wide basis;
3) increase the usage of computer systems in support of coursework and programs;
4) expand the technical capabilities of microcomputing on a college-wide basis;
5) create a new degree program with external certification and recognition;
6) improve administrative control and maintenance of software on a college-wide basis; and
7) create a computer network using a recognized software vendor.

The existing Computer Programming Associate Degree Program is oriented toward the minicomputer or mainframe computer environment. The microcomputer has evolved at a rapid pace, forcing existing technical programs to expand to include course opportunities and options using microcomputers.

In the spring of 1990, Northwest Technical College made a decision to acquire the hardware and software to establish a computer network. The sharing of common resources including hardware, software and data is possible through the use of networking software. Using $30,000 from Academic Challenge Grant Funds established by the Ohio Board of Regents, a $15,000 Grant from the Small Business Development Center, and a $5,000 Grant from Novell Inc. of Provo, Utah, a network consisting of 16 NEC computer workstations using the Novell Network Software was established. The Novell Network selected would allow for expansion up to 255 workstations, which would accommodate the demand by students, faculty and staff. The Novell Network was established in an open lab for the use by all students using application software in support of the courses and all degree programs.

In 1991, an additional 16 CBS computers were added to the existing Novell Network. The initial installation of hardware and software was completed by a third-party vendor.

The need for Computer Networking or Communications courses had been discussed for several years by our Computer Programming Advisory Committee and it became apparent that internally the college needed a trained expert to help manage the new system. The process of providing one employee with the required training to manage the Novell Network gave rise to the Novell Networking Technology Degree Program. Novell Inc. has approved Northwest Technical College as a certified Novell Education Center authorized to offer the Novell Technical Education Courses which lead to CNE (Certified Network Engineer) designation. Upon completion of coursework students may sit for an examination that, if passed, will receive the status of CNE. The Novell Training referred to is available through third party vendors presented in seminar format, ranging from two to five days at daily rates set by the authorized vendor. The 20 days of seminar coursework has been redesigned to fit in a traditional college format and packaged for delivery over three college quarters.

During the summer of 1992, the installation of 17 network communications boards and software for all Business Division Faculty and Faculty Secretary was completed. This actually represents a pilot test phase before expanding access to the entire college. Fall 1992 marked the beginning of yet another phase in the project, which included faculty and staff training and use. During the installation phases the college received from the WordPerfect Corporation a copy of the WordPerfect Office Program to enhance and strengthen the communication process for the network users. The summer expansion also included attaching 24 additional student workstations to the network, bringing the total number of workstations accessing the network to 75.

Contact:
John Richter
(419) 267-5511, ext. 225

Northwest Technical College
Box 246-A, 22-600 State Road 34
Archbold, OH 43502
Total head count enrollment-Credit: 1,833; Non-Credit: 1,162
Campuses/sites: 1; Full-time faculty: 39

FULL-TIME SYNERGISM FOR PART-TIME FACULTY

Major components of the program include assignment, mentoring, orientation, evaluation, professional development and salary upgrades

Recognizing the value added to the institution as well as the crucial staffing needs that are fulfilled by part-time faculty, Sinclair Community College increases their effectiveness by building contacts with full-time faculty, enhancing instructional capabilities and providing professional development.

Some of the components of this effort have been in place for a considerable period – for example, structured mentoring of new part-time faculty was initiated more than 15 years ago. The major responsibility for developing and overseeing the multi-faceted program has been assumed by an all-college committee.

Major components of the program include selection/assignment, mentoring, orientation, evaluation, professional development, and salary upgrade.

Selection/assignment involves departmental screening committees that set desired qualifications and interview candidates for part-time teaching positions. Recommended applicants are placed on the approved list and sent a *Part-Time Faculty Handbook,* developed by the Part-Time Faculty/Mentor Committee of Academic Council. Assignments are made by department chairpersons from this list as scheduling demands.

At the time that a part-time faculty member is assigned to a class for the first time, a full-time colleague is appointed as mentor for the first term of teaching. This formalized program ensures that the neophyte faculty member receives support and assistance during this crucial period and recognizes the contributions of the full-time faculty. Mentors must have completed a video training program and are compensated for this service.

While an in-person orientation was presented for new part-time faculty each term for several years, this crucial component is now handled by means of a campus-produced videotape available in all academic departments.

The flexibility for personal schedules offered by use of the videotape means that required information as well as a welcome from the president of the college are extended to all part-time faculty early in their career with the institution.

Part-time faculty are evaluated by students at least once each academic year using an instrument approved by the particular academic department. Results are reviewed by the chair of the department and discussed with the individual part-time faculty member.

An in-service session designed by the Part-Time Faculty/Mentor Committee to reflect interests of part-time faculty is presented one Saturday each quarter. Campus seminars and departmental meetings are open to part-time faculty as well as materials on topics relating to teaching and learning. These materials are located in the Instructional Resource Center, which houses a significant number of items selected specifically for part-time faculty in addition to videotapes of staff development activities which are offered on-campus throughout the year. Among those most in demand – and yet produced at essentially no cost to the college – are videotapes of the Saturday sessions and other on-campus professional development activities.

Part-time faculty who successfully complete 15 hours of teaching assignments and at least 12 hours of approved professional development activities are eligible for a salary upgrade. Credit for the Saturday seminars as well as for use of materials from the Instructional Resource Center can be applied toward these criteria for progression from Lecturer I at entry to Lecturer II which also includes full-time faculty teaching beyond base contract.

Activities such as these, when packaged in a dynamic program, can provide major benefits at reasonable cost for any institution.

Contact:
Eleanor Young, Assistant to the Vice President for Instruction
(513) 226-2789

Sinclair Community College
444 West Third Street
Dayton, OH 45402
Total head count enrollment-Credit: 20,417; Non-Credit: 2,621
Campuses/sites: 1; Full-time faculty: 325

LIBERAL ARTS AND SCIENCES RESOURCE CENTERS

▦ The centers offer students support in disciplines ranging from English ▦
to Math and Physics and from Psychology to Sociology

In today's society, the ability to work with and utilize technology begins as early as pre-school. As a result of this massive incorporation of computers, it has become essential that colleges and universities prepare all students to use computers. In addition, it is critical that students are also given opportunities to garner enhanced learning experiences outside of the traditional classroom.

The Liberal Arts and Sciences Division at Sinclair Community College has taken a crucial step toward offering today's high technology and enhanced learning experiences to students.

Because the college was required to work within a limited budget, Dr. Clifford V. Barr, Dean of the Liberal Arts and Sciences Division, sought additional ways to support the development of resource centers for the various disciplines in the division. As a result of Dr. Barr's diligent efforts, the state of Ohio awarded the division an academic challenge grant. Through this grant, resource centers were established and initially funded for many of the division's departments including English, Psychology, Math, Physics and Sociology. Three of these resource centers, the Writing Center, The Physics Resource Lab, and the Psychology Demonstration Lab, are truly exemplary in providing students with the "out of classroom experience" so vital for their educational progress.

Operational since 1988, the state-of-the-art Writing Center has provided more than 10,000 students with one-on-one tutorial assistance in writing as well as help or training in word processing and computer operations. The equipment the Writing Center consists of 46 NCR PC810's and 20 Epson dot matrix printers. The Center has a central tutoring area and two large computerized classrooms. While a regular English or Developmental English class is conducted in one classroom, open lab is held for drop-in students in the other classroom. The two word

processing programs used in the Center are PC-Write v3.0 and Norton Textra v2.0. Both are the full version word processing programs which will expose students to applications they are likely to see in the workplace. The result is that while students are learning the fundamentals of English or business communications, they are also acquiring the new skill of personal computer operation.

The Physics Resource Lab (PRL) currently operates as an open laboratory facility for students taking physics courses at Sinclair Community College. The laboratory serves students in four general areas: as a tutoring center; as a location for independent work among students alone or in small groups; as a computer lab where PC's are available for use in data analysis, simulation activities and as "tutors" (tutorial software); and as a facility where laboratory and demonstration equipment is available for student use. The lab is staffed by student workers who have taken the equivalent of a one-year sequence in physics, and by faculty who spend one hour of all three-hour laboratories in the lab.

Since 1985, the Psychology Demonstration Lab (PDL) has served students in Psychology classes in a multitude of ways. Unique in its existence in a two-year college setting, the lab boasts more than 125 demonstrations that provide students with outstanding additional learning opportunity. Each demonstration has an accompanying learning packet where important terms, definitions and directional steps are provided. In addition, the learning objectives each student undergoes are clearly outlined. The demonstrations are divided into three different categories consisting of videos, computers and tabletop. By choosing demonstrations in each area, students can see the world through the eyes of a schizophrenic, analyze classical conditioning or handle human and animal brains.

Contact:
Christina M. Smiley, Manager
(513) 449-5106

Sinclair Community College
444 West Third Street
Dayton, OH 45402
Total head count enrollment-Credit: 20,417; Non-Credit: 2,621
Campuses/sites: 1; Full-time faculty: 325

AUTOMOTIVE ENGINEERING TECHNOLOGY

With an eye on the future, the program already is supplying students with knowledge of federal standards coming down the pike

The Stark Technical College Automotive Engineering Technology program truly has its eye on the future.

The next phase of implementation of the Clean Air Act in 1994 will mandate automotive technician knowledge and job competency levels much above those presently required. Flexible and alternate fuel vehicles (Electric Vehicles - EVs) are scheduled for production in the late 1990's and will require an understanding of new operating principles and new components.

Stark Tech's program will be ready for these and many other changes anticipated in the automotive service and repair industry.

Integral to its readiness is the department's faculty and student involvement in a Solar Car Project which has gained national recognition. STC was one of only two two-year colleges represented in General Motors' Sunrayce '90 in which the Stark Tech team placed 13th (out of 32 colleges and universities nationwide). The student team competed in Sunrayce '93, which ran from Dallas, Texas, to Minneapolis-St. Paul, Minnesota, in June '93, and placed 23rd out of 36 competing colleges. The thousands of hours of research and application of this solar (electrical) information is enabling the department to keep the curricula current with the latest development in the field. It also provides program graduates with hands-on experience with the latest technologies prior to employment. Faculty and students continue to share their newfound information with the community to raise its environmental awareness.

The program's state of excellence can also be attributed to the department's Automotive Resource Center which provides students, graduates and faculty, with the latest equipment and resource materials to facilitate learning. This Center is being utilized by automotive professionals and vocational instructors in the college's service area. Three classroom/labs, an automobile service area, and a fleet of 30 late-model vehicles donated by automobile manufacturers also exist to enhance instruction and learning.

Contact:
Karl Tonhauser
(216) 494-6170

Stark Technical College
6200 Frank Avenue Northwest
Canton, OH 44720
Total head count enrollment-Credit: 4,537; Non-Credit: 569
Campus/sites: 1; Full-time faculty: 97

ACCOUNTING AND FINANCE TECHNOLOGY

Many graduates have passed the CPA exam and many have passed all four parts in one sitting – significant for those with only two years of Accounting education

The core accounting courses at Start Technical College meet or exceed those of most four-year programs and exceed the CPA exam requirement of pre-requisite credit hours, contributing to the 100 percent placement of program graduates.

Keeping up with changes in the field and adequately preparing new entrants into the field is a challenge, but one that is zealously accepted by STC Accounting and Finance faculty, who must keep abreast of new tax legislation, the widespread implementation of microcomputers in business applications and the number of new Financial Accounting Standards Board pronouncements.

The proof is in student and graduate performance. STC sophomore students who take the American Institute of Certified Public Accountants Level II exam consistently score higher than the median score of the test group. Another positive measure of strength occurred in 1988, when students in three STC Principles of Finance classes took a standardized proficiency test developed by the Educational Testing Service. The college's students placed third among participating colleges and universities. Many graduates continue their education to facilitate advancement in their field. To date, a large number of graduates have passed the CPA exam and many have passed all four parts in one sitting – a major accomplishment for someone with only two years of Accounting education! Textbooks used by the program are the same as those used in four-year Accounting programs. The program also offers a wide range of options for students: Corporate, CPA, and Electronic Data Processing.

Students' outstanding academic performance (nearly one-half of program completers are honors graduates) can be partly attributed to the dedicated and competent faculty whose real-world experience is balanced by education qualifications. Of the eight full-time faculty, there are four

Continues on Page 550

CPAs, four master's degrees, and one doctorate. Eleven part-time faculty who are practitioners in the field also enhance the program.

Student enthusiasm for the program is evident by active participation in a student chapter of the Institute of Management Accountants. This chapter has received recognition at national IMA meetings on more than one occasion.

Contact:
William Lucas, Department Head
(216) 494-6170

Stark Technical College
6200 Frank Avenue Northwest
Canton, OH 44720
Total head count enrollment-Credit: 4,537; Non-Credit: 569
Campus/sites: 1; Full-time faculty: 97

UNIVERSITY OF AKRON COMMUNITY AND TECHNICAL COLLEGE

AUTOMOTIVE STUDENT SERVICE EDUCATIONAL TRAINING (ASSET)

This is one of the few ASSET programs in the United States that is operated cooperatively by two separate educational institutions

A joint effort of four organizations, the ASSET (Automotive Student Service Educational Training) is implemented by a year-round calendar of alternating school and work periods.

This flexibility has become crucial in the last decade, when the automobile became extremely complex – and will in the next decade become even more complex. Electronic control of engine functions is now standard and the near future will bring electronic control of many, if not most, vehicle functions. On-the-job training of service people is no longer sufficient. Specific training is now a necessity. The mechanic of past years must yield to a true technician with real technical training, learned through such programs.

ASSET is a joint effort of The University of Akron Community and Technical College, Portage Lakes Career Center, Ford Motor Company, and area Ford and Lincoln-Mercury dealerships. After extensive planning, the program admitted its first class in 1987. The program is one of the more established of the more than 60 ASSET programs in the United States and one of the few which is operated cooperatively by two separate educational institutions.

The purposes of the ASSET program and the roles of the University of Akron Community and Technical College, Portage Lakes Career Center and the individual Ford or Lincoln-Mercury dealership in reaching these goals are:

- The University of Akron Community and Technical College general course content provides the communication, people, decision-making and learning skills which will enable the technician to effectively serve the customer, advance to supervisory roles, and understand the radically new technology which is sure to come. These courses are taught by regular university faculty.
- The technical courses taught by expert and experienced Ford technicians at the Portage Lakes Career Center train students to analytically diagnose, service and maintain Ford Motor products using recommended procedures and specified tools and Ford service information systems.
- The required cooperative employment in a dealership is invaluable in providing the student with real experience in the work ethic, work relationships, customer relations, and, of course, hands-on automotive service.

Under the year-round calendar, the eight-week school sessions have the students attending the university at its main campus in Akron in the morning and the classes at the Portage Lakes Career Center south of Akron in the afternoon. Six of these eight-week school sessions are spread across the fall, spring and summer sessions of two years. During a final "Post Second-Year" session the students finish the last two university courses. The ASSET students are university students in full standing and many of their classes are with other university students.

The technical automotive classes at the Portage Lakes Career Center are held in a large classroom and laboratory facility used only by the ASSET program. The facility and faculty are administered by the Portage Lakes Career Center. The extensive inventory of equipment and tools, more than a dozen new Ford Motor vehicles, many new out-of-vehicle engines, and components are provided by the Ford Motor Company. Ford Motor also provides and updates the extensive service information and training aids. The two faculty members attend numerous Ford service training update sessions.

A careful qualifying process for entering students has resulted in an excellent retention rate (70 percent to 85 percent). Placement testing determines a prospect's potential to do college work and his or her mechanical aptitude. Because employment in a dealership is required for the program, the hiring process is also a qualifier.

The placement rate for graduates has been 100 percent. Actually, the students are placed as they begin the program and most remain with their original dealerships. Participating dealerships have seen the ASSET Program as a means of securing for themselves the technicians needed for the future. Salaries for graduates have been excellent (for the most recent class, a $26,000 average, with a high of $42,000 – especially good for Northeast Ohio!) The

extreme demand for truly qualified automotive technicians should ensure excellent placement for any foreseeable future.

The ASSET program at the University of Akron's Community and Technical College has become quite successful and is attracting better qualified and motivated students each year.

Contact:
M. Pritchard, Associate Dean
(216) 972-7220

University of Akron Community and Technical College
Akron, OH 44325
Total head count enrollment-Credit: 4,065
Campuses/sites: 1; Full-time faculty: 90

UNIVERSITY OF TOLEDO COMMUNITY AND TECHNICAL COLLEGE

DEVELOPMENTAL EDUCATION

A strength of the program is its research base, which includes summative and formative data collection

Graduation rates among developmental students rose from 8 percent to 24 percent over a six-year period of offering strong developmental education at University of Toledo Technical College, validation that the program is meeting its twofold goals:

1) to serve under-prepared students by providing access to a college education, a meaningful curriculum, and services to enhance their preparation; and

2) to support students to the point of graduation.

In order to best accomplish the goal of developmental education, a balanced approach is essential. Today, program components include mandatory placement testing using the ASSET system, identification of students requiring two or more developmental courses as pre-majors (PREM), a dedicated PREM advisor, college-wide mandatory prerequisite courses, a sequential developmental curriculum, and a comprehensive Learning Assistance Center. In addition, DE has served as the provider of workplace literacy programs for the University's business and industry outreach.

The curriculum has been subject to ongoing evaluation and change. A strength of the program is its research base, which includes summative and formative data collection. A curriculum development model designed by an instructor and a former Director of DE espouses a cyclical approach that includes creating a curriculum model basing current literature and pedagogy, assessing the model's effectiveness through collection and analysis of student outcomes, and subsequently adjusting the model. While the approach was initiated for a reading curriculum, it is now used for initiation and revision of all developmental courses.

The Learning Assistance Center (LAC) was created in 1987. During its initial year, 400 tutorial sessions were held

in the LAC. In 1991-92, the LAC had 5,200 visits from 1,090 students for tutoring alone. In addition to tutoring for all levels of reading/study strategies, writing and mathematics courses, the LAC offers tutoring for other courses such as accounting, chemistry, and anatomy and physiology. In addition, the LAC offers Supplemental Instruction (SI) in selected high-risk courses.

An innovative component of the LAC is its program to recruit and train professional retirees from the community to mentor and tutor. Providing Athletes Study Strategies (PASS), an academic support program for student athletes at the university, also is provided as an LAC service.

The best indicator of program success is data as it relates to its goal. In addition to increased graduation rates, the subsequent quarter retention rate of developmental students increased to 80 percent, which is comparable to the retention rates of non-developmental students.

The Developmental Education Program has a budget of approximately $750,000, which is supplemented by several small grants, including an Ohio Department of Education grant and University of Toledo Foundation Program for Excellence grant. Funding for its workplace literacy programs has been supported by federal, state and local sources.

The program has been nationally recognized. Several awards include: The John Champaigne Award for Outstanding Program from the National Association for Developmental Education (1991); the Governor's Workplace Literacy Award (1991); Outstanding Program Award from the Toledo Area Private Industry Council (1991); Outstanding Woman Administrator from The University of Toledo Women's Commission (1992);

Continues on Page 552

Outstanding Administrator from the Ohio Association of Two Year Colleges (1992); and Outstanding Alumna of a Developmental Program from the Ohio Association for Developmental Education (1991). Program leaders are frequently called upon to serve as consultants to other institutions.

Contact:
Jim Gerlach, Director
(419) 537-3126

University of Toledo Community and Technical College
2801 West Bancroft
Toledo, OH 43606-3390
Total head count enrollment-Credit: 4,655
Campuses/sites: 1; Full-time faculty: 87

RESPIRATORY CARE

The Respiratory Care Laboratory is recognized as one of the most comprehensive in the nation

At the University of Toledo Community and Technical College, the Respiratory Care Program's mission is to educate respiratory care practitioners to provide quality care for those afflicted with respiratory disease, ultimately directed at the prevention and control of lung disease.

The program, founded in 1971, has produced more than 600 graduates. It enjoys a 100 percent placement rate of graduates, whose rate of completion of the national credentialing exam exceeds the national average. It was designated as a Program of Excellence recipient of special budgetary support through Academic Challenge Funding by The Board of Regents. The Respiratory Care Laboratory is recognized as one of the most comprehensive in the nation.

The program's faculty members are extensively involved in local, state and national professional activities, including the National Task Force on Professional Direction for Respiratory Care. All faculty are registered respiratory therapists possessing recent clinical experience in critical care respiratory procedures. In addition, program faculty have sponsored and conducted several regional conference including "Enhancement of Clinical Instruction" and "Multi-skilled Health Care Practitioners." Also, the program's highly motivated advisory committee comprises administrative representatives, technical directors and medical directors of local employing hospitals.

The University of Toledo uses several basic criteria for identifying programs of excellence: quality of faculty; quality of program (including facilities); ability of the program to achieve distinction; success of graduates; results of program review and professional accrediting reviews; relationship to the university mission; and service to the community. Measured against these criteria, the Respiratory Care Program has been judged to be exemplary and is a designated Center of Excellence at The University of Toledo.

Contact:
Jerome Sullivan, Chairman, Health and Human Services Department
(419) 537-3314

University of Toledo Community and Technical College
2801 West Bancroft
Toledo, OH 43606-3390
Total head count enrollment-Credit: 4,655
Campuses/sites: 1; Full-time faculty: 87

COLLEGE SCHOLARS PROGRAM

Each Scholar Program student is adopted by someone who contributes at least $600 toward the student's scholarship

The Carl Albert State College Scholars Program, designed to create opportunities for academic and social enrichment, is for students who have demonstrated superior leadership and academic performance.

In December of 1979, the Carl Albert State College Development Foundation was established to secure private funding to build a residence hall for scholars, build an endowment fund for scholarships, and an enrichment program for students and faculty.

By the spring of 1984, the foundation had raised almost $200,000 for the building fund. Bill J. Barber and W.D. Hoffman, Poteau businessmen, each donated $40,000 to the foundation. The first residents moved into the Bill J. Barber residence hall in August of 1985, with the W.D. Hoffman residents moving in after completion in August of 1987.

Funding has been, and continues to be, provided through private contributions from community members, faculty and staff. This fundraising effort is called the Human Endowment Adopt-A-Scholar Program. The goal is to provide a permanent endowment to produce an annual income of $50,000 to totally fund one-half of the housing costs of the scholar center residents.

Each Scholar Program student is adopted by an individual(s) who contributes at least $600 toward the student's scholarship. The Adopt-A-Scholar sponsors are actively involved in the program and cultivate personal relationships with the students.

The Bill J. Barber and W.D. Hoffman residence halls house 76 students, of which 40 are male and 36 female. Each room includes a 12-by-19-foot bedroom and study area; an 8-by-8-foot bathroom with a tub and shower, toilet, and vanity and a 4-by-8-foot walk-in closet.

The Scholar's Program Selection Committee, chaired by the President of CASC, evaluates an objective criteria section of each student's application. Finalists are selected and invited for a two-minute interview with the selection committee. This committee is made up of faculty, staff, foundation trustees and community members. The standard of education is being raised through this innovative program. The quality of students on campus has increased tremendously with the addition of the 76 students living in the residence halls.

Contact:
Lakeita Farmer, Dean of Students
(918) 647-8660

Carl Albert State College
1507 South McKenna
Poteau, OK 74953
Total head count enrollment-Credit: 2,000; Non-Credit: 1,000
Campuses/sites: 3;Full-time faculty: 45

SERVICES TO THE AGING

Graduates are trained for placement in many job settings, including home health, adult day care, nursing homes, private business and housing developments

In 1960, there were only 16.7-million people in the United States 65 years in age or older. This figure had almost doubled in 1990 to 31.5-million; by 2010, it will have doubled once again to 65.6-million. In 1985, Connors State College decided to stay ahead of this trend by implementing a Services to the Aging Program that has proven quite unique in the State of Oklahoma.

With main goals of providing students with the knowledge and experience to work with the elderly population in many settings and to infuse an attitude of respect for all elderly persons by a life span study of development, the program has steadily grown.

Managing to incorporate the Eastern Oklahoma area has opened many avenues. Services to the Aging classes are taught not only in Warner and Muskogee but also in Henryetta, Eufaula and Wagoner – thus offering classes to the north, south and west of the main Warner campus.

The program has grown from its first graduating class of eight in May of 1988 to 15 graduates in 1991.

The program is further enriched by workshops given throughout the year. These are given for college credit, non-credit and for Continuing Education Units. Three of these workshops are given per semester, either exclusively by the Services to the Aging Program or in conjunction with other community agencies such as Eldercare, the local Public Health Office or the Area Agency on Aging.

Involving several communities in the program is an important mission, with recruitment of local students playing an integral part of the overall program. Many of

Continues on Page 554

these students are from the non-traditional class of college freshmen and many begin the program as part-time students.

As our society ages and as the older population grows, continued interest and need for those trained in gerontological services will become more demanding. CSC graduates are trained for placement in many job settings, including: home health, private or employed; adult day care center; nursing home; senior citizen centers, nutrition sites; marketing to the older population; corporations; private business; hospitals; information and referral services; Area Agency on Aging; state and federal positions; housing developments for the elderly; and activity directors.

Many CSC graduates elect to go on to a four-year program and are justly rewarded with even higher paying positions. Connors envisions its Services to the Aging growing in the coming years and its graduates continuing to be in demand for the next decade.

Contact:
Billye Frazier
(918) 463-2931

Connors State College
Route 1, Box 1000
Warner, OK 74469-9700
Total head count enrollment-Credit: 2,400; Non-Credit: 933
Campuses/sites: 2

HIGH SCHOOL OUTREACH: MATHEMATICS AND SCIENCE

Evidence of the success of the outreach is the continuation and expansion of the projects

In 1982 Oklahoma City Community College conducted a pilot program for problem-solving in applied mathematics for high school students. Since then the college has conducted various cooperative projects in applied mathematics and in scientific inquiry skills with high schools in the Oklahoma City area and throughout the state. The projects have grown and currently consist of two summer academies for high school students, two state-wide high school problem solving competitions, and a Summer Teachers Institute.

For the third year, the Oklahoma State Regents of Higher Education have awarded through a competitive process grants funded by the state legislature for summer science and mathematics academies for high school juniors and seniors. OKCCC has been awarded five grants in three years and completed two of these in 1992. Both academies are directed by college faculty and utilize college faculty and staff as facilitators.

The purpose of the Summer Science Academy is to give students the opportunity to develop their abilities to apply scientific principles and the scientific method. The three-week academy involves 40 high school students and six high school teachers who serve as coaches. Hands-on laboratory activities plus field trips form the basis of the academy.

The Summer Math Academy offers three weeks of problem-solving techniques, statistics, computer aided design, report writing, and team dynamics centered around applied mathematics. Six high school teachers serve as coaches for the 42 student participants.

To further the development of problem solving in high schools, two statewide competitions are conducted. Applications in Mathematics for High School Students (AIM-HI) has been conducted since 1987, and in 1991 involved more than 1,000 students and 100 teachers. Applied problem-solving skills in math using real-life problems derived from Oklahoma businesses are the focus of the project. A contest problem from business is developed and materials are produced that enhance team dynamics, report writing and oral presentations. Written materials are dispersed and the on-site problem from a business is taped for airing over OETA-TV. Certificates and scholarships are awarded to students with outstanding performance.

Related to science students is a similar project called Meteorological Applied Problem Solving (MAPS). In its first year, 260 students and 52 teachers participated in the competition. In the past, these projects have been funded by various grants administered by the Oklahoma State Regents for Higher Education or by funds made available through the National Science Foundation. For 1992 AIM-HI will be funded by corporate sponsors from throughout Oklahoma.

All of the above-mentioned projects are primarily for high school students, but teachers also are participants. The feedback from teachers was positive and in 1992, OKCCC applied, and was awarded, a grant from the State Regents to offer a one-week Teachers Institute on applied problem solving. During the week, 24 math teachers and 24 science teachers participated in activities that included applications of mathematical software, field and laboratory experiences, report writing and problem-solving. Each group of teachers worked with applied problems from their own discipline and returned to their home schools with materials applicable to the classroom.

Evidence of the success of OKCCC's math and science high school outreach is the continuation and expansion of the projects. Positive evaluation from participants as well as external reviewers have been received. Faculty have been asked to speak at numerous state, regional and national meetings of professional organizations regarding these outreach projects. In addition an article about AIM-HI was published in a national journal. These successful high school outreach projects serve a need in the math and science community.

Contact:
Ann Ackerman, Dean, Science and Mathematics
(405) 682-7508

Oklahoma City Community College
7777 South May Avenue
Oklahoma City, OK 73159
Total head count enrollment-Credit: 17,129; Non-Credit: 6,912
Campuses/sites: 1;Full-time faculty: 108

OKLAHOMA CITY COMMUNITY COLLEGE

EMERGENCY MEDICAL TECHNOLOGY

The program also serves local EMS agencies, business and industry, and area health care facilities that need specialty courses

Many Emergency Medical Technology (EMT) program graduates are in leadership positions with EMS providers across the state and region, demonstrating the excellent preparation received at Oklahoma City Community College.

The EMT program began in 1972 with the opening of the college. Responding to a need within the community to improve existing pre-hospital emergency medical care, Ms. Dianna Denton, RN – with input from an advisory committee comprising experts in the fields of critical care and emergency services – started the program with approximately 20 students. Since there was no national standard curriculum available in 1972, the advisory committee provided the critical experience and input necessary for the development of the curriculum and its content.

One of approximately 12 programs nationwide to offer paramedic training for college credit in 1972, the program graduated its first paramedic students in 1974 with an Associate in Science-EMT degree.

Today, more than 200 students per semester enroll in EMT courses, with approximately 15 to 20 per semester graduating at the paramedic level. The primary goal of the EMT program is to provide the community with an excellent educational program that prepares Emergency Medical Service (EMS) providers for immediate entry into the workplace.

Graduates provide the needed skills and knowledge necessary for quality intervention and care to the ill or injured within the community, state and region. Additionally, the program serves as a resource where local EMS agencies, business and industry, and area health care facilities are able to access specialty courses meeting their respective needs.

Impacting the local, state and regional EMS community, the program provides three exit levels of EMS proficiency, thus meeting local EMS agencies as well as across the State of Oklahoma. Increasing request for additional EMS providers has resulted in an increase in program offerings to meet the demand. Graduates are recruited locally, statewide, and nationally.

The EMT program takes pride in the fact that besides the many graduates in leadership positions with EMS providers, 18 graduates have either graduated from or are currently enrolled in medical school. The EMT program is approved by the Oklahoma State Regents for Higher Education and the Oklahoma Department of Health-EMS Division. Curriculum content for each level of EMT coursework is congruent with the current national standard criteria of the Department of Transportation and the American Heart Association.

Courses are offered at three immediate job entry license levels: Basic EMT, EMT Intermediate and Paramedic. Certificates of mastery are awarded for each level as well as an Associate in Applied Science Degree at the Paramedic level.

Additional specialty courses are offered to meet EMS provider needs, along with customized training programs delivered on-site at EMS agencies, business and industry, and health care facilities. Utilizing a full-time coordinator who oversees program operations and clinical placements, the EMT program employs three full-time faculty and 16 adjunct faculty. All instructors are licensed at the paramedic level. More than 25 health care agencies are utilized to provide the clinical experiences required at the three educational levels. Adjunct faculty assigned to clinical instruction hold dual licenses as EMS providers and Registered Nurses.

During FY 1993, approximately $9,200 was utilized to fund general direct costs of program operations (not including salaries and benefits).

Achieving a solid reputation within the EMS community, the EMT program faculty are called upon frequently to present in-service lectures and programs for local and statewide agencies/facilities providing emergency services. Faculty routinely serve as consultants and evaluators for simulated disaster exercises, while also serving on statewide committees and task forces to review and develop training protocols for emergency medical services in Oklahoma.

Continues on Page 556

In 1990 the three full-time EMT faculty were given the honor of being the first group to all receive the Oklahoma EMT Association's "Instructor of the Year" award. Additionally, one of the program's adjunct faculty was honored as "Paramedic of the Year." Such recognition of the program faculty reinforces the excellence, quality and commitment to EMS education at Oklahoma City Community College.

Contact:
Richard Anglin, Dean, Health, Social Sciences and Human Services
(405)682-7573

Oklahoma City Community College
7777 South May Avenue
Oklahoma City, OK 73159
Total head count enrollment-Credit: 17,129; Non-Credit: 6,912
Campuses/sites: 1;Full-time faculty: 108

OKLAHOMA STATE UNIVERSITY/OKMULGEE

ENERGY EDUCATION MANAGEMENT PROGRAM

The program helps economically revitalize rural communities and places a positive impact on the environment

The Community Energy Education Management Program for the state's rural communities has potential to cut municipal energy expenses by 20 to 40 percent. This supports one of OSU/Okmulgee's strategic goals to "expand the institution's role in Oklahoma's economic development."

Economic development is sometimes difficult for Oklahoma's rural communities, which each year face increasing pressures that impact their ability to meet economic viability, environmental, energy and resource management. In the past decade energy prices have continued to escalate, impacting Oklahoma communities, their annual budgets, and holding them hostage to the effects of the ever-changing global markets. Many of the communities do not have the technical and/or financial means to provide self-assessment of their infrastructures to meet these increasing pressures of the cost of energy, new environmental regulations, the condition of their facilities, and the state-wide rural economic conditions. One can begin to understand the plight of Oklahoma communities, particularly considering the limited budget and staffing resources available within these small communities.

Help for many comes through the Community Energy Education Management Program (CEEMP), which primarily targets cities with populations of 3,000 to 35,000. It is funded by oil overcharge dollars through the Oklahoma Department of Commerce. Since energy expenditures represent the second largest operating expense of many rural Oklahoma local governments, a vast opportunity for energy saving exists.

The technical assistance program is designed to educate and assist communities in developing and implementing energy usage management strategies to enable future independent monitoring and management of all energy resources. Once a city applies and is accepted for the program, OSU/Okmulgee's assessment team works with individual municipal energy officers appointed by each city to collect and review energy data, evaluate their findings and identify realistic management projects.

The program conclusions identify energy resource management problems, recommend improvement projects based upon return on investment, raise environmental consciousness, educate the community in proper energy management strategies and identify solutions to be implemented in assisting the community to better manage their resources.

An earlier pilot program that included three rural Oklahoma cities, ranging from 14,000 to 45,000 in population, illustrated significant potential for savings, whether low cost/no cost improvements or substantial measures were implemented. The combined projected and actual annual energy savings for those particular cities, as a direct result of the program was $23,600 for one city that had a population of 14,000, $47,725 for a city that had 16,000 people, and $108,084 for the city having a 45,000 population base.

The overall goal of the program is to provide assistance that will economically revitalize rural communities, properly manage resources statewide, place a positive impact on the environment and achieve a sustainable and efficient energy future for Oklahoma communities.

Contact:
Anita Gordy, Director, Technology Resource Center
(918) 756-6211, ext. 204

Oklahoma State University/Okmulgee
1801 East Fourth Street
Okmulgee, OK 74447
Total head count enrollment-Credit: 2,300; Non-Credit: 250
Campuses/sites: 1;Full-time faculty: 136

TEACHING ARTS RESOURCE CENTER

As a result of the Center, cooperative partnerships involving training and production of products have begun

A Computerized Testing Center, a Multimedia Classroom and an Instructional Technology Center created a firm foundation for the infusion of a variety of learning technologies at Oklahoma State University/Okmulgee. But the need for a faculty development center, teaching-learning center, and more networked classrooms and labs prompted a reconceptualization of how to provide facilities and training for learning technologies.

The Teaching Arts Resource Center was born. Its goals include:

1) promoting excellence in teaching and learning;
2) strengthening communication and curricular links among disciplines;
3) improving institutional accessibility and utilization of academic computing; and
4) providing a regional resource for education and industry in multimedia applications.

Faculty seminars, training and customized materials along with a faculty workstation development area help keep faculty up-to-date in learning theory and management methods. Development projects which share technological resources such as laser discs, or common goals such as improved writing skills in common students improve interdisciplinary communication lines among those involved. Future development projects, both individual and institutional (i.e., orientation films, programs, etc.) will continue to foster sharing experience and expertise among faculty.

Spring of 1992 saw three networked, interactive classrooms bridged to the Learning Resource Center network, and a new Skills Center network. The result was improved student access to software available in the classrooms through the LRC and Skills Center. As a computer-intensive campus, courses requiring computer skills have been in place for years; however, all general education courses can now integrate computer information bases into their curriculum without having to install or staff separate labs. As the Skills Center is supplemented and study skills, workplace readiness, conferencing and bulletin board tools are available for integration into any class curriculum, the fusion of technology with the learning process will become more complete.

Thanks to authoring programs, the use of presentation programs, hypermedia tools and multimedia systems for classroom presentation is taking off. Re-purposing multimedia for usage in classrooms away from the Multimedia Classroom or off-campus is a new direction. The ability to create instructional materials that draw on multiple, quality resources has proven to be of great interest to local industry and schools. Cooperative partnerships involving training and production of products has begun and are expected to increase as the Teaching Arts Resource Center continues.

Contact:
Kent Roberson, Teaching Arts Resource Center
(918) 756-6211

Oklahoma State University/Okmulgee
1801 East Fourth Street
Okmulgee, OK 74447
Total head count enrollment-Credit: 2,300; Non-Credit: 250
Campuses/sites: 1;Full-time faculty: 136

ROGERS STATE COLLEGE

UNIVERSITY PREPARATORY ACADEMY

Designed to help under-prepared and at-risk students, the academy offers assessment, development education, ABE/GED classes and a learning lab

The changing demographics of its student body prompted a change in curriculum at Rogers State College, where the average age of students at the college is 29, and most students are women returning to school after an extended absence.

Many are single parent head of households with young children. Approximately 40 percent of students at the college begin their academic careers under-prepared for the rigors of college work and even more lack the confidence necessary to continue and succeed in college.

In 1989 Rogers State College developed the University Preparatory Academy (UPA) to serve its students, but particularly to assist the under-prepared and at-risk students. The purpose of the UPA is to provide under-prepared students from diverse backgrounds the opportunity to build a solid basic skills foundation from which to launch their academic endeavors.

The UPA comprises four major components designed to get students started "on the right foot." The four compo-

Continues on Page 558

nents are:

1) Assessment. The UPA serves as the assessment center for Rogers State College. All students must participate in entry-level assessment for course placement purposes. The positioning of the assessment center within the UPA serves two important functions. The UPA becomes one of the first offices on campus with which students become familiar, and students are immediately informed that help is available in areas in which they might not feel prepared.

2) Developmental education. All developmental studies courses are taught within or coordinated by the UPA. Courses are available in reading, math and English and are designed to give students the foundation needed in college-level courses. Students may enroll in as many developmental courses as needed. Enrollments are generally based upon assessment results, but students may also voluntarily enroll.

3) ABE/GED classes. The ABE/GED program at Rogers State College was one of the first daytime programs in the state. Designed to help the Department of Human Services meet the JOBS program mandates, the ABE/GED classes are open to anyone interested in participating. The 20-hour-per-week program has resulted in a 90 percent GED pass rate and 40 percent of graduates continue at Rogers State College as full-time students.

4) Learning Lab. Recognizing the value of computer-assisted instruction and the need for students to gain confidence with technology, the UPA houses a 26-station computerized learning lab. All students at the college may use the facility for homework assignments, or word processing. All developmental classes and many college-level classes have learning lab requirements imbedded within their course requirements. Software is available for basic skills instruction and supplemental course work at all levels. Students may access software that ranges from addition and subtraction to sophisticated health science and calculus instruction.

Combining all components into one division and location on campus provides Rogers State College the ability to maximize utilization of funds, facilities and staff and gives the student the confidence that they can find various types of help in one place. The design of this type of service has been described often as the "high-tech, one-room school house." The design can easily be replicated at any college with limited funds and facilities.

Contact:
Penny Coggins, Director
(918) 341-7510, ext. 295

Rogers State College
Will Rogers and College Hill
Claremore, OK 74017-2099
Total head count enrollment-Credit: 3,910; Non-Credit: 3,000
Campuses/sites: 3; Full-time faculty: 66

ROGERS STATE COLLEGE

CREATIVE WRITING

Because Americans are losing their eloquence with the language, the program reaffirms the value of each person's unique voice

More and more, individuals are relying on standardized word packages to express their feelings and insights for them. Wal-Mart even features a card section for intimate afterthoughts, disregarding the individual's responsibility and ability to frame personal responses. In other words, Americans are losing their eloquence with the written word and with each other. Countering that trend, the creative writing program at Rogers State College reaffirms the value of each individual by challenging student writers to rediscover their unique voices and by encouraging them to take pride in their own words and their own experiences. For, as Richard Hugo said, "A creative writing class may be one of the last places you can go where your life still matters."

Rogers State College offers three sophomore-level creative writing courses: the basic creative writing course, which focuses on writing as both a practical and a creative art; the advanced creative writing course, which provides an extended support framework for students working on longer projects; and a directed writing course, which is designed to accommodate students who wish to work one-on-one with the instructor/editor/mentor. The college is also developing a television version of the basic writing course for those unable to attend class sessions on campus.

Though the advanced writing courses focus more particularly on developing technical skills and submission techniques, they, along with the basic course, are keyed to four major objectives:

1) to encourage students to communicate clearly with others;

2) to encourage students to think and live creatively;

3) to encourage students to broaden their vision of the world around them; and

4) to encourage students to be their own biographers,

to discover themselves and others through words.

Working toward these objectives, Rogers State College has reached beyond the classroom by developing a weekly radio broadcast, "Writing Out Loud," which features student writers. Beginning in August 1992, the college will also sponsor a television version of that same program. Additionally, the writing program hosts a number of guest professional writers each semester, who visit with students in informal settings. And when possible, the writing courses take field trips to public lectures. One of the most successful outside activities has been the college's annual writers' weekend retreat to Eureka Springs, Arkansas.

Before the writing program was expanded in January 1991, the basic writing course was essentially a fledgling course that was often canceled due to low enrollment. With the additional activities, the course has attracted a variety of students, ranging in age from 17 to 75.

Creative writing continues to grow, not just as a course, but as a program. Not only are two writing courses offered on the main campus each semester; two courses are also offered at an extension site each semester. The program is also reaching to other disciplines. Creative writing is now an elective for broadcasting students and nursing students. The program also works closely with the art department and will be working closely with the computer/advanced technologies department.

Contact:
Teresa Miller, Instructor-in Charge
(918) 341-7510, ext. 343

Rogers State College
Will Rogers and College Hill
Claremore, OK 74017-2099
Total head count enrollment-Credit: 3,910; Non-Credit: 3,000
Campuses/sites: 3; Full-time faculty: 66

LIBRARY TECHNICAL ASSISTANT

This program offers a significant advantage for library personnel who have not had a professional or paraprofessional library science education

Because the staffs of many libraries in rural Oklahoma towns cannot attend classes in person, Rose State College offers courses via television.

The Library Technical Assistance (LTA) Program at Rose State College began in 1977 as a pilot project with HEW Title II-B grant funds. LTA classes have continued to be broadcast live since 1977 from the Rose State campus near Oklahoma City, through the Oklahoma Regents for Higher Education Televised Instruction System to 62 receiving sites throughout the state. This remote broadcasting enables students to receive an LTA certificate or associate of applied science degree without leaving their home towns. This is a significant advantage for the many library personnel who have not had a professional or paraprofessional library science education.

In the spring of 1992, another program innovation was implemented. Lecture material not requiring visual support is now recorded on audio cassette tapes, which are distributed along with other course materials by U.S. mail to remote students. This move was made to reduce the amount of time the students (90 percent of whom are working full time) would be spending in the classroom or receiving site and to allow for offering more than one LTA course per semester.

Six courses comprise the core of the program: LTA 1313 Introduction to Library Resources and Services; LTA 1323 Introduction to Library Technical Services; LTA 1333 Introduction to Audio Visual Equipment and Services; LTA 1343 Automated Library Services; LTA 1302 - Government Publications; and LTA 1312 - Library Services for Children and Young Adults

Other courses, with a heavy liberal arts emphasis, fulfill the general education and program support related requirements for the certificate and associate degree.

The LTA program is supported by members of the Oklahoma Department of Libraries and the Oklahoma Library Association which have both provided student scholarships. Individual libraries have often encouraged their employees to continue their education in the program by providing them with release time and/or by paying their tuition.

In 1992, the LTA certificate and associate degree programs were incorporated in the final draft of the Oklahoma Public Librarian Certification Manual. With this statewide support the LTA program will continue in its primary goal to advance the status of, and provide standardized training for, the paraprofessionals who play a major role in the operation of both rural and metropolitan libraries in Oklahoma.

Contact:
Kay Britton, Program Director
(405) 733-7512

Rose State College
6420 Southeast 15th Street
Midwest City, OK 73110
Total head count enrollment-Credit: 10,000; Non-Credit: 40,000
Campuses/sites: 1; Full-time faculty: 152

THE OKLAHOMA ENVIRONMENTAL TRAINING CENTER

▓ The program is coordinated with state and federal regulatory agencies ▓
in order to remain current with rules and standards

Soon after Congress passed the Clear Water Act in the 1970's, it became apparent that it was critical to educate men and women in the proper operation and maintenance of newly built facilities for cleaning up the nation's streams, lakes and rivers.

In Oklahoma, Rose State College was designated as the site for the "Oklahoma Environmental Training Center," which soon developed an appropriate training program and began holding workshops to help both the municipalities and industry. Shortly thereafter, the college received a grant from the Environmental Protection Agency to buy, renovate and equip a building near the main campus with laboratory facilities and classrooms. Today, the Environmental Training Center has expanded its role in environmental training to include a wide array of educational activities and opportunities.

The Environmental Technology program has expanded over the years. At the present time, the program offers an Associate of Applied Science Degree in either Water/Wastewater Technology, or in Environmental Technology. In addition to the regular semester classes for students working toward a degree, the program offers a series of workshops year-round for individuals wanting to become more proficient with their technical skills in the environmental field.

It is important to note that both the workshops and the degree programs have remained flexible in order to continue meeting the needs of the municipalities and industry. Environmental regulations are constantly changing or being revised. This means the program must be coordinated with state and federal regulatory agencies in order to remain current with the latest rules and standards. A close working relationship has developed between Rose State College, the Oklahoma State Department of Health, and the Environmental Protection Agency. At the same time, the program has provided a bridge between these regulatory agencies, the municipalities and industries being regulated, and other state colleges and universities offering Environmental Training. In a few instances, municipalities on the verge of receiving heavy fines from the state and/or EPA have been given the option of sending their water pollution control facilities operators to Rose State College to receive proper training. This has resulted in a better employee for the city, a plant that is properly operated and maintained, a cleaner environment and a savings of tax dollars to the citizens.

As an example of how well this program has been received, the Environmental Protection Agency, acting through the Oklahoma State Department of Health and the Office of the Governor, recently awarded Rose State College a $250,000 grant to purchase additional equipment for the program. This equipment is being used to train laboratory technicians on state-of-the-art laboratory equipment, develop training packages for self-study classes, and to further facilitate programs in rural areas of the state by providing electronic communication services directly to facilities which could not otherwise receive training information. In addition to this grant, the program has, since 1983, received more than $500,000 in funding from the EPA to provide on-site, "Over-the-Shoulder" training for the state's water pollution control facility operators.

In order to help the greatest number of communities, many innovative teaching methods have been developed. Some of the more repetitious training material (e.g., laboratory procedures) has been placed on video tape. These tapes are sent to the different communities requiring training assistance. When the field trainer arrives, the operators have already received the basics and are ready with questions. Many of the video tapes used were produced in cooperation with students and instructors from other programs on campus, and numerous other subjects and tapes are currently being developed. It is estimated that the Environmental Science program has saved millions of dollars for the industries, institutions and municipalities served through worker training, resulting in improved operation, maintenance and performance of their facilities.

The success of this program can also be measured in terms of improved environmental quality. Of the more than 150 municipalities which have participated in the "Operator Outreach" program from across the state, more than 90 percent have either been brought into compliance with the state's water quality standards or have experienced significant improvement in their operations. In our most recent EPA grant acquisitions, the Training Center has expanded the program to include assistance to several Oklahoma Indian tribes.

Environmental Technology is a very dynamic profession. As it evolves, expertise is required in an increasing number of areas. To meet this demand, the Environmental Technology program at Rose State has integrated other disciplines into a more comprehensive offering to continually meet the needs of municipalities and industry. Workshops and seminars in air quality legislation, water quality rules and regulations, solid waste handling, and hazardous material storage, treatment and disposal have been offered.

Recent trends in environmental awareness have heightened the Training Center's importance both to the community and to the state. As an example, Rose State was selected by both the State Regents for Higher Education and the Environmental Protection Agency to receive a grant for conducting a "Summer Academy for Youth and the Environment." The EPA also recognized the Training Center with an "Environmental Excellence" award for "outstanding service to the environmental profession."

Contact:
Lynn Laws, Environmental Science
(405) 733-7453

Rose State College
6420 Southeast 15th Street
Midwest City, OK 73110
Total head count enrollment-Credit: 10,000; Non-Credit: 40,000
Campuses/sites: 1;Full-time faculty: 152

COMPUTER INTEGRATED MANUFACTURING/ENTERPRISE

The college has a 10,000-square-foot training facility that, among other things, has an automated manufacturing cell on the shop floor

When Tulsa Junior College (TJC) began planning its Computer Integrated Manufacturing/Enterprise program in January 1989, Dr. Dean VanTrease, TJC president, called for a total college commitment to the program. The result: a program that incorporates computer science and engineering curriculum equally with business curriculum to more accurately reflect the integration necessary in industry application.

Computer integrated enterprise is the significant component in TJC's CIM/E Center. While computer integrated manufacturing optimizes individual areas such as technical or marketing, computer integrated enterprise maximizes the business as a whole.

TJC is one of 48 charter institutions chosen by IBM Corporation to form their "CIM in Higher Education Alliance." The result is a 10,000-square-foot training facility which includes an automated manufacturing cell, SMARTCAM, IBM CAD, MAPICS, and Office Vision/400 on the shop floor. The adjacent computer aided drafting, quality control, and business laboratories facilitate business/manufacturing simulations. The center also possesses capabilities to provide the CIM/HE training demonstration.

Both credit courses and non-credit continuing education workshops are scheduled in the CIM/E Center. Faculty develop customized, cost-effective training programs for local, regional, and national companies each semester. The program is evaluated twice yearly by an advisory committee selected from professionals in related fields and by faculty and students.

Contact:
Lonny McDonald, Coordinator/Instructor
(918) 631-7487

Tulsa Junior College
909 South Boston Avenue
Tulsa, OK 74119-2094
Total head count enrollment-Credit: 22,056; Non-Credit: 4,638
Campuses/sites: 3; Full-time faculty: 222

INTERNATIONAL LANGUAGE CENTER

In addition to classroom instruction, the Center acts as a community resource, with a translating service and information on business practices and social mores

To be multilingual in today's world is an asset. In the global world of tomorrow, it may be a necessity. The International Language Center at Tulsa Junior College is a direct response to Tulsa's growing global economy. As Tulsa businesses expand internationally, TJC expands its International Language Center capabilities.

Fourteen international languages are offered at TJC. Created in 1986, the International Language Center is designed to equip students to speak, read and write the target language effectively, interact comfortably with members of that society, be sensitive to both cultural differences and similarities, and work productively in a country of that culture group. Annual enrollments have increased from 300 in 1984, to 3,000 in 1992 .

In addition to classroom instruction, the Center acts as a community resource with information on business practices, social mores, governmental structure and translating services provided by faculty members. Other services include data banks with the names of resource people

Continues on Page 562

knowledgeable in economics, finance, trade, marketing, politics, culture and language conditions of various foreign countries; workshops, training seminars and other resources for elementary, middle school, and high school foreign language instructors; information and counseling on foreign language requirements for educational degrees at other institutions; and national and international career options.

Significant features of TJC's International Language Center include:

- a variety of instructional methods, combined with computerized electronic language laboratories on each campus capable of simultaneous instruction in 24 languages;
- a proficiency rating certificate program which assesses an individual's listening, reading, writing, and speaking language abilities;
- corporate and special group classes, intensive short-term classes, telecourses and honors courses, summer institutes, and culture comparison classes; and
- international campus and other opportunities to study abroad.

Contact:
Laura Walker, Director
(918) 631-7851

Tulsa Junior College
909 South Boston Avenue
Tulsa, OK 74119-2094
Total head count enrollment-Credit: 22,056; Non-Credit: 4,638
Campuses/sites: 3; Full-time faculty: 222

ART / HUMANITIES

▩ An art course was taken from the lecture hall ▩
and art studio into the computer lab

Humanities at Blue Mountain focuses on the study of man and culture. The Art Department has developed a three-term sequence of Introduction to Visual Art which fulfills the Humanities requirements for an AA transfer program. In 1989 the Computer Art (ART 106) course, which studies the creative process, was offered.

Although not unique in itself, the course was taken out of the lecture hall and traditional art studio and taught in the computer lab. Students were given basic instruction in a computer paint program, given the opportunity to use their skills in a creative way, and then asked to return to the class with an analysis of how they each had made creative decisions while using the tools. The students were not graded on their art work but on their analysis of the processes they went through while making creative decisions. The course, which reduced the sense of competition, generated a high demand.

Another visual arts course in the sequence, Video Film Making, investigated how people work together creatively. Groups of seven or eight students create a video film and analyze the dynamics of their own and their peers' creative endeavors.

Contact:
Bruce Guiwits, Art Department
(504) 276-1260, ext. 224

Blue Mountain Community College
PO Box 100,
Pendleton, OR 97801
Campuses/sites: 1
Full-time faculty: 75

ELECTRONIC ENGINEERING TECHNOLOGY

▩ Faculty, administration and industry take a team approach ▩
to ensuring program quality

The Electronic Engineering Technology program at Blue Mountain Community College has earned a reputation that is second to none, according to industry and research/development laboratories. The foundation for such success is the faculty's intimate relationship with industry, which enables continuous feedback and solid financial support through equipment donations and scholarships.

The program provides students with an honest evaluation of their career potential thorough grading procedures. Students are prepared technically and professionally and acquainted with the realities of the workplace to ensure a solid foundation for pursuit of a career in the field. The program is committed to providing technically competent, experienced, trustworthy, trainable, responsible technicians who are prepared to fit into their professional group. The key to linking the students and industry is the faculty, who maintain a high level of credibility in the integrity of the program. Furthermore, faculty, administration and industry take a team approach to ensure program quality.

Companies who have hired our graduates are eager to donate equipment to the program and the college. An electronics lab equipped with the latest GPIB computer controlled instrumentation and a networked computer lab serving the entire college were donated as a result of employer satisfaction with our graduates. The industry is enthusiastic about encouraging and supporting student interest in a career in this field.

Contact:
Tom Sutherland, Electronics Engineering Technology
(503) 276-1260, ext. 270

Blue Mountain Community College
PO Box 100
Pendleton, OR 97801
Campuses/sites: 1
Full-time faculty: 75

THE OPPORTUNITY CENTER FOR TEACHING EXCELLENCE

The Center enjoyed extensive faculty participation in its development
as well as input of 'affinity groups'

In 1991, Chemeketa Community College began an instruction revolution supporting:

- radical change in the valuing of teaching and learning college-wide;
- consideration of the emerging teaching and learning values in all aspects of planning and college operation;
- commitment on the part of instructors, instructional managers and instructional support staff to support these values and to make them "happen" in the classroom;
- empowerment to challenge institutional barriers to teaching and learning;
- empowerment to create opportunities that support excellence in instruction; and
- emotional, personal and financial support for innovation in teaching.

To that end, the Opportunity Center for Teaching Excellence was developed in an extensive grass roots campaign. Its mission has been to advance and celebrate the art of teaching and learning campus-wide. "Centers" focused on teaching and learning are emerging across the country in an effort to deal with problems of revitalizing instruction and faculty development at the community college level. What distinguishes the Opportunity Center has been the extensive faculty participation in its development, wide use of services within its first two years of existence, the varied efforts/products evolving out of Chemeketa's Center such as "affinity groups," dedicated staff training time, LEARN system database, and linked-course implementation, etc., which are primarily supported through the efforts of faculty volunteers.

The Center's credibility has encouraged the use of individual consulting services (more than 342 consultations in 1992 alone) and participation in faculty-generated trainings (more than 112 trainings highlighting faculty expertise and modeling core values of teaching supported by the college). The endorsement of all departments and divisions at the college including the faculty association, and the collaborative partnerships with college committees have strengthened the conversation about teaching and learning.

The Opportunity Center has met the challenge of the instructional revolution and will continue with currently successful services. New experiences acknowledging the need for dialogue and a guided approach to assessing teaching and students' learning to be implemented next year include:

- exploration of Chemeketa's core teaching and learning values;
- support for a new faculty orientation/discussion group;
- implementation of a cooperative group curriculum revision process based on teaching methodology and learning theory;
- support for a critical reflection group discussing teaching as a personal experience;
- encouragement of faculty sharing groups;
- implementation of new faculty evaluation procedures based on core teaching and learning values;
- support of in-depth training experiences; and
- expanded partnership with information technology to support instructional technology needs.

Contact:
Lowell Ford, Dean, Student Services and Extended Learning
(503) 399-5076

Chemeketa Community College
4000 Lancaster Drive NE
Salem, OR 97309
Total head count enrollment-Credit: 19,576; Non-Credit: 21,207
Campuses/sites: 5; Full-time faculty: 239

ENVIRONMENTAL SCAN

Thrice yearly, college officials 'scan' businesses firsthand to see what training
partnership scan be forged between employers and the college

In its traditional form, an environmental scan – which is meant to keep a finger on the pulse of the community – involves reading newspapers and magazines and watching television. Chemeketa Community College has created its own breed of environmental scan by choosing to visit in person those places which may benefit most from what the college has to offer local employers.

Participants include higher-level administrators at the college, including the president and representatives from the five college associations, as well as any other staff member who expresses an interest. The college began conducting scans about four yours ago, and goes on about three scans per year throughout Chemeketa's 2,600-square-mile district. The only costs involved are van transportation and lunch.

Specifically, the scans afford a firsthand look at businesses in the college district and reveal possible training partnerships that could be forged between employers and the college. The visits also illustrate the college's attempt to be responsible to the needs of local businesses and promote goodwill between educators and employers.

The scans also help sensitize the college to what business people are thinking and what their perception of the college is. In turn, the college can take the initiative when it comes to delivering services. The scans have resulted in several benefits for Chemeketa, namely that the community has begun to see the college as a prime provider of training that is custom-fit to individual needs. Businesses have learned that the college will develop new classes when needed, and won't force existing classes or training

programs into a particular work environment with a "take-it-or-leave-it" philosophy.

The most significant partnership that has resulted from an environmental scan was one forged between Chemeketa and Cascade Steel Rolling Mills, a steel-producing company in nearby McMinnville.

Administrators heard about the company's need to train employees to run a new high-tech steel melt shop, and the college responded by implementing a custom-designed series of classes that were conducted on-site during hours that were largely determined by the employees. Because of the success of the Cascade program, other companies have approached the college with an interest in specialized training for their employees.

While the particular visit to McMinnville resulted in the Cascade partnership, more often than not the scans serve as one of the most effective ways to touch base informally with the community. In-person visits also provide an opportunity to see Chemeketa graduates "in action" and gather feedback on previous or current training programs.

Contact:
Lowell Ford, Dean, Student Services and Extended Learning
(503) 399-5076

Chemeketa Community College
4000 Lancaster Drive NE
Salem, OR 97309
Total head count enrollment-Credit: 19,576; Non-Credit: 21,207
Campuses/sites: 5; Full-time faculty: 239

CLACKAMAS COMMUNITY COLLEGE

OREGON ADVANCED TECHNOLOGY CENTER

Dislocated workers, women and minorities have been specifically recruited
for the program, a training ground for the screw machine industry

The Oregon advanced Technology Center began as a training ground for screw machine industry companies and has grown into a $1.6-million, 15,500-square-foot facility.

Such growth was made possible through a partnership between the Oregon Precision Metal Fabricators Association (OPMFA), the Cooperative for Manufacturing Excellence (CME) – a group of screw machine industry companies – and Clackamas Community College (CCC). In 1988, the OPMFA and CME equipped the training center with more than $1-million worth of state-of-the-art CNC metal fabrication equipment, while CCC provided curriculum development, program recruitment and the training center itself. The equipment has either been loaned, donated or leased to the center through the associations from suppliers, vendors and manufacturers.

A $300,000 U.S. Department of Education Cooperative Demonstration Program grant in Precision Manufacturing Technology funded the development and piloting of the training programs. Industry representatives were heavily involved in every step of the process, to the point that the instructors hired to teach in the programs came from industry (one a small shop owner and the other an engineer from a local business).

Dislocated workers, women and minorities were recruited for the programs, which had an 80 percent placement rate after the first group graduated. The program continues to enjoy that level of success in job placement.

At the same time that CCC applied for the federal grant, it partnered with four other local community colleges – Chemeketa Community College, Linn-Benton Community College, Mt. Hood Community College, and Portland Community College – to form the Oregon Advanced Technology Consortium (OATC). The consortium received a state grant to fund a network of statewide advanced technology centers, beginning with Clackamas Community College's advanced technology center in Wilsonville.

The consortium's mission is to improve Oregon's competitiveness by assisting manufacturers with the adoption and implementation of state-of-the-market technologies. Since September 1990, the OATC has researched and evaluated the applications of laser-cutting technology on the manufacturing shop floor. This is done mostly through part prototyping for local businesses and collecting data regarding all aspects of production, analyz-

Continues on Page 566

ing the data, and making recommendations. Research is conducted on a 1,000-watt CNC laser-cutting machine loaned to the Center by U.S. Amada, Ltd. This project has been so successful that four Willamette Valley companies, influenced by their access to and experience with the Center facilities, have purchased lasers.

The OATC's success with the partnership has inspired similar ventures. Index Corporation, a German machine tool manufacturer, loaned the OATC a new CNC screw machine worth approximately $400,000. At the end of the academic year, Leupold & Stevens, a local company, will purchase the machine and Index will replace it with their latest technology.

All OATC programs and projects are now housed in the new $1.6-million advanced technology center in Wilsonville, OR, which was dedicated by Governor Barbara Roberts on March 19, 1992. This building is 15,500 square feet and contains a fully equipped computer lab, four classrooms (one which can be divided into two or left as a meeting room large enough to hold 100 people), two manufacturing shop floor spaces, and staff office space.

The Oregon Legislature approved another $800,000 in funding for the OATC for the 91-93 biennium. By January 1, 1992, technical project coordinators were housed on each campus to identify the advanced technology needs of industries in their districts and work toward providing those industries with the opportunity to test and evaluate those technologies. This process occurs through hands-on public demonstrations, workshops, seminars and individual consulting. The work occurring at the other campuses is in accordance with the consortium's long-term goal of enhancing its accessibility to other manufacturing and service industries. Maintaining the alliance between the partners in this effort is the key to developing and conducting successful programs. Support from the manufacturing industry has helped us gain nationwide attention.

Both the precision metal fabrication program and the advanced technology center projects have received local press coverage, nationwide industry press coverage in magazines such as *The Fabricator*, *CNC West*, and *Oregon Business*, and has been featured in the business section of a local television news program.

Contact:
Jeff Molatore, Department Chair
(503) 657-6958, ext. 4610

Clackamas Community College
9600 South Molalla Avenue
Oregon City, OR 97045
Total head count enrollment-Credit: 12,919; Non-Credit: 14,259
Campuses/sites: 3; Full-time faculty: 156

CLACKAMAS COMMUNITY COLLEGE

DRAFTING TECHNOLOGY

Through individualized instruction and attention to industry standards, the program builds skills and work habits students need to become employable

Clackamas Community College started its Drafting Technology program in 1969 and has remained a pioneer ever since.

This program was the first to develop an individualized training system that became known as Individualized Curriculum for Drafting. Also implemented was an open-entry/open-exit enrollment format where nearly every course was offered every term. Students became able to enter and graduate every term.

In recent years, the program has gained world-wide acclaim as a leading Authorized AutoCAD Training Center. Instructors have written several related text books that have become leaders in this technology. One book, *AutoCAD and Its Applications*, is a leading CAD text with both French and German translations.

The drafting department at Clackamas prepares students for jobs in industry. Through individualized instruction and close attention to industrial standards and techniques, the program builds skills, work habits and the thinking ability that students need to become employable. Students may enter any term, and are exposed to a wide range of tech-

nologies. One term of cooperative work experience is included, during which students work to acquire drafting experience.

The OIT Industrial Management Transfer Degree Program is a drafting degree option designed for the student who wants to continue working on an advanced degree. Completion of this option allows the student to enter Oregon Institute of Technology with junior standing in the Industrial Management program.

Computer-aided drafting (CAD) is rapidly becoming the drafting industry standard. Clackamas is a world-wide leader in CAD education, with one of the most comprehensive curricula available, and has been an Authorized AutoCAD Training Center since 1986. Clackamas is also the Authorized AutoCAD Teacher Training site for the State of Oregon, and Authorized Softdesk Training Center for Civil Engineering CAD Software, and an Authorized Training Center for SmartCAM software.

Students who have taken drafting classes at one of the Clackamas County high schools may be eligible for college credit.

Students whose disabilities limit or prevent use of their hands or arms can learn drafting using a voice-activated computer system. This program enables students to use the AutoCAD software by speaking the commands into a headset microphone. This pioneering program allows students to work at their own pace to complete the standard two-year degree program.

AutoCAD Level I, II, III, and 3-D are offered in a distance learning format when students are unable to attend on-campus classes.

Contact:
David Madsen, Department Chair
(503) 657-6958, ext. 2445

Clackamas Community College
9600 South Molalla Avenue
Oregon City, OR 97045
Total head count enrollment-Credit: 12,919; Non-Credit: 14,259
Campuses/sites: 3; Full-time faculty: 156

MARITIME SCIENCES

▓ *The program includes training a network of marine safety instructors* ▓
and teaching personal safety to fishermen

Clatsop Community College has expanded its one-year certificate in Maritime Sciences to address two new special maritime training needs: Marine Safety Training and Radar Observer Training. These are in addition to established classes such as Boat Handling and Vessel Safety, Marine Weather, Tides, Currents, and Waves, and Practical Navigation.

The Marine Safety Program has been developed to train a network of safety instructors and to begin the process of providing ongoing personal safety training and education classes for Oregon fishermen at their home ports. The long-term goal is to reduce the rate of injury, disability, and loss of life and property in the commercial fishing fleet.

The U.S. Coast Guard-approved curriculum meets federal requirements and is coordinated with other agencies active in marine safety. Classes are conducted coast-wide with other community colleges and Sea Grant agencies. Marine Safety classes cover first aid and CPR, preparation for an emergency, cold water near-drowning, hypothermia, cold-water survival skills, sea survival, stability, marine fire fighting and emergency procedures.

These topics can be arranged to meet the needs of specific groups in formats ranging from two days to six days. A five-day course is aimed at certifying commercial fishermen to meet or exceed international maritime organization standards as well as those of the U.S. Marine Safety Advisory Committee. The graduates of this course meet compliance criteria as set forth by the Fishing Vessel Safety Act of 1988, which in part became effective September 15, 1991, and which allows for ongoing legislation.

Other affected groups which can benefit are charter operators and crew; government agencies such as NOAA, USCG, and NMFS; local and state police; fisheries observers; park rangers; lifeguards; and the general public – especially where the CPR, first aid, cold water near-drowning and hypothermia sections are concerned.

The new U.S. Coast Guard-approved Radar Observer Program offers three different courses: five-day original endorsement, three-day re-certification, and one-day re-certification. The five-day original endorsement class is required for mariners who will be operating vessels 200 gross tons or over on an ocean route, or 300 gross tons on any route. The three-day class is designed for individuals who need to renew their endorsement and would like to practice their plotting skill before taking the renewal exam. The one-day re-certification class does not include any instruction or practice time and is limited to the exam only. The one-day re-certification class is recommended only for individuals with recent time on direct plotting radars.

The school operates a state-of-the-art computer simulator which looks like the targets operators see on the ocean. Use of a simulator allows problems to be resolved much more quickly than in actual situations. Instruction in the first two classes includes radar operation, characteristics of radar waves, target identification, plotting and rules of the road for using radar.

Cost of the classes range from $125 to $325, including books and classroom materials. Students must pay at the time of reserving their class seat. The fee is refundable up to 30 days prior to the first class. All classes are guaranteed to be taught regardless of number enrolled.

Contact:
Sharon McConnell, Marine Science Building
(503) 325-7962

Clatsop Community College
1653 Jerome Avenue
Astoria, OR 97103
Total head count enrollment-Credit: 2,756; Non-Credit: 2,817
Campuses/sites: 2; Full-time faculty: 40

NORTH COAST EDUCATIONAL CONSORTIUM / EDUCATION REFORM

The consortium aims to resolve work force problems throughout the region

More than two years ago, Clatsop Community College formed a unique consortium with seven school districts and a job corps to address work force development issues. Additionally, the college was selected as one of Oregon's six Education Reform pilot sites to resolve work force problems.

The North Coast Educational Consortium includes the college, Clatsop Education Service District, and the following school districts; Astoria No. 10, Columbia No. 5J, Jewell No. 8, Rainier No. 13, Seaside No. 10, and Warrenton-Hammond No. 30.

On March 26, 1992, CCC received notification from the Oregon Department of Education that a Workforce 2000-II grant for $190,000 was approved and funded for the consortium. The grant proposal was to develop a "feeder" program to the college with public schools involved in curriculum development. In addition, it would serve as a transition program for those in the work force. The components of the grant are:

1) 2 + 2 Tech Prep Associate Degree, which includes 2 + 2 Integrated Technologies (Tech Ed. Middle School, Community College), and Office Systems Technology (high school, community college). The grant provides coordination, staff development, curriculum development, substitute teacher pay for release time, summer pay, travel and Tech Ed classroom supplies;

2) secondary professional technical equipment, specifically, four Principles of Technology workstations to a local high school and one to the Clatsop ESD Area Center, and four AUTOCAD units at the Area Center;

3) paid internships for technology education (Integrated Technologies), Office Systems Technology, math, science and communications teachers and guidance counselors (internships are at least three weeks but may be longer); and

4) curriculum improvement, specifically coordination, staff development, curriculum development, substitute teacher pay for release time, summer pay travel and evaluation; focus on applied academics (communications, math, science) as related to integrated Technologies and Office System Technology.

The Clatsop College Industrial Technology program is being phased out to be replaced by the Integrated Technologies program. The second year of the Industrial Technology program was offered in 1992-93 to allow students to complete their associate degree program. The first year of the Associate in Applied Sciences in Integrated Technologies degree program began in fall 1992. The second year will be in place by fall 1993.

The Integrated Technologies program prepares students to gain academic and technical knowledge, skills and values required for entry into mid-level professional/technical careers. It is based on hands-on learning and will be designed to help prepare individuals for specific occupations or a range of occupational categories within the area of technology careers. The technology areas covered in the program include industrial designing, communication, computer-aided drafting (CAD), machine tools skills, computer-aided manufacturing (CAM), mechanical drive systems and industrial controls, electrical and electronic systems, and welding and fabrication. Technical courses will be coordinated with other departments to make an interdisciplinary tie with mathematics, science and communications.

Contact:
Cynthia Risan
(503) 325-0910, ext. 2248

Clatsop Community College
1653 Jerome Avenue
Astoria, OR 97103
Total head count enrollment-Credit: 2,756; Non-Credit: 2,817
Campuses/sites: 2; Full-time faculty: 40

COOPERATIVE EDUCATION

The success of the Cooperative Education program can be traced in part to its centralized model under which the program is managed by one administrator

Lane Community College (LCC) recognizes all academic instruction for the student need not take place in a formalized lecture or laboratory setting. Working cooperatively with business and industry, LCC places 2,000 students with more than 800 businesses annually in a formalized learning arrangement between the student, business community and the college. Most student placements are within commuting distance to the college; however, many students are placed at national and international work sites.

Starting with a small vocational grant in 1970, LCC has developed a Cooperative Education program available to all students in its 48 applied technical and 45 liberal art disciplines. Cooperative Education (co-op) is intended to enhance students' on-campus instruction, not duplicate or substitute for it. College statistics show an increased retention rate for co-op students. Students also tend to do better in their classroom studies after they have started a co-op assignment.

Although Cooperative Education is clearly intended to assist student academic success, additional benefits of Cooperative Education are noted by the college: students earn more than $4-million a year in their co-op placements, thus generating an alternative source of financial aid, and 65 percent of the co-op placements result in a permanent job for LCC students.

Once students have selected a major and enrolled in classes, they meet with a Cooperative Education coordinator for career guidance and placement at work sites related to their career objectives. Coordinators are responsible for determining the learning objectives to be accomplished during the placement, visiting students at the work site, evaluating student work, awarding credits and determining student grades.

LCC's Cooperative Education program success can be traced in part to its centralized model where the program is managed under one administrator with centralized record-keeping and support staff. The college has seven full-time and 28 faculty-coordinators. Co-op coordinators are housed and work directly with their academic department, providing department personnel and students with the feeling that the coordinator is "their" coordinator.

Bob Way, an internationally recognized two-year and four-year consultant on Cooperative Education, is chair of The Lane Community College Cooperative Education and president of the National Cooperative Education Association. The LCC Cooperative Education program has been recognized by the U.S. Department of Education and the U.S. Department of Labor as a model program.

Contact:
Bob Way, Department Chair
(503) 726-2203

Lane Community College
4000 East 30th Avenue
Eugene, OR 97405
Total head count enrollment-Credit: 14,522; Non-Credit: 21,829
Campuses/sites: 4; Full-time faculty: 287

GRAPHIC DESIGN

The program includes a mixture of such things as fine arts, internships, computer technology and cooperative institutional projects

As society has moved into the Information Age, the role of graphic designers – those who design and "package" that information for reproduction – has grown in importance. In addition, the recent advent of desktop publishing has created new opportunities and new challenges for this field.

The Art & Applied Design Department of Lane Community College first offered a certificate of completion in Graphic Design in 1981. In 1988 a full-time faculty/coordinator position in Graphic Design was created and filled, and shortly thereafter graphic design was approved as a professional/technical program by the state of Oregon.

The goals of the program are:
1) to prepare students for entry-level positions in graphics communications; and
2) to offer a firm foundation for those students who chose to transfer to a four-year college to continue their education.

The advertising, commercial art, publishing and printing industries are the principal employers, although many public and private organizations employee graphic designers as well.

Continues on Page 570

Although there are a number of graphic design programs at the community college level throughout the country, Lane believes that its mixture of several key components is unique. These include: a foundation in fine arts, requiring four terms of graphic design production, internships, computer technology, real-life projects, an advisory committee and cooperative institutional projects.

Because Lane considers graphic design more than just a trade, students' artistic and creative abilities are encouraged. First-year students are required to take the same basic curriculum as any art major. But to balance the picture, Lane also requires that its students – who will be expect to produce camera-ready art – take four terms of graphic design production, specializing in the technical aspects of the field.

As part of Lane's Cooperative Education Program (the largest of any community college in the U.S.) the graphic design program requires a minimum of six credits of Supervised Field Experience. This encourages students to apply the lessons and skills learned in the classroom in professional situations.

Additionally, in Oregon, where more than 80 percent of the advertised jobs specify computer experience, it is no longer sufficient to have training only in traditional design and production skills. Four years ago, Lane's Art Department joined forces with the Computer Information Technology, Business, and Media Arts & Technology departments to offer a unique, interdisciplinary Introduction to Desktop Publishing course. Since that time, two other computer classes geared specifically to graphic design students have been added to the curriculum. Although these classes are taught on the Macintosh computer, the choice of most design professionals, students are also required to take an introductory course in MicroSoft® DOS, the operating system used by IBM and IBM-compatible computers.

Students are further prepared for the "real world" through real-life projects in the classroom. In Graphic Design Production 3, students spend the entire term on real projects, handling all aspects from client contact to final production. In the Graphic Design sequence, students take on a number of real-life projects during the year, including designing the covers of Lane's four class schedules. As one of their final projects in Graphic Design 3, they each design their own four-color business card and are involved in the process all the way through printing. Also, the lectures of Graphic Design 3 are devoted entirely to the business aspects of graphic design to help prepare students to be more successful as employees, freelancers or business owners.

The graphic design program has strong support from the community and its advisory committee. Among the committee's recommendations that have been implemented are:

1) the creation of an Introduction to Graphic Design career course;
2) a 10-year anniversary exhibit of the work of graduates of the program; and
3) the inclusion of courses in keyboarding, MS DOS, and desktop publishing into the curriculum.

Finally, Lane has worked with the University of Oregon and Oregon State University to bring professional graphic design speakers to the Eugene area. Lane was instrumental in creating an association of Oregon community college graphic design instructors that meets twice a year. Lane is also working with representatives from area high schools to develop 2 + 2 Technical Professional Associate Degree programs.

Although Lane's graphic design program is always seeking to improve itself, it is already recognized by businesses and educational institutions throughout the region. Locally the program has considerable community support and its graduates are often considered better employees than graduates of four year programs. There is such demand for admission to the program each year that almost 50 percent of those who apply must be turned away.

Contact:
Thomas Rubick, Coordinator
(503) 747-4501, ext. 2887

Lane Community College
4000 East 30th Avenue
Eugene, OR 97405
Total head count enrollment-Credit: 14,522; Non-Credit: 21,829
Campuses/sites: 4; Full-time faculty: 287

STEPS TO SUCCESS

*⊠ The program is a partnership of education, industry and social services that assists ⊠
families moving from welfare dependency to economic self-sufficiency*

In March 1988, Mt. Hood Community College began an ambitious endeavor that was destined to change the face of Oregon's welfare system. MHCC was faced with an issue many community colleges share – an influx of "non-traditional" students, many of them single parents with very limited resources. These students face more challenges than the "traditional" college student: child care, low basic skills, housing, family support, self-esteem and lack of work experience.

These issues combined with Workforce 2000 issues crystallized into the development of a program called Steps To Success. Steps To Success is a partnership of education, industry and social services which assists families as they move from welfare dependency to economic self-sufficiency. The partners include: Mt. Hood Community College, Portland Community College, Adult and Family Services Division, The Private Industry Council, The Oregon Employment Division, and Portland Public Schools.

Steps To Success provides a wide range of services which ensure that its students are more successful in school and in the work force. These services include: Comprehensive Skills Assessment, Basic Education and GED Preparation, Career and Life Planning, Vocational Training, Volunteer Work Experience, Job Search and Placement Assistance, and On-The-Job Training. Steps To Success staff provides continuing support and follow-up as students move through the program and into employment.

To help ensure their success while in the program, students continue to receive their welfare benefits, as well as transportation and child care allowances. This allows students to focus their energies on being successful students and workers, and helps keep them from leaving the program due to financial difficulties.

Steps To Success expanded in October 1990 with the implementation of the federal Family Support Act, which mandates that States provide education and training services to welfare recipients. The program is funded through Oregon's Adult and Family Services Division and serves the most populous region of the state of Oregon, including Multnomah and Washington Counties. Steps To Success serves 3,500 participants per year, at an annual budget of approximately $5-million.

Steps To Success has been recognized by the American Association of Women in Community and Junior Colleges and continues to be held up as a model program of collaboration and innovation, particularly as we approach educational reform in Oregon and nation-wide.

Contact:
Nancy Poppa
(503) 667-6422

Mt. Hood Community College
26000 SE Stark Street
Gresham, OR 97030
Total head count enrollment-Credit: 12,228; Non-Credit: 17,404
Campuses/sites: 3; Full-time faculty: 169

REGIONAL COOPERATIVE CONSORTIUM

*⊠ Benchmarks of the consortium include a Vocational Inderdistrict Program, a Health ⊠
Occupations Program and expansion of principles of technology into more schools*

The Mt. Hood Regional Cooperative Consortium has firmly established a strong, effective cooperative relationship between and among the district high schools, Education Service District and Mt. Hood Community College. This cooperative spirit is pervasive at all institutional levels, from faculty members to board members.

Written articulation agreements exist between the college and each of the seven high school or elementary-secondary districts. At the program level, 65 written articulation agreements have been developed by high school and community college faculty, in 13 professional-technical areas ranging from automotive technology to video technology.

The regional consortium members who have been meeting monthly for at least five years have established a very successful Vocational Interdistrict Program (VIP), which expands professional and technical education opportunities for students by opening programs at one school to students at another school on a space-available basis. During a recent year, 114 students participated in the VIP program at no additional cost to the student, the parent or the schools.

Another benchmark which was reached was the successful completion of the first year of a VIP Health Occupations Program, which will more than double in size

Continues on Page 572

and scope during its second year of operation. Other benchmarks and milestones include upgraded electronics, drafting, manufacturing and office occupations programs and expansion of principles of technology into more schools. This improvement and expansion will continue.

Finally, a major milestone was achieved in April 1991, when Mt. Hood Community College was honored as one of the top three community colleges in the nation for Tech Prep by the American Association of Community Colleges at its annual convention in Kansas City, Missouri. This honor was shared with Tri-County Technical Institute of South Carolina and the Community College of Rhode Island.

Contact:
Jack Miller
(503) 667-6422

Mt. Hood Community College
26000 SE Stark Street
Gresham, OR 97030
Total head count enrollment-Credit: 12,228; Non-Credit: 17,404
Campuses/sites: 3; Full-time faculty: 169

THE FALL TERM TUITION AWARD

The college offers a waiver of nine credits of tuition for full-time students enrolling in the fall term immediately following high school graduation

The high school drop-out rate in Rogue Community College's district has historically been well above the state's average and the proportion of high school graduates seeking further education and training has been below the norm. Traditional areas of employment opportunity that don't require specialized training and post secondary education (such as timber products) are diminishing.

Into this bleak scenario comes Rogue Community College and a ray of hope: a unique fall term tuition award. This waiver of nine credits of tuition for full-time students enrolling in the fall term immediately following graduation from high school (or GED completion) was approved by the Board in 1987. Now serving 118 students, the fall term tuition award provides $28,098 per year in incentives for young people to finish high school and continue with a college education and job training.

Contact:
D. Thomas Bradbeer, Director, Personnel and College Information
(503) 471-3505

Rogue Community College
3345 Redwood Highway
Grants Pass, OR 97527
Total head count enrollment-Credit/Non-Credit: 11,200
Campuses/sites: 2; Full-time faculty: 64

COLLECTIVE BARGAINING

The collaborative process is based upon a negotiating team concept rather then reliance on a hired spokesperson to represent each side

For many years adversarial relations and protracted negotiations were the norm in faculty and staff collective bargaining at Rogue Community College. But in 1986 the appointment of a new college president and the call from the Board for "labor peace" set the stage for a new approach to negotiations.

The new collaborative process developed at the college is based upon a negotiating team concept rather than relying on a hired spokesperson to represent each side. The teams, consisting of an equal number of managers and faculty (or classified staff) identifies issues, carries out research, and develops consensus on recommendations for contract revisions.

The new process was well received by faculty and staff

and culminated in 1990 with the first (and only) five-year collective bargaining agreement in Oregon. More importantly, trust has been restored, cooperative relations are now the norm, and the collaborative process has permeated deliberations on all aspects of decision-making at the college.

Contact:
D. Thomas Bradbeer, Director, Personnel and College Information
(503) 471-3505

Rogue Community College
3345 Redwood Highway
Grants Pass, OR 97527
Total head count enrollment-Credit/Non-Credit: 11,200
Campuses/sites: 2; Full-time faculty: 64

SOUTHWESTERN OREGON COMMUNITY COLLEGE

HAPPE (HOLISTIC APPROACH TO PREPARING PRODUCTIVE EMPLOYEES)

HAPPE includes specially designed training units that simulate situations in which mechanical devices operate

HAPPE is an 18-week training course at Southwestern Oregon Community College that prepares students for technology-related jobs. Geared for displaced, older workers with transferable job skills and limited academic proficiency, the program incorporates both academic and job/career counseling components. Tuition is waived for participating students; recruitment is through local agencies that partner with the college in providing educational services to the region.

Hands-on applications on topics are accomplished simultaneously or within a short time following presentations. Specially designed training units simulate the situations in which mechanical devices and systems would be operated in a work setting, giving students opportunities to practice in the classroom/lab before moving into structured work experience. The goal is to relate every concept to specific applications that can be physically experienced.

All academic classes are applied and include lecture and lab components. Technology classes are supported by software and students are expected to use the software as a critical component of the program.

The program includes innovative elements designed to build on each participant's transferable skills and offer new skills to bridge the gap from the old workplace to the new. Elements of this competency-based program include:

1) portfolio development, through which trainees document their transferable skills and document their new skills with samples of work, photos of products they produce and other evidence of competency assisted by case manager;

2) a familiarity with technology use, which begins immediately using the computer-assisted basic skills brush-up, applied math and communication;

3) the use of training systems, which help provide immediate "hands-on" application experience;

4) a case manager approach to participants' need for counseling, tutoring, mentoring and progress tracking ensures that close contact with each student is maintained;

5) employability/education plans that build on the participants' strengths and skills with an individualized approach, enabling each person to move ahead as rapidly as possible; participants with significant experience may challenge the pre-tech sections and devote more time to the specialty course;

6) team learning processes (cooperative learning) with project development;

7) attention to student learning styles and success-oriented environment and positive reinforcement; and

8) computer-assisted instruction, video-disc and CD-ROM technology provide interactive learning experiences while engaging students in use of technology.

Contact:
Barbara Davey, Associate Dean, Professional/Technical Education
(503) 888-7331

Southwestern Oregon Community College
1988 Newmark Avenue
Coos Bay, OR 97420
Total head count enrollment-Credit: 6,685; Non-Credit: 3,127
Campuses/sites: 1; Full-time faculty: 56

WORK FORCE 2000 SKILLS CENTER

*▨ Collaborative efforts with education, business, industries, agencies and community ▨
organizations produce a strong program with stable funding*

The Community-Based Skills Center in Southwestern Oregon broke new ground by providing educational services not previously available to a target population that includes disadvantaged women, minorities, handicapped and at-risk youth and adults – in addition to dislocated, unemployed and under-employed workers.

The program is centrally located as a store-front educational center in downtown Coos Bay and provides an array of pre-vocational education programs and support services.

The program includes a core of 100 hours of intensive training in self-development, transitional process, career planning, employability skills, communication and basic skills development. Longer-term basic skills development is available using computer-assisted instruction.

The comprehensive program includes outreach and recruitment, orientation, assessment, instruction, employability skills, basic skill development, computer skills, employment preparation, direct placement and follow-up.

The Center, developed in 1990, features computer-assisted instruction in basic skills with new opportunities for learning provided through a PLATO Computer-Assisted Learning System. Computer-Assisted Placement Testing (CPT) and Career Information Services (CIS) are also used. Ten networked student stations served by a file-server and system manager enable students to work on individualized units keyed to individual needs and academic levels. Selections are made from more than 4,500 instructional modules available on the PLATO System.

Collaborative efforts with education, business, indus-tries, agencies and community organizations produce a strong program, coordinated efforts, stable funding and greater involvement of business and industry. The annual budget is $226,000.

Business and industry are closely involved. Representatives serve on the Advisory Committee, work in the Center, give classroom workshops on employability skills, conduct program review sessions through an Employer Roundtable and contribute matching funds.

Community and target group response to the Skills Center is phenomenal. Referrals come in from throughout the district, from families, churches, peers, agencies and organizations. Many families have three and four unemployed adults. In many cases, once one has success at the Center, the others enroll in succeeding sessions.

The program enables participants to identify their abilities, occupational interests and aptitudes, set career and academic goals and brush-up many skills. Most of them become highly motivated to attain higher skill levels and enter employment, on-the-job training or vocational education.

Follow-up telephone surveys showed the following: 35 percent entered vocational education programs at Southwestern Oregon Community College; 12 percent planned to enroll in vocational programs fall term; 22 percent entered employment; 11 percent enrolled in Adult Basic Education/GED; 10 percent were job searching; and 10 percent were in neither school or job due to health, moving, family disruption or other reasons.

Contact:
Patricia Bruneau-Gaber, Associate Dean, Extended Learning
(503) 888-7329

Southwestern Oregon Community College
1988 Newmark Avenue
Coos Bay, OR 97420
Total head count enrollment-Credit: 6,685; Non-Credit: 3,127
Campuses/sites: 1; Full-time faculty: 56

SUPERVISED FIELD EXPERIENCE

*▨ The program includes work experience placement for on-the-job training ▨
in areas where the college does have a technical program*

How does a small, rural college with a population base that limits its number of programs meet the ever-varying occupational education and training needs of its district residents? At Umpqua Community College, it's done through a Supervised Field Experience program that includes work experience placement for on-the-job training in areas where the college does have a technical program. This is particularly helpful to agencies such as vocational rehabilitation, insurance companies dealing with retraining injured workers, and some JTPA referrals.

Implemented in 1986, the program enjoys a 90 percent placement rate.

Entering students are tested for basic skill levels. Through an interview process that includes identification of career interests and job skills, a program is formulated for approval by the referring agency. The program includes college coursework for provision of needed basic and related job skills, in addition to the work experience. Since the college is not funded by the state for other than approved formal programs, the referring agencies pay the full cost of training – and are happy to do so. These costs are significantly less than those required if the agencies were to send the students out of the district for training. The students are also pleased because they are not uprooted from their place of residence.

The SFE program is administered by the college's Cooperative Work Experience Coordinator. Job placements are developed by three retired local residents who have extensive contacts in business and industry. These part-time employees find this project challenging and enjoyable, and are very successful in locating training opportunities.

One area of success is in wastewater treatment. Although the college does not have a formal program in this occupation, the SFE program has placed approximately eight persons annually. The program maintains an enrollment of 30 to 35 students each year – all of whom would not receive training locally if it were not for this program.

Contact:
Charles M. Plummer, Vice President, Instructional Services
(503) 440-4625

Umpqua Community College
PO Box 967
Roseburg, OR 97470
Total head count enrollment-Credit: 3,100; Non-Credit: 12,000
Campuses/sites: 1; Full-time faculty: 65

UMPQUA COMMUNITY COLLEGE

ANNUAL STUDENT REGISTRATION

Convenience and assurance of getting required courses are among the reasons students say they like annual registration

Umpqua Community College no longer worries as much about fluctuating enrollment, because student registration keeps the numbers consistent and the planning is much easier.

Annual Student Registration allows students to pre-register for fall, winter and spring quarters. Since 1991, annual registration has served as a logical next step to current faculty advising and student orientation programs. Annual student registration is designed to:

1) assure students who plan to graduate during the following year that they will meet their class requirements;

2) make a positive, clear commitment to returning students;

3) provide assurances that graduating and returning students will have the opportunity to complete sequence courses;

4) strengthen our faculty advising system; and

5) promote student responsibility and interest in total degree planning.

A 1992 telephone survey of students who participated in annual registration indicated that virtually all students took advantage of the opportunity to enroll for all academic terms, and those that intended to graduate would be graduating. Students most frequently cited convenience, assurances of getting required courses, and degree planning when asked what they liked the most about annual registration.

UCC has several years of experience providing student enrollment support services. These include offering required entrance student assessment testing, required faculty advising for all new students, the publishing of an annual academic schedule, and a one-credit required Orientation to College course.

In addition, successful annual registration requires program evaluation measures and support from the college president and chief academic officer, data systems management (the capacity to handle multiple term registrations), a Faculty Student Advising Committee or its equivalent.

Although implementation of the program does require staff resources, it has served as a positive rallying point for all staff who have immediate evidence of contributing to our students success.

Contact:
Dr. Jacky Hagan, Vice President, Student Services
(503) 440-4677

Umpqua Community College
PO Box 967
Roseburg, OR 97470
Total head count enrollment-Credit: 3,100; Non-Credit: 12,000
Campuses/sites: 1; Full-time faculty: 65

HISTORIC PRESERVATION

⊠ *The program integrates the theory and practice of historic preservation* ⊠
through course work and internships

"Historic preservation is an autobiographical undertaking. A person, a community, a society or a nation paints its own portrait by what it chooses to save."

-W. Brown Morton, III

Bucks County, Pennsylvania, has a rich historical tradition that extends for more than 300 years. Much of this heritage is represented in the historic downtown areas, vernacular architecture and rural landscapes that give the country its distinctive character and color. The destruction of built environments has frequently been challenged by enlightened citizenry who wish to preserve the integrity of local structures.

The community college has formally joined this interest in historic preservation by implementing a two-year Historic Preservation Certificate Program that will help residents to evaluate, document and protect their architectural heritage.

The Certificate Program is designed to serve as an important educational link between the amateur's interests and the preservation degree granted by four-year colleges. Homeowners, community planners, developers, realtors, members of historic architectural review boards, historic commissions, zoning commissions and local governments are invited to participate in this special program.

The Certificate Program integrates the theory and practice of historic preservation through course work and internships and requires the completion of twenty-four

semester credits. Three courses (nine credits) are required: History and Theory of Historic Preservation (HIS 197); History of American Architecture (HIS 198); and Methodology and Documentation (HIS 199).

Four electives can be selected from the following courses: Geography of Bucks County (GEO 115); Introduction to Historical Archaeology I (HIS 195); Material Culture in Historic Preservation (HIS 200); Building Pathology (HIS 201); and Law, Taxes and Zoning for Historic Preservation (HIS 202).

A three-credit internship is required. Internships are undertaken in county/local organizations or as a specific research project. Students must take 21 credits in the Certificate Program before the internship is begun. To receive a Certificate in Historic Preservation, 24 credits must be successfully completed in the program. Students may choose to take individual courses as they are offered or enroll in the courses necessary for the certificate. The Social and Behavioral Science Department administers the Certificate Program, a program unique in community colleges in the United States.

Workshop seminars which focus on specific preservation topics will be offered each semester through the Continuing Education Department. A Preservation Forum lecture series will also present guest speakers throughout the year on timely preservation themes.

Contact:
Lyle Rosenberger, Department of Social/Behavioral Science
(215) 968-8270

Bucks County Community College
Swamp Road
Newtown, PA 18940
Total head count enrollment-Credit: 11,000; Non-Credit: 11,000
Campuses/sites: 10; Full-time faculty: 184

FINE WOODWORKING

⊠ *The program prepares students for direct entry into careers as independent* ⊠
craftspeople or employees of woodworking companies

The Fine Woodworking Program is a career-oriented associate degree program with high expectations for its students. Program applicants must present samples of their work before admittance to the program, which is designed to develop entry-level job skills as a woodworker.

Students seeking to enter this program should be interested in manual skills and the aesthetic insights required of the fine woodworker. Woodworkers find employment as independent craftspeople and as members of large and small woodworking companies.

The Fine Woodworking Program prepares students for direct entry into careers as independent craftspeople or as employees in large or small woodworking companies. Employment opportunities include the positions of cabinetmaker, wood carver, wood finisher, finish carpenter, furniture assembler, furniture finisher, furniture maker and craftsperson of exhibitions and displays. Courses cover the tools, materials, business concepts, aesthetic concepts and general education basic to the woodworker.

The Fine Woodworking Program prepares students for:

working with machinery; working independently; seeing the results of one's work; making decisions based on information and measurements derived by self; concentrating for long periods of time; and precise manual skills and mastery of technique. The field also calls for the ability to appreciate that which is aesthetic.

Admission to the Fine Woodworking Program depends upon a pre-admission interview during which the applicant presents samples of his or her work that may be from the applicant's work as a woodworker, artist or craftsperson. It is preferred, but not necessary, that the interview pieces be examples of previous woodwork. The important part of the interview is for the applicants to show how they work with their hands.

Students may enroll in this program on either a full- or a part-item basis. Individuals with previous experience in woodworking may qualify for academic credit through successful completion of the Credit for Life Learning Experience (CLLE) Program.

The Fine Woodworking Program of the Fine Arts Departments is accredited by the National Association of Schools of Art and Design (NASAD). NASAD is the only national professional accrediting agency for education in the visual arts recognized by the Council of Post-secondary Accreditation and the United States Department of Education.

Contact:
Jon Alley and Mark Sfirri, Department of Art and Music
(215) 968-8425

Bucks County Community College
Swamp Road
Newtown, PA 18940
Total head count enrollment-Credit: 11,000; Non-Credit: 11,000
Campuses/sites: 10; Full-time faculty: 184

THERAPEUTIC RECREATION OPTION

Students in this option of the Parks and Recreation Management program must complete a minimum 200-hour, 10-week field placement experience

Students desiring a career meeting the needs of special population groups find out before graduation about the real-world demands of the job. All Butler County Community College students in the Therapeutic Recreation Option of Parks and Recreation Management program must complete at least a 200-hour, 10-consecutive-week field placement experience at an agency site. The student is supervised by a field placement supervisor who is certified by NCTRC at the Therapeutic Recreation Specialist Professional or Therapeutic Recreation Assistant level.

The Therapeutic Recreation program offers the two-year associate degree student future job placement as a certified recreation paraprofessional. The program has been designed by a Certified Therapeutic Recreation Specialist to meet the standards of the National Council for Therapeutic Recreation Certification (NCTRC). Skills acquired include: knowledge of various disabilities, client assessment, documentation and record keeping, leadership, program planning, medical terminology, and other areas needed to assist disabled persons in reaching their maximum leisure potential.

Upon completion of the degree, the Butler County Community College graduate is eligible to apply for certification as a Therapeutic Recreation Assistant through the National Council for Therapeutic Recreation Certification.

Contact:
Admissions Office
(412) 287-8711

Butler County Community College
PO Box 1203
Butler, PA 16003-1203
Total head count enrollment-Credit: 3,200; Non-Credit: 4,000
Campuses/sites: 4; Full-time faculty: 53

METROLOGY

⁂ Program courses emphasize measurement and calibration techniques, ⁂
with about half the time spent in the laboratory

Recent developments in the international community require quality measurements and assurances for precision measurements. As a result, Butler County Community College has developed a unique, nationally recognized program titled "Metrology" which prepares students for positions in research laboratories, government agencies, branches of the military and private firms.

The program has provided excellent employment for graduates. Some graduates continue studies in engineering and science programs at four-year institutions.

Metrology is a technology program designed to give a student a foundation in all types of measurement techniques and processes. It is a two-year career program developed to prepare metrology personnel for any area of industry where measurements are performed. This program emphasizes the theoretical aspects of experimentation and precise laboratory procedures. It requires

calibration of equipment and development of test procedures that has traceability to the National Institute of Standards Technology (NIST).

Graduates of the Metrology program are employed by industries and national laboratories to perform design tasks and measurements in areas including dimensional, surface analysis, optics, electrical and temperature, pressure and vacuum, nondestructive testing, chemistry, electronics, electromechanics, radiation, sound, fluids and heat transfer.

The Metrology program consists of both theory and practical applications. Approximately 50 percent of the student's time is spent in the laboratory applying the theory to laboratory calibration, precision measurements, design and modification of procedures, and testing. The courses emphasize measurement and calibration techniques.

Contact:
Admissions Office
(412) 287-8711

Butler County Community College
PO Box 1203
Butler, PA 16003-1203
Total head count enrollment-Credit: 3,200; Non-Credit: 4,000
Campuses/sites: 4; Full-time faculty: 53

EMS HAZARDOUS MATERIALS RESPONSE PROJECT

⁂ The college's operating EMS Department regularly responds ⁂
to emergencies involving hazardous materials

The Community College of Allegheny County-Allegheny Campus recruits and trains volunteer emergency medical staff for the county's 130 municipalities. Their experience gained through the college is real: During 1990-1991 alone, the college's EMS Department reacted to several near calamities resulting from accidents involving dangerous and hazardous materials.

The campus' staff has trained more than 5,000 county residents to volunteer and serve their neighbors in need of emergency care. The courses are coordinated, from design to implementation, with the Pennsylvania Emergency Management Agency, the regional office of the Environmental Protection Agency, the Commonwealth's Department of Environmental Resources, the Allegheny County's Health Department, the Emergency Management Department, the county Fire and Police Academy's and the City of Pittsburgh. This partnership permits the college to serve more constituents with an expanded range of equipment and instructional expertise.

In addition, the Bell of Pennsylvania Foundation made a grant of $20,000, to further assist the college with the capital equipment expenses involved in offering these complex instructional courses.

This productive partnership permitted the college to train 1,500 volunteers during 1991-92. More importantly, the county of Allegheny is assured of an increased level of safety, since traditional emergency competition has been reduced and the partners and teams of trained volunteers remain on call if community safety is jeopardized.

The very first Haz-Mat course was offered over a weekend. That following Monday morning a chemical spill solving Styrene, occurred at a local chemical plant. Responding to that spill was a company safety director and his team – all trained during that past weekend. The Emergency Services Training Weekend (the last weekend in April of each year) attracted 600 during 1992. More than 27 emergency management workshops (16 hours each) were offered. Each year that weekend project attracts more volunteers.

New courses in Hazardous Materials were designed in accord with Title 29 CFR 1910.120 (Federal Regulations) and the National Fire Protection Association's published Standards 471,472,473.

Contact:
Knox Walk, Department Director
(412) 237-4628

Community College of Allegheny County-Allegheny Campus
808 Ridge Avenue
Pittsburgh, PA 15212-6097
Total head count enrollment-Credit: 12,124; Non-Credit: 19,215
Campuses/sites: 5; Full-time faculty: 156

COMMUNITY COLLEGE OF ALLEGHENY COUNTY-ALLEGHENY CAMPUS

VOCATIONAL IMPROVEMENT

The program targets educationally and economically disadvantaged adults, many of whom are interested in health professions

Located in the heart of a minority community currently undergoing much-needed economic and residential revitalization, the Homewood-Brushton Branch of the Community College of Allegheny County-Allegheny Campus serves a significant percentage of educationally and economically disadvantaged students. These students too often have been unaware of the accessibility of vocational technical training programs at CCAC.

Traditionally, high attrition was attributed to the students' inability to comprehend vocational training manuals, solve simple math problems or express themselves in clear concise sentences. Low self-esteem with the absence of career guidance intensified a frustrating, failing situation. These deficiencies coupled with an inability to navigate the educational system made it difficult for these educationally and economically disadvantaged students to be retained with academic stability and eventually complete their vocational training program.

That began to change in 1986. In order to rectify the situation, a program was developed which would provide educationally and economically disadvantaged adults with additional basic skills and supportive services. To enhance their success in their chosen vocational programs, students would participate in an average of 100 hours of assessment, counseling, academic instruction, tutoring and career readiness activities. To finance this program, a grant was submitted to the Pennsylvania Department of Education and the Bureau of Vocational Education entitled the Vocational Improvement Program. Since 1986, grant funding has been renewed yearly.

Over the past six years, the grant has served more than 1,200 educationally and economically disadvantaged adults, 18 years and older, interested in enrolling in or who were already enrolled in vocational training programs. The services have been modified periodically to meet the needs of its changing population. Because many of the participants were interested in health profes-sions, a science component was added to strengthen their knowledge of the scientific approach. Computer literacy was also incorporated into the program.

Participants are recruited for 10-week sessions, both internally through other support services on the campus and through many community-based organizations. Prior to the beginning of each session, an orientation, including a testing segment, is conducted for all participants. An educational specialist evaluates the test results and an assessment is made to determine the extent and nature of supplemental support services needed. In conjunction with the basic skills instructors, an individualized educational plan is developed for each participant. Based on this plan, the students, with the guidance of the educational specialist, schedule appropriate classes in reading, math, English, science, computer and life management skills. Some students need all the basic skill classes and attend 15 hours of structured classes and five hours of individual tutoring/counseling per week over the year before entering credit classes. More advanced students take classes in only their designated weaknesses and complete these skills in a shorter period of time. To accommodate students' schedules, classes are offered in the day and the evening. The progress of all participants is monitored and regularly evaluated and all participants receive continuous intervention/support. Over the past six years, a 60 percent completion rate has been maintained with approximately 60 percent of those completing the VIP program continuing on to credit classes and 32 percent attaining employment.

A grant-funded coordinator supervises a program assistant, six instructors and tutors and an educational specialist. The staff meets weekly to discuss students' progress and to alter or revamp the program to meet the changing needs of its participants. A CCAC employed program director is responsible to the dean of the Homewood-Brushton Branch and the Assistant Dean of Educational Services for monitoring the entire program.

Continues on Page 580

Due to the success of the program, the funding has increased. Currently, the program receives $150,000, which is approximately $650 per student. The VIP program has been recognized by the local media including *The New Pittsburgh Courier* and *The New Informer*.

Contact:
Fran Howze, Dean, Homewood-Brushton Branch
(412) 371-1600

Community College of Allegheny County-Allegheny Campus
808 Ridge Avenue
Pittsburgh, PA 15212-6097
Total head count enrollment-Credit: 12,124; Non-Credit: 19,215
Campuses/sites: 5; Full-time faculty: 156

COMMUNITY COLLEGE OF ALLEGHENY COUNTY-BOYCE CAMPUS

LINKING SERVICES TO INCREASE PRODUCTIVITY IN PLACEMENT

Personnel directors from several businesses recruit on campus exclusively through Job Service

In order to maintain and even increase productivity in the college placement office in the face of impending budget cuts, public and private services merged at Community College of Allegheny County-Boyce Campus, serving as a successful model for other placement offices. This merger brought together placement functions such as job leads, recruiters on campus, advertising and additional placement counselors at virtually no cost to the institution.

The complexity of moving an outside agency such as the State Employment Office (Job Service) within the confines of the campus presented some unique problems, solutions and benefits. The marriage, to some degree, was brought about by financial and community pressures. In 1981, the state's financial problems necessitated closing the Monroeville branch location of the Monroeville Job Service. Boyce Campus was approached by the main Job Service office regarding the possibility of developing a synergistic arrangement. Because a formal relationship was being developed by two public non-profit agencies, it was decided by both parties that an exchange of services was the primary way to address the financial aspect of this mutual arrangement.

Boyce students using the Career Planning and Placement Office may use Job Service on a one-stop basis providing the students with a convenient job lead system of up-to-date listings from Southwestern Pennsylvania. Personnel Directors from several businesses recruit on campus exclusively through Job Service giving students a better opportunity for full and part-time jobs. Through Job Service, employers have increased contact with Boyce Campus, enhancing the college's image in the market place.

Job Service advertises through radio, TV, newspaper and personal employer contacts with the Boyce Campus location. This type of publicity is an excellent recruiting tool. Workshops are presented by Job Service in connection with Boyce Campus Career Week and Freshmen Orientation programs.

In terms of college retention, more students have been placed in full-time and part-time positions. In terms of recruitment alone, more than 800 non-students each month are using the placement services and many of these people become students or refer other people to Boyce Campus. Boyce Campus' Dean of Students describes the operation as "giving a real boost to our recruiting new students in bringing them to campus to be exposed to the services we have to offer." The impact becomes significant in terms of placement help, retention gain and recruitment efforts.

In addition, Job Service refers approximately 55 percent of its clients to the Admissions Department and to the Placement Office for career testing, job leads, resume writing and degree requirements. In turn, the college's Placement Office refers 20 to 25 percent of its clients to Job Service's microfiche listing of jobs available in southwestern Pennsylvania.

The services provided by the Monroeville Job Service and Career Planning and Placement are approximately 90 percent mutually related. An employer may want to see resumes from special degree and technical programs and would be contacted to help staff such a large operation. The services unique to the Career Planning and Placement are:

- career counseling;
- occupational and employer information library;
- college transfer library;
- credential service;
- resume booklets;
- career, vocational and aptitude testing;
- cooperative education, intern, experimental programs;
- academic counseling;
- career planning for employment readiness Career Week;
- workshops and seminars on careers; and
- GIS computer system for careers, scholarships and

colleges.

The Career Planning and Placement and Monroeville Job Service overlap services in these areas:
- placement of graduates and alumni;
- campus interviewing;
- resume referral; and
- placement for part-time and summer jobs.

Job Service provides Microfiche of job listings in southwestern Pennsylvania and referrals for jobs in other parts of the country.

The combining of the services of the Job Service and Placement offices presents advantages for both Job Service and Boyce Campus. The college has been able to add two placement counselors from Job Service to work five days a week at no cost to the campus, with Job Service providing their own equipment, phone system, and secretarial help.

Some institutions have conditions that would make the type of relationship with outside agencies such as the one with Boyce Campus and Job Service viable. A small college or campus in a suburban setting has certain advantages in such a relationship in attracting an agency to that location. The space arrangements must be realistic and the personnel from both school and agency must be compatible.

This approach of bringing other agencies on campus can help create a better environment to serve the community, students, and promote the college. Some agencies that might be interested in such an arrangement would be the Bureau of Vocational Rehabilitation, Comprehensive Employment Training Act Programs, Mental Health Agencies, and any social agency that deals with the unemployed. Other aspects might focus on agencies that face severe financial cutbacks. Whatever the situation might be, the attitude of the people involved must be positive in terms of the college and the outside agency working with and benefiting from each other's expertise. If this happens, the program will be successful.

Contact:
Charles Bostaph, Director, Career Planning and Placement
(412) 325-6770

Community College of Allegheny County-Boyce Campus
595 Beatty Road
Monroeville, PA 15146-1395
Total head count enrollment-Credit: 7,576; Non-Credit: 9,110
Campuses/sites: 2; Full-time faculty: 78

ENVIRONMENTAL TECHNICIAN TRAINING

The program includes an intensive practicum semester of field-oriented training

A critical need for environmental paraprofessionals prompted Community College of Allegheny County-Boyce Campus to develop the Environmental Technician Training Program. The program was initiated by a group of industrial, academic and government leaders who also established competency outcomes for training such technicians.

Working with the Commission for Workforce Excellence, the college and the Center for Hazardous Materials Research developed a program that integrates academic competencies in science, mathematics and communications with intensive applied skills needed by environmental technicians in the field. Unlike other programs, the Environmental Technician Training Program includes an intensive practicum semester offered on site at the Center for Hazardous Materials Research. The practicum consists of hands-on field-oriented training with environmental instruments and equipment, as well as applied environmental practices.

The program is an exemplary model of academic, industry and government partnership that address a critical training need by preparing students for careers as para-engineers in the environmental industry.

Contact:
Daniel Obara, Dean of Instruction
(412) 325-6680

Community College of Allegheny County-Boyce Campus
595 Beatty Road
Monroeville, PA 15146-1395
Total head count enrollment-Credit: 7,576; Non-Credit: 9,110
Campuses/sites: 2; Full-time faculty: 78

NURSING

❈ A Nursing Administrative Board, comprising Nursing administrators ❈
from four campuses, manages the system-wide program

The Community College of Allegheny County boasts Pennsylvania's largest Nursing Program, which enrolls 1,000 nursing student annually. The North Campus is one of four major campuses integral to the program.

The college conducts courses at multiple sites throughout the county for the convenience of students. The North Campus and the Allegheny, Boyce and South campuses are strategically located to serve the entire Allegheny County region. In the past, each campus offered an Associate in Science Degree with a major in Nursing. Historically, each of the four Nursing Programs developed independently, and had individual and separate Pennsylvania State Board of Nursing approval. Two campuses (Allegheny and South) also had National League for Nursing accreditation status.

The incentive for moving in the direction of a common nursing curriculum offered by all campuses stemmed from the following three major factors:

1) the attempt for NLN accreditation at two of the non-NLN accredited campuses;

2) there was a strong attempt on the part of CCAC to address inconsistencies within current college course and program offerings in order to design a common college catalog; and

3) an awareness by faculty and administration of public confusion in regard to four separate Nursing Programs.

It became apparent to administration and faculty that a united Nursing Program would improve public image, provide easier advisement and transfer, and promote articulation agreements with baccalaureate institutions in the area who accepted CCAC associate degree Nursing graduates into their BSN programs.

An activities calendar was designed to include integrated tasks and notification dates of progress for Nursing faculty, supportive disciplines, administration, and significant community agencies including clinical affiliates. Simultaneously, a broad advisory committee composed of representatives from Nursing service and education was formed and periodic meetings were scheduled in order to solicit recommendations and provide clarification regarding the program's development.

Unique to the new system-wide Nursing Program is the administrative governance structure that was conceived and implemented. A Nursing Administrative Board formed to manage the system-wide program, comprises the four campus Nursing administrators, who meet weekly to discuss procedure, policy, budget, staffing and other program needs. Although this format is atypical, it best fits the existing organizational structure at CCAC and the needs of the system-wide Nursing Program.

The development of a unified Nursing Program has allowed CCAC to collectively utilize the vast expertise of all Nursing faculty instead of fragmenting this expertise among four separate programs. The development of a cohesive, unified faculty mutually working to offer, monitor, and update a common curriculum is viewed as a valuable new resource within the ever-changing Nursing professional milieu. The Nursing Program maintained approval from the Pennsylvania State Board of Nursing and received National League of Nursing accreditation in the spring of 1992.

Contact:
Nursing Administrative Board
(412) 323-2323

Community College of Allegheny County-North Campus
8701 Perry Highway
Pittsburgh, PA 15237-5372
Total head count enrollment-Credit: 6,995; Non-Credit: 33,860
Campuses/sites: 3; Full-time faculty: 370

HEALTH UNIT COORDINATION

❈ The program not only teaches basic job duties, but also ❈
how to have a caring attitude with people under stress

Educationally disadvantaged and minority students interested in health careers are being actively recruited to become academically ready to enter the Health Unit Coordinator Program at Community College of Allegheny County-South Campus. This effort is among many that have kept CCAC-South Campus a leader in the field.

The Health Unit Coordinator Program prepares an individual to perform non-patient care activities on a nursing unit in an acute care facility. Students learn the necessary theory and skills related to transcription of physician orders, communication, organizational prioritizing, human relations and ethical/legal responsibilities. Practical application takes place in a hospital setting in the form of a practicum. Graduates of the program can earn national certification by successfully completing the National Association of Health Unit Coordinator (NAHUC) examination.

The current 30-credit program began in 1973 as a one-semester, 15-credit program called Unit Clerical Management. Through the last 20 years of advisory board input, community needs, employer evaluations and national trends, the curriculum has been updated to meet the ever-changing advances in health care.

In the fall 1983 semester a separate Pharmacology component was added to the curriculum, making the graduates comfortable in reading physician's handwritten orders for medications. More in-depth computer technology was added then to accommodate the ever-increasing upgrading of computer application in the actual clinical setting. Furthermore, in 1987, a co-operative education tract was designed to provide for direct employment opportunities for students. Likewise an Evening/Saturday option was offered for those students unable to attend in the traditional day scheduling.

Originally the position of "unit clerk" began in the 1940's with on-the-job-training; the purpose of which was to alleviate the nurses' "paperwork" at the desk. Today the majority of hospitals do not use on-the-job-training but prefer individuals who have completed a basic heath Unit Coordinator Program.

The impact of the HUC program has not just been locally. In 1983, the Program Coordinator (Kathy Korona) was the founding director of the NAHUC Certification Board. CCAC-South Campus, was the single largest certification testing site nationwide that year, with 275 examinees. More than 15,000 Health Unit Coordinators have been nationally certified.

In 1984, the Health Unit Coordinator Program was designated as Supportive Institution of the Year by the National Association of Health unit Coordinator (NAHUC). That same year, the HUC Program Coordinator received NAHUC's Educator of the Year award. Ms. Korona was also active in helping other educators start HUC Programs in other regions and states.

In its current efforts to recruit and retain educationally disadvantaged and minority students, South Campus offers pre-career planning, free job placement skills such as resume writing, job interviewing skills and once a year we invite employers on campus to meet our students.

The goal of this program is to provide the adult student with a quality program leaning to employment. Through this two-semester program, South has afforded individuals the opportunity to become self-sufficient and independent of governmental funding for food and shelter. In a recent recruitment video, the Program Coordinator said: "At CCAC, in the Health Unit Coordinating Program, we teach the students the job responsibilities, but we go a little bit further and teach them people skills, good communication skills, listening skills, a caring attitude and dealing with people during a high stress time in their life. We attempt to foster independence, good organizational skills and bolster them to go out into the job market."

In the past 20 years, the Health Unit Coordinator Program has provided southwestern Pennsylvania and the tri-state area with a competent and knowledgeable health care team member.

Contact:
Kathleen Mally, Assistant Dean, Health Sciences
(412) 469-6310

Community College of Allegheny County-South Campus
1750 Clairton Road, Route 885
West Mifflin, PA 15122-3097
Total head count enrollment-Credit: 8,857; Non-Credit: 12,156
Campuses/sites: 3; Full-time faculty: 178

COMMUNITY COLLEGE OF ALLEGHENY COUNTY-SOUTH CAMPUS

FOSSIL ENERGY TECHNOLOGY

Courses in this program are offered both at the college and at the industrial site

When the coal energy industry and the U.S. Department of Energy (DOE) saw a need to upgrade technical support staff at their facilities, they turned to the Departments of Continuing Education and Engineering Technology of the South Campus of CCAC and the Pittsburgh Energy Technology Center (PETC). Together, they designed a program for both federal and contract employees that enhances their knowledge and skills in a range of technologies related to fossil fuel research as well as the accompanying skills of mathematics and technical report writing.

The courses were offered at both the college and the industrial site. Each enrollee was required to complete six courses (21 credits) to receive a certificate in Fossil Energy Technology. Key to the program is a course in Coal Science and Technology, ERG 111 (4 credits), which centers on the present and future demands for energy of our nation and the world, the coal fuel cycle and its impact on the environment, and the efficient and responsible uses of coal.

The remaining courses are in the areas of technical

Continues on Page 584

mathematics, computer skills, technical writing, and two electives. Electives offered are chemistry, mechanical power, and electronic computer interfacing.

The program has been offered at the Pittsburgh Energy Technology Center and has 17 graduates. A new cycle of courses is being offered at the Morgantown Energy Technology Center (METC) for approximately 30 technicians. Technicians receiving the Fossil Energy Technician Certificate may apply their work toward an associate degree in a number of Engineering Technology fields at CCAC.

Contact:
Patrick E. Gerity, Director, Continuing Education
(412) 469-6363

Community College of Allegheny County-South Campus
1750 Clairton Road, Route 885
West Mifflin, PA 15122-3097
Total head count enrollment-Credit: 8,857; Non-Credit: 12,156
Campuses/sites: 3; Full-time faculty: 178

AIR TRAFFIC CONTROLLER PROGRAM

Students get practical experience at the college's working air traffic control tower

The Community College of Beaver County's Air Traffic Controller program is in day-to-day touch with the needs and trends of the profession: A working air traffic control tower at Beaver County Airport has been equipped, staffed and operated by the college since 1977.

Unique resources offered by the program include: the control tower, which provides students the opportunity to earn a Federal Aviation Administration (FAA) issued Control Tower Operator certificate with a facility rating endorsement; two 12-position non-radar/computer based instruction (CBI) labs; and a control tower lab. These specialized training facilities are all located at the Beaver County Airport.

The support staff for this AAS degree program includes eight full-time and three part-time air traffic control specialists who are certified and rated by the FAA. The majority of these employees are also National Weather Service (NWS) certified weather observers.

Throughout the years the CCBC Air Traffic Control program has received several formal awards for quality. In 1982, in recognition of the excellence of the CCBC ATC program, the FAA Eastern Region initiated a cooperative education (Co-Op) agreement with CCBC. In 1983, the program was selected by the Department of Education as the best vocational program in the state of Pennsylvania. In 1987, the FAA recognized the program as the "outstanding" aviation education program in the state of Pennsylvania. In 1989, the program was awarded the FAA Administrator award for "outstanding achievement in aviation education." In 1990, the FAA and CCBC signed a precedent-setting agreement that, for the first time in FAA history, enabled graduates of a college ATC program to be assigned directly into FAA ATC facilities, by passing the traditional FAA Academy training process.

Contact:
Robert Powell, Assistant Professor, Aviation
(412) 775-8561

Community College of Beaver County
1 Campus Drive
Monaca, PA 15061-2588
Total head count enrollment-Credit: 2,827; Non-Credit: 1,491
Campuses/sites: 1; Full-time faculty: 60

PROJECT ACCESS

High school seniors are enticed to pursue a college education with certificates of admission

Not satisfied that traditional recruiting techniques were drawing enough urban high school students to Community College of Philadelphia (CCP), the college began issuing certificates of admission to each public high school senior. The results were impressive: In one year, applicants increased by 36 percent and the participation rate of those students rose 17 percent.

The concept for "Project Access" came about in the fall of 1990. It was an idea of Dr. Ronald J. Temple, President of CCP. Dr. Temple wanted CCP to play a major role in getting more students from the Philadelphia School District to pursue college after their graduation from high school. He felt that many urban public high school students lacked the confidence to pursue college admission due to their academic and/or financial situation.

Dr. Temple shared his idea for the certificate of admission with Dr. Constance Clayton, Superintendent for Philadelphia Public Schools. After their discussion, it was decided that the two institutions would work in a partnership to make this concept, reality. After the two CEO's agreed to work together, Dr. Temple assigned Dr. Preston Pulliams, Vice President for Student Affairs and Gordon Holly, Director of Admissions and Recruitment to design and implement the concept, which was later termed "Project Access."

Dr. Pulliams and Mr. Holly designed a program which included three key parts:

1) involving personnel in the high schools to guide the students reaction once they receive the certificates;
2) providing information sessions for student and parents; and
3) sending statistical information back to the Philadelphia School District on each student's progress through the admission process.

Along with the key parts to the design, considerations for promotion, target population and project timing were included.

In November of 1990, members of Community College of Philadelphia and the Philadelphia School District met and reviewed the plan presented CCP. It was decided that the program would be done as follows.

- January 1991: CCP Director of Admissions would meet school district counselors, senior class sponsors, and senior English teachers to present certificate program.
- February 1991: Certificate mailing would be produced and include letter from Dr. Temple, Certificate for Admission, information sessions invitation, special application, and college overview book.
- March 1991: Certificate mailing would be sent to principals and school personnel who will act as CCP contacts for this event.
- April 1, 1991: Certificate mailing would be sent to all public high school students.
- April 10, 1991: Press conference with Dr. Temple and Dr. Clayton announcing "Project Access" to the Philadelphia community, along with posters being placed around the city.
- May 1, 1991/July 1, 1991: Statistical reports sent back to the high school personnel that showed who

had applied, tested and registered from their schools. (The personnel would follow-up on students they thought were completing the process, but did not.)

- August 1991: Final open house for prospective students and parents.
- October 1991: Review meeting with CCP and the Philadelphia School District regarding students who entered in fall 1991.

The reason for choosing the above format was based on a few factors. It was important to inform as many people about the project as possible, prior to mailing to the students. This gave the students many avenues to have their questions answered regarding the certificate. The target population was to be students who had no college plans after graduation. The mailing was sent only two months before graduation. This allowed all seniors to complete most of their course work and apply to other colleges without being distracted by this mailing. April was excellent timing because it would motivate those students who did not plan to go to college and have them enter the admission process early enough so that they could get a good orientation before entering.

The implementation went very well and "Project Access" created a lot of excitement in Philadelphia. It also became a very successful endeavor!

The results from our efforts were impressive. The participation rate from public high school seniors to CCP, despite the school's drop in enrollment of seniors from 1990 to 1991, was the largest single year enrollment improvement from this group of students in the last five years.

More valuable than the statistical results was the relationship that was built between the Philadelphia School District and Community College of Philadelphia. There has already been talk about the groups working together on articulation agreements, grants, and Project Access II. Because of the commitment from the "top," these Philadelphia institutions will continue to combine their efforts towards the goal of successful post-secondary attendance for the Philadelphia youth.

Most of the resources used were human resources. More than 100 people were involved in supporting "Project Access." The financial investment for the college was limited to the certificate mailing. The production and mailing cost was approximately $15,000.

Community College of Philadelphia received accolades from the Philadelphia School Board for an outstanding project. Also many other colleges have called for information on Project Access so that they can emulate the program in their areas.

Contact:
Gordon Holly, Director of Admission, (215) 751-8230
Preston Pulliams, Vice President for Student Affairs, (215) 751-8160

Community College of Philadelphia
1700 Spring Garden Street
Philadelphia, PA 19130
Total head count enrollment-Credit: 30,875; Non-Credit: 18,625
Campuses/sites: 28; Full-time faculty: 350

DENTAL HYGIENE

Expanded classrooms enable dental hygiene and dental assistant students to work together

Though relatively new, the Dental Hygiene program at Harcum College already is filling a huge need for the local dental community, which in January 1989 requested the college develop such a program.

The dental community pledged a fund-raising campaign which would match federal and state start-up grants. When the college agreed, a program director was hired and the process of developing a curriculum, building a facility and initiating the accreditation process was begun. In September 1990, the first class of 24 students entered; in May 1992, Harcum graduated its first class of 22 Dental Hygiene students.

While it is too soon to see a broad impact (the first students are just now entering the field), it was obvious from the early days of the program's creation that it would have a dramatic impact on the area dental community. There had previously been, according to local dentists, an "unparalleled shortage of hygienists."

The Dental Hygiene program provides a natural complement to Harcum's established Dental Assistant-Expanded Functions program, already well-perceived by members of the dental community, many of whom had employed Harcum-trained dental assistants or office managers.

The program's primary goal is to educate students to become licensed preventive oral health care professionals who provide a variety of patient care services, from screening and exposing and developing X-ray to oral health education, nutritional counseling, removal of calculus and plaque and application of cavity-preventive agents. While Harcum grants an Associate of Science degree in Dental Hygiene, upon completion of the program the graduate is qualified to take the necessary licensing examination.

Harcum's program consists of four semesters of course work at our Bryn Mawr, Pennsylvania, campus, with clinical experience in the second, third and fourth semesters at the University of Pennsylvania School of Dental Medicine. To accommodate the program, the campus dental building was dramatically enlarged and enhanced. An eight-chair facility is used for pre-clinical instruction and laboratory courses, and there are three X-ray rooms. Expanded classrooms offer the opportunity of doing classes for both dental assistant and dental hygiene students, emphasizing the team approach to dentistry. The new Dental Programs Center was dedicated in October 1992.

The Dental Hygiene program is directed by the former clinical director of the dental hygiene program of the University of Pennsylvania. The director has seen the program through from the planning stage and has planned the course of study, worked with architects in creating the new facility and worked to achieve accreditation. She is assisted by three full-time faculty. Members of Harcum's Dental Hygiene facility teach the students their clinical experience in a clinical environment which exposes them to state-of-the-art dentistry and teaches a "team approach" to dental care.

The full accreditation process takes two to three years to complete. In May of 1992, Harcum received a full accreditation status from the Commission on Dental Accreditation of the American Dental Association.

Contact:
Jean Byrnes-Ziegler, Program Director
(215) 526-6110

Harcum College
Morris and Montgomery Avenues
Bryn Mawr, PA 19010
Total head count enrollment-Credit: 798; Non-Credit: 247
Campuses/sites: 1; Full-time faculty: 37

VETERINARY TECHNOLOGY

No experiments are done on animals at the college, although students use them to learn restraint, husbandry, sample collecting and dosing

With the need for veterinary technicians far outpacing the supply, Harcum College created a Veterinary Technology program that today boasts graduates in private practice and in research and industry.

The profession of Veterinary Technology began in the 1960's, when Veterinary Medicine recognized the need for professionally educated assistance – a role previously filled by the veterinarian's wife. The Veterinary Technology Program at Harcum was put into place in 1972, offering students an opportunity to develop their personal, scientific and technical interest in animals into a profession. An association with the University of Pennsylvania School of Veterinary Medicine offering hands-on experience began in 1975; the program was first accredited by the American

Veterinary Medical Association in 1976. (Most states license veterinary technicians and graduation from an AVMA-accredited program is a common prerequisite to eligibility for licensing.)

Besides the traditional career venues, veterinary technicians find employment in zoos, in federal and state departments of agriculture, in animal agriculture, in pharmaceutical sales and anywhere else animal health and care is a concern.

The program's primary goal is the education of competent and professionally qualified members of the animal health care team. Harcum also works to foster in its students a desire for life-long learning (since licensing usually stipulates continuing education requirements) and to enable continued competency as veterinary medicine expands and evolves. Professionalism is emphasized; it insures that this new profession will continue and grow.

Harcum's program consists of four semesters of course work at our Bryn Mawr, Pennsylvania, campus, followed by two semesters of hands-on experience, called the practicums, in association with the University of Pennsylvania School of Veterinary Medicine. Students spend 13 weeks at the Veterinary Hospital of the University of Pennsylvania (the small animal hospital in West Philadelphia) and 13 weeks at New Bolton Center (the large animal facility in Kennett Square).

Small animal and laboratory animal experience is gained prior to the practicum in Harcum's Veterinary Services building, a USDA inspected facility for dogs, cats, rabbits and rodents. No experiments are performed on these animals; they are on campus for students to learn restraint, husbandry, sample collection and dosing.

The Veterinary Technology program faculty at Harcum consists of two full-time veterinarians and two full-time veterinary technicians. On practicum, vet tech students are supervised and taught by Veterinary School staff technicians and veterinarians.

The Veterinary Technology program is accredited by the American Veterinary Medical Association. Graduates are eligible to sit for state licensing exams as well as certification by the American Association for Laboratory Animal Science at the assistant technician and technician level.

Contact:
Nadine Hackman, Program Director
(215) 526-6055

Harcum College
Morris and Montgomery Avenues
Bryn Mawr, PA 19010
Total head count enrollment-Credit: 798; Non-Credit: 247
Campuses/sites: 1; Full-time faculty: 37

COMPUTER INFORMATION SYSTEMS

The program offers four associate degrees and four certificates in microcomputer specialist areas

Because business and industry offer many job opportunities for students who have experience with microcomputer hardware and software, Harrisburg Area Community College designed a program in Computer Information Systems with options for the full-time, part-time, novice, intermediate or advanced student.

The Computer Information Systems program offers four associate degrees and four certificates for: microcomputer communications specialist, microcomputer hardware specialist, microcomputer software specialist, and microcomputer specialist. Each one of the degrees and certificates leads directly to employment in the area of specialization.

The microcomputer communications specialist focuses on the fundamentals of communications, the administration of microcomputer networks, and the design and implementations of LANs and WANs. The microcomputer hardware specialist focuses on the installation, repair, and troubleshooting of microcomputer hardware. The microcomputer software specialist focuses on the design and creation of software applications and troubleshooting of software problems. The microcomputer specialist is a flexible program which allows the novice or advanced student to pick and choose the area of concentration best suited for them. Each one of the programs includes extensive hands-on courses with top software applications.

Enrollment in the Computer Information Systems program is steadily increasing. The success of the program is due to its flexibility. Many students with previous computer experience know they will not have to take courses in subjects they are already familiar with. The courses are diversified enough that every student can take courses in subject matter they are unfamiliar with or novices in. This appeals to all types of students who want to pursue one computer course, several computer courses,

Continues on Page 588

or an entire certificate or degree. The program offers courses in the following areas: WordPerfect, Lotus 1-2-3, Borland DBase, Aldus PageMaker, Banyan Vines, Novell, AppleWorks, MS DOS 5.0, MS Windows, and several theory courses in each one of the specific area.

Contact:
Barbara Felty, Assistant Professor
John Zales, Assistant Professor
(717) 780-2324

Harrisburg Area Community College
1 HACC Drive
Harrisburg, PA 17110
Total head count enrollment-Non-Credit: 55,000
Campuses/sites: 3; Full-time faculty: 190

DISTANCE EDUCATION VIDEO COURSES

One survey revealed that more than 60 percent of video course students would not have otherwise enrolled in college

In the beginning, Harrisburg Area Community College, like many colleges, offered video courses via broadcast over a local cable channel and the local PBS affiliate. But in the fall of 1991, the college ceased such broadcasts and instead made lessons available by rental of VHS cassettes for home viewing and by putting lessons on reserve for viewing in any of four branch location libraries.

Enrollments nearly doubled with the use of videotape rentals rather than broadcast for viewing lessons.

The college invested approximately $30,000 in an automated duplication system to permit bulk duplication of video course lessons. Annual enrollments increased from 643 for the 1990-91 academic year, to 1,235 for the 1991-92 academic year when the new rental system was implemented.

Success of the video course program has occurred mainly because of the active involvement of full-time faculty in designing and operating the Distance Education program. The design includes scheduled meetings with faculty, supplemental experiences, and videotapes of on-campus orientation and test review sessions for students unable to attend. Faculty ensure the academic integrity of the video courses and provide the invaluable assistance through routine meetings for distant students that has helped insure their success. Studies in the fall of 1988 and fall of 1991 indicated grade distributions consistent with the overall college and a high level of student satisfaction. While withdrawal rates were somewhat higher for video courses, success (grade of C or better) for completing video course students was not significantly different than for students in other courses.

Student satisfaction was high because the program design successfully addressed problems faced by growing numbers of students. The three major factors identified by students for enrolling in a video course were lack of time for class attendance (52 percent), possible to combine college with family responsibilities (47 percent), and minimized travel (42 percent). More than 60 percent of the students were first time video course students and would not have otherwise enrolled in a college course.

The decision to provide lessons via videotape rental appears to have been correct because 95 percent of the respondents own a VCR and 88 percent rent the tapes. The remainder view lessons in branch libraries.

Contact:
Larry Adams, Distance Education Coordinator
(717) 780-2306

Harrisburg Area Community College
1 HACC Drive
Harrisburg, PA 17110
Total head count enrollment-Non-Credit: 55,000
Campuses/sites: 3; Full-time faculty: 190

WEEKENDER PROGRAM

⌗ The program allows students to earn a degree in as little as 2-1/3 years ⌗
by taking three courses per term

Adults interested in pursuing an associate's degree while working full-time and maintaining family, job and social responsibilities have found hope for success through Keystone Junior College's Weekender Program.

Conveniently scheduled on a trimester basis, three terms are held throughout the year, beginning with September and continuing in January and May. Classes are held on six weekends during each four-month trimester, normally every third weekend. Students may attend each trimester or choose those that are best-suited to their needs and responsibilities.

The Weekender Program is designed to allow students to earn the Associate in Science degree in as little as 2-1/3

years by taking a maximum of three courses per term. Students attending the Weekender Program receive a minimum of six hours of classroom instruction per course each weekend that classes are held. Classes are scheduled from Friday evening through Sunday afternoon.

Students in the Weekender program may either choose to enroll in the Early Childhood Education, the Education, the Engineering, the Liberal Studies, the General Business, Pre-Nursing or the Computer Information Systems curricula, or they may choose courses for personal or career development without pursuing a particular degree or program of study.

Contact:
E. Meredith Young
(717) 945-5141

Keystone Junior College
PO Box 50
La Plume, PA 18440-0200
Total head count enrollment-Credit: 1,048;
Campuses/sites: 2; Full-time faculty: 43

EARLY CHILDHOOD EDUCATION

⌗ The program includes three options: general, in-home ⌗
and early intervention

The United States is confronted with what can best be described as a child care crisis. Nationally we have experienced an unprecedented number of women entering the labor force. In the next decade, the need for child care will continue to rise. In 1979, there were 7.22-million children younger than six with mothers in the labor force; by 1985, there were 9.6-million; and by 1995, the number will rise to almost 15-million.

In response to the crisis and emerging certification standards, Keystone Junior College expanded its training program and today offers three options to its early childhood education majors: general, in-home and early intervention.

Students can also earn their associate's degree in early childhood education, as well as a 30 credit certificate for Early Intervention, through Keystone's Weekender Program.

In recognition of great numbers of early childhood personnel with little or no training, the college began several years ago to provide off-campus training, which included:

1) Workshops for Family Day Care Providers (participants may apply for credit), funded by the

Pennsylvania Department of Welfare.

2) Professional Preparation Program (12 credit program for income-eligible individuals provided in cooperation with JTPA). Individuals are employed in the early childhood education program and attend class one or two days a week for 15 weeks. The credits earned may be applied to the Associate in Arts degree if the student matriculates at the college. Students who successfully complete the program are prepared for CDA assessment.

3) Day Care Training Project, which provides training to all employees of licensed child care centers. Keystone is developing a training program that is based on three-hour workshops. Participants can accumulate specific workshops that are equivalent to the course content of basic early childhood education courses. A procedure for awarding credit for non-credit training is being developed. It is funded by the Pennsylvania Department of Welfare.

All of these programs have been developed to meet the

Continues on Page 590

needs of untrained and minimally trained early childhood education staff. The increasing enrollment of these programs suggests that these programs – which provide professional education in non-traditional formats, off-campus or evenings or weekends – best meet the needs of this population. These programs all follow the same basic principles as Keystone early childhood degree majors: strong base in child development, observation of children in natural settings, and field experience integrated with course work in every semester.

Contact:
Lansdale Shaffmaster
(717) 945-5141

Keystone Junior College
PO Box 50
La Plume, PA 18440-0200
Total head count enrollment-Credit: 1,048
Campuses/sites: 2; Full-time faculty: 43

LEHIGH COUNTY COMMUNITY COLLEGE

CAREER DAY

This annual event draws more than 2,000 students from 17 area high schools

At Lehigh County Community College's Career Day, students are exposed to more than speeches and brochures. Each is treated special and provided an individualized schedule based on his or her career interest.

The college hosts more than 50 community professionals and more than 2,000 students from 17 area high schools for career planning workshops at each Career Day.

The event was established in 1978, when the college was faced with a decline in enrollment. The Admissions Office developed Career Day as a marketing and recruiting tool, and garnered support for the activity among superintendents of sponsoring school districts. Career Day has been an extremely successful, well-attended, and eagerly anticipated event each year since its inception.

Career Day involves the presentation of 55 occupational workshops around the interests of high school students in the community. Workshop topics vary widely. At Career Day 1992, offerings included architect, aviation, biomedical equipment technology, professional chef, lawyer, pharmacist, and respiratory care. Presenting speakers are experts in their fields, obtained primarily through referrals of college faculty and staff, advisory committees, community leaders, and business and industry contacts.

The program is marketed to high school students in a variety of ways. Some schools permit a college representative to discuss the event at an assembly. At other schools, the event is presented in study halls, English classes, or through a college-designed flyer.

Implementation of the program requires college-wide support and cooperation. Speakers are greeted by LCCC faculty hosts, who join them for a buffet breakfast. High school students are provided with an individualized schedule based upon their career interests. LCCC staff and students guide the high school students and confirm their attendance at sessions.

The program has proven to be mutually beneficial for both LCCC and participating high schools for the following reasons:

For the college:

- this is a time- and cost-effective method of bringing a large number of local high school sophomores, juniors, and seniors to campus;
- it provides an opportunity to market and promote new programs of study, especially career programs such as robotics, office technologies, and biomedical equipment;
- the involvement of the total college community facilitates an attitude of teamwork (faculty, administration and classified staff all contribute to a program designed to market the college and its programs of study);
- it provides an opportunity to provide a direct service to high school guidance programs;
- it provides an opportunity to assist vocational-technical schools in strengthening college career program articulation in related career fields such as electronics, drafting, data processing, and culinary arts;
- it draws practitioners from business, industry, government, health and social service, and the arts, who hosted by LCCC faculty, thus strengthening a valuable link between the college and employers in the community; and
- it creates an opportunity to invite LCCC graduates, Black and Hispanic professionals, and women in leadership and non-traditional occupations to serve as role models to high school and LCCC students.

For the high schools:

- a community college career day relieves them of planning and implementing their own programs;
- a college-based career day provides an excellent opportunity for high school "general" students to identify with higher education; and
- high school students are exposed to career informa-

tion directly from practitioners, which enhances the traditional textbook exposure.

Career Day has served its original purpose well, and it has also served several other purposes. It represents an important step in preparing future workers for the economic success of our community.

Contact:
David Moyer, Director of Admissions
(215) 799-1134

Lehigh County Community College
525 Education Park Drive
Schnecksville, PA 18078-2598
Total head count enrollment-Credit: 5,082; Non-Credit: 17,000
Campuses/sites: 4; Full-time faculty: 70

LEHIGH COUNTY COMMUNITY COLLEGE

OLDER ADULTS AS CHILD CARE WORKERS: A PRODUCTIVE WORK OPTION

Offering job opportunities to those over 55 also helps fill a void in the staffing of child care facilities

The Older Adults as Child Care Workers Training program did more than recognize the obvious: there is an ample supply of older adults and a growing demand for skilled and reliable child care aides. As dual-income families become the norm, and as our increasingly mobile work force separates parents from traditional family supports, this program is helping to redefine the role older Americans play in the development of the next generation.

With the annual turnover rate for child care aides nationwide exceeding 50 percent, changes in staff are beginning to have an adverse effect on children. The demand for skilled and reliable child-care aides is increasing and is likely to continue to grow.

Lehigh County Community College received funding from the University of Pittsburgh and Generations Together under the Retirement Research Foundation Grant to train older workers to be child care professionals. This program provided satisfying, important work for individuals age 55 or older, and helped fill a void in the staffing of child care facilities. Generations Together has been recognized by state and local officials, health care agencies, and the White House for its efforts to bridge the gap between old and young.

A community advisory committee comprised of leaders in older adult and child care organizations provided the review and direction needed to successfully implement the program. In addition, the course was continually evaluated by Generations Together and the students.

More than a dozen trainees were selected to take part in this 90-hour training program. The program involved 67 hours of classroom instruction and 27 hours of internship at an area child care center. The students were involved in all aspects of child care, from writing observation reports to designing activities for the children.

LCCC's program has received enthusiastic support from community agencies that work with older adults, prospective students, and child care employers. The program has been so successful that it was recognized in a video for national circulation entitled *Waking Up Vanessa. The Older Adults as Child Care Workers: A Productive Work Option* was featured on ABC's *Good Morning America* and *World News Tonight*.

Many lasting friendships were formed among the students during the program. Graduation ceremonies and reunions were held for the students to meet and exchange information.

Contact:
Ann Bieber, Director of Community Education
(215) 799-1581

Lehigh County Community College
525 Education Park Drive
Schnecksville, PA 18078-2598
Total head count enrollment-Credit: 5,082; Non-Credit: 17,000
Campuses/sites: 4; Full-time faculty: 70

HOTEL AND RESTAURANT MANAGEMENT

The program emphasizes management of food services, food preparation and middle-level hotel administration

The Luzerne County Community College Hotel and Restaurant Management program gives students significant on-the-job experience, while specialized offerings are supplemented by liberal arts and basic business courses. A close relationship exists between LCCC and the School of Hotel Administration at Cornell University.

The program is designed to prepare students for direct entry into the hotel, catering, restaurant and resort management fields. Emphasis is placed upon the management of food services, food preparation and middle-level hotel administration. Basic principles of management are stressed.

All students are required to complete a Hotel and Restaurant Work Experience Practicum that consists of 500 non-credit work experience hours in the Hospitality Industry.

William Bruce Neil, chairman of the Hotel and Restaurant Management program, is a summa cum laude graduate of LCCC, with an associate in applied science degree in Hotel and Restaurant Management. In addition,

he holds a BS in Hotel Administration from Cornell University and was recently awarded the Certified Hotel Administrator distinction from the Educational Institute of the American Hotel and Motel Association (AH&MA).

Since Neil has been active in the Hotel and Restaurant Management Program at LCCC, the number of students continuing their education at four-year institutions has increased by 45 percent.

Neil held the position of sports venue food service director during the 1980 Winter Olympics in Lake Placid, New York and was directly responsible for planning athlete and support personnel meals. Much of Neil's work during this time was documented in detail and utilized at the 1988 Winter Olympics in Calgary, Canada.

In 1991, Neil traveled to the Soviet Union with 14 other professionals as part of the Citizen's Ambassador Program's Hospitality Delegation to teach and promote the growth of tourism. He was the only educator from a community college selected for this honor.

Contact:
William Bruce Neil, Chairperson
(717) 821-1514

Luzerne County Community College
1333 South Prospect Street
Nanticoke, PA 18634-3899
Total head count enrollment-Credit: 7,000; Non-Credit: 8,000
Campuses/sites: 17; Full-time faculty: 86

COMMERCIAL ART / GRAPHIC DESIGN

The program allows students to specialize in graphic design, painting illustration, photography or computer graphics

The Commercial Art Program at Luzerne County Community College offers four separate courses of study to students interested in a career in the arts: A Graphic Design specialization, Painting Illustration specialization, Photography specialization, and Computer Graphics specialization. Each program leads to the achievement of an associate in applied science (AAS) degree.

The Graphic Design curriculum instructs students in the art principles and basic skills involved in the various art media. Students choosing this course of study may find employment in graphic design, lettering and visual communications, advertising layout packaging, illustration, typesetting, and airbrushing. There is also a great need throughout the television and publishing industries for creative individuals with a background in graphic design.

The Painting and Illustration specialization at LCCC

explores the techniques, principles, problems, and theories of art as they relate to the world of illustration in society today. Students completing this curriculum will be qualified for employment within the areas of editorial, freelance, scientific, and advertising illustration; as well as gallery painting.

The Photography concentration provides the technical training, esthetic encouragement and business practices necessary to begin or further a student's photographic career. Students in this concentration will be prepared for employment in the field of professional photography. Career options may include working in an established photo studio, opening one's own studio, freelancing, staff photographer for a large institution, advertising and photojournalism.

Computer Graphics is a new specialization within the

Commercial Art Program at LCCC. Students within this concentration will explore and experiment with graphics software packages and innovative techniques. Employment may be sought in such areas as desktop publishing, advertising, computer illustration, photo enhancement, or computer animation.

Susan Sponenberg, coordinator of the Commercial Art program, holds a bachelor of fine arts degree in Graphic Design from the College of Art at the Maryland Institute and an associate degree in Commercial Art form LCCC. She has published various articles and her work has been featured in several one-man and juried shows. In 1972, Sponenberg was the youngest member admitted to the Society of Animal Artists, and she is also a member of the American Academy of Equine Artists.

Contact:
Susan Henry Sponenberg, Coordinator
(717) 829-7319

Luzerne County Community College
1333 South Prospect Street
Nanticoke, PA 18634-3899
Total head count enrollment-Credit: 7,000; Non-Credit: 8,000
Campuses/sites: 17; Full-time faculty: 86

NORTHAMPTON COMMUNITY COLLEGE

NATIONAL TRAINING CENTER FOR MICROELECTRONICS

Electronic firms use the Center's lab to explore new technologies and solve manufacturing problems

Driven by the need for technology integration in electronics firms, the National Training Center for Microelectronics has developed innovative programs to assist manufacturers in adopting new technologies and remaining competitive.

Comprehensive services include public courses, in-plant training, custom program development, and use of state-of-the-art technical laboratory facilities. Hands-on training programs are offered in surface mount, hybrid, soldering and semiconductor technologies. Consultation and assessment are available to assist companies to evaluate their needs and implement solutions unique to their operations.

Industry has played a key role in identifying the need for programming in technical areas, assisting with the development of course content that is timely and of practical value, and supporting the development of advanced manufacturing facilities. Between 1985 and 1991, the total value of industry support for NTC Micro in the form of cash, equipment donations and loans, and in-kind support exceeded $1.25-million.

Electronics firms use NTC Micro laboratory facilities to explore new technologies and solve manufacturing problems. Sample industry projects include:
1) the evaluation and implementation of surface mount technology to allow the client to manufacture industrial controls competitive with Japanese products;
2) investigation with a start-up company of the thermal and electrical performance of hybrid microcircuits manufactured on aluminum nitride substrates; and
3) investigation of alternate atmospheres for fluxless soldering of surface mount assemblies in gas-curtained furnaces, patented by a Pennsylvania company.

The Center functions as a self-supporting operation. NTC Micro was established at Northampton in September 1985, with support from regional industry and the Northeast Tier Ben Franklin Technology Center (NET/BFTC). Seed money in the amount of $305,671 was awarded by the state over three consecutive years, with the goal that the Center become self-supporting by September 1988. This was achieved and since 1988 NTC Micro has continued to grow in response to industry demand. Additional grant funding since 1988 has enabled the Center to advance in new technology areas to better serve the electronics industry.

Recognized nationally for its unique technical expertise and laboratory facilities, NTC Micro attracts participants to its training programs from companies in the U.S. and abroad. Just a few such facilities exist in either the public or private sector, and colleges outside Pennsylvania have sought Northampton's expertise for assistance developing similar programs.

NTC Micro serves as a unique model of a self-supporting advanced technology center responsive to industry needs. Through aggressive outreach, NTC Micro is in a unique position to play a significant role in furthering the competitiveness of U.S. electronics manufacturers.

Contact:
Linda L. Erickson, Assoc. Dean, Community Education/Center Director
(215) 861-5486

Northampton Community College
3835 Green Pond Road
Bethlehem, PA 18017-7599
Total head count enrollment-Credit: 9,244; Non-Credit: 12,825
Campuses/sites: 4; Full-time faculty: 92

NATIONAL TRAINING CENTER FOR ART IN EARLY CHILDHOOD EDUCATION

The Center is developing teaching strategies for integrating art into other subjects

"Art is a way of learning" is a partnership project between Northampton Community College and Binney-Smith, Incorporated of Easton, Pennsylvania. The goal of the project is to help early childhood teachers integrate art into all areas of the curriculum.

Named the National Training Center, the project will establish three approaches: one for children, another for college students and a third for in-service training of teachers who are working in preschool to third grade classrooms. Once developed, each of these three approaches could be duplicated throughout the country.

Over the next five years, the partnership will create early childhood program models for training classroom and art teachers as well as students learning to become teachers.

The National Training Center for Art in Early Childhood Education is developing teaching strategies for the integration of art into other subjects. This program develops training materials for national distribution which document the innovations of the art-integrated curriculum and stimulate increased use of art materials in preschool through third grade. These training materials include resource booklets and seminars that document the art-integrated curriculum.

Northampton was chosen because it is the Lehigh Valley's leading trainer of early childhood education professionals. It is also the site of a newly-constructed child care center which is certified by the state to accommodate 213 children.

Contact:
Rebecca Gorton, Professor
(215) 861-5472

Northampton Community College
3835 Green Pond Road
Bethlehem, PA 18017-7599
Total head count enrollment-Credit: 9,244; Non-Credit: 12,825
Campuses/sites: 4; Full-time faculty: 92

QUALITY SERVICE MANAGEMENT

Under the initiative, 10 college-wide standards were established to meet the needs of business constituents

Declining enrollments, a changing work force, demographic changes in the Philadelphia area and the expansion of technology applications in business, mandated grand-scale changes in Peirce Junior College's approach to its business constituents. So in November 1991, Peirce Junior College began implementating college-wide Quality Services Management, under the ongoing guidance of The Orlando Consulting Group.

The initial phase of implementation of QSM included an orientation to the process, by the principals of The Orlando Consulting Group, of all full-time faculty, staff, and administration. Board of Trustees' orientation was conducted informally by the Executive Administration at regularly scheduled Board meetings.

A number of systems were implemented in support of the QSM process: a QSM Director was selected to manage the process; an interdisciplinary QSM Steering Committee, chaired by the Dean of the College in cooperation with the QSM Director, an interdisciplinary Survey Task Force, and several cross-functional issue-driven Action Teams (remediation, retention, recruitment,

student service) were activated.

In the preliminary stages of implementation, focus groups of employees identified students, employers, high school guidance counselors, and employees of the College as important constituent groups. As a result of the survey data findings from these constituents, dramatic changes were made to the existing college curriculum and new programs of study were developed and scheduled for the first time in September 1992. These new programs, and others soon to follow, reflect the current job trends, the changing needs of the work force, the opportunities available in the Philadelphia area, as well as the increasing need for a highly skilled, technologically literate population.

Ten college-wide quality standards were established to address the needs of our constituents. Internal departments were organized around a team concept and, with the guidance of the QSM Director, formulated their own quality standards and set accountability measures that supported the college-wide standards. The standards and measures were reviewed and approved by the QSM Committee.

Students, staff and faculty were surveyed using instruments prepared by the OCG and reviewed and modified by the Survey Task Force. Surveys were conducted twice the first year and will become an annual assessment tool. The OCG tabulated the results. Survey summaries were made available to all employees of the College.

Action teams summarized their activities and presented their recommendations to the QSM Committee for further review. Many of their recommendations were incorporated in changes to function and structure that were made by the Executive Administration.

In year two of QSM, Peirce has made a number of significant improvements. For instance, all action teams have been brought under the umbrella of one cross-functional Response Team that problem solves on issues identified and prioritized by the QSM Committee. The QSM Director position was elevated to a full time adminis-

trative post to facilitate the team development and continuous improvement efforts. All position descriptions were rewritten to reflect the focus on team-building and quality service to all our constituents. Additional QSM training in quality methods and professional skills has been offered to all employees in response to needs assessments. Delivery of internal services to students through tutoring efforts, job placement services and career advising has undergone improvements as well.

Additionally, a course in QSM has been developed and, as of January 1993, is being offered as part of the program requirements for all students at Peirce. The objectives of the course are twofold: to acquaint students with the philosophical orientation here at Peirce and to prepare them for the business world that is increasingly turning to quality programs to stimulate industry-wide growth and repositioning.

Contact:
Barbara Wetzler, Dean
Helen Rosenfeld, QSM Director
(215) 545-6400

Peirce Junior College
1420 Pine Street
Philadelphia, PA 19102
Total head count enrollment-Credit: 1,100
Campuses/sites: 1; Full-time faculty: 26

EDUCATIONAL ASSISTANCE CENTER

Tutoring, counseling, academic advising and placement testing are components of the Center

The Individualized Development and Educational Assistance (IDEA) Center is an integrated and comprehensive student support services area that not only includes crisis counseling and advising but also intensive academic support.

An integrated service model affords students the opportunity to receive multi-leveled assistance in one physical space. Services can be offered efficiently and economically to more students through longer periods of the day and evening. This approach is unique among Learning Resource Centers that deal with academic problems. During the first semester of operation (fall 1992), 65 percent of the student population used at least one of the services of the Center.

Tutoring is a component of the Center, as is counseling and academic advising. Educational Specialists as well as student services personnel are located in this area. Placement testing for incoming freshmen is incorporated as a function of the IDEA Center.

The educational philosophies and theories incorporated in the IDEA Center are grounded in strategies that have

been identified as critical to retaining at-risk students. PJC's student body is ethnically diverse, predominantly first-generation college students who can also be characterized as academically and economically disadvantaged. The term at-risk would describe a majority of the student body.

Retention strategies begin with the IDEA staff understanding its key role in retention. "Someone on campus knows my name" is a crucial ingredient in the retention of at-risk students. IDEA Center personnel are problem-solvers and creative thinkers. Students come in with all types of problems that need immediate answers.

Academic support is available through individual and group tutoring, supplemental computer-assisted instruction and workshops. Tutoring is conducted by professional, paraprofessional and peer tutors.

Retention strategies also include teaching students "how to do college." Students learn time management, organizational skills, note-taking, test-taking and listening skills at regularly scheduled workshop conducted by the Center's staff.

Contact:
Leslie Daughtry, Director, Developmental Education
(215) 545-6400

Peirce Junior College
1420 Pine Street
Philadelphia, PA 19102
Total head count enrollment-Credit: 1,100
Campuses/sites: 1; Full-time faculty: 26

CUSTOMER SERVICE TECHNOLOGY

The program prepares students for careers in such fields as retail sales, personnel, bookkeeping, food service and securities

The Delaware Valley, as well as the nation, is rapidly becoming a service economy, and the Pennsylvania Institute of Technology is rapidly becoming a leader in training students in Customer Service Technology.

Most opportunities for workers who have customer service skills are projected for retail sales, personnel, secretaries, office clerks, bookkeeping and auditing clerks, stock clerks on sales floors, cashiers, a host of food-service-related workers, supervisors, insurance sales workers and securities and financial services sales agents.

Several of the large employers in the region were contacted by the Pennsylvania Institute of Technology (PIT) to discuss their specific needs. A program was then developed entitled Customer Service Technology. A questionnaire was used to ask for comments on the proposed program. Those interviewed were enthusiastic about the program and offered to serve as co-op and training sites.

All were interested in technology graduates; all suggested that opportunities held promise for promotion and growth.

Many of the companies interviewed expressed growth needs at 30 to 40 positions annually. One company with 400 employees has a 20 percent annual turnover. More than 120 positions could be available from several companies interviewed. There is a concern in Delaware County about the ability to hire a trained work force. This program will help meet this need.

While there are business, secretarial and retailing programs at schools and colleges in the area, there is not a specific Customer Service Technology program available. This program, in addition to interpersonal skills and service, emphasizes applied technology at the workplace. The program is a perfect blend of PIT's expertise in computers and office technology.

Contact:
Peter J. Bachmann, Dean, Academic Affairs
(215) 565-7900

Pennsylvania Institute of Technology
800 Manchester Avenue
Media, PA 19063
Total head count enrollment-Credit: 551; Non-Credit: 64
Campuses/sites: 1; Full-time faculty: 13

PATIENT SERVICE TECHNOLOGY

This program combines aspects of medical records technology, medical assisting, unit clerk and gerontology assistant

Pennsylvania Institute of Technology's Patient Service Technology program combines aspects of medical records technology, medical assisting, unit clerk and gerontology assistant.

The program's unique design was developed after the Pennsylvania Institute of Technology (PIT) determined the needs of the Delaware Valley by contacting the following agencies: Hospitals in Higher Education, Bureau of Planning and Technological Assistance, Delaware Valley Hospital Council, Hospital Association of Pennsylvania and the Department of Labor and Industry.

The Institute wished to discern if there were specific needs in its service area that could benefit from PIT's particular expertise in office technology and the application of technology to the work environment. At about that time, the American Society of Allied Health Professions (ASAHP) published a major study, which indicated there would be critical shortages projected for allied health professions which would exceed those in nursing.

Through discussions with local care facilities, a need surfaced for an individual who: would be trained to be a support-service representative; would understand medical records, billing and credit; could handle diagnostic information and its relation to third-party payers; and as a generalist, could serve a variety of roles in medical offices, insurance companies and residential care facilities.

The Patient Services Specialist concept was developed. Research had not uncovered another program that combines aspects of many programs such as medical records technology, medical assisting, unit clerk and gerontology assistant.

The program concept, competencies and types of courses were shared with several local medical facility Personnel Directors and Vice Presidents. The agencies contacted employ the types of individuals that would be trained by this program, and currently most of their personnel learn on the job. In some medical centers turnover is very low in these areas but, in others, turnover is high. With turnover and increased growth, the medical centers in our service area could absorb all of the graduates. Regional medical facilities, physicians' offices and insurance companies all could employ graduates with this type of training. Enthusiasm was very high and all contacted offered their facilities for clinical and co-op experience and offered to serve on a program Advisory Council which has been established.

The fundamental concept of this program is to provide training in patient relations, applied technology and specifically for the health administration field. This training would provide not only entry-level positions but also could provide for distinct career ladders.

Contact:
Peter J. Bachmann, Dean, Academic Affairs
(215) 565-7900

Pennsylvania Institute of Technology
800 Manchester Avenue
Media, PA 19063
Total head count enrollment-Credit: 551; Non-Credit: 64
Campuses/sites: 1; Full-time faculty: 13

PENNSYLVANIA STATE UNIVERSITY-MONT ALTO CAMPUS

EARLY INTERVENTION

The program complements two other approaches – public awareness and curricular reform – to increasing enrollment among blue-collar residents

Historically, the southcentral region of Pennsylvania has had a very limited access to and low participation in higher education. Until recently, that didn't seem to matter. The region depended on a large blue-collar work force in stable, locally owned manufacturing industries. But as the economic base of the community changed and became more dependent on higher-tech, multinational industry, the work force could not keep pace.

The annual earnings of the county have decreased to 88 percent of the Pennsylvania state mean within the last 10 years. The relatively low skills of the work force (with only 12 percent graduating from college and 50 percent from high school) threatened the future economic viability of the region.

Campus-based research discovered very low aspirations and awareness of the benefits and opportunities for post-secondary education among the largely working-class population – school children and parents alike. The school systems tended to reinforce the blue-collar futures of all but the most promising and wealthiest students with a strong vocational program and very limited encouragement toward college participation. In 1987, the three-county area served by the campus sent fewer than 30 percent of recent high school graduates on to college – among the lowest counties in the state and the nation.

Mont Alto Campus devised a three-stage approach to increasing college participation in the region: public awareness, curricular reform, and early-intervention programs.

Public awareness of the need and potential for higher education was largely accomplished through intensive interaction with community leaders, media, and school district counselors, teachers and administrators.

Curricular reform required the development and modification of the campus curriculum from an almost exclusively two-year transfer curriculum to a combination of associate degrees and transfer curricula much more responsive to community employment and student demand.

The last stage, early-intervention programs, is the focus of this report.

Research indicated that most area school students dismissed the idea of post secondary education from their choice-set at a very early age, and many never consider the possibility of a college education in their future. To change that mindset, a series of programs brought a wide variety of K-12 students to campus for many different exposures with the same overall theme: "You, too, can go to college." Nearly 2,000 K-12 students have come annually to the campus.

Programs include: Adventures in Learning, the Equal Opportunity Program, and Next Step.

Adventures in Learning includes a Saturday experience for 300 students a year who participate in college-type experiential learning; and a weekday field trip experience with the same approach, but to which schools bring an entire seventh or eighth-grade class (the campus worried about reaching only the middle class in the Saturday program and wanted to ensure inclusion of all students, not just the self-identified, hence the requirement that a school bring an entire class). The Saturday class uses faculty volunteers and is self-funded. The weekday field-trip program is funded by a wide range of school and community-based service organizations. More than 1,500 children per year participate in Adventures in Learning field trips.

The Equal Opportunity Program is a summer and school-year program for minority junior high and high school youth which features introduction to college and a project-based, intensive-skill development and career-awareness curriculum. Field trips as well as community and campus-based activities are included, and about 60 students per year participate. Funding has come from

Continues on Page 598

community service organizations and university-based competitive grants.

Next Step is an intensive six-week summer program for ninth- and tenth-grade youth with college-going potential from poverty-level families. The program, based on an intensive project-based curriculum, includes hands-on science and communications skills and a team-building work experience. Students, teachers and families attend a once-per-month school-year program. Successful completers are guaranteed sufficient financial aid to attend Penn State University.

In the first year, 30 students participated; hereafter 50 students will. The program is funded through the local Private Industry Council with Job Training Partnership Act grant money.

As a result of the campus' intensive and extensive efforts to increase participation in college:

1) local students have doubled within four years; and
2) overall regional college attendance by recent high school graduates has risen from 29 percent to 41 percent – still well below state and national means, but nonetheless a significant and gratifying increase.

The campus plans additional programs, including two focusing on women in science and mathematics. Mont Alto Campus early intervention programs have won state-wide recognition within the university and higher education.

Contact:
Corrinne A. Caldwell
(717) 749-6000

Pennsylvania State University-Mont Alto Campus
Campus Drive
Mont Alto, PA 17237
Total head count enrollment-Credit: 910; Non-Credit: 2,000
Campuses/sites: 1; Full-time faculty: 53

WESTMORELAND COUNTY COMMUNITY COLLEGE

MEDIA TECHNOLOGY PHOTOGRAPHY OPTION

The option was created to ready students for work in commercial, industrial and educational settings

In the fall of 1992, Westmoreland County Community College added five courses and created a new program option designed to make use of current media technology. That Photography Option was created as a new associate degree, emphasizing computer-based training in state-of-the-art, digital sound and imaging.

The emphasis of the program is to keep up with changing technology in the media industry and to teach the student basic skills required to be a "lifelong learner" in a constantly changing field. Tasks that previously took hours to perform manually take only minutes using computer systems. Technologies that were "top-of-the-line" have become commonplace. The last decade, characterized by tremendous changes in technology, has resulted in computer systems that cost hundreds of thousands of dollars being out performed by desktop computers costing less than $10,000.

The Photography Option of the Media Technology program was created to prepare students for entry-level positions within commercial, industrial, and educational settings. The changes in technology have created the need for a new multimedia production specialist. They are trained to provide traditional photography and video skills that enables them to produce everything from desktop presentations and video editing to digital audio, animation, and graphic slides along with electronically manipulated photographic images.

Students acquire traditional darkroom production skills as well as state-of-the-art computer-based photographic imaging in a class such as Slide/Tape Presentation that plans and produces desktop and traditional slide shows. Individual student projects utilize presentation software such as Persuasion and PowerPoint to produce slides, speaker notes and video projected presentations from the initial idea through the storyboard, script, acquisition of photos and sound toward the final production.

Other media courses have been modified to include computerized sound, desktop video editing, and computer generated visuals. Production courses in Multimedia and Photography utilize Adobe's PhotoShop and Premiere software to produce print and video materials. In Electronic Photography students create photographs by capturing images with a still video disc camera, documenting student related campus activities. Then the image is transferred to the electronic darkroom of the Macintosh computer platform, for the creative phase of the digital production process. When image enhancement, manipulation, and editing is complete, work is out put to film and processed and printed using traditional color processors. The use of various input-output peripheral devices such as film scanners, CD-ROM, laser printers, flatbed scanners and film recorders are also explored in the development of corporate style visuals and other assignments.

The changes in technology have not only produced

course content and changes but also the technology itself is being utilized to enhance classroom instruction.

These program adaptations and changes have been made possible through grant monies secured by the college.

Contact:
Charles Sztroin, Jr., Media Instructor
(412) 925-4258

Westmoreland County Community College
Armbrust Road
Youngwood, PA 15697
Total head count enrollment-Credit: 6,748; Non-Credit: 5,056
Campuses/sites: 8; Full-time faculty: 83

WESTMORELAND COUNTY COMMUNITY COLLEGE

ELECTRONIC PUBLISHING AND IMAGING

This program fills the gap between Graphic Design and Printing Production

The Graphic industry is one of the most exciting and rapidly changing industries in America. Every day is another challenge, deadline, client or problem to resolve. Today's work force must be able to meet the known challenges of today and be prepared for the unknown challenges of tomorrow. Students must be prepared to address real-life situations as they occur in the work place.

Introduced in the fall of 1990, the Electronic Publishing & Imaging option of Graphic Communication Technology, tries to emulate the graphics industry in a classroom/laboratory setting.

EP&I is designed to ensure that WCCC graduates:

1) understand the historical development of the electronic publishing and imaging field;
2) understand the relationship between traditional and electronic production;
3) demonstrate the ability to creatively solve problems using current hardware and software, as well as tradition processes;
4) understand the relationships and limitations between the design processes and the production processes; and
5) understand the necessity of "life long learning" to remain current in a field that constantly under goes changes.

EP&I was created to fill a gap between two existing graphics programs, Graphic Design and Printing Production. The major goal of EP&I was to introduce "computer-based" technology to the more traditional-based program. To make sure that the program, its objectives and scope were reflective of the regional graphic production community, the Advisory Committee, comprising community and industry personnel, reviewed and provided guidance necessary to implement the program. In addition, the program is constantly evaluated by students and instructors, all of whom work in the graphics industry, to assure that current program content is reflective of industry trends, technology, and personnel requirements.

Students have access to: Macintosh computer workstations; flatbed scanners, both color and gray scale; film scanners; graphic tablets; laser printers; both b&w and color ink jet printers; film recorders; digital cameras; a variety of magnetic media including 45 Mb removable syquest storage drives; 128 Mb floptical drives; and CD-ROMs.

Students work with Aldus Gallery Effects, Aldus Digital Darkroom, Aldus PageMaker, Quark XPress, Adobe PhotoShop, Adobe Illustrator, Aldus Freehand, Aldus Gallery Effects, Aldus Digital Darkroom, Aldus Persuasion, and Brøderbund TypeStyler.

Also available to students for individual study is an extensive library of audio, animation, 3D and illustration software. Emphasis is placed upon solutions to classroom problems/projects that are aesthetically pleasing as well as technically correct, as they would apply to actual print production.

The program, course content and classroom instruction reflect the changes in industry and technology that are necessary to provide WCCC students with a relevant, quality education to meet today's challenges as well as tomorrow's.

The college, county and state have provided a great deal of funding for the acquisition of hardware, software and peripheral equipment that provides WCCC students with a truly unique educational experience, that rivals that of

Contact:
Gary Altemara, Assistant Professor, Graphic Communication Technology
(412) 925-4146

Westmoreland County Community College
Armbrust Road
Youngwood, PA 15697
Total head count enrollment-Credit: 6,748; Non-Credit: 5,056
Campuses/sites: 8; Full-time faculty: 83

HOTEL ADMINISTRATION

▨ The program supports tourism, which is one of ▨
Puerto Rico's most important industries

The Hotel Administration Program was established to contribute to the development of one of the most important industries in Puerto Rico today: tourism. The major goal of this program is to prepare competent, responsible and educated administrators for the hotel and restaurant industry.

This program started in August 1984 and has undergone continued evaluation and revision.

The Carolina Regional College has given top priority to this program in terms of budget assignment, laboratory construction and equipment. By January 1992 the new laboratories for this program began operating. Contacts have also been made for bringing professors, chefs and other experts in this industry from the U.S. and abroad as visiting professors or lectures to offer courses, demonstrations and lectures to Carolina Regional College professors, students and people in the local hotel and restaurant industries as well as the general public.

The chancellor and the president of the University of Puerto Rico have met with the Puerto Rico Hotel Association President and the Education Committee of the Puerto Rico Association to develop a plan for offering services to the industry and obtaining needed equipment. They also established an Advisory Board for the program. This board, which consists mainly of hotel industry members, has active participation in the program's endeavors and provides sound inputs for program and facilities development.

A proposal for the creation of a bachelors degree in Hotel and Restaurant Administration was submitted to and approved by the Academic Board, Academic Senate, Administration Board and the University Board and is waiting for approval of the Higher Council of Education. It is an initiation for academic renewal (IRA) on a three-year trial basis.

Contact:
Luz LaFontaine
(809), 257-0000, ext. 3215

University of Puerto Rico-Carolina Regional College
PO Box 4800
Carolina, PR 00984-4800
Total head count enrollment-Credit: 1,847
Campuses/sites: 1; Full-time faculty: 83

NATURAL SCIENCES TRANSFER PROGRAM

▨ Non-traditional teaching methods are used in the program, ▨
which includes Biology, Chemistry, Physics and Math

Non-traditional teaching methods are used in the Natural Sciences Transfer program at University of Puerto Rico-Carolina Regional College, which promotes the search for scientific knowledge, creativity and critical thinking while maintaining an effective transfer program to four years institutions.

The program's main goal is to provide students with experiences that fulfill their academic, intellectual and career needs in their first two years of study toward a BD in any of the following major areas: Pre-Physical Therapy, Pre-Medical, Pre-Odontology, Pre-Pharmacy, Pre-Nursing, Pre-Education in Health, Pre-Occupational Therapy, Pre-Medical Technology and Pre-Animal Health Technology.

The non-traditional teaching methods are exemplified by

the Minority Science Improvement Program (MSIP).

Five courses were offered for the first time as part of the MSIP Project: Undergraduate Research in Biology, Introduction to Instrumental Analysis, Analytical Chemistry, Statistics with Computers, and Applied Mathematics. Computer-assisted instruction (CAI) has also been utilized to improve students skills in all science fields.

For six consecutive years the Department has successfully presented a yearly Scientific Symposium, greatly accepted within the college community.

Two faculty members are actively working in research projects on the cellular regulation of amphibian regeneration. Two groups of CRC science students have had the opportunity to participate in this research. This research includes a close collaboration with the Biology Campus.

Several proposals for research in regeneration and in cell biology have been approved. The Department's goal is to establish a Cell and Development Biology Research Laboratory in the campus.

Contact:
Guillermo Castro
(809) 257-0000, ext. 3309

University of Puerto Rico-Carolina Regional College
PO Box 4800
Carolina, PR 00984-4800
Total head count enrollment-Credit: 1,847
Campuses/sites: 1; Full-time faculty: 83

PLANT PROPAGATION AND MICROPROPAGATION

This course is required of all students in Agricultural Technology minoring in horticulture

With one of the most modern and the best-equipped tissue culture laboratories in the Caribbean, the Plant Propagation and Micropropagation course at University of Puerto Rico-La Montana Regional College prepares students to deal with advanced and sophisticated technology in the science field.

Plant micropropagation or tissue culture is the multiplication of plants in vitro maintaining faithful characteristics of pattern plant using vegetative structures such as sprouts, leaves, roots and flowers. Plant tissue culture has different purposes, although two principal reasons are considered: massive plant production and virus-free plants. Other applications are induction and selection of mutation, biosynthesis products, studies of plant cell structure functions, and studies of plant development, growth and propagation in vitro.

The course, created in 1989, is a requisite for students of the Agricultural Technology Department with a minor in horticulture. This course consist of three hours of theory and three hours of laboratory weekly. Some of the objectives are:
1) to relate the students with modern techniques of propagation in plant production and its global economic importance;
2) to enable the students in chemical handling into aseptic environment;
3) to recognize the plant structure used in this technique; and
4) to relate the students with the operation use of laboratory equipment and materials.

In addition to learning, each student conduct a special project that consist of cultivating a particular plant studying the different phases of the process. Having hands-on experience, the students are trained more efficiently.

Contact:
Jose Rivera, Instructor-in-Charge
(809) 894-2828

University of Puerto Rico-La Montana Regional College
Regional Colleges Administration, Box 2500
Utuado, PR 00641
Total head count enrollment-Credit: 697
Campuses/sites: 1; Full-time faculty: 54

COMPUTERS APPLICATIONS IN AGRICULTURAL PRODUCTION

Computer simulations are used in quality control procedures, food market evaluation and consumers forecast reports

Because computers are constantly related to agriculture trends, food processing and other related fields, La Montana Regional College of the University of Puerto Rico requires the Computers Applications in Agricultural Production course for all the students enrolled at the Agricultural Technology Department.

The college introduced portable computers for the use in the Soil Analysis and Pest Control Programs because frequently laboratories are held in real field situations and these tools have demonstrated to be very helpful enhancing the instruction process. Students from the Food Processing program are involved in computer simulations for quality control procedures, food market evaluation and consumers forecast reports. Breeding cattle sites near the college are also used as laboratories for computer data

Continues on Page 602

bases applications.

In May 1992, the University of Puerto Rico provided a new computer lab with 30 IBM PS computers, plotters, scanners, letter quality printers for the students of this program. In this lab the students are trained in word processing, electronic spread sheets and electronic mail using the University of Puerto Rico Network (UPRNET). Students are discovering applications that enhance the classroom learning and the computer has become an additional tool in the field. The Office of the Academic Dean at La Montana College is encouraging faculty involvement in software evaluation for acquisition. This year the faculty will be able to use computers for curriculum update.

The Computers Applications in Agricultural Production course has been recognized from presentations at Industrial Fomentation Program of the Commonwealth of Puerto Rico, COMPUCAMPUS Conference of Puerto Rico (1992) and The First Symposium of Computers Applications in Education and Business (1991).

Contact:
Pedro L. Cartagena, Instructor-in-Charge
(809) 894-2828

University of Puerto Rico-La Montana Regional College
Regional Colleges Administration, Box 2500
Utuado, PR 00641
Total head count enrollment-Credit: 697
Campuses/sites: 1; Full-time faculty: 54

TECH PREP/ASSOCIATE DEGREE

*Since its inception, the program has grown significantly
in size, subject areas and students*

In 1987, the Community College of Rhode Island (CCRI) took the initiative and the lead in Rhode Island by establishing a 2+2 Tech Prep/Associate Degree Program. The program operates as a partnership between the community college and secondary schools and is designed to:

1) provide an alternative program of study for high school students enrolled in unfocused general education programs that prepare them for neither college nor employment;

2) keep at-risk students in school; and

3) respond to increasing demands for skilled technicians by employers; through a series of goal-oriented, hands-on courses which provide a foundation in basic academic and technical skills, students are better prepared for post secondary programs, the pursuit of an associate's degree and subsequently a career in a technical, business or health field.

A national movement is underway in the United States to implement tech prep programs in every state in order to meet the needs of a large number of undirected students as well as to meet the country's changing employment needs. Rhode Island is one of the few states to have a well-established, successful tech prep program currently in place. Since its inception, the CCRI Tech Prep Program has expanded in size, subject areas and student services.

CCRI President Edward J. Liston took the lead role in introducing the program throughout the state by hosting informational sessions for secondary school superintendents and principals, teachers and guidance counselors as well as holding discussions with public officials. Six high schools came aboard the first year by offering a course in applied technology and CCRI hosted a career development activity and orientation at the college.

Since then, the program has continued to develop and expand and now includes complete programs in technology, business, office administration and allied health. Today, 30 of the 40 secondary schools in Rhode Island are actively participating in the Tech Prep Program. More than 1,000 tech prep students are involved on the high school level and more than 300 are enrolled at the community college, with a large influx expected. Efforts are ongoing to develop articulation agreements with the remaining high schools in Rhode Island that are not participating and to expand program areas available to students. In-service training is provided for both secondary school and college faculty. "Career days" and other orientation activities are held for students and the program director visits the schools to meet with administration and faculty regularly.

In addition, the role of the business community has become increasingly important to the CCRI Tech Prep Program. With assistance from local Chambers of Commerce, a mentoring program has been developed to provide students with adult role models, guidance, support and exposure to career opportunities in a number of fields. There is also a pilot project to improve the school to work transition that includes employability skills development as well as a summer component aimed at enrichment and applied academic activities.

Program Director Judith Marmaras is responsible for the overall development and implementation of the secondary school partnerships. She is assisted by a counselor who provides student support services and retention activities for tech prep students at the post secondary level. CCRI's Cooperative Education Program provides the vehicle for job readiness training, career development and paid cooperative education placements.

The Tech Prep Program is funded by Rhode Island Workforce 2000; the Rhode Island Department of Elementary and Secondary Education, Division of Vocational and Adult Education; and the RI Office of Higher Education. Summer programs have been made possible by the Northern Rhode Island Private Industry Council and by funds allocated through the Job Training Partnership Act.

The Community College of Rhode Island has been selected as one of the three community colleges nationwide to receive the Tech Prep-Associate Degree Award for program excellence from the American Association of Community and Junior Colleges. Sponsored by AutoDesk, Inc., and the Tennessee Valley Authority, the award honors colleges and school districts that have developed exemplary working relationships while providing coordinated technical training during the last two years of high school and the first two years of post secondary education.

Additionally, the program director has been asked to deliver presentations and consult on the establishment of similar programs in almost 20 states. She was also a contributing authority for *Tech Prep: A Win Win Situation*, by Dale Parnell and Dan Hull, and serves on the Rhode Island Skills Commission.

Contact:
Judith Marmaras, Director
(401) 825-2143

Community College of Rhode Island
400 East Avenue
Warwick, RI 02886
Total head count enrollment-Credit: 17,050; Non-Credit: 25,000
Campuses/sites: 9; Full-time faculty: 305

NUCLEAR ENGINEERING TECHNOLOGY

*In addition to courses taught on campus, courses are also taught on site
for U.S. Department of Energy contractors and their employees*

Entry-level jobs as nuclear reactor operator-trainees, health physics technicians, and environmental and waste management technicians await graduates of Aiken Technical College's Nuclear Engineering Technology Program.

ATC offers both Associate Degree and Certificate programs in Nuclear Engineering Technology. The Associate Degree program offers two emphasis areas, Health Physics and Hazardous Waste Management. Certificates in Hazardous Waste Management are offered at three levels, corresponding to biological, chemical and radiological specializations.

The Associate Degree program is offered both day and evening. Students enrolled in the Certificate programs are primarily evening students. Those students enrolled in the Certificate programs must be employed in the field of waste management, or possess science and mathematics prerequisites prior to enrollment.

In addition to courses taught on the college campus, courses in Nuclear Engineering Technology are also taught

on site for the U.S. Department of Energy contractors and their employees in the local service area. Courses are taught at the Savannah River Site for Westinghouse Savannah River Company employees.

Aiken Technical College is also a member of the C2NET (Consortium of Community Colleges), recognized by the DOE as providers of Nuclear and Environment Engineering Technology programs. Participation is through network meetings and consortia newsletters, including an exchange of program syllabi.

In association with Westinghouse Savannah River Company, second-year students are offered cooperative education assignments at the Savannah River Site. Students accepted in the cooperative education program receive tuition stipends and financial incentives.

Graduates of the Nuclear Engineering Technology Associate Degree program can apply credits earned at ATC toward a baccalaureate degree at several colleges and universities.

Contact:
Alan Nelms, Chair, Health Sciences
(803) 593-9231, ext. 319

Aiken Technical College
PO Drawer 696
Aiken, SC 29802-0696
Total head count enrollment-Credit: 3,652; Non-Credit: 4,054
Campuses/sites: 1; Full-time faculty: 54

EARLY CHILDHOOD DEVELOPMENT

*Consistent with the ways children grow and develop, the program
allows for individual differences in rates and styles of learning*

The on-campus Aiken Technical College Child Development Center is one significant aspect of an Early Development Program that gives the student the option of receiving a one-year diploma with 44 semester-hour credits required or a certificate with 27 semester-hour credits required. The diploma is designed to meet the needs of the student who has had no prior experience in working with young children. The certificate is designed to meet the needs of the student who is working in an environment with young children.

The Early Childhood Development (ECD) student is taught skills necessary to plan and implement a quality, developmentally appropriate child care or preschool program for young children. In working with young children at the ATC Child Development Center and in private, church and public centers in the area, students receive many practical experiences to master the following

skills:

1) to provide activities which will stimulate the mental, emotional, social and physical development of the child;
2) to guide children in the formation of wholesome habits and attitudes;
3) to meet the physical and nutritional needs of preschool children; and
4) to help the children realize that they are purposeful, intelligent, creative, feeling, social persons who are in the lifelong process of learning.

In addition, the students learn to work and communicate with parents, fellow teachers, employers and peers.

The Aiken Technical College Child Development Center is located on the campus, but is housed in a separate building. Its purpose is to provide a safe and secure environment staffed by qualified professionals. Through well-planned, developmentally appropriate, hands-on play activities offered throughout the day, the Center promotes the development of each child physically, emotionally, socially and cognitively. Consistent with the manner in which children grow and develop, our carefully balanced program allows for individual differences in rates and styles of learning. Our focus is on the whole child.

Through this, our ultimate goal is to provide an environment in which children thrive while encouraging the formation of a positive and healthy self-concept. All staff members are experienced in early childhood and participate in a continuous program of in-service education and studies for professional advancement in order to remain alert to the ever-changing needs of today's families and to the findings of current research. The Center is open to all children, regardless of race, nationality or creed, who may benefit from our type of program. Students fulfill lab requirements each week as part of their semester-hour credits in the ECD program. A Supervised Field Experience is also required as a part of the Diploma program, in which the student plans and implements a two-week unit with the children.

The Child Development Center has been validated as a Block Grant Provider for the state of South Carolina, and the college has recently been selected as a regional training site for Block Grant Providers. The program also works closely with Head Start in providing training for their teachers and assistants. Through many planning efforts statewide, the ECD Certificate and Diploma have been approved in certifying teachers and assistants for the Head Start Program.

The program coordinator for Early Childhood Development maintains active involvement in early childhood education organizations locally, statewide and nationally. She recently organized a local affiliate chapter of the South Carolina Association for the Education of Young Children in which she serves as President-Elect. She also serves as Conference Chair for an Early Childhood Seminar held at the college in April 1993, during the Week of the Young Child. Her other involvements locally include speaking to various community groups on quality environments for young children, working on the Visions for Youth Board, and conducting parent training seminars for parents of at risk children. Statewide, she sits on the governing board of the South Carolina Association for the Education of Young Children as Public Relations Chairman. She was elected to serve as President-Elect and Conference Chairman for the state conference in October 1993. Nationally, she serves as a validator for the National Academy of Early Childhood Programs, a division of the National Association for the Education of Young Children, which accredits programs for young children.

Contact:
Judy Scurlock, Chair
(803) 593-9231, ext. 303

Aiken Technical College
PO Drawer 696
Aiken, SC 29802-0696
Total head count enrollment-Credit: 3,652; Non-Credit: 4,054
Campuses/sites: 1; Full-time faculty: 54

A DAY FOR ANDERSON COLLEGE

▨ This one-day fund-raising event replaces a fund drive ▨
that ran for several weeks each fall

In 1985, Anderson College launched "A Day for Anderson College," a one-day fund-raising event modeled after a similar program at North Carolina Wesleyan College and designed to rejuvenate a lagging Annual Fund drive.

"A-Day" marked a significant departure in style from the traditional Annual Fund drive, which ran for several weeks each fall and included a series of reporting luncheons (not unlike the United Way campaign structure).

The design for "A Day for Anderson College" was simple: after advance planning and solicitation of major gifts by a campaign chairman and his/her steering committee, scores of volunteers (approximately 100) from the business sector would gather at the college on the morning of "A-Day" to go out in pairs to solicit gifts from business and industry (about 10 calls per team) for the Annual Fund. The entire event – from the kickoff breakfast to the victory celebration – would last no more than 12 hours. Everything that previously had been completed over a period of weeks or months would be condensed into a single, dynamic day – "A Day for Anderson College."

In their discussions about improving the effectiveness of Anderson College's traditional Annual Fund campaign, institutional advancement planners reached the following conclusions:

- The volunteers and especially the leadership were showing signs of weariness long before the campaign was completed. *In a one-day blitz, the campaign would be over before volunteers would have the chance to grow weary.*
- There was a need to involve more people in the campaign and to identify new leadership for coming

Continues on Page 606

years. *"A-Day" would offer an opportunity for many more volunteers to be involved.*

- A large percentage of the volunteers, working on their own, either didn't make their calls or put little effort into soliciting a gift once they did make a call. *During "A-Day," volunteers would be strongly encouraged to work in pairs and to complete their calls in person before the day was over.*

- There were too many meetings involving too many people at too great an expense in time and money prior to the actual kickoff meeting. *With "A-Day," the only meetings for the volunteers would be the kickoff breakfast and the victory celebration-both on the same day.*

- There were too many people involved in the planning process. (The best volunteers/solicitors are not necessarily the best fund-raising technicians, just as the best fund-raising technicians are not necessarily the best solicitors.) *The planning of "A-Day" would be handled by the college advancement staff.*

- The Annual Fund drive came at a time that conflicted with the community's largest fund-raising campaign, the United Way campaign (which drew from the same pool of volunteers). *The date for "A Day for Anderson College" would be set for two weeks before the United Way campaign – a preemptive strike!*

The central organization of the "A-Day" campaign consists of a general chairman and a steering committee. The steering committee can vary in number and size, but it is imperative that each member know and understand the mission of the college, the goals of the campaign, and have proven success as a solicitor. The committee's main function is to help identify and evaluate prospects and to solicit major prospects.

It is the responsibility of the institutional advancement staff to coordinate all activities relevant to the success of the campaign, including the creation, approval and implementation of a master plan; the development and evaluation of a prospect list; recruiting and training of volunteers; assigning volunteers to teams and teams to prospects; promoting the campaign throughout the community; and making arrangements for the various meetings and special events that accompany the campaign.

The key to the success of the one-day campaign, of course, lies in the hands of the volunteers. It is imperative that a large number of volunteers be recruited and that they understand the crucial role they play. Volunteers must be encouraged to work in two-person teams and make their solicitation calls in person. No telephone calls and no one-on-one visits should be permitted except in extremely unusual circumstances.

In its first year, "A Day for Anderson College" more than doubled the amount of money that had been raised from business and industry during the previous fiscal year (from $25,000 to $50,000). The following year brought a 50 percent increase. Today, "A-Day" brings in about $100,000 annually. Although the percentage of increase has grown smaller each year (as the campaign has saturated the business/industry community), "A Day for Anderson College" provided a dramatic jump-start to an annual giving program that was languishing far beneath its potential.

Contact:
R. Dean Woods, Vice President, Institutional Advancement
(803) 231-2068

Anderson College
16 Boulevard
Anderson, SC 29621
Total head count enrollment-Credit: 1,172
Campuses/sites: 1; Full-time faculty: 62

ACADEMIC OLYMPICS

▨ This half-day academic competition allows students to take ▨ two subject tests under the multiple choice format

In 1986, the Anderson College Community Relations Office enlisted the cooperation of more than 50 faculty and staff volunteers to initiate the college's first annual Academic Olympics. After attracting a surprising 450 high school students the first year, Academic Olympics has grown into a major campus event. The Academic Olympics at Anderson College is patterned after a similar event held at Southwestern Community College in Sylva, North Carolina.

Basically, Academic Olympics is a half-day academic competition held annually on the AC campus. Students may choose to take two subject tests under the multiple choice format. The AC faculty prepares, administers and scores the tests.

There are three testing periods followed by an exciting awards ceremony. Not all tests are written. In the field of art, students bring works to be judged. In music and theatre, they perform. Tests begin at 9 a.m. and the awards ceremony is over by 12:30 p.m.

Students scoring highest on each test earn an award and up to five points for his/her respective school. Winning individuals may also be eligible for departmental scholarships form Anderson College. Team points are totaled to establish winners in both "large school" and "small school" divisions. The top three teams in each division receive a trophy. We also encourage schools to compete for a "Spirit Award."

Anderson College benefits from this event because it is an opportunity to open our campus to a large number of high school students and their sponsors. The event is an opportunity to:

1) bring our campus to the attention of academically gifted students
2) bring our academic program to the attention of high school teachers and counselors; and
3) gain media coverage for the college.

We believe that area high schools benefit by:

1) promoting the importance of academics
2) building excitement within the student body to excel in an academic area
3) giving students who might not excel in other activities a chance to be recognized for their abilities; and
4) developing school spirit.

Academic Olympics is a brief, intense event which requires excellent planning and organization in order to be successful. Currently, Academic Olympics is coordinated by the Associate Academic Dean's office.

Planning begins approximately three months before the event and includes collecting test materials and arranging test sites, distributing registration materials to high schools, and the recruitment and training of faculty/staff volunteers.

On the day of the event, college volunteers arrive on campus at 8 a.m. and the last visitor has left campus by 12:30 p.m. In 1992, more than 100 faculty, staff and AC students volunteered to help with participants in Academic Olympics. The annual budget for the event is approximately $4,000.

In 1992, more than 700 high school students from 26 area high schools registered for tests and performances in 28 subject areas. Schools from as far away as Charleston, SC, have asked to be invited to participate. And best of all, more than 45 of AC's current students competed for their high schools in Academic Olympics in 1989, 1990 and/or 1991.

Contact:
Charles Hood, Associate Academic Dean
(803) 231-2065

Anderson College
16 Boulevard
Anderson, SC 29621
Total head count enrollment-Credit: 1,172
Campuses/sites: 1; Full-time faculty: 62

CENTRAL CAROLINA TECHNICAL COLLEGE

TRANSITIONAL STUDIES

At the center of the Transitional Studies continuum is the Developmental Studies program, which allows the college's "open door" policy to become a reality

Rising adult illiteracy, increasing high school dropout rates, the need for a better-educated work force to compete in today's global marketplace, and commitment to an open admissions policy – all these things affirm the need for a systems approach in the delivery of basic skills instruction. Such an approach is offered through the Transitional Studies program at Central Carolina Technical College. Both cost-effective and educationally productive, this program offers three unique components: management of students, management of staff, and management of program.

The program is part of the college's General Education and Transitional Studies Division, which provides three "seamless" transitional progressions – from the developmental studies program to college preparatory courses to post secondary general education credit courses. Students may enter at any point along this seamless continuum wherein opportunities to reach their academic goals are offered in a variety of settings: satellite locations, industrial sites, as well as on-campus individualized and lecture-style classes.

At the center of the Transitional Studies continuum is the Developmental Studies program, which allows the college's "open door" policy to become a reality. The developmental studies curriculum is competency-based and includes a variety of learning approaches to maximize the students' potential for reaching academic goals. In addition to the use of texts, filmstrips, tapes, computer-assisted instruction and interactive videos, computer-managed instruction includes the use of the Learning Management System (LMS) based in Calgary, Canada.

In this well-structured management system, which personalizes the approach for developmental education, the student management dimension of the program distinguishes it from the typical "learning lab" approach. Not an entirely self-paced program, this systems approach to instruction involves pre-stated learning objectives, pre- and post-criterion referenced tests, sequentially designed curriculum and assignment of grades through an earned-point system. There are three separate individualized areas: reading, math and English. A department head who is responsible for the curriculum and management of each of these areas, and learning managers facilitate the learn-

Continues on Page 608

ing process of students. In addition, daily linear management meetings are held to assure a holistic view of students and to ensure accountability.

The first aspect of the program, student management, involves intricate block schedules for all sessions – morning, afternoon, evening and off-campus locations. Students are assigned to a specific section or group and are assigned specific times to attend individualized classes. Also, Learning Managers from each discipline form teams to which a specific group of students (15 to 18 per section) is assisted. Each department head serves as academic advisor for a section of students for each of the sessions. Department heads are accountable for the academic progress of each of their students in all sections, within the three areas of reading, math, and English. In order to track students progress holistically, linear management meetings are held on a daily basis with at least one team of learning managers from each session. Department heads follow these meetings with individual advising sessions with students.

The second aspect of management utilized in this system is staff management. Well-trained, competent and humanistic learning managers are the key to the success of the individualized approach to delivery of developmental education. These learning managers, who guide the student through the learning process, receive extensive training in using the system. They hold staff positions which allows for substantial savings in personnel costs.

The third component of this unique developmental studies program is program management. The primary goal of the program is to equip under-prepared students with the skills necessary to perform as well as students entering certificate, diploma, or degree programs who did not require preparation in Developmental Studies. The success of the program is measured in several ways. Detailed statistical studies of student enrollment, retention rates, academic tracking, and graduation rates are routinely performed. Historically, an average 42 percent of students who graduate from Central Carolina Technical College have completed at least one course in the Transitional Studies program.

Additionally, curricula tracking studies indicate that former developmental students at Central Carolina Technical College do perform as well as those students who were initially prepared to enter targeted entry-level post secondary courses at the college. A systematic review of the results of these and other studies provide ongoing information and data to continually revise our curricula, and to implement future planning, development and management strategies for the program.

The primary keys to success are:
1) systematic design of the total learning environment;
2) provision for multiple levels of entry into carefully ordered instructional sequences;
3) staff involvement personally and professionally; and
4) a commitment to the holistic approach to problem solving and achieving results.

Contact:
Anna T. Strange, Dean
(803) 778-6682

Central Carolina Technical College
506 North Guignard Drive
Sumter, SC 29153
Total head count enrollment-Credit: 2,333; Non-Credit: 2,586
Campuses/sites: 1; Full-time faculty: 65

CENTRAL CAROLINA TECHNICAL COLLEGE

ENVIRONMENTAL TRAINING CENTER

*▦ The Center provides training specifically designed to help industry address changes ▦
in federal and state environmental regulations*

The Environmental Training Center at Central Carolina Technical College provides a unique educational opportunity for members of the business and industrial communities of South Carolina. It provides training programs specifically designed to help industry address current changes in both federal and state environmental regulations which impact their organization's operation.

The Center was born during the 1980's, when the State Board of Technical and Comprehensive education established several Resource Centers in South Carolina. Each of the centers specializes in a specific area and offer programs on a statewide basis. For example, one focuses on Electro-Mechanical Technology, one on applied Electronics and another on Advanced Machine Tools.

The Environmental Training Center at Central Carolina

opened in 1983 as the Water Quality Institute. Its initial mission was to provide technical assistance and classroom training for water and wastewater operators in South Carolina. In 1986, in response to a growing need for additional environmental training among South Carolina industry, the Center's repertoire of courses was expanded to include training on hazardous materials handling and emergency response.

The Center's continuing mission is to provide the highest quality training programs on environmental topics. Continuing education short courses and seminars are regularly conducted on new and existing technologies for improving water and wastewater treatment operations. Other non-credit courses and seminars include the areas of waste minimization, environmental law, and hazardous materials handling. An extensive variety of seminars are conducted on specific topics concerning issues of environmental regulatory compliance. The areas addressed include, but are not limited to: The Clean Air Act, The Solid Waste Management Act and The Clean Water Act.

One of the goals of the Center is to provide environmental training support to the other 15 Technical Colleges in South Carolina. Seminars on topics which are of interest to another college's constituencies are frequently co-sponsored at that college's facility. In addition, the Center offers assistance to other college's in assessing their own facilities compliance with environmental and safety requirements. The Environmental Training Center also conducts customized environmental training programs for industry at their location.

A feature of the Environmental Training Center is the symbiotic relationship which exists between its non-credit courses and the Associate Degree program which shares the Environmental Engineering Technology Associate Degree offered in South Carolina. Graduates of the program are prepared at the technician level for entry-level positions at either water or wastewater treatment plants, or to assume positions in industry in the area of hazardous materials handling.

During a two-year period, the program experienced a tremendous growth in enrollment (more than 200 percent) of both full-time and part-time students. In the fall of 1990, 20 students were enrolled. In the spring of 1992, enrollment reached 70.

In 1991, Central Carolina, through the Training Center, formed a consortium with four other technical colleges in the state to develop a new curriculum on Environmental Restoration and Waste Minimization. The program provides industry personnel an opportunity to learn practical applications of current technologies in the areas of waste minimization and pollution prevention. The project is funded by participating Colleges and by the U.S. Environmental Protection Agency.

The Environmental Training Center first opened in 1983 as the Water Quality Institute. Its mission was to provide technical assistance and classroom training for water and wastewater operators in South Carolina. In 1986, in response to a growing need for other environmental training among South Carolina industry, the Center expanded its offerings to include hazardous materials handling and emergency response training. Its continuing mission is to provide the highest quality training on a variety of environmental topics to the business and industrial communities of South Carolina.

The Center's approximately 9,000-square-foot building was erected with an EPA construction grant. The Center and its programs are an integral part of Central Carolina Technical College. Its personnel consists of one full-time associate director, one program manager/instructor, and two support staff. The Environmental Engineering Technology Degree Program has one full-time instructor. The majority of the Continuing Education courses are taught by adjunct faculty. Frequently the Environmental Training Center utilizes experts from throughout the nation to present specific technical material.

The Center is a charter member of the National Environmental Training Association and the National Coalition of Training Centers. Most recently, it was selected as one of only four Training Centers in the United States and the only one on the East Coast, to be visited by the Director of Water and Wastewater Training for Nepal during his American tour.

Contact:
Cleta Q. Smith, Associate Director
(803) 778-6656

Central Carolina Technical College
506 North Guignard Drive
Sumter, SC 29153
Total head count enrollment-Credit: 2,333; Non-Credit: 2,586
Campuses/sites: 1; Full-time faculty: 65

CHESTERFIELD-MARLBORO TECHNICAL COLLEGE

TEACHER TRAINING "2+2" PARTNERSHIP

The success of this approach for recruiting minority teachers stems from a package of coordinated services and activities developed by two colleges

Like many rural areas, Chesterfield and Marlboro counties of South Carolina faced a problem in recruiting and retaining public school teachers, especially members of minority groups. Teacher aides and other staff members were interested in continuing their education and becoming certified teachers, but geographic isolation (the nearest senior college is an hour away) made it difficult for area school systems to provide an upgrading path.

Working in partnership with the Chesterfield County School District and Francis Marion University, Chesterfield-Marlboro Technical College has addressed this critical need through the development of a "2+2" elementary education program, offering a coordinated program of higher education for minorities and residents of rural communities; and to increase teacher recruitment and retention rates for area public school districts. Students may complete most requirements for a baccalau-

Continues on Page 610

reate degree in elementary education on the campus of Chesterfield-Marlboro Technical College.

The success of this 2+2 approach has stemmed largely from a package of coordinated services and activities developed by the two colleges, including recruitment, registration, academic advisement, course articulation, financial aid, course scheduling, facilities and faculty. The vice president for instruction from Chesterfield-Marlboro Technical College meets regularly with the dean of the School of Education at Francis Marion University to monitor the program and make any necessary adjustments.

Representatives from Francis Marion University and CMTC provide recruitment and intake services within the area school districts, which continue to provide a large portion of students entering the program. Registration is open to the general public, and many "traditional" students have also enrolled. Courses are chosen from each institution based on each student's needs, and students may be

jointly enrolled in Chesterfield-Marlboro Technical College and Francis Marion University during the same semester. Registration is coordinated between the two colleges, and financial aid eligibility may be maintained in cases of joint enrollment. The course sequence is planned and coordinated by the academic departments at both colleges to provide maximum access and flexibility.

This partnership has resulted in a site-based approach to intake, advisement and instruction for teacher education that utilizes all available resources to provide access for minorities, rural residents and traditionally under-served population groups. Students are afforded a virtually "seamless" pathway of articulation, joint enrollment and coordinated services leading to a four-year degree and teacher certification. After just two years of operation, contracts were signed with five former aides who became certified teachers through the program. Dozens more are in process.

Contact:
Sandra H. Barbour, Vice President, Instruction
(803) 537-5286

Chesterfield-Marlboro Technical College
Drawer 1007
Cheraw, SC 29520
Total head count enrollment-Credit: 974; Non-Credit: 1,512
Campuses/sites: 1; Full-time faculty: 25

RADIOLOGIC TECHNOLOGY

Students and faculty of the sponsoring institutions rotate through other local hospitals, making it a true community program

The shortages of health workers in certain disciplines have plagued providers for many years. In an effort to increase its pool of qualified workers the McLeod Regional Medical Center founded a hospital-based Radiology program. All educational, didactic and clinical experiences were provided at the hospital and upon completion of the program students received a diploma in X-Ray Technology.

Seeking to develop a stronger X-Ray Program, McLeod entered into negotiations with Florence-Darlington Technical College. From a humble beginning in 1966 an affiliated program was launched in 1969. Students who complete this program now receive an Associate in Science Degree.

The hospital provides faculty officer as well as didactic classroom and clinical space. Students return to campus for General Education courses. Faculty are employees of both institutions and program costs are shared equitably. Faculty attend meetings on campus, thus allowing for close interaction with fellow faculty members. A computer

modem connects this off-campus effort to the main computer, thus allowing easy access to student records.

The strong point of this program is that students and faculty of the sponsoring institutions also rotate through other local hospitals. This program is truly a community effort that provides quality practitioners who have been exposed to and have a working knowledge of area institutions. This exposure allows the students to get to know the health providers and in turn providers get to know and recruit the students.

This innovative approach to educational program development enabled the hospital and the college to develop and maintain a program that either one may not have been able to support alone. Joining nine other Allied Health programs, the Radiologic Technology program has allowed FDTC to cooperatively meet the staffing needs of area health providers. The visible success of this program has served as a positive model for other programs; for instance, a Practical Nursing program is being planned as a joint venture between the college and area health providers.

Contact:
Yancy Wells, Program Director
(803) 667-2804

Florence-Darlington Technical College
PO Box 100548
Florence, SC 29501-0548
Total head count enrollment-Credit: 2,610; Non-Credit: 3,051
Campuses/sites: 1; Full-time faculty: 83

INDEPENDENT STUDY

The program, begun in 1987, delivers business and general education course to about 10 percent of the student body each term

The Independent Study program at Florence-Darlington Technical College is a unique program in the two-year colleges in South Carolina, where it can effectively meet the instructional needs of a diverse student population.

For years before the program's implementation, instructors at Florence-Darlington Technical College had been working individually with students who needed to complete a course not being offered through traditional instructional methods. In the spring of 1987, with the encouragement of the administration, an English department faculty member researched Independent Study programs at more than 40 colleges. He determined that most of these programs were either a collection of correspondence courses or only offered at four year colleges. The program was begun in the summer of 1987 and currently delivers business and general education courses to an average of 250 students (almost 10 percent of the student body) each term.

Independent Study provides the structure for students to take courses under the direction of a supervising instructor available to answer questions, provide tutoring as needed, grade papers and determine course grade. During the first week of the term students obtain a course syllabi developed by the supervising instructor and the textbook, which is the same text as is used in the lecture class. The student meets with his instructor in an Orientation to Independent Study and learns how to contact this instructor for clarification of assignments and additional help. The student then must come on campus only to take tests and write a final examination administered in the testing center. Course quality is maintained by staffing courses with supervising instructors who are full-time faculty members currently teaching the same course in a lecture format. Upon completion of the course of study, students are expected to demonstrate the same competencies as in lecture format courses. Program effectiveness is monitored constantly.

The Independent Study format provides another avenue for entry into a college program for those students whose jobs, family, or distance from campus prevent them from attending classes. It also provides flexibility of scheduling classes for students who are out of sequence with their curriculum. As the student body demographics are maturing, changing from full-time students to part-time students, moving from a predominately male population to a female population, it is important that we meet their changing educational needs.

Contact:
Wilma N. Whitaker, Dean of Arts and Sciences
(803) 661-8131

Florence-Darlington Technical College
PO Box 100548
Florence, SC 29501-0548
Total head count enrollment-Credit: 2,610; Non-Credit: 3,051
Campuses/sites: 1; Full-time faculty: 83

GENERAL MANUFACTURING CERTIFICATION

The program was developed to address the need of one company's manufacturing facility

As the Cryovac Company was expanding, many of their work force were reaching retirement age, creating an anticipated need for approximately 80 employees by the end of 1988. With a critical need for qualified applicants/employees at Simpsonville, South Carolina, manufacturing facility, the company turned to Greenville Technical College (GTC). The college helped fill the work force gap through a General Manufacturing Certification Program developed by GTC and Cryovac, a manufacturer of plastics that is a Division of W. R. Grace and Company.

Cryovac, which employs 1,460 at its Simpsonville facility, has an extensive in-house training program for specific technical training. But the company needed a process to identify potential employees who could move successfully through their highly technical, in-depth training process to the highest operator level.

Cryovac and GTC personnel worked closely together to plan and implement what is now a highly successful program that has been replicated by many other companies. It was decided to measure reading comprehension, math skills and mechanical aptitude through testing. GTC tested a random sample of employees on all shifts at Cryovac to determine minimum mechanical aptitude necessary for potential employees, and reviewed Cryovac training manuals to ascertain reading and math levels necessary to successfully complete the in-house training program. Based on the above data, Cryovac determined

Continues on Page 612

minimum levels required for admission into the program.

Courses were set up by GTC to adhere to the basic educational and technical requirements of Cryovac. Individuals who fail to meet minimum levels to qualify for the program can enter the college's Adult Education program to upgrade their reading and math levels. Then they can be re-tested to determine whether they are eligible to enter the program. This provides an opportunity for all applicants to be considered.

The process and costs are as follows:

- advertisements, paid for by Cryovac, appear in the local newspaper; cost of each ad is approximately $400;
- interested potential applicants contact the college for information on the program and to sign up for the testing;
- GTC conducts a 4-1/2 hour testing session, which accommodates up to 150 people; the cost is approximately $35 per person;
- those who successfully complete the testing are invited to tour the Simpsonville plant and ask questions of both Cryovac and GTC personnel; through this point, there is no cost to the applicant;
- those who fail the testing portion are referred to GTC's Adult Education program; the cost is $25 per credit hour to the individual;
- those who enter the General Manufacturing

Certification Program must pay $200 for the courses and are given the option of making individual payments before each class; all materials are included in the price of each course; program components are registration ($15), Interpersonal Skills ($50), Materials Management ($30), Statistical Process Control ($60), Introduction to Computers ($15), and Hand Tools/Measuring Tools ($30); and

- Cryovac interviews each successful graduate of the program.

There is evidence of tremendous support for the program on the part of both Cryovac and GTC. Cryovac has expanded the program to include other plants in Texas and South Carolina. They have invited the president of Northwestern University, a representative from the Greenville Chamber of Commerce, Cryovac officials from their headquarters, and the president of GTC to participate in a presentation aimed at expanding the program to their other plants.

To date, more than 300 individuals have been hired through this program, and there is potential for many more to participate. With Greenville's relatively low unemployment rate, it is difficult for area industries to identify potential employees with the required skills, and the college is working with other companies to develop similar programs for them.

Contact:
F.M. Rogers, Director, Business and Industry Services
(803) 250-8204

Greenville Technical College
PO Box 5616
Greenville, SC 29606-5616
Total head count enrollment-Credit: 8,690; Non-Credit: 32,605
Campuses/sites: 4; Full-time faculty: 230

GREENVILLE TECHNICAL COLLEGE

ACCELERATED RESPIRATORY TECHNICIAN / THERAPIST PROGRAM

These two programs, which help fill a local need for respiratory care practitioners, was designed to be convenient for working professionals

For several years, the demand has far exceeded the supply of respiratory care practitioners. In response to this need, Greenville Technical College's Respiratory Advisory Committee formed a subcommittee in 1988 to study alternative methods for delivering respiratory care education. Their focus was to design a program that would be convenient for working professionals – accelerated, flexible and responsive to the manpower shortage of respiratory technicians and therapists.

The result has been the development and implementation of two new programs: Accelerated Respiratory Technician and Accelerated Respiratory Therapist.

The Accelerated Respiratory Technician program shortens the length of training from the traditional 15 months to

six months. To enter this academically demanding program, applicants are required to have at least an associate degree; have completed college-level courses in chemistry, anatomy and physiology, and algebra; and have at least a 2.5 GPA on previous college work. Students spend six weeks in class (eight hours per day, five days a week). The remainder of the training is in clinical, with two days per week of class. Graduates are eligible to take the Certified Respiratory Therapy Technician (CRTT) exam offered by the National Board for Respiratory Care, and upon passing the exam, they can be employed as respiratory therapy technicians.

The Accelerated Respiratory Therapist program shortens the length of training from nine months to 16 weeks. This program is designed for the working technician who does not need to suspend full-time employment. This is a very attractive and unique option for employers and potential students. Applicants must meet the same requirements listed above for the technician program, plus they must:

1) hold a CRTT credential;
2) have one full year of work experience as a technician;
3) be a graduate of an accredited respiratory therapy technician program; and
4) pass a college-administered exam assessing knowledge of respiratory care.

Students spend one week of full-time class study. The remainder of their training is clinical in the hospital where they are employed. This allows students to return home for training and keep their jobs. Graduates are eligible to take the Registered Respiratory Therapist (RRT) exam offered by the National Board of Respiratory Care.

Two full-time faculty were hired to develop and implement these curricula. These two faculty negotiate new offering sites, recruit students, teach the courses, and supervise the clinical component. Operating budgets were increased 15 percent to cover supply and material needs, faculty development and travel expenses. The largest expense was for travel needed to support faculty involvement in the clinical component over a three-state region.

The Accelerated Technician program has been offered twice since winter 1990, and has produced 21 graduates; the Accelerated Therapist program was initially offered in Summer 1991, and has produced 44 graduates. Both programs are accredited, along with the traditional programs, by the Joint Review Committee for Respiratory Therapy Education. Future plans are to continue offering the programs over a several-state area. The didactic portions of the program are being converted to a distant delivery format via telecourses, which will eventually allow the college to offer the program nationwide.

Employers in the region have been very satisfied with these programs and the graduates they have employed or promoted. Many of them have paid for their employees to complete the program, since this allows them to upgrade their respiratory staff without recruiting and/or hiring new people. The college has been contacted by numerous employers across the country for information about the programs.

Contact:
Tom Baxter, Director, Accelerated Programs
(803) 250-8493

Greenville Technical College
PO Box 5616
Greenville, SC 29606-5616
Total head count enrollment-Credit: 8,690; Non-Credit: 32,605
Campuses/sites: 4; Full-time faculty: 230

HORRY-GEORGETOWN TECHNICAL COLLEGE

TOURISM RESOURCE CENTER

The Center is the first facility in the state solely dedicated to the educational development of those in the tourism industry

Horry-Georgetown Technical College's Tourism Resource Center is a highly successful integrated system of related services located at the center of a billion-dollar-a-year tourist area – with thousands of national and local hotels, motels, restaurants, golf courses, racquet clubs, retail outlets and support industries providing a variety of training and educational programs and educational resources.

The Tourism Resource Center is the result of more than three years planning the Horry County Council, the municipal governments of the area, the Myrtle Beach Chamber of Commerce, the state's Parks, Recreation and Tourism Department, the Coastal Council and the college. It is the first facility in the state solely dedicated to the educational development of one of the state's major industries – tourism.

This integrated system of related services are as follows:

1) the Welcome Center provides information to upwards of 60,000 Grand Strand visitors per year;
2) the Business Formation Network holds workshops and Venture Capital forums involving entrepreneurs and investors;
3) the Soils Laboratory processes samples and conducts tests for businesses where turf is vital and provides a computer link-up with USGA Turfgrass Information File at Michigan State University;
4) HGTC co-sponsors the Southern Grounds and Turf Maintenance Exposition and Conference;
5) Special Schools, a start-up training assistance program is temporary and is especially designed to meet the specific needs of new or expanding operations by providing operations by providing location and specific training for a personnel pool;
6) the Southeast Manufacturing Technology Center stimulates improvements of quality and productivity in manufacturing and business by providing access to advancements in technology;
7) the Hospitality/Tourism Program provides extensive degree and/or certificate training education for students interested in the tourism industry; and
8) the two-year Culinary Arts Program, accredited by the American Culinary Federation Educational

Continues on Page 614

Institute Accrediting Commission provide Associate degree education for chefs.

Personnel requirements include: Tourism Resource Center Director; Special Schools Manager; Director of Business Formation Network; Productivity-Technology Specialist/SMTC; Soils Lab instructor/technician; Welcome Center Director, Secretary, Hospitality/Tourism and Culinary Arts Department Head and faculty.

Contact:
Bob Means, Director, Tourism Resource Center
(803) 347-3186

Horry-Georgetown Technical College
PO Box 1966
Conway, SC 29526
Total head count enrollment-Credit: 2,455; Non-Credit: 2,846
Campuses/sites: 3; Full-time faculty: 298.5

GOLF COURSE TECHNOLOGY

The program draws students from around the nation and world, but the number of graduates still are too few to meet industry's need

Tourism is the fastest-growing industry in South Carolina. That is especially true along the Grand Strand, which boasts more than 70 golf courses in operation, with other courses under construction and still more on the drawing board.

In response to the needs of this industry, Horry-Georgetown Technical College established the Golf Course Technology program in 1970. The Golf Course Technology program offers an Associate degree in Golf Course Management and a Certificate in Turf Equipment Specialist.

The program, which has in excess of 100 students enrolled, graduates approximately 25 students per year. Students from South Carolina, across the nation, and foreign countries come to HGTC specifically to enroll in Golf Course Technology. Employment opportunities continue to exceed the number of graduates of this program.

The two-year Golf Course Management program, headed by Edwin C. Zahler, includes courses in turfgrass science and general education. In addition, a summer internship is required between the first and second year. This internship blends the technical and academic with practical experience.

The one-year Turf Equipment program, headed by Bill Gaffney, teaches students proficiency in preventive maintenance and repair of turfgrass equipment. Special emphasis is placed on record-keeping for cost-effective equipment management.

Additional Golf Course Technology faculty consists of five highly qualified individuals who have experience in all phases of the golf industry: Dr. Paul Alexander, Dr. Terry Vassey, Carl Schwartzkopf, Paul Daniels and Donald Lovett

Contact:
Ed Zahler, Department Head
(803) 347-3186

Horry-Georgetown Technical College
PO Box 1966
Conway, SC 29526
Total head count enrollment-Credit: 2,455; Non-Credit: 2,846
Campuses/sites: 3; Full-time faculty: 298.5

INSTITUTIONAL EFFECTIVENESS

Among other things, the college measures its effectiveness according to its programs, student retention and community involvement

In the mid-1980's, Midlands Technical College was one of the first colleges to operationalize the institutional effectiveness concept. The college implemented a comprehensive institutional effectiveness program that incorporated an evaluation component designed to determine if the college's performance matched its purpose.

The college's administration decided a set of criteria was called for that would answer the question, "How effective is our institution in providing on-going programs and services that encourage student success and support our mission?"

After a review of several national models, including a model developed by the Sloan School of Business at MIT and DeAnza College's adaptation of that model, MTC determined that the following six broad performance characteristics are of paramount importance to the ultimate success of the college and its students:

•accessible, comprehensive programs of high quality;
•student satisfaction and retention;

- post-education satisfaction and success;
- economic development and community involvement;
- sound, effective resource management; and
- dynamic organizational involvement and development.

These six performance characteristics are called Critical Success Factors. As defined by DeAnza College, Critical Success Factors are "the key things that must go right for the organization to flourish and achieve its goals."

In order to measure how well the college is performing relative to each Critical Success Factor, Indicators of Effectiveness and a set of measurable criteria were developed for each factor. The indicators and their supporting measurement criteria are observed, quantified and qualified results of performance. They provide a structure and a mechanism for organizing the review and evaluation of MTC's effectiveness in key areas.

In determining the Indicators of Effectiveness and their corresponding criteria, two key questions were asked: What do we want the results of our college's effectiveness to be? What specific evidence are we willing to accept that the results have actually been achieved?

A set of measurement criteria was developed for each indicator. The measurement criteria vary. Some are based on comparison of MTC's performance to the performance of other colleges in the state's technical college system, or to institutions of similar size with similar missions nationwide. However, the college is very selective in the use of norms or comparative data due to the uniqueness of the college's service population. Past performance or internal trend studies are used as data become available. The Critical Success Factors and supporting Indicators of Effectiveness are reviewed annually in July to provide information on the college's overall effectiveness.

Where superior performance is demonstrated, effectiveness is assumed. If less than satisfactory performance is indicated, corrective actions can be determined and implemented.

Midlands Technical College was selected to model Institutional Effectiveness programs for the state of South Carolina's 16 two-year colleges. In 1988, MTC was one of 12 colleges nationwide to be awarded a Beacon Grant by the Kellogg Foundation to serve as an AACJC Beacon College and institutional effectiveness model. A national newsletter, *IE in Focus*, was published as a result of the Beacon grant funding.

Contact:
James L. Hudgins, President
(803) 738-7600

Midlands Technical College
PO Box 2408
Columbia, SC 29202
Total head count enrollment-Credit: 13,002; Non-Credit: 19,468
Campuses/sites: 4; Full-time faculty: 220

MIDLANDS TECHNICAL COLLEGE

PROMOTING STUDENT SUCCESS THROUGH PLANNING AND EVALUATION

Because students respond differently to an educational environment, the college uses a model to assess such things as goals, background and achievement

The effectiveness of colleges in meeting diverse student and community needs is key issue of the 1990's. Midlands Technical College has established a nationally recognized, comprehensive model of student success in which planning and evaluation are integrated to foster student goal achievement and institutional development. MTC's approach to student success focuses on how the college can effectively develop an educational environment conducive to the success of diverse student populations.

Recognizing that all students do not respond to an educational environment in the same way, the college employs a person-environment model to assess student goals, backgrounds, needs, satisfaction, achievement and personal growth. A student cohort tracking system is used to monitor and analyze patterns of student subpopulations by a number of variables. These data are combined with information obtained from student surveys, testing, interviews and focus groups collected at key points in the student's matriculation through and beyond the college. Faculty, staff and students review these findings and formulate recommendations for improvements throughout the college's planning and evaluation system to modify the college environment and enhance positive student outcomes.

Since the college began student success monitoring in 1989, initiatives have included:
- development of student educational plans at entry including information of student's goals, backgrounds, characteristics and needs;
- integrated assessment, orientation and advisement processes;
- student Orientation for Success seminars for entering students;
- college success courses;
- automated follow-up system on student needs;

Continues on Page 616

- centralized advisement centers on each campus staffed by professionals;
- developmental academic advising separated from scheduling process;
- automated tools such as on-line advisor file and degree audit system;
- college-wide training in customer service and sensitivity to diversity;
- updating student goals each term as part of registration; and
- modification to the registration process including application deadlines.

The college has also made modifications in the environment to serve the needs of targeted at-risk populations. These changes have included:

- restructuring the instructional diversity and grading systems of developmental studies courses to more closely resemble college-level courses;
- placement of undecided students into a special major which allows exploration of academic programs and advisement by career counselors;
- inclusion of Access and Equity as a major college goal with special support groups, student organizations, peer mentoring and orientation activities; and
- seminars/workshops for students with disabilities, single parents/ homemakers, minorities and other at-risk populations.

Since 1989, the college has experienced significant enrollment growth while maintaining a 90 percent student satisfaction rating in most areas. Overall retention of students toward their goals has increased 6.4 percent, with increases of 7 percent to 17 percent for at-risk student groups. In addition, more than 90 percent of graduates are employed or continuing their education within a year of graduation. More than 90 percent of sophomore-level students indicate the college has contributed to their personal growth in areas such as clearer career direction and academic autonomy.

The MTC student success model has been honored with a 1992 Pyramid Award for outstanding achievement in student development in two-year colleges and a 1992 national retention award by Noel-Levitz. The college's student success model was also featured in a 1993 national teleconference sponsored by American College Testing (ACT).

Contact:
Sandi Oliver, Associate Vice President, Student Development Services
(803) 738-1400

Midlands Technical College
PO Box 2408
Columbia, SC 29202
Total head count enrollment-Credit: 13,002; Non-Credit: 19,468
Campuses/sites: 4; Full-time faculty: 220

ORANGEBURG-CALHOUN TECHNICAL COLLEGE

NUCLEAR COOPERATIVE EDUCATION

While working, the student is enrolled in a co-op course at the college and receives a wage rate comparable to the industry standards

Qualified students enrolled in the Electronic Instrumentation Technology curriculum may work directly in the nuclear power industry, giving them a realistic view of employment in the field. This has been possible since 1983, when Orangeburg-Calhoun Technical College and South Carolina Electric and Gas Company establish a unique Cooperative Education Program.

Since its inception, more than 30 students have met the requirements for this program, taken advantage of their opportunities and are now lucratively employed in this profession.

The student must have completed at least three semesters of academic work in the curriculum, pass the company requirements for employment, including requirements of the Nuclear Regulatory Commission, and be committed to traveling up to 55 miles to the V.C. Summer Nuclear Station for this experience. Resources are made available so that all who qualify may take advantage of this opportunity.

At the conclusion of the cooperative education experience, there is no implication that employment opportunities exist with the company or that the student is compelled to accept employment if offered. However, as evidenced by the success of the program, students have availed themselves of the lucrative opportunities presented while the company has been able to obtain qualified employees with a true understanding of the nuclear power industry.

It should be noted that at all times and in all phases of the program the student is encouraged, if not required, to complete the requirements for his/her associate degree in Electronic Instrumentation Technology.

While working, the student is enrolled in a co-op course at the college and receives a wage rate comparable to industry standards.

The project is made possible by the interest that the college and the company exhibit in the program. The program is constantly monitored and periodically evaluated by all persons involved, including the participating students.

At least annually the vice president for academic affairs

of the college, the manager of organizational development and employee benefits of the company, along with their faculty and staffs meet to objectively and subjectively evaluate the progress of the program, as well as its relevance to both the academic and industrial opportunity it affords the student.

Contact:
Pat Black, Jr., Vice President, Academic Affairs
(803) 536-0311

Orangeburg-Calhoun Technical College
3250 St. Matthews Road
Orangeburg, SC 29115-8299
Total head count enrollment-Credit: 2,824; Non-Credit: 4,942
Campuses/sites: 1; Full-time faculty: 79

NURSING

The health-care community has supported the program and its students with scholarships, guaranteed loans and other financial support

In 1982, the education of area nurses moved from a health-care setting to Orangeburg-Calhoun Technical College, a move that first met with some skepticism. Today, however, the Associate Degree in Nursing program can stand soundly on its record.

The nine classes that graduated from 1984 through 1992 distinguished themselves as competent, qualified contributors to the health-care team, both in the community and in other areas of the country.

The entire health-care community, including the local hospital which serves as the primary clinical affiliate for the program, has supported the program and its students with scholarships, guaranteed loans to students, and other forms of financial support.

Through the efforts of many, this program has filled a need for nurses educated at the associate-degree level, and has made the health-care community stronger in the Orangeburg and Calhoun counties area.

While the program's primary intent is to provide bedside nurses for the health-care industry, it also provides transfer options so that students may transfer course work and continue their education toward a baccalaureate degree in nursing. Some graduates have also continued their education at graduate level.

The program was unique in that in the early 1980's the primary nursing education program was moved from a health-care institution to an educational institution.

This program has served, and continues to serve well, the nursing education and health-care needs of the South Carolina midlands area, which is largely rural in its characteristics.

The program was recently ranked first by the National League for Nursing after the NCLEX results were received.

Contact:
Pat Black, Jr., Vice President, Academic Affairs
(803) 536-0311

Orangeburg-Calhoun Technical College
3250 St. Matthews Road
Orangeburg, SC 29115-8299
Total head count enrollment-Credit: 2,824; Non-Credit: 4,942
Campuses/sites: 1; Full-time faculty: 79

TOTAL QUALITY MANAGEMENT

The college is the training source for a community-based alliance of businesses committed to quality enhancement

Piedmont Technical College is an acknowledged statewide leader in the development and delivery of training that falls within the context of "total quality management." The college has, since 1988, served as the training source for a community-based alliance of businesses and other groups committed to quality enhancement. In addition, Piedmont was designated the South Carolina Resource Center for Total Quality Education in 1991.

Involvement in the quality process began in 1987, when several college staff members and local business leaders formed M-PAQ (Managing for Productivity and Quality). The group met on a regular basis to share ideas and experiences and to learn the quality and productivity concepts as taught by Dr. W. Edwards Deming and others.

Continues on Page 618

During the next year this group broadened its focus by joining with the area chamber of commerce to organize PACE (Piedmont Area Council for Excellence). In 1989, the group's name was changed to PEP (Piedmont Excellence Process) to reflect the growing interest in the quality movement in upstate South Carolina.

Organizationally, PEP is guided by a steering committee made up of business leaders. Administrative functions are coordinated by the local chamber and the college is the training provider. In this role, the college offers a variety of quality training courses and seminars to area businesses, government agencies, and educational organizations. Among the core quality management courses and seminars developed and delivered by the college are: "Successful Teamwork," "Development of a Company-Wide Quality and Productivity Process," "Basic Statistical Process Controls," and "Basic Problem Solving." More than 1,000 industry personnel from the college's service area have participated in such programs.

As South Carolina's resource center for quality education, Piedmont is assigned responsibility for networking with the 15 other public two-year colleges in the state for the development of quality management programs. Emphasis is on helping those institutions to identify needs in their respective areas and to deliver appropriate programs to address those needs. Specifically, Piedmont enables each of the colleges to offer a basic group of core courses in quality management. This is accomplished essentially through a "train the trainer" approach. Faculty and staff from the various colleges are trained by Piedmont in the core courses, giving them the expertise needed to establish baseline quality management programs in their communities. Piedmont also provides materials and other supportive services to facilitate the trainers' efforts in establishing such programs.

Piedmont Technical College, then, is the focal point for the development and delivery of total quality management training in both its home community and around the state.

Contact:
Augustus Burgdorf
(803) 941-8350

Piedmont Technical College
PO Drawer 1467
Greenwood, SC 29648
Total head count enrollment-Credit: 3,183; Non-Credit: 18,255
Campuses/sites: 7; Full-time faculty: 78

PIEDMONT TECHNICAL COLLEGE

MANUFACTURING CERTIFICATION TRAINING

Instead of preparing students for a specific job, the program develops skills students may use in a variety of production work opportunities

The frustration experienced by American employers as they look for prospective workers who are simply "trainable" has received its due of notoriety. Any expectation that would-be employees might possess the higher order skills deemed critical to competitiveness is, generally speaking, a virtual pipe dream. The Manufacturing Certification Training Program at Piedmont Technical College is an attempt to do something about this dilemma.

The intent of the program is to provide training that will qualify individuals for possible employment by area industry. Successful completion does not guarantee employment, although it assures consideration when vacancies exist. Further, the program does not necessarily train the worker for a designated job; rather, it develops skills which make him or her trainable for a variety of production work opportunities as they come available.

Nine companies are involved with the college as sponsoring partners. In broad terms, the program offers two training tracks: an industry-specific track and a generic track. The industry-specific track – actually several distinct sub-tracks – includes training that relates to the production systems of specific industries. Classes run for six to seven weeks and feature two three-hour class meetings weekly. Day and night class options are available.

Content in all tracks includes "Communications and Interpersonal Skills," "Team Building," "Introduction to Microcomputers," "Statistical Process Control," "Industrial Economics," and other relevant subject matter. In addition, an industry-specific track would feature content that is unique to a particular firm. To illustrate, Capsugel – a major manufacturer of empty gelatin capsules for producers of pharmaceuticals – participates in the program as an industry-specific sponsor. Persons aspiring to join the Capsugel work force would pursue the Capsugel industry-specific track. In so doing, they would complete the content previously listed for the generic track, with some possible modifications, and they would complete courses in "Total Customer Satisfaction" and "Good Manufacturing Practices."

Students are generally referred to the program from a variety of sources. Qualifying tests in reading comprehension, math computation and mechanical reasoning typically lead to some 45 percent of applicants actually being accepted. Others are encouraged to consider programs and services appropriate to their needs. These services might include basic adult education or developmental education coursework offered by the college or by other providers.

Twelve programs have produced 228 graduates, with

137 (60 percent) gaining employment.

Funding to support the program is derived from two sources: student tuition and industry contributions. The program was initiated in January of 1990.

Contact:
J. Norman Wiseman
(803) 941-8413

Piedmont Technical College
PO Drawer 1467
Greenwood, SC 29648
Total head count enrollment-Credit: 3,183; Non-Credit: 18,255
Campuses/sites: 7; Full-time faculty: 78

SPARTANBURG TECHNICAL COLLEGE

CURRICULUM INTEGRATION: BLENDING JOB-SPECIFIC AND BEHAVIORAL SKILLS

All curricula now use the same three skills: problem-solving, interpersonal skills, and written and oral communication

A major role of two-year colleges is to prepare graduates who are able to meet the labor demands of business and industry. Businesses are no longer content with employees who possess job-specific knowledge only. Businesses want employees who possess other attributes, such as the ability to solve problems, work in groups and effectively communicate. To meet these demands, a curriculum model has been developed at Spartanburg Technical College to combine job-specific content with work-related skills. Innovative teaching strategies are used to bridge content and skills in such a way that content is not sacrificed, while at the same time, students' work related-skills are developed. Teaching methodologies are sequentially and strategically placed to allow students to build from basic to advanced levels of competency for each work-related skill.

The six-step model that combines behavioral and job-specific skills involves curriculum design, teaching strategy development and student evaluation. The steps are:

1) develop a chart for each course within a given curriculum that identifies major content areas and their interrelationships; consolidate these course charts into a comprehensive curriculum chart; this chart will identify all the major competencies of a curriculum and arrange them in a hierarchical manner; at STC, this step in the model is facilitated by the DACUM process, which is used as an integral component of program review;

2) develop the ultimate goal of the curriculum which will summarize what a graduate of that curriculum is capable of performing;

3) analyze the course charts to determine if all content is relevant to the ultimate goal and that there are no major gaps in continuity nor excessive redundancy;

4) identify and define the affective or behavioral skills needed to perform the ultimate goal and determine the appropriate points within the curriculum to introduce and develop these skills;

5) for each course in the curriculum, develop instructional strategies that teach content and behavioral skills simultaneously; and

6) develop assessment criteria and techniques that measure student's attainment of content/skill competencies; measure students' attainment of these skills.

After testing this process in the classroom for two years, and subsequently refining the process, all curricula now use the same three skills. These are problem-solving; interpersonal skills; and written and oral communication skills. This limitation and commonality of skills allows adequate opportunity for students to practice skills, develop competency and to carry this competency with them if they should transfer to another program.

This process offers several benefits. The students are better-prepared for the work place because they practice and develop competency in effective skills that are in demand in the work place. The students practice the type of thinking and behavior that employers look for when hiring and promoting employees. The students also receive written evaluations of their progress toward obtaining competency, which becomes part of their records maintained by their advisor. This model supports institutional effectiveness efforts since it relates directly to the mission of the college. It has also become a powerful faculty development tool. Self-examination of one's own teaching style is an essential component of the model. Faculty become coaches and facilitators, rather than just dispensers of knowledge, and students must take a more active role in their own self-development.

Continues on Page 620

This model has been outlined in more detail in an article appearing in *Community/Junior College Quarterly of Research and Practice* and has been presented at several national conventions, including the AACJC national convention in 1991.

Contact:
Susan Graham, Dean, Business Division
(803) 591-3874

Spartanburg Technical College
PO Box 4386
Spartanburg, SC 29305
Total head count enrollment-Credit: 3,860; Non-Credit: 7,534
Campuses/sites: 1; Full-time faculty: 100

COOPERATIVE PROGRAM OF THE SENSORY IMPAIRED (CPSI)

The cooperative effort spearheaded by the CPSI is helping assure the inclusion of this special population in all Tech Prep activities

Recognizing that individuals with disabilities are the "untapped work force of the 21st Century," Spartanburg Technical College (STC) and the South Carolina School for the Deaf and the Blind (SCSDB) jointly provide post secondary opportunities to deaf, hard of hearing, blind and low vision students. In doing so, the institutions address business and industry's needs due to changing demographics in the work force, and every individual's need for academic and technical training for employment opportunities.

To ensure that support services are readily available and to coordinate the cooperative effort, SCSDB employs a full-time program coordinator, a blind service specialist and a deaf service specialist whose offices are located at STC. Through this office, students may request interpreters, assistive-listening devices, note-takers, Braille and reading services, preparatory course work, assistive technology training, transportation assistance, housing on the SCSDB campus, independent living skills training, personal and vocational counseling, and job placement.

Since becoming partners in 1986, STC and SCSDB have jointly addressed the South Carolina legislators for a line-item budget to help off set the cost for providing extensive support services. Through a state grant for Innovative Technical Training, assistive technology for blind and deaf individuals was obtained by STC to enhance access to the classrooms and computers as well as to foster independence.

The Post Secondary Education Consortium (PEC) at the University of Tennessee, a federally funded project to enhance post secondary opportunity for deaf and hard of hearing individuals through the Department of Education, chose the CPSI as their South Carolina affiliate. PEC has also relocated their Resource Materials Center to the STC Library. This resource center provides books, special publications, videotapes and assistive-listening devices through the interlibrary loan process to each affiliate program, high school programs, other colleges, consumers, etc. Through the CPSI and the resource center, STC provides technical assistance to the other 15 technical colleges in South Carolina on appropriate services for students with sensory impairments.

Other cooperative efforts have grown from this program. The Industry and Business Training Division is working with the SCSDB and the South Carolina Commission for the Blind to provide a ten-week Customer Service Training Program for visually impaired individuals using assistive technology to access computer operations. Since January 1992, this program has trained 25 blind individuals with most graduates obtaining employment upon completion.

A sensor-impaired component to the Upstate Tech Prep Consortium application to the Carl D. Perkins Vocational and Applied Educational Technology Act of 1990 was developed. The networking and cooperative effort spearheaded by the CPSI is helping to assure the inclusion of this special population in all the Tech Prep activities.

The President of the SCSDB received a national award "for visionary leadership in the expansion of the post secondary programs at SCSDB" at the Conference of Education Administrators Serving the Deaf (CEASD) in 1992.

Contact:
Bonnie Martin
(803) 591-3636

Spartanburg Technical College
PO Box 4386
Spartanburg, SC 29305
Total head count enrollment-Credit: 3,860; Non-Credit: 7,534
Campuses/sites: 1; Full-time faculty: 100

HISTORY / CULTURE OF THE S.C. SEA ISLANDS

The course celebrates the heritage of the Gullah culture,
which has a blend of Creole and West African dialects

The Sea Islands, known as the Lowcountry, enjoy a unique cultural heritage. The majority of the islands' residents, both before and after the Civil War, were enslaved Africans whose descendants spoke a mixture of Creole and West African dialects known as Gullah. These descendants still live on these islands and in rural inland areas. Yet, because of the influx of outside populations caused by land development and leisure industries such as tourism, fishing and hunting. African Americans are now the minority in Beaufort County. These outside influences, which have brought with them industry, schools and the larger heterogeneous American culture, have put the Gullah culture at risk.

Technical College of the Lowcountry leadership recognizes that only through the promotion and nurturing of cultural diversity can its goal be fulfilled to be student-centered in all its endeavors and to be on the leading edge of the changing needs of the Lowcountry. With these objectives in mind, the college developed this course, which celebrates the heritage of the Sea Islands, the Gullah culture. "African American History and Culture of the South Carolina Sea Islands" is designed to be team-taught by a history instructor and a humanities instructor.

The primary objectives of the course is to invite the students to learn first-hand about African American history and the Gullah language and culture of the South Carolina Sea Islands. This course asks students to step outside the classroom and take advantage of the surrounding environment of the Lowcountry in which the college is located. Students study the origin, history, language, art, music and literature of the South Carolina Sea Islands and how these traditions are being maintained. Students develop research projects with an accompanying paper that is presented to the class at the end of the semester. Projects include:

1) collecting oral histories of the Gullah people recording folklore;
2) reporting on a variety of material culture such as homes, buildings, boat building;
3) studying the eco-culture of the Islands, which include fishing, net weaving, hunting and farming; and
4) exploring various art forms of Gullah culture such as basket weaving, indigo dying, painting, netweaving, music, literature.

Texts: Jones-Jackson, Patricia, *When Roots Die*; Lee, Willie Rose, *Rehearsal for Reconstruction*

Contact:
Renate W. Prescott, Instructor
(803) 525-8274

Technical College of the Lowcountry
PO Box 128, 100 South Ribaut Road
Beaufort, SC 29901-1288
Total head count enrollment-Credit: 1,570; Non-Credit: 3,528
Campuses/sites: 3; Full-time faculty: 42

TECHNOLOGY AND CULTURE COURSE

Students explore values and value choices in technology
and how they are influenced by culture

At many community colleges, technology students and humanities students are, like their disciplines, considered to have little in common. But at Technical College of the Lowcountry, a "Technology and Culture" course shows how false that assumption is.

The course, designed jointly by technology and humanities faculties, increases the student's awareness of the relationship between the humanities and technology through investigations of their differences and commonalities. Students explore values and value choices in technology and how they are influenced by culture. The course stimulates critical analysis of science and technological issues as they relate to society.

The student understands that:

1) the impact and use of technology is shaped by existing cultural traditions and values;
2) the issues technology address are an integral part of the reasons for and meaning of societal and cultural change;
3) technology may have its limits and may be rejected when it conflicts with human values; and
4) the ramifications of adopting a technology are usually far wider than the immediate perspective.

Some of these ramifications are that:

1) technology accelerates change within society, resulting in consequent dislocations, social anomie and uncertainty for people, along with its promise

Continues on Page 622

2) a major consequence of technological change is an increased dependency upon material culture, events and institutions with perceived loss of control; and

of progress and adaptation;

3) the benefits of technology are differential and unequal, producing social and economic differentiation.

Text: Teich, Albert H., *Technology and the Future.*

Contact:
Fred Seitz, Instructor, (803) 525-8204
Renate W. Prescott, Instructor, (803) 525-8274

Technical College of the Lowcountry
PO Box 128, 100 South Ribaut Road
Beaufort, SC 29901-1288
Total head count enrollment-Credit: 1,570; Non-Credit: 3,528
Campuses/sites: 3; Full-time faculty: 42

TRI-COUNTY TECHNICAL COLLEGE

TECH PREP

🔳 *The initiative continues to grow beyond* 🔳
the original vision and expectations

In response to local needs and the challenge presented by Dr. Dale Parnell in his landmark publication, *The Neglected Majority* (1985), the president of Tri-County Technical College, local superintendents, business leaders and key college administrators formed the Partnership for Academic and Career Education (PACE) as the umbrella organization to facilitate the programs. Through this collaboration, seven school districts, area businesses and Tri-County Technical College are linked.

With support from a U.S. Department of Education FIPSE grant in 1987, and a small administrative staff housed on the college campus, the PACE Consortium established a true collaborative working relationship between partners.

Today the PACE Tech Prep initiative, referred to locally as Preparation for Technologies, is well on its way toward accomplishing the goals established in 1987. Program objectives include: lowering dropout rates and raising the academic and vocational/technical skills of high school graduates; eliminating "gaps" and "overlaps" between secondary and post secondary curricula; developing better guidance and advising processes for non-baccalaureate bound students; and increasing the numbers of high school graduates who pursue a technical college education and increasing the numbers of skilled persons to meet the growing demands of local employers.

Various strategies and approaches have been utilized to help participating schools, career centers and the college accomplish program objectives. A key element to the success of these strategies has been the active involvement of the local business community.

The development of Tech Prep programs in Anderson, Oconee and Pickens counties is coordinated at the site level by top curriculum and vocational directors with assistance and input provided by the Consortium Coordinating Board, staff and committees. All programs at the secondary level stress curriculum change by replacing traditional general education courses with new applied academic courses, many with local enhancements. To accomplish this, one approach has involved consortium staff working collaboratively with school, college and business personnel to design modules illustrating local applications of academic concepts. These modules also provide teachers and students with information on local companies, post-secondary options and career opportunities in mid-level technology fields. Through improved guidance services and new advising publications, students select academic courses (either applied or traditional college preparatory), along with appropriate vocational/technical courses clustered into four broad areas, which provide a solid foundation for entry-level employment or post secondary study. Students also receive guidance concerning options for earning advanced standing into post secondary occupational curricula and for continued study toward the bachelor's degree.

While far from a "finished story," the PACE Tech Prep initiative continues to grow beyond the original vision and expectations. In several sites the program now includes Youth Apprenticeship options or other work-based learning activities, as well as specialized components enabling students to begin college studies while in high school. New post secondary initiatives have also begun with support of a BellSouth Foundation grant and the hiring of a post secondary coordinator. Among those initiatives are the development of advanced technology certificates for associate degree programs and expanded efforts in articulation linking the high schools, the community college and area senior colleges. As a result of these enhancements and others, staff development programs have been expanded for both secondary and post secondary personnel. During 1992, college faculty helped develop and/or teach three courses for high school instructors of applied academics as well as a summer internship program which employs high school teachers in local industries. In addition, college faculty helped coordinate the sixth annual PACE Summer Institute for academic/vocational faculty and counselors. In the 1992 academic year, a team of college faculty, recently trained in cooperative learning techniques, worked with high school teachers experienced in these strategies to implement staff development programs for faculty from several college departments.

The PACE Tech Prep initiative has been recognized in a chapter of the Hull/Parnell book, *Tech Prep/Associate Degree: A Win-Win Experience*, in numerous national publications and conferences, and in the 1991 NCRVE national Tech Prep Teleconference. In addition, PACE received the first U.S. Department of Education Excellence in Partnership Award in 1991 and was one of three recipients of the first Dale Parnell Tech Prep/Associate Degree Award.

Contact:
Diana M. Walter, PACE Executive Director
(803) 646-8361, ext. 2378

Tri-County Technical College
PO Box 587
Pendleton, SC 29670
Total head count enrollment-Credit: 4,838; Non-Credit: 18,497
Campuses/sites: 1; Full-time faculty: 96

TECHNOLOGY AND CULTURE

The course emphasizes critical thinking, sensitivity to multi-culturalism, values awareness and increased knowledge of a technical specialization

The Technology and Culture course at Tri-County Technical College relies on philosophy, history and sociology to provide context for recognizing knowledge, beliefs and values of a culture and individuals. The course has successfully used a humanities orientation to evaluate technological development. This approach resulted from the Department of Labor, SCANS Commission, which promotes foundation skills and workplace competencies that are needed for solid job performance and points out that education must not "ignore the beauty of literature, the elegance of scientific theories, or the lessons of history and geography."

The challenge of educating for a "'high-performance future" is to offer students both technological expertise and knowledge of cultural expectations, societal realities and global relationships.

Accelerating technological change is widely accepted as part of our culture. The human response to that change and the impacts on society are less acknowledged. If we are to adequately educate the future work force, technological training is only one component of that education.

As early as 1959, Lord C.P. Snow warned us in his writings in *The Two Cultures* that we were creating "half-educated" people. He saw technological complexity as leading to "educational specialization" with little opportunity for humans to acquire understanding or see any value in knowledge outside their professional field. Narrowly focused education on only specific job skills creates a gap in an individual's abilities to recognize contributions in other fields of study and to participate in making social decisions as a citizen. Yet, in today's competitive, ever-changing job market students question any course which does not immediately offer relevance for their chosen career.

This interdisciplinary course was developed to respond to both concerns. The content includes review of technological progress since early civilization. Alvin Toffler's Third Wave and Powershift theories are used to examine cultural relationships compared to technological innovation. Students follow the changes in societal structures that led to the discovery of the technology or were produced as a result of technology. Students assess technological progress in their own programs of study to compare and contrast cultural impact. These past/present relationships and comparisons offer insight into trends, patterns and implications for the future.

Additionally, a human cybernetic system is used to analyze how individuals can influence their quality of life by personal decisions. Studying self as related to societal changes offers the opportunity for self-realization in decisions both personal and professional. The human power of reasoning that led to innovation in the past must be enhanced for creative, critical thinking responsibilities of the future.

Technology and Culture offers opportunity for "student-centered learning" reflecting critical thinking, sensitivity to multi-culturalism, values awareness and increased knowledge of a technical specialization.

Finally, SCANS concludes "each community must become involved in a conversation about its place in a fast-changing world as we approach the year 2000. Our nation's ability to lead in a global economy will depend on the outcome of those conversations." Technology and Culture

Continues on Page 624

is one way of linking competencies to provide students with the opportunity for successfully competing in the next decade.

Textbook: Bradley, M. Payne, W., *Humanities and Technologies: The Humanities in a Technological World*, Kendall/Hunt Publishing Company, 1988.

Contact:
Candace Gosnell, Instructional Development
(803) 646-8361

Tri-County Technical College
PO Box 587
Pendleton, SC 29670
Total head count enrollment-Credit: 4,838; Non-Credit: 18,497
Campuses/sites: 1; Full-time faculty: 96

USER SUPPORT SERVICES

User Support Services personnel have developed procedures to routinely train all new faculty and staff in the systems they will encounter

A self-study conducted by Trident Technical College during the summer of 1989 revealed a significant need to offer faculty and staff training on a routine basis if the college was to benefit from new technologies. The college subsequently created the department of User Support Services, and charged that activity with the responsibility for providing training and technical assistance to meet identified user needs.

User Support Services at the college accomplishes the following tasks:

1) provides the ongoing opportunity for faculty and staff to attend high-quality training sessions on hardware and software products in current use or planned use at the college;

2) maintains a Faculty-Staff Computing Center with the latest in hardware and software to encourage the use of technology to improve productivity and quality, and provides coaching and assistance to faculty and staff in the use of products in the center;

3) provides system analysis and technical support to staff agencies to help them automate information processing procedures; and

4) encourages and supports the efforts of the faculty to effectively employ computer-based multimedia instructional technology in the process of teaching and learning.

Since its inception, User Support Services personnel have developed procedures to routinely train all new faculty and staff in the systems that they will encounter in daily activities, such as All-in-One, SIS, FRS, and Audix. In addition, they have developed training materials and trained several hundred persons in the use of FTterm, Lotus, dBase, WordPerfect, DOS, VMS, Windows and other computer applications.

User Support Services has also played a significant role in establishing four master classrooms at the college and equipping them with a variety of multimedia and projection systems. They have also developed three portable multimedia systems for use at the three college campuses. Training materials have been developed for use in training faculty in the use of multimedia hardware and software.

Contact:
Larry Schwartzman
(803) 572-6083

Trident Technical College
PO Box 118067
Charleston, SC 29423-8067
Total head count enrollment-Credit: 14,177; Non-Credit: 8,760
Campuses/sites: 3; Full-time faculty: 211

STUDENT SUCCESS CENTER

The Center aims to provide personalized services to students while using the latest computer technology available

Trident Technical College deals with a high attrition rate that is difficult to determine with accuracy. Are students dropping out or stopping out, or was their goal only one or two courses? There is a highly diversified student body, including many older and part-time students. Before 1990, many students needing remedial courses chose to bypass the system and enter the regular curriculum courses – then

Continues on Page 625

failed in large numbers. Students felt a lack of identity because there is no one place or person responsible for their progress. Tracking of students and follow-up of those in academic difficulty was sporadic and many were lost in the process.

Then in 1990, the Student Success Center at Trident Technical College was established to provide personalized services to students while utilizing the latest computer technology available. The Center recognized existing services into one administrative unit. This facilitates the coordination of services, the sharing of resources and the pooling of expertise.

Services offered by the Center are assessment, advising, counseling, career development, learning assistance and career placement. A brief description of each of these services follows:

1) assessment: a computerized placement test is used and students receive immediate feedback; make-up exams for students who miss scheduled classroom tests are also administered;

2) centralized advising: advisors located in the Center advise all new students and those with an undecided major; a computerized system, ON COURSE, is used in advising students;

3) counseling: the services, including the traditional functions of personal and academic counseling, are enhanced by a computerized Early-Alert-System;

4) career counseling: the Center offers individual and group career exploration; a computerized program, SIGI-PLUS, is one of the major tools used in this area;

5) learning assistance: strategies used to provide learning assistance include individual tutoring by Center staff, faculty and community volunteers and peer tutors; a variety of instructional materials are available and computer assisted instruction is used.

6) Supplemental Support Services: three federal projects – Student Support Services, Educational Opportunity Center and Single Parent Homemaker – are an integral part of the Center services and their efforts are coordinated with, and enhance and expand other counseling services offered by the Center; and

7) career placement: Career Placement Services offers Trident students and graduates as well as local, regional and national employers free employment-related services including job referrals; on-campus interviews with employers; information on resume and interview preparation; and a graduate packet with faculty evaluations and transcripts.

In three years, the Student Success Center, working with the Academic Division, grew to 50-plus employees and operates centers on all three campuses of the college. During 1991-92, the Center had more than 44,000 unduplicated student contacts. The Center strives to provide individual personalized services to students and to utilize the latest technology to ensure that the services are rendered in a timely efficient and effective manner. Preliminary data indicates that this approach works to reduce attrition.

Contact:
Donna Thigpen
(803) 572-6393

Trident Technical College
PO Box 118067
Charleston, SC 29423-8067
Total head count enrollment-Credit: 14,177; Non-Credit: 8,760
Campuses/sites: 3; Full-time faculty: 211

THE INSTITUTE FOR DAKOTA STUDIES

▦ The college's approach to teaching Native Language is an integration ▦
of Native American tradition and modern methodology

While the Institute for Dakota Studies promotes and develops Native Dakota culture and history on several levels, its innovative approach to teaching Native Language remains a highlight of the ongoing work.

The approach to teaching Native Language at Sisseton Wahpeton Community College is an integration of Native American tradition and modern methodology. This combination gives the college the ability to actively promote the subordination teaching to learning, thus simulating the extremely successful experience of learning one's first language. This approach, adopted b the Institute when founded in 1991, evolved from several years of working out successful programs in Teaching Native American Language.

Traditional Native American "pedagogy" exemplifies a high degree of respect for the ability and integrity of the individual. Students interact with the learning environment and not primarily with the teacher; modern insights into language learning allows us to incorporate the values of respect and independence into the contemporary language learning classroom.

The specific approach used is an adaptation of The Silent Way developed by Dr. Caleb Gattegno. This approach is in active use with more than 30 languages around the world. While the Language Institute at the World Trade Center in New York uses the Silent Way to teach numerous languages to people engaged in international business, only the Institute for Dakota Studies offers this training for teachers of Native Languages throughout the country. The Silent Way materials have been adapted for Lakota, Dakota, Inupiak and Canadian Ojibwe. Five other native language groups are in conversation with the Institute for training of their teachers and for possible development of materials.

Contact:
James Green
(605) 698-7879

Sisseton Wahpeton Community College
Box 689, Agency Village
Sisseton, SD 57262
Total head count enrollment-Credit: 209; Non-Credit: 11
Campuses/sites: 1; Full-time faculty: 15

ASSOCIATE DEGREE IN NURSING

▦ Equal credit is given to the liberal arts education and professional education ▦
components, thus providing the graduate with a strong foundation

The Dakota words "waunsida," meaning respectful compassion, and "awanyaka," meaning caregiver, sum up the Associate Degree in Nursing program philosophy at Sisseton Wahpeton Community College. These concepts promote an understanding of the relationship between culture and care. Preservation and accommodation of cultural values and beliefs to provide culturally congruent nursing care must be a primary concern of the nurse who is prepared at SWCC, a tribally chartered institution. The Nursing program is a tribal effort to meet the unique post-secondary educational needs of the members of the Sisseton Wahpeton Sioux Tribe and other residents of the Lake Traverse region.

The program of studies for the nursing degree is designed to meet the South Dakota State Board of Nursing guidelines, SWCC requirements, and future National League for Nursing accreditation requirements.

Specific issues which affect health care of people on the Lake Traverse Reservation are studied. Learning experiences take place on the reservation to the widest extent possible, additional settings are selected as necessary to enhance the preparation of students for providing culturally appropriate care to the Sisseton Wahpeton Sioux Tribe. Focusing on understanding the environmental context of the Lake Traverse Reservation enhances students' appreciation for the significance of the environment wherever nursing is practiced.

Equal allocation of credit is given to the liberal arts education and professional education components; thus providing the graduate with a strong foundation in the essential elements that prepare one as a critical thinker who can accept the innate dignity and worth of each individual. The comprehensively educated student has an appreciation, knowledge and understanding of the biophysical and psychosocial nature of persons and their environment.

Nursing students are prepared to give basic nursing care to children and adults in a variety of health care settings.

The graduate of the Associate Degree in Nursing is eligible to write the state examination for licensing as a Registered Nurse.

Contact:
Susan Hardin-Palmer
(605) 698-3621

Sisseton Wahpeton Community College
Box 689, Agency Village
Sisseton, SD 57262
Total head count enrollment-Credit: 209; Non-Credit: 11
Campuses/sites: 1; Full-time faculty: 15

ALTERNATIVE DELIVERY SYSTEMS

A multi-modal distance learning program uses public television,
ITFS and independent learning

Chattanooga State Technical Community College serves one urban and 10 rural counties in southeast Tennessee, north Georgia and north Alabama. Particularly in the rural counties, incomes and educational achievement are low. Residents in outlying portions of the CSTCC service area tend to be older, working adults with families. As a response to the needs of this diverse population, the college has developed a multi-modal distance learning program using three different delivery systems.

The Chattanooga State Alternative Delivery System (ADS) operation encompasses:

1) public television, broadcasting professionally produced courses via WTCI, the local Public Broadcast System affiliate, and the Chattanooga Cable Company;

2) live, interactive courses from two studios on the main campus that broadcast to five Tennessee county high schools and Chattanooga State's three main off-campus sites, via the college's four-channel Instructional Television Fixed Service (ITFS) system; and

3) both professionally and locally produced courses to students by mail through the Video Instruction Program (VIP).

All ADS courses carry the same credit, transferability, timeline and cost as on-campus courses and are selected by a committee representing all appropriate divisions and administrative units. Instructors are selected by the departments offering the courses, with approval of the Director of Distance Learning, and are either full-time or adjunct faculty. ADS courses count in the regular faculty course-load. Instructors must set aside the same number of office hours for their distant students as for on-campus classes.

Decisions regarding courses to be leased or locally developed are made based on enrollment profiles, student responses to surveys and departmental needs. A sliding-scale development fee is paid to instructors to ready courses for delivery, and developers are generally the instructor of record when the course is offered. Course licensing, instructional design and administration of all coursework are done by the Director of Distance Learning and her staff of four. Video production of in-house courses is done by the CSTCC Broadcast Center, with a television staff of four.

In fiscal year 1991-92, the program enrolled approximately 2,400 students, with more than 1,750 in the VIP mail-out option. The percent of students completing the courses with passing grades was 63.4 percent across all media, with a high of 81.6 percent for the ITFS students passing and a low of 50.3 percent for the mail-out students. Student response to these learning experiences indicated that 75.5 percent (VIP and PBS broadcast) to 84.9 percent (ITFS) rated the experience as good-to-excellent. Only 4.1 percent rated the experience as less than adequate. Repeat enrollments also indicate satisfaction, with more than one-third of the students taking an average of three courses and some taking as many as 14.

Although the initial set-up cost for the ITFS system was high ($750,000 funded by two federal grants), the program's income (generated by FTE state funding and tuition) was three times the cost of administering the program. Besides revenue, the program also provided two other advantages:

1) it has allowed students who might otherwise not have attended college to enroll; and

2) it has offered growth opportunities at a time when physical facilities on campus are at a critical stage.

By the fall 1992 semester, teachers of ITFS English composition classes could send and receive work and interact simultaneously with students at a distance via a computer bulletin board. The college also operates a video production and satellite uplink truck which can transmit broadcasts from any location across the state to any location across the world.

A presentation describing this program was made at the 1992 National Institute for Staff and Organizational Development (NISOD) Conference in Austin, Texas.

Contact:
Sue Hyatt, Director
(615) 697-4718

Chattanooga State Technical Community College
4501 Amnicola Highway
Chattanooga, TN 37406-1018
Total head count enrollment-Credit: 19,737; Non-Credit: 6,000
Campuses/sites: 5; Full-time faculty: 182

ADAPTIVE COMPUTER LABS

Under the direction of a student, who once was Olympic-bound and now is a quadriplegic,
the labs have become a model of access

Chattanooga State Technical Community College has developed a demonstration laboratory to showcase the application of adaptive devices for the disabled, provide training in their use, and assist business and industry with adaptation in the workplace.

The Center for Adaptive Technology was funded by a grant from the Tennessee Developmental Disabilities Planning Council through the Department of Mental Health-Mental Retardation. The coordinator, Jeffrey Katcher, is living proof that most obstacles in modem society can be hurdled – thanks to a positive attitude and innovative use of the latest technology.

Thirteen years ago, Jeff was a 19-year-old student at the University of Minnesota with his eye on the Olympics when he was severely injured in an accident at a training camp for gymnasts. After a period of adjustment to his new situation as a quadriplegic, Jeff enrolled at CSTCC and became an expert in the use of adaptive computers. Under Jeff's leadership, the Adaptive Computer Lab has become a model in the provision of computer access for college students with disabilities.

A workplace skills assessment provided information on career potentials for students with disabilities. Then, programs were developed to enhance the learning and productivity level of special students to prepare them for the work force. A future plan is to integrate many of the tools identified by the Adaptive Computer Lab into all CSTCC computer labs.

IBM's National Support Center for Persons with Disabilities selected the Adaptive Computer Lab to participate in an IBM conference of disabled workers. The conference demonstrated opportunities that technology can create for the disabled.

CSTCC has since obtained a second grant which allowed the college to add a Center for Assistive Technology through a partnership with the University of Tennessee at Chattanooga. This has extended services to all disabilities and to all students. The Adaptive Computer Lab and the Center for Assistive Technology provide hands-on credit courses, workshops, abilities/awareness expose, guest speakers and services to K-12 schools and the community. By combining hardware and software with other technologies, the lab can help the disabled live a more independent lifestyle. For example, computers can be used to turn switches on and off, or to perform tasks that would otherwise be impossible for the person with a disability.

The Center for Assistive Technology has added a program which integrates abled and disabled students, families and organizations to participate together in activities in the areas of sports, arts and recreations. SPARC (Sports, Arts and Recreation of Chattanooga) has been approved as a charter member of the National Handicapped Sports (NHS) organization.

Because of its active role in education and in the community, the college was named "Employer of the Year" by the Chattanooga Area Committee on the Employment of People with Disabilities. Jeffrey Katcher, coordinator of the Adaptive Computer Lab, was named "Employee of the Year" by the organization.

Contact:
Jo Ruta, Department Chair, Information Systems Program
(615) 697-4718

Chattanooga State Technical Community College
4501 Amnicola Highway
Chattanooga, TN 37406-1018
Total head count enrollment-Credit: 19,737; Non-Credit: 6,000
Campuses/sites: 5; Full-time faculty: 182

INTERNATIONAL EDUCATION

This interdisciplinary program stresses the importance of
the formulation of global strategies

Although the initial mission of the community college was to serve the local community needs, trends in the global economy have caused the community to become involved in the world of multinational corporations and the college to redefine its future existence in view of global issues. Seeking to fill emerging needs, Cleveland State Community College initiated an international education program in 1990.

The program is interdisciplinary and is sponsored by the Business and Technologies and the Humanities and Social Sciences Divisions of Cleveland State. The international program objectives include:

1) to improve knowledge of the global marketplace;

Continues on Page 630

2) to distinguish and manage cultural diversity;

3) to provide in-depth knowledge of various countries;

4) to increase awareness of the issue of international competition, trade characteristics and policies; and

5) to stress the importance of the formulation of global strategies.

The structure of the program allows for an innovative course design, thus giving the student maximum exposure to international issues. Courses include:

- International Studies. Students actually travel to a country/countries for total immersion into a diverse culture(s). Specific projects are assigned to students for academic credit. A faculty member serves as leader/instructor traveling with the group. The course is offered in the summer semester (3 credit hours).

- International Studies. A mini-course is offered for academic preparation for the trip. Analysis of cultural customs and taboos well-prepare students for the international studies trips that introduce them first-hand to cultural, historical and geographical sites.

- International Business. Historically, Japanese and European producers with small national markets have always sought global markets, while U.S.

producers tended to concentrate on their large domestic market. In the past decade, however, American producers found new product introduction a costly process which was being forced by shorter life cycles of their products. Furthermore, imports were becoming a serious threat to their market share. Like their foreign counterparts who considered international trade a way of life, Americans began to think "globally."

- International Seminars and Consultations, which are being planned through Cleveland State's Small Business Development Center to assist local business and industry in their global efforts and to aid in local economic development.

Faculty members involved in the internationalization of the curriculum are active in their research abroad. With the help of fellowships granted through major universities, faculty also are developing business and cultural case studies for use in college classes. Faculty members are invited as speakers at international conferences and participate in faculty development activities. An advisory council to the Business and Technologies Division of Cleveland State assists in the evaluation of goals and objectives set in the international program.

Contact:
Frank McKenzie, Assistant Dean, Business and Technologies
(615) 472-7141, ext. 223

Cleveland State Community College
PO Box 3570,
Cleveland, TN 37320-3570
Total head count enrollment-Credit: 3,600; Non-Credit: 1,046
Campuses/sites: 1; Full-time faculty: 71

WORLD OF WORK

The format allows students in the Office Administration program to work at their own pace, using audiovisual and tutorial software packages

Columbia State Community College has implemented the "World of Work" format for its Office Administration program, giving students the opportunity to learn in an atmosphere more akin to a work environment than a classroom. Courses offered in this manner include typing, word processing, business calculations and transcription.

The World of Work, implemented in 1985, allows students to work at their own pace, using a combination of audiovisual and tutorial software packages. Examinations are taken when the student feels he or she has mastered the course material. After an initial orientation session during the first week of classes, at which time course materials are distributed, students are expected to spend a

minimum of three hours per week in the World of Work, and are required to punch in and out on a time clock. However, students may select the particular hours they attend.

In order to provide maximum flexibility for students, department faculty maintain most of their office hours in the World of Work. This provides faculty staffing both day and night, and allows students to be tested whenever they choose. The on-campus facility is typically open and staffed 42 hours per week; students also may, upon request, use the facility on weekends. Similar facilities exist at the two off-campus sites.

This flexibility has allowed students with family and

other outside responsibilities the opportunity to complete their education with minimum disruption. It has also allowed the college to offer courses which normally would be canceled due to insufficient enrollment.

Contact:
Batty L. Kyger
(615) 388-0120

Columbia State Community College
PO Box 1315,
Columbia, TN 38402-1315
Total head count enrollment-Credit: 3,527; Non-Credit: 1,338
Campuses/sites: 9; Full-time faculty: 84

CENTER OF EMPHASIS

Among other things, the ongoing project diversifies production and delivery of interactive video and helps business and industry with employee training

When instituted at Columbia State Community College, the Center of Emphasis focused on the development of interdisciplinary, interactive video programs in biology and nursing for students to use as a supplement to traditional instruction. Today, 15 other academic and vocational disciplines have become involved with the production and delivery of interactive video and computer-assisted-instruction (CAI) programs.

These programs are tailored to the specific educational requirements of Columbia State faculty. By sharing resources, expertise and experience, Columbia State Community College developed an academic environment that enables its students to learn more effectively and efficiently both nursing skills and concepts and related biological structure and function.

This project, begun with a state grant in 1986, is unique in providing students with creative interdisciplinary teaching modules on human anatomy and physiology and related nursing skills. It combines concepts that are common to both disciplines and incorporates the related content into interactive video programs. With this interdisciplinary approach to instruction, students better understand and comprehend the relationships between human structure, function and health care.

The current goals of the Center of Emphasis include:

1) diversifying the production and delivery of interactive video and CAI programs for academic and vocational disciplines, and offering instruction primarily by CAI and interactive video formats;

2) making facilities available to students at times and locations convenient for them;

3) involving other academic institutions with the development of interactive video and CAI programs for student use; and

4) assisting businesses and industries in our service area in meeting their employment needs by providing opportunities for expeditious re-training, cross-training and upgrading of skills.

All programs are available to students in open labs located on- and off-campus as a supplement to traditional instruction. Center staff help faculty develop the programs, and faculty need to have technical knowledge or previous experience to do so. The Center's three "high-tech" instructional laboratories and two off-campus locations house 41 computer CAI workstations and 33 interactive video workstations. All labs have been fully networked to allow easy student access to all available instructional programs as well as the capability to track and test users electronically. To date, more than 375 interactive video and CAI programs are available for student use.

The Center will continue to expand program development and is currently in the process of converting video tape programs to interactive laser discs. Also, the Center plans to broaden involvement of faculty from additional disciplines to use the facilities to test students electronically and monitor their academic progress .

During the past seven years approximately $1.75-million has been spent on Center development and program delivery. These funds are allocated on a 2:1 matching basis. The Center currently employs a director, media specialist, computer specialist, two full-time laboratory assistants and two part-time laboratory aides.

The Center of Emphasis has been recognized in a chapter of The Society for College Science Teaching's *Innovations in College Science Teaching*, in *The Chronicle of Higher Education*, and EDUCOM's *Joe Wyatt Challenge Success Stories*.

Contact:
Stephen L. Stropes, Director
(615) 388-0120, ext. 349

Columbia State Community College
PO Box 1315,
Columbia, TN 38402-1315
Total head count enrollment-Credit: 3,527; Non-Credit: 1,338
Campuses/sites: 9; Full-time faculty: 84

MANUFACTURING SYSTEMS TECHNOLOGY

The delivery and presentation of certain MST courses is enhanced through the use of Hypergraphics, an advanced CAI hardware and software package

Using a variety of innovative approaches, Dyersburg State Community College focuses on close cooperation with local chambers of commerce to deliver training in Manufacturing Systems Technology to adult workers. The targeted population, those already employed in the industrial sector or who are seeking employment in a manufacturing organization, need knowledge and skills in modern manufacturing methods and technologies.

The program produces manufacturing systems technicians who would bridge the knowledge and skills gap between the vocational-technical school graduate and the four-year college engineering graduate.

One measure of students success in the program is that enrollment in the program is at an all-time high. It has grown steadily since the increased responsibility at the students' places of employment.

Other measures of students success can be seen in the MST program's reputation. Several manufacturing organizations cited DSCC's MST program as the determining factor in its choice of location. Other local manufacturing companies have stated that they will hire any and all DSCC MST program graduates. Still other companies are working closely with the college to establish Tech Prep 2+2 Cooperative Education Scholarships.

The creative and innovative approaches to serving the targeted population focus on: the curriculum itself; liaison and cooperation with area industry; close cooperation with local chambers of commerce; class scheduling; flexibility; and on-site support for area industry. The MST curriculum has been specifically designed to meet the needs of area manufacturers. The delivery and presentation of certain MST courses is also being enhanced through the use of Hypergraphics, an advanced CAI hardware and software package.

To ensure that the MST program is providing students with exactly what they need to be employed by area industry, the college relies heavily on its MST Advisory Committee. The committee is chaired by a local manufacturing manager and comprises representatives from 14 manufacturing organizations.

Area chambers of commerce frequently ask the Center of Emphasis for Manufacturing Systems Technology to assist in recruiting new industry. By having the demonstrated capability to train adult workers in state-of-the-art manufacturing systems technology, DSCC serves the targeted student population, both by helping to bring new industries to the area and by preparing workers for employment.

Flexible class scheduling is another way in which the MST program serves its student population. This is an absolute necessity since most MST students are employed shift workers. Coordination with specific companies allows for the accommodation of second-shift workers through temporary shift changes.

MST personnel also visit plants to recruit students, determine demand for specific courses and market the program.

Contact:
Ronald J. Bailey
(901) 286-3208

Dyersburg State Community College
PO Box 648,
Dyersburg, TN 38024
Total head count enrollment-Credit: 2,049
Campuses/sites: 5; Full-time faculty: 48

FOREIGN LANGUAGE INSTRUCTION

To avoid the expense of hiring qualified instructors for several languages, the college developed a way to teach French, German and Spanish students in the same hour

The pressing need for a populous that understands other cultures and speaks a language other than English prompted Dyersburg State Community College to design an innovative foreign language curriculum. A small college usually cannot afford to hire qualified instructors for several languages and, therefore, often cannot offer a variety of languages to its student body. After extensive research of various language programs in different settings, a creative and economically feasible program was designed to prepare Dyersburg students to function linguistically and socially in other languages and cultures.

The multi-instructional program utilizes one language coordinator, native speakers, external examiners, audio-cassette tapes in a language lab setting, computer software, and daily assignment sheets. On each day of class the student is given a handout which includes the objectives, homework assignments and an itemized list of the class work for the next class. Each student has an audio-cassette tape that is carefully coordinated with the text material. Students are expected to study specific grammatical structures and vocabulary and complete homework assignments prior to class. The traditional classroom is replaced by a language laboratory in which each student works at a carrel using a headset. The language coordinator assists with grammatical explanations and the native speaker assists with linguistic and phonetical problems.

This method of instruction allows multiple languages to be taught in the same period. The college offers German, French and Spanish. It is possible to teach five French students, four German students and 11 Spanish students in the same hour. An unexpected benefit of this structure is that students are exposed to three languages and three persons from other countries.

Twice weekly, in 50-minute tutorials, the students meet with the native speaker to converse in the target language, focusing on the grammatical structures and vocabulary that are currently being taught. Students may not use textbooks. As the native speakers are not responsible for assigning grades and are extremely interested in student success, camaraderie quickly develops. The students are also constantly reminded that one can speak a language perfectly without mastering complicated grammar.

Homework is checked both orally in class by conferencing through the language lab equipment and by the native speakers, who walk around the classroom individually speaking to their own students. Audio-cassette tapes are collected at the end of every chapter and checked for completion by the native speakers.

Academic credentialing of the program is achieved through the supervision and testing of students by external examiners. Dyersburg State Community College is a member of the National Association of Self Instructional Languages and adheres to its guidelines and policies. External examiners are provided by the foreign language department of a neighboring university, the University of Tennessee at Martin.

Contact:
Sara Wolfe
(901) 286-3369

Dyersburg State Community College
PO Box 648,
Dyersburg, TN 38024
Total head count enrollment-Credit: 2,049
Campuses/sites: 5; Full-time faculty: 48

ACADEMIC ADVISEMENT SYSTEM

Every student, based on academic area of interest, is assigned to one of several essential academic advisement groups

Every Motlow State Community College student, based on academic area of interest, is assigned to one of several essential academic advisement groups. By recognizing the student as the primary focus of the educational process, this Academic Advisement System helps the student fulfill educational goals and objectives.
The goals of the system are:
1) to establish a positive rapport between students and faculty;
2) to provide academic and career guidance in planning and completing a particular program of study; and
3) to create and foster a cooperative and hospitable college atmosphere.
The specific objectives designed to accomplish the college's goals are:
1) to assist students in self-understanding and self-acceptance through value clarification and understanding abilities, interests and limitations;
2) to assist students in consideration of life goals by relating interests, skills, abilities and values to careers, the world of work and the nature and purpose of higher education;
3) to assist students in developing an educational plan consistent with life goals and objectives, including alternative programs of study, alternative career considerations and selection of courses;
4) to assist students in developing decision-making skills;
5) to provide accurate information about institutional policies, procedures, resources and programs;
6) to make referrals to other institutional or community support services; and
7) to assist students in evaluation or re-evaluation of progress toward established goals and educational plans.

Academic advisement at Motlow is accomplished through the employment of a "group" concept. The college has established seven essential academic advisement groups relative to the major discipline areas of study offered by the institution. Based on a faculty member's discipline area, and/or area of special expertise or interest, he/she is assigned to one of the seven groups as an academic advisor. Every student enrolled at the college is also assigned to one of the advisement groups, contingent on the student's choice of major, area of emphasis/concentration, or special area of interest. From within the advisement group, each student is assigned a primary academic advisor whose responsibility is to assist and supervise the academic performance and progress of the student. A student receives advisement from his/her primary advisor

Continues on Page 634

or any member of the advisement group if the primary advisor is not available.

Motlow received national recognition by receiving the ACT/NACADA 1991 Certificate of Merit for the Academic Advising System. While Motlow is proud of the national recognition, positive feedback from students provides the incentive to expand and improve the system.

Contact:
Randall Bartley, Advisement Coordinator
(615) 455-8511, ext. 325

Motlow State Community College
PO Box 88100
Tullahoma, TN 37388-8100
Total head count enrollment-Credit: 3,263; Non-Credit: 4,610
Campuses/sites: 19; Full-time faculty: 71

COMPUTER INTEGRATED MANUFACTURING (CIM)

The CIM programs not only educates students, but also communities, thus fostering economic growth

Motlow State Community College – sitting in the middle of a high-tech, 11-county corridor – serves its region well through a Computer Integrated Manufacturing Center featuring classrooms, labs and a simulated factory floor.

Built on 9,000 square feet donated by an aerospace design company, the CIM Center began with seed money from a Title III Strengthening Institutions Grant, totaling approximately $1-million over a four-year period. The grant period began October 1, 1987, and ended September 30, 1991. The broad objectives of the program were:

- Year One: survey industrial needs; establish a faculty development program; install a Computer Aided Design (CAD) Lab; develop an Electronics Certificate of Credit Program supported by instructional lab units.
- Year Two: develop basic introductory courses in Robotics, Pneumatics, Hydraulics, Programmable Controllers, Computer Aided Drafting and Design, and Computer Aided Manufacturing; develop laboratory modules to support these courses; develop a Certificate of Credit Program in Microcomputer Applications.
- Year Three: design advanced courses in Servo-robotics, Process Control, Hydraulic Servos, Computer Aided Manufacturing, Computer Numerical Control, and Computer Assisted Drafting and Design to support the Automated Manufacturing Technology curriculum; develop laboratory instructional modules to support these courses.
- Year Four: integrate these modules into a Computer Integrated Manufacturing program of instruction supported by the hardware and software to run a simulated factory floor.

Motlow State Community College entered into a linkage partnership with Micro Craft, Inc., an aerospace design company in Tullahoma, Tennessee, to locate the CIM Center. Micro Craft donated the space at the corporate headquarters to house the CIM Center, which is approximately five miles from the main campus.

The CIM Center is fully operational. All program options have been developed and implemented, including:

- General Technology Major (AAS Degree);
- Computer Aided Design Concentration;
- Computer Aided Manufacturing Concentration;
- Electronics Concentration;
- Industrial Computer Applications Concentration;
- Applied Technical Studies Concentration (for students articulating from an area vocational); and
- Electronics Certificate of Credit Program.

Motlow has developed a close working relationship with its "high tech" community. The CIM programs are not designed merely to educate a student. They are designed to educate the communities in the service area which Motlow supports. The net effort is enabling economic growth, followed by an increased standard of living.

Contact:
Monty G. Thomas, Dean, Career Education
(615) 455-8511, ext. 241

Motlow State Community College
PO Box 88100
Tullahoma, TN 37388-8100
Total head count enrollment-Credit: 3,263; Non-Credit: 4,610
Campuses/sites: 19; Full-time faculty: 71

STUDENT DEVELOPMENT CENTER

▨ A partnership of Student Services and Academic Affairs, the Center ▨
exemplifies a well-organized approach to the college experience

In 1986, Nashville Tech initiated a developmental academic advising program for degree-seeking freshmen that was placed in a newly created Student Development Center and addressed the following college needs:

1) to improve the quality and accuracy of academic advisement;
2) to provide a consistent and uniform approach to advising methodology;
3) to provide a streamlined approach to the matriculation process;
4) to address the rising attrition rates of under-prepared students; and
5) to orient students to college life and activities.

The Student Development Center is a partnership between Student Services and Academic Affairs and exemplifies a successful developmental advising program which specifically assists students in developing a positive and well-organized approach to the college experience. Specific goals of the advising process allow both the student and the advisor to experience:

1) a well-organized and meaningful advising session;
2) an opportunity to discuss, and when necessary, explore educational and career objectives;
3) discussion of long-range planning, which is a must for under-prepared students who need remedial or developmental coursework;
4) a less stressful experience during the advising and registration process; and
5) a positive and meaningful "first impression" of personnel associated with the college.

All entering, degree-seeking freshmen are advised in a centralized Student Development Center. The Center uses computer-assisted advising techniques and has the capability of inputting class schedules into the computer system during the advising session.

Advising sessions are scheduled by appointment and occur after students have completed mandatory assessment. The Center is able to:

1) assure students of a class schedule which meets the needs of the student;
2) eliminate the disappointment and frustration that students experience in registration lines when informed that classes are closed or not available;
3) spend more time during the advising session in carefully planning an educational program to meet the specific needs of the student; and
4) help instruction better manage the number of specific class sections which will be needed for any particular term.

The Student Development Center received the Outstanding Institutional Advising Program Award presented by the National Academic Advising Association (NACADA) and the American College Testing Service (ACT) in 1990. The Center's *Handbook for Advising* also won one of six Outstanding Publication Awards presented by NACADA in 1990. The Center's advising program was also featured in *Recruitment and Retention in Higher Education* in January, 1991, "Developmental Advising: Hallmark of Retention," Volume 5, No. 1. The advising model has been shared with more than 150 colleges and universities in the United States, Canada, Republic of Guam, Scotland and England.

Contact:
Richard Weeks, Assistant to Vice President
(615) 353-3268

Nashville State Technical Institute
120 White Bridge Road
Nashville, TN 37209
Total head count enrollment-Credit: 6,200; Non-Credit: 200
Campuses/sites: 1; Full-time faculty: 92

QUALITY FIRST*

▨ The program, which emphasizes Total Quality Management, serves organizations ▨
throughout the local region as well as communities in nearby states

When the Mayor of Kingsport Tennessee and the Kingsport Chamber of Commerce separately but simultaneously pursued Total Quality Management (TQM) initiatives in 1985, it didn't take long for them to find common ground. Both wanted to:

1) examine quality management techniques as an

enabling tool to involve employees in teamwork and statistical thinking; and
2) provide training and education in TQM concepts that would allow local businesses to enhance their marketplace.

Continues on Page 636

A joint steering committee soon formed, leading to the 1986 establishment of Northeast State Technical Community College (then Tri-Cities State Technical Institute) as the administrative entity and delivery site for community training in TQM.

In September 1986, the institution initiated its TQM team training program with 19 teams from 14 local firms. As a result of the training, these firms experienced major organizational improvements, saw an increase in employee morale and involvement and realized $3.2-million in savings during the first nine months of the training program. These auspicious circumstances accompanied and assured the birth of the QUALITY FIRST° Program.

Since 1986, the QUALITY FIRST° Program has served a wide variety of organizations in Bristol, Tennessee/Virginia; Johnson City, Tennessee, Kingsport, Tennessee; and other locations. More than 400 teams have been trained, representing a total of 80 companies which, in turn, have realized more than $30-million in savings as result of program training activities. Also, the program has helped 11 other communities in Tennessee, Virginia, Alabama, North Carolina and South Carolina establish similar programs.

The QUALITY FIRST° Program is based on the philosophy of Dr. W. Edwards Deming, the quality and productivity improvement expert who helped to bring Japan back from the devastation of World War II. Concepts, seminars and courses are focused on Dr. Deming's approach to management philosophy, which embraces team development, team problem-solving, inter-departmental skills, data collection/analysis techniques, Statistical Process Control (SPC), and the technique of applying continuous improvement concepts to all facets of industry, service and government organizations.

The college has continued efforts to enhance the QUALITY FIRST° curriculum and has included relevant training in other programs within the college as well as within its own internal administrative operation. The college is exploring plans to offer an AAS degree and a certificate in TQM.

In 1990, the QUALITY FIRST° Program formed a part-nership with the National Center for Quality (NCQ), a Chamber-based, non-profit organization promoting quality and productivity training for the Tri-Cities region. The role of the partnership is to expand, complement and focus TQM training activities for the community at Northeast State. The partners, working in concert with the local American Society for Quality Control (ASQC) chapter, sponsor courses, seminars, forums, conferences and work-shops involving certification review courses for technicians, auditors, engineers and mechanical inspectors. Benchmarking, ISO 9000, Kaizen, Performance Management, Survey Design, Facilitation Skills, TQM in Healthcare, and Malcolm Baldridge are examples of the efforts provided throughout the year by local personnel or through satellite downlinks.

In 1992, the QUALITY FIRST°/National Center for Quality partnership grew to include the state of Tennessee, with the successful establishment of a State Quality Award based on Malcolm Baldridge criteria. The first awards were presented in October 1993.

The QUALITY FIRST° Program has received national and international attention. Visitors from New Zealand, Canada, Venezuela, Australia, Czechoslovakia, Great Britain and all parts of the United States have visited Northeast State to learn why the program is a success. The program has been cited in local and national newspapers, chamber of commerce publications and *The Keplinger Letter,* and has been featured in Mary Walton's book, *Deming Management at Work*, published by G. P. Putman's Sons. In early 1994, the program was to be featured in a 30-minute video documentary narrated by Mary Walton.

The QUALITY FIRST° Program at Northeast State, which began with one employee, continues to experience steady growth. The program now has three full-time faculty, six adjunct faculty and two support staff. The future and continued expansion of the program seems assured. The primary credit for success goes to the progressive leaders of the Tri-Cities businesses who recognize that TQM is the key to successful business competition and survival in the future.

Contact:
Al Thomas, Director
(615) 323-0222 or (615) 323-8463

Northeast State Technical Community College
PO Box 246
Blountville, TN 37617
Total head count enrollment-Credit: 4,979; Non-Credit: 4,322
Campuses/sites: 11; Full-time faculty: 70

DISTANCE LEARNING

In addition to broadcasting interactive instruction, a fiber link opens shared resources such as the UT library database

The community is greatly benefiting from increased access to post secondary education, thanks to a unique partnership involving Pellissippi State Technical Community College, the University of Tennessee, the TVA, the federal government and a wireless cable company.

In 1990, after a formal community needs assessment and help from consultants, Pellissippi entered the world of distance learning first through a partnership with the wireless cable television company. The company agreed to lease excess ITFS channel capacity from the college for use in commercial entertainment programming in exchange for the college's use of the company's main transmission tower and transmitter. This agreement saved the college a significant investment of capital funds for transmission equipment. In 1991 the wireless cable company made that investment and began operations in the Knoxville area.

In order to transmit video/audio signals from the campus to the main transmitter tower, the college was required to upgrade its TV studio equipment and install either microwave or fiber optic transmission equipment. An $85,000 equipment grant from the Department of Commerce assisted in this connection. Rather than build an unsightly 260-foot tower on campus for microwave

transmission to the main tower, an alternative was pursued. The University of Tennessee, Knoxville and TVA had previously installed 17 miles of fiber optic cable to within five miles of the PSTCC campus. By making the five-mile fiber connection and a short microwave link from UT to the main transmitter, the system was complete.

In addition to the ability to broadcast interactive instructional programming into the community, the PSTCC/UT fiber link opens up other shared data resources such as access to the UT library database, two-way video teleconferencing between the schools, national and international data networks, and satellite uplink capabilities.

In the 1992 fall semester, PSTCC began programming on this ITFS network with the transmission of three interactive credit courses at two receive sites. Plans are being made to expand the number of receive sites to 14, as well as to offer instruction to the home subscribers of wireless cable TV service. The college will also use the system to improve inter-campus communication and to provide on-site training for business and industry. Access to higher education will be improved for disadvantaged and handicapped citizens, and combining small classes at numerous locations will improve student progression toward program completion and improve efficiency of instruction.

Contact:
Fred Martin, Dean, Planning and Development
(615) 694-6587

Pellissippi State Technical Community College
PO Box 22990
Knoxville, TN 37933-0990
Total head count enrollment-Credit: 7,837; Non-Credit: 5,873
Campuses/sites: 3; Full-time faculty: 149

ENVIRONMENTAL SCIENCE

The program offers options in Air Quality Control, Waste Management, Industrial Hygiene and Health Physics

Of the many challenges facing the United States in the next decade, none may be more critical than the need to find faster, better, cheaper and safer ways to clean up the radioactive, hazardous and mixed waste that have accumulated at Tennessee Valley Authority nuclear reactors, at commercial industrial plants, and at U.S. Department of Energy (DOE) laboratories and plants.

Ground and surface water contamination, soil contamination and air pollution constitute major problems, as formerly adequate disposal practices have proven inadequate and temporary storage in aging facilities has proven unacceptable. To react to these problems, the aforemen-

tioned agencies need a trained technical work force to perform complex jobs in corrective activities, environmental restoration, waste management and technology development.

Roane State Community College, training such a technical work force through both credit and non-credit programming, is the model for Health Physics and Environmental Restoration Technology east of the Mississippi River. The AAS degree in Environmental Health offers options in Air Quality Control, Waste Management, Industrial Hygiene, and Health Physics.

Continues on Page 638

Currently the placement rate for all Roane State programs in Environmental Technology training is 100 percent.

In addition to the AAS degree, Roane State offers customized training programs for college credit. An everyday, six-month health physics training program for Martin Marietta Energy Systems (MMES) in Oak Ridge, Tennessee, has been used as a model for similar programs at other MMES installations.

A Waste Management Training Center offers short, intensive non-credit programming for Hazardous Waste Operations and Emergency Response workers and for Asbestos Remediation workers as well as other short courses such as RCRA/SARA/CERLA/NEPA Overview, CHMM Review, etc. Roane State has been recognized as a model in such nationally recognized forums as the Environmental Restoration/Waste Management Technician Education Workshop that Oak Ridge Associated Universities conducted for the Department of Energy in June 1990, in Denver, Colorado; the DOE conference in New Mexico in July 1991; and the "PETE" conferences conducted for the DOE in San Francisco in August 1991, and in San Diego in July 1992. Other DOE laboratory representatives and DOE subcontractors have contacted Roane State since the meetings requesting more information concerning our training and linkage with Oak Ridge National Laboratory and Martin Marietta Energy Systems.

Contact:
Russell Schubert, Associate Dean
(615) 882-4511

Roane State Community College
Route 8, Box 69, Patton Lane
Harriman, TN 37748
Total head count enrollment-Credit: 5,262; Non-Credit: 11,810
Campuses/sites: 7; Full-time faculty: 125

THE WRITING CENTER

Established for the college and non-college communities, the Center provides help with academic, scientific and commercial writing

Like many college writing centers across the country, the Writing Center at Roane State Community College began with the primary objective of improving students' writing abilities. But soon it developed a unique outreach, not only to students, but also to faculty and staff, community members and area businesses.

Through this commitment to all individuals in the college's service area, the Writing Center has established itself as a resource that provides assistance with academic, scientific and commercial types of writing. Although students continue to be the primary benefactors of the facility, the Writing Center staff also assist the employees of Roane State by editing journal submissions and conference papers for the faculty and by providing computer workshops as well as grammar and punctuation review for the staff during the summer.

To accommodate the needs of community members, the Writing Center offers a variety of creative writing workshops, an annual writing contest and special events throughout the year. Many budding novelists and poets from the community consult the staff of writing specialists at the Writing Center for assistance in all aspects of the writing process, from organizing material to finding markets for publication. In an effort to address the concerns of area businesses the Writing Center recognized the need for improved writing skills of employees and introduced a series of technical writing seminars which cover a range of skill levels and topics from basic editing to report and proposal writing. The Writing Center also assists area business by providing proofreading and copywriting services as well as a pool of technical writers available for hire for short- or long-term employment.

The Writing Center was established as a Center of Emphasis in 1985 and initially received equal support from both the Tennessee Higher Education Commission and the college. The Writing Center receives full support from the college while continuing to generate proceeds from corporate workshops and grant funding to assist with special programs throughout the year.

Contact:
Matt Lauer, Writing Specialist
(615) 882-4677

Roane State Community College
Route 8, Box 69, Patton Lane
Harriman, TN 37748
Total head count enrollment-Credit: 5,262; Non-Credit: 11,810
Campuses/sites: 7; Full-time faculty: 125

ECONOMIC DEVELOPMENT

The institute and Memphis Area Chamber of Commerce address the information, technology and training needs of area business and industry

A strong and dynamic partnership between the Memphis Area Chamber of Commerce and State Technical Institute at Memphis is addressing the needs of local business and industry through:

1) an economic development strategy to assist existing businesses;
2) an enticement to attract new prospects to the area;
3) state-of-the-art resources to supply a productive work force to area businesses; and
4) leadership development.

These objectives are met through the Mid-South Quality Productivity Center, the Technical Scholars program and the Supervisory Institute.

The Mid-South Quality Productivity Center (MSQPC) was established in 1988 as a community initiative to promote the use of quality management techniques in every segment of the business community. The MSQPC offers seminars, workshops, teleconferences and customized training to promote increased awareness and understanding of core quality principles, to foster the appropriate use of quality improvement tools, and to provide a balance between philosophy and hands-on experience.

To date, employees of more than 40 companies have been trained in the methods, techniques and tools of quality. Ranging in size from 35 to 2,000 employees, these companies represent the private, public and non-profit sectors as well as the manufacturing and service industries. The MSQPC is staffed by full-time instructors from the college and consultant/instructors from area businesses, offering an ideal mix of professionals for program development and implementation.

The MSQPC also sponsors a learning resource center with approximately 150 books on quality and productivity and several sets of training videos. Software includes SQCpack and Statgraphics for use with advanced SQC methods. A MSQPC Users' Group has been developed to allow informal networking and a forum for participants to share successes and problems in their continuous improvement efforts.

The Technical Scholars program pairs students with local businesses to provide significant job experience along with formal education. A Tech Scholar works part-time at the sponsoring company, training in areas relating to his/her major, rotating among departments, and becoming familiar with the overall operation of the business. This program also benefits the employer by allowing training to the company's best advantage and evaluation of potential future employees. It also offers greater potential for recruiting and training women and minorities in non-traditional job opportunities.

The Supervisory Institute was established by the Chamber and State Tech to provide needed leadership development. The institute provides management and supervisory skills for employees through a series of five courses in such areas as interpersonal skills, management skills and financial concepts. Students receive college credit for the courses, and those finishing all five courses in the program receive certificates.

U.S. News and World Report listed State Tech as one of the top 10 community colleges in America. The Mid-South Quality Productivity Center has been recognized as an exemplary program by the *Memphis Business Journal*, has been cited in numerous papers on Total Quality Management, and the MSQPC Users' Group was acknowledged as an exemplary program that should be replicated across the country by the U.S. Labor Department.

Contact:
Jim Willis, Director
(901) 575-3530

State Technical Institute at Memphis
5983 Macon Cove
Memphis, TN 38134-7693
Total head count enrollment-Credit: 11,118; Non-Credit: 43
Campuses/sites: 12; Full-time faculty: 162

WORKFORCE TRAINING CENTER

▨ Center staff provide a pre-assessment for community clients ▨
and design an individualized program for each student

As the workplace has become more technologically advanced, so have the skills required to obtain or maintain employment. By the year 2000, most jobs will require post secondary education, while more and more adults seeking employment lack the basic skills necessary to obtain jobs or ensure job security. This employability gap threatens the livelihood of a major segment of society and, consequently, of society itself.

In 1989, State Tech initiated the Workforce Training Center to address these needs. The program is designed to:

1) integrate computer-based instruction with job skills to support adults in improving their competencies in basic mathematics, writing and reading;

2) provide assistance to entering college students who have deficiencies in these areas; and

3) establish a setting which provides the constant feedback and intensive one-to-one instruction necessary for successful remediation in a cost-effective manner.

The setting for the Center is a building which was refurbished to resemble a high-tech office center rather than a tutoring lab. The new carpeting and furniture create an atmosphere that makes the adults feel valued.

The Multimedia Skills Center and the Workforce Training Center, housed together, share a Novell local area network of 40 IBM PS/2 55 Sx machines and a Model 80 fileserver, which delivers a platform of basic skills courseware ranging from third grade to GED level and advanced mathematics. Some of the primary basic skills software packages being used are IBM's basic skills series in mathematics, reading and language arts; Skills Bank II; Steck-Vaughn's GED series; WordPerfect 5.1; and the Daedalus Instructional System. Self-awareness is promoted by use of other computer-based assessment in learning styles, personality type and career selection.

In its original design, the Workforce Training Center was to serve the underemployed/employed adults in the community, and the adjoining Multimedia Skills Center was designated for college students. However, positive interactions between community adults and the students enrolled in the remedial/developmental program created more of a blending of the two areas. The relationship has fostered a realization by community clients that a college education is not beyond their reach, and college students realize that the community clients have much life and work experience to share with them.

Center staff provide a thorough pre-assessment for community clients and design an individualized program for each student. The instruction is given and managed by the computer system. For this reason, the Center can be supervised by one full-time staff person and one part-time staff person. The instructors are free to work with clients to provide extra assistance in problem areas. At the end of the predetermined blocks of instruction, the clients take a post-assessment which is compared to their original goals. Those who reach their goals go on to other training or college courses; those who need more work re-enroll in another block of training.

State Tech students come to the Center on a drop-in basis to supplement their remedial/developmental courses. Instructors may use a checklist to identify areas of needed practice. In a pilot project to study the effectiveness of the program at increasing users' basic skills, about one-half of the students who participated were able to bypass at least one college preparatory class. The potential savings in time and money to the student can serve to alleviate frustration and subsequently increase retention.

In its first year of operation, the Center served several hundred remedial/developmental students and community clients. The most recent yearly enrollment includes: 60 adults (from an inner-city neighborhood job training program) who are participating in basic skills and personal development training in preparation for technical training; more than 200 clients from JTPA and social service agencies; and more than 600 remedial/developmental students.

The Workforce Training Center was recognized by EDUCOM's Joe Wyatt Challenge in 1991 as one of the 101 outstanding technological programs for undergraduate education and has been recognized in articles in *T.H.E. Journal* (Mar 1992), *ATEA Journal* (Feb-Mar 1992), and the *Tri-State Defender* (4/25/92).

Contact:
Judith Collier
(901) 374-4107

State Technical Institute at Memphis
5983 Macon Cove
Memphis, TN 38134-7693
Total head count enrollment-Credit: 11,118; Non-Credit: 43
Campuses/sites: 12; Full-time faculty: 162

AEROSPACE TECHNOLOGY

After completing the program and becoming employed with a participating contractor, graduates work full time at NASA's Space Station Control Center

In the Fall of 1992, Alvin Community College initiated a unique two-year program in Aerospace Technology which allows graduates to work on NASA's proposed Space Station Freedom project.

With the development and deployment of the Space Station Freedom, an estimated 700 graduates with two-year degrees in Aerospace Technology will be needed by 1994 to fill newly created positions. An estimated 200 graduates will be needed per year thereafter. Alvin Community College will help provide the training for these positions.

"It came to our attention that numerous jobs in the control center were being staffed by personnel who were over qualified," said NASA's Chief, Space Station Training Branch, Dr. Frank Hughes. "To remedy the situation, we redefined the qualifications for a number of those jobs which can be performed by personnel with an associate degree."

NASA/Johnson Space Center decided that the community colleges were the appropriate place to develop the curricula, because most of the academic classes needed were already taught in the first two years of college. A Consortium of Aerospace Technology Education (CATE) was formed in March 1991, with NASA, Alvin Community College, San Jacinto College, College of the Mainland, University of Houston Clear-Lake, Rockwell Space

Operations, Omniplan, Unysis and Lockheed.

This group worked together to identify the need for an aerospace technician program and develop new curriculums at the associate degree level. Each of the three community colleges involved chose an area of expertise and designed portions of the curriculum. Alvin Community College, which is strategically located near NASA/Johnson Space Center, took the mechanical environmental area, which includes all life support systems.

Rockwell Space Operations provided the instructors for the introductory level courses and $30,000 in scholarship funds to be distributed over a three-year period to Aerospace Technology majors.

After completing the program and obtaining employment with a participating contractor, the Aerospace Technology graduate will work full-time as a Control Station Operator in the Space Station Control Center. The Control Station Operator's primary responsibility is to monitor the mechanical/environmental systems on the Space Station Freedom, identify all system malfunctions, document all of the above, and write a procedural document to refer to in the future.

An Aerospace Technology Tech/Prep program has been initiated with area high schools and a proposal has been made that the program continue through the master's degree level.

Contact:
John Bethscheider, Associate Dean, Occupational/Technology
(713) 388-4730

Alvin Community College
3110 Mustang Road
Alvin, TX 77511-4898
Total head count enrollment-Credit: 11,900; Non-Credit: 8,000
Campuses/sites: 1; Full-time faculty: 99

COURT REPORTING

The program includes an on-campus, Real-Time Courtroom, which also prepares students for employment working with hearing-impaired people

In 1975, the Alvin Community College Court Reporting program began with an initial enrollment of 70 students. Today, the program has an average enrollment of 250 students, and has achieved prominence as one of the most innovative and excellent Court Reporting programs in the country. The majority of students in the program have jobs promised them at least six months prior to graduation. ACC Court Reporting graduates are practicing in virtually every state of the union.

The ACC Court Reporting graduates can pursue a wide variety of court reporting careers such as: Official Court

Reporters, Freelance Reporters, Senate and House Reporters, Real-Time Reporters, Television Closed Captionists, Medical Transcriptionists, Rapid Text Entry Specialists, and Scopists. Reporting salaries range from $25,000 to $80,000 upward per year.

The objective of the two-year program is for the student to attain machine shorthand speed of 225 words per minute on testimony, 200 words per minute on jury charge, and 180 words per minute on literary material. The program boasts a great number of merit writers who write

Continues on Page 642

260 words per minute, and possibly the greatest number of graduates in any court reporting college who have passed the Registered Professional Reporter Examination given by the National Court Reporters Association. Twenty-one reporters trained under this program have placed on the National Reporters Championship Examination.

The ACC Court Reporting program has the only on-campus, Real-Time Courtroom for students' use in the United States. (Real-time writers find employment writing classes for the deaf in schools. Real-time writing also assures justice for hearing impaired people). In March 1993, Court Reporting students trained in "closed captioning" on campus in the ACC Radio/TV studio. The extensive training provided in the ACC Court Reporting program also guarantees that each graduate can provide full litigation support including preparation of ASCII disks, key word indexing, and researching cases for attorneys.

As an outlet for those students who must quit the program for economic reasons, students may leave the program and work as scopists after they achieve 120 words per minute. As a scopist, they work directly for a court reporter, using a computer to assist in all facets of transcript production. Although the salary for a scopist is not as high as the highest level reporter, this work assures a good living.

The program has 10 full-time instructors, two of which are English instructors. The program chairperson, Ms.

Mary Knapp, was a nationally acclaimed court reporter with 16 years of field experience when asked to re-enter education in 1965. She is one of two educators ever to receive the Distinguished Service Award from the National Court Reporters Association (NCRA). Ms. Knapp was named a Fellow of the NCRA Academy of Professional Court Reporters in 1982, and won the Distinguished Service Award from the National Court Reporter's Association in 1986. Ms. Knapp was entered into the Texas Court Reporters Association Hall of Fame in 1991.

Plans for the program include instituting an internship program whereby students nearing the end of their training can go out in the field with a practicing reporter.

The National Court Reporters Association only requires 50-hour student internships, but the ACC program will require a longer (full semester) internship of 20 hours per week to better qualify students.

So many new avenues are opening up in the reporting field since the advent of CAT (computer-aided transcription) that reporting students of ACC's innovative program can look forward to the development of more and more challenging fields of employment. Scholarships are provided on a competitive basis through Stenographic Machines, the National Court Reporter's Association, the Mike Trombatore Scholarship Fund and ACC institutional Scholarships.

Contact:
Mary Knapp, Chairperson
(713) 388-4817

Alvin Community College
3110 Mustang Road
Alvin, TX 77511-4898
Total head count enrollment-Credit: 11,900; Non-Credit: 8,000
Campuses/sites: 1; Full-time faculty: 99

AMARILLO COLLEGE

CENTER FOR ENVIRONMENTAL STUDIES

The Center provides environmental training in customized academic courses as well as community outreach concerning environmental issues

In response to enormous local, national and international concerns about the deterioration of our natural resources, the Center for Environmental Studies at Amarillo College provides environmental training in contract/customized and academic courses.

The Center was established in 1992 because of local concerns over environmental issues and legislation. Specific topics that are addressed by the Center are: Waste Management and Disposal, Manufacturing and Service Industries, State and Federal Agencies, Health Care and Education Institutions, Automotive Maintenance, Air Conditioning Refrigerants, and Alternative Fuels, Agriculture (pesticides).

The Center is partially funded by a grant from Hazardous Material Training and Research Institute (HMTRI). The grant provides contact-hour reimbursement for Waste Site Worker OSHA certifying courses. The three courses are Waste Site Worker (40 hour Haz Whopper), Emergency Spill Response (24 hour First Responder), and Refresher/Supervisor (8-hour Supplemental Training). These courses are used in conjunction with and in support of the academic courses in Hazardous Materials Technology. In addition, the Center provides other training opportunities in asbestos, waste water, land-fill and confined space entry. The HMTRI grant also provides funds for travel and teacher's aids and materials.

Other services provided by the Center are consulting, electronic bulletin board, state and federal updates, and information transfer. The Center supplies all types of information concerning environmental issues and courses to the citizens of the panhandle area.

Additional technical fields to be addressed by the Center are in areas of Health Physics (Radiation), and Industrial Hygiene. The flexibility of the Center is to provide all types of training and not necessarily confine it to the academic areas.

Contact:
Douglas L. Pickle, Director
(806) 354-6000

Amarillo College
PO Box 447
Amarillo, TX 79178
Total head count enrollment-Credit: 9,906; Non-Credit: 17,318
Campuses/sites: 3; Full-time faculty: 179

THEATRE SCHOOL FOR CHILDREN

The curriculum includes instruction for every level from age 6 to age 18, with two performing companies that tour area schools

Founded by Linda Dee Hughes in June 1983, is a self-sustained program within the departments of Fine Arts and Community Service. Its distinct purpose is to offer instruction and performance experience to young actors involved in the 11 classes offered in the after-school program.

ACTS curriculum includes theatre arts instruction for every level from age 6 to age 18. Two performing companies, The Junior and Senior Stage Players provides rehearsal and performance responsibilities for the most advanced student. Classes are offered for the aspiring dancer, the child with developmental challenges, and the young student seeking exposure to commercial work for television. The most important component is that ACTS is children's theatre. . . by children, for children.

ACTS has been noted for its work with substance-abuse education and has toured two assembly programs to all 33 elementary and middle schools in the Amarillo Independent School District. The productions are student written and produced and deal with the dangers of crack/cocaine and anabolic steroids. *Master Crack*, was sent to Mrs. Ronald Reagan for consideration as material for her "Just Say No" drug program. *Pure Strength*, a short tour show, addressed the dangers of steroids. Director Linda Hughes was presented an award of appreciation from Governor Clements for her volunteer efforts in the field of drug education.

ACTS students are well known in the community for their volunteer projects. Each year the young people involved in the program work with Special Olympics, Muscular Dystrophy Association, Don and Sybil Harrington Cancer Center, and the Ronald McDonald House.

ACTS is funded through tuition, box office receipts from productions, advertising sales and donations. Several grants have been received from Texas Commission on the Arts, Josephine Anderson Charitable Trust, and the Amarillo Area Foundation. ACTS is dependent upon these outside sources for the survival of the program. Even though there are 180 children involved, the tuition, etc. does not usually cover the increasing production costs, royalties and equipment maintenance. Community support is healthy. Three major productions are performed for the Amarillo Independent School District. Students from the fourth and fifth grades are bused to Ordway Auditorium for live theatre as part of the enrichment program. More than 5,000 young audience members delight to the antics on stage. The school system pays a small fee for each child, thus providing other necessary funding. A parental support group rounds out the fund-raising efforts, contributing several thousands of dollars each year to offset the salary of one office assistant.

ACTS has grown from an idea into a training school for young actors. Graduates are now on Broadway, in the soap operas, and studying Japanese at Brown University.

Contact:
Linda Hughes, Director
(806) 371-5353

Amarillo College
PO Box 447
Amarillo, TX 79178
Total head count enrollment-Credit: 9,906; Non-Credit: 17,318
Campuses/sites: 3; Full-time faculty: 179

CHEMICAL AND INSTRUMENTATION TECHNOLOGY

With the help of local industry and instrumentation vendors, the college developed six pilot plants instrumented with modern control systems

Brazosport College is surrounded by many of the giants of the chemical industry. This offers a unique opportunity to provide educational and training programs to support the work force needs of these diverse industries. With the cooperation of local industry and instrumentation vendors, Brazosport College has recently developed a unique process operations laboratory that offers students the opportunity to operate more than six pilot plants that are instrumented with many of the modern control systems.

The processes in these six plants are distillation, pH control, ion exchange and evaporation, liquid-liquid extraction, fixed-bed reaction, and a process control trainer. In addition, there are operating glass distillation and extraction units to allow students to see inside these processes while they are in operation.

These pilot plants use some of the most modern instrumentation including the new "smart" controls. The plants are controlled with pneumatic, electronic and digital control systems. Students are given the opportunity to simulate "real world" chemical upsets through a system of solenoid valves and programmable logic controllers. One of the plants is controlled by a computer interface system.

A chemical analysis laboratory is provided on-site to provide opportunities for sample analysis. Equipment used in analysis are titrators, gas chromatographs, polarimeters, as well as instruments used in various other bench techniques. Also included in one of the plants is an on-line gas chromatograph that allows for the continuous monitoring of the process. The laboratory also provides facilities for students to design, construct, and instrument a functioning chemical processing plant.

The college's programs train laboratory technicians, process operations technicians, and instrumentation technicians for the chemical industry. The laboratories were designed and constructed with an unusual working relationship with several area industries and vendors. The laboratory has been a showplace for training professionals from many of the companies and educational institutions in the United States as well as visitors from Europe and Asia.

In addition to the Associate of Applied Science degrees in Chemical Technology and Instrumentation Technology, Brazosport College has provided training for operations technicians for BASF Corporation, Hoffman-LaRoche, and Schnectady Chemical. The college uses advisory committees from these industries as well as Dow Chemical, Phillips, Monsanto, Shell Research, Nalco, Shintech, Rhone-Poulenc.

Contact:
Don Pugh, Dean, Academic Education
(409) 266-3232

Brazosport College
500 College Drive
Lake Jackson, TX 77566
Total head count enrollment-Credit: 3,346; Non-Credit: 1,274
Campuses/sites: 1; Full-time faculty: 685

INTERNATIONAL CENTER

For the community, the Center maintains a language bank of 65 languages to provide organizations and businesses with interpreters

Although opened to serve a growing population of English as a Second Language students, faculty and staff interested in international studies, the International Center at Brookhaven College now serves the community as well.

Student populations targeted by the Center are non-native speakers of English, bilinguals and the foreign-born. As of fall 1992, more than 10,000 students had been served. The Center provides academic assessment, advisement, tracking and mentoring for ESL students enrolled in credit ESL, Intensive English, Continuing Education ESL, and on-site language training for businesses as well as mainstreamed in academic credit programs. One hundred countries and 65 languages are represented among the Center's students, with 85 percent residents and 15 percent on non-immigrant visas. Mexico, Vietnam, Iran, Korea, India, El Salvador, Ethiopia and Nigeria are the points of origin for the majority of students.

A separate area of emphasis is services to students in the Study Abroad program, which offers an Intensive Spanish program in Cuernavaca, Mexico; a summer study abroad at the West London Institute; and occasionally, a Greece and Italy study abroad program.

For faculty and staff, the Center hosts an advisory

committee representing academic disciplines and promote internationalizing of curriculum through faculty internships or special projects. Among the highlighted disciplines are Child Development, English Composition, Human Development/Psychology, Coordinated Studies, Fashion Merchandising, World Literature, and Economics. In addition, the Center helps to provide bridge programs for ESL students in the technical-occupational programs using paired classes such as ESL for Automotive and ESL for Nursing.

For the community, the International Center maintains a language bank of 65 languages to serve organizations and businesses with interpreters. Along with a library of resources on cross-cultural communication, the Center sponsors festivals and seminars for the college and the community. The International Day draws several thousand participants each spring to a celebration of cuisine and culture in the International Courtyard.

The International Center began with funds provided for Amnesty Education by the Department of Justice, receives some assistance through Carl Perkins Vocational Education funds, and is budgeted through college operational funds under student services. Recognized in the *Wall Street Journal* (May 1991), the *Community Colleges for International Development, Inc.* (Winter 1989), and the *Leadership Abstracts/League for Innovation* (July 1990), the International Center has also been the focus of presentations at conferences of the National Institute of Staff and Organizational Development (May 1990 and 1992), American Association of Community and Junior Colleges (April 1991), and the League for Innovation (June 1989).

Contact:
Ernest L. Thomas, Vice President, Student Development
(214) 620-4801

Brookhaven College
3939 Valley View Lane
Farmers Branch, TX 75244
Total head count enrollment-Credit: 9,100; Non-Credit: 10,000
Campuses/sites: 1; Full-time faculty: 100

DEVELOPMENTAL READING IN OCCUPATIONAL AREAS

▨ *The college has completed at least four "reading resource manuals"* ▨
that have been distributed to every two-year college in the state

Brookhaven College developed occupational-specific reading resource manuals that draw from typical on-the-job and textbook materials to address a critical shortage of skilled workers plaguing the Texas economic recovery. This ambitious curriculum project, initiated in 1990, targets developmental reading in occupational areas.

Educationally and economically disadvantaged adults comprise 40 percent of the total technical-occupational enrollment in the state, a resource that had to be salvaged if the labor force is to turn from a liability to an asset. Stalled in pursuit of high demand technical fields because of insufficient basic skills, students face barriers and delays that can become insurmountable.

Advisory committees in Nursing, Computer Information Systems, Automotive Technology, Fashion Marketing, Office Technology, and Child Development isolated the core problem: reading skills. Textbooks in technical-occupational fields rank at 13th to 16th grade levels and students are arriving at eighth grade levels, at best, and frequently, at lower levels. Coupled with reading deficits are the lack of independent learning skills that permit students to monitor their own learning, set priorities, master course texts and manage time appropriately.

With the assistance of three consecutive Carl Perkins Discretionary Grants (Texas Higher Education Coordinating Board), the Instructional Development department and the reading program at the college have completed four "reading resource manuals" designed for maximum flexibility of use.

Manuals in Nursing, Computer Information System, Automotive Technology, and Fashion Marketing have been distributed to every two-year college in the state. Two more manuals, *Child Development* and *Office Technology*, are in preparation.

Besides reading samples drawn from typical on-the-job and textbook materials, each manual includes directed activities to promote development of independent reading skills. Moving through three levels, users progress from exercises that are fully supported by directions and reminders to exercises that require application of previously developed reading strategies. The manual format, in loose-leaf and indexed portfolios, permits use as primary classroom resources and as supplemental exercises in large or small group or individual instructional settings.

Materials are in use throughout the state and new manuals are in heavy demand from reading instructors. At Brookhaven, developmental reading sections are reserved for occupation-specific areas such as nursing and are taught using the manuals as a primary resource.

The impact of the materials is typified by these comments by the president of the Texas College Reading and Learning Association: "My students' greatest weakness seems to be seeing relationships between information

Continues on Page 646

presented at the beginning of an article and at the end of the same article. Relationships are also difficult in another area – it is necessary for me to spend a great deal of time showing students the connection between the reading course work and their job or other academic areas. . . Teachers of the technical/occupational courses will also benefit greatly from seeing material that objectively presents techniques and practices for tackling familiar content."

The uniqueness of the manuals is also illustrated in a letter from Dr. Nancy Wood, Chairman of the Department of English at the University of Texas at Austin: "I know of only one commercial textbook that addresses this area and it is limited compared to the material. . . (the materials) teach students to go beyond a reading textbook and to apply what they have learned about reading to actual college assignments and on-the-job print materials that they must read and understand."

Developmental Reading for Technical-Occupational Students has been featured in conferences of the Texas Association of Developmental Education (Spring 1991), the Texas College Reading and Learning Association (Fall 1991), and the National Institute for Staff and Organizational Development (May 1992).

Contact:
Linda H. Lee, Director, Instructional Development
(214) 620-4855

Brookhaven College
3939 Valley View Lane
Farmers Branch, TX 75244
Total head count enrollment-Credit: 9,100; Non-Credit: 10,000
Campuses/sites: 1; Full-time faculty: 100

FASHION MARKETING

The program emphasizes cooperative work experience, which provides students with the necessary background for successful careers

Located just 20 minutes from downtown Dallas, Cedar Valley College offers its Fashion Marketing students a unique opportunity to keep abreast of the latest developments in the fashion apparel business. That business, one of the major segments of the nation's economic structure, generates approximately $100-billion annually at retail. Marketing is the key element. Those trained in fashion marketing are involved in all aspects of the industry, from concept to point of sale. Their expertise includes product design and development, manufacturing, wholesaling, distribution, buying, advertising, sales promotion and salesmanship.

The fashion marketing program at Cedar Valley College dates to 1987, when the Texas Coordinating Board awarded the college a grant to create a model fashion marketing program. The grant, coupled with donations from the local business community, enabled Cedar Valley to create a Fashion Marketing Resource Center including a visual merchandising lab, textile library, fashion periodicals library, and retail and graphics computer lab. Provided with the latest tools in the field, students at CVC are able to gain "hands-on" experience in product development, marketing, advertising, computerized inventory management and graphic presentation.

The Cedar Valley College Fashion Marketing program is a comprehensive, two-year program consisting of 66 credit hours in both practical and theoretical training in preparation for careers in store management, buying, merchandising, wholesaling and visual merchandising. Three alternative certificate programs, each under 20 hours, are also offered. Emphasis is placed on cooperative work experience which provides students the preparation and experience necessary for successful careers in the fashion industry.

Dallas is a major regional fashion market center. Buyers from across the United States and more than 30 foreign countries visit the Dallas Apparel Mart annually to select the latest fashion merchandise for their customers. In addition, Dallas is host to more than 75 apparel manufacturing companies, a broad range of fashion retailers, and many auxiliary enterprises that promote fashion and assist the other segments of the fashion industry.

Contact:
Diane Minger, Coordinator
(214) 372-8110

Cedar Valley College
3030 North Dallas Avenue
Lancaster, TX 75134
Total head count enrollment-Credit: 3,400; Non-Credit: 1,164
Campuses/sites: 1; Full-time faculty: 54

PROJECT QUEST

*❂ Created to help under-prepared students, Project Quest features smaller classes ❂
that are scheduled in blocks of four three-hour courses*

Approximately 40 percent of the students enrolling at Cedar Valley College are academically deficient in their reading, writing and math skills. Project Quest helps them strengthen their academic skills so they can develop the self-confidence, self-discipline and motivation they need to persist in the struggle to achieve their educational and career goals.

Initiated in spring 1990, the project involves a team of three instructors, a counselor and a coordinator working together to coordinate classroom experiences that help students learn how to be academically successful. With class size limited to 22, the students enroll in a block of four three-hour courses developmental reading, writing, math and communications. In addition to the four core courses, the students also enroll in a one-hour human development course designed to help them develop student survival skills and in a one-hour writing lab course for remediating deficient grammar, mechanics, usage and rhetorical skills through prescribed individualized assignments.

And because Cedar Valley College is concerned about the whole student, the students also enroll in a PE course so that they exercise regularly and thereby are healthier and have more stamina for studying. The PE course also gives them one hour of college credit toward their degree and a semester load of 12 credit hours, so they quality as full-time students.

Developmental math is an optional course the students may choose to enroll in if they are especially interested in beginning the math sequence. Students choosing to enroll in a math course are required to meet with the math lab instructor one hour a week so they can get additional instruction as they need it, instead of waiting until they are hopelessly behind before seeking help.

Another strength of the program is the mentoring component. Each student is paired with a mentor, a faculty or staff member on campus who has expertise in the student's declared major or area of interest. The student meets with the mentor on a schedule mutually agreeable to the student and the mentor. The mentors serve as a role model and friend. Their primary functions are to listen to the students, direct them to campus services appropriate for the students' needs and/or interests, help them realize that struggling and frustration are a normal part of student life, and encourage the students to persist in striving for their goals.

Early in the semester, to promote bonding with the mentor and to help the students see the interrelationship of the oral and written communication skills, the students write a letter of introduction to their mentors in their writing class. In the communications class, they work on developing a set of questions which they use to interview their mentor; then, following the interview, they write a report on the interview for their writing class. Later in the semester, the students learn the fundamentals of making a speech of introduction and practice the skill by introducing their mentor to the class.

Interdisciplinary reading skills are emphasized through reading assignments in the reading class based on the textbook for the human development course. Exit testing at the end of the semester determines the students' course placement in the reading and writing programs for the next semester. At the end-of-the-semester lunch, the students join the Quest team and mentors to celebrate the students' successfully completing the semester.

The Dallas County Community College District Office of Research reports that income, gender race/ethnicity, and feeder high school district have no significant correlation with persistence in college. However, students taking a full-course load which includes developmental courses persist at a significantly higher rate than those not taking developmental courses and a full load in their initial course load. Developmental students need structure, additional caring support, more personal contact with faculty and counselors, an environment in which to develop positive self-images and cooperative relations with their peers, and an opportunity to clarify their goals and refine their skills. Project Quest provides these extras.

The merits of Project Quest as well as future plans for the program were shared at the North Texas Community/Junior College Consortium Fall 1990 Conference. Each successive semester since Project Quest's inception, refinements have been made in the program to improve student learning and retention. Success of the programs is evidenced by the Fall 1991 Quest class which began with 21 students. Twenty students completed the semester; 19 students returned for the Spring 1992 semester.

Contact:
Jerry Cotton, Dean, Communications/Humanities Division
(214) 372-8120

Cedar Valley College
3030 North Dallas Avenue
Lancaster, TX 75134
Total head count enrollment-Credit: 3,400; Non-Credit: 1,164
Campuses/sites: 1; Full-time faculty: 54

PROJECT BRIDGE

The project helps meet the educational and social needs of the area's estimated 75,000 adults with developmental disabilities

There has been an increased interest in the opening of community college doors to students with developmental disabilities and/or mental retardation. In 1991 the Central College of Houston Community College began a program to serve this population for three primary reasons:

1) many concerned citizens, including parents, community agency personnel and educators, approached the college asking the system to provide services to this community population, estimated to be more than 75,000 adults, aged 18 and older, living in the Houston area;

2) with the passage of the Americans With Disabilities Act (ADA), service to this population took on increasing significance for the community college; and

3) adults with developmental disabilities have traditionally been educated through high school level only; programs in the post-secondary institutions were few or non-existent.

In order to address the educational needs of this population, a task force was developed to determine what appropriate educational opportunities the college could provide. The result was the development of a phased program, which addresses both the educational and social needs of this significant student population.

In Phase One, students are self-referred or referred from the Mental Health and Mental Retardation Agency of Houston, parents, local high schools and other community agencies.

Phase Two involves evaluation and screening of students to determine academic and social abilities.

Phase Three entails placement of all entering students in the one-year Developmental Life-Skills Program. The curriculum focuses on self-esteem development, basic math, basic English, government, ethics, hygiene, appropriate social interactions, accessing community agencies, community volunteer work, career decision-making, job readiness, and appreciation of the fine arts.

In Phase Four, students who complete the Life-Skills course receive opportunity counseling and appropriate placement into either regular college courses, continuing education courses or a work place opportunity. Students already employed return to their jobs with improved self-esteem, and enhanced skills. The Mental Health and Mental Retardation Agency links with Central College to assist in locating the appropriate employment opportunities for students completing the course of study.

Approximately 220 students have been educated by the Central College since the inception of the program.

Contact:
Dennis Heller, Coordinator, Model Programs
(713) 630-1865

Central College of the Houston Community College System
1300 Holman
Houston TX 77007
Total head count enrollment-Credit: 11,395; Non-Credit: 1,000
Campuses/sites: 1; Full-time faculty: 178

PROJECT M.A.L.E.

The program aims to increase retention of African-American males, who have been disproportionately under-represented in community colleges

A special project provides support and promotes technical education opportunities for African-American males enrolled at Central College as well as those eligible participants identified through community outreach efforts. Such a project is essential today, when there is grave concern in the declining social, economic and educational status of African-American males in our society. Relatively few comprehensive program models realistically address the many barriers that limit the participation of this focus group.

In conjunction with the Black Student Union, Project M.A.L.E. was developed and implemented by Project

SOAR (Student Opportunities to Achieve Results), Central College Department of Model Programs, and the Houston Community College System. The project was facilitated by a new restructuring of the Houston Community College System, of which Central College is a part.

The transition from a multi-campus model to autonomous centers of learning permitted Central College to:

1) upgrade student services and delivery systems;

2) re-establish ongoing relationships with faculty and staff;

3) strengthen alliances with business/industry; and

4) readily respond to immediate and projected needs of the community.

Project M.A.L.E. serves as an exemplary retention model to address the problem of low enrollment and persistence among African-American males in higher education. This special population is disproportionately under-represented in our nations community colleges. In addition, vocational opportunities which exist in technical areas are seldom explored as viable, satisfying career options. This project will address the need for early intervention strategies, career and educational information, mentorship and community service activities.

The support services provided by Project M.A.L.E. facilitates the matriculation of prospective and currently enrolled African-American students within the Houston Community College System and promotes articulation within the higher educational continuum.

The following objectives demonstrate the effectiveness of this project:

- development of a system to identify, recruit, retain and graduate African-American males in academic and/or vocational/occupational programs;
- targeting of 75 African-American males, prospective and/or currently enrolled students, to participate in Project M.A.L.E for the school year;
- development and strengthening of institutional support services which promote greater sensitivity to special population's issues, with special emphasis on counseling and instructional areas;
- establishment of a project advisory council comprised of African-American leaders committed to providing technical assistance, time and talent, as well as assisting in the identification of community mentors and financial resources to accomplish project goals;
- demonstration of a "holistic" approach to retention by focusing on increasing motivation and self-esteem by providing opportunities for personal growth, self-actualization and acquisition of life-long learning skills;
- fostering academic achievement through the development of positive attitudes and behaviors and access all available college/community resources to ensure academic persistence;
- sponsoring a variety of cultural, civic, religious and educational activities to promote leadership development and create opportunities to demonstrate leadership skills through school and community service projects;
- providing increased opportunities for African-American males to regain self-worth and empowerment through education focused primarily on relevant social issues of particular interest i.e.,

male responsibility, parenting, men's movement, conflict resolution, health/wellness and stress management;

- training and assignment of adult mentors to participate; utilize both traditional one-on-one mentoring techniques as well as small group or "families" mentoring matrix;
- coordination of job readiness activities and assistance in job development for part-time and summer jobs during academic year; full-time employment once participant has earned certificate and/or associate degree; and
- establishment of an evaluation system which measures the effectiveness of the project design and strategies as well as provide baseline data on attrition and graduation rates for African-American males at Central College.

The following topics comprised the major seminar schedule for project M.A.L.E. for the 1992-93 Academic year: Motivation/Achievement; Goal Setting/Education; Cultural Heritage; Black Boys/Black Men/Black Sexism; Communications: Racism/Sexism; Health- Drugs, Aids, Alcohol, Diet; Career Development/Employment; and Celebration Of African-American Males.

Additional services include the Mentorship Program, Community/School Service projects, Readin' and Rappin' sessions, social and cultural activities, and interactive sessions to focus on self-discovery, self-sufficiency and self-empowerment.

Services include: career testing/counseling; learning style inventories/assessments; technical training programs; job-placement assistance; personal/social growth seminar series; child care assistance; transportation assistance; tutorial assistance; disabled student services; financial aid/scholarship information and assistance; transfer assistance program; and GED/ABE/remedial courses.

Extensive linkage is established with community agencies as well as faculty/staff and student body in order to provide the necessary networks to ensure academic persistence and success.

An Advisory Council – comprising community leaders representing community service organizations, churches, fraternities/sororities, local professionals, entrepreneurs and other interested individuals – assists the project staff in developing a quality and comprehensive model. The role of the Advisory Council is clearly delineated to include: serving as advisors to the project staff and Houston Community College System personnel; promoting and providing outreach/recruitment services; identifying and monitoring mentors; disseminating information on available community resources; providing indirect support staff and services; and assisting with program evaluation.

Contact:
Dennis Heller, Coordinator, Model Programs
(713) 630-1865

Central College of the Houston Community College System
1300 Holman
Houston TX 77007
Total head count enrollment-Credit: 11,395; Non-Credit: 1,000
Campuses/sites: 1; Full-time faculty: 178

EATING DISORDERS COUNSELING CERTIFICATE PROGRAM

The teaching/learning approach of the curriculum is a holistic, multi-dimensional model

In 1990, Collin County Community College became the third institution of higher education in the nation to offer an Eating Disorders Counseling Certificate Program.

The certificate is a 31-credit-hour program housed in the Social Science Division. The teaching/learning approach of the curriculum has no singular emphasis. Rather, a holistic multi-dimensional model is used seeking to include, within the instructional parameters, the content of the most effective treatment modalities now in practice. The curriculum was developed in close cooperation with the International Association of Eating Disorders Professionals, the national credentialing association. The mental health care professional provides eating disorders counseling services within the limitation of applicable state and local statues and adheres to the ethical principles of the International Association of Eating Disorders Professionals.

The Eating Disorders Counseling Certificate Program has been developed to prepare students for entry-level certification by the International Association of Eating Disorders Professionals and to provide additional training for professionals wishing to add eating disorders counseling to their credentials.

The entry-level population is 90 percent women and ethnic minorities. The program was developed to offer a paraprofessional counseling program that would meet the needs of this population in conjunction with the needs of the mental health community. The professional population is 62 percent women and 38 percent men who have masters or doctoral degrees in a variety of disciplines. Since CCCC is the only college in Texas that offers the certificate, students have come from Denton, Austin, Ft. Worth, Dallas and Abilene, as well as all of Collin County, to participate in the program.

During two academic years, 10 eating disorders counseling courses have been offered annually with an average class enrollment of 20. Eighty percent of the students completing the program are employed in the field. Fifty-five percent of the students are continuing their education at an upper-level university. The greatest success has been to track students who were terrified to attend college, complete the certificate, complete an associate's degree, and this academic year are enrolled at an upper-level university to pursue a Baccalaureate degree while working in the counseling field.

CCCC's program has established, adopted and promoted a uniform curriculum of the highest possible educational and training standards for eating disorders counselors. The certificate provides training in assessment, symptoms, treatment modalities, medical aspects, individual and group counseling and nutrition. The certificate integrates theory, skills, and an experiential field work practicum. The program is coordinated by a certified eating disorders therapist who also teaches in the program. Four adjunct faculty also teach in the program and all are professionals in the field, including a psychiatrist, dietitian, psychologist, and addictionologist. Five treatment facilities are currently practicum sites for the experiential component of the program (three facilities in Collin County, one in Dallas County and one in Denton County).

The Eating Disorders Counseling Certificate Program has received both local and national recognition from the mental health community. CCCC has the only Eating Disorders Counseling Certificate Program approved by the Texas Higher Education Coordinating Board. The International Association of Eating Disorders Professionals has recognized the program as one of only four programs in the United States to meet the educational requirements for the national certification. Due to the recognition by the Association, CCCC's program serves as a model for other colleges and universities who are attempting to start such a program. Requests have been made from colleges and universities in Arizona, Texas, Georgia, Illinois, and Connecticut. Locally, the mental health community has recognized the credibility and innovation of the program. A scholarship for a student in the program was established by a local psychiatrist. Also, students are invited to attend "professional only" seminars and workshops hosted by the mental health community. The medical directors of two treatment facilities have requested that these courses be offered at their sites to train their staff at all levels.

Contact:
Martha Ellis, Director of Staff, Program & Organizational Development
(214) 548-6606

Collin County Community College
2200 West University
McKinney, TX 75070
Total head count enrollment-Credit: 10,000; Non-Credit: 3,000
Campuses/sites: 3; Full-time faculty: 115

FULLSTREAM: EMPOWERMENT FOR LIFE

▦ Persons with challenges are assigned student mentors, who attend class ▦
with them to facilitate the learning experience

Collin County has identified a mutual education/business need to develop a program to facilitate the continued employment and education of persons with challenges, a program that empowers the people of Collin County to become employed and stay employed becoming tax-paying citizens rather than a tax burden.

The Collin County Community College District has been targeted as the natural site for the initiation of such a program. The multi-agency task force has developed the Fullstream program, a joint project of Collin County Community College, Texas Rehabilitation Commission, Collin County Mental Health/Mental Retardation, Project Move, Region 10 Education Service Center, Plano ISD, McKinney ISD, Collin County Special Education Cooperative.

Annually, public schools and local businesses collaborate to identify 25 students, ages 18 to 22 years. These students attend classes at the Collin County Community College where they are trained in skills necessary to obtain and maintain a job. They also learn basic and living skills to enable them to function as independently as possible. Each Fullstream participant is assigned a student mentor selected from CCCC students. The mentor attends class with the Fullstream student to facilitate the learning experience. The Fullstream student is placed part-time at a job

site with the assistance of a job coach. The job coach trains them to do the job at the onset and provides follow-up to ensure their continued success. Once they are able to be successfully employed full-time, the students will graduate from the program with transition services provided by Texas Rehabilitation Commission or Mental Health and Mental Retardation.

Fullstream assists the local businessman in Collin County in implementing the American With Disabilities Act. The support systems provided by Fullstream will allow them to successfully employ persons with challenges as contributing members of their work force.

Students benefit from their participation in Fullstream by being successfully included in age appropriate environments. Their basic education skills are improved, careers are identified, specific job skills are taught and appropriate employment sites are selected.

Fullstream allows students with challenges the same opportunities as their peers to graduate in a timely manner, receive further training and become successfully employed. The vision is to expand the program to include continuing education/job facilitation for all persons with challenges in Collin County, thereby ensuring their successful employment for life.

Contact:
Kathy Seei, Plano ISD, (214) 470-0777
MaryJane Wilson, Collin County Special Ed. Cooperative, (214) 442-2264

Collin County Community College
2200 West University
McKinney, TX 75070
Total head count enrollment-Credit: 10,000; Non-Credit: 3,000
Campuses/sites: 3; Full-time faculty: 115

LECROY CENTER FOR EDUCATIONAL TELECOMMUNICATIONS

▦ Telecourses, taught using video programs, textbooks and study guides, make learning ▦
possible for thousands of students unable to attend class on campus

Completed in 1991, the LeCroy Center for Educational Telecommunications provides pre-recorded and live, educational television programming to remote learning sites throughout Dallas County, the state of Texas, and the nation. The 28,000 square-foot Center is operated by the Dallas County Community College District via a sophisticated arrangement of microwave networks and satellite uplinks. The Center is located on a North Dallas site adjacent to the DCCCD's Richland College campus.

The LeCroy Center marks an educational joint venture that is both creative and cost-effective. In addition to DCCCD personnel, it houses staff for the Richardson

Independent School District Instructional Television Center, which, in association with Region 10 Education Services Center, provides services through the 60-member Regional Instructional Television Consortium. By providing advanced telecommunications resources to students from kindergarten through college, as well as to business and industry, the LeCroy Center stands as a unique model of cooperation in distance learning.

The mission of the R. Jan LeCroy Center for Educational Telecommunications is to provide greater access to learning by serving the educational and instruc-

Continues on Page 652

tional needs of students of the Dallas County Community College District and clients worldwide through the design, production and delivery of quality educational telecommunication products and services. These include telecourses, teleconferences and teleclasses via the Dallas College Network (DC-Net).

Dallas Telecourses make learning possible for thousands of students unable to attend class on campus. Telecourses are taught using the combination of video programs, textbooks and student study guides. Each course is equivalent to the on-campus sections of the same course in terms of objectives, content, rigor and transferability. During the fall 1993 semester, 4,336 students were enrolled in 20 telecourses at seven campuses in the DCCCD. Dallas Telecourses is the leading supplier of programming for the Public Broadcast System (PBS) Adult Learning Service; more than 8,000 students took Dallas Telecourses through PBS during the fall 1992 semester. Several of Dallas' award-winning telecourses are among the top 10 in use by U.S. colleges and account for approximately 38 percent of all telecourse enrollments nationally.

The LeCroy Center also offers numerous teleconfer-

ences annually to support education and training at educational institutions, businesses and governmental agencies. Specialized vocational faculty development is provided to colleges through the State of Texas Academic Resource Link (STARLINK). A number of federal and state agencies have utilized teleconferencing education and training, such as the Texas Department of Mental Health and Retardation and the U.S. Office of Personnel Management. Teleconferencing allows key elements of interactivity, access, cost effectiveness and simultaneous dispensation of information.

Teleclasses, carrying regular college credit, are offered through the three Instructional Television Fixed Service (ITFS) channels at the LeCroy Center to deliver live, interactive college credit or non-credit courses in Dallas County, including the DCCCD campuses and to specially equipped business and industry sites from the interactive television teaching studios. DC-Net is also used to distribute programming via cable television and the DCCCD's cable channel is operated 24 hours a day, featuring telecourses and informational programming.

Contact:
Pamela K. Quinn, Vice President, LeCroy Center
(214) 952-0310

Dallas County Community College District
701 Elm Street
Dallas, TX 75202

Total head count enrollment-Credit: 145,000; Non-Credit: 105,000
Campuses/sites: 8; Full-time faculty: 70

BILL J. PRIEST INSTITUTE FOR ECONOMIC DEVELOPMENT

Besides providing tailored training for businesses, Institute training consultants have counterparts on each district campus who specialize in unique cluster programs

The Bill J. Priest Institute for Economic Development, a $9.2-million, 150,000-square-foot training complex designed to play a significant role in the economic development of Dallas County, was opened by the Dallas County Community College District (DCCCD) in 1989.

Named for Dr. Bill J. Priest, founding Chancellor of the DCCCD, the Institute comprises a diverse range of programs supporting economic development efforts across the Metroplex. Programs include the Edmund J. Kahn Job Training Center, the Business and Professional Institute, the Business Incubation Center, and the Small Business Development Center.

The Edmund J. Kahn Job Training Center provides career-specific training in vocations such as office careers, accounting, data entry, medical office procedures and basic building maintenance. Enrollment opens the first week of each month, and each certificate program takes approximately six months to complete. Students attend classes five days a week from 8:15 a.m. to 3:20 p.m. Many students receive financial assistance through the Job Training Partnership Act, administered by the Private

Industry Council of Dallas. In addition to certificate programs, the Job Training Center also offers evening continuing education courses and daytime and evening courses in GED preparation. The Job Training Center places graduates in jobs across the Metroplex.

The Business and Professional Institute (BPI) provides customized training to business and industry on a contract basis. All training is tailored to meet the needs of a specific business, including curriculum development, and dates, times and location of training. Training specialties of the Business and Professional Institute include Continuous Quality Improvement, computers, workplace literacy, management/supervision, and cultural diversity, among others. In addition, BPI training consultants have counterparts on each of the DCCCD's seven campuses who specialize in a cluster of programs unique to that campus. Together, these training consultants form an extensive referral network which assures high quality training from the campus best equipped to serve the needs of a specific business. In one year, the Business and Professional Institute trained more than 9,000 employees of local businesses.

The Business Incubation Center (BIC) offers cost-shared facilities to new businesses and time-shared services for small businesses located elsewhere. Thirty-three businesses are housed in the Incubation Center, which provides a nurturing environment for growing businesses. Since the Incubation Center's opening four years ago, more that 250 jobs have been created by BIC businesses.

Four Small Business Development Center programs (made possible through a cooperative agreement with the Small Business Administration administered through the North Texas-Dallas Small Business Development Center) provide training seminars and free one-on-one counseling for small businesses in a variety of areas. The Dallas Small Business Development Center assists new businesses across Dallas County with general business concerns. The Center for Government Contracting assists businesses throughout the 49-county North Texas region seeking federal, state, county or municipal contracts. The International Business Center assists businesses across the 49-county area interested in international export. The Technology Transfer Center, which also covers the North Texas region, focuses on technology transfer, product development and commercialization, the inventions process and licensing. Over the past year alone the four small business development center programs assisted approximately 7,000 businesses.

Although the programs of the Bill J. Priest Institute for Economic Development are diverse, they are interrelated and work together to form a full-circle of business services designed to support economic development.

The Bill J. Priest Institute for Economic Development, located less than one mile from downtown Dallas, has recently been accepted as a full member of the National Coalition of Advanced Technology Centers (NCATC). The Institute has also been named Dallas's Education and Training Clearinghouse – for businesses seeking training assistance-by the Texas Department of Commerce, in conjunction with the Texas Higher Education Coordinating Board. Texas Instruments has selected the Institute to be its partner in a supplier training consortium which includes Texas Instruments, Xerox, Digital Equipment, SEMAT-ECH, Texaco, Kodak, Chrysler and Motorola. The Institute's Business and Professional Institute will be providing continuous quality improvement training – developed by consortium members – to potential suppliers.

Contact:
Kristi Day, Director, Public Information
(214) 565-5803

Dallas County Community College District
701 Elm Street
Dallas, TX 75202
Total head count enrollment-Credit: 145,000; Non-Credit: 105,000
Campuses/sites: 8; Full-time faculty: 70

DEL MAR COLLEGE

TECH PREP ASSOCIATE DEGREE

Because school districts vary in ability to provide a variety of programs, the consortium shares resources across district lines

The Coastal Bend Tech Prep Consortium is composed of 12 counties in South Texas and includes 46 independent school districts, two junior colleges two universities, and numerous business/industry members. Del Mar College serves as the fiscal agent for the consortium and provides the office space and administrative services for the consortium.

The Tech Prep program focuses on the demand occupations of the region as defined by the regional Quality Work Force Planning Association. Curriculum is being developed in Drafting Technology, Electronics Technology, Medical Laboratory, and Law Enforcement Technology. Teams of secondary educators, college instructors, and related business/industry representatives are working to develop a new curriculum that will allow high school students to earn up to 15+ college units while attending high school. The college will also have to add an equal number of credit hours for an advanced skills program. These advanced courses will reflect the current technology found in the related industry. The Texas Tech Prep model also calls for a certification examination following the completion of the new Associate Degree program to certify the graduates utilizing specific business/industry standards.

Intensive staff development will be provided for the secondary and college instructors to prepare them to teach the new curriculum content. Much of this instruction will be provided by business/industry. As each curriculum is completed, a new demand occupation project will be started following the same process.

The independent school districts in the consortium vary greatly in size and ability to provide a variety of technology preparation programs. The consortium is facilitating the sharing of resources across school district lines to provide opportunities for all students. The college will also be utilized by some school districts as the provider of technology programs for students who are still in high school. Local school superintendents are forging agreements for sending students across district lines for instruction and for

Continues on Page 654

sharing consortium resources.

The Tech Prep program will also cause Del Mar College to re-examine its responsibilities beyond its taxing district. As a partner with 46 school districts, new relationships will have to be developed to serve this regional population and to maximize the resources that are available to the educational enterprise.

Contact:
Lee W. Sloan, Project Director
(512) 886-1787

Del Mar College
101 Baldwin
Corpus Christi, TX 78404
Total head count enrollment-Credit: 11,139; Non-Credit: 10,202
Campuses/sites: 1; Full-time faculty: 265

EMPLOYEE RECRUITMENT

The program, developed to augment the number of minorities, women and disabled at the college, fills up to eight positions annually

Del Mar College in 1989 started the Academic Fellowship Program to recruit and hire more minorities, women, disabled and other professionals in the faculty and non-faculty professional ranks.

Individuals recruited and hired under this program are assigned as full-time instructors of record or administrative interns on a temporary, full-time basis with the college for a period of one (nine-month or 12-month) academic year. The program normally recruits and fills up to eight positions per year of persons who have completed a master's degree with 18 semester hours in the discipline they wish to teach or work, but need practical experience; or those professionals with specialized skills who are interested in teaching after having spent some years in other career fields. Applicants having more than one year of full-time or three years of part-time college teaching or professional experience are not eligible for the program.

These academic fellows are required to teach a minimum of 12 hours per semester or the equivalent, and no more than two class preparations. Fellows in professional support services (i.e. librarians/counselors) work a normal work week comparable to other existing professional positions. They are required to participate in a training program on teaching effectiveness designed by each department and the college's professional and organizational development coordinator, participate in the affairs of the college, hold posted office hours, attend departmental meetings, and serve on college committees.

The program is advertised widely through publications aimed at women, minorities and persons with disabilities, and written and personal contact is established with selected graduate programs revealing substantial minority populations.

The selection process utilizes a committee to screen, rank and recommend to the President candidates for hire. Included on this committee, but not limited to this list, are the Vice President of Instruction and Student Services, divisional dean, department chairperson, assigned mentor, a college counselor, the Affirmative Action Officer and a person from outside the department. This committee represents a cross section of the College community in terms of race, ethnicity and gender.

The department chairperson completes an Individualized Training Plan (ITP) for each Teaching Fellow assigned to his or her department within three weeks of the individual's arrival on campus for assignment. This plan includes all areas upon which the Teaching Fellow is to be evaluated and guidelines on how he or she will be evaluated. Each individual formal personnel file includes a copy of such Plan and all evaluations. When a full-time tenure track position vacancy occurs, the Teaching Fellow is given the opportunity to compete on an equal basis.

The Director of Equal Opportunity/Affirmative Action Officer annually develops a work force analysis outlining departments that may need assistance in meeting the goals set by the college in its Affirmative Action Plan.

The Del Mar College Academic Fellowship Program has been recognized by the Texas Higher Education Coordinating Board, Access and Equity Division, as a Model Program.

Contact:
Helen R. Gurley, Director, Equal Opportunity
(512) 886-1133

Del Mar College
101 Baldwin
Corpus Christi, TX 78404
Total head count enrollment-Credit: 11,139; Non-Credit: 10,202
Campuses/sites: 1; Full-time faculty: 265

INVASIVE CARDIOVASCULAR TECHNOLOGY

*▦ The program, established with private-sector funds, uses classroom ▦
and lab space at an area hospital*

The Invasive Cardiovascular Technology program of El Centro College was unique from the beginning, when the start-up effort combined higher education capabilities and private sector funding.

Key to this program's beginning in 1992 was Dr. Jack Schwade, Medical Director of the Cardiac Catheterization Lab at Humana Hospital-Medical City Dallas. Severe shortages in this field propelled Dr. Schwade to initiate dialogue with El Centro. Dr. Schwade spearheaded a major funding effort to enable the El Centro College Health Occupations Division to start the Invasive Cardiovascular Technology program even though no new program start-up money was available through college resources.

Because no new program start-up money was available, the funding for this program was sought through private sector donations. To date, grants have been received from Humana Hospital, $40,000; Bristol-Myers Squibb, $10,000; Pacesetter Systems, Inc., $10,000; James Sandridge, $500; and Advanced Cardiovascular Systems, $15,000. General Electric has made a $25,000 per year grant for a period of two years. Additional contributions are expected. Humana Hospital-Medical City Dallas provides classroom and lab space for the program.

Invasive cardiovascular technology students study the theory of diagnostic techniques used in diagnosis, treatment, and follow-up of cardiovascular disease in humans. The first year of the program concentrates on cardiovascular anatomy and physiology, medical electronics/instrumentation, and application of clinical skills in cardiovascular techniques. The second year of the program enables students to apply acquired cardiovascular skills in actual clinical situations in area hospital cardiovascular labs.

Invasive cardiovascular technologists work in cardiac catheterization laboratories. They assist the cardiologist in performing intracardiac pressure and electrical measurements, oximetry determination, angiocardiography, and measurement/calculation of cardiac function indices. The technologist assists in all phases of the cardiac catheterization including catheter insertion, operation of the electronic instruments, and calculation of the cardiac data used by the physician in confirming diagnosis and designing treatment for the cardiac patient. The intensive didactic and clinical training program prepares the graduates for employment in the medical specialty of invasive cardiovascular technology as invasive cardiovascular technologists. Twenty students are accepted each year.

Contact:
Sondra Flemming, Associate Dean, Allied Health
(214) 746-2271

El Centro College of the Dallas County Community College District
Main and Lamar Streets
Dallas, TX 75202
Total head count enrollment-Credit: 16,364; Non-Credit: 12,000
Campuses/sites: 1; Full-time faculty: 154

MARY CROWLEY ACADEMY

*▦ Offering the classes on site makes them accessible and minimizes problems ▦
with transportation and child care*

El Centro College goes straight to a public housing project to offer classes to women who otherwise could not attend college. The program, called Mary Crowley Academy (MCA), is a joint project between El Centro College and the STEP (Strategies to Elevate People) Foundation, a local foundation that works to improve the delivery of human services to low-income persons. This program assists low-income persons by addressing their need for improved basic skills and improved self-concept.

Started in 1985 in a Dallas housing project, it was named for the late Dallas philanthropist, Mary C. Crowley, who wanted to provide low-income mothers with opportunities to change their lives. She provided money for tuition and

books during the first year of operation; her heirs continue to provide some financial support. The program was expanded to include men in 1990. Most of the students in the Academy, however, continue to be mothers on public assistance, many of whom did not graduate from high school. Some, however, are high school graduates who have found their basic skills to be lacking. Others simply want to improve their skills to get out of dead end, low-paying jobs and make better lives for themselves and their children.

The Communications, Math and Developmental Studies Division at El Centro College provides the first level of

Continues on Page 656

developmental reading, developmental writing, developmental math, and a human development class in the housing project; one of the other colleges in the DCCCD offers a course on substance abuse since the lives of virtually all of the students are touched by this problem in one way or another. Offering the classes on site makes them accessible and minimizes problems with transportation and child care. And the students in each new "class" form a support group that makes the transition to campus classes less intimidating.

The college president, the division dean, and other campus officials visit the site at least annually to show their support for the program and to give a familiar face to the students who decide to come to El Centro College. These college officials also attend the celebration held by the academy at the end of the semester to honor the students for their work and to "graduate" those students who are coming to the campus the next semester; this celebration is held in the college performance hall.

The adjunct faculty who teach in the program are encouraged to participate in all activities held by the college or division for adjunct faculty. In addition to this, the division dean and curriculum area coordinators hold a meeting with only these adjunct faculty to discuss their particular needs or problems related to curriculum or instructional issues.

Upon completion of the first level of courses, the students make a choice about going into a training program or continuing their education at El Centro College. But for those students who choose not to pursue a college degree, their basic skills are improved so that they can function better in society.

The students are brought to the campus one time during the semester for a tour of the campus. They are encouraged to come to the campus on their own to use the Learning Center if possible.

The STEP Foundation takes a holistic view of the student's situation to try to break the cycle of poverty. In addition to raising money for tuition, books, and bus passes for on-campus students, the STEP Foundation uses volunteers, primarily from local churches, to provide parenting workshops, sex education workshops, optional Bible study, individual tutoring, an employment readiness program, enrichment seminars on diverse subjects, field trips, and "Family Share" teams. The Family Share team for each student is a group of four or more volunteers who "surround" the student to give her emotional and spiritual support. The team members stay in close touch with the student, helping her to solve problems that might prevent her from participating in the program and taking a personal interest in her and her children.

In the seven years since the program started, 10 students have completed the GED, nine have received an associate's degree, and four are enrolled in four year colleges or universities.

Of the 166 students who began the fall 1992 semester, 145 will complete the semester, a retention rate of 87.3 percent. The retention rate from one semester to the next is usually about 90 percent.

A study was conducted in 1991 to determine the effect on the children when their mothers participated in a literacy program. The study showed that the children's attitudes toward school improved, their attendance improved, and their grades improved. Some children who never thought of college as an option now plan to go to college. There have even been some children who had dropped out of high school who returned to school. It is believed that approximately 1,600 children have been affected positively because of their mothers' participation in the Mary Crowley Academy.

It is difficult to keep records on other changes that take place in the students lives. Some who get jobs don't continue to participate in the various activities available to them. But the STEP staff knows that many have been able to move out of public housing, and they estimate that 40 percent have been able to stop receiving Aid to Families with Dependent Children.

The MCA program was one of four literacy programs selected from 450 programs in 1987 to be designated an exemplary literacy program for women by Wider Opportunities for Women, Inc. (WOW). It was selected as the one outstanding adult literacy program in Dallas to be visited by Barbara Bush in spring 1990. In fall 1990 the MCA program was selected from 135 various kinds of programs to be the sole recipient of a grant of $40,000 from the Dallas Women's Foundation. It was also selected in 1990 by the Texas Governor's Commission on Women as an outstanding literacy program; leaders of the MCA then gave a workshop for other groups around the state to teach them how to start similar programs.

In 1991, the program was replicated in another housing project under the auspices of the Dallas Housing Authority (DHA). The program is a part of the DHA director's plan to turn over the management of the housing projects to the tenants. It is expected that the program will be expanded to other housing projects.

By improving basic skills and self concepts of the students, and by providing them the opportunity to get an education, the Mary Crowley Academy is affecting not only the mothers but also their children, thereby breaking the cycle of poverty.

Contact:
Georgia S. Francis, Dean, Developmental Studies Division
(214) 746-2247

El Centro College of the Dallas County Community College District
Main and Lamar Streets
Dallas, TX 75202
Total head count enrollment-Credit: 16,364; Non-Credit: 12,000
Campuses/sites: 1; Full-time faculty: 154

COOPERATIVE EDUCATION AND JOB PLACEMENT

▓ Co-op students and questions are referred to the central co-op office ▓
by placement and job developing staff

Critics of higher education and especially of student services are very alert to point out duplication of services and effort. Cooperative Education and Job Placement both contact and serve employers, but in a different way. Nevertheless, the major objective of each office is to provide services which will lead to curriculum-related, full-time employment commensurate with the student's career objectives and lifestyles. Hence, at El Paso Community College, the Office of Cooperative Education and Job Placement was initiated in March 1978.

The office serves three campuses complete with offices, scheduled pre-employment workshops, job development services, exclusive bulletin board space, and computer equipment (E-Mail). Cooperative Education staff is housed at the largest campus. Co-op students and questions are referred to the central co-op office by placement and job developing staff from the other two campuses.

Current staff includes a director, two co-op job developing staff, two placement job developers, three placement specialists, a part-time data entry clerk, a part-time assistant for data retrieval, and two student workers. A co-op administration grant coordinator is also housed in the central office. The co-op staff participates in all placement functions and activities, while the placement and job developing staff support co-op but do not become involved in working with the co-op faculty and the co-op contact

hour paper work documentation process. The director, in addition to the day to day management duties, is involved in proposal writing and working with division chairs in solving co-op class scheduling, staffing, and contact hour/site visit problems. The director and staff are active in local and regional placement/co-op professional associations, the El Paso Chamber of Commerce and the local personnel association.

The combined offices serve 400 co-op students, 20 to 25 co-op faculty and 220 co-op employers per year. Eleven hundred duplicated students are signed in each month on all three campuses. They are referred to jobs, attend pre-employment skills workshops, are referred to the co-op staff, or are seeking job search advice. Job vacancy bulletin boards are prominently located on each campus and are up-dated daily. A daily average of 45 to 55 vacant El Paso area jobs are on display throughout the year.

The combined functions and how to merge the two offices have recently been featured in the College Placement Council's *Two-Year Network News*, April 1992. The co-op program was the largest in the Texas two-year community college system in 1991, and was the only two-year school in Texas which was awarded a co-op administration grant in 1990. The office is frequently featured on local TV when out-of-town co-op and placement recruiters visit El Paso.

Contact:
Harvey S. Ideus, Director, (915) 594-2638
Roberto Reyes, Dean, Community Development, (915) 594-2133

El Paso Community College
PO Box 20500
El Paso, TX 79998
Total head count enrollment-Credit: 19,004; Non-Credit: 4,809
Campuses/sites: 5; Full-time faculty: 316

READING ACROSS THE CURRICULUM

▓ Under this faculty development program, instructors from diverse content areas ▓
work under the guidance of a reading specialist

The Reading Across the Curriculum Project is a Faculty Development Program designed to equip content area instructors with concepts and strategies to integrate reading and learning skills into their courses. Content area instructors in community colleges are typically faced with under-prepared students who can't read well enough to comprehend their required texts or organize and retain information. These reading/learning problems contribute to academic failure and attrition. This project broadens instructors' perceptions of their roles from that of a content area specialist to a facilitator of learning.

The specific objectives of the Reading Across the Curriculum Project, begun in 1988, are to:
1) encourage participants to be aware of the impact of the reading process for learning in their content areas;
2) develop an awareness of the comparable difficulty of their course materials and texts and of the factors which contribute to the complexity of these materials;
3) provide reading/learning strategies which will

Continues on Page 658

enable participants to increase the efficiency with which students are able to read and retain content information;

4) provide a forum in which participants can share problems related to reading within their content areas and find practical solutions to these problems; and

5) provide an impact on student achievement and retention in the content areas.

Some topics addressed are:

1) making purposeful assignments and using textbook organization to aid comprehension;

2) learning terminology and remembering it;

3) textbook evaluation and readability; and

4) integration of reading and writing to learn.

The project consists of five to six instructors from diverse content areas who work together under the guidance of a reading specialist. Each group meets for one academic semester or approximately 16 weeks. Participants meet in two-hour weekly sessions. In these sessions, strategies for reading/learning improvement are presented and individual problems and projects are discussed. Participants are required to implement a minimum of four different strate-

gies into their individual courses, report on these reading/learning strategies and mini-teach them to the group. Participants also take turns summarizing and reporting on distributed research articles that give background understanding to topics of discussion. Each participant receives $1,000 at the end of the semester. The coordinator receives release time or payment equal to one course. The cost of implementation is approximately $8,000. This depends on the number of participants and includes expenses for printing and travel.

The project is very popular and instructors readily volunteer to participate. The program has been recognized at many state and national conventions. The project coordinator and several participants have made presentations at the Seventh Annual Conference on Academic Support Programs sponsored by Western College Reading and Learning Association and TADE (1988) Dallas, Texas, 22nd Annual Conference of Western College Reading and Learning Association, (1989) Seattle, Wash., NISOD International Conference on Teaching Excellence, Austin, Texas 1990 and 1991, and the National Association for Business Communications Conference, Honolulu, Hawaii, 1991.

Contact:
Jenny Giron, Administrator, (915) 594-2477
Roberto Reyes, Administrator, (915) 594-2133

El Paso Community College
PO Box 20500
El Paso, TX 79998
Total head count enrollment-Credit: 19,004; Non-Credit: 4,809
Campuses/sites: 5; Full-time faculty: 316

FRANK PHILLIPS COLLEGE

PROGRAM REVIEW

Faculty responsible for a program prepare and present a formal analysis of their program to a review committee

Accountability in education has been the watch word during the last decade. Frank Phillips College believes the responsibility for program effectiveness rests primarily within the institution. The administration, faculty, and Board of Regents have bonded together to develop such an in-house process.

The college, located in a rural area, somewhat isolated in the Texas panhandle from the main population areas, has developed, implemented and revised its own program review process since 1987.

All courses and programs offered by Frank Phillips College are subject to review every three years by an informal and a formal Program Review Process. All occupational programs are reviewed twice yearly by the Occupational Advising Board for Frank Phillips College. This board, Which is composed of representatives of business and industry in the service area, review proposed changes to the curriculum and recommends both substantive and procedural changes in the occupational areas. Additional external reviews of the curriculum are

conducted by accrediting and regulating agencies.

Although external groups periodically review course and program content, the primary responsibility for this task resides with the faculty and administration. Each faculty member charged with the responsibility of insuring that the courses he/she teaches are timely and relevant. This charge to the individual faculty member insures that the syllabus and course content for each individual course are reviewed and updated on a regular basis and that substantive change is undertaken whenever necessary.

In addition to individual course review, each program of the college is subjected to a formal review on a periodic basis. This process is outlined in the Frank Phillips College Program Review Guidelines. These guidelines ensure that each program is carefully analyzed both quantitatively and qualitatively.

The Program Review requires faculty responsible for a program to prepare and present a formal analysis of their program to the FPC Program Review Committee. The

Continues on Page 659

Program Review Committee, which is composed of the Dean of Continuing/Off-Campus Instruction (Chair), and faculty, scrutinize the program analysis and present formal recommendations regarding the program to the Dean of Instruction. The Dean of Instruction. based upon committee suggestions, determines what changes or decisions should be made regarding the program.

One additional college committee, the Academic Standards and Curriculum committee, is charged with assisting in the improvement of the curriculum of the college. This committee can review new courses, survey changes in instructional programs. and supervise the implementation of state and accrediting agency guidelines relating to instruction. This committee, which is composed of six faculty and is chaired by the Dean of Instruction, also acts as an appeal body for faculty objecting to the recommendations of the FPC Program Review Committee.

Contact:
Roger Brown, Dean, Continuing/Off-Campus Education
(806) 274-5311

Frank Phillips College
PO Box 5118
Borger, TX 79008-5118
Total head count enrollment-Credit: 1,668; Non-Credit: 2,529
Campuses/sites: 1; Full-time faculty: 2

FRANK PHILLIPS COLLEGE

TRANSFER GUARANTEE

Not only do students gain confidence with a guarantee of credit transfer,
but also an increasing number of students seek academic advising

The misperception that "nothing will transfer" prompted Frank Phillips College to devise a way to guarantee transfer of credits from the community college and to publicize this "new fact."

With the approval of the FPC Board of Regents, a money-back guarantee was offered, based on certain required standards: student ability to name school of intended transfer, student participation in academic advising, and student challenge guarantee within one year of transfer.

Publicity of the program generated more positives for the college than anticipated. Not only did the students gain confidence with a guarantee of credit transfer, but also the college was recognized nationally for an innovative idea.

Senior institutions who were repeatedly asked to confirm course guarantees eventually chose to submit a "transfer equivalency;" as more and more transfer equivalencies arrived, credit transfer could be confirmed during the students registration for classes. An increasing number of students sought academic advising (formerly unheard of).

During the six years since this guarantee became available only one student has actually challenged a credit transfer, but a change of major was the "culprit." As information about the guarantee was shared among inquiring institutions, expectations grew toward the desire for guarantee from all institutions which has resulted in the common-course number system state-wide.

Contact:
Glenda K. Guyton, Dean, Student Life
(805) 275-5311

Frank Phillips College
PO Box 5118
Borger, TX 79008-5118
Total head count enrollment-Credit: 1,668; Non-Credit: 2,529
Campuses/sites: 1; Full-time faculty: 2

HOUSTON COMMUNITY COLLEGE SYSTEM-SOUTHWEST COLLEGE

THE INTENSIVE ENGLISH PROGRAM

College-bound graduates of the program develop sufficient proficiency in listening,
speaking, reading and writing to be accepted into an academic program

The Intensive English Program at the Houston Community College System is the largest of its kind in Texas and one of the largest in the United States. When established in August of 1983 as a special program to provide comprehensive English instruction to students whose native language is not English, the program was a part of the Humanities Division of Houston Community College. In February of 1992, Houston Community College was divided into six colleges, and the Southwest

Continues on Page 660

and Northeast sites of the program became separate.

The Intensive English Program-Southwest College offers adults four levels of English instruction from beginning to advanced. Within each level, students develop listening, speaking, reading and writing abilities. Instruction is given for 320 hours per semester with optional Friday computer/language laboratory instruction. The program began in 1983 with 36 students. It is staffed by six full-time faculty members and 16 adjunct instructors, who serve more than 800 full-time students per year.

The goal of the program for its college-bound graduates of the Intensive English Program is to develop sufficient proficiency in listening, speaking, reading and writing to be accepted into an academic program and complete academic courses successfully. (Eighty-five percent of all Intensive English students indicate that, after completion of the program, they will continue their academic studies at the college.) For graduates who do not plan to enter an academic course of study, it is the goal of the program to provide students with sufficient English skills to be functional, linguistically competent and confident members of the English-speaking community.

The program has been both an educational and financial success, which is due mostly to the following reasons:

1) a strong, comprehensive and organized curriculum which clearly states subject matters to be covered, yet allows for individual teacher and student teaching/learning styles and which incorporates a state-of-the-art language laboratory and Macintosh technology;

2) the structuring of the levels in blocks of developmental credit classes which qualifies the college to receive state contact-hour reimbursement funds (1991-1992 gross revenue = $1,612,380) (State reimbursement allows the college to charge tuition which is less than most programs of this kind and gives the program a competitive advantage);

3) a commitment on the part of the college administration to bear the expense of providing adequate space and funds to support the exponential growth of the program;

4) articulation with the HCCS academic program, which permits students completing the program to enter academic study at HCCS without further language proficiency testing; and

5) adherence to sound business practices: providing quality service for a fair price at a convenient location.

Both morning and afternoon sessions are offered because of the increase in demand for the program. English as a Second Language is a growth market in Houston; the ethnic diversity of the Houston area and the attraction of Houston to international students will continue to contribute to the growth of the program.

Contact:
L. Michael Evans, Coordinator
(713) 662-9226

Houston Community College System-Southwest College
5407 Gulfton
Houston, TX 77081
Total head count enrollment-Credit: 83,220; Non-Credit: 42,667
Campuses/sites: 12; Full-time faculty: 110

DESKTOP PUBLISHING

HCCS students founded the Association of Professional Desktop Publishers
to continue networking after graduation

International students have attended Houston Community College System to obtain desktop publishing training that is unavailable in their countries, taking the college's teaching as far away Nigeria. Desktop publishing became a unique part of the curriculum of the Houston Community College System in 1985. The first classes began in January 1986 with an enrollment of 35 students. The program has grown to more than 600 students.

The following is a brief history of the HCCS desktop publishing program:

- 1983: The technical communications program added three course titles: Technical Writing on Microcomputers, Technical Writing on Automated Systems, and Word Processing for Technical Personnel. Initial equipment included two stand-alone Display Writers (automated systems) and four Apple IIe computers. Fifteen Apple IIe computers were ordered.

- 1983-84 school year: Course enrollments doubled, and WordStar, Word Perfect, and Display Writer were taught on Compaq portable Computers. Apple IIe was used for Apple Writer IIe and WordStar (with a CPM card).

- Summer 1984: College officials earmarked $55,000 for the purchase of computer equipment and programs for the technical writing on computers program. Twelve PCs and XT computers were ordered, along with 15 different word processing and graphics packages.

- 1984-85 school year: The program continued using Apple IIe computers, especially in courses designed for teachers in the Houston Independent School

District and surrounding districts. Microsoft Word for PC was introduced to technical writing classes. Faculty members previewed beta-test copies of Aldus PageMaker.

- Summer 1985: Faculty seminars in desktop publishing began. Faculty members asked for 12 Apple IIe computers for teachers and 12 Macintosh computers for desktop publishing.
- 1985-86 school year: Desktop publishing courses were developed, and the first Macintosh 512K computers and Apple Laser Writer printers delivered in Houston arrived at Houston Community College's Galleria campus. A Hewlett-Packard Laserjet printer and color monitors were ordered for the PC courses. Desktop publishing courses on the Macintosh began in January 1986. The courses were so successful that the college provided more lab space at its Post Oak Boulevard location.
- 1986-87 school year: The desktop publishing program expanded to other HCCS campuses. The Texas Higher Education Coordinating Board approved HCC's desktop publishing certificate program, the first such curriculum in the United States. Students wanting a certificate were required to complete nine courses, for a total of 27 college credit hours. Students still pursued two-year degrees or certificates in technical writing.
- 1987-90: The program expanded to include 10 labs dedicated to desktop publishing on various HCCS campuses. Courses involving multimedia hardware and software were introduced. Two computer vans, one with 21 stations and another with nine stations,

were used with interchangeable Macintosh and IBM computers for a variety of programs, including desktop publishing. A transfer program was initiated with the University of Houston-Clear Lake, leading to bachelor of arts and master's degrees in communications/media.

- 1991-92 school year: HCCS developed into six separate colleges. At the newly built Southeast College, 157 networked PS/2 computers were installed with enough power for multimedia classes as well as desktop publishing on the PC. Southwest College, however, continued to lead the system in its desktop publishing expertise.
- Summer 1992: The first Quadra computers arrived at the Galleria campus of Southwest College for use in multimedia courses.

Today, HCCS supports desktop publishing labs in various parts of the system. Chancellor Charles Green and the college presidents under him are continuing to encourage expansion of the program to meet the needs of changing technology. HCCS students founded the Association of Professional Desktop Publishers (APDP) to continue networking after graduation. APDP is now a 140-member organization, comprising professional desktop publishers operating their own businesses or working in large corporations.

Students with MA's and Ph.D's enroll in the HCCS program for training. They become involved in specialized internships with service bureaus and large corporations, which offers them the opportunity to gain knowledge of the larger field of electronic publishing as it currently is being utilized.

Contact:
Arnold Goldberg, Department Head, Technical Communication
(713) 871-8930

Houston Community College System-Southwest College
5407 Gulfton
Houston, TX 77081
Total head count enrollment-Credit: 83,220; Non-Credit: 42,667
Campuses/sites: 12; Full-time faculty: 110

LAMAR UNIVERSITY-ORANGE

STUDENT LITERACY

The college and a school district developed a program to help high school students pass a required state exam

In order to address a locally identified need within a service area high school, Lamar University-Orange – in cooperation with the West Orange-Cove Consolidated Independent School District – has developed a program to assist high school students pass a required state examination. The institution obtained funding through the U.S. Department of Education's Student Literacy Corps for a program start up of fall 1992.

This effort will match community college students with high school students for the provision of remedial assistance designed to increase basic skills. Lamar

University-Orange is offering this service as part of Psychology 2340, Introduction to Learning. In this course Lamar University-Orange students receive three semester hours credit for the combination of classroom and tutorial work.

This course prepares students for the tutorial experience through a review of learning styles and theory. Classroom learning is then applied at the high school, a process which promotes real world experience and facilitates the development of altruistic behavior.

Continues on Page 662

Lamar University-Orange students receive intensive supervision by the course instructor, high school faculty, and a school district volunteer coordinator. The progress of high school students is monitored by high school faculty who provide feedback to Lamar University-Orange students.

The institution supports this and other projects which promote cooperation between the institution and local constituents.

Contact:
Joseph B. Olson, Dean, Continuing Education and Community Services
(409) 882-3321

Lamar University-Orange
410 Front Street
Orange, TX 77630
Total head count enrollment-Credit: 3,280
Campuses/sites: 1; Full-time faculty: 39

LAMAR UNIVERSITY-ORANGE

ORANGE COUNTY SUMMER YOUTH PROGRAM

The program provides at-risk juvenile probationers with learning, recreational and cultural enrichment activities

During the summer of 1992 Lamar University-Orange offered a six-week program designed to provide at-risk juvenile probationers with learning, recreational and cultural enrichment activities. The program was developed in cooperation with the Orange County Juvenile Probation Department to promote basic skills, self esteem, mentoring, and to serve as a diversion to normal probation.

With funding secured through the Texas Department of Criminal Justice, the institution utilized three classrooms to promote basic skills in computer literacy, reading, and consumer math during morning hours. In the afternoon, team sports were conducted in the institutions gym. Afternoon sessions were mixed with group counseling activities. Operating on a Monday through Thursday schedule, with classroom and gym activities on three days,

the fourth day was reserved for museum, nature or outdoor activities.

Staffing included three classroom instructors, an assistant coordinator, outside lecturers and a psychologist. The effort was overseen by a program coordinator and included intensive individual counseling. Local probation authorities were closely involved in planning and daily intervention.

The program served 21 local juveniles who attended voluntarily; each of whom completed the project. Daily attendance was never lower than 90 percent, a remarkable figure considering the level of risk, low self esteem, and reluctance to attend regular school sessions. The institution and the county prepared a more comprehensive year-round program and a summer program for 1993.

Contact:
Joseph B. Olson, Dean, Continuing Education and Community Services
(409) 882-3321

Lamar University-Orange
410 Front Street
Orange, TX 77630
Total head count enrollment-Credit: 3,280
Campuses/sites: 1; Full-time faculty: 39

LAMAR UNIVERSITY-PORT ARTHUR

HEBERT CENTER PROGRAM

A full-time Special Populations Coordinator oversees part of the program, which served physically handicapped students

Lamar University-Port Arthur has formed a unique partnership with the Hughen Center and the Hebert Adult Vocational Center of Port Arthur to serve physically handicapped students, particularly those students with mobility impairment.

Since 1927, the Hughen Center has advanced the work for crippled children between the ages 6 and 21. Children from the United States, as well as several foreign countries,

attend classes at the Hughen Center, where, in addition to dormitory facilities, there are occupational, speech, and physical therapies; 24-hour nursing supervision; augmentative communication training for the non-verbal; special apparatuses made on-site; counseling; and orthopedic clinics. Operating funds for the Hughen Center are provided by five area United Funds as well as by income from the dormitories and fees for services.

Until recently the education continuum for many students has ended at the secondary level. With funds provided by local benefactors, Effie and Wilton Hebert, the adult wing of Hughen the Hebert Adult Vocational Center has been constructed. The Hebert dormitory houses the post secondary students. Included in the facility are a kitchen, dining room, library and media center, living area, and classroom/computer lab. The Texas Rehabilitation Commission provides the funds for the students' room and board and, in most cases, the funds for the students' tuition and books. Some of the students receive scholarships from the Eagles Foundation.

Lamar University-Port Arthur is using Carl D. Perkins funds to equip a computer lab that is wheelchair accessible. Specialized equipment for students with visual, auditory, or motor impairment includes a HyperGraphics system with remote response pads, Zoom Text software to magnify screen text, and an Optelec Video Magnification System that allows students to magnify texts and class notes. Perkins funds also provide for an instructional staff to teach four courses each semester at the site. A full-time Special Populations Coordinator on the Lamar campus is an advocate for the students for special needs, such as arranging for note takers and transportation to special events, planning seminars on study habits and interpersonal relations, and providing career and job search guidance.

Although students for the post secondary program usually are referred by the Hughen Center, coordinators of secondary special education programs, or by the Texas Rehabilitation Commission, the program is open to any young adult who has a physical disability which creates a handicapping condition to employment or to obtaining training for employment. The minimum admission requirement is a high school diploma or a General Equivalency Diploma. In exceptional cases, a student's ability to benefit is the determining factor.

Currently, the students are working toward a one-year certificate in Microcomputer Support Specialist. During their first semester of classes at Hebert, the students visit the Port Arthur campus occasionally to attend tutoring sessions in the Learning Center or to attend special campus functions. After completing one or two semesters at the Hebert Center, the students begin to attend regular classes on the Port Arthur campus. For the physically handicapped student, this "school-to-school" transition prepares the student for the subsequent "school-to-work" transition.

Contact:
Janis Hutchins, Interim Dean, Technical Programs
(409) 983 4921, ext. 300

Lamar University-Port Arthur
PO Box 310
Port Arthur, TX 77641
Total head count enrollment-Credit: 5,500; Non-Credit: 900
Campuses/sites: 1; Full-time faculty: 51

SUBSTANCE ABUSE COUNSELING

The training program is particularly popular with students studying sociology, social work and criminal justice

Substance Abuse Counselors Training at Lamar University-Port Arthur quickly grew to a credit program from its non-credit, continuing-education origins designed to help counselors maintain their annual certification.

This program experienced such rapid expansion for several reasons:
- the courses also provided the education requirements needed by people who wanted to enter the field;
- the program was (and is today) the only one of its kind in Southeast Texas and attracts students from throughout the region; and
- students who became certified in Texas were able to practice in the State of Louisiana, and as a result students from Southwest Louisiana were attracted to the program.

The Texas Higher Education Coordinating Board approved a two-year Associate of Applied Science Degree Program designed around these courses, and in the fall of 1989 students could receive college credit for them. This attracted even more students into the program, and students majoring in fields such as sociology, social work, and criminal justice took one or more of these courses as electives.

Today, students who complete the two-year degree are able to enter a bachelor's degree program in counseling facility management at the University of Texas Medical School in Galveston, or use the SAC courses for a minor in several bachelor degree courses for a minor in several bachelor degree programs on the Lamar-Beaumont campus.

There is a shortage of certified/licensed alcohol and drug abuse counselors for 14,500 prisoners in state correctional institutions, which will create an even greater demand for such counselors. In the fall of 1992, a full-time instructor, with a Master's Degree in Substance Abuse Counseling, was hired. This will allow for the scheduling of additional

Continues on Page 664

sections and expansion of the program to meet the demand for these classes. The program is designed to provide the continuing education hours needed by certified/licensed counselors in Texas; to prepare students for careers as substance abuse counselors; to help meet the demand for such counselors in the region and throughout the state during the 1990's; to provide information and education for anyone personally or professionally interested in the field, such as parents, teachers, health care professionals, clergy, and criminal justice and social work professionals. The program has been very efficiently managed since its inception. As a non-credit program, it was self-supporting from the very beginning. Because of its success, the program has had the resources to provide necessary audio-visual and library materials. The program has required no expenditure of funds for capital items; none of the courses require any specialized equipment or laboratory space.

Contact:
Janis Hutchins, Interim Dean, Technical Programs
(409) 983-4921, ext. 300

Lamar University-Port Arthur
PO Box 310
Port Arthur, TX 77641
Total head count enrollment-Credit: 5,500; Non-Credit: 900
Campuses/sites: 1; Full-time faculty: 51

PHYSICAL THERAPIST ASSISTANT

The program does not require prerequisite coursework and covers four regular semesters and two summer sessions

In conjunction with Project Hope, Laredo Junior College established the Physical Therapist Assistant Program in 1985 in response to expressed community needs for physical therapist assistants in the geographical area of southwest Texas. Since 1988, at least 26 students have completed the two-year integrated curriculum, and have successfully passed the Texas State Board of Physical Therapy Examiners' licensure examination for physical therapist assistants. Ninety-six percent of the program's graduates are of Hispanic ancestry.

The Physical Therapist Assistant Program strives to provide its graduates with entry-level skills sufficient to meet the competency standards of the Commission on Accreditation in Physical Therapy Education of the American Physical Therapy Association. More specifically, program graduates complete a 72-hour curriculum designed to enable graduates to work under the supervision of a licensed physical therapist to:

- provide physical therapy services as specified in the plan of care developed by the physical therapist;
- respond to acute changes in the patient's physiological state;
- identify architectural barriers;
- interact with patients and families in a manner which provides the desired psychosocial support;
- demonstrate appropriate and effective written, oral, and nonverbal communication with patients and their families, colleagues and the public;
- demonstrate safe, ethical and legal practice;
- teach other health care providers, patients, and families to perform selected treatment procedures and functional activities;
- understand basic concepts of the health care system including multi-disciplinary team approach, quality care, governmental agencies, private sector, roles of other health care providers, health care facilities, issues, and problems; and
- understand basic principles of levels of authority, planning, time management, supervisory process, performance evaluations, policies and procedures, and fiscal consideration for both the provider and consumer.

The PTA Program, which does not require prerequisite coursework to enter the curriculum's studies, covers four regular semesters and two summer sessions over topics ranging from human anatomy and physiology, kinesiology, growth and development, and medical terminology to physical therapy procedures, physical agents, therapeutic exercise, pathophysiology, rehabilitation, and 17 weeks of clinical practicums involving patient care under the auspices of clinical instructors in local and area health care facilities. The two-year course of study allows students to acquire a cognitive data base, develop appropriate "hands-on" pyschomotor skills required for quality patient care, and formulate attitudes conducive for effective healing and promotion of their future patients' independence.

Human resource needs for effective program operation has been met through local and area support of the physical therapy community and medical facilities. The former supplies both academic and clinical faculty while the latter provide clinical education sites for the three periods of clinical practice required in the LJC PTA Program. The PTA Program has a full time coordinator/ instructor, a part-time laboratory assistant, five part-time instructors, and approximately 16 clinical adjunct faculty designated as

Continues on Page 665

clinical instructors.

The Laredo Junior College Physical Therapist Assistant Program is fully accredited by the Commission on Accreditation in Physical Therapy Education of the American Physical Therapy Association through 1993.

Contact:
J.D. Wendeborn, Coordinator
(210) 721-5263

Laredo Junior College
West End Washington Street
Laredo, TX 78040
Total head count enrollment-Credit: 5,377; Non-Credit: 2,994
Campuses/sites: 1; Full-time faculty: 166

IMPORT/EXPORT STUDIES

The program exposes students to logistical areas considered crucial to working in any business involved in international trade

Trade between the United States and Mexico in 1987 was $34-billion. It is now $65-billion. Even more spectacular is the growth of U.S. exports to Mexico – they have tripled in that same period establishing a trade surplus with that country. All this activity is due in part to a reduction or elimination of some trade barriers. Understanding this, and operating well in such an economy, is especially important to Laredo, through which more than half of the trade between the U.S. and Mexico moves (making it the largest inland port in the United States).

There are new businesses to the area such as manufacturers taking advantage of offshore production sharing (Maquiladora) opportunities; trading companies buying and selling goods on both sides of the border; transportation carriers moving the goods; freight forwarders processing exports; warehousemen providing storage services; and Customs brokers processing imports and providing some of the same export services offered by freight forwarders.

But with increased external trade has also come the challenge to meet the needs or demands of the job market for the "Gateway to Mexico." The logistical business involved in serving this trade require bilingual personnel familiar with the intricacies of import and export procedures, transportation, materials management, warehousing and distribution. Moreover, with the advent of electronic Data Interface (EDI) and the modernization of Customs procedures, automation is a must for those businesses wanting to remain competitive.

Laredo Junior College has addressed the challenge of preparing Import/Export practitioners by exposing its students to a two-year curriculum in logistical areas considered crucial to obtaining and retaining employment in any of the businesses involved. The majority of the students in the Import/Export Management Program are economically and language deficient making the challenge greater but the results even more rewarding. Development of a successful career in any of these businesses can make a world of difference to a person that grew up where unemployment rates historically are in the teens. Some students may even have experienced the local economic devastation caused when Mexico devalued its currency in 1982 and the unemployment rate in Laredo went over 20 percent.

The current program was developed by faculty and local Import/Export industry leaders that formed an advisory panel whose job it was to consider and select the competencies required of students entering the particular businesses. The advisory panel concept worked so well in selecting competencies to be addressed that it continues to be a vital source for the faculty in the design of study courses.

Once again an expected historical event will change the regional economy for decades to come, as a result of the North American Free Trade Agreement (NAFTA) between the United States, Mexico and Canada. The growth experienced after Mexico joined the GATT in 1986 is once again inevitable, in fact some believe NAFTA will launch Mexico into worldwide trade making the last economic surge seem minor. The foundation of the LJC program is being put to the test as the college enters the Free Trade Era. But high-quality instruction seems assured as plans are already being implemented in such areas as a course in Import/Export automation and a Customs Brokers Examination Review. Other areas of planned growth attributed to NAFTA will be the construction of an Import/Export Center that incorporates computer labs, telecommunications capabilities, and a consortium center for bilingual education.

Contact:
Jacinto Juarez, Vice President, Instruction
(210) 721-5142

Laredo Junior College
West End Washington Street
Laredo, TX 78040
Total head count enrollment-Credit: 5,377; Non-Credit: 2,994
Campuses/sites: 1; Full-time faculty: 166

INDUSTRIAL / EDUCATIONAL PARTNERSHIPS

▨ The college's commitment to the educational needs of employers and workers ▨
has been credited with attracting new business and facilitating expansion

Through its partnerships and programs with business and industry, Lee College helps develop a quality work force and helps ensure the economic strength and vitality of its industrial clients. Taxpaying businesses and industries contribute more than 70 percent of local tax revenue Lee College receives each year. For 1991 and 1992, these funds totaled nearly $6-million each year. Of funds Lee College receives from all sources – local, state, federal, student charges, etc. – these industrial monies comprise roughly 25 percent. Partnerships and programs that meet educational needs of industries and their employees must be a priority for institutions such as Lee College.

Lee College works closely with local employers – Brown & Root Industrial Services, Rohm & Haas, Exxon, DuPont, Northwestern Wire and Steel, Pasadena-Simpson Paper Co., Champion International Paper Co., and Union Carbide/Linde Division – to meet training needs. The college waives out-of-district fees for "industrial" students. Employers pay the remaining (in-district) tuition and fees.

Prior to the publication of each semester's class schedule, the Dean of Technical and Applied Sciences at Lee College meets with representatives from local industries to determine the types of training their employees need. The employer receives a course list for training the college can provide through credit courses. If courses are not available at times convenient to employees, Lee College alters its schedule or offers additional sections.

Students who complete these courses earn college credit. In academic year 1991-92, Lee College provided 866,432 contact hours of training in this manner. Head count for September 1991 to July 1992 totaled 5,509 students.

If Lee College cannot provide training through regular courses, the college and the employer design special courses and offer them at convenient times and places. Generally, these are not credit courses and the contact hours are not reported for funding purposes. In 1991-92, Lee College provided 73,330 contact hours of non-credit training for local industries. Enrollment totaled 2,377.

In past semesters, these educational partnerships emphasized technical skills only-welding, electronics, pipefitting and supervision. However, major employers such as Brown & Root Industrial Services have agreed to support partnerships that emphasize developmental courses in reading, mathematics and English composition as well. Lee College and the Harris County Department of Education are meeting this need for "applied academics" by integrating the teaching of academic competencies and technical skills. Lee College is also implementing self-paced, computer-assisted programs using Josten Invest or Computer Curriculum Corp. (CCC) programs targeting workplace literacy.

The Baytown Area-West Chambers County Economic Development Foundation credits Lee College's commitment to meet the educational needs of employers and workers as a factor that significantly increases the area's attractiveness for new business and expansion. The value of new and expanded business totals $200-million locally during the last three years, according to the foundation.

Mary Atlas, chairman of the Texas Higher Education Coordinating Board, has recognized Lee College's cooperation with industry in a report to the Governor on the state of higher education in Texas.

Contact:
Johnette Hodgin, Dean, Applied Sciences, (713) 425-6515
Dean Wilks, Industrial Liaison, (713) 425-6460

Lee College
PO Box 818
Baytown, TX 77522-0818
Total head count enrollment-Credit: 16,332; Non-Credit: 13,169
Campuses/sites: 9; Full-time faculty: 140

MULTICULTURAL STUDIES; AMERICAN STUDIES

▨ These two interdisciplinary programs help students understand the ▨
interrelationship among disciplines, ideas and historical periods

Helping students understand the interrelationship among disciplines, ideas and historical periods is the emphasis of two interdisciplinary programs offered at Lee College. The Multicultural Studies program is open to all freshman students who met general course prerequisites, while the American Studies program is designed for sopho-

more honors students. Courses within these programs meet general education requirements.

In its fifth year (1993), Multicultural Studies combined freshman composition and introductory sociology into a six-hour block each major semester to study the contributions and ideas of blacks, Hispanics and women, thereby representing the population of the local community. In addition to team teaching, small group discussion provides the basis for learning. Complementing the sequence is an American history class that is taught separately, using a multicultural approach.

In its 19th year (1993), American Studies combined American literature, American history and humanities into a nine-hour block each major semester. Approximately 20 students are selected for the program, based on recommendations, interviews, and English skills. Using teaching, small group discussion, and critical thinking, students study American culture and ideology as it relates to different time periods in American history; research based on original documents is required. Students making a B or better in each course within the 18-hour sequence or in combination with other honors courses will receive on their transcript a Lee College Honors Program designation.

Contact:
John Britt, Instructor
(713) 425-6375

Lee College
PO Box 818
Baytown, TX 77522-0818
Total head count enrollment-Credit: 16,332; Non-Credit: 13,169
Campuses/sites: 9; Full-time faculty: 140

INTERPRETER TRAINING

Besides interpreter training, the college also offers deaf individuals social events and coordinates various agencies that serve the hearing-impaired

It takes more than learning a language to relate to a people. McClennan Community College recognizes it also takes learning a culture. This is especially true when a person learns the second language for use in their work.

Students who plan to work in the field of language interpreting need a high level of familiarity and comfort in the cultures of the languages for which they will be interpreting. Experiencing initial contacts with a new culture within the safe structure of the college environment can help both students and members of the culture to achieve a comfort level with each other. This reduces the students' fears and anxieties, creating a better learning environment. Because of the uniqueness of the American Deaf culture and Deaf community, this approach is especially relevant for educating/training students who will work with Deaf[†] people.

Prior to establishing the Interpreter Training Program, McLennan Community College had conducted a survey, finding a clear need for such a program in the large rural area of Central Texas. In the early stages of the program, faculty members began to bring students in contact with the Deaf community in a variety of ways. Deaf individuals were hired as teaching/lab assistants for sign courses, and the program began hosting an annual social event to show appreciation to the Deaf community. (Attendance has grown from 25 to more than 300 persons.) A field trip to the state residential school for the deaf provides an exposure to the traditional "cradle" of Deaf culture. Students are encouraged and required to participate in the Deaf club and other Deaf community activities.

Even though the Deaf individuals were widely distributed in various small towns throughout the area, they had strong social and cultural ties to each other. Within this area, there were several Regional Day School Programs, a growing program for Deaf students at the State Technical College, and Baylor University, which often provides facilities for state and national conferences of Baptist Deaf people. There were also health, rehabilitation and social services agencies providing services to Deaf individuals. However, these agencies had limited contact with each other. The Interpreter Training Program, in addition to its role of teaching/training interpreters, sought to bring these agencies and organizations together into an extended community of/for Deaf people within the community at large. By doing so, job opportunities for the program's graduates would be identified and expanded.

The Central Texas Council for the Deaf/Hearing Impaired (CTCD/HI) is a non-profit, community-based organization which provides interpreting and information-referral services within the surrounding 18-county region. This organization was also interesting in promoting better access and coordination of services and better interagency cooperation.

In 1987, McLennan Community College agreed to provide CTCD/HI with office and meeting space on its campus, allowing close interaction between the interpreter training program and CTCD/HI. This provides opportuni-

[†] When capitalized, "Deaf" refers to cultural membership in the community. In lower case, "deaf" refers only to the inability to understand speech by means of hearing.

Continues on Page 668

ties for students to have practical experience in the service agency, facilitating contact with both the Deaf community and the working environment of interpreters.

As a result of this association, CTCD/HI has grown and has helped to draw the various organizations and agencies into a functioning network. The cooperation and sharing of information is beneficial to the agencies and consumers, as well as providing multi-cultural experiences and placement opportunities for students.

Contact:
Rob Granberry, Program Director
(817) 750-3648

McLennan Community College
1400 College Drive
Waco, TX 76708
Total head count enrollment-Credit: 9,630
Campuses/sites: 2; Full-time faculty: 165

Campus Camp

The summer camp features courses in art, reading, math, computers, swimming, tennis and other sports

McClennan Community College provides Central Texas with a much-needed summer children's program that provides high-quality, low-cost recreational and educational opportunities. Jointly sponsored with the Texas Council of Camp Fire, Inc., the program provides supervision for children from 7:30 a.m. until 5:30 p.m., Monday through Friday.

Since its inception in 1988, Campus Camp has grown each year. Each of the three sessions of Campus Camp lasts three weeks and may be repeated. The college enrolls campers in courses in art, reading, math, computers, swimming, tennis and various sports. The Camp Fire Council provides counselors to lead the children in traditional camp activities, including hiking, outdoor cooking, crafts and various games. The Camp Fire counselors also supervise the children between the college-offered courses and at lunch.

Because the college already offered courses for children during the regular summer children's program, campus campers would attend courses with children other than other campers.

The benefits of this program on manifold. Children have the opportunity to stay current or advance in their academic skills. They experience new and exciting educational courses and they make new friends from different backgrounds. A side benefit for many of these children is the fact they become very comfortable attending courses at "college". The benefits of a college education are shown to the children. For future first-generation college students campus camp will ease their eventual transition from high school to college.

Parents benefit from the program in that they are given another child care option for their school age children. Also, this program will bring parents, who otherwise might never visit the campus, to MCC. An unexpected side benefit has been that several parents have investigated or enrolled in MCC themselves.

MCC and the Camp Fire organization benefit by being able to maximize educational and recreational opportunities for this segment of the population in our service area.

The income derived from Campus Camp is divided between MCC and the Texas Council of Camp Fire in such a manner as both organizations meet the expenditures incurred in the operation of the camp. A letter of agreement defines the responsibilities and financial details each party assumes in the operation of this program.

Contact:
Warren Johnson, Dean, Continuing Education
(817) 750-3511

McLennan Community College
1400 College Drive
Waco, TX 76708
Total head count enrollment-Credit: 9,630
Campuses/sites: 2; Full-time faculty: 165

MERCHANDISING AND DESIGN

An important element of the AA program is the inclusion of general and advanced computer-oriented classes

Miss Wade's Fashion Merchandising College, founded in 1965, is a single-purpose institution offering an Associate of Arts degree in Merchandising and Design. The Associate of Arts program is designed to develop the competencies needed for a successful career in Fashion Design, Fashion Merchandising, or Interior Design. An added benefit to the program is the college's location – the heart of the Dallas International Apparel Mart.

This program emphasizes both general education and specialized study. The values of the former are deemed important to the development of responsible citizens; the experiences of the latter are regarded as indispensable to students preparing for active careers. The program consists of a minimum of 76 credit hours earned in 16 consecutive months. The course of study is broken down into four trimesters of 15 weeks each; two trimesters are equivalent to one academic year. All students are required to complete the general education component of the curriculum. Students are allowed to choose between Merchandising, Fashion Design, or Interior Design electives. An important element of the education received during the Associate of Arts program is the inclusion of general and advanced computer-oriented classes.

The Associate of Arts degree in Merchandising and Design is accredited by the Southern Association of Colleges and Schools (SACS). This accreditation status represents the highest degree of educational quality and recognition in the educational community.

Contact:
Charles Restivo, Vice President
(214) 637-3530

Miss Wade's Fashion Merchandising College
2300 Stemmons, Suite M5120, PO Box 586343
Dallas, TX 75258
Total head count enrollment-Credit: 302
Campuses/sites: 1; Full-time faculty: 15

COMPUTER-AIDED DESIGN AND MARKETING

The program is for students who want to continue their studies without seeking a four-year degree

In 1990, Miss Wade's Fashion Merchandising College began offering Professional Certification to those students wishing to continue their studies beyond the Associate of Arts level, but not wishing to seek a four-year degree. The Professional Certification program that is currently offered concentrates in the areas of Computer-Aided Design and Marketing; additional advanced business courses are included to enable students to more readily advance in the business world.

The CAD and Marketing certificate is comprised of 20 credit hours that are earned in one trimester. This is in addition to the four trimesters required to earn the Associate of Arts degree. In this program, 10 hours of coursework concentrate on using the computer as a design and business tool. Students are also taught Entrepreneurship, Promotional Strategy and are allowed one elective. Elective topics may be selected from the Fashion Design, Interior Design, or Marketing areas. Elective courses include: Advanced Fashion Design Techniques, Advanced Interior Design Topics, and International Marketing.

Goals for the CAD and Marketing Certification program are to provide state-of-the-art computer technology for students in the program and to emphasize the computer as a important design and business tool.

Contact:
Charles Restivo, Vice President
(214) 637-3530

Miss Wade's Fashion Merchandising College
2300 Stemmons, Suite M5120, PO Box 586343
Dallas, TX 75258
Total head count enrollment-Credit: 302
Campuses/sites: 1; Full-time faculty: 15

SELF-PACED BUSINESS LAB

The courses are individualized so that students may study, read, watch and listen to tapes of the course at their own pace

The Business Lab at Mountain View College addresses the community college challenges of part-time students and courses not offered because of low student enrollment. It provides flexibility and opportunities that would not otherwise be available for these students. The lab recognizes the potential of technology and multimedia applications for improving learning and achieving student success.

Integral to the operations of the business lab is a videodisc component. Gemmy Allen has developed an interactive videodisc to be used by the self-paced business students. The disk includes:

1) an orientation to each course offered; and
2) "Study Skills and Tips: appropriate for the student's learning style" (The Cognitive Style Map Instrument is used to assess learning style; assessing learning style helps students to determine the best course of action to succeed academically.)

As videodisc technology allows students to become more responsible for and more active in their own education, the teacher functions as a guide or facilitator, a content specialist, a learning specialist and a resource expert.

The self-paced business lab began in a renovated classroom equipped with four 3/4-inch video cassette players and monitors. Three classes (Introduction to Business, Introduction to Computer Science, and Principles of Marketing) were offered. Today the lab is equipped with VHS videotapes, videodiscs, CD-ROM, plus microcomputer and appropriate software to control and integrate it all. The lab serves 500 to 600 students per year with 10 to 12 courses offered per semester.

Courses are built around a syllabus, a textbook, a study guide, and audio/visual programs. The courses are individualized because the student may study, read, watch and listen to the tapes of the course at a pace suited to his-her personal priorities. Even though the student studies independently, an instructor for the course is available during posted office hours other times by appointment to assist students.

The courses are self-paced because the student may complete the course on or before the final deadline established for the semester. Students are evaluated by means of tests (taken in the Testing Center) and a class project.

The business Lab has been recognized in a chapter of *Technology and Teaching: Case Studies on the Use of Computers, Networks and Multimedia in the Classroom*, editor Les Lloyd, Lafayette College, Easton, Pennsylvania, 1992.

Contact:
Gemmy Allen, Business/Technology Division
(214) 333-8616

Mountain View College
4849 West Illinois Avenue
Dallas, TX 75211
Total head count enrollment-Credit: 6,090; Non-Credit: 1,200
Campuses/sites: 1; Full-time faculty: 77

SELF-PACED BIOLOGY LAB

Various levels or starting points of critical thinking are programmed into student computer work stations

The Self-Paced Biology Lab at Moutain View College allows students to practice critical thinking by testing alternatives and developing thought process in a non-threatening environment. Due to the large number of non-science major students and limited number of faculty and staff, the program employs a multimedia interactive teaching methodology.

Various levels or starting points of critical thinking are programmed into student computer work stations. Initially, students are given an hypothesis and asked to select data that will prove the hypothesis. Alternatively, students may be given data and asked to form an hypothesis. The third option is to design experiments to support their hypothesis and form a conclusion based on the process. All these methods are programmed into the multimedia interactive system by combining various authoring systems, and a profusion of media.

The use of authoring and presentation programs allows student input and record keeping. Students may try different paths or experiments until they can prove their hypothesis or suggest an alternate hypothesis. When the student chooses an hypothesis or test not anticipated by the instructor and consequently programmed into the lesson, the instructor acts as a mentor to help the students re-channel their efforts. Should the student present a valid alternative view, it can quickly be programmed into the system. Multimedia interactive offers the instructor the ability to quickly adapt to the students ever changing needs.

Computer-based multimedia instruction at Mountain View College encompasses a great variety of instructional materials, each serving a specific purpose. The use of 2-D and 3-D animations are vital to the understanding of molec-ular, chemical, cellular and physiological processes. They are also beneficial in the students' understanding of complex processes, i.e. evolution, geology and development. Most materials in use at Mountain View College have been produced locally by teaching faculty and staff without additional compensation and as part of their regular duties.

Contact:
Larry Legg, Math/Science/PE Division
(214)333-8649

Mountain View College
4849 West Illinois Avenue
Dallas, TX 75211
Total head count enrollment-Credit: 6,090; Non-Credit: 1,200
Campuses/sites: 1; Full-time faculty: 77

NORTH HARRIS MONTGOMERY COMMUNITY COLLEGE DISTRICT

CENTER FOR BUSINESS AND ECONOMIC DEVELOPMENT

The Center brings together all the business services and resources of the district and its three colleges at one central contact point

The Center for Business and Economic Development centralizes all the business services and resources of North Harris Montgomery Community College District. The Center develops and delivers quality training and provides research and technical assistance to businesses, organizations and communities in the North Harris and Montgomery counties. It brings together all the business services and resources of the district and its three colleges at one central contact point.

Specific services of the Center include business needs assessment, contract and customized training, business research, technical assistance, management development seminars, conference planning and economic development initiatives. Small business services are available through the Small Business Development Center, which has provided free counseling and training to thousands of businesses since 1986.

Ray Laughter has been named executive director of the Center. He has been with the college since 1987, serving as director of the Small Business Development Center and is the former president of Business Services Assistance Corporation and previous Chief Administrative Officer of a major international helicopter manufacturer.

The Center's staff includes a team of business training representatives, a program coordinator and job development specialists. The Small Business Development Center staff also provides complete services at each of the colleges.

Major program areas include:
- contact and customized training;
- management development programs; business research and technical assistance; and
- community and economic development programs.

Contact:
Ray Laughler, Executive Director
(713) 591-9320

North Harris Montgomery Community College District
250 North Sam Houston Parkway East
Houston, TX 77060
Total head count enrollment-Credit: 17,193; Non-Credit: 12,756
Campuses/sites: 4; Full-time faculty: 280

NORTHEAST COLLEGE-HOUSTON COMMUNITY COLLEGE SYSTEM

OWNER BUILDER CENTER

The program teaches house building students how to do their own contracting or how to work successfully with a hired contractor

Northeast College offers home improvement courses at its Scarborough Campus, where house building students learn how to do their own contracting or how to work successfully with a hired contractor. In addition, individuals planning to make a house purchase learn what to look for in a sound building structure and consumers learn the language of repair personnel to avoid rip-offs and misunderstandings. Real estate professionals also find the classes highly useful.

Continues on Page 672

The program, initiated in 1987, is franchised as an Owner Building Center. A wide range of workshops lasting from three class hours to nine class hours is available, as well as courses averaging 40 class hours. The short-term workshops cover topics such as wallpapering, door and window installation, cabinet making, roofing, drywall, deck building, and plumbing. The long-term courses focus on house building and remodeling, along with foundation repair and other major construction efforts.

Classes are offered chiefly at night and on the weekend; although there are some daytime offerings. Workshops are generally less than $100, with three-hour workshops costing about $25. Courses cost $380 for a 42-hour period of instruction, the maximum offered. Cabinet making is limited to 10 students, but most workshops have a 20-student limit. The house building courses enroll up to 30 students.

The schedule is publicized in a college publication entitled the *Home Improvement Journal*. It covers home improvement classes at the Northeast College and the other colleges which also offer the Owner Builder Program, managed by the Northeast College staff. The *Journal* contains photos of house construction and repair work completed by students, and discussion of how the Owner Builder Program influenced the construction or renovation.

The original director of the Owner Builder Program, Tom Tynan, is the host of a radio program "Home Improvement Hotline." He continues to serve in a consulting capacity to the program. The roster of instructors includes a variety of specialists. The current director, for example, is a registered architect. Classes and workshops involve considerable hands-on activity and discussion.

Contact:
Paul Titterington, Director
(713) 956-1178

Northeast College-Houston Community College System
PO Box 7849
Houston, TX 77270-7849
Total head count enrollment-Credit: 3,549; Non-Credit: 2,199
Campuses/sites: 10; Full-time faculty: 66

NORTHLINE MALL CAMPUS

The college, which began offering Student Services at the mall in 1992, now leases enough space to offer classes there

Northeast College truly placed itself in the midst of its community when it moved Student Services, and eventually classes, to a shopping mall. This move has proved immensely popular, especially considering that when Northeast College was formed as one of the Houston Community College System's regional colleges in 1992, most of its academic credit courses were being taught in sites shared with the local school district. This placed severe limitations on the college's ability to provide daytime instruction. As a result, the college conducted a search throughout the service region to identify lease space that could potentially serve the needs of a community college. Community accessibility and readily available parking were two major considerations in selecting a site. The Northline Mall, a regional mall serving the area, offered those two features and was willing to lease a generous amount of space to the college system.

In February 1992, the Northeast College made its first venture into the Northline Mall, establishing the college's Student Service Center in space that had formerly been utilized as a military recruitment station. The office layouts used by the recruiters were compatible with the center's needs, and a move-in was facilitated with little need for renovation. Among the services offered are financial aid counseling, academic and personal counseling, vocational and academic skills testing, and job development. Several of the mall student service programs receive partial Carl Perkins support for assisting students seeking technical training.

With the community reacting favorably to the student service activities, particularly the convenience of the extended hours of accessibility, the college sought additional space in the Northline Mall to provide instructional services. The college made its next move in Spring 1993 to fill space vacated by the relocation of a drugstore and utilized space awaiting the development of a food court. This temporary space was renovated in less than six weeks to provide 18 classrooms for the college, nearly tripling the college's available space for daytime academic instruction.

By fall 1993, the Northeast College expands to 71,400 square feet in the mall. A department store will be relocating from that space and a major renovation effort will need to occur. The college's temporary classroom location in the mall has limited space for any activities other than instruction. The expanded site will permit the college to house student support services in the same facility and add services such as a library and bookstore. It is expected that when the Student Service Center is absorbed into this location that another community service activity will be offered at its old site, such as a Houston Police Department Service Center or a Child Care Center.

Contact:
Raul Ortegon or Jacqueline Howard, Campus Specialists
(713) 699-9623

Northeast College-Houston Community College System
PO Box 7849
Houston, TX 77270-7849
Total head count enrollment-Credit: 3,549; Non-Credit: 2,199
Campuses/sites: 10; Full-time faculty: 66

NORTHWEST COLLEGE-HOUSTON COMMUNITY COLLEGE SYSTEM

MENTAL HEALTH ASSOCIATES DEGREE PROGRAM

The program includes preparation for careers as peer counselors and therapeutic recreation specialists

It is a daunting task, addressing such critical societal issues as substance abuse, homelessness and bereavement, and such a special challenge as mental retardation. But Northwest College boldly and effectively is doing just that through its Mental Health Associates Degree Program.

The first students were accepted into the program in the fall of 1986. The curriculum places an emphasis on basic generic counseling skills applicable to all populations. These populations include Substance Abuse Counseling, Mental Retardation, Victims of Abuse, Homeless, Bereavement, Volunteer Agencies, Nursing Home/Geriatric Care, Recreation, Group Homes, General Psychiatric and many more.

In 1990, a new certificate program, Case Manager Aide, was added to the curriculum. This innovative program trains former mental health consumers to work in the mental health community as peer counselors. The graduates are employed by the County Mental Health/Mental Retardation Association and many have continued their studies in the field.

Fall 1992 showed yet another new addition to the curriculum. By adding two Therapeutic Recreation courses to the one already offered, the Mental Health degree affords the opportunity for students to become Therapeutic Recreation Specialists.

Students, upon graduation, fill all of the academic requirements to be licensed or certified in three specialty areas: Substance Abuse Counseling, Social Work and Therapeutic Recreation. The opportunity for employment in the helping services are endless. Currently, the Mental Health Associate Program boasts a 100 percent job placement rate.

Houston Community College has received program approval for its Mental Health Associate Program from a number of licensing agencies to include:

1) the Texas Commission for Alcohol and Drug Abuse Counselors;
2) the National Association for Social Work;
3) the National Council for Therapeutic Recreation;
4) the Council for Standards in Human Services Education; and
5) the National Association of Alcohol and Drug Abuse Counselors.

Contact:
Naydean Blair, Department Head, (713) 468-6891
Manuel Reyes, Coordinator, Public Service Careers, (713) 468-0955

Northwest College-Houston Community College System
PO Box 7849
Houston, TX 77270-7849
Total head count enrollment-Credit: 8,400
Campuses/sites: 7; Full-time faculty: 103

AUDT: AUDIO AND RECORDING TECHNOLOGY

▓ *The AUDT program is closely linked with the music program,* ▓
often using the musical talent of students and faculty

The dramatic increase in the use of electronic media during the past 30 years promises to continue as the importance of recorded music, film, TV, radio, video, PA and multimedia presentations continues to grow. These technologies are similar in that they all require sound to be successful. Until recently, the knowledge needed to use these audio technologies was passed down through an apprenticeship system. But today, the rate of change in electronic and computer technologies has led the professional community and the Houston Community College System to believe that a formal education in audio technology may be required.

The Audio and Recording Technology (AUDT) program was started in 1985 and expanded yearly until 1990, when lab facilities could no longer support expansion. The AUDT program is highly successful at using community and student involvement to teach students the skills they need to compete in a competitive job market as well as the theoretical background necessary to apply these skills and adapt to changing technologies. Students study electronics, music synthesis, music theory, video, and the use and application of audio and recording technologies.

The AUDT program is closely linked with the music program, often utilizing the musical talent of students and faculty. Since 1985, music students have been required to take at least the introductory AUDT lecture and lab courses while pursuing their degrees. HCCS offers other commercial programs related to the music industry such as

Piano Tuning and Repair, Band Instrument Repair, and Arranging and Composition. Eventually, HCCS envisions these programs expanding and diversifying into areas such as music business, video technology and multimedia production.

Students enrolled in the AUDT program have access to a video and several well-equipped audio lab facilities. Each contains a Macintosh II personal computer with peripheral devices that enables it to record, sequence, and edit MIDI and sampler information. This computer use enhances classroom instruction as well as learning. Students use lab facilities while working on live and multi-track recording, editing, audio for video, mastering using a direct-to-hard-disk system, duplicating, and other projects typical of those found in a professional environment. This AUDT student lab use has a tremendous community impact. Often, members of the community are involved as "'talent." Numerous professionals and amateurs have been in the labs assisting with the student projects and accounts of their experiences and the recordings they take with them give the AUDT program and HCCS much needed visibility. Many return to take courses.

Students must complete an internship before being awarded their AUDT degree. Many businesses in the area support the program by allowing students to work under supervision in professional multi-track recording, live sound, video, remote recording, TV and sound installation situations.

Contact:
Mark C. Erickson, Department Head, (713) 468-6891
Thomas Baynum, Coordinator, Humanities, (713) 468-0955

Northwest College-Houston Community College System
PO Box 7849
Houston, TX 77270-7849
Total head count enrollment-Credit: 8,400
Campuses/sites: 7; Full-time faculty: 103

PALO ALTO COLLEGE

HONORS PROGRAM

▓ *Enrollment in honors courses is limited to 25 students, who are exposed* ▓
to more rigorous requirements than non-program students

Honors courses at Palo Alto College provide: opportunities for more in-depth subject analyses with emphasis placed on creative and critical thinking; more participatory classroom styles that stimulate critical inquiry and research; creative problem-solving; and informed decision-making. This fulfills two goals of the college Master Plan that call for measures of effectiveness that assure quality of education and services for students as well as a supportive campus environment fostering academic excellence.

The program began in August 1991 as part of the Palo Alto PLUS, a 2 + 2 Transfer Program. Following a two-week Summer Academic Camp, the 23 selected high school graduates enrolled at Palo Alto College in a program of studies consisting of honors courses, an honors seminar and regular courses. In the summer of 1992 several students enrolled in summer courses at a participating PAC PLUS senior institution. The program was broadened in the spring of 1992 to allow other qualified

Palo Alto College students to enroll in honors courses.

The curricular focus of the Honors Program is the college core curriculum. Once selected as an honors course, enrollment is limited to 25 students. The regular course syllabus is revised and augmented so as to provide additional academic rigor and to require scholarship beyond usual expectations.

Financial aid has been provided to the students in the form of work study. It is hoped that scholarships will be available in the future. A holistic, thematically-based, inter-disciplinary seminar semester (consisting of three discipline courses linked with an information/research course), independent study-mentorships, and community service components are in the planning stages. An Honors Advisory Committee with representation from students, faculty, staff and administration is reviewing the experimental phase of the program.

The Honors Program was designated to be an exemplary program by the Alamo Community College District Board of Trustees in the fall of 1991.

Contact:
Norlene M. Kunkel, Dean, Liberal Studies
(210) 921-5260

Palo Alto College
1400 West Villaret Boulevard
San Antonio, TX 78224-2499
Total head count enrollment-Credit: 6,291; Non-Credit: 1,961
Campuses/sites: 1; Full-time faculty: 83

AVIATION TECHNOLOGY

Unique among technology programs is a dedicated aviation library for use by college students, area school teachers and researchers

Established in 1988, by the ACCD Board of Trustees, the PAC Aviation Technology program was designed to serve regional aviation/aerospace industry needs in two areas: management and professional pilot.

The program will be expanding to include an option in the Federal Aviation Administration's Airway Science curriculum which provides transferability to several senior institutions. The program has a strong integration of academic courses with the technology offerings in the aviation specialization.

Aviation Technology has served as a utility for the regional aerospace industry to provide seminars, workshops and short courses to serve selected operational and support personnel needs. The program maintains an informal relationship with area military bases utilizing their equipment and research resources providing students exciting opportunities to participate in aerospace activities.

Unique among technology programs is a dedicated aviation library for use by college students, area school teachers and researchers. The Aviation Education Resource Center is one of three in the state of Texas providing aviation curriculum materials for K-12 grades and a broad range of research data for students in the college program.

Classroom and laboratory equipment are standard to math, science and physics programs. However, Aviation Technology has invested in flight simulation devices, meteorology software and CD-ROM technology all integrated into the classroom/lab experience.

Capital resources required to implement and maintain a program of this nature have been kept to a minimum by establishing a contractual relationship with a private flight training operation at a local airport. Investments in expensive aircraft, maintenance and insurance has been avoided. The contract, while lengthy and detailed, has worked quite well for four years. Quality control, competencies and high standards have not been compromised.

The program includes three full-time instructors and several adjuncts from various aviation industries.

Contact:
Robert D. Krienke, Dean, Technologies, Sciences and Business
(210) 921-5300

Palo Alto College
1400 West Villaret Boulevard
San Antonio, TX 78224-2499
Total head count enrollment-Credit: 6,291; Non-Credit: 1,961
Campuses/sites: 1; Full-time faculty: 83

FORESTRY TECHNICIAN CERTIFICATE

▨ When done with the program, a student is a qualified forestry technician, ▨
able to perform many tasks once reserved for professionals

The Forestry program at Panola College is designed for an energetic person with self-pride, character and a dedication to succeed. More and more professionals are finding that certain tasks that once were performed by the professionals can be delegated to the technician.

After the 12-month program, not only is the individual qualified as a Forestry Technician with the equivalence of two years field training, but also a representative paraprofessional.

The curriculum contains introduction to forestry, silvi-culture I and II, dendrology, forest math, forest communications, forest drafting, business machines, forest protection, surveying, mapping, forest harvesting, business methods, personnel management and safety, forest products and wildlife ecology.

For the past 19 years Panola College has produced a comprehensive curriculum as well as hands-on experience in solving actual forestry problems. Classes are conducted from 8 a.m. to 3:30 p.m., Monday through Friday.

Contact:
Jim Martin, Dean, Vocational/Technical Education
(903) 693-2034

Panola College
1109 West Panola Street
Carthage, TX 75633
Total head count enrollment-Credit: 1,374; Non-Credit: 2,000
Campuses/sites: 3; Full-time faculty: 67

TECH PREP ASSOCIATE DEGREE FOR NURSING

▨ The career ladder approach assures employers ▨
of getting a more qualified entry-level employee

Though relatively young, the Tech Prep Associate Degree for Nursing program at Paris Junior College has become a model for schools and colleges throughout Texas and the United States.

It began in the fall of 1988, when the Texas Education Agency and the Texas Higher Education Coordinating Board awarded a contract, funded by the Carl D. Perkins Vocational Education Act, Title II B, to Paris Junior College and Paris Independent School District. The overall goal for the project was to develop a "2+2 tech prep" articulated curriculum that would link the last two years of secondary and the first two years of post secondary education to prepare students for employment in the nursing profession. The curriculum was to be designed to provide for the development of salable skills in the hierarchy of nursing education at the end of grade 12 and advanced employment skills in nursing requiring less than the baccalaureate degree on completion of the curriculum at the associate degree level.

With the above contractual stipulations the project staff, along with technical assistance from the Project Advisory Committee, the tech prep curriculum for nursing was developed utilizing the career ladder concept. The tech prep associate degree curriculum was developed with the registered nurse occupation situated at the top of the ladder.

This articulated competency-based curriculum is designed so that upon completion of grade 12 students are eligible to take the Texas examination for registry as a nurse aide, and/or at the end of grade 13 be eligible to sit for the National Council Licensure Examination for practical (vocational) nurse. Utilizing the career ladder approach in the development of the TPAD nursing curriculum is beneficial to students and employers alike. For the students, it provides the opportunity to exit and re-enter the program at specified levels. For the employer, it assures a better-prepared, more qualified entry-level employee with greater skills and competencies than is available in current two-year nursing education programs.

The project staff, with confirmation by health professionals and the advisory committee, determined that a rigid base core of secondary prerequisites was essential for students preparing to enter into the TPAD nursing program. Mathematics prerequisites are a minimum of three years of math beginning with Algebra I. Science prerequisites include Physical Science; Biology I; Chemistry; and Anatomy and Physiology; or Biology II. Texas graduation requirements of four years of English/language arts and 3½ years of social studies were sufficient for students entering the TPAD program in the judgment of staff and advisory committee.

The program has been recognized in a number of ways. A chapter in the book *Tech Prep Associate Degree: A Win/Win Experience* by Dan Hull and Dale Parnell is devoted to this program. It was one of three health tech prep programs in the nation to be selected for presentation at the A.V.A. conference in Orlando in 1990. It has been presented by request at three TPAD regional workshops sponsored by the Center for Occupational Research and Development (CORD).

The program is presented as a model in a working paper *How Much Does A Youth Apprenticeship Program Cost And Who Will Pay For It*, published by Jobs for the Future, by Hannah Finan Roditi, August 1991.

The curriculum/course outlines, upon request, have been sent to 22 secondary schools in Texas, 77 post secondary institutions in Texas, and 21 organizations and/or institutions from various places throughout the United States, which includes ERIC, The National Network For Curriculum Coordination in Vocational and

Technical Education (NNCCOTE) and, the U.S. Department of Education. Additionally, presentations have been made at Deans and Directors conferences, Quality Work Force Planning seminars and to Tech Prep Planning Consortiums.

There is no doubt that this four-year program can teach more skills, in-depth training and knowledge than the current generic two-year program. Health care, particularly nursing, is currently one of the high-demand career areas, and will maintain that status in the coming decades. As the general population grows and health care becomes increasingly technically oriented, the need for health care workers will continue to soar. Programs such as this one has the potential to help fill that need with a better educated, more competent, and qualified person entering the nursing profession.

Contact:
Victoria Oglesby, Dean, Applied Science Instruction
(903) 785-7661

Paris Junior College
2400 Clarksville
Paris, TX 75460
Total head count enrollment-Credit: 2,300; Non-Credit: 3,248
Campuses/sites: 1; Full-time faculty: 87

LEARNING SKILLS CENTER

Basic skills classes are offered to traditional students as well as industrial employees needing improvement

Since its opening in the fall of 1971, the Learning Skills Center has expanded its offerings from reading and study skills classes to include basic skills development in math and tutorial services for practically all content areas. Four reading courses are now offered from literacy through college level. Twenty-five to 30 percent of the students enrolled at Paris Junior college take at least one Learning Skills course.

The Adult Basic Education/GED preparation program and the Lamar County Literacy Council are included in the Center. Classes are held on-site at local industries for employees needing to improve basic skills. More than 700 students attended ABE/GED or literacy classes last year.

Since 1978, the Center has been in the Rheudasil

Learning Center which also includes the library, counseling services, and financial aid offices. A computer lab in the Learning Skills Center utilizes an integrated learning system for reading, writing, and math skills from literacy level through college preparation.

In 1986, the Center for Development Education at Appalachian State University selected the Learning Skills Center as an Exemplary Developmental Education Program.

In 1990, the CAPPS system was added to the Learning Skills Center to provide immediate scoring of placement tests and advising of students for placement in developmental and regular college courses.

Contact:
Jimmye Hancock, Dean, Support Services and Continuing Education
(903) 785-7661

Paris Junior College
2400 Clarksville
Paris, TX 75460
Total head count enrollment-Credit: 2,300; Non-Credit: 3,248
Campuses/sites: 1; Full-time faculty: 87

ETHNIC STUDIES LEARNING COMMUNITY BLOCK

▨ Learning Community Block Psychology and Human Development classes are taught together, ▨
allowing close relationships among students and between students and faculty

Dallas County is rich in ethnic diversity, with African Americans, Asian Americans, Latinos, Native Americans and other people of color comprising 51 percent of its population. As our society approaches the year 2000, a further growth in ethnic minority populations and migrations of large groups of people are anticipated. But so is a further growth of racism. Therefore, emphasis upon a scholarly understanding of American race relations is timely, unique and distinctive.

The Ethnic Studies Learning Community Block at Richland College and other Dallas County community colleges is designed to facilitate students' appreciation of the value of cultural diversity and to promote the understanding of why and how people, events and experiences impact the values, attitudes and behaviors of racial groups in America. Students enroll in two regularly transferable classes (Psychology 101.010 and Human Development 105.004), which are taught together in a six-hour block. This format allows the students the opportunity to form close relationships with other students and with the team of faculty. Thus, students participate in a self-analytic and multicultural experience, learning and developing human relation skills through reading, exercises, journal writings and class discussions.

Psychology lectures and discussions deal with issues such as stereotypes, personality traits and behavioral patterns of various ethnic cultures. Major concepts and issues in psychology, communications and interpersonal relationships are reviewed. However, in lieu of standard texts, students read a selection of contemporary articles, novels, poems and short stories relating to Hispanic American, African American, Asian American and Native American issues.

Developing critical thinking, writing, speaking and research skills is emphasized. Students are required to write six critical analysis papers designed to promote thinking and evaluation skills whereby students demonstrate their abilities to integrate theoretical concepts with practical applications.

There is an optional Honors Program component which requires a community service commitment.

The first year of this pilot program was well-received by faculty, staff, students, and community. Alumni students serve as our best recruiters to the program. Richland College continues to refine and redefine the course based upon student and community feedback.

Contact:
Jana Flowers or Fred Martinez, Multicultural Center
(214) 238-6900

Richland College of the Dallas County Community College District
12800 Abrams Road
Dallas, TX 75243-2199
Total head count enrollment-Credit: 12,595; Non-Credit: 9,168
Campuses/sites: 1; Full-time faculty: 154

DISPLACED WORKERS

▨ In response to the often fragile emotional state of one displaced person, ▨
a 'one-stop' system was implemented to ensure simplified procedures

No one could have anticipated the impact of the first student to arrive at Richland with a Job Training Partnership Act (JTPA) letter of introduction authorized by PIC in his hand. Not only were the acronyms unfamiliar, the college was unfamiliar with what the man was authorized to do. After being told he was eligible to receive training, as a result of a layoff, he was assured he would be welcomed as a student and the college would research the program to learn the necessary steps to make his training a reality.

Although that was a few years ago, the first student became symbolic of the intense and difficult times ahead for a large sector of the Dallas population. This chance meeting led to a commitment by Richland College to meet the needs of people experiencing the consequences of a changing economy. Rather than sounding foreign, JTPA and PIC (Private Industry Council) became common terminology.

A comprehensive program has been developed to assess and meet the needs of persons dislocated from their jobs. In response to the often fragile and vulnerable emotional states of this population, a "one-stop" system was implemented to ensure a simplification of the necessary procedures, thereby increasing retention. Programs have either been developed or were already in place to create a total "package" for this target audience. The package includes: advertisement, career counseling, program planning; free job kits; free monthly 10-hour power job search seminars; use of Career and Life Planning Center; career seminars; a Job Search Center to include major U.S. newspaper, a telephone bank, computers/laser printers for resume production and video programs on employment skills; outplacement services; job fairs; business and industry testing center; and job placement.

Area industries who are experiencing downsizing are finding the availability of these services quite attractive. Counselors and staff are ready to participate as a "rapid response" team with the local PIC when called upon. Richland College has assisted with several such layoffs to date and has provided follow-up assistance in outplacement centers. Due to the success of the program, PIC is placing a counselor on campus to expedite the certification process. As the program continues to grow, new services are emerging, such as support and networking groups, job

clubs, special topic seminars, guest speakers from business and industry, and a greater emphasis in the development of internships and jobs. Special communication process workshops are being offered to give students a greater edge in securing a job in a difficult market. More individual time with students is being required as depression increases and self-esteem plummets.

Even as the numbers and the problems increase, the college's determination and dedication to serve the people and resolve problems remains steadfast. Possibly a brighter day is on the horizon and these services will be enjoyed by those simply making career changes by choice; in the meantime, those who are affected have advocates on whom they can rely.

Contact:
Judy Fiedler, Vocational Counselor
(214) 238-6005

Richland College of the Dallas County Community College District
12800 Abrams Road
Dallas, TX 75243-2199
Total head count enrollment-Credit: 12,595; Non-Credit: 9,168
Campuses/sites: 1; Full-time faculty: 154

CONTINENTAL AIR LINES PILOT DEVELOPMENT

Although no jobs are guaranteed, Continental Air Lines expects each successful graduate to be hired by Continental's commuter airline

San Jacinto College District prepares students with no flight experience for entry-level positions as co-pilots with a commuter airline. The Pilot Development Program is a joint effort with Continental Air Lines to address the need for quality trained pilots.

The objective of this "ab initio" associate degree program is to prepare a student with no prior flight experience for an entry-level position as co-pilot with a regional commuter airline. This 70-credit hour program includes a combination of ground school, flight and general education courses.

Objectives for program graduates are to pass and obtain the following Federal Aviation Administration (FAA) certificates, ratings, and examinations: Private and Commercial Pilot Certificates, Multi-Engine and Instrument Ratings, and the Flight Engineer Written Examination.

Continental provides SJCC with a full-time employee who has credentials to meet instructor requirements for teaching college level aviation technology courses. This employee assists in the coordination of the program, advises and consults with college representatives and students about the program, and provides classroom instruction as assigned by the college.

Continental tracks and evaluates students in their areas

of knowledge, attitude, aptitude and flying skills and provides airline- oriented seminars and air carrier training workshops for the students as they progress through this program.

The program was first proposed by Eastern Airlines and an agreement was reached with the San Jacinto College District and Eastern Airlines in 1987 to provide the Pilot Entry Program (PEP). The first PEP classes were offered during the fall of 1988. This agreement was terminated with Eastern Airlines on May 31, 1990, and was transferred to Continental Air Lines as the PDP on June 1, 1990.

The program includes a provision for either a full- or part-time cooperative education arrangement to be developed between PDP students and Continental. Although no jobs are guaranteed, Continental expects but does not require each successful graduate to be hired by CAL's commuter airline, Continental Express. Continental has also provided SJCC Aeronautical Technology instructors with the opportunity to further their professional development by attending First Officer training courses. This partnership between SJCC and Continental serves to provide high quality standards of training as well as the latest advances in airline-oriented flight training.

Contact:
Larry Tucker, Chairman, Aeronautical Technology Department
(713) 476-1501, ext. 1502

San Jacinto College District
4624 Fairmont Parkway, Suite 204
Pasadena, TX 77504
Total head count enrollment-Credit: 51,514; Non-Credit: 22,578
Campuses/sites: 3; Full-time faculty: 374

AEROSPACE TECHNOLOGY

🖾 *The curriculum was developed to provide technically competent employees* 🖾
to the aerospace industry upon completion of the program

In 1991, the National Aeronautics and Space Administration/Johnson Space Center recognized that numerous jobs in the control center were being staffed by personnel who were over-qualified. In order to remedy this situation, they initiated the task of redefining the qualifications for a number of those jobs which can be performed by personnel who have an associate degree. Soon, the Aerospace Technology curriculum was developed by the Consortium for Aerospace Technology Education (CATE) to provide technically competent employees to the aerospace industry immediately upon completion of an approved two-year plan of study in one of three specific fields: Data Management Systems, Electrical Systems, and Mechanical Systems.

CATE is a partnership of three community colleges (San Jacinto College Central, Alvin Community College, and College of the Mainland), NASA Space Station Systems Division, and Rockwell Space Operations Company. While the Data Management Systems Option may be obtained at San Jacinto College Central, students may also choose the Electrical Systems Option offered by College of the Mainland or the Mechanical Systems Option available at Alvin Community College. After successfully completing the two-year degree program and obtaining employment with a participating employer, the graduate will work full-time as a control station operator in the Space Station Control Center.

To develop this curricula, CATE worked throughout the academic year 1991/1992, as NASA foresaw a large market for employees with this type of training developing in the middle 1990's. In fact, they predicted that the contractor forces at the Johnson Space Center could absorb as many as 150 to 200 of this type of individual each year once the Space Station begins flying in the year 1995. This number could account for up to 10 to 15 percent of the work force in the Space Station Control Center. Should an employee choose to pursue a higher degree of education, he/she may enroll at the university level. The University of Houston-Clear Lake is developing a Bachelor of Science degree program in space operations. The employer will arrange a work schedule to avoid conflicts with class time and will reimburse the employee for tuition and books. The employee may continue in the program through graduate school provided he/she maintains satisfactory job-related work performance and meets all academic requirements set by the company.

San Jacinto College Central Campus plans to continue working with NASA/JSC to refine and update this program and, as opportunities become available, to expand its involvement in the aerospace educational program by developing new courses of study.

Contact:
Sue Rodgers, Chairman, Department of Computer Science
(713) 476-1836

San Jacinto College District
4624 Fairmont Parkway, Suite 204
Pasadena, TX 77504
Total head count enrollment-Credit: 51,514; Non-Credit: 22,578
Campuses/sites: 3; Full-time faculty: 374

THE CORNERSTONE PROGRAM

🖾 *The honors courses are team-taught, interdisciplinary* 🖾
and emphasize critical thinking skills

The Cornerstone Program at Tarrant County Junior College is a challenging, humanities-based honors curriculum designed to serve the student of high academic ability and limited financial resources. The program was developed with the aid of a $92,000 grant from the National Endowment for the Humanities. No more than 90 new Cornerstone Scholars are accepted each year on each of TCJC's three campuses. Selection criteria include grade point average, class rank, SAT or ACT test scores, letters of recommendation, an essay and a personal interview. Members of the Cornerstone faculty have established liaisons with personnel in all Tarrant County school districts, with special emphasis on Fort Worth.

The theme of The Cornerstone Program is "Beliefs, Knowledge, Creations, Institutions: Cornerstones of Character and Civilization. The program consists of a four-semester, 66-hour curriculum leading to the Associate in Arts degree. Central to the curriculum are the four Cornerstone courses, one to be taught in each of the four semesters. These courses are team-taught and interdisciplinary, relying on readings in the humanities and emphasizing critical thinking expressed in both written and oral forms.

The Cornerstone courses are: History of Ideas: Individuals and Their Beliefs; History of Thought:

Individuals and Their Search for Knowledge; Aesthetics: Individuals and Their Creations; and Human Society: Individuals and Their Institutions.

The content of the Cornerstone courses are reflected each semester in the special Cornerstone sections of English, history and government. Readings and assignments augment and are coordinated with those in the Cornerstone courses. Cornerstone Scholars also earn credit for four semesters of a foreign language, two semesters of science and two semesters of mathematics.

Each Cornerstone Scholar receives a scholarship of $300 per semester, provided a 3.0 GPA is maintained. Four area universities have agreed to provide scholarships to Cornerstone graduates.

Contact:
Bill McMurry, Cornerstone Program Director
(817) 336-7851

Tarrant County Junior College
1500 Houston Street
Fort Worth, TX 76102
Total head count enrollment-Credit: 73,346; Non-Credit: 30,565
Campuses/sites: 3; Full-time faculty: 453

CREATIVE LISTENING EXPERIENCES IN MUSIC

The course emphasizes the participatory aspect of listener involvement, as opposed to the traditional approach to music appreciation

The Creative Listening Experiences in Music course is a non-technical approach to the philosophy, analysis, creation and enjoyment of music. It places emphasis on creating an intelligent and sensitive listening and analysis procedure and is designed to familiarize the student with several new styles of music.

Unlike the traditional approach to music appreciation, this course stresses the participatory aspect of listener involvement. Various projects are assigned which demand creativity on the part of the student.

Specific goals of this course include being able to perform an intelligent music analysis; having an understanding of what a performer and composer go through when working/creating a piece of music; being able to read music on an elementary level, and having a general understanding of the history of music.

Students are expected to learn the elements of music, to write a music analysis, learn musical terms, participate in philosophical vs. practical discussions on music, write simple compositions in class, and maintain a concert journal. Additionally, a final project which creates a musical scenario involving multi-media elements is required.

The course has enjoyed great popularity as a means of satisfying a fine arts requirement toward the AA degree.

A textbook is being developed which will contain the various approaches and assignments that are contained within the course.

Contact:
Walt Paul, Vice President, Instructional Services
(817) 773 9961, ext. 202

Temple Junior College
2600 South First Street
Temple, TX 76504
Total head count enrollment-Credit: 2,249; Non-Credit: 1,250
Campuses/sites: 1; Full-time faculty: 75

BLADESMITHING

All courses in this one-of-a-kind program are taught in a replica one-room school house with an attached stable

Students are attending Texarkana College to sharpen their skills at what was nearly a lost art – bladesmiting. The Texarkana College Bladesmithing School, established in 1988, is the only one of its kind in the world.

All courses are taught in historic Old Washington, Ark. (located eight miles west of Hope, birthplace of Bill Clinton) in a replica one-room school house with an attached stable. The pioneer Washington Restoration Foundation built the facility and makes it available to the college at no cost. The American Bladesmiths' Society assisted in the curriculum development.

Courses at the Bladesmithing School run for one or two 40-hour weeks and are taught by faculty who have earned

Continues on Page 682

international reputations. The classes, with approximately 12 to 15 students each, begin in March of each year and continue through October.

Bill Moran, senior faculty member in the Bladesmithing School and resident of Maryland, rediscovered the art of forging blades from Damascus steel in 1973. Moran teaches advanced students how to layer high quality tool steel and soft iron.

The two different metals are placed in alternating layers and then heated until they are orange hot, one step higher than red hot. After reaching the orange hot temperature, they are hammered on an anvil. When the layered metal doubles in length, it is reheated, folded in half and hammered on an anvil again with the process repeated several times. The result is Damascus steel.

In addition to Damascus Steel, the school offers courses in Introduction to Bladesmithing, Knifemaking, Handles and Guards, Folding Blades and Bladesmithing Lab.

Tuition for the school, which attracts students from all over the world, averages $600 per course. But the typical student spends at least $1,500, because each must be responsible for his own transportation, meals, lodging at a nearby hotel and related expenses.

After completing coursework, a student must spend a considerable amount of time refining his skills and improving his products. In some cases, students sell the knives they make in class and thereby make back the cost of the course. Extremely skilled bladesmiths can sometimes sell their knives for as much as $20,000.

Contact:
Scotty Hayes, Director, Community Services
(903) 838-4541

Texarkana College
2500 North Robison Road
Texarkana, TX 75599
Total head count enrollment-Credit: 4, 500; Non-Credit: 10,000
Campuses/sites: 1; Full-time faculty: 117

TEXAS STATE TECHNICAL COLLEGE-AMARILLO

STRATEGIC STUDENT RETENTION PLAN

One part of the plan, a mentoring program, reduces the need for additional guidance and counseling staff

Believing that successful academic achievement and self-confidence strengthen the student's commitment and enthusiasm to stay in school, Texas State Technical College-Amarillo in 1989 implemented the multi-faceted Strategic Student Retention Plan.

The first step was the selection of an evaluation instrument that would result in an accurate profile of each entering student to be used in conjunction with a state-mandated general education entrance exam. Subsequently, this results in a more complete and accurate profile of the factors which negatively or positively may impact the individual student's ability to perform, both academically as well as socially.

Utilizing past records of student performance on the required entrance exam, the General Education Division developed a strong prerequisite system of non-credit courses. In addition, the General Education Division cooperatively utilizes numerous technical program faculty as support for students enrolled in academic courses. To further emphasize the importance of general education achievement as regards student success, both remedial and college-level academic courses were consolidated by locating them in one department located in one building.

The Counseling Department solicited personnel from every department on campus to be trained and utilized as student mentors. Based upon the profile garnered from the two instruments, students identified as at-risk are paired with an appropriate mentor. However, any student may request to participate in the mentoring program.

First-year costs of implementing the program approached $30,000, which involved the acquisition of testing materials and the utilization of a professional to train student mentors. No additional personnel were added. The estimated annual costs to continue the program should not exceed $2,500.

On the other hand, major savings occur in personnel time. The mentoring program reduces the need for additional guidance and counseling staff. Because the instrument now being administered to each new student results in a more accurate profile, an action plan to address individual student needs can be more readily developed than the previous method which often required numerous sessions with individual students.

The student wins because he has a more positive learning experience, and a greater percentage of students are achieving the personal career development/attainment goals that they sought at the time they initially enrolled. The faculty and staff benefit because the results of both programs provides a student who is more positive and more capable of learning the necessary course work required for degree completion. In the end, business and industry benefit because the graduate is more capable of performing job requirements and more able to adapt to continuous technological changes within the workplace.

Overall student retention rates in recent years have improved from a low of 58 percent to a high of 84. In light of the fact that the college consistently must remediate from 50 percent to 60 percent of its entering students, 74 percent of students successfully completed the first level of college-level academic courses in one year.

As a technical college, TSTC has been concerned about the regional decline in college enrollment in technical majors; however, the college attributes its first overall enrollment increase in a number of years to the success of this student centered program.

As a result of the Strategic Student Retention plan, TSTC-Amarillo received the Annual Texas Technical Society Institutional Award. Presentations on the plan have been made at regional conferences, and professional staff have assisted other colleges in implementing the program.

Contact:
Dawn Boyer, Director, Guidance and Counseling

Texas State Technical College-Amarillo
PO Box 11157
Amarillo, TX 79111
Total head count enrollment-Credit: 879; Non-Credit: 4,196
Campuses/sites: 1; Full-time faculty: 58

CHEMICAL TECHNOLOGY

In this quality-driven program, faculty must recruit students, develop and instruct courses and labs and place graduates in jobs

The Chemical Technology program at Texas State Technical College-Harlingen is unique in that students receive the typical chemical training offered at a four-year institution, plus detailed training in the calibration, use, standard and sample preparation for chemical analysis on approximately 40 different types of analytical instruments. The range of instrumentation on which the graduates are experienced is wide and include balances, pH meters, UV/VIS spectrophotometers, infrared spectrophotometers, atomic absorption spectrophotometers, gas chromatographs, high performance liquid chromatographs, mass spectrometry, kinametric/dynamic viscosity, killion polymer extruders, tinius olsen plastic impact testers, tinius melt plastometers, compression molding presses and other analytical equipment and instruments.

This course of study was the joint product of 13 chemical manufacturing companies and Texas State Technical College-Harlingen. These companies, which include Dow Chemical Company, Phillips Petroleum Foundation, Inc. and The Upjohn Company, contribute funds and equipment as well as representatives who serve on an Advisory Committee, ensuring a curriculum that serves the needs of the chemical industry.

Program faculty have a responsibility to recruit students for the program, develop and instruct the courses and laboratories in the curriculum, and place the graduates in jobs. Since the original 17 students began the program, TSTC has graduated approximately 150 students. Some of the program's graduates have chosen to continue their education while others have chosen to step right into the laboratory. Placement has been 100 percent for those who desired to go directly to work. Graduates have received an average starting annual salary of $30,400. The return of investment for both the student and the State of Texas has been tremendous for this two-year program.

The Chemical Technology Program's success is also attributable to the diversity in the faculty's experience and background. Instructors contribute to the needs of the program with backgrounds in research in analytical chemistry, and industry-grounded experience as a chemical engineer, an organic chemist with experience as a medial technologist and a polymer chemist. This diversity in program staff and curriculum creates the best-qualified chemical technician that any education institution could provide.

Only four years after the program graduated its first chemical technicians, 26 TSTC graduates were working in the laboratories of Shell Development Company's Westhollow Research Center in Houston.

As the demand for Chemical Technicians increases with the growth of scientific research and development and the rise in production of technical products, TSTC's Chemical Technology program continues is "partnership with industry" to offer state-of-the-art facilities, a diverse and highly skilled faculty and staff, as well as innovative cooperative training working on real-world problems to see exactly how industry wants them to perform.

Contact:
Al Guillen Jr., Program Chairman
(210) 425-0736

Texas State Technical College-Harlingen
2424 Boxwood
Harlingen, TX 78550-3697
Total head count enrollment-Credit: 2,566; Non-Credit: 7,089
Campuses/sites: 1; Full-time faculty: 130

TECH PREP

The program, formed in partnership with educators and private industry, includes a mobile training lab for manufacturing instruction

Texas State Technical College is leading Tech Prep implementation efforts in Texas' Lower Rio Grande Valley, with a curriculum spanning kindergarten through baccalaureate degree in five counties on the Mexican border. The project blends rigorous academics and highly technical instruction, targets manufacturing/engineering, business/office technologies and nursing/allied health.

The Tech Prep Project Director works closely with TSTC's Associate Dean of Economic Development and Industrial Training and the Director of TSTC's Engineering/Manufacturing Division. The curriculum includes the SCANS Competencies and principles of Total Quality Management. Tech Prep AAS graduates will be ready for employment in high-performance work organizations and will also have the option to pursue baccalaureate degrees.

Tech Prep planning began in September 1991, and implementation began in March 1992. The Tech Prep consortium includes 17 school districts, six college and university campuses, and numerous business, labor, governmental, professional and civic organizations. The project stresses active participation of business and industry, and the president of a Harlingen manufacturing company is implementation chair. The Tech Prep project follows a successful 2+2 Project in Construction Operations Technology at TSTC; the COT program is now a Tech Prep program.

Texas' Lower Rio Grande Valley is plagued with double-digit unemployment rates, a large percentage of special populations, and longitudinal dropout rates exceeding 50 percent. The area has tremendous potential, though having been one of Texas' fastest-growing areas for the past two years. To develop the work force needed to sustain the Valley's current economic growth, Tech Prep is working with the Lower Rio Grande Valley Quality Work Force Planning Committee and numerous governmental and civic leaders.

Tech Prep has formed partnerships with the Texas Business and Education Coalition on the Texas Scholars project and with the National Center for Manufacturing Sciences. Valley business leaders made Texas Scholars presentation in eighth grade classrooms in 1992-93. The consortium utilizes an NCMS-style Tech Prep mobile training lab for manufacturing instruction. The mobile lab features state-of-the-art, interactive technology and includes a multifaceted curriculum for all levels of students plus parents, teachers and counselors.

Professional development is a top priority. A series of workshops was held in June 1992 for business and industry and for teachers, counselors and administrators from kindergarten through college. Multiple professional development activities will be ongoing in the future. Parental involvement and career awareness are integral, and 1992-93 parental involvement workshops featured the Harlingen CISD's program, which was named the best parental involvement program in Texas in 1991-92.

TSTC's Tech Prep project was featured at the Fourth Commissioners' Conference on Teacher Education in February 1992 and at a Texas Senate subcommittee hearing on work force development in July. The project is funded by a grant in federal funds under the Carl Perkins Vocational and Applied Technology Act of 1990.

Contact:
Pat Bubb, Project Director
(210) 425-0729

Texas State Technical College-Harlingen
2424 Boxwood
Harlingen, TX 78550-3697
Total head count enrollment-Credit: 2,566; Non-Credit: 7,089
Campuses/sites: 1; Full-time faculty: 130

FAULCONER ACADEMIC INCENTIVE AWARD FOR ETHNIC MINORITIES

The award draws students who otherwise might not attend college and requires a student to maintain a 2.0 GPA while attending full time

The Faulconer Academic Incentive Award for Ethnic Minorities encourages students who think that college may not be a possibility for them, either because of economics or academic preparedness, to pursue a higher education at Tyler Junior College.

First preference is given to average achievers from high school who show the potential for success in completing an associate degree or certificate program leading to the completion of a baccalaureate degree.

The $2,000 award is given to each qualifying student who is accepted into the program. The award may be granted for up to five years if scholastic progress is maintained. This encourages the student to complete at least two years at Tyler Junior College and then transfer to a four-year college or university.

As a recipient of the Faulconer award, the student must maintain at least a 2.0 grade point average and be enrolled as a full-time student (at least 12 hours) at Tyler Junior College.

Additional responsibilities include maintaining close contact with their college counselor, attending Summer Freshman Orientation and transferring to a four-year college or university.

Award winners and their parents – along with the donor of the award, one of the city's leading citizens - are honored each year with a reception.

In 1990-91, the first year the Faulconer Academic Incentive Award for Ethnic Minorities was awarded, 10 students from the Tyler Independent School District were selected for the program. For 1991-92, the number doubled to 20 and continues to double each year.

Contact:
C. C. Baker, Jr., Vice President, Development
(903) 510-2497

Tyler Junior College
PO Box 9020
Tyler, TX 75711
Total head count enrollment-Credit: 8,590; Non-Credit: 23,343
Campuses/sites: 1; Full-time faculty: 190

COLLEGE / SCHOOL DISTRICT POST-GRADUATE PARTNERSHIP

A tuition scholarship requires the student to remain drug-free, maintain a 75 to 80 GPA and maintain a 95 percent attendance during high school

Every area high school graduate has a shot at a college education through a Post-Graduate Partnership Plan of the Tyler Junior College Foundation and the Winona Independent School District (WISD). Through tuition scholarships from community-based service organizations and businesses, the partnership presents an opportunity for developing the academic and occupational potential of WISD students.

The post-graduate plan first targeted high school graduates in the 1992 graduating class. The plan designates that students must be drug-free and a member of D-FY-IT (Drug-Free Youth In Texas), a state organization that began in Tyler. Membership requires a commitment that the student will remain drug-free. The eligible student must also maintain a 75 to 80 grade point average and maintain a 95 percent attendance during school.

The district envisions receiving private gifts, business and corporate donations of $235,000 over 13 years to fund the plan. The total number of scholarships awarded each year is dependent upon the interest earned from the endowment.

The purpose of the plan is to challenge all high school students to rise to the next academic level – to become informed and productive young adults, equipped to function effectively within society.

Contact:
C. C. Baker, Jr., Vice President, Development
(903) 510-2497

Tyler Junior College
PO Box 9020
Tyler, TX 75711
Total head count enrollment-Credit: 8,590; Non-Credit: 23,343
Campuses/sites: 1; Full-time faculty: 190

THE CHALLENGE FOR EXCELLENCE ENDOWED SCHOLARSHIP

The program for students in grades 7 through 12 provides for interaction among parents, teachers and administrators

The "Challenge for Excellence" Scholarship Endowment Program addresses three critical issues facing education: a lack of basic skills among high school graduates, a skyrocketing drop-out rate, and the inaccessibility of higher education because of a lack of financial resources.

The program is designed to reach students in grades 7 through 12 in the Texas Southmost College District. The essence of the program is that every student enrolled in the "grade level" courses (essentially college preparatory courses) of math, English, science, social science and a foreign language can earn his or her way to college by electing the endowment sponsored courses and by making a grade of an "A" or a "B" in these courses.

Students who make the required grades are automatically credited with tuition hour credits at Texas Southmost College and redeemable after graduation from high school or the equivalent. The innovative aspect of this scholarship program is that it begins to address the issues before developmental work is necessary. Students are directed early into the courses that will prepare them for college-level work. Achieving a grade of an "A" or a "B" determines a competence level in the coursework, immediate gratification is provided for the student each semester as he or she attains a fundable grade in these courses, and the financial reward of funding a complete Associate Degree education becomes a reality as students begin to earn "scholarship dollars" good toward tuition at Texas Southmost College.

As a departure from previous practice, scholarships were awarded upon graduation from high school. While this obviously has a major role in pursuing upper level education, it fails to address the issues of the drop out rate, lack of basic skills, and motivation. As students become aware of the skills needed to succeed in college and careers at an early age, they begin to shape their own future through their choice of coursework in junior high and high school.

The results of this program will be quantitatively shown as the 7th and 8th graders, who are the first students to begin to earn "scholarship dollars," graduate from high school and enter into college-level courses in 1994. The scholarship endowment anticipates three direct influences of the program:

1) a decrease in the drop-out rate;
2) an increase in college enrollment; and
3) a decrease in the number of students currently assessed as requiring developmental courses before entering into college level coursework.

What the program has accomplished to date is a recognition level among secondary school administrators of the importance of the availability of grade level and college preparatory courses. It has provided an opportunity for interaction among parents, teachers, and administrators in determining courses and coursework that is indeed providing students with basic skills. Courses have been added at schools as a result of parental interaction with the administrators.

Students are becoming aware of the availability of a college education and becoming familiar with the terminology associated with college semester hours. And of course, students are becoming aware of the importance of early preparation and the need to remain in school. The unexpected enthusiasm this project has generated among the citizens of our community and public and private school administrators and faculty has been overwhelming, making it possible for TSC to raise the funds needed to support the program.

This program has the potential to be replicated in any area of the country. The basic areas of need are the tracking of student grades and the funding of the "scholarship dollars."

Texas Southmost College was committed to raising the funds necessary to support the "scholarship dollars" and in doing so, applied to the Department of Education for a Title III Challenge Grant. The receipt of the matching funds, $2,000,000 was dependent on the local community, acknowledged as one of the poorest in the nation, raising $1-million to support this effort. With a median personal income of just more than $6,500 and more than 72 percent of students enrolled at the college receiving financial aid, this incredible effort is truly an inspiration.

The "Challenge for Excellence is designed for any student enrolled in 7th through 12th grades in public and private schools in the college district regardless of ethnicity or level of income. The program is anticipated to serve over 80 percent of all students, i.e. those enrolled in courses other than basic or developmental courses. With a total of 19,500 students in grades seven through 12, the immediate enrollment of 7th and 8th graders is approximately 8,000 students.

The budget is approximately $180,000 for the first group of students entering the program. This figure is based on an endowed corpus of $3-million attained from the DOE Challenge Grant referred to previously. The DOE stipulates that one half of the interest must be reinvested in the corpus, the other half is available for scholarships. Anticipated increases in enrollment in the local school districts mandates the necessity to continue to raise funds for this project to cover the expenditure of the "scholarship dollars."

In conclusion, this program has sparked the interest of educators nationwide, and the practicality of the program enhances the ability to replicate the essential aspects of the program anywhere there is a need.

Contact:
Margie Mancillas, Director, Special Programs
(210) 544-8255

University of Texas at Brownsville with Texas Southmost College
80 Fort Brown
Brownsville, TX 78520
Total head count enrollment-Credit: 19,800; Non-Credit: 8,454
Campuses/sites: 5; Full-time faculty: 200

VERNON REGIONAL JUNIOR COLLEGE

SUMMER YOUTH PROGRAM

The program allows young people to begin their college education while earning money for job training at the college and other work sites

Young people can begin their college education while earning money for job training at a number of public, non-profit work sites at Vernon Regional Junior College and in the surrounding area, through the college's Summer Youth Program. The college each summer accepts 25 to 30 disadvantaged rising seniors and spring high school graduates into its the program. These participants are chosen from among applicants from 25 counties in the North Central Texas area.

Each program participant is both pre- and post-tested to first determine his/her level of competence in English, mathematics, and reading, and second, to determine his/her degree of improvement in these three areas at the end of the program. After pre-testing, these participants are counseled into appropriate college classes and can earn from 12 to 14 hours of college credit. These classes are scheduled in the morning, so that participants can work in the afternoon at their assigned job sites. In the evenings and on weekends, the participants are offered a variety of cultural and entertainment activities designed to keep them interested and to offer them opportunities which they would not otherwise enjoy. They are housed in a college dormitory and take their meals in the college cafeteria.

The immediate college staff for the program consists of an administrator, a director, and three associate tutors. In addition, the participants have full access to all services available to any student enrolled at the college, including counseling and health care.

Since the program has been in existence, student success has been extremely gratifying. More than 95 percent of the participants have completed both semesters of the summer program. In addition, approximately 38 percent of the participants have finished or are pursuing baccalaureate degrees at senior institutions. Additional follow-up indicates that one participant is pursuing a Ph.D. in astrophysics.

Contact:
Jim D. Farber, Instructor-In-Charge
(817) 552-6291, ext. 233

Vernon Regional Junior College
4400 College Drive
Vernon, TX 76384
Total head count enrollment-Credit: 1,800; Non-Credit: 8,000
Campuses/sites: 4; Full-time faculty: 50

VERNON REGIONAL JUNIOR COLLEGE

NURSING

The college, which serves a vast area of rural Texas, is helping fill a dramatic need for qualified nurses

Vernon Regional Junior College has a 10,000-square-mile area in rural North Central Texas, where health care agencies have indicated a registered nurse shortage of more than 20 percent.

Responding to this critical shortage of registered nurses in the area, the college began to seek approval for an Associate Degree Nursing Program in the late 1980's.

However, when funding was unavailable, VRJC turned to Amarillo College and requested an extended campus (located in Vernon) transition program. This transition program ideally suited VRJC because the college has one of the largest vocational nursing enrollments in Texas and would be able to provide registered nurses in the most

Continues on Page 688

timely manner. The transition program is designed to allow advanced standing for previously learned vocational nursing content and clinical experiences, and students (after meeting course prerequisites) are able to complete the nursing portion of the program in three semesters. The extended campus request was approved, and the first Amarillo College class enrolled on the Regional Junior College campus in 1990.

During the next two years, the college began to solicit outside funding to subsidize the startup costs for its own program. Generous gifts were obtained from E. Paul & Helen Buck Waggoner Foundation, Wilbarger General Hospital, Bethania Regional Health Care Center, Wichita General Hospital, and the Electra Medical Service Corporation. Once pledges for adequate funding were received, the college proceeded with obtaining proper approval from state agencies, including permission from the Board of Nurse Examiners to assume sole ownership of the nursing program from Amarillo College. The initial VRJC nursing transition class enrolled in 1992. A generic program, designed for persons who do not have a nursing background, will be implemented in the Fall 1993 Semester.

Providing registered nurses for the North Central Texas area has been a collaborative effort — working with another community college, receiving financial support from area health care providers and a local foundation, and developing a program through input from the medical community.

Contact:
Cathy Bolton, Instructor-In-Charge
(817) 552-6291, ext. 270

Vernon Regional Junior College
4400 College Drive
Vernon, TX 76384
Total head count enrollment-Credit: 1,800; Non-Credit: 8,000
Campuses/sites: 4; Full-time faculty: 50

ELDEN B. SESSIONS HONOR RESIDENCE

The residence hall, once set aside for athletes, now houses students with academic scholarships

The most unique residence hall in Utah, "Sessions," is reserved exclusively for students attending College of Eastern Utah on a Presidential or Honors Scholarship, which covers the cost of the room. The award is made each year to a freshman with the possibility of renewal if high academic status is continued.

When the idea of a honors residence was conceived in early 1987 the hall was exclusively for athletes. With special funding the building was modernized with resource and studying support areas. In the beginning students were allowed to enter the program with a GPA of 3.0. However, the current minimum entry level is 3.5 and the 1992 cut-

off point was a GPA of 3.75, a significant change in five years.

Sessions has 94 room awards, for which approximately 200 students apply. The residents of the hall are further supported by academic learning programs.

The Sessions residence program has been considered quite a success by CEU staff and board members. The students place a high value on the scholarships that allow them a room in the "honors" residence hall. The results are quite positive for CEU students and are complimented by an approximate annual retention rate of 97 percent for Elden B. Sessions honor residents.

Contact:
Rich McCormick
(801) 637-2120, ext. 637

College of Eastern Utah
451 East 400 North
Price, UT 84501
Total head count enrollment-Credit: 7,922
Campuses/sites: 2; Full-time faculty: 72

ELECTRONICS TECHNOLOGY FOR RAILROAD SIGNAL PERSONNEL

Tailored for the Union Pacific Railroad, the program has led to a long-term commitment to share a building with UPR

Since January 1989, Salt Lake Community College (SLCC) has conducted specialized electronic technology training for signal maintainers and communication technicians for Union Pacific Railroad (UPR). It has been so successful and well-received that the college is expanding the training to serve the entire North American railroad industry.

UPR employees come to Utah from the 22 states in which UPR operates. They stay for two-week intervals, returning to Utah approximately every six months over a 2-1/2-year period. During their time away from SLCC they return to their normal jobs and also work on assignments. A dedicated phone line to their instructor ensures immediate access for questions and answers. Upon completion of the program, employees have all the core requirements for an Associate of Applied Science degree in Electronic Technology.

Approximately 100 UPR employees are involved with this training. An additional 100 employees have already completed the training. As employees complete the training, more are added to take their place. SLCC has realized a retention rate in excess of 90 percent, a remark-

able achievement given the program's length and difficulty.

In August 1991, this program was presented as a model training program to the joint North American convention of the AAR and the Railroad Systems Suppliers, Inc. signal divisions. Railroad officials and suppliers from throughout the United States, Canada and Mexico attended this annual convention. SLCC's training program was well-received as an innovative and needed training model for the railroad industry.

Since this program began, SLCC has developed two additional customized training programs for UPR in welding and construction. Each of these programs is conducted over a two-week, 80-contact-hour period.

To date, in all three programs, SLCC has trained more than 800 UPR employees.

UPR's successful experience with SLCC has resulted in a long-term commitment to share a building which will house UPR's corporate technical training center. This new building will be located on SLCC's Redwood Road Campus. Total construction costs will be approximately

Continues on Page 690

$15-million. UPR committed $5-million and will occupy one-third of the building. Working with the Utah State legislature, SLCC received a funding commitment for the balance of the building's cost. Construction began in the fall of 1993.

Contact:
John Anjewierden, Division Chair
(801) 967-4327

Salt Lake Community College
PO Box 30808
Salt Lake City, UT 84130
Total head count enrollment-Credit: 15,862
Campuses/sites: 9; Full-time faculty: 232.32

BUILDING CONSTRUCTION

Incarcerated students at the Young Adults Correctional Facility receive every aspect of building construction training

After years of teaching Building Construction to the general population, Salt Lake Community College has introduced it to the inmate population at the Young Adults Correctional Facility.

The program started in 1986 with less than 10 incarcerated students. One instructor taught all courses. Since then, the program has grown to more than 50 full-time students with two full-time instructors and two adjunct instructors.

Students in this program have the option to earn a diploma or an Associate of Applied Science degree. It took two years for the first students to complete the program. This graduating class was made up of only three individuals. In 1992, 15 individuals earned diplomas in building Construction and 11 of these went on and completed their Associate of Applied Science degree.

Students receive training in every aspect of building construction while incarcerated. Even concrete technology is covered. As a learning exercise, students in the program have produced more than 50 portable classrooms. These portable classrooms are constructed in two sections, are moved to appropriate school locations, fastened together and used as overload classrooms. Seven of these classrooms have been furnished to Salt Lake Community College's Redwood Road Campus and several school districts throughout the state have received the others. By providing free labor for these buildings, the Building Construction program has saved the state of Utah many thousands of dollars.

The goal of the Building Construction Program at the Young Adults Correctional Facility is to provide offenders with employable skills, so that when they are released they will become self-supporting, contributing members of society.

Several of the graduates from this program have been released and have become successful contractors and tradesmen. One in particular has his own siding company. He has several employees and is an excellent role model for other inmates in the program.

One of the most difficult problems for any incarcerated program is tuition funding. This problem has been solved through the use of Pell Grants. Everyone at the college has been very supportive in accessing Pell Grants and supporting our prison effort.

The college has been able to acquire Carl Perkins funding to purchase some equipment for the Building Construction lab located at the Young Adults Correctional Facility. Additional equipment has been supplied through normal college funding. The Utah State Legislature has appropriated funds to enable the Building Construction Program to manufacture four portable classrooms to be located at the prison and to serve as classrooms for the Building Construction Program and the Office Information Systems Program. The Office Information Systems Program is providing training at the women's prison facility.

When the program was officially introduced at the prison, the college had to solicit students to participate in the program. Now, Salt Lake Community College has more than 50 students on a waiting list to receive training for this program.

Contact:
Don Merrill, Division Chair, Technical Specialties
(801) 967-4074

Salt Lake Community College
PO Box 30808
Salt Lake City, UT 84130
Total head count enrollment-Credit: 15,862
Campuses/sites: 9; Full-time faculty: 232.32

SNOW'S VARSITY EXPERIENCE

*The college philosophy is that students can be "varsity" in many activities,
including internships and volunteer work*

The specific mission of Snow College is threefold:
1) to educate students;
2) to inspire them to love learning; and
3) to lead them to serve others.

Varsity Experience was created to help Snow fulfill that mission. Varsity Experience is the name given to any significant "out of classroom" activity(ies). The Varsity Experience also includes a student center on campus (the Varsity House), which provides counseling on where and how to get involved (the college actually identifies and contacts students who are not involved outside of class), as well as tracking and recognizing each student's activities.

Snow's philosophy is that students can be "varsity" in many activities, including: performing arts, volunteer organizations, work, athletics, internships, leadership positions, student government and hundreds of other opportunities. These Varsity Experiences help each student maintain a balance in life, as well as develop leadership and maturity.

After three years, the program included one full-time director and two part-time staff. This year Varsity Experience will touch the lives of nearly 90 percent of our student body.

Contact:
Jeffery Savage, Director
(801) 283-4021

Snow College
150 East College Avenue
Ephraim, UT 84627
Total head count enrollment-Credit: 2,344
Campuses/sites: 1; Full-time faculty: 75

LEARNING ENRICHMENT

*The program is designed to provide students the tools needed
to become independent learners*

Wanting to serve all students but recognizing that not all are prepared to meet the college's academic standards and requirements, Utah Valley Community College established a developmental program to address the needs of students who are academically unprepared for college work. Learning Enrichment is designed to provide students with the tools to become independent learners and to develop the skills and attributes they require for success.

The college recognizes that students who are underprepared are the most likely to drop out of college before completing their educational goals, and that personal and institutional costs related to attrition can be avoided if the institution can provide services to ensure students receive extensive and varied assistance from the beginning of their college days through the years to graduation.

Learning Enrichment offers carefully sequenced preparatory coursework in developmental mathematics, algebra, writing, reading, study skills, plus personal assistance courses in stress management, eliminating self-defeating behaviors and vocational communications. A many-faceted, centralized operation, the program also offers a learning specialist to help students understand and improve their learning styles, advisors to help students make sound educational decisions, and peer tutors to conduct study and support groups as well as one-on-one tutoring in college courses. Learning assistance labs provide tutoring in mathematics, reading and writing.

Learning Enrichment is dedicated to serving underprepared students in a caring, warm and disciplined environment. Faculty are hired for their nurturing, positive attitudes as well as teaching expertise. Courses are mastery based, and students are given the option of lecture or individualized instruction. All courses are carefully structured to make a positive difference in students' lives, to motivate students to learn, to take responsibility for their own learning to give students early successes and regular feedback, and to prepare students to think critically and analytically through their coursework as well as in life.

Although Utah Valley Community College has not instituted a policy of mandatory placement of under-prepared students, Learning Enrichment grew from a handful of

Continues on Page 692

students when the program was established in 1971, to 5,000 students in 1991-1992 taking an average of 3.8 credit hours. More than 48 percent of one year's graduates had taken courses in Learning Enrichment, testifying to its effectiveness.

Contact:
Carrol Reid, Dean, Learning Resources and Services
(801) 222-8000, ext. 8258

Utah Valley Community College
800 West 1200 South
Orem, UT 84058
Total head count enrollment-Credit: 10,510
Campuses/sites: 2; Full-time faculty: 206

ETHICS AND VALUES

▨ An interdisciplinary ethics core has been adapted ▨
as a requirement for numerous majors

In 1986, Utah Valley Community College (UVCC) developed and implemented the interdisciplinary, core course, "Ethics and Values." Since then, it has proved to be one of the most unifying, strengthening and educationally rigorous moves the college has made. An ethics core is amazingly adaptable as a requirement for numerous majors including business, nursing, trades and technologies.

Ethics became a staple in the curriculum after two years of debate among Humanities faculty on how to improve the rigor of the Humanities offerings. An interdisciplinary, core approach centered around ethics was the faculty consensus, and the National Endowment for the Humanities funded the project. The grant made possible faculty summer seminars with nationally prominent scholars, community lecture series, quarterly visits from both in-state and out-of-state scholars and library acquisitions. All of these activities took place during the three-year grant and they continue today.

In designing the course, at least five goals of national curricular reform were integrated:

1) The discussion of ethics should be important and timely. Well-educated students should know the seminal works in ethics and understand the various approaches to dilemmas – what could be called ethical literacy.

2) Interdisciplinarity is integral to student understanding. A new perspective on an ethical issue often unfolds with each discipline; sometimes these perspectives conflict. The disciplines used are philosophy, literature, religion and history. Philosophy helps one discern the complexities

involved in moral ideas; religion reminds one that each ethical dilemma has inherent moral and value implications and conflicts; literature brings the dilemma to life with characters moving through right and wrong decisions and living with the consequences of their choices; history can help one compare the values of a different time and culture with our own, and can make students aware that an unquestionable assumption today was seen quite differently at another time.

3) A strong writing component should be included. Thinking and articulating an issue becomes clearer as students format ideas in written form.

4) Self-confrontation and classroom discussion should be encouraged. Students need to share their thoughts and scholarship with others. They also need to learn from the reflections of others.

5) Critical thinking is necessary as students understand the perspectives of scholars and writers, for such understanding will shape the analysis of and recommended responses to ethical dilemmas.

Six full-time faculty teach this course. Two of the faculty have written textbooks. Elaine Englehardt with co-author Don Schmeltekopf authored *Ethics and Life: An Interdisciplinary Look at the Humanities* (1992). Joseph Grcic authored *Moral Choices: Ethical Theories and Problems*, Western Publishing Company (1988).

Core study in ethics has benefited the UVCC community. Its spill-over effects can be seen in numerous classes and programs. This demanding course and its accompanying program has enhanced the rigor of the curriculum and fits well with the college's educational reform.

Contact:
Elaine Englehardt, Program Chair
(801) 222-8000, ext. 8129

Utah Valley Community College
800 West 1200 South
Orem, UT 84058
Total head count enrollment-Credit: 10,510
Campuses/sites: 2; Full-time faculty: 206

ASSESSMENT OF PRIOR LEARNING

The program has assisted thousands of adults starting or returning to college

Because learning is an ongoing, life-long activity and the source of learning is secondary to the actual learning, the Community College of Vermont gives equal value to learning acquired on the job, in the classroom, or in the community.

Thus, since 1975, the Vermont State Colleges Office of External Programs (OEP), through the Community College of Vermont, has administered one of the largest and most successful programs in the country for the assessment of prior experiential learning. It is a statewide, non-institutional based program which awards Vermont State Colleges transfer credit to approximately 200 adults each year. Since its inception, this program has assisted more than 4,000 adults in beginning or returning to college.

Assessment is a three-step process. The first step for students is to enroll in a course titled Educational Assessment and Portfolio Preparation, which is sponsored by four of the Vermont State Colleges as well as other colleges and businesses in the state. The major activity of this course is the preparation of individual student portfolios. The portfolio is the vehicle by which students articulate and document their college-level learning. Throughout this 15-week course, there is a strict emphasis on learning, not experience. OEP awards credit for learning only. The distinction between learning and experience is often difficult for students; however, it is this strict distinction that ensures program quality.

The second step in the process is the assessment of student portfolios by an Advanced Standing Committee (ASC). At the end of each semester, student portfolios are submitted to the Office of External Programs. OEP sorts these portfolios by content area and then assembles teams of professionals to review them. ASC's are composed of two faculty members from the VSC system, one faculty member from another institution and a practitioner. Committee members review each portfolio individually about two weeks prior to the committee meeting. When the entire committee meets, the group spends about half a day working through the portfolios together. A representative from OEP facilitates each meetings. Credit award decisions are made by consensus. This committee structure has several advantages. First, working in a group of peers enables committee members to work through, problems and questions concerning various parts of the portfolio. Such group decisions strengthen the validity of credit awards and increase consistency of portfolio assessments. Secondly, group work enables assessors with varying backgrounds to combine their expertise so that in a group of four committee members, differing perspectives can be brought to the evaluation. Finally, by involving faculty members from many institutions, we assure that faculty throughout the state are familiar with the assessment process. This increases the likelihood that when our students attend their institutions, they will be aware of the validity of the prerequisite learning and serve as valuable advocates for assessed learning at their individual institutions.

The third and final step in the process is the transfer of credit awarded by the Advanced Standing Committee to a degree-granting institution. Our assessment program is not attached to any one college or university. The credits awarded are considered Vermont State Colleges transfer credits and as such, receiving institutions make final determinations about which credits they will accept. Most of the Vermont State Colleges accept OEP credits as do many other institutions in and out of Vermont.

It should be noted that the Assessment of Prior Learning's association with the Vermont State College system as opposed to association with any one institution is very deliberate. Being a system-wide program has many advantages. Most importantly, students' credit requests are not limited by the academic offerings of one institution. This allows the student more options when requesting credit and allows the committee to shift its focus from whether or not a requested area of study is offered at his/her institution together or whether a particular area of study is college level. The Vermont State Colleges Assessment of Prior Learning program has served as a model for programs throughout the U.S. and Canada.

Contact:
Office of External Programs
(802) 241-3522

Community College of Vermont
PO Box 120
Waterbury, VT 05676
Total headcount enrollment-Credit: 4,327; Non-Credit: 96
Campuses/sites: 12; Full-time faculty: 0 (600 part-time)

DIMENSIONS OF LEARNING

⬚ *The course for disadvantaged students is* ⬚
built around carefully selected literature

In 1981, CCV decided to take a chance and make a single course the centerpiece of its Special Services for Disadvantaged Students program. "Don't build a whole program around a single course" was the advice from the "experts" and from many of our colleagues in the college. Well-intentioned caveats notwithstanding, the college went ahead and created Dimensions of Learning (DOL), a course designed around liberal arts content.

While DOL's primary content is an eclectic mix of carefully selected literature, it also provides students with strong personal support and it pays systematic attention to the development of critical thinking and study skills.

The college assumed that such a course would work for disadvantaged students, returning adults and for younger students just starting out. It has. The record shows that it builds confidence, enhances learning skills, and it helps to motivate students to take more courses. "This course was incredible. It challenged me, encouraged me, and changed me, and it was fun," noted one student, a comment that is typical of many found on end-of-course evaluations.

The course goals are to develop students' reading, writing, critical thinking and study skills while building self-confidence and developing cultural, historical, social and aesthetic awareness and appreciation. The overarching goal is to challenge students intellectually while supporting them personally. Readings include *Revelations: Diaries of Women, Short Story Masterpieces*, Orwell's *1984*, and Plato's *Allegory of the Cave*.

Teachers are trained to support and encourage student growth and development. Remarks like, "For a first effort, this paper reflects hard work and serious thinking. We'll work on your spelling and grammar next," can be commonly heard from DOL instructors. Students experience early successes and as their confidence grows, the challenges get incrementally more difficult. Metacognition is emphasized. Students are continually asked to explain their thinking and to articulate what they know and how they know it.

Since its inception, the course has become so popular that CCV now typically offers more than 20 sections of DOL each semester. DOL is a course that thrives on student diversity. It has attracted a broad range of students, from recent GED recipients to people with master's degrees. It is also not uncommon to find an 18-year-old discussing Plato with a 55-year-old. DOL has been the subject of conferences. Within the college it has become a model, both in terms of course design and the training of faculty, for the development of other "super courses."

Contact:
Jack Anderson
(802) 241-3535

Community College of Vermont
PO Box 120
Waterbury, VT 05676
Total headcount enrollment-Credit: 4,327; Non-Credit: 96
Campuses/sites: 12; Full-time faculty: 0 (600 part-time)

TRANSITION TO TECHNOLOGY

⬚ *The program prepares students for the challenge* ⬚
of a two-year technical degree pursuit

For the large number of students arriving at Vermont Technical College (VTC) under-prepared for the academic rigors of a two-year technical degree program, VTC offers the "Transition to Technology" program. Transition to Technology provides a year of developmental work in reading, writing, mathematics and physics to ensure success at the freshman level.

The curriculum is made up of three courses, including Integrated Math-Physics, Integrated Language Arts and Introduction to Technology.

Integrated Language Arts teaches developmental reading, writing, oral communication and study skills. The course is team-taught and includes a two-hour laboratory where students develop proficiency in word processing, research skills and logic.

The Integrated Math-Physics course is taught by a team comprising a teacher from each discipline. Topics are presented in a logical order and integrated to the extent traditional study of math and physics will allow to facilitate learning on the formal operational level. Students attend eight lectures and two, two-hour laboratory sessions each week, including approximately one hour of supplemental instruction.

The purpose of Introduction to Technology is to provide developmental students with active learning experiences in several degree program areas. Each student attends three,

three-hour laboratories in five of seven technologies (agriculture, architecture, automotive, business, civil, electrical and mechanical) and is required to complete one library assignment which demonstrates the connection between the language arts and the technologies. Upon completing the program, students are able to make an informed choice of major.

The Transition to Technology program includes eight full-time instructors as well as several faculty from degree programs who teach part of their load in the program. More students are successful in the integrated developmental program than had been in the more traditional program which it replaced.

The program was cited as an Exemplary Program by the American Association of Community and Junior Colleges in 1991.

Contact:
Darlene Miller, Associate Professor
(802) 728-3391, ext. 305

Vermont Technical College
Randolph Center, VT 05061
Total headcount enrollment-Credit: 872; Non-Credit: 174
Campuses/sites: 2; Full-time faculty: 57

VERMONT TECHNICAL COLLEGE

WOMEN IN TECHNOLOGY (WIT) PROJECT

The project emphasizes outreach to rural populations and disadvantaged families

Alarmed at the few number of women enrolling in technical majors, Vermont Technical College in 1986 initiated the Women in Technology (WIT) Project.

The goal of the WIT Project is to encourage young women to study advanced math and science courses through high school and inspire them to pursue technical careers. To achieve this goal, WIT has specific objectives – to educate young women about technical careers; to show the relevance of math and science to professions in technology; provide female role models; to expose girls and boys to women scientists, engineers, mathematicians and technicians in order to discourage traditional occupational stereotyping; and to increase teachers' awareness and effectiveness regarding gender equity in the classroom.

The staff of the Women in Technology Project includes a full-time director, part-time assistant director and an administrative support person. During the summer the project also employs a full-time temporary camp coordinator. A non-profit program, the WIT Project relies almost exclusively on grant funding to cover the expenses of salaries and program operations. Vermont Technical College offers support by providing the office space and all related expenses, and use of facilities such as computer and engineering labs.

Because the WIT Project places a strong emphasis on outreach to the rural populations of Vermont, to include girls from economically disadvantaged families in all of its programs, seeking grant funding is an important aspect of the project's activities.

The WIT Project implements five programs in order to meet its goal and objectives: the Summer Technology Camp, Math and Science Institute, Speakers Bureau, Shadow Days and Girl Scouts Computer Badge Day.

The Summer Technology Camp is a five-day residential camp for 7th- and 8th-grade girls and a six-day camp for high school girls designed to interest them in math, science, engineering, and technology through hands-on workshops. Instructors and counselors are women employed in technical professions or majoring in these areas in college. Because camp is residential, the opportunity for role modeling is significant. Girls are selected by their schools based on their interest in the designated courses, rather than high grades. Emphasis is placed on selecting girls from rural, economically disadvantaged families who would probably be otherwise unable to participate in a summer camp. When it is necessary to charge a fee for camp, it is kept to a minimum and full financial aid is available. One hundred eighty girls attended during summer 1993.

The Math and Science Institute brings girls who attended Summer Technology Camp the previous summer back for four days of intensive math and science workshops. It follows a format and philosophy very similar to Summer Technology Camp. One session per summer is held, with approximately 35 girls in attendance.

A Speakers Bureau of about 85 women engineers, scientists and technicians give classroom presentations about their jobs specifically or technical careers in general to students throughout Vermont. All schools with grades K-12 are invited to participate. During the 1991-92 school year, Speakers Bureau volunteers gave 73 presentations, reaching approximately 200 teachers, aides and administrators, and 1,250 students.

Shadow Days take place on the VTC campus as well as at the workplace. High school girls have the opportunity to meet women studying and working in the areas of science and technology, and to experience first-hand what technical education and work encompass. This program exposes girls to role models and provides WIT the opportunity to

Continues on Page 696

network with a variety of corporations, broadening the base of community support. Approximately 25 high school women participate in Shadow Days each year.

The Girl Scouts Computer Badge Day is program designed to provide Junior and Cadet Girl Scouts (grades four to eight) with the opportunity to earn their Computer Fun Badge. Experienced faculty at VTC volunteer to assist the girls in the computer and robotics labs. Computer Badge Days occur in the fall and spring, accommodating about 75 girls at each.

In December 1991, a questionnaire was distributed to alumnae of Summer Technology Camps 1987 and 1988 for the purpose of evaluating the long-term impact and effectiveness of the camp experience. Based upon responses, 50 percent of the participants indicated that they took more math and science courses in high school as a result of camp, and 50 percent said camp helped them decide what to pursue as a career. Many of the college majors listed were related to math, science and technology.

In 1988, the Women in Technology Project received the American Association of University Women (AAUW) Legal Advocacy Fund's second annual Progress in Equity Award. In addition, the Vermont Division of AAUW awarded its state Progress in Equity Award to WIT during the same year.

Contact:
Amy Emler-Shaffer, Director
(802) 728-3391, ext. 305

Vermont Technical College
Randolph Center, VT 05061
Total headcount enrollment-Credit: 872; Non-Credit: 174
Campuses/sites: 2; Full-time faculty: 57

CONVERSATIONAL SPANISH FOR THE POULTRY INDUSTRY

After visiting poultry plants, the college developed a text
and a list of vocabulary words distinctive to the industry

Rather than try to teach English to the largely Hispanic work force in three poultry plants, Blue Ridge Community College (BRCC) teaches supervisory personnel Spanish words and gestures, vastly improving employee-employer relations.

This teaching resulted from the 1991 partnership of BRCC and the local poultry industry. It enabled the college to hire a full-time language teacher to help develop the language program at the college. A three-year grant was arranged in which three poultry companies, ROCCO, Tyson and Wampler-Longacre, would pay approximately two-thirds of the instructor's salary for the first year, one-half for the second year, and one-third for the third year, with the BRCC Foundation picking up the remainder of the salary each year.

A Spanish instructor was hired who would teach the college-level Spanish classes at BRCC, as well as teach Spanish to the poultry industry supervisory personnel. The classes at the college were traditional, requiring the usual planning and implementation, but the classes for the poultry industry required extra study to design them. The instructor consulted the officials of the industry to determine their needs and decided that the best benefits for the dollars spent would be provided if the classes took place on site at the plants. After visiting each of the plants, a list of vocabulary words distinctive to the poultry industry was developed and a text was created. An additional text was identified to teach conversational Spanish. Then an eight-week classes were established.

The result of the classes was that students who completed their first level could greet and say good-bye to their employees, ask appropriate questions in Spanish to get more Spanish words, use directions appropriate to their line of work with their employees, and isolate words and expressions enough to bring to class for clarification. They began to "hear" more words in Spanish.

From the beginning it was emphasized that not all needs for conversational Spanish could be satisfied in eight weeks. It was established that these were beginning courses to enable the students to continue learning Spanish. It also was emphasized that we were not teaching them Spanish so their employees would not have to learn English, but so they could help their employees learn English by learning together ("I'll teach you some English if you will teach me some Spanish"). The program was called Communicamos, because the college was not teaching Spanish as much as it was teaching communication skills. BRCC asked a Spanish-speaking worker to sit in the class as a resource for first-hand information about vocabulary for the particular site. He/she brought personal experience.

The students have learned some Spanish, but they also have learned gestures and culture and what is valued by Spanish speakers. In one instance, a supervisor was able to use a gesture he learned to prevent a worker from doing something dangerous. One of the most enlightening bits of information for these students has been their own feeling of oddness at saying unfamiliar words, which has allowed them to experience the emotions their international employees feel on venturing to speak English.

The course called for creative scheduling, flexibility and reassessment of teaching methods. In the first two years of the partnership, six people completed Level 3, 37 people completed Level 2, and 130 people completed Level 1. Six Hispanics completed Level 1 of the same course but learned English. There were six people of varying levels of study who completed an eight-week study. In addition to those served at the plants, three people from one plant enrolled in credit classes at BRCC.

For the 1993-94 academic year, the third year of the grant, nine people from the three companies were enrolled in Spanish 195 (Basic Communications) for two credits. After two semesters, they will have the equivalency of Spanish 101. At BRCC the language offerings have increased and now include five Spanish courses, a French for Conversation course, two German courses and a Russian course, in addition to a non-credit Russian for Conversation course.

In 1992 the Conversational Spanish for the Poultry Industry program was awarded a certificate of recognition by Virginia Polytechnic Institute & State University at its Excellence in Education Conference. The instructor has given presentations at the Community Colleges Humanities Association and the Foreign Language Association of Virginia, and was invited to introduce the program at Georgia Tech's Safety Workshop for the Poultry Industry in June 1992. The program has been highlighted in news magazines from each of the companies and was mentioned in the Virginia Community College System's Business Partnerships, 1991-92 Annual Report.

Contact:
Nell G. Tiller, Instructor
(703) 234-9261

Blue Ridge Community College
Box 80
Weyers Cave, VA 24486
Total head count enrollment-Credit: 1,391; Non-Credit: 2,671
Campuses/sites: 1; Full-time faculty: 42

QUALITY FIRST

▓ *The program has helped produce a documented savings* ▓
of at least $5-million among participating companies

The Quality First program at Central Virginia Community College (CVCC) challenges business and industry to set aside traditional ways of doing business to achieve a "quality revolution." A joint effort between Region 2000 and CVCC, Quality First is based on the management principles of Dr. W. Edwards Deming.

Organizations send project teams of four to six people to the college for a full day, every other week, for a total eight sessions over a 16-week period. The teams plan, execute and evaluate a quality-improvement project of significance to their organization. A "Quality First" class – known as a "Track" – is composed of five of these teams, so that a typical track roster numbers 25 to 30 people. Each session features "live" and videotaped lectures, demonstrations, team-building, problem-solving and project management exercises. At the conclusion of the program, each team presents a status report of its quality improvement project to its management and interested members of the Region 2000 community.

CVCC reports that 88 teams representing 513 individuals from area businesses, hospitals and public agencies have completed the program since it began in March of 1990. The program helps companies focus their quality plans on system or process improvement. A documented savings of more than $5-million has been realized by participating companies.

CVCC's program was started with seed money from the regional economic improvement group, REGION 2000, which earned an award from the Virginia Council on Vocational Education for its support of the Quality First program.

Contact:
Roger W. Beeker
(804) 386-4530

Central Virginia Community College
3506 Wards Road
Lynchburg, VA 24502-2498
Total head count enrollment-Credit: 4,077; Non-Credit: 4,468
Campuses/sites: 1; Full-time faculty: 60

CREATING A NEW EDUCATIONAL ENVIRONMENT

▓ *Business, labor, government and industrial representatives participate in development,* ▓
marketing and policy-making for the tech prep consortium

Tech Prep is creating a new cooperative educational environment for the Tech Prep Region 2000 Area Educational Consortium. Business, labor, government and industrial representatives are participating in the curriculum development, marketing efforts and policy-making committees in partnership arrangements with the local educational agencies.

These task forces are helping to develop close relationships not only with the business and industry representatives, but also with school counselors, parents, students, academic teachers, vocational teachers and school administrators. The consortium comprises the school divisions in the counties of Amherst, Appomattox, Bedford and Campbell and the cities of Bedford and Lynchburg, in full cooperation with Central Virginia Community College. "Educators must know what is needed in their product (a graduate) by the prospective employers, while the business and industry community must explain to educators how their product (the graduate) is arriving in the work force. It is essential that the product being produced meets the demands of the consumer," explains Richard B. Carter, Sr., a recently retired superintendent of schools who is now the Tech Prep coordinator for the consortium.

The atmosphere among the participants in the Tech Prep Region 2000 Area Educational Consortium is an improvement in our educational system, not, "Let's bash the educational system." Says Jeff Taylor, Program Director for Virginia's Region 2000: "What we need is to consolidate our resources to meet the changing demands of our rapidly changing technological work world."

Contact:
Richard B. Carter
(804) 386-4511

Central Virginia Community College
3506 Wards Road
Lynchburg, VA 24502-2498
Total head count enrollment-Credit: 4,077; Non-Credit: 4,468
Campuses/sites: 1; Full-time faculty: 60

PULP AND PAPER TECHNOLOGY

The program includes course work in such things as papermaking, processes of pulping, pulp and paper mill maintenance, and environmental problems

The Pulp and Paper Technology program at Dabney S. Lancaster Community College is the only one of its kind in the southeastern United States and one of only five associate degree level programs in this field in the nation. It is ideal for Virginia, where the paper industry ranks as one of the state's top 10 employers, according to a study at the University of Virginia. The three largest employers in the paper and allied products industry are Union Camp (3,000 employees), Westvaco (2,600 employees), and Chesapeake Corporation (1,900 employees). The introduction of high technology into paper and allied product processing in these and other plants has necessitated training of employees in the entire system of pulp and paper processing. The need for paper technicians has grown substantially, and has not been adversely affected by economic fluctuations in other manufacturing industries. America remains the largest producer of paper and allied products in the world.

The AAS program began as a cooperative effort with Westvaco Corporation to train workers at its 1,800 employee mill in nearby Covington. A liberal tuition reimbursement plan for employees served as an incentive for employee participation.

Students complete a 65-semester-hour program leading to an AAS. degree in Pulp and Paper Technology, which includes course work in papermaking, processes of pulping, pulp and paper mill maintenance, converting and printing, instruments and controls, environmental problems, and applied statistical quality control. The program requires 21 semester hours in general education and has an option for a cooperative education course. The program articulates with a bachelor's degree program in Paper Technology at North Carolina State University and a bachelor's degree in Environmental Sciences at SUNY-Syracuse.

A $200,000 federal grant from the Appalachian Regional Commission (ARC) has helped underwrite the cost of instructional lab equipment.

Graduates have been placed at various Virginia paper mills, including Georgia Bonded Fibers, Georgia Pacific, Virginia Fibers, Chesapeake Corporation, Union Camp, and Westvaco. Starting salaries for associate degree graduates range from $25,000 to $35,000 per year.

Contact:
Chuck Bartocci, Program Head
(703) 862-4246

Dabney S. Lancaster Community College
PO Box 1000
Clifton Forge, VA 24422-1000
Total head count enrollment-Credit: 2,599; Non-Credit: 375
Campuses/sites: 1; Full-time faculty: 31

FORESTRY TECHNOLOGY

To make the learning practical, the college operates a small-engine and large-equipment repair shop, a 10-acre farm and an operating sawmill

Forestry and forest-related industries are vital to the economy of Virginia, where 60 percent of the total land acreage is forested. The use of these resources by government agencies, forest industries and land management agencies requires forest technicians trained in forest management, protection, timber harvesting and utilization.

Thus, in 1968, the State Board of Community Colleges approved the AAS degree in Forestry Technology as a one-of-a-kind program to serve the Commonwealth of Virginia. The program is designed to produce technicians who assist forest managers, sawmill operators, wood products and timber harvesters and urban forestry professionals. Recognized nationally, the program meets the educational standards of the Society of American Foresters and enrolls more than 30 majors each year.

Students complete a 73-semester-hour program leading to the AAS degree, with course work in forest and wildlife ecology, dendrology, forest mensuration, forest fire control, timber harvesting, forest products, urban forestry, wildlife and fisheries management, applied silviculture, and sawmilling. The program requires 18 semester hours in general education courses, and a four-semester-hour summer cooperative education course.

To provide practical experience, the college operates a small-engine and large-equipment repair shop, a 10-acre farm and an operating sawmill on the campus. Students also are trained to operate a knuckleboom loader, dump trucks, backhoe loader and crawler tractor. Field trips are scheduled to area national forests and forest laboratories and demonstration sites in Virginia and West Virginia. The Student Forestry Club is one of the most active student

Continues on Page 700

organizations on campus.

Strong linkages exist with government and industry, which provide cooperative education positions and student scholarships. The program has successfully placed graduates throughout Virginia and the nation in positions with state and national forests and with the private sector. Virginia employers include the U.S. Forest Service, the Virginia Game Commission, Westvaco Corporation, Bartlett Tree Company and other private industries.

Contact:
Craig Kaderavek
Milton McGrady, Co-Program Heads
(703) 862-4246

Dabney S. Lancaster Community College
PO Box 1000
Clifton Forge, VA 24422-1000
Total head count enrollment-Credit: 2,599; Non-Credit: 375
Campuses/sites: 1; Full-time faculty: 31

PARENTS' ORIENTATION

Because 90 percent of the college's first-time freshmen were the first in their families to attend college, Danville decided to acquaint parents with the institution

In the summer of 1990, Danville Community College initiated a new program to introduce the parents of first-time students to its campus, programs and services. This program was developed after recognizing that approximately 90 percent of all first-time college freshmen at the college were the first in their families to attend college. The program's goals included:

1) introducing the parents to the mission, goals and objectives of Danville Community College;

2) providing the parents with specific information on the various academic and student support services offered by the college;

3) demonstrating the college's commitment to instruction and to maintaining quality state-of-the-art classrooms and laboratories; and

4) providing the parents with direct contact with college personnel who can assist their son or daughter in the areas of advising, counseling and financial aid.

This orientation program introduces the parents to not only what their son or daughter can expect from the college, but also the parents' role in their son's and/or daughter's ultimate success. Participants are introduced to the college's academic programs and services.

Special emphasis is placed on explaining the benefits of developmental studies in enhancing collegiate success, the objectives of the college's transfer programs and the expected outcomes for students enrolling in the college's many technical fields. The parents are provided detailed information on the cost of attending the college, various options in paying tuition and fees, and a description of available loans. A special emphasis is given to providing information on available financial aid programs and scholarships and about career planning services available through the college's Counseling Center. The parents are then provided with a complete tour of the campus and then invited to join their son or daughter for lunch at the college's Student Center.

The college holds four new student orientation sessions each summer to assist them in the matriculation into the college setting. The first session is in June, two are held in July, and one group meets in August. Each new student orientation session has a corresponding parents' orientation session. The parents are invited to sign up for one of the orientation sessions once their son and/or daughter has registered for one of the new student orientation sessions. The members of the college's administration and staff are assigned various responsibilities for parents' orientation, coordinated by the office of Student Development Services.

In 1990, 219 parents participated in orientation; 231 in 1991; and 253 in 1992. This program was featured at a session during the 1992 Virginia Community College System's deans/provosts meeting.

Contact:
Betty Jo Foster, Dean, Instruction and Student Development
(804) 797-2222

Danville Community College
1008 South Main Street
Danville, VA 24541
Total head count enrollment-Credit: 5,669 Non-Credit: 742;
Campuses/sites: 1; Full-time faculty: 58

ALLIANCE FOR EXCELLENCE

▩ The Alliance engages the leadership and influence of black churches ▩
in promoting higher education to minorities

Alliance for Excellence is a partnership developed by black churches with community colleges for the purpose of increasing opportunities for minorities in higher education. The principle interest for the partnership was how black churches and the local community college might work together in order to encourage broader participation in higher education through local educational opportunities.

Danville Community College is one of four community colleges in south-central Virginia with an Alliance for Excellence Program. Since the advent of the Alliance for Excellence in 1986, minority student participation in higher education at Danville Community College has increased by more than 100 percent. Success in this case is measured by rates of enrollment, retention, graduation and transfer to four-year colleges by black students in comparison with the same rates over the past six years and the same statistics for white majority students.

Support for Alliance for Excellence activities and projects at Danville Community College come primarily from the college in partnership with civic groups and small businesses in the service region. The program has become a model for community support for higher education and was featured in forums at annual conventions of the National Council for Black American Affairs in Atlanta in 1988 and the American Association of Community and Junior Colleges in Washington, D.C. in 1980.

Alliance for Excellence has adopted the following goals:

1) to promote the advancement of minorities through higher education;
2) to collectively engage the educational resources of community colleges, the leadership and influence of black churches, and the cooperation of other organizations for the purpose of offering support services, educational and cultural programs, and sponsoring other efforts which encourage opportunities for minorities in higher education; and
3) to enhance the quality of campus life for minority students and to encourage greater frequency and effectiveness of minority education programs and services.

To accomplish these goals, the following annual projects are implemented:

1) annual motivational seminar for grades K-12;
2) city-wide tutorial programs;
3) career expo;
4) essay Contest during February, Black History Month;
5) Academic Excellence Awards Program to recognize outstanding academic achievement by community college and high school seniors;
6) campus tours;
7) career seminars and workshops; and
8) Executive for Day youth mentoring program that pairs youth with a businessperson/professional.

Alliance for Excellence is organized under the auspices of a regional Board of Directors, who oversees the program at four community colleges. The board works through local community leaders who form an advisory group. A project coordinator is employed by Danville Community College to work with the advisory group to design suitable programs.

The local advisory group consists of representatives from the black community and the Danville Community College. The group has its own officers and program committees. One Regional Board member is designated as the support person for the local project coordinator.

Alliance for Excellence functions under a set of by-laws revised in 1988; is incorporated as a non-profit organization consistent with regulations of section 501(c)3 of the Internal Revenue Code; and is awaiting a tax-exempt determination letter from the IRS. The project coordinator is responsible for overall program planning and implementation in the college's region in cooperation with the local advisory committee.

Contact:
Andrea Burney, Administrative Assistant, Minority Concerns
(804) 797-2222

Danville Community College
1008 South Main Street
Danville, VA 24541
Total head count enrollment-Credit: 5,669 Non-Credit: 742;
Campuses/sites: 1; Full-time faculty: 58

ELECTRONICS PROGRAM ASSESSMENT

Students in their final semester of electronics classes choose a research topic,
prepare a written report and deliver an oral presentation

The Electronics Associate in Applied Science program at Eastern Shore Community College has a unique student outcomes assessment measure. Students in their final semester of electronics classes choose a research topic, prepare a written report and deliver an oral presentation at the end of the second year of studies.

The audience for these presentations is made up of electronics program freshmen and sophomores, alumni, college faculty and staff, members of the electronics community advisory committee, potential employers, and faculty from four-year institutions that accept ESCC electronics students in transfer programs.

Freshman students learn first-hand what their presentations should be like when they complete the second year.

Alumni provide support. Employers and four-year college faculty see potential employees and students present their best work. Community advisory board members serve as raters.

Several program changes have resulted from this method of assessment. More research, writing and oral presentation skills have been added to this technical major.

This capstone assessment project is quite effective in a small program, with fewer than 10 graduates each year. Because the electronics faculty comprises only one full-time faculty member and part-time lab instructor, outside raters broaden the base of evaluation. Community involvement enhances both recruitment and placement activities for the electronics program.

Contact:
Marykay Mulligan, Director, Academic Division
John Floyd, Lead Instructor
(804) 787-5900

Eastern Shore Community College
29300 Lankford Highway
Melfa, VA 23410
Total head count enrollment-Credit: 976; Non-Credit: 636
Campuses/sites: 1; Full-time faculty: 15

ADULT BASIC EDUCATION

Among the college's partners helping deliver adult basic education are Head Start,
the departments of social services and two public school systems

Eastern Shore Community College has established numerous partnerships for delivery of adult basic education, including family literacy classes and basic skills classes.

Among the partnerships are agreements with Head Start for the delivery of family literacy classes and with the departments of social services of Accomack and Northampton counties for JOBS classes. Partnerships were strengthened with the two public school systems, which provide no-cost sites for family literacy classes. The college also continued its relationships with the Virginia Department of Transportation for a basic skills class and the Virginia Employment Commission, the Community Services Board, and the Private Industry Council for GED preparation classes.

For the 1991-1992 year, 420 adults accumulated nearly 34,000 instructional hours (75 FTEF) in 27 classes taught by one full-time and 11 part-time faculty at seven sites

throughout a 22-county (620 sq. mi.) service area. The number of participants increased by 15 percent over the previous year. Based on 1990 census data, 3.4 percent of the target population was served by adult basic education (literacy), GED preparation, and ESL classes.

Students averaged 80 hours of attendance and a 1.0 grade level improvement in reading, English or math skills. The Eastern Shore Literacy Council, which uses no-cost office and tutoring space on campus that is provided by community volunteers, offers an additional 1,100 hours of individualized tutoring to 35 low-level readers.

Expenses total $105,000 for the year – or about $3.08 per student instructional hour. The program is one of a few situated at community colleges in Virginia and has received numerous recognitions and awards, including a 1990 "Award for Excellence" from the Virginia Council on Coordinating Prevention.

Contact:
Maurine Dooley
(804) 787-5900

Eastern Shore Community College
29300 Lankford Highway
Melfa, VA 23410
Total head count enrollment-Credit: 976; Non-Credit: 636
Campuses/sites: 1; Full-time faculty: 15

THE GERMANNA GUARANTEE

The tuition guarantee program is designed to insure that no qualified student is denied educational opportunity due to financial need

Germanna Community College wants to encourage young people to dream of going to college, that is, even if they don't have the money.

Under a tuition assistance program begun in 1991, Germanna enabled 28 students from eight area high schools to begin their college educations. For the 1992-93 school year, the program distributed $40,000 to 76 students.

Known as the Germanna Guarantee Program, the effort is designed to guarantee that no qualified student will be denied educational opportunity due to financial need. The program aims to inform students and parents alike as early as the sixth grade that a college education is within their financial grasp.

The program is sponsored by the Germanna Educational Foundation, which solicits donations, both large and small, from individuals and businesses. Sponsors are encouraged to become "full partners" by giving the entire amount needed to help one student. During the program's first year, a donation of $1,500 paid for a student's books and tuition. By 1992-93, the cost was $1,750.

The program is directed to students of the college's eight-county service region and the city of Fredericksburg.

Top grades are not a requirement. A student must show, however, the ability and motivation to complete a degree or certificate program at Germanna.

Aside from the financial benefits afforded by the Germanna Guarantee program, students receive a lot of personal encouragement as well.

"We hope to encourage their belief in their own abilities and to give them a concrete incentive to achieve," said Joe Daniel, president of the Germanna Educational Foundation. Daniel said he believes the program will help "catch" those students who might otherwise "fall through the cracks."

Daniel said the program also provides businesses "with a workable plan for becoming actively involved in supporting education. We'd like to see business people take a personal interest in encouraging these young folks along their way."

A report from the U.S. General Accounting Office supports the philosophy behind the Germanna Guarantee Program. According to the report, "early intervention, personal mentoring, and intensive academic help linked with tuition assistance guarantee programs appear to be key variables to increasing the chances of academic success for disadvantaged youth."

Contact:
Susan Scott Neal, Public Information Office
(703) 423-1333

Germanna Community College
PO Box 339
Locust Grove, VA 22508
Total head count enrollment-Credit: 3,420; Non-Credit: 1,238
Campuses/sites: 1; Full-time faculty: 37

THE CULPEPER ALLIANCE

The input of area major employers is regularly used when creating credit and non-credit courses, as well as seminars, for the private sector

When different industries need training for their employees, their needs are often the same. Germanna Community College helps serve those common needs via the Culpeper Alliance, an organization of industry executives whose goal is to promote economic development through training programs.

The alliance consists of representatives from 10 major employers in Culpeper County who meet regularly with Germanna's director of continuing education to discuss training needs. Out of those meetings come both credit and non-credit courses, one-day seminars and other programs designed to meet the specific needs of local business, industry and government.

In addition to a variety of business and computer classes, the college has offered courses in such subjects as personal financial planning, dealing with difficult people, hazardous waste management and cardio-pulmonary resuscitation.

Besides promoting good relations between the college and business community, the Culpeper Alliance makes it easier for Germanna to provide the types of training most needed by area businesses. "Rather than shooting in the dark and offering this class or that class, we know exactly what their needs are," said Dr. Kay Kincer, Germanna's division chair for business sciences, technologies and nursing.

Continues on Page 704

An indirect benefit to the college, she said, is that Germanna's faculty members are exposed to the actual work force that their students will enter. "The interaction gives us good ideas for our degree program and helps us better prepare our students for the work force," she said.

Contact:
Susan Scott Neal, Public Information Office
(703) 423-1333

Germanna Community College
PO Box 339
Locust Grove, VA 22508
Total head count enrollment-Credit: 3,420; Non-Credit: 1,238
Campuses/sites: 1; Full-time faculty: 37

J. SARGEANT REYNOLDS COMMUNITY COLLEGE

PAVE: PROGRAM FOR ADULTS IN VOCATIONAL EDUCATION

PAVE offers adults with mild mental disabilities a two-year, non-transferable credit, career studies program

J. Sargeant Reynolds Community College piloted for the state's community college system a continuing education program for the mildly mentally retarded. The primary focus of the project, as requested by parents and the community, was to provide job skill training. In 1987, the Virginia General Assembly funded the Program for Adults in Vocational Education (PAVE).

Studies show that there are approximately 104,500 students receiving special education, of which approximately 24,000 are 15 years of age or older. An estimated 5,000 students are exiting the system each year. Many of these students require a transfer of service responsibility from education to other agencies and need a variety of services in order to achieve employment and independence. It has become apparent that the need for vocational programs and services for special needs learners greatly exceeds the currently available resources. The social benefits, however, of providing appropriate effective opportunities will far exceed the costs of providing such services.

PAVE is a vocational training program for adults with mild mental disabilities. It is a two-year, non-transferable credit, career studies program. Application is made to the college and the program. There are no tuition stipends; however, all students may apply for financial assistance through the Financial Aid office or the Virginia Department of Rehabilitative Services (DRS). Certificates on the assistant level are currently offered in the areas of Food Preparation, General Housekeeping, Clerical, and Child Care. All of the certificate programs have an internship during the last semester and job placement assistance coordinated with DRS.

The entrance criteria require that all students complete a high school or other educational program. They should also submit a recommendation by a school or counselor, and submit a vocational assessment. They must possess social skills necessary to function independently, demonstrate mobility skills necessary to transport themselves to and from the college, and the student must demonstrate the ability to benefit.

Contact:
Norma Bolling, Program Director
(804) 371-6486

J. Sargeant Reynolds Community College
PO Box 85622
Richmond, VA 23285-5622
Total head count enrollment-Credit: 21,119
Campuses/sites: 3; Full-time faculty: 148

JOHN TYLER COMMUNITY COLLEGE

CAREER STUDIES CERTIFICATE IN FINE ARTS

The curriculum exposes students interested in a career in the arts to opportunities available and helps them develop appropriate capabilities

Many students are interested in pursuing careers in the arts but have limited understanding of either the occupational options or the skills expected in the profession. A more cohesive fine arts curriculum at John Tyler Community College exposes them to the career opportunities available while enabling them to develop appropriate capabilities.

This approach contrasted sharply with two decades of merely educating a population of persons interested solely in their personal artistic development. The emerging interest in professional training and preparation for continued study at the baccalaureate level precipitated the implementation of the Career Studies Certificate in Fine Arts program in 1992.

The purpose of this Certificate is to provide occupational and technical training and to parallel the first year of study, or Art Foundation, of a Bachelor of Fine Arts degree. This foundation is usually the same and required for all students in baccalaureate programs regardless of whether their intended major is commercial art, fashion or interior design, painting, printmaking, sculpture or mixed media.

There is an increasing number of students at John Tyler Community College interested in or actually applying to four-year art programs, notably Virginia Commonwealth University's School of the Arts, where several of John Tyler's students have already been accepted. A more coherent structure of study enhances their chances for successful transfer and encourages additional students to begin their study of art at John Tyler.

VCU has been recommending John Tyler's currently informal art program to their overflow applicants – significant evidence of their confidence in our art curriculum and instruction. The college is now better-positioned to accommodate students seeking a credentialed Art Foundation curriculum comparable to that at VCU. In fact, this curriculum has already been formally accepted by VCU's nationally ranked School of the Arts as equivalent to their Art Foundation freshman year for art majors.

As a requirement of the final Supervised Study (ART 195), students must develop and submit a portfolio of their art work for approval by the instructor, and suitable for presentation, before a Certificate is awarded. The curriculum requirements, totaling 33 credits are:

- History and Appreciation of Art I and II, 6 credits;
- College Composition I and II, 6 credits;
- Introduction to the Arts I and II, 6 credits;
- Drawing I and II, 6 credits;
- Fundamentals of Design I and II, 6 credits; and
- Supervised Study: Portfolio Development, 3 credits.

Contact:
Michelle Morris, Assistant Professor
(804) 796-4102

John Tyler Community College
Chester, VA 23831
Total head count enrollment-Credit: 8,971
Campuses/sites: 3; Full-time faculty: 72

JOHN TYLER COMMUNITY COLLEGE

INSTRUMENTATION ENGINEERING TECHNOLOGY

The instrumentation curriculum, which has changed at a harrowing rate, continues to do so with the assistance of local industry

The Instrumentation Engineering Technology Program at John Tyler Community College is designed to provide local industry with well-trained instrument technicians and technologists ready to install and maintain industrial measurement and control equipment.

It evolved from an instrumentation class that was added to the electronics program in 1980. A separate degree curriculum created in 1983 continues to the present, following many program changes designed to better train the graduating technicians for the latest in classical control technology. Day and evening classes are offered in order to provide full-time and part-time students the class times best suited to their individual schedules.

Students completing the program will have the skills to secure a well-paying job today and for the future, because control of processes by instrumentation is ever-increasing. Lifelong learning is emphasized in classes, necessary for technician knowledge and ability in an ever-changing industrial controls environment. Basic and advanced analog and digital electronics classes provide the basics for the instrumentation classes. Math, physics, English, and social sciences prepare a well-rounded individual who becomes an asset to society.

The instrumentation classes initially provided education in pneumatic and analog electronic instruments that measure and control industrial levels, pressures, temperatures, flows and product compositions. The past 10 years have seen a major shift from pneumatics to analog and digital electronics measurement and control systems. The instrument curriculum has changed at a harrowing rate along with industry. Digital measurement and control comprised 45 percent of the instrumentation class material in 1992. Change is continuing through the assistance of local industry.

A close partnership with local industry and business through advisory committees is a major hallmark at John Tyler Community College. From the inception of the instrument program the Electronics/Instrumentation Advisory Committee has provided development leadership and material support to the program. More than $150,000 in urged equipment has been given to JTCC by the committee members companies. Two technicians from ICU Americans were paid regular wages by the company for two weeks to help build a controlled process and control board. Several complete training units were

Continues on Page 706

supplied by local industry.

The committee determined in 1989 that the program needed motor and motor control classes within the curriculum to train students in the latest digital and computer control of motors. A matching grant totaling $150,000 was received from the National Science Foundation in 1991 to acquire six complete motor laboratory stations compatible with digital controllers and computer interface equipment. Computers interfaced to the motor's equipment help students plot operating and

control characteristics of AD, DC, and specialty motors. Computers and programmable controllers are used to control motor operating parameter. This enhancement is leading the way toward another degree in industrial electricity/electronics as requested by the advisory committee.

The program includes three full-time and several adjunct instructors teaching electronics and instrumentation in addition to those providing education in the related studies.

Contact:
Daniel Coake, Instructor
(804) 796-4185

John Tyler Community College
Chester, VA 23831
Total head count enrollment-Credit: 8,971
Campuses/sites: 3; Full-time faculty: 72

LORD FAIRFAX COMMUNITY COLLEGE

"ON WITH THE SHOW"

The National Collegiate Alcohol Awareness Week included substantive efforts to drive home the dangers of alcohol abuse

"On With the Show" was the theme for National Collegiate Alcohol Awareness Week at Lord Fairfax Community College. The theme was selected because many of the events held during the college's Alcohol Awareness Week activities were "performances" rather than "lectures."

Planning for the 1991 Alcohol Awareness Week was accomplished by the Drug Prevention Coordinator and PANDA (Peers Against Alcohol and Drug Abuse), the newly formed BACCHUS (Boost Alcohol Consciousness Concerning the Health of University Students) group. The group is also responsible for planning educational and social programs throughout the year.

To ensure success of NCAAW, several activities were held prior to the beginning of the fall 1991 semester:

- a one-week Group Facilitators Workshop trained 25 participants to facilitate support groups, with special emphasis on working with "at risk" youth;
- the "Spotlight on Leadership" conference, attended by more than 60 people, educated participants on topics such as burnout, stress and managing conflict;
- a team of peer educators attended the Virginia Intervention Education Weekend (VIEW) conference and learned substance abuse prevention strategies, marketing, communication and leader-

ship skills. This team developed the action plan for the 1991-1992 school year;

- highlighter pens were distributed to each new student who attended the New Student Registration Workshops. "Highlighting Your Life... LFCC" with the Drug Prevention Office number printed on the pens;
- LFCC requires all students to attend a one-credit orientation class that provides a five-hour alcohol and drug module along with viewing videos;
- "The Wall" was built with red paper bricks; on each brick was a statement of how alcohol abuse had affected the lives of students and staff; and
- a column with facts on alcohol abuse in the college student population is included in the weekly campus newsletter.

All these activities contributed to the success of LFCC's Alcohol Awareness Week.

The drug and alcohol awareness week programs at Lord Fairfax Community College received national attention for its creativity, leadership and commitment to educating students, faculty and staff of the effects of substance abuse. Lord Fairfax was one of three schools recognized for Drug Awareness Week and one of six schools recognized for outstanding alcohol awareness events. The national awards are sponsored by the Inter-Association Task Force on

Alcohol and Other Substance Abuse Issues.

The drug and alcohol prevention program was also involved in the Virginia Governor's Conference, a college drug prevention consortium, and was a member of an area drug prevention community board.

Contact:
Susan Collins, Director, Student Support
(703) 869-1120

Lord Fairfax Community College
PO Box 47
Middletown, VA 22645
Total head count enrollment-Credit: 4,020; Non-Credit: 1,830
Campuses/sites: 2; Full-time faculty: 38

MOBILE COMPUTER CLASSROOM

The mobile classroom plays a vital role in making work force training, credit courses, seminars and workshops available to area residents

Lord Fairfax Community College takes very seriously its designation as a COMMUNITY college. LFCC strives to make high quality, low-cost education accessible to all residents of the Northern Shenandoah Valley. The college expands the educational opportunities by taking classrooms to people when it is difficult or impossible for them to come to the Middletown campus.

College instructors regularly set up classrooms on the premises of businesses and institutions throughout the area and teach a variety of courses. However, a classroom for teaching the use of computers cannot be set up off-campus, for it must be designed for and equipped with computers, printers, and other equipment and materials. This kind of classroom must be mobile, and LFCC's solution is the new Mobile Computer Classroom.

Critical shortages of qualified workers are predicted for the 1990's as the American economy shifts from goods-producing to service-producing industries. There is a great need to upgrade the skills of the current work force and to train new workers in order to meet the demands of new, high-tech jobs. The LFCC Mobile Computer Classroom plays a vital role in making this training accessible to area residents by providing:

- basic literacy training programs;
- jobs training programs designed to meet the specific training needs of individual industries and businesses; and
- workplace literacy programs focused on the basic skills training that workers need to gain new employment, to retain a present job, to advance in their careers or to increase productivity.

This classroom, which is installed in a 37-foot recreational vehicle, is equipped with 12 IBM microcomputer stations, one printer, a television monitor, appropriate software, and other equipment and materials. The Mobile Computer Classroom allows LFCC to bring classes and workshops requiring computer use to businesses, industries, and other sites within the area served by the college.

The ability to present off-campus instructional programs using microcomputer technology is a tremendous asset in helping LFCC fulfill its mission to serve all the residents in its service region. Schools, businesses and individuals can all benefit from the accessibility provided by the Mobile Computer Classroom.

The Mobile Computer Classroom offers courses for college credit, short courses, and seminars and workshops.

With the Mobile Computer Classroom, Lord Fairfax Community College is continuing its partnership with area industries and businesses to help meet the challenge of developing a skilled, competitive work force.

The Lord Fairfax Community College Educational Foundation purchased the $165,000 classroom for the college. Potomac Edison donated the $64,000 computer equipment for the project.

Lord Fairfax Community College's Mobile Computer Classroom was among 10 community college programs that received recognition as 1991 Exemplary Programs and Services from the American Association of Community and Junior College's Small/Rural Community Colleges Commission.

Contact:
Ronald Ludwick, Director, Continuing Education
(703) 869-1120

Lord Fairfax Community College
PO Box 47
Middletown, VA 22645
Total head count enrollment-Credit: 4,020; Non-Credit: 1,830
Campuses/sites: 2; Full-time faculty: 38

SMALL BUSINESS DEVELOPMENT CENTER

*▓ The Center provides, among other things, networking assistance, active ▓
participation in conferences, and a business planning workbook*

The Small Business Development Center at Mountain Empire Community College enhances the economic development of southwest Virginia by providing management and technical assistance to small businesses in order to help them to prosper and increase job opportunities.

Since the Center opened in 1991, more than 250 businesses have been served. New capital investment in excess of $3-million has been made by these businesses into the local economy through assistance provided by the Small Business Development Center.

The Mountain Empire Community College SBDC is part of a southwest Virginia consortium comprising three community colleges and a research university. The program is a cooperative effort of the educational community, the private sector, and federal, state and local governments. The Center is operated by a director, volunteers and secretarial assistance. Qualified individuals recruited from professional and trade associations, the legal and banking communities, academia, chambers of commerce, and SCORE (the Service Corps of Retired Executives) are among those who donate their services.

The Small Business Development Center's assistance is tailored to the local community and the needs of individual clients. It develops services in cooperation with local Small Business Administration district offices to ensure statewide coordination of other available resources. It is a non-profit organization which offers it services at no charge. The Center is funded by the U.S. Small Business Administration, the Virginia Department of Economic Development, and the counties of Dickenson, Lee, Scott and Wise, and the City of Norton.

The goals of the Center are to:

1) provide quality, in-depth counseling to existing businesses which have the potential to impact in a positive manner upon the economy of the Commonwealth of Virginia through the creation of additional jobs and the maintenance of existing jobs;

2) provide effective and efficient assistance to pre-business and start-up ventures through the most effective means available;

3) reduce the failure rate of small businesses in the Commonwealth; and

4) assist small businesses to improve management skills and their ability to generate profit.

In carrying out its purpose, the Center engages in: providing networking assistance; active participation in conferences, symposia, and forums; providing a business planning workbook for start-up efforts; maintaining comprehensive literature sources; providing resource lists of federal and state governments and the private sector; utilizing computer software to provide sensitivity analysis of potential new ventures; and conducting workshops on innovation, entrepreneurship and new venture development. The Center also provides a package to the potential entrepreneur to evaluate the most important factors related to success of a new enterprise; assists in coordinating preliminary patent searching; provides off-the-shelf materials on how businesses can improve their productivity, quality and competitiveness; provides informative reports on numerous related topics; makes available information and techniques for the development of economic profiles and comparisons; evaluates various sources of financing; and provides training and counseling on federal procurements.

Contact:
Tim Blankenbecler, Center Director
(703) 523-2400

Mountain Empire Community College
PO Drawer 700
Big Stone Gap, VA 24219
Total head count enrollment-Credit: 3,822; Non-Credit: 3,005
Campuses/sites: 1; Full-time faculty: 50

GOVERNOR'S MATH AND SCIENCE SCHOOL

*▓ The school, part of the Young Scholars Program of the National Science Foundation, ▓
is for high school students exceptionally talented in science and math*

In 1993, Mountain Empire Community College (MECC) completed its ninth summer magnet school in math and science for area high school students. This nationally and state recognized exemplary program is the result of the cooperative efforts of secondary and post secondary educational institutions, state and federal agencies, and a dedicated directorship.

The Governor's School targets 60 high-ability high

school students from the rural, four-county service area of the college who are exceptionally motivated and talented in the fields of science and mathematics. Students participate in one of three programs of study: microbiology and environmental science, chemistry and physical science, and mathematics and computer science. More than half of the program participants are women.

Since 1988, the school has been part of the Young Scholars Program of the National Science Foundation. Mountain Empire Community College was the first community college to receive funding under this program. The program has been named as one of the exemplary programs among the Commonwealth's summer Governor's Schools. The Nelco foundation, in recognition of the program, has provided a high resolution computer system.

Three MECC professors serve as instructors, one also serving as the director of the program. Five area high school teachers and five college students assist as staff members, and three college professors serve as mentors to the students, one for each program area. Students are provided with a stipend. Program funding is provided by the Virginia Department of Education, the National Science Foundation, Mountain Empire Community College, and the local public school system.

The program is noted for its "hands-on" approach. Research activities include:

1) the study of microbial activity in various mine-soil mixes at the Powell River Project where coal mines

reclamation techniques are being studied;

2) chemical and geological study of acid-mine drainage in the coal fields of southwest Virginia, with on-site investigations of the impact on local streams conducted by the Virginia Department of Mines, Minerals and Energy; and

3) investigations in the recent mathematical discoveries in the field of dynamical systems, chaos and fractions. Students use scientific calculators and computer graphics.

Field trips include the laboratories of Oak Ridge Associated Universities at Oak Ridge, Tennessee; the Virginia Water Resources Research Center at Virginia Polytechnic Institute and State University; assimilated study of utility rate issues at the Appalachian Power Company; a tour and discussion of lake ecology at Smith Mountain Lake and Dam; and a visit to the Engineering, Mathematics and Computer Science Department at VPI & SU.

Throughout the four-week program, students keep a daily written journal of their activities. A writing workshop is conducted which emphasizes scientific writing. Formal written lab reports and a final research paper are required. Scientific photography is introduced to the students. All students are provided information on various scientific careers and students complete a career assessment inventory and develop a career preparation report. Follow-up activities are planned for the academic year which include plans for participation in science fairs.

Contact:
Chris Allgyer, Director
(703) 523-2400

Mountain Empire Community College
PO Drawer 700
Big Stone Gap, VA 24219
Total head count enrollment-Credit: 3,822; Non-Credit: 3,005
Campuses/sites: 1; Full-time faculty: 50

NEW RIVER COMMUNITY COLLEGE

COMPREHENSIVE SERVICES FOR STUDENTS WITH DISABILITIES

Among the services is a Center for the Hearing Impaired that offers support so that deaf and hard-of-hearing students may enroll in any college program

A comprehensive array of services for students with disabilities is offered at New River Community College.

The services include a Learning Achievement Program (LEAP), which provides academic, tutoring and counseling support services to some 125 students. Services are tailored to the needs of identified learning-disabled students in order that they may enroll and achieve in any existing college program of study. NRCC's program has been singled out by the University of Wisconsin and others as one of the top programs of its type in the United States.

Of equal importance and distinction, New River Community College plays a special role in providing educational access to hearing-impaired students. It is one

of only two community colleges in Virginia and one of relatively few in the United States to provide a full-fledged Center for the Hearing Impaired. The Center offers support services to deaf and hard-of-hearing students in order that they may enroll in any of the college's existing programs of study. Some 30 deaf and hearing-impaired students are currently enrolled at NRCC.

Other services available to students with disabilities include a special tutoring program staffed by volunteers, a federally funded Special Student Services (Title IV HEA) Program; remedial English, math, and reading programs; services for students with ambulatory or other physical

Continues on Page 710

disabilities; and special counseling services.

Students with disabilities receive the following academic, tutoring, and counseling support services in a supportive, caring environment:

- pre-registration advising and campus orientation;
- individual and small group counseling;
- instructional technology to support special needs (such as individualized learning through computer-assisted instruction, videotapes and self-paced media for the learning disabled);
- small group seminars focusing on time management, priority setting, study techniques, social/interpersonal skills and other topics; and
- classroom intervention strategies such as taped lectures, untimed tests, and note-takers and interpreters.

New River regularly provides technical assistance to other institutions. This includes consulting, site visitations, sharing of manuals and resource materials and other assistance.

Institutions and organizations receiving such assistance have included Blue Ridge Community College, Texas Christian University, County College of Morris (NJ), Virginia Highlands Community College, Virginia Tech, Ferrum College, St. Petersburg Junior College, Wytheville Community College and the Health Resource Center of the American Council on Education.

The college also participates in the Post Secondary Education Consortium sponsored by the University of Tennessee, through which expertise on education for the hearing impaired is shared with institutions throughout the southeastern United States. Through the consortium, each of nine affiliate programs conducts on-site peer reviews as well as on-site monitoring visits on each campus.

In 1992, NRCC was recognized by AACJC and the National Organization on Disability as one of two community colleges in the United States providing exemplary services for students with disabilities. The college has also earned recognition from several other organizations in this area.

Contact:
Douglas Warren, Dean, Instruction and Student Services
(703) 674-3600

New River Community College
PO Box 1127
Dublin, VA 24084
Total head count enrollment-Credit: 6,207; Non-Credit: 2,491
Campuses/sites: 1; Full-time faculty: 65

NEW RIVER COMMUNITY COLLEGE

TOTAL QUALITY LEARNING RESOURCES

Each summer the entire staff goes on a retreat to evaluate the year's efforts and to develop or adjust the five-year plan

A total quality management effort has fostered an atmosphere of trust and teamwork at New River Community College. This climate:

- enhances the problem-solving and decision-making capabilities of employees;
- better uses the unique skills and talents of employees;
- improves communication between employees and among departments;
- pushes decision-making down to the most appropriate level;
- improves job satisfaction;
- increases employee knowledge levels; and
- improves the level and quality of products and services.

The efforts began with a commitment to quality and the empowerment of employees. A shared vision for the program was developed by employees that describes how the organization wants to be known. Staff development is a major emphasis of the process. Seminars and workshops are conducted for staff on topics such as personality style, listening, teamwork, data collection and analysis and problem-solving. Employees are encouraged to learn more about themselves and about each other so that they can better work together as a team. Employees and depart-

ments are encouraged to take ownership of their jobs and operations while working together as a team. Teamwork is stressed and various types of teams including quality circles, project teams, action teams, cross-functional work teams and self-managed work teams have been used to attack problems and seek meaningful solutions.

Planning for success is a major component of the total quality effort and including all employees in that process is stressed. The organization collects data on its efforts and benchmarks itself against other programs and organizations. Data are analyzed and appropriate actions are taken to keep the program moving toward its vision. Each summer the entire staff goes on a retreat to evaluate the year's efforts and to develop or adjust the program's five-year plan. The organization always seeks continuous improvement of its efforts.

Since the total quality effort began, New River Community College has received 10 national and state awards for excellence in service and products provided by the Learning Resources Program. Included in these honors is the prestigious United States Senate Productivity Award. Additionally, the program was recognized as one of a select group of exemplary learning resources programs in two-year community colleges in the country. Specific results include: implementation of a tutoring and note-taking program emphasizing volunteerism, which accounted for more than 9,100 hours of tutoring and 7,490 hours of note-taking; a microcomputer-based Learning Resource Center automation system; a library collection development plan which generated $110,000 in private funding; a distance education program which utilized video stores to deliver telecourses; a self-sufficient photocopying service; nationally recognized video production efforts; and a work-study training program which saves over $42,000 annually.

Contact:
Tom Wilkinson, Director, Learning Resources & Instructional Technology
(703) 674-3625

New River Community College
PO Box 1127
Dublin, VA 24084
Total head count enrollment-Credit: 6,207; Non-Credit: 2,491
Campuses/sites: 1; Full-time faculty: 65

VALUING CULTURAL DIVERSITY

*❋ The college joined with the CIA to establish ❋
a cultural diversity course for the agency*

A workplace culture demonstrates both the dynamic and the subtle, the obvious and the elusive, the conscious and the unconscious forces that shape behaviors in the organization. Employees and managers create interrelationships and additional dynamics in accordance with their differing backgrounds of race, heritage, education, religion, economic and social circumstances. Finding a shared sense of direction for an organization of such diversity means establishing core values.

In January 1991, the Office of Information Technology (OIT) in the Central Intelligence Agency (CIA) formally announced to employees that concepts for "valuing cultural diversity" would be implemented as a core value for this technical division. To assure positive action, Theodore Clark, Director of OIT, established a Multi-cultural Task Force consisting of representatives from across management, from each ethnic classification in the Agency, and from the varying classifications of the physically challenged.

These actions brought together the unusual team of Mary Arpante, OIT education instructor, who is Cherokee, and Elizabeth Lambert Johns, behavioral scientist and chair of the Division of Social Sciences at Northern Virginia Community College, who is an American. Further established was the educational partnership between the Central Intelligence Agency and Northern Virginia Community College. The result has been a series of three credit-hour courses which show that positive productivity dynamics occur when differences in cultural background are openly explored in an intellectual setting that supports the building of self-esteem. The course explores cultural differences among peoples; the strengths of cultural heritage in a multi-cultural society; and cultural diversity in the workplace.

Classes are conducted on the governmental site. The agency provides educational release time for employee participation in this time-intensive class which runs over a period of three weeks. Because tuition, books, materials and the OIT instructor are supported by the agency, and the college assigns an administrative faculty to co-teach the course, the partnership becomes a highly cost-effective undertaking for both partners.

The end of a recent course finds: a Hispanic explaining taped ballads sung by a grandmother in Central America; a sixth-generation West Virginian proudly displaying ancestral photographs found in an old trunk; several EuroAmerican males from the mid-west sampling "real" southern cooking; African Americans explaining the roots of their linguistic differences; the native American instructor demonstrating the sun dance; and a West Indian tracing her Dutch/Spanish/Italian heritage.

The best observation of this experience was articulated by a Deputy Chief of the Agency: "Today, we are valued for who we are."

Contact:
Elizabeth Lambert Johns
(703) 845-6357

Northern Virginia Community College
4001 Wakefield Chapel Road
Annandale, VA 22003-3796
Total head count enrollment-Credit: 63,605; Non-Credit: 21,470
Campuses/sites: 5; Full-time faculty: 494

NEW PATHWAYS TO A DEGREE
THROUGH DISTANCE LEARNING

Among the students who take the telecourses are the incarcerated or disabled and those who can't reach campus because of congested traffic or professional commitments

Besides providing academic programs to people without access to campus, distance learning technologies help Northern Virginia Community College tap richer and more diverse academic resources such as remote library collections, distant experts, databases, video material and powerful software.

In 1991, the Extended Learning Institute (ELI) of Northern Virginia Community College (NVCC) received funding for a three-year grant program to support the expansion and enrichment of distance learning and collegial experiences that lead to students' attainment of an associate degree. ELI was one of seven projects chosen for funding by the Annenberg/Corporation for Public Broadcasting Project, from the 243 proposals it received from two- and four-year institutions of higher education. The Annenberg/CPB Project's purpose in its New Pathways to a Degree program is to "help colleges use technologies to develop academic programs that are accessible to the New Majority of learners – people with jobs, home responsibilities, and schedules or locations that make full-time study at the campus of their choice difficult or impossible."

To accomplish its project goals, ELI is undertaking two types of activities:
1) the mainstreaming of ELI and its students into the college environment; and
2) the development or revision of 18 courses to offer the highest quality distance education courses leading to an associate degree in either General Studies or Business Administration.

Major grant activities include: the further development of working relationships with NVCC's academic divisions; the use of technology to deliver student development services; provision of remote access to the college's library and to CD-ROM databases; and the use of voice mail, electronic mail, audio conferences and other communications methods for faculty and students.

The ultimate beneficiary of ELI's efforts in this project will be its students, who account for approximately 4,000 course registrations per semester and 3,000 per summer session. They are slightly older than on-campus students, as 46 percent of them are 25 to 44 years old, about 70 percent of them are part-time students, and 66 percent are women. Students include the typical distance learning populations that cannot attend campus classes, such as the incarcerated or disabled, as well as "gridlocked" students who cannot get to campus because of the congested traffic in Northern Virginia and the hectic nature of their professional and personal lives.

ELI's expectation is that a few students will take all of their required degree courses through ELI while the majority will mix distance courses with on-campus courses. For ELI, the college, and the students, this will be the best possible result because it will begin to mainstream ELI and its students into the college community. Students will be able to take advantage of new ELI technologies which ELI will also provide to the campuses.

ELI began in 1975 and entered the grant program with 75 distance education courses based on telecourses, computer conferencing and print-based media. ELI is staffed for its regular activities and the grant by 13.5 support and administrative positions and by 43 faculty (19 FTE) most of whom teach on campus and at ELI. Recognition of this project has included articles in the *Washington Post, Fairfax Journal, Telemedia Monitor, Community College News, Metropolitan Universities Journal*, and in the meeting proceedings of the Association for Educational Communications and Technology.

Contact:
Randal A. Lemke, Director, ELI
(703) 323-3379

Northern Virginia Community College
4001 Wakefield Chapel Road
Annandale, VA 22003-3796
Total head count enrollment-Credit: 63,605; Non-Credit: 21,470
Campuses/sites: 5; Full-time faculty: 494

INFUSING A COLLEGE-WIDE WELLNESS PROGRAM

Students taking the wellness course receive a physical and nutritional assessment using the college's computerized fitness assessment equipment

Patrick Henry Community College is so committed to making wellness a college-wide initiative that wellness has become a general education outcome. Using its curricula, faculty, student development services and physical resources, the college has introduced wellness skills and concepts to both staff and students.

A Student Alternative Life-Style program has been developed which provides a broad-brush approach to wellness for the community college student. The program includes: identifying selected courses in which to infuse wellness content; faculty development in the areas of building student self-esteem and collaborative teaching methods; and programming alternative activities for students, including the development of a "Wellness Center."

Wellness concepts have been infused into the curriculum in the form of both interpersonal skill development through collaborative learning and also through substance abuse and sexuality-related issues (such as sexual assault and AIDS). A Personal Wellness course taken by most students as their health and physical education requirement incorporates a variety of group or collaborative learning experiences which foster interpersonal skill development. Also, students taking this course receive a physical and nutritional assessment using the college's computerized fitness assessment equipment. They are then given a plan to follow for the semester to improve selected areas of fitness as cardiovascular or strength.

Faculty development focused on using collaborative/cooperative learning strategies in the classroom. Assimilating community college students into the college environment is a challenge because most students commute. Often faculty are their only contact. Research supports the notion that student retention and satisfaction is most affected by other student and faculty interaction. Consequently, it is critical that community college faculty use the classroom not only to teach their respective discipline but also to foster an environment which builds student self-esteem and wellness.

Alternative activities for students have been implemented with the help of Student Development Services. Many of these are centered around the college's fitness center. Other alternative activities for the students which have increased student involvement both at the college and in the community include the Peer Helper and Peer Theater programs. Social activities which have been well received by students include take-offs on TV game shows such as the *Dating Game*, *Family Feud* and *Hollywood Squares*, which are held in the school's cafeteria. An annual Wellness Fair brings in members from the community to the college in addition to the students and staff who attend.

Finally, so that faculty and staff have a sense of "we practice what we preach," an employee wellness program, Commonhealth, has brought a number of wellness programs to the college's staff. These programs include monthly seminars ranging from stress management to low-fat cooking. Also included are weekly aerobics classes and staff blood screenings done every 18 months to two years to look at blood cholesterol, glucose and other parameters of physical wellness. These programs have been funded over the years through a combination of college funds, state funds, Title III and FIPSE.

Contact:
Susan Shearer
(703) 638-8777

Patrick Henry Community College
PO Box 5311
Martinsville, VA 24115
Total head count enrollment-Credit: 4,249;
Campuses/sites: 1;Full-time faculty: 35

DEVELOPMENTAL COURSES

Requiring an advisor's signature on a developmental student's registration form reduced the number of misadvised students from 22 percent to 2 percent

Community colleges are the port-of-entry for the majority of first-time college students, many of whom are unprepared for on-level college courses requiring developmental coursework. Patrick Henry Community College realizes the importance of developmental courses and for years has offered students an option of enrolling in developmental courses in English, reading and math. But the college realizes that good instruction alone is not enough for developmental students. The majority of the underprepared, diverse student population served by PHCC require a strong academic support unit if they are going to

Continues on Page 714

be successful.

Therefore, in the fall of 1992, developmental education and academic support services merged, creating a centralized organizational structure. Support services consist of counseling, tutoring and multi-media instructional activities. The developmental faculty and the support staff work as a team to address the numerous needs of the diverse student clientele. Evaluation of the individual services and the process are ongoing and a part of the developmental program.

Two years earlier, in 1990, the college had begun mandatory testing and mandatory placement. The testing component has been relatively easy to implement but the placement was difficult. Approximately 40 percent of students taking the Asset placement test require developmental coursework. Advising is extremely important but many students were being allowed to go into on-level courses without first completing their developmental work. A developmental education assessment committee developed a plan to address this problem that directly affected outcomes assessment and retention.

A system was established identifying a limited number of faculty who would advise developmental students. The advisors consist of counselors, learning specialists and developmental course instructors. To ensure that all developmental students will indeed see the developmental advisors before registering, the students' computer records are coded "developmental" and require a signature of a development advisor before their selected courses are keyed into the on-line advising system. As a result of the implementation of the developmental advising procedure, the number of misadvised developmental students decreased from approximately 22 percent to 2 percent.

Contact:
Carolyn Byrd
(703) 638-8777

Patrick Henry Community College
PO Box 5311
Martinsville, VA 24115
Total head count enrollment-Credit: 4,249;
Campuses/sites: 1;Full-time faculty: 35

PAUL D. CAMP COMMUNITY COLLEGE

EMPLOYEE DEVELOPMENT

❋ *Each curriculum is unique, designed according to the work environment* ❋
and literacy skills and training needed by the employees

Through work force education, participants not only become better employees but also better citizens, consumers and more productive individuals. And when these employees gain basic skills needed to retain jobs, advance in careers or increase productivity, their employers benefit as well. Such valuable training is coordinated through the Office of Employee Development at Paul D. Camp Community College. The Employee Development program serves employers in the cities of Franklin and Suffolk and the counties of Isle of Wight and Southampton.

There is no single curriculum or format for the Employee Development programs. Each is unique in that it is designed according to the work environment and the literacy skills and training needed by the employees. Some are General Education Development (GED) driven, offering employees the opportunity to prepare for the high school equivalency examination, while others teach life skills or are geared specifically to work-related skills.

Employees' needs are assessed and individualized plans are developed based on the goals and objectives of the employees. Flexibility is built into the program. Students progress at their own pace and an open entry/open exit structure is designed to accommodate employees' schedules. Classes are usually held at the work site; enrollment is voluntary.

Costs vary widely depending on the length of the program and the number of classes being offered. For most, the employer pays all of the associated costs. Funding for the Office of Employee Development is provided through Adult Education for the State of Virginia.

The Office of Employee Development at Paul D. Camp Community College, one of five located throughout the Commonwealth, was established in August 1990. Services provided to employers include:

1) determining the educational needs of their employees;
2) developing the appropriate program to meet those needs;
3) acting as a broker for the educational providers; and
4) serving as a liaison between the employer and the educational provider(s).

The Employee Development program has not only provided much-needed educational services to area employers but also has resulted in other benefits. In addition to the increased interaction between educational providers and employers, the communication and ties among the educational providers themselves have been strengthened. A consortium involving the providers has been established and is meeting on a quarterly basis to exchange ideas and information and to explore other cooperative efforts.

Contact:
Carolyn Crowder
(804) 562-2171

Paul D. Camp Community College
PO Box 737
Franklin, VA 23851
Total head count enrollment-Credit: 1,407; Non-Credit: 170
Campuses/sites: 2;Full-time faculty: 24

THE "CAMP" CONNECTION: PARTNERSHIP AT ITS BEST

Due to an annual grant from Union Camp Corporation, about 500 educators have participated in the Educator's Environmental Institute

The "Camp" connection is an exemplary partnership between two Camps: Paul D. Camp Community College and Union Camp Corporation. Since Paul D. Camp's inception more than 20 years ago, Union Camp (a major paper-making company) has been a strong proponent of education, assisting the college in many ways.

First and foremost is their funding of a unique collaborative program – the Educator's Environmental Institute. This Institute provides area educators with information on interrelationships of people and the earth's resources. More specifically, the Institute provides teachers with a basic understanding of ecology that can be shared with the students in their classrooms; resource materials and personnel from whom they can draw information and assistance for their classes; and an opportunity to prepare a project for a specific unit to be covered in their school year.

The summer of 1993 marked the 20th year the Institute has been functioning to serve area K-12 educators with the opportunity for meaningful and useful environmental education. Participants draw on the expertise of consultants from forestry, agriculture, water quality, air quality, pine barren ecology, the Great Dismal Swamp, geology, soils and marine science.

Because of the annual grant from Union Camp Corporation, approximately 500 educators have participated with no cost to them for tuition or supplies. Based on an average of 30 students per teacher, potentially 15,000 students have been introduced to and taught about their environment and issues confronting it. Participants also can receive recertification credit for taking this six-semester class.

This unique program has received two statewide awards: The Excellence in Education Award from Virginia Tech (1988) and the Award for Outstanding Partnership from the State Department of Vocational Education (1989).

Training is another collaborative effort shared between the "Camps." Although Union Camp has an extensive training division, they call on the college for many of their training needs. Each semester, for example, the college provides on-site computer training (beginning and Advanced WordPerfect, D-Base, MS-DOS, Lotus, etc.).

This past academic year the training partnership resulted in a tailor-made Career Studies Certificate (on-site) in Supervisory Management. The eight-class certificate contains five core classes. Participants choose three more from a select list. The eight courses wrap into the college's two-year degree in Management (Industrial Specialization), providing an incentive for continuing study upon completion of the Career Studies Certificate. In fall 1992, PDCCC began teaching Introduction to Business, Human Relations, and Communication in Management on-site at UCC as part of this new program.

Because UCC donated a major portion of the cost of its satellite dish, the college provides a dedicated teleconference room for use by their employees. Subsequently, several UCC employees have earned Masters Degrees in Engineering via live interactive classes from UBA and Virginia Tech – all on-site at Paul D. Camp Community College.

Another collaborative effort with UCC includes the local school system. The idea is to prepare high school students (Tech Prep) for entry into an Industrial Technology track that will prepare the type of workers who will be employable by the paper industry. This project also focuses on assisting the high school dropouts and existing UCC employees in developing necessary skills for job promotion, enhancement and employability.

Also, the UCC/PDCCC connection resulted in a newly developed Basic Skills Program under the direction of the college's Employment Development director. This on-site program is an outstanding model of Virginia's initiative to accommodate workplace literacy needs of business and industry.

The Camp partnership also includes such joint ventures as the annual sponsorship of the Black Managers' Forum. Union Camp also provides the college with an Annual Grant to be used at the college's discretion for student scholarships, business and industry breakfasts and other

Continues on Page 716

activities.

Additionally, UCC employees work with PDCCC on advisory committees as resource people for college students, as teachers and consultants. Their employees also take advantage of on-campus courses and programs (UCC has a tuition-reimbursement program). They also provide a continuing option for cooperative education students. Many PDCCC graduates have received jobs at UCC because of their co-op experiences.

Contact:
Patsy R. Joyner, Director, Community and Continuing Education
(804) 562-2171

Paul D. Camp Community College
PO Box 737
Franklin, VA 23851
Total head count enrollment-Credit: 1,407; Non-Credit: 170
Campuses/sites: 2;Full-time faculty: 24

INTERNATIONAL FESTIVAL

This annual springtime gala includes events that both enhance classroom activities and appeal generally to the wider community

Since 1989, PVCC has celebrated the area's diversity with an international festival. This annual springtime event includes speakers, performances and a food fair. Festival planners draw on the nearby University of Virginia and the larger community for speakers and performers. Area restaurants and community and PVCC student groups participate in the food fair, which grows more popular each year.

The festival is organized by a subcommittee of the college's Curriculum and Instruction Committee. The subcommittee includes faculty from a variety of disciplines and student services staff. Events are planned to enhance classroom activities and to appeal more generally to the wider community. The festival has a budget of approximately $2,000, which provides for honoraria, supplies and a small amount of paid promotion. All events are free; there is a charge only for the food fair.

The festival aims to entertain, to inform, to celebrate and to provide an opportunity for the community to come to campus. Campus and community response clearly indicates that it has been successful.

Contact:
Office of the Dean of Instruction
(804) 977-3900

Piedmont Virginia Community College
Route 6, Box 1
Charlottesville, VA 22902
Total head count enrollment-Credit: 6,850; Non-Credit: 1,338
Campuses/sites: 1;Full-time faculty: 59

PHILOSOPHY IN THE THIRD GRADE

Besides its goal of clear thinking for the children, the program aims to make children, their parents and their teachers more aware of the college

Since 1990, PVCC philosophy instructor Marietta McCarty has visited selected third grades in the college's service region. Spending five sessions with the children at each school, she discusses topics including responsibility, freedom, happiness, fear and prejudice. Children learn to think for themselves and how valuable and powerful their minds are. Care with words and respect for others' opinions are emphasized. At the conclusion of the program, the children come to the college and attend one of Ms. McCarty's classes, sharing ideas and lunch with PVCC philosophy students. Videotapes of the philosophy sessions in the elementary schools and at PVCC are given to each school as a service provided by PVCC.

In addition to its goal of clear thinking for the children, the program aims to make children, their parents and their teachers more aware of PVCC. The program has received high marks from the community and Ms. McCarty has many more requests than she can accommodate with three hours of release time. The program was recognized in 1991 by a statewide program honoring excellence in education.

The program costs include release time and approximately $1,000 a year to pay for videotaping and other operating costs.

Contact:
Marietta McCarty
(804) 977-3900

Piedmont Virginia Community College
Route 6, Box 1
Charlottesville, VA 22902
Total head count enrollment-Credit: 6,850; Non-Credit: 1,338
Campuses/sites: 1;Full-time faculty: 59

EQUAL OPPORTUNITIES FOR EMPLOYABILITY

The program includes weekly support groups covering diverse issues such as racism and sexism, low self-esteem and interview skills

The Equal Opportunities for Employability Program (EOEP) helps reduce barriers and enhance retention for a target group of single parents and displaced homemakers. EOEP attracts prospective students who have a serious desire for life changes and a willingness to make the sacrifices necessary to achieve these changes. Participants function as regular Rappahannock Community College students, while their EOEP participation helps bring about changes in their self-perceptions, goals and lifestyles through support groups, workshops and job placement assistance.

Each campus EOEP is staffed by an 11-month administrative officer and a part-time clerk working in concert with the college student development department staff. EOEP is federally funded through the Carl D. Perkins Vocational Education Act ($75,000 per campus) and supplemented locally by the college board ($2,000 per campus). Funding for EOEP has been renewed annually since first funded in 1986.

The goal of EOEP is to aid participating students in becoming financially self-supporting, self-sufficient members of society through education and the acquisition of marketable vocational skills. EOEP primarily serves women who are single parents, widowed, divorced or separated. Because of their personal situations – often as the result of sudden changes in their lives or because of a family/social circle heritage of financial and educational deprivation – these women find that they are unable to be productive, self-sufficient members of society.

EOEP offers limited reimbursement toward travel and child care expenses as well as tuition and book assistance. The funds EOEP offers in no way approach total reimbursement but do alleviate a small portion of the burden. Financial assistance is not enough for these women to succeed. EOEP tries to look at all the barriers these women face as well as their needs and services as a "pathway with travel assistance" for those seeking changes in their self-perception and life goals.

Financial assistance overcomes only one barrier in the lives of these students. More formidable barriers come from their lack of self-confidence, illiteracy, low self-esteem and unemployment, as well as the racism and sexism they encounter. EOEP offers counseling through mandatory weekly support group sessions covering these issues and a wide variety of other topics from family relationships, academics, health, social and legal issues, and job search and interview skills.

Many of the EOEP participants who would not have been able to enter college without the program have gone on to graduate and find success in the job market. In addition to student success, the project has impacted the community, through improved economic health and gender attitudes. At the college this program helped introduce a gender-fair language policy as well as sensitivity to other aspects of gender equity and sexual harassment. The program also inspired a small annual scholarship from the local Business and Professional Women's Club.

Contact:
Pamela D. Turner, Director, Student Development
(804) 758-5324

Rappahannock Community College
PO Box 287
Glenns, VA 23149
Total head count enrollment-Credit: 3,009; Non-Credit: 886
Campuses/sites: 2;Full-time faculty: 29

INDUSTRIAL TRAINING PARTNERSHIP

The coursework, not specific to one industry, impacts the college, industry and the local labor market

An Industrial Training Partnership has expanded the breadth of vocational-technical education offerings at Rappahannock Community College and enabled it to meet an important occupational need in the community.

It began in 1990, when, recognizing the critical need for industrial maintenance mechanics, the Virginia Department of Economic Development, Chesapeake Corporation and Rappahannock Community College entered into a partnership to provide the training program. Completion of the program leads to a certificate in industrial maintenance. The primary initial purpose of the program was to train industrial mechanics to maintain equipment installed as part of a $125-million expansion at the West Point location of Chesapeake Corporation. This expansion brings not only new technology to the mill but also new products.

This program will increase the number of individuals who are qualified to perform industrial maintenance duties on advanced equipment, and it will encourage employees to see further education as a viable method of keeping pace with a changing workplace. Though initiated with Chesapeake, the coursework is not specific to this one industry. Today industry runs on high technology and the need is great for a skilled work force. On-the-job training is not the option it used to be.

Three areas this program impacts are the college, the industry and the local labor market. Chesapeake Corporation needed to hire 41 maintenance mechanics over the next three years, and the comprehensive training of 38 of those people soon was underway. The financial boost to the local labor market is an estimated payroll for the 41 slots of $1,108,640 per year.

The first class to enter the program was composed exclusively of Chesapeake employees. The next year there were several openings for students straight from high school, employees of other industrial firms, or others interested in pursuing this career. In the third year of the program, a few Chesapeake employees were joined by a majority of students from outside the company; and in the fourth year, enrollment was to be completely open.

In 1991, the partnership was recognized by the Virginia Council on Vocational Education with the presentation of the Business/Industry Partnership Community College Award.

Start-up equipment has been provided in part by Chesapeake. One faculty member's salary was split between Chesapeake, the Department of Economic Development and the college for the first three years. The college assumes full funding responsibilities after the third year for faculty and for maintenance of shops, equipment and supplies.

Contact:
Richard A. Ughetto, Director, Continuing Education
(804) 758-5324

Rappahannock Community College
PO Box 287
Glenns, VA 23149
Total head count enrollment-Credit: 3,009; Non-Credit: 886
Campuses/sites: 2;Full-time faculty: 29

DUAL ENROLLMENT

High school students, excited by the challenging coursework, gain confidence in their ability to accept the challenges of post-secondary education

The Virginia Plan for Dual Enrollment allows high school students to take college classes and apply the credits both toward high school graduation and toward college transfer. In rural school districts, where distance, small class size, and lack of a strong tax base impact negatively upon special coursework, Dual Enrollment has been of particular importance in providing a wider range of course options for high school students. It also helps avoid unnecessary duplication of facilities equipment, and programs in the academic, fine arts and vocational areas. Southside Virginia Community College's Dual Enrollment Program

has been highlighted on the national PBS series, *Restructuring to Promote Learning in America's Schools*, and won an "Excellence in Education" award from Virginia Polytechnic Institute.

Dual Enrollment classes were first offered in 1986 as needs were identified: when schools were forced to either update or abandon expensive vocational programs, the community college labs were utilized. At the same time, some academically talented young people requested more challenging coursework, and college transferable courses were offered.

Approximately 40 Dual Enrollment students are being bused to the SVCC campus and 560 are taking one or more courses at their high schools, for a total of some 2,500 credits per semester. Twenty-five different courses are offered, ranging from Automotive and Drafting to English Literature and Calculus, as 11 different school divisions take advantage of expanded academic opportunities.

College faculty may teach on campus or in the high schools. When high school instructors with advanced degrees in the appropriate field are available, they may be employed on-site for one or more class periods. In the latter instance, the college reimburses the school system for the equivalent adjunct rate of pay. The school districts apply their savings in facilities and salaries toward student tuition and books, and, for on-campus classes, toward transportation. The high school students make college class size more efficient and allow the college to make full use of technical labs and equipment. Scheduling, textbooks, transportation, discipline and academic concerns are all planned cooperatively.

High school students are excited by the challenging coursework. As they broaden their intellectual experiences, these rural students gain confidence in their ability to succeed, to plan for the future, and to accept the challenges of post secondary education. They find new role models in the college faculty and among the adult students who may share their classrooms. After their Dual Enrollment experience, some students have entered college as sophomores; others enroll in advanced classes; others put their technical skills to use on the job, and many become the first in their family to pursue a college degree.

Parents, too, have been returning to the campus for additional coursework, while high school teachers have a new incentive to upgrade their credentials. The more efficient use of classrooms, faculty, equipment and materials releases needed funds for other educational goals. The enthusiasm, willingness to cooperate and intellectual curiosity evident among the Dual Enrollment participants has had a positive effect on education well beyond the classroom.

There are other options for advanced work in Virginia: some schools offer AP courses, some design 2+2 articulation agreements, and some free students are eligible to attend Magnet Schools. None of these programs, however, has the flexibility or immediate benefits of Dual Enrollment. In rural high schools, the loss of one instructor can change the intensity and depth of the school's academic or vocational program. Dual Enrollment allows the college and high school to design and redesign the course offerings according to each school's needs and their students' interests. In effect, Dual Enrollment creates "mini-magnets" of its college classrooms.

Contact:
Nancy Carwile, (804) 736-8484
Charles Vaughan, (804) 949-7111

Southside Virginia Community College
Route 1, Box 60
Alberta, VA 23821
Total head count enrollment-Credit: 3,398; Non-Credit: 142
Campuses/sites: 3;Full-time faculty: 52

SOUTHSIDE VIRGINIA COMMUNITY COLLEGE

MINORITY OPPORTUNITY CENTER FOR SCIENCE AND MATHEMATICS

The Center's primary goal is to help identify black students interested in pursuing a teaching career in science or math

The Minority Opportunity Center for Science and Mathematics (MOCSM) at Southside Virginia Community College (SVCC) is a pilot program that works with local public school systems and community organizations to identify black students who are interested in pursuing a teaching career in science or mathematics. Hopefully, these individuals will return to the school system in the SVCC service area and teach science or mathematics after obtaining their degrees.

A unique program representing collaborative efforts between SVCC, local public schools, community organizations and senior colleges, the MOCSM impacts the college industry and the local labor market. It is funded by the National Science Foundation

At the college level, the Center provides financial assistance to black students under the science/mathematics teacher education program. Those selected to participate in this program are awarded financial support in the following areas:

1) tuition and fees to attend SVCC as full-time students;
2) travel stipends to help cover transportation costs to and from the college (the average full-time SVCC student commutes 40 miles a day, five days a week); and
3) book stipends.

Participants pursue the Associate in Arts and Science Degree through the University Parallel/College Transfer program at SVCC. Students may transfer to any senior

Continues on Page 720

college of their choice. In order to encourage and facilitate transfer, SVCC has established articulation agreements with four senior colleges.

For the last three years, at least two or more MOCSM college participants have been listed in the College Board Talent Roster of Outstanding Minority Community College Graduates.

Another goal outlined in the MOCSM grant is to identify black grade school students (8th-12th) who can benefit form remedial study or advanced study in science or mathematics. Students were taken on educational trips to science and engineering research facilities at major universities in the state. Informal science and enrichment programs were also sponsored. Students are especially encouraged to participate in science/math competitions. The MOCSM helps these students develop projects. Three MOCSM students participants were selected to present their original science research papers at the Virginia Junior Science and Humanities Symposium. Only 12 students statewide are selected to participate at this conference. Another MOCSM participant who competed in the 1990 Junior Engineering Technical Society (JETS) Academic Tests Statewide competition, placed second in mathematics.

The MOCSM also took 16 student participants to the 1990 JETS Academic Competition (TEAMS: Tests of Engineering Aptitude, Mathematics and Science). The MOCSM Varsity team won first place in Division 2. Forty-eight high school participants also competed in the conference. The MOCSM took 18 students representing five different school system to the 1991 JETS Academic Excellence Competition. Approximately 600 to 800 high school students in Virginia attend this conference each year. For the last two years, 95 to 98 percent of the black students attending were sponsored by the MOCSM. MOCSM students also competed in the 1992 JETS Academic Competition. In 1992, one MOCSM participant was selected to attend the National Junior Science and Humanities Symposium in Knoxville, TN.

The MOCSM developed and co-sponsored with the State Council of Higher Education for Virginia and Longwood College, a residential program for grade school students entitled the Microgravity Space/Science Learning Program in the summer of 1992.

Despite the fact that this Center is fairly new, there is evidence of external recognition. An article describing the MOCSM at SVCC was published in the Fall/Winter 1989 issue of the Journal of the Virginia Community Colleges Association. The MOCSM was highlighted at the 1990 Governors Conference on Education in Virginia. In addition, the MOCSM was the recipient of a competitive statewide Excellence in Education Award, and was showcased at the 1991 AACJC convention in Kansas City, Missouri. We have also received inquires from other community colleges wanting to know how to establish similar Centers of their own. According to NSF officials in Washington, D.C., several other similar model programs of community colleges have been funded based on the results of the MOCSM at SVCC.

Contact:
Donald R. Spell, Program Director
(804) 736-8484

Southside Virginia Community College
Route 1, Box 60
Alberta, VA 23821
Total head count enrollment-Credit: 3,398; Non-Credit: 142
Campuses/sites: 3;Full-time faculty: 52

COMPUTER-ASSISTED INSTRUCTION

Technological expansion has been accompanied by teacher training, careful pilot testing and responsible revision of new courses

A Computer-Assisted Instruction program at Southwest Virginia Community College gives the institution an opportunity to provide a variety of learning experiences for its diverse student population, provide computer literacy for its staff and student body, and move to the forefront of instructional technology.

Each year's focus highlights a different curricular area of the college, with the goal of improving instruction by providing alternative, technology-intensive courses. Because this kind of change must be managed responsibly, technological expansion has been accompanied by teacher training, careful pilot testing and responsible revision of new courses before they are introduced into the permanent curriculum of the institution.

The first year's activities set the stage for the wider-reaching activities that were to come in the four following years. The Computer Writing Center has established a 30-station, completely networked computer environment that serves as the hub for faculty support for academic computing and as a multi-use class and open-lab facility for students. One truth became readily apparent: in order for this program to succeed, SVCC had to make a real commitment to intensive training of its faculty. This commitment came through stipend/release time for faculty members as they develop actual CAI courses, support for those faculty from a knowledgeable CAI coordinator, a wide variety of seminars, workshops and classes acquainting the institution with the concept of CAI and training faculty in the use of CAI in their own courses.

From this groundwork, the program has gone on to implement CAI concepts on many levels. Some classes have used the lab as the meeting place for every class session, operating, in essence, a paperless classroom; some classes met for one or two sessions a week, some for every class for a two- or three-week intensive period, and some used the lab as a supplement to routine activities of the class. The lab has expanded offerings to the faculty by including CD ROM, interactive disks, Internet, equipment for scanning, color LCD projection panels for projecting computer activity to the whole class at one, and several other innovative ideas. The CAI Coordinator has presented seminars as well as one-on-one sessions for faculty. The Writing Lab staff comprised of trained part-time professionals and well-trained student workers as well

as the coordinator can assist a faculty member with a presentation or put one together for the instructor to use.

Throughout all of the activities, two concepts have guided the project:

1) SVCC will be people-centered, not equipment-centered; and

2) concentrate CAI not just on doing the same thing with a computer; rather, concentrate CAI on doing with a computer something that could not be done at all or could not be done as well without a computer.

After all, CAI isn't inherently better than traditional approaches; the success of the program has been finding the ways to offer instruction in alternative ways or by enhanced means.

Contact:
Idana B. Hamilton
(703) 964-7522

Southwest Virginia Community College
POB SVCC
Richlands, VA 24641-1510
Total head count enrollment: 7,667; Full-time faculty: 84

ARTS ACROSS THE CURRICULUM

A college gallery enhances the initiative, as do faculty workshops and expanded course offerings

Believing it is vitally important to engage community college educators and students in an understanding of art as a natural human phenomenon, Southwest Virginia Community College initiated the Arts Across the Curriculum program in August of 1992. Introduced into a rural and relatively isolated cultural environment, this program engages participants in discovering their individual capacity to perceive and utilize aspects of the arts in the context of various disciplines and daily living.

A week-long seminar to faculty conducted in August of the first two years of this initiative began the process of acquainting these educators with their own creative and aesthetic perceptions, as well as the linkage of their discipline to the arts. The seminars established four principle concepts:

1) people from different disciplines have numerous ideas, concepts and concerns in common, and by sharing them "across disciplines" through the language of art, they are able to expand their knowledge base;

2) people can share and make use of related ideas and concepts between disciplines if provided with the tools of a common vocabulary and the ability to employ the mode of "right brain" processing;

3) accessibility to the arts, mentally as well as physically, is the keystone of motivation in the engagement of students and faculty in this

program; and

4) utilizing the arts across the disciplines is a means of enhancing established course content – it is not an intrusive obligation to fit more material into already full areas of study.

These concepts have been broadly and creatively implemented across the disciplines. During the first two years of the grant, 20 faculty from a variety of disciplines (including engineering, history, office services technology, child care, foreign languages, nursing and health technologies, human services and economics) created course modules that incorporated art into their curricula on a permanent basis.

The establishment of a college gallery for exhibiting varied art forms has facilitated an expanded conceptualization of art both within the campus community and without. An annual spring-break trip for students and staff to a major metropolitan area has been established for the purpose of cultural enrichment. A forum for student debate and faculty discussion of arts issues has developed.

Arts resources have been expanded; the Learning Resources Center now makes art reproductions, videos, books and slides available to students and staff. Through teacher workshops and expanded course offerings, arts integration principles have been shared throughout the educational systems in the four-county area; workshops and courses were designed to assist primary and secondary

Continues on Page 722

school teachers to integrate the arts at the K-12 educational levels. Finally, program participants now have access to a new mode of communication through the arts, which is a source of pride and pleasure.

The Arts Across the Curriculum project, which was awarded a 1993 Excellence in Education Award from Virginia Polytechnic Institute and State University, received partial funding through a grant from the Virginia Council for Higher Education.

Contact:
Ellen Elmes, Project Director
(703) 964-7205

Southwest Virginia Community College
POB SVCC
Richlands, VA 24641-1510
Total head count enrollment: 7,667; Full-time faculty: 84

THOMAS NELSON COMMUNITY COLLEGE

STRENGTHENING THE WORK FORCE THROUGH PUBLIC SCHOOL PARTNERSHIPS

Because of the under-representation of females and minorities in scientific and technical fields, special efforts are made to include these students

MATRIX is a comprehensive series of programs designed to encourage middle school and high school students to achieve in their classes, particularly mathematics, science, and technology, and to provide exposure to high-tech workers and work settings. The problem being addressed is the preparation of students to meet the needs of the technology-based economy on the Virginia Peninsula.

In 1991, a grant from the National Aeronautics and Space Administration (NASA) to TNCC created a partnership between the college and the Virginia Peninsula Chamber of Commerce. It allowed both organizations to continue partnership activities each had previously initiated with public schools and created a continuous "pipeline" for the preparation of students.

All five public school systems in the region participate in MATRIX programs as well as most of the local premier high-technology businesses and facilities. Included in MATRIX are ATOMS, the Regional Summer Math and Science Institute, and student mentorships and internships. Because of the under-representation of females and minorities in scientific and technical fields, special efforts are made to include these students.

ATOMS is a career exploration project for 7th- and 8th-grade students designed to expose them to high-technology careers by providing role models and career information. The program targets "middle achieving" students. Teams of technical workers for NASA Langley Research Center, the Continuous Electron Beam Accelerator Facility (CEBAF), Newport News Shipbuilding, Canon Virginia, Inc., and Siemens Automotive visit students in their classrooms. Achievement in mathematics and science is stressed. A highlight of the team visit is the "hands-on" demonstration designed to stimulate interest in technology. Eighth-grade students travel to industry work sites for direct exposure to high-technology work settings. More than 3,000 7th- and 8th-grade students participated in ATOMS during the 1991-92 academic year, which was the second year of the program.

The Regional Summer Math and Science Institute (RSI) brings approximately 100 rising 9th-grade students to the TNCC campus. Students participate in four weeks of activities designed to promote an attitude of accomplishment in mathematics and science and to enhance self-esteem and communication. RSI combines classroom and laboratory experiences in biology, physics, computer science, computer graphics and mathematics with field trips to industry and local sites of interest. Because a summer program alone is not sufficient to sustain students' interest and motivation, a follow-up component has been added in which a variety of enrichment activities, including field trips, science projects, competition and the RSI Honor Roll, are offered to RSI students during the subsequent academic years.

Student mentorships match students with scientists, engineers, technicians and other professionals who serve as role models. Students are given a one-on-one introduction to the world of work and are encouraged to achieve in their classes. Middle and high school students currently participate in mentorships. Student internships provide 10th- through 12th-grade students with opportunities to explore various career through short, on-site work experiences supervised by professional mentors.

Both summative and formative data are being collected on all programs. All participants including students, teachers and industry presenters are asked to complete evaluation instruments on activities. This data is compiled and used to modify the programs. A tracking system is being developed to evaluate the long-term effect these programs have in terms of student course selection, academic achievement and career preparation. Students will be traced through graduation from high school and beyond.

Contact:
Susan M. Fincke, Coordinator
(804) 825-2982

Thomas Nelson Community College
PO Box 9407
Hampton, VA 23670
Total head count enrollment-Credit: 7,815; Non-Credit: 4,056
Campuses/sites: 1;Full-time faculty: 105

THOMAS NELSON COMMUNITY COLLEGE

SIEMEN AUTOMOTIVE PAY-FOR-KNOWLEDGE PROGRAM

The program is a non-traditional compensation plan tied to knowledge and mastery of different skills rather than to work performed on a specific job

The Pay-For-Knowledge (PFK) Program was jointly developed by Thomas Nelson Community College and Siemens Automotive to help keep Siemens Automotive globally competitive well into the 21st Century. To compete effectively in the automotive industry on a global basis, Siemens must provide customers with products of an equal or better quality than that of their competitors. To accomplish this, Siemens must have the flexibility to respond to ever-changing customer demnds. The challenge is to increase the quality, productivity and versatility of the work force.

A Pay-For-Knowledge program is generally a non-traditional compensation plan tied to knowledge and mastery of different skills in the organization rather than to work performed in a specific job. The language of a collective bargaining agreement specifies that the program is to provide an incentive for employees to increase their knowledge, skills and abilities and thereby increase the flexibility and the knowledge base of the work force. According to this language, employees retain their "home" job classification and receive pay premiums for gaining knowledge/skills associated with other job classifications.

There are two components utilized to help employees gain the knowledge and mastery of skills within different job classifications at Siemens Automotive: an educational component and an on-the-job training (OJT) component. The educational component focuses on providing the broad conceptual knowledge or theoretical foundation. The OJT component provides the practical hands-on training and experience necessary to develop and master skills needed to perform specific work operations effectively.

The results of this education and business partnership have been both tangible and intangible. The target work force for this program consists of 613 production employees. Out of this total group, 379 employees are volunteer participants in the Pay-For-Knowledge Program. This amounts to 61 percent of the current production work force. Entrance into the PFK program is through enrollment into the World Class Manufacturing I course. In this course employees are taught interpersonal team skills; concepts and applications of Just-In-Time, Total Quality Tools (SPC), Manufacturing Resource Planning (MRP 11); and provided insight into the automotive industry in general and the fuel injection (supplier) industry in particular. The results from this one course alone have exceeded expectations. Some of the salient results stemming from this course include the following: 37 active Small Group Improvement teams have been formed consisting of employees and their local supervisor. These teams come together to identify, solve, and "fool proof" quality-related issues, problems and concerns.

During a recession that has had devastating effects on the economy in general, Siemens is in a position that allows for: 1) a stable work force with no layoffs; and 2) the flexibility, due to increases in the employee knowledge base, to share human capital from one product line with another distinct product line when the need arises. Thus, they avoid the need to hire during peak demands and then, lay off employees during production slow downs.

The program has expanded TNCC's education offering by integrating Total Quality Management tools within the existing curriculum. This innovative program has married compensation to the level of knowledge and skills of the employee, thus significantly increasing overall productivity and quality at the plant. The PFK program is a model program that other firms and organizations are beginning to adopt in order to stay globally competitive. It has received numerous awards and has been featured in *Fortune* magazine.

Contact:
Roy E. Budd, Director, Center for Business and Community Services
(804) 825-2936

Thomas Nelson Community College
PO Box 9407
Hampton, VA 23670
Total head count enrollment-Credit: 7,815; Non-Credit: 4,056
Campuses/sites: 1;Full-time faculty: 105

PROJECT INTERNATIONAL EMPHASIS

The project integrates global perspectives into the curricula and career development activities in every community college in Virginia

Project International Emphasis (PIE) integrates global perspectives into the curricula and career development activities in every community college in Virginia, including Virginia Highlands Community College. The official term for this broad approach is "infusion."

For example, many two- and four-year colleges formerly offered classes in "International Business." Because virtually all business is now international, infusion encourages the discussion of global concepts in all business classes. Likewise students who are entering the work force are often unaware of the global nature of local businesses. Infusion exposes them to international concepts in a variety of courses and also introduces them to job searches with international dimensions. In two years, up to 11 faculty and counselors per campus developed three-hour global components for their courses. The PIE grant provided $100 stipends to each of these individuals.

In 1990, the State Council for Higher Education in Virginia (SCHEV) awarded a two-year $330,000 grant to PIE. This is the largest single grant ever made by SCHEV to a community college project. PIE was conceived and run by a seven-member steering committee, made up of faculty and counseling based administrators from all over the state.

Since July 1990, one faculty member, Kate Foreman, and one career counselor, Alma Rowland, acted as conduits between PIE's statewide organization and our home campus. They attended two PIE Summer Institutes, passed on relevant Institute content to our colleagues, helped initiate change on our campuses, provided support and assistance to the faculty involved in international activities and the development of curricular modules. We were also heavily involved in the planning and development of the initial College Change Plan and reported campus results to the statewide steering committee.

The first year of PIE activities saw the creation of a dynamic new committee on our campus, the beginning of course changes to include an international dimension, and a remarkable level of visibility for VHCC within our region and across the state. Out of 18 activities planned for the 1990-91 year, 16 activities were completed. VHCC's two-year Change Plan was published in the *PIE Interim Report* as one of the three best plans in the state.

The following are some of the activities undertaken that were not originally specified in the Change Plan: the presentation on Japanese Culture by Keiko Morita; participation by eight VHCC students and faculty in the World Game Institute; the purchase of support materials for VHCC faculty who developed curriculum modules (including videos, books, computer software and maps); and the creation of the Global Challenge Fund through the VHCC Foundation to upgrade the library's holdings on international topics.

An additional element of support for local activities has come through Southwest International Exchange, created by individual college representatives from seven campuses in our region, including VHCC. Through a grant from the PIE Steering Committee, Southwest International Exchange was able to sponsor a mini-conference in April 1991. The spring conference was held in conjunction with Spring International Day at Virginia Polytechnic Institute and State University, and we were able to expose four more VHCC faculty to the contacts, content and enthusiasm of our colleagues in the area. A second conference occurred in fall 1991, on grant writing. Our enhanced relationship with Virginia Western faculty, through SIE, enabled us to bring Dr. Gary Weaver to our campus at half the expense.

In spring 1992, VHCC PIE representatives wrote a proposal funded through the Virginia Community College Association to bring The African Heritage Dancers and Drummers to Southwest Virginia. A matinee performance was given for Middle School students in our region and an evening performance was given to a full house at the Paramount Center in Bristol.

Our Change Plan calls for maintaining many activities from the previous year, adding a few new projects, and continuing to expand the level of participation by faculty, staff and students at VHCC. Enthusiastic support for PIE was crucial in helping our campus have such a successful experience.

Contact:
Edwin T. Hardison, Kate Foreman or Alma Rowland
(703) 628-6094

Virginia Highlands Community College
PO Box 828
Abingdon, VA 24210-0828
Total head count enrollment-Credit: 3,228 Non-Credit: 408
Campuses/sites: 1; Full-time faculty: 78

ALLIANCE FOR EXCELLENCE

*Black churches and community colleges work together to increase enrollment
and retention of black students*

Alliance for Excellence is a partnership developed by black churches with community colleges for the purpose of increasing opportunities for blacks in higher education. The idea for this alliance was born in the Gilmer neighborhood of Roanoke, Virginia, in 1986, as a result of Virginia Western Community College's minority affairs program becoming a victim of budget cuts. Members of several black churches initiated discussions with Virginia Western as to how the black church and the local community might work together in order to encourage broader black participation in higher education through local educational opportunities.

The key element of this collaborative effort is the fact that the black church has a historic commitment to higher education, and the community college is one of the most accessible and affordable option for blacks in post secondary education. As a result, Alliance for Excellence programs have been established in the service regions of four community colleges (Danville, Central Virginia, Patrick Henry and Virginia Western). In the fall of 1991, Ferrum College joined the network as the only four-year institution in an effort to bolster transfer opportunities connected with the program.

Alliance for Excellence has adopted the following goals:

1) promote the advancement of blacks in higher education;

2) collectively engage the educational resources of community colleges, the leadership and influence of black churches, and the cooperation of other organizations for the purpose of offering support services, educational and cultural programs, and sponsoring other efforts that encourage opportunities for blacks in higher education; and

3) enhance the quality of campus life for black students and encourage greater frequency and effectiveness of minority education programs and services.

As a function of these goals, the following objectives were originally adopted by Alliance for Excellence and reaffirmed in 1991. Specifically, programs are designed to:

1) increase black enrollment at area community colleges to the same level as the percentage of the black population with the general population in each college area;

2) increase black retention and graduation rates at area community colleges to the same level as the percentage of the black population within the general population in each college area; and

3) increase transfer rates for black students between community colleges and four-year colleges and universities.

Alliance for Excellence is organized under the auspices of a regional Board of Directors. The board works through local community leaders who form an advisory group in each college area. Project coordinators are responsible for overall program planning and implementation in their college region in cooperation with the local advisory committee. Each local advisory group consists of representatives from the black community and the local community college. Each group has its own officers and committees and one board member is designated as the support person for the local project coordinator. Alliance for Excellence functions under a set of bylaws revised in 1993, and is recognized as a 501(c)3 tax-exempt organization by the Internal Revenue Service.

In 1991, the four participating community colleges agreed to match grant funds that initially had been raised from national and regional church sources. This would ensure the continued development of the program. The staffing arrangement was changed to include four part-time project coordinators who would coordinate projects in their service regions and work with the local advisory committee. Alliance for Excellence was included as one of the ministries in this area supported by the Committee on Campus Ministry of the Synod of the Mid-Atlantic, PCUSA.

Programs involve a broad variety of support efforts for black students, beginning with young children and their families in order to promote the positive "idea" of higher education at an early age. Some of the programs in recent years throughout the region included: campus-sponsored tours on each of the five campuses; essay contests; tutorial programs; workshops/seminars on such topics as motivation, preparing for college, study skills, test-taking skills, financial aid, and Christian ethics in the classroom; and annual "Academic Excellence" Awards programs.

A substantial increase in black participating in higher education has been experienced since this program began. Success heretofore has been measured by rates of enrollment, retention, graduation and transfer to four-year colleges by black student in comparison with the same rates over the past six years and the same statistics for white majority students.

Contact:
Gloria Lindsay, Project Coordinator
(703) 857-7583

Virginia Western Community College
PO Box 14045
Roanoke, VA 24038
Total head count enrollment-Credit: 6,531; Non-Credit: 168
Campuses/sites: 1;Full-time faculty: 95

THE COMMUNITY ARBORETUM

▦ This two-acre educational garden is a resource for people ▦
of all ages with various levels of expertise

The first and only educational garden in the Roanoke Valley is on the campus of Virginia Western Community College. This unique, two-acre educational facility is a living laboratory for student and the community at large. The gardens are designed to serve the interests and needs of all visitors from preschoolers to senior citizens, backyard gardeners to professional horticulturists, Sunday strollers to urban foresters. To emphasize the purpose of providing a learning resource for students and the community at large, the gardens have been named The Community Arboretum at Virginia Western Community College.

Funding for this educational resource has come solely from non-budgeted sources such as federal grants, local governments, businesses, community organizations and individuals. In 1987 the VWCC Arboretum Committee was created for the purpose of planning and fund-raising. The committee consisted of college personnel, landscape architects, professional horticulturists, Virginia Western horticulture students and representatives from plant-related community organizations. The site was selected by the committee and subsequently approved by the Virginia Western Local Board with the understanding that the arboretum would be built and maintained with private funds. In addition to providing the sites, the college agreed to supply administrative and promotional support, utilities and maintenance assistance.

After obtaining approval to develop the site, the Arboretum committee adopted the following statement of purpose: "The purpose of The Community Arboretum is to provide a living laboratory for the students and the community, thereby furthering the understanding of ecological processes, botanical relationships, and horticultural practices in an aesthetically pleasing setting." The committee also established the following objectives:

1) to provide a learning resource to be used by Virginia Western's students and other groups;

2) to promote concern for the environment through an appreciation of nature;
3) to stimulate valley-wide beautification;
4) to serve as a recreational setting for residents of the Roanoke Valley; and
5) to serve as a tourist attraction for visitors to the Roanoke Valley.

After two years of careful planning and diligent fund-raising, available funds were first used for architectural services that included the development of a conceptual master plan and a complete set of working drawings. In 1989, the Arboretum Committee was reorganized to form the Arboretum Advisory Council. The council was created for the purpose of directing construction and continuing fund-raising efforts.

The first phase of construction involved the installation of an irrigation system, planting bed layout, and soil preparation. By the end of 1991, the following components of the arboretum were completed: amphitheater/gazebo; herb garden; annual display; shade collection; and rock garden. The final two gardens, conifers and perennials, were planted in 1992. The arboretum contains more than 500 different plant taxa, each identified with permanent labels.

With construction and plantings completed, the advisory council is focusing educational outreach and maintenance strategies. The gardens are being maintained by students in the college's horticulture program, community volunteers and individuals under contractual agreements. Maintenance costs are covered by community organizations, businesses and individuals.

The Community Arboretum is fulfilling its purpose and meeting its objectives by serving as a living laboratory for the college's horticulture students and countless other students in the area. Dozens of school groups and community organizations have visited the arboretum, enhancing their knowledge of plants and appreciation of nature.

Contact:
J. Lee Hipp, Project Coordinator
(703) 857-7120

Virginia Western Community College
PO Box 14045
Roanoke, VA 24038
Total head count enrollment-Credit: 6,531; Non-Credit: 168
Campuses/sites: 1;Full-time faculty: 95

CONCERT BAND

At each of the band's performances throughout the community, the audience response is overwhelming

The Wytheville Community College Concert Band is a community service project that:

1) provides adults in the community with an opportunity to continue to develop their musical interests and their performance skills which were begun, in some cases many years ago, in school programs

2) provides the largely rural service region of the college with an important resource for cultural enrichment; and

3) promotes the development of community spirit and pride.

Under the direction of Dr. Jack O. White, retired professor of music at Elon College and currently adjunct music professor at WCC, the band grew from 45 members in the fall of 1989, to 83 members for the spring 1992 concert season. These members come from throughout WCC's service region, which includes five rural counties and one small city.

With regular Tuesday night rehearsals throughout the year, the band has developed to a remarkably high level of performance. At each of the band's numerous performances throughout the service region, the audience response has been overwhelming, with spontaneous standing ovations throughout the concerts. Typically, the band will have two fall performances in area high school auditoriums and five or six spring performances – including the college Arts and Crafts Festival, the Wytheville

Chautauqua Festival before audiences of 7,000, the college graduation ceremony, a major spring concert drawing an indoor audience of about 1,000 and at least one other service region concert in a high school auditorium.

With musicians of varying levels of ability, the band's most significant achievement has been in providing the motivation for the less proficient or rustier players to rise to the very high standard set by the director and the section leaders. The musical selections (the *1812 Overture*, for example) are exceptionally challenging for a community group.

Very importantly, the project is an excellent example of the kind of success that a cooperative effort between the college, the public schools and other community organizations can accomplish. One school division provides rehearsal space; area high school band directors freely loan music to the college band; and the high schools throughout the service region permit the use of their auditoriums to accommodate the large crowds. In addition, the Wythe County Bicentennial Committee and WCC were co-sponsors of the band's Bicentennial Concert. Because the band is a community service project and not a college course, financial support comes from the Wytheville Community College Educational Foundation, the WCC Cultural Affairs Committee, and WCC's community service budget (local funds). Approximately $1,500 has been obtained from these sources each year to cover music and travel expenses.

Contact:
Dan C. Jones, Division Chair
(703) 228-5541, ext. 235

Wytheville Community College
1000 East Main Street
Wytheville, VA 24382
Total head count enrollment-Credit: 4,102; Non-Credit: 574
Campuses/sites: 1;Full-time faculty: 52

KEGLEY LIBRARY COLLECTION

The collection covers most of western civilization, with the 18th Century frontier, particularly southwestern Virginia, being the focal point

Wythe County, the site of Wytheville Community College, was a key location in the western settlement of Virginia and in the development and expansion of the colony to the West. This fact, coupled with the renewal of interest in genealogy and the offer of an outstanding collection of books, sparked a vision of a special service that could be offered through the availability of such a book collection.

Mr. Frederick Bittle Kegley, a noted area historian, bequeathed his personal library of historically significant

items to the college in 1968. His books cover most of western civilization, with the 18th Century frontier, particularly southwestern Virginia, being the focal point. In this area, he assembled not only books, but also pamphlets, clippings, census reports, letters, family papers, church records, Works Progress Administration historical inventory papers, newspapers and maps. The maps are of special interest, as they include copies of several early maps of Virginia's western frontier and many pen and pencil

Continues on Page 728

sketches of Wythe County at various dates, showing the locations of industries, churches, schools, settlements and individual inhabitants.

Mr. Kegley felt that the college would provide a permanent repository for the collection, with qualified supervision and research assistance, and that it was so situated as to serve a great segment of the people in this section of Southwest Virginia. By being a part of the college library, the special collection allows the college another avenue for serving the community and the collection is assured of being available to all who need to use it. To maximize service potential, the materials were organized and analytic indexes were prepared for easy access and referral. The college's two librarians assist students and the general public with research projects using the collection. Patrons from Hawaii to Maine and Alaska to Florida have used the collection, some returning two and three times from distant points.

Interest from an endowment fund left with the collection is used to add appropriate items to the collection. Additions include books, maps, manuscripts, personal and business account books from the turn of the century, cemetery records, microfilmed copies of early local newspapers, court records, and census reports from each county of the college's service area (which cover the time from the formation of each county up through 1920).

As a project to enhance the usefulness of the collection, the college's librarians are making an inventory of the county's cemeteries. Birth and death records are being recorded from the area's artistically unique tombstones carved in the traditional Germanic decoration (which are suffering the effects of weathering) and from family cemeteries that are in a state of disrepair or that are disappearing completely. The publication of these records is a long-term goal of the library staff.

Contact:
Anna Ray Roberts, Coordinator, Library Services
(703) 228-5541, ext. 258

Wytheville Community College
1000 East Main Street
Wytheville, VA 24382
Total head count enrollment-Credit: 4,102; Non-Credit: 574
Campuses/sites: 1;Full-time faculty: 52

INTERDISCIPLINARY PROGRAM

Learning communities help students see and understand relationships among various disciplines and course contents

Interdisciplinary teams with their resulting projects apply annually to a Steering Committee for acceptance and scheduling during an ensuing academic year. Usually two projects are accepted and scheduled each quarter, while numerous other linked or "federated" course projects are also featured as a part of the program's offerings.

Projects include faculty and course offerings from the college's five instructional divisions as well as Human Development classes taught by faculty counselors. Concepts featured in each project are usually timely and fashioned to appeal to most community college student population groups.

By providing a holistic rather than an atomistic experi-

ence, learning communities help students see and understand relationships among various disciplines and course contents. Students are greatly facilitated in the assimilation of all learning and in laying aside organizational barriers that so often discourage students from pursuing many areas of study.

In summary, learning communities provide students with an enriched experience that adds a dimension to disparate subjects. The opportunity to get to know a group of students well, and to work with them toward achieving common goals gives our students a unique experience of community that should be an integral part of any learning experience.

Contact:
Larry Reid, Chairman, Division of Arts and Humanities
(206) 641-2041

Bellevue Community College
3000 Landerholm Circle SE
Bellevue, WA 98007
Total head count enrollment-Credit: 14,000; Non-Credit: 3,000
Campuses/sites: 2; Full-time faculty: 122

ACADEMIC TRANSFER PROGRAM

Students can satisfy most major course requirements within the curriculum content of the AA and AAS degrees

Bellevue Community College has consistently, during its entire existence, nurtured and strengthened its academic transfer program. Today it is the basis of all similar programs offered in Washington State's 28 community colleges. Approximately 52 percent of those students, initially enrolled in a transfer program, succeed in obtaining admission to a baccalaureate institution within the state. No precise data is available as to the percentage of

those who leave the state to continue higher education objectives.

Students are able to satisfy most lower division major course requirements, as well as general education, within the curriculum content of the Associate of Arts and Sciences and the Associate in Science Degrees. The latter degree is designed specifically for the non-liberal arts transfer students.

Contact:
Robert K. Hamilton, Dean of Instruction
(206) 641-2361

Bellevue Community College
3000 Landerholm Circle SE
Bellevue, WA 98007
Total head count enrollment-Credit: 14,000; Non-Credit: 3,000
Campuses/sites: 2; Full-time faculty: 122

COMMERCIAL PILOT TRAINING

The program, which normally requires seven quarters to complete, also allows for an eighth quarter to gain an additional rating

The Commercial Pilot Training program combines coursework in aviation along with other courses to prepare students for obtaining a commercial pilot certificate with instrument rating. This program normally requires seven quarters to complete. Additional ratings for flight instructor, instrument flight instructor, multi-engine, helicopter and seaplane may be earned through special arrangements (usually the eighth quarter).

Students may earn an Associate in Arts and Science degree for transfer to a four year university or an Associate in Applied Science for a career as a commercial pilot. It is possible for a student to earn both degrees.

There are special admission requirements to the program. Applications for the program are accepted on October 1 for the program beginning the next fall quarter. All aviation courses and entry requirements are subject to change as required by the Federal Aviation Administration or Big Bend Community College.

Contact:
John Swedburg
(509) 762-6256

Big Bend Community College
7662 Chanute Street
Moses Lake, WA 98837
Total head count enrollment-Credit: 2,513; Non-Credit: 736
Campuses/sites: 1; Full-time faculty: 48

PEP2

The program for disadvantaged/non-traditional adults blends individual learning styles, research and innovative instructional strategies

PEP2 is a comprehensive, learner-centered training program which prepares disadvantaged/non-traditional adult students for successful entry into the work force and/or further training. To maximize student successes, PEP2 blends individual learning styles, research, innovative instructional strategies, proven teaching techniques and individual/group counseling. Completers exit this six-month program with "how to learn" skills, motivation, a solid basic skills foundation, confidence and employment/training goals.

PEP2 integrates basic skills with occupational skills instruction in competency-based modules: career planning and decision-making; basic keyboarding and computer literacy; learning "how to learn" skills; work survival (job retention) skills; consumer and homemaking skills; non-traditional careers; applied written and oral communication skills; applied mathematics; applied science; survival Spanish (conversational); and industrial first aid.

PEP2 is funded by the progressive partnership among the Employment Security Department, the Department of Social and Health Services, the PENTAD Private Industry Council, and Big Bend Community College. For participants' success, each agency utilizes its expertise and resources and maximizes its linkages with other agencies.

Contact:
Gail Erickson
(509) 762-7287

Big Bend Community College
7662 Chanute Street
Moses Lake, WA 98837
Total head count enrollment-Credit: 2,513; Non-Credit: 736
Campuses/sites: 1; Full-time faculty: 48

WELDING TECHNOLOGY

*The program aims to train students to surpass certification standards
and to train welders who have a strong work ethic*

The Welding Technology program at Columbia Basin College is recognized world-wide, with students coming from as far away as South Africa, South Korea, New Jersey, Texas and Alaska. The program has wide recognition throughout the United States. Frequently, when CBC students apply for employment on construction sites, the welder is hired without a welding certification test.

The college facilities contain the latest technology in the industry, including computer-aided orbital pipe welding units (Dimetrics and Astro-Arc), state-of-the-art "pulse" gas tungsten arc welding units, and equipment for training in titanium welding. However, welding training programs are costly to run due to equipment upkeep, supplies and electricity, special gases, exotic metals and equipment upgrades.

The program has two main goals:

1) to train students who are able to meet and surpass certification standards as specified by the various certifying agencies; and

2) to train welders who have a high level of integrity in quality of work produced, who are proud of their profession, and who appreciate knowing the work they produce is integral to the quality of life and to the society in which they live.

Two full-time and six adjunct instructors teach the six-quarter, competency-based program to 80 students quarterly. After 220 hours of lab work and 32 hours of lecture-theory per quarter, the students are well prepared to enter the job market.

Columbia Basin College has been extremely innovative in its training methods. By utilizing automatic welding equipment and a television camera approximately two inches square fitted with appropriate filters and remote control devices, a video film of close-up, color motion pictures of welding processes has been developed. By watching this video, students are able to experience the welding process in the classroom and then emulate the procedures in the lab more quickly than those who used conventional methods.

The program trains to the maximum codes established by the industry. Some students achieve certification in welding while others graduate from CBC with an Associate Degree in Welding Technology. Those who complete the degree must pass courses in English, communications, math and psychology.

Contact:
Deanna Baalman, Instructional Director
(509) 547-0511

Columbia Basin College
2600 North 20th Avenue
Pasco, WA 99301
Total head count enrollment-Credit: 19,695; Non-Credit: 1,192
Campuses/sites: 2; Full-time faculty: 96

ENVIRONMENTAL HAZARDOUS MATERIALS MANAGEMENT TECHNOLOGY

*Grduates are prepared to perform the necessary functions required to manage
hazardous wastes in compliance with environmental laws.*

Columbia Basin College and The International Union of Operating Engineers jointly developed and operate a Hazardous Materials Emergency Response facility on the CBC campus, giving students valuable experience. This facility stemmed from the Environmental Hazardous Materials Management Technology program which graduates broadly trained environmental hazardous materials technicians.

Graduates are prepared to perform the necessary functions required to manage hazardous wastes in compliance with environmental laws, to work in the environmental remediation efforts of hazardous waste site operations, and to acquire the background necessary to matriculate to four-year institutions for advanced hazardous materials technology degrees.

In response to community need, including those articulated by the United States Department of Energy (U.S. DOE) Richland, Columbia Basin College (CBC) developed and implemented an Environmental Hazardous Materials Management Technology (Hazmat) Associate Degree program. Classes began in spring quarter 1991 with 45 students enrolled. As of fall quarter 1993, the enrollment in the degree program reached 211 students,

Continues on Page 732

with capacity enrollment every quarter since the initial offering. The student makeup of the Hazmat program is 64 percent male and 36 percent female, out of which 9 percent are minority/multicultural.

To date, 43 students have received their associate degree, and 28 students have obtained employment as Hazardous Materials Technicians, Site Safety Technicians, Technical Editors or Environmental Compliance Technicians, at the USDOE Hanford site, the Washington Department of Ecology, and in the private sector with companies providing environmental services. In addition, 20 individuals who were already employed in the environmental industry enrolled in the Environmental Hazmat program to improve their skills.

The Hazmat program staff consists of the program coordinator, a full-time Hazmat instructor, and seven adjunct instructors from local industry. Financial support has come from grants from the U.S. Department of Education, the U.S. DOE, and the Washington State Board for Community and Technical Colleges, as well as college funds. These funds have been used to initiate the program, purchase training equipment, and fund student scholar-

ships and internships.

In addition to the degree program, the Hazmat department has sponsored numerous technical workshops and videoconferences for the private sector and the Hanford U.S. DOE Site.

The CBC Hazmat program is assisting in the development of a Partnership for Environmental Technology Education (PETE) Northwest consortium of community colleges to develop coordinated curricula for training Environmental Hazardous Materials Technicians, and to provide program articulation at four-year institutions. In addition, CBC is developing a Tech-Prep program to provide high school students a head start in pursuing a technical career in hazardous materials management with the capability to link with baccalaureate degree programs in hazardous materials management technology.

The Hazmat program coordinator has been actively involved with the U.S. DOE and numerous community colleges to better prepare hazardous materials technicians to work as part of environmental remediation operations at the various U.S. DOE nuclear sites.

Contact:
Kenneth Ferrigno, Coordinator
(509) 547-0511

Columbia Basin College
2600 North 20th Avenue
Pasco, WA 99301
Total head count enrollment-Credit: 19,695; Non-Credit: 1,192
Campuses/sites: 2; Full-time faculty: 96

LOWER COLUMBIA COLLEGE

INTEGRATIVE STUDIES

Integrated curriculum programs have included 'Dilemmas in Professional Life,'
'Vietnam,' and 'Truth, Lies and Images: Power and Persuasion in American Life'

LCC's Integrative Studies program is the college's successful response to the learning communities phenomenon.

Instead of enrolling in a series of specific courses – English, drama, political science, psychology – students enroll full-time for the quarter in an integrated curriculum. They receive transcript and graduation requirement credit for traditional course work, but study is unified through a central theme. To enroll in Integrative Studies, transfer degree students must have completed 60 credits plus certain courses in math and English.

Initiated in fall of 1987, the program had been suggested by a faculty member who had participated in a linked course project while on sabbatical, researched by other departments, and discussed on campus in open forum.

The program for the first quarter was "Humanity and Nature," and included English Composition, American Literature, and a survey of biology course with a lab. Students examined the intricate web of life and matter that is the human ecosystem and read American literature touching on the issues of survival, development, expansion

and conservation. Faculty members later combined English composition, psychology and political science courses to create the "Human Matrix" series. "Dilemmas in Professional Life" addressed ethical decisions; "Humor in a Serious Age" examined personal and social functions of humor; and "Truth, Lies and Images: Power and Persuasion in American Life" examined media and its influences on modern society.

The most popular Integrative Studies theme has been "Vietnam." Through the disciplines of political science, drama, psychology and English composition, students explored Vietnam's history, the events that precipitated U.S. involvement, what happened during the war, the conflict at home, getting out of Vietnam and coming home, the psychological aftermath, and the lessons we learned. This Integrative Studies program also attempted to connect Vietnam to the broader issues of war and peace; causes of war; how wars are conducted; the effects of modern war; and the aggressiveness of man.

A grant from the Lower Columbia College Foundation brought comedian Blake Clark to LCC for a live performance. A veteran himself, Blake Clark often uses his wartime experiences for material. Besides his stand-up comedy presentation, which was open to the community, Clark met with students in the program and discussed their projects – collages, scrapbooks and "happenings" reminiscent of the 1960's.

The program included production of the play *Romulus*, written by Gore Vidal, a satirical look at the fall of Rome. Vidal wrote the play as his own comment on the Vietnam conflict. Additionally, students visited the Vietnam memorial in Portland, Oregon, and attended a two-day retreat at the close of the quarter.

The proof of the success of the Integrative Studies program has not only been its popularity among faculty members, but also among students. Instructors in remediation courses have used the format for their students and Integrative Studies has been one of the first courses to close during registration .

Contact:
Don Fuller, Dean, Instruction and Student Services
(206) 577-3425

Lower Columbia College
1600 Maple Street, PO Box 3010
Longview, WA 98632
Total head count enrollment-Credit: 6,600; Non-Credit: 1,200
Campuses/sites: 1; Full-time faculty: 83

THE CAPSTONE PROJECT

The Capstone experience allows students to demonstrate progress in developing skills and values targeted in the general degree outcomes

The Capstone Project at Lower Columbia College focuses on the educational experience, rather than a class or series of coordinated classes in a quest to link and solidify the whole learning experience. The changes are not so much in course content as in delivery. Some courses will have new requirements for entry and assignments within the syllabus, but for the most part, shared standards and expectations will be the common factor. For example, English 101 communication skill levels will be expected in other 101 classes.

The Capstone experience provides an opportunity for students to demonstrate progress in developing knowledge, skills, attitudes and values targeted in the general degree outcomes:
1) application of abstract thought in concrete situations;
2) thinking creatively or dialectically, using analogies, inductive and deductive reasoning, comparing and contrasting assumptions;
3) analysis, interpretation and evaluation of information in a variety of disciplines; and
4) synthesis of information within and among disciplines. In short: survival skills for an increasingly complex world.

This marked change from the traditional curriculum format was prompted by the stark realization that students don't relate courses on their own. It's not unusual to hear a student say, "I'm taking English Composition, but it doesn't have anything to do with my other courses." The same student is appalled when points are deducted for poor writing in a philosophy paper. While specific majors, nursing, for example, have prerequisites and a prescribed order of classes for building skills and knowledge, the general transfer degree, Associate in Arts and Science, Plan B, basically has not. All degree-seeking students take placement tests in math, reading and English to find out which level they should enter or if they need remedial help in a subject. Once launched in their academic career, however, the Plan B student is often frustrated by perceived disparate subjects and a lack of a common body of knowledge with classmates.

Their frustration has been shared by faculty, who often find that even students qualified to enter college-level classes are unable to express themselves individually or in groups or to apply critical thinking skills to a variety of subjects.

In 1987 LCC faculty members decided to address these problems and research into the Capstone project was begun by a diverse committee.

Faculty see the Capstone project as an enormously useful device as it gives a natural progression to the curriculum, creates common frames of reference for courses and gets rid of redundancies. The program is "faculty-driven," with individual instructors deciding how their subject fits into the program. Although Capstone was created for the general transfer degree, it is expected to impact other programs as well, since communications, social science or humanities credits are required for all two-year technical arts degrees.

Contact:
Don Fuller, Dean, Instruction and Student Services
(206) 577-3425

Lower Columbia College
1600 Maple Street, PO Box 3010
Longview, WA 98632
Total head count enrollment-Credit: 6,600; Non-Credit: 1,200
Campuses/sites: 1; Full-time faculty: 83

WOMEN IN TECHNOLOGIES (WIT)

*▨ The women targeted in this program want to break out of poverty but have ▨
been woefully underserved by traditional technical programs*

Women, primarily single parents and displaced home-makers at North Seattle Community College, are encouraged to seek training and job placement in the Engineering and Electronics Technologies programs through the Women In Technologies (WIT) program.

These engineering and electronics training programs are some of the best on campus, providing tremendous opportunities for moderate to high-paying first-time, professional, technical employment. The women targeted have been woefully underserved by these technical programs, and WIT is committed to the gender and ethnic balance in them and the industries they serve.

WIT recruits women who are in poverty by going directly into the community – to schools, trade and career fairs, welfare agencies and to cooperating community-based organizations. WIT facilitates pre-vocational training for its recruits; assessment for learning disabilities, math and English remediation; life management and study skills; and introduction to technologies. This phase of the program satisfies most diagnostic, remedial and technical studies preparedness for all the certificate and degree vocational/technical programs of study. The WIT women are at least equally prepared for core program study, if not more ready than their male counterparts.

The direct student services provided by the WIT coordinator assure the WIT student continued timely, responsive, support while she is in the technical phase advising, and personal and financial crisis intervention. Students also participate in "Women in Success," a program that builds community, confidence, interpersonal skills and employment readiness. All this time the WIT women are mentored by a professional in the field and serve a short internship, gaining familiarity with the workplace.

The WIT program is a focused, specialized service under the direction of the Carl Perkins Special Populations, designed to serve a very narrowly-defined population with extraordinary needs. The start-up was funded by single parent competitive grants.

Contact:
Nancy E. Verheyden, Director, Special Populations
(206) 527-3769

North Seattle Community College
9600 College Way North
Seattle, WA 98103
Total head count enrollment-Credit: 6,904; Non-Credit: 1,946
Campuses/sites: 2; Full-time faculty: 100

CULTURAL PLURALISM CLIMATE TRANSFORMATION

*▨ Evaluation relating to cultural pluralism has occurred for specific course syllabi, ▨
in an opinion survey and through a multi-cultural climate survey*

"NSCC will create a climate that affirms and endorses our diversity," according to one goal in the mission statement for North Seattle Community College. Accordingly, the college has taken on the challenge of transforming the campus climate.

In instruction, that challenge has resulted in the definition of curricular outcomes for cultural pluralism, the infusion of these outcomes in general education, and the process of curriculum transformation. Faculty/staff "training" in cultural pluralism and curriculum transformation has supported these activities. In student services, peer counseling, specialized tutoring and orientations, and a multi-cultural leadership training program have been developed. The challenge has also entailed conducted and disseminating a multi-cultural climate survey.

Another major activity was the participation of a college team consisting of faculty and administrators in an 11-day summer cultural pluralism institute conducted by the Washington Center for Undergraduate Education and the University of Washington. External funding from the State Minority Enhancement budget, the college's Title III grant and the Ford Foundation has been obtained and utilized in support of this climate transformation process. Evaluation relating to the cultural pluralism has occurred for specific course syllabi, in a survey of opinion about the multi-cultural leadership training program and through the multi-cultural climate survey. Currently the associate degree is being evaluated against multi-cultural outcomes.

Several courses have been rewritten to include significant multi-cultural outcomes and content. Tenure track faculty positions have been created and filled in American Ethnic studies and Area Studies. The Curriculum Committee has recommended that a multi-cultural component be a part of the associate degree. That component is being considered in a campus-wide curriculum governance process. A faculty member has been appointed project coordinator for cultural pluralism. Faculty and staff training in cultural pluralism is occurring in the Teaching and Learning Center. Students of color are more aware of these student services available to them, more likely to access those services and to have more confidence in their future as students and potential community leaders.

Contact:
David Mitchell, Vice President, Instruction
(206) 527-3700

North Seattle Community College
9600 College Way North
Seattle, WA 98103
Total head count enrollment-Credit: 6,904; Non-Credit: 1,946
Campuses/sites: 2; Full-time faculty: 100

MASTER STUDENT PROGRAM

Master Students are students of color who are succeeding in math and/or English well enough to tutor and lead study groups

Although free tutoring in a variety of subject areas has been offered at Seattle Central Community College for a number of years, many students fail to take advantage of this service because they feel intimidated or embarrassed. This is particularly true of students of color. To make the Tutoring Lab more inviting, SCCC created the Math Student Program wherein currently enrolled students of color tutor fellow students.

The Master Students are succeeding in math/or English, though they are not necessarily "straight A" students. Their success is based in hard work and perseverance. Master Students are assigned to work with a specific pre-college math or English class. They attend the class regularly in order to get to know all the students in the class, they arrange and lead two to three study groups to help class-mates learn in teams, and they arrange individual tutoring sessions for students who need a little more assistance.

Many of the Master Students at SCCC are African-American males. This has been a priority on campus because:

1) these young men counter the myths about African-Americans and math and English;

2) they provide excellent role models for other students of color; and

3) the tutors, themselves, find their skills are further strengthened by their tutoring experiences.

Two of our African-American students have transferred to four-year universities where they are pursuing degrees in mathematics and education in order to become math instructors.

Master Students receive hourly wages for the time they spend attending the class to which they are assigned, the study group time, the individual tutoring sessions, and any time spent meeting with the course instructors. Math and English are the only two subjects for which the Master Students are used at present. Both subjects must be completed at the college level for the Associated of Arts degree. In the last three years, the Master Student Program has involved 14 students and 14 math and English instructors. Students, tutors and instructors have given very positive evaluations of the program. In the near future, we hope to extend the program to include chemistry and accounting.

Contact:
Debra Sullivan, Director, Student Affairs and Activities
(206) 587-6924

Seattle Central Community College
1701 Broadway
Seattle, WA 98122
Total head count enrollment-Credit: 7,499; Non-Credit: 1,414
Campuses/sites: 2; Full-time faculty: 135

NURSING: COORDINATED STUDIES

The coordinated studies model integrates second-quarter Medical Surgical theory, nursing skills lab, basic concepts and a trends/issues seminar

With a student body comprising a unique cross section of the urban population, Seattle Central Community College's six quarter Associate Degree Nursing Program adopted an integrated curriculum to help increase retention. The coordinated studies model for nursing theory and lab courses also help bridge the transition of learning from classroom to clinical practice for students whose enrollment profile is 40 percent ethnic minority; 16 percent ESL; 31 percent male; and 39 percent eligible for need-based financial aid.

A team of two or three nursing faculty adopted the coordinated studies model to integrate second quarter Medical-Surgical theory, nursing skills lab, basic concepts including psychology, communication, pharmacology, and a trends/issues seminar (eight credits) linked to a four-credit medical-surgical clinical practicum. These students then enrolled in a coordinated third-quarter medical/surgical clinical practicum.

Critical and creative thinking were fostered in each of the coordinated studies classes. Classroom elements were:
1) small-group care planning based on case studies;
2) role-playing based on real clinical experiences;
3) patient case studies;
4) problem-solving labs;
5) simulation games; and
6) small-group reports and presentations.

Content lectures were presented to students but re-demonstrated in seminar, lab and clinical assignments. The faculty team also supported by an instructional technician in the skills lab and peer tutors.

The effect of the coordinated studies model can be seen in the retention rate of 80 percent at the end of the first year. The combined retention rate for first- and second-year students was 86 percent. First-time pass rate on the state nursing board exam for this group was 95 percent.

Contact:
Mary Burnett, Associate Dean, Health and Human Services
(206) 587-4161

Seattle Central Community College
1701 Broadway
Seattle, WA 98122
Total head count enrollment-Credit: 7,499; Non-Credit: 1,414
Campuses/sites: 2; Full-time faculty: 135

UNDERGRADUATE CURRICULUM DEVELOPMENT IN CALCULUS

Changing the delivery of calculus is meant to attract more students to science and mathematics

A significant collaboration between two-year and four-year institutions in Washington state has impacted more than 5,000 students studying calculus, now delivered in significantly new ways. The changes impacted curricula, methods of delivery to students, and use of technology in instruction. The goal is to attract and retain a greater number of students in science and mathematics. In addition, the Seattle Community College District VI seeks to establish an ongoing statewide network of two- and four-year college faculty members committed to calculus reform.

In a program funded by the National Science Foundation, two summer workshops for two-year and four-year mathematics faculty were held at Seattle Central. The principle authors of the Harvard Calculus Consortium materials and the Duke University's Project CALC brought their two versions of reformed calculus and presented them to participants. Faculty were able to explore these materials in-depth and develop plans for implementing curricula changes at their home institutions.

Training also was provided in a wide variety of hardware and mathematical software now available to enhance mathematics instruction. Faculty were invited to discuss the applicability of the use of technology in their particular setting and to become familiar with the resources available. They also learned about using active and collaborative learning modes in the mathematics classroom. Participants themselves provided a rich source of information on methods and significant, real-life application problems.

The result of this activity will be to prepare faculty who can reverse some of the disappointing trends in calculus education over the last few years. In particular we hope to:
•improve completion rates in calculus courses;

- improve the ability of students who pass calculus to apply the information they have supposedly learned; and
- prepare students to use technology intelligently in the solution of mathematical problems.

In the first two years alone more than 50 math faculty and 20 institutions have been directly involved. Perhaps just as significant, a network of faculty committed to and enthusiastic about curricular reform has been established and its work is ongoing.

Contact:
Herb Bryce, Associate Dean, Science and Math
(206) 587-6921

Seattle Community College District VI
1500 Harvard
Seattle, WA 98122
Total head count enrollment-Credit: 20,458; Non-Credit: 3,824
Campuses/sites: 7; Full-time faculty: 312

INTERNATIONAL TRADE INSTITUTE

▓ *Customized training is designed for specific industrial groups* ▓
such as those in customs brokerage and freight forwarding

With one out of five jobs directly related to trade, Washington State is more trade-dependent than any other state. Into this business climate came The International Trade Institute (ITI), developed in 1987 as a resource center in education, training and counseling to help small businesses compete effectively in the international marketplace.

The ITI was established as a direct response to the community demand for qualified personnel in international business. The Institute provides a number of programs and services, including a practical, 30-credit Certificate in International Trade. Courses include: Introduction to International Trade, Fundamentals of Import/Export, International Marketing, International Finance, International Operations, IM/EX Operations, Trade Geography, International Legal Issues, and Cultural Imperatives in Asia/Europe. In addition, local and international internships are established for students as an elective. The Certificate is designed for all levels of managers, professionals and entrepreneurs engaged in overseas business.

The ITI also offers a full range of non-credit workshops, seminars and conferences. Customized training is designed for specific industrial groups, such as customs brokerage and freight forwarding. Recently, the ITI has fulfilled

contracts for private industry in international business and cultural applications. The ITI was recently recognized by the Department of Education as one of the top five programs in the U.S. in trade education for a two-year college. The Institute has the most comprehensive training in international business/trade in Washington State.

One of the key services of ITI is the Export Development Specialist (EDS). The EDS counsels more than 150 new clients each year on a long- and short-term basis. The EDS assists companies who are new to export with technical advice, business planning expertise, data searches and market research. Housed at North Seattle Community College, the ITI is the international counseling center for the Washington State Small Business Development Center system.

The EDS affects the community through assisting companies in international trade, and by collecting statistics on sales, job retention and job creation. The Certificate promotes trade to local and state businesses. ITI faculty assist other faculty members in internationalizing the curricula. The ITI earns money through its self-support budget, and has a high profile in the community, which contributes to the reputation of the Seattle Community College District.

Contact:
Janis Parsley, Director, North Seattle College
(206) 527-3732

Seattle Community College District VI
1500 Harvard
Seattle, WA 98122
Total head count enrollment-Credit: 20,458; Non-Credit: 3,824
Campuses/sites: 7; Full-time faculty: 312

THE GENERAL EDUCATION CORE

The core includes outcomes, integrated learning and multicultural education, all meant to make students more well-rounded

Because understanding relationships of people, history and ideas is as important for all students as communication and critical-thinking skills are to all programs of study, Shoreline Community College created an integrated core curriculum.

In 1989, faculty representing the breadth of the curriculum designed the limited but coherent core curriculum that was driven by general education student learning outcomes and would be required of all SCC degree recipients. The 20 student outcomes include the broad categories of basic skills (communication, quantitative reasoning, critical thinking), social functioning (attitudes, values, interpersonal relations), and general knowledge (e.g. historical and social ideas, science and technology, the aesthetics of the arts across time and cultures, environmental and personal health). For most degree programs, the general education core consists of 23 credits in: College Composition (five credits); Quantitative Reasoning (five credits); Multicultural Education (three credits); and Integrated Studies (10 credits). Students in some of the applied degree and specific university transfer programs complete only 18 of the 23 core credits.

Communication and critical thinking skills, along with understanding relationships of people, history and ideas, are cultivated in a faculty-designed core that includes integrated studies courses.

Integrated Studies A courses consist of both:

1) especially developed five-credit classes that incorporate instruction in writing and critical thinking and the essential ideas and texts from broad interdisciplinary studies such as science and humanities; and

2) 10 to 15 credit learning communities that engage students in team taught combined courses focused on common outcomes and themes.

Integrated Studies B courses consist of more traditional but broadened five credit courses that integrate the ideas and information of two or more disciplines within one division such as "Appreciation of Music," which now integrates dance, drama and music, or "Literature of the American West," which integrates art and Literature. The Multicultural Education requirement can be satisfied by the specially developed three credit course "Multicultural Issues" or a limited number of other courses that meet the criteria for multicultural education, e.g., "Gender, Race, Class" and "Sociology of Minority Groups."

Recognizing that completion of a small number of courses is only a beginning to student achievement of the broad general education outcomes, the faculty have written revised master course outlines for all current courses which incorporate the 20 general education outcomes; in addition, the general education committees have reviewed and will continue to review courses proposed as satisfying the categories of the core requirements. The faculty have also assessed such fundamental outcomes as college-level writing skills and are beginning a five-year system of assessing the major categories of the 20 student learning outcomes. Outcomes assessment activities which have resulted in revisions to teaching and the core curriculum are published in our quarterly outcomes assessment newsletter.

The General Education Core has involved the majority of the full-time faculty either in its development, the teaching of courses, or in assessing student learning outcomes. The result is a renewed focus on teaching and learning at Shoreline, a clearer definition of what it means to be generally educated if you are a SCC graduate, and a stronger commitment to student success through higher academic standards, a concentration on basic skills across the curriculum, and inclusion of multicultural and integrated studies in the core curriculum.

Contact:
Marie Rosenwasser, Vice President, Academic Affairs
(206) 546 4451

Shoreline Community College
16101 Greenwood Avenue North
Seattle, WA 96133
Total head count enrollment-Credit: 8,051; Non-Credit: 900
Campuses/sites: 2; Full-time faculty: 152

AUTOMOTIVE TECHNOLOGY

▣ Each program – Toyota T Ten, GM ASEP, or Honda PACT – is ▣
seven quarters long and includes three quarters of internship

"Partnerships." "Educating for real jobs." "Work force training." These are all popular terms for what community colleges and higher education should be doing to support economic development and to secure the future for higher education and the nation. While these concepts are good, they are not easy to achieve; therefore, when a program such as Shoreline Community College's Automotive Technician Training Program operationalizes successfully major themes of the day, it is worth noting.

After operating a successful generic automotive technician training program for nine years, the college evaluated the quality of the program, the need for highly trained technicians in the Puget Sound region and state, the increasingly strong relationship it and the Shoreline College Foundation were developing with the Puget Sound Auto Dealers Association, and decided to begin factory-specific automotive technician training programs. Today the college offers the Toyota T Ten, GM ASEP, and Honda PACT automotive technician training programs. Each program is seven quarters in length, includes three quarters interning in an area dealership, leads to an Associate of Applied Arts and Science, which includes education in communication, computation, human relations, multicultural studies, and integrated studies in the liberal arts.

The partnership between the college and automotive industry is threefold:

1) every student is sponsored by a dealer with whom the student interns three quarters;
2) the PSADA donates thousands of dollars of cars for instructional use, helps promote the program, find dealer sponsors, secure advisory council members, and obtain donations of equipment;
3) the manufacturers set the minimum requirements for certification and supply training materials and substantial amounts of state-of-the-art equipment;
4) the Foundation raised more than $1-million and issued certificates of deposit to construct the new Professional Automotive Training Center on campus;
5) the college hires the faculty, admits the students, combines general education with the technical training, leases the building from the Foundation, and provides all the structure, instruction, and support services needed for these first-rate vocational programs; and
6) through continuing education the college sponsors self-support work force training courses in such areas as sales, service writing, and factory retraining for more than 3,000 employees from the local automotive industry.

Indications of the high quality of this vocational program include the quality of the facility, the success of the graduates, and the excellence of the faculty. The Professional Automotive Training Center is a model for other community college automotive training facilities, boasting a model dealership with a shop that has state-of-the-art equipment, a computer lab with automotive service software, classrooms, and a library. The faculty stay current by training two to four weeks each year. The GM ASEP instructor was named national ASEP instructor of the year in 1992. Each program is evaluated as one of the best in the region. The programs enjoy a high program completion rate. All of the students have jobs when they graduate.

Contact:
David Rosenquist, Chair, Industrial Tech Division, (206) 546-4590
Donald Schultz, Assistant Division Chair, Industrial Tech, (206) 546-4573

Shoreline Community College
16101 Greenwood Avenue N.
Seattle, WA 96133
Total head count enrollment-Credit: 8,051; Non-Credit: 900
Campuses/sites: 2; Full-time faculty: 152

ENVIRONMENTAL PRESERVATION TECHNOLOGY

▣ The program includes hands-on experience in river and stream enhancement, ▣
water quality testing, community relations and trail-building.

An innovative new program Skagit Valley College provides training for displaced timberworkers as well as environmental aid for water, our greatest natural resource.

Such a program was greatly needed in the Skagit Valley, hard-hit by massive layoffs and cutbacks in the timber industry. Timberworkers, loggers, drivers, millworkers and other Northwest Washington residents faced unemployment and welfare – and serious needs for retraining. Meanwhile, the Skagit River and its tributaries were in

Continues on Page 740

serious environmental decline. Waters once rich with salmon, steelhead and other species were dwindling. Dam construction and decades of heavy logging had taken their toll. The Skagit River, long a source of employment as well as recreation, needed restoration.

Working together with local agencies, legislators, businesspeople and millowners, Skagit Valley College created the Environmental Preservation Program to provide training for new jobs in agencies related to the upgrading of the Skagit River. As students within the existing Parks and Recreation program, students make use of the skills they learned in the woods and learn new ones they will need for future jobs.

The two-year program combines classroom study with practical, hands-on experience in river and stream enhancement, water quality testing, community relations and trail-building. Students who successfully complete the program receive an Associate of Technical Arts degree and are eligible for jobs in the field of environmental preservation.

Contact:
Claus Svendsen, Instructor
(206) 428-1679

Skagit Valley College
2405 College Way
Mount Vernon, WA 98273
Total head count enrollment-Credit: 6,000; Non-Credit: 2,000
Campuses/sites: 4; Full-time faculty: 105

STUDENT HOUSING PROJECT

College Foundation volunteers developed a plan for student housing that involved purchasing nine acres adjacent to the campus

Following a series of surveys, research projects and personal interviews, Skagit Valley College administrators determined recently that the school faced a serious housing shortage. Apartments suitable for students were scarce – and expensive. However, the statewide budget picture did not look promising. Funding for essential college services and job training were at risk; a student housing project seemed impossible.

Thanks to an active group of community volunteers involved in the Skagit Valley College Foundation (a private, non-profit organization), this dream came true. Foundation volunteers developed a plan for student housing and purchased nine acres adjacent to campus on which to build it. The cost of the project was approximately $3.3-million. Fully registered bonds, issued by a major Northwest bank, provided financing for the project.

The project consists of a cluster of seven two-story buildings situated in a park-like setting. Five of the buildings contain four apartments and two contain eight apartments. Each apartment is approximately 940 square feet and will contain four bedrooms, one bath, a kitchen and a living/dining area.

The complex will accommodate 140 students in 36 units. The buildings are designed to be secure, attractive and convenient. The apartments are close to campus, jogging trails, ball fields and campus theaters. In the future, the apartments may offer short-term housing for international delegations, business seminars, sports camps and other functions of the college.

Contact:
Patrick Kennicott, Executive Director, SVC Foundation
(206) 428-1196

Skagit Valley College
2405 College Way
Mount Vernon, WA 98273
Total head count enrollment-Credit: 6,000; Non-Credit: 2,000
Campuses/sites: 4; Full-time faculty: 105

FIRE PROTECTION TECHNOLOGY

⧉ *Students work regular 24-hour shifts every three days* ⧉
with the fire district as part of their related experience

This one-of-a-kind program for Washington partners South Puget Sound Community College with a fire district in training firefighters, students work regular 24-hour shifts every three days with the fire district as part of their related experience.

For the Associate of Technical Arts in Fire Protection Technology program, the fire district provides the facility, equipment and lead instructor; the college funds supplies, materials, part-time instructors and a small stipend to the fire district for program coordination. The partnership developed as a result of fire district personnel contacting college representatives to express the need for ways in which potential professional firefighters could be provided education and training appropriate for job entry.

Both men and women seeking careers in the fire service and/or who are already employed, but wish to earn an Associate of Technical Arts degree, are enrolled in the program. Upon completion of the program, students meet all Performance Standards for National Fire Protection Association (NFPA) Firefighter I, II and III classifications.

Students work regular 24-hour shifts every three days with the fire district as part of their related experience. In addition, they take core courses covering such subjects as hazardous materials, fire department leadership, rescue practices, fire codes and firefighter law. These classes are offered at one of the fire stations within the fire district. Students come to the college's campus to take their general education classes (communications, sciences, mathematics and humanities).

Without the strong partnership and support from the fire district, it would not be possible for us to offer a program such as this because of the prohibitively high cost of equipment necessary to provide quality educational experiences for our students.

Contact:
John Mack, Deputy Chief
(206) 866-1000

South Puget Sound Community College
2011 Mottman Road
Olympia, WA 98512
Total head count enrollment-Credit: 6,514; Non-Credit: 2,276
Campuses/sites: 1; Full-time faculty: 72

INTERPRETER TRAINING (FOR THE DEAF)

⧉ *Program graduates qualify for employment in entry-level positions* ⧉
in a variety of public- and private-sector settings

In response to an overwhelming need for certified interpreters in the lower Puget Sound area, the Washington State Board for Community and Technical Colleges granted approval to the college to offer a two-year Associate of Technical Arts degree program in Interpreter Training. The college began the program with fall quarter 1992, after first conducting a national search for a qualified instructor/coordinator.

Graduates from the program qualify for employment in entry-level interpreting positions in an educational setting and/or in a variety of public or private settings as a free-lance interpreter.

The Interpreter Training program is designed for people who enjoy variety and interaction with people, enjoy setting their own hours, who are self-motivated and flexible, and who can attend to the professional ethics involved in interpreting for the deaf.

There is a nationwide shortage of certified interpreters for the deaf. For an individual interested in free-lancing, salaries upon graduation from the two-year program can range between $14 to $20 per hour. Interpreters will be working in a variety of situations which may change daily. They can choose to work in various educational, medical, mental health, and legal settings or they may interpret theater, concert, television or religious presentations.

Students practice their newly found skills while in the program by participating in practicums where they observe or interpret in a variety of settings.

The program has been assisted by officials working for such agencies as Washington State Services for the Deaf, the Office of the Superintendent of Instruction, and the

Continues on Page 742

local Educational Service District. As the program becomes more established, our area is likely to experience an increase in deaf residents because they will be able to access qualified interpreters, which has not been the case in the past.

Contact:
Deborah Kunschik, Instructor/Coordinator
(206) 754-7711, ext. 7711

South Puget Sound Community College
2011 Mottman Road
Olympia, WA 98512
Total head count enrollment-Credit: 6,514; Non-Credit: 2,276
Campuses/sites: 1; Full-time faculty: 72

HIGH SCHOOL STUDENTS "INTRODUCTION TO COLLEGE"

▓ *Two different projects attract high school students to the college,* ▓
where the projects have caused little disruption of other activities

Many high school students graduate without a clear picture of the opportunities available to them at the community college. South Seattle Community College has instituted two different projects in which high school students spend some time on campus, seeing what is available and experiencing the atmosphere: the Summer School Project and the Pre-Collegiate Visit Project.

The Summer School Project is a cooperative effort between SSCC and the Seattle Public Schools has been established involving more than 20 high school students each summer. Students are selected from those considered at risk of dropping out before completion of high school. The project enrolls students in a computer applications course taught at the college as part of the college curriculum. The course meets five days per week (two hours per day) for eight weeks. By completing the course, students earn high school and college credit simultaneously. In addition, the students are placed in campus offices and laboratories for another four hours per day where they work alongside clerical and laboratory support staff, gaining valuable work experience and earning money.

The Pre-College Visit Project is a cooperative effort between SSCC and the SeaTac Occupational Skills Center. Begun in the fall of 1992, it involves 40 students who are enrolled in a high school electronics program at the Skills Center. Students spend every Wednesday visiting industrial sites or community college classes as part of an attempt to familiarize students with options after graduation. During their visits to community college, students sit in on classes in Basic Electronics, Avionics and Robotics. Plans are under way to extend the program to students interested in other vocational and technical fields.

Both programs have been implemented with little disruption to ongoing activities at the college. The most important effect that will be monitored over the next few years is the proportion of these students who enroll in community college courses after graduation from high school.

Contact:
Jerry Riehl, Associate Dean
(206) 763-5132

South Seattle Community College
6000 16th Avenue SW
Seattle, WA 98103
Total head count enrollment-Credit: 6,055; Non-Credit: 464
Campuses/sites: 2; Full-time faculty: 77

PROGRAM EVALUATION

▓ *The ongoing evaluation is meant to strengthen academic programs* ▓
and institutional effectiveness of the college

South Seattle Community College is implementing a comprehensive institutional assessment program using Title III Strengthening Institution resources. It is designed to:
1) do intelligent planning for the future;
2) improve existing programs, and where there are severe fiscal restraints or other causes, identify programs which are to be dropped;
3) give continued accountability of expenditures; and
4) self-validate.

An institutional planner and research analyst have been hired to assist college divisions participating in the assessment process. A three-year cycle of assessment has been established during the first year of implementation and will be repeated in the next two years. The ultimate goal is to institutionalize the process of assessment so that programs are continually receiving data related to goals attainment and are adapting based on this information. One-third of the college divisions will participate in assessment each year. An Institutional Effectiveness Advisory Committee comprised of faculty, staff and administrators facilitates the project by approving the divisions' intended outcomes and assessment strategies, as well as working as consultants with faculty and staff in the divisions. A faculty or staff member from each division will be given release-time to expedite the project at the division level.

The effectiveness project is anticipated to take four years

to fully implement. During the first year of the project, the baseline information on institutional climate was collected, and the first four divisions were selected to develop intended outcomes. Employees' feedback concerning the beginning phase of the project has been very positive. All four divisions reported that communication within their division has improved considerably since the division began their collective work to establish division goals and outcomes measures. The ultimate goal of the project is to institutionalize the process of assessment so that programs are continually receiving data related to goals attainment and are adapting based on this information. The assessment information received will be used in planning, resource allocation and curriculum revision.

Contact:
Karen Foss, Associate Dean
(206) 764-5378

South Seattle Community College
6000 16th Avenue SW
Seattle, WA 98103
Total head count enrollment-Credit: 6,055; Non-Credit: 464
Campuses/sites: 2; Full-time faculty: 77

LEARNING COMMUNITIES / COORDINATED STUDIES

Coordinated studies provide a powerful college climate for active and interactive learning

An interwoven curriculum design makes it possible for Tacoma Community College faculty and students to work together to discover a new kind of enriched intellectual ground. In this form of learning community called coordinated studies, students and faculty members experience courses and disciplines not as isolated offerings, but rather as a complementary and connected whole. The curriculum provides a powerful climate for active and interactive learning.

Coordinated studies at TCC are team-taught by two to three faculty and include 10 to 15 credits per academic quarter. This model allows part-time adult students (as well as full-time students) to take these programs. A special manifestation of coordinated studies at TCC is the

Bridge program, done in association with The Evergreen State College, Tacoma branch. The design of the program is a course of studies in which TCC teaches the first two years of the four-year program at Evergreen's Tacoma campus. The curriculum is coordinated studies in format and is designed for adults interested in completing a four-year degree at Evergreen. The program is focused for adults with limited or no previous college experience. The program typically registers about 75 to 80 percent minority students each academic quarter.

Coordinated studies at TCC have received national recognition from the AACC, national humanities organizations, the *Wall Street Journal*, and, internationally, from presentations in Canada.

Contact:
Gael Tower, Associate Dean, Humanities
(206) 566-5069

Tacoma Community College
5900 South 12th Street
Tacoma, WA 98465
Total head count enrollment-Credit: 18,000; Non-Credit: 5,200
Campuses/sites: 3; Full-time faculty: 93

STAGE (STUDENT ACCESS TO GROWTH AND EARNING)

*▦ STAGE is a leadership training program that involves placing students ▦
into on-campus, paid management positions*

It is well-documented that participation in campus activities outside of the classroom increases the likelihood of student success. The primary objective of the STAGE Program at Tacoma Community College is to aid participating students in the pursuit of their educational and career goals while enhancing their college experience.

The Student Access to Growth and Earning Program (STAGE) is a leadership training program which involves placing students into paid management positions on our campus. Some of the positions in STAGE include intramural coordinator, outdoor recreation coordinator, entertainment programmer, performing arts coordinator, publicity coordinator and club coordinator. In addition to the paid-manager positions, STAGE students attend a two-credit leadership management course throughout the year and are members of the ASTCC student government. STAGE students by their involvement in manager positions, student government and management training, have a major impact on student programs at Tacoma Community College.

The program accomplishes this objective by providing the following:
1) a comprehensive leadership training program;
2) a financial package to assist with the cost of education;
3) an opportunity to belong to a high-energy, positive group;
4) individual mentoring and advising; and
5) practical employment training and experience.

In addition to helping participating students, the program is designed to:
1) improve the quality and quantity of offerings for student programs;
2) place top-quality students into paid positions on campus;
3) increase college retention;
4) aid in the college recruitment effort; and
5) provide an opportunity for TCC to enhance its image within the high school community and the greater Tacoma community.

Contact:
Tom Keegan, Associate Dean, Student Services
(206) 566-5046

Tacoma Community College
5900 South 12th Street
Tacoma, WA 98465
Total head count enrollment-Credit: 18,000; Non-Credit: 5,200
Campuses/sites: 3; Full-time faculty: 93

RESPIRATORY THERAPY

*▦ The program was established through a consortium agreement with Walla Walla, ▦
three area hospitals and Creighton University of Omaha*

The Respiratory Therapy program at Walla Walla Community College was established through a consortium that recognized a critical need for credentialed respiratory therapists in rural Southeastern Washington. The Marcus Whitman Program of Respiratory Therapy serves local medical facilities, the immediate community, and outlying areas; hospitals are in the 40- to 200-bed size range in communities with populations of 10,000 to 80,000.

The program was established in 1982 through a consortium agreement which involved Walla Walla Community College, three area hospitals, and Creighton University of Omaha, Nebraska. The original classroom was located at St. Mary Medical Center, one of the sponsoring hospitals. Two local registered therapists were hired as instructors for the program and a staff physician served as medical director. During this initial period, the general education requirements were provided by Walla Walla Community

College, while Creighton University provided the curriculum for the second year.

In 1988 and in 1993, the program received autonomous accreditation from the Joint Review Committee for Respiratory Therapy Education following a self-study and site visitation process. The affiliates continue to support the program by allowing their staff to supervise and instruct students, providing a learning environment, and participating in the program advisory committee.

The Respiratory Therapy Program, offered at only five community colleges in the state, was one of three vocational programs on the Walla Walla Community College campus chosen in 1989 for review by the Washington State Board for Community and Technical Colleges. The program is currently one of five vocational programs on campus that are the focus of a $2.5-million Title III Strengthening Institutions Grant awarded by the U.S.

Department of Education; this five-year grant, the largest in the history of Walla Walla Community College, will provide additional support for the program.

The original mission of the program, that of providing training and education in a rural setting with the goal of retraining qualified therapists, has realized its goal. In the 11 years since its inception, the program has produced more than 100 qualified graduates, many of whom are employed in hospitals and clinics in Walla Walla and neighboring communities. The college graduated its 11th class of respiratory therapists in August of 1993.

Contact:
Bob Mitchell, Instructor
(509) 527-4230

Walla Walla Community College
500 Tausick Way
Walla Walla, WA 99362
Total head count enrollment-Credit: 5,417; Non-Credit: 1,225
Campuses/sites: 4; Full-time faculty: 101

IRRIGATION TECHNOLOGY

*❖ The program has linked into a worldwide industrial network ❖
and consists of 18 continuous months of training*

The irrigation industry has experienced a period of rapid growth in technical advancement since the late 1960's. Walla Walla Community College, positioned in the middle of the irrigated Pacific Northwest states of Washington, Oregon and Idaho, responded with the Irrigation Technology Program, the only program of its kind in the world when created in 1977.

The Irrigation Technology Program remains unique today in teaching students how to operate, maintain, repair and design sophisticated irrigation systems. It has been continuously updated through the years to give its graduates the best possible basis for employment in the trade while earning an Associate in Applied Arts and Sciences Degree.

Since its inception, the Irrigation Technology Program has taken its lead from industry needs. On-campus training takes place during fall and winter quarters of the two-year program. Spring and summer quarters of the first year are used for cooperative training, with the student receiving at least 1,000 hours of job experience at the farm, retail, wholesale, contractor or manufacturer level. Graduation occurs at the end of the second winter quarter, which coincides with the beginning of the yearly irrigation season and the hiring of new employees.

The irrigation industry is a very small but viable industry that works in a worldwide network. The Irrigation Technology Program at Walla Walla Community College has linked into this network and is respected around the globe as one of the few colleges that trains people to:
1) construct irrigation systems;
2) repair and maintain irrigation systems;
3) develop water management and conservation skills;

and
4) design and install basic farm and landscape/turf irrigation systems.

The course consists of 18 continuous months of training, specifically in irrigation, and prepares the student for a career in an industry where demand exceeds the supply of trained technicians, and advancement potential is unlimited.

The key to the success of the Irrigation Technology Program at Walla Walla Community College is the strong support industry provides through contributions of equipment, training aids and current information. Advisory committee members, representing various organizations within the irrigation community, assist by updating curriculum and assessing equipment to ensure that the program stays on the cutting edge of technology in the industry.

In 1983, the program received the Secretary's Award from the U.S. Department of Education as the outstanding vocational program in the Pacific Northwest, as well as the Award for Excellence in Ag Technology Instruction for the Western United States presented by the National Association of State Departments of Agriculture.

Walla Walla Community College's U.S. Department of Education Title III grant is expected to assist the College in strengthening its Irrigation Technology Program in 1993-94. College officials anticipate that the grant, which must be re-applied for annually, will provide funds to review the irrigation technology curriculum and to purchase additional state-of-the-art instructional resources and equipment.

Contact:
Greg Farrens, Instructor
(509) 527-4250

Walla Walla Community College
500 Tausick Way
Walla Walla, WA 99362
Total head count enrollment-Credit: 5,417; Non-Credit: 1,225
Campuses/sites: 4; Full-time faculty: 101

TREE FRUIT PRODUCTION

The partnership with industry has contributed greatly to the strength of the program, through both curriculum development and donations

Wenatchee Valley College, located in North Central Washington – the Apple Capital of the World – has been drawing students from throughout North America to its Tree Fruit Production Program ever since it began in January 1985.

The college worked with industry leaders, including an advisory committee, to develop the two-year program that combines strong horticultural science studies with practical hands-on training. The advisory committee continues to work with the college to ensure that the program continues to meet the needs of students and the industry.

In recognition of the program's quality and contributions, it has received two prestigious awards: the National Association of State Departments of Agriculture/RJR-Nabisco Award for Excellence in Agriculture Technology Instruction and the Secretary's Award for Outstanding Vocational Program, a national award from the United States Department of Education. In addition, the advisory committee was named the Outstanding Vocational Advisory Committee in the state of Washington in 1989, and Dr. Kent Mullinix, director of the program, was selected as the WVC Faculty Member of the Year in 1992.

The partnership with industry has contributed greatly to the strength of the program, not only in curriculum development, but also in obtaining substantial cash and in-kind donations for the procurement and development of two laboratory orchards, one 8.5 acres and the other 40 acres. Plantings include state-of-the-art commercial plantings, as well as variety and rootstock trials in cooperation with the state university. Students perform all orchard operations in these plantings where they learn production practices as well as scientific methodology.

The curriculum is highly specific in pomology. Even related agriculture classes emphasize pomology. For example, the entomology and soils classes have an orchard emphasis and the financial management class relates to orchard operation so that horticulture is not separate from economics. The same person who teaches the orchard business management course of study to professional orchardists teaches the financial management courses in the tree fruit degree program, bringing real-world knowledge into the classroom. In this technical program, agricultural science is taught at a college level and academic standards are not compromised. In addition to college-level agricultural science studies, students take a full complement of English, economics, speech, math and chemistry classes. What has resulted is the teaching of this applied science at a college level with a curriculum predicted upon the concept that scientific studies and production studies are not mutually exclusive but rather complementary and even synergistic in effect.

Student leadership is an integral part of the program, emphasizing professionalism and the development of affective skills and attitudes needed to function as professionals in tree fruit industry. This is done by integrating the students through activities and internships in the tree fruit industry in North Central Washington. For example, through the Tree Fruit Production Student Association, students perform many vital industry functions such as organizing and putting on, in cooperation with the Washington State Horticulture Association, the North Central Washington Fieldmen's Association and the Washington State University Cooperative Extension Services, the semiannual Washington State Post-Harvest Conference's trade show, the largest post-harvest trade show in the country.

The Tree Fruit Production Program also organizes the annual Miller Lecture Series in Agriculture, the first community college endowed lecture series in the state of Washington. In 1993, the lecture series was part of the International Dwarf Fruit Tree Association meeting in Wenatchee. This is another example of the program's cooperation with other important industry organizations.

Wenatchee Valley College and Washington State University have now developed an articulated, two-tiered AAS/BS degree program. WVC contributes its strong production-oriented pomology classes and orchard-oriented agriculture classes, such as pathology, entomology, soils, financial management, and introductory plant physiology. WSU contributes upper-division classes, such as advanced physiology and genetics. All pomology students in the state would attend WVC for a program, students will have earned associate and bachelor's degrees. Transcending mere transferability, the two institutions are contributing their respective academic strengths to create one statewide, undergraduate curriculum that is setting the standards in pomology studies for the nation.

Contact:
Woody Ahn, Dean, Technical and Applied Sciences
(509) 662-1651

Wenatchee Valley College
1300 Fifth Street
Wenatchee, WA 98801
Total head count enrollment-Credit: 2,702; Non-Credit: 662
Campuses/sites: 2; Full-time faculty: 63

ENGLISH COMPOSITION

Because teaching composition via word processing is superior to hand-drafting and chalkboard technology, the college embraced computers in the classroom

Wenatchee Valley College was one of the first community colleges in the state to start using computers on an extensive basis in its English classes, beginning in 1989. From the beginning, it was shown that teaching composition via word processing was indisputably a far superior method of instruction than hand-drafting and chalkboard technology. Wenatchee Valley College was soon known as a leader in the state using computers to facilitate the writing process.

The college's English instructors knew that word processing helps students write better faster. Revision, the most important aspect of the writing process, was no longer painful for them. The software, which is very powerful and sophisticated, allows the students to use word processing to its fullest advantage. The students leave the class with better composition skills as well as word processing skills. The faculty members know that their students will be writing in whatever profession they choose. The prime objective is to provide the students with revision and editing expertise to increase their understanding of the prime process in the development of good writing skills. The students, in evaluations, consistently say that the use of word processing is the most beneficial part of beginning college writing through research writing and technical report writing.

The equipment in the English lab and faculty offices includes freestanding PCs and a networked system of terminals. The system allows individual closed use and small- and large-group exercises for students. It also allows instructors to work in isolation and privacy while allowing access to both student and departmental files. The lab is located next to the English composition classroom, allowing an entire class to move to the lab facility. Computers have been added to the classroom as well, and the campus now has approximately 50 dedicated computers for English composition. Students may use the lab for English homework outside of the classroom. As software improves and evolves, the software in the lab and classroom is upgraded.

The program has been recognized on state and regional levels. The English faculty has been invited to give presentations on the program to regional and state professional meetings in the humanities and composition. In the last accreditation report, Wenatchee Valley College's composition program was listed as one of the institution's strengths.

Additionally, the WVC faculty have undertaken several large student learning outcomes assessment projects to determine areas their own students have the greatest strengths and weaknesses. Research is ongoing, although it has shown that the WVC English composition students are especially strong in the organization and development of their writing.

Contact:
Joann Schoen, Dean of Liberal Arts and Sciences
(509) 662-1651

Wenatchee Valley College
1300 Fifth Street
Wenatchee, WA 98801
Total head count enrollment-Credit: 2,702; Non-Credit: 662
Campuses/sites: 2; Full-time faculty: 63

STUDENT ANTHOLOGY / SOURCEBOOK

Among other things, the anthology assesses quantity and quality of student writing and thinking and promotes student success and pride of accomplishment

A unique anthology is currently being published annually at YVCC. The anthology, titled *Mainsprings*, features student coursework complemented by instructors' comments regarding the intent of each assignment and the qualities of writing and critical thinking each exemplifies.

Mainsprings is interdisciplinary in that it contains student coursework from the Arts and Sciences, Vocational, Adult Basic Education, and Developmental arenas. *Mainsprings* is intentionally designed to be aesthetically pleasing. Full color reproductions of student artwork are featured inside and on its cover. In addition, a number of the written contributions are computer scanned, rather than typeset, to emphasize the attractiveness of original handwritten work, and to show respect for the "process" of thought, rather than the "product" alone.

Besides offering a sampling of writing and critical thinking across the curriculum at YVCC, the anthology also:

1) assesses the quantity and quality of student writing and thinking;
2) provides an assignment "sourcebook" for instructors;

Continues on Page 748

3) promotes student success and pride of accomplishment;

4) encourages more writing and critical thinking across the curriculum; and

5) celebrates the value of student coursework in the academic life of the college.

Initial implementation of the anthology project required recruitment of, and release time for, a faculty project director. The director conceived the unique format of the anthology; coordinated on- and off-campus workshops for faculty on the topics of discipline-specific writing exercises, critical thinking and classroom assessment; solicited submissions; utilized a representational editorial team to choose *Mainsprings* selections; typeset (with student assistance) most of the selections; oversaw the printing and distribution of the publication and assisted in hosting a reception to honor student and faculty contributors.

Mainsprings has been very well-received by the faculty and staff who enjoy complimentary copies of it each year. Other YVCC constituents who have received and praised *Mainsprings*, include community college educators in Washington state and elsewhere, the college's Board of Trustees and Foundation members, area legislators, Washington State Community and Technical College board members, area legislators, and Washington State Community and Technical College board members. The anthology has also received acclaim from the Washington Community College Humanities Association. *Mainsprings* is currently a required text for a number of "Freshman Seminar" classes, because it demonstrates faculty expectations about student writing and critical-thinking skills.

The anthology project was originally founded through a competitive Assessment Grant awarded by the Washington State Board for Community and Technical Colleges.

Contact:
Gary Tollefson, Dean of Arts and Sciences, (509) 575-2401
Elaine Smith, Instructor-In-Charge, (509) 575-2416

Yakima Valley Community College
PO Box 1647
Yakima, WA 98907
Total head count enrollment-Credit: 5,833; Non-Credit: 106
Campuses/sites: 4; Full-time faculty: 107

CULTURALLY DIVERSE AND ECONOMICALLY DISADVANTAGED CHILDREN GO TO COLLEGE

The college targets a group of migrant and economically disadvantaged children to be adopted by the Radiologic Technology Program

"Adopt An Elementary School" is a national project which has been uniquely implemented at Yakima Valley Community College, where a group of migrant and economically disadvantaged children are adopted by the YVCC-Radiologic Technology Program. Initiated in 1991, this program was a cooperative effort between the Migrant Education Regional Office, Yakima Valley Community College, and Adams Elementary School to share a vision with children about their future learning potential. This project involved 90 children from grades three and four.

The purpose of this project was: to teach economically disadvantaged and culturally diverse children about what a community college is; to demonstrate the advantages in obtaining a college education; to show that faculty, staff and students care about our youth in the community; and to encourage children at the elementary level to become excited about college as they progress through school. Lynne Milford, Curriculum Generalist for the Migrant Education Regional Office was the primary force in bringing YVCC and Adams Elementary together.

In the fall of 1991, the children were invited to campus to visit with a variety of staff from the Radiologic Technology (RT-medical x-ray), Dental Hygiene, Early Childhood Education, Nursing, and Occupational Therapy Assistant (OTA) programs; to participate in special hands-on activities related to the program, and to see a stage play directed by Dr. George Meshke. The Radiologic students under the direction of Peggy Keller, RT instructor, successfully implemented the program. Team leaders were selected from the RT program to work with the children, in groups of 10. Each group had two team leaders to answer questions.

Special demonstrations were provided and children were allowed to participate in activities related to each program career. Activities included:

1) in RT the taking of blood pressures, handling phantom body parts, and processing an x-ray film; and

2) in OTA, the children learned how to use the large balance balls and participated in hand-coordination

tests. The visit concluded with a tour of the campus and lunch in the Student Residence Center.

Each of the children received a personal "pen-pal" letter from an RT student and/or an English student, under the direction of Shannon Hopkins, English instructor, to let the children know the YVCC students were still very interested in them and to set the stage for the YVCC staff and students to visit the children in their classrooms at Adams Elementary. Some letters were written in Spanish, by Hispanic and bilingual RT students because some of the children could not speak or write English. The RT students wanted to demonstrate, through role modeling, that people of many cultures have careers in x-ray. The English class students used this extra writing project to hone their skills. YVCC Spanish instructor, Ricardo Chama treated the children to a puppet show. The YVCC puppeteers included Perry Morrison, student; Dar Baird, Health Services nurse; and Bernal Baca, Dean for Student Development.

A total of 33 RT students, three instructors, one college counselor and one administrative assistant visited Adams Elementary in early March. Students were divided into three classrooms. One class was entirely Spanish-speaking. The RT students and the Administrative assistant were bilingual, and thus attended to the Hispanic children. Each RT student worked with a partner to share a variety of x-rays such as a horse's knee, a human knee, and a phantom knee for comparison with small groups of three to four children. A pin used for fixing fractured hips was shown,

and also, x-rays showing proper placement of the pin in the hip. RT students even brought their own children to show they were mothers and dads, in addition to being students. During this visit, the children shared letters they had written in response to the RT students' letters and presented gifts to the RT students.

The "Adopt an Elementary School" project culminated in a four-hour picnic at the end of the school year for the YVCC-RT students and the Adams Elementary children. After eating, the YVCC students and children played such games as soccer, baseball, relay races and gunny sack races. The project resulted in great benefits for the YVCC staff, RT students, and the children. The benefits included the opportunity to share with others, particularly, what the students had been learning about RT. It gave the students valuable insight about how exciting learning can be for children and about the concept of "giving to others" as part of being a part of an active learning community.

The children learned college can be fun, learning can be exciting, and we can learn together through laughing, talking and hands-on activities. But most of all, the children learned that they can go to college and learn how to get a job and have a career. Finally, the children learned that ethnic minority men and women, young and old, are students and that learning occurs throughout one's life. The contribution to the children, the college, and the community were recognized by the college president when he presented the students and the children individual certificates of appreciation.

Contact:
Peggy Keller, Instructor, (509) 575-2438
Richard Tucker, Director, Multicultural Recruitment, (509) 454-7879

Yakima Valley Community College
PO Box 1647
Yakima, WA 98907
Total head count enrollment-Credit: 5,833; Non-Credit: 106
Campuses/sites: 4; Full-time faculty: 107

IDEAS THAT BUILT AMERICA

The course creates an awareness of the impact ideas have on human behavior and an understanding of some ideas that shaped American history

The Ideas that Built America at Bluefield State College explores central ideas that have shaped American thought and behavior. The general studies course approaches American social and intellectual history from a historical perspective and not from any contemporary socio-political view. The course touches on aspects of American history not ordinarily taught in traditional survey courses.

The list of broad, seminal ideas covered is not exclusive. Other historians might offer other ideas which were important in shaping the American nation. But the ideas presented in this course are among the most important that have shaped this nation and its people. The 13 seminal ideas covered are:

1) a sense of destiny;
2) constitutional self-government;
3) the free and responsible individual;
4) fundamental human equality;
5) land of opportunity and the open class society;
6) the idea of progress;
7) Puritanism: the ethic of work and self-reliance;
8) free enterprise/capitalism;
9) pragmatism and inventiveness;
10) humanitarianism;
11) the frontier mentality/the spirit of the pioneer;
12) supreme optimism; and
13) human potential and education.

These ideas are presented by six guest lecturers; therefore, some variation of emphasis results from the various backgrounds of different instructors. The lectures are recorded on video tape. They are reviewed and discussed by the instructor and students at the intervening class meetings.

The prime objectives of this course are to 1) create an awareness on the part of students of the impact ideas have on human behavior; and 2) enable the students to understand some of the major ideas which have shaped the course of American history.

Other objectives are to enable students to see American history in a broad perspective, to see a picture painted in bold strokes, to comprehend the flow of history.

The text for the course is Ideas That Built America, by Daniel Boyd Crowder, Ph.D. It was developed in a series of state-wide consultations and workshops organized throughout West Virginia by the author to bring together scholars, teachers, and political figures to identify and explore the central ideas which have shaped American thought and behavior.

The Humanities Council of West Virginia made possible the printing of the teacher's manual. An Ideas That Built America Association has been formed with a state-wide steering committee that promotes the project. Its goal is to spread the concept nationally that these ideas are among the most important in influencing the behavior of the American people and shaping the course of the American nature.

Contact:
Donald R. Baldwin, History Professor
(304) 327-4153

Bluefield State College
219 Rock Street
Bluefield, WV 24701
Total head count enrollment-Credit: 2,931; Non-Credit: 760
Campuses/sites: 2;Full-time faculty: 93

PROGRAMMABLE CONTROLLERS

The course helps prepare students to work with Programmable Logic Controller computers

As the mining industry shrank in the 1970's and early 1980's, so did Bluefield State College enrollment. No longer did mining industry emplyees need the training for the electrical work and mining engineering required in such jobs. But the decline of one disciline brought opportunities for a new one. Bluefield State College recognized the rapid growth of the Programmable Logic Controllers in every area of industry and decided to offer such a course.

The PLC is an industrial computer using ladder logic or Boolean Algebra as a programming language. After reviewing the various brands of PLCs on the market, the Square D PLC was selected since it appeared to be the easiest to learn. It was decided that the course would be offered in the spring of 1988, with a goal of at least seven to eight students. Present enrollment in the PLC course is approximately 25 students per semester.

The Programmable Controllers course consists of

lecture and lab time. Lectures include instruction in such areas as the meaning of symbols, how to write simple programs and the application of counters and timers to the PLC. The text for the class is Understanding and Using Programmable Controllers by Thomas E. Kissell. It teaches the basic principles necessary to work with any Programmable Controller and not simply the Square D model.

Labs consist of work on six programs per student. The students are encouraged to visit local industries to find out what jobs can be computerized. Each program is then demonstrated in the lab for accuracy of operation. The programs have ranged from the operation of stop lights to assembly line productions.

Upon successful completion of the course, the student should be able to put the knowledge gained to use in successfully using a Programmable Controller. The student should have learned through simulation equipment to equate problems in industry.

As the use of the Programmable Controller continues to grow, it is Bluefield State College's desire to continually update and enlarge the course content and the number of courses being offered in this field. More people in industry in the community have taken this electrical class than any other in the department. The job market has been most favorable for students trained in the program. It is believed that only by staying abreast of current development and new technology can Bluefield State College remain an integral part of the community and assist in improving the economy and the college's own prospects for future growth.

Funding is being sought from private sources for the $2,000 industrial computers and the $3,000 software packages.

Contact:
Roy Pruett, Asst. Professor, Engineering Technology & Computer Science
(304) 327-4037

Bluefield State College
219 Rock Street
Bluefield, WV 24701
Total head count enrollment-Credit: 2,931; Non-Credit: 760
Campuses/sites: 2;Full-time faculty: 93

COOPERATIVE POLICE SCIENCE

The university and the state police jointly train state and local law enforcement officers

Increased education and training standards for individuals entering the field of law enforcement prompted Community and Technical College of Marshall University and the West Virginia Department of Public Safety (State Police), to conduct training for state and local law enforcement officers. This cooperative effort was initiated in 1977 at the West Virginia State Police Academy – a residential training facility operated by The Department of Public Safety and recognized, statewide, as the premier law enforcement training facility in West Virginia.

The State Police Academy is the only approved facility in West Virginia for the training of entry level law enforcement personnel. Local (city and county) officers who complete the 13-week Basic Officer course mayreceive up to 20 semester hours of credit toward Police Science degree requirements. Department of Public Safety personnel, completing the State Police Cadet program – which extends over a period of 30 weeks of residence at the Academy plus an additional 12 weeks of field internship experience – earn an associate degree upon completion of the internship phase of the program.

Academy staff are appointed adjunct faculty of the Community and Technical College. University faculty provide general education and related instruction while Academy staff provide technical instruction in various Police Science courses. Students who complete the Basic Officer course are encouraged to transfer credits earned through the program to their local higher education institution in order to complete degree requirements.

Approximately 160 local and 35 state-level law enforcement officers (if needed) are provided with entry-level training annually. Additionally, each member of the Department of Public Safety (400 to 500 officers) is enrolled each year to complete mandated in-service training.

This program is recipient of the "Governor's Trophy" – an acknowledgment that it was the outstanding post-secondary program in West Virginia.

Contact:
Glenn E. Smith, Chairman, Public Service/Allied Health Technology
(304) 696-3025

Community and Technical College of Marshall University
400 Hal Greer Boulevard
Huntington, WV 25755
Total head count enrollment-Credit: 1,865; Non-Credit: 2,201
Campuses/sites: 4;Full-time faculty: 30

ELECTRONICS TECHNOLOGY COOPERATION

▥ The Vo-Tech Center allows the combining of resources, avoids duplication ▥
and offers a winning situation to the students

The Marshall University Community and Technical College in cooperation with the Cabell County vocational-Technical Center is responding to the fast-paced changes occurring in the electronics industry through a two-tiered, 13th- and 14th-year-level electronics technology program. These levels include an Electronic Technology certificate issued by the Vo-Tech Center and an Associate of Applied Science Degree offered by the Community and Technical College. This cooperation with the Vo-Tech Center allows the combining of resources, avoids duplication of efforts, and offers a winning situation to both institutions and to the electronics student.

The Community and Technical College and Vo-Tech Center have successfully worked together to provide students the opportunity to participate at both training sites simultaneously. For an associate degree, students take eight electronics courses, approximately one-third of the program, at the Cabell County vocational Technical School; appropriate support courses such as communications, mathematics and physics are taken on the Marshall University campus.

Students must be accepted by both institutions in order to pursue the Associate Degree program. Once accepted, the students are eligible for all collegiate benefits and activities. The Associate of Applied Science Degree awarded by Marshall University signifies learning beyond the certificate level given by the vocational-Technical School. Graduates of this program are eligible for employment as electronics technicians in a variety of fields both locally and nationally. Program offerings include digital communications and industrial electronics; lab and lecture format; flexible schedules; communication and math skills emphasized

The general goals of the electronics technology program are:
- to keep pace with new industrial work requirements;
- to restructure course content to meet the new technology needs; and
- to offer courses at times when full- or part-time workers can access programs conveniently.

These general goals have been met by segmenting the daily schedules into blocks of time beginning conveniently in the morning and continuing during the evening hours. By offering the certificate and associate degree preparation programs over six trimester time frames, students have the option of entering the program on a part- or full-time basis.

Contact:
Randall L. Jones, Chairman, Applied Science Technology
(304) 696-3059

Community and Technical College of Marshall University
400 Hal Greer Boulevard
Huntington, WV 25755
Total head count enrollment-Credit: 1,865; Non-Credit: 2,201
Campuses/sites: 4;Full-time faculty: 30

HORIZONS: DISABLED STUDENT SERVICES CENTER

▥ In a state where disability rates are the nation's second highest, the college created ▥
a full-service center, which includes child care and job placement

In May 1991, Southern West Virginia Community College began the operation of a Disabled Student Services Center called "Horizons." The center was created out of a desperate need to provide services to disabled individuals in southern West Virginia so they could pursue an active life that could include employment.

After two years of planning by a consortium group which included Southern West Virginia Community College, the West Virginia Department of Rehabilitation Services, Vocational Schools in Logan and Mingo Counties, JTPA, and tremendous community support, the Center was funded through a grant from the Governor's Office of Employment and Training as a pilot project for West Virginia. It remains the only center of its kind in the state.

The initial grant for $171,000 would cover an 18-month period and provide for a small staff including a Director/Counselor, Vocational Evaluator, and Secretary. It also provided for evaluation equipment, supplies, travel and tuition for students, and books.

The staff would provide evaluation, counseling and guidance, education and training, outreach and disability awareness for the educational community at large. The remainder of services not provided for in the grant are provided by collaborative effort and cooperation through the service providers in the consortium.

Since the Center is located on the college campus, students have use of college services such as counseling, child care, career development, job placement, libraries, television facilities and remedial education labs.

Participation is encouraged by attendance forms and constant and continued emphasis on the need for educational enrichment. A marketing plan emphasizes heavy media promotion of services to the region.

The program has been so successful that the grant was renewed again for $125,000 for 1992-1993. Since this program is so unique and valuable, it was determined that when grant funds expired, the consortium group would continue to cover the costs.

With the current emphasis on Americans with Disabilities at the national level, the timing was perfect for such a model project in West Virginia. As a state, West Virginia faces serious problems with disabilities, lack of educational attainment and unemployment. Disability rates are second highest in the nation. An estimated 95,000 children in the state are considered to have some type of handicap. On top of these problems, there is a serious economic picture and lack of health care and medical services.

The problem becomes more complex by the disadvantagement of quality education, exposure to a technology-based society, social and cultural enrichment, and interaction leading to labor market participation.

Prior to the creation of the Center, persons living in rural southern West Virginia were required to drive or transport themselves a distance of at least 75 miles, both economically and physically impossible for the majority. The alternative in most cases had been nothing.

In rural Appalachia, the culture itself creates a mindset that persons with disabilities cannot be employed or contribute to society in general. A child is brought up to believe this, and it is reinforced many times through interactions at school or in the community.

Since Horizons began operation, it has received statewide recognition. The director of the Center has been asked to speak to many groups and organizations throughout the state. The center itself has received some attention in national publications.

It is hoped that the success of this Center will encourage other areas of the state to create similar projects, and it is the ultimate hope that Horizons will open the door to a brighter future for many West Virginians.

Contact:
Sondra Sims, Director/Counselor
(304) 792-4317

Southern West Virginia Community College
PO Box 2900, Dempsey Branch Road
Logan, WV 25601
Total head count enrollment-Credit: 3,263; Non-Credit: 1,250
Campuses/sites: 4;Full-time faculty: 54

SOUTHERN WEST VIRGINIA COMMUNITY COLLEGE

TRACK 12

The program is designed to meet the needs of non-traditional students, including unemployed miners and single heads of households

Southern West Virginia Community College, located in southern Appalachia West Virginia, covers a large geographical area of approximately 30,000 square miles and services a four-county area, an area that is one of the most severely economically depressed in the nation. Unemployment, underemployment and welfare rolls are the highest in the state.

The economy of the area is dependent on the coal industry, which has undergone downsizing, restructuring, and employee dislocation during the last decade. Several of the major mining companies have closed or experienced a reduced labor force.

Coupled with the unemployment problem is a cultural problem. Families in the Appalachian region are very close-knit and root-bound. The majority of people will not leave the area to seek other employment or even attend college. Many men will still not allow their wives to work or attend school.

Approximately 10 years ago, these very problems led the way to the creation of Southern West Virginia Community College's Track 12 program. This special program was designed to meet the needs of special people. These people, such as single heads of households, persons working full or part-time, adults with the "empty nest" syndrome, or housewives of unemployed miners, would be able to attend college with very little change in their lifestyles.

The Track 12 program, designed as a one-year transitional entry program, offers 12 credit hours on a Friday-only schedule. Participants can attend college one day per week and receive full credit. Special counseling and financial aid packages are available to students who sign up for the program, since most are older and have been out of school for a long time. Child care services on the Logan and Williamson Campuses are added benefits for those who participate.

Courses that are taken through the Track 12 program will transfer to any of Southern's degree programs at the completion of the first year. A special booklet and application form are used for those enrolling.

Approximately 100 students per semester are enrolled in

Continues on Page 754

the program. Although Track 12 originally enrolled more women, data indicates that more and more men are now entering the program. This has been an avenue of retraining since the mining industry, due largely in part to new technology, will not be increasing their work force.

Anonymous donations were used to implement the program initially. The funds were used for participant scholarships. Today, scholarships from the college's Foundation are available as well as financial aid packages.

The program has been very successful over the years, receiving attention in national publications. It was also the first program of its kind in West Virginia. Students have been tracked, and a majority have gone on to complete four-year degrees.

Contact:
Ted Williams, Assistant Dean, Williamson Campus, (304) 235-2800
Sherri Mayberry, Assistant Dean, Logan Campus, (304) 792-4300

Southern West Virginia Community College
PO Box 2900, Dempsey Branch Road
Logan, WV 25601
Total head count enrollment-Credit: 3,263; Non-Credit: 1,250
Campuses/sites: 4;Full-time faculty: 54

WEST VIRGINIA STATE COLLEGE, COMMUNITY COLLEGE DIVISION

NUCLEAR MEDICINE TECHNOLOGY

*A rotation system for clinical experience is in effect so that students
are exposed to a variety of clinical situations in local hospitals*

The Nuclear Medicine Technology program seeks to reflect institutional ideals of both quality and accessibility to under-served populations. This requires delicate balancing, because the Nuclear Medicine Technology program at West Virginia State College, Community College Division is a rigorous academic one.

Students are not admitted to the program until they have demonstrated academic competence by completing a semester of general education courses in good academic standing. Nuclear Medicine Technology is a scientific and clinical discipline concerned with the diagnosis, treatment and clinical investigation of diseases and injuries utilizing radionuclides.

The program places a substantial emphasis on clinical experience in local hospitals. A rotation system is in effect so that students are able to experience a variety of clinical situations. Currently, students spend approximately 1,360 clock hours in affiliated hospitals. Because of limits which the hospitals place upon clinical positions for students, the enrollments in the program must be kept small.

In terms of quality, concerted efforts have been directed toward the development of a high standard of competency through pinpointing critical behaviors, levels of observable achievement and broad participation of the clinical affiliates in the daily operation of the program.

While new high school graduates receive full consideration for entry into the program, older students, particularly those working in health-related occupations and in need of skills for career advancement, represent an underserved population whom the college makes a special effort to include in the program.

The program was first accredited in 1982 for a period of five years. The last accreditation site visit was in May 1987. Accreditation was again granted in January 1988. Accreditation is granted by the Committee on Allied Health Education and Accreditation of the American Medical Association upon recommendation of the Joint Review Committee on Educational Programs in Nuclear Medicine Technology.

Contact:
W. Scott Snyder, Program Director
(304) 766-3118

West Virginia State College, Community College Division
PO Box 1000
Institute, WV 25112-1000
Total head count enrollment-Credit: 4,986; Non-Credit: 416
Campuses/sites: 1; Full-time faculty: 140

ART PROGRAM FOR PHYSICALLY AND MENTALLY CHALLENGED PEOPLE

The special needs and talent of one student birthed a program of multi-agency arts training for other mentally and physically challenged persons

In the summer of 1991, West Virginia State College, Community College Division, at the request of the West Virginia Rehabilitation Services, designed an interagency art apprenticeship training program for T.W., a young man with multiple disabilities. T.W., who can neither hear nor speak, has considerable talent in art worthy of cultivation.

Special arts training programs for T.W. were run in summer-fall 1991 and spring-summer 1992. He gained much from his association with professional art teachers and practicing artists. Assessments submitted by teachers and artists indicate that T.W.'s talents, workmanship, attitudes, and personal behavior appear to be positive and conducive to his development as an artist. These assessments are testimony that T.W.'s talents are extensive, deep and multifaceted. Hence, he has greatly benefited from his instructors and supervised application of talents and interests. There is a real possibility that he has potential to develop his talents to the extent that an avocation in art could evolve into a vocation, a means of earning money. It is likely that his artistic productions are marketable for financial gain. He has already earned several monetary awards and has sold some art pieces.

Whenever possible, attention was given to enhancing T.W.'s mainstreaming and socialization, which will be important as T.W. participates more fully in the community as an artist who employs his talent for avocational and vocational purposes.

T.W. had the opportunity to experiment with oil painting, drawing, raku pottery, clay/wall mosaic, sculpting with basketry, computer graphics, acrylic painting, and printmaking, among other media.

Besides the many practicing artists who participated in this training, the following agencies and organizations joined together to administer this program: Deaf Education and Advocacy Focus, Inc.; Division of Rehabilitation Services, West Virginia Rehabilitation Services; Medley Employment Services; Shawnee Hills MH/MR Center, Creative Arts Department; Very Special Arts West Virginia, Inc.; West Virginia Advocates; and West Virginia State College, Community College Division.

West Virginia State College, Community College Division, is pleased to have played a leadership role in designing and implementing this multi-agency arts training program. This pilot program has been developed in such a way to help many other mentally and physically challenged persons.

Contact:
Frank Allen, Coordinator, Continuing Education and Community Service
(304) 766-3324

West Virginia State College, Community College Division
PO Box 1000
Institute, WV 25112-1000
Total head count enrollment-Credit: 4,986; Non-Credit: 416
Campuses/sites: 1;Full-time faculty: 140

HIGHER EDUCATION ECONOMIC DEVELOPMENT

Students in the program learn to perform all functions of an economic development program under the guidance of faculty and private enterprise

Rural communities face insurmountable odds in attracting new business and industry. Often, local governments lack resources and expertise to convince the private sector to relocate to their area.

Recognizing the problems a number of its service area counties were facing, West Virginia University at Parkersburg, in cooperation with C&P Telephone Co., began work in 1990 to develop a Higher Education and Economic Development program to directly link education and economic development. The project utilizes college students to recruit and support new and existing industry in rural areas of the state. Implemented in January of 1991, the project offered a four-course sequence designed to train students to become economic development professionals by combining classroom study and real-world exposure to rural economic development issues. Its success to date has prompted plans to expand HEED's scope to encompass additional regions in West Virginia.

The students in WVU-P's program learn to perform all the functions of an economic development program under the guidance of an advisory board of economic development professionals, college faculty, business

Continues on Page 756

representatives and state and local government officials. Members of the program's advisory committee serve as the nucleus for its guest lecturers. The committee has been directly involved in the design of the courses and the recruitment of resource contacts. C&P Telephone has made several financial contributions to the program and has representatives serving on the advisory panel.

The pilot project is already making an impact. West Virginia's northwestern county of Wirt, with a population of 5,000 has become the program's "laboratory." HEED students are involved in assisting rural Wirt County in economic development activities including the development of the county's first-ever data base of available buildings and land for consideration by potential developers and employers. They have also aided county development representatives in preliminary discussions with business/industry officials exploring the possibilities of relocating in Wirt county. The students' involvement has become such a focal point that Wirt County's Economic Development Authority changed its meeting night so as not to conflict with students' classroom time.

Through combining specialized coursework with internships and cooperative education experiences, students benefit from hands-on activities ranging from collecting and analyzing statistical research, assessing the available work force and identifying prospective employers to attending county economic sessions, developing strategies and serving on student marketing teams which visit prospects.

College officials note that while the principal beneficiaries of HEED are the communities and businesses involved in the program, it is the students who are reaping real-life experiences by preparing the way for tomorrow's jobs – even perhaps their own.

The project has been recognized by an article in *Community College Week*.

Contact:
Robert McCloy, Professor of Business,
(304) 424-8000

West Virginia University at Parkersburg
Route 5, Box 167A
Parkersburg, WV 26101
Total head count enrollment-Credit: 5,022; Non-Credit: 1,600
Campuses: 2;Full-time faculty: 73

CIM ADVANCED TECHNICAL CERTIFICATE

Courses taught in the "factory of the future" environment give the students first-hand exposure to state-of-the-art technologies

Human relations, management philosophy and data collection software are all woven into the courses in the Computer Integrated Manufacturing Advanced Technical Certificate program at Chippewa Valley Technical College. These lead to an advanced technical certificate with 12 credits of course work aimed at serving a broad range of personnel within a given manufacturing organization and stressing teamwork, quality and interdependence.

Because input from industry is that CIM training should be approached as a philosophy to be embraced by all segments of an organization, Chippewa Valley Technical College has designed the advanced certificate to meet the needs of graduates from a variety of associate degree programs who may want to become involved with companies on the forefront of CIM. Examples of background training that would be an appropriate prerequisite for CIM are Electronics, Electromechanical, Mechanical Design, Fluid Power, Materials Management, Supervisory Management, Industrial Engineering, Data Processing, and Accounting.

Courses in the program that were not previously mentioned also include a mix of automation hardware, engineering processes and practical factory floor problem-solving.

The delivery of the course content makes use of a variety of formats including lecture, field trips, and a laboratory which simulates a real-life automated manufacturing enterprise, including CIM hardware and software. Courses taught in the "factory of the future" environment give the students first-hand exposure to state-of-the-art technologies and give them the opportunity to practice the philosophy, teamwork, and problem solving techniques necessary to design and build world class quality products. There's an integration of both manufacturing and non-manufacturing personnel to promote a better understanding of each other's responsibilities within an organization.

Successful computer integration is dependent on this unified effort and common goal orientation throughout all divisions of an organization. The notion that productivity and quality can be improved by simply installing automation hardware on a production line has proved disastrous in many American companies in the last decade. This program recognizes that automation alone cannot solve America's productivity and quality problems and further recognizes the importance of an integrated human resources solution.

Contact:
Marvin A. Franson, Trade and Industrial Supervisor, (715) 833-6297
James F. Brown, Program Supervisor, (715) 833-6317

Chippewa Valley Technical College
620 West Clairemont Avenue
Eau Claire, WI 54701
Total head count enrollment-Credit: 5,408; Non-Credit: 25,647
Campuses/sites: 1;Full-time faculty: 182

FOX VALLEY TECHNICAL COLLEGE

ECONOMIC DEVELOPMENT: BUSINESS / INDUSTRY CONTRACT TRAINING

The college delivers 20 percent of the total state's activity in contract training and technical assistance

Fox Valley Technical College (FVTC) made a commitment in 1982 to help upgrade the work force within its five-county district in northeastern Wisconsin. Since that economic development initiative began, the college has formed partnerships with more than 600 companies/organizations and served more then 30,000 of their employees through technical assistance and customized training provided to employers on a contractual basis. These contracts include consultant services and specialized curriculum designed to meet the specific needs of FVTC's clients and business and industry, governmental agencies and other public and private groups involved in economic development activities.

Through these services, FVTC staff can assist employers in meeting unique technical or training needs that will result in greater productivity and improved quality in goods and services. At Fox Valley Technical College, economic development is a college-wide commitment, representing a strong level of integration with FVTC's full-time programs and more than 800 business/industry representatives who serve on its program advisory committees. The success of this approach can be measured by the number of clients served and the revenues generated

Continues on Page 758

through these contracts. In 1992-93, an estimated $3.3.-million in revenue was generated through Fox Valley Technical College's economic development contracting, which was a 74 percent increase from the 1989-90 revenue of $1.9-million.

FVTC has led the Wisconsin Technical College System in the level of economic development contract activity in business/industry.

FVTC delivers 20 percent of the total state's activity in contract training and technical assistance. In addition, Fox Valley Technical College was one of two community/technical colleges in the U.S. and Canada to receive the 1993 Business/Industry Award, co-sponsored by the American Association of Community Colleges and the IBM Corporation. The award recognizes two colleges annually for their exemplary service to the business community.

Contact:
Susan May, Dean, Marketing and Economic Development
(414) 735-2401

Fox Valley Technical College
PO Box 2277
Appleton, WI 54913-2277
Total head count enrollment-Credit: 5,900; Non-Credit: 38,767
Campuses/sites: 6;Full-time faculty: 250

COMPUTER INTEGRATED MANUFACTURING DEMONSTRATION

The live demonstration tracks an engineering change from a request for a quotation to the shop floor where a prototype part will be cut

Since January 1990, Fox Valley Technical College (FVTC) has been demonstrating to business and industry the value of having a computer system that links business operations and manufacturing. The demonstration actually shows, through role-playing, a case example with a hypothetical company, how a computer integrated manufacturing (CIM) system operates in a company. Fox Valley Technical College then provides interested companies with training in all phases of CIM. The ultimate goal is to help small and medium-sized manufacturers in the Fox Valley, the second largest metropolitan area in Wisconsin, stay globally competitive.

The CIM Business Applications Demonstration is a presentation of how a small manufacturing company uses the technologies of an integrated system to improve its management, operations and responsiveness. Both business and manufacturing applications are highlighted to give tour participants a complete picture of an integrated enterprise.

The live demonstration tracks an engineering change from a request for quotation to the shop floor where a prototype part will be cut to meet a customer's specifica-tions. Management, engineering, production, operations, marketing and manufacturing departments explain their role in this engineering change and the demonstration concludes with a final quotation being printed for the customer. The integrated environment consists of micro computers (PS/2's) connected to a mini computer (AS/400) and shows departments that work together, communicate efficiently and respond quickly as a team. FVTC's CIM Alliance partnership with IBM in 1988 provided the hardware and software needed for the demonstration.

The free demonstration lasts approximately two hours and has been seen by more than 200 industry representatives, many of whom subsequently contracted with FVTC for training in 66 separate contracts during the 18 months the demonstration was offered.

A team of nine full-time instructors manage the demonstration, role-play the parts and offer the training, functioning as an enterprise unit within FVTC under the guidance of a CIM Steering Committee. The demonstration has won national acclaim and high praise from outside evaluators.

Contact:
Virgil Noordyk
(414) 735-5783

Fox Valley Technical College
PO Box 2277
Appleton, WI 54913-2277
Total head count enrollment-Credit: 5,900; Non-Credit: 38,767
Campuses/sites: 6;Full-time faculty: 250

HAZARDOUS MATERIAL INCIDENTS RESPONSE TRAINING

Instruction is provided on-campus and in-plant regarding compliance regulations, safety, and theory in storage, handling and disposal

Almost daily the news media reports some incident involving hazardous material; and the number of incidents seems to be increasing as industries expand their use of hazardous materials. Numerous landfills have been closed and covered, and many of them contain hazardous materials and represent a serious potential for dangerous incidents.

All of this has led to a demand for proper handling and control of hazardous materials that comes only through higher standards and more training of personnel.

In response to this demand, beginning in January 1987, Lakeshore Technical College became the first school in Wisconsin to offer a Hazardous Material Handling Technician program. The program is one of only two or three training programs available anywhere across the nation.

The Wisconsin Board of Vocational, Technical and Adult Education has designated this to be a statewide program, making Lakeshore Technical College one of the few publicly supported post secondary schools in the nation to be able to provide hazardous material handling training and technical assistance to industries and organizations in Wisconsin and along the Wisconsin border. The college provides instruction on-campus and in-plant regarding compliance regulations; safety; and theory in effective use of hazardous materials and safe storage, handling and disposal.

Hazardous material training is provided through various programs. One program offers workshops on the college campus and in other locations to provide supplemental information to people who are presently working in hazardous material programs within industry. This permits Lakeshore Technical College personnel to develop customized programs and provide in-plant training upon request from individual industries.

A second program in response to the needs of industry has been developed for a two-year associate degree program in hazardous material training in order to provide a resource of trained people to be employed by industry when the needs arise.

A third training program trains public service personnel across the state, including firefighters, 11,000 law enforcement officers, and 13,500 emergency medical personnel who require hazardous material response training. In addition, a large number of city department of public works employees and county highway department employees need training. Specialized training is required for emergency government officials, city and county government officials, and command personnel in fire and law enforcement departments to include the legal ramifications and responsibilities of these agencies in an incident, the coordination necessary to minimize the effects of the hazardous material incident, overall awareness and other important factors.

Students receive a combination of classroom time and hands-on training. A building provides a place for classroom instruction and indoor training. In 1991, the size of the building was tripled in response to the demand for training. Much of the training takes place on an outdoor site, using simulators representing leaking tanks, leaking pipes and valves, leaking tanker trucks, and a railroad car dome. To make the site as realistic as possible, there are underground storage tanks, septic tanks, municipal sewer lines, a simulated waterway and simulated toxic dump and landfill sites. Smoke and water are used to simulate hazardous material incidents.

Contact:
Steve Power, Associate Dean, Emergency and Protective Services
(414) 458-4183

Lakeshore Technical College
1290 North Avenue
Cleveland, WI 53015
Total head count enrollment-Credit: 7,000; Non-Credit: 30,000
Campuses/sites: 3;Full-time faculty: 106

RADIOGRAPHY

Via live interactive, television transmission, classes are beamed to five hospitals

In January of 1991, Lakeshore Technical College embarked on a new and innovative approach in providing a Radiography program to serve the Lakeshore, Moraine Park, and Fox Valley vocational-technical districts: live, interactive television transmission of classes to five hospitals.

Lab and clinical experiences are provided through

Continues on Page 760

agreements with each of the hospitals in its respective facilities using skilled employees as adjunct faculty. The hospitals are St. Agnes Hospital, Fond du Lac; St. Elizabeth's Hospital, Appleton; Holy Family Memorial Medical Center, Manitowoc; and St. Nicholas Hospital and Sheboygan Memorial Medical Center, Sheboygan.

Through cooperative scheduling with Moraine Park Technical College, Fox Valley Technical College, and Lakeshore Technical College, students can take General Education and other supporting technical classes at a local technical college and remain in their respective communities. The technology being used to provide the Radiography program may serve as a prototype to expand educational opportunities in educational programs throughout the region and provide a new concept in sharing throughout the region as well as providing a new concept in sharing between groups of technical colleges and groups of employers.

In the fall of 1992, an accreditation visitation committee commended the Radiography program for its "innovative approach to delivery of education" after completing a two-day evaluation.

H. Ronald Griffith, radiography program director at Lansing Community College in Lansing, Michigan, and Inez Gorsuch, X-ray director of education at the Medical College Hospital in Toledo, Ohio, conducted the evaluation for the Joint Review Committee on Education and Radiologic Technology. The team visited the Cleveland Campus and the five clinical sites.

In the final report to LTC staff members and representatives from the clinical sites, committee Chairperson Griffith said, "This institution will be a leader in distance learning," adding that he foresees colleges nationwide contacting LTC to learn more about its unique delivery approach. He said that with the tremendous shortage of manpower in health careers, LTC's response to train radiographers is highly commendable.

The team listed the major strengths of the Radiography program as:

1) innovative approach to delivery of education in radiography supported by the educational institution at Lakeshore Technical College, educational institutions in other districts, and the health care community;
2) radiography administrators and staff who play an active role in the delivery of education to students;
3) continual monitoring of presentation of materials via television so as to increase effectiveness of the program; and
4) individuals at the college and the clinic sites who are not resistant to change.

In May 1992, the Committee on Allied Health Education and Accreditation (CAHEA) of the American Medical Association's Division of Allied Health Education and Accreditation awarded initial accreditation to the LTC Radiography program.

In a letter to District Director/President Dr. Dennis Ladwig, Dr. John Fauser said, "CAHEA's action was taken upon the recommendation of the Joint Review Committee on Education in Radiologic Technology." Fauser said the accreditation is for two years with the next on-site evaluation in the fall of 1993.

Contact:
Nancy Kaprelian or Jim Odau
(414) 458-4183

Lakeshore Technical College
1290 North Avenue
Cleveland, WI 53015
Total head count enrollment-Credit: 7,000; Non-Credit: 30,000
Campuses/sites: 3;Full-time faculty: 106

BIOTECHNOLOGY LABORATORY TECHNOLOGY

⌗ *The college increased interest in the program by helping create a high school elective* ⌗
course to provide an introduction to biotechnology

The steady growth of biotechnology and related industry in Wisconsin, particularly in south-central Wisconsin, has resulted in the demand for highly skilled laboratory technicians. That demand is being met through a Biotechnology Laboratory Technician program at Madison Area Technical College.

This program is designed to develop entry-level skills and competencies in persons seeking employment in biotechnology and related industries. Extensive hands-on work in conjunction with lectures and classroom discussions enables students to use state-of-the-art equipment to complete laboratory projects. The competency based curriculum was developed in early 1987, using industry input.

The curriculum has a strong basic and applied science content (chemistry, cell biology, biochemistry and microbiology) that is enhanced by specific program courses in hazardous materials, radioisotopes, instrumentation, bioseparation techniques (chromatography), fermentation technology, bioseparations module I (proteins), cell culturing, bioseparations module 11 (nucleic acids and recombinant DNA), and molecular cloning. During the final semester, students enroll in an occupational work experience. Students may choose microcomputer courses, mathematics, research concepts or additional science classes as their electives. The associate degree also requires two semesters of communication skills and introductory courses in economics, psychology, and contemporary American society.

Students entering the two-year associate degree program vary in their background and preparation for laboratory work. Many adult students enter the program because they enjoyed their science classes in previous secondary or post secondary coursework; others view the consistent employment offerings as a valuable asset to their own career changes or plans. Students entering the biotechnology program as recent high school graduates have identified a career in science as a potential goal. Program and course evaluations reveal that the majority of students view the extensive hands-on laboratory work and use of instrumentation as desirable for entry into employment. Many students are employed as laboratory helpers or laboratory assistants in companies while enrolled in their program courses.

The small number of students requesting entry into the program directly from high school caused the program staff to consider the reasons for the apparent lack of interest. The direct result was increased involvement of the Biotechnology staff of MATC with an Education for Employment Council that was also looking at career opportunities in biotechnology. Consequently, a consortium of high school biology teachers, high school vocational agriculture teachers, high school counselor and post secondary teachers worked on an appropriate high school elective course to provide an introduction to biotechnology. This course is team-taught by the high school biology and vocational agriculture teachers to students who are generally juniors or seniors. Students enrolled in the course have previous high school science and math courses. Students who successfully complete the articulated introduction to biotechnology class at their high schools with a B or better can receive advanced standing for MATC's Introduction to Biotechnology (007-100).

Graduates of the program have been employed primarily in Wisconsin. Graduates who have moved out-of-state have continued to work in biotechnology or related laboratories. An articulation agreement with the University of Wisconsin-Platteville for graduates of the program has been signed.

Contact:
Joy McMillan, Program Director
(608) 246-6581

Madison Area Technical College
550 Anderson Street
Madison, WI 53704
Total head count enrollment-Credit: 19,829; Non-Credit: 36,422
Campuses/sites: 14; Full-time faculty: 380

MADISON AREA TECHNICAL COLLEGE

CULTURAL DIVERSITY

Exposure and understanding of various cultures comes from exhibits, performances and inclusion in the curriculum

To increase awareness and appreciation for multiculturalism, the Student Life Office celebrates the diversity of our global community throughout the school year by focusing monthly on different cultures or regions of the world. Over the course of the year, the heritage of everyone at the Madison Area Technical College is featured.

The uniqueness of this four-year-old program has fostered involvement from all segments of the college (staff, students, faculty, and administration) as well as members of the community. Exposure, understanding, and appreciation is gained through a multi-dimensional approach using exhibits and displays, entertainment, art, dance, music, videos and speakers. Simulation cross-cultural activities such as *BaFa BaFa*, *Star Power*, *Collidascope*, etc., promote further acceptance and understanding of other cultures.

Students and staff bring artifacts to exhibit representing their ethnic heritage or from countries they have visited. Showcases are filled with personal treasures and descriptions that many people view daily. Posters from all over the world are displayed while music from the area is featured in the lounge. The cafeteria cooperates by offering ethnic foods, and minority networking groups hold bake sales with cultural specialties.

In cooperation with student organizations, cultural performing groups present programs on campus each month. Local speakers, community members and foreign students and teachers volunteer their services. Fashion shows, panel discussions, singers, small dance groups and other speakers are also featured. Local grade and high school groups as well as various community organizations are invited to share in these celebrations, familiarizing potential students with the college and its activities.

Each year, more and more faculty members from many disciplines (foreign languages, history, sociology, psychology, anthropology, economics, communications, drama, music and dance) include these cultural diversity programs as a part of their curriculum. For example, the Native American focus included 16 speakers (with topics ranging from tribal sovereignty to spirituality) to which instructors brought classes or offered extra credit if the lecture was

Continues on Page 762

not during class time.

Events are advertised in the local papers and special invitations are sent to a variety of community groups. We have received recognition from local schools (K-12), local press media, community groups and at national conferences. There is no admission charged for these programs, which cost approximately $6,000 per year. They are funded through the student activities fee and fundraising by campus ethnic clubs. The Native American Student Association sponsored the first annual Pow-Wow which attracted more than 1,500 people, including dancers and spectators from all over the Midwest. Almost 5,000 persons were in attendance at these multicultural programs during the 1991-92 academic year.

Minority staff, representing four major ethnic populations, work closely with the Student Life Office in coordinating the presentation of cultural awareness panels, speakers and professional ethnic performances. A significant component of the college's minority retention strategy is the minority staff's role as advisors to ethnic student organizations. These student networking groups provide important support and positive visibility for minority students. In addition to their retention value, our minority clubs bring a significant dimension of the culture and community to our campus life. Their contribution to the college is part of an integrated process that also relies on the ongoing participation of a Minority Community Forum and a proactive district-wide Minority Planning Committee. The college's systemic approach to ensuring campus diversity promotes the expanded participation of minority students and reflects the contribution of the pluralistic community that it serves.

The Cultural Diversity program affords everyone at the college the opportunity to take pride in their own ethnic heritage while learning about the cultures of others. The result is a building of community at MATC as well as a sense of unity and relationship to the global community enhancing MATC's mission "to provide innovative leadership to help build a community which is socially and economically strong, flexible, and competitive in a changing global marketplace."

Contact:
Dyan Armstrong, Program Coordinator
(608) 246-6165

Madison Area Technical College
550 Anderson Street
Madison, WI 53704
Total head count enrollment-Credit: 19,829; Non-Credit: 36,422
Campuses/sites: 14; Full-time faculty: 380

RESPIRATORY CARE PRACTITIONER

Rotation among four hospitals and one large clinic enable the student to acquire a variety of skills

The Respiratory Care Practitioner program (formerly called the Respiratory Therapist program) at Mid-State Technical College has three major goals:

1) to prepare the student as a competent entry-level respiratory care practitioner as defined by the National Board Respiratory Care (NBRC);
2) to prepare the student with those cognitive, psychomotor and affective skills necessary to be employed as a respiratory care practitioner; and
3) to meet the needs of employers in the state of Wisconsin for entry level practitioners as defined by NBRC.

The program, begun in 1975, is two academic years followed by a nine-week summer clinical rotation (four 18-week semesters and one nine-week summer session consisting of 360 clinical hours.) Program requirements include a minimum of 72 credits at the associate degree level.

The evaluation of student progress in didactic and laboratory courses consist of formative and summative written exams. Clinical evaluation is addressed via the Performance Evaluation System (PES), which was originally copyrighted in 1985 and has been updated annually. Evaluation consists of oral examination of cognitive skills related to therapeutic techniques and direct observation of psychomotor and affective skills. The validity of the PES was (is) determined by the advisory board prior to the inclusion or exclusion in the system. Reliability is assured by developing consensus among the three formal evaluators (Mid-State Technical College staff).

The clinical portion of the curriculum is based on the NBRC matrix. This matrix was chosen to ensure that graduates were prepared to meet national, as well as local, standards. A varied experience is available to students on clinical practicum. Rotation among four hospitals and one large clinic enable the student to acquire skills with such things as hospital-based respiratory care and treatment, stress testing, pulmonary function lab and neonatal experience.

The program medical director teaches seminar courses to second year students. This involves such things as arterial blood gas interpretation, x-ray interpretation, pulmonary function interpretation and pulmonary diseases. These courses also include case presentations and journal article reviews. In addition, students accompany the medical director on hospital rounds. Each student is required to attain a minimum of 92 hours of physician instruction. This instruction includes a combination of didactic, psychomotor and communication skills. Seventy-two hours of didactic instruction is provided by the medical director; the remaining hours and areas are accomplished on a one-on-one basis with individual physicians. A staff instructor verifies the time and reviews the material covered with each student.

Job opportunities have been excellent for graduates of this program. Placement continues to offer myriad opportunities not only in this area and state but nationwide.

Contact:
Wanda Wallis, Division Chair
(715) 387-2538

Mid-State Technical College
600 West Fifth Street
Marshfield, WI 54449
Total head count enrollment-Credit: 6,899; Non-Credit: 9,093
Campuses/sites: 4;Full-time faculty: 85

INSTRUMENTATION TECHNOLOGY

Ninety percent of the program is devoted to electrical and electronics courses; the other 10 percent covers hydraulics, pneumatics and mechanisms

Although careers in fields as varied as oceanography and space exploration await some students studying Instrumentation Technology at Mid-State Technical College, most will focus on the industrial manufacturing processes found in central Wisconsin.

Electrical, electronic, pneumatic, hydraulic, and mechanical systems are among the various forms of instrumentation that measure physical processes. Because application of computers in automatic control systems has increased the use of electrical and electronic instruments, about 90 percent of the Instrumentation Technology Program is devoted to electrical and electronics courses. The other 10 percent covers hydraulics, pneumatics and mechanisms.

Instrumentation technicians maintain various measuring and automatic control systems. Once a malfunction has been located in a system, the technician must have the basic skills to perform required electrical and mechanical repairs. Also, if the malfunction is not easily found, the technician must have the ability to plan troubleshooting procedures needed to isolate any difficulty. In order to perform these tasks, technicians must understand the basic laws of physical science and have the mathematical expertise to apply those laws to practical situations.

There are several entry-level jobs that graduates might seek. Instrument apprentices assist journeymen. Instrument maintenance people do repair and calibration. Process control technicians supervise the operation of instruments used in industrial processes. Installation technicians install, check, and help start new measurement and control systems. Field service technicians repair systems and serve as troubleshooters. Design specialists assist engineers or customers who design and evaluate instruments and control devices on automatic equipment. Instrument management trainees assist in managing instrument shops. Sales technicians sell instrumentation equipment and help customers solve problems. Employers include water, electric, and natural gas utilities; chemical companies; pulp and paper firms; food and dairy companies; and instrument contractors, manufacturers and sales organizations.

Because physical science and mathematical expertise are so important to practical situations arising in the instrumentation technician's career, those interested in enrolling in Instrumentation Technology would find some exposure to college preparatory mathematics and physics necessary.

Contact:
John Clark, Division Chair
(715) 423-5650

Mid-State Technical College
600 West Fifth Street
Marshfield, WI 54449
Total head count enrollment-Credit: 6,899; Non-Credit: 9,093
Campuses/sites: 4;Full-time faculty: 85

INDUSTRIAL SCREEN PRINTING

▦ The college designed and implemented a 24-week program that offers ▦
classroom and hands-on training in all facets of the business

Industrial screen printing is a unique, high-tech process for which there was no formal training in the state of Wisconsin prior to the implementation of Moraine Park's Industrial Screen Printing Program. John Torinus, CEO of Serigraph, Inc., noted that ". . .Wisconsin is arguably the worldwide center for high-tech screen printing. The two biggest companies in that business in the world are Serigraph, Inc. in West Bend, Wisconsin, and Northern Engraving Company in Sparta, Wisconsin. In addition, there are a half-dozen spin-offs from our two companies that are doing a good level of business in the state."

Industrial screen printers apply inks, adhesives, and other coatings to a wide variety of substrates including metal plastics, vinyls, paper. Products using screen printing range from multicolored circuit boards to automobile dash boards, and semi-trailer truck decals.

To prepare individuals for entry-level jobs in screen printing, Moraine Park designed and implemented a 24-week program that offers classroom and hands-on training in building screens; setting up and operating screen printing presses; finishing, drying, and curing products; and performing quality control functions. In addition, students develop related math and communication skills with special emphasis on employability skills. Moraine Park Technical College is a member of the Screen Printing Association International (SPAI) and highlights about the program appear regularly in its publications. Program faculty cooperate with SPAI to incorporate their training materials into the program materials.

Industrial Screen Printing students benefit from the unique paid internship feature of the program. From the first week of the program to its conclusion, students attend classes and labs four days per week and work in a screen printing plant one day each week. The college awards a total of four credits for this portion while students gain on-the-job experience and earn money that can be used to help pay tuition or other expenses.

Students who complete the program and go on to work at Serigraph, Inc. enter at a higher level, are offered higher starting wages, and progress up the career ladder more rapidly than those who have not had this technical training. Several smaller screen printing firms in the region also offer students internships and entry-level employment advantages.

In May 1990, John Torinus, CEO of Serigraph, Inc., wrote a letter to the Wisconsin Board Vocational, Technical, Adult Education describing his company's urgent need for formal technical training in industrial screen printing. He noted that his company hires more than 100 individuals a year for screen press jobs, and that with increasing emphasis on "zero defects" hires off the street no longer provide the quality work force that Serigraph, Inc. needs. In response, the Wisconsin Technical College System's governing board granted Moraine Park Technical College permission to develop a vocational diploma program to address these needs.

In June 1990, Moraine Park hosted representatives from Broy Company Manufacturing and Sales; Graphic Technologies, Inc.; Fabriko, Inc.; and Serigraph, Inc. in a DACUM study of the competencies/skills needed by entry-level employees. The results of the study showed a significant number of skills unique to the industrial screen printing process, justifying the development of a new technical college program. Moraine Park faculty and staff then began building a competency-based curriculum founded on the skills revealed in the DACUM study. Meanwhile, local companies led by Serigraph, Inc. and Fabriko in Green Lake Wisconsin, worked with the college staff members to acquire equipment and assemble a screen printing lab.

The program, which accommodates 16 students, has completed two sections of students since its beginning in August 1991. Many of the graduates have been offered positions in the firms in which they interned.

In August 1992, Wisconsin initiated two Printing Youth Apprenticeship pilot programs for high school juniors and seniors. John Torinus of Serigraph, Inc. has once again taken the lead to ensure that the screen printing industry is in the fore-front. West Bend High Schools and Moraine Park Technical College are working with Serigraph, Inc. to design and implement a program that integrates applied academic instruction in math, science, language arts, and training in screen and offset printing, along with pre-press operations.

Twelve West Bend High School students qualified to begin in the program in August 1992. Those who successfully complete the program receive advanced standing in Moraine Park's Industrial Screen Printing or Marketing Communications (Pre-press Graphics) programs if they choose to continue in post secondary education, or they will be prepared for a variety of entry-level screen or offset printing jobs.

The Wisconsin Printing Youth Apprenticeship program was featured during a visit from President George Bush. West Bend High School Printing Youth Apprenticeship students and their parents were honored at the occasion.

Contact:
Howard Sonnenberg, Associate Dean
(414) 334-3413

Moraine Park Technical College
235 North National Avenue, PO Box 1940
Fond du Lac, WI 54936
Total head count enrollment-Credit: 12,423; Non-Credit: 8,043
Campuses/sites: 3;Full-time faculty: 140

CORE ABILITIES

Seven core abilities are emphasized to prepare students to be marketable, productive members of the work force

Based on recent trends in education and employment as documented in studies such as the American Society for Training and Development's *Workplace Basics: The Skills Employers Want* and the *SCANS Report*, Moraine Park Technical College is among the institutions incorporating "essential elements" or "core competencies" into all programs and courses so that students develop skills that complement specific occupational skills, broaden the ability to function outside a given occupation, and connect occupational, personal and community roles and perspectives.

"Core Abilities" or transferable skills essential to an individual's success regardless of occupation or community setting, that were determined by members of the business community, students, technical college faculty and college staff include:

- work productively;
- learn effectively;
- communicate clearly;
- work cooperatively;
- act responsibility;
- value self positively; and
- think critically and creatively.

Using principles of competency-based education, Moraine Park is committed to incorporating Core Abilities across the curriculum, teaching them in all occupational programs. Posters featuring the seven Core Abilities are posted in classrooms and labs. Faculty members contextualize the Core Abilities by working with students to identify specific behaviors that characterize each of the broad core skills in their particular occupational or career area. Once students identify the Core Abilities, they practice applying them; they assess the importance of Core Abilities to both employers and employees; and finally, they demonstrate their capacity to evaluate themselves in terms of Core Abilities.

Moraine Park began implementation of Core Abilities in 1989 with a series of summer workshops led by a team of faculty and Instructional Development staff members.

College faculty and deans, along with secondary faculty from Tech Prep partner high schools participated in the four-day sessions which provided them with an overview of competency-based instructional design; assisted them in ascertaining ways in which Core Abilities relate to their programs; and helped them identify teaching and evaluation strategies that promote the application of Core Abilities.

Rather than creating rules for how Core Abilities should be incorporated into instruction, Instructional Development staff members have encouraged faculty members to build on ways they already teach Core Abilities by taking the approaches that feel most comfortable and promise to be effective for them within the unique context of their disciplines. The important difference is that Core Abilities become explicit rather than implicit in their teaching. During the workshops, faculty members work in small groups to explore how Core Abilities might impact what they teach; how they teach – including the types of learning activities and assignments they plan; how they evaluate student achievement; and how they manage their courses.

Ideas and strategies generated in the faculty workshops have been shared with the college community and with Tech Prep partner high schools. Workshop leaders have continually used the ideas to enrich subsequent Core Ability workshops and presentations. Instructional Development staff members have featured Core Ability concepts in the Moraine Park Curriculum Development Handbook and The Core Ability Booklet, which have been provided to each faculty member.

Moraine Park Core Abilities have been featured nationally in sessions at AACJC, Mid-America Conference on Competency-Based Instruction, and Eastern Regional Competency-Based Instruction conferences. In addition, they have been presented at numerous state level Tech Prep and School to Work Transition conferences and workshops.

Contact:
Judith Neill, Project Leader, Computerized Instructional Design System
(414) 929-2485

Moraine Park Technical College
235 North National Avenue, PO Box 1940
Fond du Lac, WI 54936
Total head count enrollment-Credit: 12,423; Non-Credit: 8,043
Campuses/sites: 3; Full-time faculty: 140

TEAM BUILDING CHALLENGE WORKSHOP

▨ Customized training focuses on trust, communications, cooperation, group problem solving, ▨
appreciation of differences, support and interdependence

The TeamBuilding Challenge Workshop is one of many offerings that NATC's Economic Development department provides to area business, industry and government agencies in accordance with its mission to promote economic development.

The origin of this workshop is traced to the Outward Bound program that was used to train Peace Corps volunteers. Educators carried the concept into physical education classes, calling it Project Adventure. The main component was the "Ropes" course, which is owned by the Rhinelander School District in conjunction with Forward Service Corporation. The average workshop is six to eight hours in length, with 12-team members participating. It can be combined with other team-building components such as type and team-building utilizing Myers Briggs Type Indicator.

The TeamBuilding Challenge workshop has a high impact on individuals and teams. This is one of NATC's value-added offerings which allows us to recover our full cost (direct and indirect), thus it generates revenue to support the other economic development offerings.

The workshop was introduced to area CEOs and human resource directors at a premiere workshop and marketed with a brochure. A customized training contract is written by NATC for the service recipient stating the date, time, place, and fee for the workshop.

Before attending the TeamBuilding Challenge workshop, an assessment of the team's needs is done by the facilitators. Typical areas of focus are: trust, communications, cooperation, group problem solving, appreciation of differences, support and interdependence. Based on the team's priorities, the facilitators select from myriad exercises for the team to experience. During the course of the workshop, the facilitators are constantly assessing the interactions of the team and may decide to alter the original agenda of exercises to better meet their needs. Following each exercise the facilitator helps the team to "process" their experience...and transfer it into their workplace. Four facilitators have had extensive training with nationally recognized Project Adventure. NATC rents the Project Adventure/Ropes course facility from Rhinelander School District and Forward Service Corporation.

TeamBuilding Challenge has received the national LERN, Learning Resources Network, award for outstanding Course of the Year ('92), the Exemplary Award ('92) from the Wisconsin Vocational, Technical, and Adult Education Board, and was featured as an Exemplary Program at the Community College Consortium in June 1993.

Contact:
Karen S. Isebrands, Associate Dean, Economic Development
(715) 365-4414

Nicolet Area Technical College
Box 158
Rhinelander, WI 54501
Total head count enrollment-Credit: 1,700; Non-Credit: 8,000
Campuses/sites: 2;Full-time faculty: 65

PROGRAMS FOR THE HEARING & VISUALLY IMPAIRED

▨ Visually Impaired Students are placed on job sites where they receive ▨
regular evaluations by a work experience supervisor

It's often difficult for someone to decide to go back to school or change jobs, but when they have a hearing or visual disability, the change seems almost impossible. That's where programs for the hearing impaired and visually impaired at Northcentral Technical College come in.

The Hearing Impaired Persons (HIP) and Visually Impaired Persons (VIP) programs make it possible for members of these groups to take part in prevocational as well as vocational education and, in most cases, to maintain gainful employment and independence.

NTC's hearing-impaired program helps individuals in their quest for quality education and subsequent employment. When a student wants to use the services of the program, they are assessed by a career evaluator to determine ability and desire to attend school or begin a specific major. This evaluation includes tests in reading, math, and general communication skills, vocational testing, and aptitude and general interest tests.

"Student input is very important to us," says HIP liaison instructor Crystal Anderson. "We feel it's very important to meet the needs of the student on an individual basis."

For some students, this may mean a "hands-on" approach to learning which is designed to give the student the experience of being an employee in a "true-to-life" situation. This is accomplished by placing them on a Job site where they receive regular evaluations by a work experience supervisor. Emphasis is placed on student self-evaluation of work habits and attitudes as well as overall performance.

When a student is ready to enter a major course of study, he or she enrolls in mainstreamed classes along with hearing students. It is especially important at this point to realize the intricate relationship between mainstreamed hearing impaired students, the occupational instructors, and the HIP program staff. A key to success are support services such as interpreters, tutors and note-takers made available to the student as needed during the course of their studies.

There is also an Assistive Listening Device Lab at NTC which is used by hearing impaired people throughout the state. The lab was designed as an extra means to help students succeed in their studies. It allows them to sample listening aids to find the one best suited to their individual needs.

The Visually Impaired Persons program at NTC is also unique. Such programs are not usually placed in post secondary education settings. There are many services available within the VIP area including rehabilitation, mainstreaming, individualized programs, career exploration, academic instruction and career adjustment .

As with the HIP program, the VIP program at NTC also mainstreams its students after they have mastered the skills of daily living. The instructors' experience in teaching the visually impaired and the hearing impaired enables the students the maximize their learning.

Also like the program for the hearing impaired, the visually impaired program exists to help students enter competitive employment, sheltered employment, or to become an independent homemaker. To be successful in this endeavor, career and placement specialists – as well as the school's regular student placement services and instructors – get involved.

"In the special needs area, we are interested in the total student," says Joe Mielczarek, VIP liaison instructor at NTC. "While it is the special need that brings them to us initially, it is important to remember that they share many of the same problems and concerns as sighted and hearing students."

The HIP and VIP programs are not strictly about classroom education. They offer students a chance to grow and learn as human beings by giving them the opportunity to meet people from different backgrounds – blind and sighted, deaf and hearing – so that they not only have people to relate to in regard to their problems, but also people with whom to share their unique qualities and offerings. This not only gives them a more rounded education but makes their employment and daily living outlook quite a bit brighter.

Contact:
Crystal Anderson or Joe Mielczarek
(715) 675-3331

Northcentral Technical College
100 West Campus Drive
Wausau, WI 54401
Total head count enrollment-Credit: 18,000; Non-Credit: 12,500
Campuses/sites: 5;Full-time faculty: 145

NORTHCENTRAL TECHNICAL COLLEGE

LASER TECHNOLOGY

In addition to in-depth classroom instruction, students receive hands-on training, resulting in job placement throughout the country

Wausau, Wisconsin, is known for many things. It's the home of Wausau Insurance whose ads appear regularly on *60 Minutes*. It's the site of world championship kayak races. And more and more, it's becoming known as a source for laser technicians from its local technical school.

Developed in 1978, Northcentral Technical College's laser technician program is one of the oldest two-year laser technician programs in the country and the only one recognized by the U.S. Department of Education as an exemplary vocational program.

Admission to the program is selective – only about 35 out of the 70 people who applied last year were admitted. According to NTC laser instructor Dan Sczygelski, that's a sign the college isn't just producing assembly-line technicians.

Students in NTC's laser program get solid technical training but also take related courses to give them a more well-rounded education. Courses such as laser electronics and technical physics are required, but so are courses in technical reporting and human relations. Electives in other NTC programsmicroprocessors, computer graphics and automation systems round out the course-of-study.

In addition to in-depth classroom instruction, students get plenty of hands-on experience too. Sczygelski teaches a course in laser applications where students are exposed to a wide range of uses. And a proposed Industrial Laser Applications Center offers even more opportunities for hands-on training. The Center, located in an industrial incubator off-campus, will enable companies to try out lasers to see if they're the answer to their manufacturing needs.

All the training seems to have paid off for NTC laser graduates. Some 175 grads have been placed in companies

Continues on Page 768

all over the country since the program started.

Sczygelski says NTC has a good reputation in the marketplace because students come out with a thorough understanding of laser design, operations and application.

Contact:
Dan Sczygelski
(715) 675-3331

Northcentral Technical College
100 West Campus Drive
Wausau, WI 54401
Total head count enrollment-Credit: 18,000; Non-Credit: 12,500
Campuses/sites: 5;Full-time faculty: 145

FOOD AND ENVIRONMENTAL LABORATORY TECHNOLOGY

Among other things, students learn standard lab techniques, government regulations, ecosystems, control charts and food microbiology

The Food and Environmental Laboratory Technology program at Northeast Wisconsin Technical College, which prepares technicians with entry-level skills, was developed at the request of food and environmental professionals. A survey studying the need for educated laboratory technicians was then released. As a result, experts from the industries met with a facilitator provided by NWTC and discussed the equipment, procedures and knowledge needed by laboratory technicians.

The program is designed to help NWTC graduates learn the standard lab techniques, methodologies and equipment; government regulations related to laboratories; hazardous materials and Right-to-Know laws; ecosystems; food preservation, safety, and good manufacturing practices; pests, pesticides and the watercycle; control charts; sensory evaluation methods; analytical chemistry; and food microbiology. After completing the two-year program, students will have 67 credits and an Associate Degree.

The program received international recognition during a presentation given to the American Society for Quality Control (ASQC) at its international annual meeting. An article in the *Food Protection Inside Report* highlighted the program, which is the first of its kind in the nation. The program has been endorsed by the Wisconsin Laboratory Association.

Contact:
Don Jaworski, Associate Dean
(414) 498-5659

Northeast Wisconsin Technical College
2740 West Mason Street, PO Box 19042
Green Bay, WI 54307-9042
Total head count enrollment-Credit: 14,870; Non-Credit: 33,120
Campuses/sites: 3;Full-time faculty: 213

INDUSTRIAL MODEL BUILDING

The program, in conjunction with a model building corporation, hosts an annual regional American Engineering Model Society seminar

Industry saves money when problems are found and corrected on models, which students in the Industrial Model Building program are taught to produce. There is a need by numerous industries for models: small-scale prototypes of new products in the medical, consumer, and automotive fields; buildings; and manufacturing systems. Models are also used to create special effects in the movies, to develop theme parks and museum exhibits.

Northeast Wisconsin Technical College instructors work closely with industry professionals to produce students with entry-level skills in the model building field. The program is designed to help graduates learn model construction processes and machines, foundry applications, model layout and design, CAD and CNC milling, model problems, architectural topographical models and process piping models. Students graduate with an Associate Degree.

The Industrial Model Building program, in conjunction with Bay Technologies, Inc., a Northeast Wisconsin model building corporation, hosts an annual regional American Engineering Model Society (AEMS) seminar with guest speakers from across the United States and attendees from as far away as Japan. NWTC has also co-hosted the annual national AEMS seminar. NWTC is one of the few schools in the country to have a model building program; it is the only one with a concentrated two-year study. The Ronald A. Rasmussen Memorial Scholarship in honor of the former AEMS President is awarded to a second year NWTC Industrial Model Building student.

Contact:
Pamela Mazur, Associate Dean
(414) 498-6317

Northeast Wisconsin Technical College
2740 West Mason Street, PO Box 19042
Green Bay, WI 54307-9042
Total head count enrollment-Credit: 14,870; Non-Credit: 33,120
Campuses/sites: 3;Full-time faculty: 213

INTERNATIONAL TRADE TECHNOLOGY CENTER

A comprehensive library, continuing education and a degree program
support the needs of businesses expanding to the world market

As business expands to include a world market, WCTC is making it easier to learn the language and the skills of international business.The WCTC International Trade Technology Center provides a three-pronged approach to meet the needs of business and industry competing in a growing world market:

1) the Center includes a comprehensive library exclusively dedicated to provide users with up-to-date information needed to be internationally competitive; technical assistance is also provided as part of the Center's service;

2) continuing education programming is provided for upgrade training to employed persons; and

3) an International Trade Associate Degree Program – the only one of its kind in Wisconsin – for people who want to go into international trade either at the entry level or at a more advanced level if the individual already has business experience.

Coursework is designed to instruct in the basic areas of international trade including marketing, finance and technical subject matters such as regulations and documentation.

Job opportunities will vary along the same lines as marketing job opportunities. Some may involve travel, while others can be in a domestic office of an international business. Graduates of this program can anticipate obtaining a job in companies involved in import and export of their products.

Because this field is relatively new, graduates can create or enlarge their position within an organization through the skills learned through this program.

This program was the winner of the Service Sector for the Governor's Export Achievement Award and has received more than $225,000 in federal grants.

Contact:
Barbara Moebius, Associated Dean
(414) 691-5550

Waukesha County Technical College
800 Main Street
Waukesha, WI 53072
Total head count enrollment-Credit: 10,000; Non-Credit: 25,000
Campuses/sites: 4; Full-time faculty: 160

AUTO BODY AND PAINT TECHNOLOGY

A Collision Technology Center is the result of a partnership with the
leading manufacturer of auto service and collision repair equipment

WCTC, as a partner in a pioneering arrangement with the world's leading manufacturer of automobile service and collision repair equipment, has leased approximately 13,000 square feet in a new facility developed by the Hein-Werner Corporation as a part of its world headquarters. It will be known as the WCTC Collision Technology Center.

This innovative relationship will allow WCTC use of Kansas Jack and Blackhawk equipment manufactured by Hein-Werner valued at over $250,000; adjacent to Hein-Werner's own training facility; participation in a planned instructor/curriculum joint venture that will permit merging and development of a new version of auto collision repair curriculum; and perhaps most significantly, a national visibility for WCTC's program that will make it not only state-of-the-art in equipment and instruction but

Continues on Page 770

also one of the highest profile auto body training programs in the country.

I-CAR, the Inter-Industry conference on Auto Collision Repair, an international educational organization dedicated to improving the quality, safety and efficiency of auto collision repair, has enthusiastically endorsed the venture. They feel it comes at a time when the shortage of qualified entry-level people in the collision repair industry is reaching crisis proportions, establishing new and innovative programs is welcomed.

News about this first-of-a-kind venture is spreading throughout the auto collision industry to the extent that equipment dealers are considering placing new equipment in the WCTC center at reduced or no cost to the college just to have it available to students.

Through the entrepreneurial spirit of the Hein-Werner Corporation, the WCTC Administration and Board, the Auto body faculty and regional employers, WCTC auto body graduates will offer their customer skills unmatched in the history of the industry for technology timeliness and state-of-the-art application.

Contact:
William Glasenapp, Associate Dean
(414) 691-5594

Waukesha County Technical College
800 Main Street
Waukesha, WI 53072
Total head count enrollment-Credit: 10,000; Non-Credit: 25,000
Campuses/sites: 4 Full-time faculty: 160

ADOPT-A-SCHOLAR

*⊠ Each year the program ends with a three-day summer youth conference ⊠
which gives scholars a chance to meet role models of minority descent*

Students as young as sixth grade are selected to receive a variety of benefits, including free tuition for community education and credit classes and a two-year scholarship through Eastern Wyoming College's Adopt-A-Scholar program.

The scholars were first selected in the fall of 1991 from those students in the 6th through the 12th grades in the Goshen County Schools whose parents or guardians lack college experience or whose financial support is limited. Because it is an agriculture-based economy, Goshen County, Wyoming has a high concentration of Hispanics. According to the Torrington schools, more than 20 percent of their students are Hispanic.

At high school graduation, students selected for the Adopt-A-Scholar program are presented a two-year scholarship to EWC. Other benefits to the students include recognition of academic progress; EWC hats and T-shirts; participation in EWC athletic and cultural events; and development of relationships with current EWC student role models as mentors. The scholars must maintain a minimum grade point average and sign a statement stating they will refrain from illegal drug use during the years of participation in the program. The scholars will have continuing support for seven years to consider and experience college.

A 15-member Advisory Committee from the community was established. They represent the middle school, high school, parents and the business community. The establishment of such an advisory committee raises the college's visibility within the local school district and the community.

Each year the Adopt-A-Scholar program ends with a three-day summer youth conference in June. The summer conference gives the scholars opportunities to meet regional and national role models of minority descent, and to participate in self-esteem enhancement, alcohol and drug abuse prevention, career exploration, study skills training and experience on-campus living.

While initial funding was secured from the Wyoming Education Trust Fund, Coors Brewery, National Drinks, Holly Sugar Corporation, and American College Testing (ACT) have all contributed to the program. Additional funding will be sought to ensure the continuation of this model program for minority access to higher education.

Contact:
Billy Bates, Dean of Student Services
(307) 532-8232

Eastern Wyoming College
3200 West C Street
Torrington, WY 82240
Total head count enrollment-Credit: 1,877; Non-Credit: 1,700
Campuses/sites: 2; Full-time faculty: 36

PORTALS (PROVIDING OPPORTUNITIES FOR RENEWAL TRAINING AND LEARNING SUPPORT)

*⊠ The program is designed to, among other things, decrease attrition and provide ⊠
students with long-term vocational goals and aid in job placement*

The PORTALS (Providing Opportunities for Renewal Training and Learning Support) program at Eastern Wyoming College identified five planned outcomes that were to be addressed during a three year period:

1) decrease the attrition rate from college programs;
2) provide all community college students with long-term vocational goals and plans;
3) aid students in job placement and employment retention after program completion;
4) increase student's pre-vocational and vocational skills leading to employability; and
5) increase student awareness of academic and vocational program requirements as they meet labor market and work force expectations.

It was agreed that the completion of the first two objectives would be priorities during the initial year of the program, and that the development of a comprehensive advising system for identified "high risk" students would be the first step.

As a result, the Productive Life Plan (PLP), a form designed to assist students in identifying their vocational and educational goals and how to best achieve them, was developed in order to facilitate a more comprehensive approach to advising.

An "Intake Form" was also developed to assist the advi-

Continues on Page 772

sors in becoming acquainted with his or her advisee. Ten student-oriented faculty and administrative advisors were recruited and training sessions were held regarding the use of the PLP and the Intake Form. Additional training sessions were held to: acquaint the advisors with various community human service agencies, obtain additional information regarding on-campus programs and services, promote improved advising skills – as well as the development of basic counseling skills, and becoming more adept at the art of student empowerment. Sixty students were served by the PORTALS advisors during the 1991-92 school year.

The PORTALS program, initially funded through the Wyoming Educational Trust Fund expanded during FY1992-93 to serve a greater number of students. Primary objectives included the recruitment and training of 10 additional PORTALS advisors, development of a PORTALS Advisor checklists and the provision of writing and math skills remediation.

Contact:
Marilyn J. Cotant, Assistant Dean, Student Services
(307) 532-8214

Eastern Wyoming College
3200 West C Street
Torrington, WY 82240
Total head count enrollment-Credit: 1,877; Non-Credit: 1,700
Campuses/sites: 2; Full-time faculty: 36

LARAMIE COUNTY COMMUNITY COLLEGE

DESKTOP PUBLISHING

▓ *The program's success is attributed to the classes being taught out of* ▓
the journalism department rather than the business department

Economic development has been but one successful spin-off of the Desktop Publishing program, as two publications hare based in Cheyenne because their editors learned the skills at Laramie County Community College (LCCC).

Although Cheyenne, Wyoming, might seem an unlikely home for a sophisticated desktop publishing computer lab, attracting students from other states and more than a hundred miles away and transforming an award-winning journalism department into the setting for professional development and job retraining. However, that is exactly what happened nearly five years ago at Laramie County Community College.

Prior to 1987 few people in the Cheyenne business community and government agencies had heard of desktop publishing. In the beginning students were traditional journalism majors, but these were soon augmented by community professionals. Others followed, including those who had paid relatively large sums for unproductive private instruction elsewhere. Enthusiasm for this new technology spread, leading local businesses to purchase their own software and hardware. Soon following were teachers and other employees on the LCCC campus, employees in the county's school districts and a group of Colorado community college instructors. Then those working in a journalism-related field began to enroll because their skills no longer were up-to-date.

Because of their desktop publishing experience, several journalism majors with AA degrees were immediately employed in jobs usually requiring more education and experience. One student became publications editor for the Wyoming State Library; another is the public relations director for the Wyoming State Fair; and still another became the public relations director for the Cheyenne Chamber of Commerce, competing successfully with more than 100 applicants who had more experience and education. Another received a scholarship to work on her master's degree at Northwestern University because they wanted her to publish a departmental newsletter. After the president of the local economic development agency took the class, he created a desktop publishing position and hired one of his classmates.

Economic development has been another successful spin-off of desktop publishing. At least one international publication and one national publication have headquarters in Cheyenne because the editors learned desktop publishing at LCCC. Other former students operate their own desktop publishing business or do desktop publishing free-lance consulting. One published two children's books.

LCCC's desktop publishing success in serving its student population is attributed to the classes being taught out of the journalism department rather than the business department. Desktop Publishing at LCCC has been taught with the idea that students do not need to know DOS, printing terminology, or good layout and design principles. They can jump right into desktop publishing without any background, and then they take additional classes in the art and journalism departments if necessary.

Following LCCC's lead area school districts have incorporated desktop publishing into their curricula, and school teachers have used their knowledge and access to the technology to create greatly improved visual materials for their students.

On campus, a literary magazine has been established, and, in 1992, the *High Plains Register* won first place in the Wyoming Media Professionals contest and competed nationally.

The Desktop Publishing program is technology-intensive. LCCC has upgraded the equipment four times in anticipation of the requirements of future software, the desire to develop a full-scale visual communications degree program, and the commitment to stay on the leading edge of technology for the journalism students and the business and government communities it serves.

Contact:
Rosalind Schliske, Communications and Mass Media Instructor
(307) 778-1109

Laramie County Community College
1400 East College Drive
Cheyenne, WY 82007-3299
Total head count enrollment-Credit: 10,128; Non-Credit: 6,646
Campuses/sites: 2; Full-time faculty: 86

LEARNING ASSISTANCE RESOURCE CENTER (LARC)

The Center, open to students whenever classes are offered on campus, creates a more equalized situation for students with disabilities

The Laramie County Community College Learning Assistance Resource Center (LARC) includes an 18-station computer lab with adaptive equipment for students who are physically disabled or hearing/visually impaired. Laramie CCC developed LARC in the spring of 1984 to meet the needs of students with learning disabilities, students who are disadvantaged, and/or students with physical disabilities. These students are graduating from high school in record numbers with the expectation of continuing their training and education at the post-secondary level. Additionally, many older nontraditional students are enrolling in classes at the community college and with them come unique needs and requirements.

The basic premise of the Learning Assistance Resource Center is that within the parameters of the community college system, disadvantaged students and those with learning and/or physical disabilities must be allowed the same opportunities for vocational and academic success and failure as the student who is not disabled or disadvantaged. We do not advocate "spoon feeding" these students with special needs. Rather, we advocate the removal of barriers and the provision for support services to create a more equalized classroom situation for them.

The LARC is centrally located on the LCCC campus in a newly renovated 1,292 square-foot facility specifically designed to meet the growing needs of our expanding population of students with special needs. Its computer lab is constantly utilized for remedial and tutorial reinforcement of academic skills; it includes special adaptive equipment for the physically disabled and the hearing/visually impaired. The LARC is open to students whenever classes are offered on campus. Support services include textbook taping, note-taking assistance, test administration, interpreting for the hearing impaired, personal care attendants, mobility assistance and equipment lending, as well as tutorial support, registration and advising assistance, and emotional support. The staff of the LARC also provide campus-wide assistance in the ongoing renovation of facilities, student advising/counseling, and educational programming for special needs students.

During the 1989-90 academic year, 306 students utilized LARC services on a regular basis and received 3,642 hours of small group and individualized assistance.

LARC referrals come from many sources. A student with low placement test scores in any of the basic skills areas of reading, mathematics or English is an appropriate LARC student and may benefit from tutorial and remedial services. Many students are identified by their instructors as needing tutorial assistance, study skills training, or test anxiety reduction. Other students are referred by their high school counselors and/or teachers. Because LCCC is an open enrollment community college, there are many students whose basic skills are not well enough developed to allow them success in college-level courses, or even in structured, developmental classes without the provision of remedial and tutorial support. Other students simply learn at a slower rate and require task repetition to reach skill mastery levels. As student success and retention are very important to our mission at LCCC, these high risk students are referred to the LARC.

Student success is measured in a number of ways. Types of students who are considered successful include: those who retake and pass placement tests, those who take developmental classes and go on to receive degrees and/or certificates, and those who develop job skills and gain permanent employment.

The LARC is staffed by a full-time coordinator, two 3/4-time instructors and four educational aides. Students are encouraged to set up appointments and receive assistance from LARC staff on a regularly scheduled basis in small group and individual settings. However, staff members are also available to help students who just drop in.

Since its inception, the LARC has existed on a minimum

Continues on Page 774

of 50 percent external funding.

Local, state and national conference presentations describing the LARC have included the Wyoming State Reading Conference, the Wyoming State Conferences on Transition, and the National Association of Developmental Education.

Contact:
Caron Mellblom, Center Coordinator
(307) 778-1245

Laramie County Community College
1400 East College Drive
Cheyenne, WY 82007-3299
Total head count enrollment-Credit: 10,128; Non-Credit: 6,646
Campuses/sites: 2; Full-time faculty: 86

WORKSHOP ON WHEELS

The project is designed to increase the capacity and modify the practices of child care workers through a series of training modules

Workshop on Wheels is a rural child development teacher training program providing a network to disperse child development information to the surrounding community.

Coordinated by the Child Development Department of York Technical College, the program was initiated in March of 1990 and is funded by the Close Foundation, Inc. for the sum of $40,000 annually for five years.

The specific goal of this project is to develop, implement and evaluate a series of workshops that will enhance the capacity of child care workers to facilitate the language/science development of infants and preschool-aged children.

The program is unique for several reasons. The training package is composed of "kits" that contain a training manual and a variety of toys promoting language and science development. The content of the kits focuses on developmental stages of young children, from infancy to kindergarten. The training manuals are designed to be used by paraprofessionals and persons with limited literacy skills. All participants receive continuing education credits, a packet of health and developmental information, as well as free children's books.

This project is designed to increase the capacity and modify the practices of child care workers through a series of training modules consisting of materials and activities workshops and practical training.

As an inducement to participate in these workshops, child care workers are loaned kits containing developmentally appropriate toys and descriptions of activities that are the focus of each of these training modules. Although the focus of training will be on teaching providers about how to use developmentally appropriate materials and activities in their child care settings, training also emphasizes the rationale underlying these activities, particularly as related to facilitating children's language and science development. The information is shared in a workshop format, which takes place in individual child care programs (public, private, church or family, hence the name "Workshop on Wheels").

The total number of workshops presented exceeds 100. The program has been presented to more than 400 participants locally and in nearby states. Workshop on Wheels has provided consultations for local community projects, churches and community organizations such as Cities in Schools. It was adopted as a program by the Health and Human Finance Commission statewide.

Contact:
Julie Durham
(803) 327-8000, ext. 8229

York Technical College
452 South Anderson Road
Rock Hill, SC 29730
Total head count enrollment-Credit: 3,039; Non-Credit: 8,090
Campuses/sites: 1; Full-time faculty: 95

REGIONAL ACCREDITING AGENCIES

FEATURED INSTITUTIONS INDEX

FEATURED INSTITUTIONS INDEX

FEATURED INSTITUTIONS INDEX

FEATURED TOPICS INDEX

FEATURED TOPICS INDEX

ELECTRICAL/ELECTRIC POWER TRAINING

Northwest Iowa Community College (IA), 257
Pratt Community College/Area Vocational School (KS), 271

ELECTRON MICROSCOPY

San Joaquin Delta College (CA), 97

ELECTRONICS TECHNOLOGY

Blue Mountain Community College (OR), 563
Community and Technical College of Marshall University (WV), 751
Eastern Shore Community College (VA), 702
J.F. Drake State Technical College (AL), 12
Mid-State Technical College (WI), 762
North Seattle Community College (WA), 734
Northampton Community College (PA), 593
Orangeburg-Calhoun Technical College (SC), 616
Salt Lake Community College (UT), 689
Sauk Valley Community College (IL), 226
University of North Dakota-Lake Region (ND), 528

ELEMENTARY SCHOOL, ON-SITE

Miami-Dade Community College-North Campus (FL), 150

EMERGENCY DISASTER SERVICES TECHNOLOGY

Frontier Community College (IL), 204

EMERGENCY DISPATCH TRAINING

Mohave Community College (AZ), 22

EMERGENCY MEDICAL SERVICES

Community College of Allegheny County-Allegheny Campus (PA), 578
Crafton Hills College (CA), 54
Oklahoma City Community College (OK), 554
Southeastern Community College (IA), 258

ENERGY TECHNOLOGY

Bismarck State College (ND), 525
Community College of Allegheny County-South Campus (PA), 582
Crowder College (MO), 386
Oklahoma State University/Okmulgee (OK), 556
Orangeburg-Calhoun Technical College (SC), 616

ENGINEERING SCIENCES/TECHNOLOGY

Blue Ridge Community College (NC), 493
Essex County College (NJ), 427
Kellogg Community College (MI), 342
Middle Georgia College (GA), 185
North Seattle Community College (WA), 734
North Shore Community College (MA), 327

ENGLISH

Anoka-Ramsey Community College (MN), 357
Caldwell Community College and Technical Institute (NC), 495
Chabot-Las Positas Community College District (CA), 42
College of the Siskiyous (CA), 50
County College of Morris (NJ), 424
El Paso Community College (TX), 657
Foothill College (CA), 58
Inver Hills Community College (MN), 365
Miami-Dade Community College-Kendall Campus (FL), 148
Monroe Community College (NY), 469
Monroe County Community College (MI), 346
North Arkansas Community Technical College (AR), 32
Orange County Community College (NY), 476
Paducah Community College (KY), 286
Roane State Community College (TN), 637
Rogers State College (OK), 557
Santa Fe Community College (FL), 160
Santa Rosa Junior College (CA), 100
Seattle Central Community College (WA), 735
Seminole Community College (FL), 161
Solano Community College (CA), 104
Wenatchee Valley College (WA), 746
Windward Community College (HI), 190
Yakima Valley Community College (WA), 747

ENGLISH AS A SECOND LANGUAGE

Bainbridge College (GA), 177
Bergen Community College (NJ), 419
Black Hawk College (IL), 195
Bronx Community College (NY), 450
Brookhaven College (TX), 644
Eastern Iowa Community College District (IA), 245
Eastern Shore Community College (VA), 702
Henderson Community College (KY), 278
Houston Community College System-Southwest College (TX), 659
Lake Tahoe Community College (CA), 64
Los Angeles City College (CA), 69
Los Angeles Mission College (CA), 71
Merced College (CA), 75
Mission College (CA), 77
Prairie State College (IL), 222
Truman College, Harry S. (IL), 230
Union County College (NJ), 435
Wake Technical Community College (NC), 522
Waldorf College (IA), 259

ENVIRONMENTAL SCIENCES/TECHNOLOGY

Amarillo College (TX), 642
Anne Arundel Community College (MD), 299
Bay de Noc Community College (MI), 333

FURNITURE PRODUCTION TECHNOLOGY

Rockingham Community College (NC), 517
Vincennes University-Jasper Center (IN), 242

GAMING *SEE HOSPITALITY INDUSTRIES*

GED

Cecil Community College (MD), 303
Eastern Shore Community College (VA), 702
El Centro College of the Dallas County Community
     College District (TX), 655
Henderson Community College (KY), 278
Jefferson Davis Community College (AL), 14
Mississippi Gulf Coast Community College (MS),
     384
Mitchell Community College (NC), 511
Paris Junior College (TX), 676
Rogers State College (OK), 557
Savannah Technical Institute (GA), 186
Southeastern Illinois College (IL), 227

GLASSBLOWING

Seward County Community College (KS), 273

GOLF COURSE MANAGEMENT / OPERATIONS

Horry-Georgetown Technical College (SC), 613
Lake City Community College (FL), 145

GRAPHICS/GRAPHIC DESIGN

Coahoma Community College (MS), 376
Lane Community College (OR), 569
Luzerne County Community College (PA), 592
Wake Technical Community College (NC), 522
Westmoreland County Community College (PA),
     598

GUARANTEED EDUCATION

Carl Sandburg College (IL), 196
Frank Phillips College (TX), 658
Germanna Community College (VA), 703
Henry Ford Community College (MI), 339
Prairie State College (IL), 222

HAZARDOUS MATERIALS/WASTE TECHNOLOGY
SEE WASTE MANAGEMENT/TECHNOLOGY

HISTORIC PRESERVATION

Bucks County Community College (PA), 576

HISTORY

Bluefield State College (WV), 750
Coffeyville Community College (KS), 264
Lexington Community College (KY), 282
Pima County Community College District (AZ), 25

HONORS PROGRAMS

Butler County Community College (KS), 263
Carl Albert State College (OK), 553
College of Eastern Utah (UT), 689
Corning Community College (NY), 454
Darton College (GA), 180
Gulf Coast Community College (FL), 141
Los Angeles Pierce College (CA), 72
Merced College (CA), 75
Nassau Community College (NY), 471
North Arkansas Community Technical College
     (AR), 32
Palo Alto College (TX), 674
San Bernardino Valley College (CA), 89
Tarrant County Junior College (TX), 680
Waldorf College (IA), 259

HORTICULTURE *SEE AGRICULTURE/HORTICULTURE*

HOSIERY TECHNOLOGY

Catawba Valley Community College (NC), 497

HOSPITALITY INDUSTRIES
Culinary Arts/Restaurant Operations

Cape Cod Community College (MA), 319
Central Piedmont Community College (NC), 499
City College of San Francisco (CA), 44
Columbia College (CA), 52
Delgado Community College (LA), 290
Grand Rapids Community College (MI), 338
Gulf Coast Community College (FL), 141
Jefferson State Community College (AL), 15
Lake Tahoe Community College (CA), 64
Luzerne County Community College (PA), 592
Manchester Community-Technical College (CT),
     119
Northern Essex Community College (MA), 328
Northwestern Michigan College (MI), 349
State University of NY College of Technology at
     Delhi (NY), 481

Gaming

Mohave Community College (AZ), 22

Hotel Operations & Management

Cape Cod Community College (MA), 319
City College of San Francisco (CA), 44
Lake Tahoe Community College (CA), 64
Luzerne County Community College (PA), 592
Northern Essex Community College (MA), 328
Northwestern Michigan College (MI), 349
State University of NY College of Technology at
     Delhi (NY), 481
University of Puerto Rico-Carolina Regional College
     (PR), 600

Tourism

Horry-Georgetown Technical College (SC), 613
Lake Tahoe Community College (CA), 64

FEATURED TOPICS INDEX

LITERATURE

MACHINE/MACHINERY TECHNOLOGY

MANUFACTURING

MARINE PROPULSION TECHNOLOGY

MARITIME SCIENCES

MATHEMATICS, GENERAL

MEASUREMENT

MECHANICS

MENTORING

METROLOGY

MICROELECTRONICS

MILITARY ALSO SEE: ROTC

MISSION

MOBILE PROGRAMS

MULTICULTURAL PROGRAMS/CLASSES
ALSO SEE: OUTREACH TO ETHNIC MINORITIES

Highland Community College (IL), 205
Indiana Vocational Technical College-Muncie
    Region 06 (IN), 237
Pitt Community College (NC), 514
South Georgia College (GA), 188

SERVICE ACADEMY PREPARATION
New Mexico Military Institute (NM), 441

SIGN LANGUAGE *SEE INTERPRETER TRAINING*

SINGLE PARENTS/DISPLACED HOMEMAKERS
ALSO SEE: OUTREACH TO WOMEN
Cecil Community College (MD), 303
Davidson County Community College (NC), 502
DeKalb Technical Institute (GA), 182
El Centro College of the Dallas County Community
    College District (TX), 655
Jefferson Davis Community College (AL), 14
Louisiana State University at Eunice (LA), 291
Mississippi Gulf Coast Community College (MS),
    384
New Hampshire Technical College (NH), 416
North Seattle Community College (WA), 734
Rappahannock Community College (VA), 717
Sampson Community College (NC), 518
San Diego Community College District (CA), 92
Santa Barbara City College (CA), 99
Southern West Virginia Community College (WV),
    752
Southwestern Oregon Community College (OR),
    573
Westchester Community College (NY), 489

SPACE SHUTTLE
Sierra Community College (CA), 102

SPACE TECHNOLOGY
Anne Arundel Community College (MD), 299

SPEAKERS PROGRAMS/BUREAUS
Glen Oaks Community College (MI), 336

SPECIAL EDUCATION
ALSO SEE: DISABLED PROGRAMS/SERVICES
Coastline Community College (CA), 45
Collin County Community College (TX), 650

SPECIAL TOPICS
Isothermal Community College (NC), 507

SPEECH/SPEAKING
Chipola Junior College (FL), 135
Rend Lake College (IL), 224

STAFF/FACULTY DEVELOPMENT
ALSO SEE: CONTINUING EDUCATION / IN-SERVICE TRAINING
American River College (CA), 38
Arizona Western College (AZ), 20
Broome Community College (NY), 451
Catonsville Community College (MD), 302
Chemeketa Community College (OR), 564
College of DuPage (IL), 199
College of the Canyons (CA), 48
Community College of Aurora (CO), 109
Danville Area Community College (IL), 201
Del Mar College (TX), 653
East Central College (MO), 388
Eastern Iowa Community College District (IA), 245
El Paso Community College (TX), 657
Finger Lakes Community College (NY), 459
Florida Community College at Jacksonville (FL),
    138
Golden West College (CA), 61
Hazard Community College (KY), 277
Indiana Vocational Technical College-East Central
    District (IN), 235
Jefferson Community College (KY), 279
Kentucky Community College System, University of
    (KY), 280
LaGuardia Community College (NY), 466
Las Positas College (CA), 66
Mercer County Community College (NJ), 430
Middlesex Community College (MA), 325
Moberly Area Community College (MO), 392
New River Community College (VA), 709
Norwalk Community-Technical College (CT), 124
Oakton Community College (IL), 219
Oklahoma State University/Okmulgee (OK), 556
Orange County Community College (NY), 476
Palomar College (CA), 84
Pasco-Hernando Community College (FL), 156
Pensacola Junior College (FL), 157
Porterville College (CA), 84
Red Rocks Community College (CO), 113
Santa Fe Community College (FL), 160
Santa Fe Community College (NM), 443
Schoolcraft College (MI), 351
Sinclair Community College (OH), 547
Tompkins Cortland Community College (NY), 485
Trident Technical College (SC), 624

STATISTICS
College of the Siskiyous (CA), 50
Suffolk Community College (NY), 483

SUMMER PROGRAMS
Camden County College (NJ), 423
Citrus College (CA), 43
College of the Siskiyous (CA), 50
Dutchess Community College (NY), 455

FEATURED TOPICS INDEX